The Illustrated Bible Dictionary
Part Two: Goliath-Papyri

The Illustrated Bible Dictionary

INTER-VARSITY PRESS

Co-ordination
Derek Wood

Research
Tessa Clowney (pictures)
Caroline Masom (diagrams)

Editorial
Mary Gladstone (copy-editing and proofs)
Norman Hillyer (proofs)
Rhona Pipe (proofs)
Joanne Bramwell (copy-editing)
Sue Mills (copy-editing)
Derek Wood (copy-editing)
Marie Cross (secretarial)

Maps preparation
Min Topliss
Elisabeth Pearce

Production
Michael Sims (managing)
Joanne Battisson (assistant)

Indexing
Norman Hillyer

The Illustrated Bible Dictionary

PART 2
Goliath-Papyri

Organizing Editor of *The New Bible Dictionary:*

J. D. Douglas, M.A., B.D., S.T.M., Ph.D.
Editor-at-large, *Christianity Today.*

Revision Editor:

N. Hillyer, B.D., S.Th., A.L.C.D.
Formerly Librarian, Tyndale House, Cambridge.

Consulting Editors:

F. F. Bruce, M.A., D.D., F.B.A.
Emeritus Rylands Professor of Biblical Criticism and Exegesis, University of Manchester.

J. I. Packer, M.A., D.Phil., D.D.
Professor of Systematic Theology, Regent College, Vancouver.

R. V. G. Tasker, M.A., D.D.
Formerly Professor of New Testament Exegesis, University of London.

D. J. Wiseman, O.B.E., M.A., D.Lit., F.B.A., F.S.A.
Professor of Assyriology, University of London.

Additional Consulting Editors for the revised edition:

D. Guthrie, B.D., M.Th., Ph.D.
Vice-Principal, London Bible College.

A. R. Millard, M.A., M.Phil., F.S.A.
Rankin Senior Lecturer in Hebrew and Ancient Semitic Languages, University of Liverpool.

Consulting Editor for illustrations:

D. J. Wiseman,
in association with:

A. R. Millard.

J. P. Kane, Ph.D., Dip.Ed.,
Lecturer in Hellenistic Greek, University of Manchester.

K. A. Kitchen, B.A., Ph.D.,
Reader in Egyptian and Coptic, University of Liverpool.

INTER-VARSITY PRESS

TYNDALE HOUSE PUBLISHERS

HODDER AND STOUGHTON
SYDNEY AND AUCKLAND

First published 1980

Inter-Varsity Press,
38 De Montfort Street,
Leicester LE1 7GP, England.

Published and sold in the USA
and Canada by
Tyndale House Publishers,
336 Gundersen Drive, Box 80,
Wheaton, Illinois 60187, USA.

First published in Australia
in 1980 by
Hodder & Stoughton (Australia)
Pty Limited, 2 Apollo Place,
Lane Cove, NSW 2066.

Quotations from the Bible are
from the Revised Standard Version
(copyrighted 1946 and 1952,
Second Edition 1971, by the
Division of Christian Education,
National Council of the Churches
of Christ in the USA), unless
otherwise stated.

Part Two

UK ISBN 0 85110 628 5
US ISBN 0 8423 1567 5
US ISBN (set) 0 8423 7575 2
US Library of Congress Catalog
Card Number 79–92540
Australia ISBN 0 340 25920 5

Typeset by Monophoto Lasercomp
in Times New Roman by
Richard Clay (The Chaucer Press)
Limited, Bungay,
Suffolk NR35 1ED, England.

Designed by
Thumb Design Partnership Limited,
20–21 D'Arblay Street,
London W1V 3FN, England.

Cartography by
George Philip and Son Limited,
12–14 Long Acre,
London WC2E 9LP, England.

Colour reproduction by
Vauvelle (Photo-litho) Limited,
Clayton Wood Close, West Park,
Leeds LS16 6QE, England.

Printed in the USA by
R. R. Donnelley & Sons Co.,
Willard, Ohio, USA.

Contents

Preface

The Illustrated Bible Dictionary is based on the text of **The New Bible Dictionary,** first published in 1962, which has now been completely revised using the Revised Standard Version of the Bible. While a few of the original articles have been omitted as superfluous and others amalgamated for easier reference, many new articles have been added. A large number have been completely re-written. Bibliographies have been brought up-to-date, cross references revised and a comprehensive index added at the end of the last volume.

In its original form **The New Bible Dictionary** has proved itself to be a steady bestseller through two decades. It came to be regarded by many throughout the world, echoing the verdict of the late Professor William F. Albright, as 'the best one-volume Bible dictionary in the English language'. The revised text is now published in an entirely new form, in three parts, with every advantage that accrues from extensive colour illustrations, photographs, diagrams and maps.

The illustrations have been chosen, not as mere decoration, but with a view to enhancing the value of the Dictionary, by increasing its scope as a source of information. If they make the work more attractive to a wider range of readers, a further advantage has been gained.

The New Bible Dictionary is a major product of the Tyndale Fellowship for Biblical Research, which was founded in close association with the Inter-Varsity Fellowship (now the Universities and Colleges Christian Fellowship) to foster evangelical biblical scholarship. The contributors to **The Illustrated Bible Dictionary,** as to its predecessor, are not, however, drawn exclusively from the ranks of the (mainly British) Tyndale Fellowship; we are deeply indebted to academic colleagues in many parts of the world for their generous co-operation.

The aim of the editors and contributors has continued to be to produce a work of reference, written in a spirit of unqualified loyalty to Holy Scripture, which will substantially further the understanding of God's Word to mankind. That loyalty to Holy Scripture involves treating as true and trustworthy all its statements of fact, theological, physical and historical, is an assumption basic to the whole Dictionary. We do not apologize for the fact that this book reflects the credal, confessional and evangelical convictions for which the Tyndale Fellowship stands—the triunity of God, the deity, atoning death, bodily resurrection and approaching return of Jesus Christ, the divine inspiration and authority of the Bible, the supernatural life of the Christian church, and all that these articles of faith bring with them. No attempt, however, has been made to impose a rigid uniformity upon the work as a whole, or to exclude the occasional expression of different viewpoints within the bounds of this basic loyalty. Nor, of course, are our contributors bound to endorse all the opinions expressed by their colleagues, whether in the Dictionary itself or elsewhere.

The task of organizing this huge revision has fallen on the shoulders of the Rev. Norman Hillyer, whose care, application and courtesy have been instrumental in bringing to birth the text as it now appears.

All who have been involved in the revision are conscious of our continuing debt to Dr J. D. Douglas, the Organizing Editor of the original work, and to Mr Ronald Inchley, the former Publications Secretary of the Inter-Varsity Fellowship. The new Dictionary builds upon their foundation.

As Consulting Editors we are the first to recognize that a major enterprise such as this is possible only because of the enthusiastic and dedicated effort of a large team of people. We wish to record our gratitude to the staff of the Inter-Varsity Press, including those specially engaged for this project, and to the typesetters, colour reproduction specialists, cartographers and printers. Considerable assistance in the preparation of the maps was given by Dr Colin Hemer and Dr John Bimson. A fully illustrated work owes a great deal to its designer, and we are glad to acknowledge here the skilful contribution of Philip Miles and his colleagues at Thumb Design Partnership Ltd.

Our hope is that **The Illustrated Bible Dictionary** will enable many to reach a deeper understanding of the Bible and a richer appreciation of its message.

F.F.B.

D.G.

A.R.M.

J.I.P.

D.J.W.

How to use this Dictionary

The work is divided into three parts and gives the reader the simplest possible access to the most comprehensive information.

Cross references
There are two methods of cross reference:
1. An asterisk before a word indicates that further relevant information will be found in the article under that title and is equivalent to the abbreviation *q.v.*
2. References in the margin provide a list of topics which do not carry articles under their own heading, but the relevant information can be found under another heading, *e.g.*

▬ ADVOCATE
See Counsellor, Part 1.

Index
A comprehensive index, containing every significant reference to each topic, is to be found at the end of Part Three. This includes locations on maps and an index to illustrations.

Abbreviations
A full list of abbreviations used in the Dictionary will be found on pages xii–xvi.

Authorship of articles
The authors and co-authors of articles are indicated by their initials at the foot of each article. A full index of contributors is to be found on pages viii–xi. The entries are listed in alphabetical order of initials, not of surnames.

Bibliographies
To assist those wishing to study subjects in greater detail, bibliographies appear at the end of most of the longer articles. These usually provide references to the recent general works on the subject and may include detailed studies or books which take up a position different from that of the contributor.

Picture acknowledgments
The source and/or holder of copyright for the illustrations is indicated by initials in brackets at the end of the picture caption. The full list of sources to which these initials refer is to be found at the end of this volume.

Bible versions
The Bible translation adopted for this Dictionary is the Revised Standard Version. In a few cases contributors have selected quotations from the King James (Authorized) Version, or, when available at the time of writing, the New International Version.

Maps
There is no map supplement in the Dictionary, but maps are to be found alongside the articles themselves for easy reference.

Names of regions, provinces, kingdoms, *etc.*, are printed in large roman capitals, *e.g.* BABYLONIA

Tribes and ethnic groups: large italic capitals, *e.g. AMORITES*

Towns and villages: lower case roman, *e.g.* Jerusalem

Geographical features such as mountains, rivers, lakes, seas, *etc.*: lower case italic, *e.g. Great Sea*

Modern place-names: as above but in brackets, *e.g.* (*Mediterranean Sea*). Absolute consistency has not been possible but, in general, where the modern name is clearly derived from the ancient (*e.g.* Creta = Crete, Italia = Italy) or where it would be pedantic to place modern names in brackets (*e.g.* Egypt, Jerusalem) brackets have been omitted. In a few other cases, where nearly all the place-names are modern, the principle has been abandoned for the sake of simplicity.

Features to be noted particularly, such as the subject of the article concerned, are underlined, *e.g.* Ashdod.

Where a site was known by two or more alternative names they are divided by an oblique stroke, *e.g.* Ezion-geber/Elath.

The word 'or' indicates uncertainty about the name or the location, as does a question mark.

Transliteration
The following systems have been adopted throughout the volume. In fairness to our contributors it should be said that some have disagreed on philological grounds with our transliteration of Hebrew words generally and of the divine name *Yahweh* in particular, but have graciously subordinated their convictions to editorial policy.

Hebrew

א = ʾ	ד = ḏ	י = y	ס = s	ר = r
בּ = b	ה = h	כּ = k	ע = ʿ	שׂ = ś
ב = ḇ	ו = w	כ = ḵ	פּ = p	שׁ = š
גּ = g	ז = z	ל = l	פ = p̄	תּ = t
ג = ḡ	ח = ḥ	מ = m	צ = ṣ	ת = ṯ
דּ = d	ט = ṭ	נ = n	ק = q	

Long vowels		Short vowels	Very short Vowels
(ה)◌ָ = â	◌ָ = ā	◌ַ = a	◌ֲ = ^{a}
י◌ֵ = ê	◌ֵ = ē	◌ֶ = e	◌ֱ = ^{e}
י◌ִ = î		◌ִ = i	◌ְ = ^{e} (if vocal)
וֹ = ô	◌ֹ = ō	◌ָ = o	◌ֳ = ^{o}
וּ = û		◌ֻ = u	

Greek

α = a	ι = i	ρ = r	ῥ = rh
β = b	κ = k	σ,ς = s	ʽ = h
γ = g	λ = l	τ = t	γξ = nx
δ = d	μ = m	υ = y	γγ = ng
ε = e	ν = n	φ = ph	αυ = au
ζ = z	ξ = x	χ = ch	ευ = eu
η = ē	ο = o	ψ = ps	ου = ou
θ = th	π p	ω = ō	υι = yi

Arabic

ا = ʾ	خ = ḫ	ش = š	غ = ġ	ن = n
ب = b	د = d	ص = ṣ	ف = f	ه = h
ت = t	ذ = ḏ	ض = ḍ	ق = ḳ	و = w
ث = t	ر = r	ط = ṭ	ك = k	ى = y
ج = ǧ	ز = z	ظ = ẓ	ل = l	ة = t
ح = ḥ	س = s	ع = ʿ	م = m	

List of Contributors

A.A.J. A. A. Jones, M.A., B.D., Ph.D., formerly Head of Department of Religious Studies, Avery Hill College, London.

A.C. R. A. Cole, B.A., B.D., M.Th., Ph.D., Federal Secretary, Church Missionary Society (Australia) and Lecturer in Old Testament Language and Literature, University of Sydney.

A.E.C. A. E. Cundall, B.A., B.D., Senior Lecturer in Old Testament Studies, London Bible College.

A.E.W. A. E. Willingale, B.A., B.D., M.Th., Romford, Essex.

A.F. A. Flavelle, B.A., B.D., Minister of Finaghy Presbyterian Church, Belfast.

A.F.W. A. F. Walls, M.A., B.Litt., Professor of Religious Studies, University of Aberdeen.

A.G. A. Gelston, M.A., Senior Lecturer in Theology, University of Durham.

A.J.M.W. A. J. M. Weddeburn, M.A., B.D., Ph.D., Lecturer in New Testament Language and Literature, University of St Andrews.

A.K.C. A. K. Cragg, M.A., D.Phil., D.D., Assistant Bishop of Wakefield and Vicar of Helme, Huddersfield.

A.R. The late A. Ross, M.A., B.D., D.D., formerly Professor of New Testament, Free Church College, Edinburgh.

A.R.M. A R. Millard, M.A., M.Phil., F.S.A., Rankin Senior Lecturer in Hebrew and Ancient Semitic Languages, University of Liverpool.

A.S. A. Stuart, M.Sc., Dip.R.M.S., Emeritus Professor of Geology, University of Exeter.

A.S.W. A. S. Wood, B.A., Ph.D., F.R.Hist.S., Principal, Cliff College, Calver, Derbyshire.

A. van S. A. van Selms, Th.D., Emeritus Professor of Semitic Languages, University of Pretoria.

B.A.M. B. A. Milne, M.A., B.D., Ph.D., Lecturer in Biblical and Historical Theology and Christian Ethics, Spurgeon's College, London.

B.F.C.A. The late B. F. C. Atkinson, M.A., Ph.D., formerly Under-Librarian, University of Cambridge.

B.F.H. B. F. Harris, B.A., M.A., B.D., Ph.D., Associate Professor of History, Macquarie University, New South Wales.

B.L.S. B. L. Smith, B.D., Th.Schol., Classics Teacher, Sydney Grammar School; Visiting Lecturer, Moore Theological College, Sydney.

B.O.B. B. O. Banwell, B.A., M.A., formerly Lecturer in Old Testament, Rhodes University; Methodist Minister, Fort Beaufort, S. Africa.

C.D.W. C. de Wit, Docteur en philologie et histoire orientales; Conservateur honoraire Musées Royaux d'Art et Histoire, Brussels; Emeritus Professor of the University of Louvain.

C.F.P. The late C. F. Pfeiffer, B.A., B.D., Ph.D., formerly Associate Professor of Old Testament, Gordon Divinity School, Beverly Farms, Massachusetts.

C.H.D. C. H. Duncan, M.A., B.D., Ph.D., Th.D., Lecturer in Philosophy, State College of Victoria, Australia; Canon of St Paul's Cathedral, Melbourne.

C.J.D. C. J. Davey, B.Sc., M.A., Inspector of Mines, Victoria, Australia.

C.J.H. C. J. Hemer, M.A., Ph.D., formerly Lecturer in New Testament Studies, University of Manchester.

C.L.F. C. L. Feinberg, A.B., A.M., Th.B., Th.M., Ph.D., Emeritus Professor of Semitics and Old Testament and Dean of Talbot Theological Seminary, Los Angeles.

D.A.H. D. A. Hubbard, B.A., B.D., Th.M., Ph.D., D.D., L.H.D., President and Professor of Old Testament, Fuller Theological Seminary, Pasadena, California.

D.B.K. D. B. Knox, B.A., B.D., M.Th., D.Phil, A.L.C.D., Principal, Moore Theological College, Sydney; Senior Canon of St Andrew's Cathedral, Sydney.

D.F. D. Freeman, B.A., Th.B., Th.M., Ph.D., Professor, Rhode Island Junior College.

D.F.P. D. F. Payne, B.A., M.A., Senior Lecturer and Head of Department of Semitic Studies, The Queen's University, Belfast.

D.G. D. Guthrie, B.D., M.Th., Ph.D., Vice-Principal, London Bible College.

D.G.S. D. G. Stradling, Magdalen College, Oxford.

D.H.F. D. H. Field, B.A., Vice-Principal, Oak Hill College, London.

D.H.T. D. H. Tongue, M.A., formerly Lecturer in New Testament, Trinity College, Bristol.

D.H.W. D. H. Wheaton, M.A., B.D., Principal, Oak Hill College, London; Canon of St Alban's Cathedral.

D.J.A.C. D. J. A. Clines, M.A., Senior Lecturer, Department of Biblical Studies, University of Sheffield.

D.J.V.L. D. J. V. Lane, Ll.B., B.D., Overseas Director, Overseas Missionary Fellowship, Singapore.

D.J.W. D. J. Wiseman, O.B.E., M.A., D.Lit., F.B.A., F.S.A., Professor of Assyriology, University of London.

D.K.I. D. K. Innes, M.A., B.D., Rector of Alford and Loxwood, West Sussex.

D.O.S. D. O. Swann, B.A., B.D., Minister of Ashford Evangelical Congregational Church, Middlesex.

D.R. de L. D. R. de Lacey, M.A., Ph.D., Lecturer in New Testament Studies, London Bible College.

D.R.H. D. R. Hall, M.A., M.Th, Superintendent Minister of the North of Scotland Mission Circuit of the Methodist Church, Aberdeen.

D.T. D. H. Trapnell, M.A., M.D., F.R.C.P., F.R.C.R., Consultant Radiologist, Westminster Hospital, London.

D.W. D. Wenham, M.A., Ph.D., Research Fellow, Tyndale House, Cambridge.

D.W.B. D. W. Baker, A.B., M.C.S., M.Phil., Assistant Professor of Biblical Studies, Bethel College, St Paul, Minnesota.

D.W.B.R. D. W. B. Robinson, M.A., Bishop in Parramatta, New South Wales; formerly Head of New Testament Department, Divinity School, University of Sydney.

D.W.G. D. W. Gooding, M.A., Ph.D., M.R.I.A., Professor of Old Testament Greek, The Queen's University, Belfast.

E.A.J. E. A. Judge, M.A., Professor of History, Macquarie University, New South Wales.

E.E.E. E. E. Ellis, Ph.D., Research Professor of New Testament Literature, New Brunswick Theological Seminary, New Jersey.

E.J.Y. The late E. J. Young, B.A., Th.M., Ph.D., formerly Professor of Old Testament, Westminster Theological Seminary, Philadelphia.

E.M.B. E. M. Blaiklock, O.B.E., M.A., Litt.D., Emeritus Professor of Classics, University of Auckland.

E.M.B.G. E. M. B. Green, M.A., B.D., Rector of St Aldate's Church, Oxford; Canon of Coventry Cathedral. Formerly Principal, St John's College, Nottingham.

E.M.Y. E. M. Yamauchi, B.A., M.A., Ph.D., Director of Graduate Studies and Professor of History, Miami University, Oxford, Ohio.

F.C.F. F. C. Fensham, M.A., Ph.D., D.D., Professor in Semitic Languages, University of Stellenbosch.

F.D.K. F. D. Kidner, M.A., A.R.C.M., formerly Warden, Tyndale House, Cambridge.

F.F. F. Foulkes, B.A., B.D., M.A., M.Sc., Lecturer in Biblical Studies, St John's College, Auckland, and Lecturer in Biblical History and Literature, University of Auckland.

F.F.B. F. F. Bruce, M.A., D.D., F.B.A., Emeritus Rylands Professor of Biblical Criticism and Exegesis, University of Manchester.

F.H.P. F. H. Palmer, M.A., Diocesan Missioner and Priest-in-charge of Blymhill and Weston-under-Lizard, Diocese of Lichfield.

F.N.H. F. N. Hepper, F.I.Biol., B.Sc., F.L.S., Assistant Keeper, The Herbarium, Royal Botanic Gardens, Kew.

F.R.S. F. R. Steele, A.B., M.A., Ph.D., Assistant Director North America for the North Africa Mission; formerly Assistant Professor of Assyriology, University of Pennsylvania.

F.S.F. F. S. Fitzsimmonds, B.A., B.D., M.Th., Vice-Principal, Spurgeon's College, London.

G.C.D.H. G. C. D. Howley, Consulting Editor of *The Witness*.

G.G.G. G. G. Garner, B.A., B. D., Director, Australian Institute of Archaeology, Melbourne.

G.I.D. G. I. Davies, M.A., Ph.D., Lecturer in Old Testament and Intertestamental Studies, University of Cambridge.

G.I.E. Mrs G. I. Emmerson, M.A., Dip.Or.Lang., Lecturer, Department of Theology, University of Nottingham.

G.O. The late G. Ogg, M.A., B.Sc., D.D., D.Litt., formerly Minister at Anstruther Easter, Fife.

G.R.B.-M. G. R. Beasley-Murray, M.A., Ph.D., D.D., James Buchanan Harrison Professor of New Testament Interpretation, Southern Baptist Theological Seminary, Louisville, Kentucky.

G.S.C. G. S. Cansdale, B.A., B.Sc., F.L.S., Consultant Biologist.

G.S.M.W. The late G. S. M. Walker, M.A., B.D., Ph.D., formerly Lecturer in Church History, University of Leeds.

G.T.M. The late G. T. Manley, M.A., sometime Fellow, Christ's College, Cambridge.

G.W. G. Walters, B.A., B.D., Ph.D., Professor of Ministry, Gordon-Conwell Theological Seminary, South Hamilton, Massachusetts.

G.W.G. G. W. Grogan, B.D., M.Th., Principal, Bible Training Institute, Glasgow.

H.A.G.B. H. A. G. Belben, M.A., B.D., formerly Principal, Cliff College, Calver, Derbyshire.

H.D.McD. H. D. McDonald, B.A., B.D., Ph.D., D.D., formerly Vice-Principal, London Bible College.

H.G.M.W. H. G. M. Williamson, M.A., Ph.D., Assistant Lecturer in Hebrew and Aramaic, University of Cambridge.

H.L.E. H. L. Ellison, B.A., B.D., formerly Senior Tutor, Moorlands Bible College.

H.M.C. H. M. Carson, B.A., B.D., Minister of Hamilton Road Baptist Church, Bangor, Northern Ireland.

H.R. H. N. Ridderbos, D. Theol., Emeritus Professor of New Testament, Kampen Theological Seminary, The Netherlands.

I.H.M. I. H. Marshall, B.A., M.A., B.D., Ph.D., Professor of New Testament Exegesis, University of Aberdeen.

J.A.M. J. A. Motyer, M.A., B.D., Principal, Trinity College, Bristol.

J.A.T. J. A. Thompson, M.A., M.Sc., B.D., B.Ed., Ph.D., formerly Reader in Department of Middle Eastern Studies, University of Melbourne.

J.B.J. J. B. Job, M.A., B.D., Tutor in Old Testament, Cliff College, Derbyshire.

J.B.P. J. B. Payne, Ph.D., Professor of Old Testament, Covenant Theological Seminary, St Louis, Missouri.

J.B.T. J. B. Torrance, M.A., B.D., Professor of Systematic Theology, University of Aberdeen.

J.B.Tr. J. B. Taylor, M.A., Bishop of St Albans.

J.C.C. J. C. Connell, B.A., M.A., formerly Director of Studies and Lecturer in New Testament Exegesis, London Bible College.

J.C.J.W. J. C. J. Waite, B.D., Principal, South Wales Bible College.

J.C.W. J. C. Whitcomb, Jr, Th.D., Professor of Theology and Director of Postgraduate Studies, Grace Theological Seminary, Winona Lake, Indiana.

J.D.D. J. D. Douglas, M.A., B.D., S.T.M., Ph.D., Editor-at-large, *Christianity Today*.

J.D.G.D. J. D. G. Dunn, M.A., B.D., Ph.D., Lecturer in New Testament, University of Nottingham.

J.E.G. J. E. Goldingay, B.A., Lecturer in Old Testament, St John's College, Nottingham.

J.G.B. Miss J. G. Baldwin, B.A., B.D., Dean of Women, Trinity College, Bristol.

J.G.G.N. J. G. G. Norman, B.D., M.Th., Pastor of Rosyth Baptist Church, Fife.

J.G.S.S.T. J. G. S. S. Thomson, B.A., M.A., B.D., Ph.D., Minister at Wigtown, Scotland.

J.H. J. W. L. Hoad, M.A., Clinical Supervisor, Princeton, New Jersey.

J.H.H. J. H. Harrop, M.A., formerly Lecturer in Classics, Fourah Bay College, University of Sierra Leone.

J.H.P. J. H. Paterson, M.A., Professor of Geography, University of Leicester.

J.H.S. J. H. Skilton, B.A., M.A., M.Div., Ph.D., Dean of the Reformed Bible Institute of the Delaware Valley; Lecturer in New Testament, Westminster Theological Seminary, Philadelphia.

J.H.Sr. The late J. H. Stringer, M.A., B.D., formerly Tutor, London Bible College.

J.I.P. J. I. Packer, M.A., D.Phil., D.D., Professor of Systematic Theology, Regent College, Vancouver, BC.

J.J.H. J. J. Hughes, B.A., M.Div., Assistant Professor of Religious Studies, Westmont College, Santa Barbara, California.

J.L.K. The late J. L. Kelso, B.A., Th.M., M.A., Th.D., D.D., Ll.D., formerly Professor of Old Testament History and Biblical Archaeology, Pittsburgh Theological Seminary, Pennsylvania.

J.M. The late J. Murray, M.A., Th.M., formerly Professor of Systematic Theology, Westminster Theological Seminary, Philadelphia.

J.M.H. J. M. Houston, M.A., B.Sc., D.Phil., Chancellor, formerly Principal, Regent College, Vancouver, BC.

J.N.B. J. N. Birdsall, M.A., Ph.D., F.R.A.S., Reader in New Testament and Textual Criticism, University of Birmingham.

J.N.G. The late J. N. Geldenhuys, B.A., B.D., Th.M.

J.P. J. Philip, M.A., Minister of Holyrood Abbey, Edinburgh.

J.P.B. J. P. Baker, M.A., B.D., Rector of Newick, East Sussex.

J.P.K. J. P. Kane, Ph.D., Dip.Ed., Lecturer in Hellenistic Greek, University of Manchester.

J.P.U.L. J. P. U. Lilley, M.A., F.C.A., Magdalen College, Oxford.

J.R. J. Rea, M.A., Th.D., Professor of Old Testament, Melodyland School of Theology, Anaheim, California.

J.Ru. J. Ruffle, M.A., Keeper of Archaeology, Birmingham City Museum.

J.S.W. J. S. Wright, M.A., formerly Principal, Tyndale Hall, Bristol; Canon of Bristol Cathedral.

J.T. J. A. Thompson, B.A., M.Div., Th.M., Ph.D., Research Consultant, American Bible Society.

J.T.W. J. T. Whitney, M.A., L.C.P., Ph.D., Head of Religious Studies, South East Essex Sixth Form College.

J.W.C. J. W. Charley, M.A., Warden of Shrewsbury House and Rector of St Peter's, Everton, Liverpool.

J.W.D. J. W. Drane, M.A., Ph.D., Lecturer in Religious Studies, University of Stirling.

J.W.M. J. W. Meiklejohn, M.B.E., M.A., formerly Secretary of the Inter-School Christian Fellowship in Scotland.

K.A.K. K. A. Kitchen, B.A., Ph.D., Reader in Egyptian and Coptic, University of Liverpool.

K.L.McK. K. L. McKay, B.A., M.A., Reader in Classics, The Australian National University, Canberra.

L.C.A. L. C. Allen, M.A., Ph.D., Lecturer in Old Testament Language and Literature, London Bible College.

L.M. L. L. Morris, M.Sc., M.Th., Ph.D., formerly Principal, Ridley College, Melbourne; Canon of St Paul's Cathedral, Melbourne.

M.A.M. M. A. MacLeod, M.A., Director, Christian Witness to Israel.

M.B. Mrs M. Beeching, B.A., B.D., M.Ed., formerly Principal Lecturer and Head of Department of Divinity, Cheshire College of Education, Alsager.

M.G.K. M. G. Kline, Th.M., Ph.D., Professor of Old Testament, Gordon-Conwell Theological Seminary, South Hamilton, Mass.

M.H.C. M. H. Cressey, M.A., Professor of Systematic Theology and Apologetics, Westminster College, Cambridge.

M.J.S. M. J. Selman, B.A., M.A., Ph.D., Lecturer in Old Testament, Spurgeon's College, London.

M.J.S.R. M. J. S. Rudwick, M.A., Ph.D., Sc.D., Professor of History of Science, The Free University, Amsterdam.

M.R.G. M. R. Gordon, B.D., Principal, Bible Institute of South Africa, Kalk Bay, South Africa.

M.R.W.F. M. R. W. Farrer, M.A., Vicar of St Paul's Church, Cambridge.

M.T.F. M. T. Fermer, B.A., B.Sc., A.R.C.S., Rector of Old Brampton and Loundsley Green, Derbyshire.

N.H. N. Hillyer, B.D., S.Th., A.L.C.D., formerly Librarian, Tyndale House, Cambridge; Vicar of Hatherleigh, Devonshire.

N.H.R. N. H. Ridderbos, D.D., Emeritus Professor of Old Testament, The Free University, Amsterdam.

P.A.B. P. A. Blair, M.A., Rector of Barking, Essex.

P.E. P. Ellingworth, B.A., M.A., Ph.D., Translation Consultant to the United Bible Societies, London.

P.E.H. P. E. Hughes, M.A., B.D., Th.D., D.Litt., Visiting Professor at Westminster Theological Seminary, Philadelphia; Associate Rector of St John's Episcopal Church, Huntingdon Valley, Pennsylvania.

P.H.D. P. H. Davids, B.A., M.Div., Ph.D., Head of Department of Biblical Studies and Language, Trinity Episcopal School for Ministry, Ambridge, Pennsylvania.

P.W. P. Woolley, B.A., Th.M., D.D., Emeritus Professor of Church History, Westminster Theological Seminary, Philadelphia.

R.A.F. R. A. Finlayson, M.A., Emeritus Professor of Systematic Theology, Free Church College, Edinburgh.

R.A.H.G. R. A. H. Gunner, B.A., M.Th., Lecturer in Religious Studies, Brooklands Technical College, Weybridge, Surrey.

R.A.S. R. A. Stewart, M.A., B.D., M.Litt., formerly Church of Scotland Minister.

R.E.N. The late R. E. Nixon, M.A., formerly Principal, St John's College, Nottingham.

R.H.M. R. H. Mounce, B.A., B.D., Th.M., Ph.D., Professor of Religious Studies and Dean of Arts and Humanities, Western Kentucky University.

R.J.A.S. R. J. A. Sheriffs, B.A., B.D., Ph.D., formerly Lecturer in Old Testament, Rhodes University, Grahamstown, Cape Province.

R.J.B. R. J. Bauckham, M.A., Ph.D., Lecturer in the History of Christian Thought, University of Manchester.

R.J.C. The late R. J. Coates, M.A., sometime Warden, Latimer House, Oxford.

R.J.McK. R. J. McKelvey, B.A., M.Th., D.Phil., Principal, The Congregational College, Manchester.

R.J.T. R. J. Thompson, M.A., B.D., Th.M., D.Theol., Principal, New Zealand Baptist Theological College, Auckland.

R.J.W. R. J. Way, M.A., Minister of St Columba's United Reformed Church, Leeds.

R.K.H. R. K. Harrison, M.Th., Ph.D., D.D., Professor of Old Testament, Wycliffe College, University of Toronto.

R.N.C. R. N. Caswell, M.A., Ph.D., Head of Religious Education, The Academical Institution, Coleraine, Northern Ireland.

R.P.G. R. P. Gordon, M.A., Ph.D., Lecturer in Old Testament, University of Cambridge.

R.P.M. R. P. Martin, M.A., Ph.D., Professor of New Testament, Fuller Theological Seminary, Pasadena, California.

R.S.W. R. S. Wallace, M.A., B.Sc., Ph.D., Emeritus Professor, Columbia Theological Seminary, Decatur, Georgia.

R.T.B. R. T. Beckwith, M.A., Warden, Latimer House, Oxford.

R.T.F. R. T. France, M.A., B.D., Ph.D., Warden, Tyndale House, Cambridge.

R.V.G.T. The late R. V. G. Tasker, M.A., D.D., formerly Professor of New Testament Exegesis, University of London.

S.S.S. S. S. Smalley, M.A., B.D., Ph.D., Canon Residentiary and Precentor of Coventry Cathedral.

T.C.M. T. C. Mitchell, M.A., Deputy Keeper, Department of Western Asiatic Antiquities, British Museum.

T.H.J. T. H. Jones, M.A., B.D., A.M.B.I.M., Principal, Hind Leys College, Shepshed, Leicestershire.

W.G.P. W. G. Putman, B.A., B.D., Methodist Minister, High Wycombe, Bucks.

W.H.G. W. H. Gispen, D.Theol., Doctorandus Semitic Languages, Emeritus Professor of Hebrew and Old Testament, The Free University, Amsterdam.

W.J.C. W. J. Cameron, M.A., B.D., Professor of New Testament Language, Literature, Exegesis and Theology, Free Church of Scotland College, Edinburgh.

W.J.M. W. J. Martin, M.A., Th.B., Ph.D., Professor Emeritus, Regent College, Vancouver, BC; formerly Head of the Department of Hebrew and Ancient Semitic Languages, University of Liverpool.

W.O. W. Osborne, M.A., M.Phil., Lecturer in Old Testament, The Bible College of New Zealand.

W.W.W. W. W. Wessel, M.A., Ph.D., Professor of New Testament, Bethel College, St Paul, Minnesota.

Abbreviations

I. Books and Journals

AASOR
Annual of the American Schools of Oriental Research

AB
Anchor Bible

ACA
Sir Moses Finley, *Atlas of Classical Archaeology*, 1977

AfO
Archiv für Orientforschung

AJA
American Journal of Archaeology

AJBA
Australian Journal of Biblical Archaeology

AJSL
American Journal of Semitic Languages and Literatures

AJT
American Journal of Theology

ALUOS
Annual of the Leeds University Oriental Society

ANEP
J. B. Pritchard, *The Ancient Near East in Pictures*, 1954; ^{2}1965

ANET
J. B. Pritchard, *Ancient Near Eastern Texts*, 1950; ^{2}1965; ^{3}1969

ANT
M. R. James, *The Apocryphal New Testament*, 1924

AOTS
D. W. Thomas (ed.), *Archaeology and Old Testament Study*, 1967

ARAB
D. D. Luckenbill, *Ancient Records of Assyria and Babylonia*, 1926

ARE
J. H. Breasted, *Ancient Records of Egypt*, 5 vols., 1906–7

Arndt
W. F. Arndt and F. W. Gingrich, *A Greek–English Lexicon of the New Testament and Other Early Christian Literature*, 1957

ARV
American Revised Version (see ASV)

AS
Anatolian Studies

ASAE
Annales du Service des Antiquités de l'Égypte

ASV
American Standard Version, 1901 (American version of RV)

ATR
Anglican Theological Review

AV
Authorized Version (*King James'*), 1611

BA
Biblical Archaeologist

BANE
G. E. Wright (ed.), *The Bible and the Ancient Near East*, 1961

BASOR
Bulletin of the American Schools of Oriental Research

BC
F. J. Foakes-Jackson and K. Lake, *The Beginnings of Christianity*, 5 vols., 1920–33

BDB
F. Brown, S. R. Driver and C. A. Briggs, *Hebrew and English Lexicon of the Old Testament*, 1906

Bib
Biblica

BibRes
Biblical Research

BIES
Bulletin of the Israel Exploration Society

BJRL
Bulletin of the John Rylands Library

BNTC
Black's New Testament Commentaries

BO
Bibliotheca Orientalis

BRD
W. M. Ramsay, *The Bearing of Recent Discovery on the Trustworthiness of the New Testament*, 1914

BS
Bibliotheca Sacra

BSOAS
Bulletin of the School of Oriental and African Studies

BTh
Biblical Theology

BZ
Biblische Zeitschrift

BZAW
Beiheft, Zeitschrift für die alttestamentliche Wissenschaft

CAH
Cambridge Ancient History, 12 vols., 1923–39; revised ed. 1970–

CB
Century Bible

CBP
W. M. Ramsay, *Cities and Bishoprics of Phrygia*, 1895–7

CBQ
Catholic Biblical Quarterly

CBSC
Cambridge Bible for Schools and Colleges

CD
Qumran Damascus Document

CDC
Cairo Geniza Documents of the Damascus Covenanters

CE
Chronique d'Égypte

CGT
Cambridge Greek Testament

CIG
Corpus Inscriptionum Graecarum

CIL
Corpus Inscriptionum Latinarum

CQ
Classical Quarterly; *Crozer Quarterly*

CRE
W. M. Ramsay, *The Church in the Roman Empire before AD 170*, 1903

CTJ
Calvin Theological Journal

DAC
J. Hastings (ed.), *Dictionary of the Apostolic Church*, 2 vols., 1915–18

DBS
Dictionnaire de la Bible, Supplément, 1928–

DCG
J. Hastings (ed.), *Dictionary of Christ and the Gospels*, 2 vols., 1906–08

DOTT
D. W. Thomas (ed.), *Documents of Old Testament Times*, 1958

EAEHL
M. Avi-Yonah (ed.), *Encyclopaedia of Archaeological Excavations in the Holy Land*, 4 vols., 1975–8

EB
Expositor's Bible

EBi
Encyclopaedia Biblica

EBr
Encyclopaedia Britannica

EBT
J. B. Bauer (ed.), *Encyclopaedia of Biblical Theology*, 3 vols., 1970

EEP
K. Lake, *The Earlier Epistles of St Paul*, 1911

EGT
W. R. Nicoll, *The Expositor's Greek Testament*[6], 1910

EIs
Encyclopaedia of Islam, 1954–

EJ
C. Roth (ed.), *Encyclopaedia Judaica*, 15 vols., 1971

EQ
Evangelical Quarterly

ERE
J. Hastings (ed.), *Encyclopaedia of Religion and Ethics*, 13 vols., 1908–26

ExpT
Expository Times

FRLANT
Forschungen zur Religion und Literatur des Alten und Neuen Testaments

FT
Faith and Thought (formerly *JTVI*)

GB
Ginsburg's Bible (New Masoretico-Critical Text of the Hebrew Bible), 1896

GNB
Good News Bible (= TEV)

GTT
J. Simons, *Geographical and Topographical Texts of the Old Testament*, 1959

HAT
Handbuch zum Alten Testament

HDB
J. Hastings (ed.), *Dictionary of the Bible*, 5 vols., 1898–1904

HES
Harvard Expedition to Samaria, 1924

HHT
J. Lightfoot, *Horae Hebraicae et Talmudicae*, 1658–64

HJ
Hibbert Journal

HJP
E. Schürer, *A History of the Jewish People in the Time of Christ*, 2 vols., E.T. 1885–1901; revised ed., M. Black, G. Vermes and F. Millar (eds.), 3 vols., 1973–

HNT
H. Lietzmann, *Handbuch zum Neuen Testament*

HSS
Harvard Semitic Series

HTKNT
Herders Theologischer Kommentar zum Neuen Testament

HTR
Harvard Theological Review

HUCA
Hebrew Union College Annual

IB
G. A. Buttrick *et al.* (eds.), *Interpreter's Bible*, 12 vols., 1952–7

IBA
D. J. Wiseman, *Illustrations from Biblical Archaeology*, 1958

ICC
International Critical Commentary

IDB
G. A. Buttrick *et al.* (eds.), *The Interpreter's Dictionary of the Bible*, 4 vols., 1962

IDBS
IDB, Supplement vol., 1976

IEJ
Israel Exploration Journal

IG
Inscriptiones Graecae

IGRR
Inscriptiones Graecae ad res Romanas pertinentes

Int
Interpretation

INT
Introduction to the New Testament

IOSCS
International Organization for Septuagint and Cognate Studies

IOT
Introduction to the Old Testament

ISBE
International Standard Bible Enclopaedia, 5 vols., ²1930

JAOS
Journal of the American Oriental Society

JB
Jerusalem Bible, 1966

JBL
Journal of Biblical Literature

JCS
Journal of Cuneiform Studies

JEA
Journal of Egyptian Archaeology

JEH
Journal of Ecclesiastical History

JewE
I. Singer *et al.* (eds.), *Jewish Encyclopaedia*, 12 vols., 1901–06

JHS
Journal of Hellenic Studies

JJS
Journal of Jewish Studies

JNES
Journal of Near Eastern Studies

JNSL
Journal of Northwest Semitic Languages

JPOS
Journal of the Palestine Oriental Society

JQR
Jewish Quarterly Review

JRAS
Journal of the Royal Asiatic Society

JRS
Journal of Roman Studies

JSOT
Journal for the Study of the Old Testament

JSS
Journal of Semitic Studies

JTS
Journal of Theological Studies

JTVI
Journal of the Transactions of the Victoria Institute (now *FT*)

JWH
Journal of World History

KAT
Kommentar zum Alten Testament

KB
L. Köhler and W. Baumgartner, *Hebräisches und aramäisches Lexicon zum Alten Testament*[3], 1967

KEK
H. A. W. Meyer (ed.), *Kritisch-exegetischer Kommentar über das Neue Testament*

KJV
King James' Version (= AV)

LA
Liber Annus (Jerusalem)

LAE
A. Deissmann, *Light from the Ancient East*[4], 1927

LBC
Layman's Bible Commentary

LOB
Y. Aharoni, *The Land of the Bible*, 1967

LOT
S. R. Driver, *Introduction to the Literature of the Old Testament*[9], 1913

LSJ
H. G. Liddell, R. Scott and H. S. Jones, *Greek–English Lexicon*[9], 1940

MM
J. H. Moulton and G. Milligan, *The Vocabulary of the Greek Testament illustrated from the Papyri and other non-literary sources*, 1930

MNTC
Moffatt New Testament Commentary

Moffatt
J. Moffatt, *A New Translation of the Bible*[2], 1936

NASB
New American Standard Bible, 1963

NBC
F. Davidson (ed.), *The New Bible Commentary*, 1953

NBCR
D. Guthrie *et al.* (eds.), *The New Bible Commentary Revised*, 1970

NCB
New Century Bible

NClB
New Clarendon Bible

NEB
New English Bible: NT, 1961; OT, Apocrypha, 1970

Nestle
Nestle's Novum Testamentum Graece[22], 1956

NIC
New International Commentary

NIDNTT
C. Brown (ed.), *The New International Dictionary of New Testament Theology*, 3 vols., 1975–8

NIV
New International Version: NT, 1974; complete Bible, 1978

NLC
New London Commentary

NovT
Novum Testamentum

NTD
Das Neue Testament Deutsch

NTS
New Testament Studies

OCD
M. Cary *et al.* (eds.), *The Oxford Classical Dictionary*, 1949

ODCC
F. L. Cross and E. A. Livingstone (eds.), *The Oxford Dictionary of the Christian Church*[2], 1974

Or
Orientalia

OTL
Old Testament Library

OTMS
H. H. Rowley (ed.), *The Old Testament and Modern Study*, 1951

OTS
Oudtestamentische Studiën

Pauly-Wissowa
See *RE*

PEQ
Palestine Exploration Quarterly

PG
J. P. Migne, *Patrologia Graeca*

Phillips
J. B. Phillips, *The New Testament in Modern English*, 1958; revised ed. 1972

PJB
Palästina-Jahrbuch

PL
J. P. Migne, *Patrologia Latina*

POTT
D. J. Wiseman (ed.), *Peoples of Old Testament Times*, 1973

P.Oxy.
Papyrus Oxyrhynchus

PRU
Le Palais Royal d'Ugarit

PTR
Princeton Theological Review

RA
Revue d'Assyriologie

RAC
T. Klausner *et al.* (eds.), *Reallexicon für die Antike und Christentum*, 1941–

RAr
Revue d'Archéologie

RB
Revue Biblique

RE
A. F. Pauly, G. Wissowa *et al.* (eds.), *Real-Encyclopädie der klassischen Altertumwissenschaft*, 1893–

RGG
K. Galling (ed.), *Die Religion in Geschichte und Gegenwart*[3], 7 vols., 1957–65

RHR
Revue de l'Histoire des Religions

RQ
Revue de Qumran

RSV
Revised Standard Version: NT, 1946; OT, 1952; *Common Bible*, 1973

RTR
Reformed Theological Review (Australia)

RV
Revised Version: NT, 1881; OT, 1885

SB
H. L. Strack and P. Billerbeck, *Kommentar zum Neuen Testament aus Talmud und Midrasch*, 6 vols., 1926–61

SBL
Society of Biblical Literature

SBT
Studies in Biblical Theology

Schürer See *HJP*

SHERK
The New Schaff-Herzog Encyclopaedia of Religious Knowledge[2], 1949–52

SIG
W. Dittenberger (ed.), *Sylloge Inscriptionum Graecarum*, 1915–24

SJT
Scottish Journal of Theology

SP
Samaritan Pentateuch

SPEM
G. S. Duncan, *St Paul's Ephesian Ministry*, 1929

SPT
W. M. Ramsay, *St Paul the Traveller and Roman Citizen*[4], 1920

ST
Studia Theologica

Strack-Billerbeck See *SB*

TB
Babylonian Talmud

TBC
Torch Bible Commentary

TCERK
The Twentieth Century Encyclopaedia of Religious Knowledge, 1955

TDNT
G. Kittell and G. Friedrich (eds.), *Theologisches Wörterbuch zum Neuen Testament*, 1932–74; E.T. *Theological Dictionary of the New Testament*, ed. G. W. Bromiley, 10 vols., 1964–76

TDOT
G. J. Botterweck and H. Ringgren (eds.), *Theologisches Wörterbuch zum Alten Testament*, 1970– ; E.T. *Theological Dictionary of the Old Testament*, trans. by J. T. Willis, 1974–

TEV
Today's English Version[4], 1976 (= GNB)

Th
Theology

THAT
E. Jenni and C. Westermann (eds.), *Theologisches Handwörterbuch zum Alten Testament*, 2 vols., 1971–6

THB
Tyndale House Bulletin (now *TynB*)

Them
Themelios

ThL
Theologische Literaturzeitung

THNT
Theologische Handbuch zum Neuen Testament

TJ
Jerusalem Talmud

TNT
Translators' New Testament (Bible Society)

TNTC
Tyndale New Testament Commentary

TOTC
Tyndale Old Testament Commentary

TR
Theologische Rundschau

TS
Texts and Studies

TSFB
Theological Students' Fellowship Bulletin

TU
Texte und Untersuchungen zur Geschichte der altchristlichen Literatur

TWBR
A. Richardson (ed.), *A Theological Word Book of the Bible*, 1950

TynB
Tyndale Bulletin (formerly *THB*)

TZ
Theologisches Zeitung

VC
Vigiliae Christianae

VT
Vetus Testamentum

VT Supp.
Vetus Testamentum, Supplementary vol.

UF
Ugarit-Forschungen: Internationales Jahrbuch für die Altertumskunde Syrien-Palästinas

WC
Westminster Commentary

WDB
Westminster Dictionary of the Bible, 1944

Wett.
J. J. Wettstein, *Novum Testamentum Graecum* 1751–2

Weymouth
R. F. Weymouth, *The New Testament in Modern Speech*, 1903

WH
B. F. Westcott and F. J. A. Hort, *The New Testament in Greek*, 1881

WTJ
Westminster Theological Journal

ZA
Zeitschrift für Assyriologie

ZAW
Zeitschrift für die alttestamentliche Wissenschaft

ZDMG
Zeitschrift der deutschen morgenländischen Gesellschaft

ZDPV
Zeitschrift des deutschen Palästina-Vereins

ZNW
Zeitschrift für die neutestamentliche Wissenschaft

ZPEB
M. C. Tenney (ed.), *The Zondervan Pictorial Encyclopaedia of the Bible*, 5 vols., 1975

ZTK
Zeitschrift für Theologie und Kirche

Editions are indicated by small superior figures: *LOT*[9]

II. Classical Works

ad Fam.
Cicero, *Epistulae ad Familiares*

Adv. Haer.
Irenaeus, *Adversus Haereses*

Ann.
Tacitus, *Annales*

Ant.
Josephus, *Antiquities of the Jews*

Apol.
Justin Martyr, *Apologia*
Tertullian, *Apologia*

BJ
Josephus, *Jewish Wars*

Clem. Recog.
Rufinus, *Clementine Recognitions*

Contra Pelag.
Jerome, *Contra Pelagium*

Eccles. Hist.
Sozomen, *History of the Church*

EH
Eusebius, *Ecclesiastical History*

Epig.
Martial, *Epigrammaticus Latinus*

Ep. Mor.
Seneca, *Epistulae Morales ad Lucilium*

Eus.
Eusebius

Ev. Petr.
Gospel of Peter (apocryphal)

Exc. Theod.
Clement of Alexandria, *Excerpta ex Theodoto*

Geog.
Ptolemy, *Geography*; Strabo, *Geography*

Hist.
Dio Cassius, *History*; Tacitus, *History*

Hypot.
Clement of Alexandria, *Hypotyposes*

Il.
Homer, *Iliad*

Iul.
Suetonius, *C. Julius Caesar* (*Lives of the Caesars*)

In Verr.
Cicero, *In Verrem Actio*

Jos.
Josephus

Juv.
Juvenal

Lk. Hom.
Origen, *Homily on Luke*

Magn.
Ignatius, *Magnesians*

NH
Pliny, *Natural History*

Od.
Horace, *Odes*

Onom.
Eusebius, *Onomasticon de Locis Hebraicis*

Philad.
Ignatius, *Philadelphians*

Praep. Ev.
Eusebius, *Praeparatio Evangelica*

Quaest.
Seneca, *Quaestiones Naturales*

Sat.
Juvenal, *Satires*; Persius, *Satires*

Strom.
Clement of Alexandria, *Stromateis*

Trall.
Ignatius, *Trallians*

Vesp.
Suetonius, *Vespasian* (*Lives of the Caesars*)

Vit. Mos.
Philo, *De Vita Mosis* (*Life of Moses*)

III. Biblical Books

Books of the Old Testament
Gn., Ex., Lv., Nu., Dt., Jos., Jdg., Ru., 1, 2 Sa., 1, 2 Ki., 1, 2 Ch., Ezr., Ne., Est., Jb., Ps. (Pss.), Pr., Ec., Ct., Is., Je., La., Ezk., Dn., Ho., Joel, Am., Ob., Jon., Mi., Na., Hab., Zp., Hg., Zc., Mal.

Books of the New Testament
Mt., Mk., Lk., Jn., Acts, Rom., 1, 2 Cor., Gal., Eph., Phil., Col., 1, 2 Thes., 1, 2 Tim., Tit., Phm., Heb., Jas., 1, 2 Pet., 1, 2, 3 Jn., Jude, Rev.

IV. General Abbreviations

ad loc.	*ad locum* (Lat.), at the place
Akkad.	Akkadian
Apoc.	Apocrypha(l)
Aq.	Aquila's Gk. tr. of OT, *c.* AD 140
Arab.	Arabic
Aram.	Aramaic
Assyr.	Assyrian
b.	*bar/ben* (Aram./Heb.), son of
Bab.	Babylonian
BM	British Museum
c.	*circa* (Lat.), about, approximately
ch.(chs.)	chapter(s)
cf.	*confer* (Lat.), compare
Copt.	Coptic
D	Deuteronomist
DSS	Dead Sea Scrolls
E	East, eastern; Elohist
eccl. Lat.	ecclesiastical Latin
Ecclus.	Ecclesiasticus (Apoc.)
ed. (eds.)	edited by, edition, editor(s)
Egyp.	Egyptian
Eng.	English
E.T.	English translation
et al.	*et alii* (Lat.), and others
Eth.	Ethiopic
EVV	English versions
f. (ff.)	and the following (verse(s), *etc.*)
fig.	figuratively
Ger.	German
Gk.	Greek
H	Law of Holiness
Heb.	Hebrew
ibid.	*ibidem* (Lat.), the same work
idem	*idem* (Lat.), the same author
J	Yahwist
Lat.	Latin
lit.	literally
L.L.	Late Latin
loc. cit.	*loco citato* (Lat.), in the place already quoted
LXX	Septuagint (Gk. version of OT)
Macc.	Maccabees (Apoc.)
mg.	margin
mod.	modern
MS (MSS)	manuscript(s)
MT	Massoretic text
N	North, northern
n.f.	*neue Folge* (Ger.), new series
n.s.	new series
NT	New Testament
OE	Old English
OL	Old Latin
op.cit.	*opere citato* (Lat.), in the work cited above
OT	Old Testament
P	Priestly Narrative
par.	and parallel(s)
Pent.	Pentateuch
Pesh	Peshitta
Phoen.	Phoenician
pl.	plate (illustration)
Q	*Quelle* (Ger.), source thought to be behind sayings of Jesus common to Lk. and Mk.
q.v.	*quod vide* (Lat.), which see
R.	Rabbi
Rom.	Roman
S	South, southern
Sem.	Semitic
Suppl.	supplementary volume
s.v.	*sub verbo* (Lat.), under the word
Symm.	Symmachus' Gk. tr. of OT, 2nd century AD
Syr.	Syriac
Targ.	Targum
Theod.	Theodotion's Gk. tr. of OT, 2nd century AD
TR	Textus Receptus
tr.	translated, translation
Turk.	Turkish
v. (vv.)	verse(s)
v.l.	*varia lectio* (Lat.), variant reading
vol.	volume
vss	versions
Vulg.	Vulgate
W	West, western

GOLIATH. A *giant of Gath serving in the Philistine army (1 Sa. 17:4), Goliath may have descended from that remnant of the Rephaim which, after having been scattered by the Ammonites (Dt. 2:20–21; 2 Sa. 21:22), took refuge with the Philistines. For discussion of his origin, see G. A. Wainwright, 'Early Philistine History', *VT* 9, 1959, pp. 79f. His height is given as 'six cubits and a span', *i.e.* 3·2 m, if the cubit is understood as 52·5 cm (*WEIGHTS AND MEASURES). That this, though unusual, is not an impossible phenomenon, is confirmed by the discovery in Palestine of human skeletons of similar stature and of roughly the same period.

Goliath was slain by *David at Ephes-dammim in a duel whose religious character is attested by 1 Sa. 17:43, 45; and perhaps also by the Philistines' flight, if this is directly attributed to their conviction that the God of Israel had triumphed over their god (*cf.* 2 Sa. 23:9–12, 1 Ch. 11:12ff.). Goliath's sword, which had been kept in the sanctuary at Nob, was given by the priest Ahimelech to David when the latter was fleeing from Saul to the king of Gath, for whom the weapon was likely to be an acceptable present.

Two later appearances of the name have puzzled scholars. Elhanan is recorded as having slain '(the brother of) Goliath the Gittite'—so AV of 2 Sa. 21:19, and again (without parentheses) in 1 Ch. 20:5, where the victim's name is given as Lahmi. It may be that *Elhanan was David's original name. On the other hand, some have suggested that this second Goliath could have been the son of David's adversary. For full discussion of the problem and possible emendation, see S. R. Driver, *Notes on the Hebrew Text of the Books of Samuel*, 1913; and E. J. Young, *IOT*, 1949, pp. 181f. J.D.D.

GOMER (*gōmer*, 'completion'). **1.** The eldest son of Japheth and the father of Ashkenaz, Riphath and Togarmah (Gn. 10:2–3). In Ezk. 38 the people of Gomer are closely associated with the house of Togarmah in the army of Gog, and are probably to be identified with the ancient Gimirrai (Cimmerians), an Aryan group who conquered Urarṭu (Armenia) from their Ukrainian homeland some time before the 8th cent. BC, when they appear as enemies of Assyria.

2. The daughter of Diblaim and wife of *Hosea (Ho. 1:3). She bore Jezreel, Lo-ruhamah and Lo-ammi (Ho. 1). G.W.G.

GOOD. The Hebrew word is *ṭôḇ* ('pleasant', 'joyful', 'agreeable'), signifying primarily that which gratifies the senses and derivatively that which gives aesthetic or moral satisfaction. The LXX renders *ṭôḇ* by *agathos*, the regular Greek word for good as a physical or moral quality, and sometimes by *kalos* (lit. 'beautiful'; hence, in classical as well as biblical Greek, 'noble', 'honourable', 'admirable', 'worthy'). The NT reproduces this usage, employing the two adjectives interchangeably (*cf.*, *e.g.*, Rom. 7:12–21). Paul, following the LXX, uses the noun *agathosynē* for the Christian's goodness, with the accent especially on his beneficence (Rom. 15:14; Gal. 5:22; Eph. 5:9; 2 Thess. 1:11, *etc.*, for the translation, see the commentaries). He also uses *chrēstotēs* ('goodness', AV, RV; 'kindness', RSV) for the merciful beneficence of God (Rom. 2:4; 11:22).

The common element of meaning in the many applications which the word 'good' has in every language is that of approbation, either for inherent value, or for beneficent effect, or both. There is nothing distinctive about the various non-moral senses in which the Bible speaks of things as 'good' (*e.g.* 'useful', as salt, Mt. 5:13; Lk. 14:34; 'of high quality', as gold, Gn. 2:12, or cattle, Gn. 41:26; 'productive', as trees, Mt. 7:17, ground, Lk. 8:8; *etc.*). But the biblical concept of moral and spiritual good is thoroughly theological, and stands in sharp contrast with the anthropocentric view of goodness developed by the Greeks and later thinkers in the Greek tradition. This biblical view may be analysed as follows.

a. God is good: for he is morally perfect, and gloriously generous.

The acknowledgment of God as good is the foundation of all biblical thinking about moral goodness. 'Good' in Scripture is not an abstract quality, nor is it a secular human ideal; 'good' means first and foremost what God is ('he is *good*', Ps. 100:5, *et al.*), then what he does, creates, commands and gives, and finally what he approves in the lives of his creatures. It is not that the biblical writers assess God in terms of a prior concept of goodness, but rather that, contemplating the supreme glory of God's perfections, they apply to him the ordinary word for acknowledging worth. By so doing, however, they give that word a new depth of meaning. They define good in terms of God; not vice versa. Accordingly, the biblical position is that God, and God alone, is good without qualification (Mk. 10:18 and parallels: on which see B. B. Warfield, *The Person and Work of Christ*, 1950, pp. 149ff.); and he is the arbiter and judge, as he is the norm and standard, of creaturely goodness. Man is good, and things are good, just so far as they con-

GOMORRAH
See Plain, cities of the, Part 3.

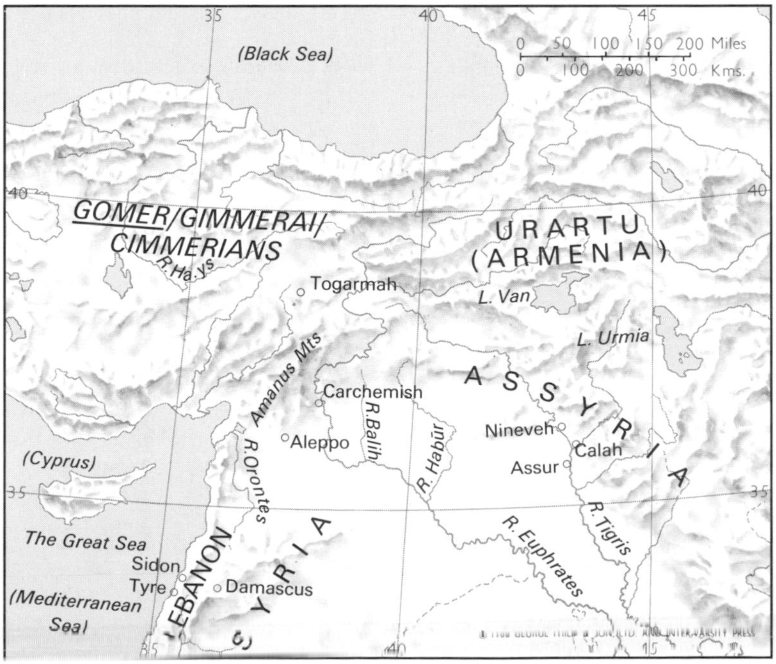

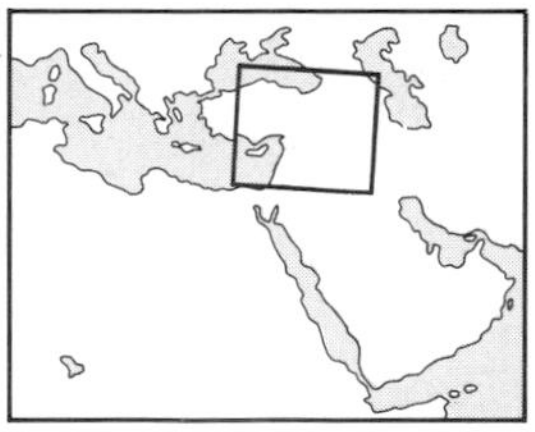

The region occupied by Gomer, known also as Gimirrai, the territory of the 'Cimmerians'.

GOOSE
See Animals, Part 1.

Opposite page: Base of a colossal statue of Rameses II from the site of Pi-Ramessē (Qantir) probably in 'the land of Goshen'. c. 1290–1224 BC. (AAI)

form to the will of God. Woe, then, to those who invert the divine scale of values, giving the name of good to what God calls evil, and vice versa (Is. 5:20).

In the OT the goodness of God is frequently invoked as a theme of praise and an argument in prayer (*cf.* 2 Ch. 30:18; Ps. 86:5). His goodness appears in the good that he does (Ps. 119:68), the beneficent activity of his good spirit (Ne. 9:20; Ps. 143:10), the many-sidedness of his cosmic generosity (Ps. 145:9); most notably, in his kindness to the needy and faithfulness to his covenant (Pss. 25:8; 73:1; La. 3:25; Na. 1:7). The Psalmists' reiterated exhortation to praise and give thanks to God, 'for he is good: for his steadfast love endures for ever' (Pss. 106:1; 107:1; 118:1; 136:1; *cf.* 100:4f.; also 1 Ch. 16:34; 2 Ch. 5:13; 7:3), is quoted by Jeremiah as the characteristic motto theme of Israel's worship (Je. 33:11).

b. The works of God are good: for they reveal his attributes of wisdom and power (see Ps. 104:24–31), and are the objects of his own approval.

When creation was done, 'God saw every thing that he had made, and behold, it was very good' (Gn. 1:31, *cf.* vv. 4, 10, 12, 18, 21, 25). The whole material order, as such, being God's handiwork, is good (1 Tim. 4:4; *cf.* Rom. 14:14). There is no room for Manichaean dualism in the Bible.

c. The gifts of God are good: for they express his generosity, and make for the welfare of their recipients.

'Beneficial', 'advantageous', is one of the standard secular meanings of 'good' as an adjective; as 'prosperity', 'well-being', is of 'good' as a noun. The Bible integrates this usage into its theology by teaching, not merely that all God's gifts are good, both in intention and in effect, but also that all good is in fact God's gift (Jas. 1:17; *cf.* Ps. 4:6). It is characteristic of God to do good to the needy, as it was of Jesus, God's anointed (Acts 10:38; Mk. 3:4). God does good to all men in his ordinary providence, showering on them the blessings of nature (Acts 14:17; Ps. 145:9; Lk. 6:35); and, as a perfect Father, he knows how to give good gifts to those who are his children through Christ (Mt. 7:11). God's promise to 'do good' to his people is a comprehensive promise of blessing (Je. 32:40, *cf.* 24:6f.), as the plea that God will 'do good' to them is a comprehensive prayer for it (Pss. 51:18; 125:4). In such passages the 'good' in question is the pledged blessing of the covenant; it is virtually 'salvation' (*cf.* Is. 52:7). 'Good' on the material level was the promised blessing of the old covenant (with 'evil', the state of blessing withdrawn, as its alternative: Dt. 30:15), and 'good' in the realm of spiritual privilege, 'good' not enjoyed under the old covenant, is the gift of the new (Heb. 9:11; 10:1). Both testaments, however, authorize God's faithful people to rest assured that in God's good time everything that is truly good for them will be made theirs (Pss. 84:11; 34:10, *cf.* 85:12; Rom. 8:32; Eph. 1:3).

'Good', as an adjective, is used in various instrumental senses in connection with God's gracious activity of doing good to men. It is used of the word of God that announces blessing, of the hand and work of God that conveys it, of the course of action that leads to enjoyment of it, and of the days in which that enjoyment is experienced (see 1 Ki. 8:56; Is. 39:8; Je. 29:10; Heb. 6:5; Ezr. 7:9; 8:18; Phil. 1:6; 1 Ki. 8:36; Je. 6:16; Ps. 73:28; 1 Pet. 3:10; *cf.* Ps. 34:12).

Even when God withdraws the 'good' of outward prosperity from his people and brings upon them 'evil' (hardship) in its place (*cf.* Jb. 2:10), there is still a sense in which he is doing them good. 'It is good' for a man to be thus afflicted; hereby he receives correction, for his own subsequent benefit (*cf.* Heb. 12:10), and is exercised and strengthened in faith, patience and obedience (Ps. 119:67, 71; *cf.* La. 3:26f.). Anything that drives a man closer to God is for his good, and the Christian's temporary distresses, under God, work for him an eternal weight of glory (2 Cor. 4:17). Paul is therefore fully entitled to insist that 'in *everything* (afflictions included) God works for good with those who love him' (Rom. 8:28). The Christian should regard every circumstance, however ungratifying, as among God's good gifts to him, the expression of a beneficent purpose and, if rightly used, a sure means to his lasting profit.

d. The commands of God are good: for they express the moral perfection of his character and, by showing us how to please him, mark out for us the path of blessing (Ps. 119:39; Rom. 7:12; 12:2).

The moral ideal in the Bible is to do the will of God, as revealed in his law. When the rich ruler asked Christ what good thing he should do to gain life, Christ immediately directed him to the Decalogue (Mt. 19:17ff.). In a lawless and unloving world, Christians must resist the temptation to do as they are done by, and in face of evil must seek out and hold fast in their conduct that 'good' which the law prescribes (Rom. 12:9, 21; 1 Thes. 5:15, 21).

e. Obedience to God's commands is good: for God approves and accepts it (1 Tim. 2:3), and those who yield it profit by it (Tit. 3:8).

Unredeemed men do not and cannot obey God's law, for they are in bondage 'under sin' (Rom. 3:9ff.; 8:7f.). The evil tree (man as he is in Adam) must be made good before its fruit can be good (*cf.* Mt. 12:33–35). But those who are in Christ have been freed from sin's bondage precisely in order that they may practise the righteousness which the law prescribes (Rom. 6:12–22). The characteristic NT phrase for this obligatory Christian obedience is 'good works'. The performance of good works is to be the Christian's life's work; it was for this that God saved him (Eph. 2:10; Col. 1:10; 2 Cor. 9:8; Tit. 2:14; Mt. 5:14–16). The Christian is called to be ready for every good work that his circumstances admit of (2 Tim. 2:21; Tit. 3:1), so that it is a damning indictment of a man's Christian profession when he is 'unfit for any good deed' (Tit. 1:16; *cf.* Jas. 2:14–26). Good works are the Christian's adornment (1 Tim. 2:10); God takes pleasure in them, and will reward them (Eph. 6:8).

Good works are good from three standpoints: they are done (i) in accordance with a right standard (the biblical law: 2 Tim. 3:16f.); (ii) from a right motive (love and gratitude for redemption: 1 Thes. 1:3; Heb. 6:10; *cf.* Rom. 12:1ff.); (iii) with a right aim (God's glory: 1 Cor. 10:31; *cf.* 1 Cor. 6:20; Mt. 5:16; 1 Pet. 2:12). They take the form of works of love towards God and men, since 'love is the fulfilling of the law' (Rom. 13:8–10; *cf.* Mt. 22:36–40). This does not, of course, mean that no more is required of a Christian than a right motive; the point is, rather, that the particular acts which the commandments prescribe are to be understood as so many expressions of love, so that without a loving heart the commandments cannot be fulfilled. It is not that a right spirit excuses lapses from the letter of the law, but that

rectitude in the letter is no fulfilling of the law where an attitude of love is lacking. The truly good man is no less than the truly righteous man; for, as the truly righteous man observes the spirit as well as the letter of the law (*cf.* Mt. 5:18–20), so the truly good man observes its letter as well as its spirit. Nor is the truly good man any more than the truly righteous man. In Rom. 5:7, where Paul for a moment sets the good man above the righteous man in value, he is speaking popularly, not theologically. The world thinks of righteousness as a merely negative rectitude, and of the kindness and generosity that mark the good man as something more than righteousness; but biblical theology effectively identifies righteousness with goodness, and goodness with righteousness, by insisting that what the law requires is, in fact, love.

Good works, then, are works of love, and the nature of love is to give to the beloved. Love to God is expressed in the gift of personal devotion, however costly (*cf.* Mary's 'good work', Mk. 14:3–6). Love to men is expressed by doing them 'good', laying out one's own resources to relieve their need, and seeking their welfare in every possible way (Gal. 6:9f.; Eph. 4:29; *cf.* Pss. 34:14; 37:3, 27). The Jerusalem church's poor-relief system (Acts 2:44f.; 4:34ff.), and Paul's collection for the saints (*cf.* 2 Cor. 7–9) illustrate this. 'Kind', 'generous' are among the ordinary secular meanings of 'good' as a description of persons (*cf.* 1 Sa. 25:15; 1 Pet. 2:18); the Bible comprehends them in the Christian ethic, making the love of God and Christ the model and standard for the kindness and generosity required of Christians (*cf.* Eph. 5:1f.; Jn. 13:14, 34).

The believer who seeks thus to fulfil the law has a 'good conscience' (Acts 23:1; 1 Tim. 1:5, 19; Heb. 13:18; 1 Pet. 3:16, 21)—not because he thinks himself sinlessly perfect, but because he knows that his relationship with God is right, being founded on true faith and repentance. Such a Christian will appear to his fellows as a 'good man' (so Barnabas, Acts 11:24).

BIBLIOGRAPHY. Arndt, *s.v. agathos, kalos*; E. Beyreuther, *NIDNTT* 2, pp. 98–107; G. Vos in *DAC*, 2, 470f.; C. F. H. Henry, *Christian Personal Ethics*, 1957, pp. 209–218. J.I.P.

GOPHER WOOD (Heb. *ʿᵃṣê-gōp̄er*), the wood of which Noah's ark was constructed (Gn. 6:14). Many commentators favour an identification with cypress wood, on the ground of the similarity in name (Gk. *kyparissos*). Others, noting the similarity with Heb. *kōp̄er* (*BITUMEN), suggest a resinous *tree. It may be that the word is connected in some way with Akkad. *gubru/gudru*, '(shepherd's) reed hut', and such a cuneiform parallel is further suggested by the construct *ʿᵃṣê* which might correspond to the determinative *giš*, which precedes the names of trees and objects of wood, and which is read *iṣu* or *iṣ* in Akkadian. See *The Chicago Assyrian Dictionary*, 5, 1956, p. 118. T.C.M.

GOSHEN. 1. The territory assigned to Israel and his descendants during their Egyp. sojourn.

Cupressus sempervirens, *a cypress tree, possibly the biblical gopher, from which Noah built the ark.* (FNH)

Top left: The cones of Cupressus sempervirens. (FNH)

Excavation in progress at a 'Canaanite' mortuary temple (No. II) at Tell el Dab'a in Goshen, Egypt. This may illustrate Semitic occupation in the patriarchal age. Middle Bronze Age, c. 1650 BC. (AAI)

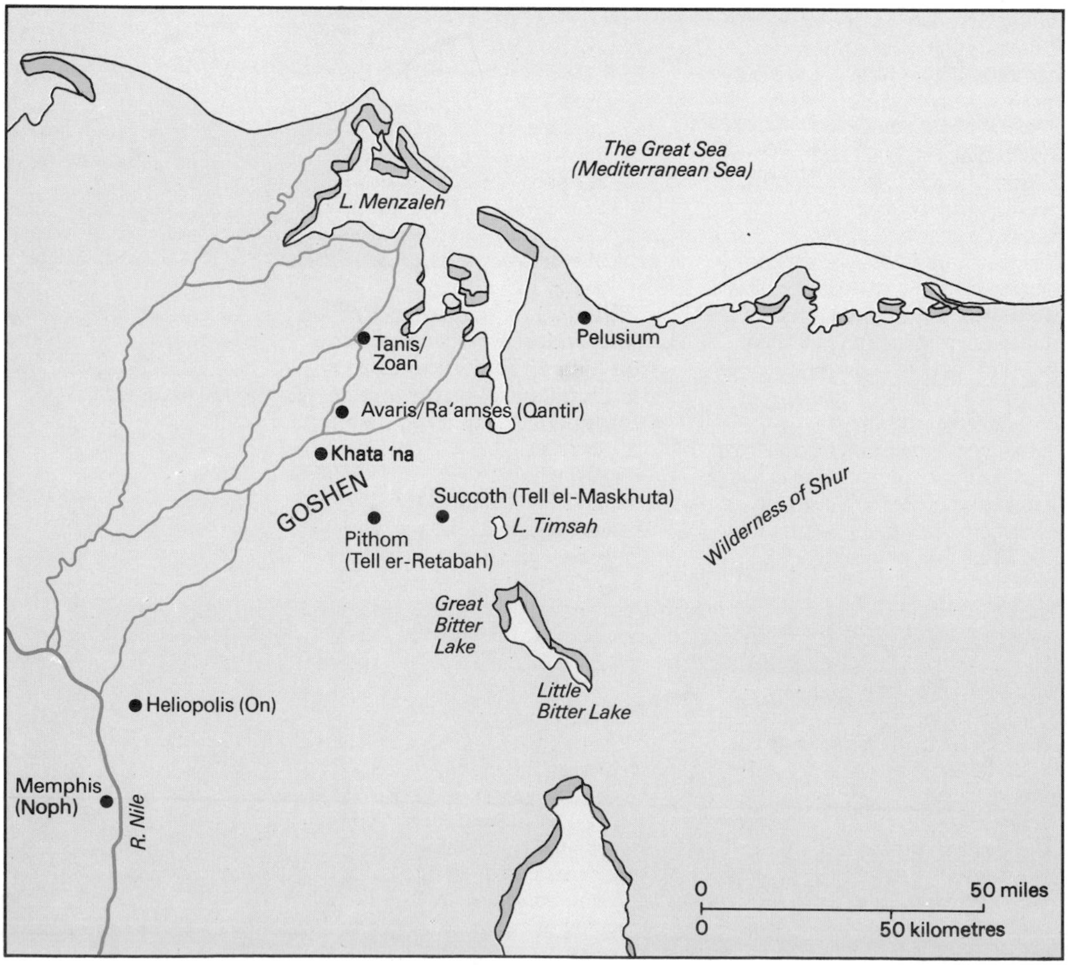

Goshen and the delta area of the river Nile.

Its exact location and extent remain uncertain, but it was certainly in Egypt (Gn. 47:6, 27), and in the E Nile Delta: Gn. 47:6 with 11 clearly equate Goshen with 'the land of Rameses', so named from the residence-city Pi-Ramessē, biblical *Ra'amses, in the NE Delta. The LXX's topographical interpretations are of uncertain authenticity. The E Delta would be suitably 'near' the court (Gn. 45:10) for Joseph serving his (probably Hyksos) pharaoh at *Memphis (near Cairo) or Avaris (NE Delta), *cf.* also Gn. 46:28–29; likewise for Moses interviewing his pharaoh at Pi-Ramessē (Ex. 7–12). Goshen was a well-favoured region suited to flocks and herds (Gn. 46:34; 47:1, 4, 6, 27; 50:8). It remained the habitat of the Hebrews until the Exodus, being therefore largely shielded from the plagues (Ex. 8:22; 9:26); nevertheless, contact was close with Egyptians living in the same general region (*e.g. cf.* Ex. 11:2–3; 12:35–36). The name *Gsmt* occurring in certain Egyp. texts, once equated with Heb. Goshen through LXX Gesem, should be read *Šsmt* and is therefore irrelevant.

2. A district in the S of Palestine (Jos. 10:41; 11:16), probably named after **3,** a town in the hills of S Palestine (Jos. 15:51), possibly near

Ẕāhiriyeh, *c.* 19 km SW of Hebron (so Abel) or else somewhat farther E (*GTT*, 1959, §§ 285–287, 497). (*GEDER.) K.A.K.

GOSPEL (Gk. *euangelion*, 'good news'). In classical literature the word designated the reward given for good tidings. It also indicated the message itself, originally the announcement of victory, but later applied to other messages bringing joy. That it is found more than 75 times in the NT indicates a distinctly Christian connotation. The gospel is the good news that God in Jesus Christ has fulfilled his promises to Israel, and that a way of salvation has been opened to all. The gospel is not to be set over against the OT as if God had changed his way of dealing with man, but is the fulfilment of OT promise (Mt. 11:2–5). Jesus himself saw in the prophecies of Isaiah a description of his own ministry (Lk. 4:16–21).

Mark defines the 'gospel of God' in 1:14 (AV, following the Byzantine text, adds 'of the kingdom') as 'The time is fulfilled, and the kingdom of God is at hand'. To believe means salvation: to reject is damnation (Mk. 16:15–16). This same gospel is proclaimed by the first heralds of Christianity, but now the essential message is made more explicit by the death and resurrection of Jesus the Christ. While the gospel came with Jesus (the Christ-event *is* the gospel), it was anticipated in God's promise of blessing to Abraham (Gal. 3:8) and promised in prophetic Scripture (Rom. 1:2).

The gospel not only comes in power (1 Thes. 1:5) but *is* the power of God (Rom. 1:16). It reveals the righteousness of God and leads to salvation all who believe (Rom. 1:16–17). Paul regards the gospel as a sacred trust (1 Tim. 1:11). Thus he is under divine compulsion to proclaim it (1 Cor. 9:16), and requests prayer that he may carry out his task with boldness (Eph. 6:19), even though this involves opposition (1 Thes. 2:2) and affliction (2 Tim. 1:8). The gospel is 'the word of truth' (Eph. 1:13), but it is hidden to unbelieving men (2 Cor. 4:3–4) who demand supernatural verification or rational proof (1 Cor. 1:21–23). Even as it was by revelation that the full theological impact of the gospel came to Paul (Gal. 1:11–12), so also it is by the response of faith that the gospel comes with saving power (Heb. 4:2).

The use of 'Gospels' as a designation of the first four books of the NT is post-biblical (2nd cent. AD).

BIBLIOGRAPHY. U. Becker, *NIDNTT* 2, pp. 107–115; C. H. Dodd, *The Apostolic Preaching and its Developments*, 1936; R. H. Mounce, *The Essential Nature of New Testament Preaching*, 1960; G. Friedrich in *TDNT* 2, pp. 705–735. R.H.M.

GOSPELS. The plural form 'Gospels' (Gk. *euangelia*) would not have been understood in the apostolic age, nor yet for two generations following; it is of the essence of the apostolic witness that there is only one true *euangelion*; whoever proclaims another, says Paul, is anathema (Gal. 1:8f.). The four records which traditionally stand in the forefront of the NT are, properly speaking, four records of the one gospel—'the gospel of God . . . concerning his Son' (Rom. 1:1–3). It was not until the middle of the 2nd century AD that the plural form came to be used; thus Justin Martyr says that the 'memoirs composed by the apostles' are called 'Gospels' (*First Apology* 66). Earlier writers use the singular, whether they are referring to a single gospel-writing or to a set of such writings (*cf. Didache* 8. 2; Ignatius, *Philadelphians* 8. 2). The traditional titles of the four records imply that in them we have the gospel or good news about Christ according to each of the four Evangelists. And the usage of the singular form to denote the fourfold record continued for long after the earliest attested instance of the plural.

I. The oral stage

Most of the material in our Gospels existed for a considerable time in an oral stage before it was given the written form with which we are familiar.

a. The words of Jesus

Jesus began his Galilean ministry by 'preaching the gospel of God'; the content of this gospel was that the time appointed had arrived and the kingdom of God had drawn near; he urged his hearers to repent and believe the good news (Mk. 1:14f.; *cf.* Lk. 4:18–21). His preaching was no bolt from the blue; it was the fulfilment of the promise of God communicated in earlier days through the prophets. Now, at length, God had visited his people; this was the burden not only of Jesus' preaching but of his mighty works (Lk. 7:16), which were signs that the domain of evil was crumbling before the onset of the kingdom of God (Mt. 12:22–29; Lk. 11:14–22). The same theme runs through the parables of Jesus, which call his hearers to decision and watchfulness in view of the advent of the kingdom.

In addition to his public ministry, Jesus took care to give his disciples systematic instruction in a form that they could easily commit to memory. His debates with the Pharisees and other opponents, too, led to pronouncements which, once heard, would not be readily forgotten, and which in fact stood his disciples in good stead later on when they were confronted with controversial issues in which it was helpful to recall their Master's ruling.

b. The apostolic tradition

There are several references in the NT Epistles to the 'tradition' (Gk. *paradosis*) received by the apostles from their Lord and delivered by them in turn to their converts. This tradition, in the fullest sense, comprises the apostles' witness to 'all that Jesus began to do and teach, until the day when he was taken up' (Acts 1:1f., *cf.* 1:21f.). This witness was borne and perpetuated in various ways—principally in missionary preaching, in the teaching of converts and in Christian worship. An outline of the basic facts of the missionary preaching is given by Paul in 1 Cor. 15:3ff.—'that Christ died for our sins in accordance with the scriptures, that he was buried, that he was raised on the third day in accordance with the scriptures, and that he appeared' to a large number of eyewitnesses, some of whom are named, and most of whom were still alive when Paul was writing. Paul adds that whether the gospel was preached by himself or by the original apostles, the basic facts of the message were the same (1 Cor. 15:11). This is confirmed by the evidence of the non-Pauline Epistles, and by the extracts from early Christian preaching summarized in Acts. In the preaching the saving events were announced; Jesus was proclaimed as Lord and Christ; men were summoned to repent and receive forgiveness through him.

Some occasional samples of the teaching of converts appear in the Epistles, from which it is plain that

Opposite page: The Gospels were among the first works of literature to be written in books with pages (codices) rather than scrolls. The last three verses of Luke and the beginning of John (1:1–16) from a 144-page papyrus codex copied early in the 3rd cent. AD are shown here. Bodmer Papyrus XIV–XV. (FMB)

the basis of this teaching was what Jesus himself had taught. Thus, in giving instruction about marriage Paul quotes Jesus' commandment forbidding divorce (1 Cor. 7:10), and similarly quotes his ruling about the maintenance of gospel preachers (1 Cor. 9:14). But there is evidence of more systematic instruction by the catechetical method; and as the number of converts increased, especially in the course of the Gentile mission, 'schools' for the training of instructors would have become almost a necessity, and digests of the teaching of Jesus would inevitably have been drawn up, orally if not in writing. We may envisage such a life-setting for the 'sayings collection' on which Matthew and Luke drew, and at a later date the Matthaean Gospel itself has been viewed as taking shape in such a school; *cf.* K. Stendahl, *The School of St Matthew*², 1968.

In worship too the works and words of Jesus were bound to be recalled. In the earliest days of the faith those who had known Jesus could scarcely avoid saying to one another, when they met informally or at the stated occasions of fellowship and worship, 'Do you remember how our Master . . . ?' In particular, the Lord's Supper provided a regular opportunity for retelling the story of his death, with the events immediately preceding and following it (1 Cor. 11:26).

The passion narrative, indeed, being told and retold both in Christian worship and in missionary preaching (*cf.* 1 Cor. 2:2; Gal. 3:1), took shape as a connected whole at an early date—a conclusion which is otherwise established by the form criticism of our existing Gospels. By the form-critical method an attempt is made to isolate and classify the various self-contained units which have been brought together in the written Gospels and to envisage the living situations in which they originated and were preserved in the oral stage of transmission. (* BIBLICAL CRITICISM, III.)

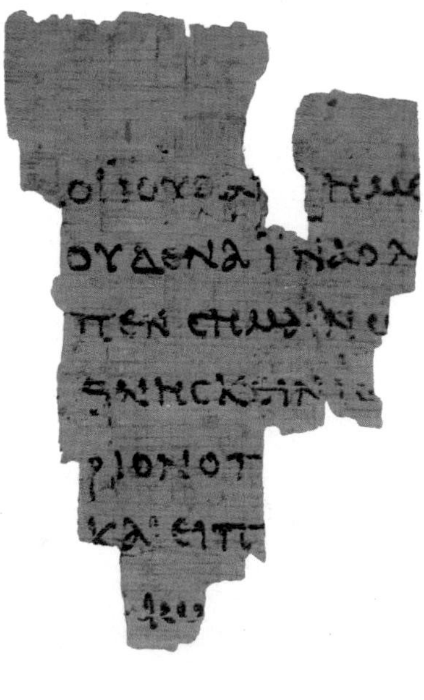

The earliest extant copy of any New Testament book, part of a papyrus page from John's Gospel (18:31–33). Greek script of c. AD 125–150. (JR)

II. The written Gospels

The beginning of gospel writing, as we might expect, coincides with the end of the first Christian generation. As those who 'from the beginning were eyewitnesses and ministers of the word' (Lk. 1:2) were removed by death, the necessity of a permanent written record of their witness would be more acutely felt than before. It is just at this point that 2nd-century tradition places the beginnings of gospel writing, and rightly so: all four of our canonical Gospels are probably to be dated within the four decades AD 60–100. We need not suppose that the transmission of the apostolic witness had been exclusively oral before AD 60—some at least of the 'many' who, according to Lk. 1:1, had undertaken to draw up an orderly account of the evangelic events may have done so in writing before AD 60—but no document of an earlier date has survived except in so far as it has been incorporated in our written Gospels.

Several strands of tradition can be distinguished in the four Gospels. In this respect, as in some others, John stands apart from the other Gospels and is best considered independently. The other three Gospels are inter-related to the point where they lend themselves excellently to 'synoptic' study—*e.g.* as when their text is arranged in three parallel columns, so that their coincidences and divergences can be conveniently examined. For this reason they are commonly known as the 'Synoptic Gospels'—a designation apparently first given to them by J. J. Griesbach in 1774.

a. The Synoptic Gospels

A comparative study of Matthew, Mark and Luke leads to the recognition that there is a considerable body of material common to all three, or to two of the three. The substance of 606 out of the 661 verses of Mark (leaving Mk. 16:9–20 out of the reckoning) reappears in abridged form in Matthew; some 380 of the 661 verses of Mark reappear in Luke. This may be stated otherwise by saying that, out of the 1,068 verses of Matthew, about 500 contain the substance of 606 verses of Mark, while out of the 1,149 verses of Luke some 380 are paralleled in Mark. Only 31 verses of Mark have no parallel in either Matthew or Luke. Matthew and Luke have each up to 250 verses containing common material not paralleled in Mark; sometimes this common material appears in Matthew and Luke in practically identical language, while sometimes the verbal divergence is considerable. About 300 verses of Matthew have no parallel in any of the other Gospels; the same is true of about 520 verses in Luke.

There is no short cut to a satisfactory account of this distribution of common and special material in the Synoptic Gospels. There is no *a priori* reason for holding one Gospel to be earlier and another later, for holding one to be a source of another and the latter to be dependent on the former. Nor will the objectivity of statistical analysis guarantee a solution. A solution can be attained only by the exercise of critical judgment after all the relevant data have been marshalled and the alternative possibilities assessed. If unanimity has not been reached after a century and a half of intensive Synoptic study, it may be because the data are insufficient for the purpose, or because the field of inquiry has been unduly restricted. Yet certain findings command a much greater area of agreement than others.

One of these is the priority of Mark and its use as a principal source by the other two Synoptic Evangelists. This finding, which is commonly said to have been placed on a stable basis by C. Lachmann in 1835, depends not merely on the formal evidence that Matthew and Mark sometimes agree in order against Luke; Mark and Luke more frequently against Matthew; but Matthew and Luke never against Mark (which could be explained otherwise), but rather on the detailed comparative examination of the way in which common material is reproduced in the three Gospels, section by section. In the overwhelming majority of sections the situation can best be understood if Mark's account was used as a source by one or both of the others. Few have ever considered Luke as a possible source of the other two, but the view that Mark is an abridgment of Matthew was held for a long time, largely through the influence of Augustine. But where Matthew and Mark have material in common Mark is fuller than Matthew, and by no means an abridgment; and time after time the two parallel accounts can be much better explained by supposing that Matthew condenses Mark than by supposing that Mark amplifies Matthew. While Matthew and Luke never agree in order against Mark, they do occasionally exhibit verbal agreement against him, but such instances mainly represent grammatical or stylistic improvements of Mark, and are neither numerous nor significant enough to be offset against the general weight of the evidence for Mark's priority.

The common Marcan element in the Synoptic tradition is the more important because of the close relation between the framework of Mark and the apostolic preaching. This relation does not depend so much on the tradition which sees in Peter the authority behind the Marcan narrative (a tradition borne out by internal evidence in certain sections of the narrative) as on the fact (demonstrated by C. H. Dodd) that an outline of the primitive preaching, comparable to those outlines which can be discerned in a few passages in the NT Epistles and in the reports of speeches in Acts, supplies the thread on which Mark has strung his several units of gospel material.

The material common to Mark and one or both of the other Synoptic Gospels consists mainly of narrative. (The principal exceptions to this are the parables of Mk. 4 and the eschatological discourse of Mk. 13.) On the other hand, the non-Marcan material common to Matthew and Luke consists mainly of sayings of Jesus. One might almost say that the Marcan material relates what Jesus did; the non-Marcan material, what Jesus taught. We have here a distinction comparable to that commonly made (albeit to an exaggerated degree) between apostolic 'preaching' (*kērygma*) and 'teaching' (*didachē*). The non-Marcan material common to Matthew and Luke may conveniently, and without prejudice, be labelled 'Q', in accordance with a custom dating from the beginning of the 20th century.

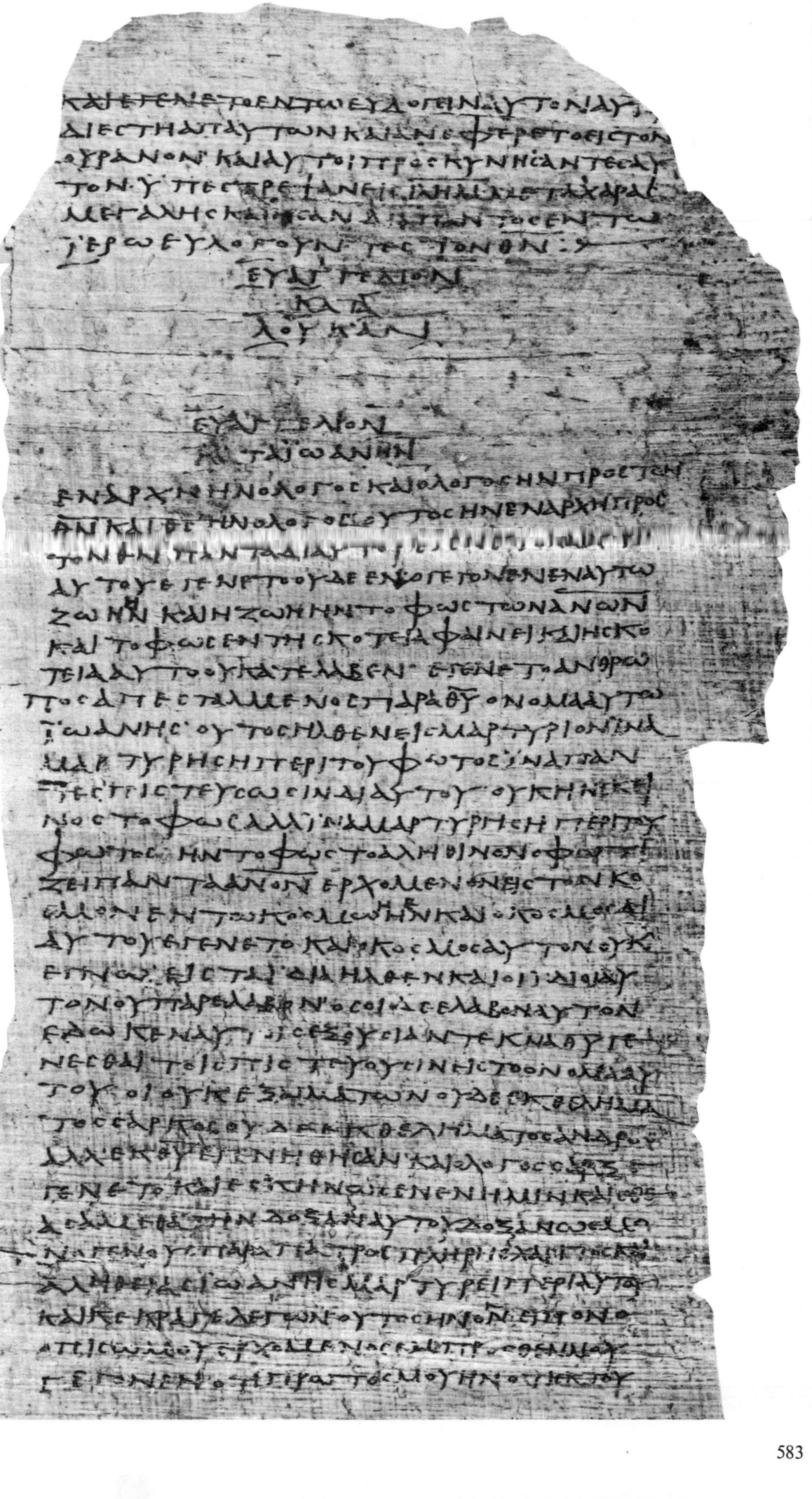

This body of material, extending to between 200 and 250 verses, might have been derived by the one Evangelist from the other, or by both from a common source. Few, if any, can be found to suggest that Matthew derived it from Luke, although some would find it easier to suppose this than to suppose that Luke derived it from Matthew. This latter supposition continues to receive widespread support, but it is specially vulnerable because it implies that Luke reduced to relative disorder the orderly arrangement in which the 'Q' material appears in Matthew, without giving any plausible reason why this should have been done.

The supposition that the 'Q' material was derived from a common source by Matthew and Luke involves fewer difficulties than any alternative supposition.

When we attempt to reconstruct this postulated common source we must beware of thinking that we can do so in anything like a complete form. Yet what we can reconstruct of it reminds us forcibly of the general pattern of the prophetical books of the OT. These books commonly contain an account of the prophet's call, with a record of his oracles set in a narrative framework, but with no mention of his death. So the 'Q' material appears to have come from a compilation which began with an account of Jesus' baptism by John and his wilderness temptations; this forms the prelude to his ministry, and is followed by groups of his sayings set in a minimum of narrative framework; but there is no trace of a passion narrative. There are four main groups of teaching, which may be entitled: (i) Jesus and John the Baptist; (ii) Jesus and his disciples; (iii) Jesus and his opponents; (iv) Jesus and the future.

Since our only means of reconstructing this source is provided by the non-Marcan material common to Matthew and Luke, the question whether Mark also made some use of it cannot be satisfactorily answered. That it is earlier than Mark is probable; it may well have been used for catechetical purposes in the Gentile mission based on Antioch. The fact that some of the 'Q' material in Matthew and Luke is almost verbally identical, while elsewhere there are divergences of language, has sometimes been explained in terms of there being two distinct strands of tradition in 'Q', but a much more probable account is that 'Q' was translated into Greek from Aramaic and that Matthew and Luke sometimes use the same translation and sometimes different ones. In this regard it is apposite to recall the statement of Papias (*apud* Eus., *EH* 3. 39) that 'Matthew compiled the *logia* in the Hebrew [Aramaic] speech, and everyone translated them as best he could'. *Logia* ('oracles') would be a specially appropriate term for the contents of such a compilation as we have tried to recognize behind the 'Q' material.

What other sources were utilized by Matthew and Luke is an even more uncertain question than the reconstruction of the 'Q' source. Matthew appears to have incorporated material from another sayings-collection, parallel to 'Q' but preserved in Judaea rather than in Antioch—the collection conveniently labelled 'M'. Luke has embodied a block of quite distinctive material (found largely between chs. 9 and 18) which may have been derived from Caesarea—the material labelled 'L'. Whether these 'sources' had a written form before they were taken over by the Evangelists is doubtful. Luke has been pictured as amplifying his copy of the 'Q' source by means of the information acquired in Caesarea and elsewhere, thus producing the preliminary draft of his Gospel sometimes called 'Proto-Luke', into which at a later date blocks of Marcan material were inserted. For an evaluation of the 'Proto-Luke' hypothesis see D. Guthrie, *New Testament Introduction*[3], 1970, pp. 175–183. In general, it may be agreed that Matthew conflates his sources while Luke combines his. The nativity narratives which introduce Matthew and Luke lie outside the general scheme of Synoptic criticism; with regard to them some dependence on Semitic documents cannot be excluded. But it must be emphasized that, fascinating and instructive as Gospel source criticism is, the Gospels themselves are much more important than their putative sources. It is good to consider what sources the Evangelists may have used; it is better to consider what use they made of their sources. In recent years it has been increasingly recognized that redaction criticism has as important a place in Gospel study as tradition criticism—the latter tracing the history of the traditions which in due course the Evangelists received, the former concentrating on the contribution of the individual Evangelists in their treatment and presentation of the traditions. Each of the Synoptic Gospels is an independent whole, no mere scissors-and-paste compilation; each has its own view of Jesus and his ministry, and each has its special contribution to make to the full-orbed picture of Jesus with which the NT presents us.

b. The Fourth Gospel

John represents a good primitive tradition which was preserved independently of the Synoptic lines of tradition, not only in the memory of the beloved disciple but in a living Christian community, quite probably in the milieu from which at a rather later date came the *Odes of Solomon*. The large area of common background which John shares with the Qumran texts, and the links binding its structure to the Palestinian synagogue lectionary, have in recent times helped to impress upon us that the Johannine tradition has its roots in Jewish Palestine, however much the requirements of a wider Hellenistic audience were borne in mind when this Gospel was given its literary form at the end of the first Christian century. And the fixed outline of the apostolic preaching can be discerned in the Fourth Gospel 'no less clearly than in Mark' (C. H. Dodd, *The Apostolic Preaching and its Developments*, 1950, p. 69). (*JOHN, GOSPEL OF.)

III. The fourfold Gospel

At an early date after the publication of the Fourth Gospel the four canonical Gospels began to circulate as a collection, and have continued to do so ever since. Who first gathered them together to form a fourfold corpus we do not know, and it is quite uncertain where the fourfold corpus first became known—claims have been made for both Ephesus and Rome. Catholic and Gnostic writers alike show not only acquaintance with the fourfold Gospel but recognition of its authority. The Valentinian *Gospel of Truth* (*c.* AD 140–150), recently brought to light among the Gnostic writings from *Chenoboskion, was not intended to supplement or supersede the canonical four, whose authority it presupposes; it is rather a series of meditations on the 'true gospel' which is enshrined in the four (and in other NT books). Marcion stands out as an exception in his repudiation of

Matthew, Mark and John, and his promulgation of Luke (edited by himself) as the only authentic *euangelion*. The documents of the anti-Marcionite reaction (*e.g.* the anti-Marcionite prologues to the Gospels and, later, the Muratorian Canon) do not introduce the fourfold Gospel as something new, but reaffirm its authority in reply to Marcion's criticisms.

In the half-century following AD 95 Theodor Zahn could find only four Gospel citations in surviving Christian literature which demonstrably do not come from the canonical four. That the 'memoirs of the apostles' which Justin says were read in church along with the writings of the prophets were the four Gospels is rendered the more probable by the fact that such traces of gospel material in his works as may come from the pseudonymous *Gospel of Peter* or *Gospel of Thomas* are slight indeed compared with traces of the canonical four.

The situation is clearer when we come to Justin's disciple Tatian, whose Gospel harmony or *Diatessaron* (compiled *c.* AD 170) remained for long the favourite (if not the 'authorized') edition of the Gospels in the Assyr. church. Apart from a small fragment of a Gk. edition of the *Diatessaron* discovered at Dura-Europos on the Euphrates and published in 1935, our knowledge of the work has until recently been indirect, being based on translations (some of them secondary or tertiary) from the Syr. text. But in 1957 a considerable portion of the Syr. original of Ephraem's commentary on the *Diatessaron* (written about the middle of the 4th century) was identified in a parchment manuscript in A. Chester Beatty's collection; this text was edited with a Latin translation by L. Leloir in 1963 and throws valuable light on the early history of the *Diatessaron*.

Tatian began his compilation with Jn. 1:1–5, and perhaps ended it with Jn. 21:25. It was the fourfold Gospel that supplied him with the material for his harmony; such occasional intrusions of extra-canonical material as can be detected (possibly from the *Gospel according to the Hebrews*) do not affect this basic fact any more than do the occasional modifications of the Gospel wording which reflect Tatian's Encratite outlook. (*CANON OF THE NEW TESTAMENT.)

The supremacy of the fourfold Gospel which Tatian's work attests is confirmed a decade or so later by Irenaeus. To him the fourfold character of the Gospel is one of the accepted facts of Christianity, as axiomatic as the four quarters of the world or the four winds of heaven (*Adv. Haer*. 3. 11. 8). His contemporary Clement of Alexandria is careful to distinguish 'the four Gospels that have been handed down to us' from uncanonical writings on which he draws from time to time, such as the *Gospel according to the Egyptians* (*Miscellanies* 3. 13). Tertullian does not even draw upon such uncanonical writings, restricting himself to the canonical four, to which he accords unique authority because their authors were either apostles or men in close association with apostles. (Like other western Christian writers, he arranges the four so as to make the two 'apostolic' Gospels, Matthew and John, precede Luke and Mark.) Origen (*c.* AD 230) sums up the long-established catholic attitude when he speaks of 'the four Gospels, which alone are undisputed in the church of God beneath the whole heaven' (*Commentary on Matthew* in Eus., *EH* 6. 25. 4). (Like Irenaeus, Origen arranges them in the order with which we are familiar.)

All four of the Gospels are anonymous in the sense that none of them includes its author's name. The first reference to Matthew and Mark as Evangelists is found in Papias, bishop of Hierapolis in Phrygia in the first half of the 2nd century AD. His statement, made on the authority of 'the elder', that 'Mark, the interpreter of Peter, wrote down accurately all the words or deeds of the Lord of which he [Peter] made mention, but not in order . . .', is certainly a reference to our second Gospel. His statement about Matthew's compilation of *logia* (quoted above, under **II**) is more problematic, and it is still disputed whether it refers to our first Gospel, or to a collection of the sayings of Jesus (as has been suggested in this article), or to a catena of Messianic prophecies, or to something else. The earliest explicit references to Luke and John as Evangelists come in the anti-Marcionite Gospel prologues (which to some extent at least draw upon Papias's lost work) and Irenaeus. The latter sums up the account which he had received as follows: 'Matthew put forth a Gospel writing among the Hebrews in their own speech while Peter and Paul were preaching the gospel in Rome and founding the church there. After their departure, Mark, Peter's disciple and interpreter, has likewise delivered to us in writing the substance of Peter's preaching. Luke, the companion of Paul, set down in a book the gospel proclaimed by that apostle. Then John, the disciple of the Lord, who reclined on his bosom, in turn published his Gospel while he was staying in Ephesus in Asia' (*Adv. Haer*. 3. 1. 1).

Without endorsing all that Irenaeus says, we may heartily agree that in the canonical Gospels we have the apostolic witness to the redemptive revelation of God in Christ preserved in a fourfold form. (See articles on the four Gospels.)

BIBLIOGRAPHY. K. Aland and others, *Studia Evangelica*, 1959; C. H. Dodd, *The Apostolic Preaching and its Developments*, 1936; *idem*, *History and the Gospel*, 1938; W. R. Farmer, *The Synoptic Problem*, 1976; T. W. Manson, *The Sayings of Jesus*, 1949; *idem*, *Studies in the Gospels and Epistles*, 1961; D. E. Nineham (ed.), *Studies in the Gospels*, 1955; B. Orchard and T. R. W. Longstaff (eds.), *J. J. Griesbach: Synoptic and Text-critical Studies*, 1978; N. Perrin, *Rediscovering the Teaching of Jesus*, 1967; J. Rohde, *Rediscovering the Teaching of the Evangelists*, 1968; J. H. Ropes, *The Synoptic Gospels*, 1934; W. Sanday, *The Gospels in the Second Century*, 1876; B. de Solages, *A Greek Synopsis of the Gospels*, 1959; V. H. Stanton, *The Gospels as Historical Documents*, 3 vols., 1903–20; B. H. Streeter, *The Four Gospels*, 1924; V. Taylor, *The Gospels*[9], 1960; *idem*, *The Formation of the Gospel Tradition*, 1933.

F.F.B.

GOSPELS, APOCRYPHAL

See New Testament apocrypha, Part 2.

GOVERNMENT.

a. In the Old Testament.

During the OT period the people of God lived under various types of government. The Patriarchs might be called semi-nomads. The father was the head of the family and its priest. His jurisdiction extended not only over the members of the immediate family but also over all who were in his employ or subject to him. This type of government was similar to that of the bedouin nomads of Arabia. In the head of the family (*i.e.* of the clan) there resided even the power of life and death as well as that of making various decisions (*cf.* Jdg. 11:11ff.).

In Egypt the descendants of Jacob were in bondage until they were brought forth from the land by Moses. Moses acted as the representative of God, and the people listened to him. At this time also there were officers of the people, although it is difficult to say just how the Israelites were organized in relationship to Egypt. The organization of Sinai was unique in that it consisted in the formation of the tribes into a theocracy (*i.e.* 'the rule of God'—*theos*, 'god'; *kratos*, 'power', 'rule'). The essence of this type of government is set forth by divine revelation in Ex. 19:5–6. Primarily it was a rule of God over a nation that was to be holy and a kingdom of priests.

In the wilderness there were elders of the people who assisted Moses in his tasks. The plan of the theocracy was presented to them and they accepted it. God was to rule and he would rule through the agency of a human judge or king. This man should 'reign in righteousness', in that he should give decisions in accordance with strict justice and manifest in his rule the righteousness of God. The people were to be separate from the rest of the world, for they were holy, belonging unto God himself.

For a time the nation was not ready to accept the full implications of the theocracy. Under Joshua it was necessary that they should obtain possession of the land that had been promised to them. For a time there were rulers or judges over them, but there was no central organization. This condition led them to realize that they must have a king. Their request for a king, however, was made in an untheocratic spirit, for they merely wanted to be like the nations round about them. For this reason Samuel reproached them with having rejected Yahweh himself (1 Sa. 8:7).

The nation therefore needed not merely to learn that it must have a king but also that it must have the right kind of king. The first king chosen was a man who did not follow Yahweh, and for that reason was rejected. In David there was found the man after God's own heart. David rendered the decisions of a more important kind, but minor decisions were left to under-officers. Some of these officers are mentioned in the Scriptures, *e.g.* the priests, officers of the household, the cup-bearer, the officer in charge of the palace (1 Ki. 4:6), scribes, recorders, counsellors, chief of the army and chief of the king's guard (2 Sa. 8:18). The ministers of the king served in the administration of the affairs of the state (1 Ki. 4:2ff.).

Solomon divided the kingdom into twelve districts, over each of which he placed a prefect to provide victuals for the king and his house (1 Ki. 4:7ff.). The Exile brought about an interruption of the theocracy, which had long before ceased to be a theocracy in actual fact. After the Exile the Jews were subject to Persia, and Judaea was reconstituted as a temple-state, with the high priest at its head. The Persian king was represented by a provincial governor, who might occasionally be himself a Jew (*e.g.* Nehemiah). This same arrangement continued under the Greek period, although at this time a council of elders is introduced. The Temple constitution was abolished by Antiochus IV in 168 BC, but restored by the Hasmonaeans who, however, combined the high-priesthood and the civil and military sovereignty in their own family. Their secular power was terminated by the Roman conquest of 63 BC but (except for the special circumstances of the rule of Herod the Great and Archelaus) the high priest was recognized by the Romans as head of the internal Jewish administration.

The central point of the theocracy was the Temple, which symbolized the dwelling-place of God in the midst of his people. Thus, Jerusalem, the city in which the Temple was located, became known as the holy city. The formal destruction of the theocracy occurred when the Temple was burned in AD 70.

E.J.Y.
F.F.B.

b. In the New Testament.

I. The situation in Palestine

The land was largely partitioned among a number of republican states (*e.g.* Caesarea and the cities of the Decapolis). This was a device used by the successive supervisory powers, and especially the Romans, to hellenize the population and thus contain Jewish nationalism. The less tractable areas (*e.g.* Galilee) were entrusted to Herodian princes, while Jerusalem itself and its neighbourhood were under the Sanhedrin, a council drawn from the religious aristocracy. The whole complex of governments was supervised in the interests of Roman frontier security by the Caesars, acting at different stages either through a Herodian client king or through a personal deputy, the prefect or procurator. Jewish nationalism found institutional expression in a series of religious sects, whose attitudes to the government ranged from terrorism (the Zealots) to detachment (the Essenes), on the one hand, and collaboration (the Sadducees), on the other. All were dedicated in their own way to the restoration of the kingdom.

a. The career of Jesus

Jesus was inextricably involved in this confusion of government. He was attacked at birth (Mt. 2:16) as a threat to Herod's throne, and denounced in death as a pretender to royal power (Jn. 19:21). He was dogged on all sides by pressures to avow this goal. The devil's advances (Mt. 4:9) were mirrored in popular enthusiasm (Jn. 6:15), the obtuse arrogance of the disciples (Mt. 16:22f.) and the fears of those who precipitated the arrest (Jn. 11:50). Faced with such a consensus of misconstruction, Jesus generally avoided the claim to kingship, but did not conceal it from the disciples (Lk. 22:29–30) and in the end owned it publicly (Jn. 18:36–37).

b. The teaching of Jesus

Three main assertions about the relation of the kingdom of heaven to temporal government may be singled out. (i) The kingdom of Jesus is not of the same order as the temporal powers. It is not established by political action (Jn. 18:36). (ii) Temporal power is not autonomous: it is enjoyed only by permission of God (Jn. 19:11). (iii) The temporal power therefore has its rights, as does God (Lk. 20:25): both must be conceded.

c. The church in Jerusalem

After the resurrection the disciples were again instructed in the nature of the kingdom (Acts 1:3). Their view of it was still narrowly political, however (Acts 1:6), and even after the ascension the preaching of Jesus' exaltation at God's right hand (*e.g.* Acts 2:32–36) was capable of political overtones (Acts 5:31), and certainly taken as politically provocative by the Sanhedrin (Acts 5:33ff.). The apostles defied a court order restraining their preaching on the grounds of their prior duty to God (Acts 5:29). The prosecution of Peter and James (Acts 12:2–3) may have been political, but in the cases of Stephen (Acts 6:11) and Paul (Acts 21:28) the offences were religious, and reflect the transformation of the Nazarenes into a regular sect of the Jewish religion, differentiated perhaps chiefly by the added sanction that the kingship of Jesus had lent to the law (Jas. 2:5, 8).

II. The Hellenistic states

All the places outside Palestine where churches were established were, along with Rome itself, republican states, either satellites of the Romans or actual Roman colonies. Christians might thus become involved either with the local administration (*e.g.* Acts 16:19–21; 17:6, 22) or with the superintendent Roman governors (*e.g.* Acts 13:7; 18:12). The tendency to refer difficult cases to the Roman authority, however, meant that the attitude of that government became the major concern.

a. Support for the government

The only case where Christians were accused of direct opposition to the Caesars (Acts 17:7) was fobbed off by the authorities responsible. In all other known cases the charges were not political, and the various governments showed a reluctance to pursue them. Christian writers reciprocated this respectful *laissez-faire* (Rom. 13:1–7; 1 Tim. 2:2; Tit. 3:1): the teaching of Jesus was elaborated to show that the 'governing authorities' (*exousiai*) not only had their authority allowed by God but that they were positively 'ministers of God' for the punishment of evil; to oppose them was to oppose God. This attitude was sustained even (as happened under Nero) when the courts were being used for fabricated charges; the legitimacy of government was studiously defended, while its victims were solaced with the innocent sufferings of Christ (1 Pet. 2:11–25). Some have held that the restrainer of antichrist (2 Thes. 2:6–8) is meant to be the Roman government.

b. Criticism of the government

Even Paul had some reservations, however. The responsibility for the crucifixion rests on 'the rulers of this age' (1 Cor. 2:8). Saints must not settle their disputes in civil courts, because their destiny is to 'judge the world' (1 Cor. 6:2). Attention is repeatedly drawn to the rule of the 'only Sovereign, the King of kings' (1 Tim. 6:15), and the citizenship of the republic that transcends all the barriers of earthly states (*e.g.* Eph 2:19). The demonic powers (*archai* or *exousiai*) over whom Christ has triumphed (Col. 2:15) and with whom we now struggle (Eph. 6:12) may well be conceived of as the forces behind human government. This is certainly the theme taken up in detail in the Revelation, which envisages a struggle for world government between God and satanic powers. The allusions to the ruler cult (Rev. 13:15) seem sufficiently plain to identify the enemy as the Roman Caesars. We know from Pliny (*Ep.* 10. 96) that attempts to induce Christians to escape condemnation by making the formal offering to the ruler met with incorrigible obstinacy. They had unmistakably decided that they were being asked to render to Caesar the things that were God's.

BIBLIOGRAPHY. A. H. M. Jones, *The Greek City from Alexander to Justinian*, 1940; A. N. Sherwin-White, *Roman Society and Roman Law in the New Testament*, 1963; O. Cullmann, *The State in the New Testament*, 1957; E. A. Judge, *The Social Pattern of the Christian Groups in the First Century*, 1960; M. Avi-Yonah, *The Holy Land from the Persian to the Arab Conquest; a Historical Geography*, 1966; D. R. Griffiths, *The New Testament and the Roman State*, 1970; A. Richardson, *The Political Christ*, 1973; E. M. Smallwood, *The Jews under Roman Rule*, 1976.

E.A.J.

GOVERNOR.

I. In the Old Testament

Since Israel through her history was involved directly or indirectly with various civilizations, each of which had its own distinctive constitutional system and titles for those in authority, it is not surprising to find a variety of Hebrew terms, and of English translations in RSV, *e.g.* 'governor', 'ruler', 'captain'. They may be classed as follows.

a. Technical words

Of these Heb. *peḥâ* (*cf.* Assyr. *paḫatu*) is the most frequent, meaning the ruler of a district under a king, *e.g.* an Assyrian provincial governor (Is. 36:9), Chaldean and Persian governors (Ezk. 23:6, 23; Est. 3:12; 8:9), the Persian Tattenai (Ezr. 5:3; 6:6), whose satrapy included Palestine, Phoenicia and Egypt; and Nehemiah and Zerubbabel as governors of Judah (Ne. 5:14; Ezr. 6:7). The latter are also called 'Tirshatha' (Ezr. 2:63; Ne. 7:65, 70), the Heb. form of a Persian title (from Avestan *tarshta*, 'reverenced').

b. General words

Nine other Heb. terms indicate authority in various spheres. *'allûp̄* (*e.g.* Zc. 9:7, of governors of Judah), *môšēl* (Gn. 45:26, of Joseph in Egypt) and *šallîṭ* (Gn. 42:6, also of Joseph) are wider terms; the others have more particular references: *pāqîḏ* ('overseer', Je. 20:1, of a priest; *cf.* Gn. 41:34, of Egyptian officers), *ḥôqēq* (of lawgivers, Jdg. 5:9, 14), *sāḡān* ('deputy', 'lieutenant', *e.g.* Dn. 3:2, not 'governors'), *nāśî'* (indicating social rank, 2 Ch. 1:2), *śar* ('governor of a city', 1 Ki. 22:26) and *nāḡîḏ* ('commander of a palace', 2 Ch. 28:7).

II. In the New Testament

Fewer Gk. words are used, and these sometimes imprecisely, sometimes with technical accuracy.

a. hēgoumai ('lead') and its derivatives occur most frequently. The term *hēgemōn* is used for governors in the general sense (Mk. 13:9; 1 Pet. 2:14) but more often describes Roman subordinate rulers, such as Pilate (Mt. 27:2; 28:14), Felix (Acts 23:26) and Festus (Acts 26:30), who were 'procurators' (or, in the case of Pilate, 'prefect') under the legate of the province Syria (the official Gk. equivalent was *epitropoi*).

b. Other terms appear at Jn. 2:8 (*architriklinos*, 'steward of the feast'), 2 Cor. 11:32 (*ethnarchēs*, *'ethnarch'), Gal. 4:2 (*oikonomos*, RSV 'trustees', *cf.* Lk. 12:42; 1 Cor. 4:2) and Jas. 3:4 (*euthynōn*, 'pilot').

B.F.H.

Coin of Felix (*AD 59*), *who was the governor* (procurator) *of Judaea AD 52–59, before whom Paul was brought for trial at Caesarea* (*Acts 23:23–24*). *Enlarged.* (BM)

GOVERNMENT, DIVINE
See Justice, Part 2.

GOVERNOR OF THE FEAST
See Marriage, Part 2.

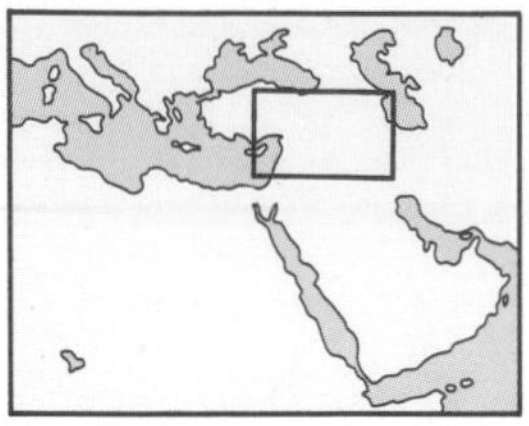

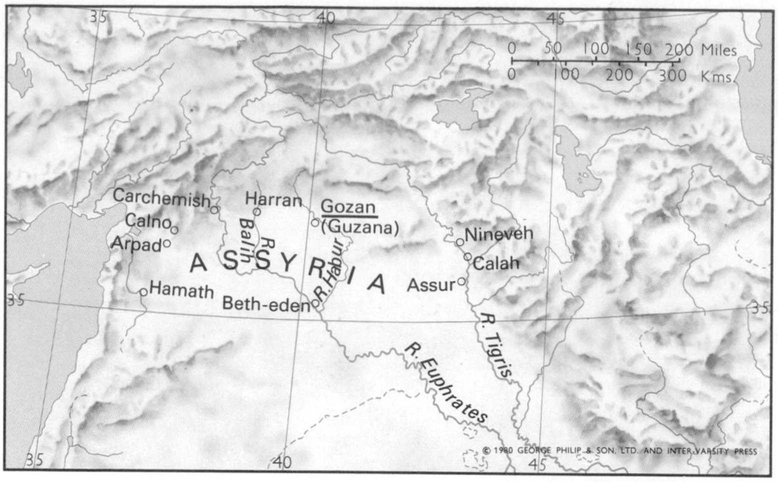

The location of Gozan.

Cavalryman with shield and sword. Relief from the palace at Gozan. Height 58 cm. 9th cent. BC. (BM)

GOZAN is identified with ancient Guzana, modern Tell Halaf, on the Upper Habur river. Israelites from Samaria were deported here in 722 BC (2 Ki. 17:6; 18:11). Sennacherib, in his letter to Hezekiah (2 Ki. 19:12 = Is. 37:12), refers to the heavy punishment inflicted on this Assyr. provincial capital when it rebelled in 759 BC. Excavations in 1899, 1911–13 and 1927 (M. von Oppenheim, *Tell Halaf*, 1933) produced tablets of the 8th–7th centuries BC, in which W Semitic names may attest, or explain, the presence of the Israelite exiles (*AfO* Beiheft 6).   D.J.W.

GRACE, FAVOUR.

I. In the Old Testament

a. Vocabulary

Grace involves such other subjects as forgiveness, salvation, regeneration, repentance and the love of God. 'There are "grace-words" which do not contain the word "grace" ' (Moffatt); see Dt. 7:7; 9:4–6. The OT 'grace-words' are:

(i) *ḥeseḏ*, in RSV usually 'steadfast love', occasionally 'loyalty'. This is translated in AV as 'mercy' (149 times), 'kindness' (38), 'lovingkindness' (30) and 'goodness' (12). Luther translates it by *Gnade*, the German word for 'grace'. Despite that, it is not quite the equivalent of grace. It is a two-way word, and can be used of God and man. Of God, it certainly implies grace. Of man, it implies steadfast love to another human being or to God. It is often found in association with the word 'covenant', and denotes the attitude of faithfulness which both parties to a covenant should observe. For God's *ḥeseḏ*, see La. 3:22; for man's, Ho. 6:6. Snaith suggests 'covenant love' as the nearest Eng. equivalent.

(ii) *ḥēn*, 'favour' (RSV). This is not a covenant word and not two-way. It is used of the action of a superior, human or divine, to an inferior. It speaks of undeserved favour; in AV it is translated 'grace' (38) and 'favour' (26). Examples of man's *ḥēn* are found in Gn. 33:8, 10, 15; 39:4; Ru. 2:2, 10. God's *ḥēn* is found in Je. 31:2 (RSV 'faithfulness', AV 'lovingkindness'). No-one can show *ḥēn* to God (as one can show *ḥeseḏ*), for no-one can do him a favour.

b. The law

(i) Jn. 1:17 puts the law into sharp antithesis with grace. See Tit. 2:11, which also states that grace came into the world with Christ. That does not mean that grace was non-existent in the OT, but merely that it is not in the foreground, and that it is concerned chiefly with Israel. The Bible often uses antithesis where we would use comparison.

(ii) The idea of promise is developed in the NT in Gal. (3:16–22) and in Hebrews. It shows that grace is prior to law. God dealt with the Patriarchs as individuals by way of promise, and with the nation as a whole by way of law. The law was not primary, but it clarified and emphasized the kind of *ḥeseḏ* that God expected of his covenant people.

(iii) Grace is found, however, in the law itself. The election of Israel to be God's people is attributed in the law to God's free choice, and not to Israel's righteousness (Dt. 7:7–8; *cf*. 8:18). The initiative in the Sinai covenant comes from God, just as much as did the covenant of grace with Abraham. Then there is the statement in Ps. 19 of the converting or restoring power of the law.

c. The prophets

Repentance is the chief point of interest in the prophetic writings. Typical passages are Am. 5:14; Ho. 2:7; 6:1; 14:1; Is. 1:16–18; Je. 3:1, 7, 12–14. The prophets are often accused of a doctrine of repentance which lays stress on human willpower, as did the Pelagian heresy. But the prophets regarded repentance as inward (Joel 2:13). Ezekiel, who demanded that the individual should make himself a new heart (18:31), also recognized that a new heart can only be a gift of God's grace (36:26). With this agrees the 'new covenant' passage in Je. 31:31–34.

d. The Psalms

The word *ḥēn* is almost absent from the Psalms, though its cognates appear. *ḥesed* is very often found, *e.g.* Pss. 5:7; 57:3 ('steadfast love', AV 'mercy'); 89:33 (AV 'lovingkindness'). In the Psalms also is found the increasing use of the cognate word *ḥāsîd*, which is found in, *e.g.*, Pss. 12:1; 86:2 ('godly man'); 79:2 ('saints'). The plural of this word (*ḥ^{a}sîdîm*) appears as 'Hasidaeans' in 1 Macc. 2:42; 7:13; 2 Macc. 14:6; it really meant those who were loyal to the covenant, the rigorous, devout, law-keeping party in Judaism, from whose ranks came the *Pharisees.

II. In the New Testament

a. Vocabulary

Gk. *charis* was the normal word used to translate Heb. *ḥēn*. The nearest corresponding verb, *charizesthai*, was used to denote forgiveness, human as well as divine (Col. 2:13; 3:13; Eph. 4:32). *eleos* represents the Heb. *ḥesed* and has the meaning of 'mercy'. It is not used very often, and occurs largely in passages based on the OT, such as Rom. 9:15–18, 23; 11:30–32. 'Grace' is preferred to 'mercy', because it includes the idea of the divine power which equips a man to live a moral life.

b. The Synoptic Gospels

Quite apart from the word *charis*, which is never placed on the lips of Jesus, the idea of grace is very prominent. Jesus says that he came to seek and save the lost. Many of his parables teach the doctrine of grace. The parable of the labourers in the vineyard (Mt. 20:1–16) teaches that God is answerable to no-one for his gifts of grace. The parable of the great supper (Lk. 14:16–24) shows that spiritual privilege does not ensure final bliss, and that the gospel invitation is to all. The prodigal son was welcomed by his father in a way he did not deserve (Lk. 15:20–24). Repentance is stressed as a condition of salvation (Mk. 1:15; 6:12; Lk. 24:47). Faith also has its place (*e.g.* Mk. 1:15; Lk. 7:50), although there is no theological statement on Pauline lines.

c. The writings of Luke

Both the Gospel and the Acts need special attention. Luke shows flexibility in dealing with the subject. Even the non-religious sense of the noun, of a favour done by one man to another, appears ([illegible] 25:3, 9). The OT sense of 'favour' is seen in Lk. 1:30; 2:52; Acts 2:47; 7:10, 46. The dynamic sense of grace resulting in fearless courage and effective witness is seen in Acts 4:33; 11:23; 13:43 and is used in the context of the universal appeal of the gospel. Luke also brings together, in a way that even Paul does not, the terms 'gospel' ('word') and 'grace' (Lk. 4:22; Acts 14:3; 20:24).

d. The Pauline Epistles

The word 'grace' has a prominent place in the opening greetings and the closing benedictions of the Epistles, being added to the conventional Jewish greeting of 'peace'. The basis of Paul's doctrine is found in Rom. 1:16–3:20. Man is shown as a sinner, but by grace he is justified (Rom. 3:21–4:25), *i.e.* God in his grace treats him, though guilty, as if he had never sinned.

*Faith is the human response to divine grace (Rom. 5:2; 10:9; Eph. 2:8). This faith is the gift of God (Eph. 2:8); the words 'not your own doing' may refer to *sesōsmenoi* ('saved'), but Paul is seeking to point out that the word 'faith' must not be thought to imply some independent action on the part of the believer. See also 2 Cor. 4:13; Phil. 1:29. This faith, although it implies that there is no salvation through the law, is not unethical. Faith is morally vital by itself. It works 'through love' (Gal. 5:6). C. A. Anderson Scott (*Christianity according to St Paul*, 1927, p. 111) says that from the moment that faith was active a transformation of

In Gozan (Guzana: Tell Halaf, Syria) the palace of Kaparu was dominated by colossal sculptures at its N entrance. The female figure standing on a lion may be a goddess or a queen. Height (head to plinth) c. 2·60 m. 9th cent. BC. (JDH)

Egyptians winnowing grain. Wall-painting from the Tomb of Nakht. c. 1415 BC. (RS)

ethical outlook was ideally there.

The believer's position in grace is explained, not by anything in himself, but by the will of God. The doctrine of *election has two functions: it checks human independence and self-righteousness, and shows that in bestowing favour God is perfectly free (Eph. 1:1–6; 2 Tim. 1:9; Tit. 3:5). Every step in the process of the Christian life is due to grace—Gal. 1:15 (call); 2 Tim. 2:25 (repentance); Eph. 2:8–9 (faith). In Rom. 8:28–30 Paul surveys the divine agency from the call to the final glory of the redeemed. He does not, however, overlook man's responsibility. Obedience (Rom. 1:5; 6:17) is a moral attitude, and cannot be made anything else. A man of himself turns to the Lord (2 Cor. 3:16). A. Stewart in *HDB* suggests that 1 Thes. 3:5 teaches that even perseverance is doubted. The two sides are brought together in Rom. 9–10. Ch. 9 contains the strongest possible statements of double predestination, while ch. 10 states that rejection by God is due to unbelief and disobedience. It must be remembered, however, that the primary subject of these chapters is not personal salvation, but the collective functions of those chosen by God to carry out his purpose.

Rom. 6 uses the figure of baptism to teach the conquest of sin by grace. See also 1 Cor. 6:11; 12:13; Eph. 5:26; Col. 2:12; Tit. 3:5. H. Wheeler Robinson (*The Christian Doctrine of Man*, 1926, pp. 124–125) holds that believers' baptism is not merely illustrative symbolism but the objective aspect of what is subjectively faith. Others would argue that infant baptism is a means of grace, because the child is a symbol of human inability and helplessness. These views seem to contradict the unvarying Pauline emphasis on faith.

e. The other NT writings

(i) 1 Pet. The apostle emphasizes grace in chs. 1–2 by means of the usual variants of covenant election and inheritance; 3:7 has the unusual phrase 'the grace of life'. Grace is also used in 5:10 in relation to the believer's future glory.

(ii) Heb. The writer uses most of the 'grace-words'. In 2:9 the grace of God is related to the sufferings of Christ. The word *charis* is used in 12:28 of human thankfulness to God. Grace is viewed as a calling to consecration in 12:14–15. The striking phrase 'the throne of grace' in 4:16 unites the divine majesty and grace. Another fresh phrase is 'the Spirit of grace' (10:29).

(iii) The Johannine writings. There is surprisingly little directly about grace, but God's love is emphasized throughout. The idea of grace must be related to that of 'eternal life'. Faith is prominent, and John uses a Gk. phrase *pisteuein eis* (believe *into*) of real *faith in Christ's person. The 'grace and truth' which characterize the glory of the incarnate Word in Jn. 1:14 (*cf.* v. 17) echo the 'mercy and truth' (*ḥeseḏ we'ᵉmeṯ*) of Ex. 34:6.

We conclude with Moffatt that the religion of the Bible 'is a religion of grace or it is nothing . . . no grace, no gospel' (*Grace in the New Testament*, p. xv).

BIBLIOGRAPHY. H. Wheeler Robinson, *The Christian Doctrine of Man*, 1926; N. H. Snaith, *The Distinctive Ideas of the Old Testament*, 1944, pp. 94–130; J. Moffatt, *Grace in the New Testament*, 1931; N. P. Williams, *The Grace of God*, 1930; C. Ryder Smith, *The Bible Doctrine of Grace*, 1956; H.-H. Esser, *NIDNTT* 2, pp. 115–124; H. Conzelmann, W. Zimmerli, *TDNT* 9, pp. 372–402; H. D. McDonald, *ZPEB*, 2, pp. 799–804.

J.H.Sr.

GRAFTING
See Olive, Part 2.

GRAIN. The commonest OT Heb. words are **1.** *dāḡān*, wheat (fully-developed grain). **2.** *bar*, grain of any kind standing in the open field (hence *bar* means also 'open country'). **3.** *šeḇer*, grain, cereal, victuals, *i.e.* broken crushed grain.

'Parched grain' (*qālî, qālâ*, 'roasted') were ears or grains of wheat (Lv. 23:14; Ru. 2:14; 1 Sa. 17:17; 25:18; 2 Sa. 17:28) roasted over a blazing fire, usually on an iron pan or flat stone.

kussemeṯ (Ex. 9:32; Is. 28:25; Ezk. 4:9), rendered 'spelt' (RSV) and 'rie', 'rye' or 'fitches' (AV), denotes the false spelt or einkorn wheat (*Triticum monoccum*) and not true spelt (*Triticum spelta*) which has not been recorded from Egypt of that time.

The Gk. word *kokkos* ('kernel', Mt. 13:31, *etc.*) denotes the singular form, *e.g.* 'a grain of mustard seed'.

By 'grain' in the Bible the cereal crops barley and wheat are usually intended. (*AGRICULTURE, *FOOD.)

F.N.H.

Grain ears surviving from Roman Egypt. (FNH)

Barley (Heb. *śᵉʿōrâ*, Gk. *krithē*). An edible grain of the genus *Hordeum*. The grass *H. spontaneum*, which still grows wild in Palestine, gave rise to the primitive cultivated 'two-row' barley (*H. distichon*), and later to the 'six-row' barley (*H. vulgare*), which was the barley of biblical times and continues to the present day.

Barley formed the major part of the staple food of Palestine (Dt. 8:8), particularly of the poorer classes (Ru. 2:17; Ezk. 4:9; Jn. 6:9). It has a shorter growing season than wheat and can flourish on poorer soil. Barley was also used as fodder for horses and cattle (1 Ki. 4:28), and for brewing, judging from evidence of Philistine drinking vessels. In Jdg. 7:13 it apparently symbolizes a reformed Israel. Barley meal as a jealousy offering (Nu. 5:15) seems to indicate that basic integrity had been disrupted. F.N.H.

Chaff. 1. Heb. *mōṣ*, the most common word, denotes worthless husks and broken straw blown away by the wind during the winnowing of grain (Jb. 21:18; Pss. 1:4; 35:5; Is. 17:13; 29:5; 41:15; Ho. 13:3; Zp. 2:2). **2.** Heb. *ḥᵃšaš*, 'hay', 'dry grass' (Is. 5:24; 33:11). **3.** Aram. *'ûr*, 'skin', 'chaff' (Dn. 2:35). **4.** Gk. *achyron*, 'chaff' (Mt. 3:12; Lk. 3:17).

In some of the above references it is applied figuratively in connection with superficial or wrong teaching, and with the inevitable fate of wrongdoers. J.D.D.

Straw (Heb. *teḇen*; Arab. *tibn*). The stalk of wheat or barley, while chaff is the wind-scattered husk of the threshed grain, and stubble remains after harvesting. Chopped straw mixed with more solid foodstuffs contributed to the provender of horses, asses and camels (Gn. 24:32; Jdg. 19:19; 1 Ki. 4:28). In Egypt straw was and is mixed with clay to make the familiar mud bricks of the poorer houses. When the Israelite brickmakers, already overworked, had to collect their own straw, their burdens were almost intolerably increased (Ex. 5).

Straw is also still used in certain kinds of hand-moulded pottery, later burnt by fire. Such was the strength of leviathan that he could bend iron like straw (Jb. 41:27). In the peace of the Messianic age the lion will cease to devour flesh, and eat straw (Is. 11:7; 65:25). The final fate of Moab is pictured as straw trampled down among dung (Is. 25:10). In the Bible, stubble (Heb. *qaš*, 'dried up') is used to typify worthless inflammable substances, since chaff and straw were often thrown on to fires to give instant heat (Ex. 15:7; Jb. 13:25; 41:28–29; Ps. 83:13; Is. 5:24; so Gk. *kalamē* in 1 Cor. 3:12). See C. F. Nims, 'Bricks without Straw', *BA* 13, 1950, pp. 22ff. R.A.S.

Wheat (Heb. *dāḡān*, Gk. *sitos*). A cereal grass of great antiquity and importance as a food of mankind. The typical wheat of OT times in the Mediterranean region was the 'emmer' wheat (*Triticum dicoccum*), which gave rise to the 'hard' wheat (*T. durum*) that was immensely important from Hellenistic times onward, thus including the NT period. Modern cultivated varieties are of the 'bread' wheat (*T. vulgare*). Owing to its physical and chemical qualities, wheat makes more palatable and better *bread than any other cereal.

Wheat formed an important part of the diet of the Israelites (Jdg. 6:11; Ru. 2:23; 2 Sa. 4:6), and the wheat harvest is used as a *calendar reference (Gn. 30:14; 1 Sa. 6:13; 12:17). Because of its importance as a food, it is a symbol of God's goodness and provision (Pss. 81:16; 147:14). It was used as a cereal offering in the Temple (Ezr. 6:9; 7:22) and forms part of the sacrifice made by David on Ornan's threshing-floor (1 Ch. 21:23).

Its botanical nature whereby one grain gives rise to several new ears of wheat, while the original grain is used up, is taken by Christ to show that spiritual fruitfulness has its origin in the death of self (Jn. 12:24; *cf.* 1 Cor. 15:36ff.). As symbolic of the children of God, it is contrasted with the valueless chaff (Mt. 3:12). Similarly, in Mt. 13:24–30 the darnel or tares (*Lolium temulentum*) in their early stages of growth appear as grass-like as wheat, but can easily be distinguished at harvest-time.

BIBLIOGRAPHY. H. Helbaek, 'Ancient Egyptian wheats', *Proceedings of Prehistory Society* 11, 1955, pp. 93–95; D. Zohary, 'The progenitors of wheat and barley . . .' in P. J. Ucko and G. W. Dimbleby, *The Domestication and Exploitation of Plants and Animals*, 1969, pp. 47–66; D. M. Dixon, 'A note on cereals in ancient Egypt' in Ucko and Dimbleby, pp. 132–142. F.N.H. *et al.*

GRASS (Heb. *ḥāṣîr*, *deše'*, *yereq*, *'ēśeḇ*; Gk. *chortos*).

Gn. 1:11 records that the earth brought forth vegetation (literally 'grass', as AV) on the 'third day' of the creation narrative. In the promised land it provided food for cattle; it would be given to the land by God in response to the people's obedience (Dt. 11:15). It was the portion of Nebuchadrezzar during his madness (Dn. 4:15, 25).

Green pastures are not of permanent occurrence in Palestine, but last only for a while after the rains, withering in the dry season. As a result, grass is a fitting symbol of the transitoriness of human life (*e.g.* Ps. 103:15; Is. 40:6–7), of the brief sway of the rich man (Jas. 1:10–11), and is a figure of weakness, of perishing enemies (Is. 37:27 = 2 Ki. 19:26), of the wicked soon to be cut down (Ps. 37:2) and of haters of Zion (Ps. 129:6).

The multitude of blades is likened to a multitude of people (Jb. 5:25; Is. 44:4) and to a flourishing people (Ps. 72:16), and the luxuriance of green pastures is likened to serenity in the spiritual life (Ps. 23:2). In tender grass can be seen a quality of the just ruler (2 Sa. 23:4), and a benevolent ruler is as refreshing and productive of good as rain upon mown meadows (Ps. 72:6).

In contrast, a barren locality without grass can indicate God's wrath (Dt. 29:23). R.A.H.G.

GREECE. Who the Greeks were is a famous crux. Their language is Indo-European and its earliest known location is in the Mycenaean states of the Peloponnesus (as established by the decipherment of the Linear B script) in the 2nd millennium BC. When they emerge into history well into the 1st millennium they belong indifferently to either side of the Aegean.

The first flowering of the two institutions that became the hallmarks of Hellenism, speculative philosophy and republican government, apparently occurred on the Ionian coast of Asia Minor. Ionia is perhaps the OT Javan (Is. 66:19). The area of Greek settlement was never static. The republics were early established throughout the Black Sea, Sicily and S Italy, and as far W as Marseilles and Spain. After Alexander there were Greek states as far E as India. Under Seleucid and more especially

GRASSHOPPER
See Animals, Part 1.

GREAT HOUSE
See Palace, Part 2.

GREAT RIVER
See Nile, Part 2.

GREAVES
See Armour, Part 1.

Aerial view of Athens, Greece, showing the Acropolis hill with the Parthenon (built 447–438 BC). (RVS)

GREEK CHRISTIANS
See Hellenists, Part 2.

GREEK COINAGE
See Money, Part 2.

GREEK NUMERICAL SIGNS
See Number, Part 2.

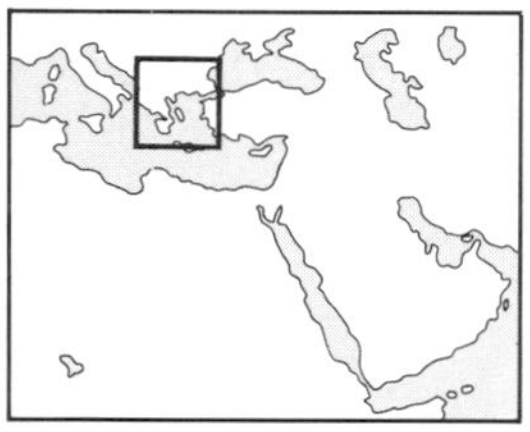

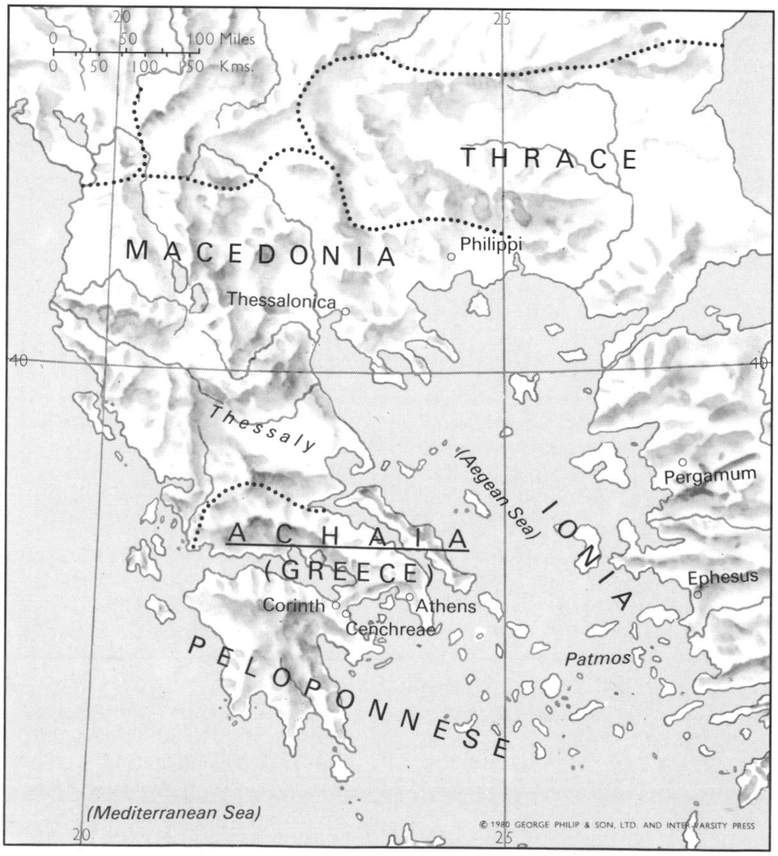

Greece (ancient Achaia) and the adjoining province of Macedonia.

Roman control the wealthy and ancient nations of Asia Minor and the Levant were systematically broken up into many hundreds of Greek republics, leaving only the most backward regions under the indigenous royal or priestly governments. This political fragmentation was always characteristic of the Greeks, as was the consequent subordination to foreign powers. Greece was never a political entity. 'The king of Greece' (*yāwān*, Dn. 8:21) must be one of the *Macedonian rulers, Alexander or a Seleucid, who controlled the affairs of many but by no means all Greek states. 'Greece' (*Hellas*) in Acts 20:2 must refer to the Roman province of *Achaia, which, while it contained many ancient Greek states, was now almost a backwater of Hellenism.

On the other hand, the ever-increasing diffusion of Greek institutions brought unification at a different level. The whole of the E Mediterranean and much beyond was raised to the common norm of civilization that Hellenism supplied. Both the opulence of the states and the degree of standardization are attested by the splendid ruins that indiscriminately litter these parts today. The ideal of a free and cultivated life in a small autonomous community, once the boast of a few Aegean states, was now almost universally accepted. *Athens was still a home of learning, but Pergamum, Antioch and Alexandria, and many others in the new world, rivalled or eclipsed her.

The states provided not only education but brilliant entertainment and a wider range of health and welfare services than most modern communities. It was membership in such a republic and use of the Greek language that marked a man as civilized (Acts 21:37–39). Such a person might be called a Greek, whatever his race (Mk. 7:26); all others were 'barbarians' (Rom. 1:14). The term 'Hellenists' in Acts 6:1; 9:29 presumably shows that this distinction applied even within the Jewish ethnic community. The term 'Greek' (*hellēn*, Acts 11:20; 19:17; Rom. 1:16, *etc.*) is, however, the regular NT usage for non-Jews, being virtually equivalent to 'Gentile'. *Greeks were frequently associated with the synagogues as observers (Jn. 12:20; Acts 14:1; 17:4; 18:4), but the exclusiveness of Israel as a nation was jealously preserved. It was the agonizing delivery of the gospel

Roman copies of original Greek busts (now lost). Left: *Socrates.* Right: *Plato.* (RS)

from this constricting matrix that marked the birth of the Christian religion in its universal form. The translation from Hebrew into Greek opened the gospel to all civilized men. It also produced the NT.

BIBLIOGRAPHY. A. H. M. Jones, *The Greek City from Alexander to Justinian*, 1940; M. I. Finley, *The Ancient Greeks*, 1963; A. Andrewes, *The Greeks*, 1967; M. Hengel, *Judaism and Hellenism*, 1974.

E.A.J.

GREEKS. Two words are used in the NT: *Hellēnes* and *Hellēnistai*. The term *Hellēnes* refers to the inhabitants of Greece or their descendants (*cf.* Acts 16:1; Rom. 1:14). It is also used, as a virtual equivalent of 'Gentile', to describe those who are not of Jewish origin (*cf.* Rom. 10:12; Gal. 3:28).

The term *Hellēnistai* is a crux. It is confined to Acts 6:1; 9:29 (where A reads *Hellēnas*); and 11:20 (as a variant reading, although *Hellēnas* is probably to be preferred). The objection to the traditional interpretation of *Hellēnistai* as 'Gk-

Head of Alexander the Great, founder of the Hellenistic Empire. c. AD *350–400.* (BM)

The Erechtheion, Athens, with female figures serving as pillars (caryatids), was built in 421–406 BC. This temple was a dominant feature of the city in the time of Paul's visit, as it is today. (BPL)

GRIEF
See Gestures, Part 1.

GRIFFIN VULTURE
See Animals, Part 1.

speaking Jews' is that Paul, who spoke Gk., called himself *Hebraios* (Phil. 3:5), which in Acts 6:1 forms the contrast to *Hellēnistai* (*cf.* C. F. D. Moule, *ExpT* 70, 1958–9, p. 100). Various alternatives have been offered: *e.g.* Jews who spoke *only* Gk. (Moule, *loc. cit.*); Gk.-speaking diaspora Jews living in Palestine (J. A. T. Robinson, *Twelve New Testament Studies*, 1962, pp. 116f.); 'non-conformist' Jews influenced by Hellenism and noted for their opposition to the Temple (O. Cullmann, *ExpT* 71, 1959–60, pp. 8–12, 39–43; also *The Johannine Circle*, 1976). S.S.S.

GREETING. Following modern idiom, RSV changes AV 'salutation' invariably to 'greeting', the verb 'salute' to 'greet' or some equivalent. The social courtesies intended have six main biblical forms:

1. An epistolary message of greeting, involving no personal encounter. Paul occasionally uses the noun *aspasmos*, more frequently the cognate verb *aspazomai*, a customary formula in contemporary Gk. correspondence, as the papyri prove (see *MM*). The greeting may be in the name of the writer, or of some other person specified by him (*cf.* Rom. 16, *etc.*).

2. A formal greeting with obeisance from subject to monarch, invoking, with oriental exaggeration, eternal life for him (*cf.* Ne. 2:3, *etc.*, Heb.; Dn. 2:4, *etc.*, Aram.).

3. A face-to-face greeting, formal, verbal, perhaps with hand gesture, but without physical contact. The Gk. descriptive terms are the same as Paul's (Mt. 10:12; Mk. 12:38, *etc.*). Note the mock homage to Jesus in Mk. 15:18. The uttered word was frequently the imperative *chaire*, plural *chairete*, 'rejoice', AV 'Hail!' (Mt. 27:29, *etc.*). The infinitive *chairein* is also used (*cf.* 2 Jn. 11; 1 Macc. 10:18, 25). The commonest Heb. terms are connected with blessing (root *bārak̲*, 2 Ki. 4:29, *etc.*), or with the invoking of peace (*šā'al lᵉšālôm*, 1 Sa. 17:22, *etc.*). Modern Heb. and Arab. greetings are based on the same vocabulary stock (*cf. šālôm*, *salaam*).

4. A formal cheek kiss, Heb. *nāšaq* and cognate noun; Gk. *philēma* (*cf.* 1 Sa. 10:1; Rom. 16:16, *etc.*). The double-cheek kiss is still daily exchanged between males in the Orient.

5. The affectionate kiss, normally on the mouth, implying greater intimacy (same words, Gn. 29:11; Ct. 1:2). **6.** The deceitful kiss (same words, Pr. 27:6; the kiss of Judas, Mt. 26:48, *etc.*).

Greetings might be forbidden through urgency (2 Ki. 4:29; Lk. 10:4) or to prevent association with error (2 Jn. 11).

BIBLIOGRAPHY. G. Finkenrath, *NIDNTT* 2, pp. 356–358; H. Windisch, *TDNT* 1, pp. 496–502.

R.A.S.

King Shalmaneser III of Assyria shakes hands with Marduk-zakir-shumi of Babylon (left-hand figure). While this may be a sign of greeting it can also denote the conclusion of a treaty. Relief from Shalmaneser's throne dais at Nimrud. Height c. 20 cm. c. 845 BC. (DO)

GRINDER (from Heb. *ṭāḥan*, 'to grind'). Grinding in the E is usually done by women (*cf.* Mt. 24:41). In Ec. 12:3 the word is used in a metaphorical sense to denote the teeth. For a full discussion of the Jewish poetic imagery employed here, see *ICC*, *Ecclesiastes*, pp. 186ff. J.D.D.

GRUDGE. Frequently found in the earliest translations, this word was altered to 'murmur' in most of the AV occurrences, then similarly changed in all but two of the RV passages. Where it is retained in AV several words are thus rendered, *viz.* Heb. *nāṭar*, 'to keep anger' (Lv. 19:18, so RSV); Heb. *lûn, lîn*, 'to murmur' (Ps. 59:15, RSV 'growl'); Gk. *stenazō*, 'to groan, sigh' (Jas. 5:9, RSV 'grumble'); Gk. *gongysmos*, 'grudging' (1 Pet. 4:9, so RSV); Gk. *ek lypēs*, 'grudgingly', 'out of grief' (2 Cor. 9:7, RSV 'reluctantly'). RSV translates 'grudge' at Dt. 28:54, 56; Mk. 6:19, *enechō* (AV quarrel); 'grudging' at Dt. 15:10, *rā'a'* (AV 'grieve'). J.D.D.

GUARD. In the OT the word translates four Heb. terms.
1. *ṭabbāḥ*. The word originally signified royal 'slaughterers' (cooks), but later came to mean guardsmen or bodyguard, being used of Pharaoh's bodyguard (Gn. 37:36; 39:1) and of Nebuchadrezzar's bodyguard (2 Ki. 25:8–10). (In Israel Aegean mercenaries [Cherethites and Pelethites] formed David's bodyguard, while Carian troops seem to have had a similar appointment in the time of Athaliah [2 Ki. 11:4, 19].) **2.** *mišma'aṯ*, from *šāma'*, 'hear', 'respond', the attitude of an obedient body of subjects, was sometimes the name given to the bodyguard (2 Sa. 23:23; *cf.* 1 Sa. 22:14). **3.** *mišmār* denotes 'guard', 'watch' or 'guardhouse' in a camp (Lv. 24:12; Nu. 15:34), or 'guard-post' (Ne. 7:3). **4.** *rāṣîm*, lit. 'runners', were the runners of the king who acted also as the royal bodyguard (1 Sa. 22:17; *cf.* 1 Ki. 1:5; 14:27). (*FOOTMAN.)

'Guard' occurs once in the AV of the NT (Acts 28:16), but the text is disputed (*CAPTAIN). The Temple had its own police department known as the Temple Guard, who were mostly Levites and whose task, among other things, was to keep out the forbidden Gentiles (*cf.* Mt. 27:65, RSV). The *spekoulatōr*, a Latinism found in Mk. 6:27, was one of ten such officers attached to a legion who acted mostly as couriers but sometimes as executioners; one such was in the employ of Herod Antipas. R.P.G.

GUDGODAH. One of the Israelite encampments in the wilderness according to Dt. 10:7. Hor-haggidgad in Nu. 33:32–33 is probably another form of the same name. Its location is not known, although its proximity to *Bene-jaakan and *Jotbathah suggests that it was somewhere in the mountains W of Wadi Arabah. The suggestion that the name survives in Wadi Ḥadaḥid, in this area, is unlikely from a linguistic point of view. Baumgartner, comparing an Arab. word, has suggested that it may be an animal name, 'a cricket': the first element of the longer form, Hor, appears to mean 'cave'.

BIBLIOGRAPHY. *KB*, pp. 169, 335 (bibl.). G.I.D.

GULF (Gk. *chasma*, 'chasm' (RSV), from *chainō*, 'to gape' or 'yawn'). Found only in the parable of Lazarus and Dives (Lk. 16:19–31, AV), this word is sometimes connected with an ill-defined rabbinical belief that the souls of righteous and wicked exist after death in different compartments of Hades (see J. M. Creed, *The Gospel according to St Luke*, 1942, pp. 212–213), with no road between them, but so situated as to allow the inhabitants of each to see those of the other. There is, however, insufficient evidence for this application of the word. Any interpretation, moreover, must take into account the oriental love of imagery, for which full scope is provided by a subject such as this (which in various forms

Wooden model of servant-girl grinding corn with a stone rubbed on a stone quern. From Egypt, c. 2500 BC. (SI)

A royal Persian guardsman. Part of a relief in glazed brick from the palace of Artaxerxes II, Memnon at Susa, Iran. 404–358 BC. (MC)

GUARANTEE
See Earnest, Part 1.

GUIDANCE
See Rod, Part 3.

GUILE
See Deceit, Part 1.

GUITAR
See Music, Part 2.

was a common feature of the writings of classical antiquity).

The passage seems to imply also that the gulf is seen in this earthly life, in which the respective conditions of Lazarus and Dives are reversed. Abraham, after outlining this aspect, is made to say, 'In all these things' (v. 26 RVmg.) '. . . there is a great gulf fixed.' It seems clear that the gulf is in character as well as in condition, otherwise the false impression would be given that some stigma attaches to riches in themselves. The story reminds us that it is of the very essence of the gospel that there is between believers and unbelievers a fundamental difference in this world and in the next. (*LAZARUS AND DIVES, *ABRAHAM'S BOSOM.) J.D.D.

GUTTER
See Siloam, Part 3.

GYPSUM
See Jewels, Part 2.

HABAKKUK, BOOK OF.

I. Outline of contents

The prophecy attributed to Habakkuk consists of six sections.

a. 1:1–4. The prophet cries to God because of the lawlessness he sees around him and asks how long it will go unpunished.

b. 1:5–11. As if in reply, God announces that he is raising up the Chaldeans and describes the fierceness of their armies and their contempt for all who stand in their way.

c. 1:12–17. But if God is holy, how can he allow the brutal inhumanity and idolatry of the Chaldeans, whose atrocities are worse than the evils that they are sent to punish?

d. 2:1–5. The prophet waits in imagination upon his watchtower to see if God will resolve his dilemma. The answer comes in the asseveration of the principle that the pride of the Chaldean will be his downfall and the faithfulness of the righteous will be his salvation.

e. 2:6–20. A taunt-song (*māšāl*) addressed to the Chaldeans, consisting of a series of five woes predicting dire consequences upon them for the acts of inhumanity for which they are responsible.

f. 3:1–19. If this psalm of Habakkuk has any connection with the theme of the earlier chapters it describes a revelation of God coming in his awful majesty to bring judgment upon the nations and salvation to his people.

II. Authorship

So little is known of the prophet Habakkuk that anything that is written about him must be conjectural and based on internal evidence. His name may be connected with a Heb. root meaning 'embrace' (*ḥbq*) or with an Assyr. plant name, *ḥambaḳuḳu*. The Gk. form of his name is *Hambakoum*. The suggestions that he was the son of the Shunammite woman of 2 Ki. 4:16, or the watchman of Is. 21:6, have as little evidence to support them as the tradition associating him with Daniel in the lions' den (so Bel and the Dragon, vv. 33ff.).

III. Date and background

There has been considerable discussion among scholars about which if any of these sections are original to Habakkuk, and there is no agreement with regard to unity, authorship and date. The only clear historical reference is to the Chaldeans in 1:6 and so the prophecy is usually dated at the close of the 7th century BC shortly after the battle of Carchemish (605 BC) when the Chaldeans routed the Egyptians under Pharaoh Neco on the fords

The river Habor (modern Ḫâbûr) flowing past the ruin of Gozan (Tell Halaf) in Syria. (JDH)

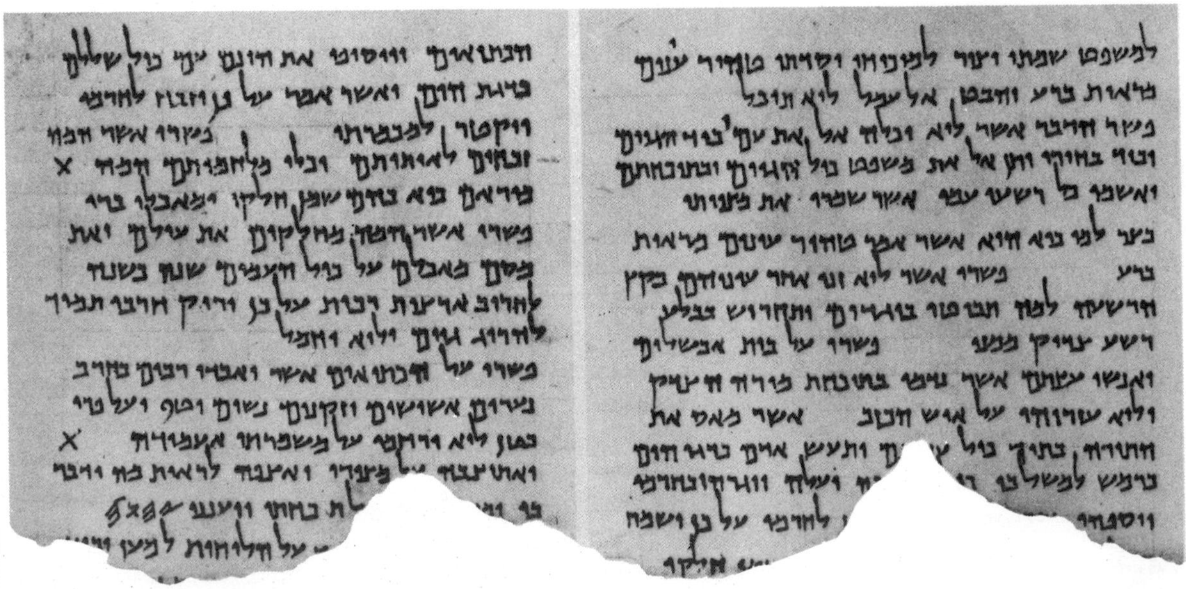

Part of a commentary on Habakkuk (1:12–2:2) found among the Dead Sea Scrolls. The commentator believed the prophecy referred to religious and political events of his own day. 1st cent. BC. (JCT)

of the Euphrates and marched W to subjugate King Jehoiakim of Judah.

The theory of Duhm and C. C. Torrey that 'Chaldeans' (Heb. *kaśdîm*) should read 'Kittim' in the sense of 'Greeks' was based on the problematical 1:9 (Heb. lit. 'the eagerness of their faces is *eastwards*'). This would fit in better with Alexander's invasion from the W (and a 4th-century date) than with Nebuchadrezzar's from the N or E. But the text of 1:9 is extremely difficult; there is no textual evidence for the reading 'Kittim' in 1:6; and the traditional dating is to be preferred.

IV. The prophet's message

A unity of theme may be observed throughout the book, though whether this is due to 'the molding influence of liturgical use' (Irwin) or to unity of authorship cannot be known. Habakkuk deals with the moral problem of God's raising up of the Chaldeans to inflict his judgment upon Judah, when their cruelty and barbarity are a denial of his righteousness. The answer given in 2:4 is that a man's arrogance carries within it the seed of his ruin, whereas the faithful man is assured of living in the light of God's favour. Clearly the full Pauline meaning of faith is not to be found in this oft-quoted scripture (*cf.* Rom. 1:17; Gal. 3:11; Heb. 10:38); indeed, it is doubtful whether Pauline faith could have been expressed by any Heb. word. But the NT gives a legitimate development of the prophet's thought through the medium of the LXX translation, *pistis*.

The Commentary on Habakkuk of the Dead Sea Scrolls interprets 1:4–2:20 only in the light of the history of the Qumran sect and gives no clue to the meaning of the prophecy. Although on 1:6 and elsewhere it reads 'This means the Kittim', there is no suggestion that the original 'Kasdim' was in need of emendation.

BIBLIOGRAPHY. Commentaries by S. R. Driver, A. B. Davidson, J. H. Eaton and standard series. C. C. Torrey, 'The Prophecy of Habakkuk', in *Jewish Studies in Memory of George A. Kohut*, 1935; W. A. Irwin, 'The Psalm of Habakkuk', *JNES* 1, 1942, pp. 10–40; W. F. Albright, 'The Psalm of Habakkuk', in H. H. Rowley (ed.), *Studies in OT Prophecy*, 1950, pp. 1–18; D. M. Lloyd-Jones, *From Fear to Faith*, 1953. J.B.Tr.

HABOR. A river (the modern Ḫâbûr) which carries the waters of several streams draining the Mardin area SW to the middle Euphrates. It ran through the Assyr. province of *Gozan (*n^ehar gôzān*, 'river of Gozan') and was one of the locations to which the Israelites were deported by the Assyrians (2 Ki. 17:6; 18:11; 1 Ch. 5:26). T.C.M.

HACHILAH (Heb. *ḥ^akîlâ*, 'drought'). A hill in the wilderness of Judah where David was hidden when the Ziphites plotted to betray him to Saul (1 Sa. 23:19; 26:1, 3). The site is uncertain, but generally regarded as being near Dahret el-Kôlâ, between Ziph and *En-gedi. J.D.D.

HADAD. The name of a Syrian deity meaning 'the Thunderer' (Heb. *h^adad*; Akkad. (*H*)*ad*(*d*)*u* or Adad) the storm-god, also named in Ras Shamra texts as *Baal. A Hadad temple at Aleppo is known. The personal names Hadad, and their dialectal variant Hadar, are probably abbreviations of names compounded with this divine element, *e.g.*, *Hadadezer, *Ben-hadad, *Hadad-rimmon. There is as yet no evidence to support the view that Hadad was a specifically Edomite name, although it was borne by four rulers of that country.

1. The grandson of Abraham, being the son of Ishmael (Gn. 25:15 = 1 Ch. 1:30). The *MT* Hadad is supported by LXX readings, while the AV 'Hadar' follows the Syr. and other MSS.

2. A son of Bedad who came from Avith and defeated the Midianites in the plain of Moab. He was succeeded as king of Edom by Samlah (Gn. 36:35–36; 1 Ch. 1:46).

3. A later king of Edom, named Hadar in 1 Ch. 1:50, whose native village was Pau.

4. An Edomite of the ruling family who lived in the time of Solomon. He was a young child and fled to Paran when Joab murdered his family after Judah's conquest of Edom. He took refuge in Egypt, where he married the pharaoh's daughter, his son Genubath being brought up at the Egyptian court. When Hadad heard of the death of David and Joab he returned to Edom and plotted against Solomon (1 Ki. 11:14–22, 25).

BIBLIOGRAPHY. S. Moscati (ed.), *Le Antiche Divinità Semitiche*, 1958, pp. 30ff. (under Adad). D.J.W.

Hadad, the Syrian storm-god, standing on a bull and holding his symbol of forked lightning. Basalt stele from Arslan Tash, Syria. Height 1·35 m. c. 740 BC. (MC)

HADADEZER. This Aramaean personal name, meaning '(the god) *Hadad is (my) helper', was borne by at least two kings of the Damascus region. It is sometimes written 'Hadarezer', perhaps reflecting an Aramaic dialectal variant, in 2 Sa. 10:16–19; 1 Ch. 18:3–8 (AV).

Hadadezer, son of Rehob, was king of Zobah, E of Hamath, whose territory at one time included part of the bank of the river

HABITATION See Naioth, Part 2.

HACHMONITE See Jashobeam, Part 2.

HADAR
See Hadad, Part 2.

HADAREZER
See Hadadezer, Part 2.

HADORAM
See Jehoram, Part 2.

HADRAMAUT
See Hazarmaveth, Part 2.

Bronze figurine of a Syrian god, possibly the storm-god Hadad or Rimmon ('the thunderer'). Height 11·4 cm. Late 2nd millennium BC. (BM)

Euphrates (2 Sa. 8:3). He was defeated by David and the gilded shields of his bodyguard taken as trophies to Jerusalem together with booty from the towns of Betah and Berothai in his territory, despite the advance of reinforcements from Damascus. Following this reversal his old enemy, Toi of Hamath, sent gifts to David (v. 10). However, Hadadezer continued to rule his territory and later supported the Ammonites in force in their war with David (2 Sa. 10:16–19; 1 Ch. 18:3–8). When the Israelites again defeated the Syrian forces *Rezon, a refugee from the court of Hadadezer, became king in Damascus and plotted against Solomon (1 Ki. 11:23).

A Hadadezer (Assyr. *Adad-'idri*), king of Damascus, is named as one of the allies who, with Ahab of Israel, opposed Shalmaneser III at Qarqar in 853 BC (*DOTT*, pp. 47–48). These kings are sometimes identified with *Ben-hadad I–II. See *Or* 34, 1965, pp. 472–473 for name. D.J.W.

HADAD-RIMMON. The mourning in Jerusalem on the death of Josiah in battle with Neco II of Egypt in 609 BC is compared with that 'of Hadad-rimmon in the plain of Megiddo' (Zc. 12:11). It is commonly supposed to be the name of a place near Megiddo and thus to be identified with modern Rummaneh, S of that city. However, the form of the name meaning '(the god) *Hadad is (the god) Rimmon', and the context, may show that it is a composite name. Both elements mean 'the thunderer' and are local names or epithets for Baal, and such a name can be compared with the deity Rashap-shalmon. The allusion would then be to the great mourning normally associated with this deity personifying the elements in ceremonies at Megiddo, and perhaps a counterpart to that described in Jdg. 11:37–40 (*DOTT*, p. 133).

D.J.W.

HADRACH. A place on the N boundaries of Syria (Zc. 9:1). Mentioned in the Aram. inscription of Zakur of Hamath, *c.* 780 BC, it is the Hatarikka of Assyr. inscriptions, once the seat of a district governor, near Qinneṣrin, 25 km S of Aleppo (*HUCA* 18, 1944, p. 449, n. 108).

A.R.M.

HAGAR. A Semitic, not an Egyptian, name and thus perhaps given to the woman by Abraham when he left Egypt. It may mean 'flight' or something similar, *cf.* Arab. *hegira.* Hagar was an Egyp. bondservant in Abraham's household, handmaid to Sarah; Abraham probably acquired her during his visit to Egypt. With the passing years Abraham felt keenly the lack of a son and heir, and, after the war of the kings (Gn. 14), with magnificent faith believed God's promise that he would indeed have a son (Gn. 15:2–6). But as time still passed, Abraham and Sarah had doubts, and sought to gain an heir by their own unsanctioned efforts: in accordance with the customary law of the period (attested in tablets from Ur and Nuzi), the childless Sarah urged Abraham to have a son by her servant Hagar—so Ishmael was born, the son of a slave-woman (Gn. 16). In conception, Hagar despised the barren Sarah, and fled into the desert from Sarah's wrath. At a well, God commanded her to return to her mistress and promised her numerous descendants. Awed by this experience of God, Hagar called the well 'the well of him who lives and sees me' (Beer-lahai-roi). In due course (Gn. 21:1–7) the promised son, Isaac, was born, the gift of God's initiative and supernatural grace. At Isaac's weaning the half-slave Ishmael mocked; God then commanded Abraham (against the custom of the day) to expel Hagar and her son (Gordon, *BA* 3, 1940, p. 3), for the line of promise was in Isaac, and God had another destiny for Ishmael (Gn. 21:9–14). In the wilderness the fugitive pair soon ran out of water, and Hagar sat apart from Ishmael to avoid witnessing his death. God then showed her a well of water. Ishmael grew up in Paran (in NE Sinai) as a hunter with the bow, and Hagar procured him a wife from her Egyp. homeland (Gn. 21:15–21).

Two millennia later, Paul had to rebuke his Galatian converts for hankering after a deceptive 'righteousness' gained by self-exertion in obeying the stipulations of the law, instead of continuing in Christ by faith (Gal. 3–5). He used the story of Hagar and Ishmael, Sarah and Isaac, as an allegory. Ishmael was the son, by earthly effort, of Hagar the slave. Similarly, the Jews (*i.e.* 'the present Jerusalem') were 'sons' of the Sinai covenant (pictured as Hagar); their failure to keep it faultlessly demonstrated the power of sin and the futility of seeking justification by self-effort. Isaac was the son of a promise received by faith, the gift of God's grace: Sarah typified the covenant of promise and grace (*cf.* Gn. 15) and all reborn spiritually in saving faith are numbered with Isaac. As Isaac was the true heir and Hagar and Ishmael were expelled, so the law as a limited phase in God's plan of redemption was in due time supplanted by the covenant of faith established finally and eternally in Christ (Gal. 4:21–5:1). K.A.K.

Hadadezer (*Adad-'idri*), *king of Damascus, is named in the Kurkh stele as supplying 1,200 chariots, 1,200 cavalry and 20,000 infantry to the allies who battled against Shalmaneser III of Assyria at Qarqar, Syria. One of his allies at the time, also named here, was Ahab of Israel* (Ahabbu māt siralaia). *853* BC. (BM)

HAGGAI, BOOK OF. This little book, as we know from the dates it contains, records messages given between August and December 520 BC. Some 18 years had elapsed since the return from Babylon permitted by Cyrus, but work on restoring the Temple had long since ceased (Ezr. 4:24). Haggai's main task was to rouse his contemporaries to action once more and in this he was assisted by the prophet Zechariah (Ezr. 5:1).

I. Contents and structure

Despite the internal evidence of chronological sequence the order of the text has been questioned and its rearrangement suggested (*cf.* NEB). The biblical order is attested by the *Scroll of the Twelve* from the caves of Murabba'at, the earliest known Heb. MS, and follows a recognizable pattern. The structure is a twofold accusation, response, assurance:

	I	II
Accusation	1:1–11	2:10–17
Response	1:12–15	2:18–19
Assurance	2:1–9	2:20–23

Though there may well have been editorial arrangement of the prophecies, the immediacy of the message and the absence of comment upon it suggest that little time elapsed between the prophet's preaching and the publication of his words.

II. Development of theme

The twofold presentation serves a specific purpose. In the first half the prophet starts with the present and looks back over the previous 18 years, whereas in the second half he works from the present to the future, though in each case the assurance section contains references to promised blessing.

Part I. 1:1–11. Catching the current mood of lethargy Haggai intersperses accusation with diagnostic comment on the economic situation. One directive (v. 8) provides a goal for the community and a test of their willingness to accept correction.

1:12–15. The response is unprecedented. Zerubbabel the prince and Joshua the priest lead their people into unanimous acknowledgment of Haggai's authority as

Dates given in the book of Haggai on which prophetic statements were made.

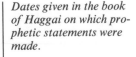

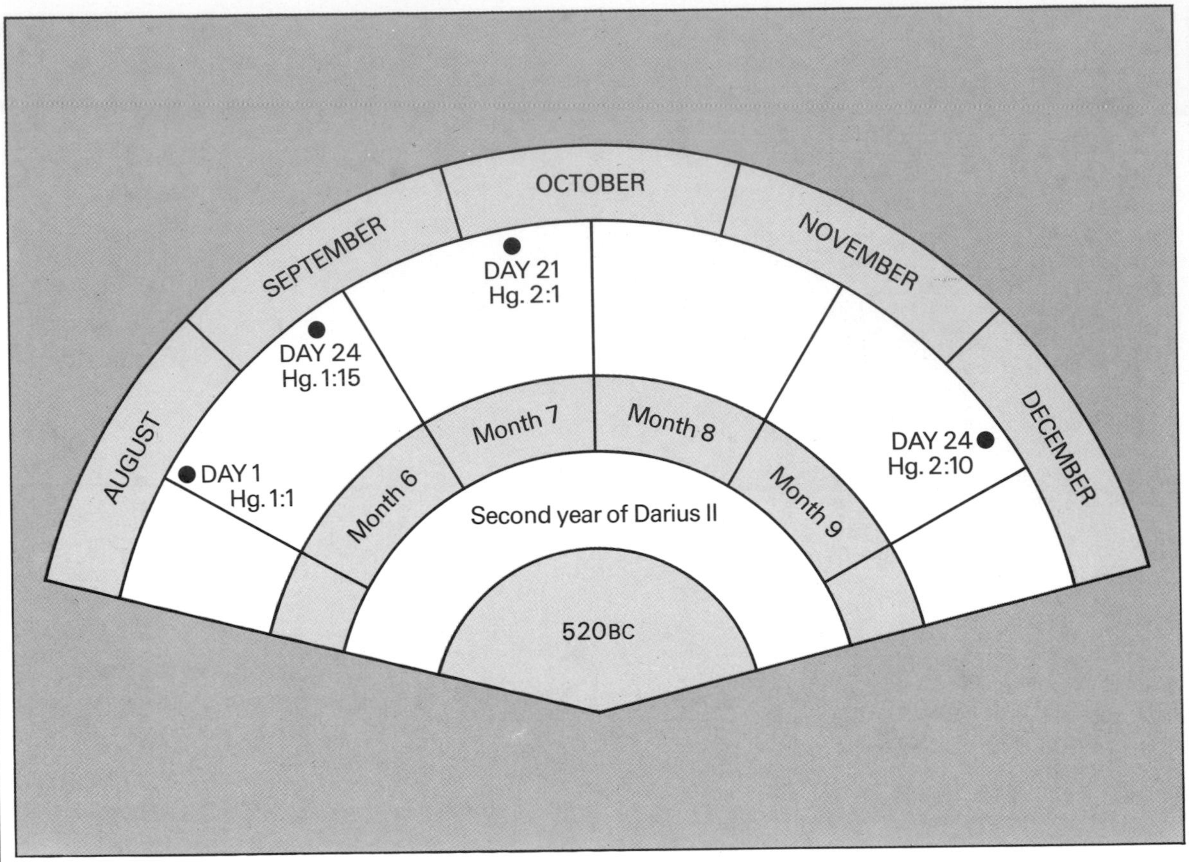

HAGIOGRAPHA
See Canon, OT, Part 1.

HAIL
See Plagues of Egypt, Part 3.

God's spokesman. With the promise of God's Spirit among them they make a start 3 weeks later on rebuilding the Temple.

2:1–9. After a further 4 weeks discouragement was again hindering progress. Because of their poverty the new building was necessarily basic, lacking the splendour of Solomon's Temple. Nevertheless it would one day be beautified with silver and gold contributed by the nations, and would then surpass even that of Solomon.

Part II. 2:10–17. It was one thing to reconstruct the Temple but quite another to remove the contamination caused by its desecration under heathen armies. The mere offering of sacrificial meat in their ritual could not ensure acceptance by the Lord. Far from being a place of cleansing, the Temple-skeleton had been a defilement. Repentance was all-important, and of that obedience to the prophet was a tangible proof. God would acknowledge this change of heart by changing shortage into abundance.

2:18–19. The people had responded and the Lord would once again give his blessing. That very December day, when no farmer could predict what next year's harvest would be, God promised prosperity as a sign of his approval.

2:20–23. There are echoes here of the imagery used in 2:1–9. In 520 BC there was little in the political scene to cheer the returned exiles. The great powers were entrenched, but the day of their overthrow was imminent. Then the Davidic prince, Zerubbabel, God's chosen servant, would be the Lord's executive, like the signet ring which was used to seal royal documents (*cf.* Je. 22:24), and would perform all his will.

According to Haggai, there is a strict correlation between commitment to God's cause and the enjoyment of his good gifts. There are priorities too. When these are observed and God has pride of place, he will see that the needs of his work and of his people are met. The promise to Zerubbabel found fulfilment in his greater descendant (Mt. 1:12; Lk. 3:27).

BIBLIOGRAPHY. H. G. Mitchell, *Haggai and Zechariah*, *ICC*, 1912; D. R. Jones, *Haggai, Zechariah and Malachi*, *TBC*, 1962; J. G. Baldwin, *Haggai, Zechariah, Malachi*, *TOTC*, 1972. J.G.B.

HAGRITES. A prosperous tribe or confederation living E of Gilead which was attacked by Israelites in the time of Saul (1 Ch. 5:10, 18–22); in Ps. 83:6–8 they are listed among the enemies of Israel. They are mentioned in association with Aramaean tribes in an inscription of Tiglath-pileser III and the name also occurs in inscriptions in Nabataean, Sabaean, *etc.* They are probably the *Agraioi* mentioned by Strabo, Ptolemy and Pliny. The resemblance to the name Hagar has inclined some to consider them as her descendants (Ishmaelites), but this is improbable. R.P.G.

HAIR. The normal Israelite custom, for both sexes, seems to have been to let the hair grow to considerable length. Absalom's luxuriant growth is recorded with apparent admiration (2 Sa. 14:26). It was only the weight of it that forced him to have it cut annually. Barbers are mentioned (Ezk. 5:1), but their function was to trim rather than to crop the hair. But by the NT period long hair was a 'shame' to a man (1 Cor. 11:14), although Paul made that statement to a church in Greece. Women, on the other hand, wore the hair long and practically uncut in both periods. The Talmud does mention women's hairdressers, but the root of the word (*m*^{e}*ḡadd*^{e}*lâ*) is 'to

plait' rather than 'to cut'. Baldness was disliked, perhaps because of its possible connection with leprosy (*cf.* Lv. 13), and evidently the youths' reference to Elisha's baldness was a studied insult. In Egypt the head and face were shaved, however, and Joseph had to comply with the local customs (Gn. 41:14). Dark hair was admired in both sexes; but grey hair was very honourable, and revered accordingly (* AGE, OLD AGE). Indeed, we find God himself portrayed as having grey (or white) hair (Dn. 7:9; *cf.* Rev. 1:14). But Herod the Great apparently preferred a youthful appearance, for he dyed his hair when it began to go grey.

The hair was treated in various ways. Samson had seven plaits, and women frequently braided or plaited their hair. Soldiers proceeding to battle let it hang loose, but to leave it unkempt was a sign of mourning; tearing it betokened fear and distress. The trimming of it had to be done in special ways; the forelock must never be cut (Lv. 19:27), since this was a feature of some idolatrous cults (*cf.* Dt. 14:1). To this day orthodox Jews observe this custom; small boys can be seen with the whole head cropped close, except for the ringlets hanging at the ears. The priests were given instructions about their hair by Ezekiel (44:20). The Nazirite had to leave his hair untrimmed so long as his vow lasted, and then shave it completely. This shaving signified purification (Lv. 14:8). Another special case was that of Samson, the secret of whose strength was his untrimmed hair.

Wigs showing Egyptian hair-styles worn by the vizier Ramose and his wife. From the tomb chapel of Ramose, Thebes. c. 1385–1380 BC. (BPL)

Hairdressing scene shown on the side of the sarcophagus of the Egyptian princess Kawit. c. 2100 BC. (PAC)

It was a sign of hospitality to anoint a guest's head (Lk. 7:46). The hair was frequently anointed on festive occasions (*cf.* Ps. 45:7). Swearing by the hair (or head) was a custom which Jesus could not commend (Mt. 5:36).

In metaphor and simile the hair was used to denote multitude, insignificance and fineness (Ps. 40:12; Mt. 10:29f.; Jdg. 20:16).

BIBLIOGRAPHY. L. Köhler, *Hebrew Man*, E.T. 1956, pp. 26ff.

D.F.P.

HALAH. A place in Assyria to which Israelites were deported from Samaria (2 Ki. 17:6; 18:11; 1 Ch. 5:26; *cf.* Ob. 20, RSV 'exiles in Halah' by small emendation). There is no doubt this was Assyr. Halahhu, a town and district NE of Nineveh, giving its name to one of the gates of that city. Other proposed locations are far less likely.

A.R.M.

HALAK (Heb. *ḥālāq*, 'smooth, bald'). A mountain (lit. 'the bald mountain') in Judaea which marked the S limit of Joshua's conquests (Jos. 11:17; 12:7). Its locality is described as 'going up to Seir'. Probably the modern Jebel Ḫalâq, W of the Ascent of Akrabbim.

J.G.G.N.

HALF-HOMER
See Weights and measures, Part 3.

HALF-SHEKEL
See Money, Part 2.

Statuette of a woman from Telloh, Babylonia. Her hair, which falls straight down her back, is held in place by crossed bands of cloth or ribbon. Height 22 cm. Gypsum. c. 2600 BC. (MC)

HALLELUJAH. This is a transliteration of the Heb. liturgical call *hall^{e}lû-yâh* = 'praise ye Yah', the shortened form of Yahweh (see * GOD, NAMES OF), which occurs 24 times in the Psalter. Though it is merely one variant of several calls to praise, the fact that with one exception (Ps. 135:3) it is always found at the beginning or end of psalms, and these all anonymous and so presumably among the later ones, suggests that it had become a standardized call to praise in the post-exilic Temple worship.

The psalms where it is found fall into groups: (1) Pss. 104–105 (at the end), 106 (at the beginning and end, the latter being part of the doxology to the Fourth Book of Psalter). (2) Pss. 111–113 (at the beginning), 115–117 (at the end), LXX is almost certainly correct in placing the repetition at the end of Ps. 113 at the beginning of Ps. 114, thus completing the series. (3) Ps. 135, at the beginning and end, but LXX correctly places the latter at the beginning of Ps. 136. (4) Pss. 146–

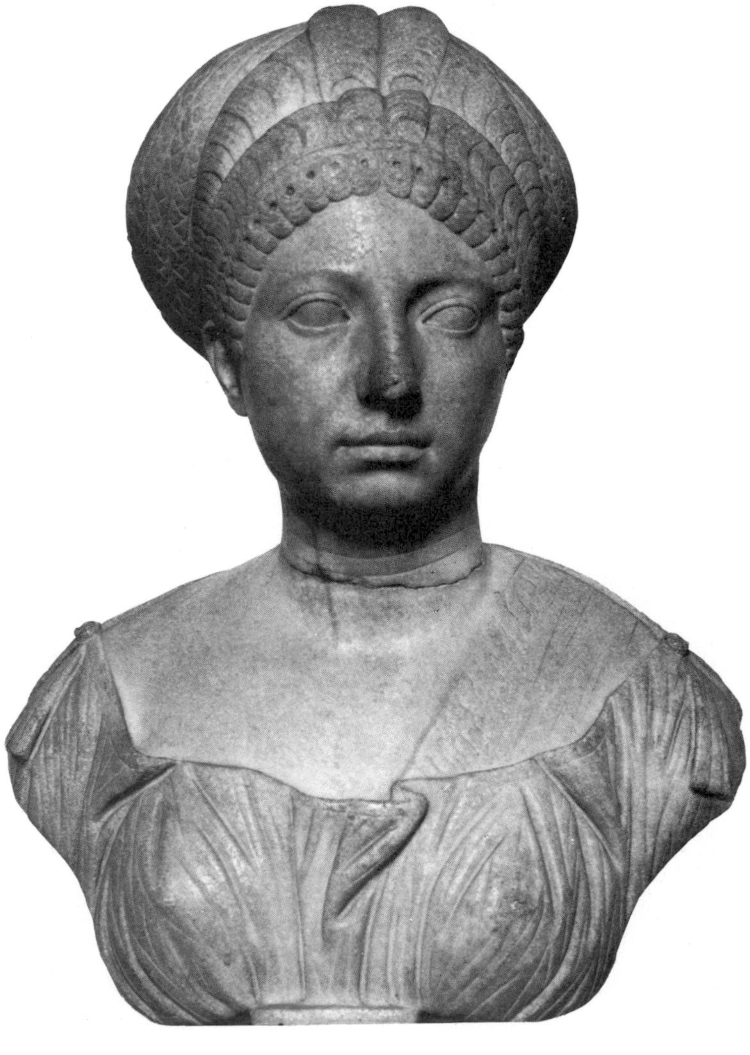

Hair elaborately arranged to resemble a turban. Roman portrait-bust of Claudia Olympias. c. AD 115. (BM)

A hair-style worn by Roman ladies of the late 1st–early 2nd cent. AD. *(Cf. 1 Pet. 3:3.) Unknown Roman woman.* (BM)

150, at the beginning and end of each.

From the NT ('Alleluia', Rev. 19:1, 3–4, 6) the call has been taken over into Christian worship. Most of the Hallelujah psalms play a special role in synagogue worship. Pss. 113–118, the Egyp. Hallel, are sung at the feasts of *Passover, *Pentecost, *Tabernacles and *Dedication, at the first Pss. 113–114 being sung before the meal, Pss. 115–118 after the third cup (*cf.* Mk. 14:26). Pss. 135–136 are sung on the sabbath, and the Great Hallel (Pss. 146–150), with Ps. 145, at all morning services. H.L.E.

HAM. 1. (Heb. *ḥām*, LXX *cham*; etymology uncertain). One of the sons of Noah, probably the second (Gn. 5:32; 6:10; 7:13; 9:18; 1 Ch. 1:4, 8; though *cf.* Gn. 9:20–24), and ancestor of many descendants (*NATIONS, TABLE OF). In 1 Ch. 4:40 and Pss. 78:51; 105:23, 27; 106:22 the name is used to indicate one section of his descent: Egypt (*MIZRAIM). From its biblical usage the term 'Hamitic' is applied by modern authors to a group of languages of which Egyptian is one, and for precision it is limited to this linguistic sense, a Hamitic 'race' not being recognized by modern anthropological classifications. In the biblical sense, however, genetic descent is all that is implied, and with the movement and intermarriage of peoples and the changes of language which took place in ancient times common descent from Ham would not necessarily imply common habitat, language, or even race in a recognizable form. At the end of the Flood when Noah was drunk Ham saw him naked and informed his two brothers, who covered up their father. In consequence of this, Noah put a curse upon Canaan (Gn. 9:20–27). Many explanations of this apparent cursing of Canaan for what Ham had done have been put forward, perhaps the most plausible being that Canaan did something not recorded which was worthy of cursing and that the phrase 'his younger son' (*b^enô haqqāṭān*, lit. 'his son/grandson, the little [one]') in v. 24 might refer to Canaan. This would be consistent with the twice-repeated statement (vv. 18, 22) that Ham was the father of Canaan.

2. *Hām.* The name of a city whose inhabitants, the Zuzim, were smitten by Chedorlaomer in the time of Abraham (Gn. 14:5). The

HALLMARK
See Seal, Part 3.

HALLUCINATION
See Resurrection, Part 3.

The head of an Assyrian dignitary with typical long curled black hair and a beard. Wall painting from the palace at Til Barsip, Syria. 8th cent. BC. (AP)

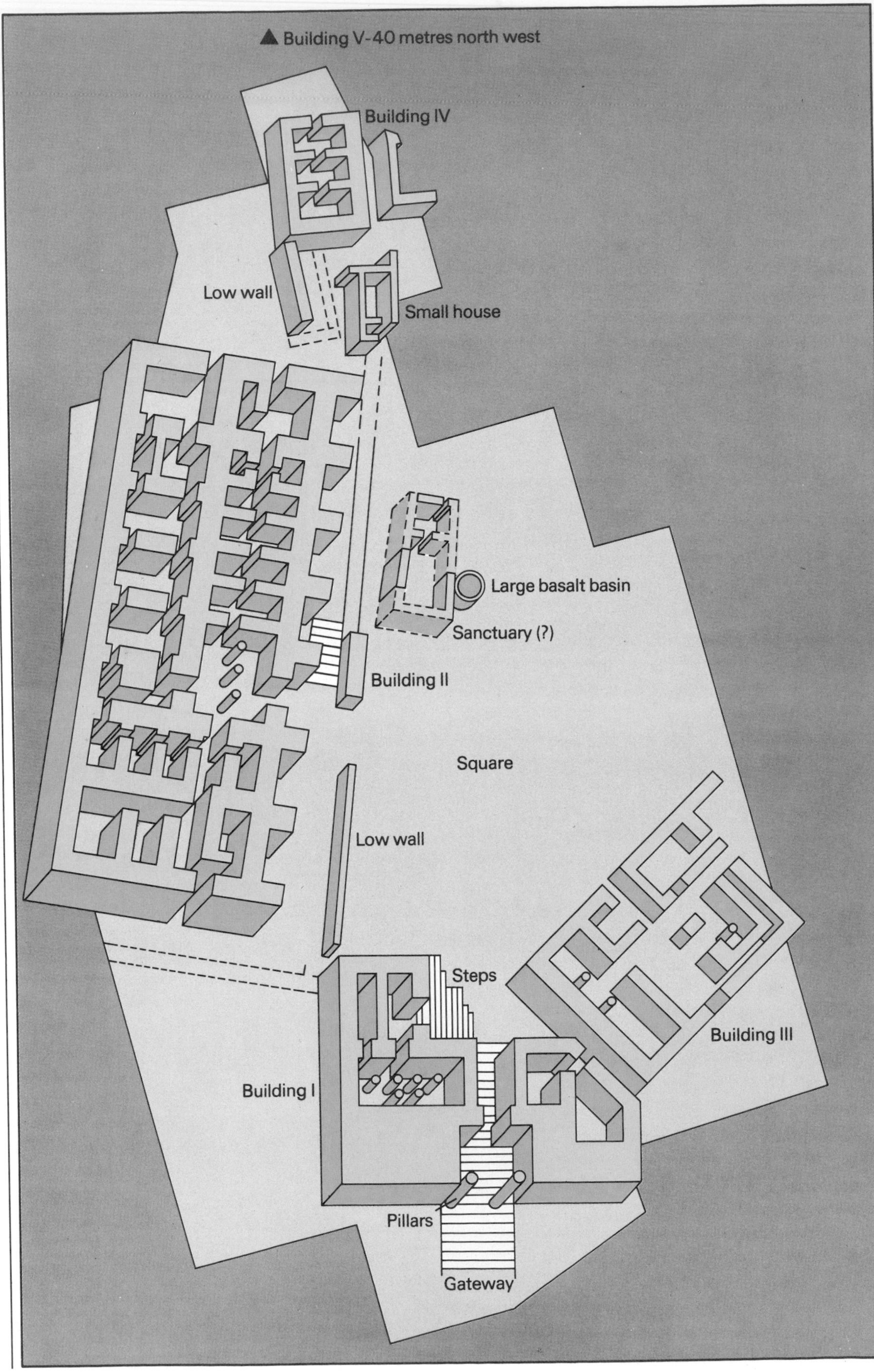

Plan of the main buildings on the citadel of Hamath before their destruction by Sargon II of Assyria.

site, though probably somewhere in Transjordan, is unknown. LXX (*hama autois*) interprets the Heb. *b^{e}hām* 'in Ham' as *bāhem*, 'with them'. T.C.M.

HAMAN. The villain of the book of *Esther, who plots to massacre the Jews when his vanity is hurt by Mordecai's refusal to bow to him. He is eventually hanged on the gallows that he has prepared for Mordecai. He is called an *Agagite. His name may be derived from the Elamite god, Hum(b)an. J.S.W.

HAMATH (Heb. *ḥ^{a}maṯ*, 'fortress, citadel'). City on the E bank of the Orontes, lying on one of the main trade-routes to the S from Asia Minor. Gn. 10:18 describes it as Canaanite. In David's time, under King Toi (or Tou), it was friendly towards Israel (2 Sa. 8:9–10; 1 Ch. 18:9–10). Toi's son is named Joram in 2 Sa. 8:10. This is probably not a Yahweh name ('Yah is exalted'), but an abbreviation of Hadoram as given in 1 Ch. 18:10. Connection of a Hamathite rebel called *Ya'u-bidi* by Sargon of Assyria with Yahweh is also unlikely (*cf. ANET*, p. 285; *DOTT*, p. 59). Solomon controlled it (2 Ch. 8:4), and it was conquered by Jeroboam II (*c.* 780 BC, 2 Ki. 14:28) and Sargon (*c.* 721 BC, *cf.* 2 Ki. 18:33f.; Is. 36:18f.; 37:13, 18f.), some of its inhabitants being settled by the Assyrians in *Samaria worshipping their deity *Ashima there (2 Ki. 17:24ff.). Palace buildings of the 9th and 8th centuries BC were excavated by a Danish team, 1931–8 (see E. Fugmann, *Hama, l'Architecture des périodes préhellénistiques*, 1958). Inscriptions in Hittite hieroglyphs, cuneiforms and Aramaic were found. According to the Babylonian Chronicle, it was at Hamath that Nebuchadrezzar overtook the Egyptians fleeing from Carchemish in 605 BC (*cf.* D. J. Wiseman, *Chronicles of Chaldaean Kings*, 1956, p. 69). The city was known in Greek and Roman times as Epiphaneia; today it is *Ḥamāh*. The ideal N boundary of Israel reached 'Labo of Hamath', formerly rendered 'the entering in of Hamath', *e.g.* Nu. 34:8; Jos. 13:5; Am. 6:14, but probably modern Lebweh, NNE of Baalbek, at the watershed of the Beqa' valley, near one source of the Orontes, so at the head of the road N to Hamath, Assyrian Laba'u in the province of Supite (*ZOBAH). For discussion see R. North, *Mélanges de l'Université S. Joseph* 46, 1970–1, pp. 71–103. J.G.G.N. A.R.M.

HAMMURAPI. (Akkad. [Amorite] Hammu-rapi, '(the god) Hammu heals'). **1.** King of Babylon *c.* 1792–1750 BC, sixth in line of First Amorite Dynasty. **2.** Name of two kings of Yamhad (Aleppo), the first *c.* 1760 BC. **3.** King of Kurda, mid-2nd millennium BC. **4.** Common 2nd millennium BC personal

Top: The fortified city of Hamath under attack by the Assyrian army of Shalmaneser III. Bronze relief from the temple gates at Balawat, near Nimrud, Iraq. c. 845 BC. (BM)

'Hamath' (hmt) *inscribed in Aramaic letters on an ivory label, probably captured by Sargon II and taken to Nimrud (Calah). 9·2 cm × 6·5 cm. 8th cent. BC.* (BSAI)

Limestone relief plaque with a representation of Hammurapi, king of Babylon, dedicated to the goddess (Ash)ratum by a provincial governor, Itur-ashdum. Width 38 cm. c. 1760 BC. (BM)

Head, found at Susa, Iran, thought to represent Hammurapi, king of Babylon (c. 1792–1750 BC*). Black granite (diorite). Height c. 15 cm.* (MC)

name especially in Upper Mesopotamia. Formerly **1** was identified with * Amraphel (Gn. 14:1).

Hammurapi (more correct than Hammurabi) as 'Governor of Babylon' was stated as having ten or fifteen kings 'going with him' as had his contemporary Rim-Sin of Larsa, while Ibal-piel of Eshnunna had twenty. The same Mari letter shows that all these were less powerful than the ruler of Yamhad.

Initially Hammurapi devoted himself to gaining control of * Babylonia and of the Euphrates waters. By 1764 BC he had defeated a coalition of Ashur, Eshnunna and Elam and the next year defeated Rim-Sin and by 1761 BC Zimrilim of * Mari. His reign was marked by a distinctive personal style which sought to unify Mesopotamia under a single ruler. He is now adjudged a weak administrator. A selection of his legal judgments (not a 'code' of laws, *e.g.* omission of homicide laws) survives on a diorite stele found at Susa in AD 1902. In this he reports to the national god Marduk on his role as 'king of justice' towards the end of his reign. The 282 sections of the Laws of Hammurapi (= LH) are roughly arranged to cover cases of theft and miscellaneous decisions (LH 1–25), property (26–49), commercial law (100–126), marriage (127–161), priestesses (178–184), adoption (185–194), assault (195–240), agricultural cases (241–267), rates and wages (268–277) and an appendix on slaves (278–282). Some of the cases and decisions are similar to earlier collections of laws (Ur-Nammu, Lipit-Ishtar, Eshnunna). A few are worded similarly to OT cases, *e.g.* false witness (LH 1, 3–4; *cf.* Ex. 23:1–3; Dt. 19:16–20), kidnapping (LH 14; *cf.* Ex. 21:1f.), loss of animals on deposit (LH 266–7; *cf.* Ex. 22:10–13), just as warning to the owner of goring ox (Ex. 21:35–36) compares with Eshnunna Law 53. Many of the specific cases concerning marriage, divorce and sexual offences, *e.g.* the death penalty for both parties in adultery with a married woman (Dt. 22:22; LH 129), have a similar approach. In other cases the offences are the same but the penalty differs, the Hebrew being seemingly the more consistently humane. In most cases the legal treatment differs, but precise comparison with OT is difficult since only the established fact (without supporting evidence) is given, followed by the oral judicial decision. These laws therefore represent a local Babylonian manifestation of the attitude to law and order common throughout much of the ancient Near East.

BIBLIOGRAPHY. C. J. Gadd, *CAH*, 2/1, 1973, pp. 176–227; D. J. Wiseman, *Vox Evangelica* 8, 1973, pp. 5–21; S. Greengus, *IDBS*, 1976, pp. 533–534, sub. 'Law in the OT'.

D.J.W.

HAMOR. '(He-)ass', see below. The ruler of Shechem in the time of Jacob (Gn. 33:19–34:31), from whose citizens (lit. 'sons', a common Sem. usage, *cf.* below) Jacob bought a plot of land (Gn. as cited; Jos. 24:32). Both Hamor and his son Shechem fell in Simeon and Levi's slaughter of the Shechemite menfolk and despoliation of the city in revenge for the humiliation of their sister * Dinah. In the period of the judges Hamor's name was still attached to Shechem (Jdg. 9:28). In the NT, in his dramatic speech to the council, Stephen telescopes Abraham's purchase of the Machpelah cave with Jacob's acquisition of the plot at Shechem—a realistic mark of the rapid flow of Stephen's impromptu, lightning exposition of Israel's history, not an error by Luke (Acts 7:16).

Animal personal names such as Hamor, 'ass', were common in biblical lands and times. *Cf.* Merānum ('pup'), the name of a doctor in the Mari tablets of patriarchal date (Bottéro and Finet, *Archives Royales de Mari*, 15, 1954, p. 152, refs.; compare Mendenhall, *BASOR* 133, 1954, p. 26, n. 3). Egypt also affords many examples.

Killing an ass was sometimes part of covenant-making (Mendenhall, *op. cit.*), but to interpret the phrase 'sons of Hamor' as 'members of a confederacy'—as suggested by Albright, *Archaeology and the Religion of Israel*, 1953, p. 113—is unnecessary. 'Son' of a place or person often means simply a citizen of that place or member of that person's tribal group. *Cf.* the common phrase 'children (sons) of Israel', 'daughter of Jerusalem', as well as Assyr. usage. K.A.K.

HANANEL. In Ne. 3:1, a *Jerusalem tower, lying between the Sheep and Fish Gates, at the NE corner of the city. It is closely connected with the Tower of the *Hundred, and some scholars would equate the two, or else make them two parts of the same fortress. AV spells the name 'Hananeel'; the Heb. is *ḥ^{a}nan'ēl*, 'God is gracious'.

The Targum of Zc. 14:10 seems to place the tower on the W of the city, by identifying it with the later Hippicus; this cannot be correct. D.F.P.

HANANIAH (Heb. 'Yahweh has been gracious'). A Heb. name occurring frequently in the OT and under its Gk. form *Ananias, in later times also.

1. A cult-prophet, son of Azur, whom Jeremiah denounced (Je. 28) for publicly declaring in the Temple that in 2 years' time, in opposition to Jeremiah's prophecy of 70 years (25:12), the booty taken from Jerusalem by Nebuchadrezzar would be restored, the captives returned and the power of Babylon broken. He confirmed his words by the symbolic action of removing from Jeremiah's neck the yoke worn as a symbol of Jeremiah's policy of submission to Babylon (27:2–3, 12), and breaking it. Jeremiah's denunciation, 'Yahweh has not sent you' (28:15), was shown to be true by the death of Hananiah 2 months later.

2. Father of a prince under Jehoiakim, king of Judah (Je. 36:12). **3.** Grandfather of Irijah, the officer of the guard who arrested Jeremiah as a traitor (Je. 37:13). **4.** One of Daniel's companions in captivity, renamed Shadrach (Dn. 1:6–7, 11, 19). **5.** Son of Zerubbabel (1 Ch. 3:19, 21). **6.** A Benjaminite (1 Ch. 8:24). **7.** Leader of one of the groups of musicians set up by David for the service of the Temple (1 Ch. 25:4, 23). **8.** A captain in Uzziah's army (2 Ch. 26:11). **9.** Commandant of the citadel whom Nehemiah put in charge of Jerusalem (Ne. 7:2). **10.** Various persons figuring in the lists of Ezra-Nehemiah (Ezr. 10:28; Ne. 3:8, 30; 10:23; 12:12, 41). J.B.Tr.

HAND. In comparison with the Gk. word *cheir* (which is translated only by 'hand', with some composite words such as *cheiropoiētos*, 'made with hands'), the two main Heb. words translated 'hand' in RSV have very wide meanings. *yāḏ* has many variant translations in RSV, and *kap̄* several, all of which are related to the primary meaning, 'hollow' or 'palm', from a root meaning 'curved' or 'bent'. *kap̄* is also the name of one of the letters of the Heb. alphabet, probably descriptive of its shape, which is somewhat like a reversed C.

In common with other parts of the body in Heb. thought, the hand is described as having apparently almost autonomous functions (1 Sa. 24:11). But the balancing of the phrases 'my power' and 'the might of my hand' in Dt. 8:17, and other examples of parallelism, indicate that this is far from absolute autonomy, the primary reference being to the action of the whole individual, although, at the same time, attention is specifically focused on the relevant functioning part (*cf.* Mt. 5:30).

Like the *arm, the hand (especially the right hand) is used as a symbol of might and power. In the case of 'hand', however, the figurative meaning has gone a step further than with 'arm'. See, *e.g.*, Jos. 8:20, where *yāḏ* is translated 'power'. There are several very common phrases in which the hand is used as a symbol of power, *e.g.* in or out of 'the hand of one's enemies' (Ps. 31:15; Mk. 14:41). Conversely, the dropping of the hands symbolizes weakness or lack of resolution, and to strengthen them is to remedy that (Is. 35:3; Jdg. 9:24). Left-handed persons are specially noted (Jdg. 3:15).

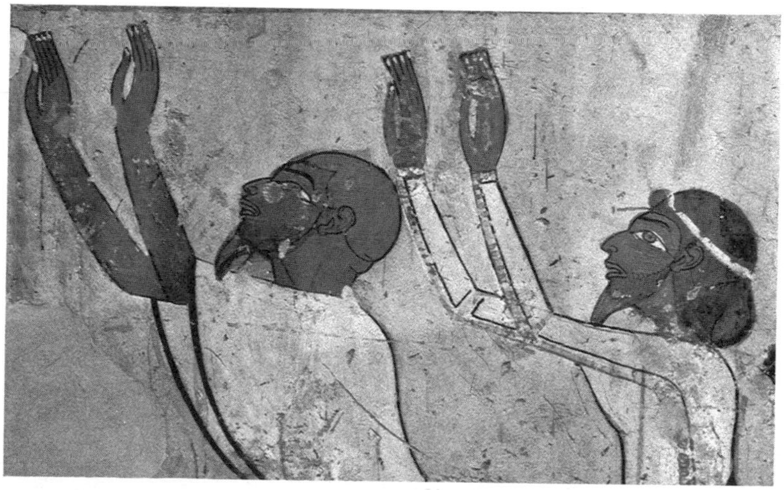

Hands raised in supplication by envoys to Egypt from Syria. Tomb of Sebek-hotep, Thebes. c. 1420 BC. (BM)

Lifting the hand is symbolic of violence (1 Ki. 11:26) as well as of supplication (Ex. 9:33; 17:11; Ps. 28:2), the *gesture being indicative of the attitude or action. The word *kap̄*, indicating the open palm, is more frequently used in the latter sense.

Clasping hands (Jb. 17:3; AV, RSV 'give surety') ratified an agreement, as did also the placing of one's hand under another's *thigh (Gn. 24:9) or raising one's hand, as in a law court today (Gn. 14:22 [RSV 'I have sworn', lit. 'I have lifted my hand']; Ex. 17:16).

HANAEANS
See Nomads, Part 2.

'Martha the daughter of Hananiah' (Mrth bt Hnnyh) *written on an ossuary from Jerusalem. Boxes used to house the bones of the dead required such identification. 40 BC – AD 70.* (JPK)

Women and children clap their hands as they follow a procession of Elamite musicians celebrating the accession of Prince Ummanigash. Relief from the palace of Ashurbanipal, Nineveh. c. 640 BC. (BM)

HANDBREADTH
See Weights and measures, Part 3.

HANGING
See Gallows, Part 1.

HANGINGS
See Tabernacle, Part 3.

The touch of a person's hands was held to communicate authority, power or blessing, the right hand being more significant in this respect than the left, but both hands were often used (Gn. 48:13–14; Dt. 34:9). Notice especially the laying of the hands of the worshipper on the head of his sacrificial beast, where the communication of authority probably signified identity with the offering (Lv. 1:4); and the NT communication of the Holy Spirit or performance of miracles by the laying on of hands (Mk. 6:5; Acts 8:17–19; 19:11). This is but another indication that in Heb. thought, and to a certain extent in the NT as well, there was a close relation between what much Gk. and modern thought would designate separately as 'body' and 'spirit'.

'Absalom's monument' (2 Sa. 18:18) is literally 'Absalom's hand'.

BIBLIOGRAPHY. A. R. Johnson, *The Vitality of the Individual in the Thought of Ancient Israel*, 1949; C. Ryder Smith, *The Bible Doctrine of Man*, 1951. B.O.B.

HANDKERCHIEF (Gk. *soudarion*, in Acts 19:12; rendered as 'napkin' in Lk. 19:20; Jn. 11:44; 20:7). It transliterates Lat. *sudarium* defined etymologically (*sudor*, 'sweat') as a cloth for wiping perspiration. Catullus, however, uses the word for 'table-napkin' (12. 14), and Nero (Suetonius, *Nero* 25) undoubtedly used *sudarium* with the meaning of 'handkerchief'. E.M.B.

HANES. Is often identified with Egyp. *Ḥ(wt-nni-)nsw*, Gk.–Lat. Heracleopolis magna, modern Ihnâsyeh el-Medîneh or Ahnâs, about 80 km upstream (*i.e.* S) of Cairo, and an important city in Middle Egypt. However, this does not really suit Is. 30:4, in the two parallel clauses: 'His officials are at Zoan, and his envoys reach Hanes.' *Zoan is Tanis in the NE Delta, the seat of the 22nd–23rd Dynasty pharaohs, and Lower Egypt advanced-headquarters of the Ethiopian 25th Dynasty, for Asiatic affairs. Hence the parallelism of the verse seems to demand that Hanes be closely linked with E Delta Tanis, not Upper Egypt Heracleopolis, far distant and irrelevant.

Two solutions are possible. W. Spiegelberg, *Aegyptologische Randglossen zum Alten Testament*, 1904, pp. 36–38, postulated a 'Heracleopolis parva' in the E Delta, arguing from Herodotus' mention of a province and city of Anysis there (2. 166, 137); this would then be Egyp. *Ḥ(wt-nni-)nsw* of Lower Egypt, Heb. *Ḥanes*, and Assyr. *Ḫininsi*. *Cf.* Caminos, *JEA* 50, 1964, p. 94. Or Hanes may merely be a Heb. transcription of an Egyp. *ḥ(wt)-nsw*, 'mansion of the king', as the name of the pharaoh's palace in Zoan/Tanis itself. Either interpretation is plausible; neither is proven. Some refer the 'his' (princes, envoys) of Is. 30:4 to the Judaean king; but the natural antecedent is pharaoh in v. 3. Hence, with É. Naville, *Ahnas el Medineh*, 1894, p. 3, these are pharaoh's officials at Zoan and his envoys who come to treat with the Jewish emissaries, either at Hanes as an advance-post for Zoan (Naville, Spiegelberg), or summoned to the 'Ha-nesu', the king's palace, in Zoan itself. K.A.K.

HANNAH (Heb. *ḥannâ*, 'grace'). The favourite of the two wives of Elkanah, an Ephraimite who lived at Ramathaim-zophim (1 Sa. 1). The other wife, Peninnah, tormented her because she had no family. She vowed that if she bore a son she would devote him to God as a *Nazirite. This she did, and named him *Samuel. Her song of thanksgiving (1 Sa. 2:1–10) suggests that she was a prophetess. It contains the first mention of the king as Yahweh's Messiah ('his anointed'). There are many echoes of it in Mary's song when Christ's birth was announced (Lk. 1:46–55; *MAGNIFICAT). She brought Samuel a robe every year when she came to Shiloh to worship. She later became the mother of three sons and two daughters (1 Sa. 2:19, 21). J.W.M.

HARA. With *Halah, *Habor and *Gozan, a place to which Tiglath-pileser III removed rebellious Israelites in 734–732 BC (1 Ch. 5:26). An Assyr. site of this name is not known. 2 Ki. 17:6; 18:11, however, interpret *hārā'* as '*cities* of the Medes' and LXX 'mountains' may represent Heb. *hārê*, 'hill-country'. D.J.W.

HARAN (Heb. *ḥar(r)an*; Akkad. *ḫarrānu*, 'cross-roads'; Gk. *charrhan*, Acts 7:4). **1.** The city *c.* 32 km SE of Urfa (Edessa), Turkey, on the river Baliḫ, lies on the main route from Nineveh to Aleppo. Terah lived there with Abram (Gn. 11:31; *cf.* Acts 7:2, 4) before the latter migrated to Canaan (Gn. 12:1). It was the home of Isaac's bride *Rebekah. Jacob fled there to escape Esau (Gn. 29:4), married Leah and Rachel, daughters of Laban, and all his children (except Benjamin) were born there (Gn. 29:32–30:24).

Harran is referred to in texts from the Ur III period *c.* 2000 BC as a temple (*é.ḫul.ḫul*) for the worship of *Sin the moon-god, and its occupation is confirmed by archaeological evidence. Its strategic position made it a focus for Amorite tribes according to *Mari texts of the 2nd millennium BC, and

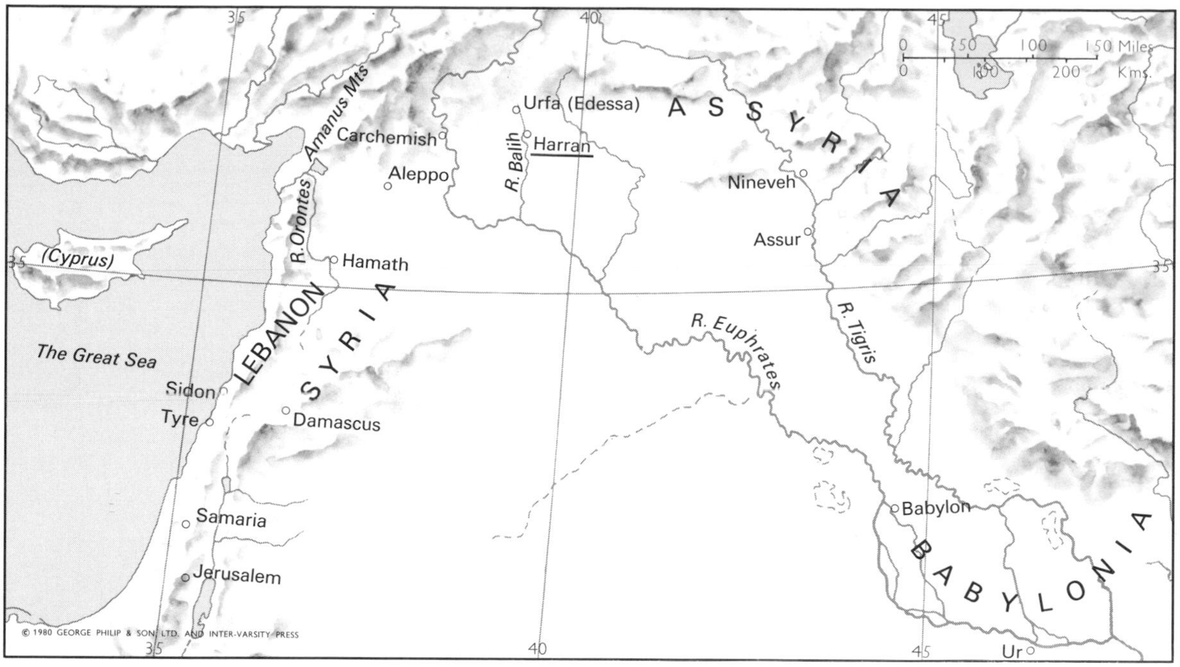

Harran ('Crossroads' or 'Highways') lies at a strategic point between Mesopotamia and the W.

This stele, found at Harran, depicts King Nabonidus of Babylon worshipping the moon (crescent = Sin), the sun (rayed disc = Shamash) and the goddess Ishtar (divine crown). The inscription below describes the rebuilding of Eḫulḫul, the Sin temple. Height 1·87 m. 555–539 BC. (SOAS)

later an Assyrian centre fortified by Adad-nirari I (*c.* 1310 BC) with a temple embellished by Tiglath-pileser I (*c.* 1115 BC). Harran rebelled and was sacked in 763 BC, an event used by Sennacherib's officials to intimidate Jerusalem (2 Ki. 19:12 = Is. 37:12). The city was restored by Sargon II, and the temple repaired and refurnished by Esarhaddon (675 BC) and by Ashurbanipal. After the fall of Nineveh (612 BC) Harran became the last capital of Assyria until its capture by the Babylonians in 609 BC. The Chaldean Dynasty's interest in the Babylonian temples led to the restoration of the Sin temples at Harran and at Ur. At the former the mother of Nabonidus (who lived to 104), and at the latter his daughter, were made the high priestesses. It was a thriving commercial city in contact with Tyre (Ezk. 27:23).

The site, excavated 1951–3, 1959, indicates clearly an occupation before the Assyrian period. The existing ruins are mainly from the Roman city near which the Parthians slew Crassus (53 BC) and from the later occupation by Sabaean and Islamic rulers in Harran, then called Carrhae. In AV of Acts 7:4 the city is named Charran.

2. Haran is also a personal name. (*a*) The son of Terah, brother of Abraham and Terah, father of Lot, Milcah and Iscah, who died at *Ur (Gn. 11:26–31); (*b*) A man of Judah, son of Caleb and his concubine Ephah (1 Ch. 2:46); (*c*) A Levite; son of Shimei, of Gershon (1 Ch. 23:9).

BIBLIOGRAPHY. S. Lloyd and W. Brice, *AS* 1, 1951, pp. 77–112; D. S. Rice, *AS* 2, 1952, pp. 36–84; C. J. Gadd, *AS* 8, 1958, pp. 35–92; K. Prag, *Levant* 2, 1970, pp. 63–94. D.J.W.

HARARITE. A designation applied to some of David's heroes: Shammah (*šammā'*) son of Agee, who was possibly the same as Shammah (*šammâ*) (2 Sa. 23:11, 33); Jonathan son of Shage (1 Ch. 11:34); and Ahiam son of Sacar (1 Ch. 11:35). The name is unknown outside the Bible, and may be that of a tribe or city, or may simply mean 'mountain dweller' from *har*, 'mountain, hill'. T.C.M.

HARMON. A place (RSV, Am. 4:3) otherwise not mentioned in OT (AV interprets as 'the palace', from vss. LXX has 'the mountains of Rimmon', possibly the hill of *Rimmon (Jdg. 20:45, 47). Various emendations, 'naked' (*'armôṯ*), 'devoted to destruction', have been suggested. More plausible is the suggestion, on the basis of Ugaritic *hrmn*, that this may be Harmel (S of *Kadesh on the Orontes).

BIBLIOGRAPHY. *BASOR* 198, 1970, p. 41. D.J.W.

HAROD (Heb. *ḥ*^{a}*rōḏ*, 'trembling'). A copious and beautiful spring at the foot of Mt Gilboa, E of Jezreel, which flows E into the Beth-shean valley. Here Gideon, confronting the Midianite hordes, reduced his army in two stages from 32,000 to 300 (Jdg. 7:1–8). Probably Saul and his army camped here prior to the fatal battle on Mt Gilboa (1 Sa. 29:1; *cf.* 31:1). Two of David's 'mighty men', Shammah and Elika

HARE
See Animals, Part 1.

HARLOT
See Prostitution, Part 3.

HAR-MAGEDON
See Armageddon, Part 1.

HARMEL
See Harmon, Part 2.

HARNESS
See Ornaments, Part 2.

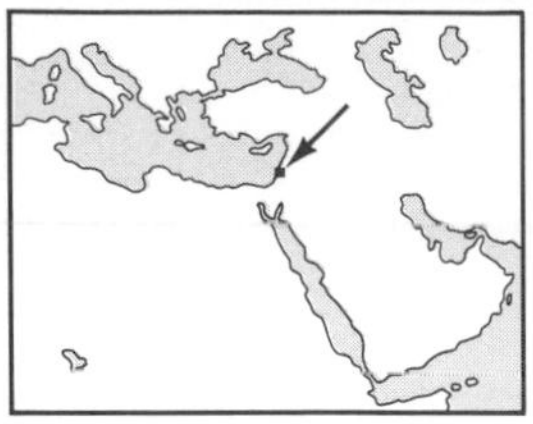

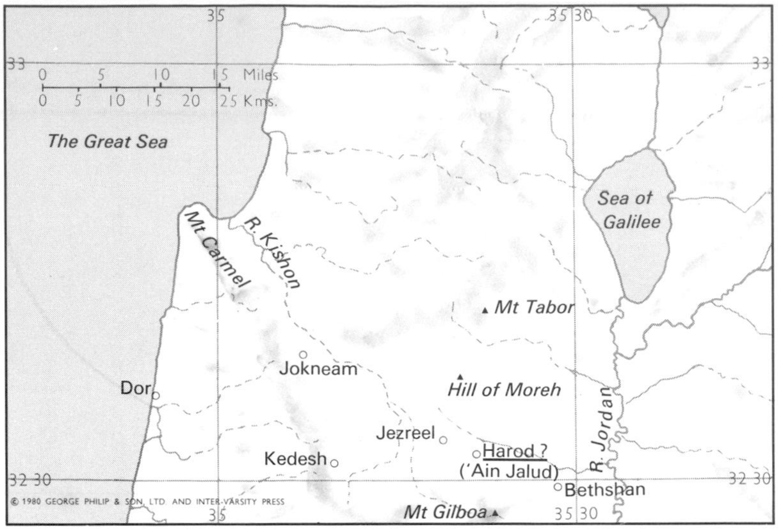

Harod, site of the spring by Mt Gilboa.

HARP
See Music, Part 2.

HARRAN
See Haran, Part 2.

HART
See Animals, Part 1.

HARTEBEEST
See Animals, Part 1.

HARVESTER ANT
See Animals, Part 1.

The spring of Harod wells up from the rocks at the foot of Mt Gilboa, near Jezreel. (SH)

Opposite page: Top right: Harosheth in upper Palestine.

Bottom right: Havvoth-Jair and its surroundings.

(2 Sa. 23:25; 1 Ch. 11:27), came from Harod, possibly to be identified with the modern 'Ain Jalud.

A.E.C.

HAROSHETH. Always occurs as 'Harosheth of the Nations' (*ḥªrōšeṯ hagôyīm*). It is found only in connection with *Sisera, a Canaanite commander who fought against Barak, and whose base it was (Jdg. 4:2, 13, 16). The battle is located in NW Palestine near the river Kishon. Mazar has suggested that a region rather than a city is implied, but v.16 would strongly suggest the latter (*cf.* Targum). Tell 'Amr NW of Megiddo and Tell el-Harbaj SE of Haifa have been suggested as possible sites, but of these the former appears to be disqualified by soundings indicating an absence of habitation before the 10th century BC. The city is not mentioned in extra-biblical documents, and the exact location remains uncertain.

BIBLIOGRAPHY. *LOB*, pp. 201, 203; B. Mazar, *HUCA* 24, 1952–3; pp. 80ff.; *GTT*, p. 288.

W.O.

HARROW. A toothed implement dragged along the ground to break clods of earth after ploughing. The verb (Heb. *śāḏaḏ*) always occurs parallel to verbs of ploughing or breaking the soil (Jb. 39:10; Is. 28:24; Hos. 10:11, AV 'break'). The actual form of the implement used is uncertain; it was drawn by a led ox (Jb. 39:10), but there is no known representation of anything corresponding to a modern harrow in form. Heb. *ḥārîṣ* (2 Sa. 12:31) denotes a sharp or pointed implement, RSV 'picks' rather than AV 'harrows'.

A.R.M.

HASIDAEANS. This is a transliteration of *Hasidaioi* in 1 Macc. 2:42; 7:13; 2 Macc. 14:6, though 'Hasmonaeans' may be the correct reading in the last case. RVmg. and modern literature prefer the underlying Heb. *ḥªsîḏîm*. This term, meaning fundamentally 'loyal ones', is used frequently in the Psalms (usually 'saints' in EVV). It seems to have been adopted by the zealots for the law, when Hellenistic ideas came flooding in early in the 2nd century BC.

Their leader seems to have been the high priest Onias III, deposed by Antiochus Epiphanes. They would have avoided armed struggle against the Syrians by withdrawing into the wilderness, but the implacable hostility of the Hellenizers drove them to support the Maccabees. As soon as they were granted a legitimate high priest they were prepared to return to normal life, but their leaders were murdered by Bacchides (1 Macc. 7:12–18). They had little sympathy with the nationalistic aims of the Hasmonaeans. Probably already under Simon, their party split in two. The majority, now known as *Pharisees, tried to win the people to their views. The minority, represented by the Essenes and Qumran Covenanters, despaired of all but divine eschatological intervention and withdrew to a greater or lesser degree from public life.

BIBLIOGRAPHY. M. Black, *The Scrolls and Christian Origins*, 1961.

H.L.E.

HATRED, HATE.

I. In the Old Testament

Hatred between brothers (Gn. 27:41; 37:4f., 8; 2 Sa. 13:22) or fellow-Israelites (Ps. 55:12f.; Pr. 14:20) is condemned (Lv. 19:17). Dt. 4:42; 19:4, 6, 11, and Jos. 20:5 distinguish between accidental and malicious manslaughter. Sexual love (2 Sa. 13:15; Dt. 22:13–16; 24:3; *cf.* Jdg. 14:16, see **III**, below) may turn to hatred. Personal enmity is sometimes tempered with mercy (Ex. 23:5; Jb. 31:29), but the enemies of Israel (2 Sa. 22:41; Ps. 129:5; Ezk. 23:28) or of the godly (Ps. 34:21; Pr. 29:10) are God's enemies too (Nu. 10:35; *cf.* Ex. 20:5; Dt. 5:9; 7:10). God hates both evil (Pr. 6:16; Am. 6:8) and evildoers (Dt. 32:41): so therefore do the righteous (Pss. 101:3; 139:21f.; 119:104, 113). God hates idolatry

(Dt. 12:31; 16:22), injustice (Is. 61:8), worship that is inconsistent with conduct (Is. 1:14), and even sinful Israel herself (Ho. 9:15; *cf.* Je. 12:8).

II. In the New Testament

The Father (Jn. 15:24), Jesus (Jn. 7:7; 15:18, 24f.), and all Christians (Mk. 13:13; Lk. 6:22; Jn. 15:18–20; 17:14; 1 Jn. 3:13) are hated by the world; but believers must not hate either fellow-Christians (1 Jn. 4:20) or enemies (Mt. 5:43f.). Hatred of evil (Heb. 1:9 = Ps. 45:7; Rev. 2:6; *cf.* Mk. 3:5), though not of persons, is attributed to Christ. (*WRATH.)

III. Contrasted with love

'Hate' as opposed to 'love' in Gn. 29:31, 33 (*cf.* 30, 'loved . . . more'); Dt. 21:15–17; Mt. 6:24 = Lk. 16:13, implies the choice or preference of another rather than active hatred of [illegible] Mal. 1:2f. = Rom. 9:13 of God's election of Israel; Lk. 14:26 (*cf.* Mt. 10:37, 'loves . . . more'); Jn. 12:25 of the overriding claims of discipleship.

BIBLIOGRAPHY. J. Denney, *ExpT* 21, 1909–10, pp. 41f.; W. Foerster, *TDNT* 2, pp. 811–816; O. Michel, *TDNT* 4, pp. 683–694; H. Bietenhard, H. Seebass, *NIDNTT* 1, pp. 553–557.

P.E.

HAVILAH (Heb. *ḥ^a^wîlâ*, 'circle', 'district'). **1.** A land (*'ereṣ*) in the neighbourhood of *Eden, through which meandered (*sābab*) the river Pishon, and in which was found gold, *bdellium and *shoham*-stone (Gn. 2:11–12). The location of the place is unknown.

2. An area mentioned in the phrase 'from Havilah to Shur'; inhabited by the Ishmaelites (Gn. 25:18) and Amalekites (1 Sa. 15:7). It probably lay therefore in the area of Sinai and NW Arabia.

3. A name that occurs twice in Gn. 10; as a descendant of Ham through Cush (Gn. 10:7; 1 Ch. 1:9) and as a descendant of Shem through Joktan, Eber, Shelah and Arpachshad (Gn. 10:29; 1 Ch. 1:23). These may be entirely distinct, but as the names associated with them indicate a possible area of settlement in S Arabia and across the Bab el-Mandeb in Africa, it may be that the name indicates one strong tribe which had absorbed a weaker group.

BIBLIOGRAPHY. J. A. Montgomery, *Arabia and the Bible*, 1934, p. 39.

T.C.M.

HAVVOTH-JAIR (Heb. *ḥawwōṯ yā'îr*), 'the camps (tent-villages) of Jair', probably in the hills between Mt Gilead proper and the Yarmuk, which were dotted with settlements called *'^a^yārîm* (Jdg. 10:4); a unique plural of *'îr*, 'town', or a diminutive (so Rashi, *Commentary*) homonymous with 'ass colts'. The area may have been known earlier as Havvoth Ham; so Nu. 32:41 (as emended by Bergman, *JPOS* 16, 1936, pp. 235ff.), since 'their villages' (*ḥawwōṯêhem*) has no plural antecedent; *cf.* Gn. 14:5. It was associated with the Argob, N of the Yarmuk, as part of Bashan, of which Og was the last king. Jair was credited with the conquest of the whole region (Dt. 3:14; 1 Ch. 2:23f.), including the Argob, to which the 'sixty cities' of Jos. 13:30; 1 Ch. 2:23 refer; *cf.* [illegible]

HAZAEL (Heb. *ḥ^a^zā'ēl*, *ḥ^a^zâh'ēl*, 'El sees' or 'whom God beholds'). A powerful king of Syria (Aram), God's scourge to Israel during the reigns of Jehoram, Jehu and Jehoahaz. Elijah was commissioned to anoint him as one of the three ordained to complete the extirpation of Baal-worship that he had begun (1 Ki. 19:15–17). Later, Hazael, as the emissary of Ben-hadad II to Elisha, learnt that he was to be king and would become an oppressor of Israel, a prophecy speedily put into effect by his murder of Ben-hadad and assumption of the throne (2 Ki. 8:7–15). He fought against Jehoram at Ramoth-gilead (2 Ki. 8:28–29; 9:14–15), and frequently defeated Jehu, devastating the country E of Jordan as far S as the Arnon valley (2 Ki. 10:32–33). He continued his attacks in the reign of Jehoahaz, and Israel was preserved from complete destruction only by God's mercy (2 Ki. 13:3, 22f.). 2 Ki. 12:17–18 reveals a Syrian incursion into SW Palestine, probably with the aim of securing the trade-routes. Gath was taken, and Jerusalem threatened, and Hazael was bought off only with a tribute from the Temple treasures. Syria's ascen-

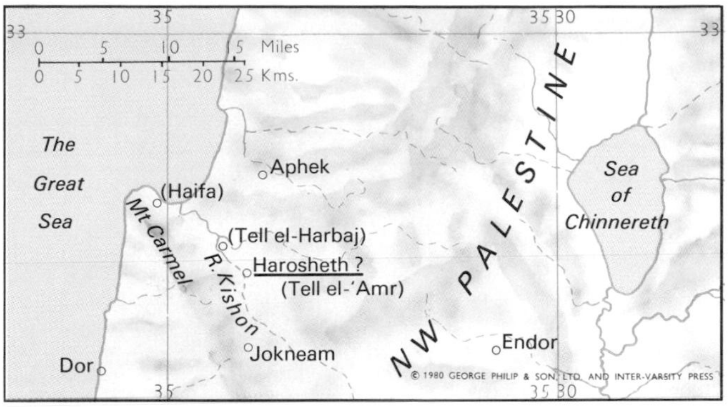

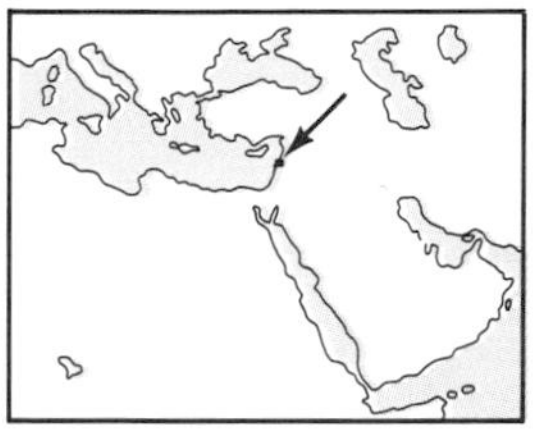

HAUGHTINESS
See Pride, Part 3.

HAWK
See Animals, Part 1.

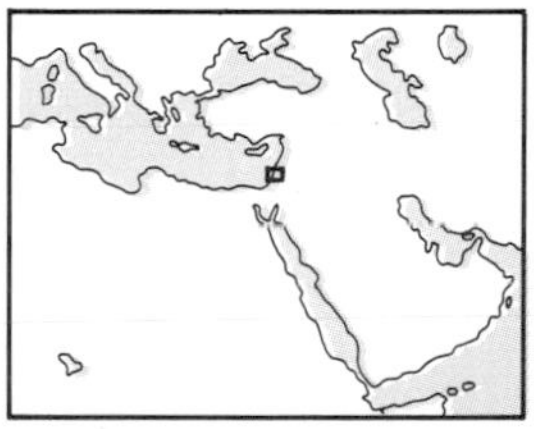

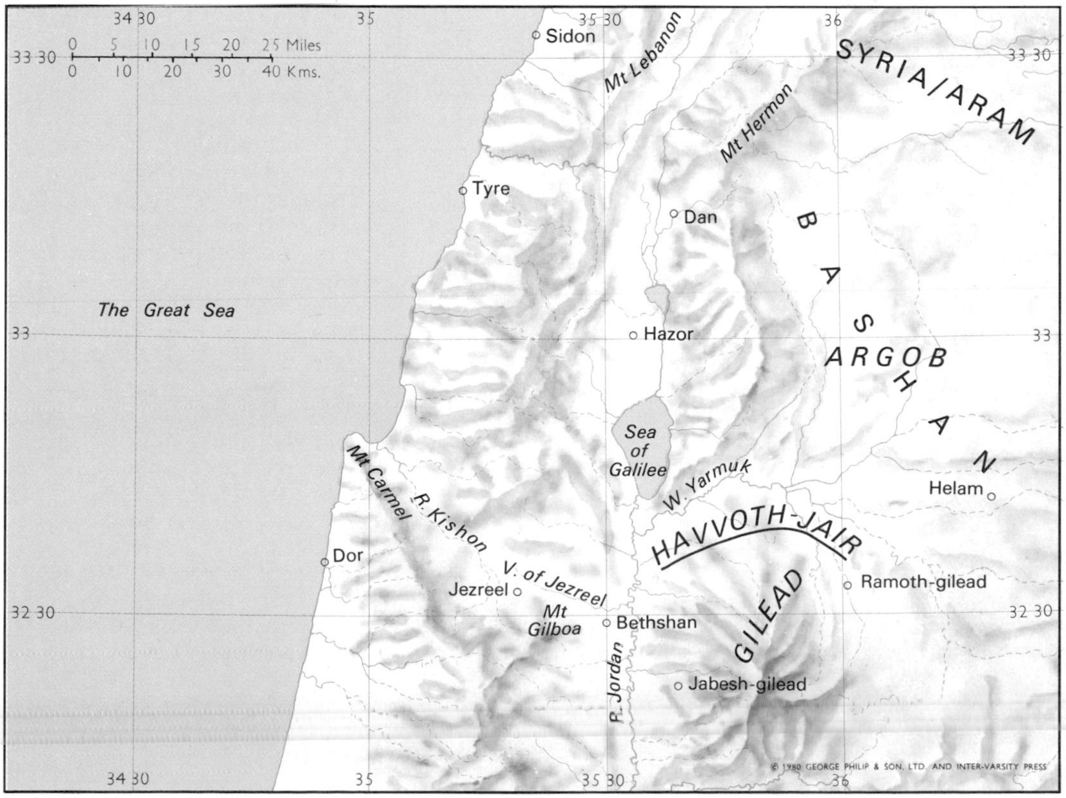

Ivory figure which may represent Hazael, king of Damascus (844–802 BC). From Arslan Tash, Syria. (MC)

dancy was checked only after Hazael's death, when his son, Ben-hadad III, was thrice defeated by Jehoash of Israel (2 Ki. 13:24–25). As one of the chief Syrian oppressors of Israel, the memory of Hazael's might lingered, so that half a century later Amos recalled his name as symbolizing the height of Syria's power which would yet feel the fire of God's judgment (Am. 1:4).

Hazael's name also occurs in Assyr. cuneiform inscriptions as an opponent of Shalmaneser III from 841 BC onwards. The wording of one text shows that the Assyrians not only knew Hazael to be a usurper ('son of a nobody', *ANET*, p. 280, text (c), 14–2:1) but that they also knew that his predecessor was the victim of foul play (Weidner, *AfO* 13, 1940, pp. 233f.).

Hazael must have attained his throne before 841 BC, as his and the Israelite Joram's forces fought in 842 at Ramoth-gilead; 843 BC, as suggested by Unger (*Israel and the Arameans of Damascus*, 1957, p. 75), is an early enough date. Shalmaneser III and Hazael fought again in 837 BC. Thereafter for 30 years no further collision of the two kingdoms is known, until Adad-nirari III in *c.* 805–802 BC cowed the now ageing Hazael into submission (*ANET*, pp. 281–282; *DOTT*, pp. 51–52), referring to him as *Marī'*, Aramaic for 'lord'. In Syria the earlier redoubtable Hazael had evidently become known as 'the lord' *par excellence*, and this current epithet was simply taken over by the Assyrian annalists. Hazael 'oppressed Israel all the days of Jehoahaz' (2 Ki. 13:22), who reigned *c.* 814/813–798 BC, and hence, at least briefly, outlived him, surviving to perhaps *c.* 797 or 796 BC.

Assyrian spoils from Hazael's Damascus included ivory-work, two pieces inscribed *l-mr'n Ḥz'l*, 'belonging to our lord Hazael', and another bearing the figure of a prince, just possibly a representation of Hazael himself.

BIBLIOGRAPHY. On Hazael and Israel generally, see R. de Vaux, *RB* 43, 1934, pp. 512–518, and A. Jepsen, *AfO* 14, 1941/4, pp. 153–172. See also *ARAM and *BEN-HADAD for further background and bibliography. J.G.G.N. K.A.K.

HAZARMAVETH (*ḥᵃṣarmāweṯ*). The third son of *Joktan (Gn. 10:26; 1 Ch. 1:20), probably to be identified with the kingdom of Ḥaḍramaut in S *Arabia, written *ḥḍrmt* and later *ḥḍrmwt* in the native inscriptions. The latter form corresponds closely to the unvocalized Heb. *ḥṣrmwt*, Heb. *ṣ* often corresponding to S Semitic *ḍ*.

BIBLIOGRAPHY. G. Ryckmans, *Les Noms propres sud-sémitiques*, 1, 1934, p. 338; C. Brockelmann, *Grundriss der vergleichenden Grammatik der semitischen Sprachen*, 1, 1908, § 46. T.C.M.

HAZEL
See Trees (Almond), Part 3.

HAZEROTH. A stopping-place on the desert journey of the Israelites (Nu. 11:35; 33:17–18), where Miriam became a leper (Nu. 12:1–16; *cf.* Dt. 1:1). Generally identified with 'Ayin Khodara, an oasis with a well on the way from Sinai to Aqabah. (*ENCAMPMENT BY THE SEA.) C.D.W.

HAZOR (Heb. *ḥāṣôr*). A place-name, probably meaning 'settlement' or 'village', and therefore used of several places in the OT, of which the most important was a fortified city in the territory of Naphtali (Jos. 19:36).

I. In the Old Testament

This city lay in N Palestine, and at the conquest it was the royal seat of Jabin (called 'king of Hazor', *meleḵ-ḥāṣôr*, Jos. 11:1), who organ-

Ivory inscribed with the name of Hazael, king of Damascus (844–802 BC). Furniture decoration from Arslan Tash, Syria. (MC)

UPPER CITY	LOWER CITY	PERIOD	REMARKS
			Citadel
I	NO LONGER SETTLED	Hellenistic (3rd–2nd cents. BC)	Citadel, farmhouses, graves
II		Persian (4th century BC)	Citadel
III		Assyrian (7th century BC)	Unfortified settlement
IV		8th century BC	Destruction by Tiglath-pileser III, 732 BC
V		8th century BC	City of Jeroboam II, destruction by earthquake
VI		8th century BC	Reconstruction of parts of stratum VIII
VII		9th century BC	Omrid dynasty
VIII		9th century BC	Conflagration (Ben-hadad I)
IX		End 10th–beginning 9th cent. BC	City of Solomon
X		Mid-10th century BC	[illegible]
XI		11th century BC	Temporary Israelite settlement, semi-nomadic
XII		12th century BC	Destruction in second half of 13th century by Israelite tribes
XIII	1a	13th century BC	Amarna period
XIV	1b	14th century BC	Thutmose III–Amenhotep II
XV	2	15th century BC	Graves in the ruined city
Post-XVI		MBA II-C transitional	Destruction by conflagration (Ahmose)
XVI	3	17th–16th cents. BC	Lower city founded in mid-18th century BC (the Mari documents)
XVII	4	18th–17th cents. BC	Unfortified. Mainly burials and some structures
Pre-XVII	NOT YET FOUNDED	Early MBA II-B	
XVIII		21st–20th cents. BC (MBA I)	Khirbet Kerak culture
XIX-XX		26th–24th cents. BC (EBA III)	
XXI		27th century BC (EBA II)	

Levels of occupation of the upper and lower cities of Hazor.

ized a coalition against Joshua. The Israelites defeated this, however, Jabin was killed, and Hazor was destroyed and burnt (Jos. 11:1–13; 12:19). Hazor was the only city thus burnt, perhaps because of its former importance (Jos. 11:10), but in spite of this destruction a later king of the same name, who this time was styled 'king of Canaan' (*meleḵ-kᵉna'an*, Jdg. 4:2, 24) threatened Israel in the time of Deborah. Though his general, Sisera, had 900 *chariots at his disposal, the Israelites under Barak were able to defeat him, and crush Jabin (Jdg. 4; 1 Sa. 12:9). Some two centuries later Hazor was fortified, together with Jerusalem, Megiddo and Gezer, by Solomon when he was organizing his kingdom (1 Ki. 9:15), but in the 8th century, in the time of Pekah of Israel, Tiglath-pileser III of Assyria came and destroyed the city and carried off its remaining inhabitants to Assyria (2 Ki. 15:29).

II. Excavation

The site of Hazor was identified in 1875 by J. L. Porter with the abandoned mound of Tell el-Qedah some 8 km SW of Lake Huleh in Galilee. J. Garstang made some trial soundings in 1928, but the first major excavations were carried out from 1955 to 1958 and 1968 to 1969 by an Israeli expedition under Yigael Yadin. The site lies on a NE facing slope, and consists of the city tell of some 100,000 sq.m extent at the S end, and adjoining this to the N a much larger area of about 0·6 sq.km with an earthen rampart on the W or uphill side. The main tell was founded in the 3rd millennium, and the lower city added to it in the early part of the 2nd millennium, probably by the Hyksos. Though Garstang assumed this lower city to be a camping enclosure for horses and chariots, excavation revealed that the whole of this area had been occupied by a

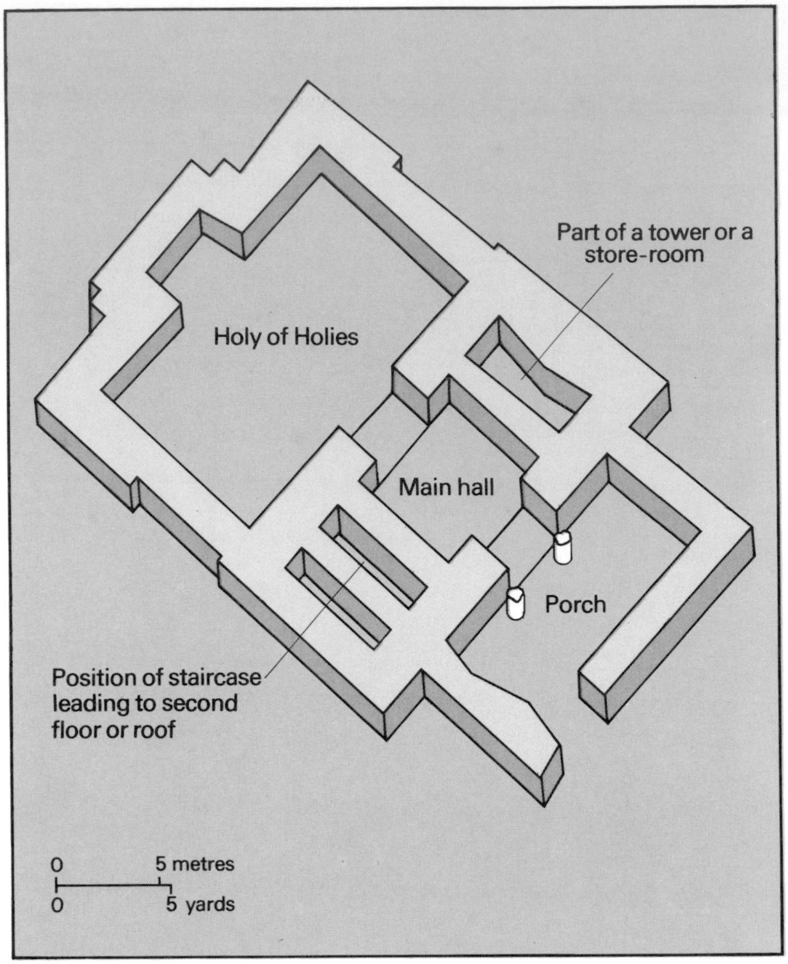

Plan of a Canaanite temple at Hazor, built in the 14th cent. BC *and destroyed, perhaps by Joshua and the Israelites, in the 13th cent.* BC.

built city, which at its height must, with the tell proper, have accommodated up to 40,000 souls. A further indication of the importance of the city at this time is given by the discovery of a pottery jug with an Akkadian inscription (the earliest known in Palestine) scratched on it. Though crudely done, the inscription has been read as *Iš-me-ilam*, an Akkadian personal name, perhaps that of a Mesopotamian merchant. This lower city was occupied for only about five centuries, having been destroyed in the 13th century (Level 13). This destruction is attributed by the excavators to Joshua. Among the remains in this destroyed city were found a Canaanite temple and a small shrine. While the lower city lay barren, the tell was reoccupied by the Canaanites, and then by the Israelites. A city gate and casemate wall from the time of Solomon, almost exactly matching those found at *Megiddo and *Gezer (*cf.* 1 Ki. 9:15), were uncovered. Evidence from the later Israelite period included a pillared public building of the time of Ahab (taken by Garstang to be stables), and a fortress containing a thick layer of ash, in which was a fragment of a wine jar bearing the name Pekah (*pqḥ*), and other signs of violent destruction, probably due to

Canaanite stele excavated at Hazor. Hands raised in prayer to the moon crescent and disc. Height c. 60 cm. 13th cent. BC. (MEPhA)

Hazor: the remains of the Israelite citadel, 9th–8th cent. BC. (RS)

Tiglath-pileser III, who took the city in 732 BC (2 Ki. 15:29).

III. In extra-biblical texts

Hazor is first mentioned in the Egyp. Execration Texts of the 19th century BC, as a Canaanite city likely to be a danger to the empire. It figures (*ḫa-ṣu-ra*) in the Mari archives of the first quarter of the 2nd millennium, and in a slightly later Bab. text, as an important political centre on the route from Mesopotamia, perhaps to Egypt. In one tablet the ruler is spoken of as a 'king' (*šarrum*), a title not usually applied to city rulers (*cf.* Jos. 11:1), and his importance is further indicated by the mention of ambassadors from Babylon travelling to see him. One king's name is given as Ibni-Adad, an Akkadian form suggesting Bab. influence, but there was also contact with the N and W, as is manifested in gifts from the king to Ugarit and Crete (*Kaptara*). Hazor is mentioned in the lists of their dominions made by the Egyp. kings Tuthmosis III, Amenhotep II and Seti I in the 15th and 14th centuries BC. The city is later mentioned in the Amarna letters, of the 14th century, the ruler still being spoken of as a king (*šar ḫa-zu-ra*). Finally, from the next century, the city is mentioned in an Egyp. papyrus (Anastasi I) in a military context. Thus the texts and excavations amply bear out the biblical testimony to the importance of the site.

IV. Other places of the same name

1. A place in the S of Judah (Jos. 15:23) whose site is unknown. **2.** (*ḥāṣôr ḥ^a^dattâ*) 'New Hazor' [illegible] whose site is unknown. **3.** Another name for Kerioth-hezron (Jos. 15:25) in S Judah, site unknown, perhaps the same as **2.**
4. A place in Benjamin (Ne. 11:33) probably modern Khirbet Hazzur. **5.** An area occupied by semi-nomadic Arabs, mentioned by Jeremiah (49:28, 30, 33).

BIBLIOGRAPHY. Y. Yadin *et al.*, *Hazor I*, 1958, *Hazor II*, 1960, *Hazor III–IV*, 1961; Y. Yadin, *Hazor* (Schweich Lectures, 1970), 1972; see also A. Malamat, *JBL* 79, 1960, pp. 12–19; E. K. Vogel, *HUCA* 42, 1971, pp. 35–36.

T.C.M.

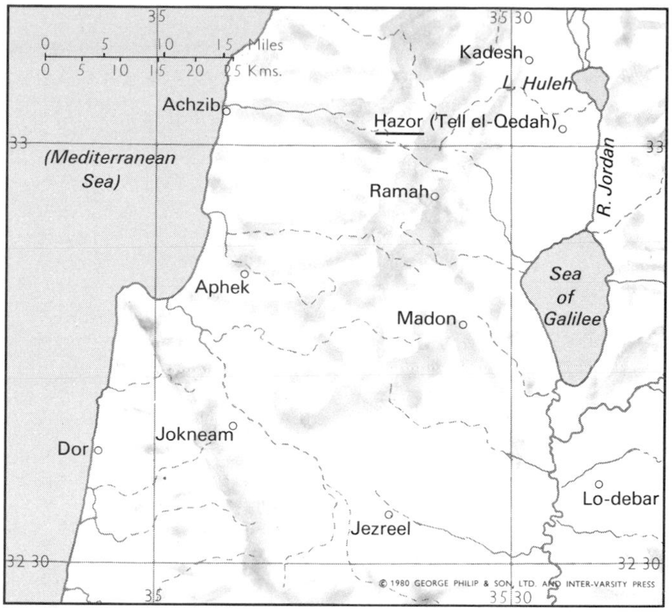

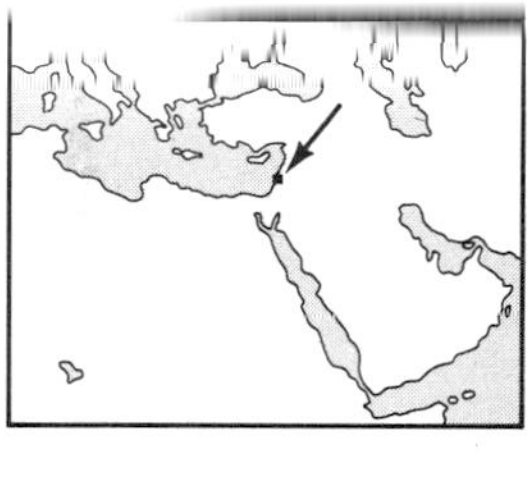

The location of Hazor.

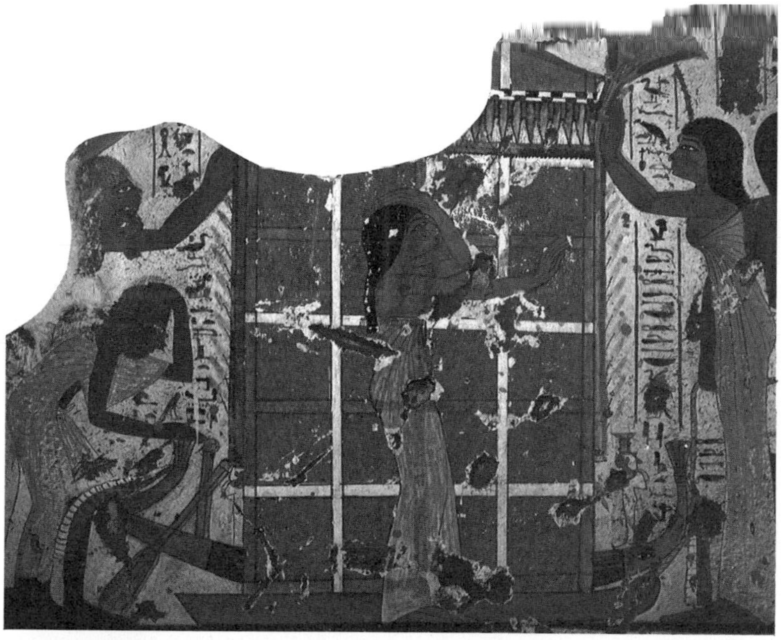

Female Egyptian mourners cover their heads with their hands as they follow the coffin of the deceased. Wall-painting in the tomb of the sculptors Nebamun and Ipuky at Thebes. c. 1350–1300 BC. (CP)

Women with their hands on their heads in a gesture of mourning, depicted on the stone sarcophagus of King Ahiram of Byblos. Length of sarcophagus c. 2·30 m. c. 1000 BC. (NMBL)

HEAD. The head (Heb. *rō'š*; Gk. *kephalē*) is not regarded as the seat of the intellect, but as the source of life (Mt. 14:8, 11; Jn. 19:30). Thus to lift up the head is to grant life in the sense of success (Jdg. 8:28; Ps. 27:6; Gn. 40:13, but *cf.* the pun in v. 19), or to expect it in God himself (Ps. 24:7, 9; Lk. 21:28). To cover the head by the hand or with dust and ashes is to mourn the loss of life (2 Sa. 13:19; La. 2:10). Figuratively, headship denotes superiority of rank and authority over another (Jdg. 11:11; 2 Sa. 22:44); though when Christ is spoken of as head of his body the church (Eph. 5:23; Col. 2:19), of every man (1 Cor. 11:3), of the entire universe (*hyper panta*, Eph. 1:22), and of every cosmic power (Col. 2:10), and when man is spoken of as the head of the woman (1 Cor. 11:3; Eph. 5:23; *cf.* Gn. 2:21f.), the basic meaning of

■ **HEADBAND**
See Magic, Part 2.

■ **HEAD-DRESS**
See Dress, Part 1.

■ **HEAD OF THE CORNER**
See Cornerstone, Part 1.

head as the source of all life and energy is predominant.

The church is Christ's body and he is her head (Eph. 4:15f.): the two cannot be severed. In this unity of head and body, Christ the head directs the growth of the body to himself: he is not merely the source of being of the body (1 Cor. 10:16f.) but also the consummation of its life (Eph. 4:15f.); *cf.* * CORNERSTONE. Hence to give allegiance to any other spiritual mediator, as was being done at Colossae, cuts the vital link between the limbs and Christ the head who is the source of all their being (Col. 2:18f.).

BIBLIOGRAPHY. F. Foulkes, *Ephesians*, *TNTC*, 1963, pp. 65f., 124, 155ff.; K. Munzer and C. Brown, *NIDNTT* 2, pp. 156–163; H. Schlier, *TDNT* 3, pp. 673–681; S. Bedale, 'The Meaning of *kephalē* in the Pauline Epistles', *JTS* n.s. 5, 1954, pp. 211 ff.

F.H.P.

HEALTH, DISEASE AND HEALING.

I. Introduction

The biblical descriptions of health, disease, healing and death are limited by:

a. The purpose of Scripture, which is theological rather than medical. Only those details which are relevant to the over-all purpose, revealing God to man, are included. Thus, for example, it is sufficient to record that a boy was 'paralysed' and 'in terrible distress' (Mt. 8:6). The object was to indicate the severity of the illness and the gravity of the prognosis against which to contrast the greatness of the cure and the divine power of Christ. This illness may have been an example of poliomyelitis with respiratory paralysis. Like most of the diseases of the Bible it was unnecessary to say so even if that had been known. There is no evidence to suggest exactly what caused that boy's illness in medical terms (the proximal cause), although some instances of disease in OT and NT do have a spiritual explanation given (the ultimate cause), *e.g.* Lk. 13:11–16.

b. Contemporary medical knowledge. Descriptions of disease were simple and were mostly confined to what could be seen (*e.g.* ulcer, swelling, haemorrhage) and/or felt by an observer (fever) or by the patient himself (dysentery, paralysis).

c. Contemporary public knowledge was even more restricted. Even if the medical knowledge of the day had been advanced, it would not have been understood by the readers.

d. Patterns of disease are constantly changing. This is particularly true of diseases of microbiological origin. 'Plague' refers to any epidemic disease and is not the equivalent of the modern infection with *Yersinia pestis*. Others may be unchanged for centuries, *e.g.* blindness from trachoma is still very common in the Middle East and was probably even more common in biblical times. In addition, the terms used to describe disease have also been greatly altered, even in the last few hundred years. No longer do doctors report that their patients suffer from the botch, the blain or the emerods, mentioned in the AV.

None the less, the biblical accounts of disease are based on observed facts. Sincere and honest men, mostly with no medical knowledge, wrote of what they saw as they understood best. The facts that they describe, therefore, can and should be treated as facts. Moreover, the standard of medical treatment (such as it was) and public hygiene (see **VII**, below) were superior to those of contemporary adjacent cultures.

II. Medical terms

a. Some general (non-medical) terms used to describe disease, healing and health

(*i*) OT. Heb. *ḥālâ* is used for 'to be sick' (nouns *ḥᵒlî* and *maḥᵃlâ*), and also *maḏweh* (Dt. 7:15; 28:61) and *dāḇār* (Ps. 41:8) meaning 'a matter' (*i.e.* evil matter). *rāpā'* (to heal) is most commonly used for healing, and is also used for 'physician' in Gn. 50:2 (twice); 2 Ch. 16:12; Jb. 13:4; Je. 8:22. Other OT terms include *ḥāyâ* (revive) and *šûḇ* (restore).

The words for health are infrequently used in the OT, and then always figuratively (*e.g.* Je. 30:17; 33:6; Ps. 42:11; Pr. 12:18).

(*ii*) NT. Disease is normally described by the Gk. nouns *astheneia* (weakness), *malakia* (misfortune)—used three times in Mt. only, or the verbs *astheneō* (to weaken) or *kakōs echein* (lit. 'to have badly') and once (Jas. 5:15) *kamnō* (to be ill, to ail). The adjective *arrhōstos* ('not robust') is used four times (*e.g.* Mk. 6:13); *mastix* (a whip) is used not only literally but metaphorically of disease—see *Plague*, below.

The commonest non-technical words for healing and health are *ischyō* (be strong) and *hygiainō* (be healthy), while *sōzō* and *diasōzō* (save) are used both of physical and spiritual healing (see *Leprosy*, below). *stereoō* (set up, make strong) is used in Acts 3:16, where *holoklēria*, 'perfect health', also occurs, possibly indicating active rehabilitation to normal life as well as to physical well-being.

b. Some more technical terms describing disease and healing in the New Testament

nosos (disease), while a specific term, was used only of disease in general rather than of any individual case. Luke and the other Evangelists employ the word in the same way (*e.g.* Mt. 4:23; 8:17; Lk. 4:40; 6:17; Acts 19:12, *etc.*). For other yet more specific words, see below.

Verbs for healing are *therapeuō*, *iaomai* and *apokathistēmi.*

The medical terminology used by Luke, as well as his discreet silence about the failures of his colleagues in treating the woman with an issue of blood (see *Menstruation*, below), indicate his medical training. Only Luke quotes 'Physician, heal yourself' (4:23). In Lk. 4:35 *ripsan*, 'thrown him down', is a medical term describing epileptic convulsions and *blaptein*, 'harm', is similarly a technical medical term (J. R. W. Stott, *Men with a Message*). In Lk. 24:11 *lēros*, 'idle tale', is a medical term used to describe the babblings of a feverish or insane patient (W. Barclay, *Commentary on Luke*).

c. Further medical terms

Barrenness. To be a wife without bearing children has always been regarded in the East, not only as a matter of regret, but as a reproach which could lead to divorce. This is the cause of Sarah's despairing laughter (Gn. 18:12), Hannah's silent prayer (1 Sa. 1:10ff.), Rachel's passionate alternative of children or death (Gn. 30:1) and Elizabeth's cry that God had taken away her reproach (Lk. 1:25). The awfulness of the coming judgment on Jerusalem is emphasized by the incredible statement, 'Blessed are the barren . . .' (Lk. 23:29). It was believed that the gift of children or the withholding of them indicated God's blessing or curse (Ex. 23:26; Dt. 7:14), as also did the barrenness or fruitfulness of the land (Ps. 107:33–34).

Blindness. Heb. *'iwwēr*, 'closed' or 'contracted', and its cognate *'iwwārôn*, *'awwereṯ* and *sanwērîm*, 'blindness'; Gk. *typhlos*. Blindness was common throughout the Middle East in biblical times. It is probable that several different diseases were responsible. Trachoma may have been common then, as it still is in some parts, causing blindness in infancy. Gonorrhoea in the mother can infect the eyes of children during their birth and lead to blindness. Blindness was sometimes seen as a punishment from God, as Dt. 28:28–29 indicates (also describing the pathetic groping gait of the blind and their propensity for being robbed).

There is one fascinating instance of a two-stage or double miracle of Jesus on a blind man (Mk. 8:22–25) in the Gentile town of Bethsaida. In the first miracle the blind man was led by Jesus out of the village, saliva was applied to his eyes and he was enabled to 'see'. However, presumably because he had never remembered seeing, his mind could not interpret the images he saw (v. 24). 'Men' looked like 'trees'; this is a well-recognized phenomenon in those who have never seen and who have sight made possible by corneal grafting or cataract surgery—see a fascinating article by R. E. D. Clark on 'Men as trees walking' (*FT* 93, 1963, pp. 88ff.) in which the subject is reviewed in depth. Jesus therefore performed a further miracle. Again a simple sign, a touch, was given and then he 'saw everything clearly' (v. 25). If the man had once learnt to 'see' and then become blind the second miracle would not have been necessary (*cf.* Mt. 9:27–31; 12:22; 20:29–34; 21:14). The sign applied for each miracle, an aid to faith, may have been the more necessary for him if he was a Gentile. See **V**, below.

Boil, botch. Heb. *šᵉḥîn*, 'burning'; *cf.* root in Arab., Aram., Eth., 'to be hot'. A generic term which the OT uses to denote different kinds of localized inflammation. For the 'boils breaking out in sores' of the sixth plague (Ex. 9:9) see * PLAGUES OF EGYPT. In Lv. 13:18–24 boils are mentioned in association with what is there termed leprosy, while the 'boils' (AV) or 'loathsome sores' (RSV) which afflicted Job (2:7), of which various diagnoses have been made, may have been tuberculous leprosy. 'The boils of Egypt', which extended from head to toe (Dt. 28:27, 35), was probably one of the cutaneous diseases peculiar to Egypt (*cf.* Pliny, *NH* 26. 5) such as an endemic boil or malignant pustule. Hezekiah's boil (2 Ki. 20:7; Is. 38:21) was probably a carbuncle.

Burn. Heb. *ṣārebeṯ*, a 'burning' or 'scorching'. Used twice of a skin disorder (Lv. 13:24, 28) and once metaphorically (Pr. 16:27). It is not clear whether the word means a literal burn from fire or simply a skin disorder producing a burning sensation.

Childbirth. See *Midwifery*, below.

Consumption. Heb. *šaḥepeṯ*, 'wasting away'. Occurs in Lv. 26:16; Dt. 28:22. In neither case is the exact medical meaning at all clear. It could mean tuberculosis, cancer or a host of other diseases producing wasting. Tuberculosis existed in Egypt when the children of Israel were there (D. Morse *et al.*, *Tuberculosis in Ancient Egypt*).

Deafness. Heb. *ḥērēš*, 'silent', Gk. *kōphos*, 'blunted, dull, dumb'. The Israelites were to be kind to the deaf (Lv. 19:14). Isaiah foretold that the deaf would be made to hear (29:18; 35:5; 42:18), a prophecy fulfilled by Jesus (Mt. 11:5; Mk. 7:37).

One man whom Jesus healed was deaf and had 'an impediment in his speech' (*mogilalos*, 'speaking with difficulty', Mk. 7:32) which was probably caused by his deafness (but obviously might have been due to a separate mechanical defect, as AV 'the string', lit. bond, 'of his tongue was loosed' might suggest). It is surely significant that his hearing was healed first. Some authorities consider that the man was deaf and dumb but the Greek does not suggest this. It is more likely that he could make noises but, because he could not hear them (or other people's words) he will not learn normal speech. Zechariah was temporarily dumb and deaf (Lk. 1:20, 22, 64). (* EAR.)

An obese harpist shown on a stele erected in a tomb-chapel at Aswan, Egypt. Height of figure 12 cm. 12th Dynasty. c. 1800 BC. (RVO)

Dropsy. Gk. *hydrōpikos*, 'full of water' (Lk. 14:2). Dropsy (ascites) is strictly not a disease in itself but rather a sign of disease of the heart, kidneys or liver, *etc.*

Dumbness. Heb. *'illēm*, 'dumb', 'bound', 'tied', *dûmām*, 'silent', *'ālam*, 'to be dumb, bound, tied'. Gk. *alalos*, 'speechless', *aphōnos*, 'voiceless', and most commonly *kōphos*, 'blunted', 'dumb' or 'deaf'. This disorder occurred throughout biblical history. It can be attributed to no specific cause. Sometimes it was a feature of *demon-possession (*e.g.* Mt. 9:32–35; 12:22). Zechariah was temporarily dumb and deaf (Lk. 1:20, 22, 64) through an act of God because of his unbelief. The deaf man of Mk. 7:32 was almost certainly not dumb even though he is called the 'deaf-mute'.

Dysentery. The RSV rendering of Gk. *dysenteria* (AV 'bloody flux'), a technical medical term used by Herodotus, Plato, Aristotle, *et al.*, the infectious disease of which Paul healed the father of Publius (Acts 28:8). It has been suggested that the 'incurable disease' of the bowels with which the Lord afflicted Jehoram was a chronic amoebic dysentery (2 Ch. 21:15, 18–19). See also *Prolapsed rectum*, below.

Emerods. (AV). See *Tumours*, below.

Epilepsy. Gk. *selēniazomai*, 'to be moon-struck', a concept from which the English word 'lunatic' is derived, occurs twice (Mt. 4:24; 17:15), translated 'lunatick' in AV, 'epileptic' in RSV. Epilepsy was thought to vary in its severity in cycle with the visible size of the moon. The boy described in Mt. 17:15 appears to have had typical *grandmal* epilepsy (*cf.* Mk. 9:17–29; Lk. 9:38–42) as well as being *demon-possessed, a condition from which epilepsy was distinguished (Mt. 4:24).

Fever. Heb. *qaddaḥaṯ*, 'burning heat' (Dt. 28:22); Gk. *pyretos*, 'fiery heat' (Lk. 4:38; Jn. 4:52; Acts 28:8, *etc.*). A generic term which in EVV covers various ailments, all of them suggesting the presence of a high temperature. Luke describes (4:38) Peter's wife's mother as having 'a great fever', indicating that he recognized degrees of fever and, probably, that he saw the grave prognosis indicated by the severity of the fever which Mt. (8:14) and Mk. (1:30) did not.

Inflammation. Heb. *dalleqeṯ* (only Dt. 28:22). The physical afflictions of consumption, fever and inflammation, and the climatic ones—heat and drought—would have combined to form an awful prospect. The terms are too vague to allow specific interpretation.

Issue; issue of blood. Apart from the more usual meanings of 'issue', the word is also used biblically in connection with disease. In Lv. 15:2ff. Heb. *zôḇ* denotes a discharge which rendered its victims ritually unclean. In Lv. 12:7; Mt. 9:20; Mk. 52:25; Lk. 8:43f.; Heb. *māqôr* and Gk. *rhysis* and *haimorrhoeō* (the latter of which is used in Lv. 15:33, LXX) refer to an issue of blood, translated by NEB as 'haemorrhages'. It is possible that the woman of Lk. 8:43, *etc*, had menorrhagia. See *Menstruation*, below.

Itch. 1. Heb. *ḥeres*, 'heat, sun, itch'. A skin condition, probably akin to eczema, included among the scourges ('which cannot be healed') which would overtake the disobedient (Dt. 28:27). No data are available for precise identification.

2. Heb. *neṯeq* (Lv. 13:30–37; 14:54). A general term, apparently meaning an irritating skin rash, sometimes regarded then as a sign of 'leprosy'. See also *Scab*.

Leprosy. The common OT word translated thus is *ṣāra'aṯ* (Lv. 13–14) which in the LXX was rendered *lepra*, the same Greek word being used in the NT. Both terms were simple, non-specific, imprecise, 'lay' ones and lacked the precision of the modern word leprosy which indicates an infection by *Mycobacterium leprae*. *sāra'aṯ* is primarily a word describing ritualistic uncleanness or defilement characterized by the presence of coloured patches. The same word was used to describe human skin disease (Lv. 13:1–46), discolouration of wool, leather, linen (vv. 47–59), and even the walls of houses (14:33–57), thus indicating that *ṣāra'aṯ* cannot have been (but it might possibly have included) true leprosy. The word *lepra* in the NT occurs only in the Gospels and was used only of human disease. The evidence for uncleanness, on which the diagnosis was based, depended on the presence of depigmented (pale) patches on the human skin or discoloured or dark patches on the surface of inanimate objects. Some of the features described in Lv. 13–14 do not occur in leprosy and some suggest other conditions such as erysipelas adjacent to a boil (Lv. 13:18), infection following a burn (v. 24), ringworm, or sycosis of the scalp or beard (v. 29), pustular dermatitis (v. 36), *etc.* Leprosy is such a slowly-changing process it could not possibly have recovered in the 7 days of Lv. 13:4–6. It is significant that in Lk. 17:11–19, ten lepers were *cleansed* (*katharizō*) (v. 14), while only the one who was grateful was *cured* (*iaomai*) (v. 15) and he was told his faith had (lit.) saved him (*sōzō*) (v. 19) which may refer to his spiritual state or simply mean 'made well' (RSV). There is no clue as to the nature of their 'leprosy'—it is possible that more than one disease process was present among them.

Undoubted leprosy existed in India by *c.* 600 BC and in Europe by 400 BC. There is no definite evidence that it is referred to in the OT or that it even existed at the time of the Exodus, although it certainly did in NT times. For a detailed study of the subject, see S. G. Browne, *Leprosy in the Bible* (good bibliography).

Madness, mental disorder. Several different words are used, all non-specific. The more significant are:

1. Heb. *hōlēlâ*, *hōlēlûṯ*, 'foolishness', 'madness' or 'boasting' (Ec. 1:17; 2:12; 7:25; 9:3; 10:13).

2. Heb. *šiggā'ôn*, 'madness', 'erring', madness inflicted as a judgment from God (Dt. 28:28; Zc. 12:4).

3. Gk. *anoia*, 'mindlessness', leading to folly (2 Tim. 3:9) or rage (Lk. 6:11). In neither case is mental disease implied but rather unbalanced behaviour.

4. Gk. *paraphronia*, 'madness' (2 Cor. 11:23; 2 Pet. 2:16).

5. Gk. *mania* (Acts 26:25). Paul said he had not got (lit.) mania after Festus had accused him of raving (*mainomai*) madly (*cf.* Jn. 10:20).

The recurrent episodes of madness of *Saul and the single severe attack suffered by *Nebuchadrezzar are described in some detail. Saul (1 Sa., *passim*) was a man who was gifted but in some respects inadequate, *e.g.* he was much at the mercy of other people's opinions; he was subject to moods of recurrent depression; and, in later life, he had the paranoid ideas and irritability characteristic of depression in older patients, though homicidal tendencies such as he had are uncommon. His suicide is probably medically unimportant and that of a defeated warrior rather than a depressed neurotic. Nebuchadrezzar, active and irascible, had a hypomanic personality, *i.e.* an inherited liability to develop a manic-depressive psychosis. His illness (Dn. 4:28–37) was long-lasting and occurred when he was perhaps in his fifties. Though he remained conscious he was totally incapable of government. There was no evidence of organic disorder. There was some perversion of appetite. He recovered from it completely (v. 36) in the end, and it would be described today as involutional melancholia.

Menstruation. Heb. *dāwā* or *dāweh*, 'sick', 'menstruous' (Lv. 12:2, 5; 15:33; 18:19; 20:18). Both RSV and AV translate the words rather inconsistently, although AV uses such expressions as 'sick of her flowers' (Lv. 15:33). This normal, physiological feature of the life of women in the reproductive phase of their lives rendered them ritually unclean.

It is probable that the woman with an issue of blood (Mk. 5:25; Lk. 8:43 *rhysei haimatos*, 'a flow of blood'; Mt. 9:20 *haimorrhoeō*, 'to suffer from a flow of blood'; the latter word was used in Greek medical writings and in LXX for Lv. 15:33 meaning 'menstruous') had menorrhagia, a disease in which the menstrual flow is abnormally prolonged—in her case continuous for 12 years—and may produce anaemia.

Midwifery. While childbirth is a normal and healthy phenomenon, it seems appropriate to include it in this 'medical' section. Midwifery was in the hands of women, who had probably considerable experience, perhaps little skill and training (Gn. 38:27–30; Ex. 1:15–21; Ezk. 16:4–5). A birthstool (Ex. 1:16, Heb. *'oḇnayim*, lit. 'double stones', probably indicating its origin) of the type used in Egypt at the time of the Exodus is described in the article *MIDWIFE.

Palsy, paralysis. The Gk. terms for a paralytic, *paralytikos* (*e.g.* Mt. 4:24; 9:2; Mk. 2:3) and to be paralysed, *paralyomai* (*e.g.* Lk. 5:18, 24; Acts 8:7; 9:33) are similar and non-specific. Some types of paralysis in biblical times were clearly non-fatal because patients managed to survive for many years in spite of being paralysed. The centurion's boy servant (Mt. 8:6) was paralysed and 'in terrible distress'. This could be a description of the frightening respiratory paralysis that is a feature of some cases of poliomyelitis.

Plague, pestilence. The AV rendering of five Heb. and three Gk. words connected with disease, death or destruction. None is to be interpreted as necessarily indicating infection with *Yersinia pestis* (the modern 'plague').

1. Heb. *deḇer*, 'pestilence, plague'. Originally meaning 'destruction', this word is used comprehensively for all sorts of disasters, and is often linked with the sword and famine (which three evils generally go hand in hand; *cf.* Je. 14:12; Ezk. 6:11, *etc.*), and with divine visitation. It describes also the virulent epidemic which, after David's numbering of the people, cut off 70,000 Israelites (2 Sa. 24:15; *cf.* Jos., *Ant.* 7. 326), and is probably the same affliction as destroyed 185,000 of *Sennacherib's men (2 Ki. 19:35; Is. 37:36). The same word is found in Solomon's dedication prayer (1 Ki. 8:37; 2 Ch. 6:28); is employed in an unusual sense to describe God's effect on death (Ho. 13:14); and, translated 'murrain', is connected with a disease of cattle (Ex. 9:3, AV; *cf.* Ps. 78:50, AVmg.).

2. Heb. *maggēpâ*, 'plague, smiting' (Ex. 9:14; Zc. 14:12, *etc.*). **3.** Heb. *makkâ*, 'a smiting, beating' (Lv. 26:21; Je. 19:8, *etc.*). **4.** Heb. *nega'*, 'a touch, smiting'. This word, associated most often with leprosy (Lv. 13–14), also denotes any great distress or calamity (Ps. 91:10, *etc.*), or inward corruption (1 Ki. 8:38). **5.** Heb. *negep̄*, 'a stumbling, plague' (Ex. 12:13; Jos. 22:17, *etc.*).

6. Gk. *mastix*, 'a scourge, whip, plague' (Mk. 3:10; 5:29, 34; Lk. 7:21). This is used as a synonym for

A sick man, and magical rites to cure him, portrayed on a cylinder-seal used as an amulet. Assyrian. Enlarged. c. 1100 BC. (MC)

disease in general. **7.** Gk. *loimos*, 'a plague, pestilence' (Mt. 24:7; Lk. 21:11; *cf.* Jos., *BJ* 6. 421). In both biblical references it is coupled with famine, but RV and RSV follow some older MSS in omitting 'pestilence' in Mt. 24:7–8. **8.** Gk. *plēgē*, 'a stroke, plague'. This word is thus translated only in Rev. (9:20; 11:6, *etc.*), in connection with the judgment that will overtake the wicked.

Prolapsed rectum. Jehoram (2 Ch. 21:15, 18–19) was smitten 'with an incurable disease' in his bowels. After 2 years of this 'his bowels came out' and he died 'in great agony' (*taḥ*ᵃ*lû'îm*—a plural noun not translated thus in any other place in RSV; it is translated 'deadly diseases' in Je. 16:4, and 'diseases' in Ps. 103:3). This was almost certainly chronic dysentery which, when very severe and prolonged, occasionally may be complicated by prolapse of the rectum or more of the large intestine, producing *intussusception* which itself produces intestinal obstruction. This could have been the cause of his painful death.

Scab, spot. Skin diseases are rife in the East, and it is often difficult both to identify precisely those mentioned in Scripture and to distinguish one from another. 'Scab', for example, represents four different Heb. words.

1. *gārāḇ*, Dt. 28:27 ('scurvy', AV, Lv. 21:20; 22:22; LXX *psora*; Vulg. *scabies*). Included among the curses that should overtake the disobedient, this was evidently not the true scurvy, but a chronic disease which formed a thick crust on the head and sometimes spread over the whole body. It was regarded as incurable.

2. *yallep̄eṯ*, 'scabbed' (LXX *leichēn*). One of the afflictions that rendered men unfit for the priesthood (Lv. 21:20) and animals unsuitable for sacrifices (Lv. 22:22), it may be another form of **1**, above.

3. *sappaḥaṯ* ('spot'), Lv. 13:2; 14:56.

4. *mispaḥaṯ*, Lv. 13:6–8. A verbal form (*śippaḥ*) is employed in Is. 3:17, 'smite with a scab'.

Tumours (RSV), **Emerods** (AV). The Philistines in Ashdod captured the *ark and the Lord 'afflicted them with tumours' (Heb. *'op̄ālîm*, 'tumours' or 'boils'), 1 Sa. 5:6. The root meaning of the Heb. word means 'to swell, bump up', hence the name of Mt Ophel at Jerusalem. The word may be a technical 'medical' one. When the ark was taken to Gath 'tumours broke out on them', 'both young and old' (5:9), and many died (5:11–12). After 7 months the ark was returned to Israel with golden models of five tumours and five 'mice' (Heb. *'aḵbār*), an inexact word meaning 'rodent' and including mice, rats and gerbils which were common in the Middle East (G. S. Cansdale, *Animals of Bible Lands*). Both rats and gerbils are known vectors of infected fleas which transmit bubonic plague. The description of a plague spreading along lines of communication and breaking out in successive communities, producing multiple boil-like swellings or tumours and an illness that was sometimes fatal and that was associated with numerous 'mice' ruining the crops (6:5), is consistent with (though not proof of) a diagnosis of bubonic plague. It is possible that the same plague caused the seventy deaths in Beth-shemesh 'because they looked into the ark of the Lord' (6:19). The explanation for the number five (mice and tumours) models is 6:16–18).

Wen (AV) (Heb. *yabbeleṯ*, Lv. 22:22; *cf.* LXX *myrmēkiōnta*). Included in a list of blemishes which made animals an unacceptable sacrifice to the Lord. According to Jewish tradition, the Heb. word applies to 'one suffering from warts'. RVmg. reads 'having sores'; RSV 'having a discharge'.

Withered hand. Gk. *xēros* (Mt. 12:10; Lk. 6:6, 8), 'dry', 'withered', denotes a hand in which the muscles are paralysed and shrunken, leaving the affected limb shorter and thinner than normal—a chronic condition in biblical times regarded as incurable. Some identify with a late complication of infantile paralysis (poliomyelitis). Luke records that it was the man's right hand.

III. The treatment of disease

The therapeutics of the Bible are those of the time, and are described in general terms, *e.g.* Pr. 17:22; Je. 46:11. Local applications are frequently referred to for sores (Is. 1:6; Je. 8:22; 51:8), and a 'cake of figs' is recommended by Isaiah for Hezekiah's boil (Is. 38:21). The good Samaritan used wine and oil as a local treatment (Lk. 10:34). Such treatment is often ineffective, however, as in the case of the woman with the issue of blood (Mk. 5:26), or conditions are apparently intrinsically incurable, as in the case of Mephibosheth (2 Sa. 4:4). In Dt. 28:27 there is a note of despair about some illnesses. It is not surprising that treatment is sometimes bound up with superstition, such as the attempt by Leah and Rachel to use mandrakes to increase sexual desire in infertility (Gn. 30:14–16). Wine is twice mentioned as a medicament and stimulant (Pr. 31:6; 1 Tim. 5:23).

The word physician is rarely used, but implies much the same as 'doctor' in English today (Heb. *rāp̄ā'*, *e.g.* Ex. 15:26; Je. 8:22; Gk. *iatros*, Mk. 5:26; Lk. 8:43). Asa is condemned (2 Ch. 16:12) for consulting 'physicians', but these may have been pagan, magically minded and worthless, and not really deserving the name of physician. The point of the condemnation is that he 'did not seek the Lord'. Job condemns his comforters as 'worthless physicians' (Jb. 13:4). In the NT physicians are twice mentioned proverbially by Christ (Lk. 4:23; 5:31). They are mentioned in the incident of the woman who had an issue of blood (Lk. 8:43). Luke is referred to by Paul as 'the beloved physician' (Col. 4:14).

The Jewish religion differed from many pagan ones in that there was almost no confusion between the offices of priest and physician. Declaration of diagnosis of, and freedom from, leprosy is an exception (Lv. 13:9–17; Lk. 17:14). Prophets were consulted about prognosis (see, *e.g.*, 1 Ki. 14:1–13; 2 Ki. 1:1–4; 8:9; Is. 38:1, 21). A primitive form of bone-setting is mentioned in Ezk. 30:21. It is remarkable that medical practice changed so little in its essentials over the centuries during which the events described in the Bible occurred that it is possible to speak of the whole time as though it were a relatively circumscribed period, and there was scarcely any element in it which could be dignified with the name of science.

IV. Demon possession

The singular phenomenon of *demon possession, rarely paralleled since apostolic times, is clearly something *sui generis*. It is recorded as having occurred at the time of Christ more frequently than at any other time. (The account of Saul—'an evil spirit from the Lord troubled him', in 1 Sa. 16:14–15—is probably to be regarded as a statement of his mental disorder rather than as a theological explanation of its origin.) It seems likely that Satan was particularly active at this time in an attempt to counter the effect of the *miracles of Christ and his apostles. Demon possession was real and cannot be 'explained' simply as the current interpretation of purely physical or mental disorders by ignorant (but sincere) people. Jesus himself made this diagnosis and accepted it when made by others. He was never deceived by contemporary error.

Those who were 'demon possessed' (Gk. *daimonizomenos* = 'demonized') could be used as a mouthpiece by the possessing spirit; they often had accompanying physical manifestations such as dumbness (Mt. 9:32), blindness (Mt. 12:22), epilepsy (Lk. 9:37–43) or mental disorder (Mk. 5:1–20). Particularly they were able to recognize the divinity of Jesus and knew they were subject to his authority. However, demon possession is definitely *not* synonymous either with epilepsy or with mental disorder in general, and is clearly distinguished by the Synoptists and in Acts (5:16) from the general run of disease. The disciples were commanded by Jesus to 'heal' (*therapeuō*) the sick but to 'cast out' (*ekballō*) demons and unclean spirits (Mt. 10:1, 8). Luke (9:37–43) describes how Jesus 'rebuked' (*epitimaō*) the unclean spirit and 'healed' (*iaomai*) the boy, suggesting that the presence of the unclean spirit (which was 'rebuked') was associated with, but distinct from, any medical or mental disease—probably epilepsy—which was 'healed'.

Different degrees of involvement were recognized as is shown (Mt. 15:22) by the girl 'severely possessed by a demon' (*kakōs daimonizetai*).

There is no significant difference between the 'man with an unclean spirit' (Mk. 5:2), 'the demoniac' (*daimonizomenos*) (Mk. 5:15–16) or the man who had been 'possessed with demons' (v. 18) as the same man was variously described.

The best authenticated modern cases seem to be those described by missionaries in China from about 1850 onwards. There is no good reason to doubt the biblical view of it as a 'possession' by an evil spiritual being of the personality and body of the person concerned. For present-day examples, see D. Basham, *Deliver us from evil*, 1972.

V. Miracles and healing

a. Healing—its meaning

Healing means the restoration of one to full health who had been ill—in body or mind (or both). This includes recovery resulting from medical treatment and spontaneous remission of a disease. It includes the improvement in a patient's outlook on his condition even if no physical amelioration is possible, and even a correction of a patient's misconception of the nature of his illness. In psychological disorders the term is used to describe an improved mental state. It is important that these different facets of the meaning of the word be realized, because the biblical miracles of healing (apart from cases of demon possession) show healing in its primary medical sense of the restoration to normal in cases of organic disease. Any cases claimed as present-day miracles must show comparably outstanding cases of the healing of organic disorders. Changes in spiritual outlook, an improved acceptance of an organically incurable condition, or the natural and spontaneous remission of disease, are all continually occurring, but do not partake of the miraculous, in the strict theological sense. There are, of course, natural recoveries from illness, as well as miracles, recorded in the Bible, and in fact probably most recoveries other than the miraculous ones were natural, because of the almost complete ineffectiveness of therapy in ancient times.

b. Healing—its Author

God is the one who heals all our diseases (Ps. 103:3; Acts 3:12–16). Even today when medical and surgical skill is so developed, God is the healer, using men (trained or untrained) to do his work for him in the same way that he uses the governing authorities to maintain order and execute justice in the world (Rom. 13:1–5).

c. Healing—the use of means

Even in biblical times, when so few treatments for disease existed (see III, above), men were encouraged and expected to use the means that were available, both in OT times (*e.g.* the fig poultice for Hezekiah's boil, Is. 38:21) and in NT times (Paul's advice to Timothy, 1 Tim. 5:23). True faith in God gladly and gratefully uses such means as are available, whether medicines, blood transfusions or surgical operations to prevent death, as much as life-jackets to prevent drowning.

d. Faith healing

Various terms are currently used to describe healing that occurs without the use of means and in response to faith. Because all true healing comes from God the term 'divine healing' is not helpful to distinguish this especial form. 'Spiritual' healing suggests more the restoration of health to the spirit than the body and moreover may be confused with the work of spiritists who, in the name of the devil, can produce spurious healing. Faith healing is a helpful term so long as the object of faith is clear (it is by no means always God).

e. Miraculous healing

A *miracle essentially consists of 'a striking interposition of divine power by which the operations of the ordinary course of nature are

Health, including diagnosis, prescriptions and omens, is the subject of numerous documents from biblical times. This Babylonian text lists things to be done when a person has been stung by a scorpion. Copy made in the mid-7th cent. BC *for the library of Ashurbanipal at Nineveh, perhaps based on an earlier text.* (BM)

overruled, suspended or modified' (*Chambers's Encyclopaedia*, 'Miracle'). So far as miraculous healing in Scripture is concerned, the essential features are that the cure is instantaneous (the incident of Mk. 8:22–26 being a notable exception), complete and permanent, and usually without the use of means (the saliva of Mk. 7:33; 8:23; Jn. 9:6 is an exception; *cf.* also Mk. 5:27–29; Acts 5:15; 19:12). Divine miracles of healing show no relapses, which typify spurious miracles, except, of course, when dead persons were raised to life who, sooner or later, subsequently died again (*e.g.* Jairus' daughter, Mk. 5:21–24, 35–43; the widow of Nain's son, Lk. 7:11–15; Lazarus in Jn. 11:1–44, *etc.*).

1. *The purpose of miraculous healing.* Like the other miracles in Scripture, they were dramatized signs and enacted parables intended to teach a double lesson. They were to *authenticate* the word of the person who performed them (*e.g.* Ex. 7:9; Lk. 5:20–24; Jn. 7:19–22; 10:37–38; Acts 2:22) and to *illustrate* the word. Thus what happened to the body of the paralytic in Lk. 5:18–26 was a proof and picture of what happened in his soul. It is important to see, therefore, that the purpose of the healing miracles was theological, not medical. The many who were healed at the beginning of the ministry of Jesus, of the early church and of individual Christians (*e.g.* Philip, Acts 8:5–8) gradually became fewer as the essential lesson was learnt. Many lay ill at the pool of Bethesda (Jn. 5:3) but Jesus healed only one because one was enough to teach the spiritual truth. If Christ's purpose had been the healing of the sick, he would have healed them all.

Thus a miracle of healing today should not be expected simply when it is medically desirable but rather where the Word of God and his servant needs to be authenticated and illustrated, and such evidence is not already available in the Bible. The fringe of an area of new evangelization on the mission field would therefore seem to be the most likely place for miraculous healing to occur today, the very place where miracles can least scientifically be proven! (But the church in general is now recovering her healing ministry as an integral part of the total gospel of wholeness, and such healings sometimes include the instantaneous as well as the more usual gradual recoveries. See J. C. Peddie, *The Forgotten Talent*, 1961; G. Bennett, *The Heart of Healing*, 1971; F. MacNutt, *Healing*, 1974; *The Power to Heal*, 1977.—N.H.)

2. *Miraculous healing in the Old Testament.* Even if medical means were also used, recovery in the OT is generally attributed to the intervention of God, *e.g.* the recovery of Moses (Ex. 4:24–26) from the illness associated with his disobedience over his son's circumcision is given an entirely spiritual significance. The healing of Miriam's leprosy (Nu. 12:1–15) and of Naaman, through Elisha (2 Ki. 5:8–14), appear to be miraculous. The healing of Jeroboam's suddenly paralysed hand (1 Ki. 13:4–6) and the raising from the dead of the son of the widow of Zarephath by Elijah (1 Ki. 17:17–24) and of the son of the Shunammite woman by Elisha (2 Ki. 4:1–37) are clearly miraculous. This boy's illness has been attributed to sunstroke; but it could equally well have been a fulminating encephalitis or a subarachnoid haemorrhage. (The Jews were conscious of the effects of the sun [see Ps. 121:6], and a case of sunstroke is reported in the Apocrypha [Judith 8:2–3].) The recovery of the Israelites bitten by the serpents when they looked on the bronze serpent is miraculous also, though individuals are not specified (Nu. 21:6–9). The salvation of the Israelites from the later plagues in Egypt is a curious example of what might be termed a 'prophylactic miracle', *i.e.* for them disease was miraculously prevented rather than miraculously healed. The recovery of Hezekiah (2 Ki. 20:1–11) was probably natural, though it is attributed directly to God (v. 8) and is accompanied by a nature miracle (vv. 9–11); the illness was probably a severe carbuncle.

Miraculous healing, even counting raising from the dead, is unusual in the OT, and the few cases seem to cluster about the two critical times of the Exodus and the ministry of Elijah and Elisha. See Ex. 7:10–12 for nature miracles performed by Moses and Aaron. The miracles performed by the Egyptian sorcerers (Ex. 7:11, 22; 8:7) mimicked the first three miraculous signs wrought by Moses and Aaron (even though their second and third attempts only added to the sufferings of their people), but they were unable to counterfeit the power of God in the subsequent signs (8:18). Thus the miracles wrought by Moses achieved their purpose (7:9) of authenticating his word of authority and finally led to the escape of the children of Israel.

3. *Miraculous healing in the Gospels.* Our Lord's miracles of healing are reported by the Synoptists as groups (*e.g.* Lk. 4:40–41) and, in greater detail and more specifically, as individual cases. *Demon possession is clearly distinguished from other forms of disease (*e.g.* Mk. 1:32–34, where *kakōs echōn* is separate from *daimonizomenos*). People came to him in large numbers (Mt. 4:23–24) and were all healed (Lk. 4:40). Doubtless cases of mental as well as of physical illness were included, and on one occasion our Lord even restored a severed part of the body (Lk. 22:50–51). At the same time, these recorded instances can represent only a small fraction of those ill in the country at this time.

In the combined narrative of the four Gospels there are over twenty stories of the healing of individuals or of small groups. Some were healed at a distance, some with a word but without physical contact, some with physical contact, and some with both physical contact and 'means', *i.e.* the use of clay made from spittle, which was a popular remedy of the time for blindness (Mk. 8:23; Jn. 9:6) and deafness (Mk. 7:32–35). This may have been to aid the patient's faith, or to demonstrate that God does not exclude the use of means, or both. In one unique instance Jesus performed two successive miracles on the same man—see *Blindness*, above.

Luke's Gospel is the only one to give the story of the good Samaritan. It also includes five miracles of healing not recorded by the other Evangelists. These are the raising of the son of the widow of Nain (7:11–16), the healing of the woman 'bowed together' (13:11–16), the man with dropsy (ascites) (14:1–4), the ten lepers (17:12–19) and the healing of Malchus' ear (22:51). More details of cases are given and the writer uses the more technical *iaomai* for healing, rather than the non-technical words.

The Fourth Evangelist, unlike the Synoptists, never refers to healing of people in large numbers, nor to demon possession (though demons are referred to, and the word *daimonizomenos* is used, Jn. 10:21). In addition to the raising of Lazarus from the dead, only three cases are described. These are the healing of the nobleman's son of a serious febrile condition (4:46–54), the man paralysed 38 years (5:1–16), and the man born blind (9:1–14). These miracles of healing in John's Gospel are not only mighty works (*dynameis*) but also signs (*sēmeia*). They demonstrate that Christ's miracles of healing have not only an individual, local, contemporary physical significance but a general, eternal and spiritual meaning also. For example, in the case of the man born blind, the point is made that individual sickness is not necessarily attributable to individual sin.

4. *Miraculous healing in apostolic times.* While the promise of healing powers in Mk. 16:18 is probably to be dismissed as being no part of the true text, Christ had commissioned the Twelve (Mt. 10:1) and the Seventy (Lk. 10:9). The Twelve were evidently commissioned for life, while the mission of the Seventy seems to have ended when they reported back (Lk. 10:17–20). In Acts there are several accounts of individual miracles, which have much the same character as those performed by Christ. The lame man in Jerusalem (3:1–11) and the one at Lystra (14:8–10), the paralytic (9:33–34), and Publius' father's dysentery ('bloody flux', AV, 28:8) are individual cases, and there are a few reports of multiple healings, including that in 5:15–16 and the unique case of the use of clothing taken from Paul (19:11–12). Two people were raised from the dead (Dorcas, 9:36–41, and Eutychus, 20:9f.) and demons were cast out on two occasions (5:16 and 16:16–18). The author distinguishes between demon possession and other illness (5:16).

Cases of illness among Christians in apostolic times are mentioned. The fact that they occur indicates that the apostolic commission to heal could not be used indiscriminately to keep themselves or their friends free from illness. Timothy had a gastric complaint (1 Tim. 5:23). Trophimus was too ill to accompany Paul from Miletus (2 Tim. 4:20). Epaphroditus was gravely ill (Phil. 2:30), and his recovery is attributed to the mercy of God (Phil. 2:27). Most striking of all is Paul's enigmatic 'thorn in the flesh' (*skolops tē sarki*), which has been variously identified (most often as a chronic eye disease), but by few convincingly and by none conclusively. Its spiritual significance far exceeds its importance as an exercise in diagnosis. Paul gives three reasons (2 Cor. 12:7–10) for it; 'to keep his feet on the ground' (v. 7), to enable him to be spiritually powerful (v. 9) and as a personal service to Christ (v. 10, 'for Christ's sake'). There is perhaps more resemblance between this 'thorn' and Jacob's shrunken sinew than has been realized (Gn. 32:24–32).

The classical passage on prayer for the sick (Jas. 5:13–20) has suffered from two misinterpretations: that which finds in it authority for the institution of anointing those who are *in extremis*, and that which regards it as a promise that all who are sick and who are prayed over in faith will recover. The oil may have been used as was Christ's clay or spittle (see above) to reinforce faith, and may in some cases even have been medicinal. Or oil may be taken as a symbol of separating the sickness from the patient on to Christ (*cf.* Mt. 8:17), after the pattern of kings, *etc.* being *anointed to separate them from others for their office. For a full discussion, see R. V. G. Tasker's commentary on James (*TNTC*). The important points are that the outlook in the passage is spiritual (*i.e.* the matter is referred to God), the distress of the individual is made the concern of the church, and what is said neither excludes nor condemns the use by doctors of the normal means of healing available at any particular time and place. The whole of this passage is really concerned with the power of prayer.

5. *Miraculous healing after apostolic times.* This is, strictly, outside the scope of this article, but is relevant in that certain texts are quoted in favour of there being a possibi-

A Syrian settler, whose leg shows deformation typical of infantile paralysis, depicted on an Egyptian stele of c. 1200 BC. (GC)

lity, and more, of miraculous healing mediated by Christians at the present day (*cf.* Jn. 14:12, above). However, there must be considerable caution in equating personal commands by Christ to the apostles with those which are generally binding upon Christians today. Such views are out of keeping with the general view of miracles as instruments and accompaniments of revelation. Great care must be exercised in avoiding the magical in a search for the miraculous. The ecclesiastical miracles of patristic times, often posthumously attributed, sometimes became absurd. It has also been shown that the frequently quoted passages in Irenaeus, Tertullian and Justin Martyr, which purport to show that miracles of healing continued well into the 3rd century, will not in fact bear that interpretation. Post-apostolic claims should therefore be treated with extreme care. But this cautious attitude should not be confused with modern materialistic unbelief and scepticism. See also 1. *The purpose of miraculous healing*, above.

Obesity as represented by the Queen of Punt. Painted relief from the temple of Queen Hatshepsut at Deir-el-Bahri, Thebes. New Kingdom, 18th Dynasty. c. 1490 BC. (MNAC)

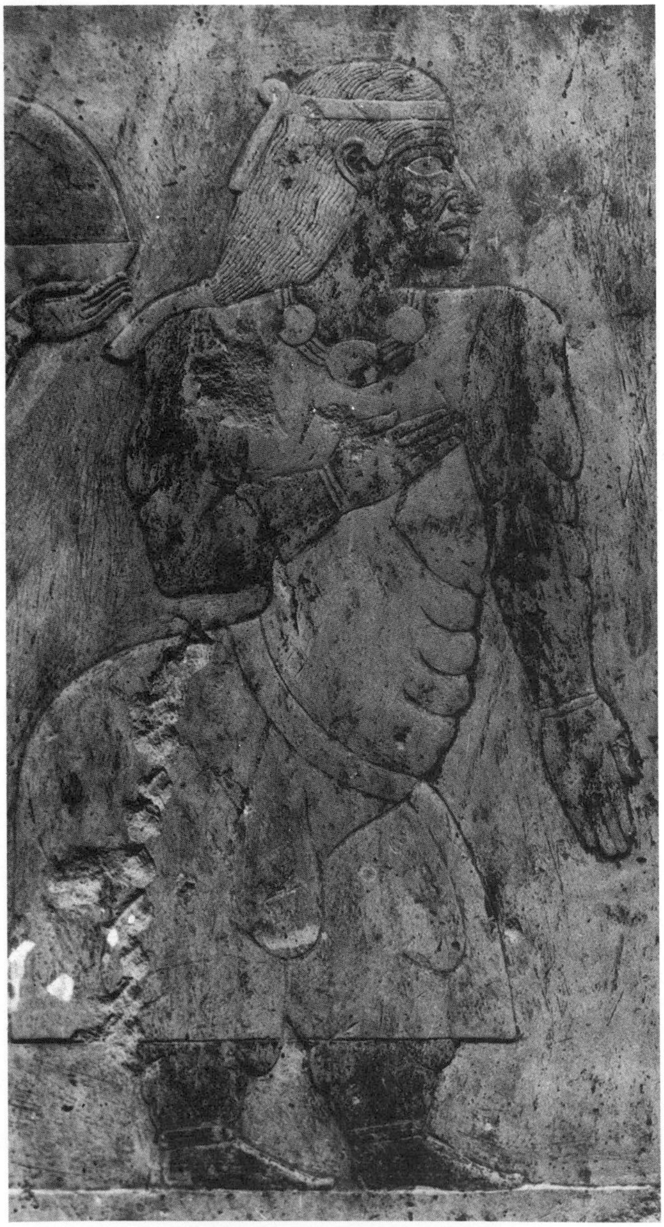

VI. The biblical outlook on disease

The topics of suffering and disease, in the Bible, are closely bound up with the questions of the nature and origin of evil itself. Suffering is a human experience, with diverse causes, and is one of the results of human sin. In the case of suffering from disease, the link is not usually obvious, though sometimes the illness is directly connected. From the account of the Fall of man in Genesis it is clear that soon afterwards man knew insecurity, fear and pain (Gn. 3:16:17). Here *'iṣṣāḇôn* (AV 'sorrow') is better rendered 'pain', and then mental anguish (Gn. 4:13). The direct connection between sin and suffering becomes rapidly more complex, but nations which obeyed God were, in general, promised freedom from disease (Ex. 15:25–26; Lv. 26:14–16; Dt. 7:12–16 and ch. 28, especially vv. 22, 27, 58–61). On the other hand, pestilence is one of the three sore judgments on the people of God (Je. 24:10; 32:24; Ezk. 14:21) and on other nations, *e.g.* Philistines (1 Sa. 5:6) and Assyrians (2 Ki. 19:35). There are passages such as Ps. 119:67, where the sinner himself is involved, and the case of the impotent man healed (Jn. 5:1–16), where his own fault is perhaps implied (v. 14). David's sin involved the afflictions of others (2 Sa. 24:15–17). On the whole, human suffering, from disease or from any other cause, is the effect on the individual of the spiritual malaise of the human society of which he is an integral part. In Job 1 something is seen of the activity of Satan. This is also apparent in Acts 10:38, where the sick are spoken of as 'all that were oppressed by the devil' and in the suggestive parable of the wheat and tares ('An enemy has done this', Mt. 13:28). Again, Christ himself spoke of 'this woman, whom Satan bound . . .' (Lk. 13:16).

God does not stand by helplessly, however. Suffering is sometimes used punitively. This may be on a national scale. Or it may be applied to individuals, as in the cases of Moses (Ex. 4:24), Miriam (Nu. 12:10), Uzziah (2 Ch. 26:16–21), Jeroboam (2 Ch. 13:20), Gehazi (2 Ki. 5:25–27), Ananias and Sapphira (Acts 5:5, 10), Herod (Acts 12:21–23) and Elymas (Acts 13:11). Much more detail is given when suffering is used constructively (Heb. 12:6–11), as in the case of Jacob, who, after a real physical injury miraculously inflicted, learnt to depend upon God, and matured spiritually to fulfil his new name of Israel (Gn. 32:24–32). Hezekiah's illness demonstrated his faith in God, and is probably in this category (2 Ki. 20:1–7). The book of Job shows that the real issue is a man's relationship to God rather than his attitude to his own suffering. It is the principal OT refutation of the view, put forward with great skill by Job's 'comforters', that there is an inevitable link between individual sin and individual suffering. After disposing of the view, which is only partially true, that the reason for the existence of suffering is disciplinary, it leads to the sublime picture of Job both comforted, vindicated and blessed. It is important to realize that the biblical picture is not a mere *dualism. Rather, suffering is presented in the light of eternity and in relation to a God who is sovereign, but who is nevertheless forbearing in his dealings with the world because of his love for men (2 Pet. 3:9). Conscious of the sorrow and pain round about them, the NT writers look forward to the final consummation when suffering shall be no more (Rom. 8:18; Rev. 21:4).

This conception is different from the Gk. notion of the body as something inherently evil, and the spirit as something inherently good. The biblical conception of the transience yet nobility of the body is best seen in 2 Cor., especially in 5:1–10 (*cf.* also 1 Cor. 6:15). It is an integral part of the complex of the individual through which the personality is expressed.

VII. Hygiene and sanitation

One respect in which Jewish medicine was better than that of contemporary peoples was the remarkable sanitary code of the Israelites in Moses' time (*e.g.* Lv. 15). A. Rendle Short gives an excellent short account of this (*The Bible and Modern Medicine*, pp. 37–46). Although generally referred to as a code, the details are, in fact, scattered through the Pentateuch. The Jews, as a nation, might not have survived their time in the wilderness, or the many other vicissitudes through which they passed, without their sanitary 'code'. It deals with public hygiene, water supply, sewage disposal, inspection and selection of food, and control of infectious disease. The most interesting thing about it is that it implies a knowledge which in the circumstances of the Exodus and the wilderness wanderings they could scarcely have discovered for themselves, *e.g.* the prohibition, as food, of pigs and of * animals which had died natural deaths, the burial or burning of excreta, *etc.*, and the contagious nature of some diseases. Burning of excreta (Ex. 29:14) was a particularly wise practice for a wandering people, since there was no time for dung to do good as manure. The spread of disease was thus effectively prevented. The origin of the word 'quarantine' in the Jewish use of the period of 40 days of segregation from patients with certain diseases (Lv. 12:1–4) adopted by the Italians in the 14th century because of the relative immunity of Jews from certain plagues. In a number of respects the biblical outlook on the sick, and on health in general, has a bearing on modern medical practice, and is perhaps more up-to-date than is generally realized. The story of the good Samaritan (Lk. 10:30–37) presents an ideal of care which has always inspired the medical and para-medical professions and typifies selflessness and after-care. There is more than a little in the Bible about what might be called 'the medicine of the family', the ideal of marriage among the Jews being a high one.

BIBLIOGRAPHY. W. Barclay, *The Gospel of Luke*, 1958; G. Bennett, *The Heart of Healing*, 1971; M. Botting, *Christian Healing in the Parish*, 1976; S. G. Browne, *Leprosy in the Bible*, 1974; G. S. Cansdale, *Animals of Bible Lands*, 1970; R. E. D. Clark, 'Men as Trees Walking', *FT* 93, 1963, pp. 88–94; R. A. Cole, *Mark*, *TNTC*, 1961; A. Edersheim, *Life and Times of Jesus the Messiah*, 1907, Appendix 16; V. Edmunds and C. G. Scorer, *Some Thoughts on Faith Healing*, 1956; J. N. Geldenhuys, *Commentary on the Gospel of Luke*, 1950; J. S. McEwen, *SJT* 7, 1954, pp. 133–152 (miracles in patristic times); F. MacNutt, *Healing*, 1974; *idem*, *The Power to Heal*, 1977; D. Morse *et al.*, 'Tuberculosis in Ancient Egypt', *American Review of Respiratory Diseases* 90, 1964, pp. 524–541; J. C. Peddie, *The Forgotten Talent*, 1961; A. Rendle Short, *The Bible and Modern Medicine*, 1953; J. R. W. Stott, *Men with a Message*, 1954; M. Sussman, 'Diseases in the Bible and the Talmud', in *Diseases in Antiquity*, ed. D. Brothwell and A. T. Sandison, 1967; R. V. G. Tasker, *James*, *TNTC*, 1956; B. B. Warfield, *Miracles: Yesterday and Today*, 1965 (reprint of *Counterfeit Miracles*, 1918); F. Graber, D. Müller, *NIDNTT* 2, pp. 163–172; on Paul's thorn in the flesh, see C. Brown, *NIDNTT* 1, pp. 726f.

D.T.

HEART (Heb. *lēḇ* or *lēḇāḇ*; Gk. *kardia*). The term is used of the centre of things (Dt. 4:11; Jon. 2:3; Mt. 12:40); the root of the Heb. word, which is obscure, may mean centre.

The references to the physical organ as such are few and by no means specific. The clearest is 1 Sa. 25:37. In 2 Sa. 18:14 and 2 Ki. 9:24 the meaning seems to be wider, indicating the internal organs generally, especially since, in the former passage, Absalom remained alive after three darts had pierced his 'heart'. But this lack of accurate physiological definition is typical of Hebrew thought, particularly in respect of the internal organs. In Ps. 104:15, for instance, the 'heart' is affected by food and drink, and though this may not be true in a direct way physiologically, it certainly is true in experience, if one takes the 'heart' to mean, as outlined below, the inner man, in a wide sense.

The Hebrews thought in terms of subjective experience rather than objective, scientific observation, and thereby avoided the modern error of over-departmentalization. It was essentially the whole man, with all his attributes, physical, intellectual and psychological, of which the Hebrew thought and spoke, and the heart was conceived of as the governing centre for all of these. It is the heart which makes a man, or a beast, what he is, and governs all his actions (Pr. 4:23). Character, personality, will, mind are modern terms which all reflect something of the meaning of 'heart' in its biblical usage. (But *cf.* * BODY where mention is made of synecdoche.)

H. Wheeler Robinson gives the following classification of the various senses in which the words *lēḇ* and *lēḇāḇ* are used.

a. Physical or figurative ('midst'; 29 times).

b. Personality, inner life or character in general (257 times, *e.g.* Ex. 9:14; 1 Sa. 16:7; Gn. 20:5).

c. Emotional states of consciousness, found in widest range (166 times); intoxication (1 Sa. 25:36); joy or sorrow (Jdg. 18:20; 1 Sa. 1:8); anxiety (1 Sa. 4:13); courage and fear (Gn. 42:28); love (2 Sa. 14:1).

d. Intellectual activities (204 times); attention (Ex. 7:23); reflection (Dt. 7:17); memory (Dt. 4:9); understanding (1 Ki. 3:9); technical skill (Ex. 28:3) (latter two = 'mind' in RSV).

e. Volition or purpose (195 times; 1 Sa. 2:35), this being one of the most characteristic usages of the term in the OT.

The NT usage is very similar, and C. Ryder Smith writes of it as follows: 'It (the heart) does not altogether lose its physical reference, for it is made of "flesh" (2 Cor. 3:3), but it is the seat of the will (*e.g.* Mk. 3:5), of the intellect (*e.g.* Mk. 2:6, 8), and of feeling (*e.g.* Lk. 24:32). This means that "heart" comes the nearest of the NT terms to mean "person".'

There is no suggestion in the Bible that the brain is the centre of consciousness, thought or will. It is the heart which is so regarded, and, though it is used of emotions also, it is more frequently the lower organs (* BOWELS, *etc.*), in so far as they are distinguished, that are connected with the emotions. As a broad general statement, it is true that the Bible places the psychological focus one step lower in the anatomy than most popular modern speech, which uses 'mind' for consciousness, thought and will, and 'heart' for emotions.

'Mind' is perhaps the closest modern term to the biblical usage of 'heart', and many passages in RSV are so translated (*e.g.* Ec. 1:17; Pr. 16:23). The 'heart' is, however, a wider term, and the Bible does not distinguish the rational or mental processes in the way that Gk. philosophy does.

C. Ryder Smith suggests that: 'The First great Commandment probably means "You shall love (*agapān*) the Lord your God with all your heart—that is with all your soul and with all your mind and with all your strength" (*e.g.* Mk. 12:30, 33).'

The heart of man does not

HEAR
See Obedience, Part 2.

always do that, however. It is not what it should be (Gn. 6:5; Je. 17:9), and the OT reaches its highest point in the realization that a change of heart is needed (Je. 24:7; Ezk. 11:19), and that, of course, is fulfilled in the NT (Eph. 3:17).

There are the exceptional people whose hearts are right with God (1 Ki. 15:14; Ps. 37:31; Acts 13:22), though it is obvious from what we know of David, the example referred to in the last passage, that this is not true in an absolute sense, but that repentance and conversion are still necessary (2 Ki. 23:25, of Josiah).

The right attitude of heart begins with its being broken or crushed (Ps. 51:17), symbolic of humility and penitence, and synonymous with 'a broken spirit' (*rûaḥ*). This brokenness is necessary because it is the hard or stony heart which does not submit to the will of God (Ezk. 11:19). Alternatively, it is the 'fat' or 'uncircumcised' heart which fails to respond to Yahweh's will (Is. 6:10; Ezk. 44:7).

Yahweh knows the heart of each one and is not deceived by outward appearance (1 Sa. 16:7), but a worthy prayer is, nevertheless, that he should search and know the heart (Ps. 139:23), and make it clean (Ps. 51:10). A 'new heart' must be the aim of the wicked (Ezk. 18:31), and that will mean that God's law has to become no longer merely external but 'written on the heart' and make it clean (Je. 31:33).

Thus it is that the heart, the spring of all desires, must be guarded (Pr. 4:23), and the teacher aims to win his pupil's heart to the right way (Pr. 23:26).

It is the pure in heart who shall see God (Mt. 5:8), and it is through Christ's dwelling in the heart by faith that the saints can comprehend the love of God (Eph. 3:17).

BIBLIOGRAPHY. A. R. Johnson, *The Vitality of the Individual in the Thought of Ancient Israel*, 1949, pp. 77ff.; C. Ryder Smith, *The Bible Doctrine of Man*, 1951; H. Wheeler Robinson, *The Christian Doctrine of Man*, 1911; F. Baumgärtel, J. Behm, *TDNT* 3, pp. 605–613; H. Köster, *TDNT* 7, pp. 548–559; T. Sorg, *NIDNTT* 2, pp. 180–184; H.-H. Esser, *NIDNTT* 2, pp. 599f.

B.O.B.

HEATH
See Plants (Shrub), Part 3.

HEBREW NUMERICAL SIGNS
See Number, Part 2.

HEAVEN. Several words are translated 'heaven', but the only important ones are the Heb. *šāmayim* and the Gk. *ouranos*. The former is plural, and the latter often occurs in the plural. But, just as in Eng., there does not seem to be any great difference between 'heaven' and 'the heavens'. The term is used of the physical heaven, especially in the expression 'heaven and earth' (Gn. 14:19; Mt. 5:18). Some suggest that the Bible writers thought of heaven in this aspect as solid, and rather like an inverted bowl (the 'firmament', Gn. 1:8). The sun makes his daily pilgrimage across it (Ps. 19:4–6), and there are windows through which the rain might descend (Gn. 7:11). Some Hebrews may well have held this idea, but it must not be forgotten that the men of the OT were capable of vivid imagery. It will never do to treat them as wooden literalists. The theological meaning of their language about heaven can be understood without recourse to such hypotheses.

Heaven is the abode of God, and of those closely associated with him. The Israelite is to pray, 'Look down from thy holy habitation, from heaven' (Dt. 26:15). God is 'the God of heaven' (Jon. 1:9), or 'the Lord, the God of heaven' (Ezr. 1:2), or the 'Father who is in heaven' (Mt. 5:45; 7:21, *etc.*). God is not alone there, for we read of 'the host of heaven' which worships him (Ne. 9:6), and of 'the angels in heaven' (Mk. 13:32). Believers also may look forward to 'an inheritance . . . kept in heaven' for them (1 Pet. 1:4). Heaven is thus the present abode of God and his angels, and the ultimate destination of his saints on earth.

Among many ancient peoples there was the thought of a multiplicity of heavens. It has been suggested that the NT bears witness to the rabbinic idea of seven heavens, for there are references to Paradise (Lk. 23:43), and to 'the third heaven' (2 Cor. 12:2; this was called Paradise on the rabbinic reckoning, *cf.* 2 Cor. 12:3). Jesus also is said to have passed 'through the heavens' (Heb. 4:14). These, however, are slender bases on which to erect such a structure. All the NT language is perfectly capable of being understood along the lines of heaven as the place of perfection.

Heaven comes to be used as a reverent periphrasis for God. Thus when the prodigal says 'I have sinned against heaven' (Lk. 15:18, 21), he means 'I have sinned against God'. So with Jn. 3:27, 'what is given him from heaven'. The most important example of this is Matthew's use of the expression 'the kingdom of heaven', which seems to be identical with 'the kingdom of God'.

Finally, we must notice an eschatological use of the term. In both OT and NT it is recognized that the present physical universe is not eternal, but will vanish away and be replaced by 'new heavens and a new earth' (Is. 65:17; 66:22; 2 Pet. 3:10–13; Rev. 21:1). We should understand such passages as indicating that the final condition of things will be such as fully expresses the will of God.

BIBLIOGRAPHY. *TDNT* 5, pp. 497–543; *NIDNTT* 2, pp. 184–196; *ZPEB*, 3, pp. 60–64. L.M.

HEBER. 1. An Asherite, the son of Beriah (Gn. 46:17; Nu. 26:45; 1 Ch. 7:31–32; Lk. 3:35). **2.** The husband of * Jael, known as Heber the Kenite (Jdg. 4:11, 17; 5:24), though he lived apart from the rest of the Kenites or nomad smiths. The context suggests him to be a man of some importance. **3.** A Judahite, the father of Soco (1 Ch. 4:18). **4.** A son of Elpaal, a Benjaminite (1 Ch. 8:17). J.D.D.

HEBREWS. In the OT *'iḇrî* is confined to the narrative of the sons of Israel in Egypt (Gn. 39–Ex. 10), the legislation concerning the manumission of Heb. servants (Ex. 21; Dt. 15; *cf.* Je. 34), the record of Israelite–Philistine encounter during the days of Samuel and Saul (1 Sa. 4; 13–14; 29), plus Gn. 14:13 and Jon. 1:9.

The patronymic 'Hebrew', *'iḇrî*, used for Abraham and his descendants, can be traced to his ancestor Aber (Gn. 10:21ff.; 11:14ff.). Accordingly, this designation serves to tie the Abrahamic revelation to the covenant promise to Shem. The Noahic doxology in praise of the covenantal union of Yahweh with the family of Shem (Gn. 9:26) is echoed in Gn. 14 in the doxology of Melchizedek (vv. 19–20) celebrating God's covenantal blessing on Abraham the Hebrew, *i.e.* of the lineage of Shem. That the divine favour is shown to Abraham the Hebrew in a conflict which finds him in military alliance with the 'sons of Canaan' against the forces of an Elamite 'son of Shem' (*cf.* Gn. 10:15ff., 22) is indicative that the covenantal election of Shem announced by Noah was being more particularly realized through the Eberite (Hebrew) Semites (*cf.* Gn. 11:10–26).

The broad significance of *'iḇrî* in Gn. 14:13 might also be plausibly assumed in the Gn. 39–Ex. 10 context (*cf.* especially Gn. 40:15; 43:32; Ex. 2:11). However, the usage there is perhaps not uniform, since there seems to be a simple equation of Hebrews and Israelites in Ex. 5:1–3 (*cf.* 3:18), for example, though in speaking of 'the God of the Hebrews' Moses possibly designates his brethren 'Hebrews' as being the Hebrews *par excellence.*

In view of this broader application of *'iḇrî*, the appearance of non-Israelite or even non-Abrahamite *'iḇrîm* need not come unexpectedly in non-biblical texts of the patriarchal and Mosaic ages. According to a popular theory, the *ḫa-BI-ru*, who figure in numerous texts of the 2nd millennium BC, are such *'iḇrîm.* The term *ḫa-BI-ru* is usually regarded as an appellative denoting a social or professional group, but some find an ethnic component in their identity. However, the phonetic equation of *'iḇrî* and *ḫa-BI-ru* is highly debatable. The *ḫa-BI-ru* presence in Canaan attested in the Amarna letters cannot be successfully identified with the Hebrew conquest.

On the basis of the interpretation of the term *ḫa-BI-ru* in Nuzi servant contracts as an appellative meaning 'foreign-servant', it has been contended that *'iḇrî* in the legislation of Ex. 21:2 and Dt. 15:12, whose terms correspond closely to the stipulations of the *ḫa-BI-ru* contracts, denotes not a specific ethnic identity but the status of an alien and, therefore, that the *'eḇeḏ 'iḇrî* is like the Nuzi *ḫa-BI-ru* a foreign servant. But that interpretation of *ḫa-BI-ru* in the Nuzi texts seems to be inaccurate, and certainly the biblical legislation is concerned with Israelite servants. Dt. 15:12 identifies the Heb. servant as 'your brother' (*cf.* v. 3; Je. 34:9, 14). It is objected that what Ex. 21 allows for an *'eḇeḏ 'iḇrî*, Lv. 25 forbids for an Israelite; but what Ex. 21:2ff. allows is a voluntary perpetuation of an agreeable type of service, while Lv. 25:43–44 forbids compulsorily permanent, rigorous slavery. The Jubilee stipulation of Lv. 25 is a supplementary privilege granted the Heb. servant, which apparently yielded precedence to the servant's further right of voluntary lifelong service (Ex. 21:5–6).

It has been maintained that the *'iḇrîm* in 1 Sa. 13 and 14 are non-Israelite mercenaries (a role characteristic of the *ḫa-BI-ru*). But in 13:3–4 'the Hebrews' are obviously the same as 'all Israel'. Moreover, it is apparently the 'men of Israel' described in 13:6 to whom the Philistines refer in 14:11, designating them 'Hebrews'. There is similar identification of the *'iḇrîm* in 13:19–20 (*cf.* also 4:5–9). In 13:6–7 the *'iḇrîm* are not, as alleged, distinguished from the 'men of Israel'; rather, two groups of Israelites are described. V. 6 refers to those who had been excused from military service (2b) and later hid in the hills W of Jordan. V. 7 refers to certain Israelites, here called 'Hebrews', who had been selected by Saul (2a) but afterwards, deserting, sought refuge E of the Jordan (note the reduction in Saul's army: 13:2, 11, 15; 14:2). Again, 14:21 even if, following EVV, the *'iḇrîm* are regarded as having fought for the enemy, they might have been Israelite traitors. The original text of v. 21, however, supports the exegesis that certain Hebrews after a lapse of courage resumed their former active hostility against the Philistines by rejoining Saul. These *'iḇrîm* are those mentioned in 13:7a. Along with the men of Israel who had hidden in the hill-country of Ephraim (14:22; *cf.* 13:6) they returned to swell the ranks of Saul's unexpectedly triumphant army.

The OT usage of *'iḇrî* is thus consistently ethnic. Most occurrences being in discourse spoken by or addressed to non-Israelites, many would see a derogatory nuance in *'iḇrî.* The suggestion that *'iḇrî* is an alternative for 'Israelite' in situations where the person is not a free citizen on free soil is perhaps not unsuitable to any of the OT passages. But even if such a connotation were intended it would be neither primary nor permanent. In the NT, 'Hebrew' is found as an exclusivist term for Jews not decisively influenced by Hellenization (Acts 6:1), but also as a term distinguishing Jews in general from Gentiles (2 Cor. 11:22; Phil. 3:5).

BIBLIOGRAPHY. M. G. Kline, 'The Ḫa-BI-ru—Kin or Foe of Israel?', *WTJ* 20, 1957, pp. 46ff.; F. F. Bruce in *AOTS*, pp. 3ff.; R. de Vaux, 'Le Problème des Ḫapiru après quinze Années', *JNES* 27, 1968, pp. 221–228; R. Mayer and T. McComiskey, *NIDNTT* 2, pp. 304–323. M.G.K.

HEBREWS, EPISTLE TO THE.

I. Outline of contents

The doctrinal theme: the superiority of Christ. 1:1–10:18

a. The Person of Christ, 1:1–4:13

(i) *Christ is superior to the Prophets* (1:1–4). The Prophets are here representative of OT revelation generally.

(ii) *Christ is superior to angels* (1:5–2:18). This is demonstrated by an appeal to various Scriptures, and Christ's apparent inferiority through suffering is then explained.

(iii) *Parenthesis* (2:1–4). Solemn warnings are given to those who neglect God's revelation.

(iv) *Christ is superior to Moses* (3:1–19). Since Moses was no more than a servant, Christ's Sonship establishes his superiority over the [illegible]. This superiority is also seen by the fact that Moses, unlike Christ, could not lead his people into rest.

(v) *Christ is superior to Joshua* (4:1–13). Although Joshua led the Israelites into their inheritance, a better rest, still future, remains for God's people.

b. The work of Christ, 4:14–10:18

This is particularly exemplified in his office as Priest.

(i) *His priesthood is divinely appointed* (4:14–5:10). In this section the sympathy of Christ as an essential qualification for the high-priestly office is emphasized.

(ii) *His priesthood is after the order of Melchizedek* (5:11–7:28). This section begins with a long digression consisting of rebuke, solemn warning and exhortation (5:11–6:8). Then the order of Melchizedek is explained. His priesthood is perpetual (7:1–3); it is anterior to, and therefore greater than, the levitical (7:4–10); it shows the imperfections of the levitical priesthood (7:11–19). Christ's priesthood is seen to be the perfect fulfilment of the order of Melchizedek because it was established by oath, is unaffected by death and unmarred by sin (7:20–28).

(iii) *His work is within the new covenant* (8:1–9:10). Every aspect of the old order has its counterpart in the new. There is a new sanctuary in which the Mediator of a new covenant has entered to minister.

(iv) *His work is centred in a perfect atonement* (9:11–10:18). Our High Priest offered a unique sacrifice (himself), and because this

Parts of the Epistle to the Hebrews, written in Greek on the back of a papyrus roll originally containing a summary of Livy's history of Rome. Part shown here unrolled. Found at Oxyrhynchus, Egypt. 3rd–4th cent. AD. (BL)

offering was made 'through the eternal Spirit' it is superior to the levitical offerings (9:11–15). The necessity of Christ's death is demonstrated by an illustration from a legal testament (9:16–22). His perfect sacrifice shows up the blemishes of the levitical system (10:1–10). His ministry, unlike the Aaronic, is complete and effective (10:11–18).

The practical application of the doctrinal theme. 10:19–13:25

a. Exhortations to hold fast, 10:19–25

b. Parenthesis, 10:26–37

(i) A serious warning against apostasy (10:26–31).

(ii) Encouragement based on the readers' former experiences (10:32–37).

c. Examples from the past, 11:1–40

The writer appeals to the heroes of faith in order to inspire his readers into heroic action.

d. Advice concerning present sufferings, 12:1–29

(i) Present trials to be regarded as chastisements (12:1–13).

(ii) Warnings based on the story of Esau (12:14–17).

(iii) A final contrast between the old and the greater glory of the new (12:18–29).

e. Christian responsibilities, 13:1–25

(i) Various exhortations affecting the social and personal life of the believer (13:1–8).

(ii) A concluding warning to the readers to go forth from the camp (of Judaism) and some final personal references (13:9–25).

II. Authorship and date

The question of authorship was of greater importance in the early church than it is today, for upon it depended the canonicity of the Epistle. Ancient tradition regarding authorship consisted of various opinions. Tertullian (*De Pudicitia* 20) attributed it to Barnabas, while Origen reports that many ancients held it to be by Paul, a view shared by Clement of Alexandria. The latter seems to have regarded it as written in the Heb. dialect but translated by Luke, and he appears to have received the tradition from his predecessor Pantaenus (the blessed presbyter). Origen mentions that some in his day ascribed it to Clement of Rome and others to Luke, but he himself regarded the thoughts as the apostle's though not the words. His own conclusion regarding authorship was that God alone knew for certain who wrote the Epistle, but this reserve was not followed by the later Alexandrians, who adhered so strongly to Pauline authorship that it became accepted as canonical not only in the E but also in the W, where earlier doubts concerning it had been strong. It was not, however, until the time of Jerome and Augustine that canonicity was settled in the W. The tradition of Pauline authorship was not again seriously challenged until the time of the Reformation, when Erasmus, Luther and Calvin all disputed it. Luther's idea that Apollos was the author has commended itself to many modern scholars, although none would regard it as any more than speculative. Grotius revived the early idea that Luke was the author, and many other suggestions have been offered by modern criticism. But it is significant that few modern scholars have attempted to support the theory of Pauline authorship. It falls down on difference of style, as Origen noted when he recognized the language as 'more Greek'; on different modes of composition, such as the absence of greetings, the manner of introducing exhortations, the method of argument, and the lack of Pauline signature; on the different historical situation in which the author places himself, for whereas Paul never tired of stating that he had received the gospel by revelation, this author makes clear his personal indebtedness to second-hand information (2:3–4); and on the difference of background clearly evident in the absence from this Epistle of any past spiritual crisis dominating the author's thought and in the absence of the familiar Pauline antitheses.

Two interesting alternative suggestions are those of Ramsay, who suggested that Philip wrote the Epistle from Caesarea after contact with Paul and sent it to the Jerusalem church, and of Harnack, who made out a case for Priscilla and Aquila as joint-authors. But at best these are only ingenious guesses, and modern criticism would do well to abide by Origen's caution and let the author remain incognito.

Although the information available for dating purposes is scanty, there is enough to enable the most probable period to be ascertained. Since it was cited by Clement of Rome (*c.* AD 95) it must have been produced some while before his time. In all probability it was written before AD 70, as no mention is made of the fall of Jerusalem and as the ecclesiastical situation suits an earlier date (*cf.* 13:7,17, where those in charge are vaguely called 'leaders'). Yet some interval is required after the foundation of the church addressed to allow for the 'former days' of persecution to be regarded in retrospect. If the persecution was that under Nero a date about AD 67–8 would be required, but probably only general opposition is meant, in which case a date before AD 64 would be possible. Some scholars date the Epistle *c.* AD 80–90 on the strength of the author's use of the Pauline Epistles, but since the date of the collection of these Epistles is shrouded in mystery, and since the author does not show the influence of them all, little importance can be attached to this line of evidence.

III. Destination and purpose

The opening sentences of the Epistle give no indication of the location or identity of the readers, but the traditional title ascribes it simply 'To the Hebrews'. Although this was not part of the original text, it cannot be entirely ignored, since it may preserve genuine tradition. If that is so it must be Jewish Christians and not simply Jews who are intended. Yet a theory which has gained some support in modern times is that the title is no more than an inference from the substance of the Epistle and that it was really sent to Gentiles. Support for this notion is claimed from the consistent citations from LXX rather than the Heb. text of the OT and from the supposed Hellenistic background to which the writer appeals. The Epistle would then set forth the absolute character of Christianity to the Gentile world, showing it to supersede all other faiths, especially the mystery cults. But there is nothing in the Epistle which corresponds to mystery religions or to unbelief in religion as a whole.

Akin to this latter theory is the suggestion that the Epistle was an answer to a pre-Gnostic heresy of a type similar to that combated in Colossians. The passage showing Christ's superiority to angels (Heb. 1:4–14) would certainly give an effective answer to the tendency to angel-worship (*cf.* Col. 2:18). T. W. Manson went so far as to suggest that Apollos wrote this Epistle to the Colossian church to answer the two main tendencies of reliance on intermediaries (answered in chs. 1–4) and on ritual practices (chs. 5–10). Yet there are no evidences of pre-Gnostic tendencies in the situation underlying Hebrews such as clearly existed at Colossae.

The more widely-held view is that the Epistle was addressed to Jewish Christians to warn them against apostasy to Judaism. This is based on the serious exhortations in chs. 6 and 10, which presuppose that there is danger of a definite falling away which would amount to nothing short of crucifying the Son of God afresh (6:6) and of profanation of the blood of the covenant (10:29). Since the author is addressing those who have once tasted the goodness of God (6:4–5) and who are therefore in danger of forsaking Christianity for their old faith, and since the Epistle sets forth the superiority of Christianity to OT ritual, it is natural to suppose that Jewish Christians are in mind. The question then arises as to whether these Jewish Christians can be any more specifically defined, and various answers have been given to this inquiry: (*a*) that the Epistle was designed generally for all Jewish Christians; (*b*) that it was designed for a small house-community of Christians who had the capacity to be teachers (*cf.* 5:12) but who were not exercising it; and (*c*) that the readers were converted Jewish priests. The first view is difficult because of the personal notes in the conclusion (13:22–25) and the direct personal approach in many places in the body of the Epistle. The second view is for this reason preferable, since a particular historic situation seems to be in mind, and the readers were evidently a group apart from the main body of the church, since 5:12 could not well apply to the whole community. Moreover, the language and concepts of the Epistle presuppose an educated group, and this lends support to the idea of an intellectual clique within the local church. As to the location of these Jewish Christians, various suggestions have been made, depending partially on theories of authorship. Palestine and Alexandria have both found supporters, the former particularly by those regarding Barnabas as the author, but Rome is more favoured, supported by the somewhat ambiguous allusion in 13:24 ('They who come from Italy send you greetings'). It is not without significance in this connection that the earliest evidence for the use of the Epistle is the writing of Clement of Rome. The third alternative mentioned above, *i.e.* that the readers were converted priests, has gained support from those who claim that the argument of the Epistle would be of great relevance to those who had just recently turned from Jewish ritual practices, and especially to those who had been connected with the Jerusalem Temple (Acts records that a great many of these people were converted through Stephen's ministry). It has been objected that no evidence of separate priestly communities exists from the primitive period, but nevertheless this Epistle may provide such evidence. There seems to be no conclusive reason against this theory, and it must remain an interesting conjecture.

Yet another view, a modification of the last, sees in the Epistle a challenge to restricted Jewish Christians to embrace the world mission. This is based on certain similarities between this Epistle and Stephen's speech, such as the conception of Christianity as superseding Judaism, and the definite call to the people addressed to leave their present position. But the resemblances must not be pressed too far, since Stephen's audience did not consist of Jewish Christians. But nevertheless it is possible that the apostasy danger was the forsaking of the divine world mission purpose. A group of Jewish Christians who regarded Christianity as little more than a sect of official Judaism would certainly have benefited from the arguments of this Epistle, and it seems possible that this view will gain more support.

IV. Canonicity

The Epistle had an interesting early history, with the West generally more reluctant to accept it than the East. Through the influence of

Origen the eastern churches came to accept it, mostly on the strength of Pauline authorship. But although certain of the early western Fathers used it (Clement of Rome and Tertullian), it suffered a period of eclipse, until the time of Jerome and Augustine by whom it was fully accepted, and their opinion settled the matter for the western churches.

V. Background

An understanding of the author's milieu is essential for a right appreciation of his thought, and there has been a great deal of discussion on this subject. It may be dealt with under five headings.

a. Old Testament

Since the whole argument of the Epistle revolves around OT history and ritual, it goes without saying that the author was deeply influenced by biblical teaching. In fact, it is to be noted that the basis of his approach is biblical and not Judaistic. His reverence for the sacred text is seen in the care with which he cites it, though always from LXX, in the manner in which he introduces his citations (*e.g.* the repetitive 'he says' in ch. 1) and in the strictly historical approach to OT history as contrasted with the contemporary allegorical tendencies. The author, well versed as he is in OT concepts, has clearly thought through the problem of the Christian approach to the OT, and his major emphasis is on the fulfilment in Christ of all that was adumbrated in the old order. This subject is further elaborated in the section on the theology of the Epistle, but for the present it should be noted that the author not only himself accepts the full authority of the Scriptures but clearly expects his readers to do the same.

b. Philonism

At the end of the 19th century a strong movement existed which assumed that the author's mind was so steeped in Philonic thought that it was only possible to understand his Epistle against the background of Philo's philosophical and allegorical expositions. The leading exponent of this view was E. Ménégoz, and one of his presuppositions was that a gap existed between this author's theology and that of Paul, and any similarities were clutched at to prove his indebtedness to Philo rather than to Paul. Yet some similarities cannot be denied. The notion of heaven as real and earth as only a place of shadows and the corresponding antitheses between the old covenant and the new show a similar tendency to Philo. Moreover, many words and phrases may be paralleled in the two authors, some of which occur nowhere else in the NT. C. Spicq finds the similarities reaching even to matters of style, schemes of thought, and psychology, and concludes that the author was a converted Philonist. Yet this opinion must be received with reserve, for the author differs from Philo on a number of important issues. His biblical exegesis is more akin to rabbinic methods than Philonic, his understanding of history is not, as Philo's, allegorical, and his idea of Christ as High Priest is far removed from Philo's abstract ideas of the Logos. A Christian Philonist would certainly transform his master's conceptions, but it is questionable whether the Christology of Hebrews stands in direct line of succession from Philo. The author may echo Philonic language and ideas, but his roots are without doubt elsewhere.

c. Primitive tradition

The question arises whether or not this Epistle is to be regarded as being a natural development from primitive Christian theology and whether it has any close connections with Pauline and Johannine theology, or even whether it stands as an unrelated attempt of an author to deal with the OT outside the main stream of development. Increasing interest is being shown in the early roots of the Epistle. The attempt to connect it with the catechesis of Stephen focuses attention on this, but further features from the primitive tradition may also be mentioned by way of illustration. The idea of the continuity between the old and new covenants, the interest in the earthly life of Jesus, the realization that his death must be interpreted, and the mixture of present and eschatological appeals, are all basic to the primitive Christian tradition. The main theme of this Epistle, with its predominant interest in man's approach to God, could not fail to find roots in the earliest preaching and teaching. The author introduces many new features, such as Christ's enthronement and heavenly high priesthood, but he brings in nothing alien to that primitive tradition.

d. Paulinism

It was inevitable under the hypothesis of Pauline authorship which held the field for so long that the Epistle should be regarded as an aspect of Pauline theology, yet with the rejection of Pauline authorship an unfortunate reaction set in against any Pauline influence. Support for this extreme position has declined; but it is undeniable that there are some differences from Paul which would support the theory of the author's belonging to an independent stream of tradition, as, for instance, the different treatment of Christ's relation to the law, for there is an absence of that wrestling with the law which is so evident in Paul's experience. Yet the differences must not be stretched into contrasts, and it remains possible to conceive of the author as having been under Pauline influence while at the same time acknowledging his debt to other influences. Thus he becomes an independent witness, in the truest sense, of early Christian reflection upon the great themes of the gospel.

e. Johannine thought

Whether there are any close connections between the Johannine literature and this Epistle will clearly depend on the dating of each. It has been argued that Hebrews stands midway between Paul and John in the line of theological development (as, for instance, by R. H. Strachan, *The Historic Jesus in the New Testament*, 1931), but in view of the increasing emphasis which is being placed on the primitive character of the Johannine catechesis, to which the evidence of the Dead Sea Scrolls has lent some support, this notion of theological development must be modified. The main points of contact between Hebrews and the Johannine theology are the common use of antithetic parallelism, the similar conception of Christ's high-priestly work, the description of Christ as Shepherd, the allusion to the propitiatory work of Christ, and the attention given to the perfect character of that work.

To sum up, the author is no antiquary whose researches into the biblical revelation possess no relevance for Christians generally, whether ancient or modern, but a writer who presents a vital aspect of Christian thought, complementary to other streams of primitive tradition.

VI. Theology

All that precedes has prepared the way for the most important consideration, the theological contribution of the Epistle. The standpoint of the author is to regard Christianity as the perfect revelation of God. This meant that Christianity not only superseded all other faiths, including Judaism, but that it could not itself be superseded. Its salvation is eternal (5:9), so is its redemption, inheritance and covenant (9:12, 15; 13:20), while Christ's offering is described as being 'through the eternal Spirit' (9:14). This idea of the perfection and abiding character of Christianity pervades the whole Epistle and furnishes the key for the understanding of all its major themes.

a. Christology

The first part of the Epistle is devoted to demonstrating Christ's superiority to all other intermediaries, to prophets, angels, Moses, Joshua and Aaron, but the opening chapter strikes the positive and exalted note of his divine Sonship. This Sonship is conceived of as unique, for Christ is heir of all and agent of creation (1:2). He is even more closely related to God in 1:3, where he is described as the bursting forth of his glory and the express stamp of his nature, and these two statements taken together exclude the twin errors of difference of nature and lack of distinct personality. The pre-existence of Christ seems to be clearly in the author's mind. The further statement in 1:3 that after effecting purification the Son sat down on the right hand of the majesty on high links this opening Christological statement with the later theme of the Epistle, *i.e.* the processes of redemption. Although some have sought, mistakenly, to trace influences of the currently held enthronement ritual of a king who becomes a god, the idea of Christ's exaltation is firmly rooted in the primitive Christian tradition and is a close corollary to the ascension of Christ. When he comes to his later high priest theme the writer clearly intends to introduce his readers to an exalted Christ who no longer needs liturgical means for the purgation of sins.

The incarnation of the Son is many times mentioned. He was made lower than the angels (2:9) in order to taste death for everyone, he partook of the same nature as man (2:14), he was made like his brethren in every respect (2:17) and is capable of sympathizing with our weaknesses because he was in all points tempted as we are (4:15). These statements are a necessary prelude to the high priest theme, since he must be shown to be truly representative (*cf.* 5:1). The earthly life of Jesus comes into focus not only in his temptations (2:18; 4:15) but also in his agony of prayer (5:7), in his perfect obedience (5:8), in his teaching ministry (2:3) and in his endurance of hostility (12:3).

But it is the priestly office of Christ which dominates the author's thought. The Aaronic order was good as far as it went, but its inadequacy is brought out strikingly in contrast to the perfect priesthood of Christ. This leads the author to introduce the mysterious *Melchizedek theme before his expositions of the weakness of the levitical economy (5:6, 10; 6:20–7:19). There is no means of ascertaining whether the writer himself innovated this theme or received it from primitive tradition, as it is nowhere else elaborated in the NT. But Ps. 110 in which the theme occurs exerted a powerful influence on primitive Christian thought, mainly through our Lord's own use of it, and it is reasonable to suppose that this Psalm provided the author with his conception of a superior order of priesthood. Philo, it is true, had already identified Melchizedek with the Logos, but there is no need to appeal to Philo to account for the usage of this Epistle. Nor is it just to maintain that the Melchizedek exposition is entirely speculative and without any modern relevance, for although the method of argument in 7:1ff. borders on the allegorical, the author is clear on the fundamental Christian position that Christ must belong to a higher order than that of Aaron, and in introducing the Melchizedek motive he justifies his contention that, although Christ is not a Priest according to the Aaronic order, he still is a Priest, and not only a Priest but a King.

b. The work of Christ

Against the background of the weaknesses of the Aaronic order the author brings out the positive superiority of Christ's atoning work, and the major factors involved are: (i) the finality of Christ's offering (7:27; 9:12, 28; 10:10); (ii) the personal character of his offering in that he offered himself (9:14); (iii) the spiritual character of the offering (9:14); and (iv) the abiding results of his priestly work achieving as it did *eternal* redemption (9:12). The Aaronic order, with its constantly repeated ritual, could offer no comparison with this. Even the arrangement of furniture in the holy place and the holiest place is brought into the argument (9:1ff.) in order to contrast this with the greater and more perfect sanctuary into which Christ entered once for all by virtue of his own blood. The climax of the soteriological argument is essentially reached at 9:14, where Christ is said to have offered himself 'through the eternal Spirit', which brings into striking contrast the helpless and hapless victims of the Aaronic ritual and the deliberate self-offering of our High Priest. The practical application of all this is found in 10:19, where confidence of approach on the basis of Christ's high-priestly work is urged upon the readers, and this leads on to the mainly practical conclusion of the Epistle.

c. Other theological concepts

One of the great words of the Epistle is 'faith', but it has a different meaning from the Pauline concept. For this writer there is little of the dynamic concept of faith which accepts God's provision of salvation (though 10:22 approximates to this and requires to be so understood). In the use of the concept in the great gallery of heroes in ch. 11, the writer does not give a formal definition of faith but rather gives a description of some of its active qualities. It is essentially practical, comprising rather an approach to life than a mystical appropriation. In various ways the author makes clear the meaning of Christian *salvation*, which has deeply impressed him with its greatness (2:3). He makes use of Ps. 8 to introduce the fact that it is through humiliation that Christ gained the right to bring 'many sons to glory' (2:5–10); he conceives of salvation as deliverance from the power of the devil (2:14–15) and also depicts it as a rest into which believers enter as an inheritance (3:1–4:13). The processes of salvation are described as sanctification (*hagiasmos*, 12:14; *cf.* 2:11; 10:10, 29; 13:12) and perfection (*teleōsis*, 7:11; *cf.* 11:40; 12:23).

BIBLIOGRAPHY. F. J. Badcock, *The Pauline Epistles and the Epistle to the Hebrews*, 1937; W. Manson,

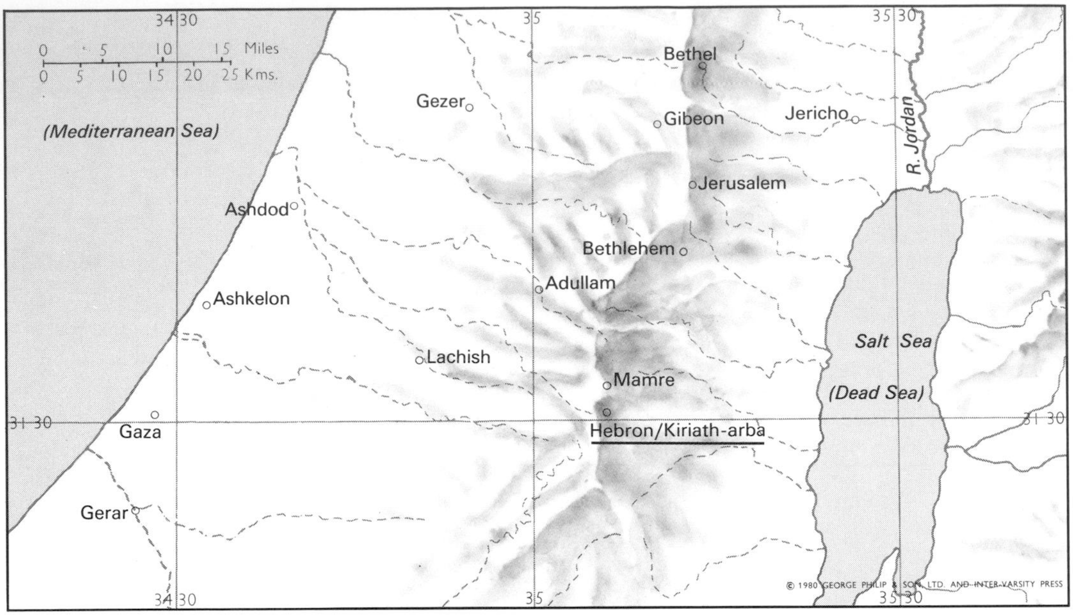

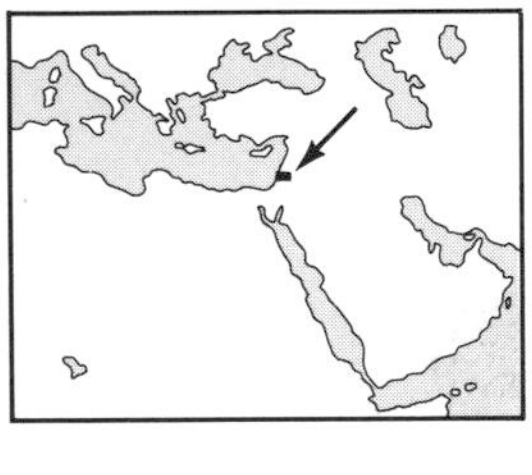

Hebron, burial-place of Abraham.

Jar-handle of the 7th cent. BC *stamped with an official emblem and the words 'royal' and 'Hebron' in Hebrew* (lmlk, ḥḇrn). (BM)

The Epistle to the Hebrews, 1951; E. Ménégoz, *La Théologie de l'Épître aux Hébreux*, 1894; O. Michel, *Der Brief an die Hebräer, Kritisch-Exegetischer Kommentar*, 1949; J. Moffatt, *The Epistle to the Hebrews, ICC*, 1924; A. Nairne, *The Epistle to the Hebrews, CGT*, 1922; F. D. V. Narborough, *The Epistle to the Hebrews, Clarendon Bible*, 1930; T. Hewitt, *The Epistle to the Hebrews, TNTC*, 1960; C. Spicq, *L'Épître aux Hébreux, Études Bibliques*, 1952; B. F. Westcott, *The Epistle to the Hebrews*, 1892; E. C. Wickham, *The Epistle to the Hebrews, WC*, 1910; E. Käsemann, *Das wandernde Gottesvolk*, 1939; R. Williamson, *Philo and the Epistle to the Hebrews*, 1970; F. F. Bruce, *The Epistle to the Hebrews*, 1964; J. Héring, *The Epistle to the Hebrews*, E.T. 1970; F. L. Horton, *The Melchizedek Tradition*, 1976; P. E. Hughes, *A Commentary on the Epistle to the Hebrews*, 1977.

D.G.

HEBRON (Heb. *ḥeḇrôn*, 'confederacy'; *cf.* its alternative and older name Kiriath-arba, 'tetrapolis'), the highest town in Palestine, 927 m above the level of the Mediterranean, 30 km SSW of Jerusalem. The statement that it 'was built seven years before Zoan in Egypt' (Nu. 13:22) probably relates its foundation to the 'Era of Tanis' (*c.* 1720 BC). Abraham lived in its vicinity for considerable periods (* MAMRE); in his days the resident population ('the people of the land') were 'sons of Heth' (* HITTITES), from whom Abraham bought the field of Machpelah with its cave to be a family burying-ground (Gn. 23). There he and Sarah, Isaac and Rebekah, Jacob and Leah were buried (Gn. 49:31; 50:13). According to Josephus (*Ant.* 2. 199; 3. 305), the sons of Jacob, with the exception of Joseph, were buried there too. The traditional site of the Patriarchs' sepulchre lies within the great *Ḥaram el-Ḫalîl*, the 'Enclosure of the Friend' (*i.e.* Abraham; *cf.* Is. 41:8), with its Herodian masonry. During the Israelites' wilderness wandering the twelve spies sent out to report on the land of Canaan explored the region of Hebron; at that time it was populated by the 'descendants of Anak' (Nu. 13:22, 28, 33). After Israel's entry into Canaan, Hoham, king of Hebron, joined the anti-Gibeonite coalition led by Adoni-zedek, king of Jerusalem, and was killed by Joshua (Jos. 10:1–27). Hebron itself and the surrounding territory were conquered from the Anakim by Caleb and given to him as a family possession (Jos. 14:12ff.; 15:13f.; Jdg. 1:10, 20). In Hebron David was anointed king of Judah (2 Sa. 2:4) and 2 years later king of Israel also (2 Sa. 5:3); it remained his capital for 7½ years. It was here too, later in his reign, that Absalom raised the standard of rebellion against him (2 Sa. 15:7ff.). It was fortified by Rehoboam (2 Ch. 11:10). Hebron is one of the four cities named on royal jar-handle stamps found at * Lachish and other sites, which probably points to its importance as a major Judaean administrative centre in the reign of Hezekiah. After the Babylonian captivity it was one of the places where returning exiles settled (Ne. 11:25; Kiriath-arba = Hebron). Later it was occupied by the Idumaeans, from whom Judas Maccabaeus captured it (1 Macc. 5:65). During the war of AD 66–70 it was occupied by Simon bar-Giora, but was stormed and burnt by the Romans (Jos., *BJ* 4. 529, 554). Under the name of el-Ḫalîl it is one of the four sacred cities of the Muslims.

BIBLIOGRAPHY. L. H. Vincent and E. J. H. Mackay, *Hébron, le Ḥaram el-Khalil, sépulture des patriarches*, 2 vols., 1923; D. Baly, *Geography of the Bible*², 1974.

F.F.B.

HEIFER (Heb. *'eglâ*, 12 times; Heb. *pārâ*, 'young cow', 6 times; Gk. *damalis*, 'tamed heifer', Heb. 9:13 only). Mixed with water, the ashes of an unblemished red heifer, burnt in its entirety 'outside the camp', imparted levitical purification (Nu. 19; Heb. 9:13). A heifer with a broken neck cleansed the nearest city from the blood-guiltiness of a corpse slain by unknown hands (Dt. 21:1–9). Jdg. 14:18; Je. 46:20; Ho. 4:16, *etc.*, give interesting metaphorical usages.

BIBLIOGRAPHY. F. F. Bruce, *The Epistle to the Hebrews*, 1965, pp. 201–204, *etc.*; C. Brown, *NIDNTT* 1, pp. 115f.; R. A. Stewart, *Rabbinic Theology*, 1961, p. 138.

R.A.S.

HELAM. A city in Transjordan, probably the modern 'Alma, the location of the defeat of Hadadezer's Syrian forces, reinforced by Syrian troops from beyond the Euphrates, by David (2 Sa. 10:16f.), following the defeat of an Ammonite–Syrian alliance by David's captain Joab. The mention of the Gk. form, Eliam, constituting part of a place-name in LXX of Ezk. 47:16, has led to a proposed alternative location on the border between Damascus and Hamath. Connection with Alema (1 Macc. 5:26) has also been suggested.

R.A.H.G.

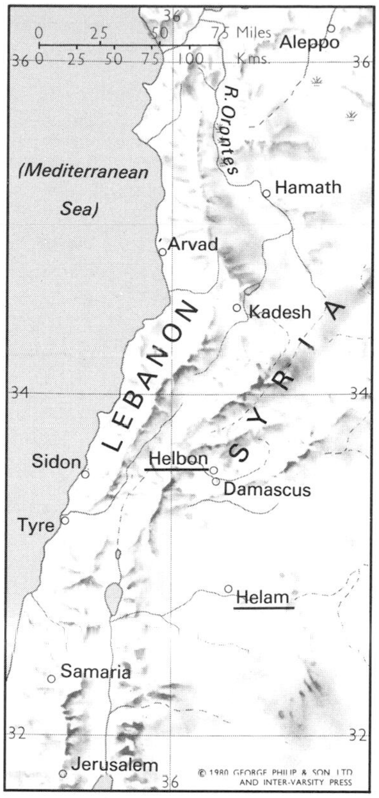

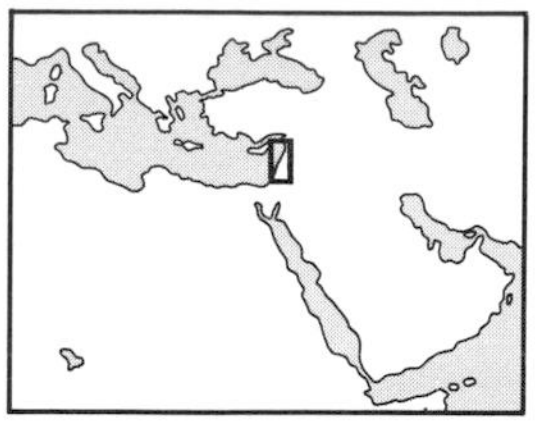

Probable locations of Helam and Helbon.

HELBON (Heb. *ḥelbôn*, 'fat', 'fruitful'). A town mentioned in Ezk. 27:18 as trading wine to Tyre. This has been identified with the village of Khalbun, 25 km N of Damascus. The author of the Genesis Apocryphon from Qumran wrote Helbon for the place-name *Hobah of Gn. 14:15, described as 'on the left hand of' or 'north of' Damascus, and this gives interesting evidence for thus identifying an otherwise unknown site.

J.B.Tr.

HELDAI. *Cf.* Heled. (Heb. *ḥeleḏ* means 'duration of life'; *cf.* Arab. *ḥalada* and *ḥuldun*.)

1. In 1 Ch. 27:15, one of David's famous soldiers who was appointed over 24,000 in the 12th month. He was a Netophathite, and thus from Judah, from the stock of Othniel (*cf.* Jdg. 1:12–15). The 'Heled' of 1 Ch. 11:30 is doubtless the same person. He is called a free man (Heb. *gibbôr ḥayil*, v. 26), one of the commanders of the army. We must probably read 'Heled' and not 'Heleb' in 2 Sa. 23:29, and he may have been the same person as the above mentioned.

2. A Heldai is mentioned in Zc. 6:10 with Tobijah and Jedaiah. After they returned from the Exile, silver and gold was taken from

HEDGE
See Gederah, Part 1.

HEDGE AROUND LAW
See Stripes, Part 3.

HEDGEHOG
See Animals, Part 1.

Clay figure of a prisoner inscribed with formulae ('execration text') intended to achieve the magical destruction of rulers, cities and lands named on the figure, possibly including Helam. Egyptian. c. 1800 BC. (ACL)

them to make a crown for Joshua, the high priest. Heldai is called Helem in v. 14 (Heb.); this may have been a nickname or may be due to a scribal error. F.C.F.

HELEB, HELED, HELEM
See Heldai, Part 2.

HELIOPOLIS
See Prostitution, Part 3.

HELEZ. The Heb. *ḥeleṣ* may mean 'loins' or perhaps 'strength'.

1. One of David's heroes. The Helez of 2 Sa. 23:26 is probably the same as the one of 1 Ch. 11:27 and 27:10. The problem is that in 2 Sa. he is described as the Paltite (Heb. *palṭî*, a man of *bêṯ peleṭ*, a place in Judah) and in 1 Ch. as the Pelonite (Heb. *p*[e]*lōnî* means 'any one'). We may have to change 'Pelonite' to 'Paltite' or to accept that Helez of 2 Sa. is not to be identified with the one of 1 Ch. 11 and 27. In 1 Ch. 27:10 he is called one 'of the sons of Ephraim'. It may be that as a descendant of Ephraim he was regarded as a Pelonite, 'one without any connection to Judah', but lived in Beth Pelet.

2. The son of Azariah, a descendant of Judah (1 Ch. 2:39). F.C.F.

HELKATH. In the border-territory of Asher (Jos. 19:25) and a levitical city (Jos. 21:31). 1 Ch. 6:75 gives Hukok as a variant for Helkath. The exact location in the Kishon valley is disputed: a likely site for it is Tell el-Harbaj nearly 10 km SE of Haifa (A. Alt, *Palästinajahrbuch* 25, 1929, pp. 38ff.), or perhaps even better, Tell el-Qasis (or Kussis) 8 km SSE of Tell el-Harbaj (Y. Aharoni, *IEJ* 9, 1959, pp. 119–120). Helkath is probably the *ḥrḳt* in topographical lists of the pharaoh Tuthmosis III, *c.* 1460 BC. K.A.K.

Possible locations of Helkath.

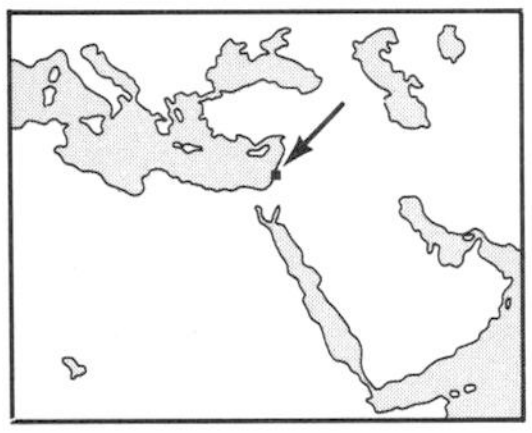

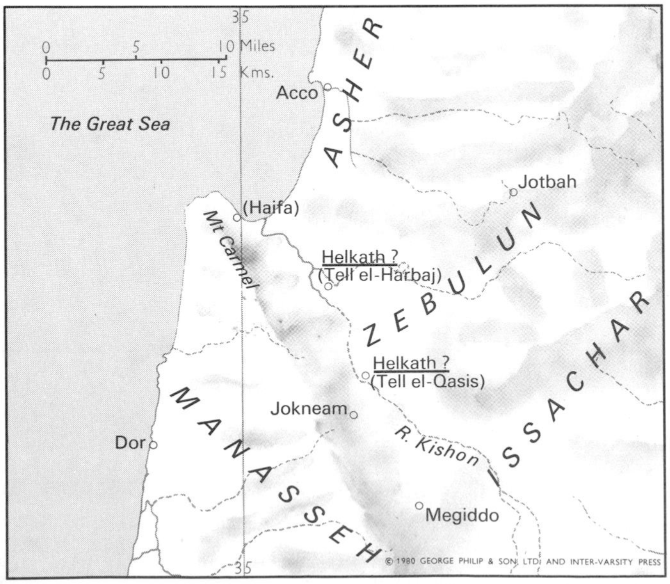

HELKATH-HAZZURIM (Heb. *ḥelqaṯ haṣṣurîm*, 'field of flints' or 'field of (sword)-edges'). This is the name given to the place in Gibeon where there was a tournament between the champions of Joab and Abner, which led on to a battle (2 Sa. 2:16). Other meanings conjectured include 'field of plotters', based on the LXX *meris tōn epiboulōn*, 'field of sides' and 'field of adversaries'. (*Cf.* S. R. Driver, *Notes on the Hebrew Text of the Books of Samuel*, 1913.) J.G.G.N.

HELL. 'Hell' in the NT renders the Gk. word transliterated as 'Gehenna' (Mt. 5:22, 29–30; 10:28; 18:9; 23:15, 33; Mk. 9:43, 45, 47; Lk. 12:5; Jas. 3:6). The name is derived from the Heb. *gê(ben)(b*[e]*nê) hinnōm*, the valley of (the son[s] of) Hinnom, a valley near Jerusalem (Jos. 15:8; 18:16) where children were sacrificed by fire in connection with pagan rites (2 Ki. 23:10; 2 Ch. 28:3; 33:6; Je. 7:31; 32:35). Its original derivation is obscure, but Hinnom is almost certainly the name of a person. In later Jewish writings Gehenna came to mean the place of punishment for sinners (*Assumption of Moses* 10:10; 2 Esdras 7:36). It was depicted as a place of unquenchable fire—the general idea of fire to express the divine judgment is found in the OT (Dt. 32:22; Dn. 7:10). The rabbinic literature contains various opinions as to who would suffer eternal punishment. The ideas were widespread that the sufferings of some would be terminated by annihilation, or that the fires of Gehenna were in some cases purgatorial (*Rosh Hashanah* 16b–17a; *Baba Mezi'a* 58b; Mishnah *Eduyoth* 2. 10). But those who held these doctrines also taught the reality of eternal punishment for certain classes of sinners. Both this literature and the Apocryphal books affirm belief in an eternal retribution (*cf.* Judith 16:17; *Psalms of Solomon* 3:13).

The teaching of the NT endorses this past belief. The fire of hell is unquenchable (Mk. 9:43), eternal (Mt. 18:8), its punishment is the converse of eternal life (Mt. 25:46). There is no suggestion that those who enter hell ever emerge from it. However, the NT leaves the door open for the belief that while hell as a manifestation of God's implacable wrath against sin is unending, the existence of those who suffer in it may not be. It is difficult to reconcile the ultimate fulfilment of the whole universe in Christ (Eph. 1:10; Col. 1:20) with the continued existence of those who reject him. Some scholars have contended that an eternal punishment is one which is eternal in its effects; in any case eternal does not necessarily mean never-ending, but implies 'long duration extending to the writer's mental horizon' (J. A. Beet). On the other hand Rev. 20:10 does indicate conscious, never-ending torment for the devil and his agents, albeit in a highly symbolic passage, and some would affirm that a similar end awaits human beings who ultimately refuse to repent. In any case, nothing should be allowed to detract from the seriousness of our Lord's warnings about the terrible reality of God's judgment in the world to come.

In Jas. 3:6 Gehenna, like the bottomless pit in Rev. 9:1ff.; 11:7, appears to be the source of evil on the earth.

NT imagery concerning eternal punishment is not uniform. As well as fire it is described as darkness (Mt. 25:30; 2 Pet. 2:17), death (Rev. 2:11), destruction and exclusion from the presence of the Lord (2 Thes. 1:9; Mt. 7:21–23), and a debt to pay (Mt. 5:25–26).

In 2 Pet. 2:4 only, we find the verb *tartaroō*, translated in RSV 'cast into hell', and rendered by the Pesh. 'cast down to the lower regions'. *Tartaros* is the classical word for the place of eternal punishment but is here applied to the intermediate sphere of punishment for fallen angels.

BIBLIOGRAPHY. J. A. Beet, *The Last Things*, 1905; S. D. F. Salmond, *The Christian Doctrine of Immortality*, 1907; J. W. Wenham, *The Goodness of God*, 1974; H. Bietenhard, *NIDNTT* 2, pp. 205–210; J. Jeremias, *TDNT* 1, pp. 9f., 146–149, 657f. D.K.I.

HELLENISTS. Gk. *hellēnistai*, people, not themselves Greeks (*hellēnes*), who 'hellenized', *i.e.* spoke the Greek language (*hellēnisti*, Acts 21:37, *etc.*) and otherwise adopted the Greek way of life (*hellēnismos*, 2 Macc. 4:10).

The earliest occurrence of the word in Greek literature is in Acts 6:1, where it denotes a group of Jewish Christians in the primitive church of Jerusalem, distinguished from the 'Hebrews' (*hebraioi*), who were probably Aramaic-speaking.

The seven almoners, including Stephen and Philip, appointed in response to the Hellenists' complaint that the 'Hebrew' widows were being favoured over theirs in the distribution of charity from the common fund, all appear by their names to have been Hellenists (Acts 6:5). Many of the Hellenists would have connections with the Diaspora, whereas most of the Hebrews would be Palestinian Jews. The line of demarcation between Hebrews and Hellenists cannot have been hard and fast, for many Jews were bilingual. Paul, for example, who spoke Greek habitually (as might be expected in a native of Tarsus), nevertheless calls himself 'a Hebrew born of Hebrews' (Phil. 3:5; *cf.* 2 Cor. 11:22). Perhaps the determinant factor with such a person was whether the services in the synagogue which he attended were conducted in Greek (*cf.* Acts 6:9) or in Hebrew.

To judge from Stephen and Philip, the Hellenists in the Jerusalem church were more forward-looking than the Hebrews, in teaching and practice alike. In the persecution which broke out after Stephen's death, it was mainly the Hellenists who were scattered, propagating the gospel wherever they went. Attempts to link these Hellenists with Essenes or with Samaritans have not been successful (apart from their antecedent improbability).

The Hellenists of Acts 9:29 were members of one or more Greek-speaking synagogues in Jerusalem.

In Acts 11:20 the MSS are divided between 'Hellenists' (*hellēnistas*) and 'Greeks' (*hellēnas*), with the weight of evidence favouring the former. Whichever reading be preferred, the context makes it plain that the reference is to Gentile residents of Antioch, to whom Christian visitors, 'men of Cyprus and Cyrene', took the initiative in preaching the gospel, whereas their associates on first coming to Antioch had preached it 'to none except Jews' (Acts 11:19). If they were not Greeks (*hellēnes*) by origin, they could have belonged to other ethnic groups in Antioch which had adopted Greek language and culture.

BIBLIOGRAPHY. G. P. Wetter, 'Das älteste hellenistische Christentum nach der Apostelgeschichte', *Archiv für Religionswissenschaft* 21, 1922, pp. 410ff.; H. J. Cadbury, 'The Hellenists', *BC* 5, pp. 59ff.; H. Windisch, *TDNT* 2, pp. 511f. (*s.v. Hellēnistēs*); E. C. Blackman, 'The Hellenists of Acts vi.1', *ExpT* 48, 1936–7, pp. 524f.; O. Cullmann, 'The Significance of the Qumran Texts for Research into the Beginnings of Christianity', *JBL* 74, 1955, pp. 213ff.; M. Simon, *St. Stephen and the Hellenists in the Primitive Church*, 1958; C. F. D. Moule, 'Once More, Who Were the Hellenists?', *ExpT* 70, 1958–9, pp. 100ff.; C. S. Mann, ' "Hellenists" and "Hebrews" in Acts VI 1', in J. Munck, *The Acts of the Apostles*, 1967, pp. 301ff.; I. H. Marshall, 'Palestinian and Hellenistic Christianity', *NTS* 19, 1972–3, pp. 271ff.; M. Hengel, *Judaism and Hellenism*, 1974.

F.F.B.

HEMAN (Heb. *hêmān*, 'faithful'). **1.** One of the sages whom Solomon excelled in wisdom (1 Ki. 4:31). Said to be a son of * Mahol; but 1 Ch. 2:6 calls him a son of Zerah, a Judahite.

2. A Kohathite Levite, son of Joel, one of David's leading singers (1 Ch. 6:33; 15:17, 19; 16:41–42; 25:1, 4–6; 2 Ch. 5:12; 35:15). Probably the 'sons of Heman' in 1 Ch. 25:4 are really the titles of parts of a prayer or anthem, the singers receiving names from their parts (*cf.* H. L. Ellison in *NBCR*, 1970, pp. 281f.; W. R. Smith, *The Old Testament in the Jewish Church*, p. 143 n.).

3. The Ezrahite named in the title of Ps. 88. Probably the same as **1**.

J.G.G.N.

HEN (Heb. *ḥēn*, 'favour'). One of the men who were to receive a symbolical crown (Zc. 6:14), this may be a figurative name for Josiah who had earlier (6:10) been similarly described as 'the son of Zephaniah'.

J.D.D.

HENA. A city whose god, the Assyrians boasted, could not save it (2 Ki. 18:34). It is identified by LXX

HELMET
See Armour, Part 1.

HEMLOCK
See Plants (Wormwood), Part 3.

HEN
See Animals, Part 1.

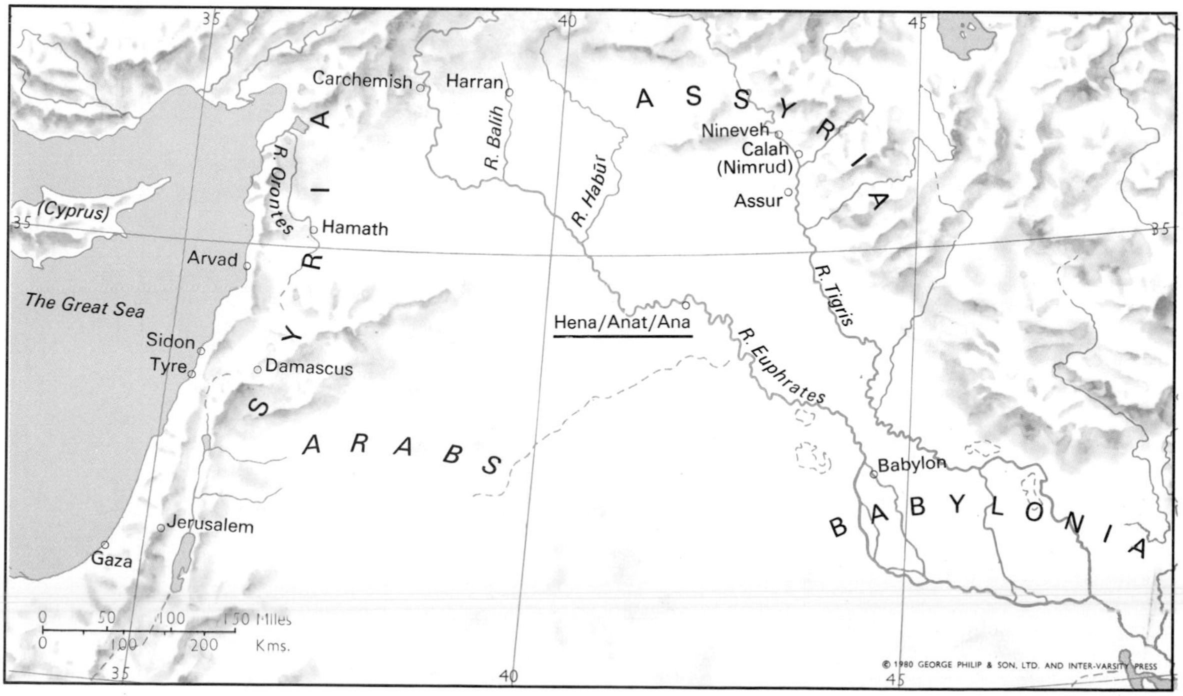

Hena (Ana) on the river Euphrates.

The bitter aloe (Aloe barbadense), *used at the burial of Jesus, is native to the Yemen and grows in dry places elsewhere in the Mediterranean region.* (FNH)

with Ana on the Euphrates. Hena and Ivvah have been identified as Arab. star names, and consequently taken as the names of deities. This is, however, unlikely, as the latter is almost certainly a place-name identical with Avva (2 Ki. 17:24, 31).

M.A.M.

HERALD. 1. Aram. *kārôz* occurs only in Dn. 3:4 with reference to the official who relayed Nebuchadrezzar's commands. *kārôz* may be derived from Old Persian *xrausa* (*KB*), 'caller', or is related to Hurrian *kirezzi*, 'proclamation'. The causative form of the associated verb *krz*, 'made a proclamation', occurs in Dn. 5:29 (see A. Shaffer, *Orientalia* 34, 1965, pp. 32–34).
2. Heb. *m[e]baśśereṯ* (Is. 40:9; masculine. Is. 41:27), 'bringing good news', is rendered in RSV as 'herald of good tidings'. The verbal form is used elsewhere in Is. in the same sense of preaching the deliverance of Yahweh (Is. 52:7; 61:1).

3. Gk. *kēryx* is translated 'herald' by RSV in 2 Pet. 2:5, but 'preacher' in 1 Tim. 2:7; 2 Tim. 1:11.

W.O.
A.R.M.

HEPATOSCOPY See Divination, Part 1.

HERBS AND SPICES. Here considered in the popular sense of edible culinary, or sometimes medicinal, plants, although strictly a herb is a non-woody plant with seasonal foliage and varying expectation of life in the root. This selection of species mentioned in the Bible is complementary to the articles on *plants, *trees, *cosmetics and individual subjects.

In the OT *deše'* normally denotes grass, *ḥāṣîr*, *'ēśeḇ*, and the less common *yārāq* (Dt. 11:10; 1 Ki. 21:2; Pr. 15:17) may mean grass, and also herbs or vegetables. *'ōrōṯ* (2 Ki. 4:39) is talmudically rendered 'garden-rocket' or 'colewort' (*Eruca*), precision perhaps exceeding the evidence (*Yoma* 18b). Is. 26:19 may speak of the dew of light (RSV) rather than the dew of herbs (AV). The NT uses *chortos* for pasturage, *lachanon* for herbs in the popular sense.

Some species of rock rose (Cistus) *become sticky to the touch and this resin was collected for medicine and perfume.* (FNH)

Spices are aromatic vegetable substances, highly esteemed by ancient Near Eastern peoples. Spice caravans pioneered the trading routes from N India to Sumeria, Akkad and Egypt at a very early period, and subsequently these routes became an important factor in cultural exchanges. While many spices were brought to Palestine from Mesopotamia and India, a number of those in common use were the product of the country itself. In OT times the Palestinian spice trade was carefully protected. Solomon derived considerable revenue by exacting tolls of the caravans passing through his realm.

Herbs and spices such as cummin, dill, cinnamon and mint were employed in the preparation of food (Ezk. 24:10) and the flavouring of wines (Ct. 8:2). The manufacture of the sacred *incense necessitated the use of frankincense, stacte, galbanum, onycha and sweet cane (Ex. 30:34), while substances such as cassia, aloes and spikenard were used as unguents for cosmetic purposes (Est. 2:12; Ct. 4:14; Mk. 14:3; Jn. 12:3).

When bodies were being prepared for burial it was customary

for spices to be placed in the grave-clothes as a form of embalming. They included mixtures of myrrh and aloes (Jn. 19:39), or, more generally, 'spices and ointments' (Lk. 23:56). While they did not significantly inhibit putrefaction, they served as deodorants and disinfectants.

Aloes (Heb. *'*^{a}*hālîm* in Pr. 7:17; Nu. 24:6, 'lign aloes'; *'*^{a}*hālôṯ* in Ps. 45:8; Ct. 4:14). Probably the modern eaglewood (*Aquilaria agallocha*) found today in E Bengal, Malaya and parts of China. From it was derived a precious spice used in biblical times for perfuming garments and beds. The perplexing question of the reference in Nu. 24:6 may suggest that the tree (or one similar) grew in the Jordan valley, but Balaam need not have actually seen the tree of which he spoke.

Aloes in Jn. 19:39 refers to a totally different liliaceous plant *Aloe barbadense*, also known as *A. vera*, wild in the Yemen and now widely naturalized. The juice of its fleshy, sword-like leaves is bitter and was used for embalming.

Balm (Heb. *ṣ*^{e}*rî, ṣ*^{o}*rî*; LXX *rhētinē*). This product of * Gilead, a somewhat vague geographical area, was exported to Egypt (Gn. 37:25; 43:11) and to Tyre (Ezk. 27:17). Celebrated for healing properties (Je. 46:11) and often used for cosmetic purposes, it was used also to symbolize deliverance from national distress (Je. 8:22; 51:8). It was probably an aromatic gum or spice, but the original meaning of the word is not clear and it cannot now be identified with any plant in Gilead, despite the claims made for a similarly-named substance prepared by the monks of Jericho from the fruit of the *zaqqûm* (*Balanites aegyptiaca*). Some understand the *ṣ*^{o}*rî* of Gn. 37:25 to be gum mastic, a product of the shrub *Pistacia lentiscus* which, common in Palestine for healing purposes, is used by the Arabs in flavouring coffee and sweets, and as a chewing-gum. Classical authors applied the name 'balm of Gilead' to what is now known as Mecca balsam or stacte (*Commiphora gileadensis*), still imported into Egypt from Arabia. The gum (Heb. *n*^{e}*kō'ṯ*, 'spicery' AV) of Gn. 37:25; 43:11 could have been the exudate from the stems of the small prickly shrub *Astragalus gummifer*. It grows on the arid slopes of Iran and Turkey and belongs to the pea family.

Mint (Mentha), *a commonly cultivated culinary herb, tithed by the Pharisees.* (FNH)

Myrrh (Commiphora myrrha). *The reddish myrrh resin was obtained by making incisions in the bark.* (FNH)

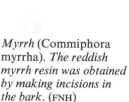

Rue (Ruta graveolens), *one of the herbs tithed by the Pharisees. It has very pungent leaves.* (FNH)

Bottom left:
Dill (Anethum graveolens), *a herb with tiny seeds regularly tithed by the Pharisees.* (FNH)

Bottom right:
Henna (Lawsonia inermis), *a fragrant shrub with leaves used for dyeing hair and skin. The identity of the ancient plant is doubtful.* (FNH)

Coriander (Coriandrum sativum), *a favourite spice seed, said to look like the 'manna'.* (FNH)

Bitter herbs (Heb. *m^{e}rôrîm*; Gk. *pikrides*). A salad composed of herbs constituted part of the Passover ordinance (Ex. 12:8; Nu. 9:11), and ordinarily was eaten after the Passover lamb had been tasted. The bitter herbs were not named individually, but are identified in the Mishna as lettuce, chicory, eryngo, horseradish and sowthistle, although all these may not have been available in biblical times. Though *m^{e}rôrîm* was used elsewhere of 'bitterness' (*cf.* La. 3:15), the Passover herbs, being easily prepared, reminded the Israelites of their haste in leaving Egypt, not their bitter persecution there.

Black cummin (Heb. *qeṣaḥ*: 'fitches' AV, 'dill' RSV). *Nigella sativa*, or nut-meg flower, is an annual closely related to the ornamental love-in-the-mist, but with greenish-blue flowers and black seeds. Its dry fruits were beaten with light sticks (Is. 28:27) to avoid damaging the aromatic, oily seeds, which were a favourite condiment of the ancient Greeks and Romans and are still used for seasoning bread and as a carminative. See also **Dill** below.

Cassia (Heb. *qiddâ*, Ex. 30:24; Ezk. 27:19; *q^{e}ṣîʿoṯ*, Ps. 45:8). These two words, identified as similar in the Pesh. and the Targ., have traditionally been considered to refer to the bark of *Cinnamomum cassia*. But, since this is a Far Eastern tree, it is unlikely to have been the fragrant aromatic substance used in the anointing oil of Ex. 30:24. The word 'cassia', like other plant products (*e.g.* ebony), was probably applied in ancient times to one substance and the application later transferred to another more easily obtainable product having properties similar to or better than the original. Cassia and cinnamon were perfumes used at Roman funerals by which time the E trade routes were established and they used the products at present known by these names.

Cinnamon (Heb. *qinnāmôn*; Gk. *kinnamōmon*). Traditionally considered to be the product of *Cinnamomum zeylanicum*, a plant of the laurel family cultivated in Ceylon and Java, but possibly cinnamon, like cassia, was obtained from an as yet uncertainly identified plant more readily available to the Israelites in Sinai. Used as one of the perfumes of the 'holy anointing oil' (Ex. 30:23), and for beds (Pr. 7:17), it was highly prized in Solomon's day (Ct. 4:14), and was listed as one of the valuable commodities of 'Babylon the Great' (Rev. 18:13).

Coriander (Heb. *gaḏ*, Ex. 16:31; Nu. 11:7). Indigenous to the Mediterranean area, this small umbelliferous annual (*Coriandrum sativum*) is known to have been used as early as 1550 BC for culinary and medicinal purposes. Its aromatic seed, to which the wandering Israelites likened *manna, is grey-yellow in colour, enclosed in a spherical fruit 4 mm in diameter.

Cummin (Heb. *kammōn*; Gk. *kyminon*). An aromatic seed from *Cuminum cyminum*, a plant indigenous to W Asia and cultivated from the earliest times. Resembling the caraway in taste and appearance, it is used to flavour dishes, particularly during fasts, and is said to have medicinal properties. The plant is still threshed with sticks to preserve the small brittle seeds which would be crushed by a wheel (Is. 28:27). The scribes and Pharisees, scrupulously paying tithes of cummin, were charged by Jesus with neglecting weightier matters (Mt. 23:23).

Dill (Gk. *anēthon*, 'anise' AV, Mt. 23:23). An annual umbelliferous plant (*Anethum graveolens*) with finely divided leaves and small greenish yellow flowers. The seeds and leaves were widely used for culinary and medicinal purposes in antiquity. See **Black cummin** above for 'dill' of Is. 28:27.

Henna. A cultivated shrub (*Lawsonia inermis*; Heb. *kōp̄er*, Ct. 1:14; 4:13, 'camphire' AV) which favours warm conditions such as prevail at Ein Gedi where Solomon had vineyards. Its fragrant white blossoms were given between friends; its pulverized leaves were made into a paste as a cosmetic by women in ancient times to impart a yellow dye to skin, especially the palms of the hands, and the men's beards, even the manes and tails of horses. Any women thus adorned who fell captive to the Hebrews were required to remove all traces of the dye (Dt. 21:11–12). The

orange or bright yellow colour probably had pagan associations.

Mint (Gk. *hēdyosmon*, Mt. 23:23; Lk. 11:42). Many species of the mint family (Labiatae) are fragrant, but the most likely one to be used was a species of *Mentha*, probably the horse-mint (*M. longifolia*). It is a perennial about 40 cm high with mauve flowers in whorls. The characteristic essential oils present in mints make the herbs a useful condiment. NT references, however, merely point out the scrupulosity of the Pharisees, who tithed even the commonest garden herbs.

Myrrh (Akkad. *murru*; Heb. *mōr*). The resinous exudate from incisions on the stems and branches of a low shrubby tree, either *Commiphora myrrha* (formerly *Balsamodendron myrrha*) or the closely related *Commiphora kataf*. Both species are native to S Arabia and adjacent parts of Africa. The gum oozes from the wounds as 'tears' which harden to form an oily yellowish-brown resin.

Myrrh was an ingredient of the holy anointing oil (Ex. 30:23–33). It was prized for its aromatic qualities (Ps. 45:8; Pr. 7:17; Ct. 3:6; 4:14; 5:5, 13), and used in female purification rites (Est. 2:12), as well as in cosmetic preparations. Myrrh was presented to the infant Jesus by the magi (Mt. 2:11); it formed part of an anodyne offered to him on Calvary (Mk. 15:23), and was one of the spices employed at his burial, together with aloes, as a form of embalming (Jn. 19:39).

The 'myrrh' of Gn. 37:25; 43:11 (Heb. *lōṭ*) carried by Ishmaelite traders to Egypt was probably a ladanum resin obtained from the rock roses *Cistus laurifolius* or *C. creticus* (= *C. villosus*). They are rounded evergreen bushes sticky to the touch, with large white or pink rose-like flowers.

Rue (Gk. *pēganon*, Lk. 11:42). A perennial herb up to 80 cm high, shrubby at the base, with grey-green leaves emitting a strong odour. *Ruta chalepensis* grows in rocky places in Palestine, and the similar *R. graveolens* is S European, having been in cultivation since ancient times. Rue was highly prized for its medicinal values, having alleged disinfectant and antiseptic properties, and for flavouring food. Christ criticized the Pharisees for their meticulous legalism in tithing it while neglecting more important matters.

Saffron (Heb. *karkōm*, LXX *krokos*, Ct. 4:14). This expensive substance is produced from the flowers of *Crocus sativus*, a native of Greece and Asia Minor. Only the orange styles and stigmas are collected, dried and packed. In antiquity saffron was used for dyeing and colouring foodstuffs. It was also a therapeutic agent, being used as an emmenagogue, stimulant and antispasmodic. The ancient Egyptians employed a different plant, safflower (*Carthamus tinctorius*), which yields a yellow dye similar to saffron for colouring the grave-clothes of mummies.

Spikenard (Heb. *nērd*; Gk. *nardos*). The fragrant essential oil referred to as a perfume in Ct. 1:12; 4:13f. is very likely to be the same as the *lardu* of Assyro-Babylonian inscriptions, which was obtained from the camel grass *Cymbopogon schoenanthus*, common in the deserts of Arabia and N Africa.

Spikenard of the NT (Mk. 14:3; Jn. 12:3) was described as 'pistic', an obscure term probably meaning 'genuine'. This perfume is considered to have been obtained from the essential oil in the roots of *Nardostachys jatamansi*, a more pleasantly scented relative of the valerian. It is native of the Himalayas and is still used for the hair.

Stacte (Hebb. *nāṭāp̄*; Gk. *staktē*). One of the ingredients of the sacred incense (Ex. 30:34). The Heb. name indicates 'dropping', from which is implied its origin as an exudate in the form of drops. Two plants are possibilities: the balm-of-Gilead (*Commiphora gileadensis*), a native of S Arabia in spite of its name, and storax (*Styrax officinale*) of the Palestinian hills. The balm-of-Gilead is also known as opobalsam and is a much-branched bush less than the height of a man, with small, three-foliolate leaves. The storax is a small tree with white flowers. The resin is obtained from both by making incisions in the branches. Another suggestion, *Liquidambar orientalis*, also known as storax, is not as likely since it is a tree of Cyprus, Rhodes and Turkey.

Sweet cane (Heb. *qāneh*, Is. 43:24; Je. 6:20). Whole dry rhizomes of sweet flag (*Acorus calamus*), a marsh plant of the arum family, were traded as sweet cane in ancient times for use as a tonic and stimulant. Native of temperate Asia, it has been introduced into a wider area. The sugar cane, with which sweet-cane has also been identified, actually spread E after OT times. F.N.H. *et al.*

HERESY. The Gk. word *hairesis* properly denotes 'choice', and this is the meaning which it always bears in the LXX; in classical authors, however, it can refer to a philosophical school which the individual chooses to follow. Similarly, the NT uses the word to denote a 'party', with the suggestion of self-will or sectarian spirit; but it must be noted that none of the parties thus described is in a state of schism from its parent body. The Sadducees (Acts 5:17) and the Pharisees (Acts 15:5; 26:5) form sects within the fold of Judaism; and the same word is used to describe Christianity as seen from outside (Acts 24:5, 14; 28:22). Josephus, however, uses the same term to describe the Essenes as well, who were in schism (*Ant.* 13. 171; 18. 18–22). When parties appear within the church they are called 'heresies' (1 Cor. 11:19, where Paul seems to imply that, though bad, they have the good result of making it clear who are the true Christians). Such divisions are regarded as a work of the flesh (Gal. 5:20), and primarily as a breach of mutual charity, so that the heretic, *i.e.* the man who stubbornly chooses to form or follow his own group, is to be rejected after two admonitions (Tit. 3:10).

The only NT use of 'heresy' in the sense of opinion or doctrinal error occurs in 2 Pet. 2:1, where it includes a denial of the Redeemer. Among incipient heresies mentioned in the NT, the most prominent are: Gnosticism of a Jewish type (Col. 2:8–23) and Docetism (1 Jn. 4:2–3; 2 Jn. 7).

BIBLIOGRAPHY. G. Forkman, *The Limits of the Religious Community*, 1972; W. Elert, *Eucharist and Church Fellowship in the First Four Centuries*, E.T. 1966; H. Schlier, *TDNT* 1, pp. 180–184. G.S.M.W. R.T.B.

HERMAS. One of a group of Christians greeted, some by name, in Rom. 16:14. They apparently belonged to a single community, perhaps a house-church. The name is a fairly common diminutive for a number of compound names. Origen's suggestion that the author of *The Shepherd* of Hermas

(*PATRISTIC LITERATURE) is indicated here has nothing to commend it. A.F.W.

HERMENEUTICS. This term, from Gk. *hermēneuō* ('interpret'), is used to denote (*a*) the study and statement of the principles on which a text—for present purposes, the biblical text—is to be understood, or (*b*) the interpretation of the text in such a way that its message comes home to the reader or hearer. In our own day this aim has been pursued by means of an existential interpretation of the text. For example, while the understanding of the parables of Jesus is greatly aided at one level by an examination of the local and contemporary setting (as in J. Jeremias, *The Parables of Jesus*, 1954), their relevance to readers today has been brought out by existential interpretation (as in G. V. Jones, *The Art and Truth of the Parables*, 1964, or E. Linnemann, *The Parables of Jesus*, 1966). There is a place for both levels of interpretation, but without the prior historical exegesis the existential hermeneutic lacks any anchorage. The task of existential hermeneutics has been seen as the re-establishment, for today's reader of (say) the parables, of that common understanding with his hearers which Jesus established when he first told them. (*INTERPRETATION, BIBLICAL.)

BIBLIOGRAPHY. G. Ebeling, *Word and Faith*, 1963; J. M. Robinson and J. B. Cobb, *The New Hermeneutic*, 1964; J. D. Smart, *The Strange Silence of the Bible in the Church*, 1970; H. G. Gadamer, *Truth and Method*, 1975; N. Perrin, *Jesus and the Language of the Kingdom*, 1976; I. H. Marshall (ed.), *New Testament Interpretation*, 1977. F.F.B.

HERMES. Originally the spirit inhabiting the *herma* or cairn, set up as a guide-mark or boundary. Hence the doorside *herms*, roughly carved phallic stones of Athens, and the god's function as guide of living and dead, as patron of road-users (including footpads), and as Zeus' attendant and spokesman (Acts 14:12). (The cultic association of Zeus and Hermes at Lystra is illustrated in that part of Asia Minor by the legend of Philemon and Baucis, preserved by Ovid, and by inscriptions in which the two deities appear together. The description of Hermes as 'the chief speaker' in Acts 14:12 is paralleled by Iamblichus' description of him as 'the leader of the utterances'.) Anthropomorphic myth made him the son of Zeus and Maia, heaven's swift messenger, patron of commerce, eloquence, literature and youth. Latinized as Mercurius (Mercury). E.M.B.
F.F.B.

HERMETIC LITERATURE. A collection of writings associated with the name of 'Hermes Trismegistos' ('Thrice-great Hermes').

I. Origin and character

The writings represent a coalescence of Egyptian and Greek modes of thought, often transfused with mystical personal religion. Hellenistic syncretism identified Thoth, the Egyptian scribe of the gods, with the Greek Hermes, whose functions were not dissimilar. In this way the name of the ancient and wise 'Hermes Trismegistos' became attached to much of the magical and astrological lore of the Egyptian temples, which was now seasoned with Greek science and presented in a revelatory form. The surviving literature of this type may go back to the early 2nd century BC.

More permanent interest attaches, however, to the more recognizably philosophical and religious treatises in Greek, of diverse but unknown authorship, in which Hermes, Tat (really a by-form of Thoth, but regarded as distinct), Asclepius and others appear as teacher and disciples. The treatises are usually dated in the 2nd and 3rd centuries AD: some may be slightly earlier. The main extant items are a body of eighteen treatises (of which one has been artificially constructed from fragments) preserved in Christian manuscript tradition, and a long tractate dedicated to Asclepius, surviving in a Latin translation, and in a Coptic version in the Nag Hammadi library (*CHENOBOSKION). In addition there are some thirty Hermetic fragments in the *Anthology* of Stobaeus, and others in other early writers. Three other tractates included in Codex 6 of the Nag Hammadi library in addition to the Coptic version of *Asclepius* 21–29 are *Authoritative Teaching*, *The Discourse on the Eighth and Ninth*, and *The Prayer of Thanksgiving*. *Asclepius* and *The Discourse* both specifically mention Hermes, but all contain similarities with the previously known Hermetic documents. *The Prayer*, although very short, is valuable for the light it sheds on Hermetic cultic practices.

Some of the tractates are in the form of epistolary discourses: others are Socratic dialogues. The most famous, the *Poimandres*, is a vision reminiscent of that of Hermas (*PATRISTIC LITERATURE).

II. Contents

In some ways the *Poimandres* may be taken as a typical Hermetic work. In it Poimandres (perhaps from the Coptic *p-emi-n-re*, 'knowledge of the [sun] god'), described as 'the Mind (*Nous*) of the Sovereignty', offers to reveal to Hermes what he longs to know: 'the things that are, and to understand their nature, and to know God'. There follows the story of the creation of the universe and the fall of man. The former has elements drawn from Gn. 1; the latter describes how archetypal man, God's image, entered into a fatal embrace with Nature, and accordingly became a mixed being, both mortal and immortal. Escape from the dead hand of Nature is, however, possible for those who repent and abandon corruption, till the ascent of the soul is completed at death, when body, passion, feeling are utterly surrendered, and man enters into God.

Not all the Hermetica are as coherent, but the aim expressed and the outlook reflected in the *Poimandres* are generally dominant. Knowledge is the goal; the mortal body the curse; regeneration (enthusiastically described in Treatise 13), the purification of the soul from the taint of matter, the *summum bonum* the soul's final liberation and absorption into God. There is a warm strain of devotion: the appeal to heedless humanity in the *Poimandres* and the still more impassioned cry of Treatise 7 are moving; and the occasional hymns are fervent and rapturous.

To this mystical piety is added rather shop-soiled philosophy, partly Platonic, partly Stoic in origin, with a free use of cosmogonic myth. Judaic sources are under tribute, and there are echoes of the language of the LXX. Indeed, it is arguable that Jewish influences originally stimulated religion of this type. The various elements do not always cohere: there are inconsistencies and contradictions of thought within the corpus. The whole tendency is monotheistic, though not polemically so. Of ceremony or sacrament little is said. Although there is no evidence of a Hermetic 'church', there is a reference in the Nag Hammadi tractate, *On the Eighth and the Ninth*, to a brotherhood consisting of Hermetic saints, and in the *Prayer* to cultic kissing and eating of food without blood.

III. The Hermetica and the Bible

The Hermetic use of the OT, as already noted, is undoubted. The relationship between Hermetic religion and the NT is more variously assessed. The Christian father Lactantius, who thought of 'Hermes' as writing in remote antiquity, delightedly notes his monotheism and his address of God as 'Father' (*Divine Institutes* 1. 6). More recent writers point to subtler parallels of thought and language with the NT, though not all of equal significance. The Logos in Hermetic thought, for instance, is both cosmic and an activity of the soul: but not personal. A statement like 'Thou who by a word hast constituted all things that are' (*Poimandres* 21) need have no other background than Gn. 1; there is no definite article in the original. More striking are phrases like 'No one can be saved before rebirth' (*Treat.* 13. 1), 'He that loveth the body, the same abideth in darkness' (*Poimandres* 19), and the 'Johannine' vocabulary of light and darkness, life and death, belief and witness. Direct influence by the NT on later Hermetica is not impossible, but unproven: direct influence of the Hermetic literature on the NT would be even harder to substantiate. However, while our extant religious Hermetica are almost certainly later than most of the NT, they clearly derive from a well-established tradition; and those may be right who suggest that John has partly in view a public with this *kind* of education and devotion. We must remember, however, that the Hermetica are but one example of contemporary piety; and the language of the Johannine writings can be paralleled also in the Judaic, and essentially biblical, dualism of Qumran.

As to content, it will be seen that the Hermetic parallels are closest with what might be called the accidentals of the NT: with the process of redemption rather than with its essential nature and the means by which it is effected. Concerned with sin as ignorance or passion to be sloughed off, rather than as rebellion requiring reconciliation, and with desire set on a salvation which involved deification through union with God, the motive forces of the Hermetists maintained a pagan, not a biblical, direction. And, while the ethical teaching of the Hermetica is insistent and lofty, its other-worldly nature does not allow for the concreteness of biblical ethics. As C. H. Dodd says, the Hermetists share the second, but not the first half of the description of 'pure religion' in Jas. 1:27. (*GNOSTICISM.)

BIBLIOGRAPHY. Best edn. by A. D. Nock and A. J. Festugière, *Corpus Hermeticum*², 4 vols., 1960 (with French translation); *cf.* also W. Scott, *Hermetica*, 4 vols., 1924–36; A. J. Festugière, *La Révélation d'Hermès Trismégiste*, 4 vols., 1944–9; C. H. Dodd, *The Bible and the Greeks*, 1935; *The Interpretation of the Fourth Gospel*, 1953, pp. 10ff. For the new Hermetica see J. Doresse, *The Secret Books of the Egyptian Gnostics*, E.T. 1960, pp. 275ff.; L. S. Keizer, *The Eighth Reveals the Ninth*, 1974; *The Nag Hammadi Library in English*, ed. J. M. Robinson, 1977. A.F.W.

HERMOGENES. Mentioned with Phygelus as representative of Asian Christians who once repudiated Paul (2 Tim. 1:15). The language indicates Roman Asia (not, as some suggest, an Asian community in Rome), and a specific action (*cf.* RV)—perhaps breaking off relations (through fear of involvement?) when Paul had a right to expect their support. For the meaning of 'turned away', *cf.* Mt. 5:42: total apostasy is not in question. The occasion, which is unlikely to have been very remote, was known to Timothy, but it is not to us (*ONESIPHORUS). A.F.W.

HERMON (Heb. *ḥermôn*, 'sanctuary'). A mountain in the Anti-Lebanon Range, and easily the highest (2,774 m) in the neighbourhood of Palestine. It is called also Mt Sirion (Heb. Sion, Dt. 4:48), and known to the Amorites as S(h)enir (Dt. 3:9). Note, however, that Ct. 4:8 and 1 Ch. 5:23 explicitly distinguish between Hermon and *Senir (*cf. GTT*, p. 41; *DOTT*, p. 49).

Regarded as a sacred place by the original inhabitants of Canaan (*cf.* 'Baal-hermon', Jdg. 3:3; 'Baal-gad', Jos. 13:5, *etc.*), it formed the N boundary of Israel's conquests from the Amorites (Dt. 3:8; Jos. 11:17, *etc.*). Snow usually lies on the top all year round, causing plentiful dews in stark contrast to the parched land of that region (hence probably the Psalmist's allusion in Ps. 133:3), and the melting ice forms a major source of the Jordan. Hermon is identified with

Snow-capped Mt Hermon, N Galilee, 2,774 m above sea level, seen from the SE. (SH)

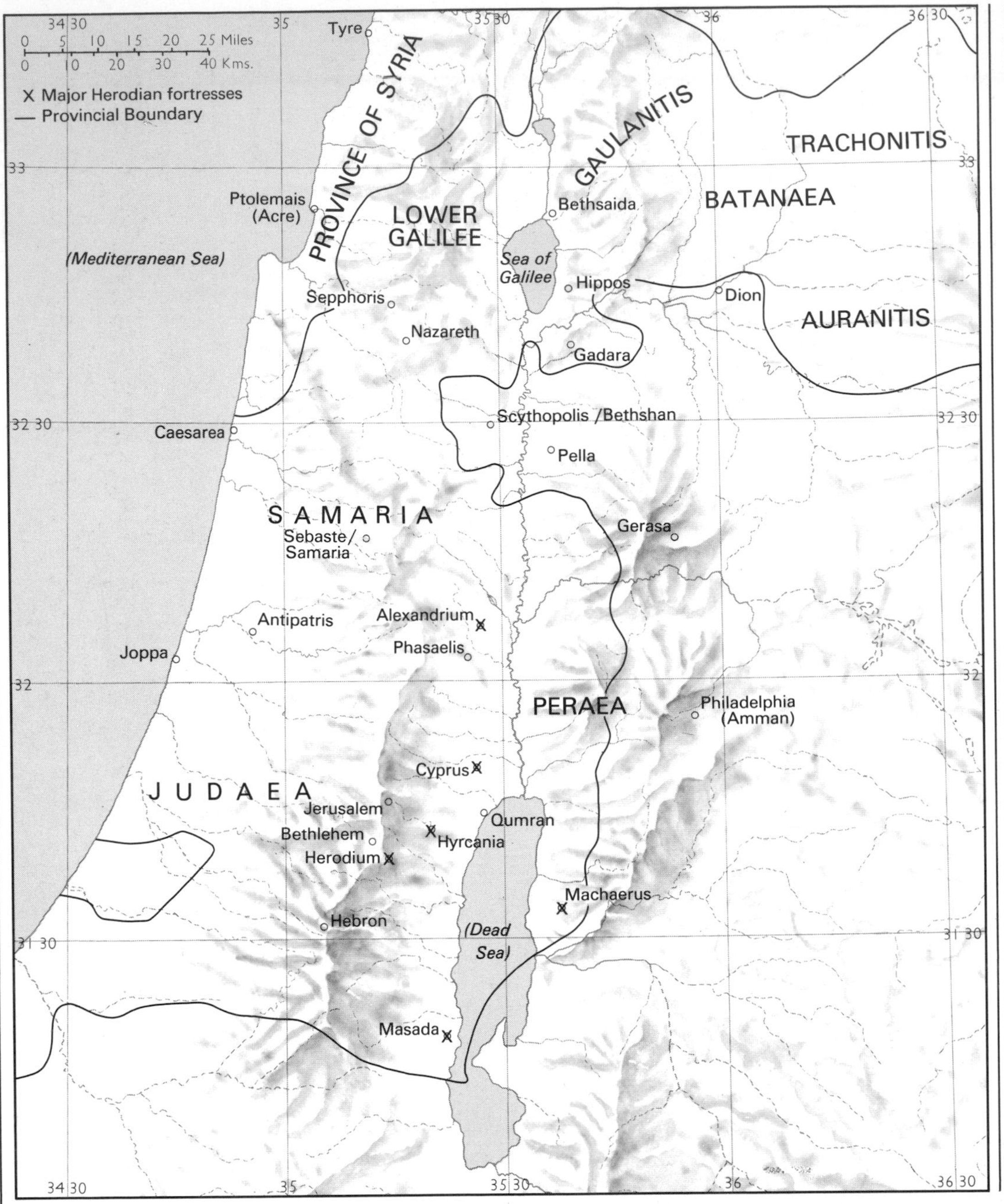

The kingdom of Herod the Great.

the modern Jebel es-Sheik, 'the Sheik's mountain', 48 km SW of Damascus (but on this point see *GTT*, p. 83). Its proximity to Caesarea Philippi has made some suggest Hermon as the 'high mountain' (Mk. 9:2, *etc.*) of the *transfiguration.

A misleading reference to 'the Hermonites' (Ps. 42:6, AV) should probably be amended to RV 'the Hermons', signifying the three summits of Mt Hermon. J.D.D.

HEROD. 1. Herod the Great, king of the Jews 40–4 BC, born *c.* 73 BC. His father Antipater, a Jew of Idumaean descent, attained a position of great influence in Judaea after the Roman conquest and was appointed procurator of Judaea by Julius Caesar in 47 BC. He in turn appointed his son Herod military prefect of Galilee, and Herod showed his qualities by the vigour with which he suppressed brigandage in that region; the Roman governor of Syria was so impressed by his energy that he made him military prefect of Coele-Syria. After the assassination of Caesar and subsequent civil war Herod enjoyed the goodwill of Antony. When the Parthians invaded Syria and Palestine and set the Hasmonaean Antigonus on the throne of Judaea (40–37 BC) the Roman senate, advised by Antony and Octavian, gave Herod the title 'king of the Jews'. It took him 3 years of fighting to make his title effective, but when he had done so he governed Judaea for 33 years as a loyal 'friend and ally' of Rome.

Until 31 BC, despite Antony's goodwill, Herod's position was rendered precarious by the machinations of Cleopatra, who hoped to see Judaea and Coele-Syria reunited to the Ptolemaic kingdom. This peril was removed by the battle of Actium, after which Herod was confirmed in his kingdom by Octavian (Augustus), the new master of the Roman world. Another source of anxiety for Herod was the Hasmonaean family, who resented being displaced on the throne by one whom they regarded as an upstart. Although he married into this family by taking to wife Mariamne, granddaughter of the former high priest Hyrcanus II, Herod's suspicions led him to get rid of the leading Hasmonaean survivors one by one, including Mariamne herself (29 BC).

Herodian coins: right: *bronze* prutah, *with anchor, inscribed in Greek, 'of King Herod'* (*Herod I, 40–4* BC). *Diameter 11mm.* left: *'of the ethnarch'* (*Herod Archelaus, ethnarch of Judaea, 4* BC *–* AD *6*) *with plumed helmet. Diameter 13 mm.* (BM)

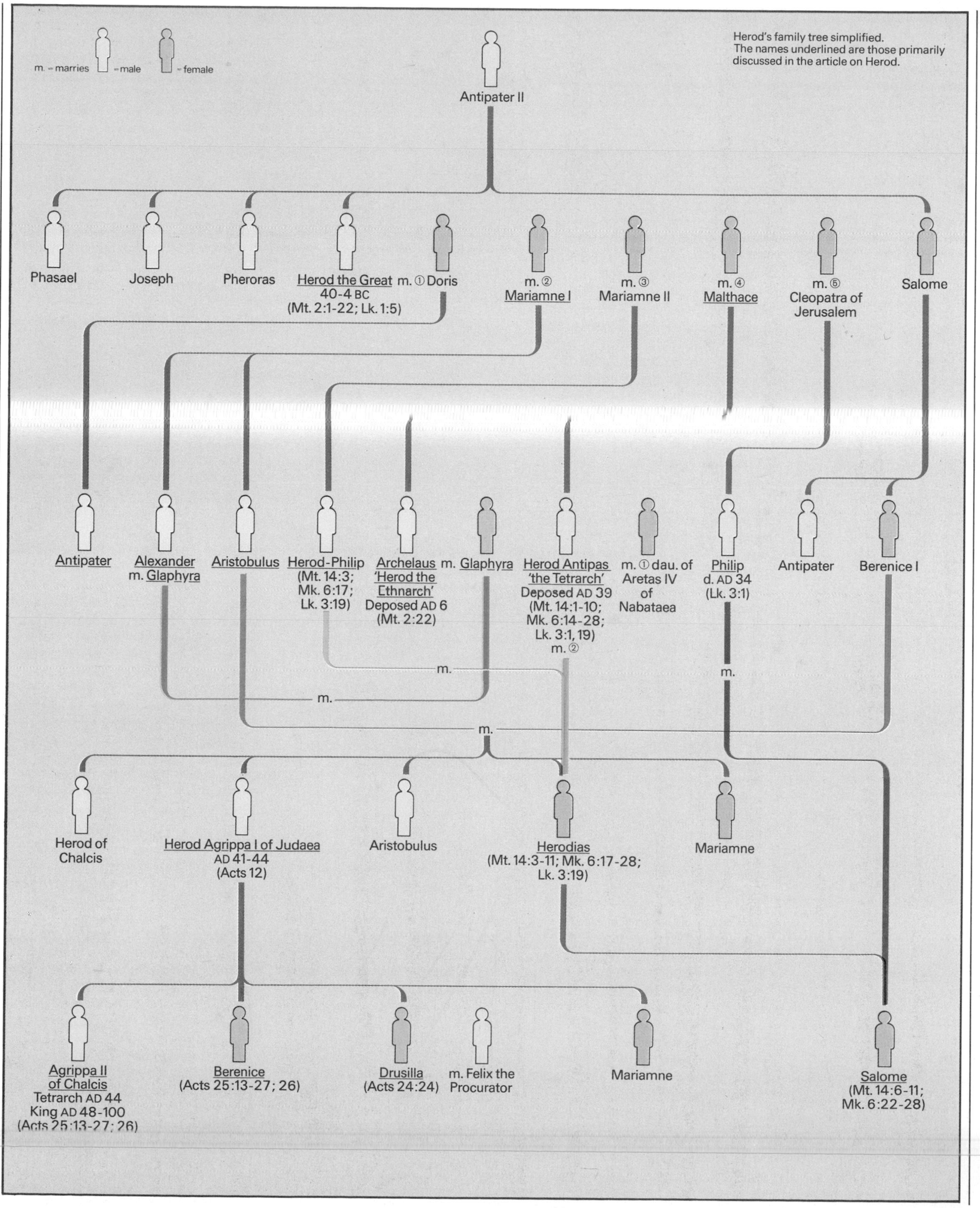
m. = marries
= male
= female
Herod's family tree simplified.
The names underlined are those primarily discussed in the article on Herod.
Antipater II
Phasael
Joseph
Pheroras
Herod the Great m. ① Doris
40-4 BC
(Mt. 2:1-22; Lk. 1:5)
m. ② Mariamne I
m. ③ Mariamne II
m. ④ Malthace
m. ⑤ Cleopatra of Jerusalem
Salome
Antipater
Alexander m. Glaphyra
Aristobulus
Herod-Philip (Mt. 14:3; Mk. 6:17; Lk. 3:19)
Archelaus m. Glaphyra 'Herod the Ethnarch' Deposed AD 6 (Mt. 2:22)
Herod Antipas 'the Tetrarch' Deposed AD 39 (Mt. 14:1-10; Mk. 6:14-28; Lk. 3:1, 19) m. ②
m. ① dau. of Aretas IV of Nabataea
Philip d. AD 34 (Lk. 3:1)
Antipater
Berenice I
m.
m.
m.
m.
Herod of Chalcis
Herod Agrippa I of Judaea AD 41-44 (Acts 12)
Aristobulus
Herodias (Mt. 14:3-11; Mk. 6:17-28; Lk. 3:19)
Mariamne
Agrippa II of Chalcis Tetrarch AD 44 King AD 48-100 (Acts 25:13-27; 26)
Berenice (Acts 25:13-27; 26)
Drusilla (Acts 24:24) m. Felix the Procurator
Mariamne
Salome (Mt. 14:6-11; Mk. 6:22-28)

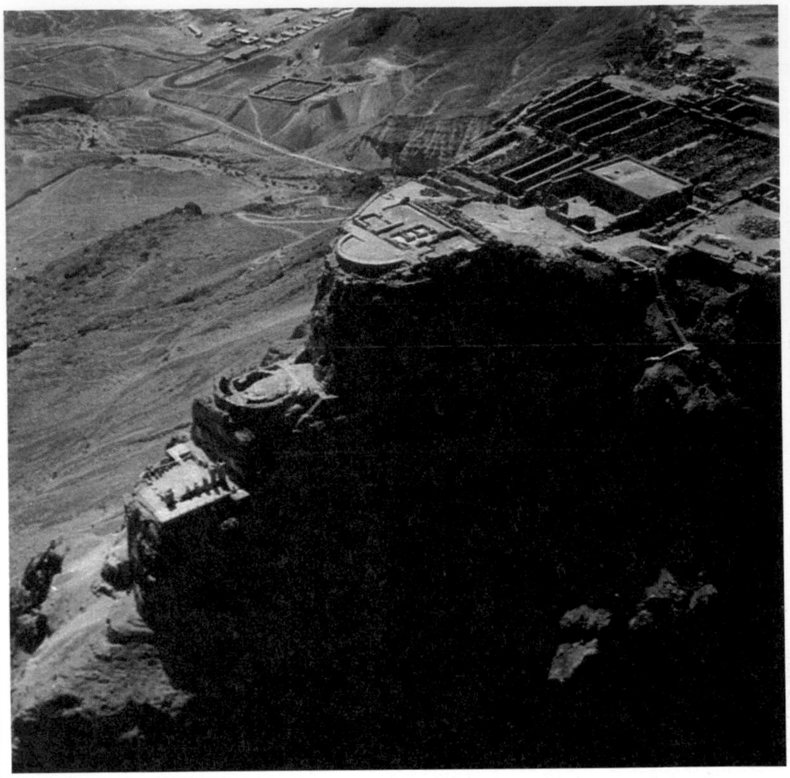

Herod the Great built one of his palaces on the rock of Masada on the W shore of the Dead Sea. The terraces contain the excavated ruins of his bath-house and store-rooms. (SZC)

Herod pacified the territories on his NE frontier in the interests of Rome, and Augustus added them to his kingdom. He furthered the emperor's cultural policy by lavish building projects, not only in his own realm but in foreign cities (*e.g.* Athens). In his own realm he rebuilt Samaria and renamed it Sebaste after the emperor (Gk. *Sebastos* = Lat. *Augustus*); he rebuilt Strato's Tower on the Mediterranean coast, equipped it with a splendid artificial harbour, and called it Caesarea, also in honour of the emperor. Other settlements and strongholds were founded throughout the land. In Jerusalem he built a palace for himself on the W wall; he had already rebuilt the Antonia fortress (called after Antony) NW of the Temple area. The greatest of all his building enterprises was the reconstruction of the Jerusalem Temple, begun early in 19 BC.

Nothing that Herod could do, not even the expenditure lavished on the Temple, endeared him to his Jewish subjects. His Edomite descent was never forgotten; if he was a Jew by religion and rebuilt the Temple of the God of Israel in Jerusalem, that did not deter him from erecting temples to pagan deities elsewhere. Above all, his wiping out of the Hasmonaean family could not be forgiven.

This drastic action did not in fact put an end to his domestic troubles. There was friction between his own female relatives and his wives, and between the children of his respective wives. His two sons by Mariamne, Alexander and Aristobulus, were brought up at Rome and were his designated heirs. Their Hasmonaean descent (through their mother) made them acceptable to the Jewish people. But their privileged position stirred the envy of their half-brothers, and especially of Herod's eldest son Antipater, who set himself to poison his father's mind against them. At last (7 BC) they were found guilty of plotting against their father, and executed. Antipater derived no advantage from their death, for 3 years later he too fell victim to Herod's suspicions, and was executed only a few days before Herod's own death (4 BC).

Herod's suspicious nature is well illustrated by the story of the visit of the Magi and the slaughter of the infants of Bethlehem (Mt. 2); although this story does not appear elsewhere, any rumour of a rival king of the Jews was bound to rouse his worst fears. This suspicion latterly grew to insane proportions, and in consequence Herod has been remembered more for his murderous outbursts than for his administrative ability.

In his will he bequeathed his kingdom to three of his sons—Judaea and Samaria to Archelaus (Mt. 2:22), Galilee and Peraea to Antipas, and his NE territories to Philip (Lk. 3:1). These bequests were ratified by Augustus.

2. Archelaus ('Herod the Ethnarch' on his coins). He reigned in Judaea 'in place of his father Herod' (Mt. 2:22) from 4 BC to AD 6, but without the title of king. He was Herod's elder son by his Samaritan wife Malthace, and has the worst reputation of all the sons of Herod. He offended Jewish religious susceptibilities by marrying Glaphyra, the widow of his half-brother Alexander. He continued his father's building policy, but his repressive rule became intolerable; a deputation of the Judaean and Samaritan aristocracy at last went to Rome to warn Augustus that, unless Archelaus were removed, there would be a full-scale revolt. Archelaus was accordingly deposed and banished, and Judaea became a Roman province, administered by prefects appointed by the emperor.

3. 'Herod the tetrarch' (Lk. 3:19, *etc.*), who bore the distinctive name of Antipas. He was Herod's younger son by Malthace, and inherited the Galilean and Peraean portions of his father's kingdom. In the Gospels he is conspicuous chiefly for his part in the imprisonment and execution of John the Baptist (Mk. 6:14–28) and for his brief encounter with Jesus when the latter was sent to him by Pilate for judgment (Lk. 23:7ff.). Jesus is recorded as having once described him as 'that fox' (Lk. 13:31f.). He was the ablest of Herod's sons, and like his father was a great builder; the city of Tiberias on the Lake of Galilee was built by him (AD 22) and named in honour of the Emperor Tiberius. He married the daughter of the Nabataean king *Aretas IV, but divorced her in order to marry *Herodias, the wife of his half-brother Herod Philip. According to the Synoptic Evangelists, John the Baptist incurred the wrath of Antipas for denouncing his second marriage as unlawful; Josephus (*Ant.* 18. 118) says that Antipas was afraid that John's great public following might develop into a revolt. Aretas naturally resented the insult offered to his daughter, and seized the opportunity a few years later to wage war against Antipas (AD 36). The forces of Antipas were heavily defeated, and Josephus says that many people regarded the defeat as divine retribution for Antipas' killing of John the Baptist. In AD 39 Antipas was denounced to the Emperor Gaius by his nephew Agrippa (see **4**) as a plotter; he was deposed from his tetrarchy and ended his days in exile.

4. 'Herod the king' (Acts 12:1), otherwise known as Agrippa. He was a son of Aristobulus and grandson of Herod the Great. After his father's execution in 7 BC he was brought up in Rome, in close association with the imperial family. In AD 23 he became so heavily involved in debt that he had to leave Rome. For a time he received shelter and maintenance at Tiberias from his uncle Antipas, thanks to his sister Herodias, whom Antipas had recently married. But he quarrelled with Antipas and in AD 36 returned to Rome. There he offended the Emperor Tiberius and was imprisoned, but on Tiberius' death the following year he was released by the new emperor, Gaius (Caligula), from whom he received the title of king, with territories NE of Palestine as his kingdom. On Antipas' banishment in AD 39, Galilee and Peraea were added to Agrippa's kingdom. When Claudius became emperor in AD 41 he further augmented Agrippa's kingdom by giving him Judaea and Samaria, so that Agrippa ruled over a kingdom roughly equal in extent to his grandfather's. He courted the goodwill of his Jewish subjects, who looked on him as a descendant of the Hasmonaeans (through his grandmother Mariamne) and approved of him accordingly. His attack on the apostles (Acts 12:2f.) was perhaps more popular than it would have been previously, because of their recent fraternization with Gentiles (Acts 10:1–11:18). His sudden death, at the age of 54 (AD 44), is recorded by Luke (Acts 12:20ff.) and Josephus (*Ant.* 19. 343ff.) in such a way that the two narratives supplement each other illuminatingly. He left one son, Agrippa (see **5**), and two daughters: Bernice (born AD 28), mentioned in Acts 25:13ff., and Drusilla (born AD 38), who became the 3rd wife of the procurator Felix (*cf.* Acts 24:24).

5. Agrippa, son of Herod Agrippa (see **4**), born in AD 27. He was adjudged too young to be made successor to his father's kingdom. Later, however, he received the title of king from Claudius, with territories N and NE of Palestine which were increased by Nero in AD 56. He changed the name of his capital from Caesarea Philippi to Neronias as a compliment to the latter emperor. From AD 48 to 66 he had the prerogative of appointing the Jewish high priests. He did his best to prevent the outbreak of the Jewish war against Rome in AD 66; when his efforts failed he remained loyal to Rome and was rewarded with a further increase of his kingdom. He died childless about AD 100. He is best known to NT readers for his encounter with Paul (Acts 25:13–26:32), whom he charged, in bantering vein, with trying to make a Christian of him (Acts 26:28).

BIBLIOGRAPHY. Josephus, *Ant.* 14–20 *passim*, *BJ* 1–2 *passim*; A. H. M. Jones, *The Herods of Judaea*, 1938; S. Perowne, *The Life and Times of Herod the Great*, 1956; *idem*, *The Later Herods*, 1958; F. O. Busch, *The Five Herods*, 1958; H. W. Hoehner, *Herod Antipas*, 1972; A. Schalit, *König Herodes*, 1968. F.F.B.

HERODIANS. They are mentioned as enemies of Jesus once in Galilee, and again at Jerusalem (Mk. 3:6; 12:13; Mt. 22:16). Their association with the Pharisees in the question regarding the paying of tribute to Caesar suggests agreement with them in the issue at stake, that is, nationalism versus submission to a foreign yoke. This fact and the formation of the word (*cf. Caesariani*) seems to prove that they were a Jewish party who favoured the Herodian dynasty. The view that they were a religious party known in rabbinical literature as 'Boethusians', *i.e.* adherents of the family of Boethus, whose daughter Mariamne was one of the wives of Herod the Great and whose sons were raised by him to the high priesthood, is not now generally held.

BIBLIOGRAPHY. H. Hoehner, *Herod Antipas*, 1972; N. Hillyer, *NIDNTT* 3, pp. 441–443. J.W.M.

HERODIAS (Mk. 6:17; Lk. 3:19), daughter to Aristobulus (son of Herod the Great by Mariamne). She married, first, her uncle Herod Philip (son of Herod the Great by a second Mariamne, and not to be confused with *Philip the tetrarch), and secondly, her uncle Herod Antipas (*HEROD, **3**). By her first husband she had a daughter Salome, who married her grand-uncle Philip the tetrarch. The identity of Herodias' daughter in Mk. 6:22ff. is uncertain. When Antipas was exiled in AD 39 Herodias chose to accompany him rather than accept the favour which Gaius was willing to show to the sister of his friend Agrippa (*HEROD, **4**). F.F.B.

HESHBON (Heb. *ḥešbôn*, 'device'). A city of Moab, taken by Sihon king of the Amorites and made his royal city (Nu. 21:26). After his defeat by the Israelites (21:21–24) it was given to Reuben (32:37), but later passed over to Gad, whose land bordered on Reuben, and was assigned by them to the Levites (Jos. 21:39). By the time of Isaiah and Jeremiah, at the height of its prosperity, Moab had retaken it (Is. 15:4; Je. 48:2, *etc.*), but by the time of Alexander Jannaeus it is once more in the hands of Israel (Jos., *Ant.* 13. 397). Remains of old pools and conduits may be seen in

HERON
See Animals, Part 1.

Aerial view of excavations at Tell Hesban (biblical Heshbon), Jordan. (AU)

Ostracon containing part of an Ammonite inventory of goods for a royal household. From Heshbon. Height 10·5 cm. 6th cent. BC. (AU)

a branch of the present Wadi Hesbān which flows by the city (*cf.* Ct. 7:4).

Excavations since 1968 at Tell Hesban have found buildings from the Iron Age, *c.* 1200 BC onwards, but no Late Bronze Age remains that might be associated with Sihon. There are a few Late Bronze Age sites nearby, however.

BIBLIOGRAPHY. L. T. Geraty, *Ann. Department of Antiquities of Jordan* 20, 1975, pp. 47–56.

M.A.M.
A.R.M.

HETHLON. (Heb. *ḥeṯlôn*). A city on the ideal N boundary of Palestine as seen by Ezekiel, near Hamath and Zedad and referred to only by him (Ezk. 47:15; 48:1). Identified with the modern Heitela, NE of Tripoli, Syria. J.D.D.

HEZEKIAH (Heb. *ḥizqîyâ* or *ḥizqîyāhû*, 'Yahweh is [my] strength').

1. The 14th king of Judah. Son of Ahaz who was 25 at the start of his reign and reigned for 29 years (2 Ki. 18:2; 2 Ch. 29:1). He was outstanding for his own piety (2 Ki. 18:5) and also cared for previous traditions and teaching (Pr. 25:1). His importance is reflected by the three accounts of his reign (2 Ki. 17–20; Is. 36–39; 2 Ch. 29–32).

There are difficulties surrounding the chronology of Hezekiah's reign, but he appears to have assumed a co-regency with Ahaz *c.* 729 BC and became king *c.* 716 BC. Thus the fall of Samaria (722 BC) occurred in the 6th year of his reign (as co-regent; 2 Ki. 18:10), while Sennacherib invaded Judah (701 BC) in the 14th year of his reign (as sole monarch; 2 Ki. 18:13). The king's illness and recovery appear to have occurred just before Sennacherib's invasion, when Hezekiah was promised an extra 15 years of rule (2 Ki. 20) (* STEPS).

After the pagan practices introduced during the period of Ahaz's submission to the Assyrians (*cf.* Is. 2:6ff.; 8:16ff.), Hezekiah undertook a major reform of religious practice in the 1st year of his sole reign (2 Ch. 29:3ff.). He re-established the true worship of Yahweh in the purified and renovated Temple, reaffirmed the covenant between Yahweh and his people, and reinstituted the Passover on a grand scale (2 Ch. 30:26), even inviting Israelites from the N to participate (2 Ch. 30:5ff.). He also destroyed the * high places in the surrounding area (2 Ki. 18:4; 2 Ch. 31:1) as well as breaking up the bronze * serpent which Moses had made in the wilderness but which had come to be regarded as an idol (2 Ki. 18:4).

Politically, Hezekiah was restive under Assyrian domination and he allied Judah with an anti-Assyrian revolt instigated by Egypt and led by *Ashdod. Judah must have listened to Isaiah's warnings (Is. 20), for although Sargon II claimed to have subdued *ia-u-di*, 'Judah' (*cf. DOTT*, p. 61; also N. Na'aman, *BASOR* 214, 1974, p. 27), no evidence of an invasion at this time is found in the OT. When Sargon died (705 BC) Hezekiah, seeing an opportunity to rebel against his son, Sennacherib, entertained envoys of the rebel Chaldean, * Merodach-baladan (2 Ki. 20:12–19; Is. 39) and received promises of support from Egypt. He also strengthened his own defences in Jerusalem, including digging the * Siloam tunnel to safeguard the water-supply (2 Ki. 20:20; Is. 22:9ff.).

Sennacherib's own records of his campaign in the W picture Hezekiah as leader of rebellion (*ANET*, pp. 287–288; *DOTT*, pp. 64–69). He claims to have taken forty-six fortified towns and imprisoned Hezekiah 'like a bird in a cage in Jeru-

Detail of Sennacherib's prism (see opposite) which relates how the king captured 46 towns and villages in Judah and then records, 'I shut up Hezekiah the Jew like a caged bird within Jerusalem, his royal city.' (BM)

Hiddekel, Hebrew name of the river Tigris. It rises in Turkey and flows past Mosul and Baghdad, Iraq. (JLH)

A six-sided clay prism inscribed in cuneiform with an account of the early campaigns of Sennacherib of Assyria, including his attack on Hezekiah of Judah in 701 BC. Height 38 cm. Nineveh. 691 BC. (BM)

salem, his royal city'. He does not claim to have conquered the city and the OT tells of Yahweh's intervention by destroying the Assyrian army (2 Ki. 19:32–36).

The mention of *Tirhakah, king of Ethiopia, in 2 Ki. 19:9, has led some to propose a second campaign by Sennacherib into Judah, *c.* 688 BC, since Tirhakah would have been too young in 701 BC to have taken part and also was not then called 'king'. It has, however, been shown that he was 20–21 at this time and that the title is in terms of the time of writing rather than of the events themselves (*cf.* K. A. Kitchen, *The Third Intermediate Period in Egypt*, 1972, pp. 385–386 and nn. 823–824).

2. The father of a clan which returned from Babylonian exile with Ezra (Ezr. 2:16; Ne. 7:21), and among those who sealed the new covenant with Yahweh (Ne. 10:17). His name is given in two forms, Ater being Akkadian. Ne. 10:17 lists the names as separate people. D.W.B.

HEZION
See Rezon, Part 3.

HIDDEKEL. The ancient name of the river *Tigris used in the account of the Garden of Eden (Gn. 2:14) and in Daniel's description of his visions (Dn. 10:4) in the 3rd year of Cyrus. The name comes from Akkadian *idiqlat*, which is equivalent to Sumerian *idigna*, *i.e.* always flowing river.

BIBLIOGRAPHY. D. O. Edzard *et al.*, *Répertoire Géographique des Textes Cunéiformes*, 1, 1977, pp. 216–217. T.C.M.

HIEL (Heb. *ḥî'ēl*, 'El lives'; but *cf.* LXX 'brother of God', from *'aḥî'ēl*). A Bethelite whose sons were (accidentally?) killed during his rebuilding of Jericho *c.* 870 BC, fulfilling Joshua's curse (1 Ki. 16:34; *cf.* Jos. 6:26). D.W.B.

HIERAPOLIS. A city in the Roman province of Asia, in the W of what is now Asiatic Turkey. It was situated about 10 km N of *Laodicea, on the opposite side of the broad valley of the Lycus. The city was built around copious hot springs, which were famed for their medicinal powers. There was also a subterranean vent of poisonous gases (the Plutonium), which was later filled in by the Christians in about the 4th century AD. When the hot water flows over the edge of the

Unusual cliff-formations at Hierapolis (Pamukkale, Turkey) formed by lime flowing from hot springs for which the place was famous. (SH)

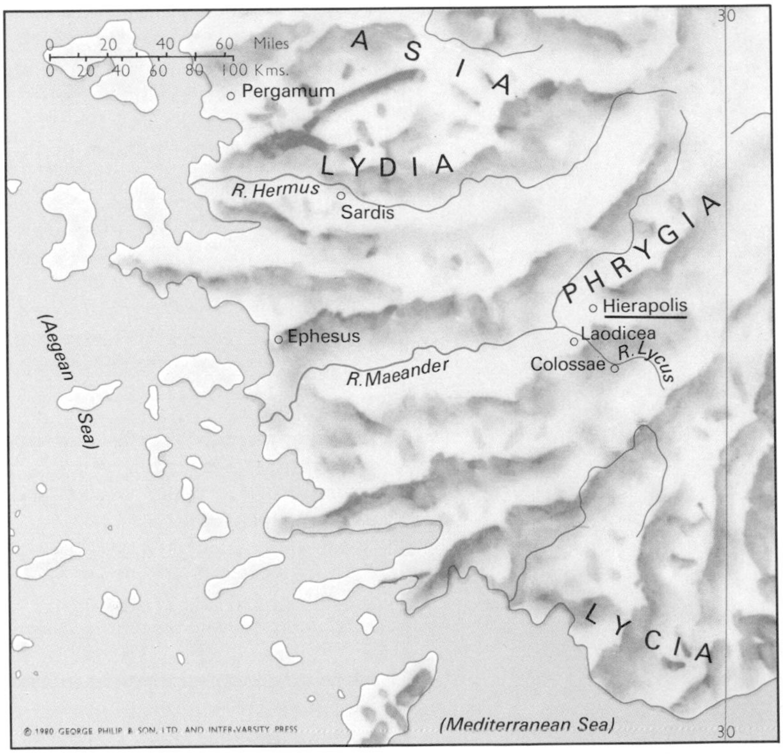

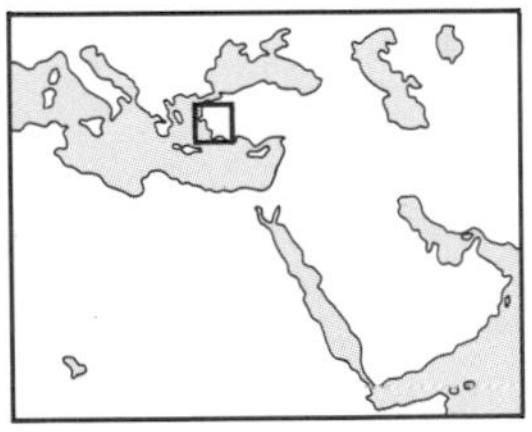

Hierapolis, in the Roman province of Asia.

city terrace it forms spectacular pools and cascades encrusted with lime. The resulting white cliffs give the site its modern name Pamukkale ('cotton castle'). These natural features made Hierapolis ('sacred city', for earlier 'Hieropolis', 'city of the sanctuary') an ancient centre of pagan cults, from which its importance and prosperity mainly derived.

The church in Hierapolis was probably founded while Paul was living at Ephesus (Acts 19:10), perhaps by Epaphras. It is mentioned only in conjunction with its close neighbours, *Colossae and *Laodicea (Col. 4:13). There may be a reminiscence of its famous hot waters in Rev. 3:15–16, in contrast with the cold waters of Colossae and the tepid of Laodicea.

According to Polycrates, bishop of Ephesus *c.* AD 190, as quoted by Eusebius (*HE* 3. 31), the apostle Philip was buried at Hierapolis, though the authorities show confusion between apostle and evangelist. Papias and the Stoic philosopher Epictetus were also connected with the city. M.J.S.R. C.J.H.

HIGGAION
See Psalms, Part 3.

HIGHER CRITICISM
See Biblical criticism, Part 1.

HIGHEST PLACE
See Meals, Part 2.

HIGH PLACE. The Heb. word *bāmâ*, rendered 'high place' by AV, RSV and JB, is used over 100 times in *MT* and in two distinct ways: of heights in a literal sense and of shrines. NEB renders 'heights' and 'hill shrine'.

The 20 non-cultic uses are all in the plural form and in poetic passages. In contrast to other height words, the plural *bāmôṯ* always carries overtones of dominance and control. Battles often took place on hill slopes; possession of heights therefore gave lordship over the land (Nu. 21:28; 2 Sa. 1:19, 25). Thus Israel asserted that God 'rides' or 'walks' on the heights (Am. 4:13; Mi. 1:3) or that he sets Israel (Dt. 32:13; Is. 58:14) or an individual (2 Sa. 22:34; Ps. 18:33; Hab. 3:19) 'upon the heights of the earth'. Cylinder seals portray *Baal astride mountains and in the Ras Shamra texts he is called *rkb rpt*, 'rider of the clouds'. Both Akkadian and Ugaritic had closely related words denoting heights or the middle region of the body (*cf.* Jb. 9:8).

The association of heights with lordship may account for their choice as locations of shrines. It has been suggested that, despite the warnings of Moses (Dt. 12, *etc.*), Israel took over the Canaanites' shrines after the conquest. Certainly loyal worshippers of God used *bāmôṯ* in the early Monarchy period. Samuel officiated at a special sacrifice when Saul was anointed before invited guests (1 Sa. 9) and later Saul went with a group of prophets coming down from a *bāmâ* led by lute, fife and drum (1 Sa. 10:5). By the time of Solomon Gibeon had risen to unique status and was known as 'the Great High Place'. The *tabernacle and the altar of bronze 'which Bezalel, son of Uri, son of Hur' had made was kept there and it was at Gibeon that God challenged Solomon in a dream about the character of his reign (1 Ki. 3; 2 Ch. 1).

After the disruption of the king-

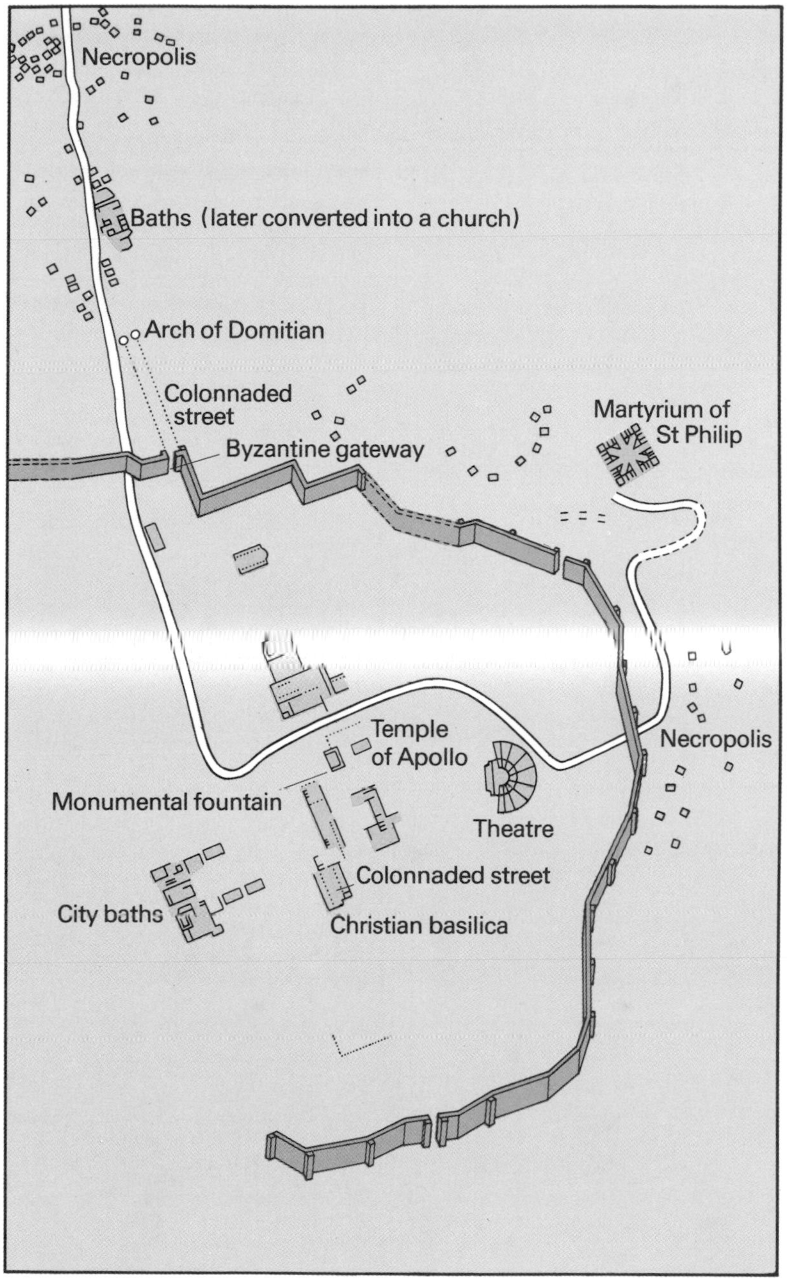

The site of ancient Hierapolis.

dom in 922 BC the *bāmôṯ* posed a new threat to the purity of Israel's faith. In the N kingdom Jeroboam built 'houses of the high places' as part of his campaign to distract his subjects' attention away from Jerusalem (1 Ki. 12). Thus 'he made Israel to sin' for the *bāmôṯ*, though often nominally dedicated to God, clearly included many Canaanite features, such as images, standing stones, Asherah poles, sacred prostitution and other fertility rites. Bloodshed, instability and apostasy characterized the two centuries of the N kingdom's existence and, as the biblical historians saw, the *bāmôṯ* were a major source of the moral and religious collapse (2 Ki. 17:9). In the S kingdom the situation was little better. *bāmôṯ* revived under Rehoboam. Attempts to suppress them by Asa and Jehoshaphat had no lasting results; Hezekiah conducted a more thorough reformation (2 Ki. 18:1–8), but his son Manasseh 'who did more evil than all the kings that were before him' again revived *bāmôṯ*. Under Josiah a far-reaching purge was undertaken (2 Ki. 23), but his successors were not of his calibre and the shrines were again reviving when the Babylonian army put an end to the Judaean kingdom. Little is known of the *bāmôṯ* thereafter.

Early study of the *bāmôṯ* reveals the embarrassment felt at the use of these shrines by Israel's heroes. The Talmud and the rabbis sharply distinguished between 'great' and 'small' *bāmôṯ* or maintained that the ban was lifted periodically. J. Wellhausen solved the problem by suggesting that the single sanctuary law was not operative until the time of Josiah; the book of Deuteronomy was but a 'pious fraud'. It seems more likely that Samuel, Saul and Solomon simply wished to claim these shrines for God without realizing the syncretistic dangers which had been plain to Moses and were all too accurately vindicated by history.

W. F. Albright proposed that the *bāmôṯ* were basically tomb-shrines, but no excavated shrine or unamended biblical reference has clear mortuary associations. P. H. Vaughan suggests that *bāmôṯ* were round or flat cult platforms on which worship was celebrated. However, although some *bāmôṯ* may have contained a platform, the term seems more naturally taken as embracing the whole cult area including altar, stones, houses, *etc.*

The 'Great High Place' at Petra, Jordan. The altar platform with offering-table before it was probably the place of blood-sacrifices. Probably Nabataean (2nd cent. BC *– 2nd cent.* AD *) on an earlier Edomite site.* (ARM)

A gradual development in the location of *bāmôṯ* is discernible. Shrines on heights were typical of the early period (Nu. 22:41; 1 Sa. 9), whereas later they are to be found in the towns (2 Ki. 17:9) or, in one instance, in a valley (Je. 7:31). By the end of the Monarchy period, the term was applied to many types of local shrine. Thus 2 Ki. 23 refers to a small gate shrine, royal centres to foreign gods, large public shrines and local rustic shrines all as *bāmôṯ*.

Widely publicized discoveries at Gezer and the 'Conway High Place at Petra' have now been discounted as *bāmôṯ*. Despite a 'wishful thinking' phase, archaeology has now revealed examples of the main types of biblical *bāmôṯ*. Shrines outside settlements are known from Naharijah, Samaria, Jerusalem and 'the Great High Place at Petra'. *bāmôṯ* in towns on heights are known from Megiddo and Arad. Shrines on lower ground in towns are known from Hazor, Dan and Jerusalem. Small gate shrines are known from Tirzah and Dan. Biblical evidence about the structures, cult and tendency of a shrine to change its status can all be illustrated from archaeological discoveries, so revealing a detailed picture of the period when Israel 'had as many gods as towns' (Je. 2:28).

BIBLIOGRAPHY. W. F. Albright, *Supplement to VT* 4, 1957, pp. 242–258; L. H. Vincent, *RB* 55, 1948, pp. 245–278, 438–445; P. H. Vaughan, *The meaning of 'bāmâ' in the Old Testament*, 1974; J. T. Whitney, *The Israelite bamah*, unpublished thesis, University of Nottingham, 1975. J.T.W.

HIGH PRIEST'S BREASTPIECE
See Breastpiece, Part 1.

HILKIAH (Heb. *ḥilqîyâhû*, *ḥilqîyâ*, 'my portion is Yahweh').

1. The father of Eliakim, Hezekiah's chamberlain (2 Ki. 18:18, 26, 37; Is. 22:20; 36:3, 22).

2. The high priest in Josiah's reign. During the repairs on the Temple, he found the book of the law, and brought it to the notice of Shaphan the scribe. Subsequently he was a member of the king's deputation to Huldah the prophetess to learn God's will in the matter, and later he helped to put Josiah's reformation into effect (2 Ki. 22–23; 2 Ch. 34; 35:8).

3, 4. Levites of the family of Merari (1 Ch. 6:45; 26:11). **5.** One who stood with Ezra the scribe when he read the law of God from a wooden pulpit (Ne. 8:4). **6.** A chief of the priests who went up to Judaea with Zerubbabel (Ne. 12:7, 21). Possibly identical with **5**.

7. The father of Jeremiah the prophet, and member of the priestly family of Anathoth (Je. 1:1). Probably a descendant of Abiathar, David's high priest who was expelled by Solomon for supporting Adonijah (1 Ki. 2:26). Hilkiah was possibly the officiating priest to the rural community at Anathoth.

8. The father of Gemariah, one of Zedekiah's ambassadors to Nebuchadrezzar (Je. 29:3). J.G.G.N.

HILL, HILL-COUNTRY. These terms translate the Heb. words *giḇʿâ* and *har*. The root-meaning of the former is convexity; bare hills, like an inverted basin, are a common feature of Palestine, notably

The valley of Hinnom (Gehenna), Wadi al-Rababi, S of Jerusalem. (SH)

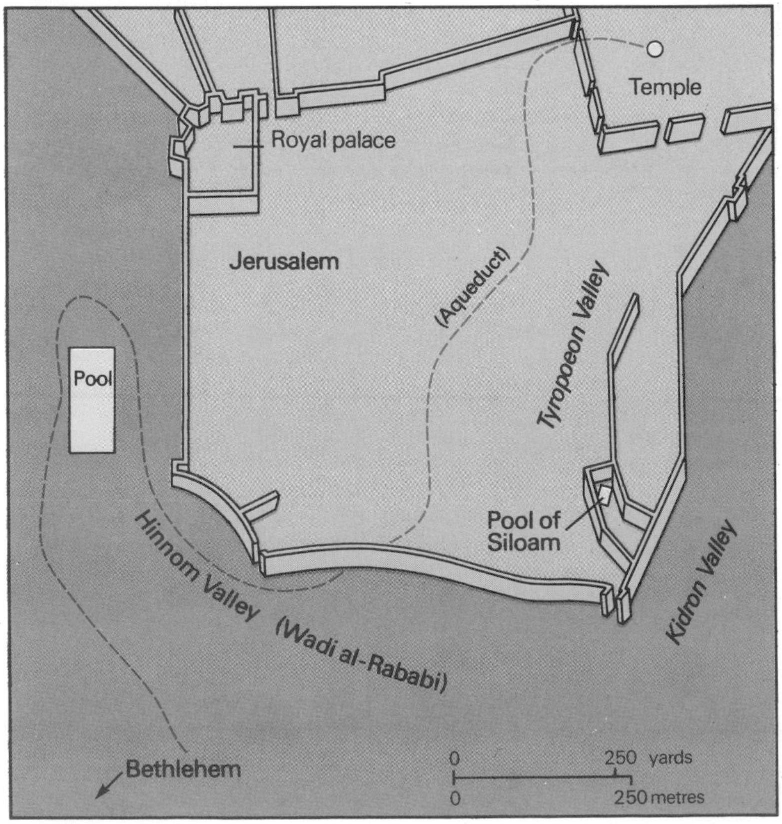

The Hinnom (Gehenna) valley, Jerusalem.

the area of Judah. But *giḇ‘â* is often a proper name (Gibeah) to indicate towns built on such eminences, coupled with a distinguishing 'surname' (*e.g.* 'of Saul', 1 Sa. 11:4).

The second word, *har*, may indicate a single eminence or a range of hills; this led to some confusion in AV, but recent EVV make it clear when a range of hills is meant. The mountainous backbone of Palestine is so styled sometimes divided into the N and S parts of it, respectively called the hill-country 'of Ephraim' and 'of Judah'. It should, however, be noted that it is not always possible to decide whether a single hill or a hilly region is meant. D.F.P.

HINNOM, VALLEY OF. A valley to the S of Jerusalem, also styled 'the valley of the son (or sons) of Hinnom'. It was associated in Jeremiah's time with the worship of Molech. Josiah defiled this shrine, and put an end to the sacrifices offered there. Later the valley seems to have been used for burning the corpses of criminals and animals, and indeed refuse of any sort. Hence the name came to be used as a synonym for *hell, the Hebrew phrase *gê* ('valley of') *hinnōm* becoming *geenna* in Greek, whence Gehenna in Latin and English. Jewish tradition at one time held that the mouth of hell was in the valley.

The identification of the valley presents problems. It formed part of the boundary between the territories of Judah and Benjamin, and lay between the 'south side of the Jebusite; the same is Jerusalem' and Enrogel (Jos. 15:7f., AV). So clearly the identification of these two localities will affect our identification of the Valley of Hinnom. If *En-rogel was the Virgin's Fountain, the Valley of Hinnom can be equated with the Kidron valley, which runs from the E to the SE of Jerusalem. But if it was what is now called Bir Eyyub, two possibilities remain: the valley was either the Tyropoeon valley, running from the centre of Jerusalem to the SE, or the valley encircling the city on the W and S, now called the Wadi al-Rababi. Each of these three valleys, at its SE extremity, terminates near Siloam. Muslim tradition supports the Kidron valley identification, but that is the least likely; the great majority of scholars accept the Wadi al-Rababi as the correct identification.

D.F.P.

HIRAM. The king of *Tyre, contemporary with David and Solomon; he reigned 979/8–945/4 BC (according to Albright, 969–936 BC).

a. Name

Heb. *Ḥîrām* (Sa. and Ki.); *Ḥîrōm* (1 Ki. 5:10, 18; LXX, *H(e)iram*); *Ḥûrām* (Ch.) is a Phoenician name possibly equivalent to, or an abbreviation for, Aḥiram (Nu. 26:38), meaning 'my brother is the exalted (god)', as Ḥiel stands for Aḥiel (1 Ki. 16:34). Hiram, or Huram(abi), was also the name of the chief technician from Tyre, married to a woman of Naphtali (1 Ki. 7:13f.) or Dan (2 Ch. 2:13) sent by King Hiram to help Solomon.

b. Relations with Judah

Hiram was a great admirer of David (1 Ki. 5:1) and sent materials and craftsmen to aid the building of his palace at Jerusalem (2 Sa. 5:11; 1 Ch. 14:1). On Solomon's accession Hiram sent ambassadors to make fresh contacts which led to a trade-treaty whereby he supplied wood from Lebanon and skilled craftsmen for the construction of the new Temple at Jerusalem, in return for an annual payment by Solomon of wheat and fine oil (1 Ki. 5:2–11) which the Phoenician cities lacked. Additional payments of barley and wine seem to have been required for the maintenance of the Tyrian workmen, who included technicians acquainted with fabric design and dyes, sent to instruct the Israelites (2 Ch. 2:3–7).

Twenty years later, on the completion of the Temple, Solomon gave Hiram twenty villages in Galilee, presumably near Tyre, and received in exchange 120 talents of gold (1 Ki. 9:10–14). Such treaties to adjust the borders between states are known from early Syrian agreements (*e.g.* Alalaḫ). These treaties, which were planned for the economic advantage of both parties, were supplemented by trading operations in which Solomon's ocean-going *ships joined the fleet of Hiram to import gold, silver and various kinds of rarities, including monkeys (1 Ki. 10:22; 2 Ch. 9:21). The vessels sailing from Ezion-geber for *Ophir were accompanied by experienced pilots provided by Hiram (1 Ki. 9:26–28; 2 Ch. 8:17–18). The trade expansion of *Phoenicia in Hiram's time included colonies in N Africa and Spain.

c. The reign of Hiram

Apart from the OT, Hiram's rule is chronicled by Josephus (*Ant.* 8. 50–54; *Contra Apionem* 1. 17f.), based on the historians Menander and Dius. According to this source, Hiram (LXX *Chiram*, Gk. *Heiramos, Heirōmos*) was the son of Abi-baal and reigned 34 years before dying at the age of 53. The building of the Temple at Jerusalem began in his 11th year, *i.e.* the 4th year of Solomon (1 Ki. 6:1). Hiram warred against Cyprus to enforce the payment of tribute and fortified the island of Tyre, where he built temples to Astarte-Melqart (later Hercules) and enriched the older temples.

Josephus, like Eupolemos and Alexander Polyhistor, recounts the letters, said to have been preserved in the state archives at Tyre, which passed between Hiram and Solomon concerning the building of the Temple. Josephus states also that the two kings engaged in an exchange of riddles until Solomon was defeated by a young Tyrian named Abdemon. Clement of Alexandria and Tatian say that a daughter of Hiram was married to Solomon; *cf.* the statement that Sidonians were among his wives (1 Ki. 11:1–2).

BIBLIOGRAPHY. *CAH*³, 3, 1978.

D.J.W.

HIRE, HIRELING. The two main classes of *wage-earner in Israel were the foreign mercenary and the agricultural labourer, typifying respectively dereliction of duty (Je. 46:21) and stinting service (Jb. 7:1f.) under exploitation (Mal. 3:5). Hence the pejoratives in Jn. 10:12–13 and Lk. 15:19. David introduced foreign mercenaries to buttress the newly adopted monarchy (2 Sa. 8:18). The agricultural labourer was debased by an enclosure movement in the 8th century (Is. 5:8) which dispossessed many freehold farmers of their patrimony and left them in *debt. By custom the ultimate discharge of debt was perpetual *slavery (2 Ki. 4:1). The law provided that an Israelite who, through poverty, had to sell himself to a fellow-Israelite should be allowed the status of an employee and be manumitted in the year of Jubilee (Lv. 25:39–55). Other laws also protected him (*e.g.* Lv. 19:13; *cf.* Dt. 24:14–15). Jacob's two contracts (Gn. 29) disclose a background of nomadic kinship and

HILLEL
See Pharisees, Part 3.

HIN
See Weights and measures, Part 3.

HIND
See Animals, Part 1.

HIP
See Leg, Part 2.

HIPPOCRATES
See Cos, Part 1.

A main entrance through the outer wall of the Hittite capital city Hattusas in the 14th–13th cent. BC. Boğaz-köy, Turkey. (JDH)

A Luwian hieroglyphic inscription of the Hittite Wasu-Sarmas (Wassurme), king of Tabal, who paid tribute to Assyrians in 738 and 732 BC. Here he records a battle against a coalition of seven Anatolian kings. From Topada, Turkey. (JDH)

The Hittite king, Warpalawas, is depicted in an attitude of prayer before the storm-god Tarhun, here shown in the form of a vegetation or fertility god. Rock relief at Ivriz in the Taurus Mts. Height of king c. 2·40 m; of god 4·20 m. Late 8th cent. BC. (JDH)

recall the great national codes of the 2nd millennium BC.

BIBLIOGRAPHY. J. D. M. Derrett, *Law in the New Testament*, 1961, ch. 1; J. Jeremias, *Jerusalem in the Time of Jesus*, 1969, ch. 6; R. de Vaux, *Ancient Israel*, 1961, p. 76.

A.E.W.

HITTITES (Heb. *ḥittîm, b^enê ḥēt*). In the OT the Hittites are, firstly, a great nation which gave its name to the whole region of Syria, 'from the wilderness and this Lebanon as far as the great river, the river Euphrates, all the land of the Hittites to the Great Sea toward the going down of the sun' (Jos. 1:4); and secondly, an ethnic group living in Canaan from patriarchal times until after the Israelite settlement (Gn. 15:20; Dt. 7:1; Jdg. 3:5), called literally 'the children of Heth' (Gn. 23:3, *etc.*) after their eponymous ancestor Heth, a son of Canaan (Gn. 10:15).

I. The Hittite empire

The Hittite empire was founded *c.* 1800 BC by an Indo-European nation which had settled in Asia Minor in city-states some two centuries before. They derived the name 'Hittite' from the Hatti, the

earlier inhabitants of the area where they settled, whose legacy is clearly traceable in Hittite art and religion and in divine and royal names and titles. With the spread of the Hittite empire the designation 'Hittites' was extended to the peoples and lands which it incorporated.

An early Hittite king, Tudhaliyas I (*c.* 1720 BC), has been identified (precariously) with 'Tidal king of nations' of Gn. 14:1. About 1600 BC Hattusilis I extended his rule over parts of N Syria. His successor Mursilis I established a new capital at Hattusas (modern Boğaz-köy), E of the Halys; it is largely to the archives uncovered there since 1906 that we owe our knowledge of Hittite history and literature. Mursilis I captured Aleppo and subsequently (*c.* 1560 BC) raided Babylon—an event which precipitated the fall of the 1st Babylonian Dynasty.

King Telepinus (*c.* 1480 BC) was the great Hittite legislator. There are some striking affinities between the Hittite law-codes and those of the Pentateuch, although affinities are found in matters of detail and arrangement rather than in general conception. Whereas the Pentateuchal codes resemble the great Semitic law-codes of the ancient Near East in employing the *lex talionis* as a basic principle, the Hittite laws are dominated by the distinctively Indo-European principle of compensation (*Wergeld*). Some analogy has also been discerned between Hittite treaty forms and OT covenant terms. Other notable points of contact are found in the levirate marriage and in the procedures for ascertaining the divine will or the unknown future by means of teraphim and *'ōḇôt* ('familiar spirits').

The Hittite empire reached the peak of its power under Suppiluliumas I (*c.* 1380–1350 BC). It was in his province of Kizzuwatna, in

SE Asia Minor, that iron was first smelted in the Near East on a scale which justifies one in speaking of the beginning of the Iron Age. He extended his empire over Upper Mesopotamia and over Syria as far S as the Lebanon. The Hittites thus collided with the N thrust of the Egyptian empire in Asia, and hostilities continued between the two powers until 1284 BC, when a non-aggression pact between Hattusilis III and Rameses II recognized the Orontes as their common frontier.

The Hittite empire collapsed around 1200 BC as the result of blows from western enemies.

II. The Hittite kingdoms

With the fall of the Hittite empire, 24 city-states of the Tabali ('Tubal' in the OT) became heirs to the Hittite home territory N of the Taurus range. In Syria seven city-states which had belonged to the Hittite empire perpetuated the name 'Hittite' for several centuries; their rulers were called 'the kings of the Hittites'. Hamath on the Orontes and Carchemish on the Euphrates were among the most important of the seven. Hamath was allied with David (2 Sa. 8:9ff.),

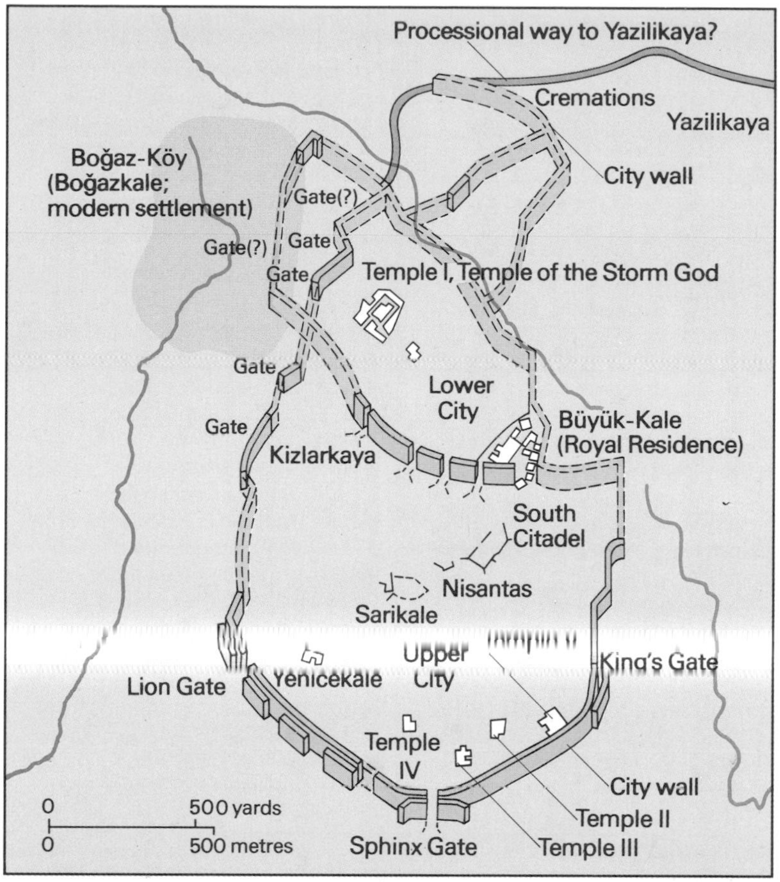

Plan of the Hittite capital city, Hattusas (modern Boğaz-köy), established by Mursilis I in the 16th cent. BC.

General view of the ruins of the great Hittite temple (Temple I) at Hattusas, perhaps dedicated to the weather god. (JDH)

whose kingdom bordered on 'Kadesh in the land of the Hittites' (2 Sa. 24:6; *TAHTIM-HODSHI). Solomon traded and intermarried with these 'kings of the Hittites) (1 Ki. 10:28f.; 11:1). In the 9th century BC their military reputation could throw the army of Damascus into panic (2 Ki. 7:6). But in the following century they were reduced one by one by the Assyrians; Hamath fell in 720 BC and Carchemish in 717 (*cf.* 2 Ki. 18:34; 19:13; Is. 10:9).

The Assyrian and Babylonian records of the period (as late as the Chaldean dynasty) regularly refer to the whole of Syria (including Palestine) as the 'Hatti-land'; Sargon II in 711 BC can speak of the people of Ashdod as 'the faithless Hatti'.

The language of the seven Hittite kingdoms is known from hieroglyphic texts which have been deciphered in recent years; bilingual inscriptions in hieroglyphic Hittite and Phoenician, discovered at Karatepe in Cilicia (1946–7), have helped considerably in their decipherment. The language of these texts is not identical with the official language of the earlier Hittite empire, which was written in cuneiform script and identified as an Indo-European language in 1917; it resembles rather a neighbouring Indo-European language called Luvian.

III. The Hittites of Canaan

The Hittites of Canaan in patriarchal times appear as inhabiting the central ridge of Judah, especially the Hebron district. It has been surmised that they were a branch of the pre-Indo-European Hatti, or early migrants from some part of the Hittite empire; the Hittite empire itself never extended so far S. They may, on the other hand, have had nothing in common with the N Hittites but their similar (though not completely identical) name. In Gn. 23 the Hittites are the resident population of Hebron ('the people of the land') among whom Abraham lives as 'a stranger and a sojourner' and from whom he buys the field of Machpelah, with its cave, as a family burying-ground. The record of the purchase is said to be 'permeated with intricate subtleties of Hittite laws and customs, correctly corresponding to the time of Abraham' (M. R. Lehmann, *BASOR* 129, 1953, p. 18; but see for another opinion G. M. Tucker, *JBL* 85, 1966, pp. 77ff.). Esau grieved his parents by marrying two 'Hittite women . . . women of the land' (Gn. 27:46; *cf.* 26:34f.)—apparently in the Beersheba region. Jerusalem, according to Ezk. 16:3, 45, had a mixed Hittite and Amorite foundation. The name of *Araunah the Jebusite (2 Sa. 24:16ff.) has been thought to be Hittite, and Uriah the Hittite, evidently a Jerusalemite, was one of David's mighty men (2 Sa. 23:39). Ahimelech, one of David's companions in the days of his outlawry, is called a Hittite (1 Sa. 26:6).

The last reference to the Hittites of Canaan is in Solomon's reign (2 Ch. 8:7); thereafter they were merged in the general population of the land.

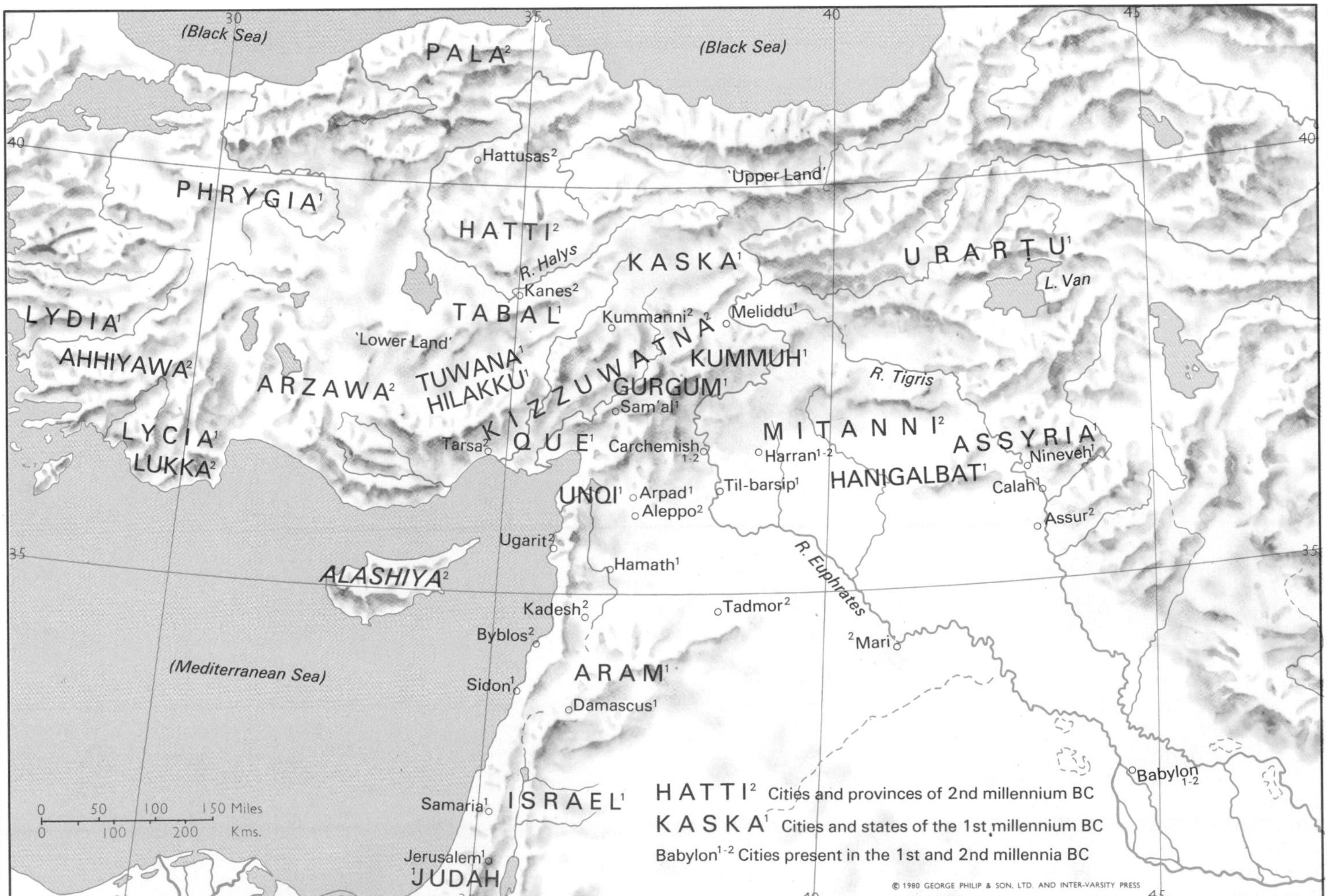

Areas under Hittite influence.

A Hittite prisoner depicted on a faience tile made in Egypt. Height 25 cm. c. 1170 BC. (OIUC)

BIBLIOGRAPHY. O. R. Gurney, *The Hittites*², 1966; *idem*, *Some Aspects of Hittite religion*, 1976; O. R. Gurney and J. Garstang, *The Geography of the Hittite Empire*, 1959; S. Lloyd, *Early Anatolia*, 1956; L. Woolley, *A Forgotten Kingdom*, 1953; E. Neufeld, *The Hittite Laws*, 1951; E. Akurgal, *The Art of the Hittites*, 1962; G. Walser (ed.), *Neuere Hethiterforschung*, 1964; H. A. Hoffner, 'Some Contributions of Hittitology to OT Study', *TynB* 20, 1969, pp. 29ff.; *idem*, 'The Hittites and Hurrians' in *POTT*, pp. 197ff.; F. Cornelius, *Geschichte der Hethiter*, 1973; J. Lehmann, *The Hittites*, 1977. F.F.B.

HIVITE. One of the sons of Canaan (Gn. 10:17; 1 Ch. 1:15); an early inhabitant of Syria and Palestine, named as distinct from the Canaanites, Jebusites, Perizzites, Girgashites and Amorites (Ex. 3:8; 23:28; Dt. 7:1), and in association with the *Arkites known to have dwelt in Lebanon (Gn. 10:17). This accords with their principal location in the Lebanon hills (Jdg. 3:3) and the Hermon range as far as the valley leading to Hamath (Jos. 11:3), where they still lived in the time of David, who lists them after Sidon and Tyre (2 Sa. 24:7). Hivites were conscripted as labourers for Solomon's building projects (1 Ki. 9:20; 2 Ch. 8:7). Others were settled in Shechem, whose founder is described as son of Hamor, a Hivite, in the time of Jacob (Gn. 34:2) and near Gibeon (Jos. 9:7; 11:19).

Many equate the Hivites (Heb. *Ḥiwwî*; Gk. *Heuaios*) with the *Horites (*Ḥorri[m]*), assuming a scribal confusion between the Heb. *w* and *r*. In Gn. 36:20–30 Zibeon is called a Horite as opposed to a Hivite in v. 2. Similarly, the LXX of Gn. 34:2 and Jos. 9:7 renders 'Horite' for 'Hivite', and some read 'Hittite' (*ḥittî*) for 'Hivite' in Jos. 11:3; Jdg. 3:3. The derivation from *ḥawwâ*, 'tent-village', is uncertain, as is the identification of the Hivites, otherwise unattested.

BIBLIOGRAPHY. H. A. Hoffner, *TynB* 20, 1969, pp. 27–37. D.J.W.

HOBAB (Heb. *ḥōḇāḇ*, 'beloved'). Nu. 10:29 speaks of 'Hobab, the son of Raguel the Midianite, Moses' father in law'—ambiguous wording which leaves unclear whether Moses' father-in-law was Hobab or Raguel (Reuel). Jdg. 4:11 (*cf.* Jdg. 1:16) says Hobab; Ex. 2:18 says Reuel; but evidence is too slight to choose between the two accounts. Islamic tradition identifies Hobab with Jethro, but others suggest an identification between Reuel and *Jethro (Ex. 2:18; 3:1). The latter would make Hobab the brother-in-law of Moses; but such an interpretation of the Heb. word (*ḥōṯēn*) is questionable. J.D.D.

HOBAH. The name of the place to which Abraham pursued the four kings who had pillaged Sodom and Gomorrah and carried off Lot (Gn. 14:15). It lay 'on the left hand of', that is (to one facing E) to the N of Damascus. Though modern sites have been suggested, the place is unknown. A district Ube is mentioned in the *Amarna letters and identified by some with Tell el-Salihiye *c.* 20 km E of Damascus. T.C.M.

HOLINESS, HOLY, SAINTS. There is probably no religion without a distinction between holy and profane, and in most, if not indeed

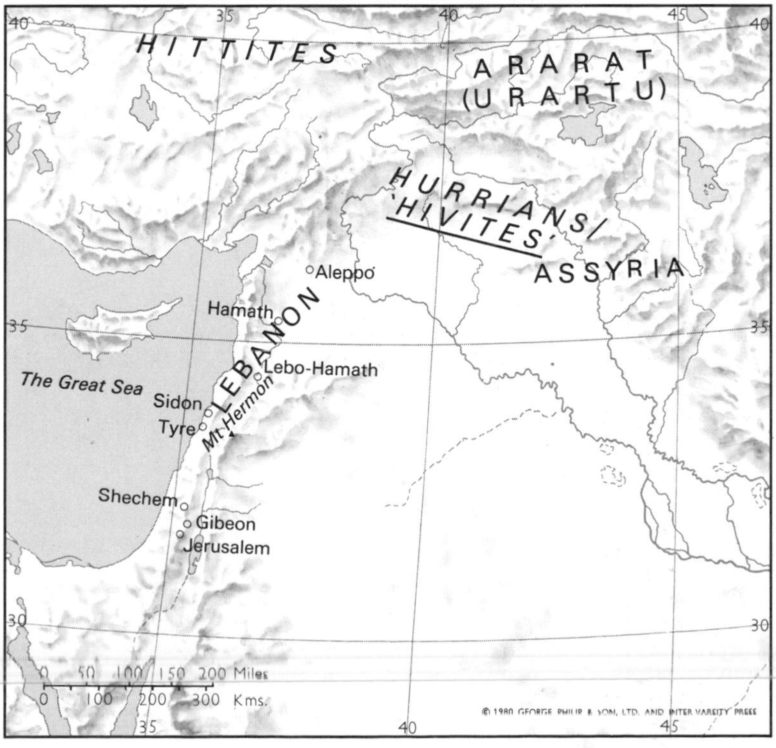

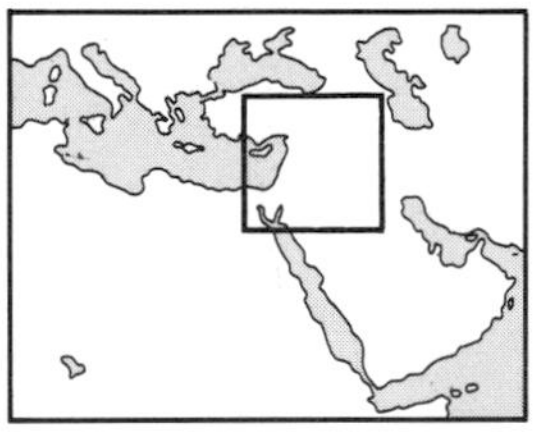

Areas of Hurrian ('Hivite') concentration.

in all, the religious man is the one to whom something is holy. This receives impressive illustration in Scripture.

The principal words are Heb. *qāḏôš* in the OT and Gk. *hagios* in the NT, both words of uncertain derivation. If the main root *qdš* is derived from the simple root *qd*, meaning to cut or separate, it denotes apartness, and so the separation of a person or thing from the common or profane to a divine use. The NT terminology suggests the distinction between the holiness which is God's very being and the holiness which marks out the character of his people. The terms *semnos*, that which invokes reverence (1 Tim. 3:8), *hieros*, sacred, having relation to deity (2 Tim. 3:15), and *hagnos*, that which is pure or chaste (2 Cor. 11:2), are used with reference to God's people, while the terms *hosios* (Rev. 15:4) and *hagios* (Jn. 17:11) are applied in the first instance to God, as denoting a character that is in absolute antithesis to that of the world.

a. Holiness as separation and ethical purity

It is clear that, in Scripture generally, holiness means separation, and the term is used with reference to persons or things that have been separated or set apart for God and his service. Thus we have in Exodus mention of holy ground (3:5), holy assembly (12:16), holy sabbath (16:23), holy nation (19:6) and holy place (29:31), to mention but a few. In these and similar cases the word does not directly imply ethical attributes, but mainly consecration to the Lord and his service, and so separation from the common sphere. It is God who causes this separation and so conveys the holiness that may be implied by the separation. For example, the 7th day was designated holy, negatively because it was separated from the other 6 days of the week, and positively because it was dedicated to God's service. When the word is applied to a certain place it is because of a divine association with that place. There was given to Moses at Horeb, before the burning bush, the injunction: 'Put off your shoes from your feet, for the place on which you are standing is holy ground' (Ex. 3:5). The ground was holy because it was at that moment the place of divine revelation. Similarly God sanctified the people of Israel by separating them from all the nations of the earth and entering into covenant with them, but this involved giving to them a knowledge of the divine law, moral and ceremonial. Thus the ethical is imparted. These two aspects of holiness are generally present, since it was understood that being holy meant not only living a separate life, but bearing a character different from that of the ordinary man. Thus the word attained a distinct ethical implication. Holiness is therefore recognized as belonging to what has been chosen and set apart by God and given a character that conforms to God's law.

b. The holiness of God's character

From what has already been said it becomes clear that holiness is not so much a relation of the creature to the Creator as of the Creator to the creature. In other words, it is the holiness of God that underlines that separation of life and distinctiveness of character that belong to God's people. This gives point to the distinction noted above, that different terms are applied to the holiness of God and that of his people. Holiness belongs to God as divine, and he would not be God without it. In that respect 'there is none holy like the Lord' (1 Sa. 2:2). The ethical quality in holiness is the aspect most commonly to the forefront when the word is applied to God. It is basically a term for the moral excellence of God and his freedom from all limitation in his moral perfection (Hab. 1:13). It is in this respect that God alone is holy and the standard of ethical purity in his creatures.

Since holiness embraces every distinctive attribute of Godhead, it may be conceived of as the outshining of all that God is. As the sun's rays, combining all the colours of the spectrum, come together in the sun's shining and blend into light, so in his self-manifestation all the attributes of God come together and blend into holiness. Holiness has, for that reason, been called 'an attribute of attributes', that which lends unity to all the attributes of God. To conceive of God's being and character as merely a synthesis of abstract perfections is to deprive God of all reality. In the God of the Bible these perfections live and function in holiness.

For these reasons we can understand why holiness is expressly attributed in Scripture to each Person in the Godhead, to the Father (Jn. 17:11), to the Son (Acts 4:30), and especially to the Spirit as the one who manifests and communicates the holiness of God to his creatures.

c. The holiness of God in relation to his people

The OT applies the word 'holy' to human beings in virtue of their consecration to religious purposes, *e.g.* priests who were consecrated by special ceremonies, and even to the whole nation of Israel as a people separated from the nations and consecrated to God. Thus it was relationship to God that constituted Israel a holy people, and in this sense it was the highest expression of the covenant relationship. This idea is not altogether absent from the NT, as in the passage in 1 Cor. 7:14, where the unbelieving husband is sanctified in virtue of his relationship to the believing wife and vice versa.

But as the conception of holiness advanced, alongside the progressive revelation of God, from the outside to the inside, from ceremonial to reality, so it took on a strong ethical significance, and this is its main, and practically its exclusive, connotation in the NT. The OT prophets proclaimed it as pre-eminently God's self-disclosure, the testimony he bears to himself and the aspect under which he wills his creatures to know him. Moreover, the prophets declared that God willed to communicate his holiness to his creatures, and that, in turn, he claims holiness from them. If 'I am holy' is the divine self-assertion, lifting God immeasurably above his creatures, so 'Be holy' is the divine call to his creatures to 'share his holiness' (Heb. 12:10). It is this imparting of the divine holiness which takes place in the soul of man in regeneration and becomes the spring and foundation of holy character.

Christ in his life and character is the supreme example of the divine holiness. In him it consisted in more than mere sinlessness: it was his entire consecration to the will and purpose of God, and to this end Jesus sanctified himself (Jn. 17:19). The holiness of Christ is both the standard of the Christian character and its guarantee: 'He who sanctifies and those who are sanctified have all one origin' (Heb. 2:11).

In the NT the apostolic designation for Christians is *saints* (*hagioi*), and it continued to be used as a general designation at least up to the days of Irenaeus and Tertullian, though after that it degenerated in ecclesiastical usage into an honorific title. Though its primary significance was relationship, it was also descriptive of character, and more especially of Christlike character. The NT everywhere emphasizes the ethical nature of holiness in contrast to all uncleanness. It is represented as the supreme vocation of Christians and the goal of their living. In the final assessment of human destiny the two categories known to Scripture are the righteous and the wicked.

d. The eschatological significance of holiness

Scripture emphasizes the permanence of moral character (Rev. 22:11). It also emphasizes the retributive aspect of the divine holiness. It involves the world in judgment. From a moral necessity in God, life is so ordered that in holiness is welfare, in sin is doom. Since the divine holiness could not make a universe in which sin would ultimately prosper, the retributive quality in the divine government becomes perfectly plain. But retribution is not the end; the holiness of God ensures that there will be a final restoration, a *palingenesia*, bringing to pass a regeneration of the moral universe. The eschatology of the Bible holds out the promise that the holiness of God will sweep the universe clean and create new heavens and a new earth in which righteousness will dwell (2 Pet. 3:13).

BIBLIOGRAPHY. A. Murray, *Holy in Christ*, 1888; R. Otto, *The Idea of the Holy*, 1946; *ERE*, 6, pp. 731–759; W. E. Sangster, *The Path to Perfection*, 1943; H. Seebass, C. Brown, in *NIDNTT* 2, pp. 223–238; *TDNT* 1, pp. 88–115, 122; 3, pp. 221–230; 5, pp. 489–493; 7, pp. 175–185.

R.A.F.

HOMOSEXUALITY. The Bible says nothing specifically about the homosexual condition (despite the rather misleading RSV translation of 1 Cor. 6:9), but its condemnations of homosexual conduct are explicit. The scope of these strictures must, however, be carefully determined. Too often they have been used as tools of a homophobic polemic which has claimed too much.

The exegesis of the Sodom and Gibeah stories (Gn. 19:1–25; Jdg. 19:13–20:48) is a good case in point. We must resist D. S. Bailey's widely-quoted claim that the sin God punished on these occasions was a breach of hospitality etiquette without sexual overtones (it fails to explain adequately both the double usage of the word 'know' (*yāḏa'*) and the reason behind the substitutionary offer of Lot's daughters and the Levite's concubine); but neither account amounts to a wholesale condemnation of all homosexual acts. On both occasions the sin condemned was attempted homosexual rape, not a caring homosexual relationship between consenting partners.

The force of the other OT references to homosexuality is similarly limited by the context in which they are set. Historically, homosexual behaviour was linked with idolatrous cult prostitution (1 Ki. 14:24; 15:12; 22:46). The stern warnings of the levitical law (Lv. 18:22; 20:13) are primarily aimed at idolatry too; the word 'abomination' (*tô'ēḇâ*), for example, which features in both these references, is a religious term often used for idolatrous practices. Viewed strictly within their context, then, these OT condemnations apply to homosexual activity conducted in the course of idolatry, but not necessarily more widely than that.

In Rom. 1 Paul condemns homosexual acts, lesbian as well as male, in the same breath as idolatry (vv. 23–27), but his theological canvas is broader than that of Lv. Instead of treating homosexual behaviour as an expression of idolatrous worship, he traces both to the bad 'exchange' fallen man has made in departing from his Creator's intention (vv. 25f.). Seen from this angle, every homosexual act is unnatural (*para physin*, v. 26), not because it cuts across the individual's natural sexual orientation (which, of course, it may not) or infringes OT law (*contra* McNeill), but because it flies in the face of God's creation scheme for human sexual expression.

Paul makes two more references to homosexual practice in other Epistles. Both occur in lists of banned activities and strike the same condemnatory note. In 1 Cor. 6:9f. practising homosexuals are included among the unrighteous who will not inherit the kingdom of God (but with the redemptive note added, 'such *were* some of you'); and in 1 Tim. 1:9f. they feature in a list of 'the lawless and disobedient'. The latter is especially important because the whole list represents an updated version of the *Ten Commandments. Paul parallels the 7th commandment (on adultery) with a reference to 'immoral persons' (*pornoi*) and 'sodomites' (*arsenokoitai*), words which cover all sexual intercourse outside marriage, whether heterosexual or homosexual. If the Decalogue is permanently valid, the significance of this application is heightened still further.

It has been suggested that the meaning of *arsenikoitēs* in 1 Cor. 6:9 and 1 Tim. 1:10 may be restricted to that of 'male prostitute' (*cf.* Vulg. *masculi concubitores*). Linguistic evidence to support this view is lacking, however, though the word itself is certainly rare in literature of the NT period. It seems beyond reasonable doubt that Paul intended to condemn homosexual conduct (but not homosexual people) in the most general and theologically broad terms he knew. His three scattered references fit together in an impressive way as an expression of God's will as he saw it. As Creator, Law-Giver and King, the Lord's condemnation of such behaviour was absolutely plain.

BIBLIOGRAPHY. H. Thielicke, *The Ethics of Sex*, E.T. 1964; D. H. Field, *The Homosexual Way—A Christian Option?*, 1976; J. J. McNeill, *The Church and the Homosexual*, 1977.

D.H.F.

HONEY, HONEYCOMB (Heb. *d^eḇaš*, 'honey', the usual word; *nōp̄eṯ*, 'juice', 'dropping'; *ya'ar*, 'comb'; *ya'raṯ had-d^eḇaš*, 'comb of honey'; *ṣûp̄ d^eḇaš*, 'a flowing of honey'; Gk. *meli*, 'honey'; *melission kērion*, 'honeycomb'). A favourite *food in biblical times (Pr. 24:13; *cf.* Ecclus. 11:3), honey was found in hollows of the rocks (Dt. 32:13; Ps. 81:16); in trees (1 Sa. 14:25–26, though the Heb. text here is obscure); in the wilderness of Judaea (Mt. 3:4; Mk. 1:6); and in animal carcasses (Jdg. 14:8).

Honey was used in cake-making (Ex. 16:31), and was regarded as having medicinal properties (Pr. 16:24). It was as acceptable gift (2 Sa. 17:29; 1 Ki. 14:3); a valuable resource (Je. 41:8); and was evidently plentiful enough to be exported (Ezk. 27:17, but some suggest that in this verse and in Gn. 43:11 grape or date syrup (Arab.

HOLM
See Trees, Part 3.

HOLY
See Holiness, Part 2.

HOLY KISS
See Kiss, Part 2.

HOLY LAND
See Palestine, Part 2.

HOLY SPIRIT
See Spirit, Holy, Part 3.

HOLY WEEK
See Jesus Christ, life of, Part 2.

HOME
See Tent, Part 3.

HOMER
See Weights and measures, Part 3.

HOMICIDE
See Crime, Part 1.

HOOPOE
See Animals, Part 1.

dibs) may be intended; *cf.* Jos., *BJ* 4. 469). It was forbidden as an ingredient of any meal-offering to Yahweh (Lv. 2:11) because of its liability to fermentation (so Pliny, *NH* 11. 15), but included in tithes and first-fruits (2 Ch. 31:5), which incidentally suggests domesticated bees (*ANIMALS). In later times bee-keeping may have been practised by the Jews.

Canaan is spoken of as a land 'flowing with milk and honey' (Ex. 3:8, *etc.*; *cf. ANET*, pp. 19–20), for a discussion of which see T. K. Cheyne's note (*EBi*, 2104). Goshen is similarly described (Nu. 16:13).

Honey as the 'chief of sweet things' has inspired many figurative allusions—*e.g.* Ps. 19:9–10; Pr. 5:3 (*cf.* Ct. 4:11); Pr. 24:13–14 (*cf.* Ecclus. 39:26); Ezk. 3:2–3; Rev. 10:9. J.D.D.

HOOK. 1. Heb. *ḥāḥ* (Ezk. 29:4; 38:4), *ḥāḥî* (Ex. 35:22; 2 Ki. 19:28; Is. 37:29; Ezk. 19:4, 9). A hook put in the nose of a tamed beast to lead it about, or of a wild one to bring it under control. **2.** *ḥōḥîm* (2 Ch. 33:11), nose rings. Assyr. monuments show this method of treating captives. NEB has 'spiked weapons'. **3.** *šᵉp̄attayim* (Ezk. 40:43); possibly a double-pronged hook used in flaying a carcase, but the meaning is uncertain. RVmg., NEB render as 'ledges'. **4.** *mazmērôṯ*, 'pruning hooks' (Is. 2:4; 18:5; Joel 3:10; Mi. 4:3). Small sickle-shaped knives employed by vinedressers, easily convertible to, and probably used as, a weapon of war. **5.** *wāw* (Ex. 26:32, *etc.*) is used only in connection with the hangings of the *tabernacle. **6.** *'agmôn* (Jb. 41:1), *ḥakkâ* (Jb. 41:2; Is. 19:8; Hab. 1:15), *ṣinnâ* and *sîrôṯ dûḡâ* (Am. 4:2) and Gk. *ankistron* (Mt. 17:27) all mean 'fish hook'. N.H.

HOPE. Hope, it would seem, is a psychological necessity, if man is to envisage the future at all. Even if there are no rational grounds for it, man still continues to hope. Very naturally such hope, even when it appears to be justified, is transient and illusory; and it is remarkable how often it is qualified by poets and other writers by such epithets as 'faint', 'trembling', 'feeble', 'desperate', 'phantom'. The Bible sometimes uses hope in the conventional sense. The ploughman, for example, should plough in hope (1 Cor. 9:10), for it is the hope of reward that sweetens labour. But for the most part the hope with which the Bible is concerned is something very different; and in comparison with it other hope is scarcely recognized as hope. The majority of secular thinkers in the ancient world did not regard hope as a virtue, but merely as a temporary illusion; and Paul was giving an accurate description of pagans when he said they had no hope (Eph. 2:12; *cf.* 1 Thes. 4:13), the fundamental reason for this being that they were 'without God'.

Where there is a belief in the living God, who acts and intervenes in human life and who can be trusted to implement his promises, hope in the specifically biblical sense becomes possible. Such hope is not a matter of temperament, nor is it conditioned by prevailing circumstances or any human possibilities. It does not depend upon what a man possesses, upon what he may be able to do for himself, nor upon what any other human being may do for him. There was, for example, nothing in the situation in which Abraham found himself to justify his hope that Sarah would give birth to a son, but because he be-

A hook through the nose holds Tirhakah of Egypt and Ethiopia and Ba'ali of Tyre on leashes as captives of Esarhaddon of Assyria. Diorite stele from Zinjirli. c. 670 BC. (SMB)

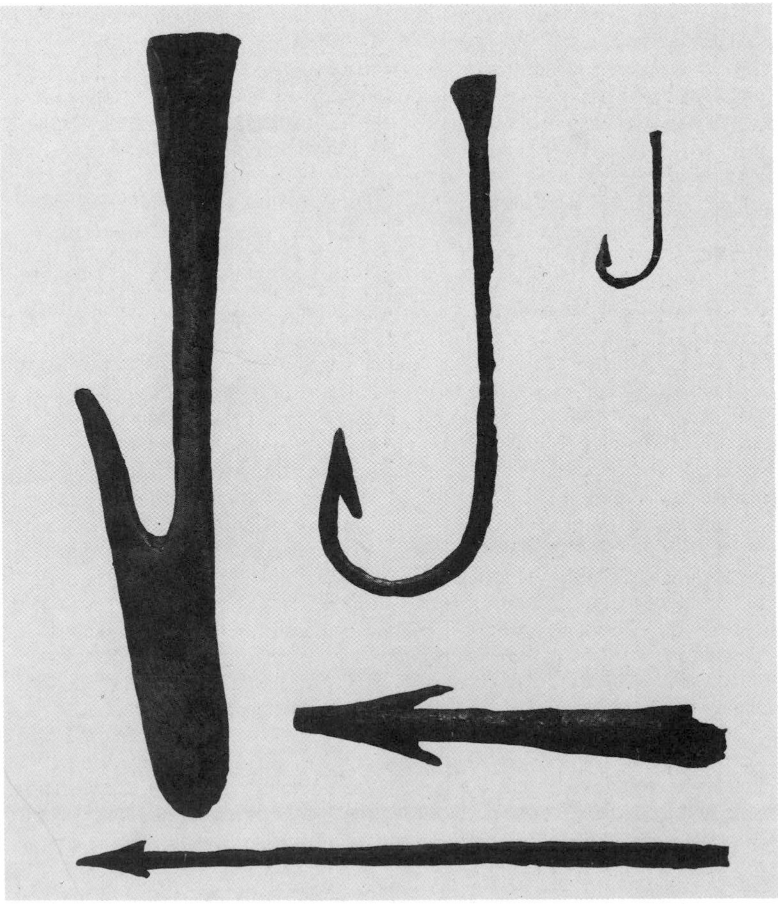

Fish-hooks and harpoons from ancient Ur near Persian Gulf. Copper and bronze. c. 2800–2500 BC. (BM)

lieved in God, he could 'in hope' believe 'against hope' (Rom. 4:18). Biblical hope is inseparable therefore from faith in God. Because of what God has done in the past, particularly in preparing for the coming of Christ, and because of what God has done and is now doing through Christ, the Christian dares to expect future blessings at present invisible (2 Cor. 1:10). The goodness of God is for him never exhausted. The best is still to be. His hope is increased as he reflects on the activities of God in the Scriptures (Rom. 12:12; 15:4). Christ in him is the hope of future glory (Col. 1:27). His final salvation rests on such hope (Rom. 8:24); and this hope of salvation is a 'helmet', an essential part of his defensive armour in the struggle against evil (1 Thes. 5:8). Hope, to be sure, is not a wind vane at the mercy of the changing winds, but 'a sure and steadfast anchor of the soul', penetrating deep into the invisible eternal world (Heb. 6:19). Because of his faith the Christian has an assurance that the things he hopes for are real (Heb. 11:1); and his hope never disappoints him (Rom. 5:5).

There are no explicit references to hope in the teaching of Jesus. He teaches his disciples, however, not to be anxious about the future, because that future is in the hands of a loving Father. He also leads them to expect that after his resurrection renewed spiritual power will be available for them, enabling them to do even greater works than he did, to overcome sin and death, and to look forward to sharing his own eternal glory. The resurrection of Jesus revitalized their hope. It was the mightiest act of God wrought in history. Before it 'panic, despair flee away'. Christian faith is essentially faith in God who raised Jesus from the dead (1 Pet. 1:21). This God towards whom the Christian directs his faith is called 'the God of hope', who can fill the believer with joy and peace, and enable him to abound in hope (Rom. 15:13). Because of the resurrection, the Christian is saved from the miserable condition of having his hope in Christ limited to this world only (1 Cor. 15:19). Christ Jesus is his Hope for time and eternity (1 Tim. 1:1). His call to be Christ's disciple carries with it the hope of finally sharing his glory (Eph. 1:18). His hope is laid up for him in heaven (Col. 1:5) and will be realized when his Lord is revealed (1 Pet. 1:13).

The existence of this hope makes it impossible for the Christian to be satisfied with transient joys (Heb. 13:14); it also acts as a stimulus to purity of life (1 Jn. 3:2–3) and enables him to suffer cheerfully. It is noticeable how often hope is associated in the NT with 'patience' or 'steadfastness'. This virtue is vastly different from Stoic endurance, precisely because it is bound up with a hope unknown to the Stoic (see 1 Thes. 1:3; Rom. 5:3–5).

In the light of what has been said it is not surprising that hope should so often be mentioned as a concomitant of faith. The heroes of faith in Heb. 11 are also beacons of hope. What is perhaps more remarkable is the frequent association of hope with love as well as with faith. This threefold combination of faith, hope and love is found in 1 Thes. 1:3; 5:8; Gal. 5:5–6; 1 Cor. 13:13; Heb. 6:10–12; 1 Pet. 1:21–22. By its connection with love, Christian hope is freed from all selfishness. The Christian does not hope for blessings for himself which he does not desire others to share. When he loves his fellow-men he hopes that they will be the recipients of the good things that he knows God longs to give them. Paul gave evidence of his hope just as much as his love and his faith when he returned the runaway slave Onesimus to his master Philemon. Faith, hope and love are thus inseparable. Hope cannot exist apart from faith, and love cannot be exercised without hope. These three are the things that abide (1 Cor. 13:13) and together they comprise the Christian way of life.

BIBLIOGRAPHY. E. J. Bicknell, *The First and Second Epistles to the Thessalonians, WC*, 1932; *RB* 61, 1954, pp. 481–532; J-J. von Allmen, *Vocabulary of the Bible*, 1958; R. Bultmann, K. H. Rengstorf, *TDNT* 2, pp. 517–535; E. Hoffmann, *NIDNTT* 2, pp. 238–246.

R.V.G.T.

HOPHNI AND PHINEHAS. The two sons of *Eli, 'priests of the Lord' at Shiloh (1 Sa. 1:3). Both names are Egyptian, meaning 'tadpole' and 'the Nubian' respectively. They are described as 'worthless men; they had no regard for the Lord' (1 Sa. 2:12). They abused their privileges as priests, claiming more than their proper share of the sacrifices and insisting on having it when and as they pleased on threat of force, so that men treated the offerings of the Lord with contempt. Because of this and their licentiousness, a curse was pronounced against the house of Eli, first by an unknown prophet (1 Sa. 2:27–36) and later by Samuel (1 Sa. 3:11–14). They died in the battle against the Philistines at Aphek (1 Sa. 4:11).

J.W.M.

HOPHRA. The pharaoh Ḥa'a'ibrē' Waḥibrē; Gk. Apries, 4th king of the 26th Dynasty, who reigned for 19 years, from 589 to 570 BC. He was an impetuous king, over-ambitious to meddle in Palestinian affairs. The Heb. form *ḥop̄ra'* is best derived from his personal name, (Wa)ḥibrē', precisely as with Shishak, Tirhakah and Neco. 'Pharaoh-hophra' is explicitly mentioned only in Je. 44:30, but several other references to 'Pharaoh' in the prophets concern him. Shortly after Hophra's accession, Zedekiah requested forces from him, presumably against Nebuchadrezzar

Pharaoh Hophra (Ḥa'a'ibre') making an offering of bowls of wine. Part of a stele. 589–570 BC. (BM)

HOREB
See Sinai, Part 3.

HOR-HAGGIDGAD
See Gudgodah, Part 2.

HORI, HORIM
See Horites, Part 2.

(Ezk. 17:11–21). Hophra duly invaded Palestine during Nebuchadrezzar's siege of Jerusalem (Je. 37:5; perhaps also Je. 47:1?), accompanied by his fleet (Herodotus, 2. 161). In 588 Ezekiel prophesied against the Egyptians (Ezk. 29:1–16) and Jeremiah prophesied Hophra's retreat (Je. 37:7). The Babylonians raised the siege of Jerusalem (Je. 37:11) just long enough to repulse Hophra; whether a battle actually occurred is uncertain. After a disastrous Libyan campaign and a revolt which resulted in Ahmose becoming co-regent, Hophra was slain in conflict with Ahmose (*cf.* Je. 44:30).

K.A.K.

HOR. 1. A mountain on the border of Edom where Aaron was buried (Nu. 20:22–29; 33:37–39; Dt. 32:50), possibly Moserah (Dt. 10:6), although Nu. 33:30, 39 distinguishes them. The place was in the region of Kadesh (Nu. 20:22; 33:37). More accurately it is 'Hor, the mountain', suggesting that it was a prominent feature.

Josephus (*Ant.* 4. 82) thought it was near Petra, and tradition has identified it with Jebel Nebi Harun, a lofty peak 1,460 m high, to the W of Edom. This, however, is far from Kadesh.

Jebel Madeira, NE of Kadesh, on the NW border of Edom has been suggested, for Israel began the detour round Edom at Mt Hor (Nu. 21:4), and Aaron could well have been buried here 'in the sight of all the congregation' (Nu. 20:22–29). However the site should be sought on 'the way of Atharim' from Kadesh-barnea to the vicinity of Arad, because it is always mentioned on the line of this journey (see references above).

2. A mountain on the N border of Israel, probably one of the N summits of the Lebanese range in the vicinity of the coast. From Jos. 13:4 the N border of 'the land that remains' included the region of Byblos and extended to Aphek on the Amorite border. Mt Hor was thus probably one of the NW peaks of the Lebanese range N of Byblos, such as Ras Shaqqah.

J.A.T.

HORESH. A place in the wilderness of Ziph (1 Sa. 23:15–19), possibly to be identified with Khirbet Khoreisa some 9–10 km S of Hebron. AV, RV 'wood' is grammatically possible but topographically unlikely; trees could scarcely have grown in this region.

R.P.G.

HORITES, HORIM. The ancient inhabitants of Edom, defeated by Chedorlaomer (Gn. 14:6), said to be the descendants of Seir the Horite (Gn. 36:20) and an ethnic group distinct from Rephaim. They were driven out by the sons of Esau (Dt. 2:12, 22). Esau himself seems to have married the daughter of a Horite chief, Anah (Gn. 36:25). The Horites (Heb. *ḥōrî*, Gk. *chorraios*) also occupied some places in central Palestine, including Shechem (Gn. 34:2) and Gilgal (Jos. 9:6–7), the LXX reading 'Horite' in both passages (AV; RSV, 'Hivite').

The E Horites cannot be identified as Hurrians either archaeologically or linguistically (Semitic personal names in Gn. 36:20–30). Some think the pre-Edomites to have been cave-dwellers (*ḥôr*) and equate this with the Egyp. name for Palestine (*hr* = *hurru*) cited

The 'Horites' are commonly identified with the Hurrians who formed part of the Mitanni Kingdom in Upper Syria and Mesopotamia. This vase of typical Mitannian style came from Alalah, N Syria. 15th–14th cent. BC. (BM)

The ram's horn (shofar), *similar to that shown here, was used as a signal in war and for heralding special festivals.* (CP)

Letter from Tushratta, king of Mitanni (a kingdom dominating the Hurrians, 'Horites') to Pharaoh Amenhotep III of Egypt. Since the non-semitic Hurrian language employing the Babylonian cuneiform script was not widely used, the correspondence is in Babylonian which was used internationally in the 2nd millennium BC. (BM)

with Israel on the Merenptah stele *c.* 1225 BC.

The pre-Israelite Jebusites ruled by Abdi-hepa during the *Amarna period seem to be Hurrians, as was *Araunah (Ornan, *'rwnh*, *'wrnh*, 2 Sa. 24:16; *'rnn* (1 Ch. 21:18), the Hurrian word for 'the king/lord' (*ewirne*).

Hurrian, a non-Semitic (Caucasian?) language was spoken by a people who formed part of the indigenous population of N Syria and Upper Mesopotamia from *c.* 2300 BC. From the 18th century they are well attested at Mari and Alalaḫ as well as in the Hittite archives where from *c.* 1500 to 1380 BC Hurrian myths and literature are found. At this time the Hurrian kingdom of Mitanni, ruled by kings with Indo-Aryan names, corresponded with Egypt (*e.g.* Tušratta–Amenophis IV) and influenced Assyria (*e.g.* *NUZI). Hurrian personal names are found throughout Syro-Palestine (*ALALAH, *TAANACH, *SHECHEM) and some biblical names may best be considered of Hurrian origin: Anah, Ajah, Dishon, *Shamgar, Toi and Eliahba (D. J. Wiseman, *JTVI* 72, 1950, p. 6).

Hori was also the personal name both of an Edomite (Gn. 36:22; 1 Ch. 1:39) and of a Simeonite (Nu. 13:5).

BIBLIOGRAPHY. I. J. Gelb, *Hurrians and Subarians*, 1944; E. A. Speiser, *Introduction to Hurrian*, 1941; E. A. Speiser, *JWH* 1, 1953, pp. 311–327; H. G. Gütterbach, *JWH* 2, 1954, pp. 383–394; F. W. Bush, *A Grammar of the Hurrian Language*, 1967; H. A. Hoffner, *POTT*, 1973, pp. 221–226.

D.J.W.

HORMAH (Heb. *ḥormâh*). An important town in the Negeb, formerly Canaanite Zephath (destroyed by Judahites and Simeonites, Jdg. 1:17); its king is listed as defeated by Joshua (Jos. 12:14). The Israelite name 'sacred' recalled the sacrifice of the captured town under a national vow made after a previous defeat (Nu. 21:1–3); there is no clear link with Nu. 14:45, though AV follows Symmachus, Vulg., *et al.*, in emending 'way of Atharim' to 'way of the spies' (see *BDB*, *s.v.* Atharim).

Hormah was certainly linked with *Arad, but is not identical; *cf.* Jos. 12:14; Jdg. 1:16f. The sequence in Jos. 15:30f.; 19:4f. suggests that it was in the N of Simeon, towards Ziklag; W. F. Albright proposed Tell es-Sheri'ah as the only site in this area with extensive Late Bronze remains (*BASOR* 15, 1924). A more S location, at the limit of Canaanite pursuit towards Kadesh, is indicated by Nu. 14:45; Dt. 1:44. J. Garstang suggested Tell el-Milh (Tel Malhata), 22 km E of Beer-sheba (so S. Talmon, *IEJ* 15, 1965, p. 239; M. Kochavi, *RB* 79, 1972, pp. 543ff.; but *cf.* *EAEHL*, p. 771); but it now seems likely that this was Canaanite Arad ([illegible]). Recent excavations at and near Kh. el-Mesas (Tel Masos), 6 km to the W, revealed an extensive Israelite settlement, and Middle Bronze fortifications to the S; this may now be the most likely site for Hormah (Y. Aharoni, *IEJ* 22, 1972, p. 243; *BA* 39, 1976, pp. 66–76). J.P.U.L.

HORN (Heb. *qeren*; Gk. *keras*).

1. Used literally of the horns of the ram (Gn. 22:13; Dn. 8:3), the goat (Dn. 8:5), and the wild ox (Heb. *r^e'ēm*, Dt. 33:17; Pss. 22:21; 92:10; AV 'unicorn'). It was used as a receptacle for oil for ceremonial anointing (1 Sa. 16:1, 13; 1 Ki. 1:39). The ram's horn (*qeren hayyôḇēl*) was also used as a *musical instrument (Jos. 6:5; *cf.* 1 Ch. 25:5).

2. The horn-shaped protuberances on the four corners of the *altars in the tabernacle and Temple, an example of which has been found at Megiddo. The sacrificial blood was smeared on these (Ex. 29:12; Lv. 4:7, 18, *etc.*) and they were regarded as places of refuge (*cf.* the respective fates of Adonijah and Joab, 1 Ki. 1:50ff.; 2:28ff.).

3. Horns symbolized power, in Zedekiah's prophetic action (1 Ki. 22:11) and in Zechariah's vision (Zc. 1:18ff.), and often the word is metaphorically used in poetic writings. God exalts the horn of the righteous and cuts off the horn of the wicked (Ps. 75:10, *etc.*). He causes the horn of David to sprout (Ps. 132:17; *cf.* Ezk. 29:21). He is spoken of as 'the horn of my salvation' (2 Sa. 22:3; Ps. 18:2; *cf.* Lk.

Horned altar from Megiddo. The projections may have served originally to hold an incense-bowl. Height 0·54 m. 10th–9th cent. BC. (RS)

HORNET
See Animals, Part 1.

HORONITE
See Sanballat, Part 3.

HORSE LEECH
See Animals, Part 1.

1:69), but this may be a metaphor based on the horns of the *altar as the place of atonement. Am. 6:13 'horns' (AV) should be read as a place-name, Karnaim (so RSV).

4. In the peculiar apocalyptic usage of Dn. 7 and 8 and Rev. 13 and 17 the horns on the creatures in the visons represent individual rulers of each world-empire.

5. For 'ink-horn', see *WRITING.

J.B.Tr.

HORONAIM. A town of Moab (Is. 15:5; Je. 48:3, 5, 34) which lay at the foot of a plateau close to Zoar. The *Moabite Stone refers to it in line 32. Some would identify it with el-'Araq, 500 m below the plateau, where there are springs, gardens and caves. It may, however, be Oronae, taken by Alexander Jannaeus from the Arabs and restored to the Nabataean king by Alexander Jannaeus (Jos., *Ant.* 13. 397; 14. 18). J.A.T.

HOSANNA. The Gk. form of a Heb. term, used at the triumphal entry of Jesus into Jerusalem (Mt. 21:9, 15; Mk. 11:9; Jn. 12:13). The Heb. consists of the hiphil imperative *hôša'*, 'save', followed by the enclitic particle of entreaty *nā'*, sometimes translated 'pray', 'we beseech thee'. It does not occur in the OT except in the longer imperative form *hôšî'â nā'* in Ps. 118:25, where it is followed by the words, also quoted at the triumphal entry, 'Blessed be he who enters in the name of the Lord.' Ps. 118 was used in connection with the Feast of Tabernacles, and v. 25 had special significance as a cue for the waving of the branches (*lûlāḇ*); see Mishnah, *Sukkah* 3. 9; 4. 5. But similar expressions of religious enthusiasm were not restricted to the Feast of Tabernacles: 2 Macc. 10:6–7 implies that psalm-singing and branch-waving were part of the festivities at the Feast of Dedication also. We may reasonably assume that the waving of palm-branches and the cries of Hosanna which welcomed Jesus were a spontaneous gesture of religious exuberance, without any reference to a particular festival and without the supplicatory meaning of the original phrase in Ps. 118.

J.B.Tr.

HOSEA, BOOK OF. This first book in the collection of twelve small prophetic writings which conclude our OT comes from the 8th century BC and, along with Amos, is addressed to the N kingdom Israel, often called by Hosea Ephraim. There is every indication that the prophet had his home in the N and loved the land and its people. It was therefore all the more painful for him to have to issue rebukes and threats when appeals went unheeded. The intensity of his emotion may be gauged from his vivid use of language. He packs metaphors and similes into allusions which in his day were no doubt extremely telling, though their exact meaning sometimes escapes the modern reader. Changes of subject-matter are abrupt and, in the absence of introductory phrases, it is by no means self-evident where one passage ends and another begins. The material appears to have been arranged in roughly chronological order, and to recognize historical situations behind the prophet's words is to find an important aid to understanding.

I. Outline of contents

1:1 Title
1:2–9 The prophet's family before 752 BC
1:10–2:1 A sermon on his children's names
2:2–15 Unfaithful Israel, prosperous now but not for long
2:16–23 The Lord's new covenant
3:1–5 The Lord's love will have its way
4:1–5:7 Sweeping condemnations of pagan worship and its consequences
5:8–7:16 Panic at the encroachment of Assyria *c.* 733 BC
8:1–14 Religious and political disintegration
9:1–9 The despised prophet warns of exile
9:10–17 Their population will decline
10:1–8 Their altars will be in ruins
10:9–15 They will reap as they have sown
11:1–11 The Lord's love recoils from punishment
11:12–12:14 A sermon on Jacob the deceiver
13:1–16 Death is inevitable, exile is imminent *c.* 724 BC
14:1–8 The Lord's pledge to forgive those who return to him
14:9 Concluding exhortation

II. Historical setting

Though Hosea prophesied in Israel the opening verse mentions only one king, Jeroboam II, who reigned in Israel. His successors were deemed unworthy of mention and the period of Hosea's ministry is marked instead by the reigns of the corresponding kings in Judah. The period covered by the prophecy is the last 30 years of the N kingdom. After years of prosperity, reflected in the prophecy of Amos but seen by him as a gross abuse of God-given resources, decline set in suddenly after the death of Jeroboam II (753 BC). The highly confident, rollicking behaviour depicted in Hosea 4 and 5 suggests the earlier period of the prophet's ministry, when politically everything seemed set fair and there was a booming economy. At that time a prophecy of destruction must have seemed incredible.

As time went on the sequence of events should have reinforced the truth of the prophet's words, but habitual attitudes were not easily changed, even under threat of invasion. The armies of Assyria marched nearer and nearer to Israel during the reign of Tiglath-pileser III (745–727 BC), until in 743 Damascus was forced to pay tribute. Before the death of Menahem of Israel in 742/1 this same king records having received tribute from Israel. On a later occasion each man paid the price of a slave to avoid deportation (2 Ki. 15:19–20).

An attempt at revolt against Assyria was made by Pekah of Israel (740–732 BC) in alliance with Syria (Is. 7); even if Judah had joined the coalition the cause would still have been hopeless. Assyrian power was too great and in 732 Damascus fell to the enemy. At the same time Israel was invaded, her Galilean territory annexed, and many of her subjects taken captive (Ho. 7:8–9). It was during Hoshea's reign (732–723/2) that an appeal was made to Egypt (2 Ki. 17:4) in an attempt to find liberation from the Assyrian yoke (Ho. 9:3; 11:5; 12:1). The attempt was abortive, Hoshea was taken captive and in 722 Samaria fell after a siege of 3 years.

Despite the worsening political situation there was no change for the better in Israel's way of life, nor was there any desire to listen to the word of the prophet.

III. Israel's way of life

Unlike his contemporary Amos, Hosea laid much of the blame for Israel's collapse on the adoption of an alien life-style borrowed from Canaanite neighbours. By going after 'Baal', the prophet's shorthand for the pagan deity and all that he stood for, Israel committed herself to a system which affected not only worship. Every part of life, from work in the fields, the use of leisure and the presuppositions of social duties and commitments to political decisions and relationships, was bound up with it. The Baals were regarded as the source of fertility (2:5; 4:10) and of financial prosperity (2:8). To worship them demanded neither self-discipline nor high moral standards. Instead, orgiastic ritual at the shrines appealed to the sensual in human nature and militated against everything that the ancient covenant morality had stood for.

The leaders of the nation, kings, priests and merchants, were the major offenders in promoting this way of life (5:1–7). It had become the norm, whereas the prophet's passion for the right was regarded as slightly mad (9:7). If the powerful in the land were to take rebuke and initiate reform, the prophet had an unenviable task ahead of him. There is evidence that at the first sign of Assyria's encroachment there was some attempt at repentance (6:1–3), but it was superficial and did not begin to result in a reformed society.

Socially lawlessness and injustice reigned. Burglary and highway robbery, murder, drunkenness, intrigue (6:7–7:7) and all the consequent evils are noted by the prophet; but his concern is not merely to list sins and point an accusing finger. What grieves him and drives him to protest is the choice Israel has made, rejecting the Lord, to whom Israel was 'betrothed', for worthless gods which, far from bestowing prosperity, could bring only ruin to the land and its people.

IV. The involvement of the prophet

To Hosea's mind it was no accident that his own personal experience had prepared him to understand the profound truth of the Lord's undying love for Israel, despite the fact that Israel had rejected him. The way Hosea expresses this (1:2) raises problems for the modern reader. Whatever explanation a biographer might have revealed, looking back Hosea could see that his experience was no accident. The Lord was in it, preparing his servant for a ministry which he could not have exercised without that particular form of suffering.

His wife Gomer bore three children whose names spoke of the Lord's judgment: 'Jezreel', the place where Jehu's sword ended the dynasty of Omri (2 Ki. 9:23–10:17), 'Not pitied' and 'Not my people' (1:4–9). It seems that subsequently Gomer left her husband for the promiscuous life that came most easily to her, and that eventually, worn and no longer attractive, she found herself forsaken, only to be bought back by the husband she had deserted. After keeping her for a while in seclusion he would restore her to her place as his wife. The story is not told explicitly, for the point is not to intrigue us with human heart-break but to demonstrate the consistency of God's love. There are therefore differences of interpretation as to the prophet's action, but as regards Israel the Lord would provide a way back to himself after the discipline of exile, and 'Not my people' would again become 'Sons of the living God' (1:10).

To help him understand the situation Hosea drew on his knowledge of God's dealings with the Patriarchs, in particular with Jacob, who strove to get his own way, even to the extent of striving with God (12:2–14). Yet the Lord had his way even with this cunning man from whom the nation was descended. Just as Jacob brought exile upon himself, so Ephraim was preparing his own destruction. As in the case of Jacob this was not the end of the story, so the prophet saw that exile would not be the last word on Israel's guilt.

Hosea also knew the Exodus story and meditated on its significance for his own time (11:1–4). Like a father with wayward sons, the Lord went on making provision for his people, though they did not realize the source of their health and progress. The Lord's love, like that of a caring parent, continued despite his son's rebellion and rejection. Still he called Ephraim 'my people' (11:7). Conflict between the Lord's love and his need to chastise and destroy tore the very heart of God (11:8). Here the prophet comes very close to the NT revelation of God's love as seen in the cross.

Opposition from the authorities is hinted at in 9:7. Not surprisingly, in the light of the treatment of earlier prophets (1 Ki. 19:2; 22:8; Am. 7:12–13), Hosea was regarded as an interfering fool, who could be passed off as a madman, to be shut away if necessary. He identified with and shared the Lord's suffering to the extent that he shared his love.

V. Hosea's theology

Whereas Amos had a message for Israel's neighbours as well as for God's people, Hosea concentrates

Quotations from Hosea 2:8–9, 10–14 with commentary (4Q p Hos [a] *). Discovered in Qumran Cave 4 (Dead Sea Scrolls). Late 1st cent. BC.* (RM)

on the relationship between the Lord and Israel, bound together as they were by a covenant of which the name Yahweh was a pledge and token (12:9). The terms of the covenant are referred to in 13:4, where reference is made to the first commandment. Evidently the Ten Commandments were known. The name Yahweh occurs most frequently, and when Elohim is used it is almost always with the possessive, 'your God' or 'our God'. Four times Hosea uses El, the Holy One (11:9, 12), the living God (1:10), the Lord of hosts (12:5). Here the emphasis is on the incomparability of Israel's God.

On another level Hosea sees that Israel has brought trouble on her own head. The natural disasters and military defeats Israel had suffered resulted from the outworking of a providential law of cause and effect, though Hosea never spoke of this as operating in any mechanical way. It is the Lord himself who is at work in circumstances, secretly eating 'like a moth' ('festering sore', JB, NEB) to destroy, or 'like dry rot' to cause collapse (5:12). This law will operate till full judgment has been worked out. Harvests will fail (9:2), riches will prove useless to save (9:6), conception will not take place and even if it does children will be born only to become war fodder (9:11–14). Men must learn that the mysterious generative powers they possess and the reproductive life of plants and animals are not ultimately under human control. There is a built-in retribution which comes into play to check abuse.

Hosea uses outrageous similes in likening the Lord to a lion, a leopard and a she-bear robbed of her cubs (13:7–8). In each case the animal is doing no more and no less than by nature it was intended to do. Such was the Lord's love that he could do no less than roar and destroy and devour. He too had been robbed of the love of his people and raging Assyrian armies would literally tear and devour and carry away their prey. Thus historical events as well as the world of nature were seen to be directed according to the Lord's will.

Did Hosea's contemporaries regard the prophet's accusations as exaggerated, so that the punishment appeared altogether out of proportion to the crime? This may well have been so, hence Hosea's insistence that throughout their history, with the possible exception of the first flush of the Exodus deliverance (2:15; 11:1). Israel had been rebellious. As soon as they encountered Baal-worship in the wilderness their true nature became apparent (9:10; 13:16). King-making had been another sign of apostasy (13:10; *cf.* 9:15), and the prophet commented on the collapse of the monarchy as kings were murdered and replaced by usurpers (7:7; 8:4). History again proved to be working out the Lord's purpose, and its meaning could be discerned by the man in tune with God's word. The apostasy of Hosea's contemporaries was the culmination of a long history of such rebellion and now the time had come for the Lord to call a halt. Israel did not in fact know the Lord, though they claimed to know him (8:2). For this reason they misunderstood his dealings with them. Such estrangement could not be resolved, largely because no estrangement was admitted on Israel's side. Neither appeals nor threats made any impression and therefore punishment had to come.

Undoubtedly Israel had set much store by public worship. The repentance formula (6:1–3) may have been a well-known 'general confession', and there was no lack of worshippers at the shrines (4:13; 8:11). Sacrifices were offered and the ritual was observed, but there was only the most fleeting consciousness of any need of forgiveness, and therefore worship bore no fruit in changed lives (6:4–6). Knowledge of God would have brought home the enormity of the people's need of forgiveness and of positive response to the Lord's steadfast love. Without these there would never be justice and right dealing between men.

In the light of all this, what hope could Hosea hold out for his own time or for the future? He knew that the next stage would be exile and the destruction of all that Israel had held dear. Then access to their idols would no longer be open

(2:6), they would not be able to hold their festivals, and poverty would bring home to them their desperate need (2:9f.). This experience would drive them back to the Lord (2:7) and cause the 'wayward wife' to listen once more to his words of love (2:14). The result would be true repentance (3:5) and an enduring betrothal relationship (2:19–20).

Later in the book, when Assyria's sword was about to complete its work, the prophet found hope in meditation on the Exodus (12:13). Israel at that time had in no way merited deliverance, yet the Lord had worked through his prophet Moses to bring it about. They still had the same Lord (13:4) in whom alone was their hope (14:4). The anguish which the prophet saw actually to be involved in God's love was ultimately to issue in the incarnation and the cross. Jesus Christ would bear the penalty of estrangement on behalf of men and so open up the way back to communion with God. The confession of 14:1–3 would then become meaningful for men and promised blessing would become a reality (14:4–8). After that the Lord would find his lovingkindness returned.

BIBLIOGRAPHY. W. R. Harper, *Hosea*, *ICC*, 1905; N. H. Snaith, *Mercy and Sacrifice*, 1953; G. A. F. Knight, *Hosea*, 1960; W. Rudolph, *Hosea*, *KAT*, 1966; J. L. Mays, *Hosea*, 1969; H. McKeating, *Amos, Hosea, Micah*, 1971; H. W. Wolff, *Hosea*, E.T. 1974. J.G.B.

HOSHEA (Heb. *hôšēaʿ*). **1.** The original name of Joshua (Nu. 13:8; *cf.* Dt. 32:44) which was changed by Moses (Nu. 13:16).

2. An official placed by David over the Ephraimites (1 Ch. 27:20).

3. The son of Elah; the 20th and last king of the N kingdom of Israel, who wrested the throne from Pekah by assassinating him (2 Ki. 15:30) and reigned for 9 years (2 Ki. 17:1). During Pekah's reign (*c.* 733 BC), Tiglath-pileser III had overrun much of Israel and claims to have established Hoshea as a vassal on his throne (*ANET*, p. 284). Expecting support from the pharaoh So, Hoshea stopped paying tribute, leading to an advance by Shalmaneser V (724 BC). When Hoshea asked him for peace, Shalmaneser arrested him and occupied the land, finally capturing Samaria in 722 BC, bringing the N kingdom to an end (2 Ki. 17:3–6). Hoshea, whose death is not recorded, apparently sought to change the religious policies of his predecessors since he receives only a qualified censure of his reign (2 Ki. 17:2).

4. A witness to the people's covenant with Yahweh after the exile (Ne. 10:23). D.W.B.

HOSPITALITY. Throughout Scripture, the responsibility of caring for the traveller and those in need is largely taken for granted. Although examples are found right through the Bible, the only specific commands about providing hospitality concern the Christian's responsibility towards his fellow believer.

I. In the Old Testament

Comparison with modern bedouin tribes, among whom hospitality is very highly regarded, suggests that the prominence of hospitality in the OT is partly due to Israel's nomadic origins. Abraham's generosity towards the three strangers (Gn. 18:1–8) provides an excellent illustration of nomadic practice, and was often remembered in later Jewish writings for its exemplary character, though settled communities were no less welcoming to the stranger (Jdg. 13:15; 2 Ki. 4:8ff.)

Hospitality in the OT was more than just a custom, however. It was also a demonstration of faithfulness to God (Jb. 31:32; Is. 58:7). One might even entertain Yahweh (Gn. 18:1–8) or his angels (Jdg. 6:17–23; 13:15–21; *cf.* Heb. 13:2), while God in his turn held a feast on the day of the Lord to which guests were invited (Zp. 1:7). The divine provision of *cities of refuge (Nu. 35:9–35; Jos. 20:1–9) and concern for the sojourner (Ex. 22:21; Lv. 19:10; Dt. 10:19) indicate the extent of OT hospitality.

Failure to provide for the traveller's needs was a serious offence, liable to punishment by God (Dt. 23:3–4) and man (1 Sa. 25:2–38; Jdg. 8:5–17). The use of *pešaʿ* (1 Sa. 25:28), a term employed for transgression of covenants, indicates the importance attached to such obligations. The unique breach of hospitality by Jael (Jdg. 4:11–21; 5:24–27) could be commended only because of her unwavering loyalty to old family ties and to Yahweh. Some invitations were better refused, however, since they might result in spiritual ruin (Pr. 9:18).

Though hospitality was extended to all, a particular responsibility existed to provide for one's own family (Gn. 29:1–14; Jdg. 19:10–12; Is. 58:7) and for God's servants (2 Sa. 17:27–29; 1 Ki. 17:10ff.; 2 Ki. 4:8ff.). A future son-in-law might be entertained as a guest, though this is known only as a Midianite custom (Ex. 2:20). The peace agreement between Heber the Kenite and Jabin of Hazor seems to have included a mutual obligation to provide hospitality (Jdg. 4:11–21).

That a host was responsible for the safety and welfare of his guests is vividly illustrated by Lot and by the old man of Gibeah (Gn. 19:8; Jdg. 19:24–25). The immorality of the communities in which both lived suggests that their disregard for their daughters was due more to the prevailing moral climate than to the requirements of the hospitality oath.

A stranger would wait at the city-gate for an offer of hospitality (Gn. 19:1; Jdg. 19:15), though the well also formed a suitable meeting-place (Gn. 24:14ff.; Ex. 2:20). Sometimes hospitality might be given in return for an earlier kindness (Ex. 2:20; 2 Sa. 19:32–40). Bread and water was the minimum provision (Dt. 23:4; 1 Ki. 17:10–11), though such meagre fare was often exceeded. A guest's feet were washed from the dust of travel (Gn. 18:4; 19:2; 24:32; Jdg. 19:21), and his head sometimes anointed with oil (Ps. 23:5; Am. 6:6; *cf.* Lk. 7:46). The best *food might be presented (Gn. 18:5; 1 Sa. 25:18), and meat, rarely eaten in the E, specially procured (Gn. 18:7; Jdg. 6:19; 13:15; *cf.* Lk. 15:23). Curds and milk also particularly refreshed the traveller (Gn. 18:8; Jdg. 5:25). Animal fodder was supplied when required (Gn. 24:14, 32; Jdg. 19:21), while Elisha even received furnished accommodation (2 Ki. 4:10).

II. In the New Testament

The Gk. terms used are *philoxenia* (lit. 'love of strangers'), *cf.* *xenizō*, 'to receive as a guest', also *synagō* (Mt. 25:35ff.) and *lambanō* (3 Jn. 8).

Many aspects of OT hospitality reappear in the NT. The courtesies of providing water for a guest's feet and oil for his head continue, though the NT also mentions a kiss of welcome and guests reclining at a meal (Lk. 7:44ff.). In fact, Simon the Pharisee's home appears to have been an open house, judging by the way in which the presence of the woman who anointed Jesus was unconsciously accepted (Lk. 7:37ff.).

A special responsibility towards God's servants is also evident, and Jesus' earthly ministry (Mk. 1:29ff.; 2:15ff.; Lk. 7:36ff.; 10:38–41) and the apostles' missionary labours (Acts 10:6ff.; 16:15; 17:7) were greatly dependent on the hospitality they received. The NT develops this by regarding the giving or refusing of hospitality to Jesus and his followers as an indication of one's acceptance or rejection of the gospel (Mt. 10:9; Lk. 10:4), even at the final judgment (Mt. 25:34–46). These Christian responsibilities, however, are no more than a pale reflection of divine generosity. Jesus both spoke of the parable of the Great Supper (Mt. 22:2ff.; Lk. 14:16ff.) and gave the disciples an example to follow (Jn. 13:1ff.). Above all, he took the obligations of hospitality to the extreme by laying down his life to redeem his guests (Mk. 10:45; 14:22ff.).

The NT letters specifically command the provision of hospitality for fellow believers (*e.g.* Gal. 6:10). The existence of certain special factors in the 1st century AD emphasized the importance of these instructions. Persecution led to Christians being scattered and driven from their homes, and in many cases there was doubtless very real material need (Acts 8:1; 11:19). Itinerant preachers were also a charge upon the church. They received nothing from the pagan world (3 Jn. 7), and therefore became the responsibility of local Christians (Acts 9:43; 16:15; 18:3, 7), even though risks might be involved (Acts 17:5–9). Sometimes

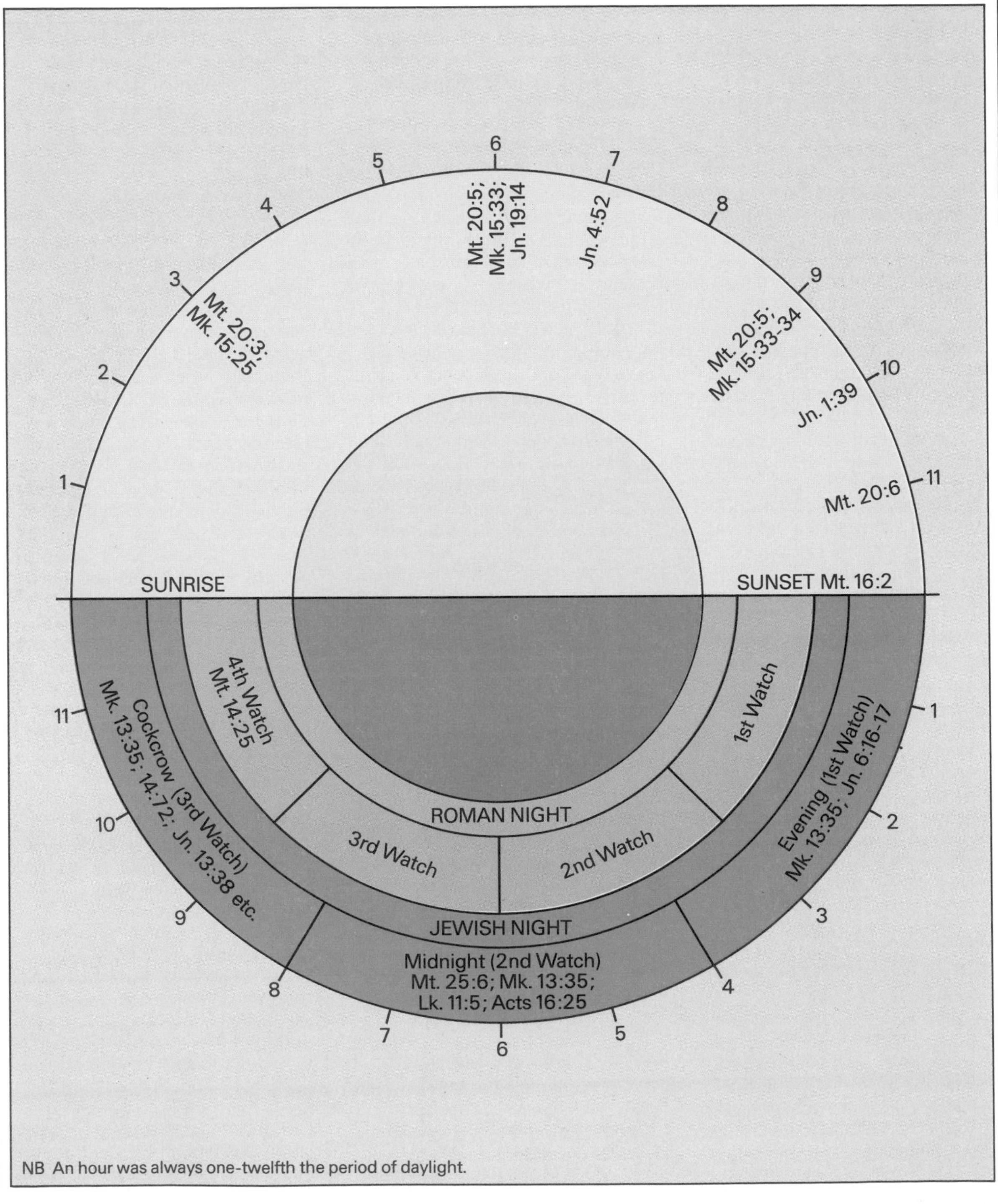

Biblical divisions of time, showing the night-watches. The hours (around the perimeter) will vary in length as they are calculated according to the times of sunrise and sunset.

the hosts would be the evangelists' own converts (3 Jn. 5–7). False teachers, however, were to be turned away (2 Jn. 10), and letters of recommendation served to identify genuine cases (Rom. 16:1; 2 Cor. 3:1). Many inns of the time were also of low standard, both materially and morally, and the Christian traveller would often have found them unattractive.

The 'pursuit' of hospitality (Rom. 12:13) was obligatory for the Christian, who must ensure that the needs of fellow believers were properly met, though hospitality was to be offered to all (Rom. 12:13–14; Gal. 6:10). Thus Paul instructs the Colossian church to receive Mark (Col. 4:10), and assumes that Philemon will prepare a room for Paul when he is released from prison (Phm. 22). The duty of providing hospitality was also one of the special qualifications of a *bishop (1 Tim. 3:2; Tit. 1:8), and of a *widow requiring support from the church (1 Tim. 5:10).

Although hospitality was a mark of civilization for the Greeks, and the NT contains an excellent example of non-Christian generosity (Acts 28:7), hospitality in the NT had a specifically Christian character. It was to be offered freely, without grudging (1 Pet. 4:9) and in a spirit of brotherly love (Heb. 13:1). Such love (*agapē*: 1 Pet. 4:8; *cf.* Rom. 12:9) is essentially outward-looking, issuing in a readiness to provide for the needs of others, and could be demonstrated only because the giver had received a gift (*charisma*) from God (1 Pet. 4:10–11). The care of others was therefore the discharge of a debt of gratitude.

III. The biblical inn

OT references to a 'lodging place' (*mālôn*) are rare (Gn. 42:27; 43:21; Ex. 4:24; Je. 9:2) and specific locations are confined to routes linking Egypt and Palestine or Midian. Nothing is known of these places, though one of them was large enough to accommodate a sudden influx of nine travellers (Gn. 42:27). The LXX equivalent *katalyma* and the cognate verb *katalyō* suggest the idea of unharnessing the animals, though it usually conveyed the general sense of lodging. Bethlehem's inn (*katalyma*) may have been a fairly simple lodging-place. It was probably not a guest-room in a private house, as no name is given, and may have been the village's common responsibility. Elsewhere *katalyma* describes a room in a private residence borrowed for the Passover meal (Mk. 14:14; Lk. 22:11; *cf.* Lk. 19:7). The *pandocheion* of Lk. 10:34 is more developed, being open to anyone and providing overnight shelter, food and attention for a recognized charge, while *xenia* is used both for Philemon's guest-room and the place of Paul's house-arrest in Rome (Phm. 22; Acts 28:23).

BIBLIOGRAPHY. J. Pedersen, *Israel* 1–2, 1926, pp. 356–358; D. W. Riddle, *JBL* 57, 1938, pp. 141–154; G. Stählin, *TDNT* 5, pp. 17–25; A. D. Kilmer, *Ugarit Forschungen* 3, 1971, pp. 299–309; W. Günther and C. Brown, *NIDNTT* 2, pp. 547–550.

M.J.S.

HOST, HOST OF HEAVEN. In RSV, the word most commonly translated 'host' is *ṣāḇā'*, used nearly 400 times. *ḥayil* is also translated 'host' a number of times (but see *ARMY), while *maḥ^aneh* ('host' in AV) is translated 'camp' or 'encampment'. Each of these words, with due regard to its special emphasis, may be used quite neutrally, for example of pharaoh's 'host' but equally of the 'host' of Israel. However, when used of the host of Israel, there are usually religious overtones, and there are two exclusively religious uses of *ṣāḇā* which ought to be noted.

a. Host of heaven

This phrase (*ṣ^eḇā' haššāmayim*) occurs about 15 times, in most cases implying the object of heathen worship (Dt. 4:19, *etc.*). The two meanings 'celestial bodies and 'angelic beings' are inextricably intertwined. The LXX translation, using *kosmos*, *stratia* or *dynamis*, does not help to resolve this. No doubt to the Heb. mind the distinction was superficial, and the celestial bodies were thought to be closely associated with heavenly beings. In fact, the implied angelology of C. S. Lewis' novels (*Out of the Silent Planet*, *etc.*) would probably have commended itself with some force to the biblical writers. The Bible certainly suggests that angels of different ranks have charge of individuals and of nations; no doubt in the light of modern cosmology this concept, if retained at all (as biblically it must be), ought properly to be extended, as the dual sense of the phrase 'host of heaven' suggests, to the oversight of the elements of the physical universe—planets, stars and nebulae.

b. Lord of hosts (*Yahweh ṣ^eḇā'ôṯ*)

This expression is used nearly 300 times in the OT and is especially common in Isaiah, Jeremiah, Zechariah and Malachi. It is a title of might and power, used frequently in a military or apocalyptic context. It is significant that the first occurrence is 1 Sa. 1:3 in association with the sanctuary at Shiloh. 'Of hosts' is rendered in LXX either by transliteration as *sabaōth* (*cf.* Rom. 9:29; Jas. 5:4) or by use of *pantokratōr* ('almighty'). It is thought by some to have arisen as a title of God associated with his lordship over the 'host' of Israel; but its usage, especially in the prophets, clearly implies also a relationship to the 'host of heaven' in its angelic sense; and this could well be the original connotation. (*GOD, NAMES OF.) M.T.F.

HOUR (Heb., Aram. *šā'â*; Gk. *hōra*) is used in Scripture in a precise sense and in a more general sense.

1. In its more precise sense (which is probably later than the more general sense), an hour is one-twelfth of the period of daylight: 'Are there not twelve hours in the day?' (Jn. 11:9). They were reckoned from sunrise to sunset, just as the three (Jewish) or four (Roman) watches into which the period of darkness was divided were reckoned from sunset to sunrise. As sunrise and sunset varied according to the time of the year, biblical hours cannot be translated exactly into modern clock-hours; and in any case the absence of accurate chronometers meant that the time of day was indicated in more general terms than with us. It is not surprising that the hours most frequently mentioned are the third, sixth and ninth hours. All three are mentioned in the parable of the labourers in the vineyard (Mt. 20:3, 5), as is also the eleventh hour (vv. 6, 9), which has become proverbial for the last opportunity. The two disciples of Jn. 1:35ff. stayed with Jesus for the remainder of the day after going home with him, 'for it was about the tenth hour' (v. 39), *i.e.* about 4 p.m., and darkness would have fallen before they concluded their conversation

HOSTAGE
See Surety, Part 3.

HOUGH
See Animals, Part 1.

with him. The third, sixth and ninth hours are mentioned in the Synoptic record of the crucifixion (Mk. 15:25, 33f.). The difficulty of reconciling the 'sixth hour' of Jn. 19:14 with the 'third hour' of Mk. 15:25 has led some to suppose that in John the hours are counted from midnight, not from sunrise. The one concrete piece of evidence in this connection—the statement in the *Martyrdom of Polycarp* (21) that Polycarp was martyred 'at the eighth hour', where 8 a.m. is regarded by some as more probable than 2 p.m.—is insufficient to set against the well-attested fact that Romans and Jews alike counted their hours from sunrise. (The fact that the Romans reckoned their civil day as starting at midnight, while the Jews reckoned theirs as starting at sunset, has nothing to do with the numbering of the hours.) The 'seventh hour' of Jn. 4:52 is 1 p.m.; such difficulty as is felt about the reference to 'yesterday' in that verse is not removed by interpreting the hour differently. In Rev. 8:1 'half an hour' represents Gk. *hēmiōrion.*

2. More generally, 'hour' indicates a fairly well-defined point of time. 'In the same hour' (Dn. 5:5, AV, RV; 'immediately', RSV) means 'while the king and his guests were at the height of their sacrilegious revelry'. 'In the selfsame hour' (Mt. 8:13, AV) means 'at that very moment (RSV) when Jesus assured the centurion that his plea to have his servant healed was granted'. Frequently some specially critical occasion is referred to as an 'hour' *e.g.* the hour of Jesus' betrayal (Mk. 14:41; *cf.* Lk. 22:53, 'your hour', *i.e.* 'your brief season of power'); the hour of his parousia, with the attendant resurrection and judgment (Mt. 25:13; Jn. 5:28f.). In John the appointed time for Jesus' passion and glorification is repeatedly spoken of as his 'hour' (*cf.* Jn. 2:4; 7:30; 8:20; also 12:23; 17:1). The present situation between the times is 'the last hour' (1 Jn. 2:18); the rise of many antichrists indicates that Christ is soon to appear.

BIBLIOGRAPHY. W. M. O'Neil, *Time and the Calendars*, 1975; H.-C. Hahn, *NIDNTT* 3, pp. 845–850. F.F.B.

HOUSE (Heb. *bayiṯ*; Gk. *oikos, oikia*). The Heb. and Gk. words are used with reference to various kinds of buildings and also in the sense of 'household, family'. Particularly in the NT, the 'house of God' is developed into an important theological concept. Architectural information in the Bible has been supplemented considerably by the results of archaeological excavation, though a complete picture of the houses people lived in is still not available for every period.

I. Old Testament

Heb. *bayiṯ*, which occurs over 2,000 times, is cognate with a nominal form occurring in many Semitic languages. It has a wide use in the OT for all kinds of dwellings, from palaces (*e.g.* Je. 39:8) and temples (*e.g.* 1 Ki. 8:13) to private houses (*e.g.* Ex. 12:7; Dt. 6:7) and possibly even tents (Gn. 33:17). Houses were usually constructed of solid materials, stone, timber and plaster (Lv. 14:37, 39, 45; Am. 5:11), and were often built into the city wall (Jos. 2:15). Some were of excellent quality (Dt. 8:12; Hg. 1:4), such as David's cedar palace (2 Sa. 7:2, 7; *cf.* 1 Ki. 7:2; Is. 22:8) or the luxurious ivory-decorated houses of Samaria (1 Ki. 22:39; Am. 3:15). *bayiṯ* is often combined with other nouns to indicate either a specialized building or part of a building, *e.g.* winter and summer houses (Je. 36:22; Am. 3:15), prisons (Gn. 39:20ff.; 2 Ki. 25:27), the Persian king's harem (Est. 2:9ff.) and above all the Jerusalem Temple ('house of God', 1 Ch. 9:11, 13, 26; 'house of Yahweh', 1 Ki. 7:12, 40–41). It is also used in other combinations to describe the quality or character of life in a house or building, *e.g.* pleasantness, mirth (Ezk. 26:12; Mi. 2:9; Ec. 7:4), mourning (Je. 16:5; Ec. 7:2, 4) and rebelliousness (Ezk. 2:5–6). By extension, *bayiṯ* can sometimes signify the 'homes' of various animals (sparrow, Ps. 84:3–4; stork, Ps. 104:17; spider's web, Jb. 8:14; moth, Jb. 27:18; wild ass, Jb. 39:5–6; calf, 1 Sa. 6:7, 10), and is also used for various receptacles such as an altar trench (1 Ki. 18:32), perfume containers (Is. 3:20) and holders for poles (Ex. 25:27). Occasionally, it refers to the transitoriness of the human body (Jb. 4:19; *cf.* 2 Cor. 5:1–10), and even to *Sheol (Jb. 38:20).

An important sense of *bayiṯ*, found in over a quarter of the total references, is that of 'household, family', which can include those living in tents (Nu. 16:32; Dt. 11:6). The frequent phrases 'father's house' and 'house of Israel' are both associated with the biblical concept by which a family, tribe or nation derives its name from an ancestor or leader. Finally, 'house' can designate both persons (including slaves) and property (Gn. 39:1–2; Ex. 20:17; 1 Ki. 13:8) belonging to a household.

II. New Testament

Much of the OT usage is continued in the NT. *oikos* has both literal and figurative meanings, with 'household, family, race' in addition to 'house'. The rarer *oikia* is largely synonymous with *oikos* in the NT, though it sometimes has the specialized meaning 'possession', notably in the distinctive phrase 'devour widows' houses' (Mk. 12:40). 'House' often occurs in the NT with reference to the Temple, both in its earthly and heavenly forms. For example, Jesus spoke in both senses of 'my Father's house' (*cf.* Jn. 2:16; 14:2), which was to be an international prayer-house (Mk. 11:15–17; *cf.* Is. 56:7; 60:7, LXX) rather than a 'house of trade' (Jn. 2:16; *cf.* Zc. 14:21).

A most important development of the idea of 'God's house' was its application to the church (*e.g.* Eph. 2:19–22; Heb. 3:1–6), whose communal character was emphasized in the concepts of the 'spiritual house' (1 Pet. 2:5) and God's temple (1 Cor. 3:16; 6:19). In contrast to the pagan temples and even the stone Temple in Jerusalem, the believers were 'living stones' (1 Pet. 2:5) in a temple built by Jesus, God's Son (Heb. 3:3, 6). In this house of God, the pillar of the truth (1 Tim. 3:15), all believers are priests (1 Pet. 2:5, 9) offering continual sacrifices (Heb. 13:15–16), obedient to God, without fear of final judgment (1 Pet. 4:17).

The theme of the 'household of God' undoubtedly owed much to the function of the house in early Christianity as a place of meeting and fellowship (*e.g.* 2 Tim. 4:19; Phm. 2; 2 Jn. 10). Whole households turned to the Lord (*e.g.* Acts 16:34; 1 Cor. 1:16), and the breaking of bread (Acts 2:46), evangelism (Acts 5:42) and teaching (Acts 20:20) were conducted 'from house to house'.

III. Archaeology

a. General

The large majority of houses in ancient Palestine were built in fortified cities, though there were also many dependent villages. Even the farmer often lived in the city, although he might camp out at harvest-time, and threshing-floors were always near the city. Large cities might cover an area of 20 acres, though most towns or villages probably did not average more than about 6 acres. Houses were usually packed closely together, particularly if the city was built on a hill, so that space was used economically. Town planning is known as early as the mid-3rd millennium BC, and during the Israelite period towns were often arranged with a central complex of houses encircled by a street and a wall with houses attached (*e.g.* Tell beit Mirsim, Tell en-Nasbeh). Larger houses were often on the W side of a city, to escape from smoke and dirt carried by the prevailing W winds.

Foundations varied according to the size and importance of the house, though they were important both because of the severe effects of heavy rain (*cf.* Mt. 7:24–27) and because Palestine is an earthquake area. The foundations sometimes went down into virgin soil, or even to the bedrock in the case of large houses, though in many instances remains of earlier walls and foundations were used in the building of new houses. If the ground was sloping, foundation layers were set on level terraces. The foundation layer often provided a ground plan for the house. The laying of foundations might be accompanied by human sacrifice (Jos. 6:26; 1 Ki. 16:34), but there is no widespread evidence of this horrific practice.

The walls of private houses were usually built of rough stone and mud-brick; where stone was scarce, the entire house was of mud-brick on stone foundations. The mud-bricks were coated with waterproof plaster on the inner faces of the wall, sometimes up to only half the height of the wall, while floors were made of marly clay, which can withstand hard use from bare feet. In the case of richer houses, the floor was sometimes paved, even in the courtyard. Strengthening of walls was sometimes achieved by placing hewn-stone pilasters at the corners and at regular intervals along the walls, or during the Divided Monarchy by stone pilasters laid horizontally, particularly in the upper parts of the wall. Walls could be up to 1 m thick, though interior walls were often thinner.

Doors were fixed in a frame of two doorposts, lintel, and still or threshold. The doorway was

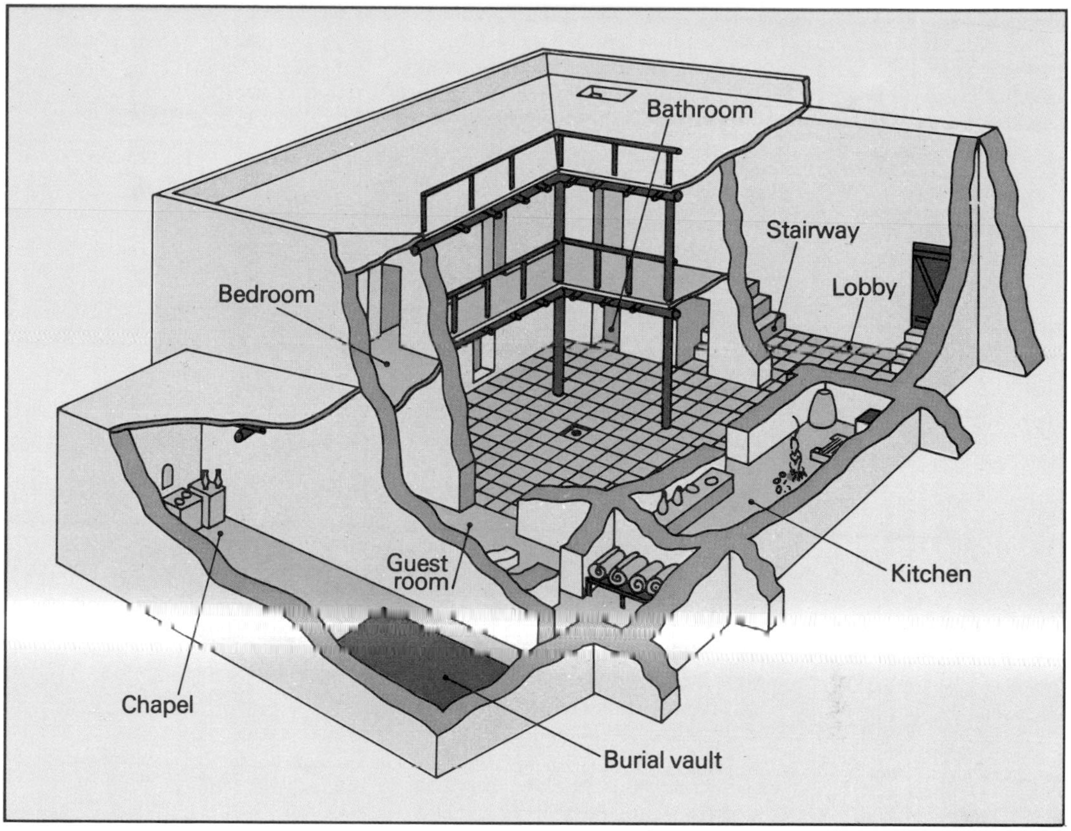

Reconstruction of a two-storey house with its paved central courtyard and flat roof surrounded by a parapet. Based on housed of c. 1800 BC, excavated at Ur, possibly contemporary with Abraham.

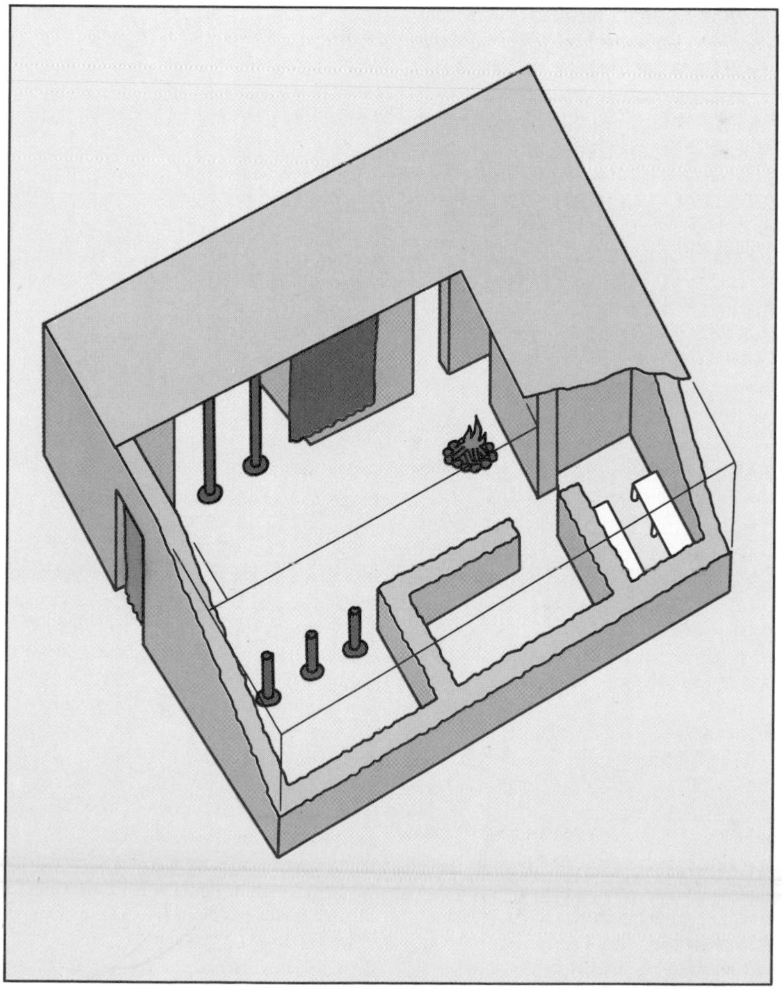

Cutaway reconstruction of a typical Israelite house with four rooms grouped round the central courtyard. Excavated at Tell el-Farah.

usually lower than a man's height, and the door usually opened inwards, being prevented from swinging outwards by ridges on the lintel and threshold. The latter also served to keep out water and dirt. Doorposts were of wood (Ex. 21:6; Dt. 15:17) or stone (Is. 6:4), and the door could be locked or bolted (*cf.* 2 Sa. 13:17–18).

Windows are known from the 4th millennium BC onwards in Palestine. They were rarely on the ground floor, as the open door furnished plenty of light during most of the year, and were usually placed in the wall opposite the entrance. Window-space was kept to a minimum to keep the temperature down in summer and up in winter. Assyrian wall-reliefs of the Israelite city Lachish show windows high in the towers of the outer wall, and such windows in city walls provided a means of escape more than once (Jos. 2:15; 1 Sa. 19:12). Ivory carvings from various sites portraying a woman's face at a balustraded window may be related to the lattice windows of the OT which were located in outside walls (Jdg. 5:28; 2 Ki. 1:2; Pr. 7:6; Ct. 2:9).

Many houses had two storeys, though, since no building in ancient Israel has yet been preserved with a complete roofed ground floor or ceiling, the original height of a building is not always certain.

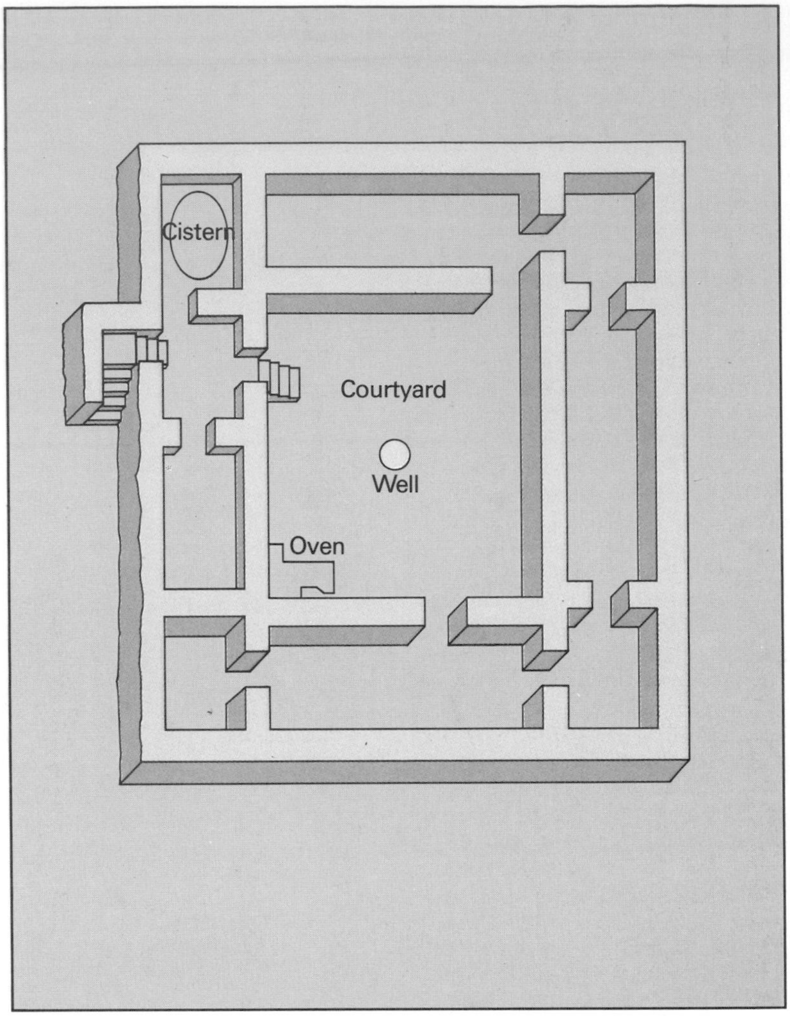

Ground plan of a villa of the early 2nd millennium BC in Palestine. Stairs lead to the upper floor and main living-rooms from the central courtyard.

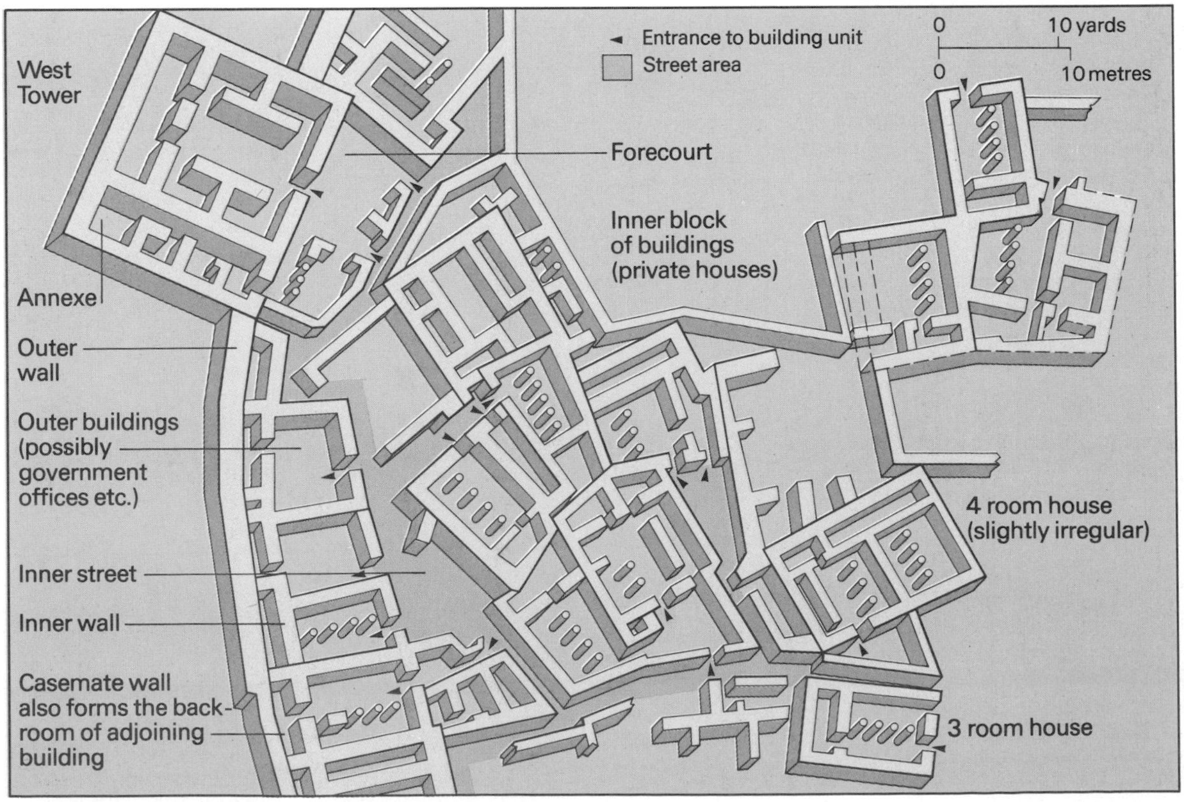

Town planning at Tell beit Mirsim in 8th–7th cent. BC Palestine. Typical four-roomed houses are grouped in blocks or ranged against the surrounding city walls.

Upper rooms were reached by stairs or ladders. These rooms provided the main living and sleeping accommodation (*cf.* 2 Ki. 9:13, 17), and guests could also be looked after there (1 Ki. 17:19; 2 Ki. 4:10–11). Roofs were constructed from beams covered with branches and a thick layer of mud plaster, though the rafters were sometimes supported by a row of pillars along the middle of the room. Cylindrical stone rollers about 60 cm long were used to keep the roofs flat and waterproof, though roofs needed to be replastered annually prior to the rainy season to seal cracks which had developed during the summer heat. The family would often sleep on the roof in summer or use it to dry raisins, figs, flax, *etc.*, in the sun. A parapet was to be built as a safety precaution according to Dt. 22:8. Vaulted roofs were certainly in use in Palestine by the Persian period, while the tiled roof also appeared before NT times. The rooftop was also a place of worship, either for Baal and especially the host of heaven (Je. 19:13; Zp. 1:5), or for the true God (Acts 10:9).

Reconstruction of furnishings in a room of the Middle Bronze Age at Jericho. (JEF)

b. Life in the house

The house during most of the biblical period was usually a dwelling-place, store-room, and even had industrial and commercial purposes. There is evidence of dyeing, weaving and corn-grinding in houses, while at Jericho there is some indication that grain was sold from narrow booths attached to exterior house-walls. The farmer lived in the house, with everything he owned. Foods sufficient for the winter, fodder for the animals, storage jars and farm tools were all kept in the house. Archaeologists have been surprised by the amount of carbonaceous matter found in these houses, especially in those destroyed by Joshua's troops. In very cold, wet weather and in times of war, the family would also have to share the house, or at least the courtyard, with the most valuable of the animals. Religious objects have also been found in many houses, such as horned altars, incense stands, braziers and figurines. Many inhabitants undoubtedly followed local practices in contrast to the official worship of Yahweh.

The furniture in the house varied with the wealth of the inhabitants. The poor could afford only kitchen equipment and bedding. The furniture in the guest-room given to Elisha would be typical of that used in the average family (2 Ki. 4:10). It

The furniture and pottery excavated in this tomb at Jericho probably represent that normally used by a typical wealthy household. (JEF)

consisted of a bed, table, chair and a lamp. The rich used a high bed, others a cot, while the poorest used a reed mat on the floor. Plenty of bedding was necessary, for Palestine's winters are cold and damp. There would be chests to hold clothes and bedding. The furniture of the wealthy was inlaid with ivory, and others sometimes imitated this in common bone inlay. The ivory inlays in turn were sometimes inlaid with gold and precious stones. The hand-loom would also be found in many homes.

In winter, to keep the house warm, the cooking was often done indoors, and in the coldest weather a pottery or copper brazier filled with burning charcoal was used, though this was not very efficient. An oven was usually built in the courtyard of the house. Hollow at the top, it could be about 60 cm in diameter at the base and about 30 cms in height, and was often shaped of alternate layers of clay and potsherds. Inside the house were stone or clay storage-silos. Large jars were employed for keeping the winter's supplies, and there was a mill for grinding the grain. Flour was kept in a wide-mouthed jar, and olive oil was stored in a specially designed vessel. Often there was a large stone mortar set in the floor, where various foods could be prepared by grinding with a pestle. If there was no cistern in the house, a large jar for storing water was at hand, with smaller jars to carry water from the spring. Wide-mouthed cooking-pots for stirring food and narrow-mouthed ones for heating liquids have been found, along with a wide variety of bowls used in serving foods. The rich used gold and silver tableware, and copper kitchen kettles. Am. 6:4–6 describes the luxurious life of Israel at its worst.

c. Developments in architecture

(i) *Pre-Israelite period.* The oldest houses in Palestine were sturdy one-room structures mainly of circular or rectangular design. Two-room houses appear *c.* 5000 BC at Jericho, while some Chalcolithic houses with artistic representations on the walls have been preserved. By the 3rd millennium BC, two-room houses, usually rectangular, were much commoner, though the largest known house of this period is at et-Tell (Ai?), being *c.* 18 m long and containing three equal rectangular rooms. Apsidal houses are also found at several sites in the early 3rd millennium, and may have been a native Canaanite type of house.

During the resurgence of urban life in the Middle Bronze Age, the courtyard-based house became widespread in Palestine, though the poor continued to live in single-room hovels. Rooms were built on one or more sides of the courtyard, though rooms on all four sides are rare in Palestine. A large house dating to *c.* 1600 BC has been uncovered at Tell beit Mirsim (Debir?), where the courtyard alone measured 11 × 6 m and the six roofed rooms on two floors covered a floor-space of *c.* 140 sq. m. A more complex example of about a century earlier from Ta'anach had good-quality walls 1 m thick, neatly-plastered floors, an internal staircase, and the ground floor measured *c.* 210 sq. m.

(ii) *Israelite period.* Where the Israelites replaced Canaanite towns, the quality of housing was noticeably poorer, though standards improved rapidly in the days of David and Solomon, partly through Phoenician influence. The most striking difference of all is the absence of Canaanite cult-objects in the period immediately following the Conquest. The poorest houses comprised a single room with a courtyard, of which many examples were found at Tell Qasile. The commonest-type house, however, of the pre-exilic period is what has become known generally as the four-room house, which appears to be an original Israelite concept. It was rectangular in design, and had a fixed arrangement of a back room, running the width of the building, which was joined to three parallel rooms stemming from it. The central 'room' was usually an enclosed courtyard through which the other rooms were entered, and the lateral rooms were often divided into two and closed off by pillars. The quality of such houses varied enormously, but the same basic plan was used for monumental and public buildings, *e.g.* at Hazor, Tell beit Mirsim.

(iii) *Hellenistic period.* Some Hellenistic cities of Palestine show a definite attempt at city planning on the rectangular pattern. The wealthy now added a bathroom to their houses. By NT times the rich were making a winter paradise out of Jericho, more luxurious than even Pompeii. It was spread over a wider area and had spacious gardens. The wealthy house of NT times in Palestine was similar to the Roman house everywhere. There was an outer court with its surrounding rooms, and behind it a second court with its adjacent rooms. In this latter area there was the utmost privacy.

(iv) *Royal palaces.* The OT gives only a brief description of Solomon's palace, but the detailed account of the building of the Temple enables us to conjecture what the palace looked like, for it was designed by the same architects and constructed by the same craftsmen. The masonry was of fine dressed stone laid in headers and stretchers. Fine woods, finished to show off their textures, were used for interior decoration. The excavation of the governor's palace at Megiddo has thrown light on Solomon's building programme. The palace of the Omri dynasty at Samaria was also built by Phoenician workmen. Here the king lived apart from his people in a citadel, built with very strong walls, and at least partially insulated from the poverty of much of his population. The beautiful ivory inlays are an indication of the luxurious style of living (*cf.* Am. 6:4–6), in marked contrast to the poorer areas of the city. Herod's palace in Jerusalem, with its extensive gardens, was the last word in luxury, as was also his winter palace at Jericho.

BIBLIOGRAPHY. H. K. Beebe, *BA* 31, 1968, pp. 38–58; Y. Shiloh, *IEJ* 20, 1970, pp. 180–190; H. A. Hoffner, *TDOT* 2, 1977, pp. 107–116; O. Michel, *TDNT* 5, 1968, pp. 119–134; S. M. Paul and W. G. Dever (eds.), *Biblical Archaeology*, 1973; A. C. Bouquet, *Everyday Life in New Testament Times*, 1955.

M.J.S.

HOUSE-ARREST
See Prison, Part 3.

HOUSE-CHURCH
See Worship, Part 3.

HOUSEHOLD
See Family, Part 1.

HOUSE OF EDEN
See Eden, house of, Part 1.

HOZAI. The name of a history, translated in RSV as 'the Seers', quoted in 2 Ch. 33:19, RV, which recorded certain of the deeds of King Manasseh, and his prayer. The translation 'the Seers' for 'Hozai' follows LXX, which presupposes a Heb. text *ḥōzim*. The *MT ḥôzai* means 'my seers'.

R.A.H.G.

HUKKOK. A town on the S border of Naphtali, listed with Aznoth-tabor (Jos. 19:34). Generally identified with Yakuk, 8 km W of the suggested site of Capernaum. 1 Ch. 6:75 gives it as a Levitical city in Asher, but this may be a mistake for Helkath as in the parallel passage, Jos. 21:31. Y. Aharoni, *LOB*, p. 378, proposed Khirbet el-Jemeijmeh. J.D.D. A.R.M.

HULDAH. This prophetess, wife of Shallum, keeper of the wardrobe (either of priestly vestments or royal robes), lived in the second (western?) quarter of Jerusalem. She was consulted (*c.* 621 BC), on behalf of King Josiah, by Hilkiah the chief priest, Shaphan the scribe and others, following the discovery of 'the book of the law in the house of the Lord' (2 Ki. 22:14; 2 Ch. 34:22). She accepted the book as the word of Yahweh, and with his authority prophesied judgment against Jerusalem and Judah after Josiah's death. It is noteworthy that, although both Jeremiah and Zephaniah were prophesying at this time, it is she who was approached on this matter of the cultus. M.B.

HUMILITY. The importance of this virtue springs from the fact that it is found as part of the character of God. In Ps. 113:5–6 God is represented as being incomparably high and great, and yet he humbles himself to take note of the things which are created, while in Ps. 18:35 (*cf.* 2 Sa. 22:36) the greatness of God's servant is attributed to the humility (gentleness) which God has displayed towards him.

Wherever the quality is found in the OT it is praised (*e.g.* Pr. 15:33; 18:12) and God's blessing is frequently poured upon those who possess it. Moses is vindicated because of it (Nu. 12:3), while Belshazzar is reproved by Daniel (5:22) because he has not profited by the experience of Nebuchadrezzar before him, which might have brought him into an attitude of humility. 2 Ch. in particular makes it the criterion by which the rule of successive kings is to be judged.

The term is closely connected in derivation with affliction, which is sometimes brought upon men by their fellows, and sometimes attributed directly to the purpose of God, but is always calculated to produce humility of spirit.

Similarly, in the NT, at Mt. 23:12 and parallels, the same word is used to express the penalty for arrogance (abasement) and the prerequisite of preferment (humility). In the first case it is a condition of low estate which will be brought

Model of the double and triple gates of Herod's Temple named after Huldah, the OT prophetess who lived in Jerusalem. (JPK) (HC)

about through the judgment of God. In the second it is a spirit of lowliness which enables God to bring the blessing of advancement. Paul too, in Phil. 4:12, uses it to describe his affliction, but goes on to make clear that the virtue lies in the acceptance of the experience, so that a condition imposed from without becomes the occasion for the development of the corresponding attitude within. In the same Epistle (2:8) he cites as an example to be emulated the humility of Christ, who deliberately set aside his divine prerogative and progressively humbled himself, receiving in due time the exaltation which must inevitably follow.

Like all virtues, humility is capable of being simulated, and the danger of this is particularly plain in Paul's letter to the Colossians. Whatever may be the true rendering of the difficult passage in Col. 2:18, it is clear that here and in 2:23 the reference is to a sham. In spite of all the appearances of humility, these false teachers are really puffed up with a sense of their own importance. Setting their own speculative system over against the revelation of God, they deny the very thing which by their asceticism they seem to proclaim. Paul warns his readers against this pseudo-humility and goes on in 3:12 to exhort them to the genuine thing.

BIBLIOGRAPHY. W. Baudel, H.-H. Esser, *NIDNTT* 2, pp. 256–264; *TDNT* 5, p. 939; 6, pp. 37–40, 865–882; 8, pp. 1–26. F.S.F.

HUNDRED, TOWER OF THE. In Ne. 3:1, a Jerusalem tower which stood between the Sheep and Fish Gates, probably near the NE corner of the city. The Hebrew is *ham-mē'â*, meaning 'the hundred'; AV reads 'Meah', omitting the definite article, while RSV translates it literally. The name may refer to its height—perhaps 100 cubits; or to the number of its steps; or to the number of the garrison it housed. (*JERUSALEM.) D.F.P.

HUNTING, HUNTER. The narratives of the patriarchal period depict the Hebrews as occupied chiefly with the raising of flocks and other semi-sedentary agricultural activities. Hunting was seldom engaged in as a pastime, and was generally resorted to only either at the promptings of hunger or when the wild *animals with which Palestine abounded in antiquity (Ex. 23:29) threatened the security of the Hebrews and their flocks (Jdg. 14:5; 1 Sa. 17:34). Certain individuals, however, were renowned for their hunting prowess, including Ishmael (Gn. 21:20) and Esau (Gn. 25:27).

By contrast the ancient Mesopotamians and Egyptians spent considerably more time in the pursuit of game. Many Assyrian monuments and bas-reliefs depict hunting-scenes, indicating a long tradition of sporting activity which may well go back as far as Nimrod, the mighty hunter of antiquity (Gn. 10:8) who colonized Assyria (Gn. 10:11). Whereas the Mesopotamians hunted lions and other ferocious beasts, the Egyptians preferred to catch game and predatory birds. In this pursuit dogs and cats frequently participated.

The austerity of the Hebrew diet in ancient times was occasionally relieved by such delicacies as par-

HUKOK
See Helkath, Part 2.

HUNDRED-WEIGHT
See Weights and measures, Part 3.

One of a series of reliefs from Ashurbanipal's palace at Nineveh. The king hunts lions, here despatching one with a spear. Mid-7th cent. BC. (BM)

Detail of the lion-hunt relief from Nineveh, showing how some hunts were staged in the palace grounds. Mid-7th cent. BC. (BM)

Hunting hippopotami in the marshes of Egypt. Bas-relief from the mastaba (tomb) of the vizier Mereruka, Saqqara, Egypt. Old Kingdom, 6th Dynasty. c. 2350 BC. (PP)

tridge (*cf.* 1 Sa. 26:20), gazelle and hart meat (Dt. 12:15). The provision for Solomon's table also included roebuck (1 Ki. 4:23). Such is the general nature of OT references to hunting that few of the animals are named, and virtually nothing is said of the methods employed or of the accoutrements of the hunter. At Hassuna in Iraq the camp of a hunter was unearthed and found to contain weapons, storage jars and tools dating back to *c.* 5000 BC. Biblical references allude to bows and arrows (Gn. 27:3), clubs (Jb. 41:29, RV), slingstones (1 Sa. 17:40), nets (Jb. 19:6), the *snares of fowlers (Ps. 91:3) and pits for larger animals such as bears (Ezk. 19:8).

While hunting was not a common occupation in ancient Palestine, its procedures were sufficiently familiar to be enshrined in figurative speech (Jb. 18:10; Je. 5:26). The NT employs few hunting metaphors (Lk. 11:54; Rom. 11:9; Mt. 22:15).

BIBLIOGRAPHY. E. W. Heaton, *Everyday Life in Old Testament Times*, 1956, pp. 112ff. R.K.H.

HUPPIM
See Manasseh, Part 2.

HUR (*ḥûr*, 'child'? or *HORITE). **1.** A prominent Israelite who with Aaron held up the arms of Moses at Rephidim in the battle against Amalek (Ex. 17:10, 12), and who also helped Aaron to judge the people while Moses went up into Mt Sinai (Ex. 24:14).

2. A descendant through Caleb and Hezron of Perez (1 Ch. 2:19–20) and grandfather of *Bezalel (Ex. 31:2; 35:30; 38:22; 1 Ch. 4:1; 2 Ch. 1:5). **3.** A son of Ephratah

Birds, deer and rabbits being hunted by Assyrians in a wood. Relief from the palace of Sargon II at Khorsabad. c. 710 BC. (BM)

Catching birds in the Egyptian marshes. Part of a wall-painting in the Tomb of Nebamun, Thebes. New Kingdom, 18th Dynasty. c. 1422–1411 BC. (BM)

and father of Caleb (1 Ch. 2:50; 4:4). **4.** One of the five kings of Midian who were killed with Balaam by the Israelites (Nu. 31:8; Jos. 13:21). **5.** The father of one of Solomon's twelve commissariat officers (1 Ki. 4:8). The son, who was over the district of Mt Ephraim, is not named, so RSV transliterates the Heb. 'son of' and names him Ben-hur. **6.** The father of Rephaiah, who helped to rebuild the walls and was ruler over half of Jerusalem in Nehemiah's time (Ne. 3:9). T.C.M.

HUSHAI. The story of Hushai the Archite (*cf.* Jos. 16:2), his devotion to his king and his readiness to undertake a dangerous errand for him, affords a model for the Christian to study and to follow (2 Sa. 15:32ff.). Hushai's arrival at the heights E of Jerusalem where David halted, and his successful mission, defeated the advice of Ahithophel and came as an answer to David's prayer (v. 31). In a list of David's officers the Chronicler includes Hushai as 'the king's friend' (1 Ch. 27:33; *cf.* 2 Sa. 15:37). Baanah, Hushai's son, appears in the list of Solomon's local officers (1 Ki. 4:7, 16). G.T.M.

HUSHIM. 'Those who hasten'. **1.** A son of Dan (Gn. 46:23), called Shuham in Nu. 26:42. **2.** A son of Aher the Benjaminite (1 Ch. 7:12). **3.** One of the two wives of Shaharaim and the mother of Abitub and Elpaal (1 Ch. 8:8, 11). G.W.G.

HUZZAB (Heb. *huṣṣaḇ*, uncertain meaning, possibly from *nāṣaḇ*, 'it is decreed'). Occurring only in Na. 2:7. LXX gives *hē hypostasis* = Heb. *maṣṣāḇ* = 'standing-place'. AV, RV read as a proper name, but no such name is known in the cuneiform texts. RSV renders 'its mistress', referring to the Assyrian queen, but J. M. P. Smith (*ICC*) thought a reference to the goddess of Nineveh more likely. W. Gesenius derived it from *ṣāḇaḇ* and put it at the end of v. 6, reading 'the palace is dissolved and *made to flow away*'. NEB renders 'the train of captives goes into exile'. J.G.G.N.

HYMENAEUS. A pernicious teacher associated with *Alexander (1 Tim. 1:19–20) and *Philetus (2 Tim. 2:17). Paul's delivery of Hymenaeus and Alexander to Satan recalls 1 Cor. 5:5; both passages have been interpreted of excommunication (*i.e.* surrender to Satan's sphere) and of the infliction of bodily punishment. These are not, of course, incompatible, but the verbal similarity with Jb. 2:6, LXX, and various other disciplinary transactions in the apostolic church (*cf.* Acts 5:3–11; 8:20–24; 13:9–11; 1 Cor. 11:30) suggest that physical effects were at least included. There are also parallels in execration texts (*cf. LAE*, p. 302). At all events the discipline, though drastic, was merciful and remedial in intention.

It had not, however, evoked repentance when 2 Tim. 2:17 was written. The error of Hymenaeus and others, described in clinical

HURAM-ABI
See Hiram, Part 2.

HUSBANDMAN
See Ploughman, Part 3.

HUSHAM
See Teman, Part 3.

HUSKS
See Plants (Pods), Part 3.

HYDROMANCY
See Divination, Part 1.

HYENA
See Animals, Part 1.

■ **HYRAX**
See Animals, Part 1.

■ **HYSSOP**
See Plants, Part 3.

■ **IBEX**
See Animals, Part 1.

Roman coin from the city of Iconium, portraying Heracles. Diameter 22 mm. (RG)

terms as 'feeding like gangrene', was still much in Paul's mind. It involved a 'spiritualization' of the resurrection (including, doubtless, the judgment), doctrine always repugnant to the Greek mind: there were similar misunderstandings at Corinth earlier (1 Cor. 15:12). Such ideas took various forms in Gnostic religion: *cf.* the claim of the false teachers in the *Acts of Paul and Thecla* 14 (combining two ideas): 'We will teach thee of that resurrection which he asserteth, that it is already come to pass in the children which we have, and we rise again when we have come to the knowledge of the true God' (tr. M. R. James, *Apocryphal New Testament*, p. 275).

The name (that of the marriage-god) is not noticeably frequent.

A.F.W.

HYMN. The Gk. *hymnos* was used by the classical writers to signify any ode or song written in praise of gods or heroes, and occasionally by LXX translators of praise to God, *e.g.* Pss. 40:3; 65:1; Is. 42:10. In the NT the word occurs only in Eph. 5:19 and Col. 3:16, with the verbal form (*hymneō*) in Mt. 26:30 and the parallel Mk. 14:26 (which refer to the singing of the second part of the Hallel, Pss. 115–118); Acts 16:25 (of Paul and Silas singing in prison); and Heb. 2:12 (a quotation from Ps. 22:22, LXX). It is clear, however, that the singing of spiritual songs was a feature of the life of the apostolic church, as is witnessed by 1 Cor. 14:15, 26; Jas. 5:13, the Christian canticles recorded by Luke, and the many doxologies found elsewhere in the NT. They were used as a spontaneous expression of Christian joy, as a means of instruction in the faith (Col. 3:16), and, on the basis of synagogue practice, as an integral part of the worship of the church.

The threefold division of psalms, hymns and spiritual songs (*ōdai*) must not be pressed too closely, as the terms overlap, but two distinct styles of composition can be observed. The first followed the form and style of the OT psalm and was a Christian counterpart of the psalmodic writing exemplified by the 1st-century BC *Psalms of Solomon* or the *Hymns of Thanksgiving* (*Hôḏāyôṯ*) of the Qumran sect. In this category may be included the canticles: Lk. 1:46–55 (* MAGNIFICAT); 1:68–79 (* BENEDICTUS); 2:29–32 (* NUNC DIMITTIS). The second group consists of doxologies (as Lk. 2:14; 1 Tim. 1:17; 6:15–16; Rev. 4:8, 11; 5:9, 12–13; 7:12, *etc.*), many of which were doubtless used in corporate worship. Some other passages have been loosely described by commentators as hymns, where the majesty of the subject-matter has driven the writer to poetical language, *e.g.* 1 Cor. 13; Rom. 8:31–39; Eph. 1:3–14; Phil. 2:5–11; but there is no certainty that they were ever set to music or recited liturgically. Fragments of liturgical or credal formulae have been detected in Eph. 5:14; 1 Tim. 3:16; 2 Tim. 2:11–13; Tit. 3:4–7.

BIBLIOGRAPHY. R. P. Martin, *Worship in the Early Church*^{2}, 1974; and (on Phil. 2:5–11) *An Early Christian Confession*, 1960; G. Delling, *TDNT* 8, pp. 489–503; K. H. Bartels, *NIDNTT* 3, pp. 668–676.

J.B.Tr.

HYPOCRITE. In English a hypocrite is one who deliberately and as a habit professes to be good when he is aware that he is not. But the word itself is a transliteration of Gk. *hypokritēs*, which mostly meant play-actor. Though it was soon in ecclesiastical Greek to take on its modern meaning, it seems impossible to prove that it bore this meaning in the 1st century AD. In LXX it is twice used to translate Heb. *ḥānēp̄*, 'godless'.

In the NT, hypocrite is used only in the Synoptic accounts of Christ's judgments on the scribes and Pharisees. Though 'Pharisaic' sources (*Soṭah* 22b) acknowledge and condemn hypocrisy in their ranks, the general tenor of the NT, the 1st-century evidences for the teaching of the Pharisees in Talmud and Midrash and their support by the mass of the people (Jos., *Ant.* 13. 298), all make it hard to accept a general charge of hypocrisy against them. A study of the actual charges against them will show that only in the rarest cases can we possibly interpret them as hypocrisy. We find blindness to their faults (Mt. 7:5), to God's workings (Lk. 12:56), to a true sense of values (Lk. 13:15), an over-valuation of human tradition (Mt. 15:7; Mk. 7:6), sheer ignorance of God's demands (Mt. 23:14–15, 25, 29), and love of display (Mt. 6:2, 5, 16). It was only Christ, the sole perfect reader of inward realities (Mt. 23:27–28), who dared pass this judgment.

BIBLIOGRAPHY. J. Jocz, *The Jewish People and Jesus Christ*, 1949; H. L. Ellison, 'Jesus and the Pharisees' in *JTVI* 85, 1953; Arndt, under *hypokritēs*; U. Wilckens, *TDNT* 8, pp. 559–570; W. Günther *et al.*, *NIDNTT* 2, pp. 467–474.

H.L.E.

IBLEAM. A Canaanite town in the N borderland of Manasseh, whose territory extended to (not 'in') Issachar (Jos. 17:11; Y. Kaufmann, *The Biblical Account of the Conquest of Palestine*, 1953, p. 38). During the Israelite settlement, its Canaanite inhabitants were subdued, not expelled (Jdg. 1:27). The site of Ibleam is now Khirbet Bil'ameh, *c.* 16 km SE of Megiddo on the road from Beth-shean (2 Ki. 9:27). It is probably the Bileam of 1 Ch. 6:70, a levitical city. Ibleam occurs in Egyp. lists as *Ybr'm*.

K.A.K.

IBZAN (Heb. *'iḇṣān*). Known only from Jdg. 12:8–10; a national judge for 7 years, following Jephthah; apparently a person of consequence, who raised a large family and arranged marriages for thirty sons. His home and burial-place was Bethlehem, probably of Zebulun (Jos. 19:15), 11 km WNW of Nazareth; Jewish commentators, assuming it was Bethlehem-judah, identified him with * Boaz.

J.P.U.L.

ICHABOD (Heb. *'îḵāḇôḏ*). The name given by the wife of Phinehas to her child, on hearing that the Philistines had captured the ark (1 Sa. 4:19–22, *cf.* 14:3). There are several possible explanations: (1) that *'î* is interrogative ('where is the glory?'); (2) *'î* is the negative particle ('no glory', *cf.* Josephus, *Ant.* 5. 360); (3) that the name stands for *'āḇî-ḵāḇôḏ* ('my father is glory').

R.P.G.

ICONIUM. A city of Asia Minor mentioned in Acts 13:51; 14:1, *etc.* and 2 Tim. 3:11 as the scene of Paul's trials, and in Acts 16:2 as a place where Timothy was commended. Standing on the edge of the plateau, it was well watered, a productive and wealthy region. It was originally Phrygian, its name Kawania: its religion remained Phrygian into Roman times, the worship of a mother goddess with eunuch priests. After being for a

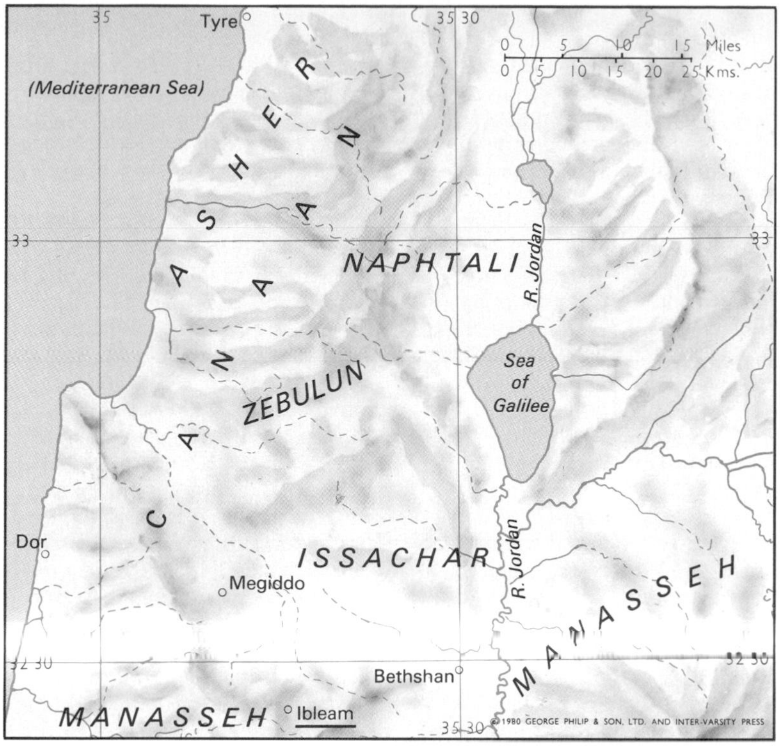

time the chief city of Lycaonia, and passing through various political fortunes, it was at length included in the kingdom of Galatia and a little later in the Roman province of Galatia. Its fame and prestige grew greatly under Roman rule: Claudius honoured it with the title of Claudiconium, and under Hadrian it became a colony in an honorary sense (since no Italians were settled there). In NT times, then, it maintained the polity of a Hellenistic city, the juridical powers of the assembly being vested in the two magistrates annually appointed.

The passage in Acts 14, though brief, gives occasion for differing interpretations. The so-called Western Text implies two attacks on Paul, one open, the second more subtle, after which the apostles flee. Two classes of Jewish leaders are mentioned, 'chief men of the synagogue' and 'rulers', a distinction epigraphically defensible. The text of Codex Vaticanus and its allies has a more difficult text with only one attack of fairly long duration implied. Here the rulers of v. 5 may plausibly be identified with the magistrates of the city, as Ramsay suggests, but whether the Old Uncial text is a bad abbreviation, or the Western Text an attempt at correction of a text perhaps corrupt, has not yet been finally decided.

Iconium is the scene of the well-known apocryphal story of Paul and Thecla, contained in the longer *Acts of Paul*. Apart from the scarcely doubtful existence of an early martyr of the name, there is no ascertainable historical content to be found in the story.

BIBLIOGRAPHY. Commentaries on Acts *in loc.*, especially *BC*, 3, pp. 129–132; 4, pp. 160–162; W. M. Ramsay, *Cities of St Paul*, 1907, part iv. J.N.B.

IDDO. The name represents seven variant spellings in the Heb. and its derivations and meanings are uncertain. **1.** The father of Ahinadab, one of Solomon's officers, 1 Ki. 4:14 (*'iddō'*). **2.** A Levite of the line of Gershon, 1 Ch. 6:21 (*MT* 6:6 *'iddô*), but called Adaiah in 6:41 (*MT* 6:16). **3.** A tribal chief of the E section of Manasseh, 1 Ch. 27:21 (*yiddô*). **4.** A seer and prophet cited as one of the sources of the Chronicler in 2 Ch. 9:29 (*ye'dî* but *Qerē' ye'dô*); 12:15 and 2 Ch. 13:22 (*'iddô*). **5.** The grandfather ('father' in Ezra) of Zechariah the prophet, Zc. 1:1, 7 (*'iddô*); Ezr. 5:1; 6:14 (*'iddô'*). **6.** One of those guilty of a mixed marriage; EVV Jaddai (AV Jadau), Ezr. 10:43 (*yiddô* or *yadday*). **7.** Head of one of the priestly families which returned to Jerusalem with Zerubbabel, Ne. 12:4 (*'iddô'*); 12:16 (*'iddoy'*). J.G.B.

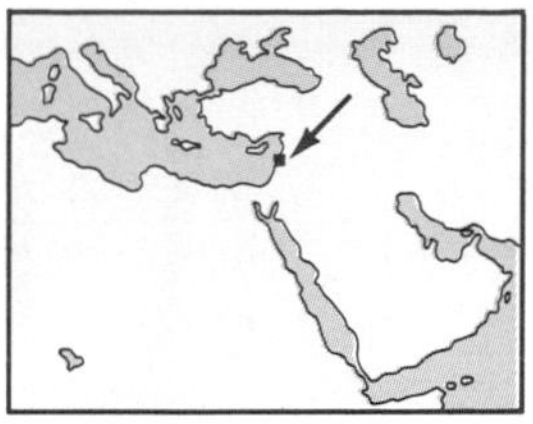

Ibleam of Manasseh (Khirbet Bil'ameh).

IDOLATRY. The story of OT religion could be told for the most part in terms of a tension between a spiritual conception of God and worship, the hallmark of the genuine faith of Israel, and various

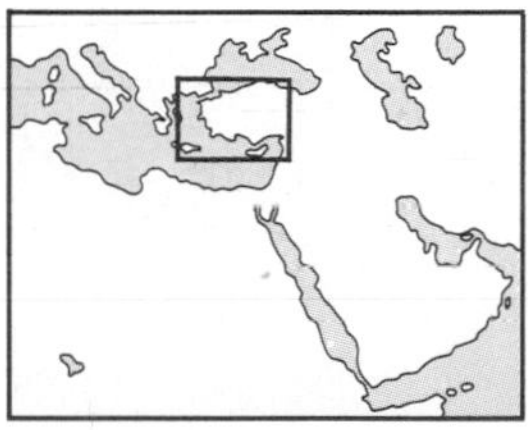

Iconium in the Roman province of Galatia, Asia Minor.

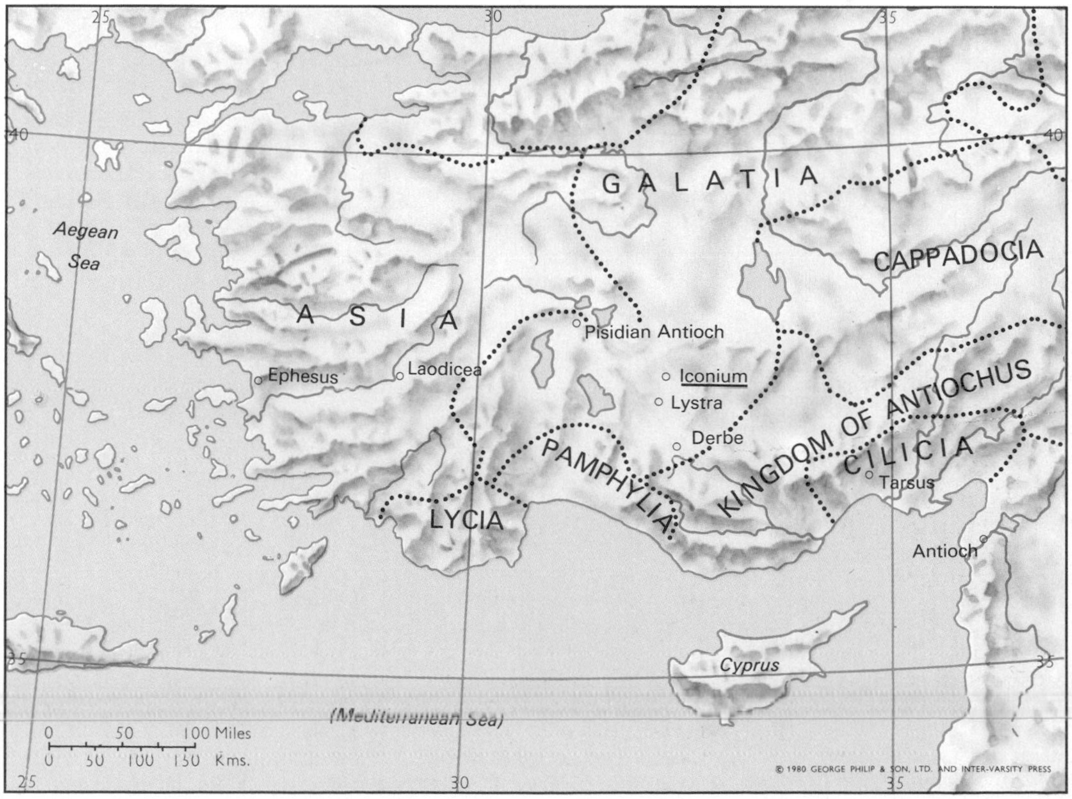

Syrian male cult-figurine of the early 2nd millennium BC (Middle Bronze IIA) flat-cast in metal. Height 23·7 cm. (BM)

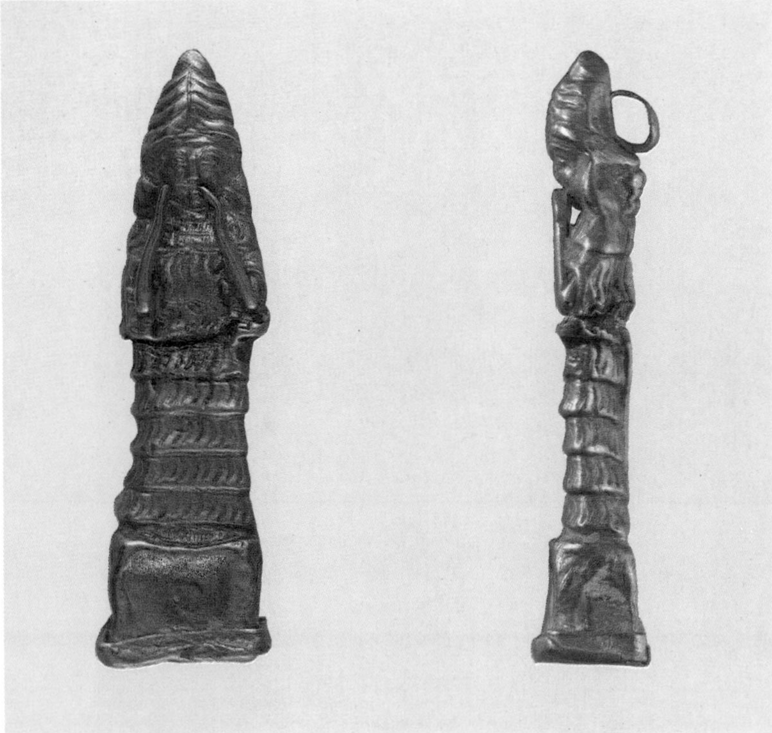

Gold figurine of the intercessory Babylonian goddess Lama, probably worn as an amulet. Early 2nd millennium BC. (BM)

pressures, such as idolatry, which attempted to debase and materialize the national religious consciousness and practice. We do not find, in the OT, an ascending from idolatry to the pure worship of God, but rather a people possessing a pure worship and a spiritual theology, constantly fighting, through the medium of divinely-raised spiritual leaders, religious seductions which, nevertheless, often claimed the mass of the people. Idolatry is a declension from the norm, not an earlier stage gradually and with difficulty superseded.

If we consider the broad sweep of evidence for patriarchal religion we find it to be a religion of the altar and of prayer, but not of idols. There are certain events, all associated with Jacob, which might appear to show patriarchal idolatry. For example, Rachel stole her father's *teraphim (Gn. 31:19). By itself, this, of course, need prove nothing more than that Jacob's wife had failed to free herself from her Mesopotamian religious environment (*cf.* Jos. 24:15). If these objects were of legal as well as religious significance, the possessor of them would hold the right of succession to the family property (*NUZI). This accords well with the anxiety of Laban, who does not appear otherwise as a religious man, to recover them, and his care, when he fails to find them, to exclude Jacob from Mesopotamia by a carefully-worded treaty (Gn. 31:45ff.). Again, it is urged that Jacob's pillars (Gn. 28:18; 31:13, 45; 35:14, 20) are the same as the idolatrous stones with which Canaan was familiar. The interpretation is not inescapable. The pillar at Bethel is associated with Jacob's vow (see Gn. 31:13), and could more easily belong to the category of memorial pillars (*e.g.* Gn. 35:20; Jos. 24:27; 1 Sa. 7:12; 2 Sa. 18:18). Finally, the evidence of Gn. 35:4, often used to show patriarchal idolatry, actually points to the recognized incompatibility of idols with the God of Bethel. Jacob must dispose of the unacceptable objects before he stands before this God. That Jacob 'hid' them is surely not to be construed as indicating that he feared to destroy them for reasons of superstitious reverence. It is allowing suspicion to govern exegesis if we do more than assume that this was the simplest as well as the most effective way of disposing of non-combustible objects.

The weight of evidence for the Mosaic period is the same. The whole narrative of the golden calf (Ex. 32) reveals the extent of the contrast between the religion which stemmed from Mt Sinai and the form of religion congenial to the unregenerate heart. These religions, we learn, are incompatible. The religion of Sinai is emphatically aniconic. Moses warned the people (Dt. 4:12) that the revelation of God vouchsafed to them there contained no 'form', lest they corrupt themselves with images. This is the essential Mosaic position, as recorded in the Decalogue (Ex. 20:4; *cf.* Ex. 34:17). The prohibition in Dt. 4:12 is in the realm of religion, it should be noted, not of theology. It is correct to speak of a 'form' of the Lord and Dt. 4:12 and Nu. 12:8 have the word *t^emûnâ* ('form') in common. But for Israel to carry this over into religious practice could only involve corruption of truth and life. This is a striking testimony to the aniconic nature of Israel's worship. The second commandment was unique in the world of its day, and the failure of archaeology to unearth a figure of Yahweh (while idols abounded in every other religion) shows its fundamental place in Israel's religion from Mosaic days.

The historical record of Judges, Samuel and Kings tells the same story of the lapse of the nation from the spiritual forms proper to their religion. The book of Judges, at least from ch. 17 onwards, deliberately sets out to picture for us a time of general lawlessness (*cf.* 17:6; 18:1; 19:1; 21:25). We should not dream of seeing in the events of ch. 19 the norm of Israelite morality. It is candidly a story of a degraded society and we have as little reason for seeing the story of Micah (Jdg. 17–18) as displaying a lawful but primitive stage in Israel's religion. The same comment from the author of Judges points in turn to the religious corruption (17:1–13; see v. 6), social unrest and lawlessness (18:1–31; see v. 1) and moral declension (19:1ff.) of the day.

We are not told in what form the images of Micah were made. It has been suggested that, since they subsequently found a home in the N Danite sanctuary, they were in the calf or bull form. This is likely enough, for it is a most significant thing that when Israel turned to idolatry it was always necessary to borrow the outward trappings from the pagan environment, thus suggesting that there was something in the very nature of Yahwism which prevented the growth of indigenous idolatrous forms. The golden calves made by Jeroboam (1 Ki. 12:28) were well-known Canaanite symbols, and in the same way, whenever the kings of Israel and Judah lapsed into idolatry, it was by means of borrowing and syncretism. H. H. Rowley (*Faith of Israel*, pp. 77f.) urges that such evidences of idolatry as exist after Moses are to be explained either by the impulse to syncretism or by the tendency for customs eradicated in one generation to reappear in the next (*cf.* Je. 44). We might add to these the tendency to corrupt the use of something which in itself was lawful: the superstitious use of the ephod (Jdg. 8:27) and the cult of the serpent (2 Ki. 18:4).

The main forms of idolatry into which Israel fell were the use of graven and molten *images, pillars, the *asherah and *teraphim. The *massēḵâ*, or molten image, was made by casting metal in a mould and shaping it with a tool (Ex. 32:4, 24). There is some doubt whether this figure, and the later calves made by Jeroboam, were intended to represent Yahweh, or were thought of as a pedestal over which he was enthroned. The analogy of the cherubim (*cf.* 2 Sa. 6:2) suggests the latter, which also receives the support of archaeology (*cf.* G. E.

The goddess Baalath, the 'lady of Byblos', receives the libation offered in worship by the king of Byblos, Yehawmilk. Phoenician text below. Height of stele 1·13 m. c. 450 BC. (MC)

Wright, *Biblical Archaeology*, p. 148, for an illustration of the god Hadad riding upon a bull). The cherubim were, however, concealed from view and were at any rate 'unearthly' in appearance. They could not point to any unacceptable affiliation of the enthroned God with earthly parallels. The bulls, on the contrary, were not (as far as the narrative suggests) concealed from view and could not but point to an involvement of Yahweh in fertility religion and theology.

The pillars and the asherah were both forbidden to Israel (*cf.* Dt. 12:3; 16:21–22). In Baal sanctuaries the pillar of Baal (*cf.* 2 Ki. 10:27) and the pole of the Asherah stood beside the altar. The pillar was thought of as a stylized representation of the presence of the god at the shrine. It was the object of great veneration: sometimes it was hollowed in part so as to receive the blood of sacrifice, and sometimes, as appears from its polished surface, it was kissed by its devotees. The asherah was wooden, as we learn from its usual destruction by burning (Dt. 12:3; 2 Ki. 23:6), and probably originated from the sacred evergreen, the symbol of life. The association of these with Canaanite fertility practice sufficed to make them abominable to Yahweh.

The OT polemic against idolatry, carried on chiefly by prophets and psalmists, recognizes the same two truths which Paul was later to affirm: that the idol was nothing, but that nevertheless there was a demonic spiritual force to be reckoned with, and that the idol therefore constituted a positive spiritual menace (Is. 44:6–20; 1 Cor. 8:4; 10:19–20). Thus, the idol is nothing at all: man made it (Is. 2:8); its very composition and construction proclaims its futility (Is. 40:18–20; 41:6–7; 44:9–20); its helpless bulk invites derision (Is. 46:1–2); it has nothing but the bare appearance of life (Ps. 115:4–7). The prophets derisively named them *gillûlîm* (Ezk. 6:4, and at least 38 other times in Ezekiel) or 'dung pellets' (Koehler's *Lexicon*), and *ᵉlîlîm*, 'godlets'.

But, though entirely subject to Yahweh (*e.g.* Ps. 95:3), there are spiritual forces of evil, and the practice of idolatry brings men into deadly contact with these 'gods'. Isaiah, who is usually said to bring the ironic scorning of idols to its peak, is well aware of this spiritual evil. He knows that there is only one God (44:8), but even so no-one can touch an idol, though it be 'nothing', and come away unscathed. Man's contact with the false god infects him with a deadly spiritual blindness of heart and mind (44:18). Though what he worships is mere 'ashes', yet it is full of the poison of spiritual delusion (44:20). Those who worship idols become like them (Ps. 115:8; Je. 2:5; Ho. 9:10). Because of the reality of evil power behind the idol, it is an *abomination (*tôʿēḇâ*) to Yahweh (Dt. 7:25), a detested thing (*šiqqûṣ*) (Dt. 29:17), and it is the gravest sin, spiritual adultery, to follow idols (Dt. 31:16; Jdg. 2:17; Ho. 1:2). Nevertheless, there is only one God, and the contrast between Yahweh and idols is to be drawn in terms of life, activity and government. The idol cannot predict and bring to pass, but Yahweh can (Is. 41:26–27; 44:7); the idol is a helpless piece of flotsam on the river of history, only wise after the event and helpless in the face of it (Is. 41:5–7; 46:1–2), but Yahweh is Lord and controller of history (Is. 40:22–25; 41:1–2, 25; 43:14–15, *etc.*).

The NT reinforces and amplifies the OT teaching. Its recognition that idols are both nonentities and dangerous spiritual potencies has been noted above. In addition, Rom. 1 expresses the OT view that idolatry is a decline from true spirituality, and not a stage on the way to a pure knowledge of God. The NT recognizes, however, that the peril of idolatry exists even where material idols are not fashioned: the association of idolatry with sexual sins in Gal. 5:19–20 ought to be linked with the equating of covetousness with idolatry (1 Cor. 5:11; Eph. 5:5; Col. 3:5), for by covetousness Paul certainly includes and stresses sexual covetousness (*cf.* Eph. 4:19; 5:3; 1 Thes. 4:6, Gk.; 1 Cor. 10:7, 14). John, having urged the finality and fullness of revelation in Christ, warns that any deviation is idolatry (1 Jn. 5:19–21). The idol is whatever claims that loyalty which belongs to God alone (Is. 42:8).

The bearing of the biblical teaching on idols on its monotheistic doctrine of God cannot be overlooked. In its recognition of the magnetism of idolatrous religion for Israel and also in such seeming recognition of 'other gods' as, *e.g.*, Ps. 95:3, the OT acknowledges not the real existence of the 'gods' but the real existence of the threat to Israel, the menace of alternative cults and claims. It thus constantly holds its monotheism (as indeed the NT also does) in the setting of the religion and religious environment of the people of God.

Bibliography. H. H. Rowley, *Faith of Israel*, 1956, pp. 74ff.; A. Lods, 'Images and Idols, Hebrew and Canaanite', *ERE*; 'Idol', in J.-J. von Allmen, *Vocabulary of the Bible*, 1958; J. Pedersen, *Israel*, 3–4, 1926, pp. 220ff., *passim*; J. B. Payne, *The Theology of the Older Testament*, 1962; Y. Kaufmann, *The Religion of Israel*, 1961; 'Image', *NIDNTT* 2, pp. 284–293; J. M. Sasson, *The Worship of the Golden Calf*, Ancient & Occident, 1973, pp. 151ff.

J.A.M.

IDOLS, MEATS OFFERED TO. Among the questions submitted by the Corinthians for the apostle's ruling was the matter of 'food offered to idols', a phrase which represents one Gk. term, *eidōlothyta.* Paul handles this subject in 1 Cor. 8:1–13 and 10:14–33. The background of the Corinthians' query may first be sketched.

I. The background

In the ancient system of sacrifice, which was the centre not only of the religious life of the Graeco-Roman world in the 1st century but also of the domestic and social life, only part of the sacrifice was presented to the god in the temple. The sacrifice was followed by a cultic meal, when the remainder of the consecrated food was eaten either in the precincts of the temple or at home. Sometimes the remaining food was sent to the market to be sold (1 Cor. 10:25).

Evidence for the practice of a meal in the temple is found in the following well-known Oxyrhynchus papyrus which Lietzmann regards as 'a striking parallel' to the reference in 1 Cor. 10:27: 'Chaeremon invites you to dinner at the table of the lord Serapis (the name of the deity) in the Serapeum tomorrow the 15th at the 9th hour' (= 3 p.m.) (quoted and discussed in Chan-Hie Kim's essay, 'The Papyrus Invitation', *JBL* 94, 1975, pp. 391–402). An invitation to a meal of this character, whether in the temple or in a private house, would be commonplace in the social life of the city of Corinth, and would pose a thorny question for the believer who was so invited. Other aspects of life in such a cosmopolitan centre would be affected by the Christian's attitude to idol-meats. Attendance at the public festivals, which opened with pagan adoration and sacrifice, would have to be considered. Membership of a trade guild, and therefore one's commercial standing, and public-spiritedness were also involved, as such membership would entail sitting 'at table in an idol's temple' (1 Cor. 8:10). Even daily shopping in the market would present a problem to the thoughtful Christian in Corinth. As much of the meat would be passed on from the temple-officials to the meat-dealers and by them exposed for sale, the question arose: was the Christian housewife at liberty to purchase this meat which, coming from sacrificial animals which had to be free from blemish, might well be the best meat in the market? Moreover, there were gratuitous banquets in the temple precincts which were a real boon to the poor. If 1 Cor. 1:26 means that some of the Corinthian church members belonged to the poorer classes, the question of whether they were free or not to avail themselves of such meals would have been a practical issue.

II. Different reactions

Conviction in the church was sharply divided. One group, in the name of Christian liberty (6:12; 10:23; *cf.* 8:9) and on the basis of a supposed superior knowledge (*gnōsis*, 8:1–2), could see no harm in accepting an invitation to a cultic meal and no possible reason why food, formerly dedicated in the temple, should not be bought and eaten.

The justification for such an attitude of religious syncretism was, first, that the meal in the temple precincts was just a social occasion. They claimed that it had no religious significance at all. And, secondly, they appear to have stated that in any case the pagan gods are nonentities. 'An idol has no real existence' and 'there is no God but one' was their plea of defence (8:4; cited probably from the Corinthians' own letter to Paul).

On the other hand, the 'weak' group (8:9; *cf.* Rom. 15:1) viewed the situation differently. With abhorrence of the least suspicion of idolatry, they believed that the demons behind the idols still exerted malign influence on the food and 'contaminated' it, thus rendering it unfit for consumption by believers (8:7; *cf.* Acts 10:14).

III. Paul's answer

Paul begins his answer to the church's inquiry by expressing agreement with the proposition, 'There is no God but one' (8:4). But he immediately qualifies this explicit confession of his monotheism by reminding his readers that there are so-called gods and lords which exert demonic influence in the world. He concedes the point, however, that 'for us' who acknowledge one God and one Lord, the power of these demons has been overcome by the cross, so that the Corinthians ought no longer to be in bondage to them (*cf.* Col. 2:15–16; Gal. 4:3, 8–9). Not all the Corinthian believers had found that freedom in Christ, and their case must be remembered and their weak conscience not outraged by indiscreet action (8:7–13). The apostle has a more serious word to say on this matter, which he takes up after a digression in ch. 9.

He comes to grips with the menace of idolatry in 10:14ff. These verses are an exposition of the inner meaning of the Lord's Table in the light of communion in the body and blood of Christ (10:16); the unity of the church as the body of Christ (10:17); the spell cast by demons over their worshippers at idol-feasts which led actually to a compact with the demons (10:20); and the impossibility of a double allegiance represented by trying to share both the table of the Lord and the table of demons (10:21–22). (*LORD'S SUPPER.)

The apostle in this section, therefore, takes a serious attitude to the implications of attendance at idolatrous banquests (*cf.* 10:14). In line with rabbinical teaching which was later codified in the Mishnah tractate *'Abodah Zarah* ('Strange Worship'), he forbids absolutely the use of food and drink in an idol-temple (10:19–20; *cf.* Rev. 2:14) on the ground no doubt that, as the rabbis said, 'as a dead body defiles by overshadowing, so also an idolatrous sacrifice causes defilement by overshadowing', *i.e.* by having been brought under a pagan roof, and by this contact becomes ritually unclean. See the Mishnah in Danby's edition, p. 649, n. 3.

But, in regard to food which has formerly been offered in the temple and is afterwards made available for consumption, Paul says that it is permitted on the basis of Ps. 24:1 (1 Cor. 10:25ff.). Although such food has been dedicated in the temple and is exposed for sale in the meat-market, it may be eaten by virtue of being God's creation (1 Tim. 4:4–5). This is a distinct departure from the rabbinical ceremonial rules (and, indeed, from the apostolic decree of Acts 15:28–29), and is the practical application of the Lord's word in Mk. 7:19, '*Thus he declared* all foods clean'; *cf.* Acts 10:15). The only qualification is that the 'law of love' (*TDNT* 2, p. 379) must be observed, and a Christian's own freedom to eat such food must be waived if the conscience of the 'weaker' believer is likely to be damaged and he is thereby caused to stumble (10:28–32), or if a Gentile is scandalized by this practice (10:32). The situation envisaged by these verses is a Christian's acceptance of an invitation to a meal in a private house (10:27). In such a circumstance the believer is free to eat the food set before him, making no inquiries as to its 'past history', *i.e.* where it comes from or whether it has been dedicated in an idol shrine. If, however, a pagan, at the meal, draws attention to the food and says, 'This has been offered in sacrifice'—using the pagan term *hierothyton*—then the food must be refused, not because it is 'infected' or unfit for consumption, but because it 'places the eater in a false position, and confuses the conscience of others' (Robertson–Plummer, *I Corinthians*, p. 219), notably his heathen neighbour (10:29). This reading differs from the suggestion of Robertson–Plummer, where they take the speaker in v. 28 to be a Gentile Christian using the terminology of his pre-Christian days; it is better, however, to regard this speaker as 'one of them that believe not' in v. 27; and then the apostle's word links up with the altruism of the rabbis, who taught that a devout Jew will not countenance idolatry lest he should encourage his Gentile neighbour in error, for which he would then be responsible (*Aboth* 5. 18; *Sanhedrin* 7. 4, 10).

BIBLIOGRAPHY. Commentaries on 1 Cor. (C. K. Barrett, J. Héring, F. F. Bruce, H. Conzelmann). Also A. Ehrhardt, *The Framework of the New Testament Stories*, 1964, ch. 12: 'Social Problems in the Early Church', pp. 275–290; C. K. Barrett, *NTS* 11, 1964–5, pp. 138ff.

R.P.M.

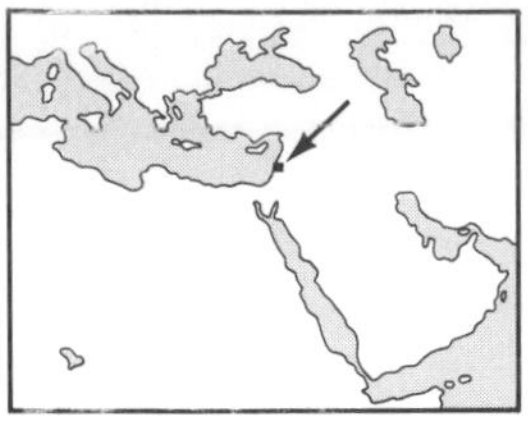

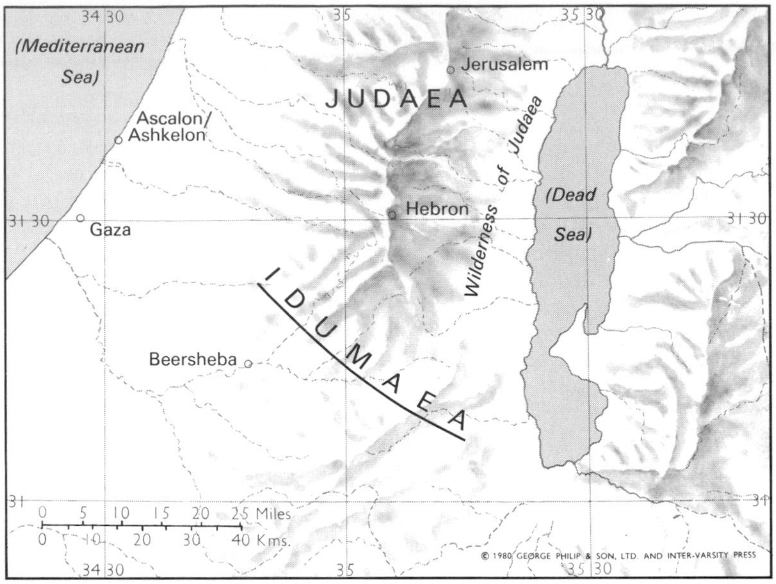

Idumaea, formerly Edom.

IDUMAEA. The Gk. form (*idoumaia*) of the Heb. *'ᵉḏôm* refers to an area in W Palestine, rather than to Edom proper. At the time of the Exodus, Edom extended to both sides of the Arabah, and the W portion reached close to Kadesh (Nu. 20:16). David subdued Edom, but there was continual conflict between *Edom and Judah. After the fall of Jerusalem in 587 BC the Edomites took advantage of the calamity to migrate into the heart of S Judah, S of Hebron. Several prophets inveighed against Edom for this (Je. 49:7–22; La. 4:21–22; Ezk. 25:12–14; 35:3; Ob. 10ff.).

Later, as various Arab groups, notably the Nabataeans, pressed into old Edom, more migrants settled in Judah, and the area they occupied became known as Idumaea (1 Macc. 4:29; 5:65). Judas Maccabaeus had successful campaigns against these people, and John Hyrcanus subdued them *c.* 126 BC, placed them under Antipater as governor and compelled them to be circumcised (Jos., *Ant.* 13. 258). Antipater was the grandfather of *Herod the Great. The word Idumaea occurs in the NT only in Mk. 3:8.

J.A.T.

IIM
See Iye-abarim, Part 2.

IGNORANCE. As is the case with *knowledge, ignorance has in Scripture a moral rather than a purely intellectual connotation, except in such casual uses as the Pauline 'I would not have you ignorant, brethren . . .' (Rom. 1:13, AV), which simply means 'I want you to know . . .' (RSV).

In the books of the Law ignorance is regarded as a palliating feature of sinful acts. For sins done in ignorance (*šᵉgāgâ*) expiation could be made by sacrifice (*cf.* particularly Lv. 4–5; Nu. 15:22–29). This idea of ignorance as an excuse is reflected in the NT uses of the verb *agnoeō*, 'to be ignorant', and its derivatives. Paul declares that he received mercy for his persecution of the church because he acted ignorantly in unbelief (1 Tim. 1:13); and at Athens he tells his Gentile audience that God overlooked the times of ignorance (Acts 17:30; *cf.* 3:17). Yet although ignorance partly excuses the sins which result from it, ignorance itself is often culpable. It may be linked with hardness of heart (Eph. 4:18; *cf.* 2 Cor. 4:4) or even be deliberate (2 Pet. 3:5; *cf.* Rom. 1:18ff.; 10:3).

Ignorance is used absolutely to refer to the condition of the Gentile world which had not received the revelation of God (Acts 17:23, 30; Eph. 4:18; 1 Pet. 1:14; 2:15). This usage is found in LXX; *e.g.* Wisdom 14:22.

The word *idiōtēs*, translated 'ignorant' in AV of Acts 4:13 (RSV 'uneducated'), implies the want of special training rather than of knowledge in general; *cf.* the modern somewhat derogatory use of 'layman'.

BIBLIOGRAPHY. R. Bultmann, *TDNT* 1, pp. 689–719; E. Schütz, *NIDNTT* 2, pp. 406–408.

M.H.C.

IJON. A town in N Naphtali taken by the Syrians under *Ben-hadad along with *Dan and *Abel of Beth-maacah (1 Ki. 15:20 = 2 Ch. 16:4). Subsequently captured by Tiglath-pileser III in 733 BC (2 Ki. 15:29). Possibly the Dan-jaan of 2 Sa. 24:6. Generally identified with Tell Dibbin, 30 km N of Lake Huleh.

D.W.B.

The region of Illyricum in the time of Paul.

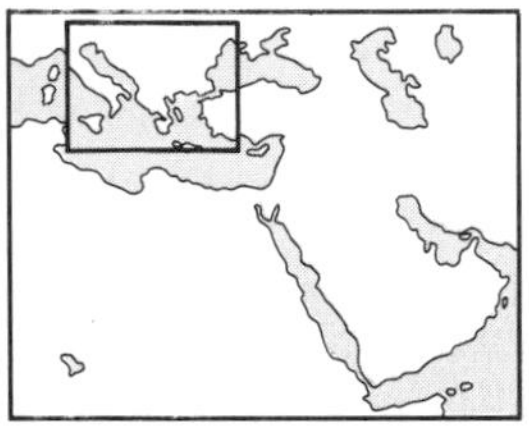

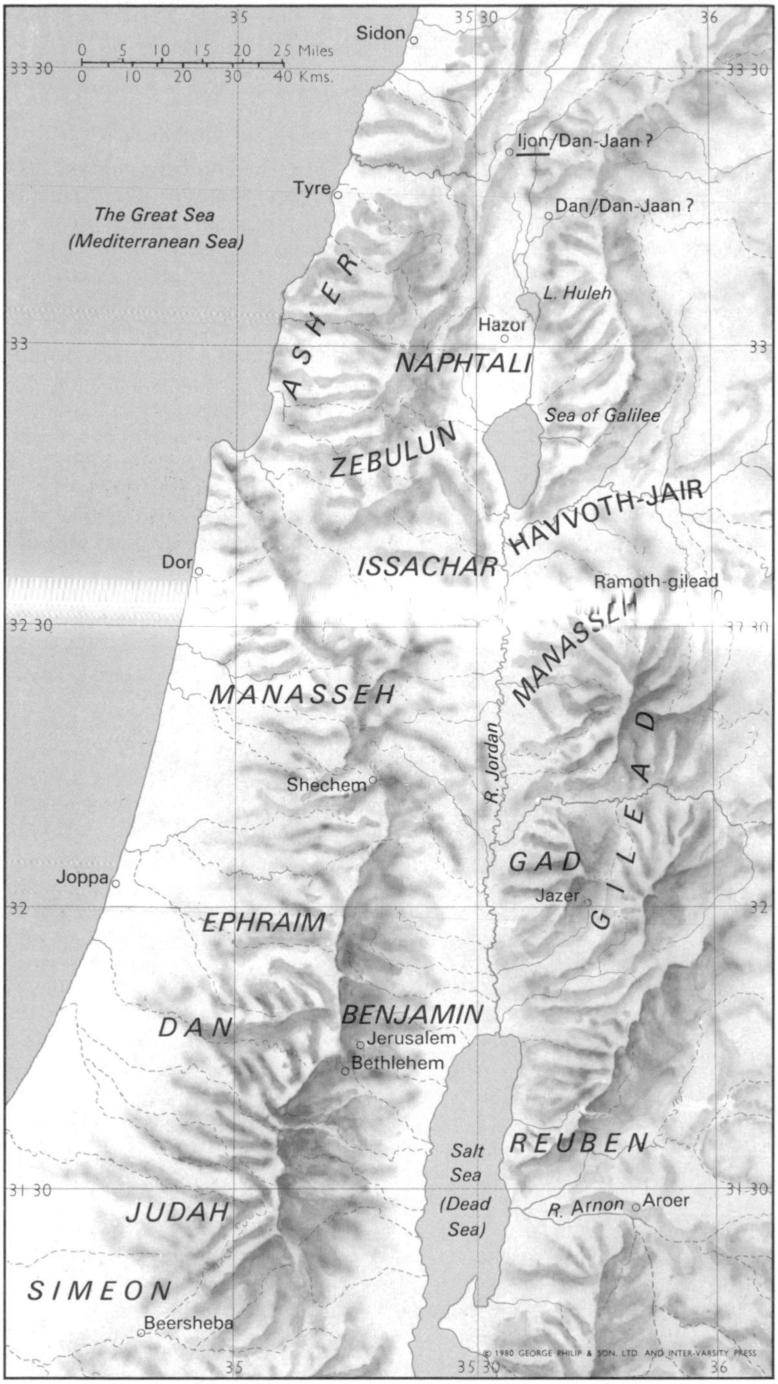

ILLYRICUM. The name of the large mountainous region on the E of the Adriatic, extending to the central Balkans in the E and reaching from NE Italy and the Celtic tribes in the N to Macedonia in the S. Its name was derived from that of one of the first tribes within its boundaries that the Greeks came across. Its inhabitants spoke dialects which were probably the linguistic ancestors of modern Albanian. The Romans had first come into conflict with some of its tribes in the 3rd century BC, but it was not finally conquered till the 1st century AD, when it was divided into the provinces of Pannonia and Dalmatia. Paul says at the time of writing the Epistle to the Romans (15:19) that it was the limit of his evangelistic activity. His reference to it appears to be inclusive, but it is not known when, or from what direction, he had entered it (possibly from Macedonia when he revisited that province after his Ephesian ministry, Acts 20:1). It was the first Latin-speaking province which he visited in the course of his apostolic ministry, and could have prepared him for his projected mission in Latin-speaking Spain (Rom. 15:24, 28). B.F.C.A.

IMAGE. The term denotes a material representation, usually of a deity. Unlike the term 'idol', which has a pejorative overtone, 'image' is objectively descriptive. Throughout the ancient Near East numerous images of various deities were to be found in temples and other holy places, such as open-air shrines; many private houses also contained a niche where the image of the protective deity of the household stood. Images were commonly anthropomorphic (in human form), though theriomorphic images (in animal form) were also widely used, especially in Egypt.

The form of the image, especially of the theriomorphic examples, frequently represented some prominent characteristic of the particular deity; thus an image of a bull (*e.g.* of El in Canaan) portrayed the god's power and fertility. The image was not primarily intended as a visual representation of the deity, but as a dwelling-place of the spirit of the deity enabling the god to be physically present in many different places simultaneously. A worshipper praying before an image would not necessarily accept that his prayers were being offered to the figure of wood or metal itself, but would probably have regarded the image as a 'projection' or embodiment of the deity. Of course, those in Israel who denied any reality to the deity represented

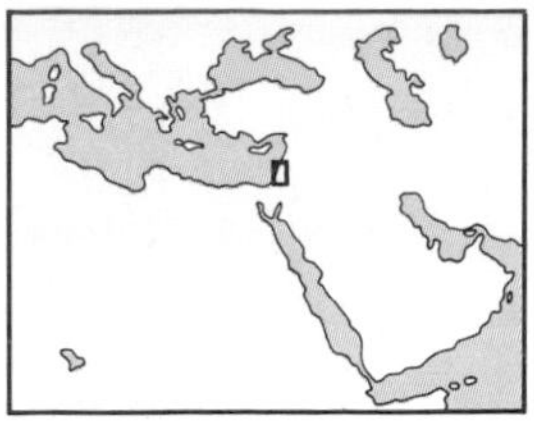

Possible location of Ijon.

ILAI
See Zalmon, Part 3.

ILIUM
See Troas, Part 3.

An Egyptian moon-god of learning, Thoth, was represented in an image taking the form of an ibis. His cult was based at Hermopolis. Saite-Ptolemaic period. c. 664–30 BC. (BM)

by the image maintained that the worshippers of foreign deities were paying homage to mere wood and stone (* IDOLATRY).

Images were made in various ways. A molten image (*massēkâ*) was cast in a mould from copper, silver or gold. A graven image (*pesel*) was carved from stone or wood; wooden images could be overlaid with precious metals (*cf.* Is. 40:19, NEB). See Is. 41:6–7; 44:12–17.

I. In the Old Testament

a. Images of foreign gods. Though the making and worshipping of images is forbidden by Pentateuchal law (Ex. 20:4–5) and condemned by the prophets (*e.g.* Je. 10:3–5; Ho. 11:2), their use in Israel throughout pre-exilic times was common (Jdg. 6:25; 1 Ki. 11:5–8; 16:31–33), even at times within the Temple itself (2 Ki. 21:3–5, 7).

b. Images of Yahweh. Standing stones (*maṣṣēḇôṯ*) erected by the Patriarchs (*e.g.* Gn. 28:18, 22; 35:14) were perhaps originally regarded as images (similarly the sacred trees; *cf.* Gn. 21:33), but were later forbidden (Asherah, Dt. 16:21) or re-interpreted as merely commemorative objects (*cf.* Gn. 31:45–50; Jos. 4:4–9). Later, images of Yahweh were denounced by pure Yahwists: the golden calf at Sinai (Ex. 32:1–8), the image (* EPHOD) made by Gideon (Jdg. 8:26–27), the golden calves at Dan and Bethel (1 Ki. 12:28–30), the calf of Samaria (Ho. 8:6).

c. Man as the image of God. In a few texts in Genesis (1:26–27; 5:2; 9:6) man is said to have been created 'in' or 'as' the image of God, 'according to his likeness'. Though many interpreters have thought to locate the 'image' of God in man's reason, creativity, speech, or spiritual nature, it is more likely that it is the whole of man, rather than some part or aspect of him, that is the image of God. The whole man, body and soul, is the image of God; man is the corporeal image of the incorporeal God. As in the ancient Near East, man as the image of God represents him through his participation in the divine breath or spirit (*cf.* Gn. 2:7; perhaps also the spirit of God is included in the 'us' of 1:26; *cf.* the reference to the spirit of God in 1:2). Man's role as ruler of the earth is established by his creation as God's image (1:27). Elsewhere in the ancient Near East it is usually the king who is said to be the image of God, but in Gn. 1 it is mankind as a whole that is God's vizier and representative. Significantly, man is still spoken of as the image of God after the Fall: the force of Gn. 9:6 depends on the belief that man represents God, so that an injury done to a man is an injury done to God himself (*cf.* also Jas. 3:9).

BIBLIOGRAPHY. *On images in general*: K. H. Bernhardt, *Gott und Bild*, 1956; E. D. van Buren, *Or* 10, 1941, pp. 65–92; A. L. Oppenheim, *Ancient Mesopotamia*, 1964, pp. 171–227. *On the image of God in man*: D. Cairns, *The Image of God in Man*, 1953; G. C. Berkouwer, *Man: The Image of God*, 1962; D. J. A. Clines, *TynB* 19, 1968, pp. 53–103; J. Barr, *BJRL* 51, 1968–9, pp. 11–26; J. M. Miller, *JBL* 91, 1972, pp. 289–304; T. N. D. Mettinger, *ZAW* 86, 1974, pp. 403–424; J. F. A. Sawyer, *JTS* 25, 1974, pp. 418–426. D.J.A.C.

II. In the New Testament

The NT teaching builds on the foundation laid in the OT. There man is described (in the seminal passage of Gn. 1:26f.) as made to be God's representative on earth and to act as God's vicegerent and steward of creation. The term is best thought of as functional, and man's destiny as man is in view (see, in particular, D. J. A. Clines' essay for details and exegetical support).

The two passages of 1 Cor. 11:7 and Jas. 3:9 re-echo this teaching, and both assert the continuance of

Bronze cat with gold earrings, an image of the Egyptian goddess representing the sun's warmth and joy, Bastet, who was worshipped at Bubastis on the Nile delta. Roman period. (BM)

man's position in the created order and as reflecting the divine 'glory', in spite of human sinfulness. The emphasis in the NT, however, falls more on the person of Jesus Christ who is called the 'image of God' (2 Cor. 4:4; Col. 1:15; both are creed-like passages, set on a polemical background, to oppose current false or inadequate notions). Christ's rank as the 'image' of the Father derives from his unique relationship as pre-existent. He is the Logos from all eternity (Jn. 1:1–18), and so he is able to reflect faithfully and fully the glory of the invisible God. See too Heb. 1:1–3 and Phil. 2:6–11 where parallel expressions are used to clarify the unique relationship of Jesus Christ to God. 'Image' (or its equivalent terms, 'form', 'stamp', 'glory') does not suggest a mere likeness to God or a paradigm of his person. Rather it connotes a sharing in the divine life and indeed an 'objectivization' of the essence of God, so that the One who is by nature invisible comes to visible expression in the figure of his Son (see the evidence in R. P. Martin, *op. cit.*, pp. 112f.).

He is thus the 'ultimate Adam' (1 Cor. 15:45) who stands at the head of a new humanity that draws its life from him. So Jesus Christ is both the unique 'Image' and the prototype of those who owe their knowledge of God and life in God to him (Rom. 8:29; 1 Cor. 15:49; 2 Cor. 3:18; 1 Jn. 3:2).

The term 'image of God' is closely connected with 'the new man' (Eph. 4:24; Col. 3:10f.; *cf.* Gal. 3:28). This is a reminder that there are important social aspects to what the 'image' means as it is reproduced in human lives, both in the fellowship of the church and in man's custodianship of nature (Heb. 2:8, referring to Ps. 8).

There is an eschatological dimension also to be recognized. The fulfilment of God's plan for humanity-in-Christ awaits the parousia when Christians' mortal existence will be transformed to a perfect likeness to their Lord (1 Cor. 15:49; Phil. 3:20–21), and in this way the image of God in man will be fully restored.

BIBLIOGRAPHY. Morton Smith, *The Image of God*, 1958; D. J. A. Clines, *TynB* 19, 1968, pp. 53–103 (bibliography); J. Jervell, *Imago Dei, Gen. 1, 26f. im Spätjudentum in der Gnosis und in den paulinischen Briefen*, 1960; F.-W. Eltester, *Eikon im Neuen Testament*, 1958; R. Scroggs, *The Last Adam*, 1966; and R. P. Martin, *Carmen Christi. Philippians 2:5–11*, 1967; *idem*, art. 'Image', in *NIDNTT* 2, pp. 284–293.

On the dogmatic issues, see G. C. Berkouwer, *Man: The Image of God*, 1962.

R.P.M.

IMMANUEL (Heb. *'immānû'ēl*, 'with us is God'). The word is found twice in OT (Is. 7:14; 8:8) and once in NT (Mt. 1:23, RSV 'Emmanuel'). It may be employed also in Is. 8:10.

To understand the significance of the word, which in itself means 'God with us', we must note the context in which it appears. Syria and Israel had desired to form a coalition with Judah in order to oppose the increasing power of Assyria. Judah had vacillated, and Syria and Israel determined to punish her. Upon hearing this news, Ahaz trembled. Isaiah was sent to him to inform him that he had nothing to fear. The power of his enemies was about played out, and they could do him no harm. Isaiah even commanded him to ask for a sign in confirmation of the divine message. This Ahaz refused to do. Hence, in reply to the hypocritical king, Isaiah announces that the Lord will give to the people of Judah a sign. In vision the prophet beholds a virgin (*'almâ, i.e.* an unmarried woman), who is with child and about to bear a son and she will call his name Immanuel.

In any interpretation of this prophecy there are three factors which must be kept in mind.

a. The birth of the child is to be a sign. It is true that in itself a sign need not be a miracle, but in this particular context, after the command issued to Ahaz to ask for a sign deep or high, one would be justified in expecting a sign such as the recession of the shadow on the sundial. There should be something unusual in the birth; a birth in the ordinary course of nature would not seem to meet the requirements of the sign. In this connection it

Assyrian soldiers carry off images of the gods of a conquered city. Drawn from a sculpture found at Nimrud (Calah). c. 730 BC.

must be noted that the question is made more difficult by the fact that there cannot be a local reference of the prophecy to Hezekiah, because Hezekiah had already been born.

b. The mother of the child is an unmarried woman. Why did Isaiah designate her by this particular word *'almâ*? It is sometimes said that had he wished to teach a virgin birth there was a good word at his disposal, namely, *bᵉṯûlâ*. But an examination of the usage of the latter word in OT reveals that it was very unsatisfactory, in that it would have been ambiguous. The word *bᵉṯûlâ* may designate a virgin, but when it does the explanatory phrase 'and a man had not known her' is often added (*cf.* Gn. 24:16). The word may also designate a betrothed virgin (*cf.* Dt. 22:23ff.). In this latter case the virgin is known as the wife (*'iššâ*) of the man, and he as her husband (*'îš*). But the word *bᵉṯûlâ* may also indicate a married woman (Joel 1:8). On the basis of this latter passage a tradition arose among the Jews in which the word could clearly refer to a married woman. Had Isaiah employed this word, therefore, it would not have been clear what type of woman he had in mind, whether virgin or married. Other Heb. words which were at his disposal would not be satisfactory. Had he wished to designate the mother as a young woman he would most likely have employed the common term *naʿarâ* ('girl'). In using the word *'almâ*, however, Isaiah employs the one word which is never applied (either in the Bible or in the other Near Eastern sources) to anyone but an unmarried woman. This unmarried woman might have been immoral, in which case the birth could hardly have been a sign. We are left then with the conclusion that the mother was a good woman and yet unmarried; in other words, the birth was supernatural. It is the presence of this word *'almâ* which makes an application of the passage to some local birth difficult, if not impossible.

c. We must note the force of the term Immanuel. A natural reading of the passage would lead us to expect that the presence of God is to be seen in the birth of the child himself. This interpretation, however, is seriously disputed, and vigorously rejected by most modern writers on the passage. The presence of God is found, rather, so we are told, in the deliverance of Judah from her two northern enemies. The infancy of the child is made the measure of time that would elapse until the two enemies are removed. Such a period of time would be short—a child learns the difference between good and evil at a tender age. Hence, within, say, 2 years, or possibly even less, Judah would have nothing to fear from Syria and Israel. In this deliverance the presence of God would be manifested, and as a token or pledge of this deliverance some mother would call her child Immanuel.

This interpretation poses tremendous problems which it does not answer. What warrant would a mother have for naming her particular child Immanuel? How could she know that her own child and no other would be a sign that in 2 years or so the presence of God would be manifested in the deliverance of Judah from Syria and Israel? Furthermore, how would Israel itself know that a particular child had been born in answer to the prophecy and that the birth of this particular child would be the promised sign? It would seem that, if the prophecy refers to a local birth, the child to be born must be someone prominent. The most prominent person, namely Hezekiah, is ruled out, and therefore we must assume that it is a child of Isaiah or some other child of Ahaz. But this is also ruled out by the word *'almâ*. Neither the wife of Ahaz nor the wife of Isaiah could properly be designated an *'almâ*, for the obvious reason that both were married women.

It seems best, then, to apply the name Immanuel to the Child himself. In his birth the presence of God is to be found. God has come to his people in a little Child, that very Child whom Isaiah later names 'Mighty God' (*'ēl gibbôr*). This interpretation is strengthened by the fact that Isaiah is seeking to dissuade men from trusting the Assyrian king. The nation's help rests not in Assyria but in God. In this dark moment God is with his people. He is found in the birth of a Child.

The infancy of the divine Child is a measure of the time that will elapse until Ahaz is freed from the fear of his two northern enemies (Is. 7:15–16). Ahaz rejects the sign of Immanuel, and turns to the king of Assyria. That king and his successors caused Judah's downfall, but for the remnant there was given the promise of Immanuel, and in Immanuel they would find their hope and salvation.

BIBLIOGRAPHY. E. J. Young, *The Book of Isaiah*, 1, 1964; E. W. Hengstenberg, *Christology of the Old Testament*, 1856, 2, pp. 26–66; J. G. Machen, *The Virgin Birth of Christ*, 1930; J. Lindblom, *A Study on the Immanuel Section in Isaiah*, 1957/8; J. S. Wright, C. Brown, *NIDNTT* 2, pp. 86f. E.J.Y.

IMPERIAL POST
See Travel, Part 3.

IMPIETY
See Wrath, Part 3.

IMPOSTOR
See Magic, Part 2.

IMPRISONMENT
See Prison, Part 3.

INCARNATION.

I. Meaning of the word

Neither the noun 'incarnation' nor the adjective 'incarnate' is biblical, but the Gk. equivalent of Lat. *in carne* (*en sarki*, 'in flesh') is found in some important NT statements about the person and work of Jesus Christ. Thus the hymn quoted in 1 Tim. 3:16 speaks of 'he was manifested in the flesh' (so RSV, following the true text). John ascribes to the spirit of antichrist any denial that Jesus Christ has 'come in the flesh' (1 Jn. 4:2; 2 Jn. 7). Paul says that Christ did his reconciling work 'in his body of flesh' (Col. 1:22; *cf.* Eph. 2:15), and that by sending his Son 'in the likeness of sinful flesh' God 'condemned sin in the flesh' (Rom. 8:3). Peter speaks of Christ dying for us 'in the flesh' (*sarki*, dative of reference: 1 Pet. 3:18; 4:1). All these texts are enforcing from different angles the same truth: that it was precisely by coming and dying 'in the flesh' that Christ secured our salvation. Theology calls his coming the incarnation, and his dying the atonement.

What does *'flesh' mean in these texts? In the Bible this word (Heb. *bāśār*, *šᵉ'ēr*; Gk. *sarx*) has fundamentally a physiological meaning: 'flesh' is the solid stuff which, together with blood and bones, makes up the physical organism of a man or animal (*cf.* Gn. 2:21; Lk. 24:39; 1 Cor. 15:50). Since Heb. thought associates bodily organs with psychical functions, we find that in the OT 'flesh' can cover the psychological as well as the physical aspects of man's personal life (*cf.* the parallelism between 'flesh' and 'heart', Ps. 73:26, and between 'flesh' and 'soul', Ps. 63:1). The word, however, bears more than a merely anthropological significance. The Bible sees physical flesh as a theologically significant symbol—a symbol, namely, of the created and dependent sort of life which men and animals share, a sort of life which is derived from

God and which, unlike God's own life, requires a physical organism to sustain it in its characteristic activity. Hence 'flesh' becomes a generic term for men, or animals, or men and animals together (*cf.* Gn. 6:12; 7:15, 21f.), viewed as creatures of God, whose life on earth lasts only for the comparatively short period during which God supplies the breath of life in their nostrils. 'Flesh' in this theologically developed sense is thus not something that a man *has*, but something that he *is*. Its mark is creaturely weakness and frailty (Is. 40:6), and in this respect it stands in contrast with 'spirit', the eternal and unflagging energy that is of God, and is God (Is. 31:3; *cf.* 40:6–31).

To say, therefore, that Jesus Christ came and died 'in the flesh' is to say that he came and died in the state and under the conditions of created physical and psychical life: in other words, that he who died was man. But the NT also affirms that he who died eternally was, and continues to be, God. The formula which enshrines the incarnation therefore is that in some sense God, without ceasing to be God, was made man. This is what John asserts in the prologue of his Gospel: 'the Word' (God's agent in creation, who 'in the beginning', before the creation, not only 'was with God', but himself 'was God', Jn. 1:1–3) 'became flesh' (Jn. 1:14).

II. Origin of the belief

Such an assertion, considered abstractly against the background of OT monotheism, might seem blasphemous or nonsensical—as, indeed, orthodox Judaism has always held it to be. It appears to mean that the divine Maker became one of his own creatures, which is a *prima facie* contradiction in theological terms. Whence came the conviction that inspired John's strange statement? How did the early church's belief that Jesus of Nazareth was God incarnate arise? On the assumption that it was not occasioned by what Jesus himself said and did, but grew up later, attempts have been made to trace its origin to Jewish speculations about a pre-existent superhuman Messiah, or to the polytheistic myths about redeemer-gods which were characteristic of Hellenistic mystery-religions and Gnostic cults. But it is now widely recognized that these attempts have failed: partly because the differences between these Jewish and Gentile fancies and NT Christology have invariably proved to be more substantial and deep-rooted than their surface similarities are; partly because it has been shown that a virtual claim to deity is embedded in the most undoubted sayings of the historical Jesus, as reported in the Synoptic Gospels, and that a virtual acceptance of this claim was fundamental to the faith and worship of the primitive Palestinian church, as pictured in the first chapters of Acts (the substantial historicity of which is now rarely disputed). The only explanation that covers the facts is that the impact of Jesus' own life, ministry, death and resurrection convinced his disciples of his personal deity even before he ascended. This, of course, is precisely the account of the matter which the Fourth Gospel itself gives (see especially Jn. 20:28ff.). In line with this, Acts tells us that the first Christians prayed to Jesus as Lord (7:59), even before Pentecost (1:21: the 'Lord' who chooses apostles is surely 'the Lord Jesus' of v. 21, *cf.* v. 3); that, beginning on the day of Pentecost, they baptized in his name (2:38; 8:16; 19:5); that they invoked and put faith in his name (*i.e.* in himself: 3:16; 9:14; 22:16; *cf.* 16:31); and that they proclaimed him as the One who gives repentance and remission of sins (5:31). All this shows that, even if the deity of Jesus was not at first clearly stated in words (and Acts gives no hint that it was), it was nevertheless part of the faith by which the first Christians lived and prayed. *Lex orandi lex credendi.* The theological formulation of belief in the incarnation came later, but the belief itself, however incoherently expressed, was there in the church from the beginning.

III. Standpoint of the New Testament writers

It is important to note the nature and limits of the interest which motivates NT thinking about the incarnation, particularly that of Paul, John and the author of Hebrews, who deal with the subject comparatively fully. The NT writers nowhere notice, much less handle, the metaphysical questions about the mode of the incarnation, and the psychological questions about the incarnate state, which have been so prominent in Christological discussion since the 4th century. Their interest in Christ's person is not philosophical and speculative, but religious and evangelical. They speak of Christ, not as a metaphysical problem, but as a divine Saviour; and all that they say about his person is prompted by their desire to glorify him through exhibiting his work and vindicating his centrality in the redemptive purpose of God. They never attempt to dissect the mystery of his person; it is enough for them to proclaim the incarnation as a fact, one of the sequence of mighty works whereby God has wrought salvation for sinners. The only sense in which the NT writers ever attempt to explain the incarnation is by showing how it fits into God's over-all plan for redeeming mankind (see, *e.g.*, Rom. 8:3; Phil. 2:6–11; Col. 1:13–22; Jn. 1:18; 1 Jn. 1:1–2:2; and the main argument of Hebrews 1–2; 4:14–5:10; 7:1–10:18).

The exclusiveness of this evangelical interest throws light on the otherwise puzzling fact that the NT nowhere reflects on the * virgin birth of Jesus as witnessing to the conjunction of deity and manhood in his person—a line of thought much canvassed by later theology. This silence need not mean that any of the NT writers were ignorant of the virgin birth, as some have supposed. It is sufficiently explained by the fact that NT interest in Jesus centres elsewhere, upon his relation to the saving purposes of God. Proof of this is given by the way in which the virgin birth story is itself told by Matthew and Luke, the two Evangelists who recount it. Each lays all his stress, not on the unique constitution of the Person thus miraculously born, but on the fact that by this miraculous birth God began to fulfil his long-foretold intention of visiting and redeeming his people (*cf.* Mt. 1:21ff.; Lk. 1:31ff., 68–75; 2:10f., 29–32). The only significance which they, or any NT writers, see in the incarnation is directly soteriological. The Scotist speculation, popularized by Westcott, that the incarnation was primarily for the perfecting of creation, and only secondarily and incidentally for the redeeming of sinners, finds not the least support in the NT.

The apostolic writers clearly see that both the deity and the manhood of Jesus are fundamental to his saving work. They see that it is just because Jesus is God the Son that they are to regard his disclosure of the Father's mind and heart as perfect and final (*cf.* Jn. 1:18; 14:7–10; Heb. 1:1f.), and his death as the supreme evidence of God's love for sinners and his will to bless believers (*cf.* Jn. 3:16; Rom. 5:5–10; 8:32; 1 Jn. 4:8–10). They realize that it is Jesus' divine Sonship that guarantees the endless duration, sinless perfection and limitless efficacy, of his high-priestly service (Heb. 7:3, 16, 24–28). They are aware that it was in virtue of his deity that he was able to defeat and dispossess the devil, the 'strong man armed' who kept sinners in a state of helpless thraldom (Heb. 2:14f.; Rev. 20:1f.; *cf.* Mk. 3:27; Lk. 10:17f.; Jn. 12:31f.; 16:11). Equally, they see that it was necessary for the Son of God to 'become flesh', for only so could he take his place as the 'second man' through whom God deals with the race (1 Cor. 15:21f., 47ff.; Rom. 5:15–19); only so could he mediate between God and men (1 Tim. 2:5); and only so could he die for sins, for only flesh can die. (Indeed, the thought of 'flesh' is so bound up with death that the NT will not apply the term to Christ's manhood in its glorified and incorruptible state: 'the days of his flesh' (Heb. 5:7) means Christ's time on earth up to the cross.)

We should, therefore, expect the NT to treat any denial that Jesus Christ was both truly divine and truly human as a damning heresy, destructive of the gospel; and so it does. The only such denial that it knows is the docetic Christology (traditionally, that of Cerinthus) which denied the reality of Christ's 'flesh' (1 Jn. 4:2f.), and hence of his physical death ('blood', 1 Jn. 5:6). John denounces this in his first two Epistles as a deadly error inspired by the spirit of antichrist, a lying denial of both the Father and the Son (1 Jn. 2:22–25; 4:1–6; 5:5–12; 2 Jn. 7, 9ff.). It is usually thought that the emphasis in John's Gospel on the reality of Jesus' experience of human frailty (his weariness, 4:6; thirst, 4:7; 19:28; tears, 11:33ff.) is intended to cut at the root of the same docetic error.

IV. Elements of the New Testament doctrine

The meaning of the NT claim that 'Jesus Christ has come in the flesh' may be drawn out under three heads.

a. The Person incarnate

The NT uniformly defines the identity of Jesus in terms of his relation to the one God of OT monotheism (*cf.* 1 Cor. 8:4, 6; 1 Tim. 2:5; with Is. 43:10f.; 44:6). The basic definition is that Jesus is God's *Son.* This identification is rooted in Jesus' own thought and teaching. His sense of being 'the Son' in a unique sense that set him apart from the rest of men went back at least to his 13th year (Lk. 2:49), and was confirmed to him by his Father's voice from heaven at his baptism: 'Thou art my beloved Son' (Mk. 1:11; *cf.* Mt. 3:17; Lk. 3:22; *agapētos*, which appears in all three reports of the heavenly utterance, carries the implication of '*only* beloved': so again in the parable, Mk. 12:6; *cf.* the similar words from heaven at the transfiguration, Mk. 9:7; Mt. 17:5). At his trial, when asked under oath whether he was 'the Son of God' (a phrase which on the high priest's lips probably signified no more than 'Davidic Messiah'), Mark and Luke report Jesus as making an affirmative reply which was in effect a claim to personal deity: *egō eimi* (so Mk. 14:62; Lk. 22:70 has: 'you say [*sc.* rightly] that *egō eimi*'). *egō eimi*, the emphatic 'I am', were words that no Jew would take on his lips, for they expressed the self-identification of God (Ex. 3:14). Jesus, who according to Mark had used these words before in a similar suggestive way (Mk. 6:50; *cf.* 13:6; and *cf.* the long series of *egō eimi* sayings in John's Gospel: Jn. 4:26; 6:35; 8:12; 10:7, 11; 11:25; 14:6; 15:1; 18:5ff.), evidently wished to make it perfectly clear that the divine Sonship to which he laid claim was nothing less than personal deity. It was for this 'blasphemy' that he was condemned.

Jesus' references to himself as 'the Son' are always in contexts which mark him out as uniquely close to God and uniquely favoured by God. There are comparatively few in the Synoptic Gospels (Mt. 11:27 = Lk. 10:22; Mk. 13:32 = Mt. 24:36; *cf.* Mk. 12:1–11), but many in John, both in Jesus' own words and in the Evangelist's commentary. According to John, Jesus is God's 'only' Son (*monogenēs*: 1:14, 18; 3:16, 18). He exists eternally (8:58; *cf.* 1:1f.). He stands in an unchanging relation of perfect love, union and communion, with the Father (1:18; 8:16, 29; 10:30; 16:32). As Son, he has no independent initiative (5:19); he lives to glorify his Father (17:1, 4), by doing his Father's will (4:34; 5:30; 8:28f.). He came into the world because the Father 'sent' him (42 references), and gave him a task to fulfil there (4:34; 17:4; *cf.* 19:30). He came in his Father's name, *i.e.* as his Father's representative (5:43), and, because all that he said and did was according to the Father's command (7:16ff.; 8:26ff.; 12:49f.; 14:10), his life on earth revealed his Father perfectly (14:7ff.). When he speaks of the Father as greater than himself (14:28; *cf.* 10:29) he is evidently referring, not to any essential or circumstantial inferiority, but to the fact that subordination to the Father's will and initiative is natural and necessary to him. The Father is greater than he because in relation to the Father it is always his nature freely and joyfully to act as a Son. But this does not mean that he is to be subordinated to the Father in men's esteem and worship. Just the reverse; for the Father seeks the Son's glory no less than the Son seeks the Father's glory. The Father has committed to the Son his two great works of giving life and executing judgment, 'that all may honour the Son, even as they honour the Father' (5:21ff.). This amounts to saying that the Father directs all men to do as Thomas did (20:28), and acknowledge the Son in the same terms in which they ought to acknowledge the Father himself—namely, as 'my Lord and my God'.

The NT contains other lines of thought, subsidiary to that of divine Sonship, which also proclaim the deity of Jesus of Nazareth. We may mention the more important of these: (i) John identifies the eternal divine *Word* with God's personal Son, Jesus Christ (Jn. 1:1–18; *cf.* 1 Jn. 1:1–3; Rev. 19:13; *LOGOS). (ii) Paul speaks of the Son as 'the *image* of God', both as incarnate (2 Cor. 4:4) and in his pre-incarnate state (Col. 1:15), and in Phil. 2:6 says that prior to the incarnation Jesus Christ was in the 'form' (*morphē*) of God: a phrase the exact exegesis of which is disputed, but which J. B. Phillips is almost certainly right to render: 'always . . . God by nature'. Heb. 1:3 (RV) calls the Son 'the effulgence of his (God's) glory, and the *very image of his substance*'. These statements, made as they are within a monotheistic frame of reference which excludes any thought of two Gods, are clearly meant to imply: (1) that the Son is personally divine, and ontologically one with the Father; (2) that the Son perfectly embodies all that is in the Father, or, putting it negatively, that there is no aspect or constituent of deity or character which the Father has and the Son lacks. (iii) Paul can apply an OT prophecy concerning the invocation of 'the Lord' (Yahweh) to the Lord Jesus, thus indicating that it finds its true fulfilment in him (Rom. 10:13, quoting Joel 2:32; *cf.* Phil. 2:10f., echoing Is. 45:23). Similarly, the writer to the Hebrews quotes Moses' exhortation to the angels to worship God (Dt. 32:43, LXX), and the psalmist's declaration: 'Thy throne, O God, is for ever and ever' (Ps. 45:6), as words spoken by the Father with reference to his Son (Heb. 1:6, 8). This shows that both writers regard Jesus as divine. (iv) The regular NT habit of referring to Jesus as 'Lord'—the title given to the gods of Hellenistic religion (*cf.* 1 Cor. 8:5), and invariably used in LXX to render the divine name—would seem to be an implicit ascription of deity.

b. The nature of the incarnation

When the Word 'became flesh' his deity was not abandoned, or reduced, or contracted, nor did he cease to exercise the divine functions which had been his before. It is he, we are told, who sustains the creation in ordered existence, and who gives and upholds all life (Col. 1:17; Heb. 1:3; Jn. 1:4), and these functions were certainly not in abeyance during his time on earth. When he came into the world he 'emptied himself' of outward glory (Phil. 2:7; Jn. 17:5), and in that sense he 'became poor' (2 Cor. 8:9), but this does not at all imply a curtailing of his divine powers, such as the so-called kenosis theories would suggest. The NT stresses rather that the Son's deity was not reduced through the incarnation. In the man Christ Jesus, says Paul, 'dwelleth *all the fullness of the Godhead* bodily' (Col. 2:9; *cf.* 1:19).

The incarnation of the Son of God, then, was not a diminishing of deity, but an acquiring of manhood. It was not that God the Son came to indwell a human being, as the Spirit was later to do. (To assimilate incarnation to indwelling is the essence of the Nestorian heresy.) It was rather that the Son in person began to live a fully human life. He did not simply clothe himself in a human body, taking the place of its soul, as Apollinaris maintained, he took to himself a human soul as well as a human body, *i.e.* he entered into the experience of human psychical life as well as of human physical life. His manhood was complete; he became 'the *man* Christ Jesus' (1 Tim. 2:5; *cf.* Gal. 4:4; Heb. 2:14, 17). And his manhood is permanent. Though now exalted, he 'continueth to be, God and man in two distinct natures, and one person, for ever' (*Westminster Shorter Catechism*, Q. 21; *cf.* Heb. 7:24).

c. The incarnate state

(i) It was a state of *dependence* and *obedience*, because the incarnation did not change the relationship between the Son and the Father. They continued in unbroken fellowship, the Son saying and doing what the Father gave him to say and do, and not going beyond the Father's known will at any single moment (*cf.* the first temptation, Mt. 4:2ff.). His confessed ignorance of the time of his return (Mk. 13:32) should no doubt be explained, not as edifying pretence (Aquinas), nor as evidence of his having laid aside his divine knowledge for the purpose of the incarnation (the kenosis theories), but simply as showing that it was not the Father's will for him to have this knowledge in his mind at that time. As the Son, he did not wish or seek to know more than the Father wished him to know.

(ii) It was a state of *sinlessness* and *impeccability*, because the incarnation did not change the nature and character of the Son. That his whole life was sinless is several times asserted (2 Cor. 5:21; 1 Pet. 2:22; Heb. 4:15; *cf.* Mt. 3:14–17; Jn. 8:46; 1 Jn. 2:1f.). That he was exempt from the entail of original sin in Adam is evident from the fact that he was not bound to die for sins of his own (*cf.* Heb. 7:26), and hence could die vicariously and representatively, the righteous taking the place of the unrighteous (*cf.* 2 Cor. 5:21; Rom. 5:16ff.; Gal. 3:13; 1 Pet. 3:18). That he was impeccable, and could not sin, follows from the fact that he remained God the Son (*cf.* Jn. 5:19, 30). Deviation from the Father's will was no more possible for him in the incarnate state than before. His deity was the guarantee that he would achieve in the flesh that sinlessness which was prerequisite if he were to die as 'a lamb without blemish or spot' (1 Pet. 1:19).

(iii) It was a state of *temptation* and *moral conflict*, because the incarnation was a true entry into the conditions of man's moral life. Though, being God, it was not in him to yield to temptation, yet, being man, it was necessary for him to fight temptation in order to overcome it. What his deity ensured was not that he would not be tempted to stray from his Father's will, nor that he would be exempt from the strain and distress that repeated insidious temptations create in the soul, but that, when tempted, he would fight and win; as he did in the initial temptations of his Messianic ministry (Mt. 4:1ff.). The writer to the Hebrews stresses that in virtue of his firsthand experience of temptation and the costliness of obedience he is able to extend effective sympathy and help to tempted and distraught Christians (Heb. 2:18; 4:14ff.; 5:2, 7ff.). (*JESUS CHRIST, LIFE AND TEACHING OF.)

BIBLIOGRAPHY. J. Denney, *Jesus and the Gospel*, 1908; P. T. Forsyth, *The Person and Place of Jesus Christ*, 1909; H. R. Mackintosh, *The Doctrine of the Person of Jesus Christ*, 1912; A. E. J. Rawlinson, *The New Testament Doctrine of the Christ*, 1926; L. Hodgson, *And was made Man*, 1928; E. Brunner, *The Mediator*, E.T. 1934; D. M. Baillie, *God was in Christ*, 1948; L. Berkhof, *Systematic Theology*[4], 1949, pp. 305–330; G. C. Berkouwer, *The Person of Christ*, 1954; K. Barth, *Church Dogmatics*, I, 2, 1956, pp. 122–202; V. Taylor, *The Person of Christ in New Testament Teaching*, 1958; O. Cullmann, *The Christology of the New Testament*, E.T. 1960; W. Pannenberg, *Jesus—God and Man*, E.T. 1968; C. F. D. Moule, *The Origin of Christology*, 1977.

J.I.P.

INCENSE. A common feature of OT ritual, incense was a costly offering and a sign essentially of the acknowledgment of deity (*cf.* Mal. 1:11). The word has a double application: it refers both to the substance used for burning and to the aromatic odour which is produced. Two Heb. words are thus rendered: (1) *l^eḇônâ*, 'frankincense'; and (2) *q^eṭōreṯ*, the 'sweet smoke' (EVV 'incense') of Is. 1:13. Among the Israelites only priests were allowed to offer incense. When the Lord gave Moses instructions for Aaron, these included strict regulations concerning the use of incense in the holy place (Lv. 16:12f.). Incense is also used in Scripture as a symbol for prayer (*e.g.* Ps. 141:2, Rev. 8:3f., Gk. *thymiama*).

Frankincense (Heb. *l^eḇônâ*). This substance consisted of the resinous exudate of certain *Boswellia* trees, the principal species being *B. frereana*, *B. carteri* and *B. papyrifera* in NE Africa, *B. sacra* in Dhofar, S. Arabia, and *B. serrata* in NW India, where they grow in semi-desert mountains. They furnished much of the wealth acquired by those traders who followed the ancient spice-routes from S Arabia to Gaza and Damascus (Is. 60:6).

The whitish-yellow aromatic resin was obtained by incising the bark, and, although acrid to the taste, frankincense was extremely odoriferous. It comprised one ingredient of the holy anointing oil (Ex. 30:34), and was also burnt with other substances during the cereal-offering (Lv. 6:15). Frankincense was placed in purified form on the showbread in the tabernacle (Lv. 24:7). While it gratified the senses (Ct. 3:6; 4:6, 14), it was also symbolic of religious fervour (*cf.* Mal. 1:11). The gift of frankincense presented to Christ by the wise men (Mt. 2:11) has been interpreted as symbolizing his priestly office.

This incense-burner was found with the supposed remains of a platform (bamah—*'high place'*) *in the gate complex at Beersheba. Strata V–VI. c. 10th cent. BC.* (TAU)

See F. N. Hepper, 'Arabian and African Frankincense', *JEA* 55, 1969, pp. 66–72.

Galbanum (Heb. *ḥelb*^{e}*nâ*; etymology uncertain). A strong-smelling spice (Ex. 30:34), usually regarded as the gum of an umbelliferous plant, *Ferula galbaniflua*, native to Persia.

The other constituents of the sacred incense were stacte and onycha (*HERBS AND SPICES).

See also *SACRIFICE AND OFFERING (OT), **IV.** *a*; *COSMETICS AND PERFUMERY, **V.** *b* (which includes bibliography). F.N.H.

INCREASE. A noun or verb meaning multiplication or growth, translating sundry Heb. and Gk. words. Primarily the term involved the natural reproduction and germination of cattle and harvest, but always under God's direction and control (Lv. 26:4; Dt. 7:13; Ps. 67:6), as acknowledged by the tithe (Dt. 14:22; *cf.* Pr. 3:9). Hence prosperity is a sign of God's favour (Dt. 6:3), adversity of his displeasure (Je. 15:8), and man's exacting gain from possessions is condemned in the same manner as usury (Lv. 25:37; Ezk. 18:8ff.; *cf.* Ps. 62:10). The term is used symbolically of Israel's relationship with God (Je. 2:3) and of the spiritual blessings God imparts (Is. 29:19; 40:29), especially by the coming of the Messiah (Is. 9:3, 7).

In the NT the term is applied to the growth of the church in numbers (Acts 6:7; 16:5; 1 Cor. 3:6) and in depth (Eph. 4:16; Col. 2:19). It is also applied to individuals generally (Lk. 2:52; Jn. 3:30; Acts 9:22), and specifically with regard to faith (Lk. 17:5; 2 Cor. 10:15), love (1 Thes. 3:12; 4:10), knowledge (Col. 1:10), or ungodliness (2 Tim. 2:16). P.A.B.

INDIA.

I. Early period

Heb. *hōddû*, from Old Persian *hindu* (*cf.* Sanskrit *sindhu*), in inscriptions of Darius I and Xerxes I of Persia. The area so designated was that part of the Indus valley and plains E of the Afghan mountains incorporated into the Persian empire by Darius I, who made it his E boundary (Herodotus, 3. 94; 4. 40, 44). In Est. 1:1; 8:9 the limits of the dominion of Ahasuerus (Xerxes I) are 'from India unto Ethiopia', *hōddû* and *kûš*; this corresponds with Xerxes I's own Old Persian inscriptions, *cf.* the list of countries including 'Sind' or India (*Hiduš*) and Ethiopia (*Kušiya*) in R. G. Kent, *Old Persian: Grammar, Texts, Lexicon*, 1953 ed., p. 151, ll. 25, 29 and § 3. But long before this, trade between India and Mesopotamia is known as early as *c.* 2100 BC (Ur III period), both in texts and by the presence of Indus Valley seals in Mesopotamia. Some think that *Ophir might be Indian (S)upāra. India was the source of the war-elephants used by Alexander and his Seleucid successors in Syria, and in the Graeco-Roman period many exotic products came from India, usually through S Arabia, either up the Red Sea or overland up the W side of Arabia. On routes and navigation, *cf.* van Beek and Hourani, *JAOS* 78, 1958, pp. 146–147; and 80, 1960, pp. 135–139. Greek principalities maintained themselves for some time in parts of NW India; *cf.* W. W. Tarn, *The Greeks in Bactria and India*, 1938. For Indians in Egypt in the Graeco-Roman period, *cf.* Sir H. I. Bell, *Cults and Creeds in Graeco-Roman Egypt*, 1953, p. 48; E. Bevan, *History of Egypt under the Ptolemaic Dynasty*, 1927, p. 155; models from Memphis: Petrie, *Memphis I*, 1909, pp. 16–17, plate 39.

II. Later period

Between the 1st century BC and *c.* AD 200, India and the Mediterranean lands entered into closer commercial and cultural relations, stimulated by the Roman market for Eastern luxuries and facilitated by the discovery of the nature of the monsoons, with the subsequent opening of a regular sea-route to the Tamil towns (mod. Cranganore and Kottayam) and even to Madras (*Sopatma*) and beyond. Against this background we must view the stories of the first introduction of Christianity to India. The unanimous tradition of the old S India church traces its foundation to Thomas the apostle. The narrative of the gnosticizing *Acts of* (Judas) *Thomas* (*NEW TESTAMENT APOCRYPHA) also sets Thomas' activities in India. In itself it is the wildest legend, but J. N. Farquhar argued that it reflects accurate knowledge of 1st-century India and postulated that Thomas worked first in the Punjab and later in the S (*BJRL* 11, 1926; 12, 1927). There seems, however, no other

Top left:
The white resin of frankincense exudes from cuts in the branches of the Boswellia *tree.* (FNH)

Left:
One of the constituents of incense was galbanum (Ferula species), *a resin obtained from a plant similar to this, growing in Persia.* (FNH)

early account of Thomas in India clearly independent of these *Acts* (A. Mingana, *BJRL* 11, 1926; 12, 1927). The peripatetic Pantaenus is said to have been a missionary in India some time before AD 180, and to have found Christians there with Matthew's Gospel in Hebrew left by Bartholomew (Eusebius, *EH* 5. 10); but a loose designation of Aden or some other part of Arabia may be involved. That the Syriac S India church is very ancient is undeniable: the question of apostolic or subapostolic foundation remains open.

A legal deed in which a brother and sister shared their mother's estate in the presence of King Niqmepa of Alalah. The cuneiform tablet is in a clay envelope sealed by the king and witnesses. c. 10 cm × 5 cm. 18th cent. BC. (BM)

BIBLIOGRAPHY. E. H. Warmington, *Indian Commerce*, 1928; L. W. Browne, *The Indian Christians of St Thomas*, 1956. K.A.K.

INHERITANCE.

I. In the Old Testament

In the OT there are two basic roots for inheritance, *nāḥal* and *yāraš*. In each case the emphasis was much more upon possession generally than upon the process of succession, though this idea is not altogether absent. The words occur only rarely in Gn. and Ex. and are most frequent in Nu. and Dt., which look forward to the allotment of land in Canaan, and in Jos. which records how it was put into effect. The law of inheritance was as follows. Land belonged to the family rather than to the individual. There was therefore a strict entail. The eldest son received a double portion and the others equal shares. If a man died leaving no sons the inheritance went to his daughters; if no daughters, to his brothers; if no brothers, to his father's brothers; if no father's brothers, to the next of kin (Nu. 27:8–11). If daughters inherited they had to marry in their own tribe (Nu. 36:6). The emphasis of the word *yāraš* is on possession, for the heir succeeded by right and not by disposition. Wills were unknown in Israel before the time of Herod. Before the giving of the law the Patriarchs were free to pass over the *first-born in favour of a younger son. Abraham, Isaac and

INGATHERING
See Tabernacles, feast of, Part 3.

INN
See Hospitality, Part 2.

Jacob were all younger sons. Joseph was preferred to Reuben (1 Ch. 5:1–2) and Ephraim to Manasseh (Gn. 48:8–20). The giving of the rights of the first-born to the first-born of a second and favourite wife was forbidden in Dt. 21:15–17. However, in the case of the royal succession David was preferred to his older brothers (1 Sa. 16:11) and Solomon to Adonijah (1 Ki. 2:15), though the normal custom was for the first-born to succeed (2 Ch. 21:3).

If a man died childless his brother had to marry his widow (Gn. 38:8–9; Dt. 25:5–10; Mt. 22:23–25). The first son of that union was regarded as the first-born of the deceased brother, and therefore if there were only one son the surviving brother would have no heir. It was accordingly possible for the brother not to marry his brother's wife, and then the right went to the nearest kinsman (Ru. 2:20; 3:9–13; 4:1–12). In the book of Ruth, Ruth plays the part of Naomi, who was past the age of marriage (Ru. 4:17). Land could not be sold in perpetuity (Lv. 25:23–24). If it was sold it could be redeemed by the next of kin (Lv. 25:25). Naboth knew Ahab's offer was against the law (1 Ki. 21:3).

The land of Canaan was regarded as the inheritance of Yahweh in a particular way (Ex. 15:17; *cf.* Jos. 22:19; Ps. 79:1), though he was God of all the earth (Ps. 47:2, *etc.*). It was for that reason that Israel was able to enjoy it as their inheritance.

The promises made to Abraham concerned a land as well as descendants (Gn. 12:7; 15:18–21, *etc.*). Abraham's faith was shown in believing that he would have descendants when he was childless and his wife was past child-bearing age, and in believing that he would have a land, though during his lifetime he was a nomad with no settled possession (Acts 7:5). The children of Israel were brought out of Egypt not only to escape from bondage but also to inherit a land (Ex. 6:6–8). This land was conquered by them, but it was the gift of Yahweh (Jos. 21:43–45). He allotted them in it an inheritance which was to last for ever (Gn. 13:15, *etc.*).

Lots were cast to discover Yahweh's disposal of portions to individual tribes (Jos. 18:2–10). Eventually it was to be a remnant who returned from exile to inherit the land (Is. 10:20–21, *etc.*). Those who formed that faithful remnant were to inherit the nations as well (Ps. 2:8).

The Levites were to have no territory because Yahweh was their inheritance (Dt. 18:1–2). Materially this meant that their portion consisted of the dues and firstfruits given by the people to Yahweh (Dt. 18:3–5). Spiritually the idea was extended to the whole of Israel (Ps. 16:5–6, *etc.*). Also Israel was to be his inheritance as the people which belonged specially to him (Dt. 7:6; 32:9). (*PROMISED LAND.)

II. In the New Testament

In the NT 'inheritance' renders Gk. *klēronomos* and its cognates, derived from *klēros*, meaning a 'lot'. The inheritance is narrowed down to the true Israel, Christ himself, who is 'the heir' (Mk. 12:7). As heir of God he enters into a possession given to him because of his relationship. He has been made heir of everything (Heb. 1:2). Believers in a sense share the divine sonship by adoption and therefore also the divine heirship (Rom. 8:17). They follow in the footsteps of faithful Abraham as heirs of the promise (Rom. 4:13–14) and like Isaac they are his children, heirs according to promise (Gal. 3:29). Their inheritance is something which is given by God's grace because of their status in his sight, and it is in no sense earned.

The object of the Christian inheritance is all that was symbolized by the land of Canaan, and more. Believers inherit the kingdom of God (Mt. 25:34; 1 Cor. 6:9–10; 15:50; Gal. 5:21; Eph. 5:5; Jas. 2:5). They inherit the earth or 'the land' (Mt. 5:5; *cf.* Ps. 37:29). They inherit salvation (Heb. 1:14), a blessing (1 Pet. 3:9), glory (Rom. 8:17–18), and incorruption (1 Cor. 15:50). These are all 'the promises' (Heb. 6:12), not received in their fulfilment by the believers of the OT (Heb. 11:39–40). In Hebrews stress is laid upon the new 'covenant' or 'testament'. It is on this that the promised inheritance is based, especially as it required the death of the testator (Heb. 9:15–17). Two men asked Jesus what they should do in order to inherit eternal life (Lk. 10:25; 18:18), and Christ spoke of that as being part of the blessing of the new world (Mt. 19:29). A Christian man and wife are joint heirs of the grace of life (1 Pet. 3:7).

The consummation of the blessings promised will not take place until the parousia. The inheritance is reserved in heaven (1 Pet. 1:4). He who overcomes is to have the inheritance of God (Rev. 21:7). However, that does not alter the fact that many of the blessings of heirship may be enjoyed in advance. The Holy Spirit is the agent who makes our position as heirs real (Rom. 8:16–17), and he is given to us 'as the guarantee of our inheritance until we acquire possession of it' (Eph. 1:14). He was sent to the church after Christ's own entry into his inheritance at his ascension.

In the NT we still see God's people as his inheritance (Eph. 1:18), and all the blessings mentioned above show that he himself is still their inheritance.

But that inheritance is not of right, it is by the free disposition of God, who is able in his sovereign pleasure to dispossess those who seem to have most title to it and give it to others of his choice.

BIBLIOGRAPHY. *TWBR*, pp. 112–114; J. Herrmann, W. Foerster, *TDNT* 3, pp. 758–785; J. Eichler, W. Mundle, *NIDNTT* 2, pp. 295–304; James D. Hester, *Paul's Concept of Inheritance*, 1968; W. D. Davies, *The Gospel and the Land: Early Christianity and Jewish Territorial Doctrine*, 1974. R.E.N.

INNER MAN. Paul uses this phrase (*ho esō anthrōpos*, in Rom. 7:22; 2 Cor. 4:16; Eph. 3:16) to denote the Christian's true self, as seen by God and known (partially) in consciousness. (For a vindication of the view that Rom. 7:14–26 pictures Paul the Christian, see A. Nygren, *Romans*, 1952, pp. 284ff.) The contrast, implicit if not explicit, is with *ho exō anthrōpos*, 'the outward man' (2 Cor. 4:16), the same individual as seen by his fellow-men, a being physically alive and active, known (so far as he is known) through his behaviour.

This contrast differs both from that which Paul drew between the new and old man (*i.e.* between man's status, condition and affinities in Christ and apart from Christ), and from that which Platonists drew between the immaterial, immortal soul (the real man) and his material, mortal body (his lodging), or, again, between the soul's rational (higher) and sensual (lower) impulses. The contrast in view is rather that between the 'outward appearance' and the 'heart' drawn in 1 Sa. 16:7: 'inner man' and *'heart' are, indeed, almost synonymous. This contrast reflects two facts. First, God, the searcher of hearts, sees things in a man that are hidden from his fellows, who see only his exterior (*cf.* 1 Sa. 16:7; Mt. 23:27f., and Peter's assertion that meekness and quietness adorn 'the *hidden* person of the heart', which God notices, if men do not, 1 Pet. 3:3f.). Secondly, God's renewal of sinners in Christ is a hidden work (Col. 3:3f.), of which human observers see only certain of the effects (*cf.* Jn. 3:8). The sphere of character, and of the Spirit's transforming work, is not the outward, but the inner man. The exact point of the contrast differs in each of the three texts.

1. In 2 Cor. 4:16 it is between the outward Paul, the Paul whom men saw, worn down by constant work, ill health, anxiety, strain and persecution, and the Paul whom God knew and who knew God, the Paul who had been recreated, and was now indwelt, by the Spirit (2 Cor. 5:5, 17), and who after physical dissolution would be 'further clothed' with a resurrection body (2 Cor. 5:1ff.). The outward Paul was going to pieces; the real Paul was daily renewed.

2. In Rom. 7:22f. the contrast is between the 'law (active principle) of sin' in Paul's 'members', influencing his outward actions, and the 'law of my mind', Paul's heart's delight in God's law and heart's desire to keep it, which desire sin constantly frustrated.

3. In Eph. 3:16–19 the contrast is only implicit. The inward man, the heart, the temple in which Christ dwells and the sphere of his strengthening operation, is the real, abiding self, the self that knows Christ's love and will be filled into God's fullness; but this self is hidden from men. Hence Paul has need to exhort his readers to show the world what God has wrought in them by the quality of their outward conduct (Eph. 4–6).

BIBLIOGRAPHY. Arndt, *s.v. anthrōpos*; R. Bultmann, *Theology of the New Testament*, 1, p. 203. J.I.P.

INSPIRATION. Noun formed from Latin and English translations of *theopneustos* in 2 Tim. 3:16, which AV rendered: 'All Scripture is given by inspiration of God, and is profitable for doctrine, for reproof, for correction, for instruction in righteousness.' 'Inspired of God' in RSV is no improvement on AV, for *theopneustos* means *out*-breathed rather than *in*-breathed by God—divinely *ex*-spired, rather than *in*-spired. In the last century Ewald and Cremer argued that the adjective bore an active sense, 'breathing the Spirit', and Barth appears to agree (he glosses it as meaning not only 'given and filled and ruled by the Spirit of God', but also 'actively out-breathing and spreading abroad and making known the Spirit of God' (*Church Dogmatics*, I. 2, E.T. 1956, p. 504)); but B. B. Warfield showed decisively in 1900 that the sense of the word can only be passive. The thought is not of God as breathing through Scripture, or of Scripture as breathing out God, but of God as having breathed out Scripture. Paul's words mean, not that Scripture is inspiring (true though this is), but that Scripture is a divine product, and must be approached and estimated as such.

The 'breath' or 'spirit' of God in the OT (Heb. *rûaḥ*, *n^esāmâ*) denotes the active outgoing of divine power, whether in creation (Ps. 33:6; Jb. 33:4; *cf.* Gn. 1:2; 2:7), preservation (Jb. 34:14), revelation to and through prophets (Is. 48:16; 61:1; Mi. 3:8; Joel 2:28f.), regeneration (Ezk. 36:27), or judgment (Is. 30:28, 33). The NT reveals this divine 'breath' (Gk. *pneuma*) to be a Person of the Godhead. God's 'breath' (*i.e.* the Holy Spirit) produced Scripture, as a means to the conveyance of spiritual understanding. Whether we render *pasa graphē* as 'the whole Scripture' or 'every text', and whether we follow RSV or RV in construing the sentence (RV has 'Every scripture inspired of God is also profitable . . .', which is a possible translation), Paul's meaning is clear beyond all doubt. He is affirming that all that comes in the category of Scripture, all that has a place among the 'sacred writings' (*hiera grammata*, v. 15, RV), just because it is God-breathed, is profitable for the guiding of both faith and life.

On the basis of this Pauline text, English theology regularly uses the word 'inspiration' to express the thought of the divine origin and quality of Holy Scripture. Actively, the noun denotes God's out-breathing operation which produced Scripture: passively, the inspiredness of the Scriptures so produced. The word is also used more generally of the divine influence which enabled the human organs of revelation—prophets, psalmists, wise men and apostles—to speak, as well as to write, the words of God.

I. The idea of biblical inspiration

According to 2 Tim. 3:16, what is inspired is precisely the biblical writings. Inspiration is a work of God terminating, not in the men who were to write Scripture (as if, having given them an idea of what to say, God left them to themselves to find a way of saying it), but in the actual written product. It is Scripture—*graphē*, the written text—that is God-breathed. The essential idea here is that all Scripture has the same character as the prophets' sermons had, both when preached and when written (*cf.* 2 Pet. 1:19–21, on the divine origin of every 'prophecy of the scripture'; see also Je. 36; Is. 8:16–20). That is to say, Scripture is not only man's word, the fruit of human thought, premeditation and art, but also, and equally, God's word, spoken through man's lips or written with man's pen. In other words, Scripture has a double authorship, and man is only the secondary author; the primary author, through whose initiative, prompting and enlightenment, and under whose superintendence, each human writer did his work, is God the Holy Spirit.

Revelation to the prophets was essentially verbal; often it had a visionary aspect, but even 'revelation in visions is also verbal revelation' (L. Koehler, *Old Testament Theology*, E.T. 1957, p. 103). Brunner has observed that in 'the words of God which the Prophets proclaim as those which they have received directly from God, and have been commissioned to repeat, as they have received them . . . perhaps we may find the closest analogy to the meaning of the theory of verbal inspiration' (*Revelation and Reason*, 1946, p. 122, n. 9). Indeed we do; we find not merely an analogy to it, but the paradigm of it; and 'theory' is the wrong word to use, for this is just the biblical doctrine itself. Biblical inspiration should be defined in the same theological terms as prophetic inspiration: namely, as the whole process (manifold, no doubt, in its psychological forms, as prophetic inspiration was) whereby God moved those men whom he had chosen and prepared (*cf.* Je. 1:5; Gal. 1:15) to write exactly what he wanted written for the communication of saving knowledge to his people, and through them to the world. Biblical inspiration is thus verbal by its very nature; for it is of God-given words that the God-breathed Scriptures consist.

Thus, inspired Scripture is written revelation, just as the prophets' sermons were spoken revelation. The biblical record of God's self-disclosure in redemptive history is not merely human testimony to revelation, but is itself revelation. The inspiring of Scripture was an integral part in the revelatory process, for in Scripture God gave the church his saving work in history, and his own authoritative interpretation of its place in his eternal plan. 'Thus saith the Lord' could be prefixed to each book of Scripture with no less propriety than it is (359 times, according to Koehler, *op. cit.*, p. 245) to individual prophetic utterances which Scripture contains. Inspiration, therefore, guarantees the truth of all that the Bible asserts, just as the inspiration of the prophets guaranteed the truth of their representation of the mind of God. ('Truth' here denotes correspondence between the words of man and the thoughts of God, whether in the realm of fact or of meaning.) As truth from God, man's Creator and rightful King, biblical instruction, like prophetic oracles, carries divine authority.

II. Biblical presentation

The idea of canonical Scripture, *i.e.* of a document or corpus of documents containing a permanent authoritative record of divine revelation, goes back to Moses' writing of God's law in the wilderness (Ex. 34:27f.; Dt. 31:9ff., 24ff.). The truth of all statements, historical or theological, which Scripture makes, and their authority as words of God, are assumed without question or discussion in both Testaments. The Canon grew, but the concept of inspiration, which the idea of canonicity presupposes, was fully developed from the first, and is unchanged throughout the Bible. As there presented, it comprises two convictions.

1. *The words of Scripture are God's own words.* OT passages identify the Mosaic law and the words of the prophets, both spoken and written, with God's own speech (*cf.* 1 Ki. 22:8–16; Ne. 8; Ps. 119; Je. 25:1–13; 36, *etc.*). NT writers view the OT as a whole as 'the oracles of God' (Rom. 3:2), prophetic in character (Rom. 16:26; *cf.* 1:2; 3:21), written by men who were moved and taught by the Holy Spirit (2 Pet. 1:20f.; *cf.* 1 Pet. 1:10–12). Christ and his apostles quote OT texts, not merely as what, *e.g.*, Moses, David or Isaiah said (see Mk. 7:10; 12:36; 7:6; Rom. 10:5; 11:9; 10:20, *etc.*), but also as what God said through these men (see Acts 4:25; 28:25, *etc.*), or sometimes simply as what 'he' (God) says (*e.g.* 1 Cor. 6:16; Heb. 8:5, 8), or what the Holy Spirit says (Heb. 3:7; 10:15). Furthermore, OT statements, not made by God in their contexts, are quoted as utterances of God (Mt. 19:4f.; Heb. 3:7; Acts 13:34f., citing Gn. 2:24; Ps. 95:7; Is. 55:2 respectively). Also, Paul refers to God's promise to Abraham and his threat to Pharaoh, both spoken long before the biblical record of them was written, as words which *Scripture* spoke to these two men (Gal. 3:8; Rom. 9:17); which shows how completely he equated the statements of Scripture with the utterance of God.

2. *Man's part in the producing of Scripture was merely to transmit what he had received.* Psychologically, from the standpoint of form, it is clear that the human writers contributed much to the making of Scripture—historical research, theological meditation, linguistic style, *etc.* Each biblical book is in one sense the literary creation of its author. But theologically, from the standpoint of content, the Bible regards the human writers as having contributed nothing, and Scripture as being entirely the creation of God. This conviction is rooted in the self-consciousness of the founders of biblical religion, all of whom claimed to utter—and, in the case of the prophets and apostles, to write—what were, in the most literal sense, the words of another: God himself. The prophets (among whom Moses must be numbered: Dt. 18:15; 34:10) professed that they spoke the words of Yahweh, setting before Israel what Yahweh had shown them (Je. 1:7; Ezk. 2:7; Am. 3:7f.; *cf.* 1 Ki. 22). Jesus of Nazareth professed that he spoke words given him by his Father (Jn. 7:16; 12:49f.). The apostles taught and issued commands in Christ's name (2 Thes. 3:6), so claiming his authority and sanction (1 Cor. 14:37), and they maintained that both their matter and their words had been taught them by God's Spirit (1 Cor. 2:9–13; *cf.* Christ's promises, Jn. 14:26; 15:26f.; 16:13ff.). These are claims to inspiration. In the light of these claims, the evaluation of prophetic and apostolic writings as wholly God's word, in just the same way in which the two tables of the law, 'written with the finger of God' (Ex. 24:12; 31:18; 32:16), were wholly God's word, naturally became part of the biblical faith.

Christ and the apostles bore striking witness to the fact of inspiration by their appeal to the authority of the OT. In effect, they claimed the Jewish Scriptures as the Christian Bible: a body of literature bearing prophetic witness to Christ (Jn. 5:39f.; Lk. 24:25ff., 44f.; 2 Cor. 3:14ff.) and designed by God specially for the instruction of Christian believers (Rom. 15:4; 1 Cor. 10:11; 2 Tim. 3:14ff.; *cf.* the exposition of Ps. 95:7–11 in Heb. 3–4, and indeed the whole of Hebrews, in which every major point is made by appeal to OT texts). Christ insisted that what was written in the OT 'cannot be broken' (Jn. 10:35). He had not come, he told the Jews, to annul the law or the prophets (Mt. 5:17); if they thought he was doing that, they were mistaken; he had come to do the opposite—to bear witness to the divine authority of both by fulfilling them. The law stands for ever, because it is God's word (Mt. 5:18; Lk. 16:17); the prophecies, particularly those concerning himself, must be fulfilled, for the same reason (Mt. 26:54; Lk. 22:37; *cf.* Mk. 8:31; Lk. 18:31). To Christ and his apostles, the appeal to Scripture was always decisive (*cf.* Mt. 4:4, 7, 10; Rom. 12:19; 1 Pet. 1:16, *etc.*).

The freedom with which NT writers quote the OT (following LXX, Targums, or an *ad hoc* rendering of the Hebrew, as best suits them) has been held to show that they did not believe in the inspiredness of the original words. But their interest was not in the words, as such, but in their meaning; and recent study has made it appear that these quotations are interpretative and expository—a mode of quotation well known among the Jews. The writers seek to indicate the true (*i.e.* Christian) meaning and application of their text by the form in which they cite it. In most cases this meaning has evidently been reached by a strict application of clear-cut theological principles about the relation of Christ and the church to the OT. (See C. H. Dodd, *According to the Scriptures*, 1952; K. Stendahl, *The School of St Matthew*, 1954; R. V. G. Tasker, *The Old Testament in the New*

*Testament*², 1954; E. E. Ellis, *Paul's Use of the Old Testament*, 1957.)

III. Theological statement

In formulating the biblical idea of inspiration, it is desirable that four negative points be made.

1. The idea is not of mechanical dictation, or automatic writing, or any process which involved the suspending of the action of the human writer's mind. Such concepts of inspiration are found in the Talmud, Philo and the Fathers, but not in the Bible. The divine direction and control under which the biblical authors wrote was not a physical or psychological force, and it did not detract from, but rather heightened, the freedom, spontaneity and creativeness of their writing.

2. The fact that in inspiration God did not obliterate the personality, style, outlook and cultural conditioning of his penmen does not mean that his control of them was imperfect, or that they inevitably distorted the truth they had been given to convey in the process of writing it down. B. B. Warfield gently mocks the notion that when God wanted Paul's letters written 'He was reduced to the necessity of going down to earth and painfully scrutinizing the men He found there, seeking anxiously for the one who, on the whole, promised best for His purpose; and then violently forcing the material He wished expressed through him, against his natural bent, and with as little loss from his recalcitrant characteristics as possible. Of course, nothing of the sort took place. If God wished to give His people a series of letters like Paul's, He prepared a Paul to write them, and the Paul He brought to the task was a Paul who spontaneously would write just such letters' (*The Inspiration and Authority of the Bible*, 1951, p. 155).

3. Inspiredness is not a quality attaching to corruptions which intrude in the course of the transmission of the text, but only to the text as originally produced by the inspired writers. The acknowledgment of biblical inspiration thus makes more urgent the task of meticulous textual criticism, in order to eliminate such corruptions and ascertain what that original text was.

4. The inspiredness of biblical writing is not to be equated with the inspiredness of great literature, not even when (as often) the biblical writing is in fact great literature. The biblical idea of inspiration relates, not to the literary quality of what is written, but to its character as divine revelation in writing.

(* Spirit, Holy; * Prophecy; * Scripture; *Authority; * Canon of the Old Testament; * Canon of the New Testament; * Interpretation, Biblical.)

Bibliography. B. B. Warfield, *op. cit.* (much of the relevant material is also in his *Biblical Foundations*, 1958, chs. 1 and 2); A. Kuyper, *Encyclopaedia of Sacred Theology*, E.T. 1899; J. Orr, *Revelation and Inspiration*, 1910; C. F. H. Henry (ed.), *Revelation and the Bible*, 1958; K. Barth, *Church Dogmatics*, I, 1, 2 (*The Doctrine of the Word of God*), E.T. 1936, 1956; W. Sanday, *Inspiration*, 1893; R. Abba, *The Nature and Authority of the Bible*, 1958; J. W. Wenham, *Christ and the Bible*, 1972; G. C. Berkouwer, *Holy Scripture*, 1975; *TDNT* 1, pp. 742–773 (*s.v. graphō*), and 4, pp. 1022–1091 (*s.v. nomos*).

J.I.P.

INTERPRETATION, BIBLICAL. The purpose of biblical interpretation is to make the meaning and message of the biblical writings plain to their readers. Some principles of interpretation are common to the Bible and other literature, especially other ancient literature; other principles of interpretation are bound up with the unique place of the Bible in the revelation of God and in the life of his people.

I. General interpretation

Each part of the Bible must be interpreted in its context, and that means not only its immediate verbal context but the wider context of time, place and human situation to which it belongs. Thus there are a number of considerations to be kept in mind if the meaning of the text is to be grasped as fully as is desirable.

a. Language and style

The idioms and constructions of the biblical languages can differ quite widely from those with which we are familiar today, and some acquaintance with these is necessary for a proper interpretation (* Language of the Apocrypha; * Language of the OT; * Language of the NT). The literary categories represented in the Bible should also be noted; this will save us, for example, from interpreting poetry according to the canons of prose narration, or vice versa. Most of the literary categories in the Bible are well known from other literature, but biblical prophecy, and still more biblical apocalyptic, have features peculiar to themselves which call for special interpretative procedures.

b. Historical background

The biblical narrative covers the whole span of Near Eastern civilization until AD 100, a period of several millennia within which a succession of sweeping changes took place. It is therefore important to relate the various phases of the biblical revelation to their proper historical context if we are to understand them aright; otherwise we may find ourselves, for example, assessing people's conduct in the Middle Bronze Age by the ethical standards of the Gospels. And we can discern the permanent principles in a biblical document only when we first of all relate that document to the conditions of its own times; we shall then be better able to reapply to our times those features of its teaching which are valid for all time.

c. Geographical setting

We should not underestimate the influence exercised by climate and terrain on a people's outlook and way of life, including its religion. The religious conflicts of the OT are interwoven with the conditions of Palestinian geography. Baal-worship, for example, arose in a land where life depended on rain. To the Canaanites Baal was the storm-god who fertilized the earth, and Baal-worship was a magical ritual calculated to ensure regular rainfall and plentiful harvests. Indeed, to such an extent have geographical conditions entered into the biblical language, literal and figurative, that some acquaintaince with these conditions is necessary for an understanding of the language. This is especially true of the OT, but even in the NT it has long been recognized, for instance, that the historical geography of Asia Minor makes an important contribution to the interpretation of Acts and the Epistles.

d. The human situation

Even more important than questions of time, place and language are questions about the everyday life of the people whom we meet in the Bible, their loves and hates,

INTERDICT
See Decree, Part 1.

INTEREST
See Debt, Part 1.

INTERMARRIAGE
See Foreigner, Part 1.

IONIA
See Javan, Part 2.

their hopes and fears, their social relations, and so forth. To read the Bible without regard to this living environment is to read it in a vacuum and to put constructions upon it which it was never intended to bear. Thanks largely to archaeological discovery, we are able to reconstruct in fair measure the private and public conditions in which the people of the Bible lived, in age after age; while a sympathetic reading of the text itself enables us in some degree to get under their skins and look at the world through their eyes. It is not unimportant to try to envisage what it must have felt like to be a servant in Abraham's household, an Israelite slave in Egypt, a citizen of Jericho when Joshua's men were marching round the city or a citizen of Jerusalem in face of Sennacherib's threats, a soldier in David's army, a captive maid waiting on Naaman's wife or a builder of the wall under Nehemiah. We may then realize that part of the Bible's perennial appeal is due to its concentration on those features of human life that remain basically the same in all times and places.

II. Special interpretation

Biblical interpretation involves not only the interpretation of the several documents but their interpretation as part of the Bible, having regard to the way in which each part contributes to the purpose of the Bible as a whole. Since the Bible records God's word to man and man's response to God, since it contains 'all things necessary to salvation' and constitutes the church's 'rule of faith and life', we may look for such a unity throughout the volume that each part can be interpreted in the light of the whole. We may look, indeed, for some unifying principle of interpretation.

In traditional Jewish interpretation of the Heb. Scriptures this unifying principle was found in the Law, understood in accordance with the teaching of the great rabbinical schools. The Prophets and the Writings were treated largely as commentaries on the Law. In addition to the surface meaning of the text, the *p^e^šaṭ*, there was the more extended application, the *d^e^raš*, derived by the use of various well-defined principles of exegesis, but sometimes appearing far-fetched by the exegetical standards of today.

In the NT and early Christian literature the OT oracles are viewed as a unity, instructing the reader 'for salvation' and equipping him with all that he needs for the service of God (2 Tim. 3:15ff.). The prophets, speaking in the power of the Holy Spirit, bear witness to Christ as the One in whom the promises of God find their fulfilment. The NT writers—whose diversity of personality, style and thought must be taken into account in the interpretation of their works—are agreed on this. In Heb. 1:1f. the 'many and various ways' in which God spoke in earlier days are contrasted with the perfect and final word which he has spoken in his Son; in the Pauline writings God's dealings with the world are traced through successive stages associated with Adam, Abraham, Moses and Christ. Biblical interpretation in the NT has Christ as its unifying principle, but this principle is not applied mechanically but in such a way as to bring out the historical and progressive nature of the biblical revelation. This creative principle of interpretation was certainly derived by the apostolic church from Christ himself.

In post-apostolic times biblical interpretation was influenced by a Gk. concept of inspiration which called for large-scale allegorization of the text. This influence was most apparent in Alexandria, where in the pre-Christian period it is found in the biblical interpretation of Philo. By allegorization, it was believed, the mind of the inspiring Spirit could be ascertained; by allegorization much in the Bible that was intellectually or ethically unacceptable in its literal sense could be made acceptable. This method, developed by the Alexandrian Fathers and taken over from them by many of the Western Fathers, in fact obscured the mind of the Spirit and obliterated the historical character of biblical revelation. In contrast to the Alexandrians the school of Antioch, while not rejecting allegorization entirely, did more justice to the historical sense of the text.

The distinction between the literal sense of Scripture and the higher or spiritual sense was elaborated in mediaeval times, and three varieties of spiritual sense were distinguished—the allegorical, which deduced doctrine from the narrative; the moral, which drew lessons for life and behaviour; and the anagogical, which derived heavenly meanings from earthly things. Yet the early Middle Ages also saw good work done in the field of literal interpretation, notably by the 12th-century school of St Victor in France.

The Reformers laid fresh emphasis on the literal sense of Scripture and on the grammatico-historical method of exegesis as the way to establish its literal sense. Grammatico-historical exegesis is fundamental, but when the foundation has been laid by its means theological exegesis and practical application are also called for. Moreover, the use of the Bible in the life of the people of God throughout the centuries continually brings fresh aspects of its meaning to light, although these fresh aspects have general validity only as they are rooted in the true and original sense. Thus, we may understand the Epistle to the Romans better because of the part it played in the lives of Augustine, Luther and Wesley; but the part it played in their lives owes its significance to the fact that these men had a rare grasp of what Paul really meant when he wrote the Epistle.

Typological interpretation, revived in our own day, must be used (if at all) with caution and restraint. Its most acceptable form is that which discerns in the biblical recital of God's acts of mercy and judgment a recurring rhythm, by virtue of which earlier stages in the recital can be viewed as foreshadowings and illustrations of later stages (*cf.* Paul's use of the wilderness experiences of Israel in 1 Cor. 10:1ff.).

Christians have an abiding standard and pattern in their Lord's use of the OT, and part of the Holy Spirit's present work for them is to open the Scriptures as the risen Christ opened them for two disciples on the Emmaus road (Lk. 24:25ff.).

BIBLIOGRAPHY. F. W. Farrar, *History of Interpretation*, 1886; B. Smalley, *The Study of the Bible in the Middle Ages*², 1952; C. H. Dodd, *According to the Scriptures*, 1952; H. H. Rowley, *The Unity of the Bible*, 1953; E. C. Blackman, *Biblical Interpretation*, 1957; R. M. Grant, *The Letter and the Spirit*, 1957; J. D. Wood, *The Interpretation of the Bible*, 1958; J. D. Smart, *The Interpretation of Scripture*, 1962; *Cambridge History of the Bible*, 1–3, 1963–70; J. Barr, *Old and New in Interpretation*, 1966; I. H. Marshall (ed.), *New Testament Interpretation*, 1977; G. W. Anderson (ed.), *Tradition and Interpretation*, 1979. F.F.B.

IRA (Heb. *'îrā'*). **1.** A Jairite, described as 'David's priest' (2 Sa. 20:26), a difficult description to understand, as he was not of the tribe of Levi. However, Pesh. reads 'of Jattir', which was a city of Levi. Alternatively, 'priest' here may mean a chief official (*cf.* 2 Sa. 8:18, AV; 1 Ch. 18:17, AV).

2. An Ithrite, one of David's mighty men (2 Sa. 23:38). May be same as **1** if Pesh. reading is correct.

3. Another of David's heroes, son of Ikkesh the Tekoite (2 Sa. 23:26). M.A.M.

ISAAC (Heb. *yiṣḥāq*, 'he laughs' or 'laughter'). At the announcement of Isaac's birth Abraham laughed (Gn. 17:17), and later [illegible] thought that she who was so old should bear a son (Gn. 18:12–15). At Isaac's birth, when Abraham was 100 years old, Sarah declares that God has made her to laugh (Gn. 21:6). On the day of Isaac's weaning Ishmael laughed (Gn. 21:9). It is difficult to discover a precise subject for the verb, and possibly it is best to take the form impersonally.

The two great features of Isaac's life centre upon his birth and marriage, and the reason for this is that he was the seed through whom the line of promise was to be continued. Abraham had been sorely tested with respect to the promise of a seed, and now, at an advanced age, when he was as good as dead, that seed came. Thus, it is seen that God is carrying out his purposes in fulfilment of the promises made to Abraham (Gn. 12:1–3), even though those promises seem to man to be incapable of fulfilment.

At the feast of Isaac's weaning the sight of Ishmael 'playing with her son Isaac' aroused Sarah's resentment. Hagar and her son Ishmael were therefore driven from the household (Gn. 21). God then put Abraham to the test, commanding him to slay his son Isaac. Abraham obeyed God and the Lord intervened, providing a ram for the sacrifice. The promise is then renewed, that Abraham shall have much seed (Gn. 22).

The second feature of Isaac's life which is of significance is his marriage. That Isaac should be born was a miracle, and soon afterwards it seemed that he must die. How, then, could he be the promised seed? He lives, however, and atten-

■ **IRON-WORKING** See Arts and crafts, Part 1.

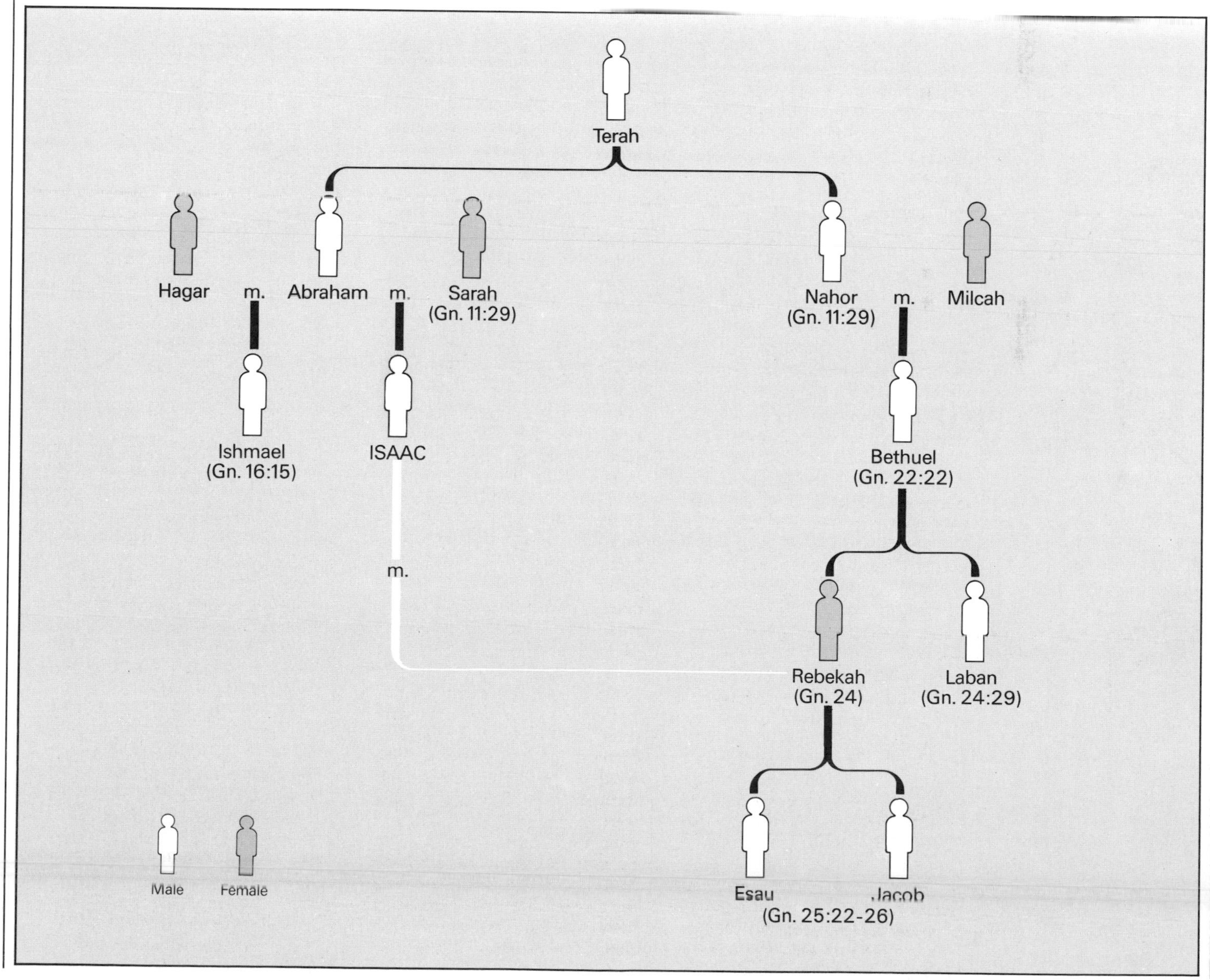

The family of Isaac.

tion is centred upon his marriage, for it is to be through him that the line of promise is to be continued. Abraham is concerned that the promised seed be continued and sends his eldest servant to take a wife for Isaac from his own country, Harran. Rebekah, the daughter of Bethuel, Abraham's nephew, is indicated as the intended bride and willingly leaves her home to accompany the servant. Isaac receives her and brings her into his mother's tent. Isaac and Rebekah are married, with love developing as a result of Isaac's considerate and courteous actions (Gn. 24).

For 20 years Rebekah was barren, and so it is again seen that the promised seed is not to come merely through the natural means of ordinary fatherhood, but through God's supernatural creative power. Rebekah's barrenness causes Isaac to entreat the Lord, and the announcement is made to Rebekah that two children are struggling in her womb (Gn. 25:22–26). These two children, representing two nations, will follow mutually hostile courses. Isaac himself is to remain a sojourner in the land and, instead of going to Egypt in time of famine, remains at Gerar. At the sign of crisis he, like Abraham, seeks to protect his wife by introducing her as his sister. After quarrels with the herdsmen at Gerar he goes to Beersheba and finally makes an agreement with Abimelech. Mutual antagonism appears between Isaac and Rebekah, occasioned by Jacob's actions. Being deceived, Isaac pronounces the paternal blessing upon Jacob and utters a devout prophetical wish upon Esau. Isaac died at the age of 180 years, and was buried by his sons, Esau and Jacob.

In the NT his birth as the son of promise is mentioned in Rom. 4:16–21; 9:7–9; the separation between him and Ishmael is allegorized in Gal. 4:22–31; his being offered up by his father is recalled in Heb. 11:17–19; Jas. 2:21–23 (for its further influence, as in Rom. 8:32a, *cf.* H. J. Schoeps, *Paul*, 1961, pp. 141ff.); his being the father of Esau and Jacob is referred to in Rom. 9:10–13; his blessing of these two sons is treated in Heb. 11:20 as evidence of his faith. E.J.Y.

ISAIAH (Heb. *y^e^šaʿyāhû*, 'Yahweh is salvation'), son of Amoz (Heb. *'āmôṣ*, to be distinguished from the prophet Amos, Heb. *ʿāmôs*), lived in Jerusalem (Is. 7:1–3; 37:2). According to Jewish tradition, he was of royal blood; it has sometimes been inferred from the narratives and oracles of his book that he was, at any rate, of noble descent; but there is no certainty about this. As appears from the superscription to the book (1:1), he prophesied under Uzziah (791/790–740/739 BC), Jotham (740/739–732/731 BC), Ahaz (735–716/715 BC) and Hezekiah (716/715–687/686 BC). (The regnal dates are those assigned by E. R. Thiele.) He was called to be a prophet 'in the year that king Uzziah died' (6:1), *i.e.* in 740/739 BC; his last appearance which can be dated with certainty was at the time of Sennacherib's campaign of 701 BC (or *c.* 688 BC, if we assume a second campaign of Sennacherib against Jerusalem). Tradition has it that he was sawn asunder in Manasseh's reign (see the late *Martyrdom of Isaiah*, ch. 5); some see a reference to this in Heb. 11:37, but the reference is dubious and the tradition appears to have no sound historical basis. It is quite possible that Isaiah survived into Manasseh's reign; the absence of Manasseh's name from 1:1 could be due to the fact that Isaiah played no public part after Manasseh became king.

Isaiah was married; his wife is called 'the prophetess' (8:3), perhaps because she too prophesied. Two sons are mentioned, both of whom bear symbolic names (8:18)—Shear-jashub, 'Remnant will return' (7:3) and Maher-shalal-hash-baz, 'Hasten booty, speed spoil' (8:1–4).

Isaiah and Micah were contemporaries (*cf.* 1:1 with Mi. 1:1). Isaiah's activity was preceded by that of Amos and Hosea (Am. 1:1; Ho. 1:1). Amos and Hosea prophesied mainly against the N tribes; Isaiah and Micah concentrated their prophecies mainly on Judah and Jerusalem (Is. 1:1).

In the first half of the 8th century both Israel, under Jeroboam II (*c.* 782–753 BC), and Judah, under Uzziah, enjoyed a time of great prosperity. This was due in large measure to the weakness of the kingdom of Aram and to Assyria's non-intervention in the W for considerable periods. Uzziah's reign may be described as the most prosperous time that Judah had known since the disruption of the Monarchy after Solomon's death. Under Uzziah and Jotham prosperity and luxury abounded in Judah; we have this state of affairs reflected in Is. 2–4. But with the accession to power of Tiglath-pileser III (745–727 BC), Assyria began once more to impose her yoke on the W lands. Pekah of Israel and Rezin of Damascus formed an anti-Assyrian coalition and tried to compel Ahaz of Judah to join them. When Ahaz refused, they threatened to depose him and place a puppet of their own on his throne (734 BC). Isaiah's action at this time is recorded in ch. 7. Ahaz committed the sinful folly of asking the Assyrian king for aid; the result was that Judah became a satellite state of Assyria. In 732 BC the Assyrians captured Damascus and annexed the territory of Israel N of the Plain of Jezreel, leaving Hoshea to rule the remainder of the N kingdom as their vassal. When he revolted, Shalmaneser V (727–722 BC) besieged Samaria, and his successor Sargon II (722–705 BC) captured it in his accession year. Even after that there were various independence movements directed against Assyrian domination. On these occasions Isaiah, who had withdrawn for a time into a smaller circle after his fruitless protest against Ahaz's foreign policy in 734 BC (8:16ff.), raised his voice again to warn Judah against participating in such movements, and particularly against relying on Egyptian aid. According to 14:28 the Philistines in the year of the death of Ahaz sent a delegation to Jerusalem to arrange an anti-Assyrian alliance; on this occasion again Isaiah uttered a warning note (14:29–32).

Under Hezekiah there were other movements of this kind, notably the revolt of Ashdod, which was crushed in 711 BC, when the Assyrians besieged and captured Ashdod (*cf.* Is. 20:1). Judah and Egypt were implicated in this revolt. It is quite possible that Is. 18 should be dated about this time; an Ethiopian dynasty was ruling in Egypt then. After Sargon's death there were widespread risings against his successor Sennacherib (705–681 BC). Judah was one of the states which revolted, and this resulted in Sennacherib's expedition of 701 BC, during which he overran Judah and besieged Jerusalem. Various oracles in chs. 28–31 may date from the years 705–701 BC, including the warnings against leaning on Egypt in 30:1–7; 31:1–3. Chs. 36–37 record Sennacherib's threat to Jerusalem, Jerusalem's liberation and Isaiah's activity throughout this time of danger. Chs. 38–39, which probably relate to the same period, tell of Hezekiah's sickness and recovery, and the mission of * Merodach-baladan. N.H.R.

ISAIAH, BOOK OF.

I. Outline of contents

a. Prophecies relating to Isaiah's own time, 1:1–35:10

(i) *Introduction* (1:1–31). Condemnation of a merely external form of worship, *etc.* Date uncertain.

(ii) *Prophecies from Isaiah's earliest period* (for the greater part) (2:1–5:30). Prophecy of the coming kingdom of peace (2:2–5; *cf.* Mi. 4:1ff.). The Day of the Lord which is to bring down everything that is proud and exalted (2:6–22). The haughty women of Jerusalem ('Isaiah's fashion-journal') (3:16–4:1). The song of the vineyard (5:1–7).

(iii) *Isaiah's inaugural vision* (6:1–13).

(iv) *The present world-empire and the coming kingdom of God* (7:1–12:6). Chs. 7:1–9:7 originate chiefly from the time of the Syro-Ephraimite war. Rebuke of Ahaz and prophecy of Immanuel (7:1–25). Isaiah's temporary withdrawal from the public eye (8:11–22). The birth of the Messiah (9:1–7). The hand stretched out to smite Ephraim (probably one of Isaiah's earliest oracles) (9:8–10:4). Assyria brought low by the Holy One of Israel (10:5–34). The Messiah and the kingdom of God (11:1–12:6); especially here a sharp contrast is drawn between the violent world-empire and the peacefulness of the coming kingdom. Ch. 12 contains a song of thanksgiving; it forms a conclusion to this section.

(v) *Mainly prophecies regarding foreign nations* (13:1–23:18). Babylon (13:1–14:23) (incorporating the impressive taunt-song in 14:4–23). Assyria (14:24–27). The Philistines (14:28–32). Moab (15:1–16:14). Aram and Ephraim (17:1–14; probably not long before ch. 7). Ethiopia and Egypt (18:1–20:6; 20, and probably 18, are to be dated *c.* 715 BC; the date of 19 is uncertain). Babylon (21:1–10). Edom ('Watchman, what of the night?') (21:11f.). Arabia (21:13–17). Jerusalem (22:1–14). Shebna and Eliakim (22:15–25). Phoenicia (23:1–18).

(vi) *The consummation: the 'Isaianic apocalypse'* (24:1–27:13). See below, under **III.** *a* (iv).

(vii) *Zion's sin, oppression and deliverance; Assyria's downfall; Egypt's vain help* (28:1–33:24). Several of the prophecies in these chapters are to be dated between 705 and 701 BC. The parable of the ploughman (28:23–29). The Messianic kingdom (32:1–8).

(viii) *A twofold future* (34:1–35:10). The judgment of Edom and the world (34:1–17). Salvation for 'the ransomed of the Lord' (35:1–10).

b. Historical chapters, 36:1–39:8

Sennacherib's invasion (36:1–37:38). Hezekiah's sickness and recovery (38:1–22). Mission of Merodach-baladan (39:1–8).

c. Prophecies which presuppose the Babylonian Exile, 40:1–55:13

These chs. foretell Israel's liberation from exile and the restoration of Zion, and in doing so they proclaim the majesty of Yahweh. They may be divided as follows:

(i) *Introduction* (40:1–31). The substance of the following chs. is presented; it consists of four parts: vv. 1–2, vv. 3–5, vv. 6–11, vv. 12–31.

(ii) *Prophecies in which those concerning Cyrus are conspicuous*

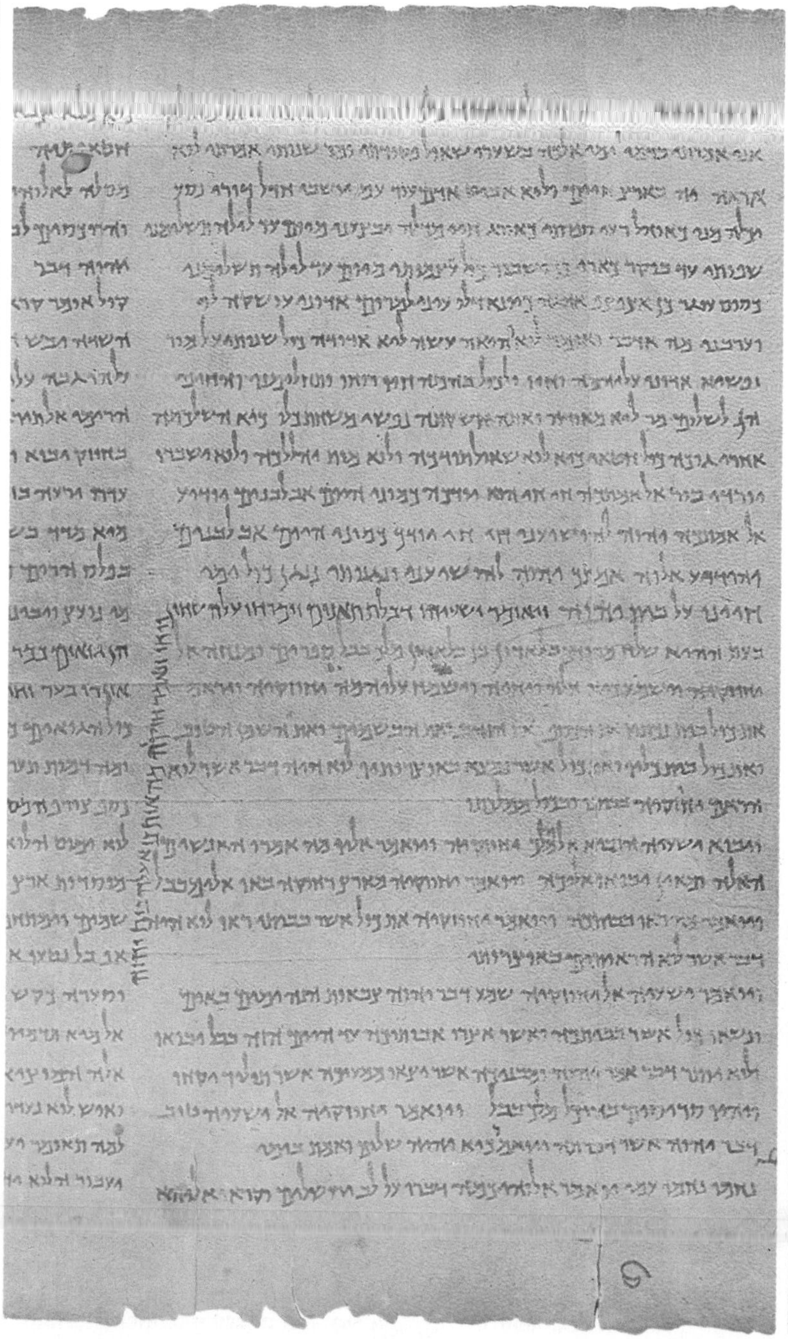

Part of the oldest complete copy of Isaiah in Hebrew that survives, a sheepskin scroll 7·34 m long found in Cave 1 at Qumran by the Dead Sea (1Q Is[a]). The column shown contains Is. 38:8–40:2. 2nd cent. BC. (JCT)

(41:1–48:22). He is mentioned by name in 44:28; 45:1. *Cf.* 41:1–16 (Cyrus' activity will make the nations tremble, but there is no need for Israel to fear), 41:21–29 (Cyrus' activity will cause Zion to rejoice), 43:9–15 (Cyrus overthrows Babylon), 44:24–45:13 (Cyrus' victory leads to the rebuilding of Zion), 46:8–13 (amidst prophecies of Babylon's downfall), 48:12–16. *Cf.* also the prophecies of Babylon's downfall, especially 46:1–47:15. There is a marked contrast drawn between the 'daughter of Babylon' (ch. 47) and the 'daughter of Zion' (49:14ff., *etc.*). Throughout these chs. Israel is comforted in her distress, her deliverance from Babylon is promised (*cf.* 41:8–20; 42:8–43:8; 43:16–44:5; 48, *passim*), Yahweh's majesty is proclaimed, and the contrast between him and the idols is emphasized (*cf.* 42:8–17; 44:6–20; 45:9–25, *passim*). In 42:1–7, the first of the 'Servant Songs', the Servant of the Lord is introduced.

(iii) *Chapters in which the restoration of Zion is prominent* (49:1–54:17). *Cf.* 49:14–50:3; 51:17–52:12; 54. We hear no more of the conquests of Cyrus or the ruin of Babylon; there is consequently less emphasis on the contrast between Yahweh and the idols. In 49:1–9a; 50:4–11 and 52:13–53:12, the second, third and fourth 'Servant Songs', there are further prophecies concerning the Servant of the Lord, his mission to Israel and the nations, his obedience and suffering, his death and vindication.

(iv) *Exhortation to accept these promises in faith* (55:1–13).

d. Various prophecies, 56:1–66:24

It is not easy to summarize the contents of these chs. The prophecies which they contain are diverse in nature and may even refer to different times. In some places Israel appears to be in exile (57:14; 58:12; 60:10ff.; 63:18; 64:10f.), in others the nation seems settled in Canaan (*e.g.* 57:3–7). Many of the ideas which are expressed in these chs. have already appeared in the preceding sections of the book.

(i) *Law-abiding proselytes and even eunuchs have a share in God's salvation* (56:1–8; see especially v. 7).

(ii) *Leaders and people alike are rebuked for their sins, particularly for idolatry* (56:9–57:13a). This section may refer to the reign of Manasseh.

(iii) *Comfort for the contrite* (57:13b–21; see especially v. 15); an affinity can be traced here with chs. 40–55.

(iv) *False and true religion* (58:1–14). Special mention is made of fasting and sabbath-observance.

(v) *Deliverance is conditional upon repentance* (59:1–21). Rebuke of sins (vv. 1–8); complaint and confession of sin (vv. 9–15a); judgment and deliverance (vv. 15b–20); Yahweh's covenant (v. 21).

(vi) *Zion's deliverance* (60:1–62:12; note again the close affinity with chs. 40–55). The glorious prospect of salvation for Zion involves blessing for the nations as well (60:1–3). The appearance of the messenger of joyful news in 61:1ff. (*cf.* 40:9; 41:27; 52:7) becomes the programme of Jesus' ministry in Lk. 4:17ff.

(vii) *Yahweh's vengeance against Edom* (63:1–6).

(viii) *Penitence and supplication.* God who wrought such wonderful deliverances for his people in the past is entreated to intervene on their behalf again (63:7–64:12).

(ix) *Rebels against God and obedient servants* (65:1–25). Idolatry rebuked (vv. 3ff., 11); new heavens and a new earth promised (v. 17).

(x) *Ch. 66:1–24.* Yahweh's repudiation of forbidden forms of sacrificial worship (vv. 1–4), Zion glorified and sinners punished (vv. 5–24).

II. Origin, construction, authorship

a. Isaiah's literary activity

We are given but little information about Isaiah's own literary activity. In 8:1 only a short inscription is involved ('Maher-shalal-hash-baz'); 8:16 should be understood in a figurative sense; 30:8 may relate to the writing down of the brief utterance of v. 7, 'Rahab who sits still', although it is possible that a more extensive passage was to be recorded. The reference to 'the book of the Lord' in 34:16 implies that the preceding prophecy of ch. 34 was written down. The 'I' style in chs. 6 and 8 tells in favour of the assumption that these chs. were written by Isaiah himself; it is noteworthy, however, that ch. 7 speaks of him in the third person (*cf.* ch. 20).

It is very likely, indeed, that more prophecies were written by Isaiah himself than the above-mentioned passages indicate. In favour of this conclusion the high standard and unity of language and style may be taken into consideration. But if Isaiah himself had had a substantial part in the composition of his book, its structure would presumably have been more straightforward than is now the case.

Chs. 36–39 are essentially parallel to 2 Ki. 18:13–20:19. In this connection it should be borne in mind that, according to 2 Ch. 26:22; 32:32, Isaiah also figured as a historical writer. The question whether Isaiah was the author of chs. 36–39 cannot be answered with certainty.

b. Construction

The book of Isaiah is decidedly not an arbitrary string of disconnected prophecies. There is a certain chronological arrangement. Chs. 2–5 consist to a large extent of prophecies from Isaiah's earliest activity. 7:1–9:7 originate mostly from the period of the Syro-Ephraimite war (734 BC). Chs. 18–20 take us to the period 715–711 BC, and various prophecies of chs. 28–37 belong to the years between 705 and 701 BC. The greater part of chs. 40–66 consists of prophecies uttered from an exilic, or perhaps even post-exilic, standpoint.

There is also a certain arrangement according to subject-matter (see **I**, Outline of contents). In this regard an outstanding feature is the group of oracles concerning foreign nations in chs. 13–23; it should also be noted here that most of the prophecies in these chapters are introduced by the words 'The oracle concerning . . .' Chs. 40–55 also, to a considerable degree, form a unity. One further point: in 39:6ff. there is clearly a transition from chs. 1–39 to chs. 40–66.

On the other hand, chronological order has certainly not been followed throughout. For example, 9:8–10:4 contains what is perhaps one of Isaiah's oldest prophecies; ch. 17 may date from the period shortly before 734 BC, *i.e.* close in time to ch. 7; 28:1–6 contains an early prophecy. It should also be noted that, while prophecies from an exilic standpoint occur chiefly in chs. 40ff., ch. 35 also presupposes the period of the Exile; and we may even be forced to the conclusion that chs. 56–66 set alongside one another prophecies whose respective standpoints are pre-exilic (*e.g.* 56:9–57:13), exilic (*e.g.* chs. 60–62) and post-exilic (*e.g.* ch. 58).

Again, it is equally plain that arrangement according to subject-matter has not been carried through with entire consistency. As we have seen, chs. 13–23 consist mainly of prophecies about foreign nations, but ch. 22 forms an exception, and elsewhere there are other prophecies against foreign nations (for example, the oracle against Assyria in 10:5–34 is similar to that in 14:24–27).

It should be noted, too, that there are superscriptions in 1:1; 2:1 and 13:1; and further, the account of the vision in which Isaiah received his call to be a prophet does not come until ch. 6.

The situation is involved—more involved, indeed, than might be gathered from the considerations which have been briefly outlined above. It may be taken as certain that our book of Isaiah has been constructed on the basis of shorter collections. But in the end we can only say that the history of its composition can no longer be reconstructed. Scholars have made various attempts to trace the stages of its composition, but have not reached convincing conclusions. Thus, some have supposed that chs. 1–12, 13–23, 24–27, 28–35 originally formed separate collections. Admittedly these divisions, lying before us in their present arrangement, do form more or less self-contained units. The song of ch. 12 or the promise of salvation in ch. 35 would form an appropriate conclusion to a collection. But we should reckon with the possibility that this is due to the work of the latest redactor.

As for chs. 40–55, they probably contain a collection of originally independent prophecies: it is hardly to be assumed that they formed a unity from the beginning. On the other hand, in these chs. the same subjects recur time and again. Their arrangement is by no means completely arbitrary; *i.e.* a certain chronological order can be observed (see **I**, Outline of contents). Many critics are of the opinion that these chs., in essence at least, come from one author.

c. Authorship

Many scholars nowadays deny great portions of the book to Isaiah—not only in the sense that he did not write them down, but in the sense that their subject-matter does not come from him at all. Even chs. 1–35 are believed by some to contain much non-Isaianic material. Some scholars go farther than others, but there is a wide measure of agreement that Isaiah cannot be credited with chs. 13:1–14:23; 21; 24–27; 34–35. In addition, critical scholars are practically unanimous in the view that chs. 40–66 do not come from Isaiah.

Chs. 40–55 are believed to be mainly the work of a prophet to whom the name Deutero-Isaiah ('Second Isaiah') has been given. It is held that his prophecies must be dated between the first victories of the Persian king, Cyrus (*c.* 550 BC), and Cyrus' conquest of Babylon, which was followed by his decree permitting the Jewish exiles to return to their own country (538 BC). Some defend the view that part of Deutero-Isaiah's prophecies should be assigned to the period after 538 BC. Babylon is mostly envisaged as this prophet's field of activity; others think of Palestine, Egypt and other lands.

As for chs. 56–66, some scholars credit Deutero-Isaiah with them too, while others ascribe them to a separate author, called Trito-Isaiah ('Third Isaiah'), who is dated either *c.* 450 BC, in the time of Malachi (*e.g.* by B. Duhm), or *c.* 520 BC, in the time of Haggai and Zechariah (*e.g.* by E. Sellin and K. Elliger). Others, again, take the view that the prophecies of chs. 56–66 do not all come from the same time; it has even been held that some come from the 8th century BC, some from the 2nd.

The following considerations are relevant to the Deutero-Isaiah question:

1. The unanimous testimony of tradition credits Isaiah with the authorship of the whole book. Chs. 1–39 and 40–66 have come down to us as a unity; ch. 39:6–8 may certainly be regarded as a planned transition from the first to the second part of the book. From Ecclus. 48:24f. it is plain that Jesus ben Sira (*c.* 200 BC) considered Isaiah to be the author of chs. 40–66 as well as of chs. 1–39. The Qumran MSS of Isaiah indicate that, at the time when they were copied (2nd or 1st century BC), the book was regarded as a unity. It is true that the testimony of extra-biblical tradition is not decisive; and in the judgment of the present author it cannot be said that the OT itself points unequivocally to Isaiah as author of the entire book. Even so, two things should be borne in mind.

First, Deutero-Isaiah is taken to be one of the greatest prophets, if not *the* greatest prophet, of Israel; it would be surprising indeed if every trace of this great prophet had been so thoroughly effaced from tradition that his very name is unknown to us. Secondly, the evidence of the NT naturally takes a special place in the testimony of tradition. The following passages from chs. 40–66 are introduced in the NT by some such words as 'that which was spoken by the prophet Isaiah': 40:3 (in Mt. 3:3); 42:1–4 (in Mt. 12:17–21); 53:1 (in Jn. 12:38 and Rom. 10:16); 53:4 (in Mt. 8:17); 65:1f. (in Rom. 10:20f.). To this it may be added that those who deny chs. 40ff. to Isaiah usually deny him ch. 13 on similar grounds; but the superscription of this chapter ascribes it to 'Isaiah the son of Amoz'.

2. The weightiest argument for ascribing chs. 40ff. to Deutero-Isaiah is no doubt the fact that these chapters have as their background the period of the Babylonian Exile—more precisely, the closing years of the Exile, from 550 BC onwards. At the very outset it is stated that Israel 'has received double for all her sins' (40:2). Babylon is the oppressing power (46–47), not Assyria, as we should expect in Isaiah's time. The Persian king, Cyrus (559–529 BC), is mentioned by name. While his conquest of Babylon is predicted in 43:14; 48:14, *etc.*, it is suggested by 41:1–7, 25, *etc.*, that he has already achieved his first successes.

It may be said in reply that the Spirit of prophecy can reveal the future to the prophets; and it is true that this fact has not always been taken sufficiently into account by adherents of the Deutero-Isaiah theory. But even those who are prepared to make full allowance for it find themselves faced with difficulties here. It is certainly inconceivable that Isaiah stood in the Temple court, comforting his people in view of a calamity which was not to come upon them until more than a century had elapsed. We may indeed suppose that Isaiah communicated these prophecies to the circle of his disciples (*cf.* 8:16)—or rather that he did not speak them but only committed them to writing. Even so, the question arises: if we credit Isaiah with these chs., must we not assume that his inspiration took a very 'mechanical' form, bearing no relation to the concepts existing in the prophet's conscious mind? The following suggestion may help in some degree to meet these objections.

Isaiah wrote down these prophecies in Manasseh's reign. He found it impossible to appear in public in those years (*cf.* 2 Ki. 21:16). Iniquity had reached such a pitch that Isaiah recognized that the divine judgment was bound to come (*cf.* 2 Ki. 21:10–15); indeed, before his mind's eye it had already come. Then the Spirit of prophecy showed him that this judgment in its turn would come to an end (see under **III.** *a* (ii), 'Judgment and salvation'). It can be said further that the judgment which Isaiah saw as already fulfilled before his mind's eye was 'delayed' by Manasseh's repentance (2 Ch. 33:12ff.) and Josiah's reformation (2 Ki. 22–23). It is, besides, important to observe that, according to Is. 39:5–7, Isaiah knew that a deportation to Babylon would take place.

And while it is true that these prophecies presuppose as their background the closing phase of the Babylonian Exile, and Cyrus is represented as having already entered upon the stage of history, yet in other respects the author expresses himself much less concretely on conditions during the Exile than might have been expected from someone who lived in the midst of it.

3. Attention has been drawn to the differences between chs. 1–39 and 40–66 in matters of language, style and conceptions. It may indeed be said that in 1–39 the language is suggestive and full of illustrations, while in 40–66 it is often more verbose; that in 40–66 the cosmological aspect of the Kingship of God is more prominent than in 1–39; that while 1–39 speak of the Messiah-King, this figure is displaced in 40–66 by the suffering Servant of Yahweh. Yet these divergences do not make it necessary to abandon belief in the unity of the book. For over against these divergences there are striking points of similarity. As examples of these it may be pointed out, first, that as chs. 1–39 do not describe only Messiah's glory (*cf.* 11:1 with 53:2), so chs. 40–66 do not describe only the Servant's suffering (*cf.* 42:1–7; 53:11f.); and secondly, that the divine appellation 'the Holy One of Israel' occurs 12 times in chs. 1–39, 13 times in chs. 40–66 and only five times in the rest of the OT. *Cf.* further J. H. Eaton, *VT* 9, 1959, pp. 138–157.

The preceding paragraphs are intended to give some idea of the lines along which the discussion of these problems proceeds and of the arguments which are adduced on either side. The conclusion is that it is both unnccessary and open to objection to deny to Isaiah any share in the composition of chs. 40–66. On the other hand, even those who desire to submit unconditionally to the testimony of Scripture may come to the conclusion that the book of Isaiah contains some parts which are not of Isaianic origin. This is perhaps the situation already in chs. 1–39. And especially with regard to chs. 40–66 there are reasons for accepting this suggestion. In the opinion of the present writer it is acceptable to hold that chs. 40–66 contain an Isaianic core, upon which the prophet's disciples (men who felt themselves closely bound to him) later worked in the spirit of the original author. It is, however, impossible for us to assess how much belongs to the Isaianic core and how much to the later elaborations.

Two final remarks will close this section.

1. There is a prevalent trend of thought nowadays which lays great emphasis on the significance of oral tradition. According to this trend of thought, a prophet's utterances were handed down orally by the circle of his disciples; in this process they were repeatedly adapted to the changing circumstances of the time. If there is an element of truth in this view it should certainly be taken into account in any attempt to explain the origin of Is. 40–66. It might lead to the conclusion that chs. 40–66 contain an Isaianic core but that the extent of this core can no longer be ascertained.

2. It should be remembered that those who deny to Isaiah the whole of chs. 40–66 frequently assume that the author or authors of these chs. belonged to the school of Isaiah. It is admitted that, alongside all the arguments for diversity of authorship, there is a close affinity between chs. 1–39 and 40–66. See, *e.g.*, what was said above about the appellation 'the Holy One of Israel'.

III. The message of the book

From ancient times Isaiah has been considered the greatest of OT prophets. He has been called 'the eagle among the prophets', 'the Evangelist of the Old Covenant', and the like. His book is not only lofty in style and conception, but rich in spiritual meaning.

a. Chs. 1–39

In endeavouring to outline the message of these chapters we may start with the divine appellation 'the Holy One of Israel' (which, as we have seen, is characteristic of Isaiah), and with the name of one of his sons, Shear-jashub, 'Remnant will return'.

That God was the Holy One was inscribed indelibly on Isaiah's heart as a result of his inaugural vision (6:3). As Amos has been called the prophet of righteousness and Hosea the prophet of loving-kindness, so Isaiah has been called the prophet of holiness (*cf.* 1:4; 5:16, 24; 8:14; 10:17, 20; 12:6; 17:7; 29:23; 30:11f.; 31:1; 37:23, *etc.*). God is the Holy One; that means he is so highly exalted above his creatures as to be totally different from them, not only in his moral perfection (*cf.* 6:5) but also in his power, his wrath, his love, his faithfulness and all his virtues (*cf.* also 29:16; 31:3). Yahweh's holiness is the very essence of his divine being, which causes men to tremble before him as they worship him.

This holy God has associated himself in a special way with Israel (1:2; 5:1ff., *etc.*), and in a pre-eminent degree with the house of David (8:13; 11:1, *etc.*). He dwells in the midst of Israel, on Mt Zion (8:18; 11:9, *etc.*).

The fact that God is 'the Holy One of Israel' involves an abiding tension in his relation to his people. On the one hand, he fulminates in a violent way against Israel's sin; on the other hand, he does not break his covenant with Israel. Hence the assurance: 'Remnant will return'. This means, first: judgment will come, only a remnant will be left. But it also means: at least a remnant will be left, a remnant will indeed return (*i.e.* to its homeland). In his wrath God remembers mercy. It is also possible to translate: 'Remnant returns to God, changes its mind'; its return and deliverance come along the path of conversion. This remnant-doctrine figures prominently in Isaiah's preaching, from the very first (6:13). And he may have seen the beginnings of the remnant in the circle of his disciples, among whom he withdrew himself from public life for a considerable time at an early stage in his ministry (8:16–18).

Some of the implications of the outlined teaching of Isaiah may now be elaborated.

(i) *God's requirements and Israel's sin.* The Holy One of Israel requires his people to sanctify him (8:13) by putting their trust in him alone, by keeping his commandments, by paying heed to the words of his prophets. Because Yahweh has entered into a covenant with Israel, Israel's sin is essentially apostasy (1:2–4; 30:1–9, *etc.*). Instead of preserving due humility in the presence of the Holy One of Israel, they are haughty and frivolous (2:6ff.; 3:8; 5:15f., 19ff.; 22:1ff.; 28:15; 29:14ff.; 32:9ff., *etc.*). Isaiah repeatedly insists that sin, in whatever sphere it may be committed, is first and foremost sin against God.

Isaiah denounces sinful worship (although this is not so prominent a feature of his preaching as of Hosea's); he inveighs against a ritual which confines itself to external matters (1:10ff.; 29:13), against the offering of sacrifices on the high places (1:29), against heathen worship (2:6–8; 17:7f.; 30:22; 31:7, *etc.*; see also 8:19).

Especially during the early years of his ministry he also spoke out sternly against sins in the social realm—oppression of the defenceless, immoderate luxury, drunkenness, *etc.* (*cf.*, *e.g.*, 1:15–17, 21–23; 3:14f., 16ff.; 5:7–8, 11ff., 14, 22f.; 10:1f.; 28:7ff.; 32:9ff.). In this connection we may think of a possible influence of Amos.

In the political domain, Isaiah's governing demand is trust in the Holy One of Israel (7:9ff.; 8:12f.; 10:20; 17:7; 28:16; 30:15, *etc.*). What did this involve in practical politics? Isaiah never advocated defencelessness, but he uttered repeated warnings against joining in coalitions, especially with Egypt (14:28–32; 18; 20; 30:1–7; 31:1–3). This abstention from active participation in world-politics would, in the circumstances, also have been a requirement of statecraft (*cf.*, *e.g.*, 36:5f.), but Isaiah's warnings should not be attributed to keen political vision, but to divine revelation (see also 30:1). Isaiah's warnings may sometimes have been heeded; we do not hear of any open conflict between Assyria and Judah during the years 714–711 BC. But often people would not listen to him. Ahaz's attitude, for example, is made quite clear in ch. 7 (*cf.* 2 Ki. 16:7ff.); and as for the time of Hezekiah, see 29:15; 30:1ff.; 31:1ff.; 36:4ff. (*cf.* 2 Ki. 18:7).

(ii) *Judgment and salvation.* It is often objected that the preaching of judgment and salvation in Is. 1–39 contains inherent contradictions. From this it is concluded that various parts of these chapters do not come from Isaiah, or else that Isaiah's views underwent a change; for example, a distinction is drawn between a pro- and an anti-Assyrian period in his ministry. But it has already been said that an inevitable tension is involved in the title 'the Holy One of Israel'. As the situation requires, this may mean that he protects Israel and Jerusalem, the Temple city, the royal city; it may mean that he enters into judgment expressly against Israel and Jerusalem. Therefore there is no need for surprise if Isaiah, in his preaching of judgment and salvation, does not always lay the emphasis in the same place (*cf.* 28:23–29; it is rightly said that this parable has a central place in the preaching of Isaiah). The persistent emphasis in his preaching is what was revealed to him at the outset, in his inaugural vision (6:11–13). A thoroughgoing judgment is to come upon Judah and upon Jerusalem as well (3:1–4:1; 5:1–7, 8–24; 32:9–14, *etc.*); in this connection the Assyrians are mentioned (5:26–30; 7:17ff.; 8:5–8, *etc.*); but through and beyond this judgment, which is consequently sometimes portrayed as a purifying judgment (1:24ff.; 4:2ff.), a remnant is saved, and for this remnant a triumphant future breaks (4:2ff.; 10:20ff., *etc.*). But this is not all that should be mentioned here. This thoroughgoing judgment on Jerusalem does not fall immediately. Isaiah is allowed to prophesy that Pekah and Rezin's attack on Jerusalem will fail (7:1–8:4), that the Assyrians will overflow Judah and cause great distress to Jerusalem, but will in their turn be struck by divine judgment and not be permitted to capture Jerusalem (8:9f.; 10:5–34; 14:24–32; 18; 29:1–8; 31:4ff.; 37:6f., 21–35). One statement does not contradict another. (It is to be noted too that before the reassuring prophecies of 37:6f., 21–35, Sennacherib has dealt treacherously, 30:1ff.; *cf.* 2 Ki. 18:14ff., and blasphemed the Holy One of Israel.) That Isaiah's prophecies on this subject are not inherently contradictory is also shown by their fulfilment. The Assyrians did cause much distress to Jerusalem in 701 BC, but were not able to capture it; later on a thoroughgoing judgment did fall on Jerusalem, at the hand of the Babylonians. Isaiah nowhere specifies the Assyrians as the executors of the thoroughgoing judgment of Jerusalem; in a later time he foretold that the Babylonians would come (39:5ff.). Finally, some prophecies, like those of 5:14ff., have their complete fulfilment only in the eschatological judgment (see below, under sub-section (iv)).

The prophet's summons to repentance should also be mentioned in this connection. In a sense his announcement of judgment and salvation is conditional; if they harden their hearts, judgment will follow; if they repent, forgiveness and salvation will be theirs (1:16ff.; 30:15ff., *etc.*). But this announcement is conditional only in a sense; for as early as Isaiah's inaugural vision it was revealed to him that Yahweh was determined to execute judgment on Judah; the broad masses of the people were sunk so deep in their sins that Isaiah's preaching would have no effect save to harden their hearts still more (6:9ff.). Equally, there is no uncertainty about the coming salvation. And, just as Isaiah's preaching, by hardening his hearers' hearts, contributed to Israel's ripening for judgment, so too it contributed to the postponement of the judgment, the rescue of Jerusalem and the formation of the remnant on which Yahweh purposed to bestow his salvation.

The salvation proclaimed by Isaiah includes the deliverance of Jerusalem from great distress, but this deliverance is not the full salvation. The promised salvation in its fullest sense is based on the remission of sins (*cf.* 1:18; 6:5f., *etc.*), and it consists further in a renewal of the heart (*cf.*, *e.g.*, 32:15ff.), a life lived in accordance with God's commandments, a life crowned with prosperity and glory. In this salvation Zion would take a central place, but the other nations would participate in it too (*cf.* 1:19, 26f.; 2:2–5; 4:2–6; 33:13ff.). Special mention should also be made here of the Messianic prophecies, which are of paramount importance (*cf.* 9:1–7; 11:1–10, where there is a marked contrast with the Assyrian empire described in 10:5ff., *cf.* also 16:5; 28:16f.; 32:1ff.; 33:17; the Immanuel prophecy of 7:14 is also Messianic, as its quotation in Mt. 1:22f. shows, but indirectly so, as v. 16 indicates). In these prophecies Isaiah naturally employs OT terms—the Messiah is portrayed as king of Israel, and the idea is raised that he will liberate his people from the Assyrians (9:3; *cf.* 11:1ff., with the preceding oracle)—but by means of these terms he gives a glorious portrayal of the coming salvation, which Christians recognize as having been inaugurated with the first advent of Christ, and as coming to its complete fulfilment with his second advent (*cf.* 11:9, *etc.*).

(iii) *The Holy One of Israel and the nations.* That Yahweh is the only true God is stated more emphatically in chs. 40ff. than in 1–39, yet it is stressed plainly enough in the first part of the book (*cf.* 2:8; 30:22; 37:16, *etc.*). Yahweh is Lord of the whole earth (6:3). All that happens is his doing, the execution of his decree (5:12, 19; 14:24, 26; 37:26, *etc.*). He directs the history of Israel and of the other nations too. Assyria is the rod of his anger (10:5ff.; *cf.* 5:26; 7:17ff.; 8:7f., *etc.*); but because of the Assyrians' pursuit of their own ambitions (10:7ff.), their haughtiness, their violence, their cruelty, their faithlessness and their blasphemy of Yahweh, they too will have to undergo his judgment (8:9.; 10:5ff.; 14:24–27; 18:4–6; 29:1–8; 30:27–33; 31:8f.; 33:1ff.; 36–37, *etc.*). See further the prophecies concerning Babylon (13–14; 21:1–10), Moab (15–16; *cf.* also 25:10ff.), Ethiopia and Egypt (18–20), Edom (21:11f.; 34), and other nations. We should observe, too, that Isaiah predicts not only disaster but also blessing for the nations—*e.g.* in the great prophecy of 19:18–25, with its promise that Egypt, Assyria and Israel will be joint witnesses for Yahweh (*cf.* 16:1ff.; 18:7; 23:15–18, and also 2:2–5; 11:10, *etc.*).

(iv) *Chs. 24–27.* These chapters, which form an epilogue to chs. 13–23, call for a special mention, because of their eloquent portrayal of world judgment (24) and the great salvation which God will accomplish (all nations will have a share in this salvation: 'He will swallow up death for ever'; *cf.* 25:6ff.) and because of their reference to the resurrection of the just (26:19).

b. Chs. 40–55

Jerusalem lies in ruins, Israel is in exile in Babylonia and the Exile has lasted a long time. The people of Israel are in great distress (42:22; 51:18ff.), Yahweh's anger lies heavily upon them because of their sins (40:2; 42:24f.; 51:17, *etc.*); they think that he has forgotten them (40:27; 49:14). Some of them have come to regard the place of their exile as their homeland (55:2). But the prophet promises that Yahweh is about to liberate his people, and he urges them to believe this promise.

(i) *The Holy One of Israel* (41:14, 16, 20; 43:3, 14f.; 45:11; 47:4; 48:17; 49:7; 55:5) *is able to help.* In view of what is said above, it is not surprising that nowhere in the OT is it asserted so emphatically as in these chs. that Yahweh is the one true God, that he alone can help (*cf.* 41:1ff., 21ff.; 43:10f.; 44:6, 8; 45:5, 14, 18, 21f.; 46:9, *etc.*) Trust in other gods is vain, image-worship is sinful folly (40:18ff.; 41:7, 29; 42:8, 17; 44:6–20, 25; 45:20; 46:1ff.; 47:9ff.). He far transcends all his creatures; he has created all things (this has more stress in chs. 40–55 than in chs. 1–39) and directs the course of all things (*cf.* 40:12–26, which forms the introduction to vv. 27–31; 41:4; 43:13; 44:7; 48:13, *etc.*). He is the eternal God (40:28; 41:4; 43:10; 44:6; 48:12); he acts in accordance with his own good pleasure (45:9ff.), and his decree is certain of accomplishment (44:28; 46:10, *etc.*). His word, spoken by the mouth of his prophets, will not return to him 'empty'—without fulfilling its mission (40:6–8; 55:10f.). Even a world-conqueror such as Cyrus is but a tool in his hand for the performance of his purpose (41:1ff., 21–29; 43:9–15; 44:24–45:13; 46:8–13; 48:12–16).

(ii) *The Holy One of Israel is willing to help.* Israel has not deserved his help; she has shown herself unworthy of it (43:22ff., *etc.*). But Israel is his people (40:1, *etc.*; *cf.* too, *e.g.*, 43:15; 44:2), and his name, his reputation, is involved in Israel's deliverance (48:1–11, *etc.*). His relation to Israel, to Zion, is compared to the marriage bond (50:1; 54:5ff.). He has chosen Israel out of all the nations (41:8f.; 48:10, *etc.*) and Israel is his servant—a title which implies both a privilege (41:8f., *etc.*) and a mission (43:10, *etc.*). His love is unchangeably set upon Israel, upon Zion (40:11; 43:3f.; 46:3f.; 49:15ff., *etc.*), and his righteousness is the guarantee of her liberation (*e.g.* 41:10; 45:24).

(iii) *The Holy One of Israel will certainly help.* The coming salvation is painted in bright colours. The basis of this salvation, and at the same time its very essence, consists in his turning away his anger, his remission of Israel's sin (40:2; 43:25; 44:22; 51:21ff., *etc.*). He uses Cyrus as his instrument to inaugurate his salvation; Cyrus is described in quite remarkable terms as Yahweh's 'anointed' (45:1), and the man whom he 'loves' (48:14, *etc.*). Babylon is overthrown by him (46–47; *cf.* 43:14; 48:14); Israel is set free, her exiled children are gathered from all the lands of their dispersion, and return to Canaan (43:1–8, 18–21; 48:20f.; 49:24–26; 52:11f., *etc.*). Yahweh returns to Zion (40:9–11; 52:7f.), Zion is once again inhabited (49:17–23; 54:1ff.), rebuilt (44:28; 45:13; 54:11f.), and protected (54:14–17).

Note especially the following points. 1. This work of deliverance is described as a new creation (41:20; 45:8; *cf.* 45:18). The miracles which marked the Exodus from Egypt are now to be repeated on a grander scale (43:16ff.; 48:21; 51:9f., *etc.*). 2. The prophet sees the whole future as a unity. Israel's liberation from exile is viewed as the beginning of the great era of salvation, in which all things will be made new. Here it can be mentioned that Israel's homeward progress is attended by a series of nature-miracles (41:17ff.; 43:18–21; 48:21; 49:9bf.; 55:12f.; *cf.* 54:13). 3. It is repeatedly emphasized that the grand aim of all this is the praise and glory of God (41:20; 43:21; 44:23; 48:9–11, *etc.*).

The prophet bends all his energies to persuade the people to accept and believe this assurance of blessing; see especially the closing ch. 55. He tries to convince them by pointing to Yahweh's majesty in nature and history. He propounds pointed questions, and challenges them to enter into debate (*cf.*, *e.g.*, 40:12–31; 49:14ff.). He also challenges the Gentile nations and their gods: can *these* gods do what the God of Israel does? It is the God of Israel who has called Cyrus into being and raised him up, in order that he may be the instrument to set Israel free. The God of Israel is therefore the only One who can foretell the result of Cyrus' actions. As certainly as Yahweh made the 'former things' come to pass—that is to say, as certainly as he fulfilled what he foretold in earlier days—so certainly will he bring the 'new things' to pass by the fulfilment of the promises which he now makes through his prophet (41:1ff., 21–29; 43:9–15; 44:6–45:25; 46:8–13; 48:12–16; *cf.* 42:9; 48:1–11). With all this the prophet does not furnish proofs in the strict sense of the word, but he makes a strong appeal to mind, heart and conscience.

All this underlines the outspoken universalism of these chapters. Yahweh, the Creator of the universe, directs world-events, including the victorious career of Cyrus. He rebukes the nations, particularly Babylon, because of their hostility to Israel and also because of their idolatry (41:11–16; 42:13, 17; 46; 47). The goal to which he is directing the course of the world is summed up in the words, 'to me every knee shall bow, every tongue shall swear' (45:23); in this serving of Yahweh lies also the salvation of the nations of the earth; *cf.*, *e.g.*, 42:10–12; 45:6, 22–24; 51:4f.

(iv) On the 'Servant Songs' (42:1–7; 49:1–9a; 50:4–11; 52:13–53:12), see *SERVANT OF THE LORD.

c. Chs. 56–66

The following features are specially noteworthy in these concluding chapters:

1. Yahweh is presented as the living God. He is fearful in his anger (59:16ff.; 63:1–6), but he bends down in kindness to his people, he shows them mercy and restores their comfort, he delights in Zion (57:15ff.; 60:10; 61:1ff.; 62:4f.; 63:7, 15; 65:1f., 8, 19; 66:2, 13). That he is no inflexible or inexorable power is movingly shown in the review of his dealings with Israel in earlier days (63:8ff.).

2. A sharp contrast is drawn between those in Israel who love God and those who disobey him (*e.g.* 57:1; 65:13ff.; 66:5; *cf.* 65:8).

3. It is frequently said, but without justification, that in some parts at least of this section of the book a legalist and nationalist spirit is manifested. True, it is clearly laid down that it is necessary to practise righteousness if one is to share in the coming salvation, and occasionally the importance of keeping the sabbath is stressed (*cf.*, *e.g.*, 56:1–8). But this is not intended to inculcate a spirit of ceremonialism and legalism; on the contrary, this very spirit is roundly condemned (*cf.* 58; 66:1, 5), and an attitude of humility is repeatedly commended (*cf.*, *e.g.*, 57:15; 61:2f.; 66:2). As to the glorifying of Zion (*cf.*, *e.g.*, 60:4ff.; 61:5ff.; 66:20), this is no mere outburst of nationalist feeling. Zion is not only the capital of Judah but the dwelling-place of God; and the Gentiles who turn to him participate in his salvation (*e.g.* 56:1–8; 60:3).

BIBLIOGRAPHY. See the Introductions to the OT and the Commentaries—*e.g.* E. J. Kissane, *The Book of Isaiah*, 1, 1941 (1960), 2, 1943, I. W. Slotki, *Isaiah*, *Soncino Bible*, 1949; R. B. Y. Scott, G. D. Kilpatrick, J. Muilenburg, H. S. Coffin, 'Isaiah', *IB*, 5, 1956; J. Mauchline, *Isaiah 1–39*, *TBC*, 1962; C. R. North, *Isaiah 40–55*, *TBC*, 1964; D. R. Jones, *Isaiah 56–66 and Joel*, *TBC*, 1964; C. R. North, *The Second Isaiah*, 1964; E. J. Young, *The Book of Isaiah*, *NIC*, 1, 1965, 2, 1969, 3, 1972; H. C. Leupold, *Exposition of Isaiah I* (chs. 1–39), 1968; J. L. McKenzie, *Second Isaiah*, *AB*, 1968; O. Kaiser, *Isaiah 1–12*, *OTL*, 1972, *Isaiah 13–39*, *OTL*, 1974; C. Westermann, *Isaiah 40–66*, *OTL*, 1969; A. S. Herbert, *Isaiah 1–39*, CBC, 1973. *Cf.*, too: O. T. Allis, *The Unity of Isaiah*, 1950.

N.H.R.

ISHBOSHETH. The name (2 Sa. 2–4) is commonly thought to have been Eshbaal originally, altered by scribes who wrote *bošeṯ* ('shame') instead of the apparently pagan divine name *Baal. In 1 Ch. 8:33; 9:39 the form Eshbaal is written. Recently a strong case has been argued against this view, *bošeṯ* being understood as a divine attribute, 'pride, strength'. Ishbosheth and Eshbaal would be alternative names for one man (so, too, Mephibosheth and Meribaal; see M. Tsevat, *HUCA* 46, 1975, pp. 71–87). A son of Saul, the Ishvi of 1 Sa. 14:49 (a corruption of Ishiah, *i.e.* Ishbaal), he was made king of Israel at *Mahanaim, out of reach of the Philistines, by Abner, his father's commander. As David's power grew, Abner began an intrigue with him but was murdered. Ishbosheth's supporters lost heart, and two of his cavalry officers, Rechab and Baanah, assassinated him during his midday rest (2 Sa. 2–4). The LXX account of this crime is more explicit than *MT* (2 Sa. 4:6, *cf.* AV with RVmg. or RSV), which may be emended to agree with the Greek. The death of Ishbosheth enabled David to gain control of all Israel from the house of Saul.

A.R.M.

ISHI (Heb. *'îšî*, 'my husband'). In Ho. 2:16 the name which the Israelites were to use for God, to supersede 'Baali' with its pagan associations.

J.D.D.

ISHMAEL (Heb. *yišmā'ē'l*, 'God hears'). **1.** The son of Abraham by Hagar the Egyptian handmaid of Sarah. When Sarah realized that she was barren, she gave her handmaid to Abraham to conceive seed for her (Gn. 16:2). An example of this ancient custom has been discovered in the *Nuzi tablets (*ANET*, p. 220). After conceiving by Abraham, Hagar began to despise Sarah, who then drove her out of the home with Abraham's reluctant consent. On her way to Egypt she was met by the angel of Yahweh, who told her to return and submit to Sarah. He also gave her the promise of a multiplied seed through her son Ishmael, who would be 'a wild ass of a man' (16:12; *cf.* Jb. 39:5–8). Ishmael was born when Abraham was 86, 11 years after his arrival in Canaan (16:15–16; *cf.* 12:4). 13 years later, both Ishmael and his father were circumcised in obedience to God's command (17:25–26). But on that same day, God had also promised Abraham a son by Sarah. The fact that he had long since centred his hopes on Ishmael caused him to cry out, 'O that Ishmael might live in thy sight!' (17:18). God then assured him that Ishmael would beget twelve princes and ultimately a great nation (17:20; *cf.* 16:10; 25:13–16). When Ishmael was about 16, a great celebration was held at the weaning of the child Isaac (21:8). Ishmael gave vent to his jealousy of 'the child of the promise' (Rom. 9:7–9) by 'mocking' him. The apostle Paul employs the verb 'persecuted' (*ediōke*) to describe this act (Gal. 4:29) and builds upon it an extended allegory of the opposition of legalistic religionists to those 'born according to the Spirit' (Gal. 4:21–31). Sarah insisted that both Ishmael and Hagar be expelled from the home, and Abraham consented only after the Lord revealed to him that 'through Isaac shall your descendants be named' (Gn. 21:12). Hagar and her son nearly perished from thirst in the desert of Beersheba, until the angel of Yahweh pointed her to a well of water in response to Ishmael's cry. He grew to be an archer, married an Egyptian and fathered twelve princes (25:12–16). Esau married one of his daughters (28:9; 36:3, 10). He joined Isaac in the burial of their father and died at the age of 137 (25:9, 17).

2. A descendant of Saul and Jonathan, and the son of Azel (1 Ch. 8:38; *cf.* 9:44). **3.** A man of Judah, father of the Zebadiah who was a high official under King Jehoshaphat (2 Ch. 19:11). **4.** The son of Jehohanan, and a captain of hundreds who took part in the conspiracy against Athaliah (2 Ch.

ISCARIOT
See Judas Iscariot, Part 2.

ISHIAH
See Ishbosheth, Part 2.

■ ISHVI
See Ishbosheth, Part 2.

23:1). **5.** A son of Pashhur the priest. He was one of those whom Ezra compelled to put away their foreign wives (Ezr. 10:22).

6. The son of Nethaniah, of the seed royal of Judah, who murdered Gedaliah 2 months after the destruction of Jerusalem in 586 BC. When Gedaliah was appointed by Nebuchadrezzar to be the governor of Judah, many Jews gathered themselves to him at Mizpah for security. Among these, however, was Ishmael, who was jealous of Gedaliah and permitted himself to be hired by Baalis the king of Ammon to plot the governor's death. In spite of Johanan's warnings, Gedaliah trusted Ishmael and invited him and ten of his men to a banquet. They used the occasion to murder Gedaliah and all the others in Mizpah. Two days later they killed a group of Jewish pilgrims and set off for Ammon with many hostages, including Jeremiah and the king's daughters. They were pursued by Johanan and other captains and were overtaken at Gibeon. The hostages were rescued, but Ishmael and eight of his men escaped to Ammon (2 Ki. 25:25; Je. 40:7–41:18).

BIBLIOGRAPHY. H. C. Leupold, *Exposition of Genesis*, 1942; C. F. Keil, *Biblical Commentary on the Old Testament*, I, *The Pentateuch*, 1949; J. J. Davis, *Paradise to Prison*, 1975; H. C. White, *ZAW* 87, 1975, pp. 267–306. J.C.W.

ISLAND, ISLE (Heb. *'î*, pl. *'iyyîm*; Gk. *nēsos*, *nēsion*). Etymologically, the Heb. term is frequently supposed to mean 'habitable land', through a cognate Arab. word, but 'coastlands' is a better translation, as usually in RSV. The general OT usage is to denote the islands and coastlands of the Mediterranean. The idea of distance is also included, *e.g.* Is. 66:19; Je. 31:10. Occasionally it appears to have the strict meaning, *e.g.* 'Kittim' or 'Cyprus' (RSV) in Je. 2:10, 'Caphtor' in Je. 47:4 (see RSV: probably Crete). Isaiah's usage is interesting. In 42:15 it denotes 'dry land' as opposed to water. In 40:15 it is parallel to 'nations'; in 41:1; 49:1 to 'peoples'; and in 41:5 to 'the ends of the earth'.

NT usage is unambiguous. Several islands are named, *e.g.* Cyprus (Acts 4:36; 13:4; 15:39), Crete and Cauda (Acts 27), Malta (Acts 28:1) and Patmos (Rev. 1:9). J.G.G.N.

ISRAEL (Heb. *yiśrā'ēl*, 'God strives'). **1.** The new name given to Jacob after his night of wrestling at Penuel: 'Your name', said his supernatural antagonist, 'shall no more be called Jacob, but Israel, for you have striven [*śārîṯā*, from *śārâ*, 'strive'] with God and with men, and have prevailed' (Gn. 32:28). With this account, assigned to J in the four-document hypothesis, *cf.* Ho. 12:3f., 'in his manhood he [Jacob] strove [*śārâ*] with God. He strove [*wayyāśar*, from the same verb] with the angel and prevailed'. The re-naming is confirmed at Bethel in Gn. 35:10 (assigned to P), where God Almighty appears to Jacob and says: 'Your name is Jacob; no longer shall your name be called Jacob, but Israel shall be your name.' 'So', adds the narrator, 'his name was called Israel.' Thenceforward Israel appears throughout the OT as an occasional synonym for Jacob; it is used most frequently when the Patriarch's descendants are called 'the children (or people) of Israel' (Heb. *bᵉnê yiśrā'ēl*).

2. The nation which traced its ancestry back to the 12 sons of Jacob, referred to variously as 'Israel' (Gn. 34:7, *etc.*), 'the people of Israel' (Ex. 1:8, *etc.*), 'the (twelve) tribes of Israel' (Gn. 49:16, 28), 'the Israelites' (Gn. 32:32, *etc.*).

The earliest reference to the nation of Israel in a non-Israelite record appears in an inscription of Merenptah, king of Egypt, *c.* 1230 BC, 'Israel is desolate; it has no seed left' (*DOTT*, p. 139). The next non-Israelite references come in inscriptions of Shalmaneser III of Assyria, *c.* 853 BC, mentioning 'Ahab the Israelite' (*DOTT*, p. 47), and of Mesha of Moab, whose victory-inscription (*c.* 830 BC) makes repeated mention of Israel, including the boast, 'Israel perished utterly for ever' (*DOTT*, pp. 196f.; *MOABITE STONE. For illustrations see *IBA*, figs. 40, 48, 50–51).

I. Israel's beginnings

Merenptah's reference practically coincides with the beginning of Israel's national history, for it is the Exodus from Egypt, which took place in his reign or his father's, that marks Israel's birth as a nation. Some generations previously their ancestors, members of a pastoral clan, went down from Canaan to Egypt in time of famine and settled in the Wadi Tumilat. The early kings of Dynasty 19 drafted them in large numbers into forced labour gangs for the building of fortified cities on Egypt's NE frontier. In these circumstances they might have been completely assimilated to their fellow serfs had not their ancestral faith been reawakened by Moses, who came to them in the name of the God of their fathers and led them out of Egypt amid a series of phenomena in which he taught them to recognize the power of that God, put forth for their deliverance.

Under Moses' leadership they trekked E by 'the way of the wilderness of the Yam Suph' until they reached the place where the God of their fathers had previously revealed himself to Moses by his covenant-name Yahweh and commissioned him to bring them out of Egypt. There, at the foot of Mt Sinai, they were brought into special covenant-relationship with Yahweh. He had already shown himself to be their God by rescuing them from bondage in Egypt; they now undertook to be his people. This undertaking involved their obedience to the 'Ten Words' in which Yahweh made his will known to them. They were to worship him alone; they were not to represent him by means of any image; they were to treat his name with due reverence; they were to reserve every seventh day for him; and in thought, word and deed they were to behave one towards another in a manner befitting the covenant which bound them together. They were to be a people set apart for Yahweh, and were therefore to have something of his righteousness, mercy and truth reproduced in their lives.

This attitude we may call practical monotheism. Whether the gods of neighbouring peoples had any sort of existence or not was a question about which neither Moses nor his followers were likely to trouble their minds; their business was to acknowledge Yahweh as supreme and sole God.

Moses was not only Israel's first and greatest legislator; in his own person he combined the functions of prophet, priest and king. He judged their lawsuits and taught them the principles of religious duty; he led them from Egypt to the Jordan, and when he died, a generation after the Exodus, he left behind him no undisciplined body of slave-labourers, such as had followed him out of Egypt, but a formidable host ready to invade

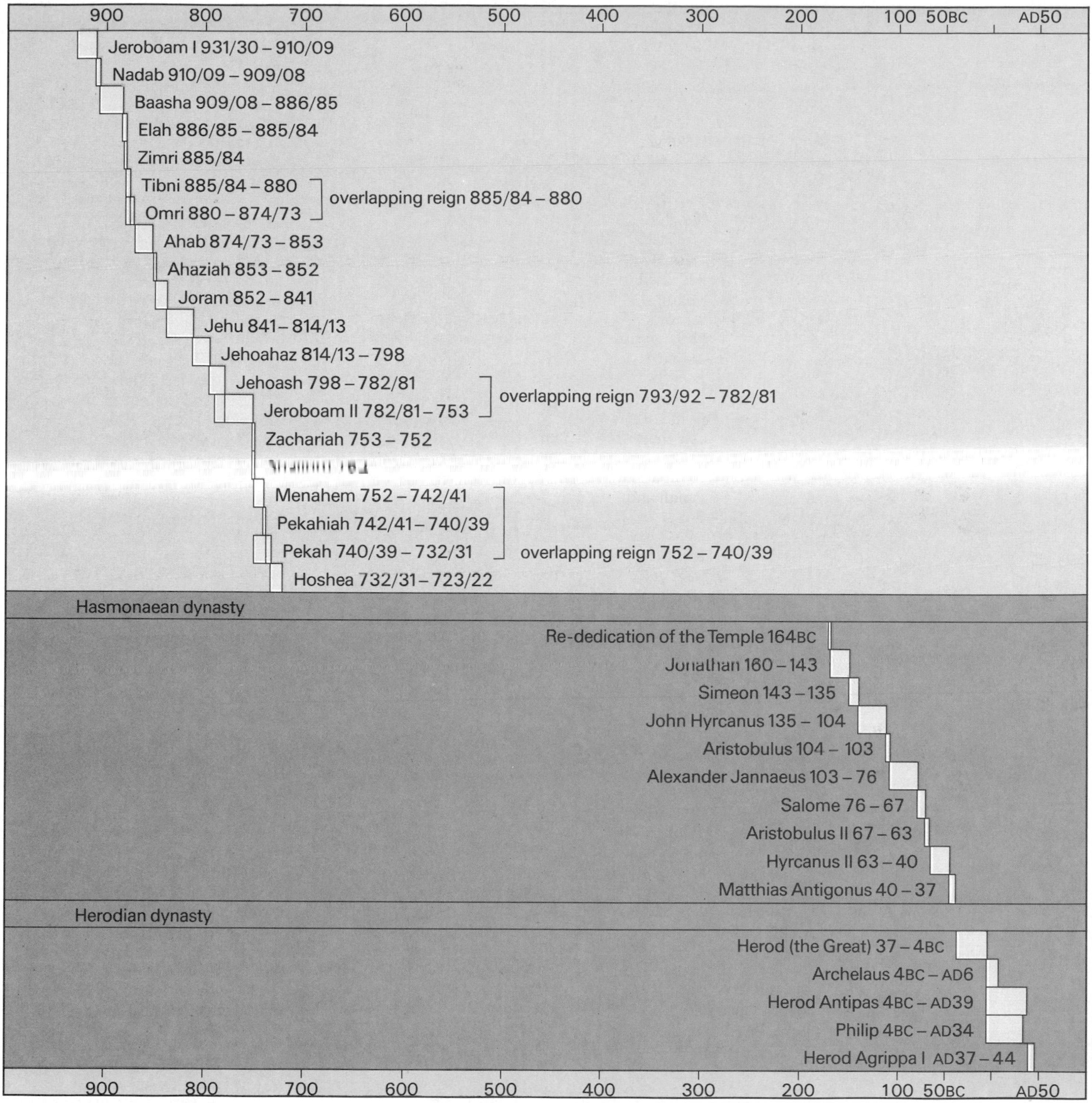

Chronological table of the rulers of Israel down to the reign of Herod Agrippa I.

Canaan as conquerors and settlers.

This host, even before its settlement in Canaan, was organized as a confederacy of twelve tribes, united in part by a common ancestry but even more so by common participation in the covenant with Yahweh. The visible token of their covenant unity was the sacred ark, housed in a tent-shrine which was located in the centre of their encampment when they were stationary, but which preceded them on the march or in battle. They formed close alliances with other nomad groups such as the Kenites (to whom Moses was related by marriage), the Kenizzites and the Jerahmeelites, who in due course appear to have been incorporated into the tribe of Judah. It was probably a breach of alliance on the part of another nomad group, the Amalekites, that was responsible for the bitter feud which Israel pursued against them from generation to generation. Alliance with such pastoral communities was very different from alliance with the settled agricultural population of Canaan, with its fertility cults so inimical to pure Yahweh-worship. Their covenant with Yahweh strictly prohibited the Israelites from making common cause with the Canaanites.

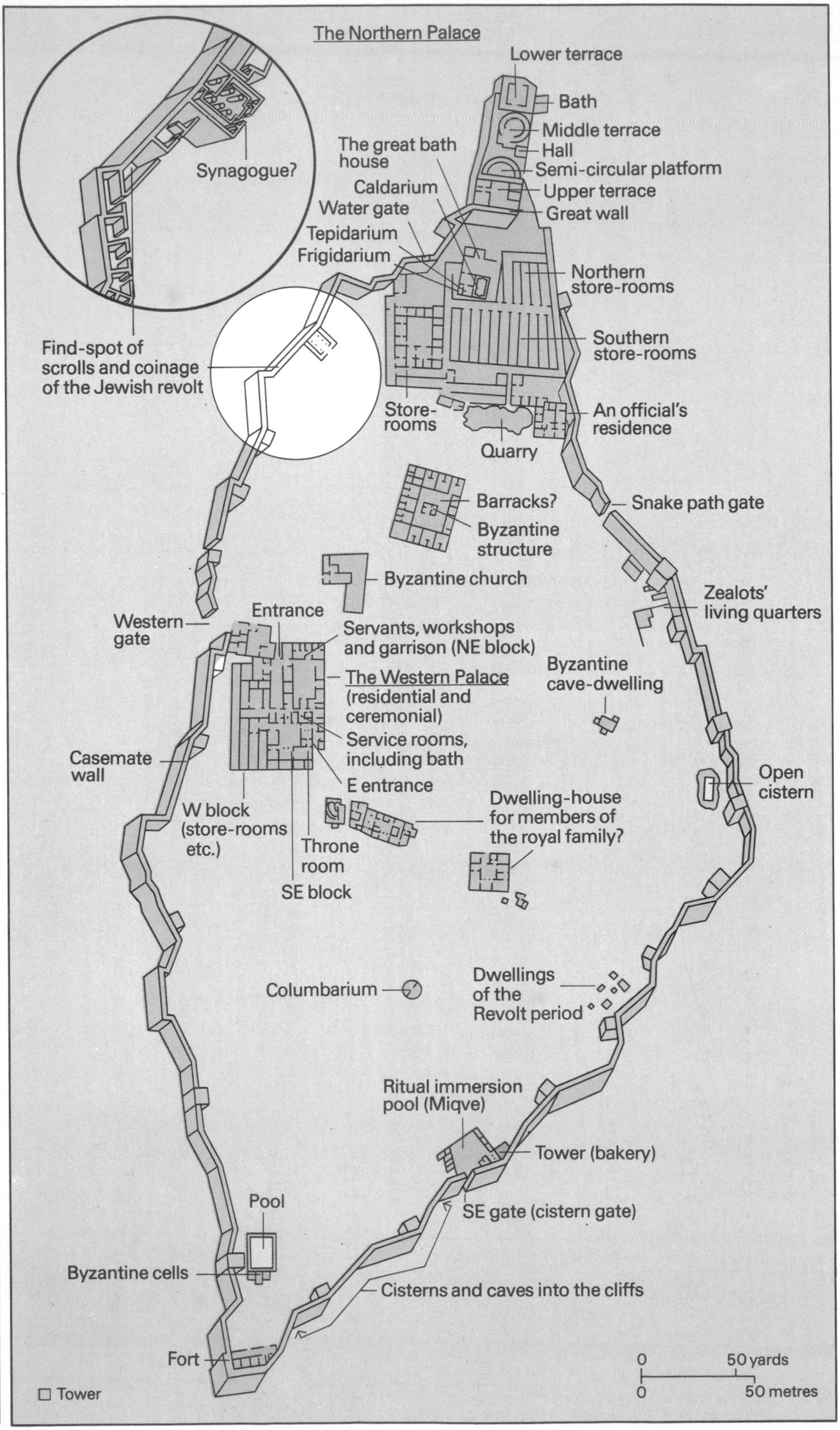

The principal centre of the tribes of Israel in their wilderness period was Kadesh-barnea, evidently (from its name) a sanctuary and also (from its alternative name En-mishpat) a place where causes were heard and judgment pronounced. When they left Kadesh-barnea some of them infiltrated N into the central Negeb, but the main body advanced S and E of the Dead Sea, skirting the territories of their Edomite, Ammonite and Moabite kinsfolk, who had very recently organized themselves as settled kingdoms. Farther N in Trans-jordan lay the Amorite kingdoms of Sihon and Og, which they entered as hostile invaders. The resisting forces of Sihon and Og were crushed, and their territories were occupied—these are the territories later known as Reuben, Gad and E Manasseh. Part at least of the Israelite community thus settled down to an agricultural way of life even before the crossing of the Jordan.

II. The settlement in Canaan

The crossing of the Jordan was followed quickly by the capture and destruction of the fortress of *Jericho. From Jericho they pressed into the heart of the land, taking one fortress after another. Egypt was no longer in a position to send help to her former Canaanite vassals; only along the W coastal road did she now exercise some control, as far N as the pass of Megiddo, and even in that region the Philistine settlement (*c.* 1190 BC) was soon to present a barrier to the extension of Egyptian power.

A coalition of five military governors of Canaanite fortresses attempted to prevent the Israelites from turning S from the central hill-country, where Gibeon and the associated cities of the Hivite tetrapolis had submitted to them as subject-allies. The coalition was completely defeated in the pass of Beth-horon and the road to the S lay open to the invaders. Although the chariot-forces of Canaanite citadels prevented them from operating in more level country, they soon dominated and occupied the central and S highlands, and also the Galilean uplands, N of the Plain of Jezreel.

The tribes which settled in the N were cut off from their fellows in central Canaan by a chain of Canaanite fortifications in the Plain of Jezreel, stretching from the Mediterranean to the Jordan.

Judah, in the S, was even more effectively cut off from the central tribes by the stronghold of Jerusalem, which remained a Canaanite enclave for 200 years.

On one notable occasion the N and central tribes joined forces in an uprising against the military governors of the Plain of Jezreel, who were steadily reducing them to serfdom. Their united rising was crowned with success at the battle of Kishon (*c.* 1125 BC), when a sudden storm flooded the water-course and put the Canaanite chariotry out of action, so that the light-armed Israelites easily routed them. But even on this occasion, while the call to action went out to all the N and central tribes, and to those in Transjordan, Judah appears to have received no summons, being too completely cut off from the other tribes.

On an occasion like this, when the tribes of Israel remembered their covenant-bond, their united strength enabled them to resist their enemies. But such united action was rare. The recession of danger was regularly followed by a period of assimilation to Canaanite ways. This assimilation involved intermarriage and the imitation of Canaanite fertility rites, so that Yahweh was thought of rather in terms of Baal, the fructifying rain-god, than as the God of their fathers who had redeemed them from Egypt to be his peculiar people. The covenant-bond was thus weakened and they became an easy prey to their enemies. Not only did Canaanite city-states try to reduce them to servitude; from time to time they suffered incursions from beyond Jordan, by their own kinsmen the Moabites and Ammonites, and much more disastrously at the hands of raiding bedouin. The leaders who rallied them in such periods of distress were the charismatic 'judges' after whom this whole settlement period is commonly named; these men not only led them forward to victory against their enemies but back to loyalty to Yahweh.

The greatest and most recalcitrant menace to Israelite independence, however, came from the W. Not long after the Israelites crossed the Jordan, bands of sea-rovers from the Aegean islands and coastlands settled on the W seaboard of Canaan and organized themselves in the five city-states of Ashdod, Ashkelon, Ekron, Gaza and Gath, each of which was governed by a *seren*—one of the 'five lords of the Philistines'. These *Philistines intermarried with the Canaanites and soon became Canaanite in language and religion, but they retained the political and military traditions of their homelands. Once they had established themselves in their pentapolis they began to extend control over other parts of Canaan, including those parts occupied by the Israelites. Militarily the Israelites were no match for them. The Philistines had mastered the art of iron-working, and kept it as a monopoly in their own hands. When the Israelites began to use iron implements in their agriculture the Philistines insisted that they must come to Philistine smiths to have them sharpened. This was a means of ensuring that

Opposite page: Plan of the fortress of Masada.

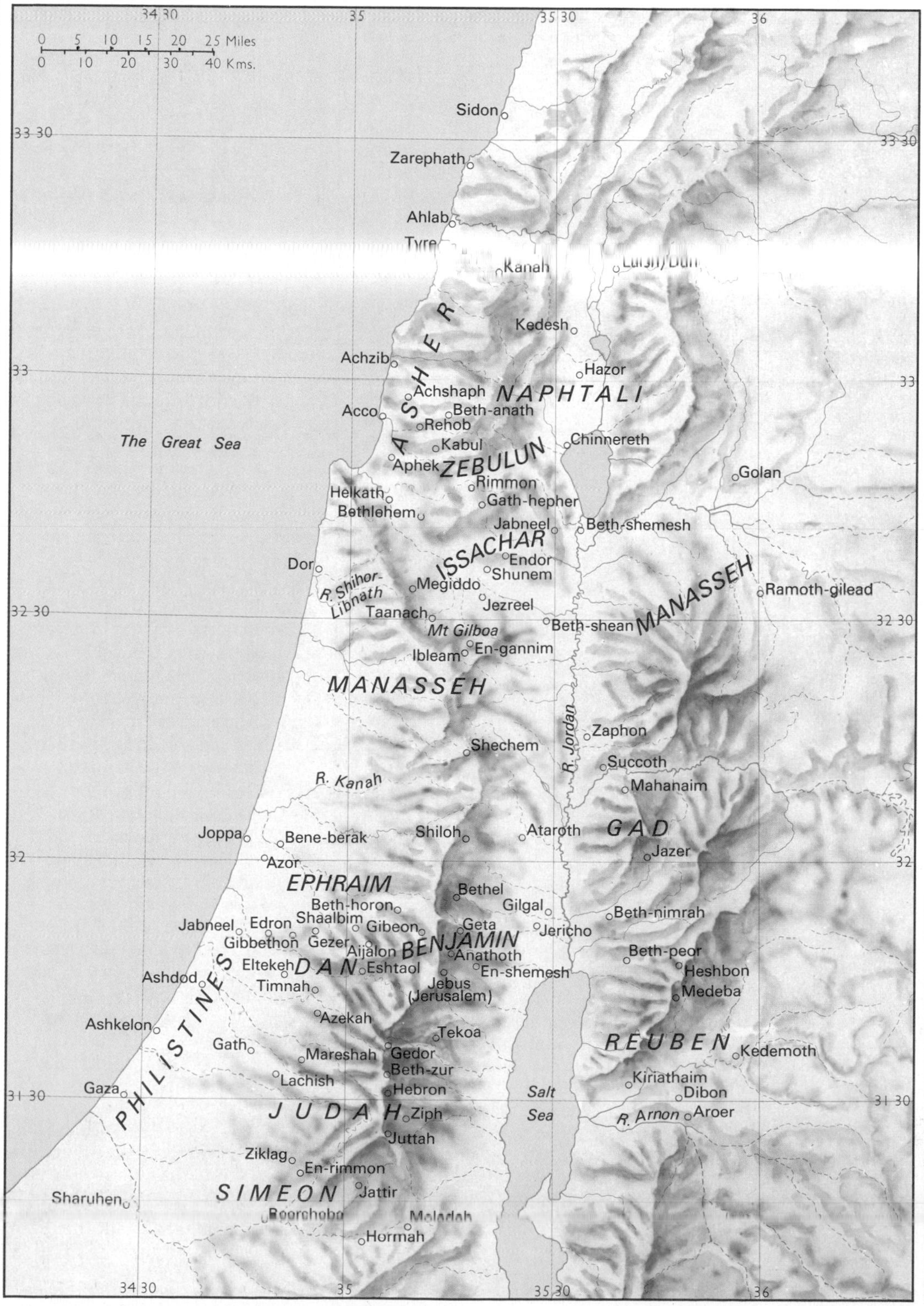

The tribes of Israel.

Israel ('Ysrail') is named on the victory stele of Merenptah, king of Egypt, c. 1215 BC. *This is the first extant reference to Israel from external sources. Black granite.* (KAK)

the Israelites would not be able to forge iron implements of war with which they might rise against their overlords.

At last the Philistines extended their domination over the Plain of Jezreel as far as the Jordan. While their suzerainty did not menace Israelite existence, it did menace Israelite national identity. The covenant shrine in those days was established at *Shiloh, in the territory of Ephraim, where the sacred ark was tended by a priesthood tracing its lineage back to Aaron, the brother of Moses. This priesthood took a leading part in an intertribal revolt against the Philistines which was an utter failure. The ark was captured, Shiloh and the sanctuary were destroyed and the central priesthood was practically wiped out (*c.* 1050 BC). All the visible bonds which united the tribes of Israel had disappeared, and Israel's national identity seemed likely to disappear with them.

That it did not disappear, but rather became more vigorous, was due to the character and enterprise of *Samuel, the greatest of Israel's charismatic leaders between Moses and David. Samuel, like Moses, combined the functions of prophet, priest and judge; and in his own person he provided a rallying-centre for the national life. Under his guidance Israel returned to its covenant loyalty, and with the return of religious devotion came a resurgence of national spirit; after some years the Israelites were able to defeat the Philistines on the very battlefield where they had been so shamefully routed.

As Samuel grew old, the question of the succession became acute. There arose a widespread demand for a king, and at last Samuel consented to this demand and anointed the Benjaminite *Saul to reign over them. Saul's reign began auspiciously with a prompt retort to a hostile show of force by the Ammonites, and this was followed by successful action against the Philistines in the central highlands. So long as Saul accepted Samuel's direction in the religious sphere all went well, but Saul's fortunes began to decline when a breach came about between them. He met his death in battle against the Philistine at Mt Gilboa, in a bold but vain attempt to bring the N tribes, beyond the Plain of Jezreel, into the unity of Israel. The Philistine grip on Israel was now firmer than ever (*c.* 1010 BC).

III. David and Solomon

The man who enabled Israel to throw off the Philistine yoke was *David, a member of the tribe of Judah, at one time a military commander under Saul and later a mercenary warrior with the Philistines. On Saul's death he was immediately acclaimed as king of Judah, and 2 years later the tribes of Israel as a whole also invited him to be their king. In a series of brilliant military actions he inflicted decisive defeats on the Philistines, who thereafter had to live as David's vassals. The capture of Jerusalem by David in the 7th year of his reign provided his kingdom with a strong and strategically situated capital and also with a new religious centre. The ark was brought back from exile and solemnly installed in a tent-shrine on Mt Zion, later superseded by Solomon's Temple.

After establishing Israelite independence and supremacy in Canaan, David went on by conquest and diplomacy to build up an empire stretching from the Egyptian border and the Gulf of Aqaba to the Upper Euphrates. This empire he bequeathed to his son Solomon, who overtaxed its resources by a grandiose building programme and the maintenance of a splendid court. For the more efficient exploitation of his kingdom's revenue, he divided it into twelve new administrative districts, which took the place of the old tribal divisions, and exacted not only heavy taxes but compulsory labour on public works, ultimately even from his Israelite subjects. The burden at last became intolerable. Towards the end of his reign most of the subject nations had regained their independence, and after his death (*c.* 930 BC) the tribes of Israel themselves split into two kingdoms—the N kingdom of Israel, which renounced its allegiance to the throne of David, and the S kingdom of Judah, consisting of the tribal territories of Judah and Benjamin, over which the descendants of David and Solomon continued to reign in their capital at Jerusalem (*JUDAH, IV).

IV. The kingdom of Israel

Jeroboam, founder of the separate monarchy in the N, elevated the two ancient sanctuaries of Dan (in the far N) and Bethel (near the frontier with Judah) to the status of national shrines. In both of these golden bull-calves provided the visible pedestals for Yahweh's invisible throne (the function fulfilled by golden cherubs in the Jerusalem Temple). Early in his reign both Hebrew kingdoms were invaded by the Egyptians under Shishak, but the S kingdom appears to have suffered the more, so that later the N kingdom had no need to fear an attempt by the Davidic dynasty to regain control of its lost territories.

A more serious threat, however, presented itself from the N. The Aramaean kingdom of Damascus, founded in Solomon's reign, began to encroach on Israelite territory about 900 BC, and this was the beginning of 100 years of intermittent war which at times reduced Israel to desperate straits.

The security of the kingdom of Israel was also impaired by frequent palace-revolts and dynastic changes. Only two dynasties—those founded by Omri (*c.* 880 BC) and

Jehu (*c.* 841 BC)—lasted for more than two generations. Jeroboam's son was assassinated by Baasha, one of his army commanders, in the year after he succeeded to the kingdom; when Baasha had reigned for 20 years his son too fell victim to a similar fate. A few years of civil war followed, from which Omri emerged as the victor.

Omri founded a new capital for his kingdom at *Samaria. Externally he strengthened his position by subduing Moab, E of the Dead Sea, and entering into an economic alliance with Phoenicia. His son Ahab married a Phoenician princess, Jezebel, and also brought the hostility between his kingdom and Judah to an end by means of an alliance which lasted until the dynasty of Omri was overthrown.

The commercial benefits of the Phoenician alliance were great, but in the religious realm it led to a revival of Baal worship, in which Jezebel played a leading part. The principal champion of pure Yahweh-worship was the prophet *Elijah, who also denounced the royal departure from the old covenant-loyalty in the social sphere (notably in the case of Naboth the Jezreelite) and proclaimed the impending doom of the dynasty of Omri.

The war with Damascus continued throughout the reigns of Omri and his descendants, apart from 3 years during the reign of Ahab, when the kings of Israel and Damascus and neighbouring states formed a military coalition to resist the invading king of Assyria, Shalmaneser III. They gave him battle at Qarqar on the Orontes (853 BC), and he did not invade the W lands again for 12 years. His withdrawal was the signal for the break-up of the coalition and the resumption of hostilities between Israel and Damascus.

The extermination of the house of Omri in Jehu's revolt (841 BC) was followed by the suppression of official Baal-worship. The revolt was supported by the prophetic guilds, who had no reason to love the house of Omri. But it gravely weakened the kingdom of Israel in face of the Aramaean assaults, and the first 40 years of the dynasty of Jehu were years of continual tribulation for Israel. Not only were Israel's Transjordanian territories overrun by the enemy but her N provinces too; the Aramaeans invaded the Plain of Jezreel and made their way along the Mediterranean seaboard as far S as Gath. Israel had been reduced to desperate straits when in 803 BC the Assyrian king Adad-nirari III invaded Syria, raided Damascus and imposed tribute on it. Damascene pressure on Israel was relaxed; and the Israelites were able to take advantage of this turn of fortune and regain many of the cities which the Aramaeans had taken from them.

Throughout the years of tribulation there was one man in Israel whose morale and confidence in Yahweh never wavered—the prophet *Elisha. Well might the king of Israel address him on his deathbed as 'the chariots of Israel and its horsemen' (2 Ki. 13:14). Elisha died with a prediction of victory over the Aramaeans on his lips.

The first half of the 8th century BC witnessed a return of prosperity to Israel, especially under Jeroboam II, the 4th king of Jehu's dynasty. Both Hebrew kingdoms were free from external molestation; Damascus was too weak after her rough handling by Assyria to renew her aggression. Jeroboam extended his kingdom's frontiers and the national wealth increased greatly.

But this increase of national wealth was concentrated in the hands of a relatively small section of the population—the well-to-do merchants and landowners, who enriched themselves at the expense of the peasantry. The smallholders who had formerly tilled their own fields were now obliged in large numbers to become serfs on the growing estates of their wealthy neighbours, cultivating the land which they had once cultivated as independent owners. This increasing disparity between two sections of Israel's freeborn citizens called forth the denunciation of such prophets as Amos and Hosea, the more so as the rich expropriators of their poorer neighbours were punctilious in the performance of what they considered their religious duties. The prophets insisted tirelessly that what Yahweh required from his people was not sacrifices of fatted beasts but righteousness and covenant-loyalty, for lack of which the nation faced disaster greater than anything it had hitherto known.

About 745 BC the dynasty of Jehu ended as it had begun, by assassination and revolt. In that year Tiglath-pileser III became king of Assyria and inaugurated a campaign of imperial conquest which in less than a quarter of a century brought an end to the existence of the kingdom of Israel and to the independence of the kingdom of Judah. Menahem of Israel (*c.* 745–737 BC) paid tribute to Tiglath-pileser, but an anti-Assyrian policy was pursued by Pekah (*c.* 736–732 BC), who allied himself for this purpose with Damascus. Tiglath-pileser took Damascus, abolished the monarchy and transformed the territory into an Assyrian province; the N and Transjordanian regions of Israel were detached and made into Assyrian provinces. The upper strata of the populations of these areas were deported and replaced by immigrants from other parts of the Assyrian empire. When Hoshea, the last king of Israel, withheld payment of tribute from Assyria at the instance of Egypt, he was imprisoned. Samaria, his capital, was stormed in 722 BC after a 3-years' siege, and became the seat of government of the Assyrian province of Samaria. A further deportation took place—according to Assyrian records 27,290 people were taken captive—and foreign settlers were sent to take their place.

V. The province of Samaria

The deportation of Israelites from the N and Transjordanian territories was so thorough that these territories quite lost their Israelite character. In the province of Samaria it was different; the immigrants in due course adopted Israelite religion—'the law of the god of the land' (2 Ki. 17:26ff.)—and were completely assimilated to the Israelites who had not been carried away; but the *Samaritans, as the population of the province of Samaria were later called, came to be despised as racial and religious half-breeds by the people of Judah farther S, especially from the end of the 6th century BC onward.

King Hezekiah of Judah attempted (*c.* 705 BC) to revive the religious unity of Israel by inviting the people of Samaria to come to Jerusalem to worship, but his attempt was rendered ineffective by Sennacherib's invasion of Judah (701 BC). Greater success attended the action of Hezekiah's great-grandson Josiah, who took advantage of the recession of Assyrian power to extend his political sovereignty and religious reformation into the regions formerly belonging to the kingdom of Israel (621 BC). The fact that he tried to bar

Pharaoh Neco's advance at Megiddo is evidence enough of the expansion of his kingdom, but his death there (609 BC) brought an end to such hopes as might have been cherished of the reunion of all Israel under a prince of the house of David. The land of Israel passed under the hegemony of Egypt, and a few years later under that of Babylonia.

The Babylonians appear to have perpetuated the Assyrian provincial organization in the W. After the assassination of Gedaliah, governor of Judah under the Babylonians, the land of Judah with the exception of the Negeb (now being occupied by the Edomites) was added to the province of Samaria (*c.* 582 BC). No great change in this respect resulted from the Persian conquest (539 BC), except that the men of Judah exiled under Nebuchadrezzar were allowed to return and settle in Jerusalem and the surrounding area, which now became the separate, if tiny, province of Judaea under a governor appointed by the Persian king (*JUDAH, **V**).

The Samaritans made friendly overtures to the restored exiles and offered to co-operate in rebuilding the Jerusalem Temple, but these overtures were not welcomed by the Judaeans, who no doubt feared that they would be swamped by the much greater numbers of the Samaritans, and also had serious doubts of the Samaritans' racial and religious purity. In consequence, a long-standing breach which might have been healed at this time became more bitter than ever, and the Samaritans seized every opportunity to represent the Judaeans to the Persian authorities in an unfavourable light. They were unable to prevent the rebuilding of the Jerusalem Temple, which had been authorized by Cyrus in 538 BC, but they had better success for a time in obstructing the Judaeans' attempts to fortify Jerusalem. When, however, Artaxerxes I sent *Nehemiah to Judah as governor in 445 BC, with express directions to rebuild the walls of Jerusalem, the Samaritans and other neighbours of Judah might betray their chagrin in various ways but could take no effective action in face of the royal edict.

The governor of Samaria at this time was *Sanballat, who continued in office for many years. In 408 BC he is mentioned in a letter from the Jewish community of Elephantine (*PAPYRI, **II.** *c*) in Egypt, who seek the good offices of Sanballat's sons in procuring permission from the Persian court for the rebuilding of their temple, which had been destroyed in an anti-Jewish riot 2 or 3 years previously. This temple had been built more than a century before to serve the religious needs of a Jewish community which the Egyptian kings of Dynasty 26 had settled on their S frontier as an insurance against Ethiopian inroads. Before writing to Sanballat's sons, the Elephantine Jews had tried to enlist the aid of the high priest in Jerusalem, but he had paid no attention to their plea; no doubt he disapproved of the existence of a rival temple to that in Jerusalem. Sanballat's sons—not unnaturally, in view of the relations between Samaria and Jerusalem—showed greater alacrity, and procured the necessary permission for the rebuilding of the Elephantine temple.

The fact that it was Sanballat's sons and not their father whom the Elephantine Jews approached suggests that, while Sanballat was still nominally governor, his sons were discharging many of his duties on his behalf, probably because of his age.

The Elephantine papyri which supply us with our information about this Jewish community in Egypt are particularly interesting because they portray a group of Jews who show no signs of having been influenced by the reformation of Josiah's days. In this they form a strong contrast to the Jews who returned from exile to Jerusalem and the surrounding territory. The latter, together with their brethren in Babylonia, had learnt the lesson of exile, and were increasingly marked by strict adherence to the Torah, including especially those features of it which were calculated to mark off the people of the law from all other communities. The emergence of the Jews as the people of the law in the most particularist sense is associated above all with the work of *Ezra, under whom the Pentateuchal law became the recognized constitution of the Judaean temple-state, subject to the overriding authority of the Persian court.

The work of Ezra (which had the whole-hearted backing of Nehemiah as governor) meant that the cleavage between the Samaritans and Judaeans was less likely than ever to be mended. Some time before 400 BC a scion of the Jerusalem high-priestly family, Manasseh by name, who had married a daughter of Sanballat, was installed by his father-in-law as high priest of the ancient holy place on Mt Gerizim, near Shechem, where a temple was built by royal permission. The rival cult thus established to that of Jerusalem has survived to the present day—based, remarkably enough, on the same law-book as that recognized by the Jews.

VI. Under the Macedonians

The conquest of the Persian empire by Alexander the Great brought no constitutional changes either to Samaria or to Judah. These provinces were now administered by Graeco-Macedonian governors in place of the former Persian governors, and tribute had to be paid to the new overlord in place of the old one. The Jewish *diaspora*, which had been widespread under the Persian empire—Haman did not exaggerate when he described them to Xerxes as 'dispersed among the peoples in all the provinces of your kingdom' (Est. 3:8)—now found new centres to settle in, especially Alexandria and Cyrene. Hellenistic influences inevitably began to give evidence of their presence among them. These influences in some directions were good; we may think in particular of the situation among the Greek-speaking Jews of Alexandria which necessitated the translation of the Pentateuch and other OT writings into Greek in the 3rd and 2nd centuries BC, and thus made the knowledge of Israel's God accessible to the Gentile world (*TEXTS AND VERSIONS, OT). On the other hand, there was a tendency to imitate features of Hellenistic culture which were inextricably interwoven with paganism and which otherwise blurred the distinction between Yahweh's 'peculiar people' and their neighbours. How far a prominent Jewish family could go in unscrupulous assimilation to the unworthier aspects of life under the Hellenistic monarchies is illustrated by Josephus's account of the fortunes of the Tobiads, who enriched themselves as tax-collectors on behalf first of the Ptolemies and then of the Seleucids.

Among the dynasties which inherited Alexander's empire, the two which chiefly affect the history of Israel are those of the Ptolemies in Egypt and of the Seleucids who dominated Syria and the lands beyond the Euphrates. From 320 to

198 BC the Ptolemies' rule extended from Egypt into Asia as far as the Lebanon range and the Phoenician coast, including Judaea and Samaria. In 198 BC the Seleucid victory at Panion, near the sources of Jordan, meant that Judaea and Samaria were now tributary to Antioch instead of Alexandria. The defeat which the Seleucid king Antiochus III suffered at the hands of the Romans at Magnesia in 190 BC, and the heavy indemnity which they imposed on him, involved an enormous increase of taxation for his subjects, including the Jews. When his son, Antiochus IV, attempted to redress the situation by imposing his sovereignty over Egypt (in the two campaigns of 169 and 168 BC), the Romans forced him to relinquish these ambitions. Judaea, on the SW frontier of his kingdom, now became a region of strategic importance, and he felt that there was grave reason for suspecting the loyalty of his Jewish subjects. On the advice of unwise counsellors, he decided to abolish their distinctive nationhood and religion, and the climax of this policy was the installation of a pagan cult—the worship of Zeus Olympios (a name metamorphosed by the Jews into 'the abomination of desolation')—in the Temple at Jerusalem in December 167 BC. The Samaritan temple on Gerizim was similarly diverted to the worship of Zeus Xenios.

Many pious Jews endured martyrdom at this time sooner than forswear their religion. Others took up arms against their overlord. Among the latter were members of the priestly family of the Hasmonaeans, headed by Mattathias of Modin and his five sons. The outstanding son, Judas Maccabaeus, was a born leader of men, who excelled in guerrilla warfare. His initial successes against the royal forces brought many of his fellow-countrymen under his leadership, including a large number of the pious people in Israel, the *ḥ^asîdîm*, who realized that passive resistance was not enough in face of the present threat to their national and religious existence. Larger armies were sent against them by the king, but they too were routed by the unexpected tactics of Judas and his men.

It became clear to the king that his policy had misfired, and Judas was invited to send ambassadors to Antioch to discuss conditions of peace. Antiochus had military plans for the reconquest of seceding territories in the E part of his kingdom, and it was important to reach a settlement on his Egyptian frontier. The basic Jewish condition was, naturally, the complete rescission of the ban on Jewish religious practice. This was conceded; the Jews became free to practise their ancestral religion. The concession was followed at once by the purification of the Temple from the idolatrous cult which had been installed in it, and its rededication to the age-long worship of the God of Israel. The dedication of the Temple at the end of 164 BC (ever afterwards commemorated in the festival of Hanukkah; *cf.* Jn. 10:22) was probably not envisaged in the terms of peace, but in itself it might have been accepted as a *fait accompli*.

It speedily became clear, however, that Judas, with his brothers and followers, was not content with the regaining of religious liberty. Having won that success by force of arms, they continued their struggle in order to win political independence. The dedication of the Temple was followed by the fortification of the Temple hill, over against the citadel or Akra (*JERUSALEM, **IV**) which was manned by a royal garrison. Judas sent armed bands to Galilee, Transjordan and other regions where there were isolated Jewish communities and brought them back to the safety of those parts of Judaea which were controlled by his forces.

Such a succession of hostile acts could not be overlooked by the Seleucid government, and further armies were sent against Judas. Judas fell in battle in the spring of 160 BC, and for a time the cause which he had led seemed lost. But events played into the hands of his successors. In particular, the death of Antiochus IV in 164 BC was followed by a lengthy period of intermittent civil war in the Seleucid empire, between rival claimants to the throne and their respective partisans. Jonathan, the brother of Judas who took his place as leader of the insurgent party, lay low until times were propitious, and then by diplomatic dealing won rapid and astounding advancement. In 152 BC Alexander Balas, who claimed the Seleucid throne on the ground that he was the son of Antiochus IV (the validity of this claim is difficult to assess), authorized Jonathan to maintain his own military force in Judaea and recognized him as high priest of the Jews, in return for Jonathan's promise to support him.

Antiochus IV had begun his intervention in Jewish religious affairs, which ultimately brought about the Hasmonaean rising, by deposing and appointing Jewish high priests at his own discretion, in defiance of ancient custom. Now a Hasmonaean accepted the high-priesthood from a man whose title to bestow it was based on his claim to be son and successor to Antiochus IV. So much for the high ideals with which the struggle had begun!

The pious groups who had lent their aid to the Hasmonaeans, at a time when it seemed that only by Hasmonaean might could religious freedom be regained, were disposed to be content when that goal was attained, and grew increasingly critical of the Hasmonaeans' dynastic ambitions. But no feature of these ambitions displeased them more than the Hasmonaean assumption of the high-priesthood. Some of them refused to recognize any high-priesthood other than the Zadokite one as legitimate, and looked forward to a day when the sons of Zadok would once more officiate in a purified Temple (*DEAD SEA SCROLLS). One branch of the Zadokite family was permitted to found a Jewish temple at Leontopolis in Egypt and function in the high-priestly office there; but a temple outside the land of Israel could not be countenanced by those *ḥ^asîdîm* who had any regard for the law.

In 143 BC Jonathan was trapped and put to death by one of the rival claimants for mastery of the Seleucid kingdom, but he was succeeded by his brother Simon, under whom the Jews achieved complete independence from the Gentile yoke. This independence was granted in a rescript from the Seleucid king Demetrius II in May 142 BC, by which the Jews were released from the obligation to pay tribute. Simon followed up this diplomatic success by reducing the last vestiges of Seleucid ascendancy in Judaea—the fortress of Gazara (Gezer) and the citadel in Jerusalem. Demetrius had embarked on an expedition against the Parthians, and could take no action against Simon, even had he so wished. Simon received signal honours from his grateful fellow-Jews for the freedom and peace which he had secured for them. At a meeting

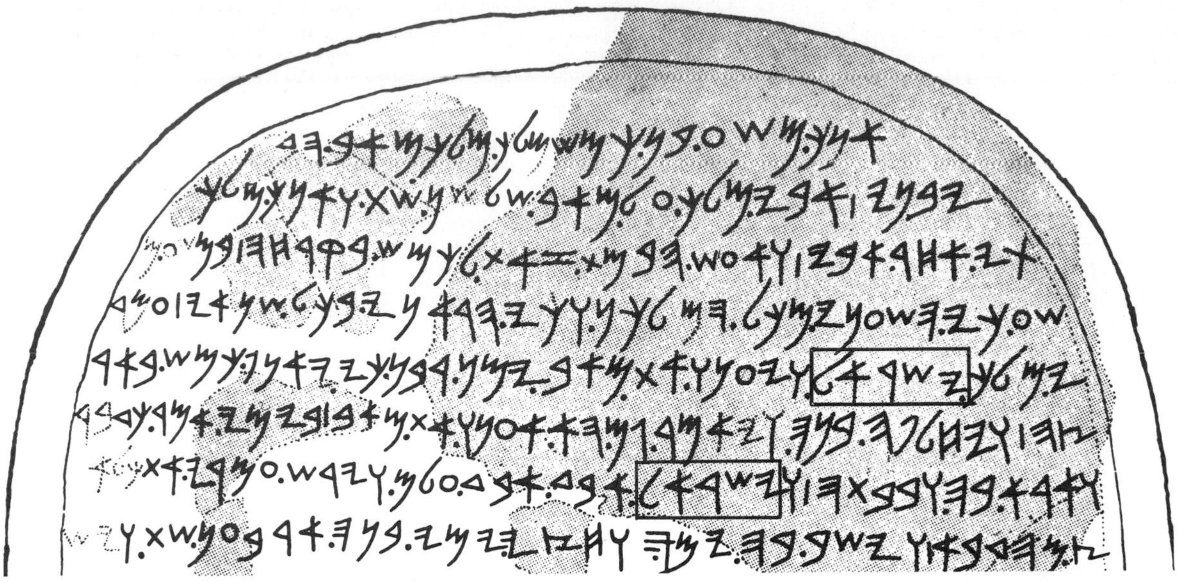

One of Israel's enemies, King Mesha of Moab, claimed in this inscription that 'Israel hath perished utterly for ever' when he attacked the country in the reign of Ahab. Part of the Moabite Stone, found at Dhiban, Jordan. c. 830 BC.

of the popular assembly of the Jews in September 140 BC, it was decreed, in consideration of the patriotic achievements of himself and his brothers before him, that he should be appointed ethnarch or governor of the nation, commander-in-chief of the army and hereditary high priest. This triple authority he bequeathed to his descendants and successors.

Simon was assassinated at Jericho in 134 BC by his son-in-law Ptolemy, son of Abubus, who hoped to seize supreme power in Judaea. But Simon's son, John Hyrcanus, thwarted the assassin's plans and secured his position as successor to his father.

The Seleucid king Antiochus VII, who had tried to reassert his authority over Judaea during Simon's later years, succeeded in imposing tribute on John Hyrcanus for the first few years of his rule. But the death of Antiochus VII in battle with the Parthians in 128 BC brought Seleucid overlordship over Judaea to a decisive end.

VII. The Hasmonaean Dynasty

In the 7th year of John Hyrcanus, then, the independent state of Judaea was firmly established, 40 years after Antiochus IV had abolished its old constitution as an autonomous temple-state within the empire. The devotion of the *ḥasîḏîm*, the military genius of Judas and the statesmanship of Simon, together with increasing division and weakness in the Seleucid government, had won for the Jews more (to all outward appearance) than they had lost at the hands of Antiochus IV. No wonder, then, that the early years of independence under John Hyrcanus were looked back to by later generations as a kind of golden age.

It was in the time of John Hyrcanus that the final breach between the majority of the *ḥasîḏîm* and the Hasmonaean family came about. John was offended by their objections to his tenure of the high-priesthood, and broke with them. From this time onward they appear in history as the party of the *Pharisees, although it is not certain that they owed that name (Heb. *perûšîm*, 'separated ones') to the fact of their withdrawal from their former alliance with the Hasmonaeans, as has frequently been supposed. They remained in opposition to the regime for 50 years. Those religious leaders who supported the regime and manned the national council appear about the same time with the name *Sadducees.

John Hyrcanus profited by the growing weakness of the Seleucid kingdom to extend his own power. One of his earliest actions after the establishment of Jewish independence was to invade Samaritan territory and besiege Samaria, which held out for a year but was then stormed and destroyed. Shechem was also captured and the Samaritan shrine on Mt Gerizim was demolished. The Samaritans appealed to the Seleucid king for help, but the Romans warned him not to interfere. The Hasmonaeans, at an early stage in their struggle, had secured a treaty of alliance with the Romans, and this treaty was renewed by John.

To the S of his kingdom John warred against the Idumaeans, conquered them and forced them to accept circumcision and adopt the Jewish religion. He reduced Greek cities in Transjordan and invaded Galilee.

His work in Galilee was continued by his son and successor Aristobulus I (104–103 BC), who forced the subjected Galileans to accept Judaism, as his father had done with the Idumaeans.

According to Josephus, Aristobulus assumed the title 'king' instead of that of 'ethnarch' with which his grandfather and (so far as we know) his father had been content, and wore a diadem in token of his royal estate. No doubt he hoped in this way to enjoy greater prestige among his Gentile neighbours, although his coins designate him, in language more congenial to his Jewish subjects, as 'Judah the high priest'.

Aristobulus died (perhaps of phthisis) after a year's reign and was succeeded by his brother Alexander Jannaeus (103–76 BC), who married his widow Salome Alexandra. A more inappropriate high priest than Jannaeus could hardly be imagined. He did go through the motions of his sacred office on occasions of high ceremony—and did so in a way that deliberately offended the sentiments of many of his most religiously minded subjects (especially the Pharisees). But the master-ambition of his reign was military conquest. His pursuit of this policy brought him many reverses, but by the end of his reign he had brought under his control practically all the territory that had been Israelite in the great days of the nation's history—at a ruinous cost to all that was of value in his people's spiritual heritage.

Greek cities on the Mediterranean seaboard and in Transjordan were his special targets for attack; one after another he besieged and conquered them, showing by his ruthless vandalism how little he cared for the true values of Hellenistic civilization. He modelled his way of life on that of the cruder Hellenistic princelings of W Asia. Feeling against him on the part of many of his Jewish subjects reached such a pitch that, when he suffered a disastrous defeat at the hands of a Nabataean force in Transjordan in 94 BC, they revolted against him and even enlisted the aid of the Seleucid king Demetrius III. But other Jewish subjects of Jannaeus, however much they disliked him, found the spectacle of a Seleucid king being called in to help a revolt against a member of the Hasmonaean family too much for their patriotism; they volunteered to support the cause of their hard-pressed king and enabled him to put down the revolt and send the Seleucid contingents packing. The barbarity of the revenge which Jannaeus took against the leaders of the revolt (who evidently included some outstanding Pharisees) was long remembered with horror.

Jannaeus bequeathed his kingdom to his widow, Salome Alexandra, who ruled it as queen regnant for 9 years. She bestowed the high-priesthood on her elder son, Hyrcanus II. In one important respect she reversed the policy of her predecessors; she befriended the Pharisees and paid attention to their counsel throughout her reign.

Her death in 67 BC was followed by civil war between the supporters of the claims of her two sons, Hyrcanus II and Aristobulus II, to succeed to supreme power in Judaea. Aristobulus was a typical Hasmonaean prince, ambitious and aggressive; Hyrcanus was a nonentity, but was easily manipulated by those who supported his claims in their own interests, among whom the dominating personality was the Idumaean Antipater, whose father had been governor of Idumaea under Jannaeus.

The civil strife between the two brothers and their respective partisans was halted by the Romans in 63 BC, in circumstances which brought Judaea's short-lived independence under the Hasmonaeans to an end.

VIII. The Roman supremacy

In 66 BC the Roman senate and people sent their most brilliant general at that time, Pompey, to bring to a successful conclusion the war which they had been waging intermittently for over 20 years with Mithridates, king of Pontus, who had carved out an empire for himself in W Asia from the lands of the decadent Seleucid kingdom and neighbouring states. Pompey was not long in defeating Mithridates (who fled to Crimea and committed suicide there); but having done that, he found himself faced with the necessity of reorganizing the political life of W Asia. In 64 BC he annexed Syria as a province of

The kingdoms of Israel and Judah.

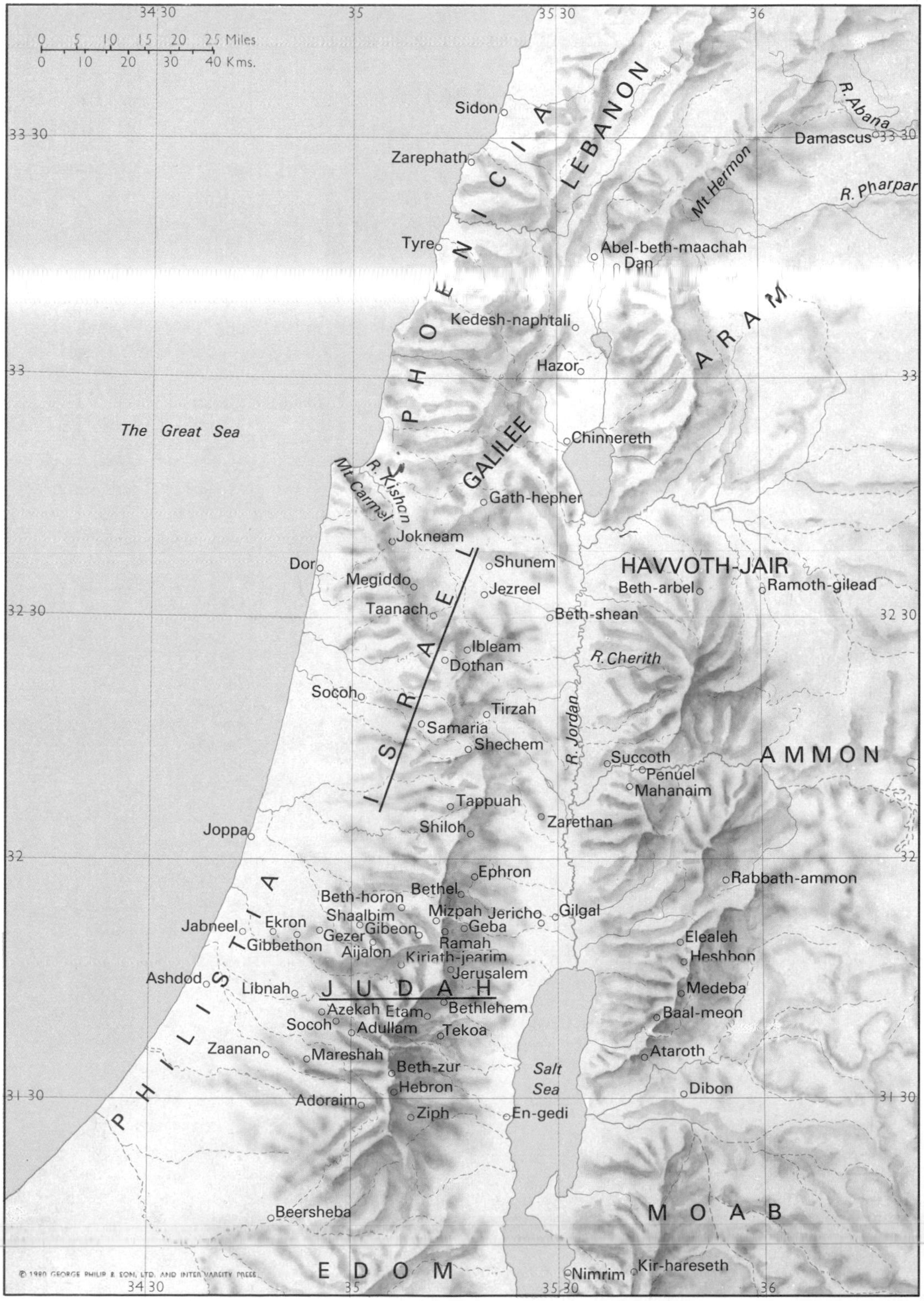

Gold aureus *of the Roman emperor Vespasian who put down a Jewish revolt in Galilee in* AD *67. He was the father of Titus who captured Jerusalem in* AD *70. Diameter 19 mm.* (RG)

Top centre:
Bronze coin (prutah) *of Hyrcanus II, son of Queen Salome Alexandra by whom he was made high priest. His coins are inscribed with the two titles of high priest and head of the Jewish community. Diameter 14 mm. 63–40* BC. (RG)

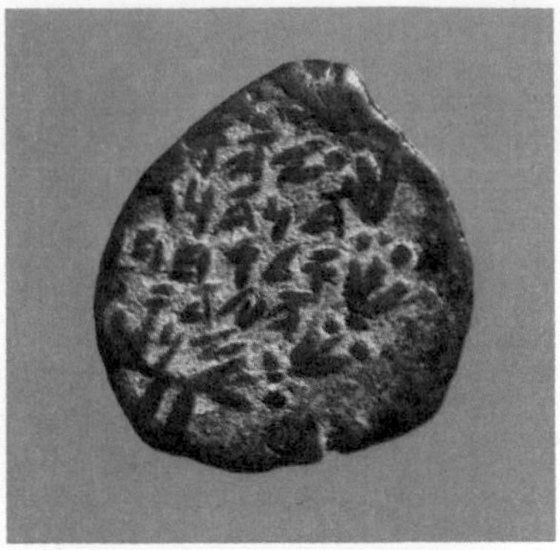

Top right:
Bronze coin (prutah) *of Aristobulus I (104–103* BC*) with an inscription 'the High Priest Jehuda and the community of the Jews'. Diameter 14 mm.* (RG)

Rome, and was invited by various parties in the Jewish state to intervene in its affairs too and put an end to the civil war between the sons of Jannaeus.

Thanks to Antipater's shrewd appraisal of the situation, the party favouring Hyrcanus showed itself willing to co-operate with Rome, and Jerusalem opened its gates to Pompey in the spring of 63 BC. The Temple, however, which was separately fortified and was held by the partisans of Aristobulus, sustained a siege of 3 months before it was taken by Pompey's forces.

Judaea now became tributary to Rome. She was deprived of the Greek cities which the Hasmonaean kings had conquered and annexed, and the Samaritans were liberated from Jewish control. Hyrcanus was confirmed in the high-priesthood and leadership of the nation; but he had to be content with the title of 'ethnarch', for the Romans refused to recognize him as king. Antipater continued to support him, determined to exploit this new turn of events to his own advantage, which (it must be conceded) coincided largely with the advantage of Judaea.

Aristobulus and his family endeavoured time after time to foment rebellion against Rome so as to secure power in Judaea for themselves. For many years, however, these attempts proved abortive. Successive Roman governors kept a firm grip on Judaea and Syria, because these provinces now lay on the E frontier of the Roman empire, beyond which was the rival empire of Parthia. The strategic importance of this area may be gauged by the number of dominant

The rocky fortress-palace of Masada, built by Herod the Great (34–4 BC*), overlooking the Dead Sea. This was the last outpost held by the Jews in their revolt against Rome in* AD *74.* (SH)

figures in Roman history who play a part in the history of Judaea in these years—Pompey, who annexed it to the empire; Crassus, who as governor of Syria in 54–53 BC plundered the Jerusalem Temple and many other temples in Syria while collecting resources for a war against the Parthians, but was defeated and killed by them at Carrhae in 53 BC; Julius Caesar, who became master of the Roman world after defeating Pompey at Pharsalus in 48 BC; Cassius, a leader of Caesar's assassins, who as proconsul of Syria from 44 BC proved financially oppressive to Judaea; Antony, who dominated the E provinces of the empire after he and Octavian had defeated Caesar's assassins and their followers at Philippi in 42 BC; and then Octavian himself, who defeated Antony and Cleopatra at Actium in 31 BC and thereafter ruled the Roman world alone as the emperor Augustus. Throughout the vicissitudes of Roman civil and external war Antipater and his family made it their settled policy to support the chief representative of Roman power in the E at any one time, whoever he might be and whichever party in the Roman state he might belong to. Julius Caesar in particular had reason to be grateful for Antipater's support when he was besieged in Alexandria during the winter of 48–47 BC, and he conferred special privileges not only on Antipater himself but on the Jews as well.

This confidence which the Romans learnt to place in Antipater's family was manifested outstandingly in 40 BC, when the Parthians invaded Syria and Palestine and enabled Antigonus, the last surviving son of Aristobulus II, to regain the Hasmonaean throne and reign as king and high priest of the Jews. Hyrcanus II was mutilated so as to be disqualified from ever becoming high priest again. Antipater was now dead, but an attempt was made to seize and liquidate his family. One son, Phasael, was captured and killed, but Herod, the ablest of Antipater's sons, escaped to Rome, where the senate nominated him king of the Jews, at the instance of Antony and Octavian. It was his task now to recover Judaea from Antigonus (who was left in peace by the Roman commander in Syria when the Parthian invaders were driven out) and to rule his kingdom in the interests of the Romans, as their

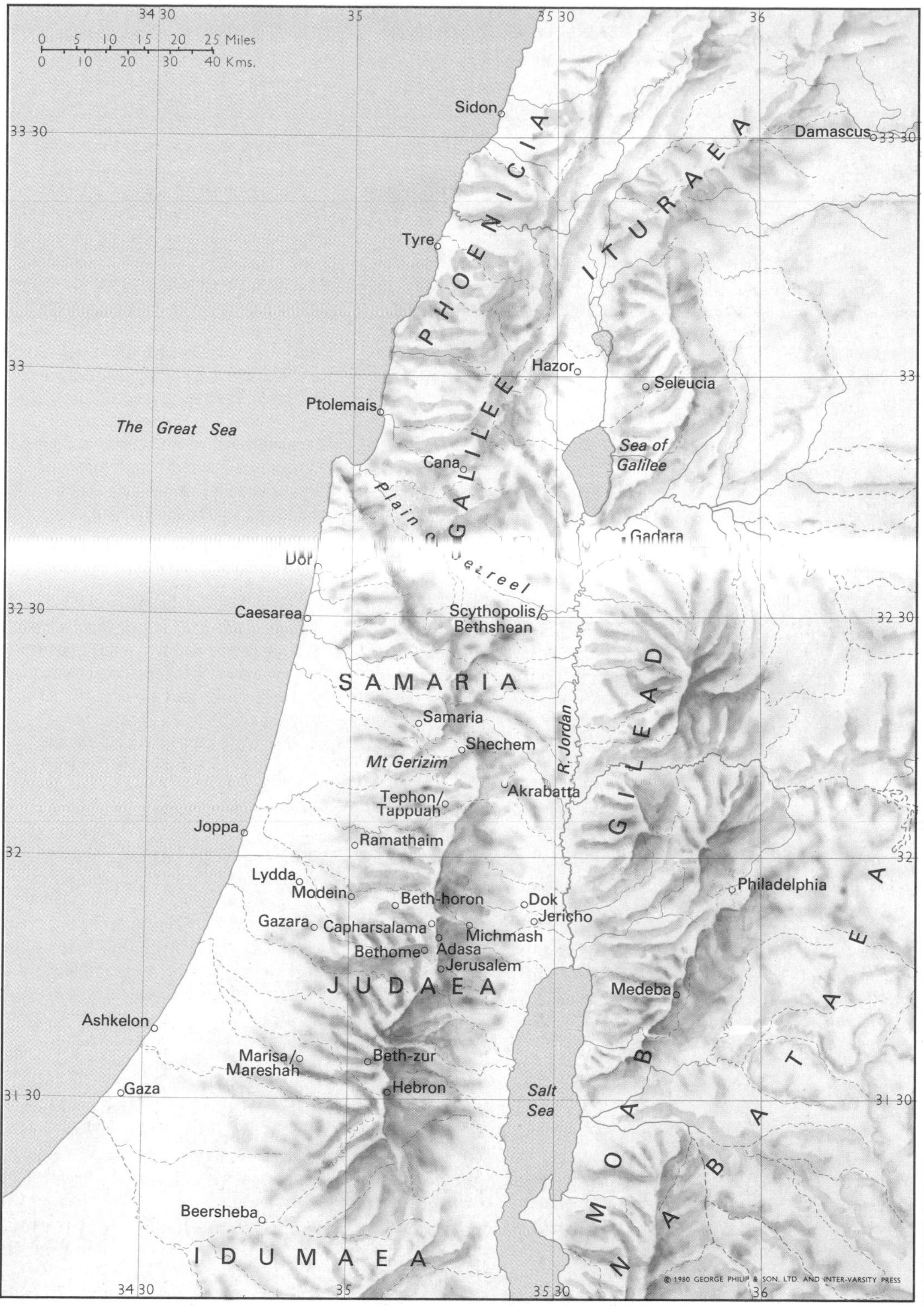

Israel in the intertestamental period.

'friend and ally'. The task was not easy, and its successful completion in 37 BC, with the storming of Jerusalem after a siege of 3 months, secured for Herod a bitter ill-will on the part of his new subjects which no effort of his could remove. Antigonus was sent in chains to Antony, who ordered him to be executed. Herod tried to legitimate his position in Jewish eyes by marrying Mariamne, a Hasmonaean princess, but this marriage brought him more trouble, not less.

Herod's position was precarious for the first 6 years of his reign. Although Antony was his friend and patron, Cleopatra longed to incorporate Judaea in her kingdom, as her earlier Ptolemaic ancestors had done, and tried to exploit her ascendancy over Antony to this end. The overthrow of Antony and Cleopatra in 31 BC, and Herod's confirmation in his kingdom by the conqueror, Augustus, brought him some relief externally, but domestic peace was denied him both in his family circle and in his relations with the Jewish people. Yet he governed Judaea with a firm hand, serving the interests of Rome even better than a Roman governor could have done. (For further details of his reign, *HEROD, **1.**)

When Herod died in 4 BC his kingdom was divided among three of his surviving sons. Archelaus governed Judaea and Samaria as ethnarch until AD 6; Antipas governed Galilee and Peraea as tetrarch until AD 39; Philip received as a tetrarchy the territory E and NE of the Sea of Galilee which his father had pacified in the emperor's interests, and ruled it until his death in AD 34. (*HEROD, **2**, **3**; *PHILIP, **2.**)

Antipas inherited a full share of his father's political acumen, and continued the thankless task of promoting the Roman cause in his tetrarchy and the surrounding regions. Archelaus, however, had all his father's brutality without his genius, and soon drove his subjects to the point where they petitioned the Roman emperor to remove him so as to prevent a revolt from breaking out. Archelaus was accordingly deposed and banished, and his ethnarchy was reconstituted as a Roman province of the third grade. In order that its annual yield of tribute to the imperial exchequer might be assessed, the governor of Syria, *Quirinius, held a census in Judaea and Samaria. This census provoked the rising of *Judas the Galilean, and, while the rising was crushed, its ideals lived on in the party of the *Zealots, who maintained that the payment of tribute to Caesar, or to any other pagan ruler, was an act of treason to Israel's God.

After the census, Judaea (as the province of Judaea and Samaria was called) received a prefect as governor. These prefects were appointed by the emperor and were subject to the general supervision of the governors of Syria. The early Roman prefects exercised the privilege of appointing the high priest of Israel—a privilege which, since the end of the Hasmonaean dynasty, had been exercised by Herod and Archelaus after him. The prefects sold the sacred office to the highest bidder, and its religious prestige was naturally very low. By virtue of his office the high priest presided over the *Sanhedrin, which administered the internal affairs of the nation.

Of the earlier prefects the only one whose name is well known is Pontius *Pilate, whose harsh and stubborn character is recorded in the pages of Josephus and Philo—not to mention the part he plays in the NT narrative. His construction of a new aqueduct to provide Jerusalem and the Temple with a better water-supply illustrates the material benefits of Roman rule; his flouting the religious scruples of the Jews by insisting on defraying the expense of it from the sacred Temple-fund illustrates an aspect of Roman rule which was largely responsible for the revolt of AD 66—the insensitivity of many of the governors and their agents to local feeling.

For a short time, between the years 41 and 44, Judaea enjoyed a welcome relief from administration by Roman prefects. Herod Agrippa I, a grandson of Herod the Great and Mariamne, to whom the emperor Gaius had given Philip's former tetrarchy as a kingdom in AD 37 (augmenting it by the addition of Galilee and Peraea in AD 39, after the deposition and banishment of Antipas), received Judaea and Samaria as further extensions of his kingdom from the emperor Claudius in AD 41 (*HEROD, **4**). Because of his descent from the Hasmonaeans (through Mariamne) he was popular with his Jewish subjects. But his sudden death in AD 44, at the age of 54, meant that the province of Judaea (now including Galilee as well as Samaria) reverted to rule by Roman governors, now called procurators, since Agrippa's son, Agrippa the Younger (*HEROD, **5**), was too young to be entrusted with his father's royal responsibility. One concession was made to Jewish sentiment, however: the privilege of appointing the high priest, which Agrippa had inherited from the prefects who preceded him, did not go back to the procurators who followed him, but was given first to his brother Herod of Chalcis, and then (after the death of that Herod in AD 48) to Agrippa the Younger.

IX. End of the second commonwealth

During the 20 years or so that followed the death of Herod Agrippa I, troubles multiplied in Judaea. The people in general found the re-imposition of procurators all the more irksome after their brief spell of government by a Jewish king; and the procurators themselves did little to conciliate the sentiments of their Jewish subjects. There was a succession of risings stirred up by pseudo-Messiahs such as *Theudas, who was killed by a cavalry detachment sent against him by the procurator Fadus (AD 44–46), or by Zealot leaders such as James and Simon (two sons of Judas the Galilean), crucified by the next procurator Tiberius Julius Alexander (AD 46–48). The fact that Alexander was a renegade Jew, scion of an illustrious Jewish family of Alexandria, did nothing to ingratiate him with the Jews of Judaea.

It was during the procuratorships of Fadus and Alexander that Judaea was hard hit by the famine of Acts 11:28. Josephus records how Helena, the queen-mother of Adiabene, E of the Tigris, bought grain in Egypt and figs in Cyprus at this time for the relief of the famine-stricken people of Judaea. The royal family of Adiabene were the most distinguished Jewish proselytes of the period; some of them actually fought on the Jewish side in the war against Rome which broke out in AD 66.

Under the procuratorship of *Felix disaffection increased in Judaea. Felix set himself energetically to rid the province of insurgent bands, and his severe measures against them were attended by temporary success, but they alienated large numbers of the population, in whose eyes the insurgents were not criminals but patriots.

The closing years of Felix's procuratorship were attended by fierce riots between the Gentile and Jewish inhabitants of Caesarea, arising out of a dispute about civic privileges. Felix sent the leaders of both parties to Rome to have the matter decided by the emperor, but was himself recalled and replaced in the procuratorship by Festus (AD 59). The Caesarean dispute was decided in favour of the Gentiles, and Jewish resentment at the decision, coupled with the Gentiles' malicious exploitation of their victory, was one of the factors in the explosion of AD 66.

*Festus was a relatively just and mild governor, but he died in office in AD 62, and his two successors, Albinus and Florus, by their persistent offending of Jewish national and religious sentiment, played into the hands of the anti-Roman extremists. The last straw was Florus' sacrilegious seizure of 17 talents from the Temple treasury. This provoked a riot which was put down with much bloodshed. The moderate elements in the nation, aided by the younger Agrippa, counselled restraint, but the people were in no mood to listen to them. They cut the communications between the fortress of Antonia and the Temple courts, and the captain of the Temple, who was leader of the war-party in Jerusalem, formally renounced the imperial authority by putting an end to the daily sacrifice for the emperor's welfare.

Matters had now escaped Florus' control, and even the intervention of Cestius Gallus, governor of Syria, with stronger military forces than Florus had at his disposal, proved ineffective. Gallus had to withdraw, and his army suffered heavy losses on its retreat through the pass of Beth-horon (November AD 66).

This success, as it seemed to the insurgent Jews, filled them with false optimism. The extremists' policy appeared to have been vindicated: Rome could not stand before them. The whole of Palestine was placed on a war footing.

But Vespasian, who was entrusted with the putting down of the revolt, set about his task methodically. In 67 he crushed the rebellion in Galilee. Some of the leaders of the Galilean revolt, however, escaped to Jerusalem, and their arrival there added to the internal strife which racked the city during its last years and months. In the summer of 68 Vespasian was approaching Jerusalem itself when news came of Nero's deposition and death at Rome. The ensuing civil war at the heart of the empire nerved the defenders of Jerusalem with fresh hope; it looked from their standpoint as though Rome and the empire were on the verge of dissolution and Daniel's 5th monarchy was about to be established on their ruins.

From Caesarea, Vespasian watched the progress of events at Rome. On 1 July, AD 69, he himself was proclaimed emperor at Alexandria by the governor of Egypt (the same apostate Jew, Alexander, who had earlier been procurator of Judaea); the example of Alexandria was swiftly followed in Caesarea and Antioch and by the armies in most of the E provinces. Vespasian returned to Rome to occupy the imperial throne, leaving his son Titus to complete the suppression of the revolt in Judaea. By the end of AD 69 all Judaea had been subdued except Jerusalem and three strongholds overlooking the Dead Sea.

Jerusalem was invested in the spring of AD 70. By May half the city was in the hands of the Romans, but the defenders refused to accept terms of submission. On 24 July the fortress of Antonia was stormed; 12 days later the daily sacrifices ceased in the Temple, and on 29 August the sanctuary itself was set on fire and destroyed. Four weeks later the whole city was in Titus' hands. It was razed to the ground, except for part of the W wall, with three towers of Herod's palace on that wall, which provided headquarters for a Roman garrison. The last centre of revolt to be crushed was the almost impregnable fortress of Masada, SW of the Dead Sea, where a Zealot force held out until the spring of AD 74 and then committed mass-suicide in preference to being captured.

Judaea was reconstituted as a province under its own imperial legate, directly responsible to the emperor and in no way subordinate to the imperial legate of Syria; unlike the procurators, the imperial legates of Judaea had legionary forces under their command. The former Temple tax, which Jews throughout the world had paid for the maintenance of the house of God at Jerusalem, was still exacted, but it was now diverted to the maintenance of the temple of Jupiter on the Capitoline hill in Rome.

With the disappearance of the Temple hierarchy and the Sanhedrin as formerly organized, the chief internal authority in the Jewish nation passed to a new Sanhedrin of rabbis, led at first by Yohanan ben Zakkai, a teacher of the school of Hillel. This religious court exercised its control through the synagogues and began the work of codifying the traditional body of oral law which was in due course committed to writing in the Mishnah towards the end of the 2nd century AD. It was in large measure due to the action of Yohanan ben Zakkai and his colleagues and their successors that Israel's national and religious identity survived the downfall of the Temple and the Second Jewish Commonwealth in AD 70 (*TALMUD AND MIDRASH.)

See also *JUDAH; *ARCHAEOLOGY; *SACRIFICE; *LAW, *etc.* and entries on individual kings and places.

BIBLIOGRAPHY. M. Noth, *The History of Israel*², 1960; J. Bright, *A History of Israel*², 1972; E. L. Ehrlich, *A Concise History of Israel*, 1962; F. F. Bruce, *Israel and the Nations*, 1963; R. de Vaux, *Ancient Israel*², 1965; *idem*, *The Early History of Israel*, 2 vols., 1977; S. Herrmann, *A History of Israel in OT Times*, 1975; J. H. Hayes and J. M. Miller (ed.), *Israelite and Judaean History*, 1977.

F.F.B.

ISRAEL OF GOD. Paul's statement that 'not all who are descended from Israel belong to Israel' (Rom. 9:6) is in line with the prophetic insistence that the true people of God, those who are worthy of the name of Israel, may be but a relatively small 'remnant' of faithful souls within the nation of Israel. In the NT the concept of such a remnant appears in the preaching of John the Baptist, who insists that descent from Abraham is valueless in itself (Mt. 3:9 = Lk. 3:8). Jesus' calling of disciples around himself to form the 'little flock' who were to receive the kingdom (Lk. 12:32; *cf.* Dn. 7:22, 27) marks him out as the founder of the new Israel; he explicitly designated the twelve apostles as judges of 'the twelve tribes of Israel' in the new age (Mt. 19:28; Lk. 22:30). The 'little flock' was to be augmented by the accession of 'other sheep' who had never belonged to the Jewish fold (Jn. 10:16).

Whether the expression 'the Israel of God' in its one appearance in the NT (Gal. 6:16) denotes believing Jews only, or believing Jews and Gentiles without distinction, is disputed; the latter is more probable, especially if the expression is to be construed in apposition to 'all who walk by this rule'. But that the community of believers in Jesus, irrespective of their natural origin, is looked upon as the new Israel throughout the NT is clear. They are 'the twelve tribes in the dispersion' (Jas. 1:1), 'the exiles of the dispersion' (1 Pet. 1:1), who are further designated, in language borrowed from OT descriptions of Israel, as 'a chosen race, a royal priesthood, a holy nation, God's own people' (1 Pet. 2:9).

But the nucleus of this new Israel is Jewish (Rom. 11:18). And while the greater proportion of 'Israel according to the flesh' is at present prevented, by a partial and temporary blindness, from recognizing their ancestral hope in Jesus, the time is coming when the veil will be removed from their eyes (2 Cor. 3:16) and they will be re-established by faith as members of the beloved community: their present estrangement will last only 'until the full number of the Gentiles come in, and so all Israel will be saved' (Rom. 11:25ff.).

BIBLIOGRAPHY. L. Gillet, *Communion in the Messiah*, 1942; M. Simon, *Verus Israel*, 1948; A. Oepke, *Das Neue Gottesvolk*, 1950; R. Campbell, *Israel and the New Covenant*, 1954; J. Munck, *Paul and the Salvation of Mankind*, E.T. 1959; *idem*, *Christ and Israel*, 1967; P. Richardson, *Israel in the Apostolic Church*, 1970. F.F.B.

ISSACHAR. 1. The fifth son of Jacob and Leah and the ninth son of Jacob (Gn. 30:18; 35:23). The name may derive from a compound of Heb. *'îš*, 'man', and *śāḵār*, 'wages', hence 'a hired worker', although others suggest a less likely connection with a verbal form, meaning, 'May (God) show mercy'.

Issachar's tribal portion fell between Mt Gilboa and the hills of Lower Galilee, at the E end of the Valley of Jezreel, but the boundaries cannot be drawn precisely. In some of the lists (*e.g.*, Jdg. 1:30) Issachar is not mentioned and may have been included with Zebulun (as Simeon was incorporated with Judah). Manasseh also seems to have expanded N into the territory of Issachar. Sixteen cities and their associated villages were assigned to Issachar (Jos. 19:17–23; *cf.* 17:10–11).

The close connection between Zebulun and Issachar is shown in their inclusion in a common blessing (Dt. 33:18–19). The mountain mentioned is undoubtedly Tabor, where there was a common sanctuary.

Issachar was involved in the campaign led by Deborah, who probably came from this tribe (Jdg. 5:15), although it is not mentioned in the prose account (ch. 4). The battle began in Issachar's territory and completely broke the Canaanite domination of the low-lying areas. The minor judge, Tola, was a man of Issachar (Jdg. 10:1) as was also the usurper, Baasha (1 Ki. 15:27). Issachar was one of the twelve administrative districts set up by Solomon (1 Ki. 4:17).

The blessing of Jacob (Gn. 49:14–15) has been viewed as evidence that part of Issachar was resident in the land in the Amarna period, maintaining its position by giving a certain amount of compulsory labour to its Canaanite overlords. But the implied reproach may be merely a statement of the fact that Issachar's material prosperity made it submissive and effete. At the time of David, however, the tribe had gained a reputation for wisdom (1 Ch. 12:32), a fact which re-emerges in the Talmudic statement that the wisest members of the Sanhedrin came from Issachar.

2. The seventh son of Obed-edom, a Levitical gatekeeper in the Davidic period (1 Ch. 26:5).

BIBLIOGRAPHY. *LOB*, pp. 200, 212, 223, 232f.: A. Alt, *PJB* 24, 1928, pp. 47ff.; W. F. Albright, *JAOS* 74, 1954, pp. 222f.; S. Yeivin, *Mélanges A. Robert*, 1957, pp. 100ff. A.E.C.

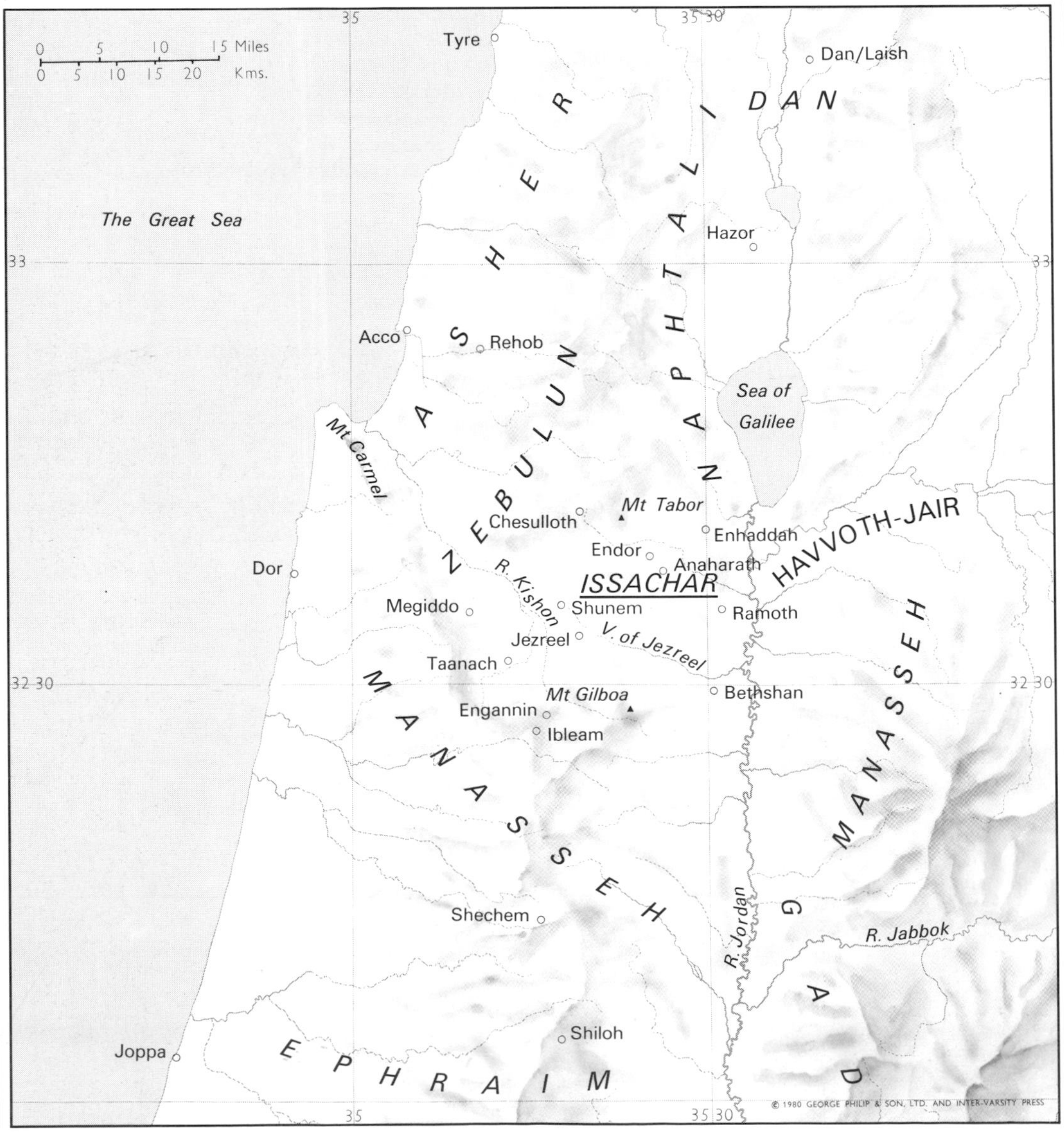

The land allotted to the tribe of Issachar.

ITALY (Gk. *Italia*). By the middle of the 1st century this name had come to have substantially its modern geographical meaning. 'All roads led to *Rome', and even before the time of Christ many Jews had resorted to Italy, especially to the metropolis. It was because the emperor Claudius had carried out a purge against the Jews that Paul met *Aquila and Priscilla (Acts 18:2). Italy was the apostle's destination when after his appeal to Caesar he and other prisoners embarked at Caesarea on what was to be his most famous journey

(Acts 27:1, 6). In Heb. 13:24 'those who come from Italy' greet the addressees. J.D.D.

ITHAMAR (Heb. *'îṯāmār*). The meaning of the name is uncertain, but may possibly be 'land of palms'. The youngest of Aaron and Elisheba's four sons (Ex. 6:23), Ithamar was ordained to the priesthood (Ex. 28:1) and directed the building of the tabernacle (Ex. 38:21). In the apostasy of Nadab and Abihu he remained faithful in all but the matter of the sin-offering (Lv. 10). He was placed over the Gershonites and Merarites (Nu. 4:28, 33). For evidence that Eli was a descendant of Ithamar, see 1 Sa. 14:3; 22:9; 1 Ch. 24:3. A man called Daniel, one of his descendants, is named among the returning exiles (Ezr. 8:2). G.W.G.

ITHIEL. Probably 'God is with me' (correcting Heb. pointing to *'ittî'ēl*). **1.** A Benjaminite ancestor of Sallu who resided in Jerusalem in Nehemiah's time (Ne. 11:7). **2.** A man mentioned with Ucal in Pr. 30:1. An altering of the word-divisions results in the more satisfactory rendering: 'I have wearied myself, O God (*lā'îṯî 'ēl*), and am consumed' (RVmg.; NEB; *BDB*). D.A.H.

ITHRA (Heb. *yiṯrā'*, 'abundance'). Husband of Abigail, David's sister, and father of Amasa, one of David's generals. Though called an Israelite in 2 Sa. 17:25, the marginal reading and 1 Ch. 2:17 describe him as an Ishmaelite and give his name as 'Jether' (*cf.* 1 Ki. 2:5). J.D.D.

ITHRITE. 'Ithrites' was the name given to one of the families descended from Kiriath-jearim (1 Ch. 2:53). Two members of David's bodyguard, Ira and Gareb, came from this family (2 Sa. 23:38; 1 Ch. 11:40) and may have originated from the town of *Jattir (1 Sa. 30:27). R.A.H.G.

ITTAI (Heb. *'ittay*, ? '(God) is with me'. **1.** The leader of 600 men from Gath, who joined David shortly before Absalom's rebellion. His fidelity was such that he refused to leave the king when he advised him to return (2 Sa. 15:19–22). 'Gittite' indicates that he was a Philistine; he was probably a soldier of fortune who found in David a leader worthy of his loyalty. With Joab and Abishai, he was subsequently one of David's 3 generals (2 Sa. 18:2).

2. A Benjaminite. One of the 'thirty' of David's mighty men (2 Sa. 23:29; 'Ithai' in 1 Ch. 11:31). J.G.G.N.

ITURAEA (Gk. *Itouraia*, Lk. 3:1). The name, mentioned in conjunction with *Trachonitis, almost certainly comes from Heb. y^e*ṭûr* (AV 'Jetur'), a son of Ishmael (Gn. 25:15–16; 1 Ch. 1:31), mentioned also as a tribe at war with the Israelites E of the Jordan (1 Ch. 5:19). Little or nothing is known of them thereafter until the time of the Jewish king Aristobulus I (105–104 BC), who is recorded as having fought against the Ituraeans and taken from them a portion of their land (Jos., *Ant.* 13. 318). Thereafter frequent allusion is made to them by classical writers (Josephus, Strabo, Pliny, Dio Cassius, *etc.*). Sometimes they are called Syrians, sometimes Arabians.

At the time of the Roman conquest they were known as a wild robber tribe especially proficient in the use of the bow, but not associated with any precisely defined geographical location. It was part of the territory ruled by Herod the Great, after whose death in 4 BC the kingdom was partitioned, and certain lands including Trachonitis and what was called 'the house of Zeno (or Zenodorus) about Paneas' formed the tetrarchy of Philip (*TETRARCH). If, as seems likely, this latter section was inhabited by Ituraeans, it may have been known as Ituraea, for migratory tribes frequently gave their name to their new home. Josephus, in defining the limits of Philip's sovereignty, does not specifically mention Ituraea—some would say because it was indistinguishable from Trachonitis (*Ant.* 17. 189).

Is Luke's reference, then, to be understood as a noun or as an adjectival form? Does he intend the place or the people? No certainty is possible. Place names of this region and time are notoriously elastic and liable to corruption, and overlapping is frequently found. The most we can safely say is that it was, in W. Manson's words (*Luke* in *MNTC*), 'a hilly country in the Anti-Lebanon range, inhabited by roving Arabs'.

Caligula gave it to Herod Agrippa I. When the latter died it was incorporated into the province of Syria under procurators.

BIBLIOGRAPHY. Discussions by

ITHAI
See Ittai, Part 2.

The Forum at Rome. (PP)

Ituraea and adjacent territories in Syria.

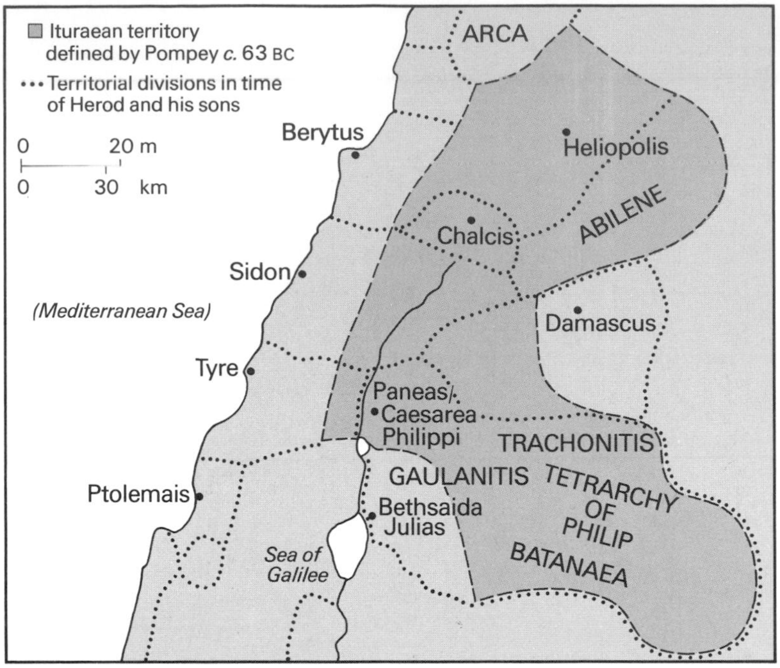

W. M. Ramsay and G. A. Smith in *The Expositor* 4, 9, 1894, pp. 51–55, 143–149, 231–238; E. Schürer, *HJP*, 1, 1973, pp. 561–573; A. H. M. Jones, *The Herods of Judaea*, 1938, pp. 9–11, *passim*. J.D.D.

IVAH. A foreign town conquered by the Assyrians during the time of Isaiah and used as an illustration of the inevitability of the defeat of Samaria (2 Ki. 18:34; 19:13; Is. 37:13). Probably the Ava of 2 Ki. 17:24. The location is unknown. D.W.B.

IVORY (Heb. *šēn*, 'tooth', or *šenhabbîm* (1 Ki. 10:22; 2 Ch. 9:21) thought by some to be 'tooth of elephant' (so LXX), but possibly meaning 'ivory (and) ebony' as in Ezk. 27:15; *cf.* Akkad. *šin piri*).

Ivory was a form of wealth and a mark of luxurious and fine goods (1 Ki. 10:18–22; Rev. 18:12, Gk. *elephantinos*). It was used for thrones and sometimes overlaid with gold (1 Ki. 10:18), for couches (Am. 6:4), and for furnishing and panelling rooms or palaces, hence Ahab's 'house of ivory' in *Samaria (1 Ki. 22:39; *cf.* Ps. 45:8) condemned by Amos (3:15). Its commonest use was in the manufacture of small objects and in composite models, where it simulated human flesh and thus was employed figuratively in poetry (Ct. 5:14; 7:4; in the latter, 'tower of ivory' may, however, be a reference to a specific locality).

Most ivory in use in Syria and Palestine came from Syrian (so-called 'Asiatic') elephants (*Elephas maximus*) which inhabited the upper Euphrates until hunted to extinction in the late 1st millennium BC. Other sources were India, from which tusks (*qarnôṯ šēn*) were imported by ocean-going ships (2 Ch. 9:17, 21) to Babylonia (Ur) by Phoenicians who decorated their vessels with plaques of ivory (Ezk. 27:6), or overland from the Nilotic

Canaanite ivory from Megiddo showing a celebration of victory with feasting and music and a procession of prisoners. Length 26 cm. 1350–1150 BC. (OIUC)

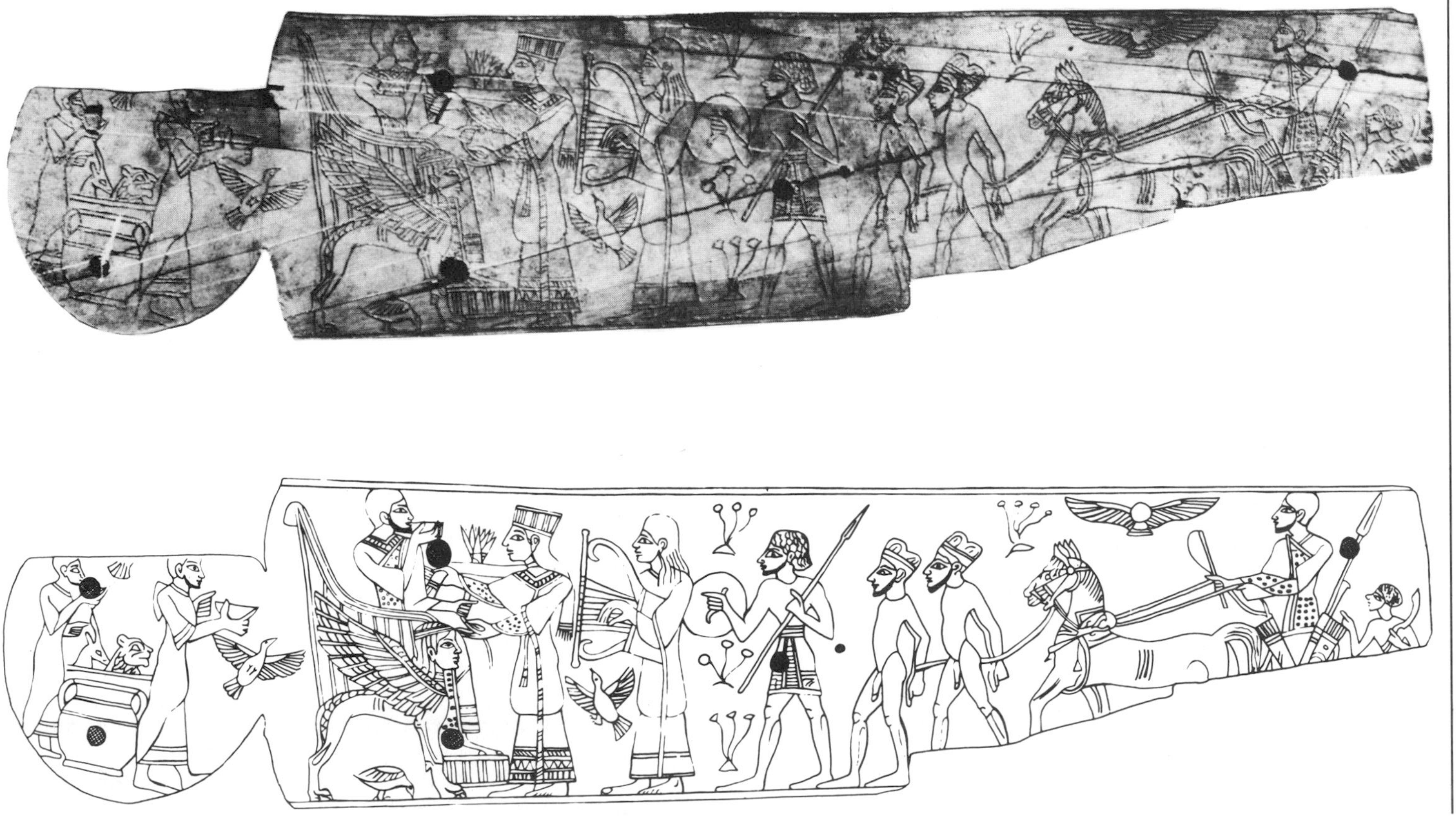

Sudan *via* Dedan in central Arabia (v. 15). Five tusks were found in the excavations at *Alalaḫ (Syria).

In the early 3rd millennium ivory was used for carving small figurines (Beersheba area), animal heads (Jericho), or for silhouettes for inlay, in the early Mesopotamian fashion, in wooden objects (El-Jisr). By the following millennium the trade flourished. Tusks are shown on Egyp. paintings and Assyr. sculpture as valued trophies of war. The Syro-Phoenician trade and guilds of ivory-workers under Egyptian influence sought to meet a growing export market to Assyria, making use of inlay, appliqué, ajouré, veneer and fretwork techniques. Furniture, especially chairs, beds, caskets and round boxes (pyxides), are found, some showing foreign influences in design. Remarkable caches of

Canaanite ivory comb from Megiddo, found in a treasury beneath the level VII palace. The scene, a dog attacking an ibex, is repeated on both sides. c. 1350–1300 BC. (RS)

Carved ivory plaque with gold leaf and inlays of cornelian and lapis lazuli on the papyrus and lotus flowers. Probably the work of a Phoenician craftsman using Egyptian motifs, it was one of a pair which may have formed part of the decoration of a throne. It depicts the overthrow of a Nubian by the lion (representing Assyria?). NW palace of Ashurnasirpal II, Nimrud. 9th cent. BC. (BM)

Ivory bed-head or chair-back, made up from six carved panels. These formed part of the largest cache of worked ivories found in the ancient Near East. Over-all dimensions, c. 84 cm × 60 cm. Fort Shalmaneser, Calah (Nimrud). 8th cent. BC. (BSAI)

Top right:
An ivory tusk carried with other tribute from Nubia to Rekh-mi-rē‘, vizier of Egypt. Wall-painting, tomb of Rekh-mi-rē‘, Thebes. c. 1470–1445 BC. (PAC)

An ivory carving from Nimrud showing a woman's head framed in the recess of a window. Height 10·7 cm. Early 8th cent. BC. (BM)

ivories have been recovered from Ras Shamra and Megiddo (*c.* 1200 BC) and Nimrud (* CALAH) in Assyria (*c.* 700 BC). In the Israelite period ivories from Samaria and Hazor attest its use for ladies' hair combs, unguent vases, flasks and elaborate spoons supported by figures of maidens as well as furniture. See also * PHOENICIA, * ARTS AND CRAFTS.

BIBLIOGRAPHY. R. D. Barnett, *A Catalogue of the Nimrud Ivories*, 1975; 'Phoenicia and the Ivory Trade', *Archaeology* 9, 1956, pp. 87–97; J. V. and G. M. Crowfoot, *Early Ivories from Samaria*, 1938; I. J. Winter, 'Phoenician and North Syrian Ivory Carving in Historical Context', *Iraq* 38, 1976, pp. 1–22.

D.J.W.

IYE-ABARIM, a stopping-place on the Exodus journey on the borders of Moab (Nu. 21:11; 33:44–45). Iye-abarim (Heb. *'iyyê hā'ᵃḇārîm*, ruins of Abarim, or of the regions beyond) is abbreviated in Nu. 33:45 AV to Iim. Abel identifies it with the ancient site of Maḥaiy to the SE of Moab, Glueck places it farther W, and du Buit chooses a site near the river Arnon. Its position is still debatable.

J.A.T.

IYYAR
See Calendar, Part 1.

IZHAR
See Kohath, Part 2.

JAAR (Heb. *ya'ar*, 'forest') in the OT usually means 'forest', but once only it may be a proper name (Ps. 132:6) as a poetical abbreviation for * Kiriath-jearim (city of forests). The allusion in this psalm is to the bringing of the ark to Jerusalem from Kiriath-jearim, where it had lain for 20 years or more after it was recovered from the Philistines (1 Sa. 7:1–2; 1 Ch. 13:5). Some take the word here, as elsewhere, to mean forest and refer 'it' to the oath in the preceding verses. M.A.M.

JA-AZANIAH (Heb. *ya'ᵃzanyah(u)*, 'Yahweh hears').
1. The Judaean army-commander, son of Hoshaiah, who supported Gedaliah at Mizpah (2 Ki. 25:23; Je. 40:8). Jezaniah (Je. 40:8) may be the same as the brother of Azariah (Je. 43:2, LXX). A seal found at Mizpah (Tell en-Nasbeh) inscribed 'Ja'azaniah, servant of the king' may be ascribed to this man, but the name was common, occurring on ostraca from Lachish (1) and Arad (39).

2. Son of Jeremiah, a Rechabite leader (Je. 35:3). **3.** Son of Shaphan, an Israelite elder, seen in a vision by Ezekiel (8:11) offering incense to idols in Jerusalem.
4. Son of Azur, seen by Ezekiel at the E gate of the Temple (Ezk. 11:1). D.J.W.

JABAL. A son of Adah, wife of Lamech, and ancestor of those 'who dwell in tents and have cattle (*ûmiqneh*)', or perhaps better 'who dwell in tents and places of reeds' (*m* [local] + *qānеh*, 'reed'). See Gn. 4:20. J.D.D.

JABBOK. A river flowing W into the river Jordan, some 32 km N of the Dead Sea. It rises near Amman (*RABBAH) in Jordan and in all is over 96 km long. It is today called the Wadi Zerqa. It marked a boundary line between Ammonite and Gadite territory (Dt. 3:16), once the Israelites had defeated the Amorite king Sihon S of the Jabbok (Nu. 21:21ff.). It was also the river forded by Jacob (Gn. 32:22) on the occasion of his wrestling with the angel and subsequent change of name. There may well be a play on words here: 'Jabbok' is in Heb. *yabbōq*, while '[and] . . . wrestled' is [*way*]*yē'āḇēq*. In the unvowelled text there is just an extra letter, an aleph, in the latter word. D.F.P.

JABESH-GILEAD (Heb. *yāḇēš gil'āḏ*). An Israelite town E of the Jordan which kept out of the war against Benjamin and suffered severe reprisals (Jdg. 21). Here Saul

The onyx scaraboid seal and imprint inscribed in Old Hebrew script (as described in the accompanying article). c. 600 BC. (IM) (PSR)

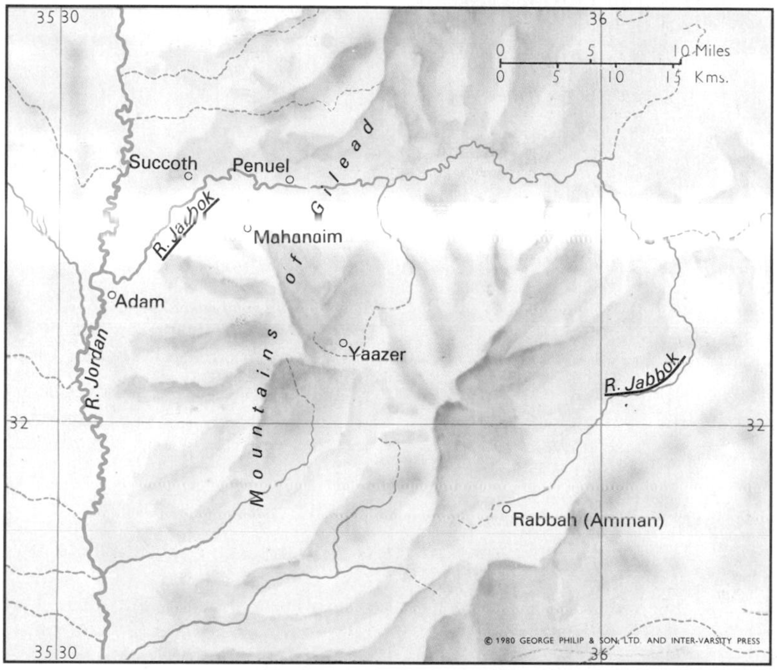

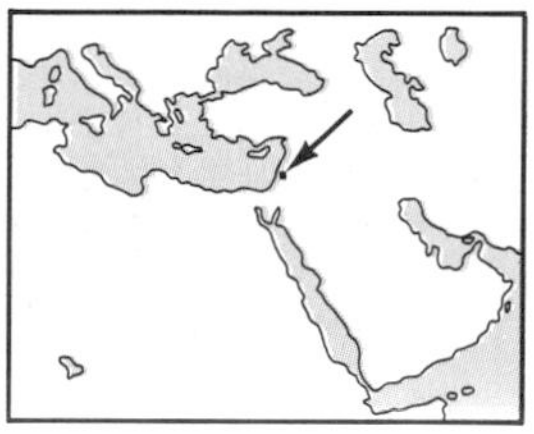

The river Jabbok.

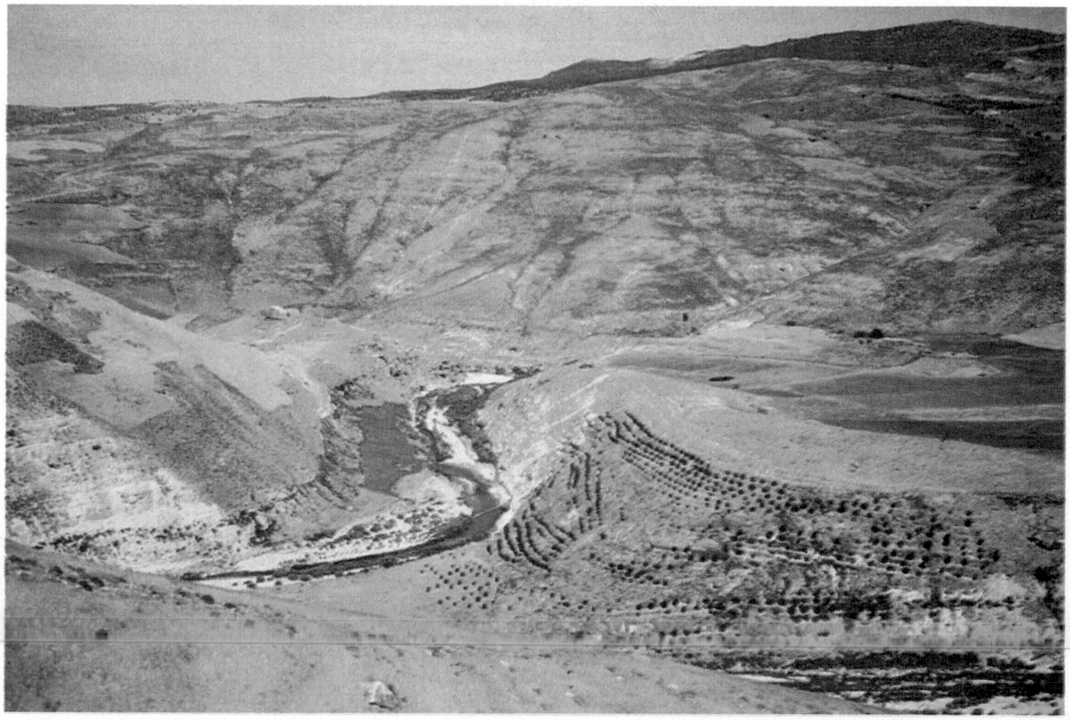

The river Jabbok (modern Zerqa) near its source at Amman, Jordan. (MEPhA)

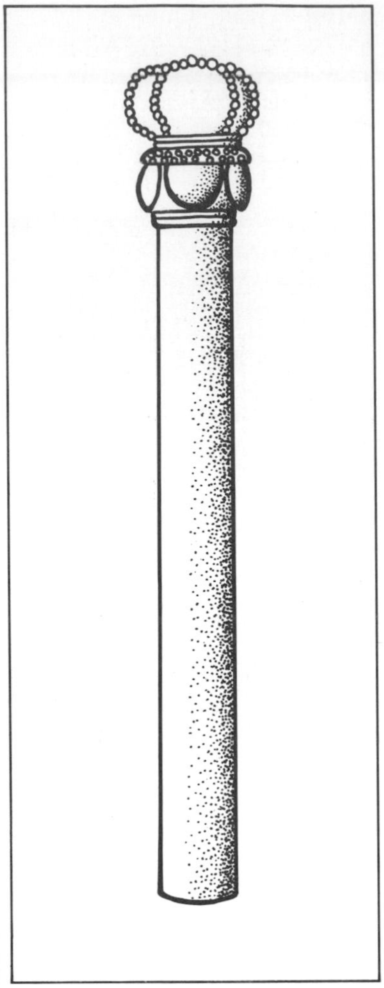

A reconstruction of one of the two free-standing pillars named Jachin and Boaz which stood at the entrance to Solomon's Temple.

JABESHITE See Tishbite, Part 3.

proved his kingship, routing the Ammonites who were besieging it (1 Sa. 11). The citizens rescued Saul's body from the walls of Beth-shan after the battle of Gilboa (1 Sa. 31; 1 Ch. 10).

Tell abu-Kharaz, on the N side of the Wadi Yabis where it reaches the plain, is the probable site (N. Glueck, *BASOR* 89, 91, 1943; *The River Jordan*, 1946, pp. 159–166). This isolated hill, 3 km from the Jordan and 15 km from Beth-shan, dominates the area and was heavily fortified in Israelite times. Earlier writers located Jabesh smaller sites upstream, but only Tell el-Maqlub is pre-Roman; this Glueck identifies with Abel-meholah. M. Noth (*ZDPV* 69, 1953, p. 28) disputes some of Glueck's arguments, but the fact that Tell abu-Kharaz exists makes Maqlub an unlikely location for Jabesh. J.P.U.L.

JABEZ (Heb. *ya'bēṣ*, 'he makes sorrowful'). **1.** A city, evidently in Judah, inhabited by 'the families of the scribes' (1 Ch. 2:55). **2.** The head of a family of the tribe of Judah (1 Ch. 4:9–10), an 'honourable' man whose prayer God answered. For discussion of a play on the Heb. words here, see C. F. Keil, *Chronicles*, p. 88; J. M. Myers, *I Chronicles*, 1965, pp. 28f. J.D.D.

JABIN (Heb. *yāḇîn*, possibly '[God] perceives'). **1.** A king of *Hazor, leader of an alliance of N princes defeated in battle by Joshua, who afterwards slew Jabin (Jos. 11:1–14). **2.** Another king of Hazor (called 'king of Canaan' in Jdg. 4:2) who for 20 years 'cruelly oppressed' the Israelites, who had been reduced thus to vassalage because of idolatry. Liberation came when Barak and Deborah defeated Jabin's general *Sisera (Jdg. 4:3–16), a notable victory immortalized in the Song of Deborah (Jdg. 5) and leading to the destruction of Jabin (Jdg. 4:23–24), which is briefly referred to also in Ps. 83:9. J.D.D.

JABNEEL (Heb. *yaḇnᵉ'ēl*, 'God (El) causes to build'), a name, of which a comparable form *Jabni-ilu* occurs in the Amarna letters, which is used of two places in the Bible.

1. A city on the SW boundary of Judah (Jos. 15:11) and probably to be identified with Jabneh, a Philistine city which was captured by Uzziah (2 Ch. 26:6). Jabneh was called Jamnia in the Gk. and Rom. periods, and it was at this city that the Sanhedrin was re-formed after the destruction of Jerusalem in AD 70.

2. A town of Naphtali (Jos. 19:33), possibly to be identified with modern Khirbet Yamma.

BIBLIOGRAPHY. M. Avi-Yonah, *Gazetteer of Roman Palestine* (Qedem, 5), 1976, p. 67; S. Z. Leiman, *The Canonization of Hebrew Scripture*, 1976, pp. 120–124. T.C.M.

JACHIN and BOAZ. The names of the decorated bronze pillars or columns which flanked the entrance to the *Temple of Solomon in Jerusalem (1 Ki. 7:21; 2 Ch. 3:15–17). When Nebuchadrezzar captured Jerusalem in 587 BC, they were broken up and taken to Babylon (2 Ki. 25:13).

I. Description and construction

The columns were 18 cubits high (*c.* 9 m) and 12 cubits in circumference (*c.* 1 m diameter) and were topped with capitals which were 5 cubits high (*c.* 2·5 m) (1 Ki. 7:15–16). The Chronicler gives the height as 35 cubits (2 Ch. 3:15) which is thought to indicate the combined height of both columns allowing 1 cubit for inserting the columns into their bases and capitals. At the time of the destruction of the Temple the capitals are said to be 3 cubits high (2 Ki. 25:17); this reduction in height may have occurred when Jehoash (2 Ki. 12:6ff.) or Josiah (2 Ki. 22:3ff.) undertook renovations in the Temple (*cf.* Je. 52:22). This is preferable to the view that the earlier figure was mis-read or that there has been an error in the transmission of the text.

Various attempts have been made to visualize the decoration as it is described (1 Ki. 7:17–22, 41–42; Je. 52:22–23). It would appear that the capital had four opened and inverted lotus petals (*šûšān*, RSV 'lily-work') 4 cubits in width (*bā'ûlām*, 1 Ki. 7:19, RSV 'in the vestibule', so Yeivin) and above this an inverted bowl (*gullā*). This bowl or pommel was encircled by a network (*śᵉḇāḵâ*) fringed with two rows of pomegranates.

The columns and capitals were cast by Hiram, a craftsman from Tyre (1 Ki. 7:13–14), who worked in the ground between Succoth and Zarethan (1 Ki. 7:46). They were hollow (Je. 52:21) and may have been cast with a technique similar to that used by Sennacherib when he had large mythical beasts cast in bronze (*ARAB*, 2, 1927, p. 169; also see Underwood, *Man* 58, 1958, p. 42), or some method akin to the casting of mediaeval cannon barrels may well have been adopted for this immense task.

II. Purpose

Although it has been suggested that the columns supported the roof of the porch, the OT description includes them with the furnishings of the Temple rather than with the architectural element and says that they were placed 'at' or 'near' (1 Ki. 7:21) and 'before' (2 Ch. 3:17) the porch. There is considerable evidence for free-standing columns at the entrances of temple sanctuaries. Bases for columns have been found in 13th-century BC temples at *Hazor, and Kamid el-Loz in a Phoenician temple at Kition and an Israelite temple at *Arad, but whether these were free-standing is impossible to determine. The appearance of the columns can be gauged from clay model shrines found in Palestine and Cyprus (13th–9th centuries BC) and from ivories found at Arslan Tash and Nimrud. Impressions of temples on Greek and Roman coins from Cyprus and Phoenicia and descriptions made by Herodotus (2. 44), Strabo (3. 4. 170) and Lucian (*de dea Syria* 15. 27) reveal that pairs of columns continued to be placed at the entrances of temples until at least the 2nd century AD.

While it is clear that the columns did not serve an architectural function, any religious significance that they may have had is obscure. They may indicate the divine presence, as did the pillars of fire and smoke during the desert wanderings (Ex. 33:9; Dt. 31:15). Various stones and pillars in use from prehistoric times to the present seem to have a similar portent.

III. Names

The names of the columns may enshrine the memory of David's ancestry through his mother (Jachin occurs as a Simeonite name [Nu. 26:12] and in a priestly family [1 Ch. 24:17]) and through the paternal line (*BOAZ). However, a more likely theory is that the names may be the first words of oracles giving power to the Davidic dynasty: perhaps 'Yahweh will establish (*yaḵîn*) thy throne for ever' and 'In the strength (*b^e'ōz*) of Yahweh shall the king rejoice' or something similar.

BIBLIOGRAPHY. R. B. Y. Scott, *JBL* 57, 1939, pp. 143ff.; H. G. May, *BASOR* 88, 1942, pp. 19–27; S. Yeivin, *PEQ* 91, 1959, pp. 6–22; J. Ovellette, *RB* 76, 1969, pp. 365–378.

D.J.W.
C.J.D.

JACOB. It is fitting that almost a quarter of the book of Genesis should be devoted to the biography of Jacob, the father of the chosen people. Written documents of the 2nd millennium BC have provided extensive material corroborating the background to the stories of Gn. 26–50. While this does not prove the existence of the Patriarch or the historicity of the narrative, it does show that they are not late compositions from the time of the Exile with imaginative and anachronistic details. Rather it suggests that the stories were recorded in writing at an early date (*PATRIARCHAL AGE). A collection of stories with details apparently discrediting the hero is unlikely to be centred on a mythical figure.

I. Date

The exact limits of the lifetime of Jacob cannot be fixed because of a lack of explicit correlations between the biblical accounts and the surviving secular records (*CHRONOLOGY OF THE OLD TESTAMENT). Evidence at present available suggests approximately the 18th century BC. Such a date would place his settlement in Goshen, not far from the Egyptian court, early in the period of the Hyksos domination, centred on Tanis (*EGYPT, *ZOAN). This date also allows *Abraham's life to be placed in the 20th and 19th centuries BC, as suggested by biblical and archaeological evidence.

II. Biography

Jacob was born clutching the heel (Heb. *'āqēḇ*) of his elder twin Esau (Gn. 25:26), so the name given to him was 'he clutches' or, on another plausible interpretation, 'he clutched' (Heb. *ya'^{a}qōḇ*). This may have been intentional punning on a current name *ya'^{a}qōḇ-il*, 'may God protect' or 'God has protected'. Cuneiform and Egyptian documents of the period contain personal names from the same root (*'qb*), including some of parallel form, in use among people of the W Semitic group (*AMORITES).

Jacob 'supplanted' (this is a nuance developed from 'to take by the heel, to overtake', Heb. root *'qb*) his brother, first obtaining the birthright of the elder son by taking advantage of his brother's hunger and then beguiling Isaac into giving to him the blessing which was by custom that of the first-born. The first-born son normally inherited more of the paternal estate than each of the other children (twice as much later, *cf.* Dt. 21:16). As well as the special legacy, it seems that the chief heir was marked out for a social and religious position as head of the family. The bestowal of

Two free-standing pillars, similar to Jachin and Boaz, surmounted by capitals, outside a clay model of a temple. Idalion, Cyprus. Height 21 cm. Iron Age. c. 10th–9th cent. BC. (MC)

JACINTH
See Jewels, Part 2.

a blessing by the father, and the possession of the household gods, probably symbolized this. These customs may be deduced from contemporary deeds of adoption and legal records as well as from the biblical accounts. The brief narrative of the sale of Esau's birthright for a meal does not tell how the exchange was confirmed or whether it was recorded officially. A document of the 15th century BC records the sale of the patrimony of a man in Assyria. A document from the same milieu shows that the oral promise of a man to his son could be upheld in a court of law (see *ANET*, p. 220). So Isaac's blessing was irrevocable, as the text emphasizes (Gn. 27:33f.). Thus Jacob became the bearer of God's promise and the inheritor of Canaan (*cf.* Rom. 9:10–13). Esau received the less fertile region, which became known as *Edom. Rebekah, the mother, obtained Isaac's permission for Jacob to flee from Esau's anger to her home in *Paddan-aram (Gn. 28:1ff.). She used as excuse the need for Jacob to marry a member of the same clan and so avoid mixed marriages such as Esau had contracted with the local people.

The central event of Jacob's life took place during his flight N. At the end of a day's journey, perhaps the first, he had arrived in the hill-country near *Bethel, some 100 km from Beersheba. This is a reasonable distance for a fast camel to cover in one day. The first stage of the flight would obviously finish as far from home as possible. There is no indication that Jacob had any knowledge of a particular sanctity attaching to the area, although he may have known of the site of his grandfather's altar (Gn. 12:8). As he slept he was granted the vision of a ladder between heaven and earth and of the God of his family standing above it. The promise given to Abraham was confirmed to him and he was given a promise of divine protection. Jacob commemorated his dream by setting up the stone on which he had rested his head and pouring a libation of oil over it (Gn. 28:11ff.). Such simple monuments were often erected in sacred places (*PILLAR). This one marked the place where, for Jacob, God was known to be present.

The narrative leaps from Bethel to the district of Harran at the time of Jacob's arrival. As had Eliezer (Gn. 24:11), so Jacob came first to the well outside the city. Here he was met by his cousin Rachel and taken to Laban, his uncle, who accepted him as his kinsman. When a month had elapsed, Jacob agreed to work for his uncle and, after 7 years, to take Rachel as his wife (Gn. 29:1ff.). The wedding was duly celebrated in the presence of witnesses to the oral or written marriage contract, legally required in Babylonia to give a woman the status of wife. Laban claimed a local custom as his excuse for actually giving his elder daughter Leah to Jacob. That the elder daughter should be married first is a custom not otherwise known. Jacob acquiesced in Laban's action and a new agreement was made allowing Jacob to marry Rachel after the week (presumably of celebrations) was completed. Seven more years' service were required in place of the money given by a man to his father-in-law (*MARRIAGE).

Eleven sons and one daughter were born to Jacob in Laban's house during the 20 years he stayed there. Leah bore four sons while Rachel remained barren. Her chagrin was partly overcome by giving her maid Bilhah to Jacob and adopting her two sons (*NUZI). Leah did likewise with her maid Zilpah, who also bore two sons. The knowledge that adoption might lead to conception by the adoptive mother may have prompted this (*cf.* Sarah and Hagar, Gn. 16:2). Two more sons and a daughter were borne by Leah before Rachel bore Joseph. Several of the names given to Jacob's children also occur in contemporary texts, although there is no mention of the biblical characters known.

Harran was an important trading centre as well as a fertile agricultural and pastoral district. Laban, it may be assumed, had a town house where he lived during the summer harvest season, taking his flocks to pasture on the hills during the winter. As head of what was evidently a fairly wealthy family, he would have had authority over his own household and perhaps in the city council. Jacob's request to be allowed to return to his home was, perhaps, made at the end of the 14 years' service for his two wives, and after Rachel had borne her first son, Joseph. His management of Laban's flocks had been so successful that Laban was unwilling to let him go (Gn. 30:25ff.). An agreement was made whereby Jacob should continue to work for Laban in return for all the beasts of Laban's flocks and herds which were of impure colour. In this way Jacob would build up a capital from which to support his family. Laban, again breaking his agreement, removed all the animals to which Jacob might lay claim, but Jacob, following advice received in a dream, ingeniously turned his father-in-law's trickery to his own advantage without infringing the agreement. His prosperity aroused the envy of Laban's sons, who felt that he was robbing them of their lawful inheritance (Gn. 31:1). A divine command overcame any reluctance Jacob may have had at leaving Harran without Laban's approval. Rachel and Leah supported his plan, since, they claimed, their father had spent the dowry they should have received (*MARRIAGE). The flight was accomplished while Laban was away from home for sheep-shearing. A 2-day start enabled Jacob and his flocks to travel as far as Gilead in N Transjordan before he was overtaken by Laban (Gn. 31:22ff.). Seven days for Laban's pursuit, covering about 400 miles, is well within the reach of a riding camel. Laban complained of Jacob's furtive departure but his particular concern was for the theft of his gods (*TERAPHIM, *NUZI). If possession of these images did mark the head of the family, then Rachel's deed was intended to exalt Jacob. She managed to retain them by a ruse. Jacob in turn reminded Laban of how well he had served him, complying with all the current requirements of a good herdsman, and how ill he had been rewarded. A pact was made, Laban using his authoritative position to dictate the terms: his daughters were not to be maltreated, nor should Jacob take another wife. A pillar was erected to commemorate the covenant and a cairn was built. These also served as points of demarcation beyond which neither party should go; possibly a recognition of the extent of Jacob's territorial rights under the promise. Each party called upon God to be witness and punish whoever might break the covenant. A sacrifice was made and the two parties shared a meal as a sign of their goodwill.

Jacob proceeded to *Mahanaim, where an angelic host met him, and then he sent scouts to discover Esau's attitude (Gn. 32:1ff.). At his approach, Jacob took care to safe-

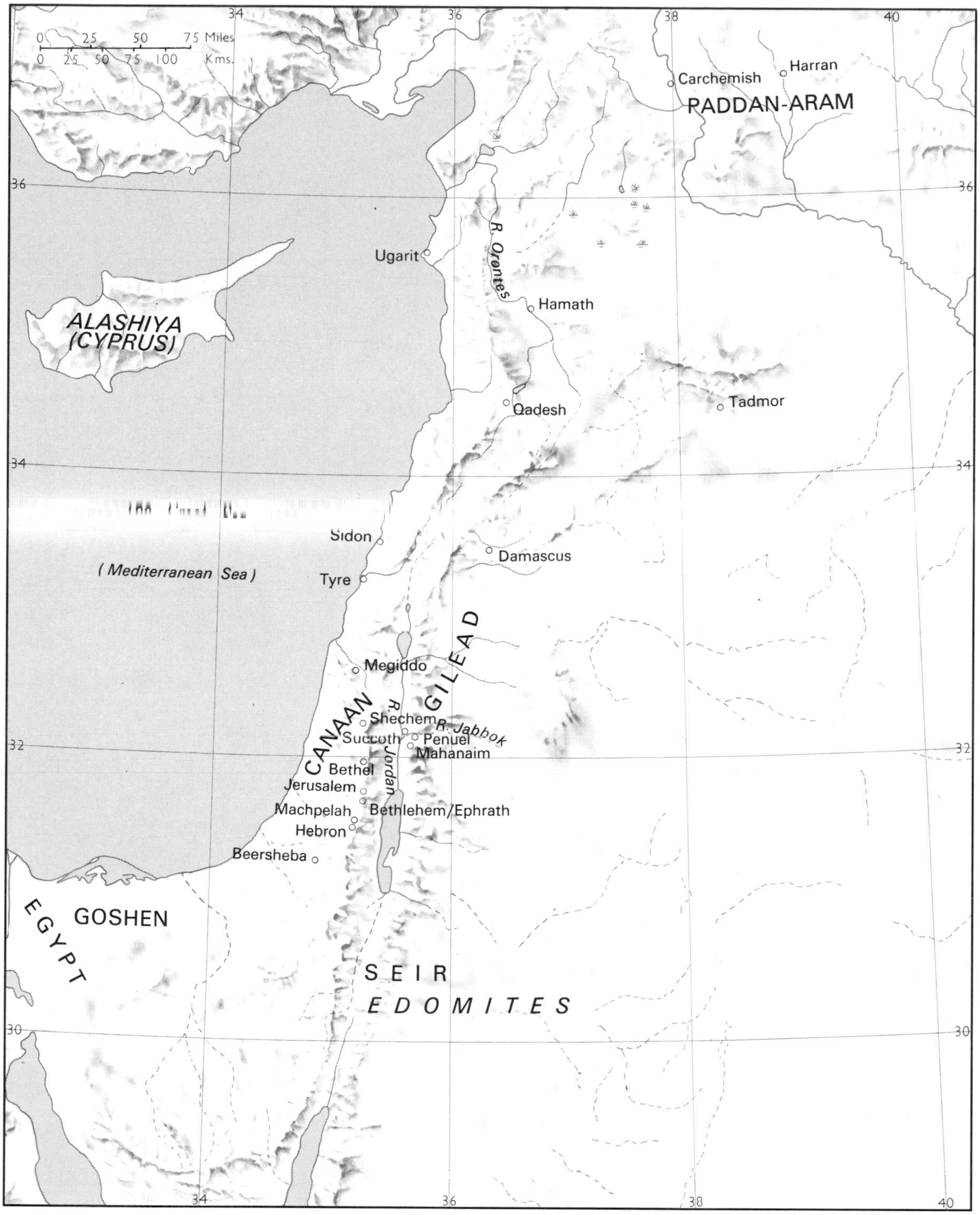

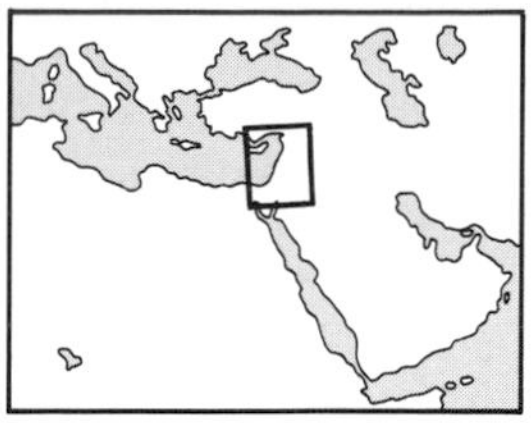

Palestine and Syria in the time of Jacob.

guard half of his possessions and also sent a large gift to his brother. After he had asked for divine protection, and as he was about to ford the river Jabbok at *Penuel, he was engaged in a struggle with a stranger who prevailed only by dislocating Jacob's thigh. This incident was regarded as Jacob's redemption 'from all evil' (Gn. 48:16), the new name Israel showing that he was able to contend with God (*cf.* Ho. 12:4), his disability displaying his subordination. Esau's friendly greeting did not overcome Jacob's qualms. He turned down to *Succoth instead of following Esau. From Succoth he moved up to a town in the territory of Shechem and purchased a piece of land. The rape of Dinah and the vengeance taken by her brothers made the area hostile to him (Gn. 34:1ff.). God instructed him to go to Bethel, presumably outside the jurisdiction of Shechem, to worship. The various pagan symbols brought from Paddan-aram were buried before the family could proceed. As before, Jacob erected a pillar to commemorate his communion with God and poured a libation. He did the same to mark Rachel's tomb at *Ephrath but without a libation (Gn. 35:1–20). After Isaac's death (Gn. 35:28–29) he settled in the region of Hebron and there lived as he had in Harran, by herding and by cultivation.

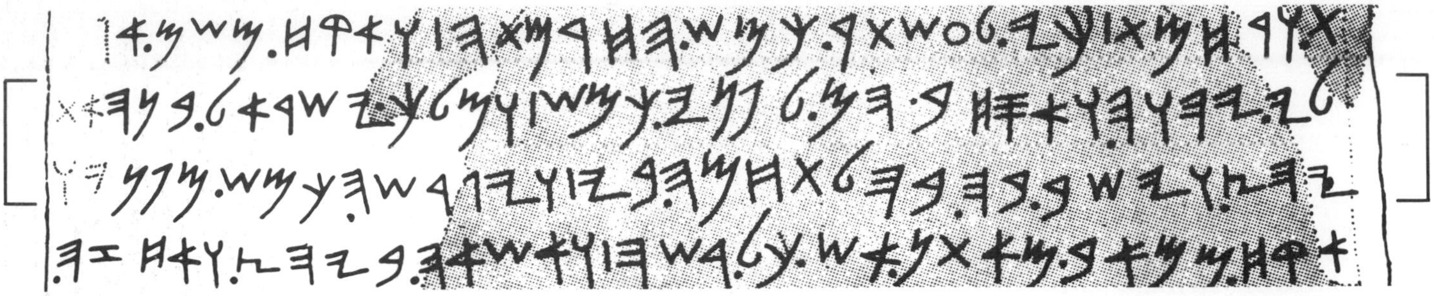

According to King Mesha of Moab, 'the king of Israel had built Jahaz and he dwelt in it while fighting aginst me'. The Moabites here claim to have recaptured Jahaz from Ahab. Lines 18–19 from the Moabite Stone, found at Dhiban, Jordan. c. 830 BC.

When the famine struck and he was invited to Egypt, he first sought assurance that it was right for him to go S of Beersheba (Gn. 46:1ff.).

Before his death he adopted the two sons of Joseph and gave them a special blessing, preferring the younger over the elder (Gn. 48). The blessings of the twelve sons are recorded in a poetic composition that plays upon the meanings of their names (Gn. 49:1–27). Jacob died, over 130 years old, and was buried in the family tomb at *Machpelah near Hebron (Gn. 50:13).

His descendants called themselves by his name *Israel (paralleled by Jacob in poetry). As the chosen people they had the privilege of striving with God. A.R.M.

III. New Testament references

Jacob the son of Isaac is listed in the genealogies (Mt. 1:2; Lk. 3:34). More significant is the recurring conjunction, Abraham, Isaac and Jacob, where Jacob stands with the other two as a type of the eternally blessed (Mt. 8:11; Lk. 13:28). All three Synoptists record Jesus' quotation of Ex. 3:6, 'I am the God of Abraham, and the God of Isaac, and the God of Jacob' (Mt. 22:32; Mk. 12:26; Lk. 20:37; also Acts 7:32). This sonorous formula (taken up in the Jewish liturgy, *cf.* the Eighteen Benedictions) gives emphasis and solemnity to the character of God as the one who entered into covenant relation with the Patriarchs of old, and who honours his promises. Peter uses nearly the same formula to heighten his declaration of what God has done in Christ (Acts 3:13). Stephen mentions Jacob several times (Acts 7:12, 14–15, 46). The last time he speaks of 'the God of Jacob', thus giving this Patriarch central importance in the history of religion. Paul refers to Jacob twice, the first time to bring out God's purposes in election (he chose Jacob before the two children were even born, Rom. 9:11–13), and the second time as a way of symbolizing the nation (Rom. 11:26). Finally, this Patriarch figures in Hebrews as one of the heroes of faith (Heb. 11:9, 20f.).

A Jacob also occurs as the name of the father of Joseph in the Matthean genealogy of our Lord (Mt. 1:15–16). L.M.

JACOB'S WELL
See Sychar, Part 3.

JADAU, JADDAI
See Iddo, Part 2.

JADE
See Jewels, Part 2.

JADON
See Meronothite, Part 2.

JAFFA
See Joppa, Part 2.

JAHAZIAH
See Jahzeiah, Part 2.

JAHLEEL
See Zebulun, Part 3.

JAEL (Heb. *yā'ēl*, 'wild goat'). The wife of Heber the Kenite and murderess of Sisera (Jdg. 4:17–21). At that time the Canaanites, under the leadership of Jabin, king of Hazor, and Sisera dominated Israel. In a parenthetical note (Jdg. 4:11) the presence of the Kenites as far N as Za-anannim, on the border of Naphtali (Jos. 19:33), is explained; normally they were associated with the tribe of Judah. Their skills in metal-working would make them useful allies to the Canaanites (Jdg. 4:17).

After the Israelites, under Deborah and Barak, had inflicted a crushing defeat upon the Canaanites, the main part of the defeated army fled W. Sisera, however, evidently having abandoned his command, headed N, probably to seek sanctuary at Hazor. Jael, appreciating his vital importance (*cf.* Jdg. 4:22), offered him hospitality, which, according to contemporary custom, guaranteed protection. Her treachery was increased by her attempt to convey a sense of security (Jdg. 4:18). Since the erection of tents was women's work, Jael was able to despatch Sisera efficiently by driving a tent peg into his temple. To be killed by a woman would be considered a disgrace (*cf.* Jdg. 9:54). So Deborah's prophecy, that the principal honour of slaying Sisera would be a woman's, was fulfilled (Jdg. 4:9).

This victory gave permanent relief from Canaanite oppression and allowed Israel control of the strategic Esdraelon valley. It was immortalized in the Song of Deborah (Jdg. 5), reckoned to be contemporary, which shows a barbaric exultation in Jael's vicious act (Jdg. 5:24–27). But, whilst not approving, we must not overlook the natural human reaction of these long-oppressed Israelites at the death of their arch-enemy.

Various unlikely emendations have been suggested to remove the surprising reference to Jael in Jdg. 5:6. The point made is probably that, although Shamgar and Jael were living when Israel was persecuted, neither was able to effect deliverance. Deborah gains full credit for this.

BIBLIOGRAPHY. A. E. Cundall, *Judges and Ruth*, 1968, pp. 81–101.
A.E.C.

JAHAZ (Heb. *yahaṣ*). A site in the plains of Moab where Israel defeated Sihon, the Amorite king (Nu. 21:23; Dt. 2:32; Jdg. 11:20). The name occurs in several forms—Jahzah, Jahaza (Jos. 13:18), and Jahazah (Jos. 21:36; Je. 48:21). It fell in the portion of Reuben, and was assigned to the Merarite Levites (Jos. 13:18; 21:34, 36). The area was later lost to Israel, but Omri reconquered the land as far as Jahaz. The *Moabite Stone (lines 18–20) states that the Israelites dwelt there while they fought Mesha. Finally, Mesha drove them out and added Jahaz to his domains.

M. du Buit would place the site just off the central highlands road on the right of the Wadi Wali. Y. Aharoni has proposed Khirbet el-Medeiyineh on the fringe of the desert (*LOB*). The city was still in Moabite hands in the days of Isaiah and Jeremiah (Is. 15:4; Je. 48:21, 34). J.A.T.

JAHZEIAH (Heb. *yaḥz*^{e}*yâ*, 'Yahweh sees, reveals'; AV 'Jahaziah', Ezr. 10:15). One of four men mentioned in connection with the controversy over foreign wives. AV regards the four as supporting Ezra, 'being employed about this matter'; but the same Heb. phrase can be translated also as 'opposed this' (so RSV, *BDB*, *etc.*). The con-

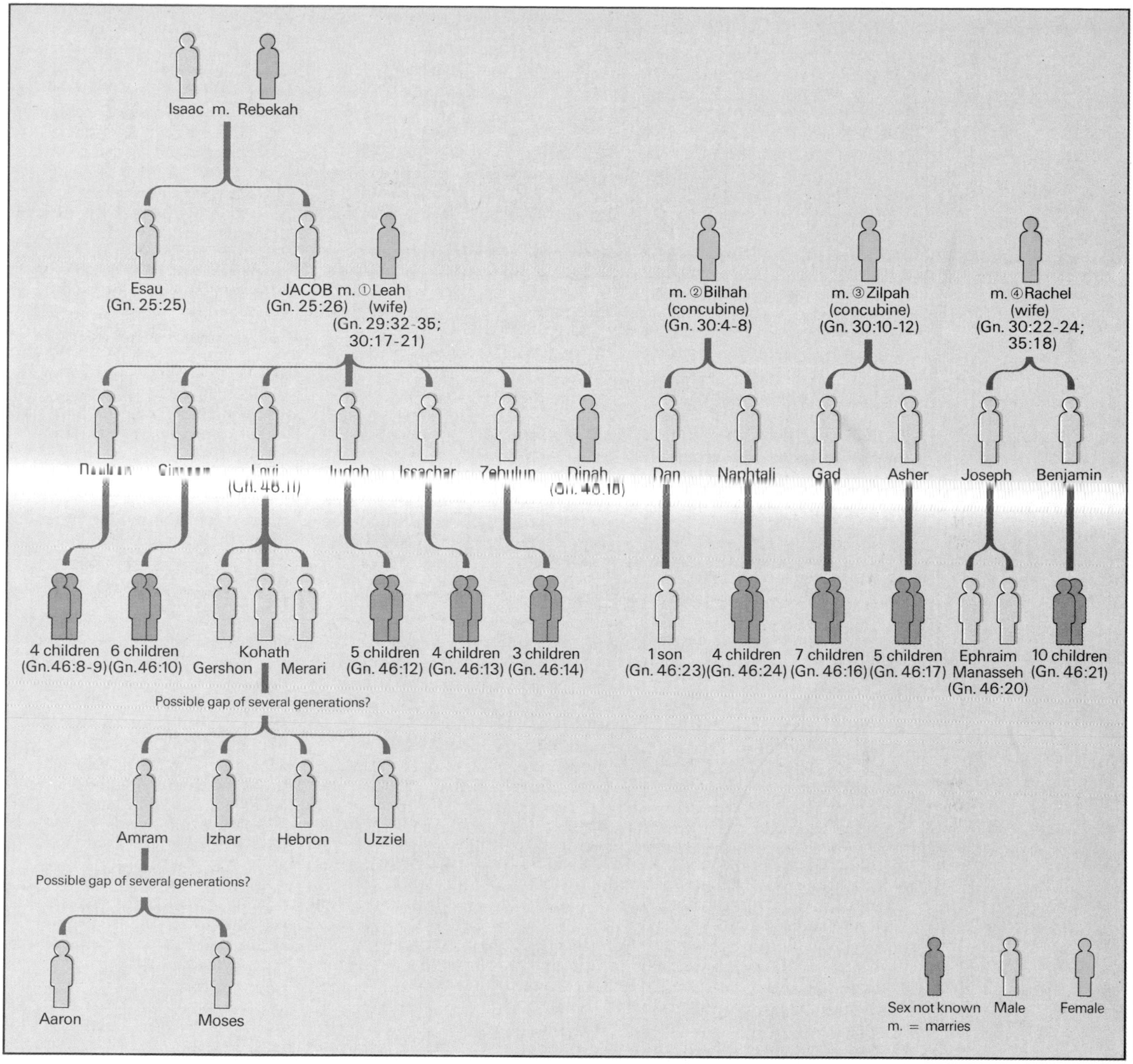

Jacob and his descendants.

text would seem to support the AV rendering. J.D.D.

JAIR (Heb. *yā'îr*, 'he enlightens'). **1.** Descendant of Manasseh who, during the conquest E of the Jordan under Moses, took several villages on the border of Bashan and Gilead (Nu. 32:41) and named them *Havvoth-jair. **2.** A judge who judged Israel for 22 years (Jdg. 10:3, 5). His thirty sons had thirty cities in Gilead, the name Havdoth-jair being associated with them. **3.** Father of Mordecai (Est. 2:5). **4.** (*yā'îr*, 'he arouses'.) Father of *Elhanan (1 Ch. 20:5), one of David's heroes; he is called Jaare-oregim (2 Sa. 21:19) by a scribal error. M.A.M.

JAIRUS. A ruler of the synagogue whose daughter was healed by Christ (Mk. 5:21–43; Lk. 8:41–56; *cf.* Mt. 9:18–26). The name may be derived from Heb. *yā'îr*, 'Yahweh enlightens' (*cf.* Jair, Jdg. 10:3). He is named by Mark and Luke but not by Matthew. His duties included the conducting of the synagogue worship and the selection of those who were to lead the prayer, read the Scriptures, and preach in it. There was generally only one *archisynagōgos* to each synagogue (Matthew describes him simply as *archōn*, which here has the same significance).

Jairus came to Jesus after he had crossed the sea of Galilee from the Decapolis and landed near Capernaum. His daughter, aged 12, was at the point of death, and he asked him to come and heal her. On the way to his home Jesus healed the woman with a haemorrhage. Then the news came that the girl was dead. Most of those present felt it unnecessary to trouble Christ any further, and they were scornful of his statement that the girl was not dead but asleep. When all but Peter, James, John, Jairus and his wife had been dismissed, Jesus took her by the hand and she came back to life. He ordered her to be fed and enjoined strict secrecy upon them.

From a literary point of view it is interesting to see how Matthew compresses the story, so much so as to give the impression that the child was dead when Jairus first approached Jesus. It is also noteworthy that the Aramaic phrase t^{e}*lîṯâ qûm(î)* is retained by Mark.

R.E.N.

JAMB
See Door-post, Part 1.

JAMBRES
See Jannes, Part 2.

JAMES (Gk. *Iakōbos*, Heb. *ya‘*^{a}*qōḇ*, 'heel-catcher', 'supplanter').

1. The son of Zebedee, a Galilean fisherman who was called with his brother John to be one of the twelve apostles (Mt. 4:21). These two along with Peter formed the inner core of three among the twelve, being present at the raising of Jairus' daughter (Mk. 5:37), the transfiguration (Mk. 9:2), and the agony in Gethsemane (Mk. 14:33) to the exclusion of the others. James and John, whom Jesus nicknamed 'Bo-anerges, that is, sons of thunder' (Mk. 3:17), were rebuked by Jesus when they suggested that they should 'bid fire come down from heaven' to destroy a Samaritan village which had refused to receive the Jerusalem-bound Jesus (Lk. 9:54). The pair also caused envy among the disciples by requesting a place of honour in Christ's kingdom; while not promised this advantage, they were told they would drink the cup their Master was to drink (Mk. 10:39), a prophecy which was fulfilled for James when he was 'killed . . . with the sword' by Herod Agrippa I, *c.* AD 44 (Acts 12:2).

2. The son of Alphaeus, another of the twelve apostles (Mt. 10:3; Acts 1:13). He is usually identified with 'James the younger', the son of Mary (Mk. 15:40). The description 'the younger' (Gk. *ho mikros*, 'the little') distinguishes him from the sons of Zebedee as either younger or smaller in stature.

3. An otherwise unknown James who was the father of the apostle Judas (not Iscariot) in the Lucan writings (Lk. 6:16; Acts 1:13; the other Gospels have Thaddaeus instead of Judas).

4. The brother of Jesus who, along with his brothers Joses, Simon and Judas (Mt. 13:55), apparently did not accept the authority of Jesus before the resurrection (see Mk. 3:21 and Jn. 7:5). After the risen Jesus had appeared to him (1 Cor. 15:7), he became a leader of the Jewish-Christian church at Jerusalem (Gal. 1:19; 2:9; Acts 12:17). Tradition stated that he was appointed first bishop of Jerusalem by the Lord himself (Eusebius, *EH* 7. 19). He presided at the first Council of Jerusalem, which considered the terms of admission of Gentiles into the church, formulated the decree which was promulgated to the churches of Antioch, Syria and Cilicia (Acts 15:19–23), and remained as sole leader of the Jerusalem church, working to maintain its unity with Paul and his mission when Paul visited Jerusalem for the last time (Acts 21:18ff.). A few years later James suffered martyrdom by stoning at the instigation of the high priest Ananus during the interregnum after the death of the procurator Festus in AD 61 (Josephus, *Ant.* 20. 9). Hegesippus' largely legendary tradition claims that James was known as 'the Just' because of his (Jewish) piety (Eusebius, *EH* 2. 23). Jerome (*De viris illustribus* 2) records a fragment from the lost apocryphal *Gospel according to the Hebrews* (*NEW TESTAMENT APOCRYPHA) containing a brief and probably unhistorical account of the appearance of the risen Jesus to James. James is the traditional author of the canonical Epistle of James, where he describes himself as 'a servant of God and of the Lord Jesus Christ' (Jas. 1:1).

BIBLIOGRAPHY. J. B. Lightfoot, *Galatians*, 1896.

P.H.D.

JAMES, EPISTLE OF.

I. Outline of contents

a. Introduction
Greeting 1:1
Statement and restatement of themes 1:2–27
(Test of faith, speech and spirit, piety and poverty)
b. Development
Piety and poverty 2:1–26
Speech and spirit (Wisdom) 3:1–4:12
Test and result 4:13–5:6
c. Conclusion (with restatement of themes) 5:7–20

II. Authorship and date

Due to uncertainty about the identity of the author, who describes himself as 'James, a servant of God and of the Lord Jesus Christ' (1:1), this Epistle did not receive general acceptance in the W until the 4th century. Most Christians recognized that James the son of Zebedee was martyred too early to have been the author, and there is no evidence that the early church ever attributed the Epistle to any other James, *e.g.* 'James the younger', Mk. 3:18; 15:40; Luther's attribution to some unknown James was the result of his dogmatic devaluation of the work as 'a right strawy epistle', since it apparently contradicted Paul on the matter of justification and did not set forth the central doctrines of salvation.

Some modern scholars, noticing the almost complete lack of references to distinctively Christian doctrines, the apparently disjointed nature of the moral axioms in which the Epistle abounds, and the fact that Jesus Christ is explicitly mentioned only twice, have rejected the idea that it was composed by any Christian, suggesting instead that an originally pre-Christian Jewish homily was adapted for Jewish-Christian use by the insertion of 'Jesus Christ' at 1:1 and 2:1. Other scholars, noticing doctrinal and church situations which could point to a date later than the life of the Lord's brother, regard the Epistle as a late Christian homily written to meet the needs of the more settled Christian communities after early evangelistic fervour had subsided (AD 70–130).

The first theory, which sometimes attributes the work to an unknown James or pseudonymously to the patriarch Jacob, might account for such expressions as 'Abraham our father' (2:21) and 'the Lord of hosts' (5:4), and the emphasis laid upon works in justification (2:14–26). It could also explain the phenomena that the writer speaks like a second Amos when he denounces the rich (5:1–6), and cites Abraham (2:21), Rahab (2:25), Job (5:11) and Elijah (5:17) as examples of virtue, but not Jesus. Yet these and similar features do not *demand* such an explanation, especially if the Epistle were written before the wide circulation of the Gospels, for the OT was the Bible of the early Christians. As has been pointed out, 'there is no sentence in the

Epistle, which a Jew could have written and a Christian could not'. Moreover, the Christianity of the Epistle is much more extensive than it appears on the surface, and it is difficult to suppose that the imaginary Christian interpolator would have been capable of exercising such great restraint!

The second theory, which normally assumes that the work was pseudonymously attributed to the Lord's brother to give it authority, gains credence from the quality of Greek in the Epistle and the argument that 2:14–26 was written to counteract an antinomian perversion of Paul's doctrine of justification by faith. But it fails to account for the primitive features of the Epistle (*e.g.* the mention of elders and not bishops in 5:14) and the Palestinian colouring (*e.g.* 'the early and the latter rain' in 5:7). Furthermore, were the Epistle pseudepigraphic, it is hard to explain why the author did not use a clearer and more exalted title (*e.g.* 'James the apostle' or 'James the brother of the Lord').

The address 'to the twelve tribes in the Dispersion' (1:1), probably referring to scattered Jewish-Christian congregations (it is the reason why the letter is included among the general or catholic Epistles), the homiletic character of the work, its Jewish-Christian flavour, its concern with a communal ethic and community solidarity, its echoes of the later Jewish Wisdom literature ('wisdom', probably meaning the Spirit, is one of its key-words, see 1:5; 3:17), of nonconformist Jewish theology (it contains striking parallels to the *DEAD SEA SCROLLS), and of the sayings of Jesus which became embodied in the Sermon on the Mount (*cf.* 2:13 and Mt. 5:7; 3:12 and Mt. 7:16; 3:18 and Mt. 7:20; 5:2 and Mt. 6:19; 5:12 and Mt. 5:34–37), and the note of authority with which the author speaks are all consistent with the tradition that he was James the Lord's brother, first 'bishop' of the church in Jerusalem. Moreover, although the Epistle contains some curious non-biblical literary phrases (*e.g.* 1:17, 23; 3:6), its Hebraic features coupled with the frequent use of rhetorical questions, vivid similes, imaginary dialogues, telling aphorisms and picturesque illustrations make it reasonable to suppose that we are listening to the completely bilingual Palestinian Jewish-Christian James, who resided at Jerusalem, a cosmopolitan centre for both Jews and Christians, for some 30 years after the resurrection of Jesus. The resemblances in Greek words and phrases between the Epistle and James' speech at the Council of Jerusalem (*cf.* 1:1 and Acts 15:23; 1:27 and Acts 15:14; 2:5 and Acts 15:13; 2:7 and Acts 15:17) may afford possible supporting evidence. It seems logical to suppose that either James himself composed the work, or else a secretary or later redactor compiled it from James' sermons. The situation of the church in the Epistle fits an early date of origin for much, if not all, of the contents: a date before the Council of Jerusalem (AD 48/49) would best explain the data, including the seeming conflict with Paul in 2:14–26.

III. Teaching

The Epistle concerns itself with the need for Christians to resist the pressure to compromise with the world, especially with respect to the use of wealth. It supplements and in no way contradicts the teaching of Gal. and Rom. on the matter of justification. James does not use the word 'justified' in 2:21 with reference to the occasion in the Abraham narrative to which Paul refers, *viz.* Gn. 15:6, but with reference to Gn. 22, a declaration of justification on the occasion of the binding of Isaac, itself the crown of a life of charity and faithfulness *flowing from* the faith of Gn. 15:6.

Roman Catholics have always valued the Epistle highly as affording evidence for the doctrines of justification by works, auricular confession (5:16), and extreme unction (5:14). On the other hand, Protestants—unduly influenced by Luther—have tended to regard it as somewhat sub-Christian. But Calvin pointed out that this Epistle contains nothing unworthy of an apostle of Christ, but on the contrary gives instruction on numerous subjects, all of which are important for Christian living, such as 'patience, prayer to God, the excellency and fruit of heavenly truth, humility, holy duties, the restraining of the tongue, the cultivation of peace, the repression of lusts, the contempt of the world, and the like'. Many modern evangelicals have begun to see the folly of underemphasizing the ethical implications of justification and the place which good works should occupy in the Christian life. As R. V. G. Tasker has said in *TNTC*, 'Whenever faith does not issue in love, and dogma, however orthodox, is unrelated to life; whenever Christians are tempted to settle down to a self-centred religion, and become oblivious of the social and material needs of others; or whenever they deny by their manner of living the creed they profess, and seem more anxious to be friends of the world than friends of God, then the Epistle of James has something to say to them which they reject at their peril.'

In an age when evangelicals are again concerned about social righteousness, the use of wealth and communal life, this Epistle calls for special study, for it draws attention to community-building virtues and to the destructive social force of improperly used wealth. In an age when the severity of the divine nature and the transcendence of God tend to be forgotten, the balance needs to be redressed by the emphasis laid in this Epistle on the unchangeable God (1:17), the Creator (1:18), the Father (1:27; 3:9), the Sovereign (4:15), the Righteous One (1:20), who must not be tested by evil men (1:13), to whom humanity must submit in humility (4:7, 10), the Lawgiver, the Judge, the Saviour and Destroyer (4:11–12), who will brook no rivals (4:4–5), the Giver of wisdom (1:5) and grace (4:6), who promises a crown of life to those who stand the test of faith and love him alone (1:12).

BIBLIOGRAPHY. Commentaries by J. B. Mayor, 1913; R. V. G. Tasker, *TNTC*, 1956; C. L. Mitton, 1966; F. Mussner, 1964; and M. Dibelius, 1975.

P.H.D.

JANNES AND JAMBRES. Paul speaks of certain false and morally dangerous teachers as resisting the truth as 'Jannes and Jambres' resisted Moses (2 Tim. 3:6–8). These names do not occur in OT, but extra-biblical allusions show that the Egyp. magicians of Ex. 7–8 are intended. Like them, the teachers played on superstitious susceptibilities with a plausibly presented parody of the truth.

The names, of unknown age, occur in various forms. The so-called 'Zadokite Work', now known to belong with the Qumran literature, has Belial raising up 'Yoḥaneh and his brother' against Moses and Aaron (7.19 in R. H. Charles, *Pseudepigrapha*, 1913;

5.19 in C. Rabin, *The Zadokite Documents*², 1958, p. 21); the Babylonian Talmud 'Yoḥanē and Mamre' (*Menaḥoth* 85a; *cf.* the spelling 'Mambres' in most Lat. and some Gk. MSS of 2 Tim. 3:8). Jewish legend made much of them, even attributing their paternity to Balaam. Pagan sources refer, not always perspicuously, to one or both (*cf.* Pliny, *NH* 30. 1. 11; Apuleius, *Apology* 90; Numenius of Apamea in Eusebius, *Praep. Ev.* 9. 8. 1), reflecting the story's celebrity. Origen knew a book on the subject (*Comm. in Mt.* 23:37; 27:9), and the Gelasian Decree a *Penitence of Jannes and Jambres*, of which M. R. James identified a fragment in a Saxon MS (*JTS* 2, 1901, pp. 572ff.). It is improbable, however, that Paul is alluding to the book: he would employ the names simply as being then in common use, with Ex. 7–8 alone in mind.

BIBLIOGRAPHY. *HJP*, 2. 3, pp. 149ff.; *SB*, 3, pp. 660ff. A.F.W.

JANOAH (Heb. *yānôaḥ, yānôḥâ*, 'rest'). **1.** A town of Naphtali seized by Tiglath-pileser during Pekah's reign (2 Ki. 15:29). Possibly modern Yanūḥ, NW of Acco (*LOB*, p. 379). **2.** A town of Ephraim, SE from Shechem, used in defining Ephraim's border with Manasseh (Jos. 16:6–70; AV 'Janohah'). Modern Khirbet Yānun. J.G.G.N.

JAPHETH (Heb. *yep̄eṯ*). One of the sons of Noah, usually mentioned last of the three (Gn. 5:32; 6:10; 7:13; 9:18, 23, 27; 1 Ch. 1:4), but his descendants are recorded first in Gn. 10 (and 1 Ch. 1:5–7). He was the ancestor of a number of tribes and peoples, most of whom had names which in historical times are associated with the regions to the N and W of the Middle East, especially Anatolia, and the Aegean (*NATIONS, TABLE OF). Japheth and his wife were among the eight people who escaped the Flood, and in a later incident he and Shem covered the nakedness of their father, Noah. In Noah's prophetic declaration after this episode he prayed that God might enlarge Japheth, and that *he* might dwell in the tents of Shem, and have Canaan as a servant (Gn. 9:27). Many commentators take *he* to refer to God rather than Japheth, though either interpretation is possible.

If the latter alternative is followed the reference may be to the benefits of the gospel which, coming first to the descendants of Shem, were later extended to the N peoples. In the above verse the word used for 'may he enlarge' is *yap̄t*, but this is probably only a play on words and does not have anything else to do with the name Japheth (*yep̄eṯ*), which does not occur elsewhere in the Bible or in the ancient inscriptions. Some have connected Japheth, however, with

The family of Japheth according to Gn. 10:1–4.

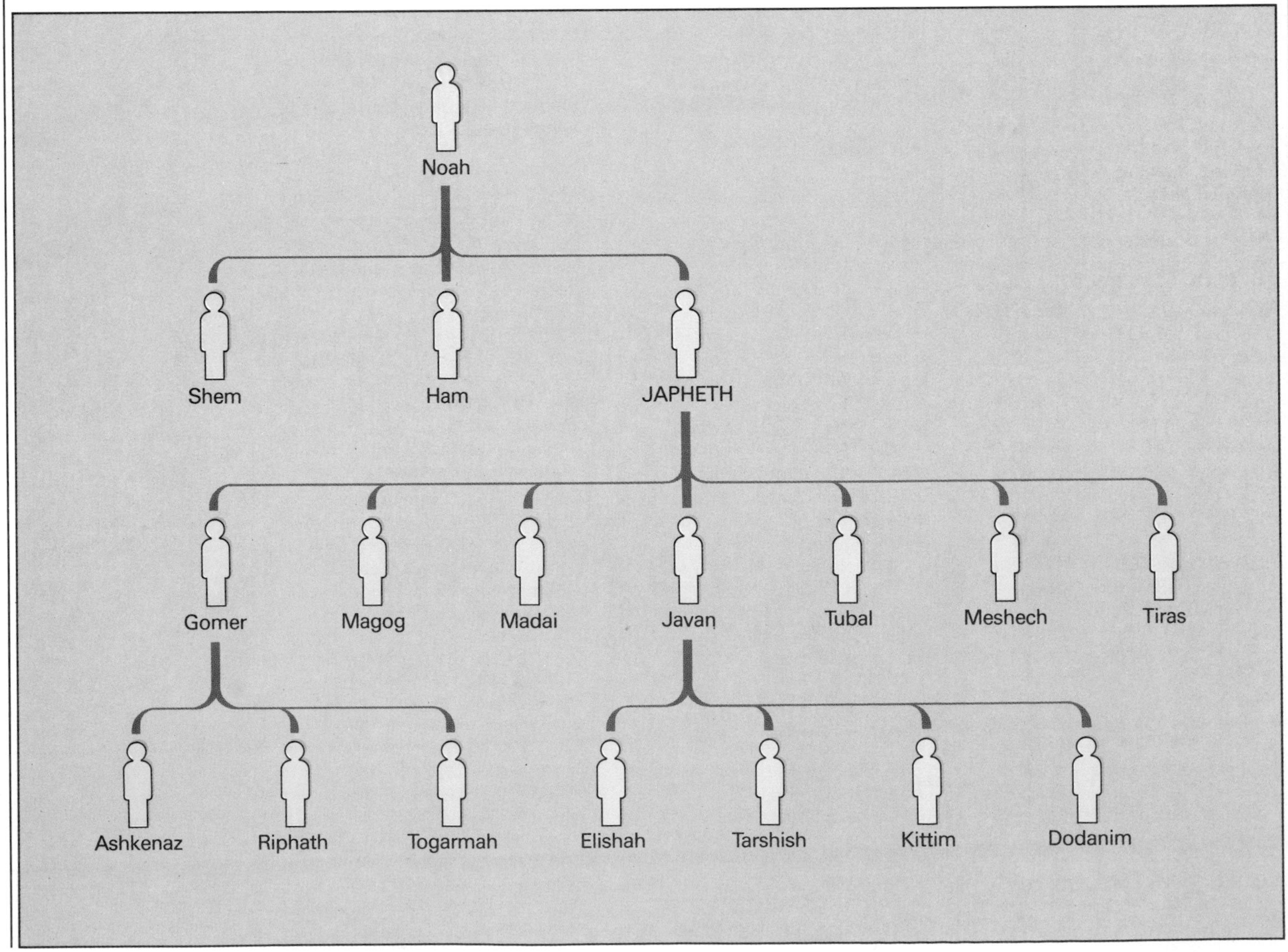

the Gk. mythological figure *Iapetos*, a son of earth and heaven, who had many descendants. The name is not Gk., so may be a form of the biblical name.

Bibliography. P. Dhorme, 'Les Peuples issus de Japhet, d'après le Chapître X de la Genèse', *Syria* 13, 1932, pp. 28–49; D. J. Wiseman, 'Genesis 10: Some Archaeological Considerations', *JTVI* 87, 1955, pp. 14ff.; D. Neisman, 'The Two Genealogies of Japheth', in H. A. Hoffner (ed.), *Orient & Occident*, 1973, pp. 119ff. T.C.M.

JAREB. The AV name or epithet of a king of Assyria who received tribute from Israel (Ho. 5:13; 10:6). If taken as a personal name it is assumed that the reference is to Tiglath-pileser III and Menahem's attempt to buy off the Assyrians in 738 BC (2 Ki. 15:19) or to the plea by Ahaz for his help against Rezin of Syria and Pekah of Israel (2 Ki. 16:7–10). Sayce's suggestion that it is Sargon II, conqueror of Samaria in 722 BC, is unlikely because of the date and circumstances.

It is more probable, since the customary definite article is here omitted, that *meleḵ yārēḇ* is a title to be translated 'warlike (or contending) king' or, taking *malki raḇ* as an old form for *meleḵ raḇ*, the usual Assyr. royal title of 'great king'. *Cf.* RVmg., RSVmg., 'a king that contends'; AVmg., 'the king that should plead'. On either interpretation the historical reference would be that quoted above. D.J.W.

JARMUTH (Heb. *yarmûṯ*). **1.** Tel Yarmut (Khirbet Yarmuk), in a commanding position above the Wadi Surar 5 km S of Beth-shemesh. Late Bronze walls and pottery indicate occupation of 6–8 acres by a population of 1,500–2,000 before the Israelite invasion, when Jarmuth was a leading Amorite city. See Jos. 10:3; 15:35; Ne. 11:29.

Bibliography. J. Garstang, *Joshua–Judges*, 1931, p. 171; *LOB*, p. 195.

2. A levitical town in Issachar, Jos. 21:29, otherwise Remeth (Jos. 19:21; *cf.* LXX(B) Jos. 21:29), Ramoth (1 Ch. 6:73); but the Egyptians called the district 'the hills of Yarmuta'. Aharoni (*LOB*) suggests Khokav-hayyarden, the Crusader Belvoir, 10 km N of Beth-shan. J.P.U.L.

JASHAR, BOOK OF. In Jos. 10:13 and 2 Sa. 1:18 the book of *yāšār* ('the upright one') is mentioned. Solomon's words in 1 Ki. 8:12–13, according to LXX, who put them after 8:53, are to be found in 'the book of the song'. As 'song', *šyr*, closely resembles *yšr*, perhaps the same book is meant here. All three quotations are in poetic style. It is possible that more quotations from ancient poetry came from this lost book. Some scholars identify it with 'the book of the wars of the Lord' (Nu. 21:14). As the quotations differ in metre, style and general contents, and date from different times, it is not probable that the book was a 'national epic'; it was rather a collection of songs with short historical introductions, *cf.* Arab anthologies as *e.g.* Hamasa. It must have been composed under Solomon's reign or later. The name *yāšār* is probably related to *Jeshurun. Printed books of Jashar are modern fabrications.

Bibliography. S. Mowinckel, 'Hat es ein israelitisches Nationalepos gegeben?', *ZAW* n.f. 12, 1935, pp. 130–152; R. K. Harrison, *IOT*, 1970, pp. 669f. A. van S.

JASHOBEAM. 1. '. . . a Hachmonite, was chief of the three', 1. Ch. 11:11; 'son of Zabdiel', 1 Ch. 27:2. He is to be identified with 'Josheb-basshebeth, a Tahchemonite' (2 Sa. 23:8), which might be read 'Josheb-bashebeth the Hachmonite' (*haḥaḵmōnî* for *taḥkᵉmōnî*, meaning unclear). LXX *Iebosthe*, *Iesebada*, Lucian *Iesbaal* imply a form 'Ishbaal'. David's leading warrior, who slew 'three hundred' (1 Ch.) or 'eight hundred' (2 Sa.), which is more likely, as it gives him superiority over Abishai (2 Sa. 23:18). (*Captain.)

2. Another warrior, who joined David at Ziklag (1 Ch. 12:6). A.R.M.

JASON. 1. Paul's host at Thessalonica (Acts 17:5–9). A rabble instigated by Jews raided his house, and, not finding Paul and Silas, seized Jason with some converts, and accused him before the politarchs (local magistrates) of harbouring seditious agitators. The prisoners were released on giving security for good behaviour. Luke does not say whether this involved a promise not to shelter the missionaries (*cf.* T. W. Manson, *BJRL* 35, 1952–3, p. 432), or simply to keep the peace. In either case the effect was the hasty departure of Paul (Acts 17:10) in circumstances which precluded an early return (*cf.* 1 Thes. 2:18). Jason was no doubt a Jew (*cf.* Acts 17:2 with 18:2–4) and probably a Christian (*cf.* Acts 17:7).

2. A Christian at Corinth, sending greetings in Rom. 16:21. 'Kinsman' here probably means 'fellow Jew' (*cf.* vv. 7, 11 and Rom. 9:3). Jason may be identical with **1**; if Sosipater is the *Sopater of Acts 20:4, Paul may be linking two fellow-Macedonians.

The name—that of the leader of the Argonauts—was very widespread, and Greek-speaking Jews seem to have sometimes used it instead of the similar-sounding, but conspicuously Jewish, name Jesus, *i.e.* Joshua (Deissmann, *Bible Studies*, p. 315n.). A.F.W.

JATTIR (Heb. *yattir*). Hurvat Yatir (Khirbet Attir) on the SW escarpment of the Hills of Judah, 21 km from Hebron; assigned to the priests (Jos. 21:14). David shared the spoils of the Amalekites with its inhabitants (1 Sa. 30:27). J.P.U.L.

JAVAN. One of the sons of Japheth (Gn. 10:2; 1 Ch. 1:5) and father of a group of peoples, *Elishah, *Tarshish, *Kittim and *Dodanim (Gn. 10:4; 1 Ch. 1:7), whose associations are with the regions to the N and W of the Middle East. It is generally accepted that this name (Heb. *yāwān*) is to be identified with Gk. *Iōnes*, which occurs as *Iaones*, probably for *Iawones*, in Homer (*Iliad* 13. 685), and refers to the people who later gave their name to Ionia. The name also occurs in Assyr. and Achaemenian inscriptions (*Iâmanu* and *Yauna* respectively). Isaiah mentions the descendants of Javan (LXX *Hellas*) beside Tubal as one of the nations (*gôyīm*) inhabiting distant islands and coastlands (*'iyyîm*, Is. 66:19). In the time of Ezekiel the descendants of Javan (LXX *Hellas*) were known as traders in men, bronze vessels and yarn, with Tyre (Ezk. 27:13, 19; in v. 19 RSV prefers to read *mē'ûzāl*, 'from Uzal', for *mᵉ'ûzzāl*, 'that which is spun, yarn'). The name Javan (RSV Greece) is used in the prophecies of Daniel to refer to the kingdom of Alexander of Macedon, and in Zc.

JAPHIA
See Lachish, Part 2.

JASPER
See Jewels, Part 2.

Jebusite terraces which supported houses on the E side of Jerusalem were repaired by the Israelites in the 10th cent. BC *with the massive stone blocks shown here.* (KK)

■ **JAVELIN**
See Armour, Part 1.

9:13 the term (EVV Greece, LXX Hellēnes) is probably used of the Seleucid Greeks.

BIBLIOGRAPHY. P. Dhorme, *Syria* 13, 1932, pp. 35–36; W. Brandenstein and M. Mayrhofer, *Handbuch des Altpersischen*, 1964, p. 156.

T.C.M.

JAZER. A town of the Amorite kingdom of Sihon captured by Israel (Nu. 21:32) and part of the pasture-lands allotted to the tribe of Gad. It was later given to the Merarite families of the tribe of Levi. During David's reign, Jazer furnished 'mighty men of valour' (1 Ch. 26:31) and was one of the towns on the route of the census-takers (2 Sa. 24:5). The Moabites gained control of it, probably a little before the fall of Samaria (Is. 16:8–9; Je. 48:32, where 'sea of' has been considered a scribal error). Judas Maccabaeus captured and sacked the town *c.* 164 BC (1 Macc. 5:7–8). The site may be Khirbet Gazzir on the Wadi Ša'īb near es-Salt.

A.R.M.

JEALOUSY. The principal OT term rendered as jealousy in the English Bible is *qînâ* from the verb *qānā'*, root meaning 'become dark red' (Nu. 5:14; Pr. 6:34; Ezk. 16:42; *etc.*). The normal LXX translation of *qînâ* and its cognates is *zēloō* or the cognate *parazēloō* (Dt. 32:21; *cf.* Rom. 10:19), and these are the principal terms used in the NT (Acts 7:9; Rom. 11:11; 1 Cor. 10:22; 13:4). Both Heb. and Gk. words refer to an exclusive single-mindedness of emotion which may be morally blameworthy or praiseworthy depending on whether the object of the jealousy is the self or some cause beyond the self. In the former case the result is envy, or hatred of others (Gn. 30:1; Pr. 3:31; Ezk. 31:9), which for the NT is the antithesis of love and hence the enemy of true Christian fellowship (1 Cor. 13:4; 2 Cor. 12:20; Jas. 3:14). The Bible however also represents the other possibility, of a '*divine* jealousy' (2 Cor. 11:2), a consuming single-minded pursuit of a good end (1 Ki. 19:10; Ex. 20:5; 1 Cor. 12:31). This positive usage is frequently associated with the marriage relationship where a jealousy for the exclusiveness of the relationship is the necessary condition of its permanence (Nu. 5:11ff.; Ezk. 16:38; 2 Cor. 11:2). Jealousy is referred to God as well as men (Ex.

'Jehoahaz of Judah' is named on this cuneiform inscription as paying tribute to Tiglath-pileser III of Assyria (2 Ki. 16:7–8). From Nimrud. c. 734 BC. (BM)

20:5; 34:14; Na. 1:2). Difficulty is sometimes felt with this, due principally to the way in which the negative connotations of the term have come to predominate in common English usage. Scripture however also witnesses to a positive application of jealousy and finds in this idea a highly relevant term to denote God's holy zeal for the honour of his name and the good of his people who are bound to him in the marriage of the covenant (Dt. 32:16, 21; 2 Ki. 19:31; [illegible] this sense the jealousy of God is of the essence of his moral character, a major cause for worship and confidence on the part of his people and a ground for fear on the part of his enemies. B.A.M.

JEBUSITE. The ethnic name of a people dwelling in the hills (Nu. 13:29; Jos. 11:3) round about Jerusalem (Jos. 15:8; 18:16). Descended from the third son of Canaan (Gn. 10:16; 1 Ch. 1:14), they are, however, listed as a distinct, but minority, group of people living alongside such peoples as Amorites and Heth. Jebus was a name given to *Jerusalem, the principal city in their territory (Jdg. 19:10–11; 1 Ch. 11:4–5; called Jebusi in Jos. 18:16, 28, RSV), and 'Jebusite' described the inhabitants of the city (Gn. 15:21; Ex. 3:8). Later the term is used of the former inhabitants (Ezk. 16:3, 45; Zc. 9:7).

Unless Melchizedek was ruler of Jerusalem (*SALEM), its earliest king named in the OT is Adonizedek (Jos. 10:1), who raised his local Amorite allies (v. 5) to protect the city from the Israelites entering the area. He met his death at Bethhoron (vv. 10–11). According to the *Amarna tablets (*c.* 1400 BC), *Urusa-limmu* was under Abdiḫepa, whose name, like that of a later Jebusite ruler *Araunah (2 Sa. 24:24) or Ornan (1 Ch. 21:15), is non-Semite, probably Hurrian or *Horite. Jebus was burnt after its capture by the men of Judah (Jdg. 1:8), but its original inhabitants regained control at least until the attack by David (2 Sa. 5:6). The Jebusites were allowed to remain on the temple hill until their ground was bought over or the Jebusite minority absorbed by the Judaeans who built a new quarter on Zion (Jdg. 1:21; 19:11). D.J.W.

JEDUTHUN (Heb. *yᵉdûṯûn*). A Levite appointed by David to conduct the music of the Temple along with Heman and Asaph (1 Ch. 25:1, 3, 6, *etc.*). He is also known as *Ethan (1 Ch. 6:44, *etc.*), which [illegible] appointment. A variation of the name, Jedithun (*yᵉḏîṯûn*), appears several times in the *Kᵉṯîḇ* (Ps. 39, *etc.*). The name appears in the titles of three psalms: 39, 62, 77. In the first of these the title is simply 'to (*lᵉ*) Jeduthun', but in the other two it is '*'al* Jeduthun', which may mean 'according to' or 'over'; if the latter, Jeduthun there means the family or guild of singers called after him. The family continued to officiate after the Exile (Ne. 11:17). M.A.M.

JEHOAHAZ (Heb. *yᵉhô'āḥāz*, 'Yahweh has grasped').

1. A variant of the name of *Ahaziah, Jehoram's son, 6th king of Judah (*c.* 848–841 BC; 2 Ch. 21:17; 25:23) in which the divine element comes first rather than last.

2. Son of Jehu; the 11th king of the N kingdom of Israel, who reigned for 17 years after his father's death (*c.* 814–798 BC; 2 Ki. 13:1). His reign saw the repeated advances of Syria under *Hazael and *Ben-hadad II, recorded as a result of his misdeeds (13:2–3). These included toleration of pagan worship (v. 6). His forces were so depleted (v. 7) that finally he had to call on Yahweh for aid (v. 4; *cf.* v. 22).

3. An inscription of *Tiglath-pileser III records tribute being received from *ia-u-ḫa-zi* (*māt*)*ia-u-da-a*, 'Jehoahaz of Judah' (*DOTT*, p. 57). This is the full form of the abbreviated name *Ahaz, 13th king of Judah, who sent gifts to the Assyrian king (2 Ki. 16:7–8).

4. 4th son of Josiah (1 Ch. 3:15) who became the 18th king of Judah upon his father's death at Megiddo (*c.* 609 BC; 2 Ki. 23:30). After reigning 3 months, he was deported by the pharaoh Neco to his headquarters at Riblah in Hamath and then to Egypt, where he died (23:33–34). Jeremiah called him *Shallum (Je. 22:11–12), an indication that Jehoahaz was his throne name (*cf.* A. M. Honeyman, *JBL* 67, 1948, p. 20). D.W.B.

JEHOIACHIN (Heb. *yᵉhôyāḵîn*, 'Yahweh will establish'; 'Jeconiah' in 1 Ch. 3:16; *cf.* Mt. 1:11–12; 'Coniah' in Je. 22:24, 28).

Jehoiachin was appointed king of Judah by the Babylonians following the revolt and death of his father Jehoiakim (6 December 598 BC). His brief reign of 3 months and 10 days (2 Ch. 36:9; Jos., *Ant.* 10. 98) is described in 2 Ki. 24:8–6; 2 Ch. 36:9–10. It was marked by evil, and the prophet Jeremiah foretold the end of both his rule and dynasty (Je. 22:24–30). According to Josephus (*Ant.* 10. 99) Nebuchadrezzar changed his mind about the appointment and returned to besiege Jerusalem and carried off the 18-year-old king, with his mother Nehushta, his family, and fellow Jews, to exile in Babylon. This famous historical event is also described in the OT and in the Bab. Chronicle. The city fell on 16 March 597, and Jehoiachin's young uncle Mattaniah (Zedekiah) was appointed to succeed him (2 Ki. 24:17; Je. 37:1).

In Babylon Jehoiachin was treated as a royal hostage. He is named (*Ya'u-kîn*) in Bab. tablets, dated between 595 and 570 BC, as receiving rations at the court in company with his five sons (E. F. Weidner, *Mélanges Syriens offerts à M. René Dussaud*, 2, 1939, pp. 923ff.; *DOTT*, pp. 84–86). While he was in exile, a steward, *Eliakim, may have continued to manage his estates in Judah, if the seal inscribed 'Eliakim, servant of Yawkin' is correctly understood (*DOTT*, p. 224). The Jews in Babylonia reckoned the years by those of Jehoiachin's captivity (Ezk. 1:2). After Nebuchadrezzar's death his successor Amēl-Marduk (*EVIL-MERODACH) in 561 BC showed Jehoiachin special favour and removed him from prison to the royal palace (2 Ki. 25:27–30; Je. 52:31–34). Jehoiachin's eldest son Shealtiel, the father of Zerubbabel, was born in 598 BC. Another son

JEBUS
See Jerusalem, Part 2.

JECONIAH
See Jehoiachin, Part 2.

JEDIDIAH
See Solomon, Part 3.

JEHDEIAH
See Meronothite, Part 2.

JEHOASH
See Joash, Part 2.

On this tablet found in Babylon 'Jehoiachin, king of Judah' and his sons are named among recipients of rations given to prisoners held at Babylon. Width 9·5 cm. 593 BC. (SMB)

Shenazar is named in 1 Ch. 3:18.

BIBLIOGRAPHY. D. J. Wiseman, *Chronicles of Chaldaean Kings*, 1956, pp. 33–35. D.J.W.

JEHOIADA (Heb. *y^{e}hôyāḏā'*, 'Yahweh knows') was a popular name in OT times. **1.** The father of Benaiah (2 Sa. 8:18), a valiant man from Kabzeel in the Negeb (1 Ch. 11:22); the son was one of David's officers. **2.** The leader of the Aaronites, who supported David at Ziklag (1 Ch. 12:27). **3.** The son of Benaiah, and grandson of Jehoiada, one of David's counsellors (1 Ch. 27:34).

4. The chief priest of the Temple in Jerusalem during the reigns of Ahaziah, Athaliah and Joash was also named Jehoiada. He married Jehoshabeath, sister of King Ahaziah, and played a prominent part in political affairs. On the death of Ahaziah he frustrated the queen-mother Athaliah's attempt to destroy all 'the seed royal'. He and his wife hid their nephew, Joash, for 6 years in the Temple precincts, while Athaliah usurped the throne. Then in a *coup d'état* he brought him out of hiding as the rightful ruler of Judah. A covenant was made for his protection, and another on his proclamation as king (2 Ki. 11:17). During Joash's minority, Jehoiada virtually ruled on his behalf. He destroyed the shrines of Baal and organized the Levites. He helped in the selection of Joash's two wives to ensure the royal succession (2 Ch. 24:3). After a rebuke from Joash himself he repaired the Temple (2 Ki. 12:7). When he died at the age of 130, he was buried in the royal tomb, in recognition of his service to the community.

5. A priest in Jerusalem before the Exile, during the lifetime of Jeremiah, who was replaced by Shemaiah (Je. 29:26). **6.** The son of Paseah who returned from the Exile with Nehemiah and played his part in the rebuilding programme (Ne. 3:6). M.B.

JEHOIAKIM (Heb. *y^{e}hôyāqîm*, 'Ya(h)w has established'; *cf.* Joakim, 1 Esdras 1:37–39). King of Judah (609–598 BC), a son of *Josiah and elder brother of *Jehoahaz, whose place he took at the command of Neco II of Egypt. His name was changed from Eliakim as a mark of vassalage. The reign is recorded in 2 Ki. 23:34–24:6; 2 Ch. 36:4–8, and as the last-named entry in the 'book of the Chronicle of the Kings of Judah' (2 Ki. 24:5). To pay the Egyp. dues Jehoiakim imposed heavy land taxes (2 Ki. 23:35). He built costly royal buildings, using forced labour (Je. 22:13–17), and is described as an oppressive and covetous ruler. The religious decay during his reign is noted by the contemporary prophets Jeremiah and Habakkuk. Josiah's reforms were forgotten in the reversion to idolatry and introduction of Egyp. rites (Ezk. 8:5–17). Jehoiakim shed much innocent blood (2 Ki. 24:4) and had the prophet Uriah murdered for opposing him (Je. 26:20–21). He opposed Jeremiah (36:26) and personally burnt the scroll from which Jehudi read the words of the prophet to him (v. 22). He was 'unjust and wicked by nature, and was neither reverent toward God, nor kind to man' (Josephus, *Ant.* 10. 83), that is, he followed in the tradition of Manasseh's sin (2 Ki. 24:3).

In Jehoiakim's fourth year (605 BC) Nebuchadrezzar defeated the Egyptians at *Carchemish and won control of Palestine as far as the Egyp. border (Je. 25:1; 46:2), but it was not until the following year that Jehoiakim, with other rulers, went before Nebuchadrezzar to submit to him as vassal (Je. 36:9–29; Bab. Chronicle). Three years later, doubtless encouraged by the Egyptian defeat of the Babylonians in 601 BC, but against the advice of Jeremiah, Jehoiakim rebelled (2 Ki. 24:1). Nebuchadrezzar did not at first intervene but sent local Babylonian garrison troops with

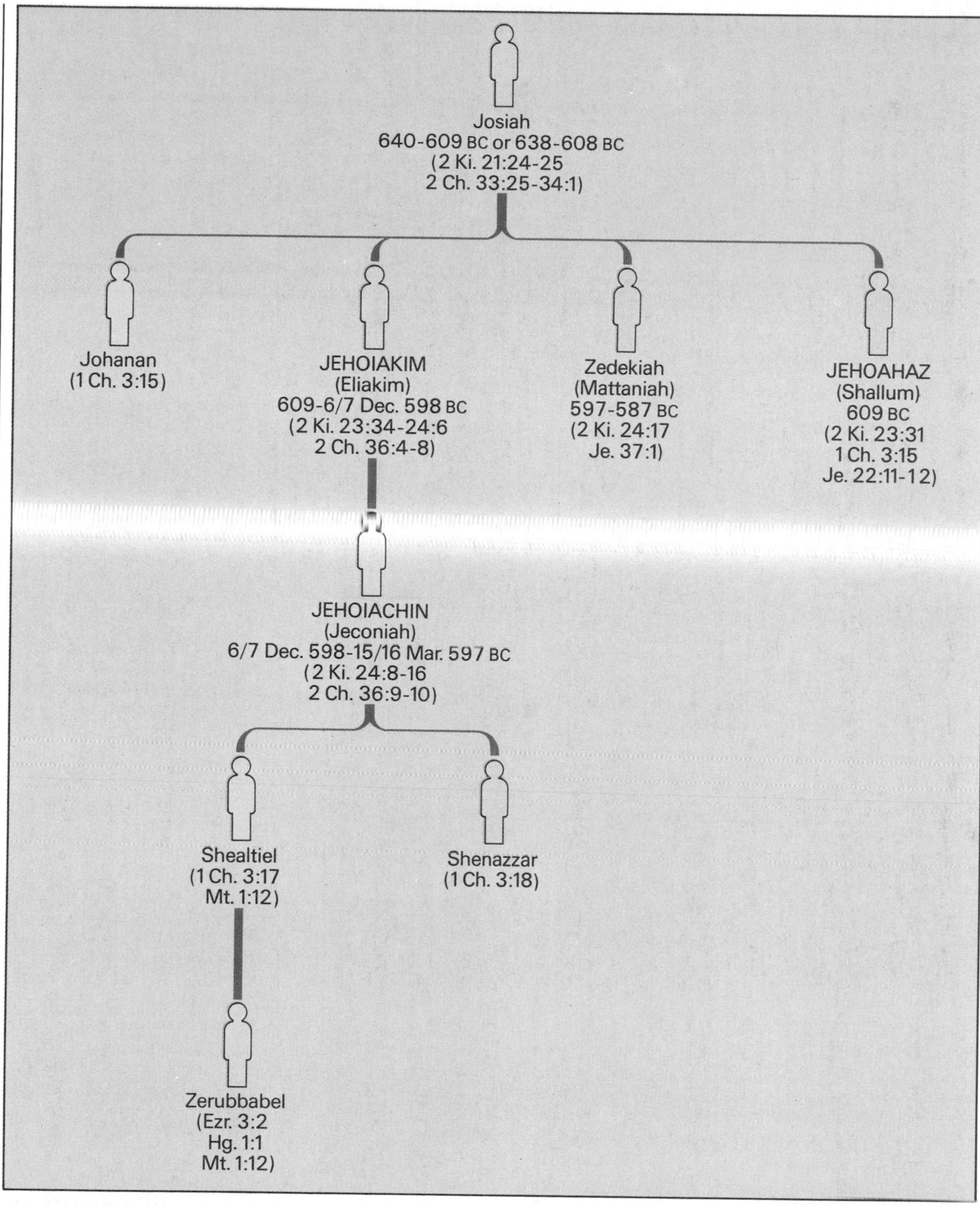

Chart showing how Jehoahaz, Jehoiachin and Jehoiakim were related.

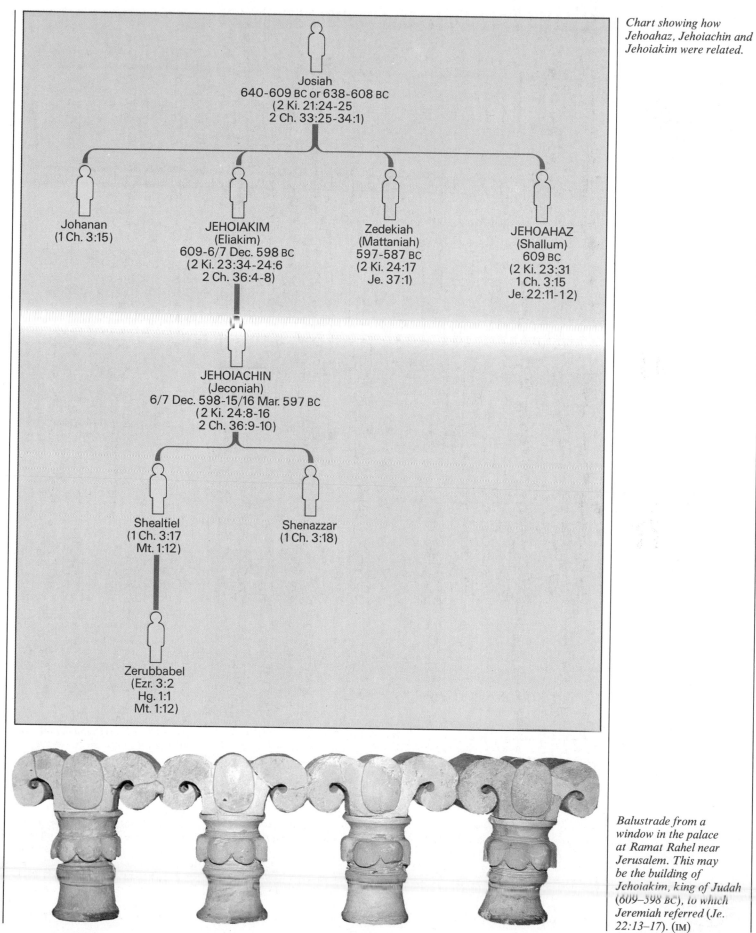

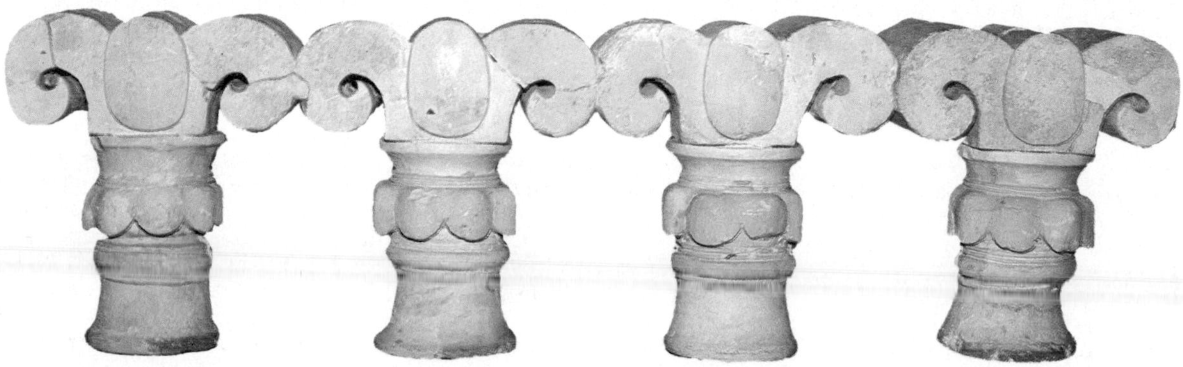

Balustrade from a window in the palace at Ramat Rahel near Jerusalem. This may be the building of Jehoiakim, king of Judah (609–598 BC), to which Jeremiah referred (Je. 22:13–17). (IM)

Family tree of Jehoram and Jehoshaphat.

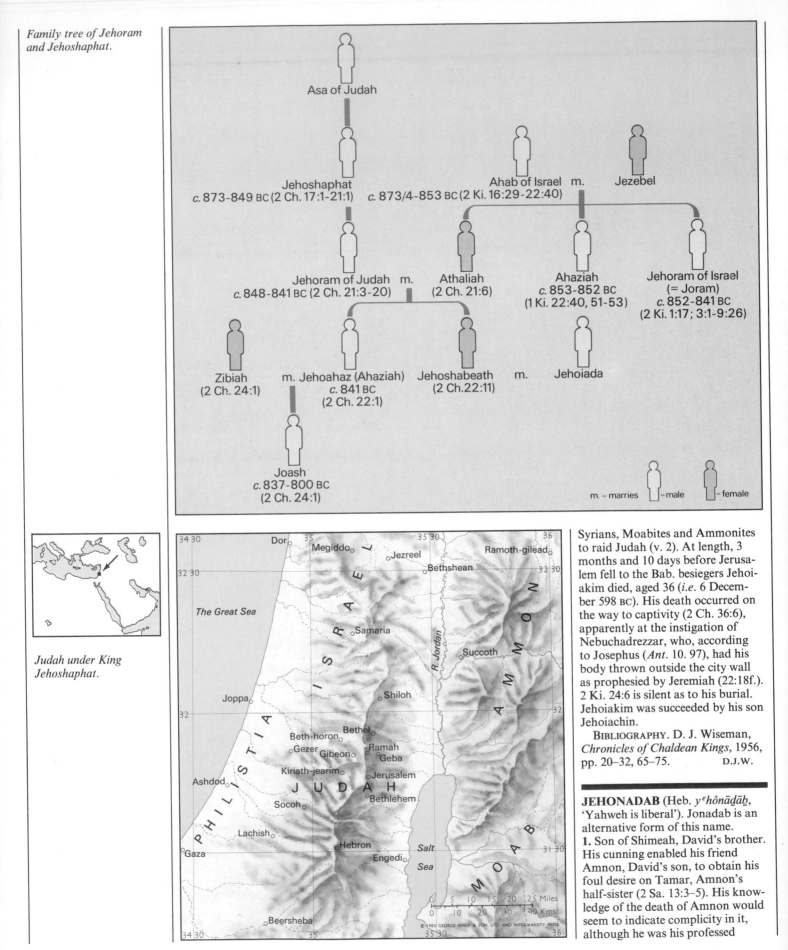

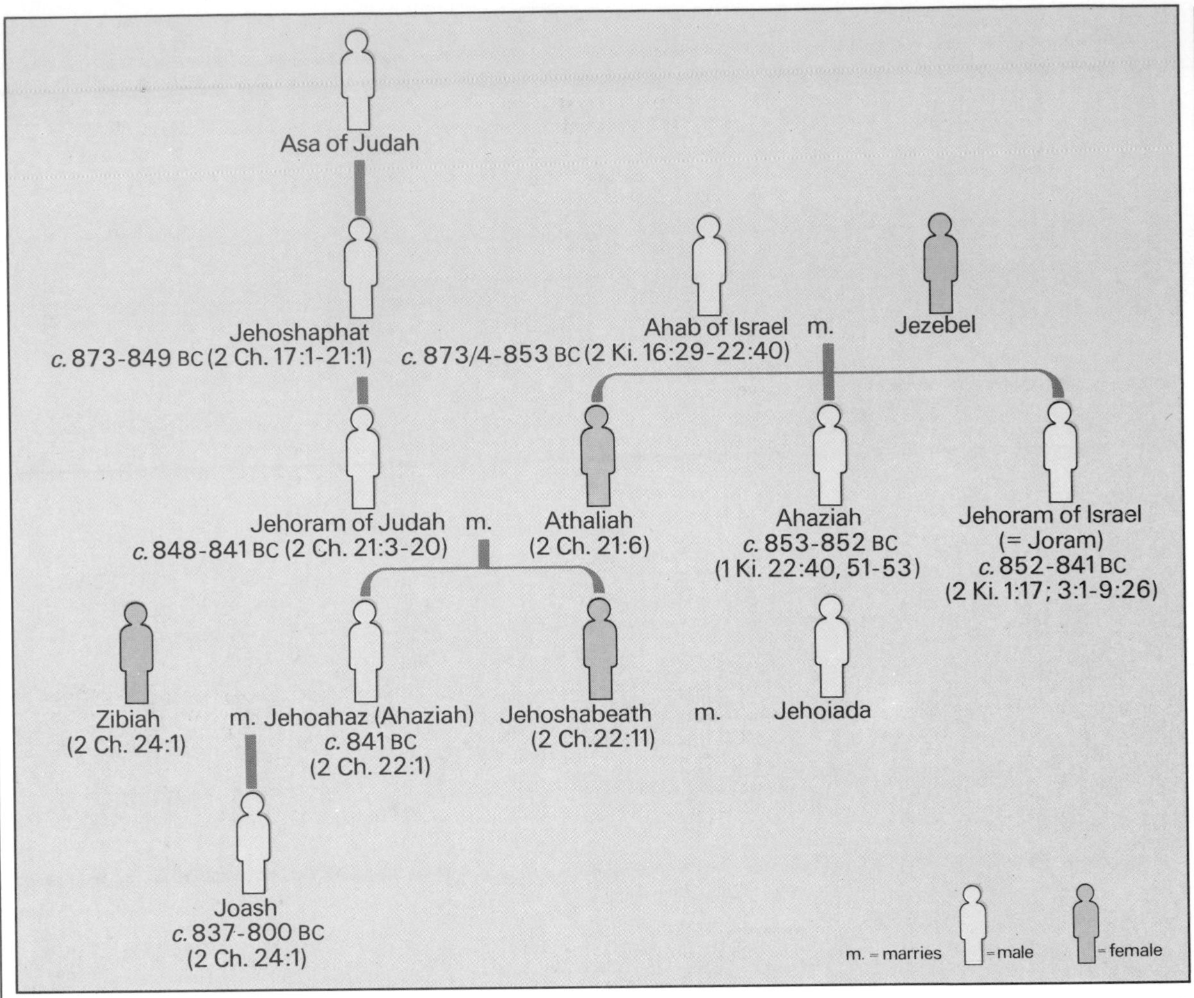

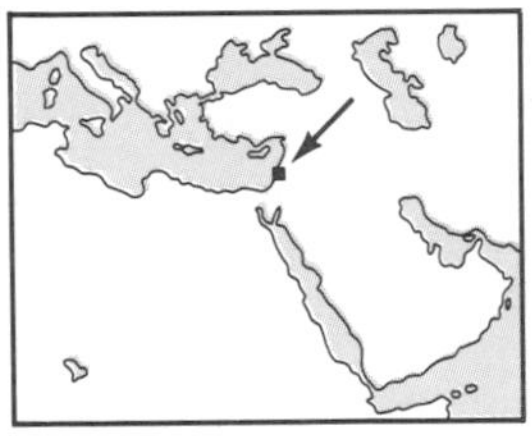

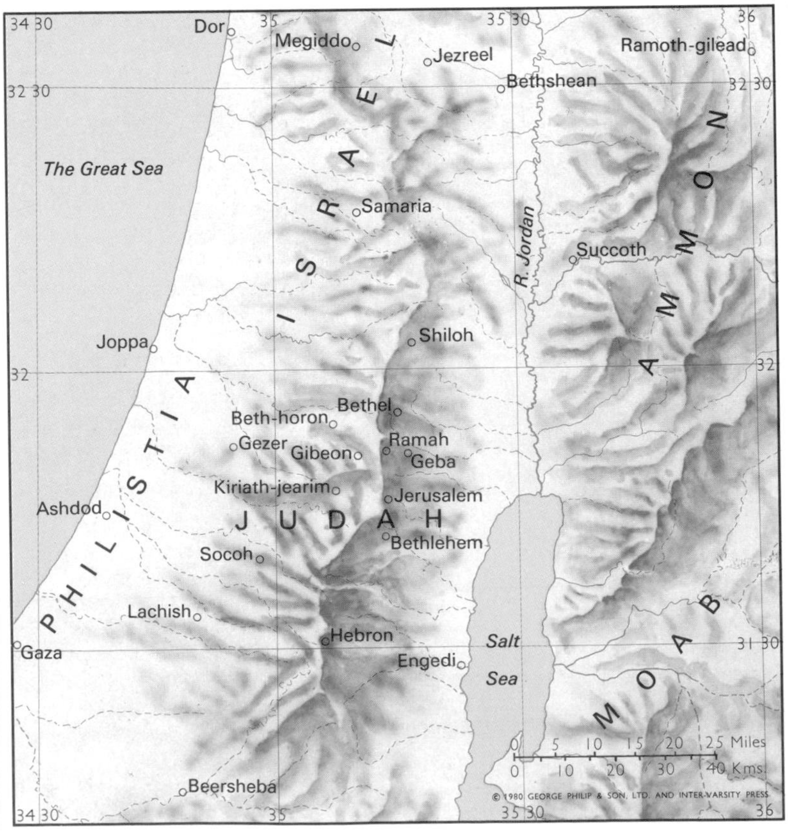

Judah under King Jehoshaphat.

Syrians, Moabites and Ammonites to raid Judah (v. 2). At length, 3 months and 10 days before Jerusalem fell to the Bab. besiegers Jehoiakim died, aged 36 (*i.e.* 6 December 598 BC). His death occurred on the way to captivity (2 Ch. 36:6), apparently at the instigation of Nebuchadrezzar, who, according to Josephus (*Ant.* 10. 97), had his body thrown outside the city wall as prophesied by Jeremiah (22:18f.). 2 Ki. 24:6 is silent as to his burial. Jehoiakim was succeeded by his son Jehoiachin.

BIBLIOGRAPHY. D. J. Wiseman, *Chronicles of Chaldean Kings*, 1956, pp. 20–32, 65–75. D.J.W.

JEHONADAB (Heb. *yᵉhônāḏāḇ*, 'Yahweh is liberal'). Jonadab is an alternative form of this name.

1. Son of Shimeah, David's brother. His cunning enabled his friend Amnon, David's son, to obtain his foul desire on Tamar, Amnon's half-sister (2 Sa. 13:3–5). His knowledge of the death of Amnon would seem to indicate complicity in it, although he was his professed friend (2 Sa. 13:30–33). **2.** A son of Rechab, a Kenite (1 Ch. 2:55; Je. 35:6). He prohibited his clan from engaging in agriculture, possessing vineyards and using their produce, and dwelling in settled communities (Je. 35:6–10). But this may have been codifying what was already general practice. He was a zealous worshipper of Yahweh and assisted Jehu in suppressing the worship of Baal Melqart (2 Ki. 10:15, 23). M.A.M.

JEHORAM (Heb. *y^ehôrām*, 'Yahweh is exalted'). Sometimes abbreviated to Joram. **1.** A Levite in the time of David (1 Ch. 26:25). **2.** A prince of Hamath (2 Sa. 8:9–12). 1 Ch. 18:9–11 suggests his real name was Hadoram. **3.** A priest in the time of Jehoshaphat (2 Ch. 17:8).

4. King of (N) Israel, 852–841 BC; the last ruler of the dynasty of Omri (2 Ki. 1–9). Jehoram was a son of King Ahab and Jezebel, and although he is said to have removed one pagan feature of Israel's worship, in general he followed the unorthodox ways of other N kings (2 Ki. 3:1–3). He had to deal with the Moabites' rebellion against their position as vassals of Israel (*MOABITE STONE) and won a spectacular, though not conclusive, victory over the Moabites (3:4–27). He was later wounded in battle with the Syrians (8:28–29). Some of the other Elisha stories also have as their background the conflict between Israel and Syria, and refer to 'the king of Israel' (5:1–8; 6:8–23; 6:24–7:20; *cf.* 8:1–6), but we cannot be sure whether or not this king was Jehoram. Jehoram was killed and succeeded by *Jehu when recovering from injury in his capital, Jezreel (9:1–37). It was Elisha who instigated this deed; he saw it as a beginning to God's final act of judgment on Ahab and Jezebel, who were still alive and active for evil in Jezreel (9:7–10, 22). It was thus also the further fulfilment of Elijah's prophecy concerning Ahab and Jezebel (9:24–26, 30–36; *cf.* 1 Ki. 21:17–29).

5. King of Judah, 848–841 BC (2 Ki. 8:16–24; 2 Ch. 21). He was son of and successor to Jehoshaphat, but reversed his father's Yahwist policies. He married Athaliah, who was a daughter of King Ahab of Israel and thus a sister of King Jehoram of Israel, and led Israel in the pagan and bloody ways of Ahab and Jezebel. Edom and Libnah both successfully threw off their vassal status in relation to Judah in his day, and the Philistines and Arabians invaded and plundered his kingdom. He died of illness 'and he departed with no one's regret' (2 Ch. 21:20); he was succeeded by his son Ahaziah. J.E.G.

JEHOSHABEATH, JEHOSHEBA. Daughter of Jehoram, sister or half-sister of Ahaziah. She saved the life of Joash (2 Ki. 11:2) when Athaliah sought to kill all the royal seed. Her marriage to Jehoiada (2 Ch. 22:11) is the only recorded instance of a union between a princess of the royal house and a high priest. M.A.M.

JEHOSHAPHAT (Heb. *y^ehôšāpāṭ*, 'Yahweh has judged').

1. An official clerk under David and Solomon (2 Sa. 8:16; 20:24; 1 Ki. 4:3; 1 Ch. 18:15). **2.** One of twelve officers appointed over Israel by Solomon (1 Ki. 4:17; *cf.* v. 7).

3. Son and successor of Asa as 4th king of Judah (*c.* 873–849 BC). Jehoshaphat strengthened Judah against aggression by fortifying and placing standing garrisons in N towns (2 Ch. 17:2, 12–19). He also broke with previous practice in entering into a parity treaty with Ahab of Israel by taking one of Ahab's daughters, Athaliah, to marry his son, Jehoram (2 Ch. 18:1; *cf.* 21:6; 2 Ki. 8:18). This new alliance had its effect on other peoples, including the Philistines and Arabs, who brought tribute to Jehoshaphat (2 Ch. 17:10–11), but the association with apostate Israel almost proved Judah's undoing after Jehoshaphat's death (2 Ki. 11:1–3).

Jehoshaphat's reign is noted for its adherence to Yahweh's instructions (1 Ki. 22:42; 2 Ch. 20:32). He eradicated much of the pagan worship (1 Ki. 22:43, 46) and provided itinerant teachers of Mosaic law (2 Ch. 17:7–9). He reorganized the legal system by appointing judges in key cities, with an appeal court in Jerusalem (2 Ch. 19:4–11).

4. Father of *Jehu, 10th king of Israel (2 Ki. 9:2; 14:20). D.W.B.

JEHOSHAPHAT, VALLEY OF. The name which Joel gives to the place of the final judgment in Joel 3:2, 12. In both of these verses 'Jehoshaphat' (meaning 'Yahweh has judged') is associated with statements that God will judge (Heb. *šāpaṭ*). Therefore it is probable that 'the valley of Jehoshaphat', like 'the valley of decision' in v. 14, is a term symbolic of the judgment, not a current geographical name.

The valley of Jehoshaphat has been variously identified. Some have thought that Joel had no definite place in mind; *e.g.* Targum Jonathan translates this name 'the plain of the decision of judgment', and Theodotion renders 'the place of judgment'. Since Joel uses the geographical term 'valley', most students have thought that some location was intended. Ibn Ezra suggests the valley of Berachah S of Bethlehem, where Jehoshaphat's forces gathered after the destruction of enemies (2 Ch. 20:26), but Zc. 14 locates the judgment near Jerusalem, and according to *1 Enoch* 53:1 all people gather for judgment in a deep valley near the valley of Hinnom. Jewish, Christian and Muslim traditions identify the place of final judgment as the Kidron valley, between Jerusalem and the mount of Olives. Therefore many have been buried there, Muslims especially on the W slope and Jews especially on the E slope of the valley. A Graeco-Roman tomb on the E slope has been called mistakenly the tomb of King Jehoshaphat. As early as the Bordeaux pilgrim (AD 333) and Eusebius' *Onomasticon* (*s.v. Koilas*), the name Jehoshaphat was associated with this valley. Some object that Joel uses the word *'ēmeq*, 'broad valley', while the Kidron valley is called *naḥal*, 'ravine' (2 Sa. 15:23). Other identifications are 'the king's dale' (2 Sa. 18:18), which runs into the Kidron valley from the NW (so C. F. Keil, E. G. Kraeling) and the valley of Hinnom, W and S of Jerusalem (so G. W. Wade).

BIBLIOGRAPHY. E. Robinson, *Biblical Researches in Palestine*, 1, 1856, pp. 268–273; J. A. Bewer in *ICC*, 1912, on Joel 3 (*MT* 4):2; E. G. Kraeling, *Rand McNally Bible Atlas*, 1956, p. 342. J.T.

JEHU (Heb. *yēhû*, meaning uncertain. Possibly an abbreviation of *y^ehôhû'*, 'Yahweh is he').

1. An ambidextrous Benjaminite warrior who aided David at Ziklag (1 Ch. 12:3).

2. A seer, son of Hanani, who foresaw the end of Baasha's

JEHOSHEBA See Jehoshabeath, Part 2.

JEHOVAH See God, names of, Part 1.

JEHOVAH-JIREH See God, names of, Part 1.

JEHOVAH-SHALOM See God, names of, Part 1.

JEHOVAH-SHAMMAH See God, names of, Part 1.

JEHOVAH-TSIDKENU See God, names of, Part 1.

Jehu, king of Israel, or his ambassador, bowing before Shalmaneser III, king of Assyria. Behind him Israelite porters bring in tribute. This limestone stele ('The Black Obelisk') was originally set up at Nimrud. c. 840 BC. (BM)

dynasty (1 Ki. 16:1–7). He also prophesied to Jehoshaphat (2 Ch. 19:2) and chronicled his reign (20:34).

3. Son of Jehoshaphat (2 Ki. 9:2), who reigned as the 10th king of the N kingdom of Israel for 28 years (*c.* 842–815 BC; 2 Ki. 10:36), where he founded its 4th dynasty.

Religious apostasy reached such an extent in Israel during the reigns of Ahab and Jehoram (2 Ki. 8:27) that a revolt was instigated by Elisha's appointing a prophet to anoint Jehu king (9:1–13). This rebellion was also supported by elements among the people, *e.g.*, the Rechabites (10:15–16). Jehu, receiving the acclamation of the army of Jehoram which he commanded, went to Jezreel, where the king lay wounded following a battle at Ramoth-gilead (8:28–29). He there killed both Jehoram and Ahaziah, king of Israel, who came out to meet him (9:21–27; *cf.* 2 Ch. 22:9). The new king entered Jezreel and had Jezebel put to death. He then eradicated all opposition by executing Ahab's family and followers (2 Ki. 10:1–11) as well as 42 visiting members of Ahaziah's family (vv. 12–17; 2 Ch. 22:8). He then proceeded to stamp out worship of Baal by tricking the god's followers into meeting together and then slaughtering them, also destroying their temple (2 Ki. 10:18–28).

Jehu himself continued in apostasy by worshipping golden calves at Bethel and Dan (vv. 29–31), for which he was punished by the Syrians, under *Hazael, annexing parts of his territory (vv. 32–33).

The Black Obelisk of *Shalmaneser III mentions tribute paid by *'ia-ú-a mar ḫu-um-ri*, '*Yâw*, son of *Omri' (*DOTT*, pp. 48–49). This is generally taken to refer to an action of Jehu of Israel not mentioned by the OT. He, or his representative, is pictured bowing before the king. *Yâw* might also be an abbreviated form of the name Jehoram (P. K. McCarter, *BASOR* 216, 1974, pp. 5–7). In either case the date would be 841 BC (E. R. Thiele, *BASOR* 222, 1976, pp. 19–23). D.W.B.

JEHUDI (Heb. y^{e}*hûḏî*). Normally means 'a Jew', as in Zc. 8:23, but in Je. 36:14, 21, 23 it is the name of an officer of Jehoiakim's court, who commanded Baruch to read the roll of Jeremiah's prophecies to the princes, and later himself read it to the king, until Jehoiakim personally destroyed it. J.G.G.N.

JEPHTHAH. One of the later (*c.* 1100 BC) Hebrew judges (Jdg. 11:1–12:7), whose name *yip̄tāḥ* is 'probably shortened from *yip̄taḥ-'ēl*, "God opens (*sc.* the womb)", which is cited as a proper name in Sabean' (*NBCR*, p. 267). The son of a common heathen prostitute (*zônâ*) and the then childless Gilead, Jephthah felt he had been illegally disinherited by the younger legitimate sons of Gilead. He fled to the land of *Tob. From there he and the renegades he gathered raided settlements and caravans and, like David's gang (1 Sa. 22:2; 27:8–9; 30), may have protected Israelite villages from marauding tribes, perhaps including the Ammonites.

Thus when the Israelites in Transjordan were threatened by a full-scale invasion of the Ammonites, the elders of Gilead invited Jephthah to be their commander. He consented only when they promised he would continue as their head (*i.e.* judge) after fighting ceased. This pact was confirmed with oaths taken at Mizpeh (Gn. 31:48–49). Jephthah's attempted diplomacy to dissuade the Ammonites failed (Jdg. 11:12–28).

Given courage and ingenuity for his task by the Spirit of God, Jephthah passed through Gilead and Manasseh to raise additional troops. He then passed over the Jabbok to Israelite headquarters at Mizpeh. There, before moving against the Ammonites, he vowed a vow (*neḏer*) unto his God, a common practice before battle among ancient peoples. Jephthah intentionally promised Yahweh a human sacrifice, probably intending a slave, because a single animal would have been as nothing from a people's leader. The LXX translation of *hayyôṣē'*, *ho emporeuomenos*, 'whoever comes by the way', long ago indicated that this is the proper interpretation. V. 31 should read: 'Then whoever comes forth . . . shall be the Lord's, and I will offer him up for a burnt offering.' Jephthah was living among heathen who offered human sacrifices to pagan deities (*cf.* 2 Ki. 3:27) and in a day when the law of Moses was little known or practised. Jephthah might sincerely (although wrongly —Lv. 18:21; Dt. 12:31) suppose 'that Jehovah would need to be propitiated by some offering as costly as those which bled on the altars of Chemosh and Moloch' (F. W. Farrar).

After subduing the Ammonites by faith (Heb. 11:32) Jephthah returned triumphantly to his headquarters house, only to meet his daughter, his only child, leading a victory procession (*cf.* 1 Sa. 18:6; Ex. 15:20). With utter grief, Jephthah felt he must fulfil his vow by offering her as a burnt-offering (*'ôlâ*, which always was burnt). He did not devote her to a life of celibacy (a view not introduced until Rabbi Kimchi), for there is no record that female attendants in tabernacle or Temple had to be virgins (Anna had been married, Lk. 2:36).

Jephthah showed himself as stern with his brethren the Ephraimites as he was with his enemies the Ammonites and with himself concerning his daughter. Offended because they had no share in his victory, the Ephraimites threatened his life. Jephthah answered harshly and slaughtered them relentlessly at the Jordan (Jdg. 12:1–6). J.R.

JERAH. One of the sons of *Joktan (Gn. 10:26; 1 Ch. 1:20), some of whom can be connected with tribes of S Arabia. The name (*yeraḥ*) is identical in form with the Heb. for 'month' or *'moon', and the word occurs in the S Arabian inscriptions (*yrḥ*) with this meaning, so it may be concluded that the descendants of Jerah had likewise settled in S Arabia. The site of Beth-Yerah (Khirbet Kerak) on the Sea of Galilee is probably unrelated.

BIBLIOGRAPHY. J. A. Montgomery, *Arabia and the Bible*, 1934, p. 40. T.C.M.

JERAHMEEL (Heb. *y^eraḥm^e'ēl*, 'may God have compassion').
1. The ancestor of the Jerahmeelites, a clan on the S frontier of Judah, 'the Negeb of the Jerahmeelites' (1 Sa. 27:10; *cf.* 30:29), related to the Calebites (*cf.* 1 Sa. 25:3) and bordering on the Kenites. Like the Calebites, they were absorbed into the tribe of Judah; their adoptive relationship to other branches of that tribe is given in 1 Ch. 2:9ff., together with the sub-divisions of the Jerahmeelite clan itself. They play a very minor part in the OT record, but by dint of large-scale textual emendation T. K. Cheyne concluded that they occupy a position of major importance in the narrative—a theory which retains interest only as a notable aberration in the history of biblical criticism (*cf. EBi*, *s.v.* 'Jerahmeel', *etc.*).

2. In 1 Ch. 24:29 the son of one Kish, a member of the Merarite clan of the tribe of Levi. **3.** In Je. 36:26 a member of the royal family of Judah who occupied an official position at the court of Jehoiakim. F.F.B.

JEREMIAH.

I. His background

Jeremiah's history covered a span of 40 years—from his call in the 13th year of King Josiah (627 BC) until the fall of Jerusalem in 587 BC. In those 4 decades he prophesied under the last five kings of Judah—Josiah, Jehoahaz, Jehoiakim, Jehoiachin and Zedekiah. While he was preaching, important personalities and events were shaping history beyond his native Judah. It was one of the most fateful periods in the history of the ancient Near East and it affected Judah's history too.

The Assyrian empire disintegrated and Babylon and Egypt were left to struggle against each other for the leadership of the E. The chronology of the last quarter of the 7th century BC has been greatly clarified by the publication of some tablets which were excavated years ago but which had lain in obscurity in the vaults of the British Museum in London. In 1956 D. J. Wiseman made these Chaldean documents available to students of the ancient Near East, thus making possible a reappraisal of the chronology of the last quarter of the 7th century BC.

Jeremiah's life and times which fall within this all-important period are remarkably well documented, and the intimacies of his personality are more vividly portrayed than those of the more spectral Minor Prophets or even of Isaiah and Ezekiel.

When Jeremiah was called to the prophetic office he was still 'a child' (*na'ar*, 1:6), an ambiguous term descriptive of infancy (Ex. 2:6) and advanced adolescence (1 Sa. 30:17). If the demure Jeremiah simply meant he was spiritually and socially immature the word might indicate that he was not the average age of a prophet, say between 20 and 30, if we may argue from the rules laid down for Levites (Nu. 8:24; 1 Ch. 23:24). Assuming, then, that at his call Jeremiah was in his early 20s his boyhood was spent in the reigns of Manasseh and Amon. When the call came to Jeremiah nearly a century had passed since the N kingdom of Israel (Samaria) had fallen to the Assyrians. Judah in the S, however, contrived to survive. By a miracle it weathered the storm of Sennacherib's invasion as Isaiah had predicted. King Hezekiah initiated reforms in Judah's religion and morals (2 Ki. 18:1ff.),

'Jerahmeel, the king's son' (lyrhm'l bn hmlk) *named on a seal impression in clay dating from the late 7th cent. BC. He may be identified with the Jerahmeel who burnt Jeremiah's scroll (Je. 36:26). 12 mm × 10 mm.* (NA)

JERBOA
See Animals, Part 1.

*The situation of Judah and the appearance of Hebrew writing in the age of Jeremiah are revealed in the * Lachish ostraca, letters to Yaush the military governor of Lachish. In this example an anonymous prophet (Heb.* nābī*), identified by some with Jeremiah himself, acts as a messenger to Yaush from Hoshayahu, who was in charge of an outpost. Lachish ostracon III. c. 590 BC.* (IA)

but these had been nullified by the long apostasy of his son Manasseh (2 Ki. 21:1ff.) and the short idolatrous reign of Amon (2 Ki. 21:19ff.). While Judah was wallowing in the slough of idolatry the Assyrians under Esarhaddon and Ashurbanipal conquered Egypt. Under Psammetichus (664–610 BC) Egypt reasserted herself and began afresh to intimidate Judah, who found herself vacillating between now the blandishments, now the menaces of the two world powers, Egypt and Babylon. In this atmosphere of international political tension and national religious declension Jeremiah grew up into boyhood.

Doubtless many in Judah yearned for the dawn that would end the night of 60 years' moral degeneracy. Jeremiah grew up in a pious priestly home (1:1). His name, 'Yahweh exalts' or 'Yahweh throws down', might well symbolize both his parents' prayers for the disconsolate nation and their aspirations for young Jeremiah. They would communicate to him their anxiety over the religious persecutions and apostasies of Manasseh and Amon, educate him in Israel's laws, and fill his fertile mind with the teachings of Isaiah and other prophets of the previous century.

II. The five reigns

a. Josiah

When God called Jeremiah, Josiah (638–608 BC), who had been on the throne of Judah for 12 years, had already introduced religious reforms (2 Ch. 34:4–7). But it was not until 621 BC, the 18th year of his reign, that he initiated a systematic reformation in Judah's religion and morals (2 Ki. 23). The impulse to reform was generated by the momentous discovery in the Temple of 'the book of the law' by Hilkiah. Jeremiah had already been a prophet for 5 years. Probably chs. 1–6 describe conditions in Judah before Josiah's main reforms in 622–621 BC. The nation is incorrigibly corrupt, insensible to God's offer of pardon, and oblivious to the menace of an invincible enemy. Apart from 11:1–8, which may contain hints of Jeremiah's enthusiasm for Josiah's reforms, the prophet has left no reference to the last 12 years of Josiah's reign. In 608 BC the king was killed at Megiddo (2 Ki. 23:29) in an abortive attempt to resist Pharaoh Neco (610–594 BC), successor to Psammetichus. Naturally Jeremiah mourned the early death of Josiah (22:10a) of whom he thought kindly (22:15f.).

b. Jehoahaz

Neco continued to meddle in the affairs of Judah. Jehoahaz (or Shallum, Je. 22:11) succeeded Josiah, but 3 months later was deposed by Neco, who imposed on Judah a heavy tribute (2 Ki. 23:31–33) and appointed Jehoiakim (or Eliakim), brother of Jehoahaz, to the throne (2 Ki. 23:34; 2 Ch. 36:2, 5). Jeremiah lamented Jehoahaz's deposition and exile to Egypt (22:10–12).

c. Jehoiakim

In this reign (607–597 BC) an event of great political significance occurred—the battle of Carchemish (Je. 46) in 605 BC. The Egyptians under Neco were crushed by the Chaldeans under Nebuchadrezzar at the battle of Carchemish, on the right-hand bank of the Euphrates NW of Aleppo, and at Hamath. Politically this event was pivotal because it marked the transference of the hegemony of the Middle East to Babylon. Therefore Carchemish also had considerable significance for Judah. Since all routes to the Egyptian border were now under Nebuchadrezzar's control, it was inevitable that the whole Middle East should come under his rule (Je. 25:15ff.). From that moment, therefore, the prophet advocated Judah's submission to Babylonian suzerainty. In 604 BC Nebuchadrezzar sacked the city of Ashkelon, against which Jeremiah (47:5–7) and Zephaniah (2:4–7) prophesy judgment. In Je. 36:9ff. a fast in Judah is proclaimed. This doubtedly points to an approaching national calamity; and indeed the date of Nebuchadrezzar's campaign against Ashkelon coincides with the date of this fast in Judah. Jeremiah anticipates that from Ashkelon Nebuchadrezzar will come against Judah; hence the fast and the proclamation of Jeremiah's message in Jerusalem. But Jeremiah's policy opposed Jehoiakim's domestic and foreign strategy. The king favoured idolatrous usages (2 Ki. 23:37), and his selfishness and vanity aggravated Judah's misfortunes (Je. 22:13–19). Jehoiakim had scant respect for the prophet's person (26:20–23) or message (26:9). His vacillating policy of alliance with Egypt, then with Babylon, was probably due to the fact that the outcome of the fighting between Babylon and Egypt in the year 601/600 BC was inconclusive. Three years later he rebelled against Babylon, but failure only brought him under the Babylonian yoke more completely, and this exacerbated Judah's anguish (2 Ki. 24:1f.). Jeremiah reprimanded the king, the prophets and the priests, and the hostility which this rebuke engendered is mirrored in his oracles. He was persecuted (12:6; 15:15–18), plotted against (11:18–23; 18:18), imprisoned (20:2), declared worthy of death (26:10f., 24; *cf.* vv. 20–23; 36:26). His prophecies in written form were destroyed (36:27). But in these depressing circumstances Jeremiah persisted in his ministry—interceding for Judah (11:14; 14:11; 17:16), expostulating with God (17:14–18; 18:18–23; 20:7–18), unmasking the time-serving prophets (23:9–40), predicting the destruction of the Temple (7:1–15) and nation (chs. 18f.), and lamenting the doom of his people (9:1; 13:17; 14:17). Eventually Jehoiakim's life ended violently in Jerusalem at the close of 598 BC, the 11th year of his reign, as Jeremiah had foretold (22:18; *cf.* 2 Ki. 24:1ff.). On the other hand, 2 Ch. 36:6f. speaks of Nebuchadrezzar's binding Jehoiakim in fetters to take him to Babylon. Dn. 1:1f. also speaks of Jehoiakim's exile in the 3rd year of his reign.

d. Jehoiachin

Jehoiachin (or Coniah, 22:24, 28, or Jeconiah, 24:1) succeeded Jehoiakim in 597 BC and reaped what his father had sown. This immature youth of 18 reigned only 3 months (2 Ki. 24:8). The rebellion of Jehoiachin's father compelled Nebuchadrezzar in the 7th year of his reign to besiege Jerusalem, and the youthful king of Judah 'went out' (2 Ki. 24:12), *i.e.* gave himself up. He, along with the majority of Judah's aristocracy, artisans and soldiers, was exiled to Babylon (as Je. 22:18f. implies and the Temple was plundered (2 Ki. 24:10–16). In the Babylonian Chronicle we now find for the first time confirmation of this information from an extra-biblical contemporary source. Jeremiah had already predicted Jehoiachin's fate (22:24–30). 36 years later, however, he was released by the son and successor of Nebuchadrezzar (2 Ki. 25:27–30).

e. Zedekiah

Zedekiah, the new appointee of

Nebuchadrezzar to the throne of Judah, was Josiah's youngest son (Je. 1:3) and uncle of Jehoiachin (2 Ki. 24:17; 2 Ch. 36:10). This OT account of Zedekiah's appointment by Nebuchadrezzar to succeed Jehoiachin is fully verified by the Babylonian Chronicle. His reign (597–587 BC) sealed Judah's doom (2 Ki. 24:19f.). He was weak and vacillating, and his officers of state were men of humble station. Having superseded the exiled aristocracy, they now looked upon them with contempt, but Jeremiah had his own convictions concerning the 'bad' and the 'good' figs (24:1ff.). It was to the latter that the prophet sent his famous letter (29:1ff.). But both in Babylon and Judah false prophets sought to have Jeremiah executed (28:1ff.; 29:24ff.). The main point at issue between them was the length of the captivity. Jeremiah foretold an exile of 70 years, while the false prophets argued that it would last only 2 years.

Jeremiah's main conflict with Zedekiah was over the question of rebellion against Nebuchadrezzar. A revolt was planned in the 4th year of the reign in conspiracy with neighbouring states which the prophet violently opposed (chs. 27f.). However, Zedekiah seems to have succeeded in allaying Nebuchadrezzar's suspicions by visiting Babylon the same year (51:59).

Finally, however, in the 7th or 8th year of his reign Zedekiah compromised himself irrevocably in the eyes of Nebuchadrezzar by entering into treasonable negotiations with Pharaoh Hophra. The die was cast, and in Zedekiah's 9th year (589) the Babylonians besieged Jerusalem for the second time. But before (21:1–10) and during the siege (34:1ff., 8ff.; 37:3ff., 17ff.; 38:14ff.) Jeremiah had only one message for Zedekiah—surrender to the Babylonians, for Jerusalem must fall into their hands. Jeremiah's interpretation of the battle of Carchemish 17 years earlier (605) was being fully vindicated. At one point during the siege, the Egyptian army's advance compelled the Babylonians to withdraw, but hopes that Jeremiah was mistaken were quickly disillusioned. His warning that the Babylonians would annihilate the Egyptians was soon fulfilled and the siege was immediately resumed (37:1–10). The perfidy of some Jews towards their slaves at this juncture roused Jeremiah's withering scorn and severest condemnation (34:8–22). Thanks to the cowardly vacillations of Zedekiah, the prophet was so rigorously maltreated by his enemies during the siege that he despaired of his life. Arrested on the charge of deserting to the enemy, he was thrown into a dungeon (37:11–16), but was later removed to a prison in the guard-court close to the palace (37:17–21). He was then accused of treason and thrown into a disused cistern, where he would have died but for the timely intervention of Ebed-melech. He was later transferred to the prison court (38:1–13), where the king secretly conferred with him (vv. 14–28).

During the last stages of the siege Jeremiah, in a great act of faith, bought the land belonging to his cousin in Anathoth (32:1–15). At this moment too he proclaimed promises of restoration (32:36–44; 33:1–26). To this period may be assigned his great prophecy of a new covenant (31:31ff.), ultimately fulfilled in Christ the Mediator of that covenant. But Judah's cup of iniquity was now full and in 587 judgment engulfed the doomed city of Jerusalem (ch. 39). Here also it is instructive to notice that the account of the captivity of Jerusalem in the Bab. Chronicle agrees in general with the OT account in 2 Ki. 24:10–17; 2 Ch. 36:17; Je. 52:28. The date of this event is 597 BC, the 7th year of Nebuchadrezzar's reign. Thus the destruction was in 587 BC, not 586 BC as has for so long been accepted.

Nebuchadrezzar treated Jeremiah kindly, and when he appointed Gedaliah governor of Judah Jeremiah joined him at Mizpah (40:1–6). The murder of Gedaliah soon followed (41:1ff.), and the remnant in Mizpah resolved to flee into Egypt in spite of the earnest protestations of Jeremiah, who, along with Baruch his secretary, was compelled to accompany them (42:1–43:7). The last scene in the aged Jeremiah's stormy ministry shows him at Tahpanhes in Egypt still unbowed. He prophesies the conquest of Egypt by Nebuchadrezzar (43:8–13) and rebukes the idolatrous worship of the Jews then residing in Egypt (44:1ff.). Of subsequent events in his life or the circumstances of his death nothing is known.

III. Jeremiah's personality

Jeremiah's personality is the most sharply etched of any of the OT prophets. Indeed, it is no exaggeration to say that in order to understand what the OT means by the term 'prophet' it is necessary to study the book of Jeremiah. Jeremiah's call, his vocation as a bearer of the word of God, the authority which this communicated to him, the manner in which the word was revealed to him, his clear-cut distinctions between the true prophet and the false, his message and the agonizing dilemmas in which his fidelity to it entangled him—all are delineated in Jeremiah's oracles with an authority that is irresistible. This is because of the correlation between the prophet's spiritual and emotional experience and his prophetic ministry.

His emotions are vividly exhibited even in his discourses. From the content of his preaching it is plain that Jeremiah was a man of marked contrasts. He was at once gentle and tenacious, affectionate and inflexible. In him the frailties of the flesh contended with the energies of the spirit. The natural aspirations of youth were to the youthful prophet denied. He insisted on repentance from a people who were incapable of contrition. He unmasked the nation's sins and broadcast its judgment knowing that it would end in futility. Those whom he loved hated him. A loyal patriot, he was branded a traitor. This prophet of undying hope had to exhibit the fallacy of his people's hope. This priestly intercessor was commanded to intercede no more. This lover of Judah was by Judah maligned.

It is impossible to plumb the depths of grief into which Jeremiah was plunged. Despairing of comfort (8:18, 21), he desired to dissolve in tears for doomed Judah (9:1; 13:17) and abandon her to her self-inflicted fate (9:2). Convinced of ultimate failure, he cursed the day he was born (15:10; 20:14–18), accused God of having wronged him (20:7a), complained of the ignominy that had befallen him (20:7b–10), invoked imprecations upon his tormentors (18:18, 21–23). It is in this sense that the emotional, highly-strung Jeremiah was a tragic figure. The tragedy of his life springs from the conflicts which raged within and around him—his higher self wrestling with the lower, courage conflicting with cowardice, certain triumph struggling with apparent defeat, a determination to abandon his calling defeated by an inability to evade it (*cf.* 5:14; 15:16,

19–21 with 6:11; 20:9, 11; 23:29). But these fierce internal conflicts and the ignominy in which his calling involved him (15:17f.; 16:2, 5, 8) compelled him to find in God a refuge. Thus the OT ideal of communion with God comes to its finest expression in Jeremiah. And it was in this fellowship with God that Jeremiah was able finally to withstand the erosive effects of timidity, anguish, helplessness, hostility, loneliness, despair, misunderstanding and failure.

IV. His message

a. Jeremiah's concept of God

God is Creator and sovereign Lord who governs all things in heaven and earth (27:5; 28:23f.; 5:22, 24; 10:12f.). While the gods of the nations are nonentities (10:14f.; 14:22), Israel's God disposes all things according to his will (18:5–10; 25:15–38; 27:6–8). He knows the hearts of men (17:5–10) and is the fountain of life to all who trust in him (2:13; 17:13). He loves his people tenderly (2:2; 31:1–3), but demands their obedience and allegiance (7:1–15). Sacrifices to pagan gods (7:30f.; 19:5) and oblations offered to him by a disobedient people (6:20; 7:21f.; 14:12) are alike abominations to him.

b. Jeremiah and idolatry

From the outset the prophet was a proclaimer of judgment. The sinfulness of Judah made this inevitable. The particular evil against which Jeremiah inveighed was idolatry. His many references to the worship of heathen deities confirm that the practice was widespread and diverse. Baal, Moloch and the queen of heaven are mentioned. Idols were found in the Temple (32:34), and in the vicinity of Jerusalem children were sacrificed to Baal and Moloch (*cf.* 7:31; 19:5; 32:35). Josiah had suppressed the idolatrous practices which his grandfather Manasseh had promoted, but the nation had apostatized after Josiah's death.

c. Jeremiah and immorality

Throughout the OT immorality was a concomitant of idolatry. This principle is powerfully exemplified in Jeremiah's idolatrous generation (5:1–9; 7:3–11; 23:10–14). Inescapably moral corruption followed the elimination of the fear of God and reverence for his law. Profligacy and improbity were common even among the priests and prophets (5:30f.; 6:13–15; 14:14). Instead of arresting immorality, they contributed to its spread. Ironically, idolatrous and immoral Judah was still zealously religious! This explains Jeremiah's oft-reiterated contention that before God the moral law takes precedence over the ceremonial. This principle Jeremiah applies to Judah's reverence for the ark (3:16), the tablets of the Torah (31:31f.), the covenant sign of circumcision (4:4; 6:10; 9:26), the Temple (7:4, 10f.; 11:15; 17:3; 26:6, 9, 12; 27:16) and the sacrificial system (6:20; 7:21f.; 11:15; 14:12).

d. Jeremiah and judgment

Naturally, then, the inevitability of judgment was prominent in Jeremiah's message. Judah's punishment at the hands of God took many forms, such as drought and famine (5:24; 14:1–6) and invasion by a foreign power (1:13–16; 4:11–22; 5:15–19; 6:1–15, *etc.*). And inexorably the great day of doom dawned when God's instrument for punishing apostate Judah appeared (25:9; 52:1–30). The history of the background against which these oracles of judgment should be set has become much clearer with the publication of *Chronicles of Chaldaean Kings* (*626–556* BC), to which reference has already been made. It describes a number of international events which took place in Jeremiah's lifetime, and hints of these are found in his oracles against the foreign nations. Doubtless his oracles against the nations in ch. 25 were written under the influence of Nebuchadrezzar's first advance W (Je. 25:1; *cf.* v. 9). Ch. 46 opens with a reference to the battle of Carchemish in 605. Then comes an oracle relating to Nebuchadrezzar's campaign against Egypt (46:13–26). The Bab. Chronicle also provides a factual basis for Jeremiah's oracles against Kedar and Hazor (49:28–33) and Elam (49:34–39). It also relates how Nebuchadrezzar in 599 made raids against the Arab tribes (*cf.* Je. 49:29, 32), while in 596 he campaigned against Elam. Hitherto this oracle has had no historical basis. See further for the light shed by the Bab. Chronicle on the dating and authenticity of the oracles in Jeremiah 46–51 in *JBL* 75, 1956, pp. 282f.

e. Jeremiah and the false prophets

Jeremiah's elevated conception of, and total committal to, his call evoked within him an uncompromising antagonism towards the professional prophets and priests, and they in turn were his sworn enemies. Jeremiah's major polemic with the priests was over their policy of making gain of their office and their contention that the Jerusalem Temple would never fall to the Babylonians (6:13; 18:18; 29:25–32, *etc.*). The false prophets confirmed the duped people of Judah in this facile optimism (8:10–17; 14:14–18; 23:9–40, *etc.*).

f. Jeremiah's hope

By contrast Jeremiah was an uncompromising preacher of judgment. However, his announcement of judgment was shot through and through with hope. Judah's exile in Babylon would not last for ever (25:11; 29:10). Indeed, Babylon herself would be overthrown (50f.). This word of hope concerning Judah's survival of judgment was present in Jeremiah's message from the start (3:14–25; 12:14–17), but as the situation became more ominous Jeremiah's confidence shone brighter (23:1–8; 30–33). And it was this hope that gave birth to his great act of faith in the darkest days (32:1–15).

g. Jeremiah and Judah's religion

Jeremiah could therefore anticipate the destruction of the Temple, the fall of the Davidic dynasty, the cessation of the sacrificial system and the ministry of the priesthood with perfect equanimity. He even proclaimed that the covenant sign of circumcision was largely meaningless without the circumcision of the heart (4:4; 9:26, *cf.* 6:10). Confidence in Temple, sacrifice, priesthood, was vain unless accompanied by a change of heart (7:4–15, 21–26). Even the ark of the covenant would be dispensed with (3:16). Knowledge of the law without obedience to the law was valueless (2:8; 5:13, 30f.; 8:8). Jeremiah therefore sees the necessity of having the law written not on stone but on the heart, thus prompting all to spontaneous and perfect obedience (31:31–34; 32:40). The passing away of the outward symbols of the covenant signified not the end of the covenant but its renewal in a more glorious form (33:14–26).

h. Jeremiah and the ideal future

Thus Jeremiah looks far beyond Judah's return from exile and the resumption of life in Palestine (30:17–22; 32:15, 44; 33:9–13). In the ideal future Samaria will have a part (3:18; 31:4–9), abundance will prevail (31:12–14), Jerusalem will be holy unto the Lord (31:23, 38–40), and be named 'the Lord is our righteousness' (33:16). Its inhabitants will return to the Lord penitently (3:22–25; 31:18–20) and with their whole heart (24:7). God will forgive them (31:34b), put his fear within them (32:37–40), establish the rule of the Messianic Prince over them (23:5f.) and admit the Gentile nations to a share of the blessing (16:19; 3:17; 30:9).

V. His oracles

The oracles in Jeremiah's book are not presented to the reader in chronological sequence. His ministry was spread over five reigns, and following C. Lattey, the chapters may be arranged in this order:
(i) Josiah: chs. 1–20, except 12:7–13:27. (ii) Jehoahaz: nothing.
(iii) Jehoiakim: chs. 26; 22–23; 25; 35–36; 45; 33; 12:7–13:27.
(iv) Jehoiachin: chs. 13:18f.; 20:24–30; 52:31–34, and see discussions on Jehoiachin's reign of 3 months in *JBL* 75, 1956, pp. 277–282; and *IEJ* 6, 4, 1956. (v) Zedekiah: warnings: chs. 24; 29; 27–28; 51:59–60; promises of restoration: chs. 30–33; the siege: chs. 21; 34; 37–39.
(vi) Following the fall of Jerusalem: chs. 40–44. (vii) Prophecies against the nations: chs. 46–51. (viii) A historical appendix: ch. 52.

Since, then, the chapters are not arranged chronologically, probably their subject-matter has determined their present order. Ch. 36 would seem to confirm this suggestion. When Jeremiah's oracles were first committed to writing in the 4th year of Jehoiakim (604 BC) they covered a period of 23 years—from the 13th year of Josiah (626 BC) until 604 BC. These oracles Jehoiakim destroyed in the 5th year of his reign, but Baruch rewrote them at Jeremiah's dictation, and 'many similar words were added to them' (36:32). What these additions were is uncertain, as is also the contents of the original roll which Jehoiakim destroyed. But clearly the original oracles and the additions formed the nucleus of the book of Jeremiah as it has come down to us; although how the whole was given its final form can only be conjectured. But the disorderly arrangement of the oracles strengthens the conviction that they are the words Jeremiah's inspired lips uttered and were then put together during days of danger and turmoil.

The question of the order of Jeremiah's oracles is also bound up with the relation between the *MT* and LXX text of his book. The Gk. translation deviates from the Heb. text in two respects. (i) It is shorter than the Heb. text by approximately one-eighth (*i.e.* about 2,700 words). This is the more remarkable when it is recalled that on the whole the text of the LXX corresponds fairly closely to the *MT*. The main exceptions are Jeremiah, Job and Daniel. (ii) In the LXX the oracles against the foreign nations (46–51) are placed after 25:13, and their sequence is also altered. These divergences go back to Origen's time, but it is difficult to believe that the Heb. and Gk. texts represent two different recensions of the book of Jeremiah. Because of Jeremiah's prophetic stature and spiritual calibre, these oracles in his book must have existed from a very early date, since no text which differed so radically from the received text as the Gk. differs from the Heb. would have been able to gain a foothold if it had been produced centuries after Jeremiah's death.

In the debate on the superiority of one text to the other those who favour the LXX version argue that it gives the oracles against the foreign nations a more natural context, and that some of the omissions (*e.g.* 29:16–20; 33:14–26; 39:4–13; 52; 28–33, *etc.*) could not have been accidental. But the foregoing references to the Bab. Chronicle have shown how it now enables us to recreate the historical background against which some of these oracles have to be set, especially those against Kedar, Hazor, Elam and the Arabs. Those who support the claims of the Heb. text emphasize 'the arbitrary character of the renderings' (Streane), which according to Graf makes it 'altogether impossible to give to this new edition—for one can scarcely call it a translation—any critical authority'. The impression too is that the omissions are not motivated by scholarly interests. And the fact remains that the men of the 'great synagogue' who did so much in determining the Canon of the OT preferred the Heb. text to the Gk. version.

VI. Conclusion

In summarizing the greatness of Jeremiah, several things should be stressed. He recognized that Josiah's reforms were in reality a retrograde movement because they threatened to undo the work of the prophets. Reformation in worship without reformation of heart was useless. He also perceived that religion in Judah would continue even though the Temple and Jerusalem were destroyed. In his famous letter to the exiles in Babylon (ch. 29) he affirmed that in a pagan land Jews could still worship God although denied the ministry of priesthood and the service of sacrifice. Indeed, they could be closer to God in Babylon than were their brethren in Jerusalem, who made the outward trappings of religion a substitute for inward faith.

He saw too that, since religion was essentially a moral and spiritual relation with God (31:31–34), its demands must also be moral and spiritual. With this insight goes also that of the importance of the individual. Individual responsibility was to be the foundation of character and spiritual life. And individuals were to be punished for their own sins, not for those of their fathers. Jeremiah's insight into the importance of the individual was important also because it proved to be a decisive step forward in men's search for a basis for the hope of immortality.

It was no exaggeration on Adam Welch's part, then, when he made Jeremiah the connecting link between Hosea and our Lord. It is significant that Jeremiah borrowed from Hosea and that Christ quotes most frequently from both. It was pre-eminently in the prophecy of the new covenant that Jeremiah spiritualized and individualized religion and insisted upon the primacy of the individual's relation with God. The new law was to be a spiritual bond between God and the individual, a law written on each heart and obeyed in love and loyalty. All this was finally fulfilled in the incarnation of Christ and the gospel he came to proclaim. He was the righteous Branch. He it was who spelt out the name, 'The Lord is our righteousness'.

BIBLIOGRAPHY. A. Bentzen, *IOT*, 1948; A. B. Davidson, 'Jeremiah' in *HDB*; A. F. Kirkpatrick, *The Doctrine of the Prophets*, 1906; J. Skinner, *Prophecy and Religion*, 1922; J. G. S. S. Thomson, *The Old Testament View of Revelation*, 1960, ch. 4; A. Condamin, *Le Livre de Jérémie*, 1920; C. Von Orelli, *The Prophecies of Jeremiah*³, 1905; A. C. Welch, *Jeremiah*, 1928; J. P. Hyatt, *IB*, 5, 1956; D. J. Wiseman, *Chronicles of Chaldaean Kings*

(*626–556 BC*), 1956; H. L. Ellison, articles in *EQ* 31–40, 1959–68; Commentaries by J. Bright, 1965; R. K. Harrison, *TOTC*, 1973.

J.G.S.S.T.

JEREMOTH
See Naphtali, Part 2.

Excavations at Jericho (Trench I) showing the pre-pottery Neolithic B levels at bottom, with the 'Mount of temptation' in the background. (JEF)

JERICHO.

I. Name

The original meaning of the name Jericho is open to doubt. It is simplest to take Heb. *y*^{e}*rîḥô* as from the same root as *yārēaḥ*, 'moon', and to connect it with the early W Semitic moon-god *Yariḥ* or *Yeraḥ*. *Cf.* remarks by Albright in *Archaeology and the Religion of Israel*, 1953 edn., pp. 83, 91–92, 197 note 36, and in *AASOR* 6, 1926, pp. 73–74. Some suggest *rwḥ*, 'fragrant place' (*BDB*, p. 437b, after Gesenius), or as 'founded by (deity) Ḥô' (*PEQ* 77, 1945, p. 13), but this is improbable.

II. Sites

OT Jericho is generally identified with the present mound of Tell es-Sultan *c.* 16 km NW of the present mouth of the Jordan at the Dead Sea, 2 km NW of er-Riḥa village (modern Jericho), and about 27 km ENE of Jerusalem. The imposing, pear-shaped mound is about 400 m long from N to S and roughly 200 m wide at the broad N end, and some 20 m thick. Herodian and NT Jericho is represented by the mounds of Tulul Abu el-'Alayiq, 2 km W of modern er-Riḥa, and so is S of OT Jericho. The mountains of Judaea rise abruptly from the plains of Jericho a little distance to the W.

III. History

a. Before Joshua

(i) *Beginnings.* The story of Jericho is virtually a précis of the whole archaeological history of Palestine between *c.* 8000 and *c.* 1200 BC. (For the special abbreviations used here, see bibliography at the end of this article.) Every settlement at Jericho has owed its existence to the fine perennial spring there and the 'oasis' which it waters (*DUJ*, pl. 1); in the OT Jericho is sometimes called 'the city of palm trees' (Dt. 34:3). Already *c.* 9600/7700 BC, food-gathering hunters may have had a shrine there, and Palestine's earliest-known agriculturists built huts by the spring (*AHL*, pp. 41–43; pl. 5A). Early in the 8th millennium BC (Carbon-14 date), the oldest *town* of Jericho was built with a stone revetment-wall that included at least one tower (with built-in stairway) and round houses. Subsequently, spacious rectangular houses became fashionable and skulls of venerated ancestors (?) were embodied in clay-moulded portrait heads of remarkable realism (*DUJ*, pp. 67–73 and pls. 25, 29–30, or *AHL*, pp. 43–47 and pl. 7, for 'prepottery Neolithic, phase A'; *DUJ*, pp. 51–67 and pls. 20–22, or *AHL*, pp. 47–57, 60 and pls. 13ff., for 'phase B'). In the 5th and 4th millennia BC later Jericho citizens learnt to make pottery, but eventually abandoned the place ('Pottery Neolithic A and B', 'Jericho IX and VIII' of older books, *DUJ*, pp. 79–94, *AHL*, pp. 60–70). Ancient Jericho is currently the primary source of information on the earliest settled life of Palestine; *cf.* also *W*, chs. 2–4 and *GSJ*, pp. 55–72.

(ii) *Early historical period.* From *c.* 3200 BC Jericho was again inhabited as a walled and towered town of the Early Bronze Age, when towns famous later (*e.g.* Megiddo) were first founded, contemporary with Egypt's Pyramid Age and the Sumerian civilization in Mesopotamia (*DUJ*, pp. 167–185; *AHL*, pp. 101–134; *W*, ch. 5; *GSJ*, pp. 75–88, cities I and II). But *c.* 2300 BC Jericho perished violently at the hands of uncultured newcomers who eventually resettled the site (Albright's Middle Bronze Age I; K. M. Kenyon's Intermediate Early/Middle Bronze Age, *cf. DUJ*, pp. 186–209; *AHL*, pp. 135–161). These coalesced with the Canaanites of the Middle Bronze Age proper (*c.* 1900–1600/1550 BC). Biblically this was the period of Abraham, Isaac and Jacob; the remains from contemporary Jericho throw a vivid light on the daily life of Abraham's Canaanite/Amorite town-dwelling neighbours. The tombs have preserved more

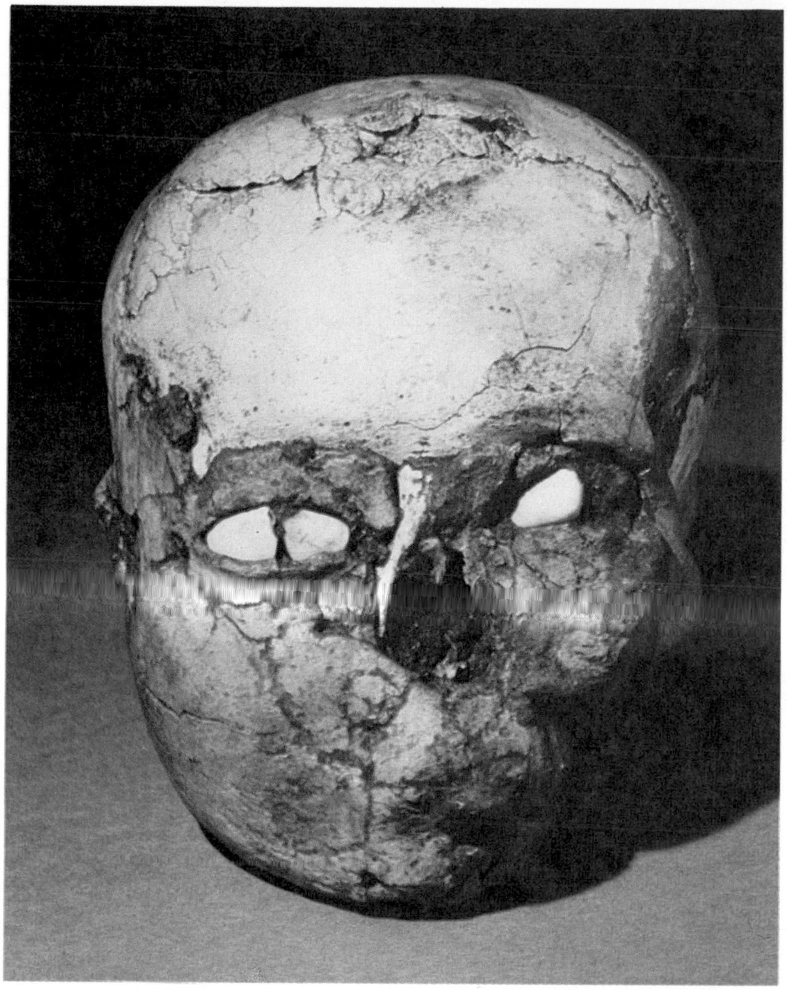

One of several plastered and painted skulls found at Jericho, probably connected with early ancestor worship. (BM)

than the badly-denuded town buildings. Splendid pottery, wooden three- and four-legged tables, stools and beds, trinket-boxes of bone inlay, basketry, platters of fruit and joints of meat, metal daggers and circlets—all have been preserved by peculiar atmospheric conditions (*DUJ*, pp. 210–232 [city], 233–255 [tombs]; *AHL*, pp. 162–194; *GSJ*, pp. 91–108). For restoration of a Jericho house-interior, see *DUJ*, endpapers. For reconstructions of the walled city on its mound, see *Illustrated London News*, 19 May 1956, pp. 554–555; *cf. AHL*, p. 188, fig. 45.

b. Jericho and the Old Testament

(i) *Joshua's invasion.* After *c.* 1600 BC Jericho was violently destroyed, probably by Egypt's 18th Dynasty imperial pharaohs. After this the only (Late Bronze) occupation found at Jericho dates mainly between *c.* 1400 and 1325 BC; from the 13th century BC, the date of the Israelite conquest (* CHRONOLOGY OF OT), virtually nothing is known (*DUJ*, pp. 259–263; *AHL*, pp. 197–198, 209–211). Garstang's 'Late Bronze Age' walls (*GSJ*, ch. 7) actually date from the Early Bronze Age, over 1,000 years before Joshua, because of the associated Early Bronze remains, and they are overlaid by Middle Bronze mater-

Simplified cross-section of K. M. Kenyon's main excavation at Jericho, showing the extent of erosion of the Middle Bronze Age and later levels, from the top of the mound.

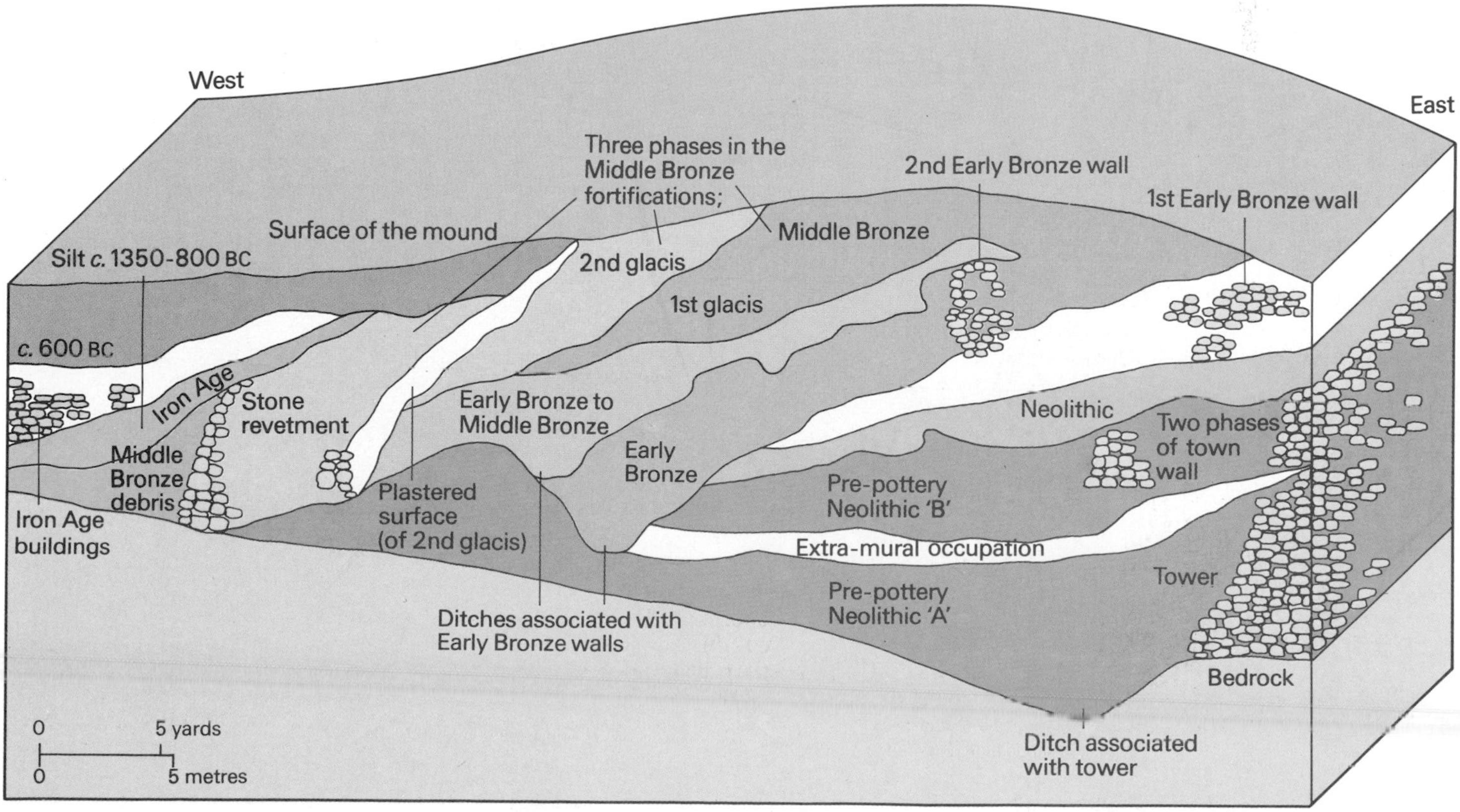

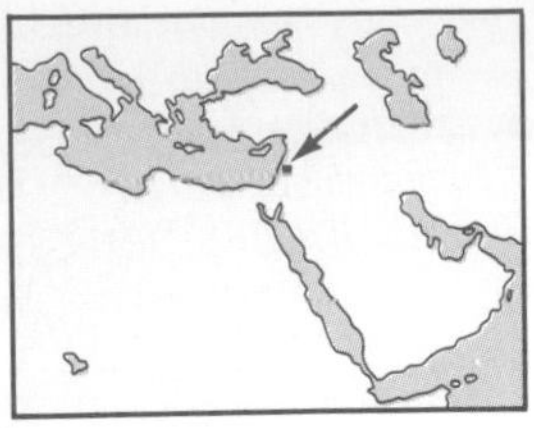

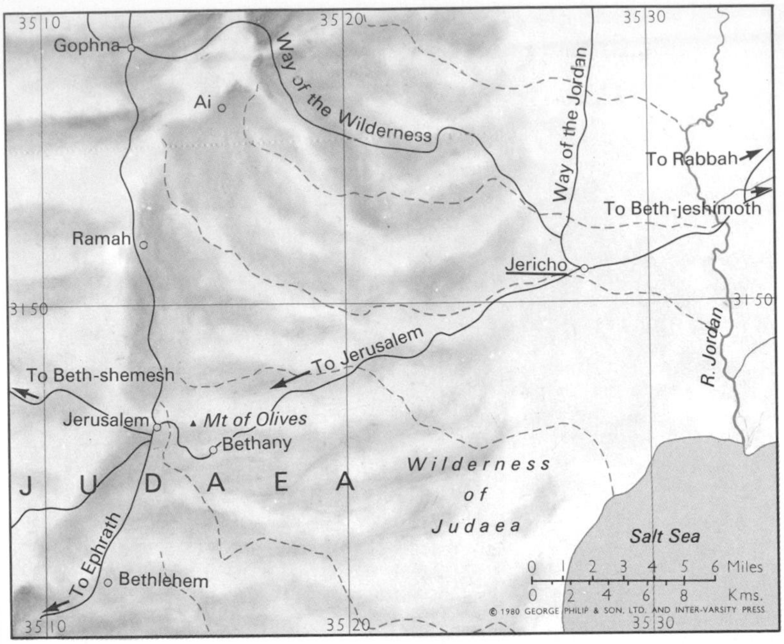

The highways running through Jericho.

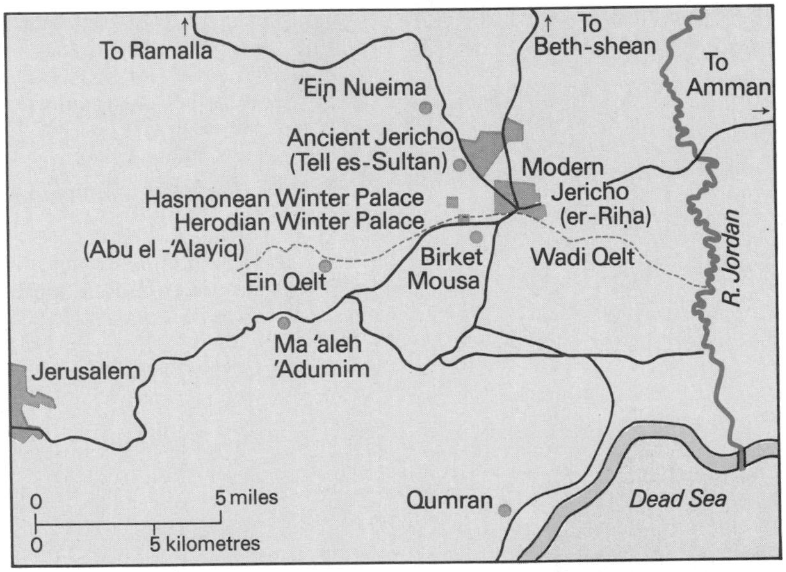

Jericho and adjacent ancient sites.

Jericho seen from Tulul Abu el-'Alayiq, site of the magnificent Hasmonaean and Herodian winter palace complexes. (JPK)

ial, only subsequently identified in Miss Kenyon's excavations (*e.g. DUJ*, pp. 170–171, 176–177, and especially 181). It is possible that in Joshua's day (13th century BC) there was a small town on the E part of the mound, later wholly eroded away. Such a possibility is not just a 'harmonistic' or heuristic view, but one suggested by the evidence of considerable erosion of the older settlements at Jericho. The tombs conclusively prove the importance of Middle Bronze Age Jericho (patriarchal period), although on the city mound most of the Middle Bronze town—and even much of the Early Bronze one before it—was eroded away between *c.* 1600 and *c.* 1400 BC (*cf. DUJ*, pp. 170–171, and also 45, 93, 259–260, 262–263). When so much damage was done by the elements in barely 200 years it is easy to see how much havoc natural erosion must have wrought on the deserted mound in the 400 years that separated Joshua from Jericho's refounding by Hiel the Bethelite (1 Ki. 16:34) in Ahab's reign. It seems highly likely that the washed-out remains of the last Late Bronze Age city are now lost under the modern road and cultivated land along the E side of the town mound, as the main slope of the mound is from W down to E. It remains highly doubtful whether excavation here (even if allowed) would yield much now. The narrative of Jos. 3–8 within which the fall of Jericho is recounted is known to reflect faithfully conditions in, and topography of, the area, while Joshua's generalship is recounted in a realistic manner. On terrain, *cf.* J. Garstang, *Joshua-Judges*, 1931, pp. 135–148 (his earth-tremors, providentially sent, remain a valid suggestion, even though his 'Late Bronze' (actually Early Bronze) walls do not now count as direct evidence for Joshua's day). On Joshua's generalship, *cf.* Garstang, *op. cit.*, pp. 149–161, and Y. Kaufmann, *The Biblical Account of the Conquest of Palestine*, 1953, pp. 91–97.

(ii) *From Joshua to Nehemiah.* For centuries no attempt was made to rebuild the town-mound of Jericho in awe of Joshua's curse (Jos. 6:26), but the spring and oasis were still frequented, perhaps supporting a hamlet there. In the time of the judges, Eglon king of Moab temporarily occupied the oasis (Jdg. 3:13) and David's envoys tarried there after being outraged by Hanun of Ammon (2 Sa. 10:5; 1 Ch. 19:5); the 'blockhouse' may have been a guard-post in this period (10th century BC: so Albright and Wright, cited by Tushingham, *BA* 16, 1953, p. 67). Then in Ahab's reign (*c.* 874/3–853 BC) Hiel the Bethelite refounded Jericho proper and finally fulfilled the ancient curse in the loss of his eldest and youngest sons (1 Ki. 16:34). This humble Iron Age Jericho was that of Elijah and Elisha (2 Ki. 2:4–5, 18–22), and it was in the plains of Jericho that the Babylonians captured Zedekiah, last king of Judah (2 Ki. 25:5; 2 Ch. 28:15; Je. 39:5; 52:8). The remains of this Jericho (9th–6th centuries BC) are very fragmentary (erosion again to blame), but quite definite: buildings, pottery and tombs; probably the Babylonians destroyed the place in 587 BC (see *BA* 16, 1953, pp. 66–67; *PEQ* 85, 1953, pp. 91, 95; *DUJ*, pp. 263–264). After the Exile, a modest Jericho still existed in Persian times. Some 345 Jerichoans returned to Judaea with Zerubbabel (Ezr. 2:34; Ne. 7:36), and their descendants in Jericho helped with repairing Jerusalem's walls in 445 BC under Nehemiah (Ne. 3:2); a pottery jar-stamp (*c.* 4th century BC) 'belonging to Hagar (daughter of) Uriah' is the last memento of OT Jericho (Hammond, *PEQ* 89, 1957, pp. 68–69, with pl. 16, corrected in *BASOR* 147, 1957, pp. 37–39; *cf.* also Albright, *BASOR* 148, 1957, pp. 28–30).

c. New Testament Jericho

In NT times, the town of Jericho was sited S of the old mound. In that region, Herod the Great (40/37–4 BC) and his successors built a winter palace with ornamental gardens, near the famous palm and balsam groves that yielded lucrative revenues. Fragmentary ruins that may be connected with these great buildings have been excavated. See Kelso and Baramki, 'Excavations at New Testament Jericho' in *AASOR* 29/30, 1955, and *BA* 14, 1951, pp. 33–43; Pritchard, *The Excavation at Herodian Jericho* in *AASOR* 32/33, 1958, and *BASOR* 123, 1951, pp. 8–17. Herod brought water by aqueduct from the Wadi Qilt (Perowne, *Life and Times of Herod the Great*, 1956, plates opposite pp. 96–97).

The environs of NT Jericho witnessed Christ's healing of blind men, including Bartimaeus (Mt. 20:29; Mk. 10:46; Lk. 18:35). Zacchaeus (Lk. 19:1) was not the only wealthy Jew who had his home in this fashionable district. The immortal story of the good Samaritan is set on the narrow, bandit-infested road from Jerusalem down to Jericho (Lk. 10:30–37).

IV. Bibliography

Sir Charles Warren sank shafts at Jericho in about 1868 with little result. The first scientific excavation there (1907–9) was by Sellin and Watzinger (*Jericho*, 1913), but they could not date their finds properly. Apart from his errors over 'Joshua's Jericho' (see above), Garstang in 1930–6 put the archaeology of the site on a sound basis. See J. and J. B. E. Garstang, *The Story of Jericho*, 1948 (*GSJ*). Detailed preliminary reports are in *Liverpool Annals of Archaeology and Anthropology* 19, 1932, to 23, 1936, and in *PEQ* for the same years. Miss Kenyon reviewed Garstang's results in *PEQ* 83, 1951, pp. 101–138. Further older bibliography is in Barrois, *Manuel d'Archéologie Biblique*, 1, 1939, pp. 61, 63.

Detailed preliminary reports of Miss Kenyon's excavations from 1952 to 1958 are in *PEQ* 84, 1952, to 92, 1960; *BASOR* 127, 1952, pp. 5–16; *BA* 16, 1953, pp. 45–67, and 17, 1954, pp. 98–104. For an instructive (and humorous) general account, see *W* = M. Wheeler, *The Walls of Jericho*, 1956 (paperback, 1960). Best detailed over-all account is *DUJ* = K. M. Kenyon, *Digging Up Jericho*, 1957 (fully illustrated), supplemented for the earliest periods by *AHL* = K. M. Kenyon, *Archaeology in the Holy Land*, 1960. The first volume of the definitive publication is K. M. Kenyon and others, *Jericho I*, 1960 (on tombs). General background and a summary in G. L. Harding, *The Antiquities of Jordan*, 1960, pp. 164–174. For NT Jericho, see above (**III.** *c*) and good background by L. Mowry, *BA* 15, 1952, pp. 25–42. Over-all bibliography, *cf.* E. K. Vogel, *Bibliography of Holy Land Sites*, 1974, pp. 42–44; survey, *cf. EAEHL*, 2, pp. 550–575.

K.A.K.

JEROBOAM (probably 'may the people increase'; possibly 'may he contend for the people', *i.e.* against Rehoboam's oppressions).

1. First king of Israel (*c.* 931–910 BC; 1 Ki. 11:26–14:20; 2 Ch. 10:2–12:20). Jeroboam, son of Nebat, seems to have been a wealthy land owner (*gibbôr ḥayil*, 1 Ki. 11:28), able to equip himself and others for war, despite the fact that his mother was a widow. *Solomon, building the Millo, placed Jeroboam, an Ephraimite, in charge of the work-force of the N tribes. The king's oppressive practices led Jeroboam to foment a revolt, resulting in his exile to Egypt until Solomon's death. The LXX contains an unreliable midrash (based partly on Hadad's experiences, 1 Ki. 11:14–22) which attempts to complete the sketchy biblical picture of Jeroboam's flight. His friendship with *Shishak was short-lived, for the pharaoh's subsequent invasion (*c.* 925 BC) proved costly to both Judah and Israel (including the destruction, as archaeological evidence indicates, of Gezer, Taanach, Megiddo, Beth-shean, *et al.*). Rehoboam's rash refusal to initiate a more clement policy than his father's brought the fulfilment of Ahijah's prophecy (1 Ki. 12:29ff.): the kingdom was rent asunder. Benjamin alone remained loyal to Judah and became a battleground for a series of border skirmishes between the two kings (1 Ki. 14:30). The conflict with Judah (1 Ki. 15:6–7; 2 Ch. 13:2–20) along with repeated pressures from Damascus and the Philistine cities, prompted Jeroboam to fortify key cities like Shechem, Penuel and Tirzah, which had served in turn as his capitals (1 Ki. 12:25; 14:17).

Jeroboam incurred divine wrath by building, in Dan and Bethel, shrines that rivalled the Jerusalem Temple and were staffed by a newly formed, non-levitical priesthood.

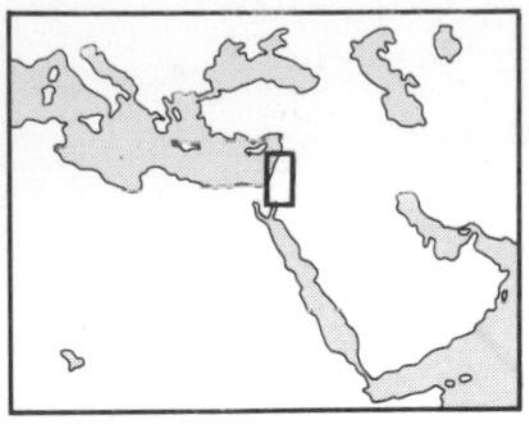

Israel and Judah in the reign of Jeroboam II.

The date of the Feast of Tabernacles was changed in the process (1 Ki. 12:31–32). The infamous calves were probably not representations of deity but pedestals on which the invisible Yahweh was supposed to stand (*cf.* W. F. Albright, *From the Stone Age to Christianity*², 1957, pp. 299–301). They threatened the covenant faith by encouraging a syncretism of Yahweh worship with the fertility cult of Baal and thus drew prophetic rebuke (*e.g.* the man of God, 1 Ki. 13:1ff.; Ahijah, 1 Ki. 14:14–16). Jeroboam's ascent to the throne by popular choice rather than hereditary right doomed the N kingdom to dynastic instability from the beginning. His royal cult set the pattern for his successors, who are customarily evaluated as perpetuating his sins (*e.g.* 1 Ki. 16:26).

Bibliography. M. Aberbach, L. Smolar, in *IDBS*, 1976, pp. 473–475; J. Bright, *A History of Israel*², 1972, pp. 226–235; J. Gray, *1 and 2 Kings*², 1970; *EJ*, 9, cols. 1371–1374; M. Noth, *The History of Israel*², 1960, pp. 225ff.; M. Haran, *VT* 17, 1967, pp. 266ff., 325ff.

2. Jeroboam II (*c.* 793–753 BC) was the 4th king of Jehu's dynasty and one of Israel's most illustrious rulers (2 Ki. 14:23–29). Co-regent with his father for a decade, Jeroboam II carried on Jehoash's policies of aggressive expansion. Aided by Adad-nirari's campaigns (805–802 BC) which broke the back of the Aramaean kingdom and by the Assyr. preoccupation with Armenia, he was able to restore Israel's boundaries virtually to their Solomonic scope and thus fulfil Jonah's prophecy (2 Ki. 14:25).

Jeroboam's administrative skills combined with comparative freedom from foreign attack to bring unparalleled economic prosperity. Excavations in *Samaria, including the discovery of the Samaritan ostraca, have demonstrated the grandeur of Jeroboam's fortress city together with the luxury and false worship which vexed Amos' righteous soul (*e.g.* Am. 6:1–7; 5:26; 8:14). Extreme wealth and poverty (Am. 2:6–7), empty religious ritual (Am. 5:21–24; 7:10–17) and false security (Am. 6:1–8) are among the characteristics of Jeroboam's lengthy reign. Amos' gloomy prophecy (7:9) was verified when Shallum's successful *coup* against Zechariah (whose name shows that Jeroboam retained some regard for Yahweh, 2 Ki. 15:8–12) wrote *finis* to Jehu's house. See J. Bright, *op. cit.*, pp. 254–256; *EJ*, 9, cols. 1374–1375; M. F. Unger, *Israel and the Arameans of Damascus*, 1957, pp. 89–95. D.A.H.

JERUBBAAL
See Gideon, Part 1.

JERUEL (Heb. *yᵉrû'ēl*, 'founded by El'; LXX 'Jeriel'). Mentioned by the prophet Jahaziel as the wilderness where Jehoshaphat would meet and conquer the Moabites and Ammonites (2 Ch. 20:16). Possibly identical with, or a part of, the wilderness of *Tekoa, the country extending from the W shores of the Dead Sea N of En-gedi. J.D.D.

JERUSALEM.

I. Introduction and general description

Jerusalem is one of the world's famous cities. Under that name, it dates from at least the 3rd millennium BC; and today is considered sacred by the adherents of the three great monotheistic faiths, Judaism, Christianity and Islam. The city is set high in the hills of Judah, about 50 km from the Mediterranean, and over 30 km W of the N end of

A seal inscribed 'belonging to Shema, servant of Jeroboam' (lšm' 'bd yrbm), *probably Jeroboam II (793–753* BC*). The roaring lion was used as a symbol for Judah. Length 3·8 cm. Megiddo.* (IM)

the Dead Sea. It rests on a none-too-level plateau, which slopes noticeably towards the SE. To the E lies the ridge of Olivet. Access to the city on all sides except the N is hampered by three deep ravines, which join in the Siloam Valley, near the well Bir Eyyub, SE of the city. The E valley is Kidron; the W is now called the Wadi al-Rababi, and is probably to be equated with the Valley of Hinnom; and the third cuts the city in half before it runs S, and slightly E, to meet the other two. This latter ravine is not mentioned or named in Scripture (although Maktesh, Zp. 1:11, may well have been the name of part of it), so it is usually referred to as the Tyropoeon Valley, *i.e.*, the Valley of the Cheesemakers, after Josephus.

Eminences rise each side of the Tyropoeon Valley, and the city can at once be divided into W and E halves. Ignoring lesser heights, we may subdivide each of these two sections into N and S hills. When considering the growth and development of the city (see **IV**) it will be important to visualize these details. In discussing the respective heights and depths of these hills and valleys, it must be realized that they have changed considerably over the centuries. This is inevitable in any city continuously inhabited for centuries, and particularly when periodic destructions have taken place. Layer after layer of rubble and debris piles up, amounting here and there to more than 30 m in parts of Jerusalem. In the case of Jerusalem there is also the factor that deliberate attempts have been made at various periods to fill in valleys (especially the Tyropoeon) and diminish hills.

Jerusalem's water-supply has always presented problems. Apart from Bir Eyyub, the well mentioned above, there is only the Virgin's Spring, which is connected by an aqueduct with the Pool of Siloam. There are, and have been, other reservoirs, of course, such as Bethesda in NT times and Mamilla Pool today, but they all depend on the rains or else on aqueducts to fill them. Bir Eyyub and the Virgin's Spring are in all probability the biblical En-rogel and Gihon respectively. Bir Eyyub lies SE of the city, at the junction of the three ravines mentioned above. The Virgin's Spring is due N of Bir Eyyub, E and a little S of the Temple area. Thus it is evident that only the SE part of Jerusalem has a reliable water supply. (See A. Mazar, 'The Aqueducts of Jerusalem', in Yadin, *Jerusalem Revealed*, pp. 79–84.)

II. Name

The meaning of the name is not certain. The Heb. word is usually written *yᵉrûšālaim* in the OT, but this is an anomalous form, since Heb. cannot have two consecutive vowels. The anomaly was resolved in later Heb. by inserting the letter 'y', thus giving *yᵉrûšālayim*; this form does in fact occur a few times in the OT, *e.g.*, Je. 26:18. This may well have been understood to be a dual (for the ending *-ayim* is dual), viewing the city as twofold. (Similarly, the Heb. name for 'Egypt', *miṣrayim*, appears to be dual.) But there can be little doubt that the original form of the word in Heb. was *yᵉrušālēm*; this is evidenced by the abbreviation *šālēm* (Eng. 'Salem') in Ps. 76:2, and by the Aramaic form of the name *yᵉrûšlēm*, found in Ezr. 5:14, *etc.*

The name is pre-Israelite, appearing in the Egyp. Execration Texts (19th–18th century; the form appears to be Rushalimum) and in later Assyrian documents (as *Urusalim* or *Urisalimmu*). The name also occurs in the * Ebla archive, *c.* 2500 BC. The first part of the name is usually thought to mean 'foundation'; the second element, though cognate with the Heb. word for 'peace', probably originally referred to a Canaanite deity Shalem. Thus 'foundation of Shalem' is probably the original sense of the name; in course of time, however, the second element will have been associated with 'peace' (Heb. *šālôm*) in Jewish minds; *cf.* Heb. 7:2.

In NT Greek the name is transliterated in two different ways, *Hierosolyma* (as in Mt. 2:1) and *Hierousalēm* (as in Mt. 23:37). The latter is evidently a close approximation to the Heb. pronunciation, and incidentally an additional evidence for an '*e*' as the original final vowel in Hebrew. The former is deliberately Hellenized, to make a Greek-sounding word; the first part of the word at once recalls the Greek word *hieros*, 'holy', and probably the whole was understood to mean something like 'sacred Salem'. LXX has only the form *Hierousalēm*, whereas Greek classical writers use *Hierosolyma* (*e.g.* Polybius; so too Latin, *e.g.* Pliny).

Jerusalem is described in Is. 52:1 as the holy city, and to this day it often receives this title. The Heb. phrase is *'îr haq-qōḏeš*, literally 'the city of holiness'. Probably the reason for this title was that Jerusalem contained the Temple, the shrine where God deigned to meet his people. Hence, the word *qōḏeš* came to mean 'sanctuary' as well as 'holiness'. To Judaism, then, Jerusalem was the holy city without a rival. It was natural for Paul and John, seeing that the earthly city was far from perfect, to designate the place where God dwells in true holiness as 'Jerusalem which is above' (Gal. 4:26) and 'new Jerusalem' (Rev. 21:2).

For other names the city has borne, see **III**, in historical sequence.

III. History

Traces of prehistoric settlement at Jerusalem have been found, but its early history cannot be traced. After a bare mention in the Egyp. Execration Texts early in the 2nd millennium, it reappears in the 14th-century el-Amarna letters, ruled by a king named Abd Khiba. At that time it was under the suzerainty of Egypt, and was probably little more than a mountain fortress. Possible pentateuchal references to it are as Salem (Gn. 14:18) and the mountain in the 'land of Moriah' of Gn. 22:2. According to very ancient tradition, the latter was the place where later the Temple was built, but there is no possible proof of this. As for Salem, it is almost certainly to be identified with Jerusalem (*cf.* Ps. 76:2); if so, it was ruled in Abraham's day by an earlier king, Melchizedek, who was also 'priest of God Most High' (*'ēl 'elyôn*).

When the Israelites entered Canaan they found Jerusalem in the hands of an indigenous Semitic tribe, the Jebusites, ruled over by a king named Adoni-zedek. This ruler formed an alliance of kings against Joshua, who soundly defeated them; but Joshua did not take the city, owing, doubtless, to its natural strength of position. It remained in Jebusite hands, bearing the name Jebus. Comparing Jdg. 1:8 with Jdg. 1:21, it appears that Judah overcame the part of the city

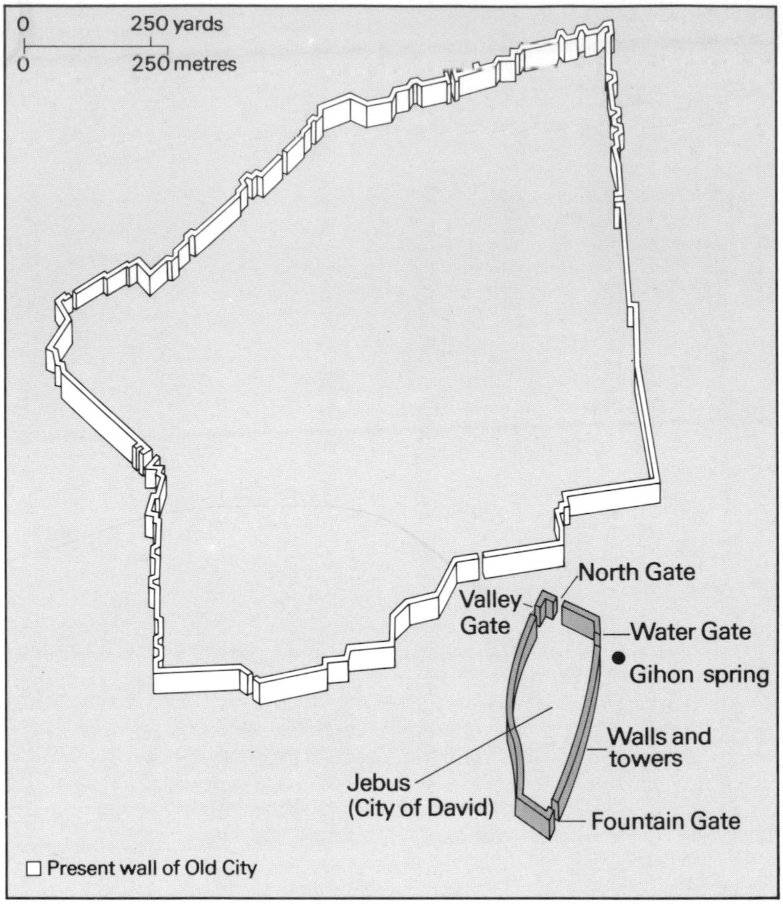

Jebus, the site of the City of David, Jerusalem, on the SE hill, Mt Zion.

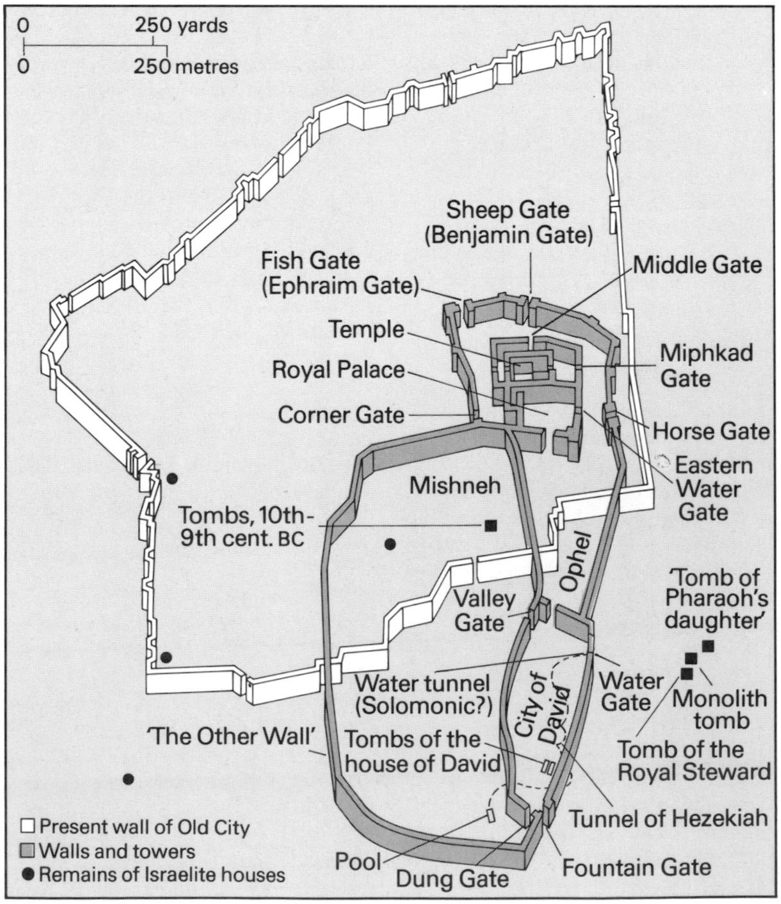

Jerusalem from Solomon to Hezekiah, showing extensions to the N and W, including the Temple area.

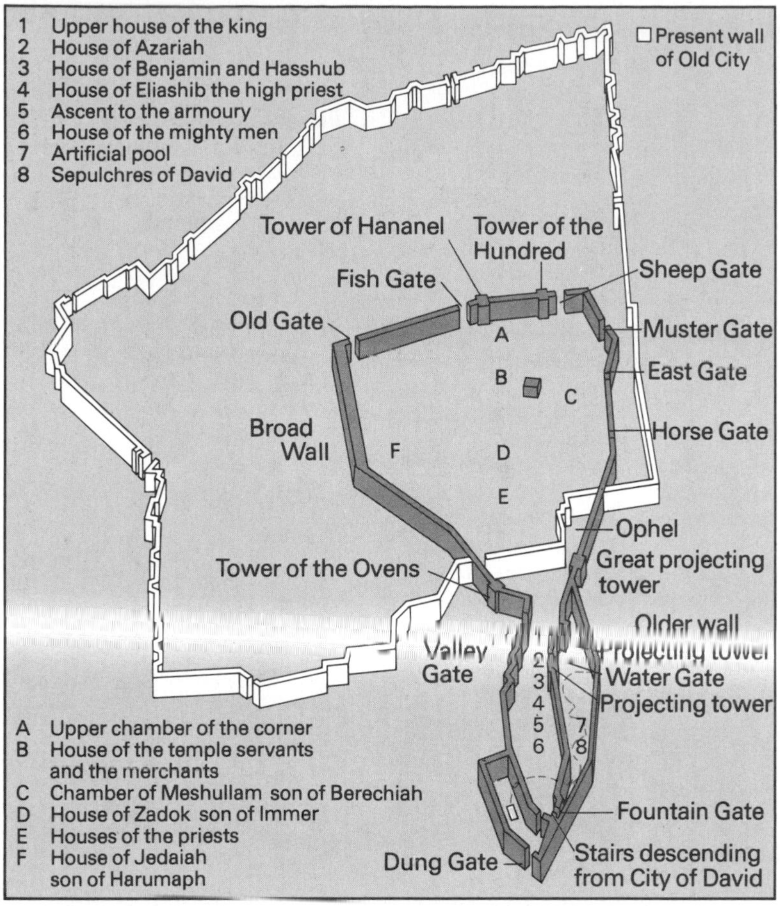

Probable reconstruction of Jerusalem as rebuilt by Nehemiah in the 5th cent. BC.

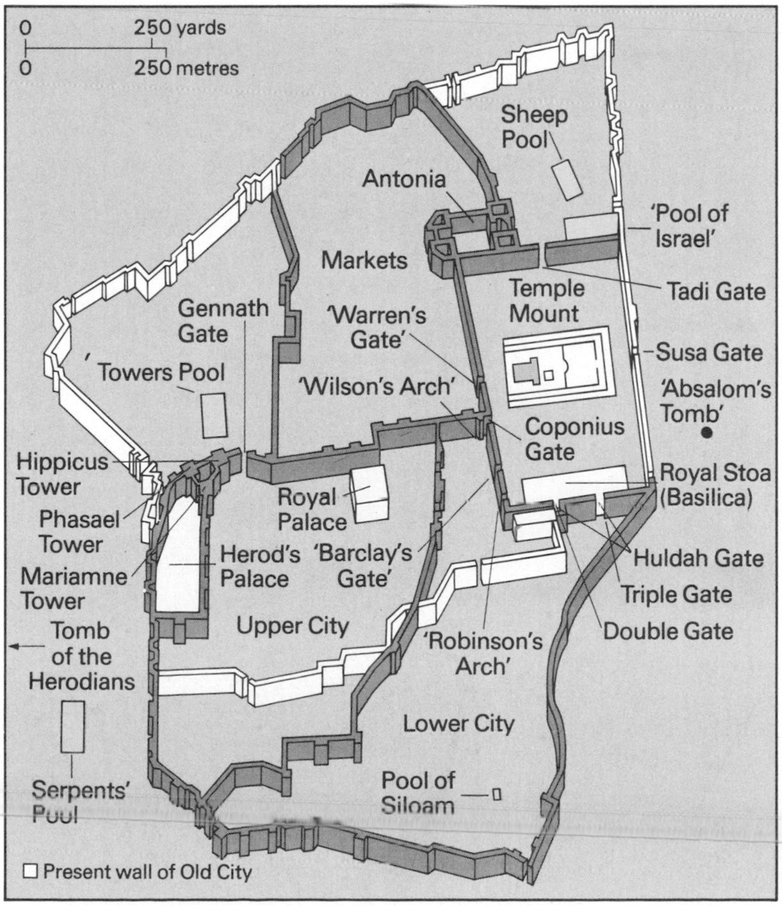

Jerusalem in the time of Herod the Great.

outside the fortress walls, and that Benjamin occupied this part, living peaceably alongside the Jebusites in the fortress.

This was the situation when David became king. His first capital was Hebron, but he soon saw the value of Jerusalem, and set about its capture. This was not only a tactical move but also a diplomatic one, for his use of a city on the Benjamin–Judah border would help to diminish the jealousy between the two tribes. The Jebusites felt confident of their safety behind the fortress walls, but David's men used an unexpected mode of entry, and took the citadel by surprise (2 Sa. 5:6ff.). In this passage we meet a third name, 'Zion'. This was probably the name of the hill on which the citadel stood; Vincent, however, thinks the name originally applied rather to the fortress building than to the ground it occupied.

Having taken the city, David improved the fortifications and built himself a palace; he also installed the ark in his new capital. Solomon carried the work of fortification further, but his great achievement was the construction of the Temple. After his death and the subsequent division of the kingdom, Jerusalem naturally declined somewhat, being now capital only of Judah. As early as the 5th year of Solomon's successor, Rehoboam, the Temple and royal palace were plundered by Egyp. troops (1 Ki. 14:25f.). Philistine and Arab marauders again plundered the palace in Jehoram's reign. In Amaziah's reign a quarrel with the king of the N kingdom, Jehoash, resulted in part of the city walls being broken down, and fresh looting of Temple and palace. Uzziah repaired this damage to the fortifications, so that in the reign of Ahaz the city was able to withstand the attacks of the combined armies of Syria and Israel. Soon after this the N kingdom fell to the Assyrians. Hezekiah of Judah had good reason to fear Assyria too, but Jerusalem providentially escaped. In case of siege, he made a conduit to improve the city's water-supply.

Nebuchadrezzar of Babylon captured Jerusalem in 597 and in 587 BC destroyed the city and Temple. At the end of that century the Jews, now under Persian rule, were allowed to return to their land and city, and they rebuilt the Temple, but the city walls remained in ruins until Nehemiah restored them in the middle of the 5th century BC. Alexander the Great ended the power of Persia at the end of the 4th century, and after his death his general Ptolemy, founder of the Ptolemaic dynasty in Egypt, entered Jerusalem and included it in his realm. In 198 BC Palestine fell to Antiochus II, the Seleucid king of Syria. About 30 years later, Antiochus IV entered Jerusalem, destroying its walls and plundering and desecrating the Temple; and he installed a Syrian garrison in the city, on the Akra. Judas the Maccabee led a Jewish revolt, and in 165 BC the Temple was rededicated. He and his successors gradually won independence for Judaea, and the Hasmonaean dynasty ruled a free Jerusalem until the middle of the 1st century BC, when Rome intervened. Roman generals forced their way into the city in 63 and 54; a Parthian army plundered it in 40; and 3 years after that Herod the Great had to fight his way into it, to take control. He first had to repair the damage created by these various incursions; then he launched a big building programme, erecting some notable towers. His most renowned work was the rebuilding of the Temple on a much grander scale, although this was not finished within his lifetime. One of his towers was Antonia, commanding the Temple area (it housed the Roman garrison which came to Paul's aid, Acts 21:34).

The Jewish revolt against the Romans in AD 66 could have but one conclusion; in AD 70 the Roman general Titus systematically forced his way into Jerusalem, and destroyed the fortifications and the Temple. He left three towers standing; one of them, Phasael, still remains, incorporated in the so-called 'Tower of David'. But further disaster awaited the Jews: another revolt in AD 132 led to the rebuilding of Jerusalem (on a much smaller scale) as a pagan city, dedicated to Jupiter Capitolinus, from which all Jews were excluded. This was the work of the emperor Hadrian; he called the newly constructed city Aelia Capitolina (the name even found its way into Arabic, as Iliya). It was not until the reign of Constantine (early 4th century) that the Jews were again permitted to enter the city. From his reign on, the city became Christian instead of pagan, and many churches and monasteries were built, notably the Church of the Holy Sepulchre.

Jerusalem has suffered many vicissitudes since the 2nd century, and has been captured and held at various times by Persian, Arab,

An aerial view of Jerusalem. (RC)

Turkish, Crusader, British and Israeli troops and administrations. The most important building developments in the Old City (as opposed to the rapidly growing modern suburbs) were due to the early Muslims, the Crusaders and finally the Turkish sultan Suleiman the Magnificent who in 1542 rebuilt the city walls as they can be seen today. The Israelis give the city its ancient Heb. name, *y^{e}rûšālayim*; the Arabs usually call it *al-Quds* (*al-Sharîf*), 'the (noble) Sanctuary'.

IV. Growth and extent

It must be stated at the outset that there is a good deal of uncertainty about the physical history of Jerusalem. This is, of course, partly due to the periodic disasters and destructions, and to the layers upon layers of rubble that have piled up over the centuries. These factors have caused difficulty elsewhere, of course, but archaeologists have often been able to surmount them to a large extent. The particular problem with Jerusalem is that it has been continuously inhabited and still is, so that excavations can be made only with difficulty. Archaeologists here have to dig where they can, not where they think it might be profitable. On the other hand, there is an abundance of traditions, Christian, Jewish and Muslim; but in many cases it is not easy to evaluate them. So uncertainty and controversy remain; however, much valuable archaeo-

Part of the wide set of steps leading up to the double doorway in the S wall of Herod's Temple mount at Jerusalem (see below). The steps continue beyond the later wall shown here. (JPK)

Reconstruction of the SW approach to Herod's Temple following recent excavations. A monumental stairway leads to the portal of the Royal Stoa at the junction of the W and S walls. To the right are the Huldah Gates.

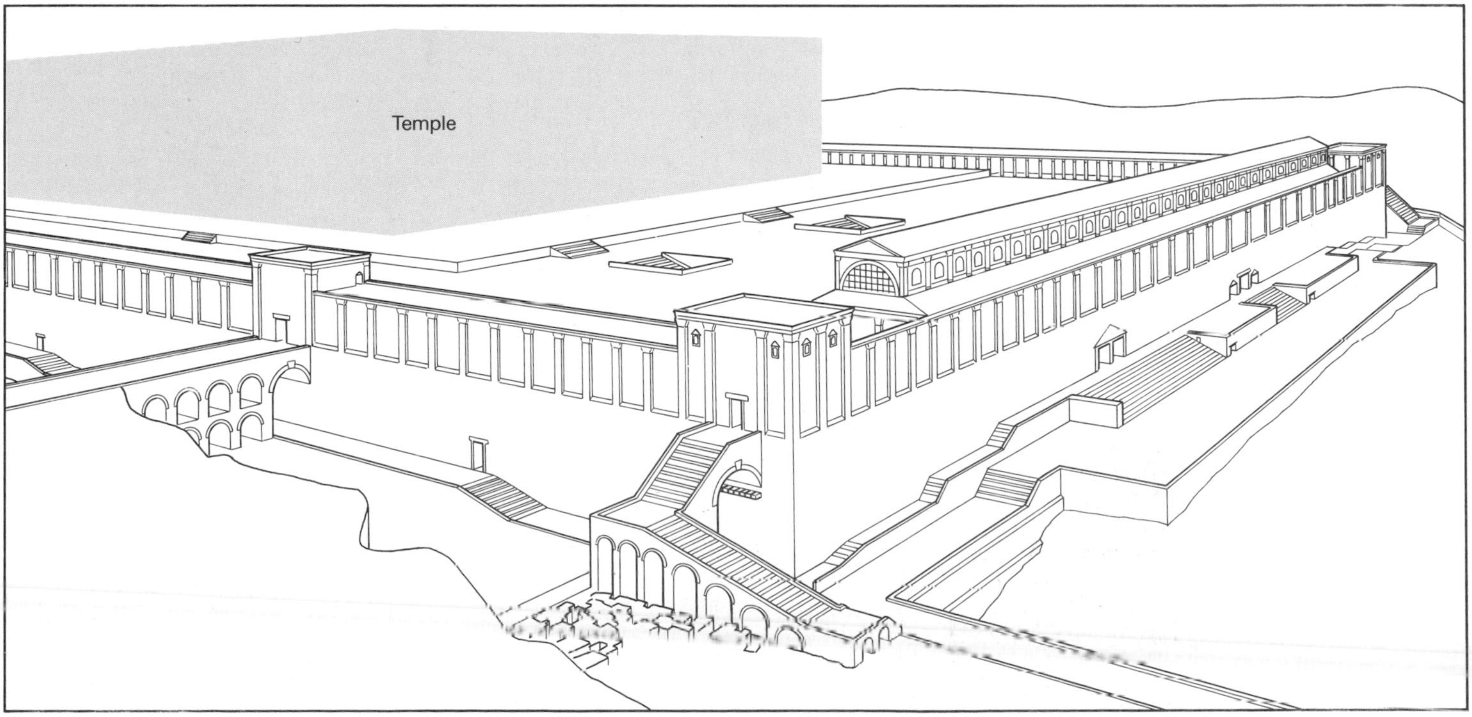

Excavations showing the crowded remains of the different occupation layers up to the present day in the Old City of Jerusalem. (DJW)

logical work has been done during the last century, and it has solved some problems.

Scripture nowhere gives a systematic description of the city. The nearest approach to such a description is the account of the rebuilding of the walls by Nehemiah. But there are a great number of references giving some information. These have to be pieced together, and fitted in with the picture we get from archaeology. Our earliest description of the city is that of Josephus (*BJ* 5. 136–141); Josephus is here laying a background for his account of the gradual capture of the city by Titus and the Roman armies. This too has to be fitted into the picture.

Excavations have conclusively shown that the earliest city was on the SE hill, an area now wholly outside the city walls (the S wall was retracted N in the 2nd century AD). It must be clearly borne in mind that the original Zion lay on the E ridge; the name was by the time of Josephus already erroneously attached to the SW hill.

Few traces remain from the pre-Jebusite period, but it may be inferred that a small town grew on the SE ridge, within easy reach of the spring Gihon in the valley to the E. The Jebusites enlarged the city to a limited extent, most notably by the construction of terraces E, so that their E wall lay well down the slope towards the spring. This terracing and E wall seem to have needed frequent maintenance and repair till their final destruction by the Babylonians in the early 6th century BC, after which the E wall was again retracted to the ridge. Present opinion is inclined to consider the word *'Millo' (*e.g.* 2 Sa. 5:9; 1 Ki. 9:15), which derives from a Heb. root meaning 'fill', to refer to this terracing.

In times of peace it was common practice for houses to be built outside the walls, which from time to time necessitated new walls and fortifications. David's and Solomon's city extended N, in particular, the Temple being built on the NE hill; the royal palace was probably situated in the area between the older city and the Temple area.

This intermediate area is probably the 'Ophel' of such passages as 2 Ch. 27:3 (the name means 'swelling', and was used of the citadel of other cities too, *e.g.* Samaria, *cf.* 2 Ki. 5:24, NEB); but some scholars apply the term to the whole E ridge S of the Temple. The Jebusite city, or perhaps more strictly the central fortress of it, already bore the name 'Zion' (the meaning of which is uncertain, perhaps 'dry area' or 'eminence') at the time of David's capture, after which it was also called 'the city of David' (*cf.* 2 Sa. 5:6–10; 1 Ki. 8:1). The name 'Zion' became, or remained, synonymous with Jerusalem as a whole.

It was in the prosperous days of the 8th century BC that the city first spread to the W ridge; this new suburb seems to have been called the Second Quarter or Mishneh (2 Ki. 22:14). A wall later enclosed it, built either in Hezekiah's reign (*cf.* 2 Ch. 32:5) or somewhat later. It is certain that this extension included the NW hill, but whether the SW hill was now occupied is as yet unresolved. Israeli archaeologists conclude that it was, and that the Pool of Siloam was inside the city walls in Hezekiah's reign; but K. M. Kenyon still maintains otherwise.

Jerusalem was sacked by Nebuchadrezzar's troops in 587 BC; most of the buildings were destroyed, and the city walls were demolished. The Temple was rebuilt at the end of the century, and Jerusalem had a small population once again; but it was not until the mid-5th century that the Persian authorities permitted the rebuilding of the city walls, by Nehemiah.

No doubt Nehemiah rebuilt earlier walls so far as was practicable but it is clear from excavations that the W ridge was abandoned, and also the E slopes of the SE hill. The Jebusite terracing had been too thoroughly demolished for repair, and Nehemiah therefore retracted the E wall to the ridge itself.

Nehemiah's description of contemporary Jerusalem unfortunately presents numerous problems. For one thing, it is not clear which gates were in the city wall and which led into the Temple. For another, there are numerous textual difficulties in the relevant passages of Nehemiah. Again, Nehemiah gives no indication of direction or changes of direction. Add to that the fact that names of gates changed from time to time. Earlier attempts to interpret Nehemiah's data now all require revision in the light of recent excavations. It is fairly clear, however, that the circuit described in Ne. 3 is in an anti-clockwise direction, and begins at the N of the city.

There is little evidence that the city spread to the W ridge again until the 2nd century BC. After the Maccabaean revolt, the city began to grow once more. Herod the Great was responsible for a major building programme in the late 1st century BC, and the city continued to develop until its destruction at the end of the Jewish War (AD 66–70). Our major literary source for this whole period is Josephus; but his information leaves us with a number of problems as yet unresolved.

The first of these problems is the position of the 'Akra', the Syrian fortress set up in Jerusalem in 169 BC. Its purpose was plainly to keep the Temple courts under close surveillance, but neither Josephus nor 1 Maccabees makes it clear whether the garrison was located N, W or S of the Temple. Opinions remain divided, but the most recent excavations tend to support the third of these possibilities. (See *BASOR* 176, 1964, pp. 10f.)

A second problem concerns the course of the 'Second Wall' and the 'Third Wall' mentioned by Josephus, who tells us that the Romans penetrated Jerusalem in AD 70 by progressively breaching three N walls. Josephus describes the termini of the three walls, but he does not give information as to the line followed by any of them. Excavations have supplemented his information here and there, but many uncertainties remain.

Thus, the remains of an ancient wall at the present-day Damascus Gate have been identified by K. M. Kenyon as part of the Third Wall, but by Israeli archaeologists as part of the Second Wall; and finds considerably further N have been linked with the Third Wall by the latter, but with a wall of circumvallation (erected by Titus, during the siege of Jerusalem) by Kenyon. The Third Wall was begun by Agrippa I (AD 41–44), and scarcely finished by the outbreak of the Jewish War AD 66, so that stratigraphical methods would scarcely serve to distinguish Agrippa's Wall from Titus' Wall.

One special point of interest concerning the Second Wall, which must have been built in the 2nd or 1st century BC (Josephus does not

This Babylonian Chronicle records events in 605–594 BC, including Nebuchadrezzar's accession, campaigns in Syria–Palestine and capture of Jerusalem 15/16 March 597 BC. (BM)

Part of a model of ancient Jerusalem, showing buildings of the New Testament period on the Ophel between the Temple and the area of the earliest city. (JPK) (HC)

date its construction) is its relationship to the Church of the Holy Sepulchre. If the church has any claim to marking the authentic site of the crucifixion and burial of Christ, its site must have lain outside the city walls; but for many years it was considered doubtful whether the site lay inside or outside the line of the Second Wall (the Third Wall was not then in existence). It has now been established that this area lay to the N of the wall; the site may therefore be authentic.

The city lay in ruins between AD 70 and the Bar-Kokhba revolt 60 years later. The emperor Hadrian then rebuilt the city, naming it Aelia Capitolina; his city was much smaller than its predecessor, with the permanent retraction of the S wall. During the Christian era, the size of Jerusalem has been by no means constant. The present-day walled area ('the Old City') was given its definitive shape by Suleiman the Magnificent in the 16th century.

V. Theological significance

By natural metonymy, the names 'Zion' and 'Jerusalem' frequently stand for the body of citizens (even when far away in exile), the whole of Judah, the whole of Israel, or the entire people of God.

Jerusalem plays an important theological role in both Testaments; in this respect too it is not readily distinguishable from the wider perspective of the whole land. Two motifs predominate: Jerusalem is at the same time the place of Jewish infidelity and disobedience, and also the place of God's election and presence, protection, and glory. The process of history demonstrated the former, which inevitably provoked divine anger and punishment; the glories of the city can only lie in the future. (See especially Is. 1:21; 29:1–4; Mt. 23:37f.; and Ps. 78:68f.; Is. 37:35; 54:11–17.) The contrast between the actual and the ideal naturally gave rise to the concept of a heavenly Jerusalem (*cf.* Gal. 4:25f.; Heb. 12:22; Rev. 21).

BIBLIOGRAPHY. On history and archaeology, see especially K. M. Kenyon, *Digging up Jerusalem*, 1974, and bibliography there listed; Y. Yadin (ed.), *Jerusalem Revealed*, 1975; B. Mazar, *The Mountain of the Lord*, 1975; *EAEHL*, 2, pp. 579–647. On economic and social conditions, see J. Jeremias, *Jerusalem in the Time of Jesus*, 1969. On theology see *TDNT* 7, pp. 292–338; W. D. Davies, *The Gospel and the Land*, 1974. D.F.P.

JERUSALEM TARGUM
See Targums, Part 3.

JESHIMON (Heb. *y*^{e}*šîmōn*, 'waste', 'desert'). Apparently used as a proper noun in Nu. 21:20; 23:28; 1 Sa. 23:19, 24; 26:1, 3. G. A. Smith, followed by G. E. Wright and F. V. Filson, identifies the name simply with the Wilderness of Judaea, but there is reason to think that in the Nu. references a location NE of the Dead Sea is indicated. See *GTT*, pp. 22f. R.P.G.

JESHUA. This is a late form of the name Joshua (the same individual is called Jeshua in Nehemiah and Ezra, and Joshua in Haggai and Zechariah). There is doubt about how many Jeshuas there are, but the following may perhaps be distinguished.

1. The head of a course of priests (1 Ch. 24:11, AV 'Jeshuah'). **2.** A Levite mentioned in Hezekiah's reorganization (2 Ch. 31:15). **3.** The high priest also called Joshua (Ezr. 2:2, *etc.*). **4.** A man of Pahath-moab who returned from the Exile with Jerubbabel (Ezr. 2:6). **5.** A head of a house of priests associated with 'the sons of Jedaiah' (Ezr. 2:36). **6.** A Levite, Jeshua son of Azaniah (Ne. 10:9). **7.** One of the chief of the Levites, the son of Kadmiel (Ne. 12:24; the text here may be corrupt). **8.** The father of Ezer, ruler of Mizpah (Ne. 3:19). **9.** The son of Nun (Ne. 8:17) (*JOSHUA).

It is clear that the name was a common one at the time of the return from the Exile. But little is told us of the various bearers of the name, and it is possible that some of those in the list ought to be identified with others.

Jeshua is also the name of a place in Judah (Ne. 11:26), usually taken as identical with Shema (Jos. 15:26), and Sheba (Jos. 19:2). The original form would be Shema, *m* becomes *b*, then *w*, and finally *j* is prefixed. L.M.

JESHURUN (Heb. *y*^{e}*šurûn*, 'the upright one'; LXX 'the beloved one'). A poetic variant of the name Israel (Dt. 32:15; 33:5, 26, AV 'Jesurun'). Used of the chosen Servant (Is. 44:2), the same Gk. word of LXX is used of Jesus (Eph. 1:6) and the church (Col. 3:12; 1 Thes. 1:4; 2 Thes. 2:3; Jude 1). Possibly to be interpreted 'People of the Law' (*cf.* D. J. Wiseman, *Vox Evangelica* 8, 1973, p. 14). D.W.B.

JESSE (Heb. *yišay*). Grandson of Boaz and father of David. He lived in Bethlehem and is commonly termed 'the Bethlehemite', but once the 'Ephrathite of Bethlehem-Judah'. He was the father of eight sons (1 Sa. 16:10–11), but the names of only seven are known (1 Ch. 2:13–15). The eighth is omitted, probably as he had no issue, unless the Elihu of 1 Ch. 27:18 is other than Eliab.

Ancient Jewish tradition (Targ. Ruth 4:22) followed by later interpreters (*cf.* AVmg.) identifies Nahash (2 Sa. 17:25) with Jesse. Two other solutions are more probable. Either Abigail and Zeruiah were daughters of Jesse's wife by a former marriage to a Nahash (*cf.*

A. P. Stanley, *Jewish Church*, Lect. 22) or Nahash may be a feminine name and taken as the mother of the daughters. Jesse's last appearance is at the cave of Adullam, whence David sent his parents for safety to Moab (1 Sa. 22:3–4). M.A.M.

JESUS CHRIST, LIFE AND TEACHING OF. A general article on the life and teaching of Jesus can touch only briefly on individual incidents and issues. Full use should therefore be made of the numerous references (at the end of sections and by asterisks in the text) to articles on specific points.

I. Sources

a. Non-Christian sources

Very few early references to Jesus with any claim to be independent of Christian sources have survived. The only direct mention by a Roman historian is a bare record of his execution by order of Pontius Pilatus in Judaea in the reign of Tiberius (Tacitus, *Annals* 15. 44). Other early Roman references to Christians do not refer to Jesus as a historical figure. The Jewish historian * Josephus has one brief account of Jesus, which is generally agreed to have been rewritten by Christians; it is likely that the original text referred to him as a reputed miracle-worker and teacher who attracted a considerable following and was executed by crucifixion under Pilate, though even this content is disputed (*Ant.* 18. 64). A number of rather obscure passages in the Talmud, whose reference to Jesus is in most cases only conjectural, add no clear historical detail, beyond the statement that he was hanged on Passover Eve, after due trial, as a sorcerer and one who 'led Israel astray' (*Sanhedrin* 43a). Non-Christian evidence therefore substantiates the fact of Jesus' existence, his popular following, his execution and the rough date (Pilate was in office in Judaea AD 26–36).

b. Christian sources

1. Outside the NT there are numerous accounts of the life and teaching of Jesus in early Christian writings (* New Testament Apocrypha). Some are clearly legendary, aiming to fill the gaps in the narratives of the canonical Gospels or to heighten the miraculous element. Others are apparently written to propagate

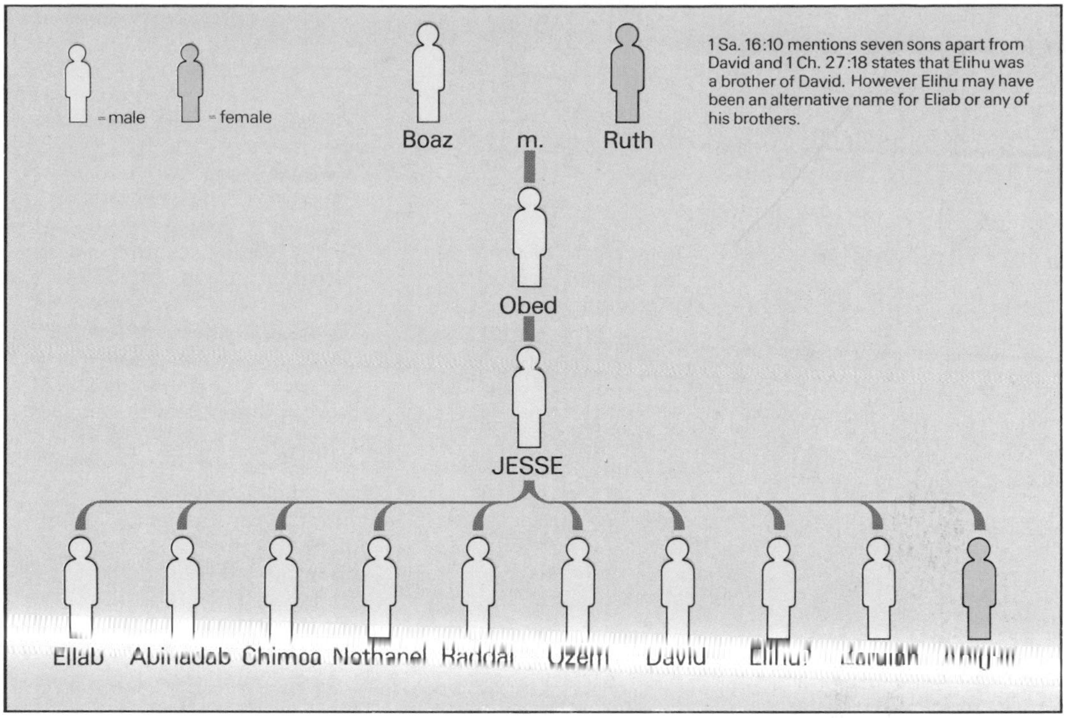

Jesse's family tree according to 1 Ch. 2:13–17.

Gnostic and other deviant views. While some of these works are quite early (early 2nd century), most of their historically credible material is clearly based on the canonical Gospels; only the *Gospel of Thomas* is generally treated seriously as possibly preserving independent authentic tradition, and many even of its sayings are influenced by Gnosticism, while many of the rest are paralleled in the canonical Gospels.

2. Thus in practice we are almost entirely restricted to the four canonical Gospels for evidence about Jesus. The rest of the NT contributes only a few isolated sayings and traditions (*e.g.* Acts 20:35; 1 Cor. 11:23–25).

The reliability of the Gospels as historical sources is hotly debated. Their primary purpose is clearly more than a mere recounting of facts, but it is not so clear that their avowedly 'propagandist' purpose necessarily calls in question their historical accuracy. If the Gospels are studied in the light of comparable literature of the period, and particularly of what is known of Jewish ideas of tradition, it appears that, while there was considerable freedom in the selection and wording of sayings and narratives, so that each writer's individual thought and purpose come out in the way he presents his material, they were essentially concerned to pass on a carefully preserved tradition of the words and deeds of Jesus. See further * Gospels, and the articles on the Gospels individually; also * Tradition.

Bibliography. F. F. Bruce, *Jesus and Christian Origins outside the New Testament*, 1974. On *b.* 2: G. E. Ladd, *The New Testament and Criticism*, 1967; G. N. Stanton, *Jesus of Nazareth in New Testament Preaching*, 1974; R. T. France in C. Brown (ed.), *History, Criticism and Faith*, 1977.

II. Setting

a. Time

Jesus was born shortly before the death of * Herod the Great in 4 BC (Mt. 2:1, 13–15); the exact date cannot be determined. His public ministry began when he was 'about thirty years of age' (Lk. 3:23); this was some time after the beginning of John the Baptist's mission in, probably, AD 28 (Lk. 3:1ff.). The length of his ministry is again impossible to determine exactly, but a period of roughly 3 years is generally agreed (based on the two springtimes indicated in Mark before the final Passover, Mk. 2:23; 6:39, and the three Passovers of Jn. 2:13; 6:4; 12:1). This would suggest a date of about AD 33 for the crucifixion, and if the Gospels indicate that the Passover (Nisan 14/15) fell on a Friday in the year of the crucifixion (though this too is disputed: see * Lord's Supper), the astronomical data for AD 33 would support this date. But certainty on the precise dates is impossible.

(*CHRONOLOGY OF THE NEW TESTAMENT.)

BIBLIOGRAPHY. G. Ogg, *The Chronology of the Public Ministry of Jesus*, 1940; H. Hoehner, *Chronological Aspects of the Life of Christ*, 1977.

b. Place

Practically the whole of Jesus' public ministry took place within Palestine. Only a few journeys outside Palestine are recorded, *e.g.* into Phoenicia and Decapolis (Mk. 7:24, 31), and to Caesarea Philippi on the slopes of Mt Hermon (Mk. 8:27). Jesus first came to the notice of John the Baptist in the Jordan valley, and John's Gospel records some early ministry in that area and in Judaea (Jn. 1:28–42; 2:13–4:3, dated before John's imprisonment, 3:24; 4:1–3, after which the Galilean ministry began, Mk. 1:14). Thereafter the main scene of ministry was Galilee, punctuated by visits to Jerusalem recorded by John in connection with festivals, until the final Passover visit.

c. Historical situation

1. Palestine had been under *Roman rule* for some 60 years when Jesus was born. It was indirect rule, through local princes, of whom *Herod the Great was the most famous. The division of his kingdom among his sons resulted in three regional rulers, of whom *Herod Antipas, tetrarch of Galilee and Peraea, held office throughout the period of Jesus' ministry; he is the Herod whom we meet in the Gospels outside the infancy stories. Archelaus, who took over Judaea and Samaria, was deposed after 10 years of misrule, and here direct rule was imposed, in the person of a Roman prefect, responsible to the governor of the province of Syria. The prefect during the period of Jesus' ministry was Pontius *Pilate.

Roman rule brought real benefits to the subject nation, but it was not popular. A special grievance was the system of taxation under which the already high official taxes were swollen by the unofficial rake-off of the *tax-collectors (AV 'publicans') who thus became a feared and hated group, both as extortioners and as collaborators with the occupying power. But the chief cause of resentment was the mere fact of political subjection, a position felt by many to be incompatible with Israel's status as the people of God.

2. The varying *Jewish reactions* to this situation may be seen in the attitudes of the 'parties' which had by this time emerged within Judaism. The priestly *Sadducees, who with the lay 'elders' exercised the effective leadership of the Jews under Roman rule (*SANHEDRIN) seem to have been more concerned with the maintenance of the *status quo* and the proper observance of the Temple ritual than with any ideological resistance to Roman rule. The *Pharisees, though in some cases willing to support insurrectionary movements, busied themselves with the law and the complex business of its rigorous application to everyday life. The *Essenes went further and opted out of all political and social involvement in favour of a monastic withdrawal. (The *DEAD SEA SCROLLS provide vivid documentation of such a separatist group at Qumran.) But there was a strong and popular movement towards political activism (*'ZEALOT', the name of one such group later in the century, is often used loosely to denote the various groups who took this stance), particularly since the abortive revolt of Judas of Galilee, provoked by the *census of AD 6. Sporadic outbreaks of insurrectionary activity, particularly in Galilee, led up eventually to the devastating Jewish War AD 66–70.

3. **Galilee*, Jesus' home province, stood to some extent apart from the Jewish heartland of Judaea. Its population, until quite recently largely Gentile, and geographically separated from Judaea by the hostile territory of Samaria, was despised by Judaean Jews as of questionable religious orthodoxy, if not still half-pagan. The pronounced N accent made a Galilean conspicuous in Jerusalem society. This difference of background may be a significant factor in Jesus' dealings with the Jewish authorities. It is also relevant to his reputation with the Romans, to whom 'Galilean' was almost tantamount to 'revolutionary'.

4. The *languages* of Palestine in the 1st century AD are a complex problem. It seems clear that Aram., Heb. and Gk. were all spoken. Aram. was most probably Jesus' vernacular, but a Galilean would almost certainly also have a working knowledge of Gk., and Heb. (in a form akin to the later Mishnaic) may well have been the medium for his debates with the religious authorities in Jerusalem.

BIBLIOGRAPHY. F. F. Bruce, *New Testament History*, 1969, chs. 1–9; P. E. Hughes, 'The Languages spoken by Jesus', in R. N. Longenecker and M. C. Tenney (eds.), *New Dimensions in New Testament Study*, 1974, pp. 127–143; G. Vermes, *Jesus the Jew*, 1973, ch. 2 (on Galilee).

III. Birth and childhood

The details of the birth of Jesus are recorded only in the Gospels of Matthew and Luke, each Gospel clearly using different sources, that of Matthew concentrating more on Joseph's side of the story, while Luke shows an intimate knowledge of Mary's experiences (and of those of her relative Elizabeth, mother of John the Baptist) which it is generally agreed could only have been derived, directly or indirectly, from Mary herself. It is therefore the more remarkable that on the crucial fact of the supernatural origin of Jesus' birth, without a human father, the two Gospels with their independent sources are agreed (*VIRGIN BIRTH).

The circumstances of Jesus' birth and childhood were in striking contrast to the supernatural mode of his conception. He was born in the animal quarters of a crowded village inn, and brought up in a very ordinary home in the obscure Galilean village of *Nazareth, which had achieved no mention in earlier literature. His family may have been what we would call 'middle class', the 'carpenter' (actually more a building contractor) being a skilled craftsman, perhaps employing labour, and a respected figure in village life (*ARTS AND CRAFTS, **III.** *c*). But the Gospel records make it clear that they were not affluent (Lk. 2:24; *cf.* Lv. 12:8), and Jesus' parables sometimes reflect experience of a home where comfort and money were limited (*e.g.* Lk. 11:5–7; 15:8–10). The fact that Joseph is not mentioned after the birth and childhood stories, and that Jesus was referred to in the village as 'Mary's son' (Mk. 6:3), is often taken to mean that Joseph died while Jesus was young, leaving Jesus as the oldest son to run the family business and provide for his four younger brothers and unknown number of sisters (Mk. 6:3).

In such circumstances Jesus could not aspire to a higher education. His full knowledge of the OT Scriptures attests to his having received the normal Jewish child's education at the village * synagogue-* school, and the one story of his childhood preserved in the Gospels indicates an abnormal aptitude in matters of religious debate (Lk. 2:42–50). Beyond this we know nothing of his childhood, though his later teaching shows a mind well stocked with the incidents and characters of daily life in a country village.

IV. The beginning of public ministry

a. John the Baptist

The occasion of Jesus' emergence from obscurity was the mission of * John the Baptist, a Judaean relative of Jesus who had grown up as an ascetic in the Judaean desert, and whose call for repentance in the light of God's imminent judg[illegible] to be baptized by him in the Jordan. It was among these followers of John that Jesus found his first disciples, with John's active encouragement (Jn. 1:35–42). John recognized in Jesus the judge whose coming he had predicted (Mt. 3:11f., *etc.*), and while the later style of Jesus' mission apparently caused him some doubts (Mt. 11:2–3), he does not seem to have withdrawn that recognition, even though some of his disciples maintained a separate existence throughout the NT period (Acts 18:24f.; 19:1–5).

b. The baptism of Jesus

Jesus' baptism by John was the event which most clearly inaugurated his mission. Why Jesus chose to submit to a baptism whose explicit significance was of repentance with a view to the forgiveness of sin has been much debated. Christians have agreed, following the lead of the NT (*e.g.* Jn. 8:46; Heb. 4:15; 1 Pet. 2:22), that it was not consciousness of personal sin which prompted him. More plausible is the suggestion that his intention was to identify himself with what John stood for, a 'vote' for the purified and reformed Israel which John demanded, and whose ideals were to form an important element in Jesus' own preaching. Further, in identifying himself with those who responded to John's call for repentance, he put himself in a position to be their representative. His own enigmatic explanation, 'thus it is fitting for us to fulfil all righteousness' (Mt. 3:15), may reflect an understanding of his role in line with that of the Servant of the Lord, who by his suffering on behalf of his people was to 'make many to be accounted righteous' (Is. 53:11).

Whatever Jesus' own intention, his baptism in fact led to a decisive revelation of his future role (Mk. 1:10f.). A visible descent of the Holy Spirit upon him marked him as the promised deliverer of, *e.g.*, Is. 11:2; 42:1 and 61:1, while a voice from heaven addressed him in terms reminiscent of Ps. 2:7 and Is. 42:1, the former greeting the Lord's anointed as his Son, and the latter introducing the Servant, chosen by God to deliver his people. Thus several important strands in OT Messianic hope are woven together, and the decisive role of Jesus in God's redemptive purpose is marked out.

c. The temptation of Jesus

The 'temptation (Mt. 4:1–11, Lk. 4:1–13), which followed quickly, was essentially an exploration of what it meant to be 'Son of God', as he had just been proclaimed at his baptism. 'If you are the Son of God . . .' is the theme of the challenges, and a study of Jesus' replies to them shows that their focus was not primarily on the way his mission should be accomplished, but on his own relationship with God. The temptation to turn stones into bread was to doubt his Father's care and wisdom in providing this period of abstinence. The temptation to leap from the Temple wall was to force his Father's hand to prove that he would protect his Son, rather than accept his care on trust. The third temptation was to compromise the Son's necessarily absolute loyalty to his Father. Jesus' three replies are drawn from verses in Dt. 6–8, and refer to the lessons the nation Israel was intended to learn from its experiences in the wilderness, suggesting that Jesus now takes up the nation's role as son of God, and by his success where Israel failed proves to be the true Son.

The encounter with Satan, concluding a long period of withdrawal in the desert area around the Jordan valley, thus served to strengthen Jesus' understanding of his unique status as Son of God which was to be the key to his mission. There is no suggestion that these were the whole of the temptations Jesus ever faced (*cf.* Heb. 4:15), or even that they were typical. They were the focal point of a vital period of preparation.

BIBLIOGRAPHY. G. H. P. Thompson, *JTS* n.s. 11, 1960, pp. 1–12; J. A. T. Robinson, *Twelve New Testament Studies*, 1962, pp. 53–60; R. T. France, *Jesus and the Old Testament*, 1971, pp. 50ff.

d. The move to Galilee

Jesus' public ministry now began, apparently at first in the Jordan valley with a focus on baptism parallel to that of John (Jn. 3:22f.; 4:1f.). Jesus appeared to many as a second Baptist, and a certain amount of rivalry soon arose between the two groups of disciples, though John refused to countenance this (Jn. 3:26–30). But this style of activity was soon brought to an end both by Jesus' increasing popularity coming to the notice of the authorities, and especially by the arrest of John the Baptist by Antipas, partly, as the Gospels record, due to his [illegible] Antipas' marriage, but also, according to Josephus, on suspicion of arousing political unrest, a charge which could easily affect the parallel ministry of Jesus. In this situation Jesus withdrew into his own region of Galilee, and his style of ministry changed to an itinerant preaching and healing mission. We do not hear of him baptizing again. (See **II.** *b* for the geographical location of the ministry.)

V. Features of Jesus' public ministry

a. Life-style

Despite Jesus' 'middle-class' background (above, **III**), his chosen style of life from this point was one of no financial security. He and his disciples lived on the contributions and hospitality of those who supported his mission (Mt. 10:8–11; Lk. 8:3; 10:38–42). He taught them to rely on God for all material needs (Mt. 6:24–34), and demanded that one would-be disciple should give away all his possessions (Mk. 10:17–22). Their money was held in common (Jn. 12:6; 13:29), but it sufficed only for their basic needs. Poverty, for Jesus, was not a disaster (Lk. 6:20f., 24f.; Mk. 10:23–31). Unmarried, and with no settled home (Lk. 9:58) or material ties, he was free to travel around Palestine preaching and healing.

In the early part of his ministry he was invited to speak in * synagogues as a visiting teacher (Mk. 1:21, 39; Mt. 9:35; Lk. 4:16–27), but later synagogue teaching is not mentioned (because his radical teaching was unacceptable?), and Jesus is found teaching the crowds in the open air, and devoting an increasing proportion of time to the instruction of his closest disciples.

b. Disciples

Like other Jewish teachers, Jesus gathered a group of *disciples. The 'crowds' came and went, listening to Jesus eagerly, but not committed to follow him; the 'disciples' were those who to a greater or lesser degree threw in their lot with him, and accompanied him on his travels. From among these disciples, an inner circle of 'the twelve' (often called the 'apostles', though the term 'apostle' is not confined to them in the NT) was selected by Jesus; and within the Twelve the special group of Peter, James and John were selected as Jesus' most intimate companions on a number of significant occasions.

To be a disciple involved an unreserved and exclusive commitment to Jesus. It involved, at least for the inner circle, the acceptance of his style of life (though not the permanent abandonment of home and family, as the case of Peter illustrates, Mk. 1:29–31; 1 Cor. 9:5), and a readiness to suffer persecution and ostracism for his sake (Mt. 10:16–39). It is an indication of the authority and attractiveness of Jesus and his teaching that he could nonetheless call people to follow him and expect to be taken seriously.

The majority of his disciples were Galileans. Of the inner circle it is probable that all except *Judas Iscariot (if his name means 'man of Kerioth') were from Galilee. But in character and background they varied from *Thomas the pessimist to *Peter the extrovert, and from *Matthew the tax-collector (and therefore in the employment of the pro-Roman government) to *Simon 'the Zealot'. To have held together such a group, and made them the foundation of the world's greatest religion, is no mean part of the achievement of Jesus.

c. Social attitudes

One of the most persistent objections to Jesus on the part of the Jewish establishment was his habit of keeping doubtful company, particularly that of 'tax-collectors and sinners', the outcasts of respectable society. That he even took meals with them was especially scandalous. But Jesus defended his actions as essential to his mission, which was to those in need, whatever their social standing (Mk. 2:17; *cf.* Lk. 15:1–2 and the sequel). He would welcome and talk with women of doubtful morals whom others shunned (Lk. 7:36–50; Jn. 4:7ff.), and even found a welcome among *Samaritans, the traditional enemies of the Jews (Jn. 4:39–42; Lk. 17:11–19). His story of the Good Samaritan (Lk. 10:29–37) is a daring challenge to the traditional Jewish taboo. His direct contacts with Gentiles were few but positive (Mt. 8:5–13; 15:22–28), and his teaching made it clear that he did not regard Gentiles as an inferior category, but gave them a place alongside Jews in God's purpose (*e.g.* Mt. 8:11–12; Lk. 4:25–27).

This unwillingness to be restricted by conventional social barriers is seen also in his relations with rich and poor. Most of his closest disciples seem to have been from the same social class as himself (particularly fishermen, owning boats and employing men, Mk. 1:20), but his preaching met with a favourable response among the poor (*e.g.* Mt. 11:5), while he also had rich and influential followers (*e.g.* Nicodemus and Joseph of Arimathaea, Jn. 19:38–42), and was at home in more affluent company (Lk. 7:36; 14:1ff.). He was apparently unimpressed by wealth or poverty as such: it was the attitude to wealth which mattered (Mk. 12:41–44; Lk. 12:13–21). He required of his followers a similar unconcern for artificial barriers (Lk. 14:7–14), and sternly condemned a callous neglect of the less fortunate (Lk. 16:19ff.).

In all this Jesus' concern was with the real needs of those he met, physical and spiritual, and in meeting those needs he cared little if conventions and taboos were overridden.

BIBLIOGRAPHY. M. Hengel, *Property and Riches in the Early Church*, 1974; R. T. France, *EQ* 51, 1979, pp. 3ff.

d. Disputes about the law

Debates with the Jewish religious leaders, especially the *scribes and *Pharisees, take up a good part of the Gospel narratives. Jesus lacked a formal scribal education (Jn. 7:15), but his style of teaching and his group of disciples cast him in the role of a *rabbi, and he was sometimes so addressed. The content of his teaching at many points, however, inevitably set him apart from scribal orthodoxy, and was a major factor in the hostility which eventually led to his death.

Central was the issue of authority. The authority of the OT *law itself was not in question, but rather the authority to interpret it. Scribal *tradition had evolved a complex and constantly growing body of oral teaching on the precise application of the law to the most minute areas of everyday life, and this tradition too was regarded as authoritative. Points of dispute were settled by appeal to previous teachers. In contrast, Jesus paid little attention to traditional rules not clearly found in the OT, and never quoted an authority other than himself (and, of course, the OT); note his formula, 'You have heard . . . but *I* say to you . . .' (Mt. 5:21f., 27f., 31f., *etc.*).

The issues are seen most clearly in the debate on defilement (Mk. 7:1–23), where Jesus explicitly accuses the Pharisees and scribes of evading OT requirements on the basis of man-made rules, and dismisses the issue of ritual defilement as relatively trivial; and in the numerous clashes on the observance of the *sabbath (*e.g.* Mk. 2:23–3:6; Lk. 13:10–17), one of the most elaborately legislated areas in scribal tradition, where Jesus cut through the tangle of legislation to the original intention of the sabbath, and asserted his own right to determine its proper observance.

The series of six 'antitheses' in the Sermon on the Mount (Mt. 5:21–48) further illustrates Jesus' radical approach to the law, going beyond the literal rule to the thought behind the act, and putting principles before precepts even to the extent of apparently setting aside the latter (Mt. 5:38f.). This radical attitude to legal questions made Jesus a danger to the scribal establishment, and the popularity of his views made it essential to get rid of him. The conflict was apparently heated, with very strong language being used by both sides (Mk. 3:22; Mt. 23:1–36). It was the legalistic attitude of the scribal authorities, more than their actual traditions, which Jesus found necessary to denounce.

BIBLIOGRAPHY. R. J. Banks, *Jesus and the Law in the Synoptic Tradition*, 1975.

e. Miracles

Christian and non-Christian sources attest that Jesus was known to his contemporaries as a worker of *miracles. The vast majority of those recorded are cases of miraculous healing, and the Gospels

Opposite page: Map showing the places prominent in the ministry of Jesus Christ.

present healing, often of large number of people, as a regular feature of Jesus' ministry (Mk. 1:32–34; 3:7–12; 6:55f.; Lk. 7:21f.). Often coupled with his healing miracles (though usually carefully differentiated from them, *e.g.* Mk. 1:32–34; Lk. 13:32) are his exorcisms (*DEMON POSSESSION). Both of these activities were expected also of his disciples when they went out in his name (Mk. 6:13; Mt. 10:8), and they are integrally related with his preaching, as aspects of a total onslaught on the powers of evil, in their physical as well as their spiritual manifestation.

Healing and exorcism were an accepted part of the activity of godly men within 1st-century Judaism, but nothing approaching the intensity of Jesus' healing ministry is recorded of any contemporary figure (*HEALTH, V). The range of complaints he healed is very wide, from paralysis to blindness, and from leprosy to a severed ear. Three cases of restoring to life those who had recently died are also recorded. Unlike some contemporary exorcists, he used little or no ritual, a mere word of command being often the only means employed (Mt. 8:8f., 16). The overwhelming impression was of his simple authority over physical and spiritual evil, and his compassion for those in need. His healing ministry was not a bid for recognition, nor was it primarily designed to prove anything, but it was the automatic response of his compassion to human need when he met it.

Jesus' other ('nature') miracles are comparatively few, but again the same pattern of an automatic and unselfconscious response to a pressing need can be seen in most of them, feeding hungry crowds, supplying wine in an emergency, providing fish after a night of fishing in vain, and calming a storm on the lake. That Jesus solved such problems by miraculous means was not so much a deliberate display of power as a natural result of who he was. Only the walking on water and the sudden withering of the fig-tree seem to have been performed more to teach the nature of his person and mission than to meet a definite need.

The miracles, then, are not *the* proof of Jesus' divine nature, though they imply it. They are an inevitable part of a total ministry of deliverance and of the conquest of evil.

f. Political stance

The charge on which Jesus was finally condemned was of political sedition (Lk. 23:2): he had claimed to be 'king of the Jews'. While the title never occurs in his sayings, he did often speak about the *'kingdom of God' as the object of his mission (see below, **VII.** *d*), and such language, particularly in Galilee, was open to nationalistic interpretation. Much of his early support was probably due to hopes that he would lead a revolt against Rome, culminating in the unsuccessful attempt to force him to accept the title of 'king' (Jn. 6:14f.). After this

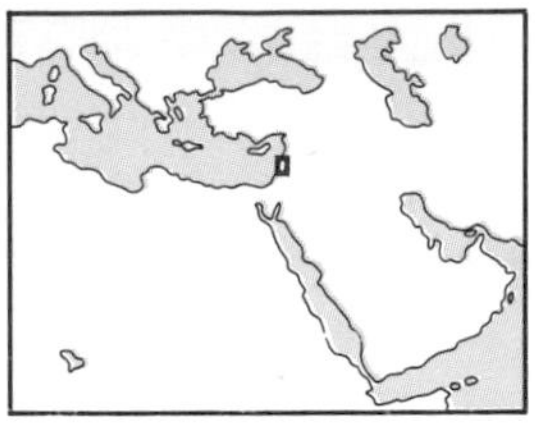

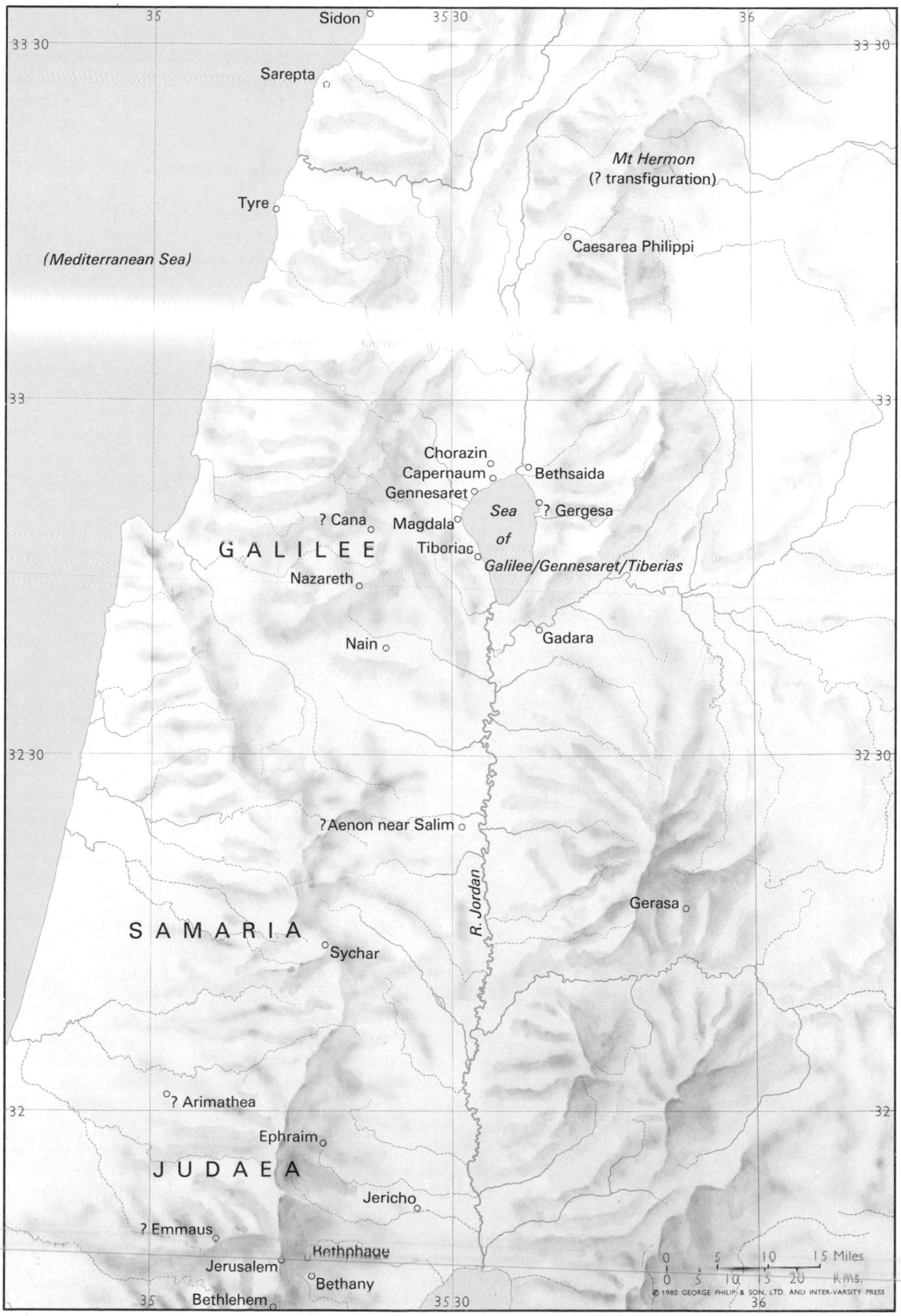

episode his support seems to have decreased, and more of his time was spent instructing his disciples on the true nature of his mission.

Some modern writers (especially S. G. F. Brandon, *Jesus and the Zealots*, 1967) have tried to show that Jesus' intentions were in fact political, and that the spiritual nature of his kingship is a later invention in the Gospels to gloss over his real revolutionary aim. While Jesus was certainly not as blind to political and social problems as more pietistic Christians have suggested, Brandon's view involves a wholesale rewriting of the Gospels on very flimsy grounds. The Jesus of the Gospels was at pains to correct misunderstandings of the nature of his mission (Mk. 8:27–38; 12:35–37; 14:61f.), avoided publicity and popular demonstrations until the last week of his ministry, refused to affirm the nationalist position when asked about the validity of Roman taxation (Mk. 12:13–17), and was declared innocent of sedition by the Roman prefect (Lk. 23:13–16). His declared attitude to the Jewish nation of his day, which he regarded as approaching its final punishment for its rejection of God's messengers in the imminent destruction of Jerusalem (Lk. 11:47–51; 13:25–35, *etc.*), is quite incompatible with nationalist sympathies. The circumstances of his ministry inevitably laid him open to political suspicion, but there is ample evidence that his own intentions were otherwise, even though some of his followers undoubtedly expected him to adopt a nationalist role. (*MESSIAH, **II.** *a.*)

BIBLIOGRAPHY. M. Hengel, *Victory over Violence*, 1973; J. H. Yoder, *The Politics of Jesus*, 1972; A. Richardson, *The Political Christ*, 1973; M. Langley, 'Jesus and Revolution', *NIDNTT* 3, pp. 967–981.

g. Jesus' authority

The Gospels tell us that the dominant impression of Jesus' ministry was that of authority. This is true both of his boldly self-authenticating teaching (Mk. 1:22) and of his miraculous activity (Mk. 1:27; Mt. 9:8). It was his personal authority which impressed the Gentile centurion (Mt. 8:8f.), which caused his disciples to leave their homes and jobs to follow him, and which carried all before him when he strode into the Temple court and threw out the traders (Mk. 11:15–17). While Jesus himself refused to state openly the source of this authority (Mk. 11:27–33), the implication is clear that it derived from God, and his own claim to be Son of God carried the same implication. After his resurrection he declared openly his universal authority (Mt. 28:18; *cf.* Jn. 17:2).

VI. The close of the ministry

a. The last week in Jerusalem

Jesus' last visit to Jerusalem was deliberately undertaken with the knowledge that it would lead to the final confrontation with the authorities, culminating in his own death (Lk. 13:33; 18:31–33). It was made at *Passover time, when Jerusalem would be crowded with pilgrims, and when the themes of death and redemption were in mind. Certain incidents are of special importance.

1. *The entry.* Jesus' arrival in Jerusalem was deliberately dramatic. Instead of arriving unnoticed among the thousands of other pilgrims, he staged a conspicuous ride into the city on a donkey, while his disciples and other pilgrims greeted him with shouts of *'Hosanna' (Mk. 11:1–10). It was a visible allusion to Zc. 9:9–10, the prophecy of the king coming to Jerusalem on a donkey. Its intention was clearly to make a Messianic claim, and it was so interpreted by the crowds, who would include many of his former supporters from Galilee. The prophecy is of a king of peace, but many probably interpreted the gesture in a more militantly nationalistic sense.

2. *Cleansing the Temple.* One of Jesus' first acts on arrival was equally deliberately symbolic. He threw out from the Temple precincts the traders in sacrificial animals and in the special Temple coinage, whose market was officially established there at Passover time by the priestly authorities (Mk. 11:15–18). This action not only expressed his repudiation of the current religious leadership and their attitude to worship. It also inevitably called to mind passages such as Mal. 3:1–4 and Zc. 14:21, and thus further reinforced his Messianic claim. (It should be noticed, incidentally, that the object of Jesus' 'violence' was not the Roman government, but the Jewish authorities; this was not an expression of nationalistic militancy.)

3. *Debates.* The week was marked by a continuing dialogue with the religious authorities. Several specific debates are recorded, covering the source of Jesus' authority (Mk. 11:27–33), his attitude to Roman taxation (Mk. 12:13–17), the question of resurrection of the dead (Mk. 12:18–27), the greatest commandment (Mk. 12:28–34) and the status of the Messiah as 'son of David' (Mk. 12:35–37). Such debates were held in public, as Jesus was teaching in the Temple precincts, and their object was to elicit from him either blasphemous or politically damaging statements which could be used against him. Jesus avoided incriminating answers, but none the less succeeded in imparting some important teaching. He went further to make clear his repudiation of the current leadership in Israel, in his parable of the tenants in the vineyard (Mk. 12:1–12), and in his continuing polemic against the scribes and Pharisees in particular (especially Mt. 23). He also predicted in more detail the coming destruction of Jerusalem and its Temple (Mk. 13).

4. *The Last Supper.* This 'farewell meal' was also a pre-arranged (Mk. 14:13–16) and deliberate act. It was in some sense a *Passover meal, though possibly held a day before the official celebration, in the knowledge that the next evening would be too late. (See *LORD'S SUPPER, **I.** *a* for details of the date.) At the meal Jesus gave some vital last instructions to his closest disciples in view of his imminent departure, and also revealed that he was to be betrayed by one of their number (though without apparently identifying the traitor explicitly, except perhaps to John, Jn. 13:23–26). But the focus of the meal was the symbolic sharing of bread and wine which he gave as tokens that his coming death was to be for the benefit of his disciples (and beyond them of 'many'). This symbolic act (performed in the context of the Passover celebration of redemption) was the clearest statement Jesus ever made of the redemptive purpose of his death, and it has fittingly become, as he himself directed, the focus of worship among his followers. (See further *LORD'S SUPPER, **I.** *b* for the significance of the words used on this occasion.) It finally put an end to any doubts his disciples may have had of his commitment to death, as the will of the Father for him.

b. Trial and death

Jesus was arrested quietly at night on the slopes of the Mount of *Olives. Judas' action as inside informer enabled the authorities to locate him among the thousands of pilgrims camping on the slopes, and Jesus himself refused to evade or resist arrest, accepting, after his prayer of surrender in *Gethsemane, that this was God's purpose.

A series of hearings during that night and the following (Friday) morning make up the so-called *'Trial of Jesus'. A first, probably quite unofficial, hearing before *Annas, the deposed high priest (Jn. 18:12–23), produced no formal result. There followed two hearings before *Caiaphas and the *Sanhedrin, one at night and the other early in the morning, the former probably a hastily summoned preliminary hearing, the latter a meeting of the full Sanhedrin, ratifying the findings of the first meeting, and passing a formal verdict that Jesus was guilty of blasphemy. Precisely what his blasphemy was held to be is not certain, but his acceptance of the Messianic title and his further allusions to Ps. 110:1 and Dn. 7:13 to predict his future vindication and power (Mk. 14:61f.) were certainly the deciding factors.

The sentence for blasphemy under Jewish law was death. But capital powers were at this period limited to the Roman prefect (see *TRIAL OF JESUS), while blasphemy was not a charge admissible in Roman law. Jesus was therefore brought to *Pilate on a charge of sedition, based on the use of the title 'King of the Jews'.

Pilate's reluctance to try, and still more to convict, Jesus is primarily to be explained by his disdain for his Jewish subjects and their religious concerns (see *PILATE for details of other incidents). A realization that the charge was an artificial one, and that Jesus' career had not been that of a political revolutionary, would only add to his reluctance. But attempts to evade the issue by referring the case to Herod Antipas (Lk. 23:6–12), by offering to release Jesus in accordance with a customary Passover amnesty (Mk. 15:6–15), by sending him for *scourging without the full capital punishment (Jn. 19:1–5), and by a simple declaration of Jesus' innocence (Lk. 23:22, *etc.*) all proved unsuccessful in the face of a carefully orchestrated expression of popular hostility to Jesus. The deciding factor was the insistence of the Jewish authorities that a threat to the Roman government could not be ignored; the implication was that failure to convict Jesus would be reported to Pilate's superiors (Jn. 19:12). Jesus was condemned to be crucified.

For details of crucifixion as a method of execution see *Cross. It was the death of a delinquent slave, and also of a rebel against the imperial power. The public and prolonged agony was a deliberate deterrent to other would-be rebels.

Jesus' crucifixion was not unusual in its method. What was unusual was the bearing of the victim. Despite the savage cruelty of the Roman scourging and the soldiers' mockery, the carrying of the heavy crossbeam and the crucifixion itself, Jesus' recorded words during his crucifixion are of forgiveness and concern for others, and prayer to his Father (*SEVEN WORDS). His bearing impressed the Roman centurion (Mk. 15:39; *cf.* Lk. 23:47), and even his fellow-victim (Lk. 23:40–42), as unique.

Also unusual was the speed and suddenness of his death; crucified men very seldom died the same day, and then only after a long period of increasing loss of consciousness. Jesus died quickly, and apparently by a deliberate act of will (Lk. 23:46; *cf.* Jn. 19:30). His final cry of 'It is accomplished' (Jn. 19:30) shows him not as the victim of circumstances, but as in control of the situation, the purposeful actor in a drama of crucial significance.

Jesus' burial was another unusual feature, and indicates the support he still enjoyed in influential circles; crucified bodies were normally left unburied. The rock-cut tomb of *Joseph of Arimathaea was probably one of many in the vicinity (*BURIAL AND MOURNING).

BIBLIOGRAPHY. J. Blinzler, *The Trial of Jesus*, 1960; A. N. Sherwin-White, *Roman Society and Roman Law in the NT*, 1963; P. Winter, *On the Trial of Jesus*, 1961; E. Bammel (ed.), *The Trial of Jesus*, 1970; D. R. Catchpole, *The Trial of Jesus*, 1971.

c. Resurrection and ascension

That Jesus' tomb was found to be empty on the Sunday morning following his crucifixion is asserted in different ways by all four Gospels, and cannot be seriously disputed on historical grounds. Explanations of this fact which dispense with a literal *resurrection of his body are entirely speculative, and open to more palpable objections than the fact they aim to discredit.

The Gospels and Paul (in 1 Cor. 15) together attest also to probably eleven separate encounters with the risen Jesus in the period immediately following that Sunday morning. Their varied and generally quite unexpected character, and the different groups involved (from single individuals to a group of more than 500), make it impossible to dismiss them as hallucinations, and the difficulty of fitting them all together (as with the accounts of finding the empty tomb) only makes it the more unlikely that there was any deliberate collusion in perpetrating a well-intentioned deception.

On these grounds, Christians have concluded that Jesus rose bodily from the tomb, with a body which, while set free from some of the limitations of time and space (he could pass through closed doors, and appear and disappear suddenly), was solidly physical, able to break bread and to eat, and to be mistaken for a gardener or a fellow traveller.

For some weeks Jesus continued to appear in this way to his disciples, not living or travelling with them, but in single encounters. Having thus convinced them of his victory over death, and assured them that they could continue to rely on his presence and help even when he was physically removed, he left them in a way which showed clearly that his bodily presence was no longer necessary (Acts 1:9–11; *ASCENSION). It was for them in future to continue the mission which he had begun, and in which he would always be spiritually present with them (Mt. 28:18–20).

BIBLIOGRAPHY. E. M. B. Green, *Man Alive!*, 1967; E. L. Bode, *The First Easter Morning*, 1970; J. N. D. Anderson, *A Lawyer among the Theologians*, 1973, chs. 3–4.

VII. The teaching of Jesus

The teaching of Jesus is not easily set out in systematic form; it was not delivered as an ordered treatise, but in a wide variety of real-life situations and encounters. In an article of this nature we can only pick out certain key themes and emphases of his teaching, concentrating on those which were most distinctive and unexpected in the environment of 1st-century Judaism.

a. Forms of teaching

Formally, Jesus' teaching has much in common with the methods traditionally employed by Jewish teachers. His arguments from and about scriptural texts, his ethical exhortations, his rules of conduct, his parables and his eschatological predictions can all be paralleled, in terms of teaching method, in rabbinic or sectarian Judaism of the period. So also can the rhythmic and sometimes poetic form in which much of his teaching is cast, and which was an aid to memorization. It is in the tone and content of his teaching that its uniqueness lies. For instance, while *parable was a known and accepted teaching form, there is nothing in Jewish literature to match the vividness, the variety and the sheer quantity of Jesus' parables, still less the doctrinal and ethical emphases which they convey.

It is a characteristic of Jesus' teaching that it was not delivered in an academic lecture-type setting. It arose out of personal encounters, questions from enquirers, debates with the religious authorities (usually initiated by them), and the need to instruct his disciples in the light of his own imminent suffering and death, and of their role in continuing his ministry afterwards. While Jesus did 'lecture' to the crowds, often for long periods (*e.g.* Mk. 6:34f.), such carefully structured discourses as we find in the Gospels (*e.g.* the *Sermon on the Mount and the discourses in the Gospel of *John) bear the marks of a later compilation of sayings of Jesus rather than of verbatim transcripts of actual addresses.

Particularly characteristic of Jesus' teaching are epigrams, striking expressions often using deliberate exaggeration and paradox to drive home his point (*e.g.* Mk. 10:25; 12:17; Lk. 9:24, 58, 60, 62). Illustrations are frequent and graphic. Sometimes he used visual aids or acted parables (*e.g.* Mt. 18:2; Jn. 13:1–15). Jesus' teaching can never have been dull, and it is consequently far more memorable than more formal or stylized teaching. Above all, it is not merely theoretical, but life-related.

b. Use of the Old Testament

Jesus based his teaching firmly on the OT. His recorded words in the Gospels contain more than 40 verbatim quotations, about 60 clear verbal allusions or other references to OT passages and well over 100 other possible allusions, where it is hard to say whether a specific allusion is intended or Jesus' mind was so full of OT words and ideas that he inevitably expressed himself in ways reminiscent of the OT.

He used the OT in every aspect of his teaching. He discussed its legal and ethical requirements, and used these as the basis for his own moral teaching (*e.g.* Mt. 5:17–48; Mk. 10:2–9; 12:28–31). He used its historical narratives to illustrate aspects of his own teaching (*e.g.* Mk. 2:25f.; Mt. 12:40–42; 24:37–39). In debate with the religious leaders he normally turned to the OT as the final authority, and sometimes chided them over their failure to grasp its basic principles (*e.g.* Mk. 7:6–13; 12:24; Mt. 12:3–7). But it is especially in his teaching about the nature of his own person and mission that Jesus uses the OT, and that in a variety of ways.

Sometimes he simply quotes clear OT predictions as finding their fulfilment in him. Many of these are predictions of the coming *Messiah, and these cause no surprise to the Christian (for details see *g*, below). But many of the passages he alluded to in this connection make no mention of a Messiah, but only of God himself coming to judge and save (*e.g.* Mt. 11:5, alluding to Is. 35:5f.; Lk. 19:10 to Ezk. 34:16, 22; Lk. 22:20 to Je. 31:31); these also Jesus sees as fulfilled in his coming. Even more remarkably, many passages which are not predictive at all, but are simply accounts of historical persons, events, *etc.*, are none the less taken up as patterns which are 'fulfilled' in Jesus' mission (*e.g.* Mt. 12:40–42 referring to Jonah and Solomon; Mt. 4:4, 7, 10 referring to Israel's wilderness experience in Dt. 8:3; 6:16, 13; Mk. 12:10f. quoting Ps. 118:22f.). This last method of using the OT is more fully developed in the rest of the NT (especially Heb.), and is generally known as *'typology'. Numerous incidental allusions throughout Jesus' teaching show that he saw his ministry as 'fulfilling' not only the explicit predic tions of the OT, but the whole pattern of God's working in the history of Israel which it records.

Bibliography. R. T. France, *Jesus and the Old Testament*, 1971; J. W. Wenham, *Christ and the Bible*, 1973.

c. The time of fulfilment

Jesus' first recorded words in his Galilean ministry are a concise statement of the basic presupposition of all his teaching: 'The time is fulfilled, and the kingdom of God is at hand' (Mk. 1:15). In Luke's Gospel Jesus' first public appearance focuses on the claim, 'Today this scripture (Is. 61:1f.) has been fulfilled in your hearing' (Lk. 4:21). Throughout his ministry this note of present fulfilment is of central importance. This was the arrival of the Messiah, the coming of the Day of Yahweh long expected by the Jews, the fulfilment of all the hopes of the OT (see *b*, above). While he did not openly use the title 'Messiah' (see *g*, below, and *Messiah, **II.** *a*), he never denied that this was his role, and when John the Baptist asked him directly, he replied with a clear affirmative (Mt. 11:2–6, alluding to Is. 35:5f.; 61:1).

The coming of Jesus thus introduces, according to his own teaching, a new era. The many centuries of expectation now give way to fulfilment. Jesus' use of typology (see *b* above) does not simply see his ministry as a *repetition* of the previous patterns of God's working, but as their *climax*. This is now the final and definitive act of God which brings in the promised days of salvation (and of judgment). It is in Jesus himself, his teaching, and especially his saving ministry of suffering, death and vindication, that God's dealings with men are henceforward focused.

A recognition of this emphasis is vital to a grasp of the significance of much of Jesus' teaching. He is not simply reaffirming what was already there in the OT, but bringing that to which the OT pointed forward, and in which it finds its role fulfilled. From now on the OT itself can only truly be understood *Christologically*.

Thus Jesus gives no sanction to a search for the fulfilment of prophecy in world events unrelated to his ministry. He himself is the focus of fulfilment, and that fulfilment has already arrived in his coming.

This emphasis is summed up in his announcement at the Last Supper of a 'new *covenant' (Lk. 22:20; 1 Cor. 11:25). The covenant made with Israel at Sinai (Ex. 24, *etc.*) is now, as Jeremiah had predicted (Je. 31:31–34), replaced by a new covenant, established by the sacrificial death of Jesus. A new era has begun.

d. The kingdom of God

This idea of present fulfilment and

of a new age comes out particularly in the teaching of Jesus about the *kingdom of God, one of his central themes. He used the term in a wide variety of contexts, so that its essential meaning needs careful definition. It means the *sovereignty* of God, the situation in which God is in control, his rule or reign. Now while in one sense God is always in control, it is also a fact that man rejects his sovereignty and rebels. The 'coming of the kingdom' therefore denotes the practical implementation of God's rule in human affairs, and it was this coming of the kingdom which Jesus announced as he began his ministry (Mk. 1:15). Other sayings reinforce the message that his coming already brought into operation the rule of God (*e.g.* Mt. 12:28; Lk. 17:20f.). Thus he could already speak of people 'entering' or 'receiving' the kingdom (Mk. 10:15, 23–25; Lk. 12:31; 16:16), and assure his disciples that 'Yours is the kingdom of God' (Lk. 6:20; *cf.* Mt. 5:3, 10).

At the same time, there is an important sense in which the kingdom is still future, when it will 'come with power' (Mk. 9:1; *cf.* Mt. 6:10; Lk. 19:11; 22:18); for the acceptance of God's sovereignty which was open to all men in Jesus' ministry, and which was realized in the experience of those who followed him (in that sense the kingdom was already present), would one day become a universal fact, when all men everywhere would recognize the rule of God.

That future consummation is the ultimate horizon of Jesus' proclamation of the kingdom, but it is the final completion of a process already begun in his earthly ministry. The new era which Jesus came to bring is the era of the rule of God. As individuals respond to his message, that rule is progressively established. The 'already' and the 'not yet' combine in a grand panorama of history, of which we have yet to see the culmination. But at the centre of it stands Jesus himself, for it is in response to his teaching and through faith in his saving work that a man can be restored to a true relationship with God, and so 'enter the kingdom of God'.

BIBLIOGRAPHY. G. E. Ladd, *Jesus and the Kingdom*, 1966 (rev. ed., *The Presence of the Future*, 1973).

e. God the Father

To enter the kingdom of God, then, is essentially to accept God's rule. And as such it involves a new relationship with God. So Jesus taught his followers, those who through his ministry entered the kingdom of God, to regard God as their Father. This very personal image of the disciple's relationship with God occurs very frequently in the Gospels, and is one of the most distinctive and novel features of Jesus' teaching. He taught them to address God as 'Our Father who art in heaven' (Mt. 6:9; *LORD'S PRAYER), and to rely on his fatherly care and provision in the very practical matters of food and clothing, because 'your heavenly Father knows that you need them all' (Mt. 6:25–34). Their Father could be relied on to protect them (Mt. 10:28–31) and to provide them with all good things (Mt. 7:7–11). As sons of their Father they must try to be like him, perfect (Mt. 5:43–48).

Jesus' teaching of the Fatherhood of God is not, therefore, a general statement of God's benevolence to his creation, but a specific relationship of love and trust open only to those who have entered the kingdom. It is totally opposed to either a vague universalism or a formal religiosity. It is an exclusive and intimate relationship.

But if Jesus' teaching on God as the Father of his disciples was novel, even more remarkable was his claim to be, in a still more exclusive sense, himself the Son of God. He regularly addressed God as 'Father' or 'my Father', assuming an intimacy never before heard in Jewish religion. (See J. Jeremias, 'Abba', in *The Prayers of Jesus*, 1967, pp. 11–65.) In the Gospel of John the overwhelming majority of references to God as Father (and there are well over 100) are specifically to him as the Father of *Jesus*. The exclusiveness of this relationship is shown by the fact that Jesus never coupled himself with even his disciples as being *in the same sense* sons of God; he never referred to God as 'our Father', including himself in the 'our'. Mt. 11:27 sums up the relationship: 'All things have been delivered to me by my Father; and no one knows the Son except the Father, and no one knows the Father except the Son and any one to whom the Son chooses to reveal him.'

Thus there are two distinct ways of being related to God as Father. There is the essential Father/Son unity which is exclusively the prerogative of Jesus; and there is the disciple's privilege, into which Jesus alone can introduce him, of knowing and depending on God as his Father in heaven. There is no suggestion in Jesus' teaching of a more general Fatherhood of *God embracing all men.

BIBLIOGRAPHY. J. Jeremias, *New Testament Theology*, 1, 1971, pp. 56–68, 178–203.

f. Ethics of the kingdom

Jesus' attack on legalism and his tendency to place personal need before conventional rules (see above, **V.** *c*, *d*) are reflected in the ethics he laid down for his disciples. There is no weakening of the moral demand; the standard is perfection (Mt. 5:48). The righteousness he requires is greater than that of the most scrupulous legalists (Mt. 5:20). But its greatness consists not in a further proliferation of rules of conduct (in fact Jesus made no attempt to lay down a complete ethic for all areas of life), but in a more searching critique of motives and attitudes. There are still rules (the *SERMON ON THE MOUNT contains many of them), but Jesus' demand focuses on the thought behind the act (*e.g.* Mt. 5:21–28; Mk. 7:14–23). Most striking in his teaching is the focal place given to *love* (Mk. 12:28–34; *cf.* Lk. 6:27–35; Mt. 7:12; Jn. 13:34f.; 15:12–17, *etc.*); and lest this demand should be weakened into sentimentality, the Good Samaritan is held up as an example of how love works (Lk. 10:25ff.), and unselfish service is made the criterion of true greatness (Mk. 10:42–45).

Such a practical love must inevitably have its effect on social attitudes and action. Jesus did not, as far as the Gospels record, make specific proposals for the reform of society, any more than he engaged in political agitation (see above, **V.** *f*). But both his life (see above, **V.** *a*, *c*) and teaching tend to undermine a comfortable acceptance of the socio-economic *status quo*. In particular his recommendation of poverty (Lk. 6:20–25; Mk. 10:17–31; Mt. 6:19–24) and his call for unstinting generosity (Lk. 6:34f.; 12:33; 14:12–14; Mk. 10:21) provide the foundation, if not the framework, for a quite radical social ethic. (See R. T. France, 'God and Mammon: the practical relevance of the teaching of Jesus', *EQ* 51, 1979, pp. 3ff.)

Discipleship is, then, a serious and total commitment, which may demand drastic renunciation not only of material possessions but of reputation and relationships (Mk. 10:28–31; Mt. 10:34–39). It is not for the dilettante (Lk. 9:62). It requires a complete reorientation whereby God and not man becomes the point of reference for a man's life and thought (Mt. 6:33, and the whole thrust of Mt. 6), and the ruling motive is not the prospect of reward from man or even from God but gratitude for the forgiving grace of God (Mt. 18:23–35; Lk. 7:36–47).

It is this reorientation rather than specific ethical rules which marks out the ethic of Jesus as radical in comparison with either the legalism or the humanitarianism which marked the best religious systems of his day.

g. The mission of Jesus

We have seen that Jesus regarded himself as playing the central role in bringing in the kingdom of God. It was in his ministry that the hopes of the OT were to find their fulfilment. In other words, he was the * Messiah.

Yet Jesus hardly ever claimed to be Messiah, using that term. The only occasion when he took the initiative in making this claim was outside Jewish territory (Jn. 4:25f.). When others referred to him as Messiah ('Christ') he accepted the idea, but was clearly anxious to avoid the title itself, and substituted his regular title 'Son of man' (Mk. 8:29–33; 14:61f.; * MESSIAH, **II.** *a*). Popular Jewish Messianic hope was firmly committed to a political and nationalistic understanding of the coming day of liberation, and Jesus had no such political intentions (see above, **V.** *f*). His own conception of his mission as Messiah was such that popular Judaism would not have recognized it under that name, and so the title itself was an embarrassment.

But if Jesus avoided the *title* 'Messiah' (and with it the still more politically loaded 'Son of David', which others used of him but which he never used of himself), he did refer specifically to several figures of OT prediction as fulfilled in his ministry. Four or five such figures stand out in his teaching, and the selection is instructive. He was David's lord, as portrayed in Ps. 110:1 (Mk. 12:35–37; 14:62); the humble and rejected shepherd/king who recurs several times in Zc. 9–13 (Mt. 21:1–11; 24:30; 26:31); the suffering Servant of the Lord in Isaiah 53 (Mk. 10:45; 14:24; Lk. 22:37; * SERVANT OF THE LORD, **II.** *a*), with the related figure of the Lord's anointed in Is. 61:1 (Lk. 4:18ff.; Mt. 11:4f.); and the vindicated and enthroned 'son of man' in Dn. 7:13f. (Mk. 8:38; 13:26; 14:62; Mt. 19:28; 25:31; 28:18). The emphasis, therefore, except in the case of Dn. 7:13f. (on which see below, *i*), is strongly on a role of suffering, rejection and death, and a humble rather than a commanding status. Even the discussion of Ps. 110:1 in Mk. 12:35–37 is specifically designed to dissociate Jesus from the title 'Son of David' with its political implications; the dominant figure of OT Messianism, a king like David, does not otherwise appear in Jesus' selection, but is superseded by the picture of suffering and humiliation.

It is for this reason, probably, that Jesus regularly referred to himself as the 'Son of man'. Other titles already had a clearly defined, and usually nationalistic, content, but 'Son of man' was not current as a Messianic *title* in mainstream Judaism (though Dn. 7:13f. was widely referred to as a Messianic prophecy, without use of the title as such), and this rather enigmatic phrase (*cf.* Jn. 12:34) enabled Jesus to define his own conception of his Messianic role. (See further * MESSIAH, **II.** *a*; * JESUS CHRIST, TITLES OF.)

The necessity of his suffering and death is a constant theme of Jesus' teaching (especially Mk. 8:31; 9:31; 10:33f.; but also Mk. 9:12; 10:38, 45; 12:6–8; 14:8, 21–25; Mt. 26:54; Lk. 9:31; 12:50; 13:32f.; 17:25; 22:37; Jn. 10:11–15; 12:23–25; *etc.*), and it is frequently stressed that this *must* be so, because it is written.

The purpose of this suffering and death is most clearly spelt out in some of the references to Isaiah 53, which speaks of the Servant's role of suffering for the sins of his people, dying on their behalf, and thus 'making many to be accounted righteous'; thus Jesus would 'give his life as a ransom for many' (Mk. 10:45), and his 'blood of the covenant' would be 'poured out for many for the forgiveness of sins' (Mt. 26:28). This is sacrificial language, and the goal of Jesus' death is to be the final sacrifice which would make possible the forgiveness of sins and the restoration of fellowship between man and God, thus ending man's rebellion and bringing in the kingdom of God. This redemptive theology appears seldom and allusively in Jesus' teaching, but its direction is unmistakable, and is subsequently taken up into the more developed theology of Paul and the other NT writers. (* ATONEMENT; * REDEMPTION.)

BIBLIOGRAPHY. V. Taylor, *Jesus and his Sacrifice*, 1937; J. Jeremias, *The Eucharistic Words of Jesus*, 1966; R. T. France, *Jesus and the Old Testament*, 1971, ch. 4.

h. The people of God

It is often asserted that Jesus did not intend to found a church. If by 'church' is understood a formal, hierarchical organization, this is no doubt true. But the conception of his mission outlined above inevitably involved the creation of a new community of those who through his redemptive sacrifice entered the kingdom of God. This community, focused at first in his immediate group of disciples but destined to embrace all who responded to his teaching of whatever racial or social background, figures significantly in his teaching.

The word 'church' (*ekklēsia*) occurs only twice in the Gospels. In Mt. 18:17 it refers to the local group of followers of Jesus gathered together to settle disputes among its members, while in Mt. 16:18 it foreshadows the NT view of the universal church as Jesus' continuing representative on earth. But other terms imply the same idea of a defined community: they are, *e.g.*, God's 'little flock' (Lk. 12:32; *cf.* Mk. 14:27; Jn. 10:16), his family (Mk. 3:34f.; 10:29f.; Mt. 10:25), and the guests at his banquet (Mk. 2:19; Mt. 8:11f.; 22:1–14).

Hitherto Israel, the nation, had been the special people of God. Now, Jesus taught, the true people of God will be both wider and narrower than Israel: Gentiles will find a place at the banquet, while some Jews will not (Mt. 8:11f.; *cf.* Mt. 22:1–10). John the Baptist had warned that to be Jewish was not in itself a guarantee of salvation (Mt. 3:8–10), and Jesus took up the same theme. In numerous metaphors and allusions the impression is given that the true Israel is now focused in himself (see above, *c*; also **IV.** *c*) and in those who respond to his call to repentance. This conviction, symbolized in his choice of twelve disciples as his foundation group (see especially

Mt. 19:28), and expressed in his establishment of a 'new covenant' (Lk. 22:20, *etc.*), explains why, while his own ministry was deliberately limited to Israel (Mt. 10:5f.; 15:24), he could send out his disciples after his resurrection to make disciples of all nations (Mt. 28:19; Lk. 24:47; Acts 1:8), to form a people of God drawn from all corners of the earth (Mk. 13:27). (*ISRAEL OF GOD.)

BIBLIOGRAPHY. J. Jeremias, *Jesus' Promise to the Nations*, 1958; G. B. Caird, *Jesus and the Jewish Nation*, 1965; C. H. Dodd, *The Founder of Christianity*, 1970, ch. 5; R. T. France, *TynB* 26, 1975, pp. 53–78.

i. The future

Jesus looked for a future 'coming of the kingdom' (see above, *d*). But precisely how and when he expected it to come is not systematically spelt out, and a number of different interpretations are possible. The following stages in this consummation seem, however, to be clearly taught.

1. Jesus several times predicted that after his suffering he would receive the power and dominion of the 'son of man' of Dn. 7:13f. (see above, *g*). When this vindication is expected is not always clear, but in Mt. 28:18, after the resurrection, he claimed that it was already accomplished. Mk. 14:62 also seems to envisage an imminent vindication, which his judges will themselves witness.

2. One future event which is clearly and repeatedly predicted by Jesus is the destruction of Jerusalem and its Temple (Mk. 13:2 and the following discourse; Lk. 21:20ff.; *cf.* also Mt. 23:37–39; Lk. 23:28–31). This is presented as the inevitable result of the Jewish rejection of God's final appeal (Lk. 13:34f.; 19:41–44; *cf.* Mt. 22:7), and it will come upon that generation (Mt. 23:36; Mk. 13:30). It is likely that some of Jesus' sayings about the 'coming of the Son of man' (again echoing Dn. 7:13f.) relate at least in part to this event rather than to his second coming, particularly as they too envisage a fulfilment within the living generation (Mk. 8:38–9:1; Mt. 10:23; Mk. 13:26, 30). This act of judgment would then be a further manifestation of his vindication. It is not agreed how much of the *Olivet Discourse refers to the question about the destruction of the Temple with which it opens and how much to a more ultimate future, but certainly the fate of Jerusalem holds a prominent place in Jesus' expectations for the future, and is viewed in relation to his own ministry.

3. A further application of Dn. 7:13f. is to the final judgment (Mt. 25:31–34; *cf.* Mt. 19:28). Most fully portrayed in Mt. 25:31ff., this 'day of judgment' is mentioned frequently in Jesus' teaching, applying both to individuals and to communities or nations (*e.g.* Mt. 10:15, 32f.; 11:22–24; 12:36, 41f.). In this final judgment too Jesus plays a central role.

4. Jesus also predicted his own second coming, or *parousia* (the term occurs in the Gospels only in Mt. 24:3, 27, 37, 39), sometimes called the 'day of the Son of man'. It will be as unmistakable and as universally visible as a flash of lightning (Lk. 17:24). It will be sudden and quite unexpected (Mt. 24:37–44; Lk. 17:26–35), demanding constant readiness (Mt. 24:42–51; 25:1–13). Its date cannot be calculated; indeed Jesus himself disclaimed any knowledge of when it would be (Mk. 13:32).

These four aspects of Jesus' teaching about the future merge into one another, so that it is not always possible to be sure which is referred to. In general, while 1 represents a constant state of affairs from the resurrection on, 2 relates to a specific future event expected within the generation, and 3 and 4 are two aspects of the final consummation when the kingdom is fully established; but all are related to Jesus' continuing role as the vindicated and enthroned 'Son of man'. Exegetical disagreement over the reference of specific passages should not be allowed to obscure this over-all pattern in Jesus' vision of the coming of the kingdom of God. Such an understanding of his teaching gives no support to the allegation that Jesus expected the end of the world in the very near future; and it ensures that his call for constant readiness is as binding on us today as on those who first heard him. (*ESCHATOLOGY.)

GENERAL BIBLIOGRAPHY. In addition to the works listed under individual sections above, the following more general works on the life and teaching of Jesus are of value. Older works are listed only where they have a special contribution to make.

A. Edersheim, *The Life and Times of Jesus the Messiah*, 2 vols., 1883 and subsequent eds. (valuable for Jewish background); J. Klausner, *Jesus of Nazareth*, 1929 (a Jewish study); T. W. Manson, *The Teaching of Jesus*², 1935; V. Taylor, *The Life and Ministry of Jesus*, 1954; H. E. W. Turner, *Jesus, Master and Lord*², 1954; G. Bornkamm, *Jesus of Nazareth*, 1960; E. Stauffer, *Jesus and His Story*, 1960; J. Jeremias, *The Parables of Jesus*², 1963; C. K. Barrett, *Jesus and the Gospel Tradition*, 1967; D. Guthrie, *A Shorter Life of Christ*, 1970; C. H. Dodd, *The Founder of Christianity*, 1970; J. Jeremias, *New Testament Theology*, 1: *The Proclamation of Jesus*, 1971; E. Schweizer, *Jesus*, 1971; H. Conzelmann, *Jesus*, 1973 (a translation of the article in *RGG*³); A. M. Hunter, *The Work and Words of Jesus*², 1973; E. Trocmé, *Jesus and His Contemporaries*, 1973; G. Vermes, *Jesus the Jew*, 1973; F. F. Bruce, *Jesus and Christian Origins outside the New Testament*, 1974; G. E. Ladd, *A Theology of the New Testament*, 1974, part 1; G. N. Stanton, *Jesus of Nazareth in New Testament Preaching*, 1974; R. T. France, *The Man They Crucified: a Portrait of Jesus*, 1975.

R.T.F.

JESUS CHRIST, TITLES OF.

A title is a designation which describes or refers to some particular function or status of a person and hence may indicate the honour which is to be ascribed to him. For example, John was known as 'the Baptist' because this term described his characteristic function. Such a function need not be a unique one; there were many people who could be designated by such formulae as 'Z the prophet' or 'Y the king'.

Names and titles are closely related. Sometimes what began as a name could become a title, and vice versa. This is well illustrated in the case of the Roman emperors. Originally Caesar was the family name of Julius Caesar and his adopted nephew Octavian who became the first Roman emperor; after that it became a title meaning 'the Emperor' (Phil. 4:22; although it is mostly used without the article in the NT, *e.g.* Mk. 12:14–17, it still remains a title). Octavian himself was given the title 'Augustus' by the Roman senate in 27 BC, it means 'worthy of reverence' and was translated into Gk. as *sebastos*.

As such it could be used of later emperors (Acts 25:21, 25), but to most people today it is the name of the first emperor, since it was the name by which he was known from the time of its presentation.

The meaning of a title can be altered by the character and deeds of a particular person who holds it and gives it a new stamp. The functions of a king in the UK have been drastically altered over many centuries, so that the title no longer conveys the same meaning as it did when it was first used. The simple title of 'the Leader' (*der Führer*) has been so much coloured by the particular character of Adolf Hitler who used it as a political title in Germany as to render it quite unsuitable for further use in politics.

Finally, there may be cases where a person can be described in such a way that it is clear that he holds the status, or performs the functions, associated with a particular title even though the title itself is not applied to him in that context. Thus we might say 'Z was king in all but name' of somebody who usurped a throne.

These rather general considerations are relevant to a consideration of the titles given to Jesus in the NT, and will help us to avoid some of the pitfalls in the study of this topic.

I. Titles used for Jesus during his lifetime

The name *Jesus* is not strictly a title for the person who bore it. It is, however, a name with a meaning, being a Greek form of 'Joshua', *i.e.* 'Yahweh is salvation'. The NT writers were well aware of this meaning (Mt. 1:21). The name thus indicated the function which was ascribed to Jesus, and this later found expression in the title *Saviour*, which was at first simply a *description* of the function of Jesus (Acts 5:31; 13:23; Phil. 3:20) but then became part of his solemn title (2 Tim. 1:10; Tit. 1:4; 2 Pet. 1:11). Jesus was the personal name of the Saviour, and while its titular significance remains present for informed hearers, it is probable that to many people it is now no more than a name (compare how the fact that 'John' means 'gift of God' is not usually in mind when the name is used).

Jesus was a common enough name in the first half of the 1st century AD, although it is significant that by the end of that century it was beginning to drop completely out of use: it was too sacred for use as a personal name by Christians, and it was abhorrent to Jews. To distinguish Jesus (Christ) from other bearers of the name he was known as *Jesus from Nazareth* or *Jesus the * Nazarene*. The use of this phrase may have acquired some theological significance in view of the similarity of the word 'Nazirite'.

As a result of his characteristic activity Jesus was known as a *Teacher*, and addressed by this title just like any other Jewish teacher (Mk. 4:38; 9:17, 38; 10:17; *et al.*). Occasionally, when there was no danger of confusion with other teachers, he could be called simply 'the Teacher' (Mk. 5:35; 14:14; Jn. 11:28). Jewish teachers were regularly addressed as *Rabbi* (literally, 'my great one'), a mark of respect which came to mean 'the revered (*sc.* teacher)'. This form of address was used by the disciples for Jesus (Mk. 9:5; 11:21; 14:45), although it was not used to refer to him in the third person. In Luke Jesus is sometimes addressed as *Master* (*epistatēs*; Lk. 5:5; 8:24; *et al.*), a term which suggests respect for Jesus by his disciples and sympathizers, and which perhaps was used of his relationship to groups of people rather than to individuals. A further respectful term was *Lord* (*kyrie*, the vocative form of *kyrios*). In the Gospels this probably represents an original Aramaic *rabbî* or *mārî* ('my lord') used as a respectful title (Mk. 7:28; Mt. 8:2, 6, 8; *et al.*). Although this form of address may simply refer to Jesus as a teacher worthy of respect (Lk. 6:46; Jn. 13:13f.), there is a case that Jesus was sometimes addressed in this way in his capacity as a person with miraculous powers (G. Vermes, *Jesus the Jew*, pp. 122–137). The term is not used in Mt. and Mk. as a means of referring to Jesus by a third person (except Mt. 21:3; Mk. 11:3), but Luke calls Jesus 'the Lord' not infrequently in narrative passages (Lk. 7:13; 10:1, 39, 41; *et al.*). This usage suggests that Luke was well aware that the full significance of the title was not realized until after the resurrection, but that he wanted to show that Jesus acted during his lifetime with something of the same authority which he possessed in full measure after the resurrection.

The fact that Jesus was regarded as more than an ordinary Jewish teacher is expressed in the term *Prophet* (Mt. 21:11, 46; Mk. 6:15; 8:28; Lk. 7:16, 39; 24:19; Jn. 4:19; 6:14; 7:40; 9:17). This understanding of his own position was recognized and expressed by Jesus (Mk. 6:4; Lk. 4:24; 13:33f.). In themselves neither of the titles, 'teacher' and 'prophet', distinguished Jesus from other teachers and prophets of his time, whether from Jewish religious leaders or from some groups of early church leaders (*e.g.* Acts 13:1), although naturally the early church would have claimed that Jesus was *the* Teacher and Prophet *par excellence*.

It is probable, however, that in some cases the term *The Prophet* was used in a unique sense. Jewish thought expected the coming of Elijah, or a person like him, to usher in the End, and there was some speculation whether John the Baptist or Jesus was to be identified as this so-called eschatological or final prophet (*cf.* Jn. 1:21, 25). There is some apparent confusion on the matter, since John denied that he was the prophet, while Jesus claimed that John was in fact Elijah (Mt. 17:12f.). The confusion would disappear if the reference in Jn. 1:21, 25 was to the coming of a final prophet like Moses (Dt. 18:15–19); Peter identified Jesus as this 'Mosaic' prophet (Acts 3:22–26), and this would leave the way clear for John to be regarded as a separate forerunner of the End, a prophet like Elijah. The difficulty may have arisen because Jewish thought did not keep the two figures quite separate. It is probable that Jesus himself saw his role as that of the Mosaic prophet. He did not use the title in this connection, but he regarded himself as reenacting the work of Moses and as fulfilling the role of the prophet who speaks in Is. 61:1–3. He used passages from Is. 29:18f.; 35:5f. and 61:1 to describe his own work (Lk. 4:18f.; 7:22) in terms of a new creation of the paradisial conditions of the Exodus period and the wilderness wanderings, *i.e.* in terms of the work of Moses. From this point of view the teaching of Jesus in which he reinterpreted the law of Moses may also be significant.

Just as Jesus saw his work in terms of the law-giver and the prophets (Moses and Elijah/Elisha; *cf.* Lk. 4:25–27), so it is probable that the Jewish concept of wisdom affected his thinking, although the actual title of *Wisdom* is not applied to him in the Gospels (see, however, 1 Cor. 1:24, 30). In the OT and the intertestamental literature we find the personified concept of Wisdom as the assistant of God at creation and (in the form of the law) as the guide of God's people (Pr. 8:22–36). The wise man *par excellence* was Solomon, and it is no accident that Jesus claimed that in his ministry something greater than Solomon was present (Mt. 12:42). Wisdom was regarded as sending her emissaries to men to reveal God's ways (Pr. 9:3–6). At times Jesus spoke as if he were such an emissary (Lk. 11:49–51) or as if he himself were to be identified with Wisdom (Lk. 13:34; *cf.* Mt. 23:34–37).

Jewish hopes were centred on the establishment of God's rule or kingdom, and this hope was often associated with the coming of an agent of God to exercise his rule. Such a person would be a king, anointed by God and belonging to the line of David. The term *Anointed One*, which could be used to describe a king, priest or prophet, came to be used as a technical term in the intertestamental period for this expected agent of God. The Heb. word was *māšîaḥ*, from which was derived the *transliterated* Gk. form *Messias*, anglicized as * *Messiah*; the corresponding Gk. word *meaning* 'anointed' was *Christos*, from which comes the alternative English form *Christ*. Since the expected ruler was expected to be a *King* and a *Son* (*i.e.* descendant) *of David*, these two terms were also used as titles or designations for him.

It stands beyond all doubt that Jesus was put to death by the Romans on a charge of claiming to be the king of the Jews (Mk. 15:26). The question is whether he explicitly claimed this office and implicitly acted in this role. The actual term 'Messiah' is only rarely found on the lips of Jesus. In Mk. 12:35 and 13:21 (*cf.* Mt. 24:5) he speaks about the Messiah and claimants to Messiahship without directly identifying himself as Messiah. In Mt. 23:10 and Mk. 9:41 he is represented as teaching his disciples, apparently with reference primarily to the situation in the early church. Mt. 16:20 merely echoes v. 16. It follows that Jesus did not refer to himself as Messiah in his public teaching to the crowds and that at best he used the title rarely in speaking to his disciples (*cf.* Jn. 4:25f.). The situation is the same with regard to 'Son of David'; the question in Mk. 12:35–37 does not explicitly identify Jesus as the Son of David. Nor did Jesus publicly claim the title of 'King' (Mt. 25:34, 40 is addressed to the disciples). On the other hand, many of Jesus' actions could be regarded as those of the Messiah. His baptism with the Spirit was regarded by both himself (Lk. 4:18) and the early church (Acts 4:27; 10:38) as an anointing. He proclaimed the coming rule of God, associated its coming with his own activity (Mt. 12:28), and acted with an authority that suggested that he stood in the place of God (Mk. 2:7). It is not surprising that the question whether he was the expected king was in the air (*cf.* Jn. 4:29; 7:25–31) and that the people would have made him king (Jn. 6:15). At his trial he was asked whether he was the Messiah, and on this occasion he did publicly admit the fact (Mk. 14:61f.; *cf.* Jn. 18.33–38). At an earlier point Peter named him as the Messiah, and Jesus did not reject the identification (Mk. 8:29f.); people who hoped that he would mercifully help them in their need addressed him as 'Son of David' (Mk. 10:47f.).

The evidence shows that while Jesus implicitly acted as Messiah he was reticent on the matter and indeed tried to hush down suggestions that he was the Messiah (Mk. 8:30). Various explanations have been offered for his attitude. We can dismiss the view that the Gospels have misrepresented the situation, and that Jesus was not recognized by himself or anybody else to be the Messiah; only after the resurrection did the church give this title to him (so W. Wrede, *The Messianic Secret*, E.T. 1971; *contra*: J. D. G. Dunn, *TynB* 21, 1970, pp. 92–117). One important element in explanation is certainly that Jesus' concept of Messiahship was markedly different from that of many Jews who expected the Messiah to inaugurate a political upheaval and liberate the country from the Romans; even if there were Jews with a more spiritual ideal of the Messiah's work, Jesus had to guard against this misrepresentation. (It should go without saying that Jesus in no way associated himself with the advocacy of violence by the political revolutionaries of his day; on this subject the last word has been spoken by M. Hengel, *Was Jesus a Revolutionist?*, 1971.) Another element may be that Jesus did not wish to claim Messiahship until he had shown himself to be Messiah by what he did, or until people recognized the real significance of his ministry. In so doing he freed Messiahship from its this-worldly political associations and reinterpreted it in terms of the OT concept of God's mighty act of salvation.

Undoubtedly, however, the Gospels give the impression that Jesus preferred to use another description, *Son of man* (note the shift in terminology in Mk. 8:29f./31 and 14:61/62). This unusual Gk. expression can have arisen only as a translation of an idiomatic Semitic phrase (Heb. *ben 'āḏām*; Aram. *bar 'enāš(â)*) which means either a particular member of the species 'man' (*e.g.* Ezk. 2:1) or mankind in general (*e.g.* Ps. 8:4). In Dn. 7:13f. the phrase describes 'one like a man' (NEB) or 'what looked like a human being' (TEV) who comes with the clouds to the Ancient of Days and receives everlasting dominion over all peoples from him. In the language of Jesus' time it appears to have been possible to use the phrase as a modest way of referring to oneself in certain situations, although opinions differ whether it was used to make a statement true of mankind in general and hence of the speaker in particular or to make a statement applying only to the speaker.

The phrase occurs quite often on the lips of Jesus, and its occurrences in the Synoptic Gospels have led to much debate.

1. On the one hand, it has been assumed that the significance of the phrase is derived from Dn. 7:13f., in which case it refers to the future coming of a heavenly being described with apocalyptic symbolism (Mk. 13:26; 14:62) and to the role played by this figure at the last judgment (Mk. 8:38; Mt. 10:23; 19:28; 25:31; Lk. 12:8f.; 17:22–30; 18:8). Some scholars think that the early church was the first to use this concept to describe the future role of Jesus (so N. Perrin, *A Modern Pilgrimage in New Testament Christology*, 1974); others argue, on the basis of Lk. 12:8f., that Jesus looked forward to the coming of an apocalyptic figure *other than himself* who would vindicate his work, and that it was the early church which later identified Jesus himself with this coming figure (so H. E. Tödt, *The Son of Man in the Synoptic Tradition*, 1965); others again argue that Jesus looked forward to his own future coming as the Son of man (so O. Cullmann, *The Christology of the New Testament*², 1963).

Alongside these 'future' statements there are others which speak of the present authority and humiliation of the Son of man (Mk. 2:10, 27f.; Lk. 6:22; 7:34; 9:58; 12:10; 19:10) and prophesy his suffering, death and resurrection (Mk. 8:31; 9:9, 12, 31; 10:33f., 45; 14:21, 41; *cf.* Lk. 24:7). It is hard (but not impossible: see below) to see how statements like these could be made about the Son of man described in Dn. 7, and accordingly many scholars think that the use of Son of man in such sayings derives from the early church which, having identified Jesus as the coming Son of man, proceeded to use the same title with reference to his earthly ministry and his passion. Other scholars hold that Jesus produced his own creative reinterpretation of the role of the Son of man under the influence of the prophecy of the suffering Servant of Yahweh (Is. 52:13–53:12).

2. On the other hand, various scholars take the use of *bar ᵉnāš(â)* as a self-designation in Aram. as their starting-point, and hold that Jesus used it simply as a means of referring to himself. On this view, the statements in the Gospels which are non-apocalyptic in content and refer to Jesus simply as a man are most likely to be authentic. Later, the use of the term by Jesus led the church back to Dn. 7, and it proceeded to reinterpret the teaching of Jesus in apocalyptic terms (G. Vermes, *op. cit.*, pp. 160–191).

3. It is probable that scholars have been led astray by insisting on one basic origin for all the sayings and not taking the ambiguity of the term sufficiently seriously. Clearly it could be used as a self-designation, even although the precise circumstances in which this was felt to be proper remain uncertain. At the same time it cannot be denied that the term could have a titular force. C. F. D. Moule rightly observes that the use of the article in the phrase may give the force of '*the* human figure' (*sc.* the one mentioned in Dn. 7:13f.; 'Neglected Features in the Problem of "the Son of Man" ', in J. Gnilka (ed.), *Neues Testament und Kirche*, 1974, pp. 413–428). The fact that this figure played a role in some areas of Jewish thought is shown by the allusions in *1 Enoch* and *4 Ezra* (although the dating of the crucial portions in *1 Enoch* is notoriously insecure). The most probable approach, therefore, is still that which takes Dn. 7:13f. as its starting-point and sees there a figure, perhaps the leader and representative of Israel, with whom Jesus identifies himself. This figure is one possessing authority and destined to rule the world, but the way to that rule is by humility, suffering and rejection. It is not too difficult to understand Jesus speaking in this way, provided that he can be assumed to have looked forward to his own rejection and subsequent vindication by God. This assumption is wholly probable when we take account of: (a) Jesus' recognition of the realities of the situation in which he carried on a ministry that brought him into collision with the hostile Jewish authorities; and (b) Jesus' acceptance of the way of life of the godly man described in the OT, according to which the godly can expect rejection and persecution and must put their trust in God to deliver them. This pattern can be traced in certain of the Psalms (especially Pss. 22; 69), in the prophecies of the suffering Servant and in the career of 'the saints of the Most High' in Dn. It is also to be found in the book of Wisdom (although it is doubtful whether this book could have influenced Jesus himself) and in the popular legends in which the Jews glorified the fate of the Maccabean martyrs. Against this considerable background it would be strange if Jesus had not understood his career in such terms. At the same time, his manner of speaking certainly mystified his hearers: 'Who is this Son of man?' (Jn. 12:34). It was probably a deliberate means of concealing his own claims to some extent so as not to lead to false expectations. It laid claim to authority but an authority which was largely rejected by men. Thus by his use of this phrase Jesus laid claim to being the final representative of God to men, destined to rule but rejected by Israel, condemned to suffer but vindicated by God.

One of the elements which contributed to Jesus' understanding of his role as Son of man was the figure of the *Servant of Yahweh.* The actual title was not used by Jesus, and the nearest approach to its use is when it occurs in a quotation from Is. 42:1–4 in Mt. 12:18–21. Nevertheless, there is good evidence that Jesus saw himself as fulfilling the role of one who came to serve and give himself as a ransom for many (Mk. 10:45; *cf.* 14:24; Is. 53:10–12) and who therefore 'shared the fate of criminals' (Lk. 22:37, TEV; *cf.* Is. 53:12; R. T. France, *TynB* 19, 1968, pp. 26–52).

If the above titles express the role of Jesus, his status and relationship to God find expression in the title of *Son of God.* The use of this title for angels and other heavenly beings does not seem to be of central significance for its application to Jesus. More important is the way in which it was used in the OT to refer to the people of Israel as a whole and to their king in particular and to express the relationship which they had to God in terms of divine care and protection on the one hand and human service and obedience on the other. It is possible that by NT times the Messiah was beginning to be regarded as in some special sense the Son of God, and the thought that godly individuals were the special objects of God's fatherly care and concern had also developed.

Jesus himself was undoubtedly conscious of a particular relationship to *God whom he addressed in prayer by the intimate name of *Abba (Mk. 14:36). It is against this background that we should understand his use of the term 'Son' to express his relationship to God as his Father (Mt. 11:27; Lk. 10:22). Here he claims that the same intimacy exists between himself and God as between a son and his father, so that he alone is qualified to reveal God to men. Yet there are secrets of the Father's purpose hidden even from the Son (Mk. 13:32). Although the allusion may well not have been clear to the crowds, it is likely that the reference to the owner's son in the parable of the vineyard (Mk. 12:6) was a veiled way of pointing to Jesus himself and to his fate. This sense of a unique Sonship goes beyond the general sense of a filial relationship to God which might have been held by a pious Jew. It is further to be seen in the way in which God himself addresses Jesus as his Son in the stories of the baptism and the transfiguration (Mk. 1:11; 9:7), and also in the manner of address used by Satan and the demons (Mt. 4:3, 6; Mk. 3:11; 5:7). The evidence shows that Jesus himself was extremely reticent to express his sense of unique personal relationship to God; nevertheless it is clear that the Jewish authorities suspected that he was making claims of this kind (Mk. 14:61; Lk. 22:70), claims which were perhaps made more openly on occasion than the Synoptic Gospels suggest (in Jn.

Jesus' self-revelation is more public, but this may be due to the way in which John has deliberately brought out more clearly the full implications of Jesus' teaching for his readers). It is in this title that the fullest expression of who Jesus was is to be found (see I. H. Marshall, *Int* 21, 1967, pp. 87–103).

II. The use of titles in the earliest period of the church

A period of some 20 years separates the death and resurrection of Jesus from the earliest NT documents (the earliest letters of Paul) which can be reliably dated. By Paul's time the use of various titles to refer to Jesus was well established; he manifestly used an existing, fully developed terminology which he could take for granted [illegible] plain to his readers. It is, however, difficult to trace the use of the various titles and the associated theological understanding of Jesus during this pre-literary period. We have to proceed by attempting to recognize occurrences of the titles in the NT writings which can plausibly be regarded as reflecting traditional usage; this is a subjective process and leads to hypotheses of varying credibility. We can also make use of the account of the early church given to us in Acts, but it has to be recognized that Luke wrote some years after the events which he described, and that there would be an inevitable tendency to adopt the terminology with which his readers were familiar. We may compare how a well-known public figure tends to be described by his later title even when his earlier career is being discussed; there is a temptation to say 'Queen Victoria spent her earlier years in Kensington Palace' rather than more pedantically 'Princess Victoria (who later became Queen) spent her earlier years . . .'. Nevertheless, with due caution we can make some progress in tracing the early development of titles to describe Jesus.

Some scholars have admittedly shown considerable boldness in postulating a series of stages in the Christological thinking of the early church on the assumption that an original understanding of Jesus in purely Jewish terms was succeeded by an understanding that was increasingly affected by Hellenistic ways of thinking mediated to the church first by Diaspora Judaism and then more directly by the Gentile world (F. Hahn; R. H. Fuller). While some *broad* developments of this kind no doubt occurred, the hypothesis cannot be used to trace stages of development with any precision, since it is clear that influences of all kinds affected the church from its earliest days and also that we have to do with the Christological thinking of a number of different semi-independent churches. There is no possibility of tracing a simple evolutionary line of development through the complex thought-processes of the first 20 years or so of the Christian church. What we can say is that this period was one of unparalleled creative thinking in the development of Christology (I. H. Marshall, *NTS* 19, 1972–3, pp. 271–287).

It is sometimes suggested that the early church's interest in Jesus was originally purely functional rather than ontological (O. Cullmann). It was concerned with what Jesus did rather than who he was, and did not ask metaphysical questions about his status. But to put the alternatives so sharply is probably to separate what originally belonged together: function and status cannot be so easily separated. The early church was no doubt concerned with what Jesus had accomplished, but the very nature of what he had accomplished inevitably raised the question of his relationship to God from the very start, and this is reflected in the titles used to describe him.

During this period most of the ordinary 'human' terms used to describe Jesus during his ministry fell out of use, except in so far as they were preserved in narrative material about his career. Terms such as *Rabbi* and *Teacher* were no longer appropriate. The term *Prophet* which had represented a higher level of popular insight into the function of Jesus likewise dropped out of use; although the term was still applied to him (Acts 3:22f.; *cf.* 7:37), it does not occur as an actual title of Jesus. What is surprising is the virtually complete disappearance of *Son of man* from circulation. The phrase is found as a title only on the lips of the dying Stephen (Acts 7:56). Elsewhere it has survived only in a citation from the OT (Heb. 2:6; quoting Ps. 8:5) and in a description of Jesus in Rev. 1:13; 14:14 (*cf.* Dn. 7:13f.). But the thought was probably still alive. On the one hand, it is possible that we have a translation of 'Son of man' into more intelligible Gk. as 'the Man' in one or two passages where Jesus is placed over against Adam, the first man (Rom. 5:15; 1 Cor. 15:21, 47; *cf.* 1 Tim. 2:5). On the other hand, the Gospels have preserved the use of the term on the lips of Jesus. As we observed, there are scholars who claim that the use of the term originated in the early church, or that at least the majority of examples of its use were developed by the early church on the basis of a small number of actual sayings of Jesus. While these suggestions are highly unlikely, we cannot exclude the possibility that the inclusion of the title in a few sayings may be due to the early church; this is most probably the case in Jn. where the teaching of Jesus has come down to us in a form where it is impossible to disentangle the actual words of [illegible] Evangelist's interpretative commentary. But it is important that John's fuller expression of the implicit significance of the title takes place within the confines of a Gospel, and as teaching which is ascribed to Jesus himself and which ultimately rests on his own words (see **IV**, below). There is no indication that the early church used the title independently. Clearly it was regarded as a term that was appropriate only on the lips of Jesus as a self-designation, with the one exception of Acts 7:56. It never became a term for use in confessional statements (with the possible exception of Jn. 9:35).

Although the title of *Servant* did not occur in the Gospels, we saw that the associated motifs were present in the description of the work of Jesus as service for 'the many'. This same motif reappears in the thinking of the early church. It is most obvious in 1 Pet. 2:21–25, where the passion and death of Jesus are described in language drawn from Is. 53; it is not quite so clearly present in a number of traditional formulae in Paul which express the significance of the death of Jesus (Rom. 4:25; 8:34; 1 Cor. 11:23–25; 15:3–5; Phil. 2:6–11; 1 Tim. 2:6; J. Jeremias, *TDNT* 5, pp. 705–712). The title itself (*pais*) is to be found in Acts 3:13, 26; 4:27, 30 where Jesus is declared to be God's Servant who was delivered up by the Jews to death, but raised and glorified by God to be the source of blessing for his people. If Jesus is designated here by a title also borne by David (Acts 4:25, *pais*) and the prophets (Rev. 11:18; 22:9, *doulos*), here it is above all the thought of Is. 42:1–4; 52:13f. which has influenced the early church. Although the title does not reappear until the Apostolic Fathers and has therefore been suspected to be a Lucan rather than a primitive designation for Jesus, it is more likely that the term was used in the Palestinian church and then fell out of use because of its ambiguity in the form *pais* (which can mean 'child' or 'servant') and its subordinationist colouring in the form *doulos* ('slave').

According to the speech attributed to Peter on the day of Pentecost the significance of the resurrection was that God had made the Jesus whom the Jews crucified to be both Lord and *Christ* (Acts 2:36). This text gives the key to the development of the Christological titles. The resurrection was the decisive event which led the followers of Jesus to a new evaluation of his person, and this was confirmed for them by the gift of the Spirit coming from the exalted Jesus (Acts 2:33). Jesus' claims to be a 'Messianic' figure of some kind had now been vindicated by God in raising him from the dead and thereby attesting the truth of these claims. The One who died under Pilate's sarcastic placard as 'The King of the Jews' had now been shown to be king in a deeper sense. The actual title of 'king' does not seem to have been used overmuch. It is true that the king replaced the 'kingdom' in the apostolic preaching, but the word was perhaps politically dangerous (Acts 17:7) and use of it was restrained (Rev. 17:14; 19:16); note, however, that the title of 'Lord' which was equally dangerous politically was in frequent use. 'Messiah'—a word meaningless outside Heb.-speaking circles—was replaced not so much by 'king' as by 'Christ'. In this form the title tended to lose its original meaning of 'anointed one' (see, however, 2 Cor. 1:21) and to take on more the sense of 'Saviour'. It was particularly used in statements about the death and resurrection of Jesus (Rom. 5:6, 8; 6:3–9; 8:34; 14:9; 1 Cor. 15:3–5; 1 Pet. 3:18; W. Kramer, *Christ, Lord, Son of God*, 1966). It was as the One who died and rose again that Jesus was the Christ. Although 'Christ' tended to become more and more a name for Jesus, rather than a title, it continued to have a sense of dignity about it, so that it was scarcely ever used alone with the title 'Lord' (*i.e.* in the combination 'the Lord Christ'; Rom. 16:18; Col. 3:24) but rather in the form 'the Lord Jesus Christ'.

In Acts 3:20f. Jesus is represented as the One who is designated to appear as the Christ at the end of time. Accordingly it has been claimed (especially by F. Hahn) that the earliest Christology of the church was concerned with the future coming of Jesus, and that the various titles of Son of man, Christ and Lord were originally used to indicate what his function would be at the end of time; only later (though still within this pre-literary period) was it realized that the One who would come as Christ and Lord at the end was *already* Christ and Lord by virtue of his resurrection and exaltation (and that the resurrection and exaltation confirmed an existing status). This theory lacks substantiation. Acts 3:20f. can only mean that the One who has already been ordained as the Christ will return at the end of time. Jesus is not the Messiah-designate, but is already the Messiah. It was indeed only because of the resurrection and what it implied concerning the person of Jesus that the early church could look forward with confidence to his parousia as the Son of man. It was, accordingly, the death and resurrection which established the meaning of the term Christ: the Christian message in Paul's view was exclusively oriented to 'Christ crucified' (1 Cor. 1:23; 2:5).

The other title which figures in Acts 2:36 is *Lord*. By the resurrection God had demonstrated that Jesus was indeed the Lord, and the early church applied the words of Ps. 110:1 to him in virtue of this event: 'The Lord said to my Lord, Sit at my right hand, till I make thy enemies a stool for thy feet' (Acts 2:34f.). This text had already been used by Jesus when he taught that the Messiah was David's Lord (Mk. 12:36) and in his reply to the high priest at his trial (Mk. 14:62). If Jesus was now Lord, it followed that the task of the early church was to lead people to recognize the status of Jesus. New converts became members of the church by acknowledging Jesus as Lord: 'If you confess with your lips that Jesus is Lord and believe in your heart that God raised him from the dead, you will be saved' (Rom. 10:9; *cf.* 1 Cor. 12:3). The great significance of this confession is seen in Phil. 2:11 where the climax of God's purpose is that all creation will acknowledge Jesus Christ as Lord. In this confession there may well be a polemical note, since it places Jesus over against other 'lords' recognized by worshippers in the Hellenistic world. Certainly Jews recognized only one God and Lord, but pagans worshipped 'gods many and lords many'; over against them both Christians acknowledged 'one God, the Father, . . . and one Lord, Jesus Christ' (1 Cor. 8:6). The Roman emperor too was acclaimed as lord (*dominus*) by his subjects and successive emperors increasingly claimed their total allegiance; this was to lead to keen conflicts of conscience for Christians at a later stage.

An important piece of evidence for the early Christian use of the title for Jesus is the phrase preserved in Aramaic in 1 Cor. 16:22: *'*Maranatha*'. This is a combination of two words and means 'Our Lord, come' or 'Our Lord has/will come'. Scholars debate whether it was originally a prayer for the parousia of Jesus as Lord (*cf.* Rev. 22:20) or a promise that his coming was at hand (*cf.* Phil. 4:5). The fact that the phrase was preserved in a Gk.-speaking church in Aram. indicates that it was originally used in an Aram.-speaking church, *i.e.* it most probably arose in the earliest days of the church in Palestine. Evidence from Qumran has helped to confirm the possibility of this development in an Aram.-speaking environment (J. A. Fitzmyer, *NTS* 20, 1973–4, pp. 386–391).

The final term to be discussed in this section is *Son of God*. It may well have been especially associated with the preaching of Paul: it is significant that Acts 9:20 links the title with his preaching, and that it appears only once elsewhere in Acts, namely in a citation of Ps. 2:7 in Paul's sermon in Pisidian Antioch (Acts 13:33). Here the promise, 'Thou art my Son, today I have begotten thee', is applied by Paul to the resurrection which is regarded as the begetting of Jesus to new life. The thought, however, is not that Jesus became God's Son by being raised from the dead, but rather that *because* he was his Son, God raised him from the dead (*cf.* Wisdom 2:18). The same thought reappears in Rom. 1:3f., generally regarded as a pre-Pauline formula, where Jesus is said to have been declared to be Son of God with power by the resurrection from the dead. In 1 Thes. 1:9f. the sonship of

Jesus is again connected with the resurrection, and this fact is made the basis for the hope of his parousia.

Two further elements appear to be associated with the title of 'Son' in this early period. One is the thought of the pre-existence of the Son; a number of texts speak of God sending his Son (Jn. 3:17; Rom. 8:3; Gal. 4:4f.; 1 Jn. 4:9f., 14), and clearly presuppose that the Son came from being with the Father into the world. This line of thought is expressed quite explicitly without the actual use of the term 'Son' in the pre-Pauline hymn in Phil. 2:6–11 (R. P. Martin, *Carmen Christi*, 1967). Here Jesus is a divine figure, existing in the image of God and equal with God, who exchanged his heavenly mode of existence for a human, earthly form of existence in humility. Although the hymn speaks of his 'emptying himself' so that he exchanged the form of God for that of a slave, the fact that Paul regarded Jesus as God's Son during his life and death indicates that he did not interpret the hymn to mean that Jesus surrendered his divine nature in order to become incarnate. Rather, 'He emptied Himself in that He took the servant's form . . . ; and this necessarily involved an eclipsing of His glory as the divine Image in order that He might come, in human flesh, as the Image of God incarnate' (R. P. Martin, p. 194).

The other element associated with the title of Son is that God gave him up to suffer and die (Rom. 4:25; 8:32; Gal. 2:20; *cf.* Jn. 3:16). There may be some connection here with the OT example of Abraham who was prepared to give up his son, Isaac, to show his faith and obedience (Gn. 22:12, 16). Nor did God withhold his only Son, but gave him up freely to take away our sins. By the use of the title 'Son' the greatness of the divine sacrifice is made all the more plain.

It is not certain at what point the tradition of the virgin birth of Jesus began to influence the Christological thinking of the church. The implication of both the birth stories is that the circumstances of Jesus' birth were kept quiet (*cf.* Mt. 1:19; Lk. 2:19, 51), and there is very little evidence that the tradition influenced the church before it was given expression in the Gospels. In both accounts Jesus is presented as the Son of God (Mt. 2:15; Lk. 1:32, 35) whose birth as the son of Mary is due to the influence of the Holy Spirit; it is as the Son of God that he is qualified for the office and task of the Messiah (Lk. 1:32f.). Not only so, but as the Son of God he can be designated *Emmanuel*, 'God with us'; his presence on earth is tantamount to that of God himself. The two accounts do not take up the question of the relation between the Spirit-conception of Jesus and his identity with the pre-existent Son of God; their concern is exclusively with the way in which the son of Mary could be born as the Son of God.

III. Paul's use of Christological titles

In the preceding section we have seen that the essential stages in the development of the Christological vocabulary of the church had already taken place before the writing of Paul's letters. He used an existing vocabulary in them, and he can assume that the terms which he uses are generally familiar to his Christian readers. Consequently, there is little to be said about the use of the titles which is distinctive of Paul. This may well be because he himself was closely involved in the development of the theology of the early church and had already made his own contribution to the common store of Christological thinking before he came to write his letters. In conscious opposition, therefore, to the scheme adopted by R. Bultmann (*Theology of the New Testament*, 1, 1952, ch. 3), L. Goppelt rightly refuses to discuss 'The kerygma of the Hellenistic Church aside from Paul' because this simply leads to 'unhistorical abstractions'; while recognizing that there were many currents of thought in the early church, he prefers to discuss the theology of Paul in the light of the traditions which he received and the situations in which he worked (*Theologie des Neuen Testaments*, 2, 1976, pp. 360f.).

Two titles which we might have expected to find in Paul's letters are conspicuously absent or rare. Paul never uses *Servant* with respect to Jesus, and he uses the motifs associated with the title only when alluding to traditional material. He does, however, think of himself and his fellow workers as slaves of God (*doulos*), and just once he can speak of Jesus as a *minister* (*diakonos*; Rom. 15:8) for the circumcision (*i.e.* for the Jews). He also sees the role of the Servant as being fulfilled in the missionary witness of the church (Rom. 10:16; 15:21; *cf.* Acts 13:47).

The actual name *Jesus*, used by itself, is quite rare in Paul (about 16 occurrences), although it is of course common in combinations. Half of these occurrences are in 2 Cor. 4:10–14 and 1 Thes. 4:14 where Paul is discussing how the death and resurrection of Jesus are repeated in the lives of believers. Otherwise he mainly uses 'Jesus' when he is discussing what other titles should be predicated of its bearer (1 Cor. 12:3; *cf.* 2 Cor. 11:4; Phil. 2:10).

For Paul *Christ* has become the main designation by which he refers to Jesus. His message was the 'gospel of Christ' (*e.g.* Gal. 1:7), and a study of the occurrences of 'Christ' produces a Pauline theology in miniature (see the excellent treatment by W. Grundmann, [illegible] 561). He takes over the traditional uses of the title with respect especially to the death and resurrection of Jesus, but he also uses it in many other ways. The distinctively Pauline element comes out in the use of the phrase 'in Christ', by which Christ is described as the determining circumstance which conditions the life of the believer (J. K. S. Reid, *Our Life in Christ*, 1963, ch. 1). This means that the phrase does not refer so much to a mystical union with a heavenly figure but rather to the historical facts of the crucifixion and resurrection which condition our existence. Thus justification takes place 'in Christ' (Gal. 2:17); the individual Christian is 'a man in Christ' (2 Cor. 12:2), and the churches are 'in Christ' (Gal. 1:22, Gk.); Christian witness takes place 'in Christ' (1 Cor. 4:15; Phil. 1:13, Gk.; 2 Cor. 2:17). At every point the Christian life is determined by the new situation brought about by the fact of Christ.

Paul frequently uses the combination 'Jesus Christ' as a title. Sometimes the words occur in the reverse order 'Christ Jesus', but a satisfying explanation for the variations in word order has not been discovered: grammatical reasons may contribute to the variation, and it has also been suggested that Paul wished to emphasize the human Jesus or the heavenly, pre-existent Christ by placing one or the other first. In any case, there does not appear to be any difference in the use of the compound title from that of the simple 'Christ', except that the compound title was felt to be more emphatic and dignified.

Paul's usage of *Lord* is essentially the same as that of the pre-Pauline church. Here especially there is no need to invoke the influence of pagan worship of cult deities in order to account for the distinctive features of Pauline usage. This thesis—along with the associated claim that much of Paul's theology was derived from transfer of originally pagan ideas to Christianity—has been increasingly shown to be unnecessary and untenable (O. Cullmann, *op. cit.*, ch. 7). Of course Christians who already acknowledged Jesus as Lord had to define more closely what they meant by this title over against pagan worship of other lords (1 Cor. 8:6), but this is quite different from saying that the Christian usage was derived from the pagan.

Since confession of Jesus as Lord was the mark of the Christian, and since for Christians there was no other Lord, it was natural for Paul to speak simply of 'the Lord' when he wished to refer to Jesus. It is true that the same title was used to refer to God the Father, and that this can lead to a certain ambiguity as to whether God or Jesus is meant (this is especially the case in Acts; J. C. O'Neill, *SJT* 8, 1955, pp. 155–174); generally, however, 'Lord' is used for God by Paul almost exclusively in quotations from the OT, so that there is little risk of confusion.

If the title 'Christ' had come to have the connotation of 'Saviour', that of 'Lord' primarily expresses the exalted position of Jesus and his rule over the universe and especially over believers who accept his Lordship. It is thus especially used when the responsibility of Christians to obey Jesus is being expressed (*e.g.* Rom. 12:11; 1 Cor. 4:4f.). But Paul also uses it quite freely to refer to the earthly Jesus (1 Cor. 9:5), especially with reference to what came to be known as 'the supper of the Lord' (1 Cor. 10:21; 11:23, 26f.) and also when referring to instructions given by the earthly Jesus (1 Cor. 7:10, 25; 9:14; *et al.*). It is not surprising that the formula 'in Christ' is altered to 'in the Lord' when it occurs in the context of exhortations and commands (Eph. 6:1; Phil. 4:2; Col. 4:17; *et al.*). Nevertheless, the use of the two titles is quite fluid, and sometimes Paul uses the one where we might have expected him to use the other.

Compound titles including the title of Lord are frequent in Paul, and are evidently used in order to exalt the person thus designated. The early Christian confession 'Jesus (Christ) is Lord' lies behind the development of 'the Lord Jesus (Christ)' (2 Cor. 4:5), and Paul often speaks of *our* Lord, thereby emphasizing both the need for personal commitment to Jesus and also the saving care and concern of Jesus for his people. This formula is found in the introductory salutations of Paul's letters where 'God our Father and the Lord Jesus Christ' are associated together as the source of spiritual blessings. W. Grundmann (*TDNT* 9, p. 554) has suggested that behind this formula there lies the OT phrase 'the Lord God' which was transformed in Christian worship into 'God the Father' and the co-ordinated 'Lord Jesus Christ', indicating that the person who has Jesus as his Lord also has God as his Father. Whether or not this explanation is correct, two facts are noteworthy. The one is that here God the Father and Jesus are placed quite naturally alongside each other in a way that indicates an equality of status; to be sure, the subordination of Jesus to the Father is always carefully preserved (1 Cor. 15:28; Phil. 2:11), but no other being is ever placed alongside the Father in this way. The second fact is that the OT usage of 'Lord' as a title for God has undoubtedly influenced Christian usage. This is clear from Phil. 2:10f. which takes up the language of Is. 45:22–25 and applies what is said there about God to Jesus. Similarly, in Rom. 10:9, 13 a citation from Joel 2:32 about calling on the name of the Lord (*i.e.* Yahweh) has been applied to Jesus. This usage is by no means peculiar to Paul (*cf.* Jn. 12:38; Heb. 1:10; 1 Pet. 3:14f.; Jude 24f.; Rev. 17:14; 19:16). When, finally, Paul refers to 'the day of the Lord', he undoubtedly understands the Lord here to be no longer Yahweh but Jesus (1 Cor. 1:8; 2 Cor. 1:14).

If statistics were our guide, it would appear that *Son of God* (15 occurrences) was much less important for Paul than *Lord*, which appears at least ten times more frequently in his writings. Nevertheless, as M. Hengel (*The Son of God*, 1976, ch. 3) has shown, Paul uses this title for Jesus when he is summing up the content of his gospel (Rom. 1:3–4, 9; Gal. 1:15f.), and tends to reserve it for important statements. He uses it when the question of the relationship between God and Jesus is particularly in his mind, and, as we saw earlier, took up the traditional statements which spoke of God sending his pre-existent Son into the world and giving him up to die for us. He brings out especially the fact that it is through the work of the Son that we can be adopted as God's sons (Rom. 8:29; Gal. 4:4–6).

A number of other expressions are used by Paul in this connection. Jesus is described as the * *Image* of the invisible God (Col. 1:15; *cf.* 2 Cor. 4:4); he is the * *Firstborn* of all creation (Rom. 8:29; Col. 1:15–18) and the *Beloved* (Son) of God (Eph. 1:6). These, however, should be regarded more as descriptions of Jesus than as titles. The same is true of other phrases which describe various functions of Jesus, such as * *Head* (Eph. 1:22) and even *Saviour* (Eph. 5:23; Phil. 3:20).

It is a moot point whether the title *God* is applied to Jesus by Paul. The interpretation of Rom. 9:5 (see RSV and mg.) is debatable, but the text should probably be understood as a doxology to the Christ as God (B. M. Metzger, in B. Lindars and S. S. Smalley (ed.), *Christ and Spirit in the New Testament*, 1973, pp. 95–112). Equally ambiguous is 2 Thes. 1:12 (see TEV and mg.; NIV and mg.).

By the time that we reach the Pastoral Epistles the rich diversity of titular usage characteristic of the earlier Pauline writings is beginning to disappear. *Son of God* is not used at all. Neither *Jesus* nor *Christ* is used independently (except in 1 Tim. 5:11) but only in combination, usually in the order *Christ Jesus*. *Lord* is, however, used as an independent title and also in combinations. In several cases we probably have examples of formal, credal statements expressed in a dignified style and based on traditional material (1 Tim. 1:15; 2:5f.; 6:13; 2 Tim. 1:9f.; 2:8; Tit. 2:11–14; 3:6). There is no doubt that here Jesus is given the title of God (Tit. 2:13), and he shares with God the title of *Saviour* (2 Tim. 1:10; Tit. 1:4; 2:13; 3:6).

IV. The titles of Jesus in the Johannine literature

In Jn. the pattern of usage is similar to that in the other Gospels. The Gospel is concerned with the activities of the human person *Jesus*, and the compound form *Jesus Christ* is used only a couple of times when the total significance of Jesus is viewed from a post-resurrection standpoint (Jn. 1:17; 17:3—the latter passage being uttered from the perspective of one who has 'accomplished the work' which the Father gave him to do). Although the term *Lord* is frequently used in the vocative to address Jesus, it is scarcely used in narrative to refer to Jesus (only in Jn. 4:1; 6:23; 11:2) until after the resurrection which established the new status of Jesus. Nevertheless, it is significant that Jesus himself describes his status as that of a 'master' (Jn. 13:13f., 16; 15:15, 20) who can give commands to his slaves—although he regards his disciples as friends rather than slaves.

One of the key questions in Jn. is whether Jesus is the *Messiah* of both Jewish and Samaritan expectation; the purpose of the Gospel is to lead to belief that this is the case (Jn. 20:31). Despite the rarity of its use in the other Gospels, Jesus is confessed as Messiah in Jn. (Jn. 1:41; 4:29; 11:27), but it is interesting that the word never appears on the lips of Jesus himself. Other quasi-titular descriptions of Jesus which are used in Jn. include the *Coming One* (Jn. 11:27; 12:13; *cf.* Mt. 11:3); the *Holy One of God* (Jn. 6:69; *cf.* Mk. 1:24), the *Saviour* (Jn. 4:42), the *Lamb of God* (Jn. 1:29, 36), the *Prophet* (Jn. 6:14; 7:40) and the *King of Israel* (Jn. 1:49; 12:13; 18:33–38; 19:3, 14–22). Several of these are also found in the Synoptic Gospels.

Jesus' characteristic self-designation of *Son of man* also figures prominently in Jn., but here there is a new stress on the heavenly origin of the Son of man, his descent into this world, his glorification on the cross and his significance as the giver of life (Jn. 3:13; 5:27; 6:27, 53, 62; 12:23, 34; 13:31) which is absent from the Synoptic Gospels. While it is unnecessary to assume that foreign influences have contributed to the use of the title in Jn., the language used is sufficiently different from that in the Synoptic Gospels to suggest that, although the sayings in Jn. ultimately rest on the actual teaching of Jesus, they have been to some extent rewritten by the Evangelist or his sources (S. S. Smalley, *NTS* 15, 1968–9, pp. 278–301).

The most fundamental title for Jesus in Jn. is undoubtedly *Son of God.* It indicates the closeness of the relationship between the Father and his pre-existent, only Son (Jn. 3:16–18); this relationship is one of mutual love (Jn. 3:35; 5:20), and it is expressed in the way in which the Son obeys the Father (Jn. 5:19) and is entrusted by him with his functions as the judge and the bringer of life (Jn. 5:17–30). The unique filial relationship of Jesus to God which we find in the Synoptic Gospels is here most clearly expressed (Jn. 11:41; 12:27f.; 17:1). Essentially the same ideas are conveyed by the title * *Logos* (or *Word*) which figures in the prologue to the Gospel. So closely is the Logos identified with God, that it is not surprising to find that Jesus is actually given the title of *God*; this is clearly the case in Thomas' confession in Jn. 20:28, where it is the appearance of the resurrected Jesus which leads to recognition of his divine status, but it is then probable that Jesus is described as 'the only Son, who is the same as God and is at the Father's side' (TEV) in Jn. 1:18 (the text, however, is uncertain).

Finally, it should be noted that there are various 'I am' sayings in Jn. which apply such descriptions as 'the Good Shepherd' and 'the true Vine' to Jesus. Sometimes we simply have the words 'I am he' (Jn. 4:26; 6:20; 8:24, 28, 58; 13:19). Since these words echo the self-affirmation of Yahweh found in Is. 43:10; 48:12, it is likely that we should see them as a veiled indication of the deity of Jesus.

The use of titles in the Johannine Epistles is similar to that in the Gospel, although of course there is a difference between the way in which the earthly Jesus is described in a Gospel and that in which the risen Lord is described in an Epistle. It is a curious but no doubt unimportant fact that 3 Jn. is the only NT book which never refers to Jesus. In 1 Jn. *Jesus* is often the subject of statements in which his significance as *Christ* or *Son of God* is expressed (1 Jn. 2:22; 4:15; 5:1, 5). While the question raised here may be simply whether Jesus was indeed the Messiah of Jewish expectation, scholars generally agree that the issue was rather whether there had been a true and lasting incarnation of God in Jesus. The opponents of John appear to have denied that there was a true and lasting union between the Messiah or Son of God and Jesus (1 Jn. 4:2; 2 Jn. 7), and John had to emphasize that *Jesus Christ* had truly come in both water and blood, *i.e.* in his baptism and his death. He therefore uses the full title 'his Son Jesus Christ' (1 Jn. 1:3; 3:23; 5:20) to indicate the object of Christian belief. Only the Son of God can be the *Saviour* of the world (1 Jn. 4:14). The term *Lord* is absent from the Epistles of John.

In Rev. *Jesus* figures prominently as a designation, in the same way as in Heb. The fuller title *Jesus Christ* is used only as a solemn designation in the introduction to the book (Rev. 1:1f., 5), but there are four references to (the) *Christ* or to *his* Christ (Rev. 20:4, 6; 11:15; 12:10), which show that the thought of the Messiah as God's agent in the establishment of his rule was very much alive for John. This idea is further seen in the way in which the divine titles of *King* and *Lord* are used of both God and Jesus (Rev. 15:3; 17:14; 19:16). But undoubtedly the most distinctive title of Jesus in Rev. is that of * *Lamb* which is used 28 times here and nowhere else (the Gk. word used in Jn. 1:29, 36; Acts 8:32; 1 Pet. 1:19 is different). The Lamb combines the paradoxical features of being slain or sacrificed (Rev. 5:6) and yet being the Lord who is worthy of worship (Rev. 5:8). He displays his wrath against evil (Rev. 6:16) and leads the people of God in battle (Rev. 17:14), and yet it is his blood which acts as a sacrifice for sin (Rev. 7:14) and through which his martyred people emerge victorious (Rev. 12:11).

V. The titles of Jesus in the rest of the New Testament

Of the remaining books of the NT, Heb. is perhaps the most distinctive in its use of titles. Thus it reverts to the use of the simple *Jesus* to designate the One who suffered humiliation and death and yet has been exalted by God (Heb. 2:9; 13:12). It can also refer to him simply as the *Lord* (Heb. 2:3; 7:14) or as *Christ* (Heb. 3:6, 14; *et al.*). But although the writer is no doubt conscious that Christ means 'anointed' (Heb. 1:9), he uses it more as a name which needs to be explained by other titles. He describes Jesus as a *Pioneer* of salvation and faith (Heb. 2:10; 12:2), using a phrase which may have had a wider currency as a Christological title (Acts 3:15; 5:31). But above all he thinks of Jesus as the *High Priest* and expounds his work in terms of this category drawn from the OT sacrificial legislation. If this term is more a description than a title of Jesus, the term *Son* is the significant title which underlies it. It is only after he has established the identity of Jesus as the Son of God, exalted above the angels and Moses, that the writer goes on to demonstrate how this position qualified Jesus to be the high priest and mediator between God and man. The writer makes careful use of Pss. 2:7 (Heb. 1:5; 5:5) and 110:4 to define the status of Jesus. He stresses the enormity of rejecting the salvation achieved by so exalted a Saviour (Heb. 6:6; 10:29).

Jas. is remarkable for referring only twice to the *Lord Jesus Christ* (Jas. 1:1; 2:1), but when he speaks of the coming of the Lord (Jas. 5:7f.) he is no doubt thinking of Jesus.

In 1 Pet. the use of *Jesus* as an independent name is missing, and the writer prefers *Jesus Christ*. He uses *Lord Jesus Christ* once (1 Pet. 1:3) in a traditional phrase. But he refers frequently to *Christ*, and it is interesting that he does so particularly in the context of suffering and death (1 Pet. 1:11, 19; 2:21; 3:18; *et al.*) which we saw to be characteristic of the primitive use of the title. He also speaks of confessing Christ as *Lord* (1 Pet. 3:15; *cf.* 2:13) in a way which is again reminiscent of early usage.

2 Pet. is characterized by the use of *Lord Jesus Christ*. The title of *Saviour* is also frequent here (2 Pet. 1:1, 11; 2:20; 3:2, 18), and in 2 Pet. 1:1 Jesus is described as 'our *God* and Saviour'. The usage of Jude is generally similar; both writers use the unusual form *despotēs*, 'Lord', for Jesus (2 Pet. 2:1; Jude 4), possibly because the background thought is that of the redemption of slaves; the term was not a popular one because it suggested arbitrary despotism.

VI. Conclusion

The teaching of the NT about the person of Jesus is not confined to what is expressed by the titles whose use has been rapidly sketched above. We should also need to take into account what is said about the character and activity of Jesus both during his earthly life and in his heavenly state; it is also important to consider the kinds of credal statement and literary works which were created to express his significance. Nevertheless, the titles themselves sum up much of the NT teaching. Study of them enables us to see how the thinking of the disciples was moulded by their first contact with Jesus during his lifetime, and then decisively fixed by their experience of him as the risen Lord, and finally elaborated in the course of their evangelism and teaching in the Jewish and Hellenistic world. In differing ways the titles express the supreme worth of Jesus as the Son of God, his saving function as Messiah and Saviour, and his honourable position as the Lord. The early church drew on a rich source of material to explain who Jesus was; basically it took its material from the OT, which it saw as the divinely given prophecy of the coming of Jesus, but at the same time it did not shrink from using titles which would be meaningful in the wider world. Some titles proved less adequate than others, but collectively they all bear testimony to the fact that in Jesus God has acted decisively to judge and save the world, and they summon all to acknowledge that this Jesus is indeed one with God and worthy of the worship that is fitting for God himself.

BIBLIOGRAPHY. See the relevant articles in *DBS*; *NIDNTT*; *TDNT*; F. H. Borsch, *The Son of Man in Myth and History*, 1967; W. Bousset, *Kyrios Christos*, 1970; O. Cullmann, *The Christology of the New Testament*[2], 1963; R. H. Fuller, *The Foundations of New Testament Christology*, 1965; F. Hahn, *The Titles of Jesus in Christology*, 1969; M. Hengel, *The Son of God*, 1976; A. J. B. Higgins, *Jesus and the Son of Man*, 1964; M. D. Hooker, *Jesus and the Servant*, 1959; *idem*, *The Son of Man in Mark*, 1967; W. Kramer, *Christ, Lord, Son of God*, 1966; I. H. Marshall, *The Origins of New Testament Christology*, 1977; S. Mowinckel, *He That Cometh*, 1956; N. Perrin, *A Modern Pilgrimage in New Testament Christology*, 1974; V. Taylor, *The Names of Jesus*, 1953; *idem*, *The Person of Christ in New Testament Teaching*, 1958; H. E. Todt, *The Son of Man in the Synoptic Tradition*, 1965; G. Vermes, *Jesus the Jew*, 1973. I.H.M.

JESUS JUSTUS
See Justus, Part 2.

JESUS' MINISTRY, LENGTH OF
See Chronology of NT, Part 1.

JETHER
See Ithra, Part 2.

JETUR
See Ituraea, Part 2.

The Judaean (Jewish) inhabitants of Lachish leave the city for exile after the siege by the Assyrians under Sennacherib in 701 BC. *Sennacherib's palace. Nineveh. c. 690* BC. (BM)

JETHRO. Moses' father-in-law *Reuel, called Jethro in Ex. 3:1; 4:18. He brought Zipporah and her sons to meet Moses at Mt Horeb, and held a sacrifice to Yahweh in thanksgiving for the deliverance of Israel. Here he also advised Moses to delegate the administration of justice (Ex. 18). Moses persuaded Jethro's son Hobab to join the Israelites. In Jdg. 4:11 'Hobab the Kenite' is called Moses' *ḥōṯēn*, perhaps a broad term for 'in-law'; this, with Jdg. 1:16, is the only evidence for Jethro's Kenite descent. The name may mean 'preeminence'. J.P.U.L.

JEW (Heb. y^{e}*hûḏî*; Aram. y^{e}*hûḏai*; Gk. *joudaios*; Lat. *judaeaus*). Originally a member of the state of *Judah (2 Ki. 16:6; Ne. 1:2; Je. 32:12) and so used by foreigners from the 8th century BC onwards (*e.g.* Assyr. *Yaudaia*, *ANET*, pp. 287, 301). Non-Jews used this term of the former inhabitants of the province of Judah as opposed to other nations in post-exilic times (Est. 9:15; Dn. 3:8; Zc. 8:23) or of proselytes to *Judaism (Est. 8:17). 'Jewess' occurs in 1 Ch. 4:18; Acts 16:1; 24:24 and 'Jewish' in Gal. 2:14 (Gk.); Tit. 1:14. The 'Jew's language' describes the local Semitic dialect spoken in Judah which, like 'Jew' (Je. 34:9), becomes synonymous with 'Hebrew'. AV 'Jewry' (Dn. 5:13; Lk. 23:5; Jn. 7:1) stands for Judah.

In the NT, 'Jews' is used of members of the Jewish faith or their

Jewellery of the Egyptian 12th Dynasty (c. 1850 BC*). The decoration of the girdle includes electrum cowrie shells and silver fish pendants. The flying scarab beetle and the fish amulet are both inlaid.* (BM)

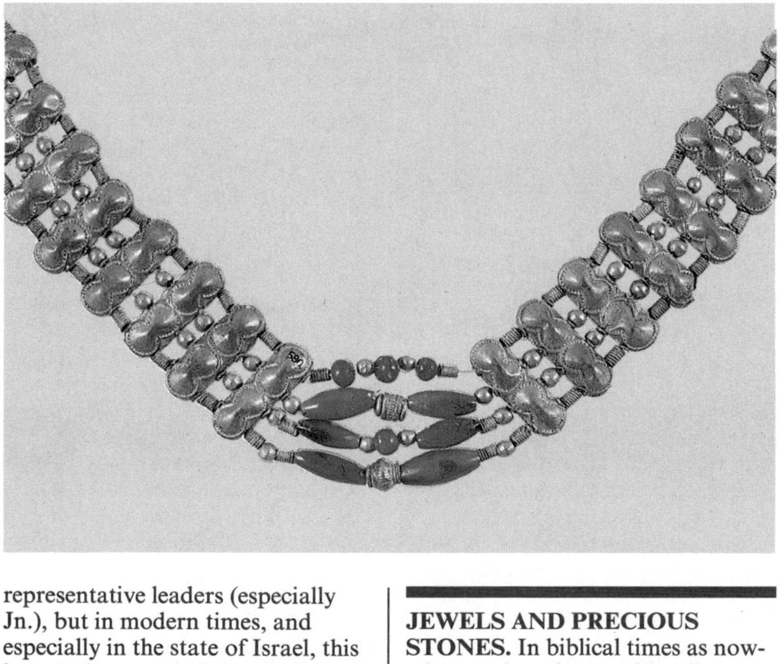

Gold and cornelian necklace found in a tomb at Enkomi, Cyprus. 14th–13th cent. BC. (MH)

representative leaders (especially Jn.), but in modern times, and especially in the state of Israel, this is sometimes extended to denote ethnic birth but not necessarily religion. Its precise connotation is therefore now often a matter of debate.

BIBLIOGRAPHY. *EJ*, 10, 1971, pp. 22–26. D.J.W.

JEWELS AND PRECIOUS STONES. In biblical times as nowadays various forms of jewellery were worn and highly esteemed by both men and women (Ex. 11:2; Is. 3:18–21). They were given as presents (Gn. 24:22, 53), and were an important item of spoil in war (2 Ch. 20:25). They were a form of wealth, especially before the use of coins (2 Ch. 21:3), and were used as a standard of value (Jb. 28:16; Pr. 3:15; Rev. 21:11). Among the various types of jewellery used we find mention of bracelets for the arm (Gn. 24:22, 30, 47; Ezk. 16:11), ornaments for the ankles (Is. 3:18, 20), necklaces (Gn. 41:42; *cf.* Lk. 15:8, where the ten pieces of silver may have been coins strung together to form a necklace), crowns (Zc. 9:16; here the Lord's people are likened to shining jewels in a crown), ear-rings (Gn. 24:22), nose-rings (Is. 3:21) and rings for the fingers (Gn. 41:42; Est. 3:10; Lk. 15:22). These might be made of gold, silver or other metals (Ex. 3:22).

A considerable number of precious and semi-precious stones were known and used in jewellery. Inscribed seals have been found in cornelian, chalcedony, jasper, agate, onyx, rock crystal, haematite, jade, opal and amethyst (D. Diringer, 'Seals', in *DOTT*, pp. 218–226). The stones were valued for their rarity, beauty and durability. The modern method of faceting was not employed; instead

Sumerian court jewellery from the Royal Tomb of Queen Pū-abi, Ur, S Iraq. Gold, lapis lazuli and cornelian are among the precious stones used most frequently. c. 2500 BC. (BM)

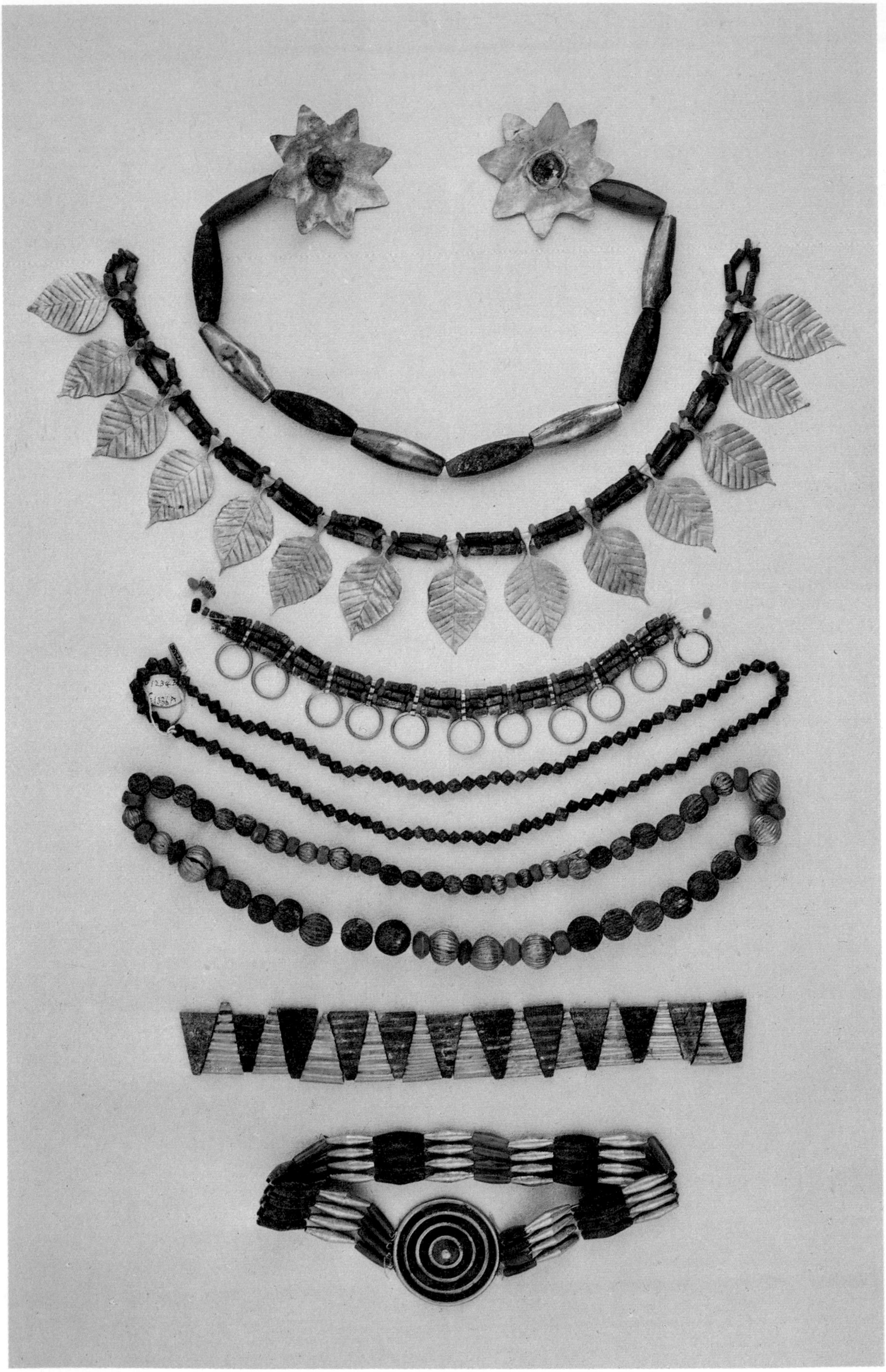

the stones were rounded and polished, and often engraved and carved.

In general, the ancients were more familiar with semi-precious than with precious stones. Since many species of stone occur in a variety of colours and since a scientific terminology had not been developed, the identification of the various stones mentioned in the Bible is not always easy, and in some cases we can only guess at the meaning of the terms used. Etymology is not much help, since many of the roots simply mean 'sparkle', 'gleam' or the like. The following list is geared to the RSV translation.

Agate (*š^{e}ḇô*, Ex. 28:19; 39:12) was probably modern agate, a type of translucent quartz with layers of different colours, or the very similar onyx. In Is. 54:12; Ezk. 27:16 (*kaḏkoḏ*), a red stone, possibly carbuncle, red jasper (NEB) or ruby (JB), may be meant (*cf.* Ezk. 27:16, where Symmachus has *karchēdonion*, *i.e.* carbuncle). For Rev. 21:19, RSV, TEV, see **Chalcedony**, below.

The word **Alabaster** (*alabastron*, Mk. 14:3 = Mt. 26:7; Lk. 7:37), originally the neuter form of the adjective *alabastros*, was used to mean an alabaster flask with a long neck for storing perfume, the neck being broken off when the contents were used; but the word was also used for flasks of this shape of *any* material. Ancient alabaster was a banded variety of calcium carbonate produced by gradual deposition from solution in water, as in stalactites; modern alabaster is a softer stone, a variety of gypsum (calcium sulphate).

Amethyst (*'aḥlāmâ*, Ex. 28:19; 39:12) was the well-known stone of that name, a purple variety of transparent, crystalline quartz. (NEB 'jasper' identifies it as an Egyp. stone.) So also in Rev. 21:20 (*amethystos*, so called because it was supposed to prevent intoxication).

Beryl (*taršîš*, Ex. 28:20; 39:13; Ct. 5:14; Ezk. 1:16; 10:9; 28:13; Dn. 10:6) was associated with Spain (Tarshish), and was probably Spanish gold topaz, known to the ancient world as chrysolith. In Rev. 21:20 (*bēryllos*) ordinary green beryl is meant.

Carbuncle (*bāreqeṯ*, Ex. 28:17; 39:10; *bār^{e}qaṯ*, Ezk. 28:13) was probably a green stone in view of the LXX translation as 'emerald' (*smaragdos*) in the Ex. references; possibly green felspar (NEB) is meant. (The modern carbuncle is a red stone.) In Is. 54:12 (*'eqdaḥ*) a red stone is meant in view of the derivation from *qāḏaḥ*, 'to kindle', possibly garnet (NEB).

For **Carnelian** (better spelt 'cornelian', the common form being due to confusion with Latin *caro*), see **Sardius**, below.

Chalcedony (*chalkēdōn*, Rev. 21:19, NEB; RSV 'agate') is usually taken to have been a green stone, since Pliny refers to a kind of emerald and jasper as Chalcedonian (from Chalcedon in Asia Minor). (The word is used in modern writers for various types of translucent quartz, including agate, onyx, cornelian and chrysoprase.)

Chrysolite (*chrysolithos*, Rev. 21:20) is the ancient term for yellow topaz (alminium fluo-silicate) or yellow quartz. (Note that ancient chrysolite is modern topaz, and vice versa.) For Ezk. 1:16; 10:9; 28:13, RSV, see **Beryl**, above. For Ex. 28:17 NEB see **Topaz**.

Chrysoprase (*chrysoprasos*, Rev. 21:20) is in modern usage an apple-green form of chalcedony, but the identification here is uncertain. The name suggests a golden-tinted variety.

Coral (*rā'môṯ*, Jb. 28:18; Ezk. 27:16) may be either black or red coral. It is, of course, not strictly a precious stone, being the skeleton of innumerable small marine polyps. *rā'môṯ* also occurs in Pr. 24:7, *MT*, but this is probably to be read as *rāmôṯ*, 'high'. The RSV translates *p^{e}nînîm* as coral in La. 4:7, where some red stone is meant (see **Pearl**, below).

Crystal (*gāḇîš*; Jb. 28:18a) is a translucent substance (*cf. 'elgāḇîš*, 'hail') but G. R. Driver thinks that gypsum is meant (*cf.* NEB 'alabaster'). The word *z^{e}ḵôḵîṯ* ('crystal', Jb. 28:17, AV) was applied in the ancient world not simply to rock crystal (pure transparent crystalline quartz) but to any hard, transparent, colourless substance. Glass may be meant (RSV). *qeraḥ* (Ezk. 1:22) is elsewhere translated 'frost' or 'ice'. In Rev. 4:6; 21:11; 23:1 (*krystallon, krystallizō*), either ice or rock crystal may be the rendering.

Diamond (*yāh^{a}lôm*, Ex. 28:18; 39:11; Ezk. 28:13) is of uncertain identification. The modern diamond was probably unknown in OT times, the first certain reference to it apparently being in Manilius (1st century AD). Probably a white, opaque stone is meant (possibly moonstone); G. R. Driver suggests jadeite or nephrite (*cf.* NEB). In Je. 17:1 (*šāmîr*) adamant or emery, a form of corundum (the hardest substance known except for diamond), is meant (*cf.* Ezk. 3:9; Zc. 7:12).

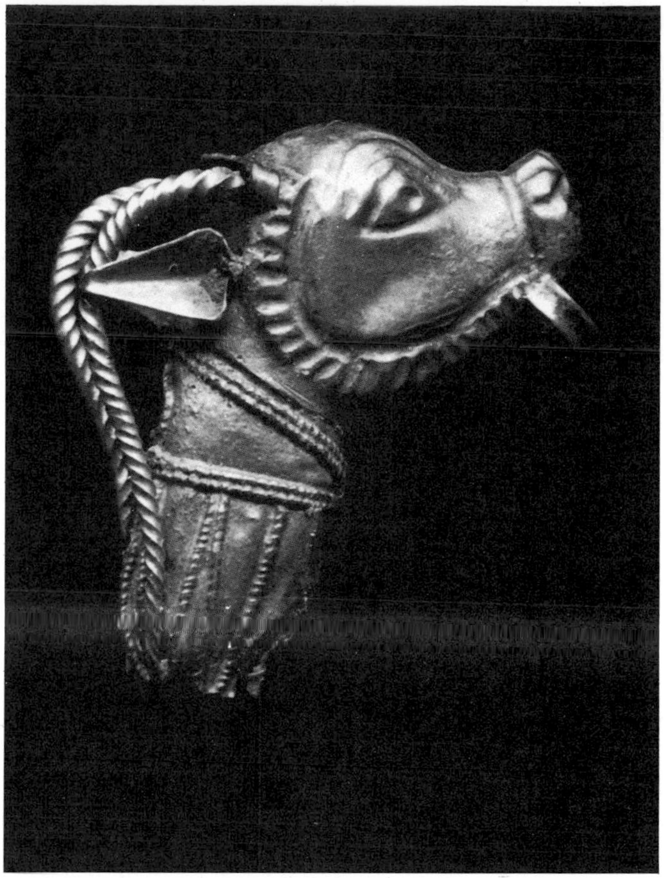

Gold ear-ring excavated at Ashdod (Philistia). Probably Achaemenid Persian. 2·0 cm × 1·5 cm. 6th–4th cent. BC. (IM)

Emerald (*nōp̄eḵ*, Ex. 28:18; 39:11; also Ezk. 27:16, where various scholars consider the text uncertain) may have been a green stone like the modern emerald, but in view of the LXX translation (*anthrax*, 'a burning coal'), some authorities prefer the purple almandine garnet (NEB). In Rev. 4:3 (*smaragdinos*) and 21:19 (*smaragdos*), the green emerald is meant.

For **Glass**, see **Crystal**.

For **Hyacinth**, see **Jacinth**.

Jacinth (*lešem*, Ex. 28:19; 39:12; AV 'ligure') is usually thought to have been a yellow stone; G. R. Driver prefers a blue stone such as turquoise (NEB). In the NT jacinth (*hyakinthos*, Rev. 21:20) is a blue stone, aquamarine (the blue variety of beryl), sapphire or turquoise. (Modern jacinth is quite different.) The name was used to indicate a blue colour (in classical Greek as a noun it means the hyacinth or bluebell), as in Rev. 9.17 (*hyakinthinos*), where RSVmg. has 'hyacinth' and RSV has 'sapphire'.

Jasper (*yāš^{e}p̄eh*, Ex. 28:20; 39:13;

Sandstone mould for making jewellery. Found at Nimrud. Assyrian. 9th–7th cent. BC. (BM)

Ezk. 28:13) is a translucent, green stone. In Rev. 4:3; 21:11, 18–19 (*iaspis*), green quartz may be meant. In 21:11 the reference to crystal suggests that a transparent stone may be intended.

For **Lapis lazuli**, see **Sapphire**.

Onyx (*šōham*, Gn. 2:12; Ex. 25:7; 28:8, 20; 35:9, 27; 39:6, 13; 1 Ch. 29:2; Jb. 28:16; Ezk. 28:13) has been identified as a green stone (*cf.* LXX 'beryl' in some of these verses) or as onyx (translucent agate with layers of black and white. The word means finger-nail, the stone being so called because of its appearance. S. R. Driver prefers red carnelian. For Rev. 21:20, see **Sardonyx**, below.

Pearl is found in the OT in Jb. 28:18a (*gāḇîš*) AV, where RSV has 'crystal'. In the RSV 'pearl' is found as the translation of *p^enînîm* in Jb. 28:18b (AV, 'rubies'). The same Heb. word occurs in Pr. 3:15; 8:11; 20:15; 31:10 and La. 4:7 (it is also accepted by some scholars as an emendation in Ps. 45:14). In all these references AV has 'rubies'; RSV has 'jewels' or 'costly stones', except in La. 4:7, where it has 'coral'. *BDB* prefer 'corals' (*cf.* NEB), but E. Burrows (*JTS* 42, 1941, pp. 53–64) argues that the word properly means 'pearls' but also has the generic sense of 'jewels'. *Unger's Bible Dictionary* (1957, p. 742) suggests that the pink pearls found in the Red Sea are meant, and this would solve the difficulty of La. 4:7, where a reddish stone is indicated.

There is no doubt that in the NT *margaritēs* means 'pearl'. Pearls are noted as articles of feminine ornament (1 Tim. 2:9, where they are frowned upon; Rev. 17:4) and of merchandise (Mt. 13:45f.; Rev. 18:12, 16). The gates of the New Jerusalem are each made of a single large pearl or possibly of mother-of-pearl (Rev. 21:21). The kingdom of heaven is like a fine pearl which a man will seek to obtain at the cost of all that he has (Mt. 13:45f. In view of the context it is unlikely

Examples of typical stones used by seal-cutters. These include serpentine, haematite (iron-ore), lapis lazuli, agate, cornelian, shell and marble. (DJW)

References in the Old Testament (jewels in the High Priest's breastplate). Ex. 28:17–20 = 39:10–13 = Ezk. 28:13 (omitting nos. 7–9)							
	MT	LXX	RSV	NEB	JB	GNB	NIV
1.	*'ōḏem*	*sardion*	sardius	sardin	sard	ruby	ruby
2.	*piṭᵉḏâ*	*topazion*	topaz	chrysolite	topaz	topaz	topaz
3.	*bāreqeṯ*	*smaragdos*	carbuncle	green felspar	carbuncle	garnet	beryl
4.	*nōp̄eḵ*	*anthrax*	emerald	purple garnet	emerald	emerald	turquoise
5.	*sappîr*	*sappheiros*	sapphire	lapis lazuli	sapphire	sapphire	sapphire
6.	*yāhᵃlōm*	*iaspis*	diamond	jade	diamond	diamond	emerald
7.	*lešem*	*ligyrion*	jacinth	turquoise	hyacinth	turquoise	jacinth
8.	*šᵉḇô*	*achatēs*	agate	agate	ruby	agate	agate
9.	*'aḥlāmâ*	*amethystos*	amethyst	jasper	amethyst	amethyst	amethyst
10.	*taršîš*	*chrysolithos*	beryl	topaz	beryl	beryl	chrysolite
11.	*šōham*	*beryllion*	onyx	carnelian	beryl	carnelian	onyx
12.	*yašᵉp̄eh*	*onychion*	jasper	green jasper	jasper	jasper	jasper
Other Old Testament references							
			RSV	NEB	JB	GNB	NIV
	zᵉkûkîṯ	Jb. 28:17	glass	crystal	glass	[illegible]	[illegible]
	rā'môṯ	Jb. 28:18	coral	black coral	coral	coral	coral
		Pr. 24:7 *MT*					
		Ezk. 27:16					
	gāḇîš	Jb. 28:18	crystal	alabaster	crystal	crystal	jasper
	pᵉnînîm	Jb. 28:18	pearls	red coral	pearls	rubies	rubies
		La. 4:7	coral	branching coral	coral	–	rubies
		Pr. 3:15 *et al.*	jewels	red coral	pearls	jewels	rubies
	kaḏkōḏ	Is. 54:12	agate	red jasper (*mg.*carbuncle)	rubies	rubies	rubies
		Ezk. 27:16	agate	red jasper	rubies	rubies	rubies
	'eqdaḥ	Is. 54:12	carbuncle	garnet (*mg.*firestone)	crystal	–	sparkling jewels
	qeraḥ	Ezk. 1:22	crystal	ice	crystal	crystal	ice

References in the New Testament Rev. 21:19–20 (Gk.)

1.	*iaspis*	jasper (RSV, NEB, GNB, NIV, TNT); diamond (JB)
2.	*sappheiros*	sapphire (RSV, GNB, NIV, TNT); lapis lazuli (NEB, JB)
3.	*chalkedōn*	agate (RSV, GNB); chalcedony (NEB, NIV, TNT); turquoise (JB)
4.	*smaragdos*	emerald (RSV, NEB, GNB, NIV, TNT); crystal (JB)
5.	*sardonyx*	onyx (RSV, GNB); sardonyx (NEB, NIV, TNT); agate (JB)
6.	*sardion*	carnelian (RSV, GNB, NIV); cornelian (NEB); ruby (JB); sardius (TNT)
7.	*chrysolithos*	chrysolite (RSV, NEB, NIV, TNT); gold quartz (JB); yellow quartz (GNB)
8.	*bēryllos*	beryl (RSV, NEB, GNB, NIV, TNT); malachite (JB)
9.	*topazion*	topaz (RSV, NEB, JB, GNB, NIV, TNT)
10.	*chrysoprasos*	chrysoprase (RSV, NEB, NIV, TNT); emerald (JB); chalcedony (GNB)
11.	*hyakinthos*	jacinth (RSV, NIV, TNT); turquoise (NEB, GNB); sapphire (JB)
12.	*amethystos*	amethyst (RSV, NEB, JB, GNB, NIV, TNT)

①	②	③
④	⑤	⑥
⑦	⑧	⑨
⑩	⑪	⑫

Arrangement of the twelve stones in the High Priest's breastplate.

Jewels, precious and semi-precious stones as translated in some versions of the Bible.

that this parable refers primarily to Christ giving his life for men, although in fact Christ himself is the supreme example of giving up all for the sake of the kingdom.) On the other hand, it is as foolish to put the Christian message before men who refuse to appreciate it as to cast pearls before swine (Mt. 7:6; *cf. Didache* 9. 5, where Christ's saying is used to justify exclusion of the unbaptized from the Lord's Supper).

Ruby is found in AV as a translation of *pᵉnînîm* in six places (see **Pearl**, above). RV also has 'ruby' in Is. 54:12 and Ezk. 27:16 for *kaḏkōḏ* (see **Agate**, above).

Sapphire (*sappîr*, Ex. 24:10; 28:18; 39:11; Jb. 28:6, 16; Ct. 5:14; Is. 54:11; La. 4:7; Ezk. 1:26; 10:1; 28:13) was the ancient name for lapis lazuli (*cf.* RSVmg.), a deep blue stone with golden flecks of iron pyrites (*cf.* 'dust of gold', Jb. 28:6). Lapis lazuli is also meant in Rev. 21:19 (*sappheiros*). The modern sapphire (blue corundum) was scarcely known to the ancients. For Rev. 9:17, RSV, see **Jacinth**, above.

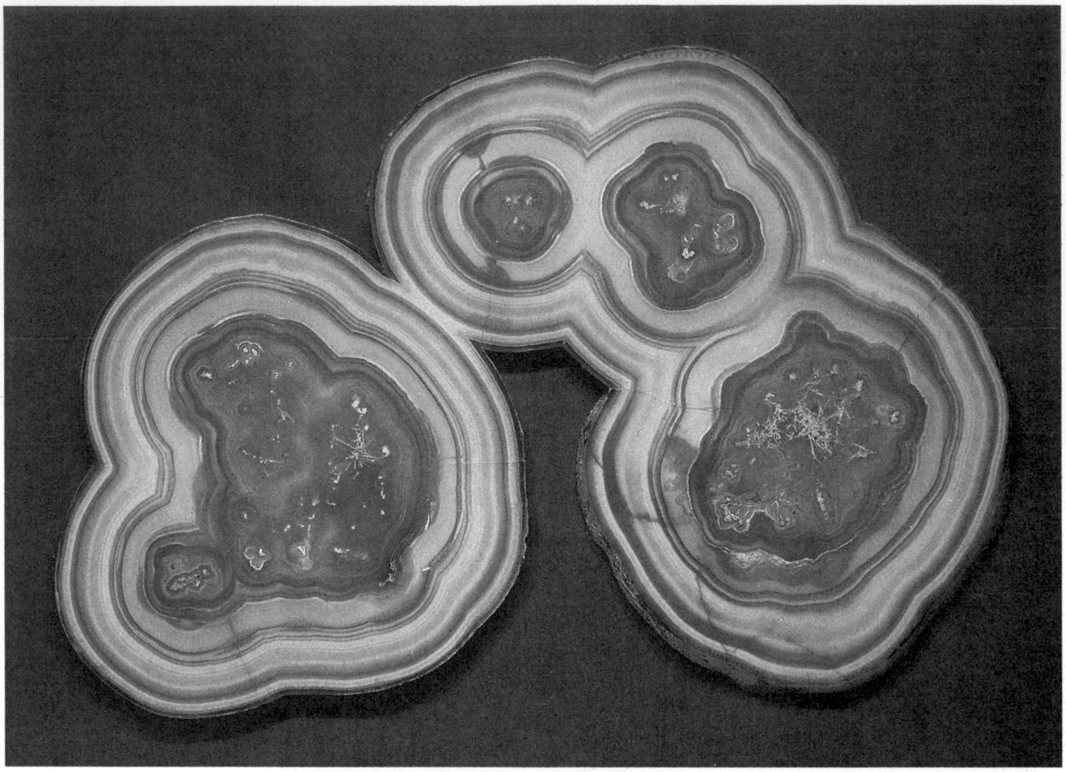

Agate, cut to show the different bands of colour. (IGS)

Amethyst (purple crystalline quartz) lining an agate stone. (IGS)

Sardius (*'ōḏem*, Ex. 28:17; 29:10; Ezk. 28:13) was certainly a red stone (from *'āḏam*, 'to be red'), probably modern sard (a form of cornelian; *cf.* Ezk. 28:13, RSV), *i.e.* a deep brown or red form of quartz. It is also mentioned in Rev. 21:20 (*sardios*) and is the sardine stone of Rev. 4:3 (*sardinos*): RSV and NEB have carnelian/cornelian in both places.

Sardonyx (*sardonyx*, Rev. 21:20, RV, NEB; RSV 'onyx') is in modern usage a form of agate with layers of brown and white; but, according to *LSJ*, in ancient usage a stone was called 'onyx' when the dark ground was simply streaked or spotted with white, and 'sardonyx' when the different colours were arranged in layers.

Topaz (*piṭᵉḏâ*, Ex. 28:17; 39:10; Jb. 28:19; Ezk. 28:13) was a yellow stone, probably yellow rock crystal or chrysolite (a pale yellow variety of peridot); *cf.* Ezk. 1:16; 10:9; 28:13, NEB (*taršîš*). So also in Rev. 22:20 (*topazion*).

The fullest list of stones in the OT is given in the description of the high priest's breastpiece (Ex. 28:17–20, repeated in 39:10–13). This contained four rows of three stones, each stone engraved with the name of one of the twelve tribes of Israel. Later authors commenting on the OT regarded these twelve stones as symbolic of the months of the year or the signs of the zodiac (Philo, *Vit. Mos.* 2. 124ff.; Jos., *Ant.* 3. 186), but it is impossible to work out any correlations. Some scholars have rearranged the order of the stones in the *MT* on the basis of the LXX translation, but this is a dubious procedure.

An abbreviated version of the same list of stones is found in Ezk. 28:13 as a description of the covering of the king of Tyre when, according to the poetic imagery used here, he was in Eden, the garden of God. Nine of the stones are mentioned, the jacinth, agate and amethyst being omitted. In the LXX version of this verse, however, the full list of twelve stones is substituted.

A list of twelve stones is given in Rev. 21:19f. as decorations of the foundations of the New Jerusalem. The basis of this description is clearly Is. 54:11f. (*cf.* also Tobit 13:16–18). The number twelve is clearly significant for John, and various attempts have been made to ascertain whether the twelve stones have any special meaning. It

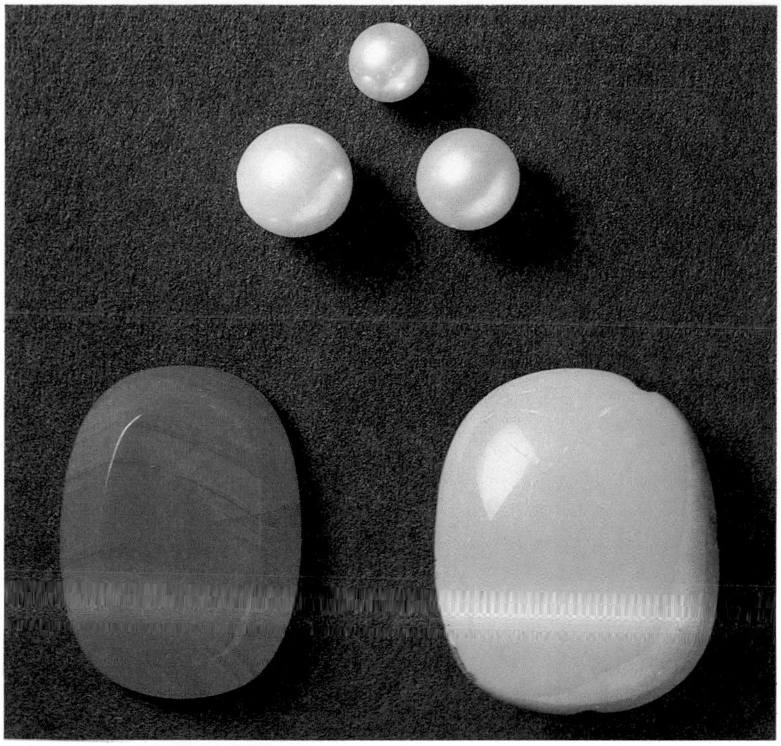

Top left:
1. *Pearls.*
2. *Cornelian, probably the biblical sardius, cut and polished.*
3. *Turquoise.* (IGS)

Centre left:
Garnet, cut en cabuchon. (IGS)

Lapis lazuli unpolished. (IGS)

is likely that the form of the vision has been influenced by the description of the twelve stones of the high priest's breastpiece; scholars have attempted to relate the two lists of stones more closely to each other, but in view of the difficulties of translation from Heb. to Gk. and the fact that John was probably not quoting verbatim from Ex., it is very doubtful whether we can say more than that he was generally influenced by the description in Ex. R. H. Charles (*ICC*, *ad loc.*) has taken up the symbolism of the signs of the zodiac mentioned above and holds that the stones represent these signs arranged in precisely the opposite order to that in which the sun travels through the zodiac, thus portraying the truth that the New Jerusalem and Christianity bear no relation to those religions in which men worship the sun; this theory is implausible (T. F. Glasson, *JTS* n.s. 26, 1975, pp.95–100). It is further

Green aventurine quartz. (IGS)

Jewellers in their workshop. From the tomb of Sebek-hotep, Thebes, c. 1420 BC. (BM)

■ **JEWISH COINAGE**
See Money, Part 2.

possible that the stones, like the twelve gates of the city, are symbolical of the tribes of Israel (A. M. Farrer, *A Rebirth of Images*, 1949, pp. 216ff.), but again it is impossible to work out convincing identifications of individual stones with individual tribes. In the light of 21:14 there is perhaps more to be said for the suggestion that the stones represent the twelve apostles, in which case individual identifications are clearly not to be attempted. What is beyond dispute in the symbolism is that in the New Jerusalem we see the fulfilment of the OT prophecy of the perfect city of God in which the saints of the old and new covenants find a place. (*MINING AND METALS, *ORNAMENTS.)

The name Jezebel (yzbl) *has been added in Phoenician characters on this Egyptian-style scarab seal. Grey opal. 1·3 × 2·2 × 1·0 cm. 9th–8th cent.* BC. (IM)

BIBLIOGRAPHY. H. Quiring, *Sudhoffs Archiv* 38, 1954, pp. 193–213; G. R. Driver, *HDB*², pp. 497–500; J. S. Harris, *ALUOS* 4, 1962–3, pp. 49–83; 5, 1963–5, pp. 40–62; U. Jart, *ST* 24, 1970, pp. 150–181; *RAC*, 4, pp. 505–535; C. Aldred, *Jewels of the Pharaohs*, 1971; N. Hillyer, 'Precious Stones in the Apocalypse', *NIDNTT* 3, pp. 395–398. I.H.M.

JEZANIAH (Heb. *yᵉzanyāhû*). One of the Judaean military commanders who joined Gedaliah at Mizpah (Je. 40:8). He was among those who sought counsel from Jeremiah concerning going down to Egypt (Je. 42:1—LXX here has 'Azariah', *cf.* 43:2). In 2 Ki. 25:23 his name appears as *'Jaazaniah'. J.C.J.W.

JEZEBEL. 1. The daughter of Ethbaal, priest-king of Tyre and Sidon. She was married to Ahab, to ratify an alliance between Tyre and Israel, by which Omri, Ahab's father, sought to offset the hostility of Damascus towards Israel (*c.* 880 BC). Provision was made for her to continue to worship her native god Baal in Samaria, her new home (1 Ki. 16:31–33).

She had a strong, domineering character, and was self-willed and forceful. A fanatical devotee of Melqart, the Tyrian Baal, her staff numbered 450 of his prophets, and 400 prophets of the goddess Asherah, by the time Ahab was king (1 Ki. 18:19). She clamoured for her god to have at least equal rights with Yahweh, God of Israel. This brought her into conflict with the prophet Elijah. A battle between Yahweh and Baal was fought on Mt Carmel, when Yahweh triumphed gloriously (1 Ki. 18:17–40). Even so, this and the massacre of her prophets, instead of diminishing her zeal, augmented it.

Her conception of an absolute monarchy was at variance with the Heb. covenant-relationship between Yahweh, the king and the people. She took the lead in the incident of Naboth's vineyard with high-handed, unscrupulous action, affecting the whole community as well as undermining the throne of Ahab. It resulted in the prophetic revolution and the extermination of the house of Ahab. She had written letters and used her husband's seal (1 Ki. 21:8), but that she had a seal of her own is suggested and illustrated by N. Avigad, *IEJ* 14, 1964, pp. 274–276.

After Ahab's death, Jezebel continued as a power in Israel for 10 years, in her role as queen-mother, throughout the reign of Ahaziah, then during Jehoram's lifetime. When Jehoram was killed by Jehu she attired herself regally (2 Ki. 9:30), and awaited him. She mocked Jehu, and went to her fate with courage and dignity (842 BC).

It is remarkable that Yahweh was honoured in the naming of her three children, Ahaziah, Jehoram and Athaliah (if indeed she was Athaliah's mother), but they may have been born before her ascendancy over Ahab became so absolute.

2. In the letter to the church at Thyatira (Rev. 2:20), 'that Jezebel of a woman' is the designation given to a seductive prophetess who encouraged immorality and idolatry under the cloak of religion (*NICOLAS). This could refer to an individual, or to a group within the church. It indicates that the name had become a byword for apostasy. M.B.

JEZREEL (Heb. *yizrᵉʿeʾl*, 'God sows'). **1.** The town in the mountains of Judah (Jos. 15:56); the native place of Ahinoam, one of David's wives (1 Sa. 25:43).

2. A city in Issachar and the plain (*ESDRAELON for location) on which it stood (Jos. 19:18; Ho. 1:5). The city and general neighbourhood are associated with several notable events. By its fountain the

Israelites assembled before engaging the Philistines at Gilboa (1 Sa. 29:1). It was a part of Ish-bosheth's short-lived kingdom (2 Sa. 2:8ff.), an administrative district of Solomon (1 Ki. 4:12); and the scene of the tragedy of Naboth and his vineyard (1 Ki. 21:1). Here Joram, who had earlier come to convalesce from war wounds (2 Ki. 8:29), was slain by Jehu, and his body significantly cast into the vineyard so cruelly appropriated by Ahab and Jezebel (2 Ki. 9:24–26). Thereafter at Jehu's instigation Jezebel herself (2 Ki. 9:30–37) and the remnant of Ahab's household (2 Ki. 10:1–11) were slain. Jezreel is identified with the modern Zer'in, about 90 km N of Jerusalem.

3. The name symbolically given to Hosea's eldest son (Ho. 1:4) and to Israel (Ho. 2:22).

4. A Judahite (1 Ch. 4:3).

J.D.D.

JOAB (Heb. *yô'āḇ*, 'Yahweh is father'). **1.** Son of Zeruiah, half-sister of David (2 Sa. 2:18). His father's name is not recorded here, but Josephus (*Ant.* 7. 11) gives it as Suri, whose sepulchre was in Bethlehem (2 Sa. 2:32).

Joab is first heard of when, with his brothers Asahel and Abishai, he led David's army to victory at Helkath-hazzurim against Ish-bosheth's rebel forces under Abner (2 Sa. 2:12–17). In fleeing, *Abner reluctantly killed *Asahel in self-defence and was himself later treacherously slain by Joab, ostensibly in blood-revenge (2 Sa. 2:23; 3:27, 30), but probably also because Abner's new-found loyalty to David confronted Joab with a potential rival for the king's favour.

David was angry with his nephew for this murder, greatly mourned Abner as 'a prince and a great man', and prophesied that God would punish the killer (2 Sa. 3:31–39). Nevertheless, after taking the Jebusite stronghold, Joab was made commander-in-chief of all Israel (2 Sa. 5:8; 1 Ch. 11:6, 8), of which David was by this time king.

Joab proved himself a skilful general who greatly helped the establishment of the monarchy, but his character was a strange mixture. Apart from his personal deeds of violence and his opportunism, his cruelty can be seen in the way he swiftly comprehended and carried out David's plan to kill Uriah (2 Sa. 11:6–26). Yet he could be magnanimous also, as when he gave David the credit after the capture of Rabboth-ammon (2 Sa. 12:26–31). Perhaps most notably and surprisingly, he tried to dissuade David from numbering the people (2 Sa. 24:2–4).

Joab is found in the role of peacemaker, reconciling David and Absalom on one occasion (2 Sa. 14:23, 31–33), but later when Absalom's guilt was clearly seen he had a hand in his death (2 Sa. 18:14–33), despite David's injunction that the young man's life should be spared. After this David superseded Joab by Amasa as commander (2 Sa. 19:13), but the resourceful Joab subdued Sheba's revolt and seized the first opportunity to slay the new commander, who had proved inefficient (2 Sa. 20:3–23). Thereafter for a time Joab seems to have been restored to favour (2 Sa. 24:2).

In David's last days Joab's loyalty to the king faltered, and with Abiathar and others he supported Adonijah as claimant to the throne (1 Ki. 1:5–53), in defiance of David, who had resolved that Solomon should succeed him (1 Ki. 2:28). For once Joab supported the wrong side, and it eventually cost him his life (1 Ki. 2:34), when with the connivance of Solomon he was slain by Benaiah before the altar at Gibeon, where he had fled for sanctuary.

2. Son of Seraiah (1 Ch. 4:14; *cf.* Ne. 11:35), a Judahite. **3.** A family which returned with Zerubbabel (Ezr. 2:6; Ne. 7:11). Probably the 'Joab' of Ezr. 8:9 is the same person.

J.D.D.

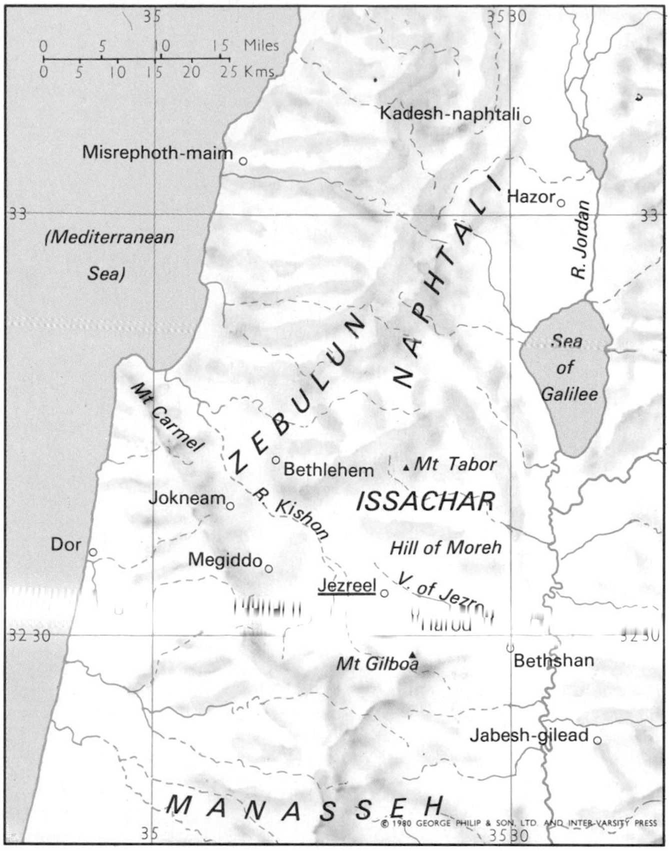

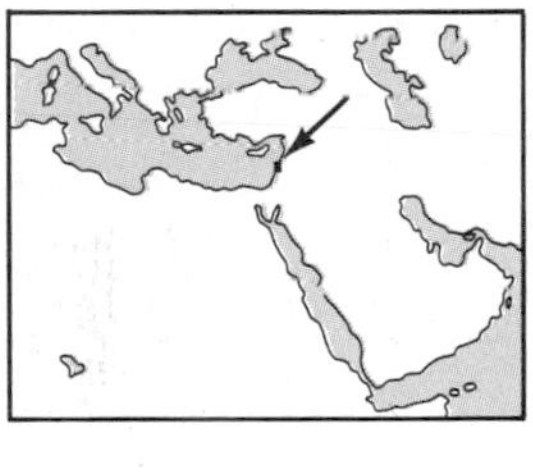

The land around Jezreel.

Top left: The plain of Jezreel viewed from Mt Tabor. (SH)

JOANNA. One of several women, healed by Jesus, who assisted in maintaining the Lord's itinerant company. Her husband, Chuza, was a responsible official of Herod Antipas: whether in the household ('a steward of Herod's', NEB) or in government ('the chancellor', Moffatt) is uncertain (Lk. 8:1–3). She sought also to share in the last offices to the Lord's body, and became instead one of those who announced the resurrection to the Twelve (Lk. 24:1–10). Luke's notes may indicate personal acquaintance with, and possibly indebtedness for information to, these women.

A.F.W.

JOASH, JEHOASH (Heb. *yô'āš*, *y^ehô'āš*, 'Yahweh has given').

The 'Joash' stele as found to the left of the altar base or podium. (BSAI)

Stele bearing the name of King Joash (Ya'asu) *the Samaritan, which shows that Israel paid tribute, with other city-states, to Adad-nirari III of Assyria about 796* BC. *From Assyrian temple at Tell Rimah, NW Iraq.* (BSAI)

1. Father of *Gideon; member of the Abiezrite branch of the tribe of Manasseh living at Ophrah (Jdg. 6:11–32). A Baal worshipper who had his own altar and *Asherah, which Gideon replaced by an altar to Yahweh (vv. 25–27). He told those who would defend him that Baal could take care of himself (v. 31). It was possibly he who renamed Gideon Jerubbaal (v. 32).

2. An ambidextrous Benjaminite warrior who, although a relative of Saul, aided David in his revolt (1 Ch. 12:1–3).

3. A 'son' of King *Ahab to whom the prophet Micaiah was to be taken in order to be imprisoned after angering Ahab by prophesying unfavourably (1 Ki. 22:26; 2 Ch. 18:25f.). Possibly 'son of the king' was an official's title rather than a kinship form.

4. Son of *Ahaziah, 8th king of Judah (*c.* 837–800 BC). When Athaliah annihilated the royal line at the death of her son Ahaziah, his aunt Jehosheba hid him in the Temple for 6 years under the protection of her husband *Jehoiada, the high priest (2 Ki. 11:1–6; 2 Ch. 22:10–12). At 7 years of age he was proclaimed king by Jehoiada and Athaliah was executed (2 Ki. 11:7–20; 2 Ch. 23:1–15).

Joash's reign lasted 40 years (2 Ki. 12:1), although the 6 years of Athaliah's reign might be included in this number. He rebuilt the *Temple with the help of Jehoiada (2 Ki. 12:5–16; 2 Ch. 24:4–14) but allowed the re-emergence of pagan practices upon Jehoiada's death (2 Ch. 24:17–18). When reprimanded for this by Zechariah, son of Jehoiada, he killed him (2 Ch. 24:20–22). In order to forestall a Syrian invasion under *Hazael, Joash bribed him with the Temple's treasure (2 Ki. 12:18–19). Joash was killed in a plot by his officers to replace him (2 Ki. 12:21–22; 2 Ch. 24:25–26).

5. Son of *Jehoahaz; 12th king of Israel who reigned 16 years (*c.* 801–786 BC; 2 Ki. 13:10). Israel was under external pressure from three sources during his reign. A stele of Adad-nirari III from Rimah records him receiving tribute from 'Iu'usu the Samaritan' in 796 BC (S. Page, *Iraq* 30, 1968, pp. 139ff.; *cf.* A. Malamat, *BASOR* 204, 1971, 37ff., concerning the reading of the name). The Aramaeans were oppressing them, but he was able to regain territory from them which had previously been lost (2 Ki. 13:22–25). Joash was helped in this by the ageing Elishah (vv. 14–19). He was also challenged by *Amaziah, king of Judah, whom he defeated. He sacked Jerusalem, taking hostages to ensure good conduct (2 Ki. 14:8–14; 2 Ch. 25:17–24).

BIBLIOGRAPHY. A. Malamat in *POTT*, pp. 145ff. D.W.B.

JOB (Heb. *'iyyôḇ*). Apart from the book bearing his name and the passing references to him in Ezk. 14:14, 20; Jas. 5:11 we have no reliable information about Job. It is impossible to show that the Jewish, Christian and Muslim legends about Job (the latter summarized in W. B. Stevenson, *The Poem of Job*, 1947, ch. 6) have any firm roots in a pre-biblical form of the story. Apart from the tradition of the location of Job's home (see below), which may be no more than intelligent deduction from the Bible, we have the impression of popular or pious fancy.

If we identify the Daniel (*dānī'ēl*) of Ezk. 14:14 not with the Daniel (*dāniyyē'l*) of the Exile but with the person mentioned in Ugaritic inscriptions, we can with some confidence give all three names in Ezk. 14:14 a very early date. If we do not accept this clue we have no indication of his date. The location of the land of Uz, where he lived, is uncertain. The modern tendency is to regard it as on the borders of Edom, certain indications in the book being regarded as Edomite; but the traditions placing it in the Hauran (Bashan) are far more probable. Job was a man of great wealth and high social position, but the book is so concerned with stressing his position among the Wise that it avoids precise details; we can, however, unhesitatingly reject the legends that make him a king.

As a result of divine permission Satan robbed him of his wealth, his ten children and finally his health. There is no agreement on what disease he was smitten with, the main suggestions being elephantiasis, erythema and smallpox. This wide disagreeement is due to the symptoms being given in highly poetic language. His relations and fellow-townsmen interpreted his misfortunes as a divine punishment for gross sin and threw him out of the town, the rabble taking a particular pleasure in this. His wife accepted the common opinion and urged him to expedite the inevitable end by cursing God.

Job was visited by three friends, Eliphaz, Bildad and Zophar, also members of the Wise, and rich and affluent, as he had been. When they saw his plight they shared popular opinion and could only sit in silence with Job on the dunghill outside the city gate for the 7 days of mourning for a man as good as dead. Job's outburst of agony led to a long, vehement discussion, ending with a wordy intrusion by a younger man, Elihu. All this only revealed the bankruptcy of traditional wisdom and theology when faced with an exceptional case like Job's. Though his friends' lack of comprehension drove Job almost to distraction, it also turned him to God and prepared him for the revelation of divine sovereignty, which brought him peace. The mob was confounded by his healing, the doubling of his wealth, and the gift of ten children.

H.L.E.

JOB, BOOK OF.

I. Outline of contents

Ch. 1 and 2 (in prose) introduce us to the encounter in heaven between God and Satan and its effects on earth. Ch. 3 is Job's great 'Why?'; Eliphaz gives his views in chs. 4–5 and Job replies in chs. 6–7. Bildad continues in ch. 8, Job replying in chs. 9–10. The first round of the discussion is completed by Zophar's contribution in ch. 11 and Job's reply in chs. 12–14. In the second round we hear Eliphaz (15), Bildad (18) and Zophar (20), with Job's replies in chs. 16–17, 19, 21. As the text stands (see **III**, below), the third round is incomplete, only Eliphaz (22) and Bildad (25) speaking, with Job's replies in chs. 23–24, 26–27. After an interlude in praise of wisdom (28), Job sums up the debate (29–31). Elihu's intervention follows in chs. 32–37, and then God replies to Job in chs. 38–42:6. The book ends with a prose epilogue telling of Job's restored prosperity (42:7–17).

II. Authorship and date

The book is anonymous. The 'official' Talmudic tradition, followed by many earlier Christian writers, is that the book was written by Moses (*Baba Bathra* 14b, *seq.*), but the continuation of the passage and other statements show that this is merely a pious pronouncement, based presumably on a feeling of fitness, and not to be taken seriously. The simple fact is that we have no purely objective evidence to guide us either in the question of authorship or of date. The evidence for a very early date lies mostly in the non-mention of any of the details of Israelite history, but this is sufficiently explained by the author's wish to discuss the central problem outside the framework of the covenant. Other evidence, such as the mention of the Chaldeans as nomadic raiders (1:17) and of the archaic *qᵉśîṭâ* (42:11), point merely to the antiquity of the story and not to that of its present written form.

Moderns have varied in their dating from the time of Solomon to about 250 BC, dates between 600 and 400 BC being most popular, though there is a growing tendency to favour later dates. A Solomonic date, accepted by Franz Delitzsch and E. J. Young, is the earliest we can reasonably adopt. The arguments from subject, language and theology probably favour a somewhat later date, but since the book is *sui generis* in Heb. literature, and the language is so distinctive (some even regard it as a translation from Aramaic, or consider the author lived outside Israel), while the theology is timeless, any dogmatism derives from subjectivism or preconceptions.

III. Text

The fact that we are dealing with some of the most difficult poetry in the OT, and that in the vocabulary we have some 110 words (W. B. Stevenson, *The Poem of Job*, p. 71) not found elsewhere, has made the scribe's task very difficult. Unfortunately the versions are no great help in checking the Heb. text. The LXX must be used with great caution. In its earlier form about 17–25% of the Heb. is missing, probably because the translators were daunted by their task; the rendering is often free and periphrastic, and not seldom incorrect.

The main textual problem concerns chs. 26–27. As they stand they are Job's answer to Bildad's third speech. No objection can be raised to Zophar's failure to speak a third time; it is in keeping with his character, and would be the most obvious proof of Job's verbal triumph over his friends. Indubitably we hear Job speaking in 27:2–6, but in its context it is virtually impossible to ascribe 27:7–23 to him. It is probably part of Zophar's third speech or possibly of Bildad's. If that is so, no entirely satisfactory reconstruction of the text has been suggested and it may be that part of the original ms has been lost, something that could easily happen with a brittle papyrus roll.

IV. Integrity

Most scholars separate the prose prologue and epilogue from the poetry of 3:1–42:6. Where this is interpreted as meaning that they are older than the poem, and that the author transformed the heart of the old story into magnifient verse, the theory is unobjectionable and quite possibly correct. There are no objective proofs for the suggestion that the prose was added later to the verse by another hand, whether it is earlier or later in composition. In the hands of W. B. Stevenson (*op. cit.*) this theory has been used to impose a non-natural interpretation on the book.

Very many scholars regard certain portions as later insertions. In descending order of importance the chief are: Elihu's speeches (32–37), the praise of divine wisdom (28) and certain parts of God's answer (39:13–18; 40:15–24; 41: 1–34). In every case the linguistic arguments are very tenuous. The argument from their contents is liable to take the passages in isolation. A very reasonable defence of them in their actual setting can be made.

V. As Wisdom literature

R. H. Pfeiffer, *IOT*, 1948, pp. 683f., says very well: 'If our poet ranks with the greatest writers of mankind, as can hardly be doubted, his creative genius did not of necessity rely on earlier models for the general structure of his work. . . . We may regard it as one of the most original works in the poetry of mankind. So original in fact that it does not fit into any of the standard categories devised by literary criticism . . . it is not exclusively lyric . . . nor epic . . . nor dramatic . . . nor didactic nor reflective . . . unless the poem is cut down to fit a particular category.' The convention that calls Job part of Heb. Wisdom literature and aligns it with Proverbs and Ecclesiastes and compares it with certain Egyp. and Bab. 'Wisdom' writings is justified only if we are careful to keep Pfeiffer's warning in mind. For all that, it is clear that Job and his friends are depicted as, and speak primarily as, members of the Wise, and they are so addressed by Elihu (34:2).

The Wise in Israel sought to understand God and his ways by studying the great uniformities of human experience by reason illuminated by 'the fear of the Lord'. Proverbs is a typical example of their understanding of life. Job is a flaming protest, less against the basic concept of Proverbs that a God-fearing life brings prosperity, godlessness suffering and destruction, than against the idea that thereby the ways of God are fully grasped. Job is not a type; he is the exception that makes folly of the assumption that through normal experience the depths of God's wisdom and working can be fully grasped.

VI. The problem of Job

The poem is so rich in its thought, so wide in its sweep, that much in human experience and its mysteries has been found mirrored there. Mostly, however, it has been regarded as concerned with the problem of human suffering. Though he has overstated his case, W. B. Stevenson (*op. cit.*, pp. 34ff.) makes it clear that in the poem there is far less allusion to Job's physical sufferings than has often been assumed. Job is concerned less with his physical pain than with his treatment by his relations, his fellow-townsmen, the mob and finally his friends. But these are merely evidence that God has forsaken him. In other words, Job's problem is not that of pain, nor even suffering in a wider sense, but the theological one, why God had not acted as all theory and his earlier experiences demanded he should. Being a child of his age, he had naturally built up his life on the theory that God's justice implied the equation of goodness and prosperity.

Taken out of their context, the words of his friends and Elihu are more acceptable than many of the rasher utterances of Job. They are rejected by God (42:7), not because they are untrue, but because they are too narrow. This is made especially clear by the discussion on the fate of the wicked. With all Job's exaggeration we recognize at once that his friends are in fact producing an *a priori* picture of what the fate of the wicked should be. They create their picture of God only by a careful selection of evidence. Job's agony is caused by the breakdown of his theological world-picture.

This explains the apparently unsatisfactory climax in which God does not answer Job's questions or charges, but though he proclaims the greatness of his all-might, not of his ethical rule, Job is satisfied. He realizes that his concept of God collapsed because it was too small; his problems evaporate when he realizes the greatness of God. The book does not set out to answer the problem of suffering but to proclaim a God so great that no answer is needed, for it would transcend the finite mind if given; the same applies to the problems incidentally raised.

BIBLIOGRAPHY. S. R. Driver and G. B. Gray, *The Book of Job, ICC*, 1921; G. Hölscher, *Hiob*, 1937; J. C. Rylaarsdam, *Revelation in Jewish Wisdom Literature*, 1946; W. B. Stevenson, *The Poem of Job*, 1947; H. L. Ellison, *From Tragedy to Triumph*, 1958; E. Dhorme, *The Book of Job*, 1967; H. H. Rowley, *Job, NCB*, 1970; F. I. Andersen, *Job, TOTC*, 1976. H.L.E.

JOCHEBED (Heb. *yôkebed*, probably 'Yahweh is glory', though M. Noth [*Die israelitschen Personennamen*, 1928, p. 111] thinks it may be of foreign origin.) The mother of Moses, Aaron and Miriam (Ex. 6:20; Nu. 26:59). She was a daughter of Levi, and married her nephew Amram. However, according to the LXX of Ex. 6:20 they were cousins, though S. R. Driver (*CBSC*, 1918) thinks that *MT* preserves a genuine ancient tradition. J.G.G.N.

JOEL, BOOK OF.

I. Outline of contents

Joel discusses four main topics: (*a*) the appalling devastations of successive plagues of locusts, literal enough, yet symbolizing deeper meanings; (*b*) the renewed fruitfulness of the land on the repentance of Israel; (*c*) the gifts of the Spirit; (*d*) final judgment on the nations which have wronged Israel, and the blessedness-to-be of the land of Judah. In all these, primary and eschatological references intertwine.

a. The locust plague, 1:1–12

For locusts in the OT, *cf.* also Ex. 10:12–15 *et passim*, with Pss. 78:46; 105:34; also Pr. 30:27; Na. 3:15, 17, *etc.* (*ANIMALS.)

(i) Joel claims in customary prophetic manner that he has received the word of the Lord, giving his own name and that of his father, both otherwise unknown (1:1).

(ii) The burden of his message is prodigious—a locust plague in successive swarms, of frightening dimensions (1:2–4; *cf.* Ex. 10:14). Full etymological, entomological

Devastation caused by a swarm of locusts like this is described in the book of Joel (1:1–12). (S)

and figurative discussion of v. 4 will be found in commentaries.

(iii) The effects of the plague are vividly described (1:5–12). The first to be mentioned, perhaps in derision, is the loss to the drunkard of his solace. The teeth of the locust host are fearsome (*cf.* Pr. 30:14, *etc.*)—the very fig-bark is devoured, the white, sappy interior uncovered to the world. Temple priests should mourn with the bitterness of an aged virgin whose betrothed died in her youth before marriage, for the very materials of sacrifice are cut off (*cf.* Dn. 8:11; 11:31; 12:11; contrast Is. 1:11–15; Mi. 6:6; *etc.*). The devastation in cornfield, vineyard and orchard is vividly described.

b. The fruits of repentance, 1:13–2:27

(i) The priests in sackcloth are to lament, with fasting and prayer, the day of God's wrath, the 'conquest from the Conqueror', to reflect palely the striking Heb. assonance (1:13–15; see Ne. 9:1; Est. 4:3, 16; Dn. 9:3, *etc.*, contrasted with Is. 58:4ff.; Je. 14:12; Zc. 7:5; *etc.*). The OT views on sacrifice and fasting are not contradictory; much depended on circumstance and particular usage. Joel need not stand condemned because he is more ritualistic than Amos or Isaiah.

(ii) It seems reasonable to regard the next section (1:16–20) as a prayer, despite the vivid initial delineation of locust ravage. V. 18 should read 'What shall we put in them?'—*i.e.* the flimsy barns not rebuilt through lack of need. The fire and flame of v. 19 may be heat and drought, or even the vivid red colouring in the locust bodies.

(iii) The prophet now reverts from the devastation of the locusts to their initial onslaught, likening it to the Day of the Lord (2:1–11). V. 2b is typical oriental idiom (*cf.* Ex. 10:14). Vividly accurate is the likening of the swarm to an advancing fire. The fruitful earth before them becomes a black desolation as they pass over it (v. 3). First-hand experience is reflected also in the likening of the separate locusts to horsemen, and the parallel drawn between the noise of their advance and the sound of a rapidly spreading bush fire (vv. 4–5). People are horror-stricken before the unswerving, unjostling, accurate advance of myriads of myriads of these insects, invincible through sheer numbers (vv. 6–9). The real locusts could be symbols of the Gentiles in the valley of decision, before their judgment.

(iv) In the hour of horror it is not too late to repent, with mortification of the flesh (2:12–14). Official rending of the garments may be hypocritical; real repentance is in the heart. This may even make God 'repent' of his recently appropriate judgment, and provide sacrificial materials again. This is oriental symbolism, implying no 'sinful' deity.

(v) A fresh call to special temple worship is given (2:15–17). This embraces priests and people, with specific mention of suckling babes, tottering greybeards and newlyweds, who normally enjoyed far-reaching exemptions from public duties. J. A. Bewer (*ICC*, 1911) ingeniously points the imperatives as perfects, without consonantal change, making v. 15, not v. 18, the turning-point of the book, and the beginning of continuous narrative.

(vi) The devastation of the locust will be surpassed by the plenty that the Lord will grant on repentance (2:18–25). V. 20 means that the physical bodies of the locusts in Judaea will be wind-driven into the Dead Sea and the Mediterranean Sea, and this will be followed by a stench of decay (18–25).

c. The gifts of the Spirit, 2:28–32

The outpouring of the Spirit described in this passage is the apex of prophetic utterance. Vv. 28–29, and 32 were clearly fulfilled at Pentecost; aspects of vv. 30 and 31 were fulfilled in the passion of our Lord. Ecstatic prophesying might include the gift of tongues. The pillars of smoke might be sand columns raised by desert whirlwinds, or the conflagration of doomed cities. A solar eclipse can make a blood-red moon. What more saving name could be foreshadowed in v. 32 than that of Jesus? Everything here has a meaning—yet there is a deeper meaning belonging to the days when the last sands of human time will sink for evermore.

d. God's enemies judged, 3:1–21

The surface meaning of this section is the prediction of divine vengeance on the nations which have scattered and persecuted the Jews. The references of vv. 3–8 are clearly historical. The locusts might foreshadow these armies of Gentiles in their brief hour of victory. Vv. 9–11 are biting in their sarcasm as the prophet urges the heathen to make war on God. God alone will judge the assembled nations in the valley of decision (vv. 12, 14; *JEHOSHAPHAT, VALLEY OF). The full horror of vv. 15ff., 19a, and the full benediction of v. 18, are both alike as yet unrealized. Earthly prophecy and eschatology are wedded in a chapter of rich prefiguring. The Christian church is the heir of the OT, and the sure word of prophecy, be it about Egypt or anything else, will come to pass in God's good time.

II. Authorship and date

This is superb extrovert literature, betraying a Judaean flavour, but intrinsically concerned with bigger issues than contemporary politics. This makes dating exceptionally difficult. Most scholars maintain (*cf.* W. Nowack, 1922; K. Marti, 1904), some (e.g. Bewer, *ICC*) that Joel is a literary unity. Older conservatives dated the book in the 8th century BC, the time of Amos and Hosea. Oesterley and Robinson adopt the extreme late dating of 200 BC, others assign between these limits. R. K. Harrison (*IOT*, 1970, pp. 874–882) discusses the issues thoroughly, but, stressing the book's timelessness, will not commit his dating beyond 'in advance of 400 BC'. Were the early dating to be taken as correct, certain familiar prophetic battle-cries would then find their first known utterance in Joel. Ploughshares might have been considered the fathers of swords before the hope of the reverse transformation was born (Joel 3:10; Is. 2:4).

III. Special characteristics

Joel was the vehicle of a divine revelation which has a significance perhaps beyond his full understanding. In his book the impinging of the eternal on the temporal, which is the hallmark of genuine inspiration, is undeniably in evidence. This is especially true in his arresting description of locust-plague havoc, symbolic of God's wrath and punitive visitation of sin. Vividly portrayed also is God's gracious restoration of his people following upon repentance. There are factual prophecies linked with our Lord's death, with the coming of the Holy Spirit, with both the horror and the hope of the end-times. This is one of the briefest and yet one of the most disturbing and heart-searching books of the OT.

BIBLIOGRAPHY. S. R. Driver, *Joel and Amos*, *CBSC*, 1915; A. S.

Kapelrud, *Joel Studies*, 1948; J. A. Thompson, 'Joel's Locusts in the Light of Near Eastern Parables', *JNES* 14, 1955, pp. 52 ff.; *IB*, 6, pp. 727–760; L. C. Allen, *Joel, Obadiah, Jonah and Micah, NICOT*, 1976.

R.A.S.

JOGBEHAH (Heb. *yoḡbᵉhâ*, 'height'). A town in Gilead assigned to Gad (Nu 32:35), named also in Gideon's pursuit of the Midianites (Jdg. 8:11). It is the modern Jubeihât, about 10 km NW of Amman and 1057 m above sea-level. J.D.D.

JOHANAN (Heb. *yôḥānān*, 'Yahweh is gracious'). A number of men are so called in the OT, the most notable being the son of Kareah. A Jewish leader who supported Gedaliah on the latter's appointment as governor of Judah (2 Ki. 25:23; Je. 40:8) after the fall of Jerusalem, Johanan offered to kill Ishmael, who was plotting Gedaliah's assassination (Je. 40:13–16). The offer rejected and the warning ignored, Ishmael succeeded in his purpose. Johanan pursued him, rescued the people captured by him (Je. 41:11–16), and took them and the protesting Jeremiah to Tahpanhes in Egypt (Je. 43:1–7).

Others possessing the same name include the eldest son of Josiah, king of Judah (1 Ch. 3:15); a son of Elioenai (1 Ch. 3:24); a grandson of Ahimaaz (1 Ch. 6:9–10); a Benjaminite recruit of David at Ziklag (1 Ch. 12:4); a Gadite who likewise joined David (1 Ch. 12:12); an Ephraimite chief (2 Ch. 28:12, where Hebrew has 'Jehohanan'); a returned exile in Artaxerxes' time (Ezr. 8:12); and a priest in the days of Joiakim (Ne. 12:22–23). J.D.D.

JOHN, THE APOSTLE. Our information about John comes from two sources: NT and Patristic.

I. New Testament evidence

a. In the Gospels

John was the son of Zebedee, probably the younger son, for except in Luke–Acts he is mentioned after his brother James. Luke gives the order Peter, John and James, probably because in the early days of the church John was closely associated with Peter (Lk. 8:51; 9:28; Acts 1:13). That John's mother's name was Salome is an inference from Mk. 16:1 and Mt. 27:56; for the third woman who is said to have accompanied the two Marys to the tomb is designated Salome by Mark, and 'the mother of Zebedee's children' by Matthew. Salome is usually regarded as the sister of Mary the mother of Jesus, because in Jn. 19:25 four women are said to have stood near the cross, the two Marys mentioned in Mark and Matthew, the mother of Jesus, and his mother's sister. If this identification is correct, John was a cousin of Jesus on his mother's side. His parents would appear to have been well-to-do, for his father, a fisherman, had 'hired servants' (Mk. 1:20); and Salome was one of the women who 'provided for Jesus out of their means' (Lk. 8:3; Mk. 15:40). John has often been identified with the unnamed disciple of John the Baptist, who with Andrew was directed by the Baptist to Jesus as the Lamb of God (Jn. 1:35–37); and if *prōtos* is read in Jn. 1:41, it is possible that Andrew was the first of these two disciples to bring his brother Simon to Jesus, and that the unnamed disciple (John) subsequently brought his own brother James. This is not certain, however, as there are textual variants (see *TNTC*). After their subsequent call by Jesus to leave their father and their fishing (Mk. 1:19–20), James and John were nicknamed by him *Boanērges*, 'sons of thunder' (Mk. 3:17), probably because they were high-spirited, impetuous Galileans, whose zeal was undisciplined and sometimes misdirected (Lk. 9:49). This aspect of their character is shown by their outburst after a Samaritan village had refused their Master entrance (Lk. 9:54). Moreover, their personal ambition was, it would seem, untempered by a true insight into the nature of his kingship; and this lingering trait of selfishness, together with their readiness to suffer for Jesus regardless of self, is illustrated in the request they made to him (a request encouraged by their mother [Mt. 20:20]) that they should be allowed to sit in places of special privilege when Jesus entered into his kingdom (Mk. 10:37).

On three important occasions in the earthly ministry of Jesus, John is mentioned in company with his brother James and Simon Peter, to the exclusion of the other apostles: at the raising of Jairus' daughter (Mk. 5:37), at the transfiguration (Mk. 9:2) and in the garden of Gethsemane (Mk. 14:33); and, according to Luke, Peter and John were the two disciples sent by Jesus to make preparations for the final Passover meal (Lk. 22:8).

John is not mentioned by name in the Fourth Gospel (though the sons of Zebedee are referred to in 21:2), but he is almost certainly the disciple called 'the disciple whom Jesus loved', who lay close to the breast of Jesus at the Last Supper (13:23); who was entrusted with the care of his mother at the time of his death (19:26–27); who ran with Peter to the tomb on the first Easter morning and was the first to see the full significance of the undisturbed grave-clothes with no body inside them (20:2, 8); and who was present when the risen Christ revealed himself to seven of his disciples by the sea of Tiberias. In the account of that last incident in ch. 21, support is given to the later tradition that John lived on to a great age (21:23). The evidence of Jn. 21:24 for the Johannine authorship of this Gospel is capable of different interpretations (see *TNTC*).

b. In the Acts

According to the early narratives of Acts, John, together with Peter, with whom he remained closely associated, had to bear the main brunt of Jewish hostility to the early Christian church (Acts 4:13; 5:33, 40). Both men showed a boldness of speech and action which astounded the Jewish authorities, who regarded them as 'uneducated, common men' (Acts 4:13). John, it would seem, continued for some years to play a leading part in the church at Jerusalem. On behalf of the other apostles he and Peter laid hands on the Samaritans who had been converted through the ministry of Philip (Acts 8:14); and he could be described as a reputed 'pillar' of the Jerusalem church at the time when Paul visited the city some 14 years after his conversion (Gal. 2:9). We do not know when John left Jerusalem, nor where he went after his departure. Assuming that he is the seer of the book of Revelation, he was presumably at Ephesus when he was banished to Patmos 'on account of the word of God, and the testimony of Jesus' (Rev. 1:9), though the date of this exile is uncertain. There is no other mention of John in the NT, though some think that he refers to himself as 'the elder' in 2 Jn. 1; 3 Jn. 1.

II. Patristic evidence

There is a certain amount of late but probably unreliable evidence, that John the apostle died as a martyr early in his career, perhaps at the time his brother James was slain by Herod (Acts 12:2). A 9th-century chronicler, George Hamartolos, reproduces, as we can now see, a statement contained in the history of Philip of Side (*c.* 450), a relevant fragment of which was discovered by de Boor in 1889, to the effect that Papias, bishop of Hierapolis in the middle of the 2nd century, in the second book of his *Expositions* asserted that *both* the sons of Zebedee met a violent death in fulfilment of the Lord's prediction (Mk. 10:39). Though some scholars accept this testimony as genuine, most regard Philip of Side as an unreliable witness to Papias, and are impressed by the absence from Eusebius of any reference to the early martyrdom of John, and also by the failure of Acts to mention it, if both the sons of Zebedee in fact suffered in the same way at approximately the same time. It is true that some support for Philip of Side's statement seems to be obtainable from a Syr. martyrology written about AD 400, in which the entry for 27 December is 'John and James the apostles at Jerusalem'; and also from a calendar of the church at Carthage, dated AD 505, in which the entry for the same date reads 'John the Baptist and James the apostle whom Herod killed', for it is pointed out by those who accept this evidence that, as the Baptist is commemorated in this calendar on 24 June, the probability is that the entry for 27 December is a mistake for 'John the Apostle'. It is, however, very doubtful whether the Syr. martyrology preserves an ancient tradition independent of the Gk.-speaking church; nor does it follow that, because the two brothers were commemorated on the same day, they were commemorated as being both martyrs in *death* who had been slain at the same time. Nor again does the reference to the sons of Zebedee as 'drinking the cup' and 'being baptized with the baptism of Christ' necessarily imply that both were destined to come to a violent end.

Against this partial and weakly attested tradition must be set the much stronger tradition reflected in the statement of Polycrates, bishop of Ephesus (AD 190), that John 'who reclined on the Lord's breast', after being 'a witness and a teacher' (note the order of the words), 'fell asleep at Ephesus'. According to Irenaeus, it was at Ephesus that John 'gave out' the Gospel, and confuted the heretics, refusing to remain under the same roof as Cerinthus, 'the enemy of truth'; at Ephesus that he lingered on 'till the days of Trajan', who reigned AD 98–117. Jerome also repeats the tradition that John tarried at Ephesus to extreme old age, and records that, when John had to be carried to the Christian meetings, he used to repeat again and again 'Little children, love one another'. The only evidence that might seemingly conflict with this tradition of John the apostle's residence at Ephesus is negative in character. It is alleged that if, as the writers at the end of the 2nd century assert, John resided long at Ephesus and exercised such influence, it is remarkable that there should be an entire absence of any reference to John in the extant Christian literature which emanated from Asia during the first half of the century, particularly in the letters of Ignatius and the Epistle of Polycarp. But, even if the absence of allusions to John in these documents is significant, it may merely be an indication that 'there was a difference between his reputation and influence at the beginning and at the close of the century' (so V. H. Stanton, *The Gospels as Historical Documents*, 1, p. 236). On any score the objection, it would seem, is insufficient to overthrow the tradition which later became so firmly established. Westcott concluded that 'nothing is better attested in early church history than the residence and work of St John at Ephesus'. It is true that Westcott wrote before the evidence for John's early martyrdom had accumulated, but as we have seen, that evidence is not adequate enough or reliable enough to confute the definite statements of the man who occupied the see of Ephesus at the close of the century, and of the man who at the same period made it his primary aim to investigate the traditions of the apostolic sees.

(*JOHN, EPISTLES OF; *JOHN, GOSPEL OF; *REVELATION, BOOK OF).

BIBLIOGRAPHY. S. S. Smalley, *John: Evangelist and Interpreter*, 1978; F. F. Bruce, 'St John at Ephesus', *BJRL* 60, 1977–8, pp. 339–361. See also the Commentaries listed under *JOHN, GOSPEL OF.

R.V.G.T.

JOHN THE BAPTIST. Born (*c.* 7 BC) to an elderly couple, Zechariah a priest and his wife Elizabeth, he

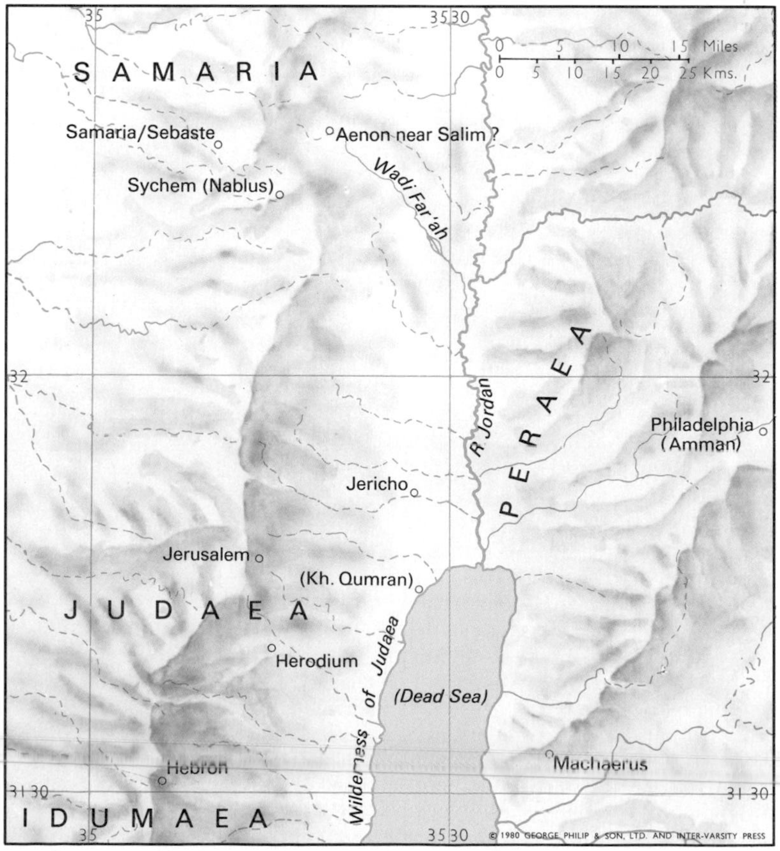

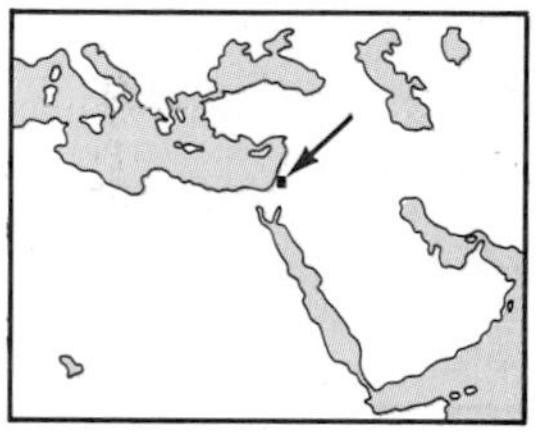

The area of John the Baptist's ministry.

John ('Yehohanan'), a Jewish name, inscribed on an ossuary from Jerusalem between 40 BC *and* AD *135.* (JPK)

grew to manhood in the wilderness of Judaea (Lk. 1:80), where he received his prophetic call, *c.* AD 27 (Lk. 3:2). The view that his wilderness period was spent in association with the Qumran community or a similar Essene group must be treated with caution; even if it could be substantiated, it was a new impulse which sent him forth 'to make ready for the Lord a people prepared' (Lk. 1:17), and his prophetic ministry must have involved a break with any Essene or similar group with which he may previously have been connected. After the Spirit of prophecy came upon him, he quickly gained widespread fame as a preacher calling for national repentance. Crowds flocked to hear him, and many of his hearers were baptized by him in the Jordan, confessing their sins.

His attitude to the established order in Israel was one of radical condemnation; 'the axe', he said, 'is laid to the root of the trees' (Mt. 3:10; Lk. 3:9). He denounced the religious leaders of the people as a brood of vipers, and denied that there was any value in the bare fact of descent from Abraham. A new beginning was necessary; the time had come to call out from the nation as a whole a loyal remnant who would be ready for the imminent arrival of the Coming One and the judgment which he would execute. John thought and spoke of himself as a mere preparer of the way for this Coming One, for whom he was unworthy, he said, to perform the lowliest service. Whereas John's own ministry was characterized by baptism with water, the Coming One's ministry would be a baptism with the Holy Spirit and fire.

That John aimed at giving the loyal remnant a distinct and recognizable existence is suggested by the statement in Josephus (*Ant.* 18. 117) that John was 'a good man who bade the Jews practise virtue, be just one to another, and pious toward God, and come together by means of baptism'; these last words seem to envisage the formation of a religious community which was entered by baptism. This is probably an accurate assessment of the situation. But when Josephus goes on to say that John 'taught that baptism was acceptable to God provided that they underwent it not to procure remission of sins but for the purification of the body, if the soul had first been purified by righteousness', he differs from the NT account. The Evangelists say quite plainly that John preached a 'baptism of repentance for the remission of sins'. Josephus is probably transferring to John's baptism what he knew to be the significance of Essene washings; the Qumran *Rule of the Community* gives an account of the significance of such washings almost identical with that which Josephus gives of John's baptism. But John's baptism, like his preaching, may well represent a deliberate turning away from Essene beliefs and practices.

Among those who came to John for baptism was Jesus, whom John apparently hailed as the Coming One of whom he had spoken—although later, in prison, he had doubts about this identification and had to be reassured by being told that Jesus' ministry was marked by precisely those features which the prophets had foretold as characteristic of the age of restoration.

John's ministry was not confined to the Jordan valley. The statement in John 3:23 that he left the Jordan valley for a time and conducted a baptismal campaign (presumably of brief duration) 'at Aenon near Salim', where there was abundance of water, has implications which are easily overlooked. For W. F. Albright (*The Archaeology of Palestine*, 1956, p. 247) is probably right in locating this place NE of Nablus, near the sources of the Wadi Far‘ah—that is to say, in territory which was then Samaritan. This could explain certain features of Samaritan religion attested for the early Christian centuries, but it also illuminates the words of Jesus to his disciples in John 4:35–38, spoken with regard to the people in this very area, and ending with the statement: 'others have laboured, and you have entered into their labour'. The harvest which they reaped (Jn. 4:39, 41) had been sown by John.

After this period of ministry in Samaria John must have returned to the territory of Herod Antipas (*HEROD, **3**), probably Peraea. He aroused Antipas' suspicion as the leader of a mass movement which might have unforeseen results; he also incurred his hostility, and still more that of Herod's second wife *Herodias, by denouncing their marriage as illicit. He was accordingly imprisoned in the Peraean fortress of *Machaerus and there, some months later, put to death.

In the NT John is presented chiefly as the forerunner of Christ. His imprisonment was the signal for the start of Jesus' Galilean ministry (Mk. 1:14f.); his baptismal activity provided a starting-point for the apostolic preaching (Acts 10:37; 13:24f.; *cf.* 1:22 and Mk.1:1–4). In Jesus' estimation, John was the promised Elijah of Mal. 4:5f., who was to come and complete his ministry of restoration on the eve of 'the great and terrible day of the Lord' (Mk. 9:13; Mt. 11:14; *cf.* Lk. 1:17). Jesus also regarded him as the last and greatest member of the prophetic succession: 'the law and the prophets were until John: since then the good news of the kingdom of God is preached' (Lk. 16:16). Therefore, while unsurpassed in personal stature, he was (in respect of privilege) less than the least in the kingdom of God; he stood on the threshold of the new order as its herald (as Moses viewed the promised land from Pisgah) without entering in. His disciples preserved their corporate existence for a considerable time after his death.

BIBLIOGRAPHY. C. H. Kraeling, *John the Baptist*, 1951; J. Steinmann, *Saint John the Baptist and the Desert Tradition*, 1958; A. S. Geyser, 'The Youth of John the Baptist', *NovT* 1, 1956, pp. 70ff.; W. H. Brownlee, 'John the Baptist in the New Light of Ancient Scrolls', in *The Scrolls and the New Testament*, ed. K. Stendahl, 1958, pp. 33ff.; C. H. H. Scobie, *John the Baptist*, 1964. F.F.B.

JOHN, EPISTLES OF.

I. Background and circumstances of 1 John

1 John is headed as an Epistle, but there is nothing 'epistolary' in the strict sense about it (contrast 2 and 3 John), and it is more like a tract addressed to a particular situation.

It was called forth by the activities of false teachers who had seceded from the church (or churches) to which John is writing and who were attempting to seduce the faithful (2:18f., 26). They formed an esoteric group, believing that they had superior knowledge to ordinary Christians (cf. 2:20, 27; 2 Jn. 9) and showing little love to them (*cf.* 4:20).

They were forerunners of the later heretics generally known as 'Gnostics' (from Gk. *gnōsis*, meaning 'knowledge') and claimed a special knowledge of God and of theology. On the basis of their new doctrine they appear to have denied that Jesus was the Christ (2:22), the pre-existent (1:1) Son of God (4:15; 5:5, 10) come in the flesh (4:2; 2 Jn. 7) to provide salvation for men (4:9f., 14). But the precise form which this heresy took is uncertain. It is generally regarded as having had some affinity with the views held by Cerinthus in Asia Minor at the end of the 1st century, although it was not fully identical with what we know of his teaching. According to Cerinthus, Jesus was a good man who was indwelt by the heavenly Christ from the time of his baptism until just before his crucifixion (Irenaeus, *Adv. Haer.* 1. 26. 1, in J. Stevenson, *A New Eusebius*, 1957, No. 70)—a view which is apparently contradicted in 5:6 and in various verses where belief that Jesus *is* (not simply *was*) the Christ, the Son of God, is emphasized (2:22; 5:1, 5). Such teaching was probably bound up with the common gnostic distinction between spirit and matter, according to which a real incarnation of God in man was impossible and was only apparent (as in Docetism) or temporary (as in Cerinthianism).

The false teachers further claimed that they were 'sinless' (1:8, 10) and possibly also that they did not need redemption through the death of Jesus Christ, while they were in fact morally indifferent, following the ways of the world (*cf.* 2:15), ignoring the commandments of Christ (2:4), and freely doing what they pleased (without, however, indulging in gross sin). They did not realize that sin is a moral category, *i.e.* lawlessness (3:4, 7f.), and consequently they felt quite consistent in claiming sinlessness while indulging in selfishness and lack of love. Probably we are to see here also the influence of the gnostic distinction between spirit and matter: since the body (matter) was evil anyhow and only the (divinely implanted) spirit or soul mattered, their bodily behaviour was irrelevant to their Christian belief.

John writes to provide an antidote to this teaching, and the progress of the argument in his tract is best understood when this is kept in mind. Attempts to explain its difficult structure in terms of source criticism (R. Bultmann; W. Nauck; J. C. O'Neill) have met with little favour.

II. Outline of contents of 1 John

John begins by stating that his purpose is to explain to his readers what he has heard and seen as regards the word of life manifested in Jesus Christ, so that there may be joyful fellowship between himself, his readers and God (1:1–4).

He then states the fundamental proposition, *God is light*, and on the basis of this universally acceptable truth proceeds to take up certain erroneous slogans of his opponents (1:6a, 8a, 10a; 2:4a). In opposition to them he asserts that only those who walk in the light can have fellowship with God and cleansing through the blood of Jesus. To deny that one is a sinner in need of cleansing is to commit self-deceit, but sinners can be sure of forgiveness from a faithful God through the righteous Advocate, Jesus Christ. To claim a true knowledge of God without obeying his commandments is to be a liar (1:5–2:6).

Christians, then, are called to obey God's new commandment. Although it is really an old one, yet it is now presented anew as the law of the new era of light which has already begun to shine in the darkness of the old, sinful world. John feels able to address his readers in this way because they have already entered into this new era and enjoy the privileges of forgiveness, knowledge and power, and he further exhorts them not to cling to the sinful world which is doomed to pass away (2:7–17).

One of the marks of the arrival of the new era is the rise of these false teachers who have now left their temporary home in the church. Their teaching is a denial that Jesus is the Christ, the Son of God, and this really means that they are denying God the Father himself. They claim special knowledge, to be sure, but John assures his readers that in view of their anointing by God (*i.e.* with the Spirit or perhaps with the Word of God) all Christians have true knowledge (2:18–27).

He now counsels them to abide in Christ, the holy and righteous One, and to test themselves and their teachers by their likeness to him. This leads to the thought of the great privilege of Christians as children of God, and the even greater privilege that at the advent of Christ they will become altogether like him—all of which constitutes a powerful incentive to holy living (2:28–3:3).

What, then, is the character of children of God in contrast with those who are the children of the devil? Since Christ came to take away sin, it follows that God's children do not, and in fact cannot, sin, while the children of the devil neither do what is right nor show love. By this uncompromising statement, which must be considered in the light of 1:8, John means that the Christian *as a Christian* cannot sin: he is speaking of the ideal character of the Christian, in contrast with the false teachers who made no attempt to emulate this ideal (3:4–10).

In fact, Christians can expect to be hated by children of the devil, just as Abel was murdered by Cain; by contrast, the mark of the true Christian is love, seen not in murder but in self-sacrifice and practical charity (3:11–18).

Through such deeds of love a man knows that he is a Christian, so that, even if his conscience at times condemns him, he can still have perfect confidence before his Judge, the God who knows his desire to love and serve him (*cf.* Jn. 21:17); indeed, armed with this confidence, he can be bold in prayer, since he knows that he is pleasing

God by keeping his commandment of love, and, further, he will receive inward assurance from the Spirit of God (3:19–24).

But how can a Christian be sure that he has the Spirit of *God*? For the false teachers also claim to have the Spirit. John replies that correct belief about Jesus Christ come in the flesh is the sure sign of true inspiration. The false teachers, however, are motivated by the spirit of antichrist (4:1–6).

After this digression, John returns to the theme of love. Love, he repeats, is the token that a man is born of God, for, as was shown in the sacrifice of Christ, *God is love*. (This is John's second great declaration about the nature of God.) Even if men cannot see God, they can know that he dwells in them if they show love (4:7–12).

John now summarizes the grounds of Christian assurance—possession of the Spirit, confession of Jesus Christ and the practice of love. These are signs that God dwells in us and give us confidence for the day of judgment, since there can be no fear where there is love. Yet, to avoid any antinomian or 'spiritualistic' misunderstanding, John emphasizes that such love for God is inevitably accompanied by love for the brethren. All who truly confess Jesus Christ love God and their fellow-men. Nor is it difficult to keep this commandment, for by faith those who are born of God can overcome the forces arrayed against them (4:13–5:4).

This leads John back to the theme of faith. True Christian faith is centred on Jesus Christ, who not only submitted to the water of baptism but also shed his blood on the cross, and to whom the Spirit bears witness (Jn. 15:26). These three—the Spirit, water and blood—are God's sure testimony to confirm faith in Christ. John possibly also means that the saving activity of the Spirit in the church (or the individual believer) and the sacraments of baptism and the Lord's supper continue this testimony. To disbelieve this testimony is to make God a liar and to reject the eternal life which he has given to men in his Son (5:5–12).

In conclusion, John states that his purpose has been to assure his readers of their salvation. Since they can be sure of divine response to their prayers, they are to win back erring brethren through prayer (although prayer is of no avail in the case of mortal sin, whatever that may be). Finally come three great declarations—that Christians have power not to sin, that they belong to God, and that they are in Jesus Christ who is their great instructor—and a final admonition to avoid idolatry (*i.e.* worship of pagan gods, but the meaning is not certain) (5:13–21).

III. Background and contents of 2 and 3 John

2 and 3 John are real letters, each long enough to be accommodated on a standard size sheet of papyrus (25 by 20 cm) and conforming to the pattern of letter-writing of the time. (For a remarkably close parallel to the structure of 3 John, see C. K. Barrett, *The New Testament Background: Selected Documents*, 1956, No. 22.)

2 John is addressed from 'the elder' to 'the elect lady and her children'. This is in all likelihood a symbolic manner of addressing a church (*cf.* 1 Pet. 5:13), perhaps intended to baffle any hostile people into whose hands the letter might fall (1–3). The occasion of the letter is similar to that of 1 John (*cf.* 2 Jn. 7 with 1 Jn. 4:3); false teachers were travelling from church to church and denying that the Son of God had really been incarnate. The elder issues a warning against such teaching; those who 'go on' to accept this new or higher teaching are abandoning their faith in God, the Father of Jesus Christ. He cautions his friends not to extend hospitality to the false teachers, and he encourages them to follow after the truth which already abides in them and to fulfil the command of love (4–11). Finally, he expresses the hope of seeing them soon and adds greetings from his own church (12f.).

3 John is a private letter (like Philemon) addressed to the elder's friend Gaius, who was a leading member in another church. He is commended for his attachment to the truth and for showing practical love to travelling preachers who depended on the churches for their keep (1–8). His attitude is the reverse of that of Diotrephes, who was seeking to be the leader in his church (probably a neighbouring church to that of Gaius), resisting the advice of John and perhaps withholding a previous letter of his from the church, refusing to welcome the travelling preachers and excommunicating those who did welcome them. It is likely that we see here the difficulties caused by the development of a settled local church leadership alongside the existence of apostolic overseers and travelling teachers, and that Diotrephes was aspiring to the position of 'bishop' in his own church and resented any interference from outside. Such difficulties were no doubt bound to arise as the apostles passed on, but it is clear that Diotrephes was not handling matters in a Christian manner. The elder warns that he will come and deal personally with Diotrephes if necessary (9–11). Finally, a word of commendation is added for Demetrius (probably the bearer of the letter and a travelling teacher), and the letter concludes with warm greetings (12–14).

IV. External attestation of the Epistles

1 John was used by Papias (*c.* 140) according to Eusebius, and is quoted by Polycarp (*c.* 110–120) and very probably by Justin (*c.* 150–160). It was accepted as the work of the fourth Evangelist, John the apostle, by Irenaeus (*c.* 180), the Muratorian Canon (*c.* 180–200), and Clement of Alexandria (*c.* 200). According to Eusebius, there was never any questioning of its authenticity. 2 and 3 John are probably listed in the Muratorian Canon (J. Stevenson, *op. cit.*, No. 124 and note); 2 John is quoted by Irenaeus, and both Epistles were probably commented on by Clement of Alexandria. Lack of mention and doubts about their canonicity, reflected in Eusebius, who quotes Origen (J. Stevenson, *op. cit.*, No. 289), were due to their slight nature.

V. Provenance, authorship and date

The Asian provenance of all five Johannine writings is still the most likely. For the Epistles this is supported by the Cerinthian teaching which is opposed and by the traditions which connect their author with Ephesus.

The authorship of the Epistles and of the Johannine writings presents problems which are not yet fully solved.

First, it is certain that one author is responsible for the three Epistles, although this was denied by Jerome and more recently doubted by R. Bultmann (*op. cit.*, pp. 1f.). 1 John is anonymous, but we may now assert that its author was also 'the elder'.

Second, it is reasonably certain that John's Gospel and 1 John are by the same author. This is disputed by C. H. Dodd (pp. xlvii–lvi; more fully in 'The First Epistle of John and the Fourth Gospel', *BJRL* 21, 1937, pp. 129–156) and C. K. Barrett (*The Gospel according to St. John*, 1955, pp. 49–52), but convincing proof is given by A. E. Brooke (pp. i–xix), W. F. Howard (*The Fourth Gospel in Recent Criticism and Interpretation*⁴, 1955, pp. 281–296), and W. G. Wilson (*JTS* 49, 1948, pp. 147–156). There can really be no doubt that John and 1 John represent the same mind at work in two different situations. John is a profound study of the incarnation of Christ addressed primarily as an apologetic to the outside world; 1 John is a tract called forth by a particular situation in the church. The differences between the two can largely be explained by this difference in audience and purpose. Logically John precedes 1 John, but whether this was the order of composition is hardly possible to determine; John is obviously the work of many years of meditation, and 1 John may have been written in that period.

Third, the relation of Revelation (which is ascribed to John the apostle by strong external evidence) to John and 1–3 John must be considered. The theory of common authorship of all five books is very difficult to maintain, as was seen quite early by Dionysius of Alexandria (J. Stevenson, *op. cit.*, No. 237). There are considerable theological differences between Revelation and the other Johannine writings, although there are also close similarities. Further, the Greek of Revelation is unlike that of any other book in the NT; despite suggestions that it was originally written in *Aramaic*, and so possibly by the same person who wrote John and 1–3 John in *Greek*, the theory of common authorship must remain doubtful.

In view of these facts, various theories of authorship have been put forward, of which three deserve attention.

First, the traditional theory, which is supported by D. Guthrie (*New Testament Introduction*), attributes all five books to John the apostle. He was known as 'the elder' *par excellence* in Asia Minor on account of his age and authority (*cf.* 1 Pet. 5:1 for a similar title). Against this theory must be reckoned the problems raised by Revelation and the uncertainty which some scholars find in the external evidence for the apostolic authorship of John's Gospel.

A second solution, which avoids the first of these difficulties, is that John's Gospel and 1–3 John are by John the apostle and Revelation by another John who is otherwise unknown to us. This was essentially the theory of Dionysius of Alexandria, and is supported today by A. Wikenhauser (*New Testament Introduction*, E.T. 1958, pp. 547–553). On this view, some connection between the two Johns must be presupposed to account for the theological similarities between the writings.

A third solution, which avoids the second of the difficulties in the traditional theory, sees a close disciple of John the apostle as the author of John's Gospel and 1–3 John and John himself as possibly the author of Revelation. (There are various forms of this theory.) On this view, it was John's disciple who was known as 'the elder'.

Support for this third solution has often been sought in a well-known passage in Papias (J. Stevenson, *op. cit.*, No. 31); Papias refers to certain of the apostles, including John, who are apparently dead, as 'elders' and then to two living disciples of the Lord, Aristion and the elder John. Some scholars think that this elder John was a disciple of John the apostle and was the author of John's Gospel and 1–3 John. But this is extremely conjectural. It is not certain whether Papias is here referring to one John (the apostle) twice or to two separate Johns, and weighty names can be quoted for both interpretations. Further, Papias clearly applied the title of 'elder' to more than one person (including John the apostle in any case), and it is not certain that he used the title in the same sense as the author of 2 and 3 John. Finally, Papias does not state that the hypothetical 'elder John' was a disciple of John the apostle. We cannot, therefore, be certain on this theory that the elder of 2 and 3 John was called John or that he was the 'elder John' of Papias.

On the whole, it still remains most plausible that the Gospel and the three letters are the work of John the apostle or of a close disciple of his.

The date of 1–3 John cannot be rigidly determined. The evidence from Qumran *allows* the possibility of an earlier development of the kind of theology found in the Johannine literature than was formerly believed possible. The chief clue, however, is the nature of the heresy attacked and the church situation, both of which suggest a date between the 60s and 90s of the 1st century; our knowledge of the church in this period is so meagre that a closer dating is impossible.

BIBLIOGRAPHY. Commentaries by B. F. Westcott, 1883, reprinted 1966; A. E. Brooke, *ICC*, 1912; C. H. Dodd, *MNTC*, 1946; R. Schnackenburg, *HTKNT*, 1963²; J. R. W. Stott, *TNTC*, 1964; R. Bultmann, *Hermeneia*, 1973; J. L. Houlden, *BNTC*, 1973; M. de Jonge (in Dutch, 1973²); I. H. Marshall, *NIC/NLC*, 1978.

W. Nauck, *Die Tradition und der Charakter des ersten Johannesbriefes*, 1953; J. C. O'Neill, *The Puzzle of 1 John*, 1966; E. Haenchen, *Die Bibel und Wir*, 1968, pp. 235–311 (= *TR* n.f. 26, 1960, pp. 1–43, 267–291; survey article).

I.H.M.

JOHN, GOSPEL OF.

I. Outline of contents

a. The revelation of Jesus to the world, 1:1–12:50

(i) Prologue (1:1–18).
(ii) The manifestation of Jesus (1:19–2:11).
(iii) The new message (2:12–4:54).
(iv) Jesus, the Son of God (5:1–47).
(v) The bread of life (6:1–71).
(vi) Conflict with the Jews (7:1–8:59).
(vii) The light of the world (9:1–41).
(viii) The good shepherd (10:1–42).
(ix) The resurrection and the life (11:1–57).
(x) The shadow of the cross (12:1–36a).
(xi) Epilogue (12:36b–50).

b. The revelation of Jesus to his disciples, 13:1–17:26

(i) The Last Supper (13:1–30).
(ii) The farewell discourses (13:31–16:33).
(iii) Jesus' prayer for his disciples (17:1–26).

c. The glorification of Jesus, 18:1–21:25

(i) The passion of Jesus (18:1–19:42).
(ii) The resurrection of Jesus (20:1–31).

(iii) The commission to the disciples (21:1–25).

II. Purpose

A clear statement of the purpose of John is given in Jn. 20:30f. (*Cf.* W. C. van Unnik, *TU* 73, 1959, pp. 382–411.) John has made a selection out of a large number of available 'signs', and his purpose in narrating them is to bring his readers to the belief that Jesus is the Christ (*i.e.* the Messiah) and the Son of God, and thus to bring them into an experience of eternal life.

From this statement we can draw certain conclusions which are amply attested by the substance of the Gospel. First, it is basically an evangelistic document. Second, its explicit method is to present the work and words of Jesus in such a way as to show the nature of his person. Third, the description of this person as Messiah indicates that a Jewish audience is probably in mind. Since, however, John appears to be writing for an audience outside Palestine and in part ignorant of Jewish customs, it is an attractive hypothesis that he wrote especially for Jews of the Diaspora and proselytes in Hellenistic synagogues. (*Cf.* J. A. T. Robinson, *Twelve NT Studies*, 1962, pp. 107–125.) This naturally does not exclude a Gentile audience from his purview, although the view that the Gospel was written primarily to convert the thoughtful Gentile (*cf.* C. H. Dodd, *The Interpretation of the Fourth Gospel,* 1953) is unlikely.

This main purpose does not exclude other, subordinate aims. Thus, first, John consciously stresses points which would refute the false or antagonistic views about Jesus held by Jews in his time. There may also be an attempt to correct an over-zealous veneration for John the Baptist. Second, particularly in 13–17, John addresses Christians and gives teaching about life in the church. But the view that a principal aim of John was to correct the church's eschatology (so C. K. Barrett) is not tenable, although this is not to deny that the Gospel contains eschatological teaching. Third, it is often alleged that John was written as a polemic against gnosticism. This view gains some plausibility from the purpose of 1 John, but is not so self-evident as is sometimes supposed; nevertheless, John was no doubt aware of the danger of gnosticism while he wrote, and his Gospel is in fact an excellent weapon against gnosticism.

III. Structure and theological content

a. The historical structure

As a historical work, John is selective. It begins with the incarnation of the pre-existent Word of God in Jesus (1:1–18), and then passes straight to the early days of Jesus' ministry—his baptism by John and the call of his first disciples (1:19–51), and his return from the Jordan to Galilee (1:43). But the scene of his work is not confined in the main to Galilee, as in the Synoptic narrative. Only a few of the incidents related take place there (1:43–2:12; 4:43–54; 6:1–7:9). Once the scene is Samaria (4:1–42), but most frequently it is Jerusalem, usually at the time of a Jewish feast (2:13; 5:1; 6:4; 7:2; 10:22; 11:55; *cf.* A. Guilding, *The Fourth Gospel and Jewish Worship*, 1960). The last of these incidents is the raising of Lazarus, which provoked the Jewish leaders to do away with Jesus (11:45ff.), although, as in the Synoptic Gospels, their enmity had been mounting for some time (*e.g.* 7:1). From this point the narrative follows lines familiar to us from the Synoptic Gospels—the anointing at Bethany (12:1–11), the triumphal entry (12:12–19), the Last Supper (13), recorded with no reference to its sacramental features, the arrest (18:1–12), trials and Peter's denial (18:13–19:16), the crucifixion and resurrection (20–21). Yet in this section also there is much material not found in the Synoptic Gospels, especially the last discourses and prayer (14–16; 17), the details of the trial before Pilate (18:28–19:16), and the resurrection appearances.

There is no need to doubt that this historical outline corresponds broadly to the actual order of events, although it must be remembered that John has recorded only a few incidents and arranged them from the standpoint of his presentation of Jesus as the Messiah.

b. The theological content

(i) *John as revelation.* This historical outline is the vehicle of a theological presentation of Jesus. John's purpose is to reveal the *glory* of Jesus as the Son of God. As the pre-existent Son he shared the glory of the Father (17:5, 24), and in his earthly life his glory was demonstrated to the world—or rather to those who had eyes to see (1:14)—in the series of signs which he wrought (2:11). Yet in these signs Jesus was seeking not his own glory but that of the Father (5:41; 7:18). This revelation of Jesus before the world is the theme of chs. 1–12, which concludes with a summarizing passage and a clear break in thought (12:36b–50). Since the world had largely not believed in him (12:37), Jesus turned to his disciples, and in chs. 13–17 we have a revelation of his glory, seen in humble service, to the disciples, who were themselves also called to a life in which God is glorified (15:8; 21:19). But a theme which had been hinted at earlier also finds expression here, namely that Jesus is supremely glorified in his passion and death. Thus the third section of the Gospel (chs. 18–21) shows us that the hour has come in which Jesus is glorified as the Son of God and glorifies God.

At the same time the Gospel may be regarded as a revelation of *truth* (1:14, 17). In the Gospel the world is characterized by error, imperfection and sin, because it has lost contact with God who is the true One (7:28); to it Jesus brings the truth of God (18:37). He himself is the incarnation of truth (14:6) and will be succeeded by the Spirit of truth (14:17). He leads men to a true worship of God (4:23f.) and frees them from the errors of the devil (8:44) through knowledge of the truth (8:32). In contrast to the empty satisfactions of the world he brings true, real bread for the souls of men (6:32, 55).

(ii) *Signs and witnesses.* The way in which this revelation is brought to men is twofold. First, there are the *signs* or *works* performed by Jesus, seven of which (excluding the resurrection) are related at length. They are signs not simply because they are evidence of a miraculous, supernatural power (4:48) but rather because by their character they show that their author is sent by God (9:16) as the Messiah and Son of God (3:2; 6:14; 7:31); they thus authenticate his person to those who have eyes to see (2:23; 12:37).

Usually these signs are the basis of a discourse or dialogue in which their spiritual significance is brought out. There is, however, what may be regarded as a further series of signs in words. Seven times (6:35; 8:12; 10:7, 11; 11:25; 14:6; 15:1; to which 8:24 is perhaps to be added) Jesus says, 'I am . . .'. A number of concepts, all of them already current in religious language, are here taken over by Jesus and used to explain who he is and what he has come to do. What is especially significant is that this use of 'I am' contains a veiled claim to deity.

Second, the glory of Jesus is attested by *witnesses*. Jesus himself came to bear witness to the truth (18:37), and witness is borne to him by John the Baptist, the woman of Samaria, the crowd who saw his signs (12:17), the disciples (15:27), the witness at the cross (19:35), and the Evangelist himself (21:24). Witness is also given by the Scriptures (5:39), by the Father (5:37), and by Jesus' signs (10:25). Such witness was meant to lead men to faith (4:39; 5:34).

(iii) *The Person of Jesus*. These signs and witnesses are thus meant to show that Jesus is the Son of God who offers life to men. Right at the beginning of the Gospel he is affirmed to be the *Word* (*LOGOS) of God (1:14, 17). Although this technical term does not recur in John, it is plain that the rest of the Gospel is an exposition and justification of the doctrine that the Word became flesh. The use of 'Word' is singularly happy, for by it John was able to speak to Jews who had already taken some steps towards regarding God's creative Word (Ps. 33:6) as in some sense a separate being from God (*cf.* the figurative description of Wisdom in Pr. 8:22ff.), to Christians who preached the Word of God and virtually identified it with Jesus (*cf.* Col. 4:3 with Eph. 6:19), and to educated pagans who saw the Word as the principle of order and rationality in the universe (popular Stoicism). But what John says goes far beyond anything that had previously been said.

Second, Jesus is the *Messiah* from the house of David awaited by the Jews (7:42). In fact, the great question for the Jews is whether Jesus is the Messiah (7:26ff.; 10:24), and the confession of the disciples is that this is precisely who he is (1:41; 4:29; 11:27; 20:31).

Third, he is the *Son of man*. This term is the key to Jesus' understanding of himself in the Synoptic Gospels, where it is connected with three ideas, the 'hiddenness' of his Messiahship, the necessity of his suffering, and his function as judge at the parousia. These ideas are latent in John (*cf.* 12:34, 3:14, 5:27), but the emphasis falls on the two ideas that the Son of man has been sent from heaven as the revealer of God and the Saviour of men (3:13; 9:35) and that he is glorified by being 'lifted up' to die (12:23–34).

Fourth, he is the *Son of God*. This is probably Jesus' most important title in John. Since the heart of the gospel is that God sent his Son as Saviour (3:16), John's purpose is to lead the reader to recognize the claim of Jesus (19:7) and make the confession of the disciples (1:34, 49; 11:27) that he is the Son of God. As Son, he reveals the Father (1:18), whose activities of life-giving and judgment he shares (5:19–29). Through belief in him men receive salvation (3:36) and freedom (8:36).

But to say that Jesus is the Son of God is, fifth, to ascribe full deity to him. Thus he who as the Word of God is himself *God* (1:1), is also confessed by men on earth as Lord and God (20:28), which is the climax of the Gospel; *cf.* also 1:18, RSVmg.).

(iv) *The work of Jesus*. A further set of titles expresses what Jesus came to do for men and what he offers them. These are summed up in 14:6, where Jesus claims to be the way, the truth, and the life. The last of these words, *life*, is the favourite word in John for salvation. The world of men is in a state of death (5:24f.) and is destined for judgment (3:18, 36). What Jesus offers to men is life, defined by John as knowledge of God and Jesus Christ (17:3). Jesus himself can thus be called the life (1:4; 11:25; 14:6), the giver of *living water* (*i.e.* life-bestowing water, 4:14), and *living bread* (6:33f.). To receive Jesus by believing in him (3:36; 6:29) is to receive the bread of life, and to eat the flesh and drink the blood of Jesus (an expression in which many scholars see an allusion to the Lord's Supper) is to partake of eternal life (6:54).

This same truth is presented in the picture of Jesus as the *light* of the world (8:12), developed especially in ch. 9. The state of men is now regarded as blindness (9:39–41) or darkness (3:19; 12:46), and Jesus is the one who cures blindness and gives the light of life to those who walk in darkness. He is also depicted as the *way* to God (14:1–7). This idea is hinted at in 10:9, where he is the *door* of the sheepfold, but here another idea becomes prominent—that Jesus is the *good shepherd* who gives his life for the sheep and gathers them into his sheepfold. Three vital ideas are contained in this description. First, Jesus is the true fulfilment of the OT promise of a shepherd for the people of God. (Note that life and light are Jewish descriptions of the Law which finds its fulfilment in Jesus.) Second, his death is not simply due to the opposition of his enemies, but is a saving death on behalf of men (10:11) by which they are drawn to God (12:32). Only through a sacrificial death can sin be removed (1:29) and life be given to the world (6:51b). Third, the picture of a flock introduces the idea of the church.

(v) *The new life*. Jesus is thus portrayed as the *Saviour* of the world (4:42). In his presence men face the decisive moment in which they either accept him and pass from death to life (5:24) or remain in darkness until the day of judgment (12:46–48).

[illegible] when the Father draws men to his Son (6:44). Through the work of the Spirit of God, whose movement is beyond human comprehension, there then takes place the radical change known as the *new birth* (3:1–21) by which a man becomes a son of God (1:12).

From the human side this change is the product of *faith*, which is centred on the Son of God who was lifted up on the cross to save the world (3:14–18). A distinction is drawn between two kinds of faith—intellectual acceptance of the claims of Jesus (11:42; 8:24; 11:27; 20:31), which by itself is not sufficient, and full self-committal to him (3:16; 4:42; 9:35–38; 14:1).

Such faith is closely related to *knowledge*. Whereas ordinary men have no real knowledge of God (1:10; 16:3), through knowledge of Jesus men can know the Father (8:19; 14:7). The content of this knowledge is not stated in John; there is no place here for the esoteric revelations characteristic of the mystery religions. Our only clue is that the way in which men know God and are known by him is analogous to the way in which Jesus knows God and is known by him (10:14f.).

One thing, however, can be said. This new relationship is characterized by *love*. Disciples share in a relationship of mutual love with God like that which exists between the Father and the Son (3:35; 14:31), though it is to be noted that their love is directed towards the Son rather than towards the Father (14:23; 15:9; 17:26; 21:15–17; *cf.* 5:42; 1 Jn. 4:20f.).

John's Gospel, in Greek (6:58–64 and 6:64–71). Papyrus Codex Bodmer II, copied about AD *200.* (FMB)

Other expressions are also used to express this communion of disciples with Jesus. They are said to *abide* in him (6:56; 15:4–10), and he abides in them (6:56; *cf.* 14:17). The preposition *in* is also important in describing the close relationship of mutual indwelling between God and Jesus and between Jesus and his disciples (14:20, 23; 17:21, 23, 26).

(vi) *The people of God.* Although the word 'church' is not found in John, the idea is most certainly present. To be a disciple is automatically to be a member of the *flock* whose shepherd is Jesus. Jesus also uses the concept of the *vine* (15:1–8). A new vine is to replace the old vine (*i.e.* the earthly people of Israel); Jesus himself is the stem, and from him life flows to the branches and enables them to bear fruit.

The life of disciples is characterized by a *love* which follows the example of Jesus, who humbly washed his disciples' feet (13:1–20, 34f.). Such love is in contrast with the attitude of the world which *hates* and *persecutes* the disciples (15:18–16:4, 32f.), and its result is that the church shows that *unity* for which Jesus prays in ch. 17.

But the church is no closed fellowship; others are to come to belief through the word of the disciples (17:20). This is confirmed in ch. 21, where the idea of *mission* or sending (20:21) is developed. The 153 fish are symbolic of the spread of the gospel to all men, and the task of the good shepherd is handed on from the Master to the disciples.

(vii) *Eschatology.* Jesus thus looks forward to the continuing life of the church after his glorification (14:12). In anticipation of his second advent he promises to come to the church (14:18) in the person of the *Spirit*. The Spirit comes to the individual disciple (7:37–39) and to the church (14:16f., 26; 15:26; 16:7–11, 13–15), and his function is to take the place of Jesus (as '*another* Counsellor') and glorify him.

It may thus be said that in John the future is 'realized' in the present; Jesus comes again through the Spirit to his disciples, they already partake of eternal life, and already the process of judgment is at work. Yet it would be wrong to conclude that in John the future activity of God is replaced by his present activity. No less than in the rest of the NT is the future coming of Jesus (14:3; 21:23) and the future judgment of all men (5:25–29) taught.

IV. Textual problems and source criticism

Two passages found in the AV of John do not belong to the original text and have been removed to the margin in modern VSS. These are the *Pericope de Adulteria* (7:53–8:11), a genuine story about Jesus which has been preserved outside the canonical Gospels and found its way into certain late MSS of John, and the explanation of the moving of the water (5:3b–4), which is omitted in the best MSS.

A special problem is raised by ch. 21. While E. C. Hoskyns held that it was an integral part of the original Gospel, the majority of scholars think that it was either a later addition of the author or (less probably) that it was added by another hand. The main argument is that 20:31 reads like the conclusion of a book; some scholars also find stylistic differences between ch. 21 and chs. 1–20, but in the opinion of C. K. Barrett these are not in themselves decisive.

Some scholars (*e.g.* R. Bultmann) believe that the present

order of the material in John is not that of the author but has been seriously altered, perhaps by loose sheets of papyrus being combined in the wrong order. There is, however, no objective textual evidence for this, although the phenomenon is not unknown in ancient literature. The displacements found in ch. 18 in certain MSS are clearly secondary, and Tatian (*c.* 170), who made some alterations in order when he was combining the Gospels in a single narrative, does not support modern reconstructions. Most recent commentators find that the Gospel makes good sense as it stands.

Attempts have also been made, most comprehensively by R. Bultmann, to trace the use of written sources and editorial activity in John. While the use of sources is probable, there is little unanimity regarding their extent. It is likely that the Gospel went through several stages of composition, a fact which makes analysis extremely difficult.

V. The background of thought

After a period in which John was regarded as a Hellenistic book, to which the closest parallels were to be found in a strongly Hellenized Judaism, mystery religions and even Greek philosophy, there is at present a rediscovery of the essentially Jewish background of the Gospel.

Much evidence has been found of Aramaic traditions behind the Synoptic Gospels and John (M. Black, *An Aramaic Approach to the Gospels and Acts*[3], 1967). An Aramaic sayings source may lie behind John—Aramaic being, of course, the mother tongue of Jesus. The thought in John is often expressed with the parataxis and parallelism which are well-known features of Semitic writing. All the indications are that the linguistic background of John is Aramaic, although the theory that it was originally written in Aramaic is unconvincing.

This naturally means that the thought of John is likely to be Jewish, which is in fact the case. Although there are comparatively few quotations, most of the key ideas in John are taken from the OT (*e.g.* word, life, light, shepherd, Spirit, bread, vine, love, witness) and Jesus is portrayed as the fulfilment of the OT.

Parallels with contemporary Jewish thought, especially with orthodox rabbinic Judaism, may also be found, it being only natural that Jesus and his followers should often have agreed with the OT scholars of their time and been influenced—both positively and negatively—by them (*cf.* 5:39; 7:42). Since Palestinian Judaism had been subject to Hellenistic influences for about two centuries, there is no need to look wider for Hellenistic influence upon John. The degree of resemblance between ideas found in John and in Philo of Alexandria is variously estimated.

The Jewish sectarian texts from Qumran also help to fill in the background of John, although their importance for the understanding of the NT tends to be exaggerated. Attention is usually drawn to the dualism of light and darkness and to the Messianic hopes found in the texts, but the roots of these ideas lie in the OT, and it is doubtful whether a direct influence from Qumran upon John requires to be postulated. (See F. M. Braun, *RB* 62, 1955, pp. 5–44); J. H. Charlesworth (ed.), *John and Qumran*, 1972).

Other possible formative influences are discussed in detail by C. H. Dodd. He rightly rejects Mandaism, a pagan-Christian syncretism whose earliest literature is considerably later than John. But he devotes considerable attention to Hellenistic mystery religion, especially as depicted in the *Corpus Hermeticum* (*HERMETIC LITERATURE), a series of tracts probably emanating from Egypt in the 3rd century in their present form. But, while there are interesting parallels of thought which demonstrate that John would be intelligible to pagans and not merely to Jews, a close affiliation of thought is unlikely. (*Cf.* G. D. Kilpatrick in *Studies in the Fourth Gospel*, ed. F. L. Cross, 1957.)

In the 2nd century there was a developed Christian *gnosticism, and we must certainly think of some kind of 'pre-gnosticism' in the 1st century, reflected in the polemic in Col. and 1 Jn. The theory that John was influenced by the gnostic heretics whom he opposes (*cf.* **II**, above) was propounded by E. F. Scott (*The Fourth Gospel*[2], 1908, pp. 86–103); more recently than this R. Bultmann and E. Käsemann have argued that in John Jesus is presented in terms of gnostic myths. The view of C. H. Dodd that Johannine Christianity is entirely different from gnosticism in spite of a common background (*op. cit.*, p. 114) does much greater justice to facts.

Within the early Christian world the Johannine literature occupies a unique place and represents an independently developed strand of thought. Nevertheless, its teaching is that of the Christian church generally, and the differences from, say, Paul are more of form than of content. (*Cf.* A. M. Hunter, *The Unity of the New Testament*, 1943.)

VI. External attestation

The existence of John's Gospel is attested in Egypt before AD 150 by the Rylands Papyrus 457, the earliest known fragment of a NT MS.

The use of John as an authoritative Gospel alongside the other three is attested by the Egerton Papyrus 2, also dated before 150 (C. H. Dodd, *New Testament Studies*, 1953, pp. 12–52). It was also used by Tatian in his *Diatessaron*, and Irenaeus (*c.* 180) speaks of a four-Gospel canon. John was certainly also known and used in heretical gnostic circles—*e.g.* by Ptolemaeus, a disciple of Valentinus, by the *Gospel of Peter* (*c.* 150), and (fairly certainly) by the author of the Valentinian *Gospel of Truth*. Knowledge of John by other writers in this period is difficult to attest. There are traces of Johannine language in Ignatius (*c.* 115) and Justin (*c.* 150–160), but it is questionable whether literary dependence is indicated.

Traditions about the authorship of John are given by Irenaeus, who states that John, the disciple of the Lord, gave out the Gospel at Ephesus. This tradition is repeated by Clement of Alexandria (*c.* 200) and the anti-Marcionite prologue to John; the 2nd-century date of the latter is, however, suspect. The Muratorian Canon (*c.* 180–200) gives a legend in which John the apostle is the author, and the apostolic authorship was accepted by Ptolemaeus. But Papias, who had close access to apostolic traditions, is silent on the matter, and Polycarp, who was an associate of John according to Irenaeus, quotes the Epistles but not the Gospel. Nor do the apocryphal *Acts of John* say anything about the Gospel. At the beginning of the 3rd century there was some opposition to the apostolic authorship of John, possibly because of the use made of it by the gnostics.

VII. Authorship

At the end of the 19th century the view that John the apostle wrote the Fourth Gospel was widely accepted on the basis of the external evidence set out above and the internal evidence. The latter received its classical formulation from B. F. Westcott and from J. B. Lightfoot (*Biblical Essays*, 1893, pp. 1–198), who demonstrated that the Gospel was written by a Jew, by a Palestinian Jew, by an eyewitness of the events recorded, by an apostle, and, in particular, by the apostle John, who is referred to as the 'beloved disciple'.

A number of arguments have been raised against this chain of reasoning. First, there is the theory that *John died as a martyr at an early age, but this is rightly rejected by the majority of scholars.

Second, the alleged geographical and historical inaccuracy of John is held to militate against authorship by an eyewitness. The most recent archaeology has, however, confirmed the geographical accuracy of John in a striking way (*cf.* R. D. Potter, *TU* 73, 1959, pp. 329–337). For the historical problem, see below.

Third, it is alleged that the apostle John was incapable of writing such a Gospel. He was an unlearned man—a view which finds its only and inadequate basis in a questionable exegesis of Acts 4:13 and ignores such analogies as Bunyan, the Bedford tinker. As an apostle he could not have written a Gospel so different from the other three—a view which does not take into account the special purpose of John and the fact that we have no other Gospel directly written by an apostle for comparison. As a Jew he could not have the mastery of Hellenistic thought seen in the Gospel—see, however, **V**, above. Finally, nobody would presume to call himself the 'beloved disciple'—which is, however, no more than a subjective argument (those who find it weighty can attribute the use of the title to John's scribe).

Fourth, the weightiest argument is the slowness of the church to accept John's Gospel. The reliability of Irenaeus has been called in question (but with uncertain justification), and it has been observed that the people who might be expected to know John and quote from it fail to do so. Against this must be pointed out the general weakness of arguments from silence (*cf.* W. F. Howard, *The Fourth Gospel in Recent Criticism and Interpretation*[4], 1955, p. 273) and the fact that the evidence for the acceptance and use of the other three Gospels is almost equally scanty before the period in which we find all four Gospels accepted together. Further, we are completely ignorant of the circumstances of publication of John except for the brief note in 21:24.

It may be taken as quite certain that we can safely disregard any theory which denies a connection between John the apostle and the Gospel. Three possibilities then arise. First, John may have composed it himself with the aid of an amanuensis. Second, a disciple of John may have used the memoirs of John or a Johannine tradition as the basis for the Gospel. A third possibility, which is a variant of the second, is that there was a Johannine 'school', possibly to be linked with S Palestine, in which the characteristic Johannine theology was developed and whose members produced the Johannine literature. It is, however, difficult to bring forward decisive evidence for or against such a theory. (One may compare K. Stendahl's hypothesis of a Matthean school, the evidence for which is still flimsy.)

It is difficult to decide between these theories. But the tradition that John dictated the Gospel is widespread (*cf.* R. V. G. Tasker, *TNTC*, 1960, pp. 17–20) and bears the marks of genuineness. There are still good grounds for maintaining a close association of John the apostle with the actual writing of the Gospel.

(See also *JOHN, EPISTLES OF.)

VIII. Provenance and date

Early tradition connects John the apostle with Asia Minor and in particular with Ephesus. A connection with Asia Minor is most suitable for 1–3 Jn. and is demanded by Rev.; whether the author of the latter be the Evangelist or an associate of his, this strengthens the case for Asia.

The claims of other places cannot, however, be ignored. The apparent lack of knowledge of John in Asia gives weight to the claims of Alexandria: here John was certainly used very early by the gnostics (*cf.* also the papyri), the climate of thought (Hellenistic Judaism) could be regarded as suitable, and the general remoteness of Alexandria would explain the Gospel's slow circulation. There is, however, no tradition connecting John with Alexandria. The claims of Antioch have also been pressed, but they are hardly strong. Some would connect the Gospel of John with S Palestine in view of its background of thought, but this only confirms that for part of his life the author was resident in Palestine.

John is usually dated in the 90s. This view is based on the assumed dependence of John on the Synoptic Gospels (but see **IX**, below) and the alleged post-Pauline character of its theology. While there is no need to regard John as dependent on Paulinism, it is difficult to avoid the impression that it is not an early writing. If it is connected with Ephesus it must be placed after the activity of Paul there; this is confirmed by the date of 1–3 Jn., which is hardly earlier than the 60s. If John is connected with some other place of composition, *e.g.* Palestine, an earlier date is possible but remains unlikely. The real point of the 'Palestinian background' argument is that the date no longer needs to be put extremely late in order to account for the development of thought. (*Cf.* J. A. T. Robinson, *op. cit.*, pp. 94–106.)

IX. Relation to the Synoptic Gospels

a. Knowledge of the Synoptic tradition

The accepted opinion until about 40 years ago was that John knew the Synoptic Gospels, or at least Mark and Luke, and that he wrote in order to correct, supplement or replace them. Sharp criticism of this view came from P. Gardner-Smith (*St. John and the Synoptic Gospels*, 1938), B. Noack (*Zur Johanneischen Tradition*, 1954) and C. H. Dodd (*Historical Tradition in the Fourth Gospel*, 1963), who argued that John was dependent on the oral tradition behind the Synoptics, and wrote independently of them. The closest contacts are between John and Luke, especially in the passion narrative, but it is doubtful whether these prove literary dependence; Luke may well have had access to the traditions recorded in John or even had personal acquaintance with its author (*cf.* G. W. Broomfield, *John, Peter and the Fourth Gospel*, 1934).

The external evidence must also be taken into account. Papias' information about Mark and the Logia came from [John] 'the elder', who *may* be connected with the composition of the Gospel of

John. Clement of Alexandria wrote, 'Last of all, John, perceiving that the external facts had been made plain in the Gospel, being urged by his friends, and inspired by the Spirit, composed a spiritual Gospel.' We can, of course, accept this description of John as the spiritual Gospel without believing that John wrote out of a knowledge of the other Gospels, but it is difficult to believe that he did not have some idea of their contents, even if he did not have copies of them before him as he wrote. The question, then, must be regarded as still open.

b. Comparison of the narratives

Two problems arise here. The first is whether the Synoptic and Johannine narratives are compatible with each other and can be worked into a single account. It is a fact that attempts can be made to fit the two together in a reasonably convincing manner and thus to shed new light on both. (E. Stauffer, *Jesus and His Story*, 1960.) This is possible because the two accounts describe the activity of Jesus at different periods and in different localities; the old-fashioned idea that the Synoptic Gospels leave no room for a ministry in Jerusalem (other than in the passion narrative) is now quite discredited. It must be remembered, of course, that none of the Gospels pretends to give an exact chronological narrative, so that a detailed reconstruction of the order of events is impossible.

The second problem concerns the cases where historical contradictions appear to arise between the Gospels, including cases where it is held that John is consciously correcting data given in the Synoptic Gospels. Examples of this are the reason for Jesus' arrest (in particular, the question why the raising of Lazarus is omitted in the Synoptic narrative; see a possible answer in J. N. Sanders, *NTS* 1, 1954–5, p. 34); the date of the cleansing of the Temple; and the date of the last supper and crucifixion (see N. Geldenhuys, *Commentary on the Gospel of Luke*, 1950, pp. 649–670). The extent of such difficulties can be exaggerated, but it must be admitted that some real problems exist to which answers have yet to be found. In any case the substance of the Gospel records is not affected by these differences.

c. The discourses in John

The teaching ascribed to Jesus in John differs markedly in content and style from that in the Synoptic Gospels. Such familiar ideas as the kingdom of God, demons, repentance and prayer are missing, and new topics appear, such as truth, life, the world, abiding and witness. At the same time there are close and intricate connections between the two traditions, and common themes appear, *e.g.* Father, Son of man, faith, love and sending. The style and vocabulary also differ. There are no parables in John, and Jesus often speaks in long discourses or dialogues which are unparalleled in the Synoptic Gospels.

Many scholars, therefore, believe that John gives us his own thoughts or his own meditations upon the words of Jesus rather than his *ipsissima verba*. This conclusion is strongly supported by the fact that a very similar style and content is found in 1 Jn. Nevertheless, it must be carefully qualified. First of all, the Gospel of John contains many sayings which are similar in form and content to Synoptic sayings (*cf.* B. Noack, *op. cit.*, pp. 89–109; C. H. Dodd, *op. cit.*, pp. 335–349) and which have equal right to be regarded as authentic. Second, there is, on the other hand, at least one famous 'bolt from the Johannine blue' in the Synoptic Gospels (Mt. 11:25–27) which is a standing warning against the facile assumption that the Synoptic Jesus did not speak the language of the Johannine Jesus. Third, the same traces of Aramaic speech and the same conformity to Jewish methods of discussion are to be found in John as in the Synoptic Gospels.

Thus we can say with considerable confidence that the sayings recorded in John have a firm historical basis in the actual words of Jesus. They have, however, been preserved in a Johannine commentary from which they can be separated only with great difficulty. (*Cf.* the problem of Gal. 2:14ff.; where does Paul's speech to Peter end and his meditation upon it begin?) This is no radical conclusion. So conservative a scholar as Westcott saw, for example, the words of John rather than of Jesus in 3:16–21.

X. History and interpretation in John

The purpose of John (see **II**, above) demands that, in broad outline at least, the contents of John be regarded as history; it completely falls of attainment if John gives us a legendary construction devised to substantiate the church's preaching of Jesus as the Messiah instead of the historical facts which lie behind and authenticate that preaching. (See C. F. D. Moule, *The Phenomenon of the NT*, 1967, pp. 100–114.)

It has already been suggested that many of the difficulties commonly raised against the historicity of John are by no means so serious as they are often made out to be. There is in fact a growing tendency to recognize that John contains important historical traditions about Jesus and that an adequate understanding of his earthly life cannot be obtained from the Synoptic Gospels alone (*cf.* T. W. Manson, *BJRL* 30, 1947, pp. 312–329; A. M. Hunter, *According to John*, 1968).

On the other hand, the total impression given by John after a reading of the Synoptic Gospels is that here we have an interpretation of Jesus rather than a strictly literal account of his life. The teaching which he gives is different and the picture of his person is also different, particularly as regards his Messianic and filial self-consciousness. Yet it would be unwise to over-emphasize these differences. Jesus is no less human in John than in the other Gospels, and even the 'Messianic secrecy' of the Synoptic Gospels is not altogether absent from John. F. F. Bruce can go so far as to say that there is no fundamental discrepancy between the Jesus of the Synoptic Gospels and of John (*The New Testament Documents*[5], 1960, pp. 60f.).

What this amounts to is that John does not contradict the other Gospels but interprets the Person who is depicted in them. While the other Evangelists have given us a photograph of Jesus, John has given us a portrait (W. Temple, *op. cit.* below, p. xvi). Consequently, in the light of what has been said, John can be used as a source for the life of Jesus and for John's interpretation of that life, even if it is impossible to separate these two rigidly from each other. The earthly life of Jesus cannot be completely understood in isolation from his revelation of himself as the risen Lord to his church. Under the inspiration of the Spirit (*cf.* 14:26; 16:14) John has brought out the meaning of the earthly life of Jesus; he interprets the story of Jesus, and in doing so he gives us, in the words of A. M. Hunter, 'the true meaning of the earthly story' (*Introducing New Testament Theology*, 1957, p. 129).

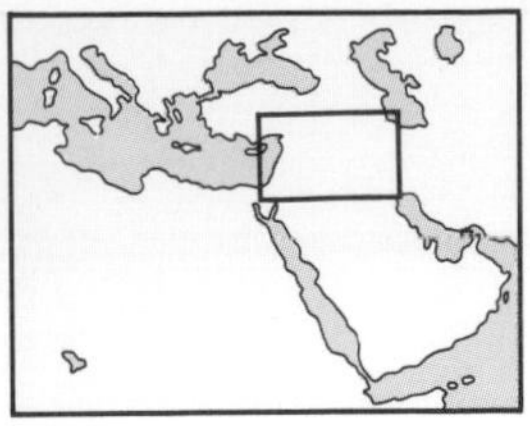

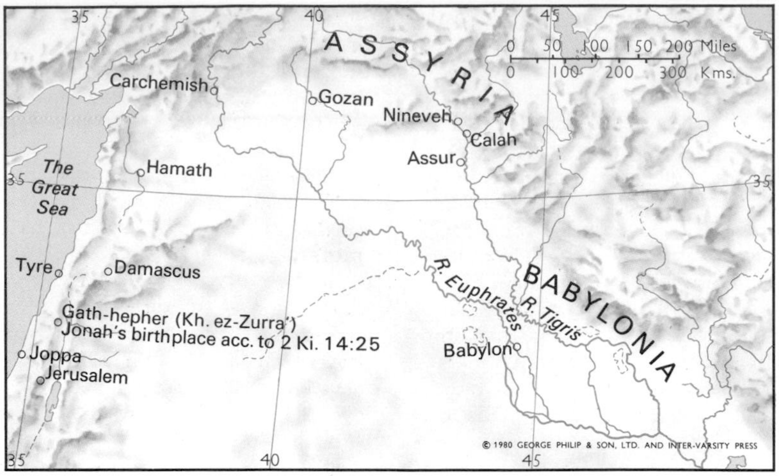

Map showing the area covered by the mission of Jonah.

BIBLIOGRAPHY. *Commentaries on the English text*: B. F. Westcott, 1882 and later (also on the Gk. text, 1908); E. C. Hoskyns and F. N. Davey, ²1947; W. Temple, 1945; R. H. Lightfoot, 1956; R. V. G. Tasker, *TNTC*, 1960; G. A. Turner and J. R. Mantey, 1964; J. Marsh, *Pelican*, 1968; J. N. Sanders and B. A. Mastin, *BNTC*, 1968; R. E. Brown, *AB*, 1971; L. Morris, *NIC/NLC*, 1971; B. Lindars, *NCB*, 1972; *on the Greek text*: J. H. Bernard, *ICC*, 1928; C. K. Barrett, 1955; R. Schnackenburg, Vol. 1, 1968; R. Bultmann, 1971; *in German*: R. Schnackenburg, *HTKNT*, Vol. 1, 1965 (see above); Vol. 2, 1971; Vol. 3, 1976.

W. F. Howard, *The Fourth Gospel in Recent Criticism and Interpretation*⁴, 1955; C. H. Dodd, *The Interpretation of the Fourth Gospel*, 1953; *idem*, *Historical Tradition in the Fourth Gospel*, 1963; E. Malatesta, *St John's Gospel 1920–1965*, 1967; J. L. Martyn, *History and Theology in the Fourth Gospel*, 1968; A. M. Hunter, *According to John*, 1968; E. Käsemann, *The Testament of Jesus*, 1968; R. T. Fortna, *The Gospel of Signs*, 1970; C. K. Barrett, *The Gospel of John and Judaism*, 1975; J. Painter, *John: Witness and Theologian*, 1975; S. S. Smalley, *John: Evangelist and Interpreter*, 1978. I.H.M.

JOHN MARK
See Mark (John), Part 2.

JOKTHEEL
See Sela, Part 3.

The location of Jokneam in Zebulun.

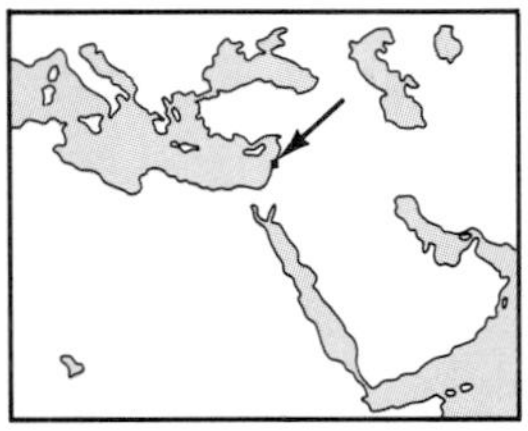

JOKNEAM, JOKMEAM (Heb. *yoqnᵉʿām, yoqmᵉʿām*). **1.** A Canaanite city (Jos. 12:22), no. 113 in the list of Tuthmosis III; modern Tel Yoqneam (Tell Qeimun), 12 km NW of Megiddo. 'The brook east of (*'al pᵉnê*, facing) Jokneam' (Jos. 19:11) could be the Kishon (J. Simons); M. Noth and Y. Aharoni think it ran in from the opposite side of the plain; but the boundary must have included Jokneam, which was a levitical city in Zebulun (Jos. 21:34). In 1 Ki. 4:12, the district boundary appears to have been similar; but the text is uncertain.

BIBLIOGRAPHY. J. Garstang, *Joshua-Judges*, 1931, p. 91; J. Simons, *GTT*, pp. 206, 350; Y. Aharoni, *LOB*, pp. 237, 278; M. Noth, *Josua*², (German) 1953, p. 115.

2. A levitical city in Ephraim (1 Ch. 6:68), possibly Kibzaim of Jos. 21:22. J.P.U.L.

JOKSHAN. A son of Abraham and Keturah, and father of Sheba and Dedan (Gn. 25:2–3; 1 Ch. 1:32). The name is sometimes assumed to be another form of *Joktan (Gn. 10:25–29; 1 Ch.1:19–23), but bearers of these names are kept distinct in the genealogical lists. R.J.W.

JOKTAN. A son of Eber of the family of Shem, and father of Almodad, Sheleph, Hazarmaveth, Jerah, Hadoram, Uzal, Diklah, Obal, Abimael, Sheba, Ophir, Havilah and Jobab (Gn. 10:25–26, 29; 1 Ch. 1:19–20, 23), many of whom have been connected with tribes in S Arabia. The name is unknown outside the Bible, but on the basis of the descendants a region of occupation in S or SW Arabia may be postulated. The modern tribes of S Arabia claim that the pure Arabs are descended from Joktan.

BIBLIOGRAPHY. J. A. Montgomery, *Arabia and the Bible*, 1934, pp. 37–42; W. Thesiger, *Arabian Sands*, 1960, p. 77. T.C.M.

JONAH. Hebrew personal name, meaning 'dove'. The NT form of the name in AV is normally Jonas, twice Jona. **1.** A Heb. prophet of the reign of Jeroboam II of Israel, in the 8th century BC. He came from Gath-hepher, a Zebulunite town, located in the vicinity of Nazareth. His father's name was Amittai. He predicted the territorial expansion achieved by Jeroboam at the expense of Syria (2 Ki. 14:25). This Jonah is also the hero of the book that bears his name, the fifth of the twelve Minor Prophets. The book differs considerably from the other OT Prophets in that it is almost entirely narrative and contains no long prophetic oracles. (See the following article.)

2. The father of Simon Peter, according to Mt. 16:17. Some MSS of Jn. 1:42; 21:15ff. also call him Jonah (*cf.* AV rendering), but the best attested reading here is 'John'. D.F.P.

JONAH, BOOK OF.

I. Outline of contents

The book is divided into four chapters, which neatly divide the subject-matter. The first chapter relates that Jonah, bidden by God to go to Nineveh and protest against its wickedness, rebelled and took ship in the opposite direction. A storm arose, and the sailors eventually threw Jonah overboard, at his own suggestion. A great fish then swallowed the prophet. Ch. 2 gives the text of his prayer, or rather psalm of thanksgiving, from the fish's belly. The fish presently disgorged Jonah on to the shore. Ch. 3 shows Jonah going to Nineveh, after all. His preaching of doom led the citizens to repent of their evil ways. In ch. 4 we find Jonah angry at their repentance and subsequent escape from destruction; whereupon God, by inducing Jonah's pity on a plant, taught him that he must have compassion for all men.

II. Authorship and date

The book gives no indication who its author was. Jonah himself may have written it, but the book nowhere uses the first person (contrast, for example, Ho. 3:1); and the probability of a date later than the 8th century is indicated by the implication of Jon. 3:3 that Nineveh [illegible] 612 BC). If Jonah was not the author, nobody can say who did write it. The date of writing, then, may have been in the 8th century, but was more probably not earlier than the 6th century. The twelve Minor Prophets were known and venerated by the end of the 3rd century (*cf.* Ecclus. 40:10), so a 3rd-century date for the book is the latest it can possibly be allowed. The universalistic emphasis of the book is frequently considered to be a protest against the ultra-nationalistic spirit of the Jews after the time of Ezra; however, universalistic passages occur as early as the 8th century (*cf.* Is. 2:2ff.). Various features of the Heb. of Jonah constitute the strongest argument for post-exilic date; but the brevity of the book permits no certainty. (See also D. W. B. Robinson in *NBCR* on this issue.)

III. Interpretations

The nature of the book is a very [illegible] It has been variously explained as mythology, allegory, commentary (or Midrash), parable and history. The mythological and allegorical approaches are no longer in vogue, and may safely be set aside. Most present-day scholars see the book as primarily parabolic, but partly midrashic, *i.e.* relating traditions about Jonah additional to the bare details of 2 Ki. 14. The parabolic interpretation views the book as a moral tale, comparable with Nathan's story to David (2 Sa. 12:1ff.) or with our Lord's parable of the Good Samaritan (Lk. 10:30ff.) which, of course, sought to teach the same lesson as the book of Jonah. The parabolic viewpoint is not merely an expedient to avoid believing in the miracle of Jonah's emerging alive from the fish's belly, as has sometimes been claimed. Such parables are frequent in Scripture; the chief argument against this interpretation is the unparalleled length of the story.

The historical interpretation is based on the obvious sense of the text, and the fact that the story is applied to a definite and historical figure, Jonah the son of Amittai (whereas the characters in the above-mentioned parables are anonymous). Certainly Jewish tradition accepted the book as history, and our Lord's references to it, quoted above, probably, though not necessarily, imply that he did so too. The historical interpretation is, however, challenged on several points, notably the miracle of the fish, the vast size attributed to Nineveh, the statement that its king and citizens not only listened to a Heb. prophet but without hesitation or exception repented, and lastly, the unnaturally fast rate of growth of the gourd. However, it may be that the first was a genuine miracle; in any case the story may have modern parallels (see A. J. Wilson). The growth of the gourd might again be miraculous; or, more simply, one can claim that Jon. 4:10 is not intended to be strictly literal. As for the size of Nineveh (Jon. 3:3), it is possible that the author intended a much bigger area than the city itself; confirmation of this may be seen in the fact that he refers to a 'king of Nineveh' (3:6), whereas other OT writers speak of kings of Assyria, of which country Nineveh was the last capital. (But see * NINEVEH.) It can also be asserted that in the low fortunes of Assyria prior to the accession of Tiglath-pileser III (745 BC) the Ninevites would readily have listened to a prophet who forecast disaster unless they

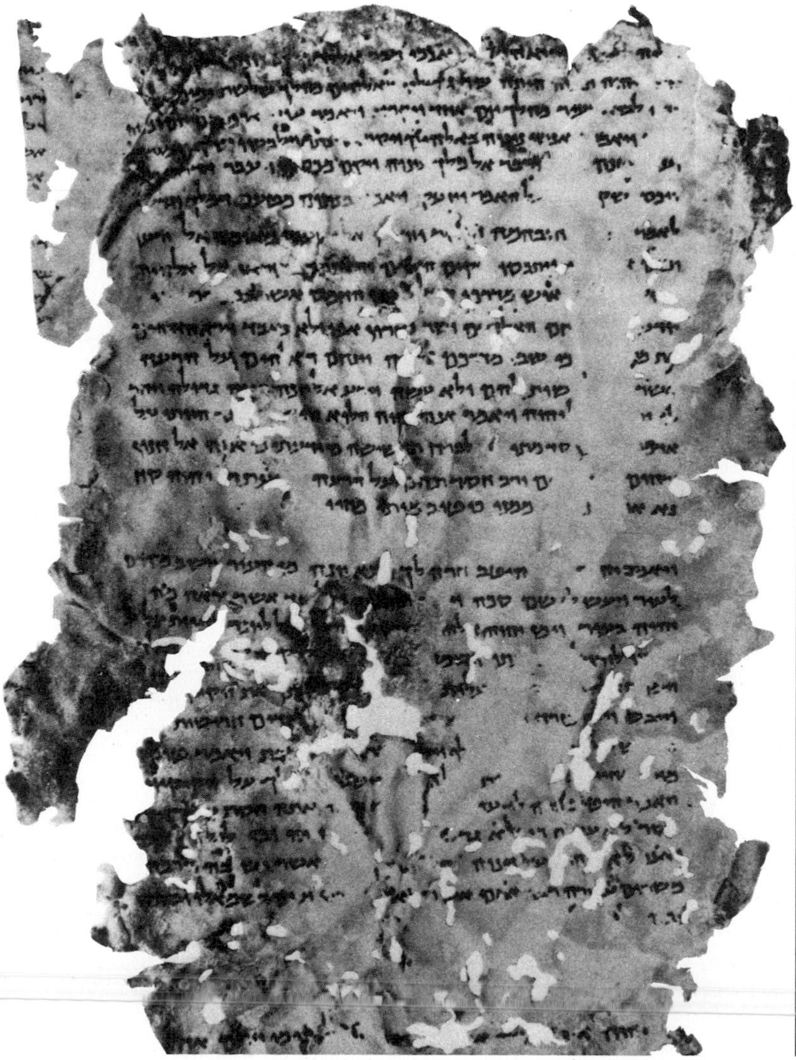

Jonah (3:2–4:1), part of the scroll of the twelve Minor Prophets (Mᵉgillah). *Found at Murabba'at, Judaea. Original length of roll c. 4·9 m. 1st cent. AD.* (RM)

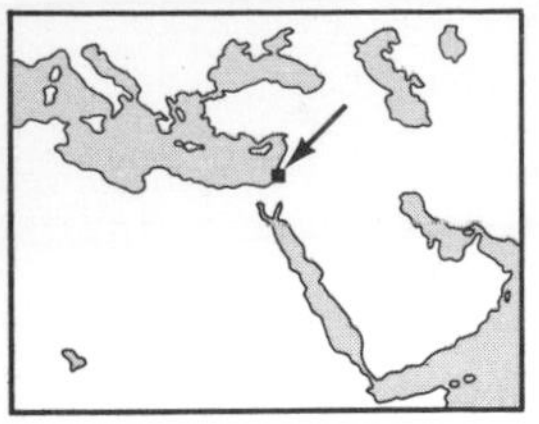

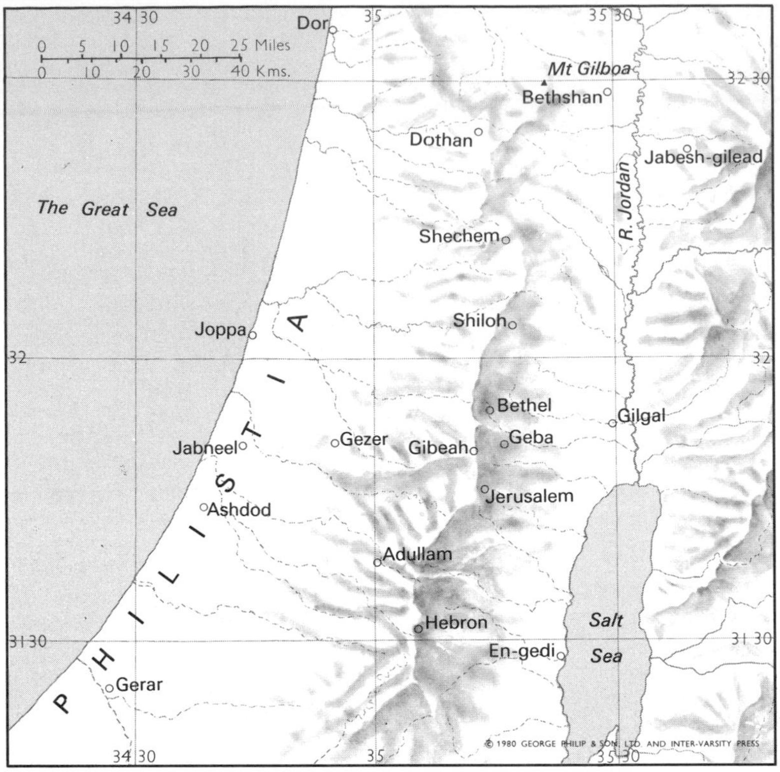

Towns of the time of the Jonathan narratives.

repented. Theirs was a polytheistic religion, so they might well have sought to avoid offending even a foreign unknown deity.

It is fair to say that none of the objections to the historical interpretation is insuperable. The same might be said about the parabolic interpretation. The choice seems to rest, therefore, between these two.

IV. Purpose

It is generally agreed that the purpose of Jonah is didactic; it ends with a challenging question (*cf.* Lk. 10:36). It is disputed whether the intention was a protest against a narrow, exclusivistic Judaism; a challenge to missionary endeavour; or an explanation for the apparent non-fulfilment of earlier prophetic oracles against foreign nations. Without knowing the exact circumstances in which the book was issued, we cannot easily decide the question; in any case, these possibilities are not mutually exclusive. The book undeniably stresses the universal powers of God, over individuals and nations east and west, and over life and death; and also the universal mercy and love of God, towards disobedient Jews and cruel Gentiles alike.

V. Composition

The book is widely accepted as a unity, apart from the psalm (2:2–9), which many scholars have held to be an interpolation. The present trend may be towards its acceptance, however (*cf.* Kaiser, *IOT*, p. 196). The psalm is not so inapposite as has often been claimed; Jonah had been rescued from a watery grave—even if he had yet to be released from the fish's belly—and the use of traditional language depicting death in marine metaphors is therefore remarkably fitting. At the same time, it is noteworthy that the more usual frame of reference of such a psalm lays the basis for the NT interpretation of its significance (*cf.* Mt. 12:39ff.).

BIBLIOGRAPHY. A. J. Wilson, *PTR* 25, 1927, pp. 636ff.; G. Ch. Aalders, *The Problem of the Book of Jonah*, 1948; L. C. Allen, *The Books of Joel, Obadiah, Jonah and Micah, NICOT*, 1976, pp. 173–235; D. W. B. Robinson, in *NBCR*; F. D. Kidner, 'The Distribution of Divine Names in Jonah', *TynB* 21, 1970, pp. 126ff.; A. R. Johnson, 'Jonah II. 3–10; A Study in Cultic Phantasy', in *Studies of OT Prophecy presented to T. H. Robinson*, ed. H. H. Rowley, 1950; and entries in standard dictionaries and introductions. See O. Kaiser, *IOT*, 1975, for recent bibliography.

D.F.P.

JONATHAN (Heb *yᵉhônāṯān* or *yônāṯān*, 'Yahweh has given').

1. Son of Gershom, descendant of Moses (AV 'Manasseh'). He was hired by Micah to officiate as priest before an idol in Ephraim, then became priest and progenitor of a line of priests to the Danites 'until the day of the captivity of the land' (Jdg. 17; 18:30–31).

2. Eldest son of King Saul by his only wife (1 Sa. 14:49–50), he was his father's heir, which makes his loyalty and affection for David, who succeeded Saul, the more wonderful (1 Sa. 20:31). Jonathan first appears in the biblical record as the victor at Geba, a Philistine stronghold, though his father's strategy at that time suggests by analogy that he may have taken part in the relief of Jabesh-gilead (1 Sa. 11:11; 13:2). His prowess and courage as a warrior, recalled in David's elegy (2 Sa. 1:22), are clearly seen in his lone attack on another Philistine garrison, an incident which also shows his ability to inspire loyalty as well as to offer it (1 Sa. 14:7). It is for his own loyalty to David, however, that he is chiefly remembered; a loyalty made more difficult because it conflicted with his filial duty to and affection for Saul, his father and sovereign. As the king, deserted by the Spirit of God and a victim to increasing fears and passions, showed ever greater hatred to 'the man after God's own heart' who was to succeed him, so Jonathan, in fealty to the brotherhood pact sworn with David after the death of Goliath (1 Sa. 18:1–4), was driven into defiance and deception of his father, even to the jeopardizing of his own life (1 Sa. 19:1–7; 20). The parting scene between the two friends is most moving. It does not appear that Jonathan accompanied his father on the two expeditions against David, to En-gedi and Hachilah, and he disappears finally in the tragic Philistine victory at Mt Gilboa, along with his father and brothers (1 Sa. 31:2). Gifted physically and morally, he is a model to those of a more favoured dispensation of loyalty to truth and friendship, as well as of that peacemaking which is the role of the sons of God.

3. Others who bore this name are an uncle of David, a counsellor and scribe, perhaps to be identified with the nephew of David who slew a giant (1 Ch. 27:32; 2 Sa. 21:21–22); a son of the high priest Abiathar, who was involved in the attempts on David's throne by Absalom and Adonijah, though not as a rebel (2 Sa. 15:36; 17:15–22; 1 Ki. 1:41–49); one of David's 'mighty men'

(2 Sa. 23:32; 1 Ch. 11:34); a son of Kareah associated with Gedaliah during the domination of Jerusalem by Nebuchadrezzar (Je. 40:8); and a scribe in whose house Jeremiah was imprisoned (Je. 37:20). The same name occurs at the time of the restoration (Ezr. 8:6; 10:15; Ne. 12:11, 14, 35). T.H.J.

JOPPA. The name in Heb. is *yāpō*, Gk. *Ioppē*, Arab. *Yâfâ* (whence mod. Eng. 'Jaffa'). As the only natural harbour between the Bay of Acco (near mod. Haifa) and the Egyp. frontier, Joppa has a long history; excavations have shown that it dates back to the 17th century BC or earlier, and it is mentioned in several Egyp. records of 15th and 14th centuries BC. After the Israelite occupation of Canaan, it was a border city of Dan (Jos. 19:46), but soon fell into Philistine hands; it was rarely under Israelite control thereafter, though it must have served as the seaport for Jerusalem, about 55 km away. In the 2nd century BC Simon wrested it from the Syrians and annexed it to Judaea (1 Macc. 13:11). It features in the story of Acts 10. Today it forms the S part of the municipality of Tel Aviv–Jaffa.

Parts of Joppa have been excavated in several archaeological campaigns since World War II. Of special interest is a pre-Philistine temple (13th century BC), dedicated to a lion cult.

BIBLIOGRAPHY. M. Avi-Yonah, *EAEHL*, 2, pp. 532–540.

D.F.P.

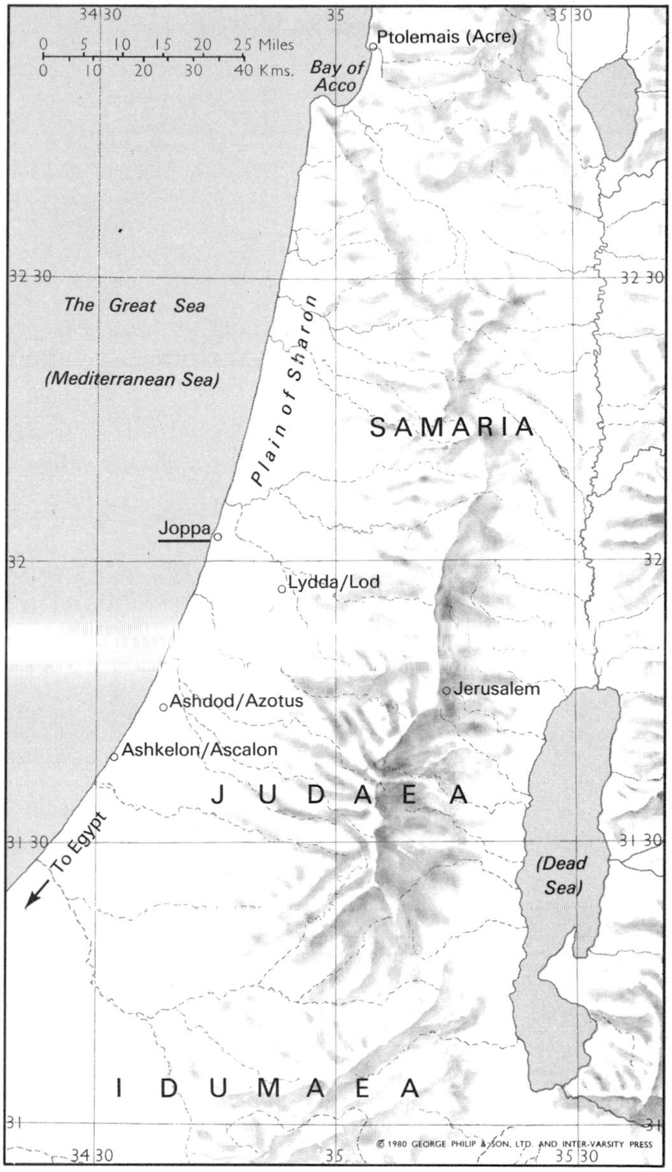

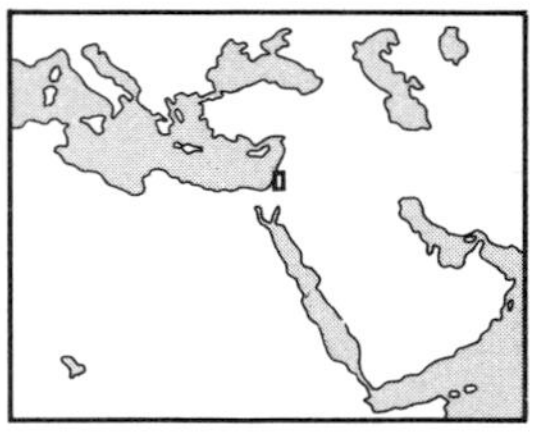

Joppa, a major harbour on the Palestinian coast from the 17th cent. BC.

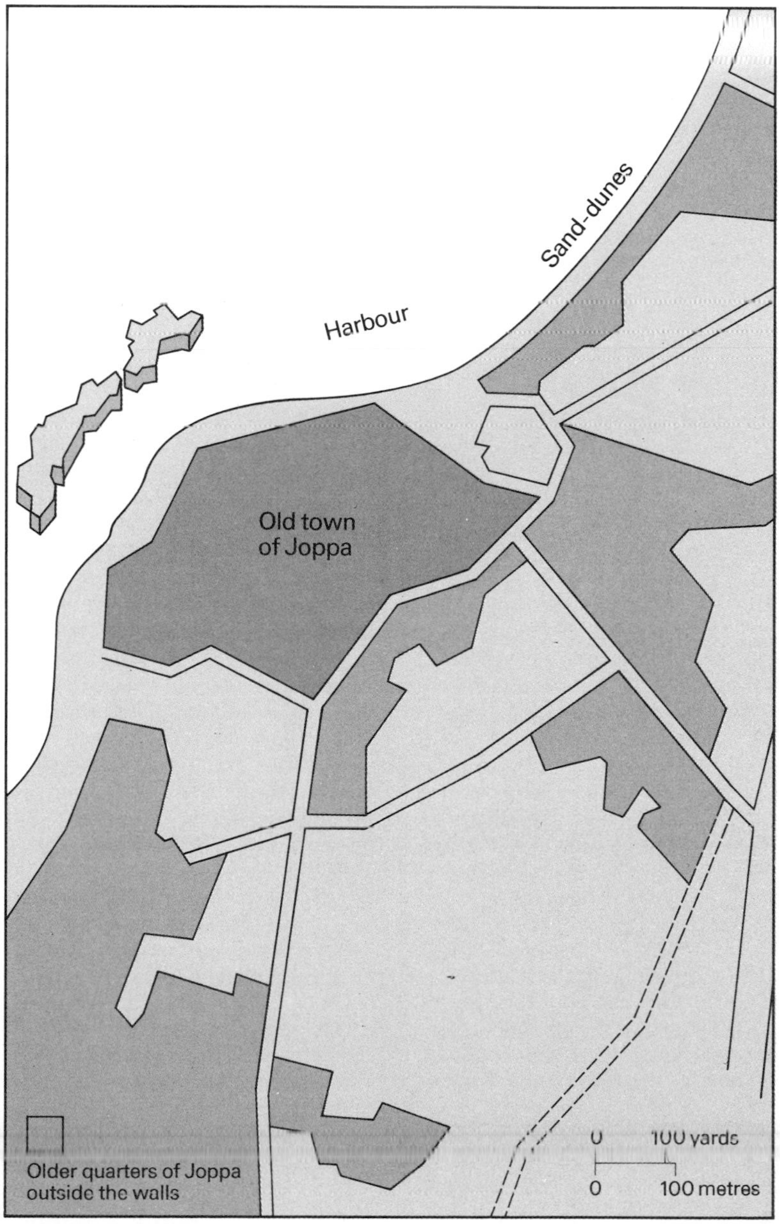

Joppa, showing the site of the harbour and old town.

JORDAN. The Jordan depression is unique among the features of physical geography. Formed as a result of a rift valley, it is the lowest depression on earth. The headwaters of the river Jordan, fed by springs, collect into Lake Huleh, 70 m above sea-level. Ten km S at Lake Tiberias the river is already nearly 200 m below the Mediterranean, while at the N end of the Dead Sea the floor of the trench has dropped a further 177 m and the river has plunged to 393 m below sea-level. Thus the name 'Jordan' (Heb. *yardēn*) aptly means 'the descender'. The river is the largest perennial course in Palestine, and its distance of some 120 km from Lake Huleh to the Dead Sea is more than doubled by its meander. No other river has more biblical allusions and significance.

JORAM
See Jehoram, Part 2.

Aerial view of the flood plain of the river Jordan, the Zor. The river meanders through thickets of tamarisk and thorn scrub called in the OT 'the jungle of the Jordan' (e.g. Je. 12:5). (P)

Opposite page: The Jordan valley in OT times.

I. Archaeological sites

Archaeological sites in the Jordan valley have revealed it to be one of the earliest loci of urban settlement in the world. The Natufian transition from hunting to urban life at Jericho may be as old as 7000 BC. A pottery-making people arrived about 5000 BC, and with the later pottery (Neolithic B culture) the first evidence occurs of links with other Jordan valley sites and the N Fertile Crescent. Copper was introduced in the Chalcolithic period (4500–3200 BC), such as at Teleilat Ghassul, just N of the Dead Sea. At Ghassul, three city levels existed from the 4th millennium onwards, with evidence of irrigation farming. This Ghassulian culture is identified widely in Palestine, but it was especially prevalent in the Jordan valley, at Mefjar, Abu Habil, Jiftlik Beth-shan, En-gedi and Tell esh-Shuneh, S of the Sea of Galilee.

At the end of the 4th millennium at least three groups of peoples entered the Jordan valley from the N, to settle in unwalled villages in the plains of Esdraelon, or from the E via Jericho. This period K. M. Kenyon has called proto-urban. City-states then began to appear in the Jordan valley, such as Jericho in the S, Beth-shan in the centre and Beth-yerah (Khirbet Kerak) in the N, and these traded with Egypt and Mesopotamia.

About 2200 BC Amorite nomads invaded the valley and destroyed many of the urban centres. They may have been part of a vast general eruption of peoples that went on from 2300 to 1900 BC, that is, to the beginning of the Middle Bronze Age. Abraham may have come into the Jordan valley in association with this period of nomadic unrest. This was followed by the N invasion of the Hyksos culture, when elaborate urban defences in depth were built at such towns as Jericho. Following the defeat of the Hyksos by the Egyptians, the great fortress towns of the Jordan valley, such as Beth-shan and Hazor, were rebuilt and equipped with Egyptian garrisons. Then later in the Bronze Age, at least by 1220 BC, the Israelites entered Palestine through the Jordan valley. There is evidence of the destruction of the cities of Hazor, Debir and Lachish. But the archaeological evidence for Joshua's capture of Jericho is obscure.

II. Topographical features

a. The Huleh basin

The Jordan valley begins below Mt Hermon (2774 m), out of whose limestone springs issue the headwaters of the Jordan. Banias, later called Caesarea Philippi, may have been the centre of Baal-gad in the valley 'of Lebanon' (Jos. 12:7). It was the territory of Dan, the N limit of Israel, whose inhabitants controlled the vital trade route into Syria and were likened to a nest of vipers (Gn. 49:17). Moving down the upper valley is the Huleh area, a depression some 5 × 15 km, where ancient lava flows blocked the valley, so that the Jordan plunges 280 m in 15 km of gorges. On the plateau overlooking the Huleh plain stands the site of Hazor, the great Canaanite town.

b. The Tiberias district

Beyond the Huleh gorges, at about 2130 m below sea-level, the Jordan enters the Sea of Galilee, a harp-shaped lake, 21 km long, and about 13 km across. Fed by numerous thermal springs, its fresh waters are well stocked with fish, the maximum depth of 50 km permitting vertical migrations of the fish with the seasonal temperatures. It was, therefore, probably in the hot summer season when the normal winter temperature of 13° C. lies 37 m below the surface of the lake, that Jesus advised the fishermen to 'cast into the deep' (Lk. 5:4). The methods of catching *fish referred to in the Gospels are still practised: the single-hook line (Mt. 17:27); the circular fishing net (Mt. 4:18; Mk. 1:16); the draw-net cast out by a boat (Mt. 13:47f.); deep-sea nets (Mt. 4:18f.; Mk. 1:19f.); and deep-sea fishing undertaken with two boats (Lk. 5:10).

A dense population clustered round the lake in our Lord's day, and it was the sophisticated city folk of Chorazin, Bethsaida and Capernaum that he condemned (Mt. 11:20–24). 'There is no spot in the whole of Palestine where memories heap themselves up to such an extent as in Capernaum' (G. Dalman). Jewish life throbbed in its synagogues (Mt. 12:9; Mk. [illegible] There lived Jairus, the chief of the synagogue (Mk. 5:22), the centurion who built a synagogue (Lk. 7:5) and Levi the customs official (Mt. 9:9; Mk. 2:14; Lk. 5:27). E of Capernaum was Bethsaida from which Philip, Andrew and Peter came (Jn. 1:44), and beyond that the less populous district of the Gadarenes, where the heathen reared their pigs (Lk. 8:32). The lake, plains and steep rocky slopes, interspersed with boulders and thistle-fields, provide the setting for the parable of the sower (Mk. 4:2–8), while in spring the flowered carpets of asphodels, anemones and irises are also telling sermons.

Dominating this lake environment are the surrounding mountains, especially those of the NW, which played so vital a part in the prayer-life of our Lord, where he taught his disciples (Mt. 5:1) and from which he appeared as the risen Lord (Mt. 28:16). The NE corner of the lake is supposedly the scene of the miracle of the feeding of the five thousand (Lk. 9:10–17).

c. The 'Ghor' or Jordan valley

This runs for over 105 km between Lake Tiberias and the Dead Sea. The Yarmuk, entering the left bank of the Jordan 8 km downstream from the lake, doubles the volume of flow, and the valley is progressively deepened to as much as 50 m below the floor of the trough. In this sector, three physical zones are distinguishable: the broad upper terrace of the Pliocene trough, the Ghor proper; the lower Quaternary terrace and the flood plain of the river, the Zor; and between them the deeply dissected slopes and badlands of the Qattara. It is the Qattara and the Zor together, rather than the river Jordan, which have created the frontier character of this obstacle (Jos. 22:25). The N half of the Ghor is a broad, well-cultivated tract, but the Judaean–Gilead dome, crossing the trough, narrows the valley S of Gilead. Beyond it, the trough becomes increasingly more arid, until at the head of the Dead Sea there is scarcely more than 5 cm mean annual rainfall. The Qattara badlands, carved grotesquely in soft marls and clays, create a steep, desolate descent to the valley floor. The Zor, making its way in vivid green vegetation cover, stands out in sharp contrast below, hence its name *gā'ôn* ('luxuriant growth') of Jordan (Je. 12:5; 49:19; 50:44; [illegible] 16:18). The haunt of wild animals (Je. 49:19), it is partly flooded in spring (Jos. 3:15). Thus the question can be understood, 'And if in a safe land you fall down, how will you do in the jungle of the Jordan?' (Je. 12:5).

Between the Yarmuk in the N and the Jabbok are nine other perennial streams entering the left bank of the Jordan, and their water supply explains why all the important settlements were located on the E side of the Ghor, towns such as Succoth, Zaphon, Zaretan, Jabesh-gilead and Pella. With the aid of irrigation, this was probably the view Lot saw 'like the garden of the Lord' (Gn. 13:10). The brook Cherith may well have been a seasonal tributary of the Jabesh farther N, where Elijah, a native of Jabesh-gilead, hid himself from Ahab (1 Ki. 17:1–7). Between Succoth and Zarthan (identified by Glueck as Tell es-Saidiyeh) Solomon had his copper cast in earthen moulds, using local clay and fuel (1 Ki. 7:46; 2 Ch. 4:17). In this section of the valley, there are a number of fords, though the river was not bridged until Roman times. Near the mouth of the Jabbok, both Abraham and Jacob crossed it (Gn. 32:10). Somewhere here, the Midianites crossed pursued by Gideon (Jdg. 7:24; 8:4–5). Twice David crossed it in the rebellion of Absalom (2 Sa. 17:22–24; 19:15–18). But between the Jabbok confluence and the Dead Sea, crossings are more difficult, owing to the swift current. The miraculous crossing of the Israel-

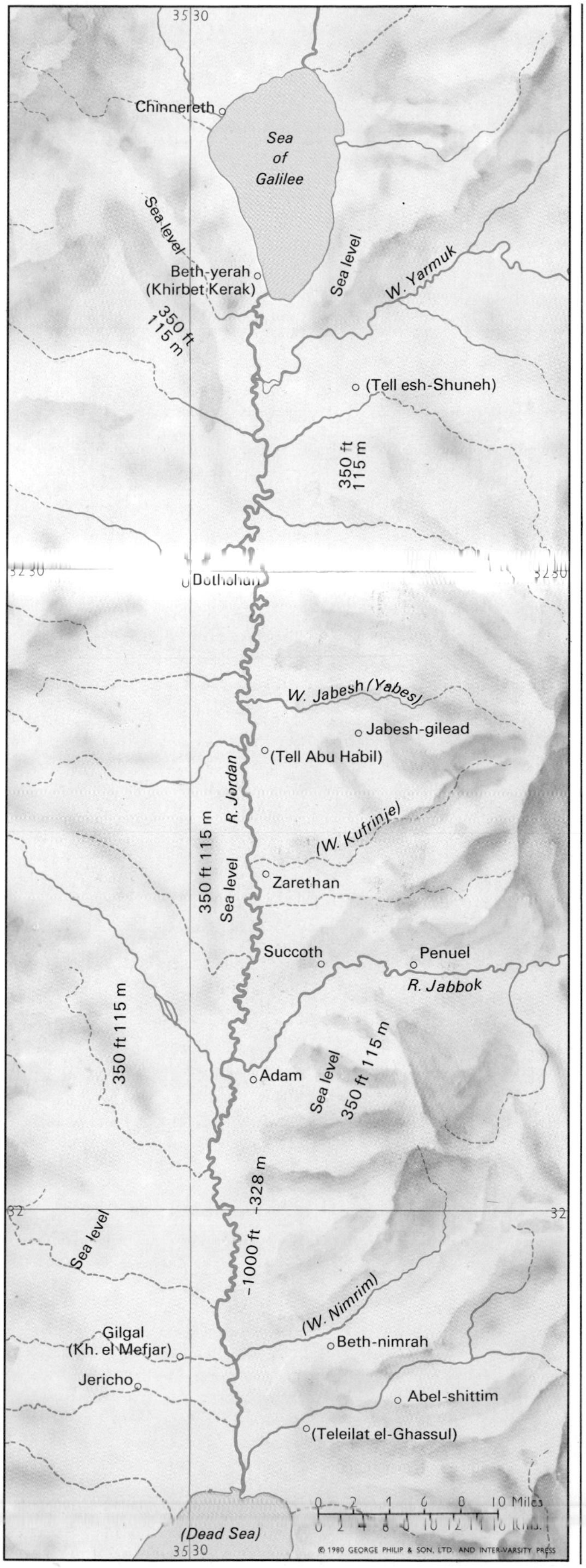

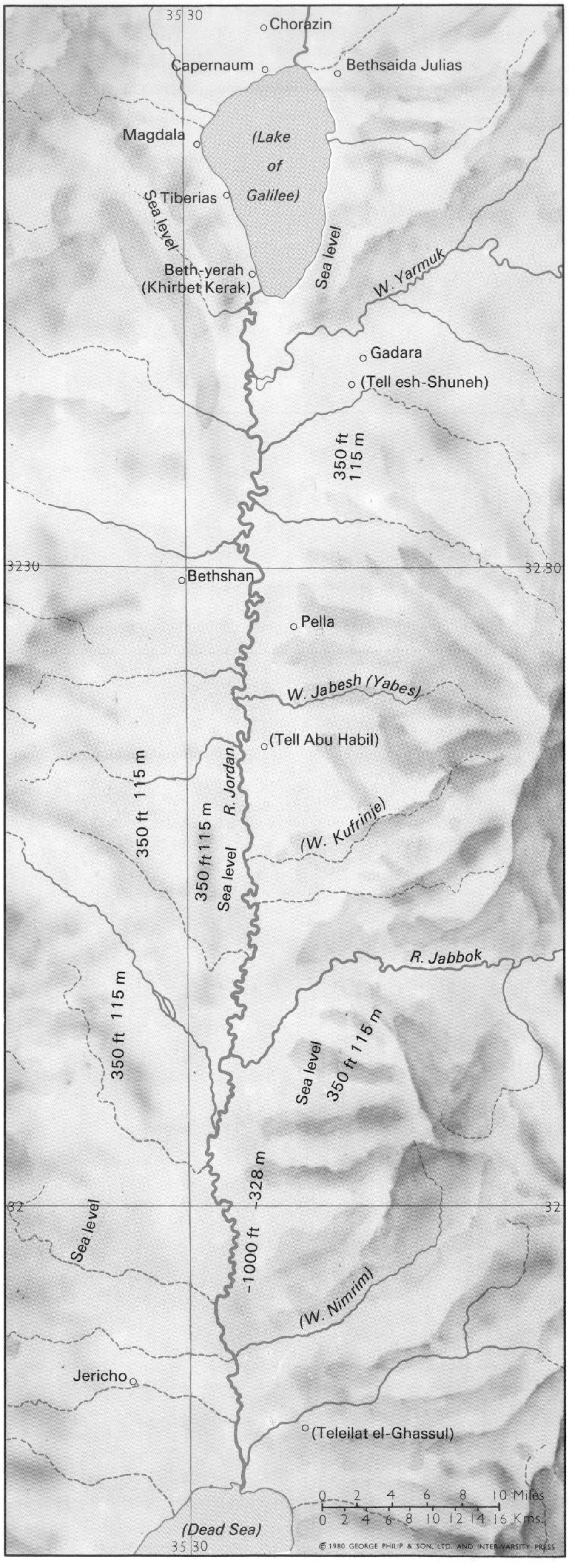

ites appears to have taken place at Adam (modern Tell Dâmiyeh), 26 km N of Jericho (Jos. 3:1–17; 4:1–24; Ps. 114:3, 5).

Between the Jabbok and Beth-nimrah for 26 km (Is. 15:6) there are no streams entering the Jordan, and little settlement. Oasis towns occur near springs, such as Jericho W of the Jordan, and in the plains of Moab (Nu. 20:1) to the E was Shittim, where the spies were sent (Jos. 2:1–7).

BIBLIOGRAPHY. D. Baly, *The Geography of the Bible*², 1974; G. Dalman, *Sacred Sites and Ways*, trans. by P. P. Levertoff, 1935; J. and J. B. E. Garstang, *The Story of Jericho*, 1948; N. Glueck, *The River Jordan*, 1946; K. M. Kenyon, *Jericho I*, 1960; E. B. Smick, *Archaeology of the Jordan Valley*, 1973.

J.M.H.

JOSEPH.

1. In the Old Testament

I. Name

Joseph is a jussive form of the verb *yāsap̄*, 'to add'; the name *yôsēp̄* means 'may he (God) add (sons)'; *cf.* Gn. 30:24. A Palestinian place-name *yšp-ỉr* (*i.e. y-š-p-'El*) in Egyp. topographical lists of the 15th and 14th centuries BC has been compared with Heb. *yôsēp̄*. But the 's'-sounds are different and the two names are almost certainly not related (so W. F. Albright, *JPOS* 8, 1928, p, 249). For the Egyp. *y-š-p-El*, compare biblical place-names such as Iphtahel (Jos. 19:14, 27).

II. History

a. Background

Joseph was the eleventh son of Jacob, his first by Rachel (Gn. 30:24; 35:24), and his favourite son (Gn. 37:3; *cf.* 33:2, 7). The story of Joseph is one of the most graphic and attractive in the OT: a spoilt boy sold into Egyp. slavery by jealous brothers, who makes good in adversity, and from an unjust imprisonment rises to the highest offices of state. By wise planning he averts the scourge of famine, thereby saving Egypt, Canaan and his own family from starvation. Reconciliation with his brothers follows and the family settles in the pastures of Goshen in the NE Delta. After burying Jacob in Canaan, Joseph commands that his bones too should be carried there when Israel's descendants eventually leave Egypt for the land of promise. The story as told in Genesis cannot be bettered; the following paragraphs will therefore merely present some Egyp. and related background material and deal with some textual points.

b. Date

The most likely date for Joseph is the period of the Hyksos pharaohs, *c.* 1720–1550 BC (*CHRONOLOGY OF THE OLD TESTAMENT). These were Semitic rulers who had infiltrated from Canaan, but scrupulously observed Egyp. conventions. At first they took over the existing Egyp. bureaucratic administration, but later appointed naturalized Semites to high office. For the historical background, see *EGYPT: History.

c. The 'coat of many colours'

Jacob's partiality for Joseph was marked by the 'coat of many colours' (AV, RV) or 'long robe with sleeves' (*cf.* RVmg., RSV). Archaeologically either rendering of the Heb. *k^eṯōneṯ passîm* is possible. For Semites in multicoloured garb, see *IBA*, p. 29, fig. 25, right, or in colour, E. W. Heaton, *Everyday Life in Old Testament Times*, 1956, dust-jacket; later examples in *IBA*, p. 35, fig. 29, or *ANEP*, p. 17, fig. 52. These same garments, especially the last cited examples, are also often long and sleeved. In favour of the meaning 'varicoloured', *passîm* has been compared with Assyr. *paspasu*, 'brightly coloured bird' and Arabic *fasafisa*, 'mosaic' (Eisler, *Orientalistische Literaturzeitung* 11, 1908, pp. 368–371, and *cf. ibid.*, 14, 1911, p. 509). The rendering 'long robe with sleeves' is attained by taking *pas* as flat of hand or foot, hence *k^eṯōneṯ passîm* is a 'tunic of (= reaching to) palms and soles' (*BDB*, p. 821a). On dreams, see below.

d. Joseph sold into Egypt

The text records that, when Joseph was sent to visit his brothers pasturing the flocks, they at first planned to kill him, but instead put him in a cistern at the suggestion of the more scrupulous Reuben, who secretly hoped to rescue him. After the brothers had sat down to a meal, a caravan of Ishmaelite merchants from Gilead appeared in the distance; so they quickly decided to rid themselves of Joseph by selling him off. When the caravan came near, 'they'—Joseph's brothers—sold him to the first of the travellers that they met: 'Midianite traders'

(Gn. 37:28). When the caravan had passed on, Reuben returned to the pit and was distraught at finding Joseph gone. This directly suggests that Reuben had been absent from the first appearance of the caravan until it (and Joseph) had passed on.

Certain points require comment. Why should Reuben be absent? Of many possible reasons, the simplest is that when the foreign caravan was sighted, Reuben, the most conscientious of the brothers (and true to character), went off to mount guard among the sheep: passing foreigners could not be trusted not to filch a few choice animals. Reuben would have to wait till they had passed. By the time Reuben could safely return, Joseph was sold and gone; they then sent his blood-stained robe to Jacob.

Who sold Joseph into Egypt? In Egypt the Midianites (or rather Medanites, see below) sold Joseph to Potiphar (Gn. 37:36), who bought him from the Ishmaelites (Gn. 39:1). The caravan was Ishmaelite, including under this designation Midianites or Medanites; the terms overlap. This interchange of terms is most plainly exhibited by Jdg. 8:24, which explicitly states that the Midianites beaten by Gideon 'had golden earrings, because they were Ishmaelites'. The spelling Medanites in the Heb. of Gn. 37:36 may indicate an overlap of a third term; compare Gn. 25:2 (= 1 Ch. 1:32), where both Medan and Midian are sons of Abraham by Keturah. The use of multiple terms in a narrative is indicative not of disparate documents but of typical Near Eastern stylistic usage. For similar use of three terms within a few lines compare the Egyp. stele of Sebekkhu (*c.* 1850 BC), who refers to the one general foe of his pharaoh's Palestinian campaign as *Mntyw-Stt*, 'Asiatic bedouin'; as *Rntw ḫst*, 'vile Syrians'; and as *'mw*, 'Asiatics'. There can be no question of separate documents behind this little stone stele, executed as a unit at one man's volition; such examples could be multiplied.

Who sold Joseph to the caravan? 'They drew' (Gn. 37:28) is at first sight ambiguous, able to refer either to the brothers or to the Midianites. In Gn. 45:4–5 Joseph plainly charges his brothers in private with having sold him into slavery (simple form of the verb), which would refer the 'they' of Gn. 37:28 to his brothers, not the Midianites. This accords with the syntax of Heb. and parallel literatures. In Egypt, a text records that when King Tuthmosis II 'flew to heaven', *i.e.* died, his son Tuthmosis III ascended the throne and 'his sister' Hatshepsut governed the land. This latter 'his' refers back, not to Tuthmosis III, but to Tuthmosis II (Schott, *Krönungstag d. Königin Hatschepsut*, 1955, p. 197). Note that 'Midianites' in Gn. 37:28 has no article, and can mean either just 'Midianites' (undefined) or else '(some) Midianites', *i.e.* part of the main body, there being no indefinite article in Heb. Finally, there is Gn. 40:14–15, where Joseph tells the butler that he 'was stolen out of the land of the Hebrews'. Why did he not openly admit that he had been sold into slavery? The reason is perfectly plain. Joseph here desperately pleads his innocence of any offence, seeking to persuade the butler to get him out of prison; it would have wrecked his plea to have revealed the humiliating fact that he had been sold into slavery by his own blood brothers. With his brothers in private (Gn. 45) Joseph could be frank; but the butler would be bound to think they had had some good reason to rid themselves of him, and Joseph's appeal would be in vain. Joseph therefore said vaguely that he was 'stolen', which was true in so far as his brothers had no right to sell him for gain. This is not a question of harmonization at any price, but of common sense and practical psychology. The truth is that Gn. 37; 39–40; 45 read plainly when put in their proper setting of exact exegesis, Heb. and other Near Eastern syntax and literary usage, and the motivated actions of individuals.

e. Joseph in Egypt

Joseph was but one of many young Semites who became servants in Egyp. households between 1900 and 1600 BC. Papyrus Brooklyn 35.1446, part of a prison-register (see below), bears on its reverse a list of 79 servants in an Egyp. household *c.* 1740 BC, of whom at least 45 were not Egyptians but 'Asiatics', *i.e.* Semites like Joseph.

Opposite page: The Jordan valley in NT times.

Like Joseph, Asiatics from Palestine entered Egypt with traders. This wall-painting depicts Ibsha, 'ruler of a foreign country', wearing a multi-coloured, knee-length garment, leading a caravan bringing eye-paint to Khnum-hotep III of Egypt. Tomb of Khnum-hotep, Beni Hasan. c. 1890 BC. (PAC)

Joseph was invested with high office by Pharaoh in the traditional Egyptian manner (Gn. 41:42). The ceremony is illustrated by the investiture of Paser as vizier of Sethos I. Drawing after a carving in the tomb of Paser, Thebes. c. 1300 BC.

Many of these have good NW Semitic names linguistically related to those of Jacob, Issachar, Asher, Job (Ayyabum) and Menahem. Some were 'domestics' (*ḥry-pr*) just like Joseph in Gn. 39:2 ('in the house'). See Hayes, *A Papyrus of the Late Middle Kingdom*, 1955, and Albright, *JAOS* 74, 1954, pp. 222–233.

There are ample scattered indications of numbers of Asiatics in Egypt at this period, some of whom reached high and trusted positions under their masters (Posener, *Syria* 34, 1957, pp. 145–163), rather like Joseph, who became Potiphar's steward (*imy-r pr*, a common Egyp. title). Potiphar's title (*śar-haṭṭabbāḥîm*) 'captain of the guard', *i.e.* of Pharaoh's bodyguard, would render the Egyp. *sḥḏ-šmsw*, 'Instructor of Retainers'. However, Vergote (*Joseph en Égypte*, 1959, pp. 31–35) has put up a plausible case for interpreting his title as actually 'butler'. For the Egyp. original of Potiphar's name, see *POTIPHAR, *POTIPHERA. Both Potiphar and the 'butler' and 'baker' of Gn. 40 are termed *sārîs*, usually rendered 'officer', but in Semitic it often means 'eunuch'. However, eunuchs are not prominent in Egypt, and *sārîs* in early times meant generally 'courtier, dignitary' as much as 'eunuch' (though this was the main meaning later). See *JEA* 47, 1961, p. 160.

The incident of Potiphar's covetous wife, who turned the tables on Joseph by asserting the opposite of the truth, is often compared with a very similar incident in the Egyp. *Tales of Two Brothers*. However, there is no other point of contact at all between these two narratives: Joseph's is pure biography, while everything else in the *Two Brothers* is pure fantasy. For a full translation see, *e.g.*, Erman-Blackman, *Literature of the Ancient Egyptians*, 1927, pp. 150–161, as the extracts in *ANET*, pp. 23–25, are abbreviated. More prosaic Egyp. documents reveal that Potiphar's wife was not unique in her sin.

Egyp. prisons served a threefold purpose: as local lock-ups like modern prisons, as forced-labour reserves for state corvée and as centres for remanded prisoners awaiting trial (*cf.* Joseph). Trials were sometimes conducted in the prisons, whose administration was highly organized, as the Papyrus Brooklyn (Hayes, *op. cit.*) vividly shows; each prisoner's record was filed under seven separate headings, from initial arrest to completion of the sentence. The 'keeper of the prison' (Gn. 39:21–23, *etc.*) probably represents the Egyp. title *s'wty n ḫnrt* which has the same meaning.

The 'butler' of Gn. 40 should be rendered *'cup-bearer', Heb. *mašqeh* being the exact equivalent of Egyp. *wdpw*, later *wb'*, 'cup-bearer' (*cf.* Gn. 40:11, 13). Bakers, too, are well known in Egypt, but chief bakers apparently were not explicitly so called. Perhaps the Egyp. title *sš wdḥw nsw*, 'Royal Table-scribe', is the nearest equivalent. For bread-baskets carried on the head, see *IBA*, p. 33, fig. 28. *Dreams (Gn. 37; 40–41) were considered important also in the non-biblical East. The 'magicians of Egypt' (*ḥarṭummîm*, an Egyp. word) were familiar figures, and special manuals were used for interpreting dreams. For details, see under *MAGIC AND SORCERY, **2. II.**

Joseph had to be properly shaved and robed in linen to appear at court (Gn. 41:14). His practical approach to the threat of famine impressed the pharaoh, who invested him with high office in traditional Egyp. manner, bestowing signet, fine linen and gold necklace. Joseph's exact rank is disputed; it seems most probable that he was actually vizier, second only to the pharaoh (so Vergote); but some would make him a minister for agriculture directly responsible to the king in person (Ward, *JSS* 5, 1960, pp. 144–150). The mention of chariots (Gn. 41:43) and horses (Gn. 47:17) fits the Hyksos period and decades immediately preceding, but not earlier. Remains of horses from the period just before the Hyksos have been excavated near Wadi Halfa (Faulkner, *JEA* 45, 1959, pp. 1–2). For the Egyp. names of Joseph and his wife, see *Zaphnath-paaneah and *Asenath.

Egypt was famed for her great agricultural wealth; *cf.* reckoning of grain, *IBA*, p. 32, fig. 27. But Egypt also suffered periodic famines; one oft-quoted biographical text reads 'When famine came for many years, I gave grain to my town in each famine' (Vandier, *La Famine dans l'Égypte ancienne*, 1936, p. 115). The Egyptians would not eat with the Hebrews (Gn. 43:32) for fear of transgressing various ritual taboos on food (Montet, *L'Égypte et la Bible*, 1959, pp. 99–101). It is possible that Gn. 44:5 on divination should be rendered 'is it not from this (= the silver cup) that my lord drinks and *concerning* which he will assuredly divine?' (*cf.* Gn. 44:15); for possible cup-divination, see *Magic and Sorcery, **2. II.**

When pharaoh invited Joseph's family to settle in Egypt (Gn. 45:17–21; 46:5), he sent wagons and told them to leave all, for they would have sufficiency in Egypt. Judging from Egyp. scenes 200 years later, such wagons were probably large, two-wheeled ox-carts. (For an excellent picture and discussion of these, see Aldred, *JNES* 15, 1956, pp. 150–153, pl. 17.) Sinuhe, a fugitive Egyptian in Syria *c.* 1900 BC, was also told to leave all by the pharaoh who recalled him to Egypt. Different customs again explain an allusion in Gn. 46:34b; by this means Joseph's family could be settled in secluded security in Goshen. Joseph's economic policy in Gn. 47:16–19 simply made Egypt in fact what it always was in theory: the land became pharaoh's property and its inhabitants his tenants. The priests were exempt not from taxation but only from Joseph's one-fifth levy, and the temple estates were separately managed (Gn. 47:22, 26). Gn. 47:21 merely indicates that throughout Egypt Joseph brought the people of each district into their nearest cities where the granaries were, the better to feed them; the unsavoury emendation in RSV ('he made slaves of them') is unnecessary. Gn. 48–49 reflects purely Asiatic usage within the patriarchal family; such oral blessings as Jacob's were legally binding in W Asia in the first half of the 2nd millennium BC (*cf.* Gordon, *BA* 3, 1940, p. 8).

f. Death of Joseph

Both Joseph and his father were embalmed in the Egyp. manner (Gn. 50:2–3, 26), and Joseph was 'put in a coffin in Egypt'. Coffins at this period were anthropoid, wooden ones with a conventional portrait-face at the head-end. The period of embalming varied in length; 40 days is one possibility among many. But 70 days' mourning was characteristic. Joseph's age at death, 110 years, is also significant: this was the ideal life-span in Egyp. eyes, and to them would signify divine blessing upon him.

For background, detailed discussion, and full source references, see J. Vergote, *Joseph en Égypte*, 1959; on D. B. Redford, *A Study of the Biblical Story of Joseph,* 1970, see K. A. Kitchen, *Oriens Antiquus* 12, 1973, pp. 233–242.

III. Joseph's descendants

The tribes of Ephraim and Manasseh, descended from Joseph's two sons, were sometimes termed '(the tribe of) Joseph', or house of Joseph; 'sons of Joseph' is common (Nu.; Jos.). So, Joseph is blessed as progenitor of the two future tribes by Jacob (Gn. 49:22–26; *cf.* Gn. 48), and Moses also blesses 'Joseph', meaning Ephraim and Manasseh (Dt. 33:13, 16). Compare also Nu. 13:11; Dt. 27:12; Jdg. 1:22–23, 35; Ps. 80:1 (poetic); and Ezk. 47:13. K.A.K.

2. In the New Testament

The husband of Mary. He is not mentioned in Mark and the references in Jn. 1:45 and 6:42 are indirect. According to Matthew, he was a descendant of David (Mt. 1:20). It seems that the genealogy in Lk. 3 is not that of Joseph but of Mary (but see *Genealogy of Jesus Christ). Luke had already shown that Jesus was not the son of Joseph. Matthew is tracing the legal relationship back to David and Abraham.

Matthew and Luke both record that Jesus was conceived by the Holy Spirit at a time when Joseph was betrothed to Mary, but before he had intercourse with her (Mt. 1:18; Lk. 1:27, 35). Luke records the revelation by an angel to Mary, Matthew that to Joseph. It seems that Matthew drew his information from Joseph (possibly *via* James, the Lord's brother) and that Luke obtained his from Mary.

Joseph acted as a father towards Jesus, taking him to Jerusalem for the purification (Lk. 2:22) and fleeing with him to Egypt to escape Herod. He returned to Nazareth and settled there (Mt. 2). He took the boy Jesus to Jerusalem each year for the Passover (Lk. 2:41). Perhaps his words in Lk. 2:49 indicate that Jesus knew when he was 12 years old that he was not Joseph's son.

It is almost certain that Joseph was not alive during the ministry of Jesus. There is no direct mention of him, and it is hard to explain otherwise the word to John from the cross (Jn. 19:26–27) and the reference to Mary and his brothers seeking Jesus (Mt. 12:46; Mk. 3:31; Lk. 8:19). It is natural to assume that the brothers of Jesus were subsequent children of Joseph and Mary.

Others mentioned in the NT who bear this name are three ancestors of Joseph the husband of Mary (or ancestors of Mary?) (Lk. 3:24, 26, 30); Joseph called Barsabbas, surnamed Justus, the unsuccessful candidate for the apostleship of Judas (Acts 1:23); and one of the brothers of the Lord (Mt. 13:55). It was also the natal name of *Barnabas (Acts 4:36). R.E.N.

JOSEPH OF ARIMATHEA.

A Jew of *Arimathea, 'a good and righteous man, . . . and he was looking for the kingdom of God' (Lk. 23:50–51), 'a disciple of Jesus, but secretly, for fear of the Jews' (Jn. 19:38), and a member of the Sanhedrin who had not voted for Jesus' death. He was rich and, having asked Pilate for Jesus' body, provided fine linen for the burial, laying it in his own, unused, rock tomb (Mt. 27:57–60). (In this Matthew perhaps sees the fulfilment of Is. 53:9.) In a legend which first appears in William of Malmesbury he is sent by Philip from Gaul to Britain in AD 63 and founded the first Christian settlement in this country, afterwards the site of Glastonbury. There is no reference

JOSEPH BARSABBAS
See Justus, Part 2.

to this story in Gildas and Bede. J. A. Robinson, in his *Two Glastonbury Legends*, 1926, says that the passages are interpolations. A still later legend, probably composed by Walter Map in 1200, tells how Joseph brought the Holy Grail to England. J.W.M.

JOSEPHUS, FLAVIUS. A Jewish historian, who was born AD 37/38, and died early in the 2nd century. He was the son of a priest named Matthias, of the order of Jehoiarib (1 Ch. 24:7), and claimed kinship with the Hasmonaeans, who belonged to that order. After a brief period of association with the Essenes, and with an ascetic wilderness-dweller named Banus, he joined the party of the Pharisees at the age of 19. On a visit to Rome in AD 63 he was impressed by the power of the empire. He was strongly opposed to the Jewish revolt against Rome in AD 66, and although he was given a command in Galilee in which he manifested considerable energy and ability, he had no confidence in the insurgent cause. After the Roman seizure of the stronghold of Jotapata, which he had defended until further resistance was useless, he escaped with forty others to a cave. When this refuge in turn was about to be stormed the defenders entered into a suicide pact, and Josephus found himself one of the last two survivors. He persuaded his fellow-survivor that they might as well surrender to the Romans, and then he contrived to win the favour of Vespasian, the Roman commander, by predicting his elevation to the imperial purple. This prediction came true in AD 69. Next year Josephus was attached to the Roman general headquarters during the siege of Jerusalem, acting as interpreter for Titus (Vespasian's son and successor in the Palestinian command), when he wished to offer terms to the defenders of the city. After the fall of Jerusalem Josephus went to Rome, where he settled down as a client and pensioner of the emperor, whose family name, Flavius, he adopted.

Not unnaturally, Josephus' behaviour during the war won for him the indelible stigma of treason in the eyes of his nation. Yet he employed the years of his leisure in Rome in such a way as to establish some claim on their gratitude. These years were devoted to literary activity in which he shows himself to be a true patriot according to his lights, jealous for the good name of his people. His first work was a *History of the Jewish War*, written first in Aramaic for the benefit of Jews in Mesopotamia and then published in a Gk. edition. The account of the outbreak of the war is here preceded by a summary of Jewish history from 168 BC to AD 66. His two books *Against Apion* constitute a defence of his people against the anti-Jewish calumnies of an Alexandrian schoolmaster named Apion; in them, too, he endeavours to show that the Jews can boast a greater antiquity than the Greeks, and in the course of this argument he has preserved for us a number of valuable extracts from ancient writers not otherwise extant. His longest work is his *Jewish Antiquities*, in twenty books, relating the history of his people from earliest times (in fact, he begins his narrative with the creation of the world) down to his own day. This work was completed in AD 93. Finally, he wrote his *Autobiography* largely as a defence of his war record, which had been represented in unflattering terms by another Jewish writer, Justus of Tiberias. It is impossible to reconcile the account of his war activities given in his *Autobiography* with that given earlier in his *History of the Jewish War*.

For the history of the Jews between the reign of Antiochus Epiphanes (175–164 BC) and the war of AD 66–74, and especially for the period beginning with the Roman occupation of 63 BC, the works of Josephus are of incomparable value. He had access to first-rate sources, both published and unpublished: the work of Nicolas of Damascus, historiographer to Herod the Great, supplied a detailed record of that monarch's career; official Roman records were placed at his disposal; he consulted the younger Agrippa (*HEROD, **5**) on various details concerning the origin of the Jewish war, and of course could rely on his own immediate knowledge of many phases of it. He can indeed be thoroughly tendentious in his portrayal of personalities and presentation of events, but his 'tendency' is so obvious that the reader can easily detect it and make necessary allowances for it.

The works of Josephus provide indispensable background material for the student of late intertestamental and NT history. In them we meet many figures, both Jewish and Gentile, who are well known to us from the NT. Sometimes his writings supply a direct commentary on NT references, *e.g.* on the mention of Judas of Galilee in Acts 5:37 and of the *'Egyptian' in Acts 21:38. It is unlikely, however, that his works were known to any NT writer. Of special interest are his references to John the Baptist (*Ant.* 18. 116ff.), to James the Lord's brother (*Ant.* 20. 200), and to our Lord (*Ant.* 18. 63f.)—a passage which, while it has been subjected to some Christian editing, is basically authentic.

BIBLIOGRAPHY. The standard edition of Josephus' works in Greek is that by B. Niese (1887–95). The Loeb edition (1926–65), in Greek and English, begun by H. St J. Thackeray and completed by R. Marcus and L. H. Feldman, comprises 9 volumes. The best-known English translation is that by W. Whiston (1736); this has been revised by A. R. Shilleto (1889–90) and (less thoroughly) by D. S. Margoliouth (1906). A most readable new translation of the *Jewish War*, by G. A. Williamson, has appeared in the Penguin Classics (1959). See also H. St J. Thackeray, *Josephus, the Man and the Historian*, 1929; F. J. Foakes-Jackson, *Josephus and the Jews*, 1930; J. M. Creed, 'The Slavonic Version of Josephus' History of the Jewish War', *HTR* 25, 1932, pp. 277ff.; R. J. H. Shutt, *Studies in Josephus*, 1961; H. W. Montefiore, *Josephus and the New Testament*, 1962; G. A. Williamson, *The World of Josephus*, 1964; F. F. Bruce, *Jesus and Christian Origins outside the NT*, 1974, pp. 32–53. F.F.B.

JOSHEB-BASSHEBETH See Jashobeam, Part 2.

JOSHUA, 1. Joshua ben Nun, grandson of Elishama chief of Ephraim (1 Ch. 7:27; Nu. 1:10), was called by his family *hôšea'*, 'salvation', Nu. 13:8 (AV 'Oshea'); Dt. 32:44 Heb.; this name recurs in the tribe of Ephraim (1 Ch. 27:20; 2 Ki. 17:1; Ho. 1:1). Moses added the divine name, and called him *y^ehôšua'*, normally rendered in Eng. 'Joshua'. The Gk. *Iēsous* reflects the Aram. contraction *yešu'* (*cf.* Ne. 3:19, *etc.*).

At the Exodus Joshua was a young man (Ex. 33:11). Moses chose him as personal assistant, and gave him command of a detachment from the as yet unorganized tribes to repel the raiding Amalekites (Ex. 17). As the Ephraimite representative on the reconnaissance from Kadesh (Nu. 13–14) he backed Caleb's recommendation to go ahead with invasion. *Caleb, the senior and leading figure, sometimes is mentioned alone in this connection; but it is unlikely that there was a version of the episode excluding Joshua, or that any later historian denied, or was unaware, that he too escaped the curse on the unbelieving people.

While Moses was alone before God at Sinai, Joshua kept watch; in the Tent of Meeting also he learnt to wait on the Lord; and in the years following, something of Moses' patience and meekness was doubtless added to his valour (Ex. 24:13; 32:17; 33:11; Nu. 11:28). In the plains by the Jordan he was formally consecrated as Moses' successor to the military leadership, co-ordinate with *Eleazar the priest (Nu. 27:18ff.; 34:17; *cf.* Dt. 3 and 31, where Joshua's position is naturally emphasized). He was then probably about 70 years old; Caleb was a remarkably vigorous 85 when he began to occupy the Judaean hills (Jos. 15:13–15).

Joshua occupied and consolidated the area of Gilgal, fought successful campaigns against Canaanite confederacies and directed further operations as long as the united efforts of Israel were required. Settlement of the land depended on tribal initiative; Joshua sought to encourage this by a formal allocation at Shiloh, where the national sanctuary was established. The time had come for him to dissolve his command and set an example by retiring to his land at Timnath-serah in Mt Ephraim. It was perhaps at this time that he called Israel to the national covenant at Shechem (Jos. 24). Ch. 23, his farewell, may refer to the same occasion; but the substance is different, and seems to imply a later period. Joshua died aged 110, and was buried near his home at Timnath-serah.

For *JOSHUA, BOOK OF, see the following article, which also discusses some modern theories of the invasion of Canaan and of Joshua's role.

2. Joshua ben Josedech was high priest of the restoration in 537 BC. Under him the altar was rebuilt and the Temple dedicated. Progress was hindered by opposition, however, until in 520 BC he was strengthened by the prophecies of Haggai and Zechariah, including a remarkable pattern of justification by the grace of God (Zc. 3). He was named prophetically the 'Branch' (or, 'shoot'; *ṣemaḥ*, Zc. 6:12). See J. Stafford Wright, *The Building of the Second Temple*, 1958, for a review of the problems in Ezra and Haggai.

3. Joshua of Beth-shemesh, owner of the field to which the ark was brought when the Philistines sent it back to Israel (1 Sa. 6:14).

J.P.U.L.

JOSHUA, BOOK OF. The book of Joshua records the invasion of Canaan by Israel and its partition among the tribes. It tells in detail how they crossed the Jordan and secured a bridgehead, describes more briefly two campaigns which broke the power of the Canaanites and summarizes Israel's further military progress. The account of

Palestine, showing the regions of Israelite settlement under Joshua.

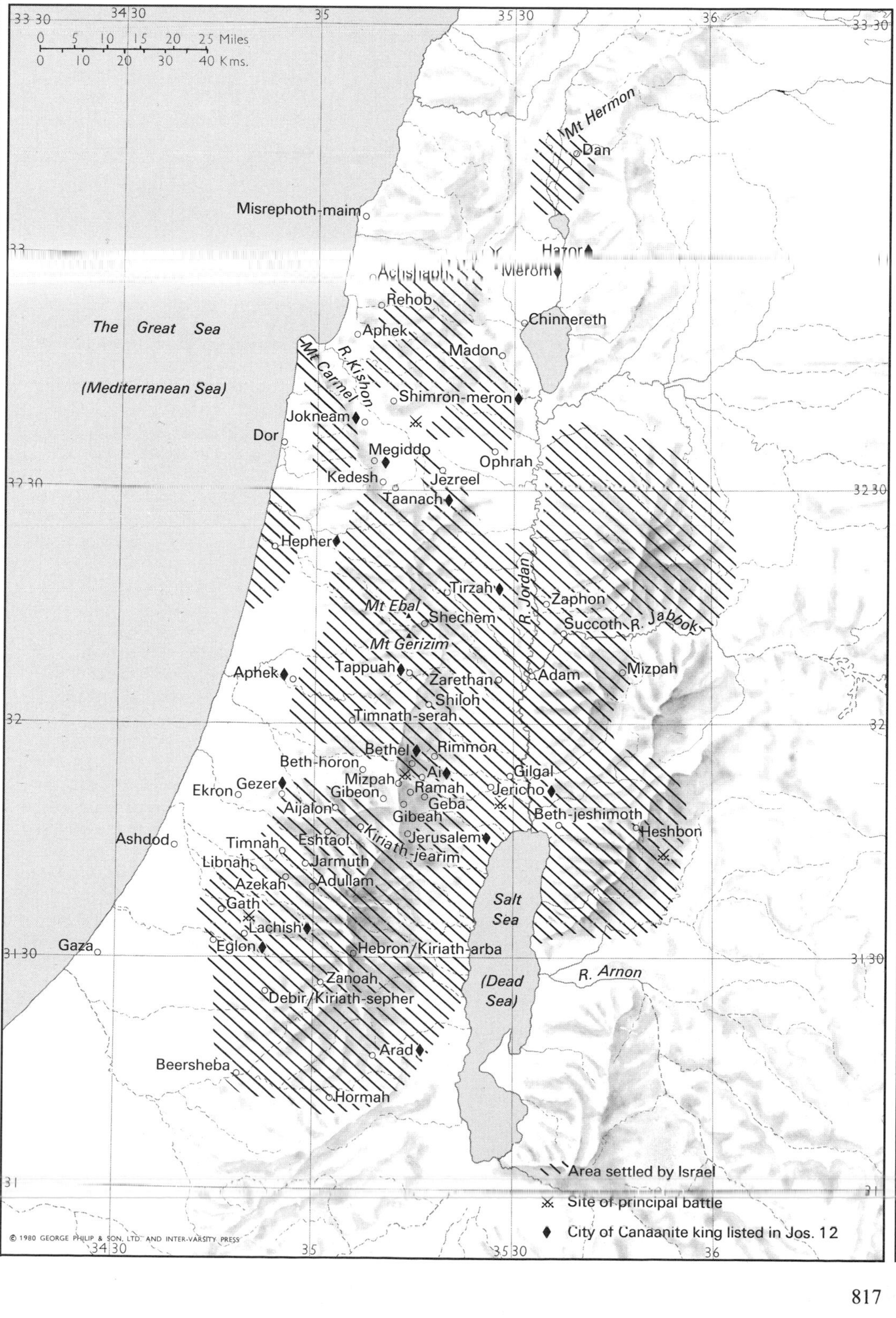

the partition includes a full description of Judahite territory, and notes on the Kenite settlement of Hebron and the difficulties experienced in N Manasseh. After referring to the levitical settlements and the problem of the Transjordanian tribes, the book closes with an account of Joshua's spiritual testament, the climax being the national covenant at Shechem.

I. Outline of contents

a. The invasion of Canaan (1:1–11:23)

(i) *Change of command* (1:1–4:24). Commission; reconnaissance; the river crossing.

(ii) *The bridgehead* (5:1–8:35). Gilgal to Ai.

(iii) *Campaign in the south* (9:1–10:43). The Hivite cities; defeat of the Jerusalem confederacy; cities captured.

(iv) *Campaign in the north, and further progress* (11:1–23).

b. The settlement in Canaan (12:1–24:33)

(i) *List of defeated enemies* (12:1–24).

(ii) *The early settlements* (13:1–17:18). Unfinished tasks; Transjordan; Caleb; the land of Judah; allotments for Ephraim and Manasseh.

(iii) *Later settlements* (18:1–21:45). Shiloh conference; cities of refuge; levitical towns.

(iv) *The way ahead* (22:1–24:33). The Witness Altar; Joshua's charge; the covenant at Shechem.

II. Composition and purpose

In the Heb. Bible, Jos. heads the 'Former Prophets', which cover Israelite history from the invasion to the Exile. In immediate and natural sequence to Dt., the book extends from Joshua's assumption of command to his passing and the death of Eleazar. Chs. 1–11 form a continuous narrative, though the treatment is progressively more summary, ending with a general evaluation of Joshua's achievement (11:15–23). In whatever form the author found his material, he has made of it a story of the highest dramatic quality, alike in treatment of the subject and in narrative technique. This is no mere editing of pre-existing work; but much is omitted or generalized to get the broad picture, in due proportions, into a limited space.

A climax is reached at the end of ch. 11, but the story is not finished. The book is about Joshua's work, and about the fulfilment of God's promises in that Israel was in possession of the land 'which I swore to their fathers to give them' (1:6, *cf.* 23:14; 24:13). For both purposes it must give an account of the settlement, and show the position of strength in which Joshua left the nation. In this part there is much use of sources, some of which reappear elsewhere (Nu., Jdg., Ch.), The author keeps firm control of his material, editing heavily in places (*e.g.* ch. 20, and probably in most of the boundary lists). Joshua's 'farewell to the nation' is recorded in ch. 23; but from the prophetic viewpoint his work was really crowned by the Shechem Covenant, though this may have been much earlier (24:28; RSV 'then', v. 1, is intrusive).

III. Authorship, sources, date

Dt. echoes strongly in Jos., both in its purpose and its language. There is also much (especially in the second part) of quite another stamp. It was therefore natural that Pentateuchal source-analysis was projected into Jos., and the concept of a 'Hexateuch' has been promoted. The theory has been largely unsuccessful because (*a*) insecure criteria have bred disagreement and increasing confusion in the analysis; (*b*) the 'priestly source' (P) is especially difficult to identify, and Jos. raises in an acute form the disputed question whether such a source was ever an independent narrative (see C. R. North, *The Old Testament and Modern Study*, 1951); (*c*) in its general form and concept, Jos. is much more one of the Former Prophets than part of the Law.

A fresh approach was made by M. Noth, stressing the importance of traditions and trying to see how they were developed. Noth concluded that an author belonging to a 'deuteronomic school' had edited old compilations of sanctuary traditions and settlement records to form the 'Joshua' part of a complete deuteronomic history, subsequently retouched by P. This lead has been widely taken, and is accepted in the main by Gray and Soggin (latest commentaries in English). Implications for dating depend on the view taken of Dt. itself. The term 'deuteronomistic' becomes assimilated to 'prophetic', and the theory fails to explain why there is so little 'deuteronomic style' in Jdg. (*cf.* S. R. Driver, *LOT*[9], pp. 112, 126ff.; C. F. Burney, *Judges*, 1920, pp. xliff.).

Noth emphasized the extent of aetiology (stories explaining names and monuments) in the traditions, and took an extremely sceptical view of its value (criticized by J. Bright, *Early Israel in Recent History Writing*, 1956). Others have explored the role of religious festivals in tradition-history, but the reconstructions are largely speculative.

IV. Historical evaluation

The account of the invasion has often been criticized as 'unrealistic', presenting a 'total reduction' of Canaan in contrast to the 'more sober account' in Jdg. 1 (Gray, p. 43). This assessment misinterprets both books. Jos. does not say that all was over in two campaigns (11:18), and it preserves hints of trouble (15:63; 17:12–18) which could easily have been omitted; but it is primarily concerned with the great measure of success in the invasion, and with the reasons for it. On the other hand, Jdg. 1 is not an account of the invasion; it highlights the beginnings of failure, but the whole book would be pointless if there had not been great success.

Many scholars have imagined an invasion by independent tribes (see H. H. Rowley, *From Joseph to Joshua*, 1948). Noth went so far as to claim that Israel was formed in Canaan as an 'amphictyony' (holy alliance, on the Gk. analogy); *cf.* Bright, *op. cit.*, pp. 83ff., for criticism; and B. D. Rathjen, *JNES* 24, 1965, pp. 100–104. Archaeological evidence is still very incomplete, and its interpretation often uncertain, but there is enough proof of the destruction of Canaanite society (*e.g.* Hazor, Tell Beit Mirsim) to demand that the invasion be taken seriously. Theories of a piecemeal invasion must restrict Joshua's role to that of a local leader, or at most an arbitrator (Soggin, pp. 14–18). The ground of such theories lies not so much in any analysis of Joshua–Judges as in the devaluation of Moses' work.

The crux of the biblical account is that the 'Sinai tradition' is the authentic tap-root of Israel's faith and hence of her political being (see Jos. 24). G. E. Mendenhall (*BA* 25, 1962, pp. 66–87) sees it as precipitating a liberation movement in Canaan, but he overstates the case. Biblical evidence of the absorption of non-Israelite elements into the tribal system presupposes the system itself, based ultimately on kinship.

V. Spiritual content

The importance of Joshua for Christians lies chiefly in that it (*a*) shows God's faithfulness to his covenant (*cf.* Dt. 7:7; 9:5f.); (*b*) records the development of his purpose for the nation; (*c*) gives reasons for a failure, already foreshadowed (17:13; 18:3), to carry out the divine plan; (*d*) provides analogies for discipleship, since the spiritual issues of faith, obedience and purity were clearly at stake in the invasion.

Israel under Joshua showed better morale than their fathers, but were no less susceptible to polytheism and nature-religion (Nu. 25; Dt. 4:3, 23). Determination to extirpate the Canaanites and their religion was therefore of prime importance (*cf.* Gn. 15:16; Ex. 20:2–6; 23:23–33; 34:10–17; Nu. 31:15ff.; Dt. 7). The Israelites could not understand or give effect to a redemptive approach, while daily contact with Canaanite culture would jeopardize their own faith in a unique, all-powerful God, as well as their moral standards, as the sequel showed. Moreover, salvation by grace could not be generally offered (as under the NT) before its necessary judicial ground had been publicly set out in Christ's death; but we see a pattern of it in God's dealing with Rahab (*cf.* Heb. 11:31). God's purpose at the time was not to teach Christianity, but to prepare the way for Christ through Israel.

The experiences of Israel in Canaan, as in the deserts, were 'written for our admonition' (1 Cor. 10:11). The chief theme of the book is that God gave Israel rest, which their unbelieving fathers had failed to obtain (Ps. 95:11). In Heb. 4:1–11 it is shown that this is a 'type'; the principle, which the Psalmist applied in his own generation, is equally valid for the Christian, while the promise is completely fulfilled (v. 8) only in the rest which God has provided for us in Christ (*cf.* J. N. Darby, *Synopsis*, 1, p. 328). If this is the primary application of the invasion story, there is also much to be learnt from the successes and failures, and from Joshua's leadership.

VI. Text and translations

Apart from topographical problems, the Heb. text contains few obscurities. The LXX maintains an average standard; its Heb. original does not appear materially different from the *MT*.

BIBLIOGRAPHY. *Text:* Benjamin, *Variations between the Hebrew and Greek texts of Joshua*, 1921. *Commentaries:* J. A. Soggin, *Joshua*, E.T. 1972; J. Gray, *Joshua, Judges and Ruth*, 1967; J. Bright, *Joshua, IB*, 2, 1953; M. Noth, *Josua*[2] (German), 1953. *Historical:* S. Yeivin, *Israelite Conquest of Canaan*, 1971; *LOB*; W. F. Albright, *Archaeology and the Religion of Israel*, 1956; and relevant portions of general works. J.P.U.L.

Passages in Numbers and Deuteronomy recalled in Joshua

Joshua	Numbers	Dt.	Subject	Notes
1:1–9		31	Joshua commissioned	Especially Dt. 31:6, 7f., 12b, 23.
1:3–4		11:24	Extent of promises	Slight differences in phrasing.
1:12–15	32	3:18f.	Eastern tribes	Phrasing echoes Dt., with variations.
8:30–35		11:29–32; 27	Reading the Law at Shechem	Jos. abbreviates, but also mentions ark and foreigners.
12:1–16	21:21–35	2:26–3:17; 4:45–49	Conquests in Transjordan	Dt. 3:1f. = Nu. 21:33f.; Jos. phrases occur in various places in Dt.
13:6–7	34:13, 17		'divide this land'	Verbs differ.
13:8–12, 15–31	32:33–42	2:36; 3:8ff.	Settlement in Transjordan	Distinctive description of Aroer in Jos. and Dt.
13:14, 33	18:24	14:27	No territory for Levi	*Cf.* Dt. 18:1f.
14:1	34:17		Joshua and Eleazar	*Cf.* Jos. 19:51.
14:6ff.	14:24	1:28–36	Caleb's inheritance	
15:1–4	34:3–5		South frontier	'Your,' Jos. 15:4, as Nu. 34:3.
17:3–6	27:1–11		Women's inheritance	
18:4–10	34:13–29		Commission for the partition	10 supervisors nominated in Nu., 21 scribes in Jos.
20	35:9–29	19:1–13	Sanctuary towns	Joshua expands on acceptance procedure, but is otherwise brief.
20		4:41–43	Transjordan towns	
21	35:2–8		Levitical towns	
23:3		1:30	'God fights for you'	*Cf.* Ex. 14:14.
23:6		5:32	'turn not . . .'	
23:8		10:20 *etc.*	'cleave to him'	v. 7 'make mention' *cf.* Ex. 23:13.
23:13	33:55		'thorns in your side'	*s^e^nînîm* only here.

Passages in Numbers and Deuteronomy recalled in Joshua.

JOSIAH (Heb. *yō'šiyyāhû*, **2** as *yō'šiyyā*, 'May Yahweh give').

1. The 17th king of Judah. As son of Amon and grandson of Manasseh, the 'people of the land' enthroned him at the age of 8 upon the assassination of his father. He reigned for 31 years (*c.* 640–609 BC; 2 Ki. 21:24–25:1; 2 Ch. 33:25–34:1).

Assyria, while still Judah's overlord, was weak enough for the vassal to take cautious steps towards freedom. In 633/2 BC, Josiah, in turning back to Yahweh (2 Ch. 34:32), was turning away from an imposed dependence on Assyria and its gods. By 629/8 BC, Ashurbanipal being aged, Josiah was able to free the country of Assyrian as well as residual native cultic practices (2 Ch. 34:3b–5). Not only was this carried out in Judah, which Josiah must have taken from the control of the weakening Assyrians, but also extended into Israel (2 Ch. 34:6–7).

Left: *the smallest letter in the Hebrew alphabet,* y (*Heb.* yôḏ, AV *'jot'*). Centre and right: *the letters* r (*Heb.* rēš) *and* d (*Heb.* dālet), *distinguished from each other by the addition of a 'tittle' to the latter. Hebrew script of the 1st cent.* AD.

This period of religious reform and political emancipation also produced the great prophet Jeremiah a year later (Je. 1:2).

In 622/1 BC, the 'book of the law' was found during the course of Temple repairs (2 Ki. 22:8–10; 2 Ch. 34:8–18). It is commonly accepted that this scroll was, or contained, the book of Deuteronomy, although this is not proven. This collection of ancient law, fanning the already burning feeling of nationalism, led to further political and religious reform. On the basis of this book, Josiah obliterated pagan worship (2 Ki. 23:4–14), including the false priests (*k^{e}mārîm*, Akk. *kumru*; 2 Ki. 23:5) and the altar at Bethel (2 Ki. 23:15; *cf.* 1 Ki. 13:2). He and the people made a new covenant with Yahweh (2 Ki. 23:1–3; 2 Ch. 34:29–33) which would make this book the law of the land. He also celebrated the Passover in such a grand style as had not been seen since the days of Samuel (2 Ki. 23:21–23; 2 Ch. 35:1–19).

In 609 BC, *Neco II of Egypt went from the Egyp. outpost in Megiddo to Harran in aid of the Assyrians (A. K. Grayson, *Assyrian and Babylonian Chronicles*, 1975, p. 96, ll. 66–69), whose king had been driven out of his capital by Babylonia and the Medes. Seeing Egypt as a threat to his own kingdom, in spite of Neco's denial, Josiah met him in Esdraelon, and was severely wounded, dying in Jerusalem (2 Ki. 23:29–30; 2 Ch. 35:20–24).

2. An Israelite during the time of Zechariah who had not been exiled to Babylon (Zc. 6:10).

BIBLIOGRAPHY: A. Malamat, *Journal of the Ancient Near Eastern Society of Columbia University* 5, 1973, pp. 167–179; *Josiah und das Gesetzbuch*; John McKay, *Religion in Judah under the Assyrians*, 1973, pp. 28–44; M. Cogan, *Imperialism and Religion*, 1974, pp. 71–72.

D.W.B.

JOT AND TITTLE. In Mt. 5:18 (AV) 'jot' is a transliteration of *iōta* (RSV), the name of the Gk. *i*; here, however, it stands for the corresponding Heb. *yôḏ*, the smallest letter of the alphabet, the use of which is frequently optional. 'Tittle' is a variant spelling for 'title', which in older Eng. meant a stroke above an abridged word, and then any minor stroke. Here and in Lk. 16:17 it represents *keraia*, meaning a horn, and refers to the minor strokes which distinguish one letter from another, *e.g.* in Heb. *bêṯ* and *kap̄*, *dāleṯ* and *rēš*.

H.L.E.

JOTBAH. Birthplace of Manasseh's wife (2 Ki. 21:19). Conquered by Tiglath-pileser III (*ANET*, p. 283). Called Jotapata during the Roman period (Jos., *BJ* 2. 573). Tentatively identified with Khirbet Jefat (W. F. Albright, *JBL* 58, 1939, pp. 184f.), *c.* 20 km E of Sea of Galilee.

D.W.B.

JOTBATHAH. A stopping-place in the Israelites' wilderness wanderings (Nu. 33:33–34; Dt. 10:7). Described in Dt. as 'a land of brooks of water', it is identified with either 'Ain Ṭābah in the Arabah N of Elath or perhaps more accurately with Ṭabeh, about 11 km S of Elath on the W shore of the Gulf of Aqabah (*LOB*, p. 183).

W.O.

JOTHAM (Heb. *yôṯām*, 'Yahweh is perfect'). **1.** The youngest of the 70 legitimate sons of Jerubbaal (Gideon), and sole survivor of Abimelech's massacre of the other brothers. Through the parable of the trees selecting the bramble to be their king (an honour previously declined by the cedar, the olive and the vine), Jotham warned the Shechemites against Abimelech (Jdg. 9:5ff.). The warning was ignored, and the curse that he uttered was fulfilled 3 years later (v. 57).

2. Son of Uzziah (Mt. 1:9), and 12th king of Judah. He began his reign as co-regent *c.* 750 BC when his father was found to be a leper (2 Ki. 15:5), and was sole monarch *c.* 740–*c.* 732 BC (*CHRONOLOGY OF THE OLD TESTAMENT). A man who feared God, Jotham built the high gate of the Temple, fortified and extended the land of Judah and subdued the Ammonites (2 Ch. 27:3–6). **3.** A son of Jahdai and descendant from Caleb (1 Ch. 2:47).

J.D.D.

JOY. The biblical words are: Heb. *śimḥâ*, verb *śāmēaḥ*, which imply also its outward expression (*cf.* the Arab. cognate, meaning 'to be excited'), and less usually *gîl* (verb and noun); Gk. *chara* (verb *chairō*), and *agalliasis* (frequently used in LXX, and corresponding to *śimḥâ*), meaning intense joy.

In both OT and NT joy is consistently the mark both individually of the believer and corporately of the church. It is a quality, and not simply an emotion, grounded upon God himself and indeed derived from him (Ps. 16:11; Phil. 4:4; Rom. 15:13), which characterizes the Christian's life on earth (1 Pet. 1:8), and also anticipates eschatologically the joy of being with Christ for ever in the kingdom of heaven (*cf.* Rev. 19:7).

I. In the Old Testament

Joy is related to the total national and religious life of Israel, and is particularly expressed in terms of noisy, tumultuous excitement at festivals, sacrifices and enthronements (Dt. 12:6f.; 1 Sa. 18:6; 1 Ki. 1:39f.). Spontaneous joy is a prevailing feature of the Psalter, where it is a mark both of corporate worship (largely centred on the Temple, Pss. 42:4; 81:41) and of personal adoration (Pss. 16:8f.; 43:4). Isaiah conceives of joy in other than simply ritual terms (*cf.* Ps. 126), and he associates it with the fullness of God's salvation, and therefore (in terms of a cosmic rejoicing) with the anticipation of a future state (Is. 49:13; 61:10f.). In later Judaism, as a result, joy is a characteristic of the last days.

II. In the New Testament

The Synoptic Gospels record the note of joy in connection with the proclamation, in its varied forms, of the good news of the kingdom: for example, at the Saviour's birth (Lk. 2:10), at the triumphal entry (Mk. 11:9f.; Lk. 19:37), and after the resurrection (Mt. 28:8). In the Fourth Gospel it is Jesus himself who communicates this joy (Jn. 15:11; 16:24), and it now becomes the result of a deep fellowship between the church and himself (*cf.* 16:22).

In Acts joy marks the life of the early church. It accompanies the gift of the Holy Spirit to the disciples (Acts 13:52), the miracles performed in the name of Christ (8:8), and the fact and report of the conversion of the Gentiles (15:3); it also characterizes the eucharistic meal (2:46).

Paul uses the term *chara* in three ways. First, progress in the faith on the part of the members of the body of Christ, and particularly those he has led to Christ, is a cause for joy—he describes them, indeed, as *hē chara hēmōn*, 'our joy' (1 Thes. 2:19f.; *cf.* Phil. 2:2).

Secondly, Christian joy may paradoxically be the outcome of suffering and even sorrow for Christ's sake (Col. 1:24; 2 Cor. 6:10; *cf.* 1 Pet. 4:13; Heb. 10:34, *etc.*), since it is produced by the Lord and not by ourselves. Joy is in fact, finally, a gift of the Holy Spirit (Gal. 5:22), and is therefore something dynamic and not static. Moreover, it derives from love—God's and ours—and is therefore closely associated with love in Paul's list of the fruit of the Spirit. But since it is a gift which may be interrupted by sin, every believer is called upon to share in the joy of Christ by a daily walk with him and a daily practice of rejoicing in the knowledge of him and his salvation (1 Thes. 5:16; Phil. 3:1; 4:4; 1 Pet. 1:8).

BIBLIOGRAPHY. The standard work on the subject is E. G. Gulin, *Die Freude im Neuen Testament*, 1932; see also J. Moffatt, *Grace in the New Testament*, 1931, p. 168, for the relation between *chara* and *charis*; E. Beyreuther, G. Finkenrath, *NIDNTT* 2, pp. 352–361; *TDNT* 1, pp. 19–21; 2, pp. 772–775; 9, pp. 359–372.

S.S.S.

JOZACHAR (Heb. *yôzāḵār*, 'Yahweh has remembered'). A servant of Joash who took part in his assassination (2 Ki. 12:21–22) but was subsequently executed by Amaziah (2 Ki. 14:5). Some MSS read 'Jozabad' in 2 Ki. 12:22, abbreviated to 'Zabad' in 2 Ch. 24:26, by confusion with the similar name of the other assassin, Jehozabad.

D.W.B.

JUBAL. A son of Adah, wife of Lamech, and ancestor of those who 'handle the harp (*kinnôr*) and pipe (*'ûgāḇ*)' (Gn. 4:21). (*MUSIC AND MUSICAL INSTRUMENTS.)

T.C.M.

JUBILEES, BOOK OF. A Jewish intertestamental work, extant completely only in Ethiopic and partly in Latin, though fragments in the original Heb. have now been found at Qumran. It was probably written in the late 2nd century BC in (proto-) Essene circles shortly before the Qumran sect came into existence. It was popular at Qumran, where its special legal precepts and calendar were observed. (It is cited by name in CD 16. 13f.)

Jubilees is a midrash or legendary rewriting of Genesis and the early chapters of Exodus. It gives the biblical history a detailed chronology, calculated in jubilee periods of 49 years, each divided into 7 weeks of years, each year a solar year of 364 days. The revelation at Sinai occurs in the 50th jubilee since the Creation. (Several texts from Qumran employ jubilee periods in historical and eschatological speculation.)

Jubilees supplements the biblical narrative with legends about the Patriarchs, passages of eschatological prophecy and legal material endorsing a strict sectarian interpretation of the Law. In opposition to hellenizing influences, the author glorifies the Law as distinguishing Israel from the Gentiles. The solar calendar has the same effect of setting Israel apart from the Gentiles, and faithful Israel from apostate Israel, only this calendar ensures the observance of the festivals on the correct dates.

The *Jubilees* *calendar derives from *1 Enoch* and was observed at Qumran. A day of the month falls on the same day of the week every year; *e.g.* New Year's day always falls on a Wednesday. Some scholars have suggested, as a solution to the problem of the date of the Last Supper, that Jesus celebrated the Passover according to this calendar, *i.e.* on a Tuesday evening.

BIBLIOGRAPHY. R. H. Charles, *The Book of Jubilees*, 1902; G. L. Davenport, *The Eschatology of the Book of Jubilees*, 1971; A. Jaubert, *The Date of the Last Supper*, 1963.

R.J.B.

JUDAEA. The Gk. and Rom. designation of the land of *Judah. The word is actually an adjective ('Jewish') with *gē* ('land') or *chōra* ('country') understood. After the Roman conquest (63 BC) it appears both in a wider sense, denoting all

JOZABAD
See Jozachar, Part 2.

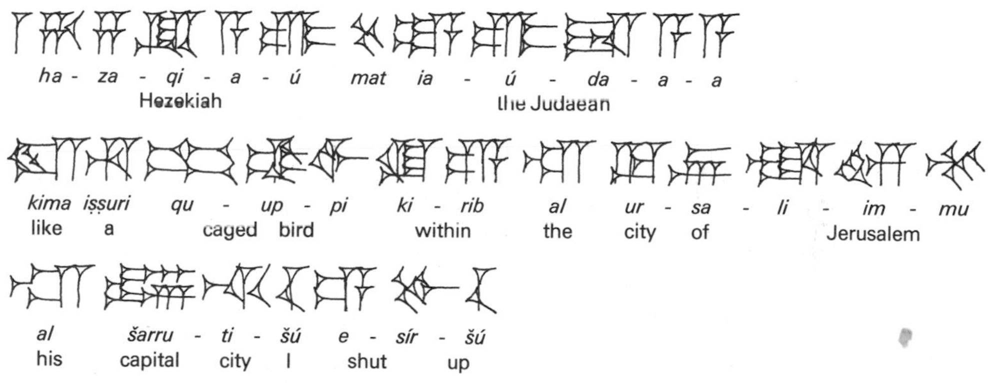
ha - za - qi - a - ú mat ia - ú - da - a - a
Hezekiah the Judaean
kima iṣṣuri qu - up - pi ki - rib al ur - sa - li - im - mu
like a caged bird within the city of Jerusalem
al šarru - ti - šú e - sír - šú
his capital city I shut up

Hezekiah 'the Judaean' (ḫazaqiau māt Yaudaya) *named on the clay prism which describes the early campaign of Sennacherib (Taylor prism), including the siege of Jerusalem in 701 BC.* (ZR)

The barren hills of the 'wilderness of Judaea' between Jerusalem and the Dead Sea.

Palestine, including Galilee and Samaria, and in the narrower sense, which excludes these two regions. Herod's kingdom of Judaea (37–4 BC) included all Palestine and some districts E of the Jordan. Archelaus' ethnarchy of Judaea (4 BC–AD 6) embraced Judaea in the narrower sense and Samaria, and the same is true of the Rom. province of Judaea from AD 6 to 41. After the death of Herod Agrippa I in AD 44 the Rom. province of Judaea included Galilee also. (* ISRAEL.)

The 'wilderness of Judaea' (Mt. 3:1), associated with John the Baptist, is probably identical with the 'wilderness of Judah' (Jdg. 1:16, *etc.*), *i.e.* the desert to the W of the Dead Sea. J.D.D.

JUDAH.

I. The son of Jacob

The 4th son of Jacob by Leah (Gn. 29:35) was called Judah (*y^{e}hûḏâ*); the name is there explained as meaning 'praised', as derived from the root *ydh*, 'to praise'. Gn. 49:8 contains a play on this meaning. The derivation is widely rejected, but no other suggested etymology has been generally accepted (for literature, see *KB*). Judah early took a leading role among his brothers, as is shown by the story of Joseph (Gn. 37:26–27; 43:3–10; 44:16–34; 46:28). Gn. 38, though throwing light on the beginnings of the tribe of Judah, clearly stands in its present position to contrast Judah's character with that of Joseph. Though Gn. 49:8–12 is not strictly a promise to Judah of kingship, but rather of leadership, victory and tribal stability, the promise of * Shiloh involves kingship ultimately. The genealogies of Judah's descendants are found in 1 Ch. 2–4.

II. Other individuals of the same name

After the Babylonian Exile Judah became increasingly one of the favourite names among the Jews. Five men of this name are mentioned in the OT, *viz.* a Levite, ancestor of Kadmiel (Ezr. 3:9), possibly the father or son of Hodaviah (Ezr. 2:40); a Levite of the return under Zerubbabel (Ne. 12:8); a levitical contemporary of Ezra (Ezr. 10:23); a leading Benjaminite under Nehemiah (Ne. 11:9); a priest under Nehemiah (Ne. 12:36). In Ne. 12:34 probably members of the tribe in general are meant by 'Judah'. In the NT the name is represented by its Hellenized form *Judas (shortened to Jude in Jude 1).

III. The tribe of Judah

a. From the Exodus till Saul

Judah plays no special role in the story of the Exodus and of the wilderness wanderings, though it is to be noted that he was the leader of the vanguard (Nu. 2:9). There is no significant change in the two census figures from this period (Nu. 1:27; 26:22).

Judah's family tree according to 1 Ch. 2:3–6.

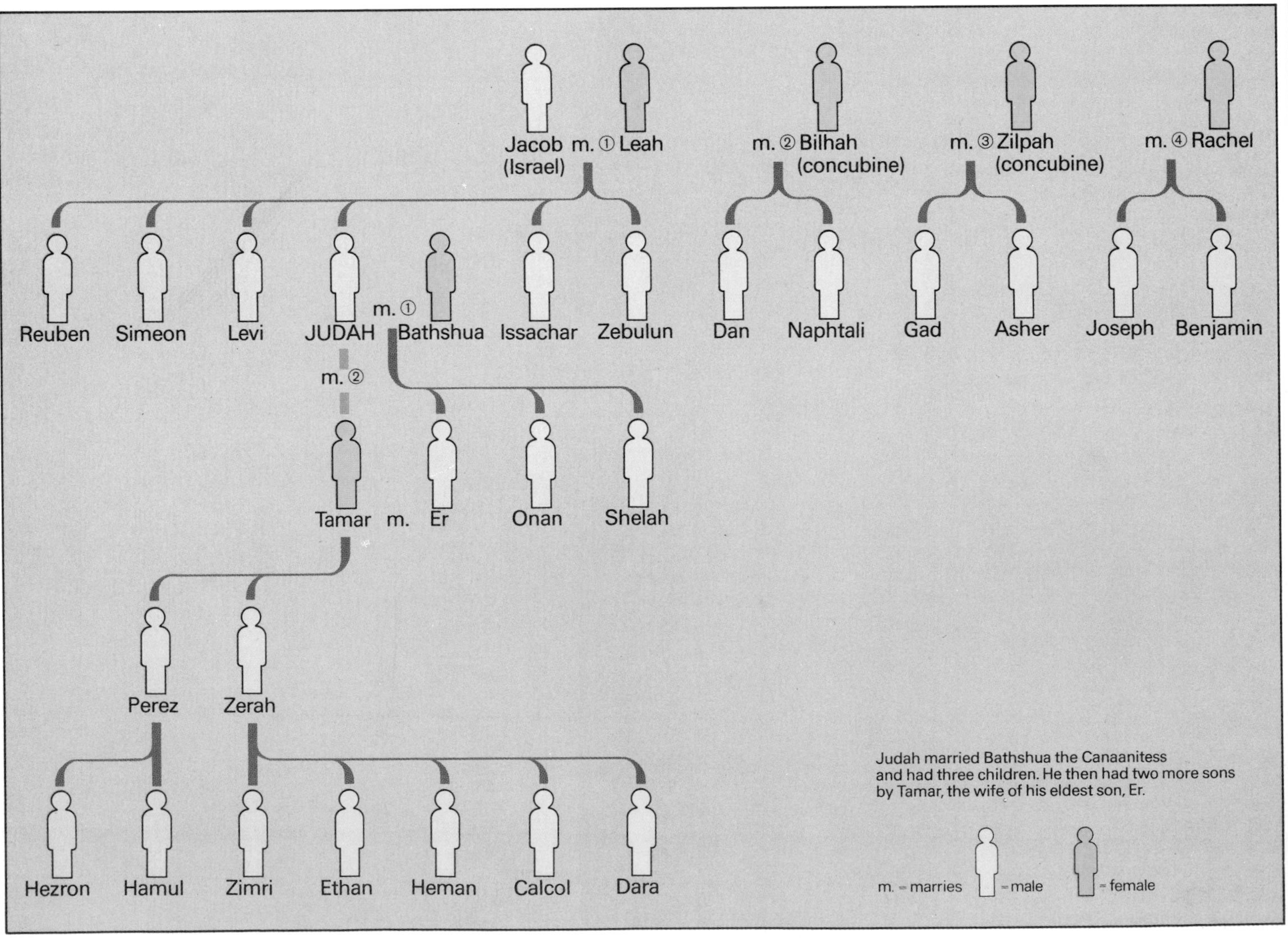

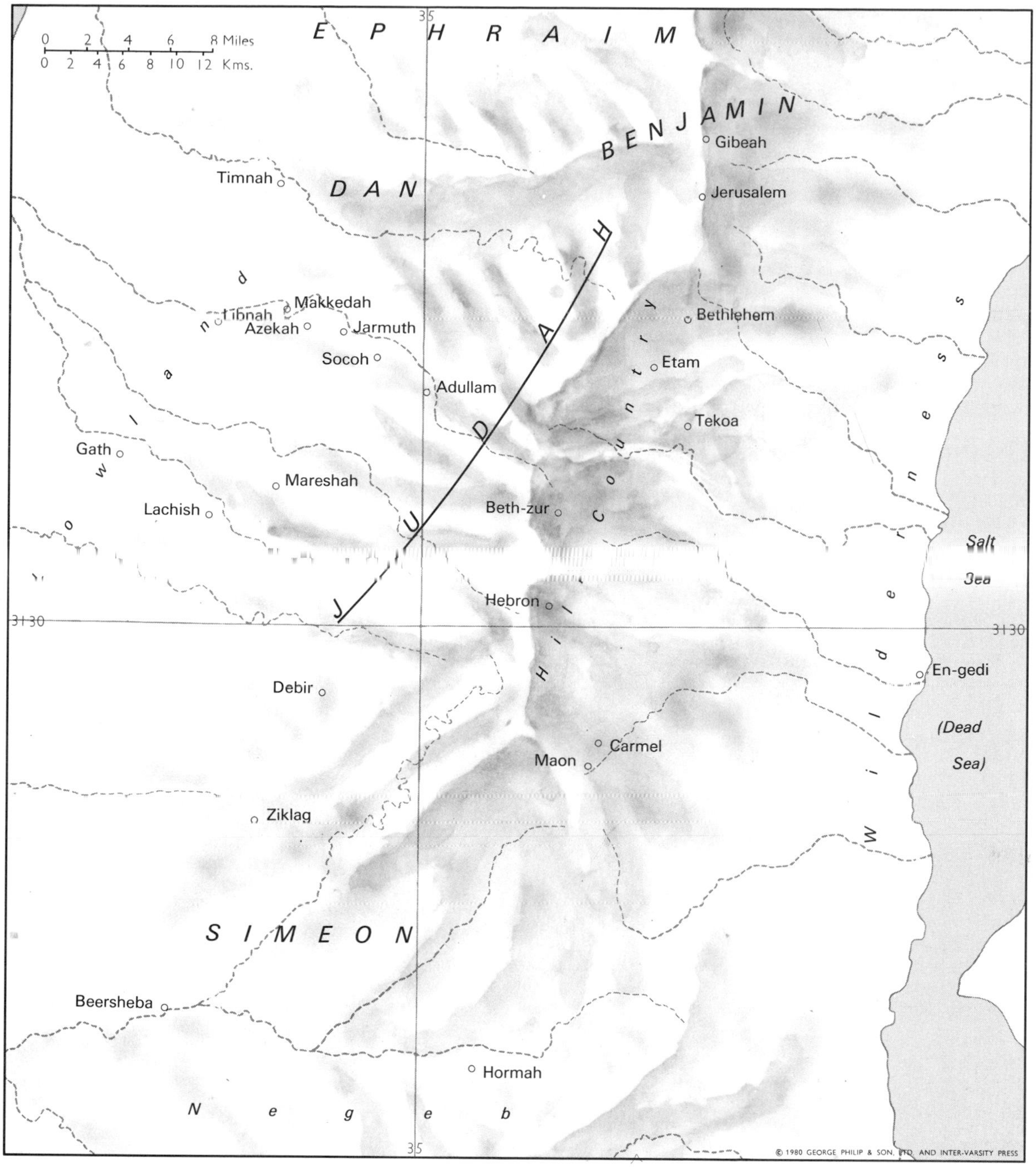

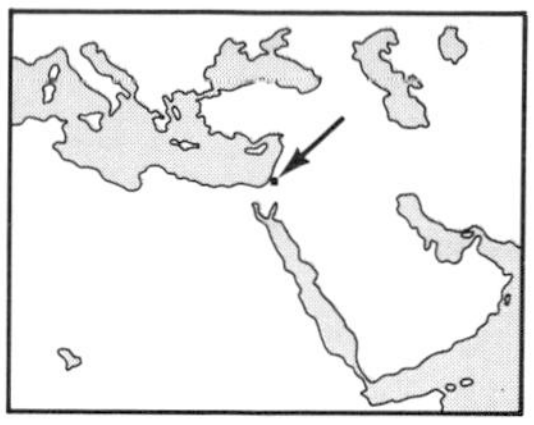

The land allotted to Judah.

Achan, a member of the tribe, was the cause of the defeat of Israel before Ai (Jos. 7). This may be the reason for the special task laid on Judah to lead an independent attack on the Canaanites (Jdg. 1:1–2). No explanation is given, but it is clear that Judah's portion was allocated not by lot in Shiloh (Jos. 18:1–10) but before its conquest (Jdg. 1:3); *cf.* the similar treatment of Ephraim and half Manasseh (Jos. 16–17). It was bounded on the N by the portions of Dan and Benjamin, and ran approximately E and W from the N end of the Dead Sea, S of Jerusalem and the Gibeonite tetrapolis to the Mediterranean. Its W and E frontiers were the Mediterranean and the Dead Sea, and it extended S as far as cultivation permitted (*cf.* Jos. 15).

Judah first overran most of the coastal plain, soon to be occupied by the Philistines (Jdg. 1:18), but evidently quickly withdrew from the struggle (Jdg. 1:19; 3:3; Jos. 11:22; 13:2–3). Since it was the best of the land apportioned to him that Judah voluntarily abandoned to Simeon (Jos. 19:1, 9), it is reasonable to suppose that he hoped to have Simeon as a buffer between him and the unconquered coastal plain.

The story of the conquest of the S in Jdg. 1:1–17 has been very widely interpreted to mean that Judah (and other tribes) entered the land from the S *before* the invasion under Joshua (*cf.* H. H. Rowley, *From Joseph to Joshua*, 1950, pp. 4f., 101f., 110ff., with literature), but the whole trend of modern archaeological discovery seems to be unfavourable to the theory, which is unacceptable on other, general grounds.

The failure to maintain a hold on Jerusalem (Jdg. 1:8, 21), combined with the existence of the semi-independent Gibeonite tetrapolis (Jos. 9; 2 Sa. 21:1–2), created a psychological frontier between

Judah and the central tribes. Though there was no barrier to communications (*cf.* Jdg. 19:10–13), Judah will increasingly have looked S to Hebron rather than to the sanctuary at Shiloh. While Judah provided the first of the judges, Othniel (Jdg. 3:9–11), and shared in the early action against Benjamin (Jdg. 20:18), he does not seem even to have been expected to join against Jabin and Sisera (Jdg. 5). As a result, when Judah became tributary to the Philistines (Jdg. 15:11), he appears not to have appealed to the other tribes, nor do they seem to have been concerned.

The fact of this division seems to have been generally recognized, for by Saul's time we find the contingent from Judah separately enumerated (1 Sa. 11:8; 15:4; 17:52; 18:16).

b. Under David and Solomon

After Saul's death this growing split was perpetuated by David's being crowned as king in Hebron over Judah (2 Sa. 2:4). A. Alt is probably correct in maintaining ('The Formation of the Israelite State in Palestine', in *Essays on Old Testament History and Religion*, 1966, pp. 216ff.) that the crowning of David as king over 'all Israel' (2 Sa. 5:1–5) made him king of a dual kingdom in which Judah kept its separate identity. Certainly during Absalom's rebellion Judah seems to have maintained its neutrality, while the N followed the rebel.

There is no evidence that Solomon showed any favouritism to Judah compared with the other tribes, for 'and one officer, which was in the land' (1 Ki. 4:19, RVmg.) will refer to Judah (RSV).

IV. The kingdom of Judah

a. Its relations with Israel

If A. Alt's view is correct, Judah and Israel in accepting different kings were acting in accordance with their rights as separate political entities. Apart from Jeroboam himself, the kings of Israel do not seem to have sought the destruction of Judah (*cf.* 2 Ki. 14:13–14), and the prophets never questioned the right of Israel to exist, though they foresaw the time when it would return to its allegiance to 'David'.

The heritage of Solomon's riches seemed to give Judah the advantage at the disruption, despite its less fertile land and smaller population compared with the N. In spite of claims to the contrary, there is no evidence that Rehoboam later disregarded the command of Shemaiah (1 Ki. 12:22–24) and attacked Jeroboam. The suggestion that Shishak's attack on Judah (1 Ki. 14:25–26) was in support of his ally Jeroboam lacks positive evidence in its support. The resultant loss of the wealth Solomon had amassed, even though Israel seems to have suffered from Shishak's attack as well, meant that Judah now stood permanently in a position of material inferiority compared with Israel. The evidence suggests that Judah needed a prosperous Israel for its own prosperity.

One effective test of the absolute, rather than relative, prosperity of Judah was its ability to control Edom, or as much of it as was necessary for the safeguarding of the trade-route to the Gulf of Aqabah. Rehoboam made no effort to maintain his father's precarious hold on the area. Jehoshaphat evidently completely subdued the country (1 Ki. 22:47), but later he had to install a vassal king (2 Ki. 3:9). Edom regained its independence under his son Jehoram (2 Ki. 8:20–22). Amaziah, about half a century later, reconquered Edom (2 Ki. 14:7). This time the conquest was more effective, and not until the troubles of Ahaz' reign 60 years later was Edom finally able to free itself (2 Ki. 16:6). After this Judah does not seem even to have attempted conquest.

It was only a decisive victory by Abijah (or Abijam) that restored a measure of parity between the kingdoms (2 Ch. 13). Asa, faced with the capable Baasha, could maintain it only by allying himself with Ben-hadad, king of Damascus (1 Ki. 15:18–20). The dynasty of Omri, disturbed both by the increasing power of Damascus, and even more by the threat from *Assyria, made peace with Judah, which was later sealed by the marriage of Athaliah, Ahab's daughter, or perhaps sister (2 Ki. 8:26), with Jehoram. It is widely held that at this time Judah was Israel's vassal. So far from this being true, the evidence suggests that Jehoshaphat used Israel as a buffer between him and Assyria. This is the most likely explanation why Judah does not figure on Shalmaneser's list of his enemies at the battle of Qarqar, nor for that matter on the 'Black Obelisk'. He seems to have looked on, with the sole exception of the battle of Ramoth-gilead (1 Ki. 22:1–38), while Israel and Damascus tore at one another's vitals. Hence, by the end of his long reign, he felt himself strong enough to refuse Ahaziah's request for a joint venture to Ophir after the first had failed (1 Ki. 22:48–49 compared with 2 Ch. 20:35–37). The relative equality between the kingdoms at this time is seen in the fact that Jehu, though he had killed Ahaziah of Judah (2 Ki. 9:27), did not venture to carry his anti-Baal campaign into Judah, nor, on the other hand, did Athaliah try to avenge her son's death.

In the century between the accession of Jehu and the deaths of Jeroboam II and Uzziah the fortunes of Judah seem to have kept pace with those of Israel both in affliction and prosperity. Probably the latter came more slowly to the S, even as the hollowness of its prosperity was revealed somewhat later than in Israel.

b. Earlier foreign enemies

Until the collapse of Israel the history of Judah is singularly uninfluenced by foreign threats. Shishak's invasion was a last stirring of Egypt's ancient power until the Assyr. advance forced it to measures of self-defence. The Philistines had been so weakened that we find them as aggressors only when Judah was weakest, *viz.* under Jehoram (2 Ch. 21:16) and Ahaz (2 Ch. 28:18). At the height of Hazael's power, when he had almost destroyed Israel, Jehoash was forced to become tributary to Damascus, but this cannot have lasted long. In fact, the only two major threats of this period were from those sudden movements that the nomads and semi-nomads of the desert have periodically thrown up. Zerah 'the Cushite' (2 Ch. 14:9) is more likely to have been an Arabian (*cf.* Gn. 10:7) than an Ethiopian, *i.e.* a Sudanese. The second was from a sudden movement of the inhabitants of the Transjordan steppe-land (2 Ch. 20:1, 10).

c. Judah and Assyria

As stated above, the earlier advances of Assyria do not seem to have affected Judah. When Damascus and Israel attacked Ahaz (2 Ki. 16:5), it was a last desperate attempt to unite the remnants of the West against the advance of Tiglath-pileser III. There are no grounds for thinking that Judah was threatened by the Assyrians, for until they wanted to challenge

Egypt they would hardly alarm it by advancing prematurely to its desert frontier. By accepting the suzerainty of Assyria Ahaz virtually sealed the fate of Judah. On the one hand, it remained a vassal until the approaching doom of Assyria (612 BC) could be foreseen; on the other, it was caught up in the intrigues stirred up by Egypt, for which it duly suffered. Hezekiah's revolt in 705 BC, crushed by Sennacherib 4 years later, reduced Judah to a shadow of its former self, at least two-thirds of the population perishing or being carried away captive, and a large portion of its territory being lost. For details, see J. Bright, *A History of Israel*[2], 1972, pp. 282–286, 296–308; *DOTT*, pp. 64–70.

d. Revival and downfall

A revival of religious and nationalistic feeling under the young Josiah began just after Ashurbanipal's death (631 BC), when the weakness of Assyria was already becoming manifest. The steps in reform indicated in 2 Ch. 34:3, 8 suggest how closely interwoven religion and politics had become, for each step was in itself also a rejection of Assyr. religious and therefore political control. By the height of the reform in 621 BC Josiah, though probably still nominally tributary to Assyria, was in fact independent. With or without the approval of his nominal overlord he took over the Assyr. provinces of Samaria and E Galilee (2 Ch. 34:6) and doubtless recovered the territory that Hezekiah had lost as a punishment for his rebellion. There is no reliable evidence that the Scythian inroad, which did so much to give Assyria its mortal wound, affected or even reached Judah.

There is no indication that Josiah offered any opposition to Pharaoh Psammetichus' expedition in aid of Assyria in 616 BC, but when Pharaoh Neco repeated the expedition in 609 BC Josiah evidently felt that in the new international position his only chance of maintaining Judah's independence was to fight, but in the ensuing battle at Megiddo he met his death. There is no evidence for the suggestion that he was acting in alliance with the rising star of * Babylon, though the possibility must not be rejected.

Egypt marked its victory by deposing Josiah's son Jehoahaz and replacing him by his brother Jehoiakim, who had, however, to accept Babylonian overlordship soon after Nebuchadrezzar's victory at Carchemish (605 BC) (Dn. 1:1; 2 Ki. 24:1). In 601 BC Nebuchadrezzar was checked by Neco in a battle near the Egyp. frontier, and on his withdrawal to Babylon Jehoiakim rebelled. Judah was ravaged by Bab. troops and auxiliary levies (2 Ki. 24:2). Jehoiakim died an obscure death in December 598 BC, before he could suffer the full penalty of rebellion, and Jehoiachin, his 18-year-old son, surrendered Jerusalem to Nebuchadrezzar on 16 March 597 BC.

His uncle Zedekiah became the last king of Judah, but revolted in 589 BC. By January 588 BC the Bab. armies were before the walls of Jerusalem. In July 587 BC the walls were breached and Zedekiah was captured to meet a traitor's fate (2 Ki. 25:6–7); a month later the city was burnt down and the walls razed.

e. Religion under the Monarchy

Popular religion in Judah was probably as degraded by concepts of nature-religion as in Israel, but its relative isolation and openness to the desert will have made it less influenced by its Canaanite forms. Its lack of major sanctuaries—only Hebron and Beersheba are known to us, with Gibeon in Benjamin—increased the influence of Jerusalem and its Solomonic Temple. It is questionable whether any king of Israel could even have attempted the centralizing reforms of Hezekiah and Josiah. The Davidic covenant (2 Sa. 7:8–16), far more than the general atmosphere of the 'Fertile Crescent', made the king the undisputed leader of the national religion, even though cultic functions were denied him (2 Ch. 26:16–21).

The power of the king might be used for good, as in the reformations, but where national policy seemed to demand an acceptance of Baal-worship, as under Jehoram, Ahaziah and Athaliah, or a recognition of the Assyr. astral deities, as under Ahaz and Manasseh, there was no effective power that could resist the royal will. The royal authority in matters of religion will also have helped to make the official cult for many merely an external and official matter.

f. Exile (597–538 BC)

Apart from an unspecified number of ordinary captives destined to slavery, Nebuchadrezzar deported the cream of the population in 597 BC (2 Ki. 24:14; Je. 52:28—the difference in figures is doubtless due to different categories of captives being envisaged). A few, including the royal family, became 'guests' of Nebuchadrezzar in Babylon; others, *e.g.* Ezekiel, were settled in communities in Babylonia, where they had apparently full freedom apart from the right to change their domicile; the skilled artisans became part of a mobile labour force used by Nebuchadrezzar in his building operations. The destruction of Jerusalem added to the general total of captives (2 Ki. 25:11), and Je. 52:29 shows there was another group of designated deportees. The murder of Gedaliah, whom Nebuchadrezzar had made governor of Judah, led to a large-scale flight to Egypt (2 Ki. 25:25–26; Je. 41:1 –43:7). This, in turn, was followed in 582 BC by another, obviously punitive, deportation to Babylonia (Je. 52:30).

As the result of deportation and flight Judah was left, and remained, virtually empty (see W. F. Albright, *The Archaeology of Palestine*[2], 1954, pp. 140–142). The land S of a line between Beth-zur and Hebron seems to have been detached from Judah in 597 BC; into it the Edomites gradually moved. As a result, this area was lost to Judah until its capture by John Hyrcanus after 129 BC and the forcible Judaizing of its population. The remainder was placed under the governor of Samaria and deliberately kept virtually empty; there is no evidence for the infiltration of other peoples. It may be presumed that Nebuchadrezzar intended to follow the normal Assyr.–Bab. practice of bringing in settlers from other conquered areas (cf. 2 Ki. 17:24), but for some reason refrained.

V. Post-exilic Judah

a. Restoration

Babylon fell to Cyrus in 539 BC, and the next year he ordered the rebuilding of the Jerusalem Temple (Ezr. 6:3–5); he accompanied this with permission for the deportees and their descendants to return (Ezr. 1:2–4). The list of names, involving a total of some 43,000 persons, in Ezr. 2 may well cover the period 538–522 BC, but there are no solid grounds for doubting that there was an immediate and considerable response to Cyrus' decree.

Sheshbazzar, a member of the Davidic royal family, seems to have been Cyrus' commissioner to oversee the rebuilding of the Temple; he

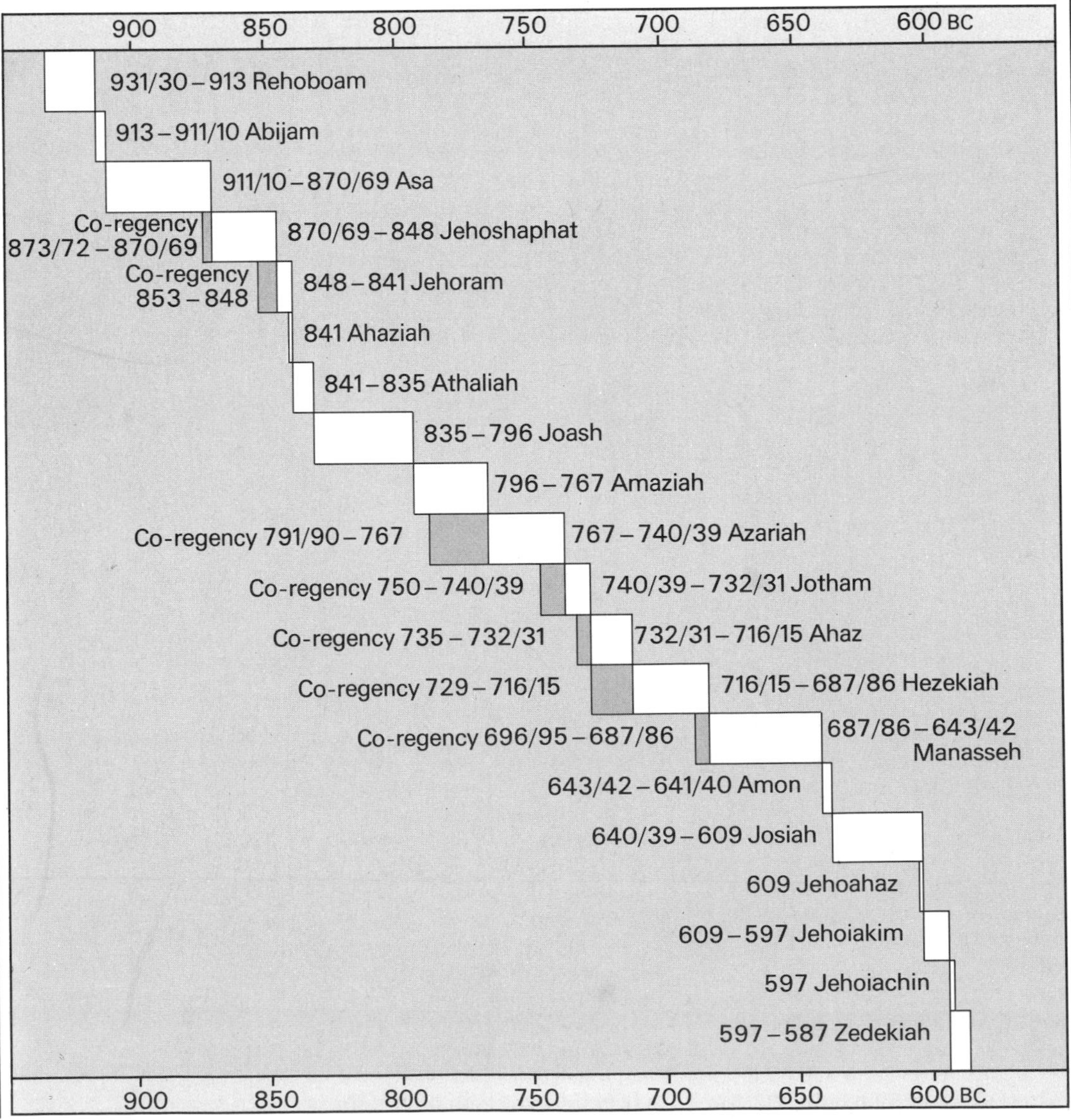

Dates of the kings of Judah.

will have returned (or died?) after the laying of the foundations (Ezr. 5:14, 16). There is no evidence that Judah was detached politically from the district of Samaria until the time of Nehemiah; the title 'governor' given Sheshbazzar is too specific a rendering for *pēḥâ*. Zerubbabel, probably heir-apparent of the royal house, does not seem to have held any official position, the title of *pēḥâ* in Hg. 1:1; 2:21 being probably honorific —note his non-appearance in Ezr. 5:3–17. Other Jewish leaders bore the title *pēḥâ* in the following decades, appointed by the Persians.

By the time of Ezra in the second half of the 4th century it had become apparent to most that political independence and the restoration of the Davidic monarchy were no more than a hope for the more distant future. Ezra transformed the Jews from a national state into a 'church', making the keeping of the Torah the purpose of their existence. The political insignificance of Judaea under the Persians and the relatively peaceful conditions of the country favoured the steady instruction of the mass of the people in the Torah. The only political upheaval of the period may have been a deportation to Babylonia and Hyrcania, though many doubt it (*cf.* Jos., *Contra Apionem* 1. 194).

b. The end of Judah

The campaigns of Alexander the Great will hardly have affected Judaea, but his founding of Alexandria provided a centre for a western, and for the most part voluntary, dispersion, which soon rivalled that of Babylonia and Persia in numbers and surpassed it in wealth and influence. The division of Alexander's empire among his generals meant that Palestine became a debatable land between Syria and Egypt. Till 198 BC it was normally in the hands of the Egyp. Ptolemies, but then it became part of the Syrian Seleucid empire.

The extravagances of the rich Hellenized upper classes of Jerusalem, in large proportion priests, and the unbalanced efforts of Antiochus Epiphanes (175–163 BC) to Hellenize his empire, which led him to forbid circumcision and Sabbath-keeping and to demand the worship of Greek deities, created an alliance between religious zeal and dormant nationalism. The Jews achieved first religious autonomy and then political freedom (140 BC) for the first time since Josiah. By 76 BC their boundaries extended virtually from the traditional Dan to Beersheba. For the history of this meteoric rise and sudden collapse, see *ISRAEL.

When the Romans destroyed the last vestiges of political independence in AD 70, and especially after the crushing of Bar Kochba's revolt in AD 135, Judaea ceased to be a Jewish land, but the name of Judah in its form of Jew became the title of all dispersed through the world who clung to the Mosiac law, irrespective of tribal or national origin.

BIBLIOGRAPHY. Archaeological discovery has put all earlier treatments of the subject to a greater or less degree out of date. John Bright, *A History of Israel*[2], 1972, gives an up-to-date and balanced presentation with a mention of the most important literature. See A. R. Millard, 'The Meaning of the Name Judah', *ZAW* 86, 1974, pp. 246f. For the text of *Kings*, see J. A. Montgomery and H. S. Gehman, *The Books of Kings*, *ICC*, 1951. For extra-biblical texts naming Judah, see J. B. Pritchard, *ANET*[3], 1969; and *DOTT*. For the post-exilic period, see W. O. E. Oesterley, *A History of Israel*, 2, 1932; F. F. Bruce, *Israel and the Nations*, 1963.

H.L.E.

JUDAISM.

I. Definition

Judaism is the religion of the Jews in contrast to that of the OT. In any full study of it, it would be natural to start with the call of Abraham; this would be solely as an introduction. Judaism should be regarded as beginning with the Babylonian Exile, but for the period up to AD 70 the term is best reserved for those elements which are either modifications or extensions of OT concepts. In German works we frequently find the misleading expression 'late Judaism' used for Jewish religion in the time of Christ. It is derived from the theory that the Priestly Code and history in the Hexateuch are exilic or post-exilic and the true beginnings of Judaism.

But it is better to regard Judaism as coming into full existence only after the destruction of the Temple in AD 70 and, except when dealing with those phenomena that continued after this catastrophe, to use the term 'intertestamental religion' for the period between Ezra and Christ. One important reason for this is that, while primitive Christianity did not reject or ignore all the historical developments in the 4 centuries after Ezra, it turned its back on precisely that element in Judaism, viz. its attitude to and interpretation of the Law, that separates it both from Christianity and the OT.

Judaism reached full development by AD 500, *i.e.* about the same time as Catholic Christianity, and like its sister religion has grown and modified ever since. This article, however, rarely goes beyond AD 200, when with the completion of the Mishnah the main concepts of Judaism had become clear. For later periods the reader is referred to articles on Judaism in *ERE*, *JewE*, *EJ*, *etc.*

II. The rise of Judaism

Judaism was made inevitable by Josiah's reformation, which reached its climax in 621 BC. The restriction of legitimate sacrifice to the Temple in Jerusalem inevitably meant that the religion of many became increasingly detached from the sanctuary and sacrifice. This tendency was powerfully reinforced by the Babylonian Exile, the more so because modern research suggests that the blow of divine judgment was too stunning for any formal non-sacrificial worship to have been developed in exile.

The Exile was a time of waiting for restoration; the refusal of the majority to return in 538 BC made a modification in their religion vital, if they were to survive as Jews. It was not enough to develop non-sacrificial worship (this in its official, formulated expression seems to have come later); an outlook on life completely divorceable from sanctuaries was needed. This was found in the Torah or Law of Moses. This was interpreted less as a law code and more as a set of principles which could and should be applied to every area of life and which were binding on all who wished to be known as Jews (Torah means 'instruction' rather than 'law').

Ezra was the true 'Father of Judaism', for he returned from Babylonia to introduce and enforce not a new law but a new way of keeping the old one.

The centuries that followed saw determined opposition to Ezra's policy from the richer priests and others, who by the reign of Antiochus Epiphanes (175–163 BC) were the leaders of the Hellenizers. The majority of the common people (*'am hā-'āreṣ*) tried to evade anything but the clear meaning of the

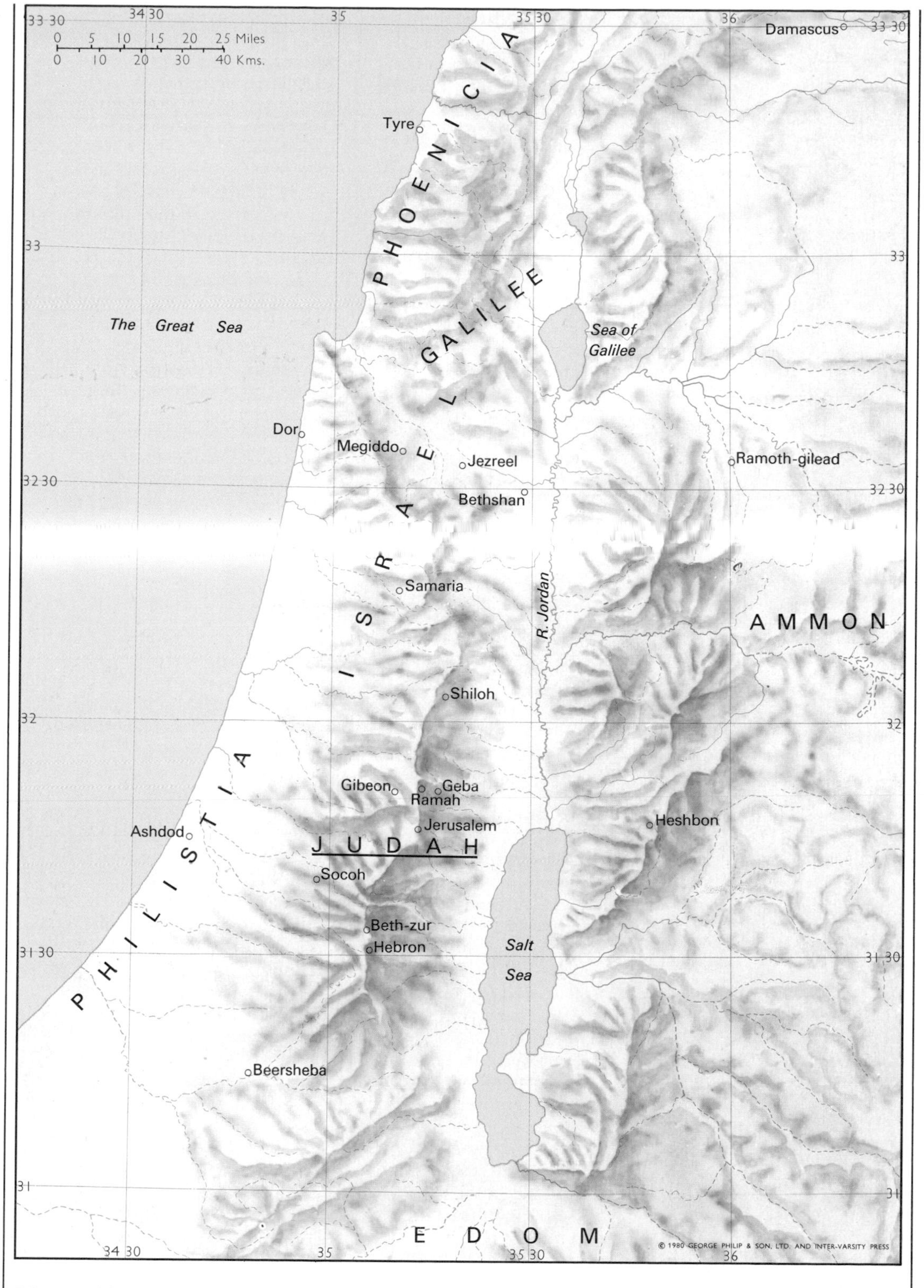

The kingdom of Judah.

Torah. In the W *diaspora* there was a growing assimilation to Greek modes of thought, helped by the prevalent allegorical interpretation of Scripture.

The next milestone in the development of Judaism was the Hellenization of the leading priests of Jerusalem and the subsequent degeneration of the victorious Hasmonean priest-kings (especially Alexander Jannaeus). Temple-worship for the pious became a duty rather than a joy. While the Qumran Covenanters seem to have turned their backs on the Temple, until God should purge it of its evil priests, the *Pharisees exalted the synagogue as the chief means whereby God could be worshipped and his will discovered through the study of the Torah. As a result, by the time of Christ, there were some hundreds of synagogues in Jerusalem itself.

Though the destruction of the Temple in AD 70 came as a shock to the Pharisees and their admirers, they had been prepared for it by its frequent desecration in varying ways from the time of Antiochus Epiphanes onwards, and their synagogue-centred religion was able to adapt itself to the new conditions with great rapidity, the more so as the other religious groups had been destroyed or reduced to impotence. By *c.* AD 90 the Pharisaic leaders, the rabbis, felt strong enough to exclude those they considered heretics (the *mînîm*), including Hebrew Christians, from the synagogue. By AD 200, after a bitter struggle, they had forced the *'am hā-'āreṣ* to conform, if they wished to be regarded as Jews. From then onwards, until Judaism began to be influenced by modern thought, the terms Jew and normative, rabbinic, orthodox or traditional Judaism were essentially coterminous.

It should be noted that, though the Pharisees were always a minority group, there is nothing surprising in the triumph of their views. Even though they were often unpopular, their views seemed the most logical adaptation of the OT to the post-exilic scene, and they became common property by their skilful use of the synagogue.

III. The doctrines of Judaism

It should be clear to the reader of the NT that, however bitter the clash between Christ and Paul on the one hand and their chief opponents on the other, the area of the battle-field was strictly circumscribed. Both sides accepted the same Scriptures—unlike the Sadducees—and, superficially at least, interpreted them in very much the same way. A deep similarity between the teaching of Christ and of the early rabbis has long been recognized, and the discovery of the Qumran MSS has speeded the recognition that the influence of Hellenism on the NT is marginal. Therefore it is sufficient to say here that much of the doctrine of Judaism does not vary significantly either from that of the OT or from that of conservative Christianity. It may therefore be assumed that in matters not mentioned here there was no essential difference down to AD 500. It must be remembered, however, that Judaism's long fight for existence in the face of victorious Christianity has often led to a significant shift of emphasis, which diminishes the apparent area of agreement.

a. Israel

Basic to Judaism is the existence and call of Israel, membership of which is primarily by birth, though the proselyte was normally welcome. The latter was conceived of as born into God's people by circumcision, baptism and sacrifice. There is no evidence of any real understanding of the OT doctrine of the 'remnant'. The aphorism 'All Israel has a share in the world to come' was generally accepted; apostasy (an elastic term) being normally regarded as the only bar to its enjoyment.

Within Israel all were regarded as brothers. Though the natural distinctions of society were never denied, before God rank depended on knowledge of the Torah and its fulfilment. Hence in the synagogue services the only qualifications for leadership were piety, knowledge and ability. The rabbis were neither priests nor ministers, and their 'ordination' was merely a recognition of their knowledge of the Torah and their consequent right to act as judges. They were simply those who knew the Torah well enough to teach it, and recognition by several recognized rabbis, or even in exceptional cases by the community, was sufficient to make a man a rabbi.

The woman was looked on as man's inferior because she was under her husband's authority and not able to carry out certain prescriptions of the Torah. But fundamentally Judaism has always maintained the truth of Gn. 2:18 and woman's essential dignity.

b. Resurrection

Though later, under the influence of Christianity and Greek philosophy, Judaism was to give a somewhat reluctant assent to the doctrine of the immortality of the soul, it has always remained sufficiently true to the spirit of the OT to consider bodily resurrection necessary for true life after death. 2 Tim. 1:10 is no denial of Judaism's hope of resurrection, for it, unlike the Christian faith based on the resurrection of Christ, was deduced from the few indications of the OT and forged in the spiritual anguish that was the lot of the pious from the time of Antiochus Epiphanes.

A clear distinction was made between the *'ôlām ha-zeh* ('this world') and the *'ôlām ha-bā'* ('the world to come'), the latter being always regarded (apart from the more Hellenized members of the W Dispersion) as belonging to this earth. They were linked by the 'Days of the Messiah', always looked on as a limited period of time.

c. The Torah

The Pharisees seem to have occupied a middle position between the Sadducees, who rejected the authority (though not necessarily the value) of the prophetic books, and the Qumran Covenanters, who gave them high authority when in the hands of a competent expositor. The Pharisees looked on them as divinely inspired commentaries on the Torah, the Pentateuch, which was for them the perfect and final revelation of God's will. The main reason for their rejection of Christ, and their demand for a sign from him, was because he appealed to the authority entrusted to him and not to that of Moses.

The rabbis so exalted the role and value of the Torah that the keeping of it became the explanation and justification of Israel's existence. It was only later, as Judaism faced a politically triumphant church, that the Torah was given a cosmic position and an existence before the creation of the world, so that it might play the part in Judaism that Christ plays in Christianity. It is easy to understand why Paul, with his doctrine of the addition of the law to bring out the sinfulness of sin, has always been obnoxious to the orthodox Jew.

In Judaism, however, the Pentateuch is only the *tôrâ še-bikᵉṯāḇ* (the written Torah). If the keeping of the Torah was to become the personal concern of every pious Jew, and if its enactments were to be extended to cover the whole of life, so as to create an essential unity within Israel, then there would have to be agreement on the principles of approach and exegesis. These had probably already been fixed in main outline by the time of Ezra. Together with some customs of immemorial antiquity, *e.g.* the washing of hands, they were attributed to tradition reaching right back to Moses on Mt Sinai. These principles and their application to everyday life form the *tôrâ še-bᵉʿal-peh* (the oral Torah or law). It has equal authority with the written Torah, for the latter cannot be understood correctly without it.

The development of the oral Torah was approximately as follows. The written Torah was studied to find out the actual commandments in it; they were calculated at 613 in all—248 positive and 365 negative. These were then protected by the making of new laws, the keeping of which would guarantee the keeping of the basic commandments—this is known as 'making a hedge about the Torah'. Finally, the enlarged laws were applied by analogy to all conceivable spheres and possibilities of life.

While in one sense the oral Torah can never be regarded as completed, for with the changes in civilization there are always new situations to which it has to be applied, it is generally considered to have received its definitive form in the Talmud, and to a lesser extent in the Midrashim (sing. Midrash), the official, mainly devotional expositions (*'aggāḏâ*) of the OT books.

The *Talmud falls into two parts. The Mishnah is a codification of the oral Torah for which Rabbi Yehuda ha-Nasi (*c.* AD 200) was mainly responsible. In contrast to most Midrashim it consists of *hᵃlāḵâ*, *i.e.* the laws governing life, and is virtually a commentary on the legal side of the Pentateuch. The Gemara is a prolix commentary on the Mishnah. It not only gives precision to points left unclear but also throws a flood of light on all aspects of early Judaism. The longer Babylonian version was virtually completed by AD 500, the unfinished Palestinian form was broken off about a century earlier. It is much fairer to compare the Talmud with the church Fathers than with the NT.

d. Man and the keeping of the Torah

It would be most unfair to write off Judaism as mere legalism, though this was bound to be prevalent. The favourite passages quoted from the Talmud to prove legalism are typical of any manual seeking to make a casuistic application of law to life. The tendency to legalism was tempered by the rabbis' insistence that the keeping of the Torah must have the right intention (*kawwānâ*), and that it must be done for its own sake (*lišmâ*) and not for the reward it might bring. They regarded the giving of the Torah as a supreme act of grace, and our keeping of it should be the response of love.

Such a system is bound to stress our measure of success and not failure in the keeping of the Torah. Hence the heinousness of 'respectable' sin and man's inability perfectly to do the will of God were minimized, and this tendency was reinforced by the disappearance of sacrifice in AD 70. Judaism knows nothing really comparable to the Christian doctrine of original sin. It is true that man was conceived of as born with an evil inclination (*yēṣer hā-rā'*), but this was balanced by an equally innate good inclination (*yēṣer ha-ṭôḇ*), which if reinforced by the study of Torah would gain the ascendancy. This over-optimistic view of sin and human nature is found throughout Judaism.

More serious is the implicit claim for the autonomy of the man versed in the Torah. Though this claims complete authority over him, God leaves it to the learned to discover what its claims may be. This went so far that in the Talmud (*Menaḥoṯ* 29b) Moses is depicted as unable to grasp Rabbi Akiba's exposition by which he discovered things Moses had never thought were in his laws. On the other hand, direct commands were occasionally deliberately circumvented, for it was felt to be to the common good. The best-known instance is Dt. 15:1–3—the example in Mk. 7:9–13 was not taken up into the Mishnah, possibly because Christ's rebuke was recognized as just. There was an invariable tendency to decrease the burden of any enactment that seemed to press too hardly on the masses (this is no contradiction of Mt. 23:4; it is the learned man's privilege to use his knowledge to lighten his burdens!). It is probably this attitude of self-confident assurance as controllers and moulders of the revelation of God's will that above all lies behind Christ's charge against the Pharisees of hypocrisy (see *HYPOCRITE and H. L. Ellison, 'Jesus and the Pharisees', *JTVI* 85, 1953). In spite of constant rabbinic admonitions to humility the note of Jn. 7:49 is all too often heard in the literature of Judaism.

Since Judaism lays all its stress on serving God by keeping the Torah, and all its intellectual subtlety was used to find the full scope of God's commands, it has been very little troubled with the type of theological dispute that has been the bane of Christendom. Provided a man accepted the perfect unity and uniqueness of God, the absolute authority and finality of the Torah and the election of Israel, he could, if he kept the demands of the law, hold what philosophical and mystic theories he chose. So much is this true that it has been rightly claimed that orthopraxy rather than orthodoxy is the correct word to apply to Judaism. The only serious schism in Jewry between the triumph of the Pharisaic viewpoint and modern times was that of the Karaites (8th century), and this was concerned with the principles of interpreting the Torah.

Judaism's historic development largely shielded it from Greek influence at its most critical stage. As a result it has preserved a much more even balance between the individual and society than is evident in much Christian practice.

*e. The *Messiah*

Though there was considerable variety of outlook, there are no traces in Judaism down to AD 200 that there would be any supernatural element in the Messiah. He is first the great deliverer from foreign oppression and then the enforcer of true Torah observance. The Days of the Messiah are the link with the world to come, but they are limited in length. For a summary, see J. Klausner, *The Messianic Idea in Israel*, 1956, Part 3.

f. The doctrine of God

Any anthology of rabbinic sayings about God will quickly show that in the vast majority of cases they are true to the OT revelation. They will be found to differ from the Christian concept mainly in the following points. Since a world to come on earth does not imply as close a contact with the Eternal as the concept of a hereafter in heaven, there is less concern with the implications of the absolute holiness of God. Since there is more stress on service than on communion, except among the frequent mystics, the problem of 'at-onement' is seldom met. In any case there is no understanding that Israel needs to be reconciled to God. The concept of incarnation is ruled out *a priori*; the gulf between Creator and creation is too great.

The conflict between Judaism and the triumphant church made it so stress the transcendence of God as to make a real immanence almost impossible. The immanence constantly stressed in Jewish devotion has always something semi-pantheistic about it. God's unity was defined in terms that made Trinitarian doctrine an abomination. Increasingly he was described by negations which made him unknowable except through his works. In spite of this the OT basis of Judaism has been too strong for the pious Jew to be happy with such a position for long, and he has repeatedly sought to circumvent it by mysticism.

BIBLIOGRAPHY. H. Danby (tr.), *The Mishnah*, 1933; I. Epstein (ed.), *The Talmud*, E.T. in 35 vols., 1935–1952; H. L. Strack, *Introduction to the Talmud and Midrash*, E.T. 1931; G. F. Moore, *Judaism in the First Centuries of the Christian Era*, 3 vols., 1927, 1930; E. Schürer, *HJP*, 1, 1973; *SB*; C. G. Montefiore and H. Loewe, *A Rabbinic Anthology*, 1938; J. Parkes, *The Foundations of Judaism and Christianity*, 1960; R. A. Stewart, *Rabbinic Theology*, 1961; L. Jacobs, *Principles of the Jewish Faith*, 1964; S. Safrai and M. Stern (eds.), *The Jewish People in the First Century*, 2 vols., 1974, 1976. H.L.E.

JUDAS. 1. The Lord's brother (Mt. 13:55 = Mk. 6:3). Perhaps the author of the Epistle of *Jude, who styles himself 'brother of James' (*BRETHREN OF THE LORD).

2. The son of James, and one of the Twelve (Lk. 6:16), called also Lebbaeus (Mt. 10:3, AV) and Thaddaeus (Mk. 3:18), who asked Jesus a question in the upper room (Jn. 14:22). Some regard him as the author of the Epistle of Jude.

3. For Judas Iscariot, see below.

4. The Galilean who stirred up a rebellion against the Romans (Acts 5:37). Josephus says he was born in Gamala (*Ant.* 18. 3), and places the rebellion in AD 6. *Quirinius defeated the rebels and Judas was slain. **5.** A Jew at whose house in Damascus Paul lodged (Acts 9:11). **6.** A prophet surnamed Barsabbas, who with Silas was chosen by the Jerusalem Christian leaders to accompany Paul and Barnabas to Antioch to convey the apostles' decision regarding circumcision (Acts 15:22–33). J.D.D.

JUDAS ISCARIOT.

I. Name and origin

In the Synoptic lists of the Twelve whom Jesus called 'to be with him' (Mk. 3:14) the name of Judas always appears last, and usually with some description which brands him with an infamous stigma (*e.g.* 'who betrayed him', Mk. 3:19; Mt. 10:4; Lk. 6:16; *cf.* Jn. 18:2, 5). We may compare the case of Jeroboam I, in the OT, who is mentioned with horror as the one 'who made Israel to sin'.

The term 'Iscariot' is applied to his name, in the Synoptic texts and in Jn. 12:4; while in the other Johannine references the textual tradition shows considerable variation, with the name of Simon being given as Judas' father (Jn. 6:71; 13:2, 26), and Iscariot being further explained by the addition *apo Karyōtou* (in certain readings of 6:71; 12:4; 13:2, 26; 14:22). These additional facts supplied by John would confirm the derivation of 'Iscarioth' from Heb. *'îš q^{e}rîyôṯ*, 'a man of Kerioth'. Kerioth is located in Moab, according to Je. 48:24, 41; Am. 2:2; but there is another possible identification, Kerioth-hezron (Jos. 15:25), which is 19 km S of Hebron. This geographical explanation of 'Iscarioth' is preferable to the view which traces the word to *sikarios*, by way of an Aramaicized *'isqaryā'ā*, 'an assassin' (*cf.* Acts 21:38), as suggested by Schulthess and O. Cullmann, *The State in the New Testament*, E.T. 1957, pp. 15f. But see, to the contrary, M. Hengel, *Die Zeloten*, 1961, p. 49.

II. Career

In the apostolic band Judas was treasurer (Jn. 13:29), while another Johannine text speaks of him as a thief (12:6), mainly, we may suppose, on the ground that he 'pilfered' the money which was entrusted to him. For this sense of the verb translated 'used to take' in 12:6, as attested in the papyri, see A. Deissmann, *Bible Studies*, E.T. 1901, p. 257.

The closing scenes of the Gospel story are shadowed by the treachery of this 'one of the twelve', as he is repeatedly called (Mk. 14:10, *cf.* 14:20; Jn. 6:71; 12:4). He raises the voice of criticism against the action of Mary, who anointed the Master's feet with the precious ointment (Jn. 12:3–5). The comment of the Evangelist is intended to stress the avarice of Judas, who saw in the price of the ointment nothing of the beautiful deed which Jesus praised (Mk. 14:6) but only a means by which the apostolic fund would be increased, and thereby his own pocket lined. And even this motive was cloaked under a specious plea that the money could be given away to relieve the poor. Thus to covetousness there is added the trait of deceit. Immediately following this incident at Bethany he goes to the chief priests to betray the Lord (Mt. 26:14–16; Mk. 14:10–11; Lk. 22:3–6). Mark records simply the fact of the treachery, adding that money was promised by the priests.

'Judas (Yehuda) *the son of John* (Yehohanan)*' son of Jethro* (*Yethua*) *inscribed on an ossuary from Jerusalem 40 BC – AD 70.* (JPK)

Matthew supplies the detail of the amount, which may have been a part-payment of the agreed sum (with an implicit allusion to Zc. 11:12, and possibly Ex. 21:32; *cf.* Mt. 27:9). Luke gives the deep significance of the act when he records that Satan entered into the traitor and inspired his nefarious sin (*cf.* Jn. 13:2, 27). All Synoptists agree that Judas determined to await a favourable opportunity when he might deliver Jesus up to his enemies 'privately', *i.e.* secretly, by craft (for this rendering in Lk. 22:6; Mk. 14:1–2, see J. Jeremias, *The Eucharistic Words of Jesus*², E.T. 1966, p. 72).

That opportunity came on the evening when Jesus gathered in the upper room for the last meal with the Twelve (Mk. 14:17ff. and parallels); and this fact is perpetuated in the church's eucharistic tradition which dates from the time of St Paul (1 Cor. 11:23: 'on the night when he was betrayed'). The Lord, with prophetic insight, foresees the action of the traitor whose presence is known at the table. In the Marcan account Judas is not mentioned by name, and there seems to be a general air of bewilderment as to the traitor's identity. The conversation of Mt. 26:25 with the question-and-answer dialogue is best understood as spoken in whispered undertones, while the Johannine account preserves the first-hand tradition of the beloved disciple's question and Jesus' action with the Paschal sop, both of which may have been said and done in a secretive fashion. At all events, this is the Lord's final appeal to Judas—and the traitor's final refusal. (See F. C. Fensham, 'Judas' Hand in the Bowl and Qumran', *RQ* 5, 1965, pp. 259–261, for Judas' rejection of Jesus.) Thereafter Satan takes control of one who has become his captive; and he goes out into the night (Jn. 13:27–30).

The pre-arranged plan for Jesus' arrest was carried through. The secret which Judas betrayed was evidently the meeting-place in Gethsemane later that night; and to our Lord at prayer there came the band of soldiery, led by Judas (Mk. 14:43). The sign of identification was the last touch of irony. 'The one I shall kiss is the man' ; and with that the traitor's work was completed.

The last chapters of Judas' life are beset with much difficulty. Of his pathetic remorse the Scripture bears witness, yet the only Evangelist to record this is Matthew (27:3–10). To this account of his agony of remorse and suicide, the account of Acts 1:18–19 must be added; and also, to complete the evidence, the grotesque testimony of Papias, *Frag.* 3, preserved by Apollinarius of Laodicea. This last-named text may be conveniently consulted in the series *Ancient Christian Writers*, 6, translated and annotated by J. A. Kleist, 1957 edn., p. 119. Papias relates how Judas' body swelled (this may be a possible meaning of Acts 1:18 for the EVV 'falling headlong'; see Arndt, *s.v. prēnēs*), and dies on his own land. There have been various attempts at harmonization (*e.g.* Augustine's suggestion that the rope broke and Judas was killed by the fall, in the manner of Acts 1:18, thus conflating the Matthean and Acts accounts). But even more terrifying than the gruesome details of these accounts is the plain, stark verdict of Acts 1:25: 'this ministry and apostleship, from which Judas turned aside, to go to his own place'. The apostle had become an apostate; and had gone to the destiny reserved for such a man.

III. Character

This reference invites the question of the true character of Judas. If 'his own place' is the place he chose for himself, what motives led him to his awful destiny and fate? How can we reconcile this statement with those scriptures which give the impression that he was predetermined to fulfil the role of traitor, that Jesus chose him, knowing that he would betray him, that he had stamped on him from the beginning the inexorable character of 'the son of perdition' (Jn. 17:12)? Psychological studies are indecisive and not very profitable. Love of money; jealousy of the other disciples; fear of the inevitable outcome of the Master's ministry which made him turn state's evidence in order to save his own skin; an enthusiastic intention to force Christ's hand and make him declare himself as Messiah—de Quincey's famous reconstruction; a bitter, revengeful spirit which arose when his worldly hopes were crushed and this disappointment turned to spite and spite became hate—all these motives have been suggested. Three guiding principles ought perhaps to be stated as a preliminary to all such considerations. 1. We ought not to doubt the sincerity of the Lord's call. Jesus, at the beginning, viewed him as a potential follower and disciple. No other presupposition does justice to the Lord's character, and his repeated appeals to Judas. 2. The Lord's foreknowledge of him does not imply fore-ordination that Judas must inexorably become the traitor. 3. Judas was never really Christ's man. He fell from apostleship, but never (so far as we can tell) had a genuine relationship to the Lord Jesus. So he remained 'the son of perdition' who was lost because he was never 'saved'. His highest title for Christ was 'Rabbi' (Mt. 26:25), never 'Lord'. He lives on the stage of Scripture as an awful warning to the uncommitted follower of Jesus who is in his company but does not share his spirit (*cf.* Rom. 8:9b); he leaves the Gospel story 'a doomed and damned man' because he chose it so, and God confirmed him in that dreadful choice.

BIBLIOGRAPHY. The difficulties associated with the variant details of the death of Judas are discussed in *BC*, 1.5, pp. 22–30; *cf.*, too, Arndt, *loc. cit.* and *s.v.* 'Ioudas', 6; K. Lüthi, *Judas Iskarioth*, 1955; D. Haugg, *Judas Iskarioth in den neutestamentlichen Berichten*, 1930; J. S. Stewart, *The Life and Teaching of Jesus Christ*, 1933, pp. 166–170; P. Benoit, art. 'La mort de Judas' in collected works, *Exégèse et Théologie*, 1961; B. Gärtner, *Iscariot*, E.T. 1971.

R.P.M.

JUDE, EPISTLE OF. One of the *'Catholic Epistles'.

I. Outline of contents

The Epistle falls into five parts:

a. Salutation (vv. 1–2).
b. Jude's purpose in writing (vv. 3–4).
c. False teachers denounced and their doom foretold (vv. 5–16).
d. Exhortation to Christians (vv. 17–23).
e. Doxology (vv. 24–25).

II. Authorship, date and canonicity

The author of this little tract identifies himself as 'Jude, a servant of Jesus Christ and brother of James'. In the early church there was only one James who could be referred to in this way without further specification—'James the Lord's brother' (as he is called in Gal. 1:19). This points to an identification of the author with the Judas who is numbered among the brothers of Jesus in Mt. 13:55 and Mk. 6:3, the Judas whose two grandsons, according to

JUDAS THE GALILEAN
See Zealot, Part 3.

JUDAS, SON OF JAMES
See Thaddaeus, Part 3.

JUDAS THOMAS, ACTS OF
See New Testament apocrypha, Part 2.

JUDEA
See Judaea, Part 2.

Hegesippus, were examined and dismissed by Domitian when he was informed that they belonged to the house of David (Eusebius, *EH* 3. 19–20). Its date cannot be fixed with certainty; it may be tentatively assigned to the second half of the 1st century AD, after the fall of Jerusalem (v. 17 refers to the apostles in the past). We have express references to it towards the end of the 2nd century, in the Muratorian list and elsewhere; but there are probable allusions to it earlier in that century, in the *Didache* and the *Shepherd* of Hermas. Although its canonicity was long disputed, we may be glad that it was finally established, for (as Origen says) 'while it consists of but a few lines, yet it is full of mighty words of heavenly grace'.

III. Occasion and purpose

Jude had projected another treatise, concerning 'our common salvation', when he found himself obliged to take up a more controversial line, in vigorous defence of the apostolic faith. This defence was made necessary by the alarming advances made by an incipient gnosticism in the circle of Christians to which Jude addresses himself—not in this case an ascetic form of teaching like that attacked by Paul in Colossians, but an antinomian form which may have appealed to Paul's teaching about Christian liberty, misinterpreting that liberty as licence and using it 'as an opportunity for the flesh' (*cf.* Gal. 5:13). This is suggested by Jude's description of the false teachers in question as 'perverting the grace of our God into licentiousness' as well as 'denying our only Master and Lord, Jesus Christ' (v. 4).

IV. Argument of the Epistle

False teaching requires to be exposed; it is not enough to set the truth alongside it in the expectation that everyone will recognize which is which. The refutation of error is an essential correlative to the defence of the faith 'once for all delivered to the saints' (v. 3).

The doom of these false teachers has been pronounced of old. God's judgment, if slow, is sure, and once executed it abides for ever. This appears from the examples of the disobedient Israelites who died in the wilderness (*cf.* 1 Cor. 10:5; Heb. 3:17; this was evidently a commonplace of primitive Christian 'typology'), of the rebellious angels of Gn. 6:1–4, and of the cities of the plain (*cf.* Gn. 19). Like those prototypes, the false teachers defy divinely constituted authority, unlike the archangel Michael, who would not use insulting language even to the devil (vv. 8–10). (Clement and Origen tell us that the incident of Michael's dispute with the devil was related in the *Assumption of Moses*, but the part of this work containing the incident is no longer extant.) The examples of Cain, Balaam and Korah also point the lesson of doom for these latter-day followers of theirs (v. 11).

These false teachers introduce trouble and disgrace into the church's fellowship, into its very love-feasts; they are shepherds who feed themselves and not the flock ('blind mouths', in Milton's phrase), clouds which blot out the sun but send down no refreshing rain, trees which produce only Dead Sea fruit (v. 12). They are ineffectual as roaring waves whose rage expends itself in froth and foam; they are stars wandering out of their orbits into eternal night (v. 13). The judgment which awaits them at the parousia was foretold by Enoch (vv. 14f.; *cf. 1 Enoch* 1. 9).

True believers, however, need not be alarmed at the activity of such people, of whose rise and fall the apostles had given them warning in advance. Let them safeguard themselves by being built up in faith, praying in the power of the Spirit, continuing steadfastly in the fellowship of divine love, and looking forward to the consummation of mercy and life at the appearing of Christ (vv. 17–21). While they must abhor and avoid all false teachers, they should pity and rescue those who are led astray by them (vv. 22–23).

The Epistle ends with an ascription of praise to God as the One who is able to guard his people from stumbling until they stand without blemish 'before the presence of his glory with rejoicing'.

BIBLIOGRAPHY. J. B. Mayor, *The Epistle of Jude and the Second Epistle of Peter*, 1907; M. R. James, *2 Peter and Jude, CGT*, 1912; J. Moffatt, *The General Epistles, MNT*, 1928; E. M. Sidebottom, *James, Jude and 2 Peter, NCB*, 1967; M. Green, *2 Peter and Jude, TNTC*, 1968. F.F.B.

JUDGES. The Heb. word (*šōp̄ēṭ*) means one who dispenses justice, punishing the evil-doer and vindicating the righteous. The corresponding word for 'judgment' is used to describe a rule by which he must be guided (Ex. 21:1).

I. The Mosaic institution

In the wilderness period Moses wore himself out by sitting to judge the cases brought to him (Ex. 18:13–27, and *cf.* Ex. 2:14). On Jethro's advice he appointed deputies to judge ordinary cases, bringing to him only the most important (see also Dt. 1:9–18).

The Deuteronomic law provides for the appointment of judges, and *officers to assist them (Dt. 16:18); 'in all your towns'. So the more primitive rule of the nomadic period is adapted to the future settlement.

There is insistence upon the need for scrupulous fairness, and impartial justice (Dt. 1:16f.; 16:19f.; 24:17f.; 25:13–16). Since the book of the law was in the charge of the priests, the more important cases were to be tried by a judge with priests as assessors (Dt. 17:8–13). During the period of the conquest we find judges taking part in assemblies of the nation (Jos. 8:33; 24:1).

II. The period of the Judges

After the death of Joshua there followed the period of disorganization, tribal discord and defeat, which is described in the book of Jdg. But when the people cried to the Lord, the author tells us, he 'raised up judges, who saved them' (Jdg. 2:16). These national heroes are sometimes called 'deliverers' (AV 'saviours') (3:9, 15), and of most of them it is said that they 'judged Israel' for a stated period of years, Othniel being the first (3:9) and Samson the last (16:31).

It is clear that this imparts a new meaning into the word 'judge', namely, that of a leader in battle and a ruler in peace. We may see in them a type of Christ, who came to be our Saviour, is with us as our Leader, and will come to be our Judge.

In 1 Sa. there is a transition to the time of the monarchy. Eli 'had judged Israel forty years' (1 Sa. 4:18), and 'Samuel judged Israel all the days of his life', going in circuit to Bethel and Gilgal and Mizpeh; and appointed his sons also as judges (7:15–8:1).

Texts from *Mari (*c.* 1800 BC) describe the activities of leaders termed *šāpiṭum*, generally similar to the work of Israelite 'judges'.

These acted as local provincial 'governors' working with other neighbouring 'governors' under the Great King (A. Marzal, *JNES* 30, 1971, pp. 186–217). Their responsibilities included the exercise of justice, maintenance of order, collection of taxes and tribute, and provision of information and hospitality. Thus the Heb. *šōpēṭ* should probably be better translated 'governor' than 'judge' since the latter describes only part of his function. Similar officials are named in the earlier tablets from *Ebla.

III. Under the Monarchy

Under the kings we find judges engaged in both judiciary and other administration. Among David's officers 'Chenaniah and his sons were appointed to outside duties for Israel, as officers and judges' (1 Ch. 26:29).

After the disruption, Jehoshaphat displayed zeal for 'the book of the law of the Lord' (2 Ch. 17:9), appointed judges and officers city by city (19:5), and charged them to deal faithfully (2 Ch. 19:9f.; *cf.* Dt. 16:19f.).

Finally, on the return from exile, the decree of Artaxerxes bade Ezra set magistrates and judges to administer justice and to teach the people (Ezr. 7:25).

Later rulers of Phoenician cities took the title *šōpēṭ*; *cf.* the Carthaginian *suffetes*, mentioned by Roman writers (*PHOENICIA).

BIBLIOGRAPHY. W. Richter, *ZAW* 77, 1965, pp. 40–72; D. J. Wiseman, *BS* 134, 1977, pp. 233–237.

G.T.M.
D.J.W.

JUDGES, BOOK OF. Judges follows chronologically upon the Pentateuch and Joshua and describes the history of Israel from Joshua's death to the rise of Samuel. It takes its name from its leading characters, the *šōp^{e}ṭîm* (Jdg. 2:16). These *'judges', however, were more than judicial arbiters; they were 'deliverers' (AV 'saviours') (3:9), charismatically empowered by God's Holy Spirit for the deliverance and preservation of Israel (6:34) up to the establishment of the kingdom (*cf.* the use of this same word for the chief magistrates of Carthage, and as a synonym for 'king' in ancient Canaanitish Ugarit, *Anat* 5. 40). Yahweh himself is the chief *šōpēṭ* (Jdg. 11:27).

I. Outline of contents

a. Events following the death of Joshua (1:1–2:5)

With initial obedience the tribes of Judah and Simeon advanced S to the conquest of Bezek, Jerusalem (not held, 1:21), Hebron and Debir (reoccupied since their devastation in Jos. 10:36, 39), Hormah, and three of the Philistine cities (not held, Jdg. 1:19). The Joseph tribes likewise captured Bethel (1:22–26), which had revolted (*cf.* Jos. 8:17; 12:9). But then came failure: Israel ceased to remove the Canaanites, no more cities were taken (Jdg. 1:27–36), and the tribe of Dan actually suffered eviction from its allotted territory (1:34). Such tolerance of evil necessitated the extended period of chastening that followed (2:1–5).

b. Israel's history under the judges (2:6–16:31)

(i) *The writer's prophetic understanding of history* (2:6–3:6). This book teaches divine retribution: that God in his providence recompenses a nation in direct correspondence to the faithfulness of its people. Israel at this time suffered under constant temptation to adopt the fertility rites of their Canaanitish neighbours, along with their confessedly superior agriculture. Many recognized that Yahweh had guided Israel in the wilderness, but Baal seemed better able to make the crops come out of the ground! Jdg. thus exhibits a repeated cycle of sin (Baal-worship), servitude (to foreign aggressors), supplication (to the merciful God, for relief) and salvation (through divinely raised up judges).

(ii) *Six successive periods of oppression and the careers of twelve deliverer-judges* (3:7–16:31).

1. *Invasions of Cushan-rishathaim* (3:7–11). After adopting the ways of Canaan, Israel suffered for 8 years under the depredations of Cushan-rishathaim, an invader who came from Hittite-controlled Mesopotamia (Jdg. 3:8). The cause, however, lay in Israel's sin (3:7) (see below, part *c*). But when they 'cried to Yahweh, Yahweh raised up a deliverer for the people of Israel, . . . Othniel, . . . Caleb's younger brother' (3:9). The 40 years of peace that followed may correspond to the parallel period of Hittite overlordship, until some years after the death of Suppiluliuma in 1346 BC (*CAH*, 2, 2:19).

2. *Oppression under Eglon* (3:12–31). Just prior to the days of international confusion coincident with the rise of Egypt's aggressive 19th Dynasty, 'Israel again did what was evil . . .; and Yahweh strengthened Eglon the king of Moab against Israel' (3:12). 'But when (they) cried to Yahweh, (he) raised up for them a deliverer, Ehud, . . . the Benjaminite' (3:15), and granted them 80 years of peace, perhaps dating from the time of the treaty of 1315, between Seti and Mursil, *cf.* its renewel in 1284 by Rameses II. Neither Egypt nor the Hittites seem to have comprehended their providential function, but the years in which either succeeded in bringing peace to Palestine do seem to correspond to the very periods that God had ordained for granting 'rest' to his people (*cf.* J. Garstang, *Joshua–Judges*, 1931, pp. 51–66). Shamgar next achieved a limited success against many Philistines, who were better equipped than he (3:31).

3. *Deliverance by Deborah* (4:1–5:31). With the decay of the empires and the rise of local Canaanitish oppression under Jabin II of Hazor (4:2–3), God raised up the fourth of the judges, the woman Deborah. Her military commander, Barak, proceeded to muster the N-central tribes to the Valley of Esdraelon for war with Jabin's troops led by Sisera. But, 'From heaven fought the stars, from their courses they fought against Sisera' (5:20): a divinely sent cloudburst immobilized the Canaanitish chariotry, and Sisera was slain in flight by a Kenite woman. The 40 years of peace that followed upon Deborah's victory may parallel the strong rule of Rameses III, the last great pharaoh (1199–1168 BC).

4. *Deliverance by Gideon* (6:1–8:32). Next there appeared out of the E desert, Midianites and Amalekites to plunder sinful Israel (Jdg. 6:2–6; *cf.* Ru. 1:1). But Israel was cleared of the nomadic raiders (7:19–25; 8:10–12; *cf.* the peaceful background of Ru. 2–4, some 20 years later).

5. *The rise and fall of Abimelech* (8:33–10:5). The turmoil that resulted from the attempt of Gideon's son Abimelech to make himself king over Israel (Jdg. 9) was rectified by the sixth and seventh judges, Tola and Jair (10:1–5).

6. *Oppression under Ammon and the Philistines* (10:6–16:31). But with the apostasy that subsequently arose, God gave up his land to

simultaneous oppressions by the Ammonites in the E and the Philistines in the W (10:7). After 18 years E Israel was freed by Jephthah, the eighth judge (ch. 11), who was succeeded by the three minor judges. W Israel, however, remained subject to the rising power of the Philistines, despite the spectacular exploits of Samson, the twelfth and last judge of the book of Judges (chs. 13–16).

c. An appendix (17:1–21:25)

This provides details on two events from Israel's very first period of apostasy (before Othniel; *cf.* the appearance of Phinehas in 20:28 and the mention of the events of ch. 18 in Jos. 19:47, the author of which seems contemporary with the conquest, Jos. 5:1; 6:25, though see *JOSHUA, **II**). The purpose of the appendix is to illustrate the depth of Israel's sin, whereby almost every standard of the Decalogue was transgressed. The section on Micah and the Danites (chs. 17–18) relates, *e.g.*, how Micah stole from his mother and then converted the proceeds into an idol for his house of gods (17:5). God's Levite, meanwhile, wandered unsupported, until hired by Micah. But he in turn proved false to his employer when offered a position of leadership by the covetous, idolatrous and murderous Danites (18:25). Yet this Levite was Jonathan, a direct descendant of Moses (18:30). Nothing, admittedly, is said respecting the seventh commandment (on purity); but the following chapters (19–21, the Benjaminite outrage) describe not simply civil war and the harbouring of criminals but also harlotry and marital desertion by a Levite's concubine (19:2), homosexuality, rape and adultery (19:22–24), and finally mass abduction (21:23). Such were the results when 'every man did what was right in his own eyes'.

II. Authorship and date

The book of Jdg. makes no direct statement about the date of its writing. The song of Deborah (5:2–31) does claim contemporary composition (5:1), and its authenticity is generally accepted. But the book as a whole could not have been compiled for another 2 centuries. It refers to the destruction and captivity of Shiloh (18:30–31) during the youth of Samuel (1 Sa. 4; *c.* 1080 BC); and the last event that it records is the death of Samson (Jdg. 16:30–31), which occurred a few years before Samuel's inauguration as judge (*c.* 1063). Furthermore, the repeated explanation that 'in those days there was no king in Israel' (17:6; 18:1; 21:25) suggests that the book was written *after* the accession of Saul as king in 1043 BC. Yet the popular appreciation for the kingship is still fresh; and the book seems to have been composed before the sack of Gezer in 970 BC (1 Ki. 9:16; *cf.* Jdg. 1:29) or David's capture of Jerusalem in 1003 (2 Sa. 5:6–7; *cf.* Jdg. 1:21).

The writer of Jdg. must therefore have been a man who was active during the early reign of Saul (before 1020 BC). He must also have been a prophet; for in the Heb. Bible, Jdg. takes its place in the prophetic division of the canon (the 'former' prophets: in Josephus, *Against Apion* 1. 8, the historical books, Jos.–Jb.), *cf.* the sermonic tone of 2:10–14; 3:7–8, *etc.* The most likely possibility is Samuel the prophet, who is indeed identified as the author of Jdg.–Ru. according to the Jewish Talmud (*Baba Bathra* 14b). But since this traditional account goes on to make the improbable assertion that Samuel also wrote 'the book which bears his name', we seem justified in concluding only that the author must, at least, have been one of Samuel's prophetic associates.

III. Sources of the book

The writer of Jdg. may have relied upon oral and written sources that are now lost, *e.g.* hero–anthologies, such as 'the book of the *yāšār* [upright]' (Jos. 10:13). Modern critics are accustomed to assert that the writer's sources consisted of largely independent materials (later perhaps a 'J' and 'E' document) and edited by an exilic Deuteronomist ('D') and post-exilic Priestly ('P') redactors; but this analysis runs counter to the evidence of the book itself and unnecessarily discredits the unity and authenticity of its contents. It seeks, for example, to equate God's call to Gideon at the winepress and his resulting sacrifice (Jdg. 6:11–24, said to be 'J') with his subsequent command to Gideon to destroy the Baal altar and to replace it with one to Yahweh (6:25–32, said to be 'E'), as if these were two conflicting versions of one call. Or again, it confuses Gideon's taking of the Midianite princes Oreb and Zeeb at the fords of the Jordan (7:24–25, 'E') with his final capture of the *kings*, Zeba and Zalmunna, farther east (8:10–11, 'J'), though it must then eliminate the words in 8:10, 'all who *were left* of the army', as being an attempt by some later editor to harmonize the supposedly conflicting stories. (*PENTATEUCH.)

The Heb. text of the book of Jdg. is better preserved than that of any of the other Former Prophets and is generally free from errors of scribal transmission. Its ancient LXX translation, however, exhibits inner-Greek variations to the extent that Rahlfs' edition of the LXX now presents on each page two divergent forms of Gk. text, according to codices A and B.

IV. Historical background

The historical background to the period of Jdg. concerns, locally, the presence of the Canaanites. Prior to the Heb. conquest, Moses had ordered their 'destruction' (Dt. 7:2; *cf.* Jos. 6:17), both because of long-standing immorality (Dt. 9:5; *cf.* Gn. 9:22, 25; 15:16) and because of their debasing religious influence upon God's people (Dt. 7:4); for on countless 'high places' the Canaanites worshipped local gods of fertility, Baalim, with rites that included sacred prostitution and even child sacrifice (11:31). Joshua had thus subdued the whole of Canaan (Jos. 11:16; *cf.* 21:43). But its native inhabitants had not yet lost their potential for resistance. Indeed, Moses himself had anticipated a gradual occupation of the land (Ex. 23:28–30; Dt. 7:22); and much still remained to be possessed (Jos. 13:1). On the international scene, the relevant facts may be outlined as follows: (1) At the time of Joshua's death, perhaps soon after 1400 BC, 18th Dynasty Egyptian imperial control over Palestine had become ephemeral: Amenhotep III was content to rule in decadent luxury; and his successor, Amenhotep IV (Akhenaten, *c.* 1379–1362 BC; *CAH*, 2. 2, p. 1038), devoted his exclusive attention to monotheistic religious reforms. The contemporary *Amarna letters from the Canaanitish city-states contain futile pleas for help against the plundering Habiru. This designation embraces the biblical *Hebrews, though it was also used for various Hurrian (?) aggressors from the N (descendants of Eber, Gn. 10:21, 25; *cf.* M. G. Kline, *WTJ* 19, May 1957, p. 184; 20, November 1957, p. 68). For this era was marked, at the same time, by revived Hittite activity from beyond Syria. King Suppiluliuma (*c.* 1385–1346 BC), the greatest of the Hittites, at the first encouraged anarchy among the states farther S and later achieved their practical domination for himself and his son Mursil II.

(2) But Egypt, under the new 19th Dynasty (1320–1200 BC), in turn experienced revival. Seti I retook Galilee and Phoenicia in 1318, defeated the Hittites, and 3 years later concluded a treaty with Mursil, by which Syria was assigned to Hittite control and Palestine and Phoenicia to Egyptian. Young Rameses II (1304–1237) indeed broke the treaty and invaded the Hittite territory. But after years of costly fighting the former division of power was re-established by the treaty of 1284; and peace was kept until the decline of the Hittite empire, due to the barbarian invasions in the latter part of the century.

(3) With the fall of Crete to the barbarians in 1200 BC the ousted Philistines, 'the remnant of the coastland of Caphtor' (Je. 47:4) fled E to reinforce their older settlements on the coast of Palestine (*cf.* Gn. 21:32; Dt. 2:23). Driven back from Egypt in about 1191 by Rameses III of the 20th Dynasty, they proceeded to consolidate their position in Canaan. Before the end of the century they were thus able to mount the first of their great offensives against Israel, with which event the history of the book of Judges comes to a close.

V. Chronology

The over-all chronology of Jdg. is indicated by the statement of Jephthah, near the conclusion of the period, that Israel had by his time been occupying Palestinian territory for some 300 years (Jdg. 11:26; *cf.* the similar figure drawn from 1 Ki. 6:1). The calculation of a more precise chronology, however, depends upon two other facts that appear in the biblical record. First, since the lapse of time from the termination of the conquest to the commencement of the first (Mesopotamian) oppression is not stated, one must count backward from the accession of Samuel, *c.* 1063 BC (reckoning, from the probable date of 930 for the division of the kingdom, with 113 years for Solomon, David (over all Israel), and Saul and his successors [1 Ki. 11:42; 2:11; Acts 13:21], plus 20 years for Samuel [1 Sa. 7:2; *cf.* *HDB*, 1, p. 399]). Second, since some of the judges overlapped each other (*cf.* Ehud and Shamgar, Jdg. 3:30–4:1), the chronology is best gathered from the dated oppressions and subsequent deliverances. Of particular significance is the fact that the 40-year Philistine oppression (13:1) in W. Palestine continued uninterruptedly from the deaths of Tola and Jair (10:7), through the judgeships of Jephthah, the three minor judges, Eli and Samson, down to the victorious advent of Samuel. The following picture results:

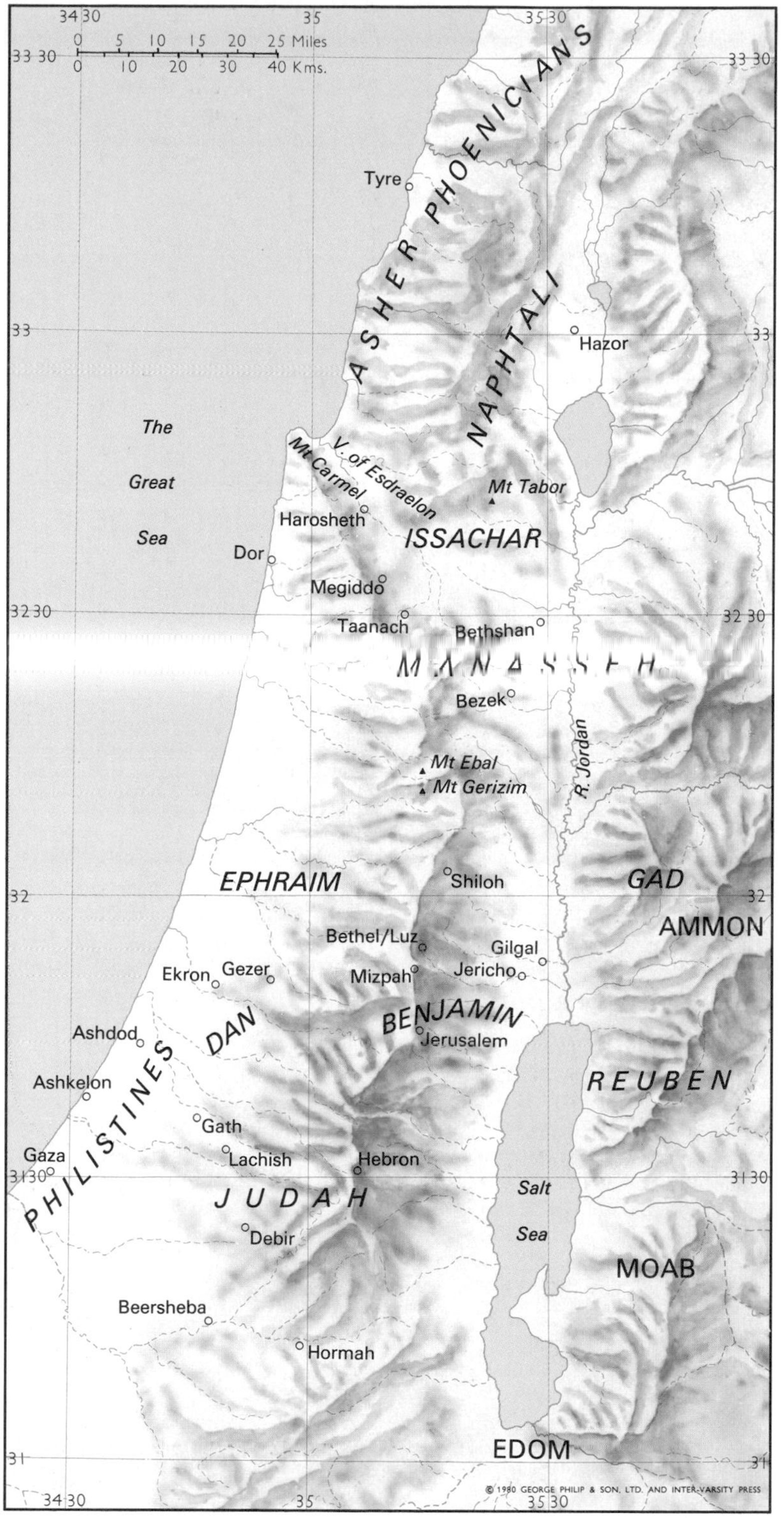

Palestine in the time of the Judges.

Oppressions

		yrs	
3:8	Mesopotamian	8	1382–1374
3:14	Eglon, Moab	18	1334–1316
4:3	Canaanite	20	1236–1216
6:1	Midianite	7	1176–1169
9:22	Abimelech	3	1129–1126
13:1	Philistine	40	1103–1063

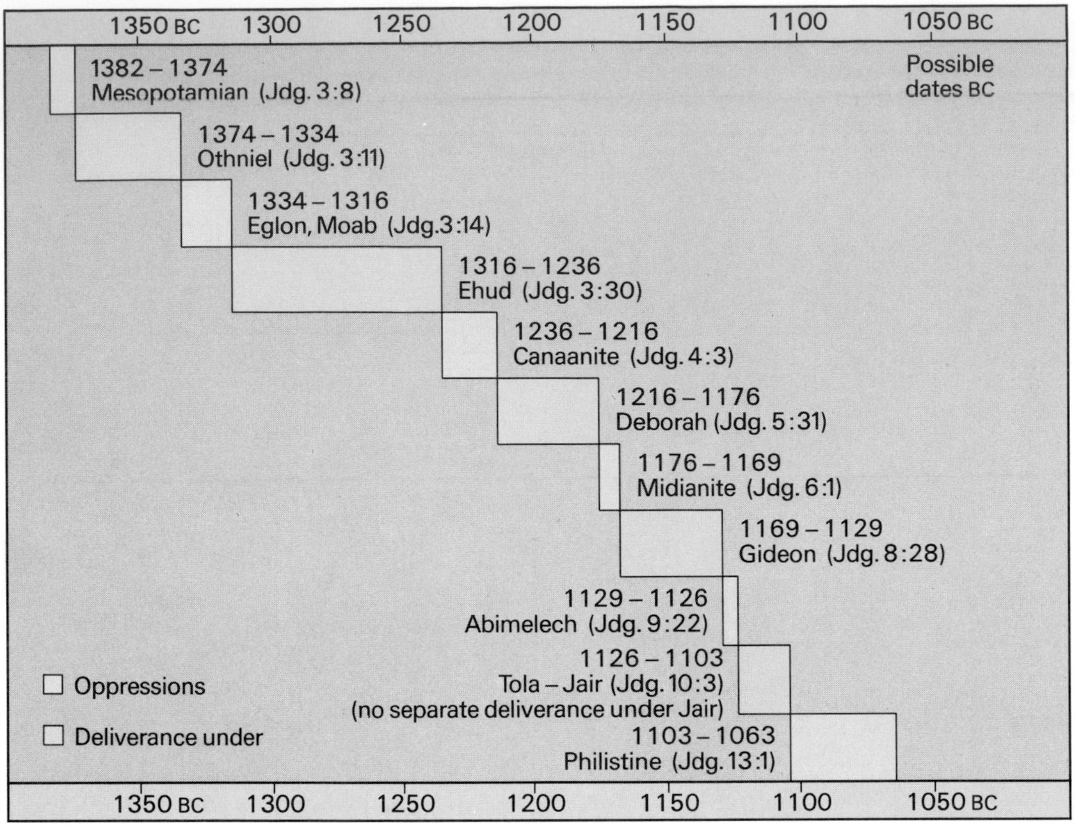

A chronology of the Judges period based on the years of oppression and peace. (For a different interpretation see Chronology of the Old Testament, Part 1.)

Deliverances

3:11	Othniel	40	1374–1334
3:30	Ehud	80	1316–1236
5:31	Deborah	40	1216–1176
8:28	Gideon	40	1169–1129
10:3	Tola-Jair	23	1126–1103

(no separate deliverance under Jair)

Confirmation of 1216 for Deborah's victory now arises from pottery types found in the last Canaanite city at Hazor, so that 'Barak is to be dated in the second half of the 13th century' (*CAH*, 1, 1:239). 319 years (1382–1063) would thus seem to elapse between the first oppression and Samuel's rise, which suggests a conquest dating 1406–1400 BC. An alternative date *c.* 1240 would require greater compression of the Judges' data.

(*Chronology of the Old Testament.)

VI. Teaching

From the principles stated in Jdg. 2:6–3:6 and the concrete historical examples furnished by the remainder of the book, its teaching may be summarized as follows.

a. God's wrath at sin (2:11, 14). Israel's hope for survival was dependent upon their intertribal unity, yet such co-operative effort arose only from a common dedication to their God (*cf.* 5:8–9, 16–18). Loss of faith meant extinction.

b. God's mercy upon repentance (2:16). Even foreign oppression served as a medium of divine grace, for Israel's edification (3:1–4).

c. Man's total depravity. For after each deliverance, 'whenever the judge died, they turned back and behaved worse than their fathers' (2:19). Individualistic society had demonstrated its inherent inadequacy, for man on his own inevitably goes wrong (17:6). Israel needed a king, though indeed only such a king as should accomplish the ultimate will of God (*cf.* 8:23; 9:6, 56). The author of Jdg. was thus one of civilization's first true historians, not simply recording events, but then interpreting the facts on the basis of an explicit philosophy of history. As to the permanent validity of his deuteronomic philosophy of retribution, one must grant that in those early days, when revelation was more limited, providence operated more obviously than at present. But his basic principles remain eternally sound: the sinning nation shall be punished, the repentant shall be saved, and all man-created systems must ultimately fail. The only valid hope of history lies in the coming of Christ, the King.

Bibliography. G. L. Archer, Jr., *A Survey of Old Testament Introduction*, 1974, pp. 274–279; A. E. Cundall and L. Morris, *Judges–Ruth, TOTC*, 1968; G. Fohrer, (Sellin's) *IOT*, 1968, pp. 196–215; J. Garstang, *Joshua–Judges*, 1931; R. K. Harrison, *IOT*, 1968, pp. 680–694; J. D. Martin, *The Book of Judges, CBC*, 1975; J. B. Payne, 'Chronology of the Old Testament', *ZPEB*, 1, pp. 833–836; *idem*, *An Outline of Hebrew History*, 1954, pp. 78–91; John H. Raven, *The History of the Religion of Israel*, 1933, pp. 156–202; L. T. Wood, 'Date of the Exodus', pp. 66–87 in J. B. Payne (ed.), *New Perspectives on the Old Testament*, 1970.

J.B.P.

JUDGMENT

JUDGMENT (Heb. *šāp̄aṭ*; Gk. *krima, krisis*).

I. Biblical teaching

God appears in the OT very commonly in the role of 'Judge of all the earth' (Gn. 18:25), or more generally as a 'God of justice' (Mal. 2:17; *cf.* Dt. 1:17; 32:4; Pss. 9:8; 94:2; 97:2; Is. 30:18; 41:1; 61:8; Je. 12:1; Ezk. 7:27; Mi. 6:1f.; *etc.*). Judgment does not simply imply an impartial and detached weighing up of good and evil but rather the thought of vigorous action against evil. It is on this understanding that the people of God are summoned to exercise judgment in turn (Is. 1:17; Mi. 6:8; Zc. 8:16). The judgment of God is not impersonal, the operation of some undeviating principle, it is a strongly personal notion. It is closely linked to the thought of God's character of mercy, lovingkindness, righteousness, truth, *etc.* (Ps. 36: 5f.; Ezk. 39:21; Ho. 2:19). It is the working out of the mercy and wrath of God in history and in human life and experience. Thus the judgment of God can bring deliverance for the righteous (Dt. 10:18; Ps. 25:9–10) as well as doom for the wicked (Ex. 6:6; Nu. 33:4; Dt. 32:41; Is. 4:4; Je. 1:10; 4:12; Ezk. 5:10; 23:10; 28:22). Judgment is a particularly rich idea in the OT and a variety of other terms are used with this meaning (*cf. dîn*, Gn. 30:6; Jb. 36:17; *pll*, 1 Sa. 2:25; Ps. 106:30; *pqd*, Je. 14:10; 51:47; *ykḥ*, Is. 1:18; Mi. 6:2; *rîḇ*, Ex. 23:2f.; Ps. 43:1). As the OT draws towards its close the thought of God's judgment becomes increasingly bound up with the eschatological expectation of the coming Day of the Lord (Joel 2:1f.; Am. 5:18f.; 8:9f.; Ob. 15 and *passim*; Zp. 1:7, 14f.; Mal. 4:1f.).

The NT, as we should expect,

continues the OT stress upon judgment as belonging to the nature of God and as part of his essential activity (Rom. 1:18; Heb. 12:23; 1 Pet. 1:17; 2:23; Rev. 16:5f.;). As in the OT, God's judgments are not confined to the future but are already at work in man's life in the present age (Jn. 8:50; Rom. 1:18, 22, 24, 26, 28; Rev. 18:8). Judgment is associated even now with Christ who exercises the Father's judgments (Mt. 3:11f.; 10:34; Jn. 3:19; 5:30; 8:12, 16; 9:39). The light of God's word is already shining into the world through his self-revelation in man's moral experience, and supremely in the incarnate Word, Jesus Christ. The judgment of men is therefore already in operation, for they show by their evil deeds that they 'love darkness rather than light' (Jn. 3:19).

The spotlight in the NT, however, falls upon the 'judgment to come', a future and final judgment which will accompany the return of Christ (Mt. 25:31–46; Jn. 5:22, 27f.; Rom. 3:5f.; 1 Cor. 4:3–5; Heb. 6:1f.). This is the coming Day of judgment (Jn. 6:39; Rom. 2:15f.; 1 Cor. 1:8; 5:5; Eph. 4:30; Phil. 2:16; 2 Thes. 1:10; 1 Pet. 2:12; 2 Pet. 3:12; 1 Jn. 4:17; Jude 6; Rev. 6:17; 16:14). Christ himself will judge (Jn. 5:22; 12:47f.; Acts 10:42; 17:31; 2 Tim. 4:8). All men will be judged; none will be absent (2 Tim. 4:1; Heb. 12:23; 1 Pet. 4:5). Even the angels will be passed under judgment (2 Pet. 2:4; Jude 6). Every aspect of life will come into account, including the 'secrets of men' (Rom. 2:16), 'the purposes of the heart' (1 Cor. 4:5; *cf.* Mk. 4:22; Lk. 12:2f.), and 'every careless word' (Mt. 12:36). The judgment will not be confined to unbelievers. Christians too (see **III**, below) will face a judgment (Mt. 7:22f.; 25:14–30; Lk. 19:12–28; 1 Cor. 3:12–15; 2 Cor. 5:10; Heb. 10:30; Jas. 3:1; 1 Pet. 1:17; 4:17; Rev. 20:12f.). There can be no avoiding this coming judgment (Heb. 9:27); it is as certain as death (Rom. 2:3; Heb. 10:27). Nowhere is this fact more clearly asserted than in the teaching of the parables of Jesus (Mt. 13:24–30, 36–43, 47–50; 21:33–41; 22:1–14; 25:1–13, 31–46; *etc.*).

II. The basis of judgment

The basis of judgment will be man's response to the revealed will of God. It will therefore include the entire range of human experience, thoughts, words and deeds, and will be such as to allow account to be taken of different degrees of knowledge of God's will, and hence of different degrees of ability to fulfil it (Mt. 11:21–24; Rom. 2:12–16). It will be utterly just and completely convincing (Gn. 18:25; Rom. 3:19). The judge of all the earth will do right and every mouth will be stopped in acknowledgment of the justice of his judgments (*cf.* Jb. 40:1–5; 42:1–6). Like Job we can cling to the justice of God (Jb. 13:13f.; 16:18f.; 19:23f.; 23:1–17; 31:1–40). In face of the frequent injustices of life in the present age we can rest in the certainty that God knows all, that he is not mocked and that he has appointed a day in which he will judge the world in righteousness (Acts 17:31). We can trust him to act in his future work of judgment with the same perfection and triumph which he manifests in the present in his works of grace and sovereignty.

Sometimes a difficulty is alleged as far as the basis of judgment is concerned in that Scripture appears to speak with two voices at points. On the one hand our *justification before God is said to rest on faith alone apart from our good works (Rom. 5:1f.; 3:28), and yet judgment is elsewhere declared to be on the basis of human works (Mt. 16:27; 25:31–46; Rom. 2:6; 1 Cor. 3:8; Rev. 22:12). The difficulty is more apparent than real. The following points need to be borne in mind.

i. Justification is an eschatological idea; *i.e.* it means that we are declared righteous before God at his judgment seat. It anticipates precisely the issue under discussion here, the final judgment of God. The man of faith who is trusting in the perfect merit and finished work of Christ has a guarantee of acquittal at the last day (Rom. 5:1; 8:1; 1 Cor. 1:30). The meaning of faith in Christ is nothing less than the truth that Christ's 'good works', *i.e.* his perfect obedience in life and death, are imputed to us here and now and will stand to our account on the judgment day. In this fundamental sense there can be no justification for anyone apart from 'works', *i.e.* the obedience of Christ in life and death which represents the only basis for human standing before God.

ii. This relationship to the perfect character and works of Christ is not merely judicial. We are not simply declared to be righteous. Our union with Christ implies a real incorporation into his death and resurrection (Rom. 6:1ff.; Gal. 2:20; Eph. 2:5f.; Col. 2:20; 3:1f.). Hence the character of Christ will inevitably be reproduced in a measure in the lives of his people. This is the insistence of James (*cf.* 2:18ff.). Faith without works is spurious because there is no such thing as a faith in Christ which does not incorporate us into union with him in his whole redeeming mission, including his death and resurrection, with all the radical implications of that for subsequent moral character. Putting this point more technically, justification which does not lead to sanctification is shown to have been no justification at all. In the words of a Puritan writer we must 'prove our pedigree by daring to be holy' (W. Gurnall). *Cf.* Rom. 6:1f.; Heb. 2:10f.; 1 Jn. 3:5f. Of course the Christian will remain a sinner in this life as far as his moral practice is concerned. Indeed it is only 'in Christ' that he begins to see sin in its true proportion and discover the depth of his moral depravity (1 Jn. 1:8–2:1f.). Yet alongside this he is 'being changed into his likeness from one degree of glory to another' (2 Cor. 3:18). Thus if a person is truly reborn by the Spirit (Jn. 3:1ff.) the scrutiny of God will certainly uncover evidences of this in their 'works'. But these works are the direct fruit of the Christian's having been regenerated by the Holy Spirit. They are in no sense a human ground of self-justification, but are simply elements of God's gift and grace towards us in Jesus Christ.

iii. When Jesus was asked 'What must we do, to be doing the works of God?' he replied, 'This is the work of God, that you believe in him whom he has sent' (Jn. 6:28f.). It is a mistake at this point to distinguish between Father and Son. God's supreme work and claim upon man, and his perfect will for his creature are expressed in Jesus Christ. God's will for us is therefore that we recognize and make response to the person and mission of Jesus. To believe in him is accordingly to work the works which God requires.

iv. Particular difficulty has been found with respect to the parable in Mt. 25:31–46, and recent interpreters have made all sorts of points on the basis of this parable, *e.g.* the idea of the so-called 'anonymous Christian' (J. A. T. Robinson, K. Rahner). This expresses the notion that some people, including atheists who have spurned God and his witness to them, agnostics who aspire to sit on the fence with respect to God's witness to them, and men and women of other faiths who have repudiated to a greater or lesser degree Christian claims for Christ, because they feed the hungry, visit the prisoners, minister to the needy, even fight in wars of liberation from political oppression, are unconsciously followers of Christ and will be acquitted at the end because in ministering to the needy in this way they have actually ministered to Christ. Such interpretations, however, suffer from a crucial weakness; they require us to interpret one parable (which is not a straightforward piece of Scripture teaching anyway since it *is* a parable) in a manner which yields conclusions at plain variance with many other clear sections of the Bible in general and the teaching of Jesus in particular. Conversely, if we are able to interpret this parable in a manner which does not involve any basic contradictions but which enables it to be integrated harmoniously into Jesus' other teaching, then clearly that ought to be the course to follow on any sound hermeneutic. This second course is entirely possible if we keep before us Jesus' statement that the acts of mercy which are in question in the parable are done to his 'brethren' (25:40). Here is a reflection of a truth which he states elsewhere that the church as the instrument of his mission to the world is so identified with him that men's response to the disciples of Jesus and their testimony becomes their response to him (Mt. 10:9–14, 40; 12:48–50; 18:18; Mk. 9:37; Jn. 20:21ff.) 'He who receives you receives me.' 'The deeds of the righteous are not just casual acts of benevolence. They are acts by which the mission of Jesus and his followers was helped, and helped at some cost to the doers, even at some risk' (T. W. Manson, *The Sayings of Jesus*, 1949, p. 251; *cf.* G. E. Ladd, *A Theology of the New Testament*, 1974, pp. 116–119). All this is not to deny the fact that many non-Christians perform deeds of love and mercy, or even that Christians are sometimes put to shame by their 'good works'. These works however need to be evaluated biblically. They are evidences of God's 'common grace' operating within fallen society restraining evil and promoting goodness. We ought to give thanks for this to God, and identify our Christian compassion where possible with all such efforts for the well-being of our human neighbours. Such action, however, even when carried to the limits of self-sacrifice, cannot claim to be atoning or justifying. These people too are fallen sinners who at many points in their lives are resisting God's will and claim, and these too can have hope at the coming judgment only in the righteousness of Christ. There are no 'anonymous Christians'. 'There is salvation in no one else (than Jesus Christ), for there is no other name under heaven given among men by which we must be saved' (Acts 4:12). The basis of judgment remains our response to God's will as embodied in his general and special revelation focused in Jesus Christ.

There is one further view of the basis of judgment which requires comment. This is the notion that the *only* basis upon which a man or woman may be exposed to the final judgment and condemnation of God is their explicit rejection of the gospel of Christ. In support of this, scriptures such as Mk. 16:15f.; Jn. 3:18, 36; Rom. 10:9–12; Eph. 4:18; 2 Pet. 2:3f.; 1 Jn. 4:3 are cited which represent *unbelief* as the ground of condemnation. However, we note the following: (*a*) these passages only prove that faith in Christ is the one way of salvation, which is not the same as proving that conscious rejection of Christ is the only ground of condemnation. No doubt unbelief is a great and serious matter and the form in which sin expresses itself when men spurn the one hope of their redemption, but it is not the only form of man's revolt against God, and hence it is certainly not the only possible ground on which man stands condemned before God. (*b*) In fact the Bible represents men as already under condemnation before the gospel is preached to them, and it is precisely this prior condemnation which represents the need of man to which the gospel comes as God's gracious answer. The effect of the gospel is not first to create and then to remove man's condemnation, but to deal with the condemnation which already hangs over man's head (*cf.* Rom. 1:18; 2:12; 5:16, 18; Eph. 2:4; 5:3–6; Col. 3:5f.). (*c*) The view that the gospel creates the possibility of man's condemnation as well as of his deliverance cannot but have a most debilitating effect upon evangelistic and missionary zeal, since, if it is only by rejecting the gospel men are finally condemned, and if, as statistics show, the majority of those who hear the gospel do not accept it, then on purely utilitarian grounds it is in the interests of the greatest happiness of the greatest number not to preach the gospel at all, and indeed to do all in our power to stop its being preached. This ludicrous and patently unbiblical conclusion shows how mistaken is the original premise.

The germ of truth in this position is that increased knowledge and increased opportunity do imply increased responsibility. Scripture certainly does recognize that men are not equal as far as their opportunity to know God is concerned, and this factor will be taken into account when God exercises his judgment (Mt. 11:20–24; Rom. 2:1–24; 2 Pet. 2:21). The principle of Lk. 12:48, 'to whom much is given, of him will much be required', is applicable at this point. Thus the general comment that those who have never heard the gospel will be judged by the light they have is correct. However, we need to add that the light they have had has not been followed by them. Only in Jesus Christ is there hope of salvation (Jn. 14:6; Acts 4:12; Eph. 2:12).

Scripture witnesses to a division at the final judgment between the 'righteous' and the 'wicked', the 'elect' and the 'non-elect', *i.e.* 'those whose names were found written in the book of life' and those whose names were 'not found written in the book of life' (Dn. 12:1–3; Mal. 3:18; Mt. 13:30, 39–43, 49f.; 25:32f., 41, 46; Mk. 13:27; Jn. 5:28f.; 1 Cor. 1:18f.; 2 Cor. 2:15f.; Rev. 20:11–15). The future existence of those who are acquitted at the final judgment is referred to in the Bible as *heaven; that of those not acquitted as *hell.

III. The judgment of Christians

Scripture speaks also of a judgment of Christians. Christ at his coming will judge his people (Mt. 25:14–30, 31–46; Lk. 19:12–28; 1 Cor. 3:12–15; 2 Cor. 5:10; 1 Pet. 1:17; Rev. 20:12f.). Christians will be judged by their Lord in respect of their stewardship of the talents, gifts, opportunities and responsibilities granted to them during the course of their lives. The reference to this judgment in 1 Pet. 1:17 is particularly significant in conveying its character. The divine judgment of the people of God will be a fatherly judgment. It will not be such as to place in peril the Christian's standing within the family of God; it will have all of a father's understanding and compassion; and yet it is not therefore to be lightly or carelessly regarded. This fatherly judgment will be exercised by Christ at his coming.

IV. Human judgment

Here as elsewhere man is called upon to imitate God. Just as God is a righteous judge, so men are called upon to judge righteously (Lk. 12:57; Jn. 7:24) in the constant recognition that ultimately the judgment is God's (Dt. 1:17). The Christian is expected to show discrimination and judgment in moral matters, and the ability to do so is a sign of true maturity (Lk. 12:57; Jn. 7:24; Rom. 15:14; 1 Cor. 2:15; Gal. 6:1; [illegible] 2 Cor. 13:5; Phil. 1:10; Col. 1:9; 1 Jn. 4:1). However, the Christian is also given frequent warnings against the danger of passing judgment on others in a way which attempts to anticipate the final divine judgment (Mt. 7:1; Lk. 6:41f.; Jn. 8:7; Rom. 2:1; 14:4; Jas. 4:1). All human judgments are provisional in the light of the coming judgment (1 Cor. 4:3–5). When the new age is fully manifest at the return of Christ, Christians, according to 1 Cor. 6:2f., will be called upon to exercise judgment with respect to the world (v. 2), and angels in particular (v. 3).

V. Present attitudes

There are few points at which the teaching of the Bible is more sharply in conflict with the assumptions of our age than in its teaching concerning God's future judgment of all men. It is correspondingly one of the most serious contemporary expressions of Christian intellectual and spiritual capitulation that this particular truth should be so little reflected in current preaching and writing. The world has been permitted at this point only too clearly to squeeze the church into its own mould (Rom. 12:1f., Phillips). Thus a theological commentator can complain with full justice that today the notion of final judgment 'figures so little in the theology and preaching of the Church' (T. Preiss, *Life in Christ*, 1954, p. 79). This theological neglect is the more inexcusable in that this century has witnessed an unprecedented recovery of the biblical eschatological perspective. This particular aspect of eschatology, however, *viz.* future divine judgment, quite unwarrantedly, has been largely left on one side.

Man today rejects out of hand the idea that he must one day render account for his life and its decisions. His loss of conviction concerning an after-life, combined with the erosion of the notion of moral responsibility on the basis of popular understanding of psychological and psycho-analytical theories, has contributed to the moral indifference and pragmatism of our times. Moral issues, in so far as they matter at all, relate only to the present moment and to considerations of personal happiness. The thought that they might relate to some transcendent divine dimension, or that all men will one day be inescapably summoned to accept responsibility for these very moral decisions in the answering presence of their Creator, is anathema. Unfortunately for modern man it happens to be true. Judgment is inevitable and awaits us all. In face of this modern tendency to dismiss future judgment there is the greater and more urgent responsibility placed upon the Christian church tenaciously to maintain the biblical perspective.

BIBLIOGRAPHY. L. Morris, *The Biblical Doctrine of Judgment*, 1960; N. Q. Hamilton, *The Holy Spirit and Eschatology in Paul*, 1957; F. Büchsel, V. Herntrich, *TDNT* 3, pp. 921–954; W. Schneider, H. Beck, T. McComiskey, *NIDNTT* 2, pp. 361–371. B.A.M.

JUDGMENT SEAT. In Greek states the assembly met in front of a dais (*bēma*) from which all official business was conducted. Thus Herod Agrippa I sits on the dais (RSV 'throne') to address the republics of Tyre and Sidon (Acts 12:21). The Gk. term is otherwise used in the NT for the *tribunal* (Acts 18:12, *etc.*), the platform on which a Roman magistrate sat, flanked by his counsellors, to administer justice. It was traditionally erected in some public place, as apparently in the case of Pilate (Jn. 19:13), or alternatively in an auditorium (Acts 25:23). That it was the solemn integrity of Roman justice that prompted the image of the judgment seat of God (Rom. 14:10) or Christ (2 Cor. 5:10) seems likely from the fact that Paul is in either case addressing an audience familiar with direct Roman government.

BIBLIOGRAPHY. E. Weiss, *RE*, 6.A.2. 2428–30, *s.v. tribunal.* E.A.J.

Roman coin showing the Emperor Vitellius seated on a judgment seat 'tribunal'. Bronze sestertius, *minted at Rome AD 69. Diameter 33 mm.* (RG)

JUDGMENT HALL See Praetorium, Part 3.

JULIUS. The family name of the Caesars, which must have become widespread since their rise to power due to the custom of conferring on new citizens the name of the magistrate under whose auspices they were enfranchised. The centurion who escorted Paul to Rome (Acts 27:1) presumably belongs to this class of Julii, since no aristocratic member of the house would serve in that rank. His unit (the 'Augustan Cohort', see *ARMY) has been thought (by Mommsen and Ramsay) to be the Caesar's regular staff of couriers. The term corresponds exactly, however, to the *cohors Augusta* known from epigraphic evidence. That this was an auxiliary (*i.e.* non-citizen) force, and therefore not likely to supply the escort for a Roman, is not a serious objection, since the centurion himself is manifestly a citizen. Whether enfranchised on promotion, or seconded to the *auxilia* from the legions, he belongs with Paul to the proud and growing body of new citizen families that Roman statesmanship created in the East.

BIBLIOGRAPHY. T. R. S. Broughton, *BC*, 1.5, pp. 427–445. E.A.J.

JUNG CODEX See Chenoboskion, Part 1.

JUNGLE CAT See Animals, Part 1.

JUNIA, JUNIAS See Andronicus, Part 1.

JURISPRUDENCE See Crime, Part 1.

JUSTICE. The word 'justice' occurs 115 times in RSV OT, usually for *mišpāṭ*, 'judgment', the rule that should guide *judges. In the AV, however, it represents *mišpāṭ* only once (Jb. 36:17); elsewhere it translates *ṣeḏeq* or *ṣᵉḏāqâ*. The more frequent rendering of these latter nouns is 'righteousness'; but when *mišpāṭ* and *ṣᵉḏāqâ* appear together AV translates the whole phrase as 'judgment and justice' (*e.g.* 2 Sa. 8:15; *cf.* Gn. 18:19), though RSV renders the same combination as 'justice and righteousness'. In AV, therefore, 'justice' must be understood as being the same word as *'righteousness', and seldom as denoting the specialized concept of 'fair play', or legal equity, with which the term justice is presently associated. The expression, 'to do (someone) justice', occurs twice, being taken from the corresponding Heb. verbal root, *ṣāḏaq*, causative, which means 'to declare one right' (2 Sa. 15:4; Ps. 82:3). Similarly, the adjective *ṣaddîq*, 'righteous', is over 40 times rendered by the adjective 'just', in both vss. In RSV NT, the noun 'justice' represents both *krisis*, 'judgment', and *dikaiosynē*, 'righteousness'. In AV it does not appear; but at over 30 points the adjective *dikaios*, 'righteous', is likewise translated by the English term 'just'.

This biblical concept of justice exhibits development through nine, generally chronological stages.

1. Etymologically, it appears that the root of *ṣ^{e}ḏāqâ*, like that of its kindred noun *yōšer*, 'uprightness' (Dt. 9:5), signifies 'straightness', in a physical sense (*BDB*, p. 841).

2. But already in the patriarchal age *ṣ^{e}ḏāqâ* has the abstract meaning of conformity, by a given object or action, to an accepted standard of values, *e.g.* Jacob's 'honest' living up to the terms of his sheep-contract with Laban (Gn. 30:33). Moses thus speaks of just balances, weights and measures (Lv. 19:36; Dt. 25:15) and insists that Israel's *judges pronounce 'just (AV; righteous, RSV) judgment' (Dt. 16:18, 20). Arguments that are actually questionable may seem, at first glance, to be 'just' (Pr. 18:17; RSV, 'right'); and Christian masters are cautioned to treat their slaves 'justly and fairly' (Col. 4:1). Even inanimate objects may be described as *ṣeḏeq*, if they measure up to the appropriate standards. The phrase, 'paths of *ṣeḏeq*' (Ps. 23:3), for example, designates walkable paths.

3. Since life's highest standard is derived from the character of deity, 'justice', from the time of Moses and onwards (*cf.* Dt. 32:4), comes to distinguish that which is God's will and those activities which result from it. Heavenly choirs proclaim, 'Just and true are thy ways' (Rev. 15:3). Recognizing the ultimacy of the will of the Lord, Job therefore asks, 'How can a man be just before God?' (Jb. 9:2; *cf.* 4:17; 33:12). But even though God stands answerable to no man, still 'to justice . . . he doeth no violence' (37:23, RVmg.); for the actions of the God who acts in harmony with his own standard are always perfect and right (Zp. 3:5; Ps. 89:14). *ṣ^{e}ḏāqâ* may thus describe Yahweh's preservation of both human and animal life (Ps. 36:6) or his dissociation from vain enterprise (Is. 45:19). In both of the latter verses the EVV translate *ṣ^{e}ḏāqâ* as 'righteousness'; but it might with greater accuracy be rendered 'regularity' or 'reliability'.

4. By a natural transition, 'justice' then comes to identify that moral standard by which God measures human conduct (Is. 26:7). Men too must 'do justice' (Gn. 18:19) as they walk with deity (Gn. 6:9; Mt. 5:48); for not the hearers, but the doers of the law, are 'just (AV; righteous, RSV) before God' (Rom. 2:13). The attribute of justice is to be anticipated only in the hearts of those who fear God (Lk. 18:2), because justice in the biblical sense begins with holiness (Mi. 6:8; Mk. 6:20; 1 Thes. 2:10) and with sincere devotion (Lk. 2:25; Acts 10:22). Positively, however, the wholehearted participation of the Gadites in the divinely ordered conquest of Canaan is described as 'executing the just decrees of the Lord' (Dt. 33:21; *cf.* S. R. Driver, *ICC*). The need for earnest conformity to the moral will of God lies especially incumbent upon kings (2 Sa. 8:15; Je. 22:15), princes (Pr. 8:15), and judges (Ec. 5:8); but every true believer is expected to 'do justice' (Ps. 119:121, AV; Pr. 1:3; *cf.* its personification in Is. 59:14). Justice constitutes the opposite of sin (Ec. 7:20) and serves as a marked characteristic of Jesus the Messiah (Is. 9:7; Zc. 9:9; Mt. 27:19; Acts 3:14). In the poetry of the OT there do arise affirmations of self-righteousness by men like David ('Judge me according to my righteousness, and establish the just', Ps. 7:8–9, AV; *cf.* 18:20–24) or Job ('I am . . . just and blameless' Jb. 12:4; *cf.* 1:1), that might appear incongruous when considered in the light of their acknowledged iniquity (*cf.* Jb. 7:21; 13:26). The poets' aims, however, are either to exonerate themselves from particular crimes that enemies have laid to their charge (*cf.* Ps. 7:4) or to profess a genuine purity of purpose and single-hearted devotion to God (Ps. 17:1). 'They breathe the spirit of simple faith and childlike trust, which throws itself unreservedly on God . . . and they disclaim all fellowship with the wicked, from whom they may expect to be distinguished in the course of His Providence' (A. F. Kirkpatrick, *The Book of Psalms*, 1906, 1, p. lxxxvii). As Ezekiel described such a man, 'He walks in my statutes . . . he is righteous (AV, just), he shall surely live, says the Lord God' (Ezk. 18:9).

5. In reference to divine government, justice becomes descriptive in a particular way of punishment for moral infraction. Under the lash of heaven-sent plagues, Pharaoh confessed, 'The Lord is *ṣaddîq*, and I and my people are wicked' (Ex. 9:27; *cf.* Ne. 9:33); and the one thief cried to the other as they were crucified, 'We indeed justly . . .' (Lk. 23:41). For God cannot remain indifferent to evil (Hab. 1:13; *cf.* Zp. 1:12), nor will the Almighty pervert justice (Jb. 8:3; *cf.* 8:4; 36:17). Even the pagans of Malta believed in a divine nemesis, so that when they saw Paul bitten by a viper they concluded, 'This man is a murderer . . . justice has not allowed him to live' (Acts 28:4). God's punitive righteousness is as a consuming fire (Dt. 32:22; Heb. 12:29; *WRATH), and condemnation is just (Rom. 3:8).

6. From the time of the judges and onward, however, *ṣ^{e}ḏāqâ* comes also to describe his deeds of vindication for the deserving, 'the triumph of the Lord' (Jdg. 5:11). Absalom thus promised a petitioner he 'would give him justice' (2 Sa. 15:4; *cf.* Ps. 82:3), and Solomon proclaimed that God 'blesses the abode of the righteous (AV, just)' (Pr. 3:33; *cf.* Ps. 94:15). Divine vindication became also the plea of Isaiah's contemporaries, 'They ask of me the ordinances of justice' (Is. 58:2–3, AV); for though God's intervention might have been delayed (Ec. 7:15; 8:14; *cf.* Is. 40:27), he yet 'became jealous for his land, and had pity on his people' (Joel 2:18).

7. Such words, however, introduce another aspect, in which divine justice ceases to constitute an expression of precise moral desert and partakes rather of divine pity, love and grace. This connotation appears first in David's prayer for the forgiveness of his crimes over Bathsheba, when he implored, 'Deliver me from bloodguiltiness, O God, thou God of my salvation, and my tongue will sing aloud of thy *ṣ^{e}ḏāqâ*' (deliverance)' (Ps. 51:14). But what David sought was not vindication; for he had just acknowledged his heinous sin and, indeed, his depravity from birth (Ps. 51:5). His petition sought rather for undeserved pardon; and *ṣ^eḏāqâ* may be translated by simple repetition—O God of my salvation: my tongue shall sing of thy 'salvation'. *ṣ^eḏāqâ*, in other words, has become redemptive; it is God's fulfilling of his own graciously promised salvation, irrespective of the merits of men (*cf.* David's same usage in Pss. 31:1; 103:17; 143:1). David's counsellor Ethan thus moves, in the space of two verses, from a reference to God's 'justice [*ṣeḏeq*, according to sense **4** above] and judgment' (Ps. 89:14, AV) to the joyful testimony, 'In thy *ṣ^eḏāqâ* [promised grace] shall Israel be exalted' (Ps. 89:16, AV; *cf.* a similar contrast within Is. 56:1). When Isaiah, therefore, speaks of 'a just [AV; righteous, RSV; *ṣaddîq*] God and a Saviour' (Is. 45:21), his thought is not, 'A just God, and yet at the same time a Saviour', but rather, 'A *ṣaddîq* God, and therefore a Saviour' (*cf.* the parallelism of * 'righteousness' with salvation in Is. 45:8; 46:13). Correspondingly, we read in the NT that 'if we confess our sins, he is faithful and just [*dikaios* = faithful to his gracious promise, not, demanding justice] and will forgive our sins' (1 Jn. 1:9). Such concepts of non-judicial 'justice', however, must be limited to those passages in which this usage is specifically intended. In Rom. 3, on the contrary, with its contextual emphasis upon the wrath of God against sin and upon the propitiatory sacrifice of Christ for the satisfaction of the Father's justice, we must continue to understand *dikaios* (Rom. 3:26) in its traditional sense: 'That he [God] might be just [exacting punishment, according to sense **5** above], and [yet at the same time] the justifier of him which believeth in Jesus' (AV; see Sanday and Headlam, *ICC*; *JUSTIFICATION).

8. As a condition that arises out of God's forgiving 'justice', there next appears in Scripture a humanly possessed *ṣ^eḏāqâ*, which is simultaneously declared to have been God's own moral attribute (*ṣ^eḏāqâ* in sense **4** above), but which has now been imparted to those who believe on his grace. Moses thus describes how Abraham's faith served as a medium for imputed righteousness (Gn. 15:6), though one must, of course, observe that his faith did not constitute in itself the meritorious righteousness but was merely 'reckoned' so. He was justified *through* faith, not *because of* it (*cf.* John Murray, *Redemption, Accomplished and Applied*, 1955, p. 155). Habakkuk likewise declared, 'The just shall live by his faith' (Hab. 2:4, AV), though here too the justification derives, not from man's own, rugged 'faithfulness' (RSVmg.), but from his humble dependence upon God's mercy (contrast the self-reliance of the Babylonians, which the same context condemns; and *cf.* Rom. 1:17; Gal. 3:11). It was God's prophet Isaiah, however, who first spoke directly of 'the heritage of the servants of the Lord . . . their *ṣ^eḏāqâ* from me' (Is. 54:17). Of this 'righteousness', A. B. Davidson accurately observed, 'It is nót a Divine attribute. It is a Divine effect . . . produced in the world by God' (*The Theology of the Old Testament*, [illegible] That is to say, there exists within Yahweh a righteousness which, by his grace, becomes the possession of the believer (Is. 45:24). Our own righteousness is totally inadequate (Is. 64:6); but 'in Yahweh' we 'are righteous' (*ṣāḏaq*) (Is. 45:25), having been made just by the imputed merit of Christ (Phil. 3:9). A century later, Jeremiah thus speaks both of Judah and of God himself as a 'habitation of justice' (Je. 31:23; 50:7, AV), *i.e.* a source of justification for the faithful (*cf.* Je. 23:6; 33:16, 'Yahweh our righteousness', Theo. Laetsch, *Biblical Commentary, Jeremiah*, 1952, pp. 191–192, 254).

9. But even as God in his grace bestows righteousness upon the unworthy, so the people of God are called upon to 'seek justice' (Is. 1:17) in the sense of pleading for the widow and 'judging the cause of the poor and needy' (Je. 22:16). 'Justice' has thus come to connote goodness (Lk. 23:50) and loving consideration (Mt. 1:19). Further, from the days of the Exile onward, Aram. *ṣiḏqâ*, 'righteousness', becomes specialized into a designation for alms or charity (Dn. 4:27), an equivalent expression for 'giving to the poor' (Ps. 112:9; *cf.* Mt. 6:1) One might therefore be led to conceive of biblical 'justice', particularly in these last three, suprajudicial senses, as involving a certain tension or even contradiction: *e.g.* *ṣ^eḏāqâ* in its 7th, gracious sense seems to forgive the very crimes that it condemns in its 5th, punitive sense. The ultimate solution, however, appears in the person and work of the Lord Jesus Christ. The ethical example furnished by his sinless life (Heb. 4:15) constitutes the climax of biblical revelation on the moral will of God and far exceeds the perverted though seemingly lofty justice of the scribes and Pharisees (Mt. 5:20). Yet he who commanded men to be perfect, even as their heavenly Father is perfect (Mt. 5:48), exhibited at the same time that love which has no equal, as he laid down his life for his undeserving friends (Jn. 15:13). Here was revealed *ṣ^eḏāqâ*, 'justice', in its ethical stage **5**, in its redemptive stage **7**, and in its imputed stage **8**, all united in one. He came that God might be just and yet the justifier of him that believeth in Jesus (Rom. 3:26) and that we might be found in him, who is made our righteousness and sanctification and redemption (1 Cor. 1:30).

Bibliography. H. Conzelmann, 'Current Problems in Pauline Research', in R. Batey (ed.), *New Testament Issues*, 1970, pp. 130–147; W. Eichrodt, *Theology of the Old Testament*, 1, 1961, pp. 239–249; D. Hill, *Greek Words and Hebrew Meanings*, 1967, pp. 82–162; J. Jeremias, *The Central Message of the New Testament*, 1965, pp. 51–70, G. E. Ladd, *A Theology of the New Testament*, 1975, pp. 437–450; J. B. Payne, *Theology of the Older Testament*, 1962, pp. 155–161, 165f.; G. Quell and G. Schrenk, *TDNT* 2, pp. 174–225); Norman H. Snaith, *Mercy and Sacrifice*, 1953, pp. 70–79; and *The Distinctive Ideas of the Old Testament*, 1946; J. A. Ziesler, *The Meaning of Righteousness in Paul*, 1972; H. Seebass, C. Brown, *NIDNTT* 3, pp. 352–377. J.B.P.

JUSTIFICATION.

I. Meaning of the word

'Justify' (Heb. *ṣāḏaq*; Gk. [LXX and NT], *dikaioō*) is a forensic term meaning 'acquit', 'declare righteous', the opposite of 'condemn' (*cf.* Dt. 25:1; Pr. 17:15; Rom. 8:33). Justifying is the judge's act. From the litigant's standpoint, therefore, 'be justified' means 'get the verdict' (Is. 43:9, 26).

In Scripture, God is 'the Judge of all the earth' (Gn. 18:25), and his dealings with men are constantly described in forensic terms. Righteousness, *i.e.* conformity with his law, is what he requires of men, and he shows his own righteousness as Judge in taking vengeance on those who fall short of it (*cf.* Ps. 7:11, RV; Is. 5:16; 10:22; Acts 17:31; Rom. 2:5; 3:5f.). There is no hope for anyone if God's verdict goes against him.

Because God is King, the thought of him as justifying may have an executive as well as a judicial aspect. Like the ideal royal judge in Israel, he will not only pass a verdict in favour of the accused, but actively implement it by showing favour towards him and publicly reinstating him. The verb 'justify' may focus on either aspect of God's action. For instance, the justifying of Israel and the Servant, envisaged in Is. 45:25; 50:8, is a public vindication through a change in their fortunes. The justification of sinners that Paul expounds, however, is simply the passing of a favourable verdict. Paul certainly believes that God shows favour to those whom he has acquitted, but he uses other terms to describe this (adoption, *etc.*).

'Justify' is also used for ascriptions of righteousness in non-forensic contexts. Men are said to justify God by confessing him just (Lk. 7:29; *cf.* Rom. 3:4, quoting Ps. 51:4), and themselves by claiming to be just (Jb. 32:2; Lk. 10:29; 16:15). Jerusalem is ironically said to have 'justified' Sodom and Samaria by outdoing them in sin! (Ezk. 16:51). The passive can denote being vindicated by events against suspicion, criticism and mistrust (Mt. 11:19; Lk. 7:35; 1 Tim. 3:16; *cf.* Jas. 2:21, 24f., for which see below).

Lexical support is wanting for the view of Chrysostom, Augustine and the Council of Trent that when Paul and James speak of present justification they refer to God's work of *making* righteous by inner renewal, as well as of *counting* righteous through remission of sins. James seems to mean neither, Paul only the latter. His synonyms for 'justify' are 'reckon righteousness', 'remit sins', 'not reckon sin' (see Rom. 4:5–8, RV)—phrases expressing the idea, not of inner transformation, but of conferring a legal status and cancelling a legal liability. Justification, to Paul, is a judgment passed on man, not a work wrought within man. The two things go together, no doubt, but they are distinct.

II. Justification in Paul

Out of the 39 occurrences of the verb 'justify' in the NT, 29 come in the Epistles or recorded words of Paul; so do the two occurrences of the corresponding noun, *dikaiōsis* (Rom. 4:25; 5:18). This reflects the fact that Paul alone of NT writers makes the concept of justification basic to his soteriology.

Justification means to Paul *God's act of remitting the sins of guilty men, and accounting them righteous, freely, by his grace, through faith in Christ, on the ground, not of their own works, but of the representative law-keeping and redemptive blood-shedding of the Lord Jesus Christ on their behalf.* (For the parts of this definition, see Rom. 3:23–26; 4:5–8; 5:18f.) Paul's doctrine of justification is his characteristic way of formulating the central gospel truth, that God forgives believing sinners. Theologically, it is the most highly developed expression of this truth in the NT.

In Romans, Paul introduces the gospel as disclosing 'the righteousness of God' (1:17). This phrase proves to have a double reference: **1** to the righteous man's status, which God through Christ freely confers upon believing sinners ('the *gift* of righteousness', Rom. 5:17; *cf.* 3:21f.; 9:30; 10:3–10; 2 Cor. 5:21; Phil. 3:9); **2** to the way in which the gospel reveals God as doing what is right—not only judging transgressors as they deserve (2:5; 3:5f.) but also keeping his promise to send salvation to Israel (3:4f.), and justifying sinners in such a way that his own judicial claims upon them are met (3:25f.). 'The righteousness of God' is thus a predominantly forensic concept, denoting God's gracious work of bestowing upon guilty sinners a justified justification, acquitting them in the court of heaven without prejudice to his justice as their Judge.

Many scholars today find the background of this phrase in a few passages from Is. 40ff. and the psalms in which God's 'righteousness' and 'salvation' appear as equivalents (Is. 45:8, *cf.* vv. 19–25; 46:13; 51:3–6; Ps. 98:2; *etc.*). This may be right, but since Paul nowhere quotes these verses, it cannot be proved. It must also be remembered that the reason why these texts call God's vindication of his oppressed people his 'righteousness' is that it is an act of faithfulness to his covenant promise to them; whereas Romans deals principally with God's justifying of Gentiles, who previously were not his people and to whom he had promised nothing (*cf.* 9:24f.; 10:19f.)—quite a different situation.

E. Käsemann and others construe God's righteousness in Paul as a gracious exertion of power whereby God keeps faith with both his covenant people (by fulfilling his promise to save them) and his captive creation (by restoring his dominion over it). Both thoughts are Pauline, but it is doubtful whether (as is argued) 'righteousness' in Rom. 3:25–26 and 'just' in v. 26 point only to gracious faithfulness saving the needy and not to judicial retribution (*cf.* 2:5; 3:5) saving the guilty by being diverted upon the One set forth to be a *propitiation. The latter exegesis fits the flow of thought better; the former cannot explain why 'and' appears in the phrase 'just *and* the justifier' (AV), for it finds in these words only one thought, not two.

It has been questioned whether Paul's doctrine of justification by faith without works is any more than a controversial device, developed simply as a weapon against the Judaizers. But the following facts indicate that it was more than this.

1. The Epistle to the *Romans is evidently to be read as a full-dress statement of Paul's gospel, and the doctrine of justification is its backbone.

2. In three places Paul writes in personal terms of the convictions that had made him the man and the missionary that he was, and all three are couched in terms of justification (Gal. 2:15–21; 2 Cor. 5:16–21; Phil. 3:4–14). In Rom. 7:7ff. Paul describes his personal need of Christ in terms of the law's condemnation—a need which only God's justifying sentence in Christ could relieve (*cf.* Rom. 8:1f.; Gal. 3:19–4:7). Paul's personal religion was evidently rooted in the knowledge of his justification.

3. Justification is to Paul God's fundamental act of blessing, for it both saves from the past and secures for the future. On the one hand, it means pardon, and the end of hostility between God and ourselves (Acts 13:39; Rom. 4:6f.; 5:9f.). On the other hand, it means acceptance and a title to all blessings promised to the just, a thought which Paul develops by linking justification with adoption and heirship (Gal. 4:4ff.; Rom. 8:14ff.). Both aspects appear in Rom. 5:1–2, where Paul says that justification brings both peace with God (because sins are remitted) and hope of God's glory (because the sinner is accepted as righteous). This hope is a certainty; for justification has an eschatological significance. It is the judgment of the last day brought into the present, a final, irreversible verdict. The justified man can accordingly be sure that nothing will ever separate him from the love of his God (Rom. 8:33–39; *cf.* 5:9). His glorification is certain (Rom. 8:30). The coming inquisition before Christ's judgment-seat (Rom. 14:10ff.; 2 Cor. 5:10) may deprive him of particular rewards (1 Cor. 3:15), but not of his justified status.

4. Paul's doctrine of salvation has justification as its basic reference-point. His belief about justification is the source from which flows his view of Christianity as a world-religion of grace and faith, in which Gentiles and Jews stand on an equal footing (Rom. 1:16; 3:29ff.; Gal. 3:8–14, 28f., *etc.*). It is in terms of justification that he explains grace (Rom. 3:24; 4:4f., 16), the saving significance of Christ's obedience and death (Rom. 3:24f.; 5:16ff.), the revelation of God's love at the cross (Rom. 5:5–9), the meaning of redemption (Rom. 3:24; Gal. 3:13; Eph. 1:7) and reconciliation (2 Cor. 5:18f.), the covenant relationship (Gal. 3:15f.), faith (Rom. 4:23ff.; 10:8ff.), union with Christ (Rom. 8:1; Gal. 2:17, RV), adoption and the gift of the Spirit (Gal. 4:6–8; Rom. 8:10, *cf.* v. 15), and Christian assurance (Rom. 5:1–11; 8:33ff.). It is in terms of justification that Paul explains all hints, prophecies and instances of salvation in the OT (Rom. 1:17; Gal. 3:11, quoting Hab. 2:4; Rom. 3:21; 4:3–8, quoting Gn. 15:6; Ps. 32:1f.; Rom. 9:22–10:21, quoting Ho. 2:23; 1:10; Is. 8:14; Joel 2:32; Is. 65:1, *etc.*; Rom. 11:26f., quoting Is. 59:20f.; Gal. 3:8, quoting Gn. 12:3; Gal. 4:21ff., quoting Gn. 21:10; *etc.*).

5. Justification is the key to Paul's philosophy of history. He holds that God's central overarching purpose in his ordering of world-history since the Fall has been to lead sinners to justifying faith.

God deals with mankind, Paul tells us, through two representative men: 'the first man Adam', and 'the second man', who is 'the last Adam', Jesus Christ (1 Cor. 15:45ff.; Rom. 5:12ff.). The first man, by disobeying, brought condemnation and death upon the whole race; the second man, by his obedience, has become the author of justification and life for all who have faith (Rom. 5:16ff.).

From the time of Adam's fall, death reigned universally, though sin was not yet clearly known (Rom. 5:12ff.). But God took Abraham and his family into covenant, justifying Abraham through his faith, and promising that in Abraham's seed (*i.e.* through one of his descendants) all nations should be blessed (*i.e.* justified) (Gal. 3:6–9, 16; Rom. 4:3, 9–22). Then through Moses God revealed his law to Abraham's family. The law was meant to give, not salvation, but knowledge of sin. By detecting and provoking transgressions, it was to teach Israelites their need of justification, thus acting as a *paidagōgos* (the household slave who took children to school) to lead them to Christ (Gal. 3:19–24; Rom. 3:20; 5:20; 7:5, 7–13). This epoch of divine preparatory education lasted till the coming of Christ (Gal. 3:23–25; 4:1–5).

The effect of Christ's work was to abolish the barrier of exclusivism which Israel's possession of the law and promise had erected between Jew and Gentile (Eph. 2:14ff.). Through Christ, justification by faith could now be preached to Jew and Gentile without distinction, for in Christ all believers were made Abraham's seed, and became sons of God and heirs of the covenant (Gal. 3:26–29). Unhappily, in this situation most Jews proved to be legalists; they sought to establish a righteousness of their own by works of law, and would not believe that faith in Christ was the God-given way to righteousness (Rom. 9:30–10:21). So many 'natural branches' had been cut off from the olive-tree of the historic covenant community (Rom. 11:16ff.), and the church was for the present predominantly Gentile; but there was hope that an elect remnant from fallen Israel, provoked by the mercy shown to undeserving Gentiles, would itself come to faith and find remission of sins in the end (Rom. 11:23–32). Thus both Jew and Gentile would be saved, not through their own works and effort, but through the free grace of God justifying the disobedient and ungodly; and all the glory of salvation will be God's alone (Rom. 11:30–36).

These considerations point to the centrality of justification in Paul's theological and religious outlook.

III. The ground of justification

As stated by Paul in Romans, the doctrine of justification seems to raise a problem of theodicy. Its background, set out in 1:18–3:20, is the solidarity of mankind in sin, and the inevitability of judgment. In 2:5–16 Paul states his doctrine of the judgment day. The principle of judgment, he says, will be 'to every man according to his works' (v. 6, RSV). The standard of judgment will be God's law, in the highest form in which men know it (if not the Mosaic law, then the law of conscience, vv. 12–15). The evidence will be 'the secrets of men' (v. 16). Only law-keepers can hope to be justified (vv. 7, 10, 12f.). And there are no law-keepers. None is righteous; all have sinned (3:9ff.). So the prospect is of universal condemnation, for Jew as well as Gentile, for a law-breaking Jew is no more acceptable to God than anyone else (2:17–27). All, it seems, are doomed. 'No human being will be justified in his sight by works of the law' (3:20, echoing Ps. 143:2).

But now Paul proclaims the present justification of believing sinners (3:21ff.). God reckons righteousness to the unrighteous and justifies the ungodly (3:23f.; 4:5f.). The (deliberately?) paradoxical quality of the last phrase is heightened by the fact that these very Greek words are used in the LXX of Ex. 23:7 ('I will not justify the wicked') and Is. 5:22f. ('Woe unto them . . . which justify the wicked . . .'). The question arises: on what grounds can God justify the ungodly without compromising his own justice as the Judge?

Paul maintains that God justifies sinners on a just ground: namely, that Jesus Christ, acting on their behalf, has satisfied the claims of God's law upon them. He was 'born under the law' (Gal. 4:4) in order to fulfil the precept and bear the penalty of the law in their stead. By his *'blood' (*i.e.* his death) he put away their sins (Rom. 3:25; 5:9). By his obedience to God he won for all his people the status of law-keepers (Rom. 5:19). He became 'obedient unto death' (Phil. 2:8); his life of righteousness culminated in his dying the death of the unrighteous, bearing the law's penal curse (Gal. 3:13; *cf.* Is. 53:4–12). In his person on the cross, the sins of his people were judged and expiated. Through this 'one act of righteousness'—his sinless life and death—'the free gift came unto all men to justification of life' (Rom. 5:18, RV). Thus believers become 'the righteousness of God' in and through him who 'knew no sin' personally, but was representatively 'made sin' (treated as a sinner, and judged) in their place (2 Cor. 5:21). Thus Paul speaks of 'Christ Jesus, whom God made . . . our righteousness' (1 Cor. 1:30). This was the thought expressed in older Protestant theology by the phrase 'the imputation of Christ's righteousness'. The phrase is not in Paul, but its meaning is. The point that it makes is that believers are made righteous before God (Rom. 5:19) through his admitting them to share Christ's status of acceptance. In other words, God treats them according to Christ's desert. There is nothing arbitrary or artificial in this, for God recognizes the existence of a real union of covenantal solidarity between them and Christ. For Paul, union with Christ is not fiction, but fact—the basic fact, indeed, of Christianity; and his doctrine of justification is simply his first step in analysing its meaning. So it is 'in Christ' (Gal. 2:17; 2 Cor. 5:21) that sinners are justified. God accounts them righteous, not because he accounts them to have kept his law personally (which would be a false judgment), but because he accounts them to be 'in' the One who kept God's law representatively (which is a true judgment).

So, when God justifies sinners on the ground of Christ's obedience and death, he acts justly. So far from compromising his judicial righteousness, this method of justification actually exhibits it. It is designed 'to show God's righteousness, because in his divine forbearance he had passed over former sins [*i.e.* in OT times]; it was to prove at the present time that he himself is righteous and that he justifies him who has faith in Jesus' (Rom. 3:25f.). The key words are repeated for emphasis, for the point is crucial. The gospel which proclaims God's apparent violation of his justice really reveals his justice. By his method of justifying sinners, God (in another sense) justified himself; for by setting forth Christ as a propitiation for sins, in whom human sin was actually judged and punished as it deserved, he revealed the just ground on which he was able to pardon and accept believing sinners in OT times (as in fact he did: *cf.* Ps. 130:3f.), no less than in the Christian era.

IV. The means of justification

Faith in Christ, says Paul, is the means whereby righteousness is received and justification bestowed. Sinners are justified 'by' or 'through' faith (Gk. *pistei, dia* or *ek pisteōs*). Paul does not regard faith as the ground of justification. If it were, it would be a meritorious work, and Paul would not be able to term the believer, as such, 'one who does not work' (Rom. 4:5); nor could he go on to say that salvation by faith rests on grace (v. 16), for grace absolutely excludes works (Rom. 11:6). Paul quotes the case of Abraham, who 'believed God, and it was reckoned to him as righteousness', to prove that a man is justified through faith without works (Rom. 4:3ff.; Gal. 3:6; quoting Gn. 15:6). In Rom. 4:5, 9 (*cf.* vv. 22, 24) Paul refers to the Genesis text as teaching that Abraham's faith was 'reckoned . . . as righteousness'. All he means, however, as the context shows, is that Abraham's faith—wholehearted reliance on God's promise (vv. 18ff.)—was the occasion and means of his being justified. The phrase 'reckoned *eis* righteousness' could either mean 'as' (by real equivalence, or some arbitrary method of calculation), or else 'with a view to', 'leading to', 'issuing in'. The latter alternative is clearly right. Paul is not suggesting that faith, viewed either as righteousness, actual or inchoate, or as a substitute for righteousness, is the *ground* of justification; Rom. 4 does not deal with the ground of justification at all, only with the means of securing it.

V. Paul and James

On the assumption that Jas. 2:14–26 teaches that God accepts men on the double ground of faith and works, some have thought that James deliberately contradicts Paul's teaching of justification by faith without works, supposing it to be antinomian (*cf.* Rom. 3:8). But this seems to misconceive James' point. It must be remembered that Paul is the only NT writer to use 'justify' as a technical term for God's act of accepting men when they believe. When James speaks of 'being justified', he appears to be using the word in its more general sense of being vindicated, or proved genuine and right before God and men, in face of possible doubt as to whether one was all that one professed, or was said, to be (*cf.* the usage in Mt. 11:19). For a man to be justified in this sense is for him to be shown a genuine believer, one who will demonstrate his faith by action. This justification is, in effect, a manifesting of the justification that concerns Paul. James quotes Gn. 15:6 for the same purpose as Paul does—to show that it was faith that secured Abraham's acceptance. But now, he argues, this statement was 'fulfilled' (confirmed, shown to be true, and brought to its appointed completion by events) 30 years later, when 'Abraham (was) justified by works, when he offered his son Isaac upon the altar' (v. 21). By this his faith was 'made perfect', *i.e.* brought to due expression in appropriate actions; thus he was shown to be a true believer. The case of Rahab is parallel (v. 25). James' point in this paragraph is simply that 'faith', *i.e.* a bare orthodoxy, such as the devils have (v. 19), unaccompanied by good works, provides no sufficient grounds for inferring that a man is saved. Paul would have agreed heartily (*cf.* 1 Cor. 6:9; Eph. 5:5f.; Tit. 1:16).

BIBLIOGRAPHY. Arndt; G. Quell and G. Schrenk in *TDNT* 2, pp. 174–225; Klein in *IDBS*, pp. 750–752; commentaries on Romans: especially C. Hodge[2], 1864; C. E. B. Cranfield, *ICC*, 1, 1976; A. Nygren, E.T. 1952; and on Galatians: especially J. B. Lightfoot[10], 1890; E. D. Burton, *ICC*, 1921; J. Buchanan, *The Doctrine of Justification*, 1867; C. Hodge, *Systematic Theology*, 1874, 3, pp. 114–212; V. Taylor, *Forgiveness and Reconciliation*, 1946; L. Morris, *The Apostolic Preaching of the Cross*, 1955; K. Barth, *Church Dogmatics*, 4. 1, E.T. 1956, pp. 514–642; A. Richardson, *Introduction to the Theology of the New Testament*, 1958, pp. 232ff.; J. Murray, *Romans 1–8*, 1959, pp. 336–362; J. A. Ziesler, *The Meaning of Righteousness in Paul*, 1972; H. Seebass, C. Brown, *NIDNTT* 3, pp. 352–377. J.I.P.

JUSTUS. A Latin name. Lightfoot (on Col. 4:11) notes its frequency among Jews and proselytes, often combined with a Jewish name (*cf.* **1** and **3** below, and see Deissmann, *Bible Studies*, pp. 315f.), and suggests that it was meant to denote obedience and devotion to the Law.

1. A name of Joseph Barsabbas, one of the two conceived as the possible apostolic successor to Judas Iscariot (Acts 1:23). By the context he was thus a consistent disciple from John the Baptist's time. Papias had a story of his survival of a heathen ordeal by poison

(Eusebius, *EH* 3. 39. 9; *cf.* Lightfoot, *Apostolic Fathers*, 1891, p. 531, for another authority). On the name 'Barsabbas' ('son of—*i.e.* born on—a Sabbath'?), see H. J. Cadbury in *Amicitiae Corolla*, ed. H. G. Wood, 1933, pp. 48ff. If it is a true patronymic, Judas Barsabbas (Acts 15:22) could be a brother.

2. Gentile adherent and neighbour of the synagogue in Corinth. When Christian preaching split the synagogue, the house of Justus became Paul's centre (Acts 18:7). The MSS variously render his other name as Titus or Titius, or omit it altogether (accepted as the original reading by Ropes, *BC*, 3, p. 173). Following the hint of Rom. 16:23, Ramsay, and, more fully, E. J. Goodspeed (*JBL* 69, 1950, pp. 382ff.) identify him with * Gaius of Corinth, rendering his name 'Gaius Titius Justus'. The guess that he was the Titus of Paul's letters has nothing but its antiquity to commend it.

3. Alias Jesus, a valued Jewish co-worker of Paul (Col. 4:11). Nothing more is known of him. It has been conjectured that his name has accidently dropped out from Phm. 24 (*cf.* E. Amling, *ZNW* 10, 1909, p. 261).

A.F.W.

JUTTAH (Heb. *yûṭṭâh*). A walled town on a hill 8 km due S of Hebron, 5 km SW of Ziph, assigned to the priests (Jos. 15:55; 21:16; *cf.* 1 Ch. 6:59, where Juttah appears in LXX as *Atta*, and is required to make the count); modern Yatta. In Lk. 1:39 some commentators would read Juttah, in apposition to *polin*, for 'Judah'; F.-M. Abel emphatically disagrees (*Géographie de la Palestine* 2, 1938, p. 367).

J.P.U.L.

KABZEEL. A town in S Judah; birthplace of Benaiah ben-Jehoiada (2 Sa. 23:20); resettled in Nehemiah's time (called Jekabzeel in Ne. 11:25). Khirbet Hora, site of an Israelite fortress 13 km E of Beersheba, is a possible identification. See F.-M. Abel, *Géographie de la Palestine*, 2, 1938, pp. 89, 353; Y. Aharoni, *IEJ* 8, 1958, pp. 36–38.

R.P.G.

KADESH. 1. Kadesh-barnea. A location apparently in the NE of the Sinai peninsula: a well, a settlement, and a wilderness region (Ps. 29:8). When Chedorlaomer and his allies marched S through Transjordan they penetrated Mt Seir as far as El Paran, turned back to the NW, came to En-mishpat (*i.e.* Kadesh) and subdued the Amalekites, before returning to defeat the kings of the Cities of the (Dead Sea) Plain (Gn. 14:5–9). In the narrative of the fugitive Hagar's experience of God, the well Beer-lahai-roi is 'between Kadesh and Bered', on the way to Shur (Gn. 16:7, 14); Kadesh is also associated with the way to Shur in Gn. 20:1. Journeying through the Sinai wilderness, the Israelites stayed in the region of Kadesh on the edges of the wilderness of Paran and Zin more than once (Nu. 13:26; 20:1; Dt. 1:19, 46); from here Moses sent his spies into Canaan. From Horeb or Sinai to Kadesh was 11 days' journey *via* Mt Seir (Dt. 1:2). From the traditional Mt Sinai to Dahab on the E coast of Sinai and up the coast and across to Kadesh (Qudeirat) is indeed 11 days' travel, as observed by Y. Aharoni (*The Holy Land: Antiquity and Survival*, 2, 2/3, pp. 289–290 and 293, fig. 7; Dahab).

At Kadesh, after doubting God's ability to give them the promised land, Israel was condemned to wander for 40 years until a new generation should arise (Nu. 14:32–35; *cf.* Dt. 2:14). After some time, Israel returned to Kadesh (Nu. 33:36–37), Miriam being buried there (Nu. 20:1). At this time, too, for failing to glorify God when striking water from the rock (Nu. 20:10–13; 27:14; Dt. 32:51) Moses was denied entry to the promised land; thence, also, he sent messengers in vain to the king of Edom, to grant Israel permission to pass through his territory (Nu. 20:14–21; Jdg. 11:16–17). Kadesh-barnea was to be the S corner of the SW boundary of Judah, turning W then NW to reach the Mediterranean along the 'River of Egypt' (Nu. 34:4; Jos. 15:3); it was also included as a boundary-point by Ezekiel (47:19; 48:28). The SE to SW limits of Joshua's S Canaanite campaign were marked by Kadesh-barnea and Gaza respectively (Jos. 10:41).

Kadesh-barnea is often identified with the spring of 'Ain Qudeis, some 106 km SW from the S end of the Dead Sea, or about 80 km SW of Beersheba. However, the water supply at 'Ain Qudeis is insignificant; see the unflattering but realistic comments by Woolley and Lawrence ('The Wilderness of Zin', in *Palestine Exploration Fund Annual* 3, 1914–15, pp. 53–57, and plates 10–12, also Baly, *Geography of the Bible*, 1974, p. 250). The name Qudeis may, indeed, have no connection with 'Kadesh' (*cf.* Woolley and Lawrence, *op. cit.*, p. 53 and note*). 'Ain Qudeirat, roughly 8 km NW of 'Ain Qudeis, has much more water and vegeta-

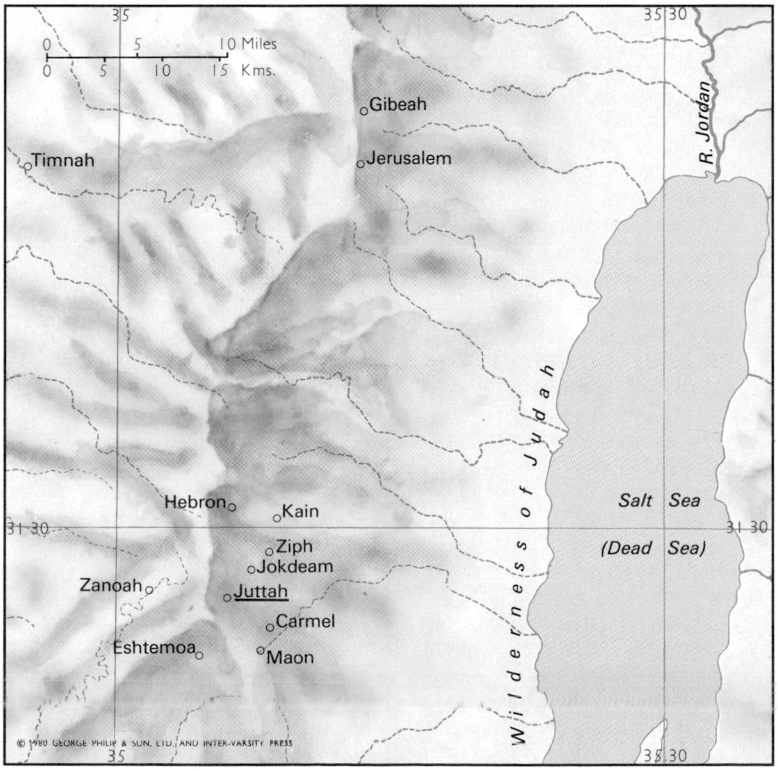

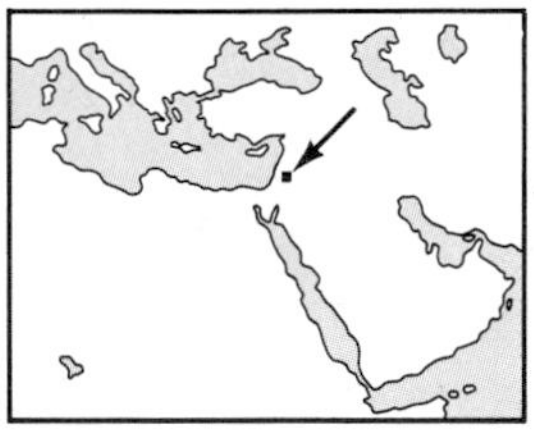

The location of Juttah, modern Yatta.

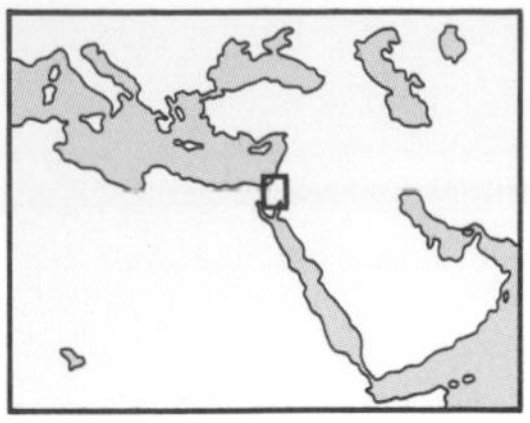

The probable location of Kadesh-barnea (modern 'Ain Qudeirat).

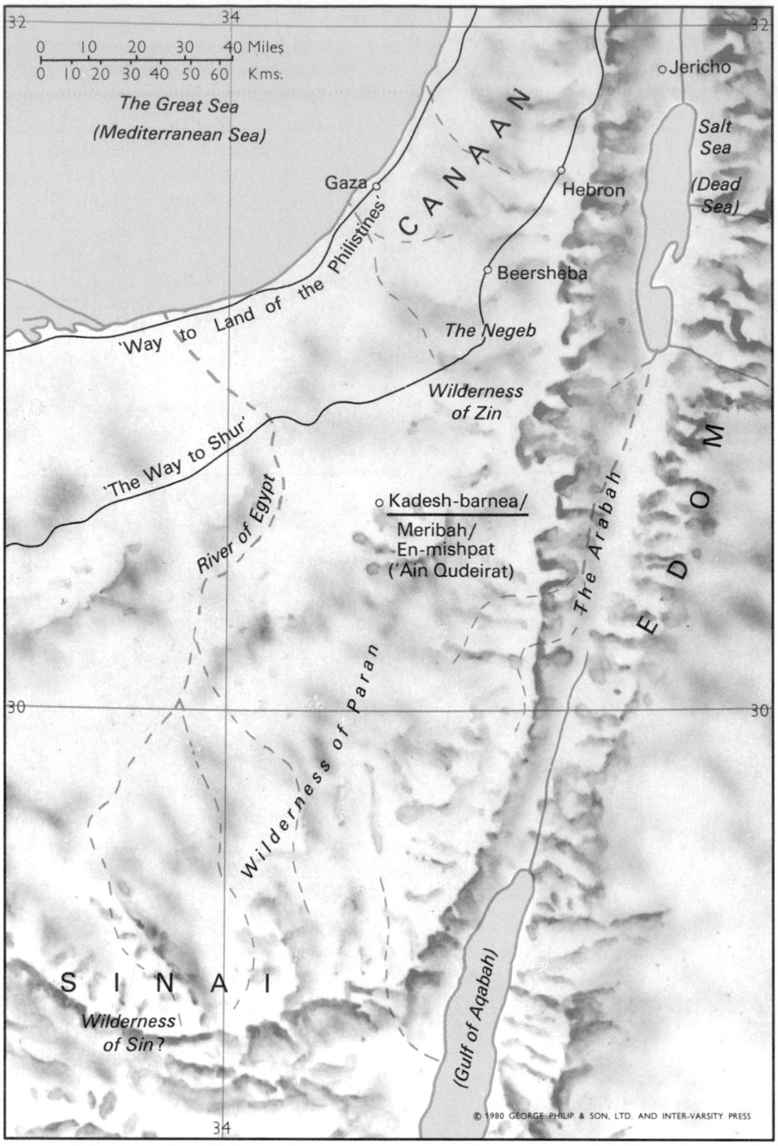

KADESH-BARNEA
See Kadesh, Part 2.

tion and is a more suitable location for Kadesh-barnea (for this see Aharoni, *op. cit.*, pp. 295–296 and figs. 1–3 opposite p. 290; and Woolley and Lawrence, *op. cit.*, pp. 59–62, 69–71 and plates 13–15). Probably the whole group of springs was used by the Israelites, Qudeirat being the main one. The general location of Qudeirat/Qudeis sufficiently suits the topographical requirements of the biblical narratives. See refs. in E. K. Vogel, *Bibliography of Holy Land Sites*, 1974, p. 6, esp. Y. Aharoni in B. Rothenberg, *God's Wilderness*, 1961, pp. 121ff. Also T. L. Thompson, *The Settlement of Sinai and the Negev in the Bronze Age*, 1975, p. 101: 0900. 11, refs. See further, *WILDERNESS OF THE WANDERING.

2. Kedesh in Jos. 15:23, in the southernmost territory of Judah, is either another otherwise unknown Kadesh, or else is probably identical with Kadesh-barnea (*cf.* 15:3).

Finally, the emendation of *Tahtim-Hodshi in 2 Sa. 24:6 to 'the land of the Hittites towards Kadesh' is not very convincing, particularly as the Kadesh on Orontes thus referred to had long passed from history by David's day. K.A.K.

KADMIEL (Heb. *qaḏmî'ēl*, 'God/El is the first/ancient one'). A Levite who returned with Zerubbabel (Ezr. 2:40; Ne. 7:43; 12:8, 24), and was concerned with the commencement of the Temple rebuilding (Ezr. 3:9), with the day of national repentance (Ne. 9:4–5) and with the sealing of the covenant (Ne. 10:9). L. H. Brockington (*Ezra, Nehemiah and Esther*, *NCB*, 1969) suggests that the name appears mainly, if not entirely, limited to the designation of a levitical family. J.G.G.N.

KADMONITES. A people whose name, *qaḏmōnî*, is identical in form with the adjective *qaḏmōnî*, 'eastern' (*e.g.* Ezk. 47:18), and for this reason may simply mean 'Easterners' and be another designation for the *b^e^nê-qedem* *'(children of the) East'. The word occurs but once as a name however (Gn. 15:19, with the article), in the list of peoples to be given to Abraham's seed. It may therefore well be the name of a tribe. T.C.M.

KAIN. A town to the S of Hebron (Jos. 15:57). Khirbet Yaqin has been suggested, but its antiquity is uncertain. LXX takes as one name with Zanoah, altering the count (*ZANOAH, **2**). J.D.D.

KAIWAN (Heb. *kiyyûn*), AV **CHIUN** (Am. 5:26). Earlier scholars thought it meant 'pedestal' or 'image-stand' (see W. R. Harper, *Amos*, *ICC*, 1910, pp. 139f.). Vulg. has *imaginem*, RVmg. 'shrine'. Most now believe that it represents Assyr. *kaiwanu*, a name of Ninurta, god of the planet Saturn, but that the Massoretes have changed the

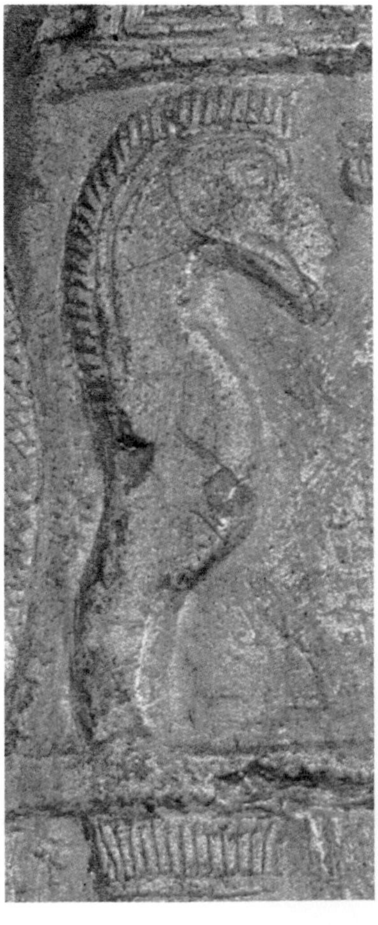

Kaiwan, usually identified with the Assyrian god Ninurta, who is represented by an eagle-headed sceptre on the boundary stone of Nebuchadrezzar I. 12th cent. BC. (BM)

original vowel-points of *kaiwan* to those of *šiqqûṣ* (= 'abomination'). LXX *Rhaiphan* (*REPHAN, AV Remphan) seems to support this view.
D.W.G.

KANAH (Heb. *qānâh*). **1.** A wadi running W from the watershed at the head of the Michmethath valley, 8 km SW of Shechem; its lower course was the boundary of Ephraim with Manasseh (Jos. 16:8).

2. A town in the Lebanon foothills, assigned to Asher (Jos. 19:28); probably modern Qana, 10 km SE of Tyre.
J.P.U.L.

KEDAR (Heb. *qēḏār*, probably 'black', 'swarthy'). **1.** A son of Ishmael (Gn. 25:13; 1 Ch. 1:29), forebear of like-named tribe.

2. Nomadic tribesfolk of the Syro-Arabian desert from Palestine to Mesopotamia. In 8th century BC known in S Babylonia (I. Eph'al, *JAOS* 94, 1974, p. 112), Isaiah prophesying their downfall (Is. 21:16–17). They developed 'villages' (Is. 42:11), possibly simple encampments (H. M. Orlinsky, *JAOS* 59, 1939, pp. 22ff.), living in black tents (Ct. 1:5). As keepers of large flocks (Is. 60:7), they traded over to Tyre (Ezk. 27:21). Geographically, Kittim (Cyprus) W in the Mediterranean and Kedar E into the desert were like opposite poles (Je. 2:10). Dwelling with the Kedarites was like a barbaric exile to one psalmist (Ps. 120:5).

Alongside Arabian tribes, Nebaioth, *etc.*, Kedarites clashed with Ashurbanipal in the 7th century BC (M. Weippert, *Welt des Orients* 7, 1973–74, p. 67). Likewise they suffered attack by Nebuchadrezzar II of Babylon in 599 BC (*cf.* D. J. Wiseman, *Chronicles of Chaldaean Kings*, 1956, p. 32), as announced by Jeremiah (Je. 49:28). By the Persian period, a regular succession of kings of Kedar controlled a realm astride the vital land-route from Palestine to Egypt, regarded as its guardians by the Persian emperors. Such was *Geshem (Gashmu)—opponent of Nehemiah (Ne. 6:1–2, 6)—whose son Qaynu is entitled 'King of Kedar' on a silver bowl from a shrine in the Egyp. E Delta. On this and these kings, see I. Rabinowitz, *JNES* 15, 1956, pp. 1–9, pl. 7; W. J. Dumbrell, *BASOR* 203, 1971, pp. 33–44; A. Lemaire, *RB* 81, 1974, pp. 63–72.
J.D.D.
K.A.K.

KEDEMOTH. Probably present-day ez-Za'ferān, *c.* 16 km N of the Arnon, just inside Sihon's territory and near the Amorites' E border. A levitical city (Jos. 21:37; 1 Ch. 6:79) from the inheritance of Reuben (Jos. 13:18), giving its name to a nearby desert area (Dt. 2:26).

BIBLIOGRAPHY. F. M. Abel, *Géographie de la Bible*, 1938, p. 69; *LOB*, p. 186.
N.H.

KEDESH, KEDESH IN NAPHTALI. 1. A former Canaanite royal city (Jos. 12:22) which became a principal town in Naphtali (Jos. 19:37). It was sometimes designated 'of Naphtali' (Jdg. 4:6) to distinguish it from **2.** It was assigned to the Levites (Jos. 21:32) and made a city of refuge (20:7). Kedesh was also marked by its location in Galilee (Jos. 20:7; 1 Ch. 6:76).

This Kedesh may well be the home of Barak where he collected his forces from Naphtali and Zebulun for war against Sisera (Jdg. 4:9–11). When Tiglath-pileser III of Assyria invaded N Israel in 734–732 BC Kedesh, being on the route S from Hazor, was one of the first cities to fall to him (2 Ki. 15:29). It was the scene of the great battle fought between the Maccabees and Demetrius (1 Macc. 11:63, 73). Kedesh is the modern Tell Qades, NW of Lake Huleh, where soundings and surface finds show it to have been occupied during the early and late Bronze Ages.

2. A town of Issachar given to Gershonite Levites (1 Ch. 6:72). Its place is taken by Kishion in the list of Jos. 21:28. It is identified with the modern Tell Abu Qedes, SSW of Megiddo.

3. A town in S Judah near the Edomite border (Jos. 15:23), probably to be identified with Kadesh-barnea, so *Kadesh.

BIBLIOGRAPHY. *LOB*, pp. 115, 204, 266.
D.J.W.

KEILAH (Heb. *qᵉʿîlâh*). A town in the Shephelah (Jos. 15:43), probably Kelti of Amarna Letters 279–280, 290 (*ANET*, pp. 289, 487). In Saul's time, David relieved it from a Philistine attack, but found Saul's influence too strong for his safety (1 Sa. 23). At the Restoration its territory formed two districts (Ne. 3:17f.). Khirbet Qila, on a hill 10 km E of Beit Guvrin, commands the ascent to Hebron S from Socoh, in the valley between the Shephelah and the hills.
J.P.U.L.

KENATH (Heb. *qᵉnāṯ*, 'possession'). A city in N Transjordan taken from the Amorites by *Nobah, who gave it his name (Nu. 32:42), and later taken by *Geshur and Aram (1 Ch. 2:23). The name appears in several Egyp.

KARNAIM
See Ashteroth-karnaim, Part 1.

KARNAK
See Thebes, Part 3.

KARTAN
See Kiriathaim, Part 2.

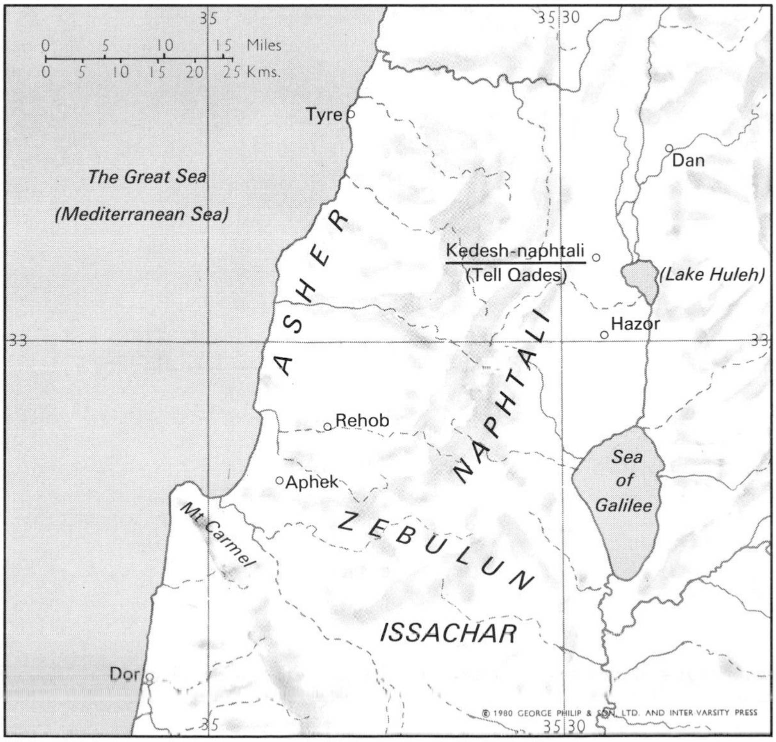

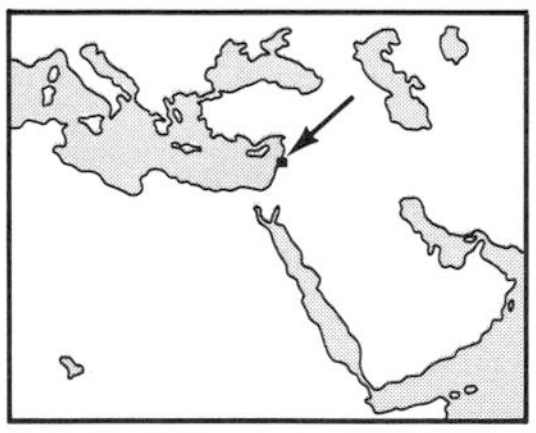

Kedesh in Naphtali (modern Tell Qades).

texts of the 2nd millennium (*cf. LOB*, index). It is usually identified with the extensive ruins at Qanawât, some 25 km NE of Bozrah; but see F.-M. Abel, *Géographie de la Palestine*, 2, p. 417, and M. Noth, *Numbers*, p. 241 (*cf. PJB* 37, 1941, pp. 80–81), who prefers a location W or NW of modern Amman, comparing Jdg. 8:11. J.D.D. G.I.D.

KENAZ. 1. A grandson of *Esau and an *Edomite chief (Gn. 36:11, 15, 42). Some commentators consider these vv. indicate Kenaz was the ancestor of the *Kenizzites. **2.** The brother of *Caleb and father of *Othniel and *Seraiah (Jos. 15:17; Jdg. 1:13; 3:9, 11; 1 Ch. 4:13). **3.** A grandson of Caleb (1 Ch. 4:15). Uknaz (AVmg.) results from Heb. word for 'and' being read as part of the name of Kenaz. R.A.H.G.

KENITES. The Kenites were a Midianite tribe (Nu. 10:29; Jdg. 1:16; 4:11). The name means 'smith', and the presence of copper SE of the Gulf of Aqabah, the Kenite–Midianite region, confirms this interpretation. The Kenites first appear as inhabitants of patriarchal Canaan (Gn. 15:19). Subsequently Moses becomes son-in-law of Reuel (Ex. 2:18), and invites Hobab his son to accompany the Israelites, coveting his nomadic skill (Nu. 10:29). Kenites accompanied Judah into their inheritance (Jdg. 1:16; 1 Sa. 27:10). They were spared by Saul in his Amalekite war (1 Sa. 15:6), and David cultivated their friendship (1 Sa. 30:29). The Rechabites were of Kenite stock (1 Ch. 2:55), and were prominent in post-exilic times (Ne. 3:14).

The 'Kenite hypothesis' gives this Midianite clan importance in the religion of Israel. It purports to answer the question: Where did Moses learn the name Yahweh? Rejecting pre-Mosaic knowledge of the name in Israel, some reply that he learnt the name from Jethro, the Kenite–Midianite. The later Yahwistic zeal of the Rechabite–Kenites cannot support this theory: it is not unknown for converts to be more zealous than traditional believers! Nor does Jethro's sacrifice (Ex. 18:12) bear the weight placed upon it, that Jethro was instructing Moses how Yahweh should be worshipped, for the chapter shows him as the learner, led to faith by Moses' testimony (v. 11). Apart, therefore, from the unconvincing observation that 'the Kenites were the smiths of the ancient nomad tribes, . . . and undoubtedly Yahweh is a fire-god' (Oesterley and Robinson, *History of Israel*, 1, p. 92), the sole support of the Kenite hypothesis is that their ancestor Cain bore the mark of Yahweh (Gn. 4:15). This hypothesis is advocated, *e.g.*, by L. Koehler, *Old Testament Theology*, p. 45; contested by M. Buber, *Moses*, p. 94. The testimony of Genesis is that the name Yahweh was known to the Patriarchs, and indeed from the earliest times (Gn. 4:1, 26). The hypothesis is a fruit of the application of documentary analysis, and well merits being called 'the acme of liberal inventiveness' (U. E. Simon, *A Theology of Salvation*, 1953, p. 88).

BIBLIOGRAPHY. H. H. Rowley, *From Moses to Qumran*, 1963, pp. 48ff.; *Joseph to Joshua*, 1950, pp. 149ff.; Y. Kaufmann, *The Religion of Israel*, 1961, pp. 242ff. J.A.M.

KENIZZITES (Heb. *qᵉnizzî*). A leading Edomite family, tracing descent from Eliphaz, Esau's eldest son (Gn. 36:11, 15, 42; 1 Ch. 1:36, 53). Part of them joined the Judahites; their contribution to Israel's history is indicated in 1 Ch. 4:13ff. V. 15 is difficult; perhaps it read originally '. . . [names lost]; these were the sons of Kenaz'. Caleb's Kenizzite descent is always expressed through Jephunneh (Nu. 32:12, Jos. 14:6, 14). 'Othniel, son of Kenaz' may simply mean 'Othniel, the Kenizzite'; otherwise, this Kenaz would have been Caleb's younger brother, and Othniel his nephew. Caleb's history implies that his family was well established in Judah before the Exodus (*cf.* Nu. 13:6); so it may have been Jephunneh's ancestors who first joined the tribe.

The Kenizzites are mentioned in Gn. 15:19 with nine other nations as occupying the land promised to Abraham; this, apparently defined in terms of settlements made after his time, included the Negeb but no part of Edom proper (*cf.* Dt. 2:5). J.P.U.L.

KENOSIS. This Gk. term is formed from the verb *heauton ekenōsen*, 'he emptied himself', which the AV of Phil. 2:7 renders 'he made himself of no reputation'. As a substantive it is used, in the technical sense, of the Christological theory which sets out 'to show how the Second Person of the Trinity could so enter into human life as that there resulted the genuinely human experience which is described by the evangelists' (H. R. Mackintosh). In its classic form this Christology goes back no farther than the middle of the last century, to Thomasius of Erlangen in Germany.

The essence of the original kenotic view is stated clearly by J. M. Creed. 'The Divine Logos by His Incarnation divested Himself of His divine attributes of omniscience and omnipotence, so that in His incarnate life the Divine Person is revealed and solely revealed through a human consciousness' (art. 'Recent Tendencies in English Christology' in *Mysterium Christi*, ed. Bell and Deissmann, 1930, p. 133). This Christological statement is open to damaging theological objections; and, on exegetical grounds too, there is little support for it.

The verb *kenoun* means simply 'to empty'. In the literal sense it is used, for example, of Rebekah's emptying the water from her pitcher into the trough (Gn. 24:20, LXX: the verb is *exekenōsen*). In Je. 14:2; 15:9 the LXX uses the verb *kenoun* to render the *pu'al* of *'āmal*, which the RV translates as 'languish'; and this translation points to a metaphorical usage which prepares the way for the interpretation of the Philippians text. The use of *kenoun* there in the active voice is unique in the NT, and the whole phrase with the reflexive is not only un-Pauline but un-Greek too. This fact supports the suggestion that the phrase is a rendering into Gk. of a Sem. original, the linguistic solecism being explained by the literal translation from one language into another. Recent scholars (H. W. Robinson, J. Jeremias) have found this original in Is. 53:12: 'He poured out his soul to death'. On this reading of Phil. 2:7, the 'kenosis' is not that of his incarnation but the final surrender of his life, in utter self-giving and sacrifice, on the cross. Even if this novel interpretation is regarded as somewhat forced (for a critique, see R. P. Martin, *Carmen Christi*, 1967, ch. 7) it puts us on the right track. The words 'he emptied himself' in the Pauline context say nothing about the abandonment of the divine attributes, and to that extent the kenotic theory is an entire misunderstanding of the scriptural words. Linguistically the self-emptying is to be interpreted in the light of the words which immediately follow. It refers to the 'pre-incarnate renunciation coincident with the act of "taking the form of a servant"' (V. Taylor, *The Person of Christ in New Testament Teaching*, 1958, p. 77). His taking of the servant's form involved the necessary limitation of the glory which he laid aside that he might be born 'in the likeness of men'. That glory of his pre-existent oneness with the Father (see Jn. 17:5, 24) was his because from all eternity he existed 'in the form of God' (Phil. 2:6). It was concealed in the 'form of a servant' which he took when he assumed [illegible] likeness; and with the acceptance of our humanity he took also his destiny as the Servant of the Lord who humbled himself to the sacrifice of himself at Calvary. The 'kenosis' then began in his Father's presence with his preincarnate choice to assume our nature; it led inevitably to the final obedience of the cross when he did, to the fullest extent, pour out his soul unto death (see Rom. 8:3; 2 Cor. 8:9; Gal. 4:4–5; Heb. 2:14–16; 10:5ff.).

BIBLIOGRAPHY. The fullest modern treatment of the kenosis doctrine, both historically and theologically, is that by P. Henry, art. 'Kénose' in *DBS*, Fasc. 24, 1950, cols. 7–161; D. G. Dawe, *The Form of a Servant*, 1964; T. A. Thomas, *EQ* 42, 1970, pp. 142–151. For a modern theological discussion, see R. S. Anderson, *Historical Transcendence and the Reality of God*, 1975. R.P.M.

KERCHIEFS (AV trans. of Heb. *mispāḥōṯ*, only in plur. Ezk. 13:18, 21, RSV 'veils'). A word associated with the practice of divination, and found in this obscure passage. Some understand the word as denoting long drapes or coverings put over the heads of those who consulted false prophetesses. These coverings for 'persons of every stature' reached down to the feet, and were connected with the introduction of the wearer into the magical circle. Others suggest that the word means a close-fitting cap (*cf.* Heb. *sāpaḥ*, 'to join'), which also fulfils the condition of certain forms of divination or sorcery that the head should be covered. See also *AMULETS, *MAGIC AND SORCERY, **II.** *b*; and, for full discussion of the context and possible interpretations, G. A. Cooke, *Ezekiel*, *ICC*, 1936, pp. 144ff. J.D.D.

KEREN-HAPPUCH (Heb. *qeren happûḵ*, 'paint-horn', *i.e.* 'beautifier'; LXX *Amaltheias keras*). The name given to the third and youngest daughter of Job after his prosperity had been restored (Jb. 42:14). For discussion of the name, *COSMETICS AND PERFUMERY, **III.***a*. J.D.D.

KERIOTH. 1. A town in the extreme S of Judah, known also as Kerioth-hezron or Hazor, possibly the modern Khirbet el-Qaryatein (Jos. 15:25). **2.** A city of Moab (Je. 48:24), formerly fortified (Je. 48:41), and possessing palaces (Am. 2:2). Probably El-Qereiyat, S of Ataroth. Some writers identify it with Ar, the ancient capital of Moab, because when Ar is listed among Moabite towns Kerioth is omitted (Is. 15–16), and *vice versa* (Je. 48). There was a sanctuary there for Chemosh, to which Mesha dragged Arel the chief of Ataroth. (*MOABITE STONE.) J.A.T.

KESITAH (Heb. *qᵉśîṭâ*, probably 'that which is weighed', 'a fixed weight', from an Arab. word meaning 'to divide, fix'). A unit of unknown value, evidently uncoined money used by the Patriarchs. LXX, Onkelos and Jerome render as 'lambs', early weights often being modelled in animal-forms (*WEIGHTS AND MEASURES). Possibly it may represent the value of a sheep in silver. It occurs only in Gn. 33:19 and Jos. 24:32 of Jacob's land-purchase at Shechem, and in Jb. 42:11 of a congratulatory present. RSV translates as 'piece of money', but NEB as 'sheep'. J.G.G.N.

KETURAH (Heb. *qᵉṭûrâ*, 'perfumed one'). Abraham's second wife after the death of Sarah who bore him Zimran, Jokshan, Medan, Midian, Ishbak and Shuah, who in their turn became the ancestors of a number of N Arabian peoples (Gn. 25:1–4; 1 Ch. 1:32–33). (*ARABIA.)

BIBLIOGRAPHY. J. A. Montgomery, *Arabia and the Bible*, 1934, pp. 42–45. T.C.M.

KEY (Heb. *mapṯēaḥ*, 'opener'; Gk. *kleis*, 'key'). In its literal sense the word is found only in Jdg. 3:25; the key was 'a flat piece of wood furnished with pins corresponding to holes in a hollow bolt. The bolt was on the inside, shot into a socket in the doorpost and fastened by pins which fell into the holes in the bolt from an upright piece of wood (the lock) attached to the inside of the door. To unlock the door one put one's hand in by a hole in the door (*cf.* Ct. 5:4) and raised the pins in the bolt by means of the corresponding pins in the key' (F. F. Bruce in *NBCR*, p. 260). The more usual biblical sense of the word is a symbol of power and authority (*e.g.* Mt. 16:19; Rev. 1:18; Is. 22:22).

See also *POWER OF THE KEYS. J.D.D.

Bronze 'knee' or 'elbow' key, so named after its form. The 'teeth' were inserted into corresponding indentations in a bolt. From the Cave of letters, Nahal Hever, W of the Dead Sea. AD 132–135. (IM)

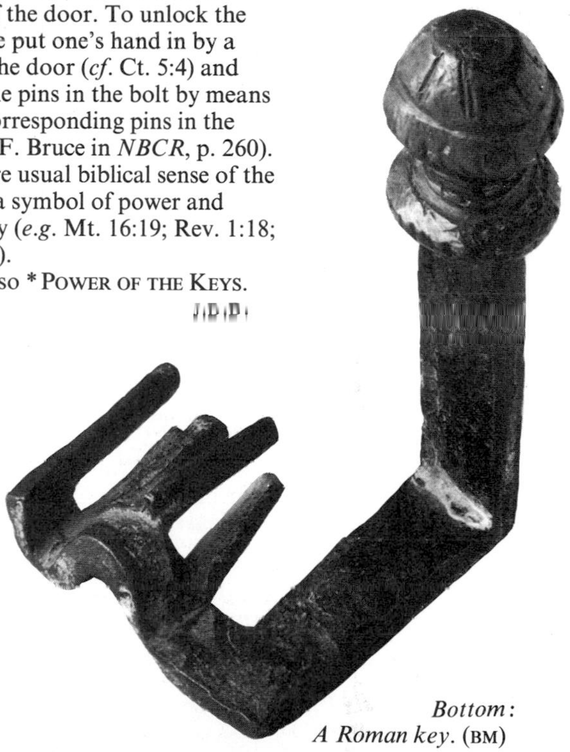

Bottom: A Roman key. (BM)

KIBROTH-HATTAAVAH (Heb. *qiḇrôṯ hatta'ᵃwâ*, 'graves of craving'). A camp of the Israelites a day's journey from the wilderness of Sinai. There the people, having craved flesh to eat and been sent quails by the Lord, were overtaken by plague, which caused many fatalities (Nu. 11:31–34; 33:16; Dt. 9:22; *cf.* Ps. 78:27–31). Some have suggested that the incident at Taberah (Nu. 11:1–3) had the same location as that at Kibroth-hattaavah, but Dt. 9:22 seems to argue against this. Grollenberg makes an identification with Ruweis el-Ebeirig, NE of Mt Sinai.

J.D.D.

KIDNEYS. In the RSV the Heb. word *kᵉlāyôṯ* is translated by 'kidneys' when it refers to the physical organ of sacrificial beasts, principally in Leviticus (3:4; 4:9; 7:4, *etc.*). The practice was that the two kidneys, together with the fat and part of the liver, were burnt on the altar as Yahweh's portion, while the worshippers no doubt consumed the rest. The kidneys along with the blood and other internal organs were held to contain the life, and the kidneys were regarded as a choice portion, perhaps because of their coating of fat; *cf.* Dt. 32:14, where the RSV translates *ḥēleḇ kᵉlayôṯ*, lit. 'fat of the kidneys of', as 'the finest of' (the wheat).

The same Heb. word is translated variously where it refers, generally figuratively, to the human organs, which were held to possess psychical functions. RSV renders it as 'the heart' which is 'troubled' (Jb. 19:27; Ps. 73:21), and 'tried' by God (Je. 11:20). In Pr. 23:16 RSV uses 'soul', which 'rejoices'. In NT Gk. *nephros* (lit. kidneys) occurs once, but RSV renders 'mind' (Rev. 2:23).

The parallelism reveals how the heart and the other internal organs (*BOWELS, *HEART) were held to be the centre of the personality and will, without clear distinction between them.

The reference to the *kᵉlayôṯ* (RSV 'heart') instructing one (Ps. 16:7) (with a parallel in the Ras Shamra texts, 'his inwards instruct him') is a further similar usage, with which compare the late Jewish concept that one kidney prompts a man to do good and the other prompts him to do evil (TJ, *Berakhoth* 61a).

B.O.B.

KIDRON. The brook Kidron, the modern Wadi en-Nar, is a torrent-bed, which begins to the N of Jerusalem, passes the Temple mount and the Mount of Olives *en route* to the Dead Sea, which it reaches by way of the wilderness of Judaea. Its modern name means 'the Fire wadi', and this bears witness to the fact that it is dry and sun-baked for most of the year. Only for short periods during the rainy seasons is it filled with water. It was also called 'the Valley of *Jehoshaphat'.

On the W side of the Kidron there is a spring known as the Gihon ('Gusher') or 'Virgin's Fountain', the flow of which was artificially diverted under Hezekiah's orders to serve the needs of Jerusalem and to protect its water-supply from the enemy. This was the latest of several tunnels and shafts connected with the spring.

As its name would suggest, the water does not come through in a steady flow, but accumulates underground in a reservoir and breaks out from time to time. In 1880 a Heb. inscription was discovered in which information was recorded concerning the making of Hezekiah's tunnel (*SILOAM). For the archaeology, see K. M. Kenyon, *Digging up Jerusalem*, 1974, pp. 84–89, 151–159.

David passed over the brook Kidron on his way out of Jerusalem during Absalom's revolt (2 Sa. 15:23). The reforming kings, such as Asa, Hezekiah and Josiah, used the valley as a place of destruction where heathen idols, altars, *etc.*, were burnt or ground to powder (1 Ki. 15:13, *etc.*). It seems to be taken as one of the boundaries of Jerusalem in 1 Ki. 2:37 and Je. 31:40.

Some suggest a reference to the Kidron in Ezk. 47, where the prophet sees a stream of water issuing from the threshold of the Temple and pursuing its way towards the Dead Sea, making the land fertile in the process. See especially G. Adam Smith, *The Historical Geography of the Holy Land*, 1931, pp. 510ff.; W. R. Farmer, 'The Geography of Ezekiel's River of Life', *BA* 19, 1956, pp. 17ff. That Ezekiel was thinking of the filling-up of the dry bed of the Kidron by the healing stream of water seems probable, but cannot be maintained with any degree of certainty.

G.W.G.

KIN, KINSMAN. Israel was originally tribal in nature. The idea was never entirely lost, although as the centuries passed the distinctions became less well marked, until today they have all but disappeared (*cf.* Scots' clans). Many of Israel's family relationships are to be understood in terms of tribal customs known all over the world. Kinship consisted basically in the possession of a common blood and was strongest nearest to its origin in the father's house, but it was not lost in the further reaches of family relationship. At the head of the family (*mišpāḥâ*) stood the father (*'āḇ*), a word which expressed kinship and authority. The father founded a father's house (*bêṯ 'āḇ*), which was the smallest unit of a tribe. But the strong cohesion of the family extended upwards from the father to the fathers, and downwards from the father to the sons and daughters. Hence the term family could mean the father's house (*bêṯ 'āḇ*), and also the house of the fathers (*bêṯ 'āḇôṯ*). Indeed, at times the whole of Israel was called a family.

A picture of tribal relationships which is more or less contemporary with the patriarchs comes from the Middle Bronze Age society at *Mari on the Euphrates. Here semi-nomadic and urban peoples of the same general stock lived side by side in a dimorphic society. The village-pastoral group were not marauding peoples but sheep-breeders who moved their encampments periodically in search of water and pastures, living in tents but settling at times. These peoples were tribally organized into 'paternal houses' or 'families' (*bit abim*; *cf. bêṯ 'āḇ* in Gn. 12:1, *etc.*). Recent studies provide several detailed comparisons between Mari and the patriarchal society. The texts from Mari provide literary evidence for such a comparison.

The word brother (*'āḥ*) also connoted various things. In its simplest meaning it referred to those who had common parents. In polygamous Israel there were many brothers who had only a common father. These too were brothers, though the brotherhood was not the same as that of men who had a common mother. Thus in Gn. 42:4 there are two kinds of brothers, full and half. The full brother was defined by the phrase 'his brother, Benjamin, his mother's son' (Gn. 43:29). However, the term extended as far as the feeling of consanguinity extended. Wherever there was a family there were brothers, for all were bearers of kinship (Gn. 24:4, 27, 38; Jdg. 14:3). At times all Israelites were called brothers (Ex. 2:11; Lv. 10:6; 2 Sa. 19:41–42).

There were limits to the closeness of relationship permitted when a man came to seek a wife. Abraham would seek a wife for his son Isaac from his kindred (*mišpāḥâ*) and from his father's house (*bêṯ 'āḇ*), not from the daughters of Canaan (Gn. 24:38, 40). She had to be someone of the same flesh and blood. But she could not be of such close relationship as a sister, mother, child's daughter, *etc*. The forbidden areas are defined in Lv. 18.

There were significant obligations laid on kinsmen. Among the more important we may mention the following.

Since a woman, married to a man, would normally have the privilege of bearing his son and heir, in the case of the untimely death of the husband without a son, the law of levirate (Lat. *levir*, 'husband's brother') *marriage came into force, and progeny was raised up to the dead man who had died 'without a name in Israel' by his next of kin (Dt. 25:5, 10). There is a good illustration of this in the book of Ruth.

Then in the matter of inheritance, a man's property was normally passed on to his son or sons. Failing these, it went to his daughters, and then in order to his brethren, to his father's brethren, and finally to his kinsman who was nearest to him (Nu. 27:1–11).

Again it was obligatory on a kinsman to redeem the property of a fellow kinsman who had fallen into the hands of creditors (Lv. 25:25ff.).

In the special circumstances where a man's life was taken by another, since this was part of the life of the family, an obligation rested on the son, or the brother, or the next of kin in order, to take vengeance (*cf.* Gn. 9:5–6). Where kinship ends, there is no longer any *avenger (*gō'ēl*).

BIBLIOGRAPHY. W. G. Dever, 'Palestine in the Second Millennium BC: The Archaeological Picture', in J. H. Hayes and J. Maxwell Miller (eds.), *Israelite and Judaean History*, pp. 70–120, with a good bibliography; D. Jacobson, *The Social Background of the Old Testament*, 1942; L. Kohler, *Hebrew Man*, 1956, pp. 75ff.; A. Malamat, 'Mari and the Bible: Some Patterns of Tribal Organization and Institutions', *JAOS* 82, 1962, pp. 143–150; *idem*, 'Aspects of Tribal Societies in Mari and Israel', in J. R. Kupper (ed.), *La civilization de Mari*, XVe Rencontre Assyriologique Internationale, Paris, 1967; J. Pedersen, *Israel I–II*, 1926, pp. 49, 52, 58ff., 284ff., *etc.*; C. R. Taber, 'Kinship and Family', *IDBS*; F. I. Andersen, 'Israelite Kinship Terminology and Social Structure', *Bible Translator* 29, 1969, pp. 29–39.

J.A.T.

View across the Kidron valley showing the Mount of Olives with tomb monuments dating from Hasmonaean times to the 1st cent. AD. (RS)

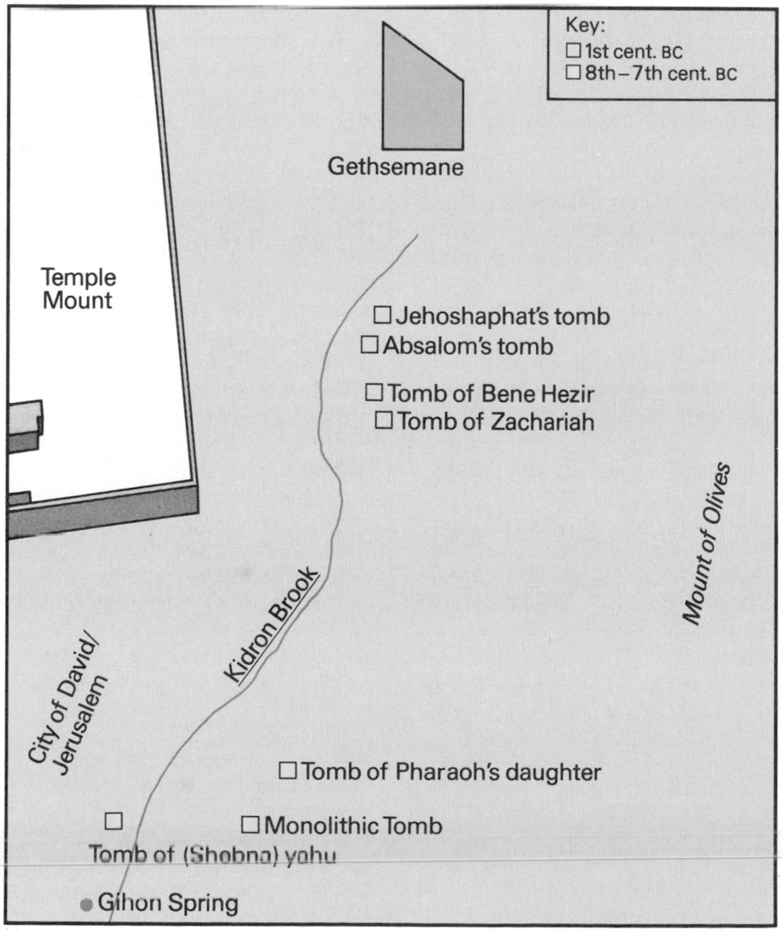

The Kidron valley E of Jerusalem. Its eastern slope was a favourite burial-ground.

KING, KINGSHIP. Heb. *meleḵ*; Gk. *basileus*. Both words are of obscure origin; the former, common to all Semitic languages, is possibly connected either with an Arab. root meaning 'possess' or an Assyr. and

'The investiture of the king.' Part of a large wall-painting from the palace at Mari, Syria. The king receives the rod and ring, symbols of authority, law and justice, from the goddess Ishtar. 18th cent. BC. (AP)

Aram. word meaning 'counsel'. The latter is probably taken over from an early Aegean language.

The office was common in the Middle East from the earliest times, the general pattern apparently being of a ruler who held sway over a settled region, often centred on a city (Gn. 14:1–2; 20:1ff.). His authority seems to have been hereditary (but *cf.* Gn. 36:31ff.), and to have derived from the divine-king or god of the land (see J. A. Soggin, *Protestantismo* 17, 1962, pp. 85–89), often spoken of as the ancestor or father of the ruling king (*e.g.* Ras Shamra—Legend of King Keret). In Egypt the tendency was for the king or pharaoh to be regarded as identical with the god; in Assyria, rather as representing the god.

In classical Greek *basileus* denotes the legal hereditary ruler, guiding the life of the people by his justice or injustice, but contrasted with the tyrant or usurper. The king's power is traced back to Zeus. Later, under Plato, we find a movement towards the idea of the king as 'benefactor', whose will is law, leading up to the idea of 'divine-king' in Alexander and the Caesars.

I. Early ideas in Israel

In the history of Israel the early nomadic tribes were ruled by the clan Patriarch. During the Exodus from Egypt rule was exercised by Moses, succeeded by Joshua, in what was a virtual theocracy, with the non-hereditary leader elected by divine call and acknowledged by the people, though not without some protest (Ex. 4:29ff.; Nu. 16:1ff.). When Israel first settled in Palestine the tribes were ruled largely by village fathers (Jdg. 11:5), who would call on a certain man to lead the militia against an enemy. Jephthah (Jdg. 11:9) demanded that he be made 'head' if he took the lead in this way, but his son did not succeed him. Gideon was asked to rule (*mālaḵ*) over Israel (8:22) and refused, but his son Abimelech seized a temporary and local kingship after him (9:6ff.). The book of Judges ends on a note of social chaos (chs. 19–21), and this is attributed to the lack of a king (19:1; 21:25).

II. From Eli and Samuel

The following period was one of improvement under the religio-judicial lead of Eli and Samuel. Eli was chief priest at the central sanctuary in Shiloh (1 Sa. 1:3; 4:13); Samuel was a non-hereditary leader (after the style of Moses and Joshua) who, after the destruction of Shiloh, judged Israel from several places which he visited in circuit (7:15f.). Finally, Samuel became the king-maker of Israel, though at the insistence of the people (1 Sa. 8:4ff.). This seems to have been regarded as a measure of apostasy from the theocracy (1 Sa. 8:7). The request was probably made largely in view of the continual Philistine threat, necessitating a sustained army (8:20), and Saul's success as a warrior was his main qualification for the role as the first king of Israel. Under his reign, however, Samuel, while he lived, preserved the religious leadership (1 Sa. 13:9ff.), and Saul never quite established his position, nor his dynasty.

III. Development under David

David, however, was eminently successful, and was ever afterwards regarded as the ideal king. He established a dynasty that lasted for over 400 years, until the break-up of the state in 587 BC. The security of David's dynasty seems to have been based largely on what has been called the Davidic covenant (Ps. 132:11f.). The capital city, centrally situated between what became later the N and S states, was Jerusalem (2 Sa. 5:5ff.). It may be that David assumed something of the role of priest-king after the style of the Jebusite kings, whose priesthood apparently dated back to the time of Abraham (Gn. 14:17ff.; Ps. 110), since he seems to have taken a lead in the cult (2 Sa. 6:13ff.; *cf.* also 1 Ki. 8:5).

The Davidic covenant may have been an extension of the Mosaic covenant, particularly if G. E. Mendenhall is right in suggesting that the form of the Mosaic covenant was analogous to Hittite treaty patterns. Under these a Hittite overlord granted an enduring dynasty to his vassal, if the vassal king was a relation, but otherwise he was always personally responsible for the appointment of a successor. The reference to the king as the son of God (Ps. 2:6–7) and the promise to maintain the dynasty in terms of the covenant (1 Ki. 9:4–5) make the suggestion easily credible.

The main responsibility of the king was the maintenance of righteousness (Is. 11:1–4; Je. 33:15), possibly signified by the possession of the testimonies or law or *tôrâ* (Dt. 17:18ff.; 1 Sa. 10:25; 1 Ki. 9:4ff.; 2 Ki. 11:12), with the duty not only to act as judge (1 Ki. 3:28) but to preserve justice and proclaim the law (2 Ki. 23:2; *cf.* 2 Ch. 17:7ff.; *cf.* also Jdg. 17:6).

But many of the kings were wicked themselves and encouraged injustice and wickedness to flourish, not only in the schismatic N kingdom but in the S too (1 Ki. 14:16; 2 Ki. 21:16). The reform under Josiah (2 Ki. 22–23) may have been an attempt to revive the Mosaic precepts in connection with the Davidic covenant, but it was above all the prophetic movement which provided a check upon the waywardness of the kings (2 Sa. 12:1ff.; 1 Ki. 18:17–18; Je. 26:1ff.) (*PROPHECY; see also **IV**, below).

It will be noticed that several so-called Messianic passages have been applied above to the Davidic dynasty (Pss. 2; 110; 132; Is. 11:1–4; Je. 33:15), and it is the considered view of many modern scholars that this is their primary reference, the psalms referred to being, among others, probably coronation psalms used in the Jerusalem Temple. The failure of the kings to live up to the ideal, however, tended to cast the hope for a righteous ruler more and more into the future. With the fall of the S kingdom, and later the failure of the Davidic prince, Zerubbabel (1 Ch. 3:19; Hg. 2:23; Mt. 1:12) to restore the dynasty on the throne of the post-exilic state, the expectation crystallized into what is technically known as the Messianic hope, though many scholars believe it began earlier. (* MESSIAH.)

IV. The king's ministers

But it should be noted that the prophets were not apparently appointed by the king, though the priests were (1 Ki. 2:27). Both officiated in the installation of a king (1:34), but the prophet sometimes took the greater initiative, especially with a change of dynasty, as in the N kingdom (1 Ki. 19:16). Other servants of the king were the commander of the army (2 Sa. 19:13); the secretary (2 Sa. 8:17; 2 Ki. 12:10), and the recorder, plus sundry others (1 Ki. 4:3ff.). The recorder (*mazkîr*, literally one who causes to remember) was perhaps connected with the chronicling of state events (*cf.* 2 Ki. 21:25), or the term may signify the advisory and executive position of a prime minister or grand vizier. Another possibility is that it was a vocal office, parallel to the Egyp. *whm.w*, 'court announcer' or 'king's herald'.

V. Later developments

During the period 104–37 BC certain of the Maccabean high priests assumed the title of king, and some were proclaimed as the fulfilment of the Messianic hope, but it is essentially the message of the NT that this hope was fulfilled only in Jesus Christ (Mt. 1:1–17; 21:5, with which compare Zc. 9:9 and the coronation procedure in the case of Solomon, 1 Ki. 1:33; also Jn. 1:49). Jesus' message began with the proclamation, 'The kingdom of God is at hand' (Mk. 1:15), and announced to the Pharisees that the kingdom was in their midst (Lk. 17:21). He pointed out that it was not a kingdom of this world (Jn. 18:36), and so was not on the same plane as that of the Roman governor, Pilate, or of Herod, the Idumaean king of Judah and vassal of Rome (*cf.* Mt. 2:16).

Though the word translated 'kingdom' (*basileia*) is used in the sense of realm or domain (Mt. 12:25), the dominant sense is 'sovereignty' or 'kingly rule'. The sovereignty of God is absolute, but not recognized by sinful man, who thus merits destruction. The 'gospel of the kingdom of God' means that men are given an opportunity to receive the kingdom by repentance and faith (Mk. 1:15). This is achieved through Christ the Messiah-King, to whom every knee must bow, whether in willing loyalty or under judgment (Rom. 14:10–11; Phil. 2:9–11).

The rule of earthly kings is limited, and Christ claims the first allegiance (Mt. 6:33). His subjects are delivered from the power of darkness (Col. 1:13), and thus are set free to live righteously (Rom. 14:17). Christ's kingdom is an everlasting kingdom (2 Pet. 1:11), but [illegible] 1 Cor. 15:24–28). (* KINGDOM OF GOD.)

BIBLIOGRAPHY. S. Mowinckel, *He that Cometh*, 1956; A. R. Johnson, *Sacral Kingship in Ancient Israel*, 1955; G. E. Mendenhall, *Law and Covenant in Israel and the Ancient Near East*, 1955; H. Frankfort, *Kingship and the Gods*, 1948; K. L. Schmidt *et al.*, *TDNT* 1, pp. 564–593; B. Klappert, *NIDNTT* 2, pp. 372–390; R. de Vaux, *Ancient Israel*, 1961; J. Bright, *The Kingdom of God*, 1953; *idem*, *A History of Israel*², 1972.

B.O.B.

KINGDOM OF GOD, KINGDOM OF HEAVEN.

KINGDOM OF GOD, KINGDOM OF HEAVEN. The kingdom of heaven or kingdom of God is the central theme of Jesus' preaching, according to the Synoptic Gospels. While Matthew, who addresses himself to the Jews, speaks for the most part of the 'kingdom of heaven', Mark and Luke speak of the 'kingdom of God', which has the same meaning as the 'kingdom of heaven', but was more intelligible to non-Jews. The use of 'kingdom of heaven' in Matthew is certainly due to the tendency in Judaism to avoid the direct use of the name of God. In any case no distinction in sense is to be assumed between the two expressions (*cf.*, *e.g.*, Mt. 5:3 with Lk. 6:20).

I. In John the Baptist

John the Baptist first comes forward with the announcement that the kingdom of heaven is at hand (Mt. 3:2) and Jesus takes this message over from him (Mt. 4:17). The expression 'kingdom of heaven' (Heb. *malᵉḵûṯ šāmayim*) originates with the late-Jewish expectation of the future in which it denoted the decisive intervention of God, ardently expected by Israel, to restore his people's fortunes and liberate them from the power of their enemies. The coming of the kingdom is the great perspective of the future, prepared by the coming of the * Messiah, which paves the way for the kingdom of God.

By the time of Jesus the development of this eschatological hope in Judaism had taken a great variety of forms, in which now the national element and now the cosmic and apocalyptic element is prominent. This hope goes back to the proclamation in OT prophecy concerning both the restoration of David's throne and the coming of God to renew the world. Although the OT has nothing to say of the eschatological kingdom of heaven in so many words, yet in the Psalms and prophets the future manifestation of God's royal sovereignty belongs to the most central concepts of OT faith and hope. Here too various elements achieve prominence, as may be clearly seen from a comparison of the earlier prophets with the prophecies regarding universal world-sovereignty and the emergence of the Son of man in the book of * Daniel.

When John the Baptist and, after him, Jesus himself proclaimed that the kingdom was at hand, this proclamation involved an awakening cry of sensational and universal significance. The long-expected divine turning-point in history, the great restoration, however it was conceived at the time, is proclaimed as being at hand. It is therefore of all the greater importance to survey the content of the NT preaching with regard to the coming of the kingdom.

In the preaching of John the Baptist prominence is given to the announcement of divine judgment as a reality which is immediately at hand. The axe is already laid to the root of the trees. God's coming as King is above all else a coming to purify, to sift, to judge. No-one can evade it. No privilege can buy exemption from it, not even the ability to claim Abraham as one's father. At the same time John the Baptist points to the coming One who is to follow him, whose forerunner he himself is. The coming One comes with the winnowing-fan in his hand. In view of his coming the people must repent and submit to baptism for the washing away of sins, so as to escape the coming wrath and participate in the salvation of the kingdom and the baptism with the Holy Spirit which will be poured out when it comes (Mt. 3:1–12).

II. In the teaching of Jesus

a. Present aspect

Jesus' proclamation of the kingdom follows word for word on John's, yet it bears a much more comprehensive character. After John the Baptist had watched Jesus' appearance for a considerable time, he began to be in doubt whether Jesus was, after all, the coming One whom he had announced (Mt. 11:2f.). Jesus' proclamation of the kingdom differs in two respects from that of the Baptist. In the first place, while it retains without qualification the announcement of judgment and the call to repentance, it is the saving significance of the kingdom that stands in the foreground. In the second place—and here is the pith and core of the matter—he announced the kingdom not just as a reality which was at hand, something which would appear in the immediate future, but as a reality which was already present, manifested in his own person and ministry. Although the places where Jesus speaks explicitly of the kingdom as being present are not numerous (see especially Mt. 12:28 and parallels), his whole preaching and ministry are marked by this dominant reality. In him the great future has already become 'present time'.

This present aspect of the kingdom manifests itself in all sorts of ways in the person and deeds of Christ. It appears palpably and visibly in the casting out of demons (*cf.* Lk. 11:20) and generally in Jesus' miraculous power. In the healing of those who are demon-possessed it becomes evident that Jesus has invaded the house of 'the strong man', has bound him fast and so is in a position to plunder his goods (Mt. 12:29). The kingdom of heaven breaks into the domain of the evil one. The power of Satan is broken. Jesus sees him fall like lightning from heaven. He possesses and bestows power to trample on the dominion of the enemy. Nothing can be impossible for those who go forth into the world, invested with Jesus' power, as witnesses of the kingdom (Lk. 10:18f.). The whole of Jesus' miraculous activity is the proof of the coming of the kingdom. What many prophets and righteous men desired in vain to see—the breaking in of the great epoch of salvation—the disciples can now see and hear (Mt. 13:16; Lk. 10:23). When John the Baptist sent his disciples to ask, 'Are you he who is to come, or shall we look for another?' they were shown the wonderful works done by Jesus, in which, according to the promise of prophecy, the kingdom was already being manifested: the blind were enabled to see, the lame to walk, the deaf to hear; lepers were being cleansed and dead people raised to life, and the gospel was being proclaimed to the poor (Mt. 11:2ff.; Lk. 7:18ff.). Also in the last of these—the proclamation of the gospel—the breaking through of the kingdom is seen. Since salvation is announced and offered as a gift already available to the poor in spirit, the hungry and the mourners, the kingdom is theirs. So too the forgiveness of sins is proclaimed, not merely as a future reality to be accomplished in heaven, nor merely as a present possibility, but as a dispensation offered today, on earth, through Jesus himself; 'Son, daughter, your sins are forgiven; for the Son of man has power on earth to forgive sins' (see Mk. 2:1–12, *et passim*).

As appears clearly from this last-quoted word of power, all this is founded on the fact that Jesus is the Christ, the Son of God. The kingdom has come in him and with him; he is the *auto-basileia*. Jesus' self-revelation as the Messiah, the Son of man and Servant of the Lord, constitutes both the mystery and the unfolding of the whole gospel.

It is impossible to explain these sayings of Jesus about himself in a future sense, as some have wished to do, as though he referred to himself only as the future *Messiah, the Son of man who was to be expected on a coming day on the clouds of heaven. For however much this future revelation of the kingdom remains an essential element in the content of the gospel, we cannot mistake the fact that in the Gospels Jesus' Messiahship is present here and now. Not only is he proclaimed as such at his baptism and on the Mount of Transfiguration—as the beloved and elect One of God (plain Messianic designations)—but he is also endowed with the Holy Spirit (Mt. 3:16) and invested with full divine authority (Mt. 21:27); the Gospel is full of his declarations of absolute authority, he is presented as the One sent by the Father, the One who has come to fulfil what the prophets foretold. In his coming and teaching the Scripture is fulfilled in the ears of those who listen to him (Lk. 4:21). He came not to destroy but to fulfil (Mt. 5:17ff.), to announce the kingdom (Mk. 1:38), to seek and to save the lost (Lk. 19:10), to serve others, and to give his life a ransom for many (Mk. 10:45). The secret of belonging to the kingdom lies in belonging to him (Mt. 7:23; 25:41). In brief, the person of Jesus as the Messiah is the centre of all that is announced in the gospel concerning the kingdom. The kingdom is concentrated in him in its present and future aspects alike.

b. Future aspect

There is a future aspect as well. For although it is clearly stated that the kingdom is manifested here and now in the gospel, so also is it shown that as yet it is manifested in this world only in a provisional manner. That is why the proclamation of its present activity in the words, 'The blind receive their sight; the dead are raised; the poor have good news preached to them', is followed by the warning: 'Blessed is he who takes no offence at me' (Mt. 11:6; Lk. 7:23). The 'offence' lies in the hidden character of the kingdom in this epoch. The miracles are still tokens of another order of reality than the present one; it is not yet the time when the demons will be delivered to eternal darkness (Mt. 8:29). The gospel of the kingdom is still revealed only as a seed which is being sown. In the parables of the sower, the seed growing secretly, the tares among the wheat, the mustard seed, the leaven, it is about this hidden aspect of the kingdom that Jesus instructs his disciples. The Son of man himself, invested with all power by God, the One who is to come on the clouds of heaven, is the Sower who sows the Word of God. He is depicted as a man dependent upon others: the birds, the thorns, human beings, can partially frustrate his work. He has to wait and see what will come of his seed. Indeed, the hiddenness of the kingdom is deeper still: the King himself comes in the form of a slave. The birds of the air have nests, but the Son of man (Dn. 7:13) has no place to lay his head. In order to receive everything, he must first of all give up everything. He must give his life as a ransom; as the suffering Servant of the Lord of Is. 53, he must be numbered with the transgressors. The kingdom has come; the kingdom will come. But it comes by the way of the cross, and before the Son of man exercises his authority over all the kingdoms of the earth (Mt. 4:8; 28:18) he must tread the path of obedience to his Father in order thus to fulfil all righteousness (Mt. 3:15). The manifestation of the kingdom has therefore a history in this world. It must be proclaimed to every creature. Like the wonderful seed, it must sprout and grow, no man knows how (Mk. 4:27). It has an inward power by which it makes its way through all sorts of obstacles and advances over all; for the field in which the seed is sown is the world (Mt. 13:38). The gospel of the kingdom goes forth to all nations (Mt. 28:19), for the King of the kingdom is also Lord of the Spirit. His resurrection brings in a new aeon; the preaching of the kingdom *and* the King reaches out to the ends of the earth. The decision has already come to pass; but the fulfilment still recedes into the future. What at first appears to be one and the same coming of the kingdom, what is announced as one indivisible reality, at hand and at close quarters, extends itself to cover new periods of time and far distances. For the frontiers of this kingdom are not coterminous with Israel's boundaries or history: the kingdom embraces all nations and fills all ages until the end of the world comes.

III. Kingdom and church

The kingdom is thus related to the history of the church and of the world alike. A connection exists between kingdom and church, but they are not identical, even in the present age. The kingdom is the whole of God's redeeming activity in Christ in this world; the church is the assembly of those who belong to Jesus Christ. Perhaps one could speak in terms of two concentric circles, of which the church is the smaller and the kingdom the larger, while Christ is the centre of both. This relation of the church to the kingdom can be formulated in all kinds of ways. The church is the assembly of those who have accepted the gospel of the kingdom in faith, who participate in the salvation of the kingdom, which includes the forgiveness of sins, adoption by God, the indwelling of the Holy Spirit, the possession of eternal life. They are also those in whose life the kingdom takes visible form, the light of the world, the salt of the earth; those who have taken on themselves the yoke of the kingdom, who live by their King's commandments and learn from him (Mt. 11:28–30). The church, as the organ of the kingdom, is called to confess Jesus as the Christ, to the missionary task of preaching the gospel in the world; she is also the community of those who wait for the coming of the kingdom in glory, the servants who have received their Lord's talents in prospect of his return. The church receives her whole constitution from the kingdom, on all sides she is beset and directed by the revelation, the progress, the future coming of the kingdom of God, without at any time being the kingdom herself or even being identified with it.

Therefore the kingdom is not confined within the frontiers of the church. Christ's Kingship is supreme above all. Where it prevails and is acknowledged, not only is the individual human being set free, but the whole pattern of life is changed: the curse of the demons and fear of hostile powers disappears. The change which Christianity brings about among peoples dominated by nature-religions is a proof of the comprehensive, all-embracing significance of the kingdom. It works not only outwardly like a mustard seed but inwardly like leaven. It makes its way into the world with its redeeming power. The last book of the Bible, which portrays Christ's Kingship in the history of the world and its advancing momentum right to the end, especially illuminates the antithesis between the triumphant Christ-King (*cf.*, *e.g.*, Rev. 5:1ff.) and the power of Satan and antichrist, which still survives on earth and contends against Christ and his church. However much the kingdom invades world-history with its blessing and deliverance, however much it presents itself as a saving power against the tyranny of gods and forces inimical to mankind, it is only through a final and universal crisis that the kingdom, as a visible and all-conquering reign of peace and salvation, will bring to full fruition the new heaven and the new earth.

IV. In the rest of the New Testament

The expression 'kingdom of heaven' or 'kingdom of God' does not appear so frequently in the NT outside the Synoptic Gospels. This is, however, simply a matter of terminology. As the indication of the great revolution in the history of salvation which has already been inaugurated by Christ's coming, and as the expected consummation of all the acts of God, it is the central theme of the whole NT revelation of God.

V. In theological thought

As regards the conception of the kingdom of heaven in theology, this has been powerfully subjected to all kinds of influences and viewpoints during the various periods and trends of theological thought. In Roman Catholic theology a distinctive feature is the identification of the kingdom of God and the church in the earthly dispensation, an identification which is principally due to Augustine's influence. Through the ecclesiastical hierarchy Christ is actualized as King of the kingdom of God. The area of the kingdom is coterminous with the frontiers of the church's power and authority. The kingdom of heaven is extended by the mission and advance of the church in the world.

In their resistance to the Roman Catholic hierarchy, the Reformers laid chief emphasis on the spiritual and invisible significance of the kingdom and readily (and wrongly) invoked Lk. 17:20f. in support of this. The kingdom of heaven, that is to say, is a spiritual sovereignty which Christ exercises through the preaching of his word and the operation of the Holy Spirit. While the Reformation in its earliest days did not lose sight of the kingdom's great dimensions of saving history, the kingdom of God, under the influence of the Enlightenment and pietism, came to be increasingly conceived in an individualistic sense; it is the sovereignty of grace and peace in the hearts of men. In later liberal theology this conception developed in a moralistic direction (especially under the influence of Kant): the kingdom of God is the kingdom of peace, love and righteousness. At first, even in pietism and sectarian circles, the expectation of the coming kingdom of God was maintained, without, however, making allowance for a positive significance of the king-

KING JAMES' VERSION
See English versions of the Bible, Part 1.

KING OF ISRAEL
See Jesus Christ, titles of, Part 2.

dom for life in this world. Over against this more or less dualistic understanding of the kingdom we must distinguish the social conception of the kingdom which lays all the stress on its visible and communal significance. This conception is distinguished in some writers by a social radicalism (the 'Sermon on the Mount' Christianity of Tolstoy and others, or the 'religious-social' interpretation of, *e.g.*, Kutter and Ragaz in Switzerland), in others by the evolutionary belief in progress (the 'social gospel' in America). The coming of the kingdom consists in the forward march of social righteousness and communal development.

In contrast to these spiritualizing, moralistic and evolutionary interpretations of the kingdom, NT scholarship is rightly laying stress again on the original significance of the kingdom in Jesus' preaching—a significance bound up with the history of salvation and eschatology. While the founders of this newer eschatological direction gave an extreme interpretation to the idea of the kingdom of heaven, so that there was no room left for the kingdom's penetration of the present world-order (Johannes Weiss, Albert Schweitzer, the so-called 'thoroughgoing' eschatology), more attention has been paid latterly to the unmistakable present significance of the kingdom, while this significance has been brought within the perspective of the history of salvation, the perspective of the progress of God's dynamic activity in history, which has the final consummation as its goal.

BIBLIOGRAPHY. The literature on the kingdom of God is immense. For the use of the term in the Gospels, see G. Dalman, *The Words of Jesus*, 1902; *SB*, pp. 172–184; for the interpretation of the kingdom in the history of earlier theology see A. Robertson, *Regnum Dei* (Bampton Lectures), 1901; for the older liberal approach, see E. von Dobschütz, 'The Eschatology of the Gospels', *The Expositor*, 7th Series, 9, 1910; for the 'social' interpretation, see N. J. van Merwe, *Die sosiale prediking van Jezus Christus*, 1921; L. Ragaz, *Die Botschaft vom Reiche Gottes*, 1941; for the newer eschatological interpretation (since J. Weiss, *Die Predigt Jesu vom Reiche Gottes*, 1892; Albert Schweitzer, *The Quest of the Historical Jesus*, 1910), see H. M. Matter, *Nieuwere opvattingen omtrent het koninkrijk Gods in Jezus' prediking naar de synoptici*, 1942. More general works: F. Holmström, *Das eschatologische Denken der Gegenwart*, 1936; H. D. Wendland, *Die Eschatologie des Reiches Gottes bei Jesus*, 1931; G. Gloege, *Reich Gottes und Kirche im Neuen Testament*, 1929; J. Jeremias, *Jesus der Weltvollender im Neuen Testament*, 1929; *idem*, *New Testament Theology*, 1, 1970; C. H. Dodd, *The Parables of the Kingdom*, 1935; W. G. Kümmel, *Die Eschatologie der Evangelien*, 1936; *idem*, *Promise and Fulfilment*, 1957; R. Otto, *The Kingdom of God and the Son of Man*, 1943; W. A. Visser 't Hooft, *The Kingship of Christ*, 1947; S. H. Hooke, *The Kingdom of God in the Experience of Jesus*, 1949; O. Cullmann, *Christ and Time*, 1951; G. Vos, *The Teaching of Jesus concerning the Kingdom and the Church*, 1951; J. Héring, *Le royaume de Dieu et sa venue*, 1959; H. Ridderbos, *The Coming of the Kingdom*, 1962; G. Lundström, *The Kingdom of God in the Teaching of Jesus*, 1963; R. Schnackenburg, *God's Rule and Kingdom*, 1963; G. E. Ladd, *Jesus and the Kingdom*, 1964; *idem*, *A Theology of the New Testament*, 1974; H. Flender, *Die Botschaft Jesu von der Herrschaft Gottes*, 1968; R. Hiers, *The Kingdom of God in the Synoptic Tradition*, 1970; W. Pannenberg, *Theologie und Reich Gottes*, 1971; K. L. Schmidt *et al.*, *TDNT* 1, pp. 564–593; B. Klappert, *NIDNTT* 2, pp. 372–390.

H.R.

KINGS, BOOKS OF. The closing part of the narrative which begins in Genesis and focuses on the story of Israel from her origins in Egypt to the ending of her political independence by the Babylonians. The division of the books of Kings from the books of Samuel is an artificial one, as is the further division of Kings itself into two books, which was introduced by the LXX.

I. Outline of contents

Kings consists of an account of the Israelite monarchy written from a theological perspective and taking the history from its high point in the united monarchy to its low point in the Exile.

(*a*) The reign of Solomon (1 Ki. 1–11): his accession (1–2), his successes (3–10), his failures (11).

(*b*) The divided kingdom (1 Ki. 12–2 Ki. 17): Judah under Rehoboam, and the majority N tribes under Jeroboam who retain the title Israel, separate from each other. Israel comes under considerable pagan influence from the beginning and experiences many bloody coups before finally being exiled. Judah is less paganized, though only preserved because of Yahweh's faithfulness to his promise to David. The prophets Elijah and Elisha are heavily involved, especially in the story of Israel.

(*c*) The kingdom of Judah (2 Ki. 18–25): despite the reforms of Hezekiah and Josiah, the paganizing policy of Manasseh finally bears fruit in the fall of Judah too. But the conclusion of the books sounds a possible note of hope (25:27–30).

II. Origin

The last event to which Kings refers is the exiled king Jehoiachin's release from prison in Babylon in 561 (2 Ki. 25:27), and clearly the books in their final form must come from after this time. There may be elsewhere hints of even later situations: notably, the dating of the building of the Temple (1 Ki. 6:1) perhaps reflects a chronological scheme which places that event midway between the Exodus and the rebuilding of the Temple after the Exile.

The main composition of the work is to be dated earlier, however. This may have been in the early years of the Exile (P. R. Ackroyd, *Exile and Restoration*, *OTL*, 1968, ch. 5). Alternatively, it may have been after the release of Jehoiachin in 561 (R. K. Harrison, *IOT*, 1970, pp. 730f., following M. Noth). Another view dates the 'first edition' of Kings in the reign of Josiah (J. Gray, *I and II Kings*², *OTL*, 1970). But while much of the material in Kings dates from long before the Exile, and some reflects its pre-exilic perspective, the evidence for an actual 'first edition' of Kings in the reign of Josiah, or for a pre-Deuteronomistic earlier version of the history, is scant.

Any pre- or post-exilic work on the books must have taken place in Palestine. Work during the exilic period itself might have taken place in Babylon or Palestine (the arguments for each location are discussed by Ackroyd, pp. 65–68, and by E. W. Nicholson, *Preaching to the Exiles: A Study of the Prose Tradition in the Book of Jeremiah*, 1970, pp. 117–122).

We do not know the name of the author(s) of Kings, though the group which was responsible for the work is often described as the

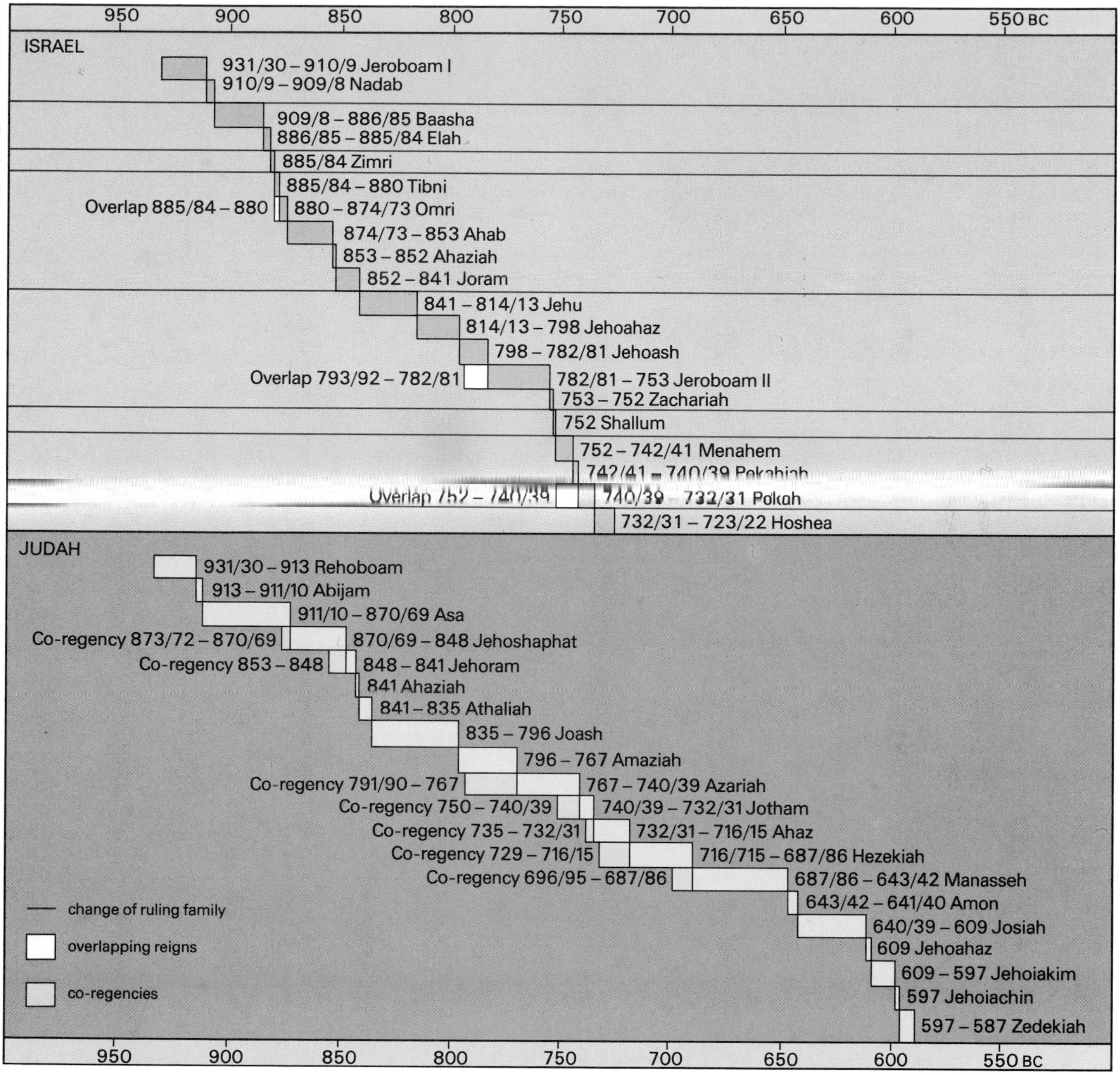

'Deuteronomists'. This description reflects the view that Kings is not merely the last part of the story begun in Genesis; it is more specifically the last part of the 'Deuteronomistic history', which begins with the book of Deuteronomy. On this view, the story from Joshua to Kings, known in the Hebrew Bible as the 'Former Prophets', has been written or edited as a whole to show how principles declared in Deuteronomy worked out in Israel's history from the conquest, via the period of the judges and the united monarchy, to the Exile. The view usually presupposes a belief that Deuteronomy itself was written in the late pre-exilic period, though it need not involve this. It is to be noted, however, that the emphases of the Deuteronomic law by no means coincide with those of Kings. On the one side, the humanitarian, social and moral concerns of Deuteronomy are not reflected in Kings. Conversely, while Deuteronomy stresses the central sanctuary (though without referring explicitly to Jerusalem) and refers to the monarchy (though without ascribing to it the theological significance it receives in Judah), these do not have the importance they receive in Kings.

III. Literary characteristics

The formal structure of Kings is provided by a reign-by-reign treatment of the history. During the period of the divided monarchy, the accounts of N and S kings are allowed to interweave in order to preserve a broadly chronological treatment. Each king is summarily

Chronological table of the kings of Israel and Judah.

described and evaluated according to a fairly consistent pattern, which may be perceived by examining the short accounts of the reign of Jehoshaphat (1 Ki. 22:41–50) or Amon (2 Ki. 21:19–26). Usually, however, this summary description and evaluation is the framework within which other material is enclosed, so that its opening and closing elements may be separated by several chapters (see, *e.g.*, the account of the reign of Hezekiah, 2 Ki. 18–20). Thus the accounts of Solomon, Rehoboam, Ahab, Jehoram, Jehu and Joash, for instance, include considerable narrative material centring on royal and political matters. Other narratives centre on prophets, especially Elijah, Elisha and Isaiah. Sometimes these prophets are involved in royal and political matters (revealingly, however, the Israelite king is not even named in 2 Ki. 5–7: he is not the real centre of interest). Other narratives concern the prophets' personal lives and ministries (*e.g.* 2 Ki. 4). The 'Deuteronomistic' perspective of the work as a whole is expounded most systematically in Kings in an extensive theological comment which closes off the history of the N kingdom (2 Ki. 17).

Various views are held as to the historical value of Kings. Clearly it is no attempt to write 'objective' or 'critical' history of a post-Enlightenment kind. It is history with a message, and the events it relates are chosen in accordance with their relevance to the message. It is thus not a political history, and some periods of great political significance (such as the reign of Omri) are passed over relatively briefly because they are of little significance in relation to the writer's concern with the history of Israel's relationship with Yahweh.

Within the Deuteronomistic framework, however, material of recognized historical value is included. The summary frameworks refer the reader to 'the book of the acts of Solomon' and to the annals of the kings of Judah and of Israel for further information on the various reigns, and it seems likely that these were the sources of many of the bare historical facts passed on by Kings (such as the name of a king's mother and the brief references to specific events). Complex chronological problems are raised by the dates provided for the kings (one basic solution for these is provided by E. Thiele, *The Mysterious Numbers of the Hebrew Kings*², 1965; *cf.* *CHRONOLOGY OF THE OT). Beyond these royal annals, it is widely accepted that 1 Ki. 1–2 forms the original ending of an account of how Solomon came to the throne, which extends back at least to 2 Sa. 9. As for the other narratives incorporated into Kings, Gray (for instance) accepts the fundamental historical value both of the material more concerned with political and military events and that concerned with the prophets, though he regards the more personal stories about Elijah and Elisha in 1 Ki. 17 and 2 Ki. 1–6 as folk-loristic, in part simply because of the miraculous element in them. But the precise nature of the author's sources, beyond the royal annals to which they actually refer, is not clear (*cf.* Gray, pp. 14–35). Considerable archaeological material from the Iron Age in Israel and Judah is relevant to Kings (*ARCHAEOLOGY).

The authors' method of composition means that their work is not a smooth literary whole, but it both gives us access to the material they pass on from their sources in a largely unredacted form, and impresses a degree of unity on the whole by the distinctive framework in which they set this material. Sometimes the source material, or the collected form of a section of the material, may fruitfully be treated by a literary critical approach, and this is likely to be a subject of increasing study (*Semeia* 3, 1975; 8, 1977).

The text of Kings in *MT* presents relatively few problems. But the Qumran discoveries (combined with evidence from Chronicles and the LXX) have implications for the state of the pre-*MT* textual traditions of Kings, as of other books (*TEXTS AND VERSIONS).

IV. Emphases

(*a*) We have noted that Kings begins at the high point of the period covered by the Deuteronomistic history, the united monarchy. The fact that this is the high point reflects the importance of the Davidic monarchy and the Temple of Solomon. Yahweh's commitment to David (2 Sa. 7:11–16) is often referred to by Yahweh and by the narrator as the explanation for Yahweh's faithfulness to Judah and to David's successors (1 Ki. 6:12; 11:12–13, 36; 2 Ki. 8:19; 19:34), and David's loyalty to Yahweh is frequently (and slightly surprisingly) a standard by which later kings are judged (*e.g.* 1 Ki. 9:4; 2 Ki. 22:2). But the repercussions of one king's reign in later times can also be negative: the sins of Manasseh are ultimately the cause of the Exile (2 Ki. 24:3–4). Thus the well-being of the people as a whole is tied up with the behaviour of the king (2 Ki. 21:11–15).

The building of the Temple is the climax of the opening chapters of Kings. 1 Ki. 8 focuses the Kings' theology of the Temple, which is the dwelling-place of Yahweh's name. W. Eichrodt (*Theology of the OT*, 2, 1967, pp. 23–45) sees Yahweh's name as the most sophisticated OT form of 'the spiritualization of the theophany'—a way of talking of the real revelatory presence of God without compromising his transcendence. The importance of the Temple makes it a crucial touchstone for the evaluation of the kings. Jeroboam I is condemned for devising alternative places and forms of worship for the N kingdom (1 Ki. 12–13), and his successors are condemned for continuing to have recourse to these. Josiah, the antitype to Jeroboam, appearing near the end of the story as Jeroboam appears near its beginning, is commended for his reform of temple worship and for his destruction of high places generally and of the shrine at Bethel in particular (2 Ki. 22–23).

(*b*) Kings' attitude to the monarchy and to the Temple, however, shows that these are not to be seen as absolutes. They are subject, first of all, to the Torah. 'The Deuteronomist sees the main problem of the history of Israel as lying in the question of the correct correlation of Moses and David' (G. von Rad, *Old Testament Theology*, 1, 1968, p. 339). The Davidic promise can be relied on only as long as the Mosaic covenant demand is accepted. Thus the great villain of the story of Judah in Kings is Manasseh; the list of his acts corresponds closely to what Deuteronomy says Israel should not do (*cf.* 2 Ki. 21:2–9 with Dt. 17:2–4; 18:9–12). Conversely in the story of its great hero Josiah, Kings emphasizes the significance of his discovery of the 'book of the covenant' by giving it first mention in its account of his reign (contrast the account in 2 Ch. 34), and the list of his acts corresponds closely to what Deuteronomy says Israel should do. Thus the requirements and the sanctions of the Torah (specifically of Deuteronomy) provide the principles for understanding Israel's history. When kings obeyed the Torah (especially its demand for faithful worship at the central shrine), they generally prospered. When they ignored it, they did not.

But the spoken word of the prophet is thought of as succeeding and supporting the written word of Moses (*cf.* the role of Huldah after the discovery of the lawbook in 2 Ki. 22:13–20), and also demanding the attention of king and people. 'What fascinated [the Deuteronomist] was, we might say, the functioning of the divine word in history' (*cf.* 1 Ki. 8:24) (G. von Rad, 'The Deuteronomistic theology of history in the books of Kings', in 'Studies in Deuteronomy', *SBT* 9, 1961, p. 91). Thus Kings pictures 'a course of history which was shaped and led to a fulfilment by a word of judgment and salvation continually injected into it' (von Rad, *Old Testament Theology*, 1, p. 344). This point is made by including lengthy stories about various prophets, especially as regards their involvement in the nation's political life. 'In the decisive political events the initiative stems from prophets, who change the gears of history with a word of God' (*ibid.*, p. 342). It is also made by criss-crossing the story with prophecies and their fulfilment (*e.g.* 1 Ki. 11:29–39 and 12:15; 1 Ki. 13:1–10 and 2 Ki. 23:15–18; 2 Ki. 20:16–17 and 24:13). The stress on how true prophecies were fulfilled may reflect concern with the problem of false prophecy during the Exile. Thus a king's attitude to the prophet's word forms another index of his attitude to God (Hezekiah, Josiah).

(*c*) One of the characteristic emphases of the covenant as expounded in Deuteronomy is that God blesses those who are faithful to him but brings trouble to those who disobey him (Dt. 28–30). Thus in Kings the material concerning Solomon's reign is arranged so that Solomon's setbacks are seen as consequences of his association with foreign women (1 Ki. 11). On the other hand, Kings recognizes that God's justice does not work out in this way in every reign. Manasseh enjoys a long reign, and his apostasy only brings its fruit decades later (2 Ki. 21; 24:3–4). Josiah is responsive to Yahweh's word, but dies an early and tragic death (2 Ki. 23:29).

V. Message and purpose

The function of Kings' review of the history which led up to the Exile is to explain why the Exile came about and to express an admission that there was ample cause for God to judge Israel. It is a form of confession, or 'an act of praise at the justice of the judgment of God'; 'this statement with its apparent lack of hope for the future lays the only possible foundation for the future' (Ackroyd, p. 78, following von Rad) because it throws the people of God totally back on the grace of God.

The possibility of hope for the future is hinted at in the way the theological emphases of Kings, described above, remain open to the future. Perhaps God's commitment to David still holds: it may be that the release of Jehoiachin, related in the final paragraph of Kings makes this hope explicit. Although the Temple has been pillaged and burnt, prayer is still possible in the Temple, or towards it on the part of people who are cut off from it, and God has undertaken to hear such prayer (see 1 Ki. 8–9). Although judgment has come in accordance with the sanctions of the covenant, the same covenant allows for the possibility of repentance and restoration after judgment (see 1 Ki. 8:46–53; *cf.* Dt. 30). Although the prophetic words which Israel ignored form a further reason for her punishment, the fact that those prophetic words of judgment have come true may encourage the hope that the prophetic promises of restoration (*e.g.* those of Jeremiah) may come true, too.

Thus the aim of Kings is in part didactic, 'to present the divine view of Israelite history' (R. K. Harrison, p. 722). Beyond this, there are at least hints of the kerygmatic (*cf.* E. W. Nicholson, p. 75). Kings does open up the possibility of there being a future. On the basis of this possibility it further seeks to be paraenetic, in that it implicitly challenges the generation of the Exile to turn back to Yahweh in repentance, faith and commitment to obedience (*cf.* 1 Ki. 8:46–50). For 'the judgment of 587 did not mean the end of the people of God; nothing but refusal to turn would be the end' (von Rad, *Old Testament Theology*, 1, p. 346).

VI. Context and implications

Kings is thus one of the several responses to the fall of Judah and the Exile. It bears comparison especially with * Lamentations (five psalms which express the feelings and tentative hopes of people in Judah after the fall of Jerusalem) and with the book of Jeremiah (whose material was collected and assembled in this same period and manifests many literary and theological points of contact with Kings; see E. W. Nicholson, *op. cit.*). Kings may also be studied in the light of parallel treatments of events it narrates as these appear in Chronicles, Isaiah and Jeremiah (see, *e.g.*, B. S. Childs, 'Isaiah and the Assyrian Crisis', *SBT* 2. 3,1967).

In a volume of expositions of passages from 2 Kings, *The Politics of God and the Politics of Man* (1972, pp. 13–21), J. Ellul suggests that Kings makes a twofold distinctive contribution to the Canon of Scripture. First, it pictures God's involvement in political life, and thus warns both against undervaluing the importance of politics, and against absolutizing this realm (since it shows how God brings judgment on politics). Secondly, it displays the interplay of the free determination of man (who in various political situations makes his decisions and puts his policies into effect) and the free decision of God (who nevertheless effects his will through or despite these deliberate human acts).

In reaction to an overstress in recent biblical study on the idea of God as the one who acts in history, the importance of this motif in the Bible is in danger of being understressed. Kings is a book which itself particularly emphasizes this motif (see J. E. Goldingay, ' "That you may know that Yahweh is God": A study in the relationship between theology and historical truth in the Old Testament', *TynB* 23, 1972, pp. 58–93; and on the application of this idea today, see D. N. Freedman, 'The biblical idea of history', *Int* 21, 1967, pp. 32–49). God *is* one who works out a purpose in history, and his people may use the marks of his footsteps in past history to see what he may be doing in the present.

Bibliography. For detailed textual study, still worth using are C. F. Keil, *The Books of the Kings* (in C. F. Keil and F. Delitzsch, *Commentary on the Old Testament*), 1872; C. F. Burney, *Notes on the Hebrew Text of the Books of Kings*, 1903; J. A. Montgomery (ed. H. S. Gehman), *The Books of Kings*, *ICC*, 1951.

J.E.G.

KING'S VALLEY
See Shaveh, Part 3.

KINSMAN, KINSWOMAN
See Kin, Part 2.

KIRIATH-BAAL
See Kiriath-jearim, Part 2.

The route of the ancient 'King's Highway'.

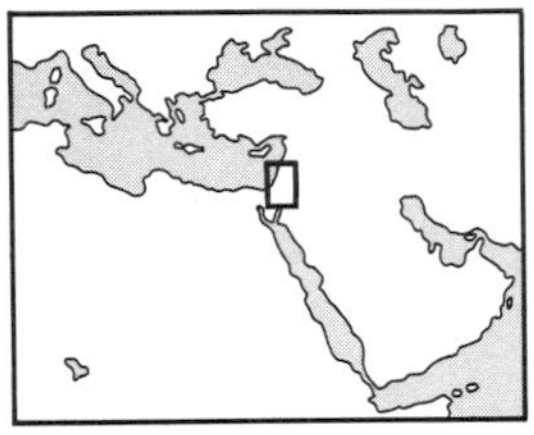

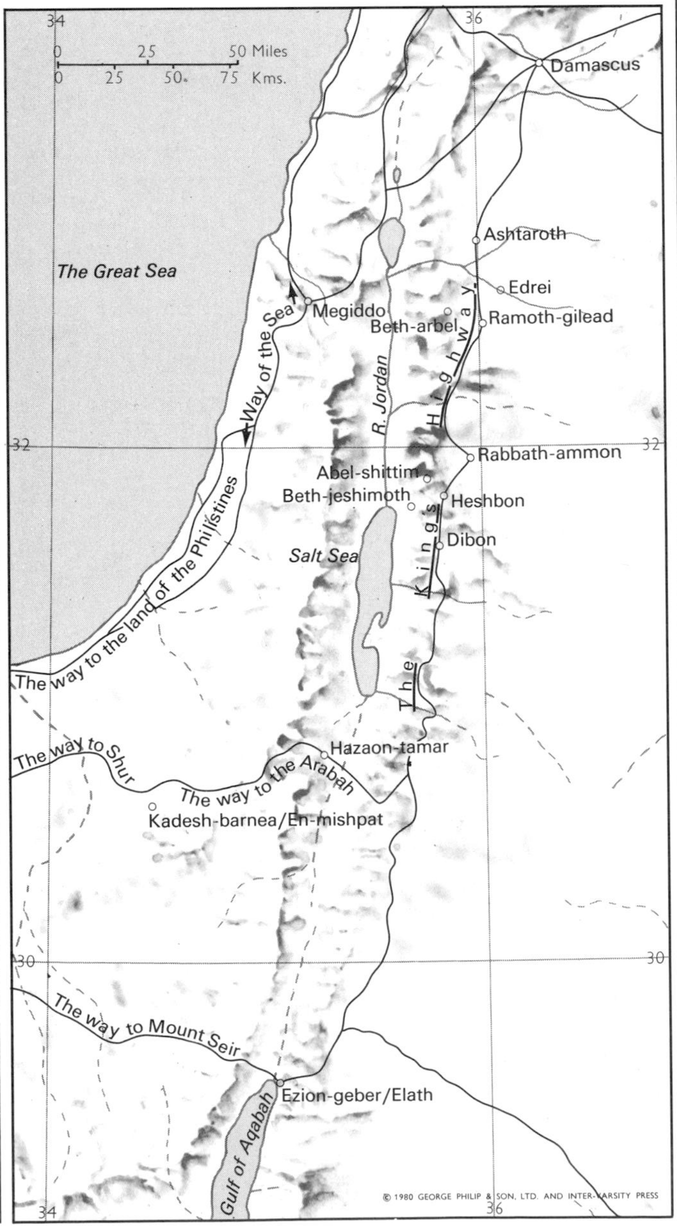

KING'S GARDEN. An open space in Jerusalem near 'the gate between the two walls' (2 Ki. 25:4; Je. 39:4; 52:7) and close to the Pool of *Siloam (Ne. 3:15). The 'two walls' (*cf.* Is. 22:11) were probably those below the 'Fountain Gate', SE of Ophel, running along the W side of the E hill of Jerusalem, and along the E side of the W hill (S. R. Driver, *Jeremiah*, 1918, p. 239; N. Grollenberg, *Atlas*, Maps 24B & C). J.D.D.

KING'S HIGHWAY. The name given to the direct road running from the Gulf of Aqabah to Damascus in Syria, E of the Dead Sea and Jordan valley. The route was in use between the 23rd and 20th centuries BC, being marked along its length by Early Bronze Age settlements and fortresses. It was, therefore, likely that Chedorlaomer and his allies approached Sodom and Gomorrah by this way and were pursued up it by Abraham (Gn. 14). Its further use in the 13th–6th centuries BC is also marked by datable ruins showing that the road was occupied at the time that the Edomites and the Ammonites prevented Moses and the Israelites from using it (Nu. 20:17; 21:22; *cf.* Dt. 2:27). In Solomon's reign the highway played an important part as a trade-link between Ezion-geber, Judah and Syria. Roman milestones show that it was incorporated into Trajan's road built in the 2nd century AD and was used by the Nabataeans. The modern motorway follows part of the old track, which is still called Tarīq es-Sulṭan.

BIBLIOGRAPHY. N. Glueck, *The Other Side of the Jordan*, 1945., pp. 10–16; J. A. Thompson, *Archaeology and the Old Testament*, 1957, pp. 57–58; Y. Aharoni, *LOB*, pp. 49–52. D.J.W.

KIR. In the Heb. text the name of the place of exile of the Syrians (2 Ki. 16:9; Am. 1:5), and a country, not necessarily the same, from which Yahweh brought them (Am. 9:7). This is perhaps not their original home, but a land occupied at some earlier stage in their history, parallel to Israel in Egypt and the *Philistines in *Caphtor (*ARAM). In Is. 22:6 Kir is parallel to Elam. No ancient place of this name is known; however, as it simply means 'city', it need not be specific. The LXX does not use a proper name in any of these passages, but translates 'from a pit' (Am. 9:7, Gk. *ek bothrou*), 'called as an ally' (Am. 1:5, Gk. *epiklētos*) and 'congregation' (Is. 22:6, Gk. *synagōgē*), feasible translations of an unpointed Heb. text. Vulg. follows the mistaken identification with Cyrene made by Symmachus. Kir has been altered to read Koa' (by Cheyne), and said to be Gutium in the Kurdish hills (*cf.* Ezk. 23:23; Is. 22:5–6). The problem is not yet solved. A.R.M.

KIRIATHAIM. The dual form of Heb. *qiryâ*, 'city, town', and meaning therefore 'double city', a name applied to two cities in the Bible.

1. A place in the territory allotted to Reuben (Jos. 13:19) which had already been conquered and rebuilt by the Reubenites (Nu. 32:37). It is possible that Shaveh Kiriathaim, which is mentioned in the account of the invasion of Chedorlaomer in the time of Abraham (Gn. 14:5), refers to this locality, as the 'plain' of Kiriathaim (RVmg.), though *šāwēh* is a rare word of uncertain meaning. The city was later in the hands of the Moabites (Je. 48:1, 23; Ezk. 25:9), and is mentioned in the 9th-century inscription of King Mesha of Moab (*qrytn*, line 10) as having been rebuilt by him, so it cannot have remained under Israelite control for more than about 3 centuries. The site is possibly near to modern El Quraiyāt about 10 km NW of Dibon in Jordan, but the place has not yet been located (*cf.* H. Douner and W. Röllig, *Kanaanäische und aramäische Inschriften*, 1962–4, pp. 174–175).

2. A levitical city in Naphtali (1 Ch. 6:76), possibly to be identified with Kartan (*qartān*) of Jos. 21:32. The site is unknown, though various suggestions have been made (see *GTT*, §§ 298, 337, 357). T.C.M.

KIRIATH-ARBA (Heb. *qiryaṯ 'arba'*, 'city of four', *i.e.* 'tetrapolis'), an earlier name of *Hebron. According to Jos. 14:15, it was 'the metropolis of the Anakim' (so LXX; *MT* makes the numeral *'arba'*, 'four', into a personal name). The name Kiriath-arba occurs once in the story of Abraham (Gn. 23:2) and a few times in the narrative of the Conquest (Jos. 14:15; 15:54; 20:7; Jdg. 1:10); thereafter it evidently fell into disuse. Some attempt may have been made to revive it in the post-exilic age (Ne. 11:25), but with the Idumaean occupation of the place soon afterwards the old name was completely discontinued. F.F.B.

KIRIATH-JEARIM (Heb. *qiryaṯ-yᵉ'ārîm*, 'city of forests'). A chief city of the Gibeonites (Jos. 9:17), on the Judah–Benjamin border (Jos. 18:14–15; *cf.* Jdg. 18:12), assigned first to Judah (Jos. 15:60), then, assuming an identification with 'Kiriath', to Benjamin (Jos. 18:28). It is called also Kiriath-baal (Jos. 15:60, suggesting that it was an old Canaanite high place), Baalah (Jos. 15:9–10), Baale-judah (2 Sa. 6:2) and Kiriath-arim (Ezr. 2:25).

Here the ark was brought from Beth-shemesh and entrusted to the keeping of Eleazar (1 Sa. 7:1), whence after 20 years David took it to Jerusalem (2 Sa. 6:2; 1 Ch. 13:5; 2 Ch. 1:4). The home of Uriah the prophet was in Kiriath-jearim (Je. 26:20).

Its precise location has not been determined, but the consensus of opinion favours Kuriet el-'Enab (commonly known as Abu Ghosh), a flourishing little village 14 km W of Jerusalem on the Jaffa road. It is a well-wooded district (or has been in the past) and it meets other geographical requirements. J.D.D.

KIRIATH-SEPHER (Heb. *qiryaṯ-sēp̄er*). The name used for * Debir in the story of Othniel and Achsah (Jos. 15:15ff., Jdg. 1:11ff.). J.P.U.L.

KIR OF MOAB, KIR-HARESETH. A fortified city of S Moab, attacked but not taken by the kings of Israel, Judah and Edom (2 Ki. 3:25). During the siege, Mesha, king of Moab, offered up his eldest son 'for a burnt offering upon the wall'.

The Hebrew name (*qîr ḥ^a^reśeṯ*) means 'the wall of potsherds'. The LXX rendering of Is. 16:11 presupposes the Hebrew *qîr ḥ^a^ḏešeṯ*, 'the new city'. Normally the town is called Kir of Moab (Is. 15:1). Some writers see in Je. 48:36–37 a play on words in which Kir Heres is parallel to 'bald' (Heb. *qorḥâ*). It is suggested that the original Moabite name was QRḤH, probably the town referred to in the * Moabite Stone (lines 22ff.), where Mesha established a sanctuary for Chemosh and carried out a building project. This would place it near Dibon.

Most writers, however, identify it with Kerak, following the Targum rendering, Kerak of Moab. If that is so, the place was built on a strategic rocky hill 1,027 m above sea-level, surrounded by steep valleys, some 18 km E of the Dead Sea and 24 km S of the Arnon River. Today a mediaeval castle crowns the hill.

BIBLIOGRAPHY. F. M. Abel, *Géographie de la Palestine*, 2, 1933, pp. 418–419; Nelson Glueck, *AASOR* 14, 1934, p. 65. J.A.T.

KISH (Heb. *qîš*, 'bow', 'power'). 1. A Benjaminite, the son of Abiel and father of King Saul (1 Sa. 9:1;

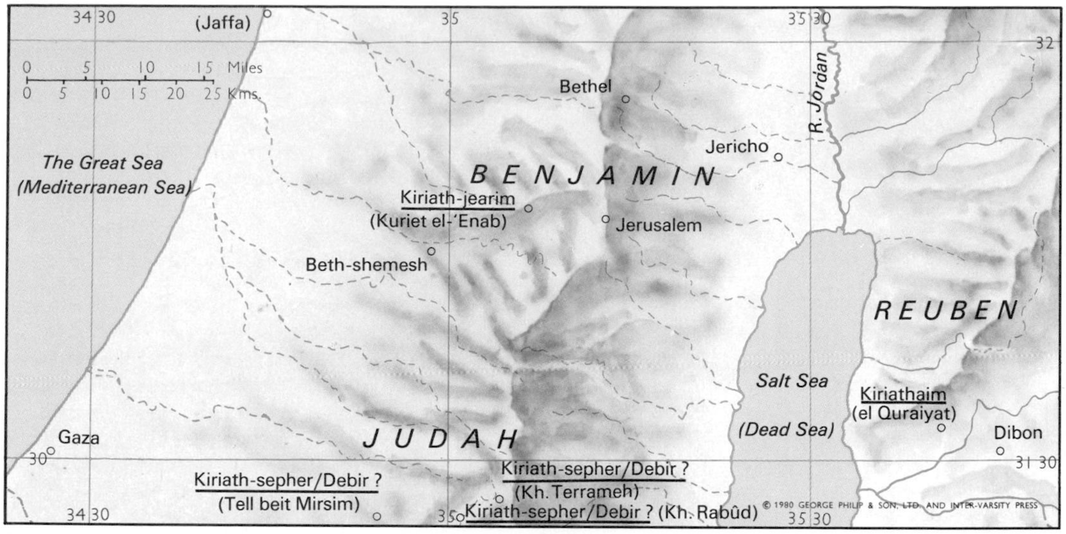

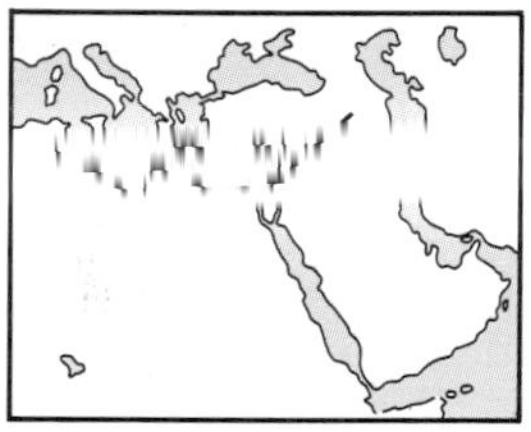

The possible locations of Kiriathaim, Kiriath-sepher and Kiriath-jearim.

KIRIATH-SANNA See Debir, Part 1.

In ancient Kish was found a baked clay figurine of Papsukkal, messenger of the gods. 7th cent. BC. (AMO)

Pair of gold ear-rings excavated at Tell Ingharra one of the mounds of ancient Kish. Probably Parthian (3rd cent. BC *–1st cent.* AD*).* (AMO)

14:51; *cf.* Acts 13:21). **2.** The son of Jehiel and Maacah (1 Ch. 8:30), perhaps the uncle of **1. 3.** A Levite, grandson of Merari (1 Ch. 23:21). **4.** Another Levite and Merarite who assisted in the cleansing of the Temple in Hezekiah's time (2 Ch. 29:12). **5.** A Benjaminite, great-grandfather of Mordecai (Est. 2:5). J.D.D.

6. Name of the capital of a city-state *c.* 20 km SE of Babylon (mod. Tell el-Ukheimer) where, according to Sumerian tradition (King List), the first dynasty after the *Flood ruled. It flourished *c.* 3200–3000 BC as a rival of *Erech when it was linked with the legendary Etana and with King Agga who opposed Gilgamesh. Documents from the earlier occupation and from the 2nd millennium are extant. It was excavated by the French (1914) and by a joint Oxford (Ashmolean Museum) and Chicago (Field Museum) expedition (1922–33). Finds include early palaces, tablets and a major flood-deposit level dated *c.* 3300 BC.

BIBLIOGRAPHY. L. C. Watelin, S. H. Langdon, *Excavations at Kish*, 1925–34; *cf. Iraq* 26, 1964, pp. 83–98; 28, 1966, pp. 18–51. D.J.W.

KISHON. The river, modern Nahr el-Muqaṭṭa‘, which, rising in the hills of N Samaria, drains the plain of Esdraelon and debouches in the bay of Acre, E of Mt Carmel. Though it winds about, in a general sense it flows in a NW direction parallel with, and to the NE of, the mountain range which runs from Samaria to Carmel and in the NE passes of which lay Taanach, Megiddo and Jokneam. The name Kishon is not often used, the river sometimes being indicated by reference to one of the towns overlooking it. Thus it is probably first mentioned in Jos. 19:11, where the 'brook which is east of Jokneam' is given as part of the boundary of Zebulun, though in this case it is only a small section of the river in the vicinity of Jokneam that is referred to.

The best-known reference to the river is that connected with the victory of the Israelites under Barak over the Syrians under Sisera (Jdg. 4–5; Ps. 83:9). The forces of Sisera, fully armed with chariots, were deployed in the plain, and the Israelites made their attack from the mountains SW of the river. The success of the Israelites was in large measure due to the river, which was running high, and must have made the surrounding plain too soft for Sisera's chariots, which became bogged down and useless.

The river is referred to in the Song of Deborah as 'the waters of Megiddo' (Jdg. 5:19), and the fact that Megiddo is not otherwise referred to in this account has been taken by Albright to indicate that it was at this time lying in ruins, while Taanach was flourishing. The excavations of *Megiddo have shown a gap in occupation about 1125 BC between Levels VII and VI, and it may be that the Israelite victory occurred during that period of abandonment, or about 1125 BC.

The river is next mentioned as the scene of the slaughter by Elijah of the prophets of Baal, after the contest on Mt Carmel (1 Ki. 18:40). It is referred to here as a brook (*naḥal*), suggesting that the long drought preceding these events had reduced the river to a low level. The rains which followed must have washed away the traces of the execution.

BIBLIOGRAPHY. G. A. Smith, *The Historical Geography of the Holy Land*[25], 1931, pp. 394–397; W. F.

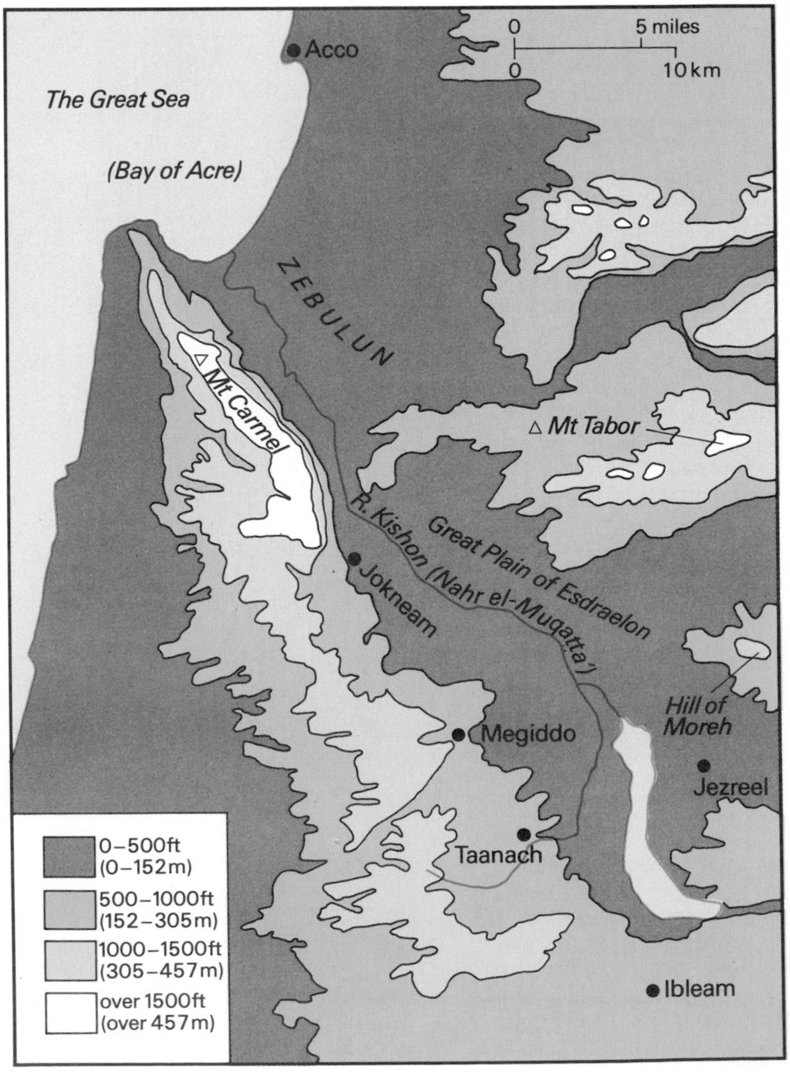

The course of the river Kishon.

Albright, *The Archaeology of Palestine*, 1960, pp. 117–118; *LOB*, pp. 204f. T.C.M.

KISS. A common salutation in the E, this word occurs in the OT as a sign of affection between relatives (*e.g.* Gn. 29:11; 33:4), an expression of love (Ct. 1:2), or lust (Pr. 7:13), and perhaps as a token of homage (1 Sa. 10:1). The last, kissing 'God's anointed', possibly may be, as Ps. 2:10, a religious or cultic rite analogous to that found among idol cults: to kiss the hand (Jb. 31:27), or an image (1 Ki. 19:18; Ho. 13:2), is an act of religious worship. In the NT *phileō* is used as a sign of friendship or affection (*e.g.* Judas, Mt. 26:48), as is the stronger form *kataphileō* (*e.g.* Lk. 7:38; 15:20; Acts 20:37). The 'holy kiss' (Rom. 16:16; 1 Pet. 5:14), which soon entered into the church's liturgy, was an expression of Christian love and presumably was restricted to one's own sex (*cf. Apostolic Constitutions* 2. 57, 12). See W. Günther, C. Brown, in *NIDNTT* 2, pp. 547–550. E.E.E.

KITTIM. One of the sons of Javan (Gn. 10:4 = 1 Ch. 1:7; Heb. *kittîm*) whose descendants settled on the island of Cyprus where their name was given to the town of Kition, modern Larnaka, which is referred to in the Phoenician inscriptions as *kt* or *kty*. They engaged in sea trade (Nu. 24:24), and the name seems to have come to apply to the whole island of Cyprus (Is. 23:1, 12), and then in a more general way to the coastlands and islands of the E Mediterranean (*'iyyê kittiyyîm*: Je. 2:10; Ezk. 27:6). The ostraca of *c.* 600 BC from Arad refer to *ktym*, probably mercenaries, principally perhaps Greeks, from the islands and coastlands. In Daniel's fourth vision, which probably deals with the period from Cyrus to Antiochus Epiphanes, the latter's failure to conquer Egypt, due to the intervention of Rome, is probably referred to in 11:30, where 'the ships of Kittim' must be Rome. The author probably saw in Rome's intervention the fulfilment of Nu. 24:24, where Vulg. translates Kittim by 'Italy' (so also in Dn. 11:30) and the Targum of Onkelos by 'Romans'. The name occurs in the Dead Sea Scrolls, also probably with reference to Rome, being used, for instance, in the commentary on Habakkuk as an interpretation of the 'Chaldeans' of that prophet (Hab. 1:6).

BIBLIOGRAPHY. A. Lemaire, *Inscriptions hébraïques*, 1, 1977, p. 156; Y. Yadin, *The Scroll of the War of the Sons of Light Against the Sons of Darkness*, 1962, pp. 22–26. T.C.M.

KNEADING-TROUGH. A large shallow bowl, made of pottery or wood, in which dough was prepared. Modern Arab nomads often use wooden bowls for this purpose. Heb. *miš'ereṯ*, Ex. 12:34; *cf.* Dt. 28:5, 17 (AV 'store'). For a model, *c.* 700 BC, see *ANEP*, no. 152. (*BREAD.) A.R.M.

KNEE, KNEEL. The concrete imagery of the OT expresses weakness or fear as 'feeble knees' (Jb. 4:4; Is. 35:3) or as 'the knees tremble', 'knock together' (Na. 2:10; Dn. 5:6).

The fifteen references in the NT are, with the exception of Heb. 12:12, always used in connection with bowing. The action may indicate a sign of respect (Mk. 1:40; *cf.* 2 Ki. 1:13; Mk. 15:19), or subjection (Rom. 11:4; 14:11; *cf. 1 Clement* 57:1, 'bending the knees of your heart'), or of religious adoration or worship (Lk. 5:8). In the latter sense kneeling is sometimes the posture of prayer (Lk. 22:41; 1 Ki. 8:54, *cf.* 18:42). The universal recognition of Christ's Lordship is thus signified: 'every knee should bow' (Phil. 2:10; *cf.* Rom. 14:10f.; 1 Cor. 15:25). *Cf. TDNT* 1, pp. 738–740; 3, pp. 594–595; 6, pp. 758–766. E.E.E.

KNIFE. The primitive flint knife was current until recent times beside metal forms in the Near East. In the OT it is specified for the *circumcision of Moses' son and of Israel (Ex. 4:25; Jos. 5:2–3), perhaps for hygienic reasons, the once-used flint being discarded without cost. The Heb. *ḥereḇ* used in these passages, and for the self-mutilation of the frenzied priests of Baal (1 Ki. 18:28), usually denotes a short sword. In Pr. 30:14 this is parallel to Heb. *ma'ᵃḵeleṯ*, a knife used in eating. It was such a short sword that Abraham took to kill Isaac and the Levite used to dismember his concubine (Gn. 22:6, 10; Jdg. 19:29). Heb. *śakkîn* (Pr. 23:2) is to be connected with Aram. *sakkîn*, Arab. *sikkîn*, 'knife'.

AV and RV follow Vulg. *cultri* in rendering the unique Heb. *maḥᵃlāpîm*, 'knives' (Ezr. 1:9; *cf.* Syr. *ḥlāpâ*). RSV 'censers' is taken from 1 Esdras 2:9 (Gk. *thyiskai*). The LXX 'of a different sort' (Gk. *parēllagmena*) translates the Hebrew but does not throw light on the meaning. A.R.M.

A Canaanite knife or dagger of bronze with silver-plated handle. (ZR)

KNOWLEDGE. The Gk. ideal of knowledge was a contemplation of reality in its static and abiding being; the Heb. was primarily concerned with life in its dynamic process, and therefore conceived knowledge as an entry into relationship with the experienced world which makes demands not only on man's understanding but also on man's will.

I. In the Old Testament

Thus it is that the OT speaks of knowing (*yāḏa'*) the loss of children (Is. 47:8), grief (Is. 53:3), sin (Je. 3:13), God's hand and his might (Je. 16:21), his vengeance (Ezk. 25:14). The intimate sexual relationship is spoken of as knowing a man or a woman (*e.g.* Gn. 4:1; Jdg. 11:39). Above all, to know God is not simply to be aware of his existence; for the most part this is taken for granted in Heb. writings. To know him is to recognize him for what he is, the sovereign Lord who makes a demand on man's obedience and especially upon the obedience of his people Israel, with whom he has made a covenant. He is the God whose holiness and loving-kindness are 'known' in the experience of nation and individual. The criterion of this knowledge is obedience, and its opposite is not simply ignorance but rebellious, wilful turning away from God (*cf.* 1 Sa. 2:12; 3:7; 2 Ch. 33:13; Is. 1:3; Je. 8:7; 24:7; 31:34). Furthermore, the acknowledgment of the Lord's claims involves a rejection of the heathen gods, knowing that they are not gods (*cf.* Is. 41:23).

On God's side of the relationship between himself and man there is also knowledge. Here especially there can be no question of theoretical observation; for man and all things are God's creation. It is from this fact that God's omniscience springs: he knows the world and man within it because it is at his command that they come to be (Jb. 28:20ff.; Ps. 139). In particular, God knows those whom he has chosen to be his agents: his know-

KISLEW
See Calendar, Part 1.

KITE
See Animals, Part 1.

KOR
See Weights and measures, Part 3.

ledge is spoken of in terms of election (Je. 1:5; Ho. 13:5; Am. 3:2).

II. In the New Testament

To speak of knowledge in these ways is natural in addressing a people who all formally believe that God exists but fail to acknowledge his claims. In Hellenistic Judaism and in the NT use of *ginōskein, eidenai*, and their derivatives we find Heb. thought modified by the fact that the Gentiles were ignorant even of God's existence (* IGNORANCE). In general, however, the Heb. conception is retained. All men ought to respond to the revelation in Christ which has made possible a full knowledge of God, no more intellectual apprehension but an obedience to his revealed purpose, an acceptance of his revealed love, and a fellowship with himself (*cf.* Jn. 17:3; Acts 2:36; 1 Cor. 2:8; Phil. 3:10). This knowledge of God is possible only because God in his love has called men to it (Gal. 4:9; 1 Cor. 13:12; 2 Tim. 2:19). The whole process of enlightenment and acceptance may be called coming to the knowledge of the truth (1 Tim. 2:4; 2 Tim. 2:25; 3:7; Tit. 1:1; *cf.* Jn. 8:32).

Both Paul and John write at times in conscious contrast with and opposition to the systems of alleged esoteric knowledge purveyed by the mystery cults and syncretistic 'philosophy' of their day (*cf.* 1 Tim. 6:20; Col. 2:8). To these knowledge was the result of an initiation or illumination which put the initiate in possession of spiritual discernment beyond mere reason or faith. Against them Paul (particularly in 1 Cor. and Col.) and all the Johannine writings stress that knowledge of God springs from committal to the historic Christ; it is not opposed to faith but forms its completion. We need no revelation other than that in Christ. (* GNOSTICISM.)

BIBLIOGRAPHY. R. Bultmann, in *TDNT* 1, pp. 689–719; E. Schütz, E. D. Schmitz, in *NIDNTT* 2, pp. 390–409. M.H.C.

KOA. Ezekiel (23:23) prophesies that this people, together with other dwellers in Mesopotamia, will attack Jerusalem. Koa has been identified by some with the people called in Assyr. texts *Qutu*, who lived E of the Tigris in the region of the upper 'Adhaim and Diyala rivers. Assyr. records often couple them with another tribe hostile to Assyria, the *Sutu*, perhaps to be equated with Shoa in Ezk. 23:23. Some (*e.g.* O. Procksch) find Koa in Is. 22:5, but only by a doubtful emendation of the word usually translated 'walls'. Vulg. misinterpreted Koa as *principes*, 'princes', an interpretation which was followed by Luther.

BIBLIOGRAPHY. F. Delitzsch, *Wo lag das Paradies?*, 1881, pp. 233–237; G. A. Cooke in *ICC*, 1936, on Ezk. 23:23. J.T.

KOHATH, KOHATHITES. Kohath, second son of Levi, was founder of one of the three great Levite families. His family was subdivided into the houses of Amram, Izhar, Hebron and Uzziel, and Moses and Aaron were Amramites (Ex. 6:20). In the wilderness the Kohathites carried the tabernacle furniture and vessels. They camped on the S side of the tabernacle. Their males over a month old numbered 8,600; those who actually served (age-group 30–50), 2,750 (Nu. 3:27–32; 4:36). In the land the Kohathites who, being sons of Aaron, were priests, were allotted thirteen cities, the rest ten cities (Jos. 21:4–5). Under David's reorganization the Kohathites held a wide variety of offices, including a share in the Temple singing (1 Ch. 6:31–38; *cf.* 9:31–32; 26:23–31). Kohathites are mentioned again under Jehoshaphat, Hezekiah and Josiah (2 Ch. 20:19; 29:12; 34:12), and at the return from the Exile (*cf.* Ezr. 2:42 with 1 Ch. 9:19; Korahites were Kohathites). See also * KORAH. D.W.G.

KORAH (Heb. *qōraḥ* = baldness?). **1.** Chief (AV 'Duke') of Edom, son of Esau (Gn. 36:5, 14, 18; 1 Ch. 1:35). **2.** Chief of Edom, son of Eliphaz (Gn. 36:16). As the name is omitted from Gn. 36:11 and 1 Ch. 1:36, some think this to be a gloss. **3.** A son of Hebron (1 Ch. 2:43). **4.** A grandson of Kohath and ancestor of a group of sacred musicians ('sons of Korah') who are mentioned in the titles of Ps. 42 and 11 other psalms (1 Ch. 6:22).

5. A Levite ('Core' in Jude 11, AV), a Kohathite of the house of Izhar, perhaps identical with **4.** With Dathan, his brother Abiram and another Reubenite, On, Korah rebelled against Moses and Aaron. Three grounds of revolt are stated, and although these have led some commentators to assume composite authorship according to the documentary hypothesis, the narrative reads naturally as a harmonious unity. Nu. 16 records discontent on the grounds: first, that Moses and Aaron have set themselves above the rest of Israel (vv. 3, 13); secondly, that Moses has failed to bring Israel to the promised land (v. 14); and thirdly, that he and Aaron have arrogated the priesthood to themselves (vv. 7–11). That different grievances should be used unitedly is not unfamiliar in both ancient history and modern. As the rebels prepare to offer incense, the wrath of God is kindled, and after Moses has interceded for the congregation of Israel the rebels and their followers are destroyed by the earth opening to swallow them, and by fire. *Cf.* Nu. 26:9; Dt. 11:6; Ps. 106:17. It has been argued that this narrative contains two differing versions which reflect variant traditions of the struggle for religious leadership among the Levites. T.H.J.

LABAN (Heb. *lāḇan*, 'white'). **1.** A descendant of Abraham's brother Nahor (Gn. 22:20–23), son of Bethuel (Gn. 28:5), Rebekah's brother (Gn. 24:47ff.) and uncle and father-in-law of Jacob (Gn. 27:43; 28:2). Laban's branch of the family had remained in Harran, but the close ethnic affinity was maintained by both Isaac and Jacob, who found their wives there. Nevertheless, notable differences existed between the Harran and Palestinian groups. Laban is described as an Aramean (Gn. 28:5; 31:20), he spoke Aramaic (Gn. 31:47), practised marriage customs unknown to Jacob (Gn. 29:26) and worshipped other gods (Gn. 31:19ff., *cf.* v. 53), though he did acknowledge Yahweh's activity (Gn. 24:50–51). Though generous in his hospitality, Laban's chief characteristics were duplicity and self-interest, as demonstrated in his dealings with Jacob. Taking advantage of Jacob's love for Rachel, he made him work 14 years for his bride, though Jacob responded with his own brand of trickery (Gn. 29–30). When Jacob eventually left with his family for Palestine, Laban, being warned in a dream not to harm them, made a covenant or treaty with Jacob (Gn. 31:44–54). Laban was thwarted ultimately not by Jacob's cunning, but by God's overruling grace. Earlier, Laban rather than Bethuel had arranged Rebekah's marriage (Gn. 24:50ff.), though no usurping of the father's authority need be assumed here (*cf.* Gn. 31:18–28).

BIBLIOGRAPHY. D. Daube and R. Yaron, *JSS* 1, 1956, pp. 60–62; M. Greenberg, *JBL* 81, 1962, pp. 239–248.

2. An unknown place (Dt. 1:1), probably in the plains of Moab, or perhaps to be identified with *Libnah, a stopping-place in the wilderness (Nu. 33:20–21). M.J.S.

LACHISH (Heb. *lāḵîš*, LXX *Lachis*). A large fortified city identified with modern Tell ed-Duweir 40 km SW of Jerusalem. This site was excavated by the Wellcome–Marston Archaeological Expedition 1932–38 and since 1966 by the University of Tel Aviv.

While the area is known to have been inhabited by cave-dwellers from at least as early as the 8th millennium BC it was not until *c.* 2500 BC that the hill which is now Tell ed-Duweir was first settled. By *c.* 1750 BC the city was strongly fortified with a wall built on the crest of a steep rampart which sloped down to a ditch or fosse at the base of the tell. Throughout this period the surrounding caves previously used for habitation served as tombs.

Letters from two rulers of Lachish, Yabni-ilu and Zimrida (nos. 328–329) were found at *Amarna. In another letter (no. 288) from there, Abdi-Ḫeba, king of Jerusalem, accuses Zimrida of conspiring with the Ḫapiru, while a letter found at Tell el-Ḥesi says that he has made a treaty with another king, Šipti-Ba'lu. The religious practices of the Canaanites have been illustrated by a series of temples in use between 1550 and 1200 BC and situated in the fosse NW of the tell. The altar was constructed of unhewn stones (*cf.* Jos. 8:31) and had a flight of stairs ascending it (*cf.* Ex. 20:24ff.). Offerings had been placed in bowls which were deposited on the benches in the temple and over 100 lamps were found scattered around the building. Bones of young sheep or goats were plentiful and practically all the identified specimens were from the right foreleg which in Hebrew religion formed part of the priests' portion of the peace offering (Lv. 7:32).

Japhia, king of Lachish, was a member of the Amorite coalition that fought Joshua at Gibeon (Jos. 10:3, 5) and was executed at Makkedah (Jos. 10:22–27) after Joshua's victory. Lachish subsequently fell to Joshua (Jos. 10:31f.) and although there is evidence of destruction of the city at *c.* 1200 BC, the OT does not explicitly state that Joshua was responsible for it (*cf.* Jos. 11:13). An Egyp. raid into Palestine is one possible explanation for the ash layer which covers the site.

The Israelites probably occupied the site some time during the period of the Judges, and although evidence from the tell at this time is scant, tombs of the period have been found. One tomb of *c.* 1000 BC contained two occupants with many objects; one of these was an iron trident which may be an example of the 'three pronged fork' (*mazlēḡ*, 1 Sa. 2:13) used when offering a sacrifice. A small room dated to *c.* [illegible] has been excavated on the tell and found to contain a large number of religious objects including an altar, a *maṣṣēbâ* and incense burners, which together with figurine fragments found nearby indicate the presence of Canaanite religion in Israel. These practices at Lachish may have been referred to later by the prophet Micah (1:13), who said that the city was 'the beginning of sin to the daughter of Zion'.

Rehoboam rebuilt the city (2 Ch. 11:5–10) to a completely new plan as part of a comprehensive system of defence against the Egyptians. The city had a large administrative building. Amaziah took refuge at Lachish when fleeing from rebels in Jerusalem, who pursued and slew him there (2 Ki. 14:19; 2 Ch. 25:27). Two walls surrounded the city; the inner one was erected on the crest of the tell and was 6 m thick, while the second was built

LABO
See Hamath, Part 2.

LABOUR
See Work, Part 3.

The family of Laban

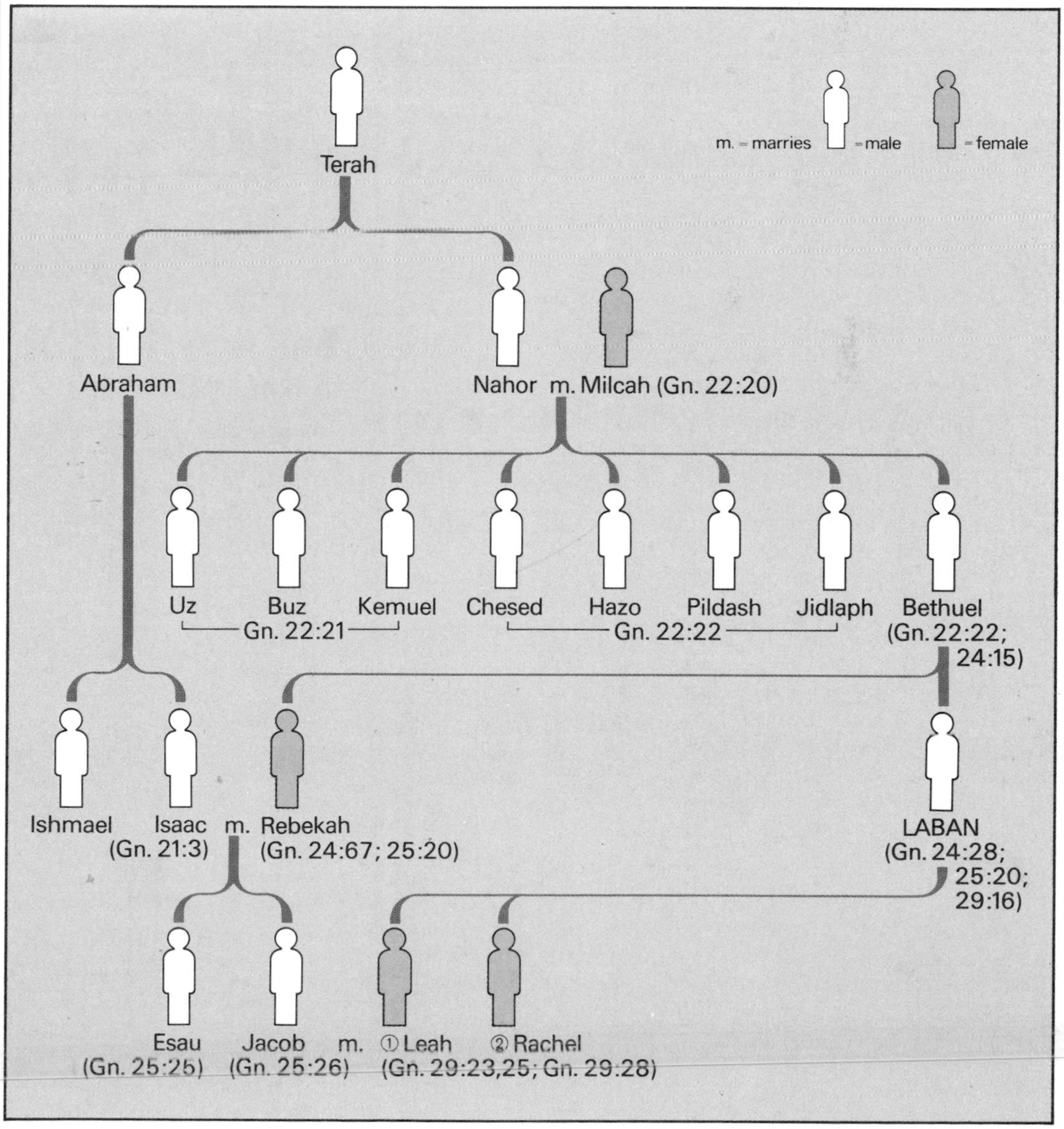

16 m down the slope. A large three-chambered gate in the inner wall led to a walled ramp which ran down the slope of the tell to a second gate. These defences are portrayed in relief sculpture from Sennacherib's palace at Nineveh (now in the British Museum) which relate his siege and capture of Lachish in 701 BC. Arrowheads, scale armour, sling-stones and an Assyrian helmet crest were found in the vicinity of the gate, testifying to this battle. The city itself was razed by the Assyrians, leaving an ash and destruction layer over the site. By capturing Lachish, Sennacherib prevented any Egyptian assistance reaching Jerusalem where he sent his messengers to demand Hezekiah's surrender (2 Ki. 18:17; 19:8; Is. 36:2; 37:8).

After its fall Lachish was administered by an Assyrian governor who had as one of his tasks the collection of levies from Philistia. A large building previously thought to belong to the Persian period has been redated on the grounds of architectural analogy to the 7th century BC and may have been the governor's residence. The walls and gates were rebuilt, but very little of the city itself has been found by archaeologists. Scythian warriors are believed to have been present in the city later in the century and this may partly account for the absence of domestic remains.

Neither the Bible nor the Babylonian Chronicle mentions a destruction of Lachish in Nebuchadrezzar's early campaigns in Palestine. It was, however, destroyed with the remainder of Judah in 588–587 BC when it was the only fortified outpost from Jerusalem (Je. 34:7) in addition to Azekah.

Lachish was resettled by returning Israelites (Ne. 11:30) and although very little of the dwellings of this period have been found, two temples notable for their similarity in plan to each other and with a much earlier example at *Arad have come to light. The city was walled during the Persian and

Lachish ostracon IV: a letter from Hoshayahu, in charge of an outpost, to Yaush, the commanding officer at Lachish. Hoshayahu reports that he is watching for signals from Lachish as he can no longer see those from Azekah (cf. Je. 34:7). c. 588–587 BC. (IA)

Lachish under seige by King Sennacherib of Assyria in 701 BC. Stone carving from Sennecherib's palace, Nineveh. Height c. 1·77 m. c. 690 BC. (BM)

Reconstruction of the late 8th–early 7th cent. BC Assyrian governor's residence, Lachish, previously thought to date from the Persian period.

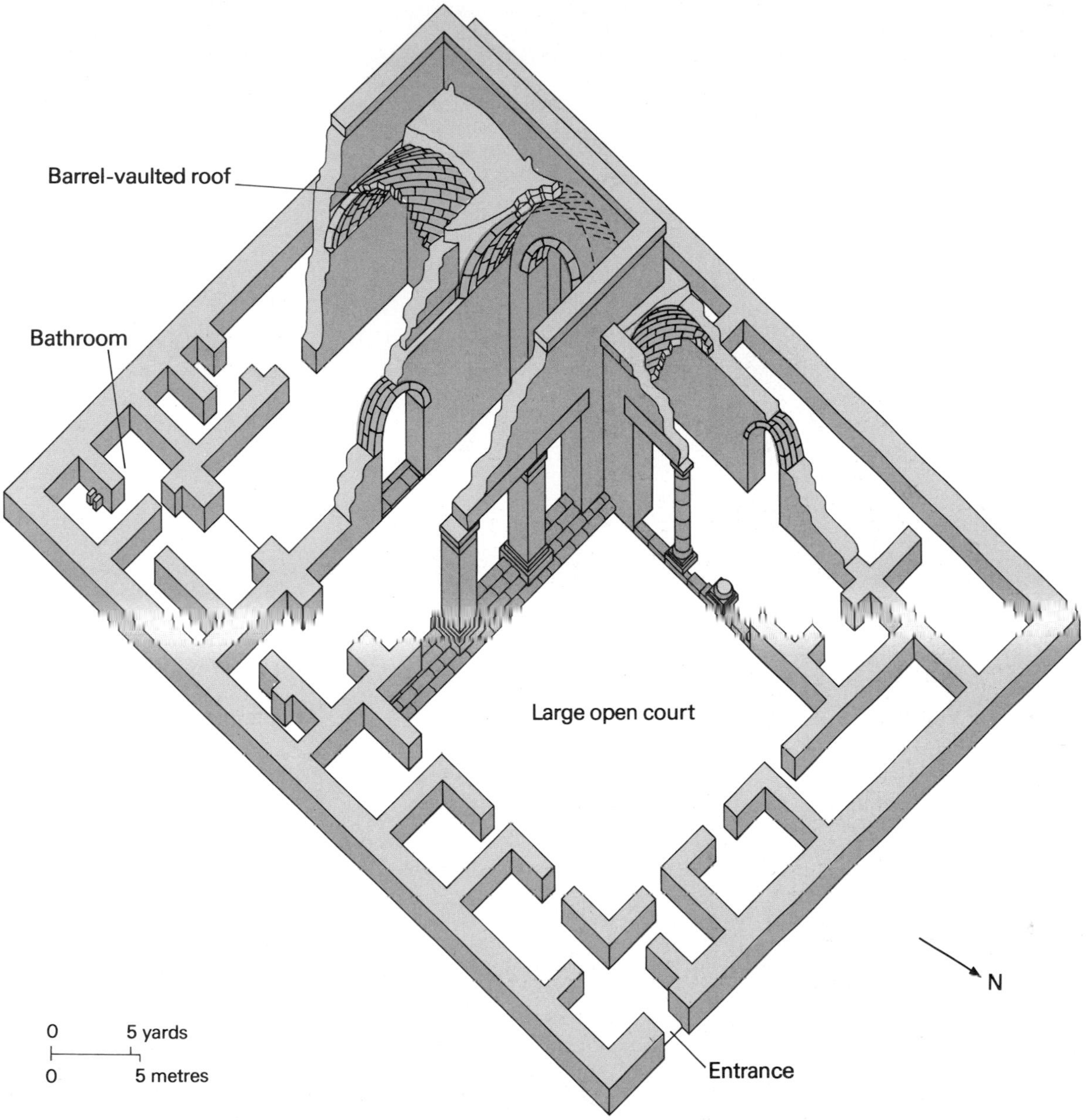

Reconstruction and plan together showing the development of the Canaanite 'Fosse Temple' at Lachish. c. 1550–1200 BC.

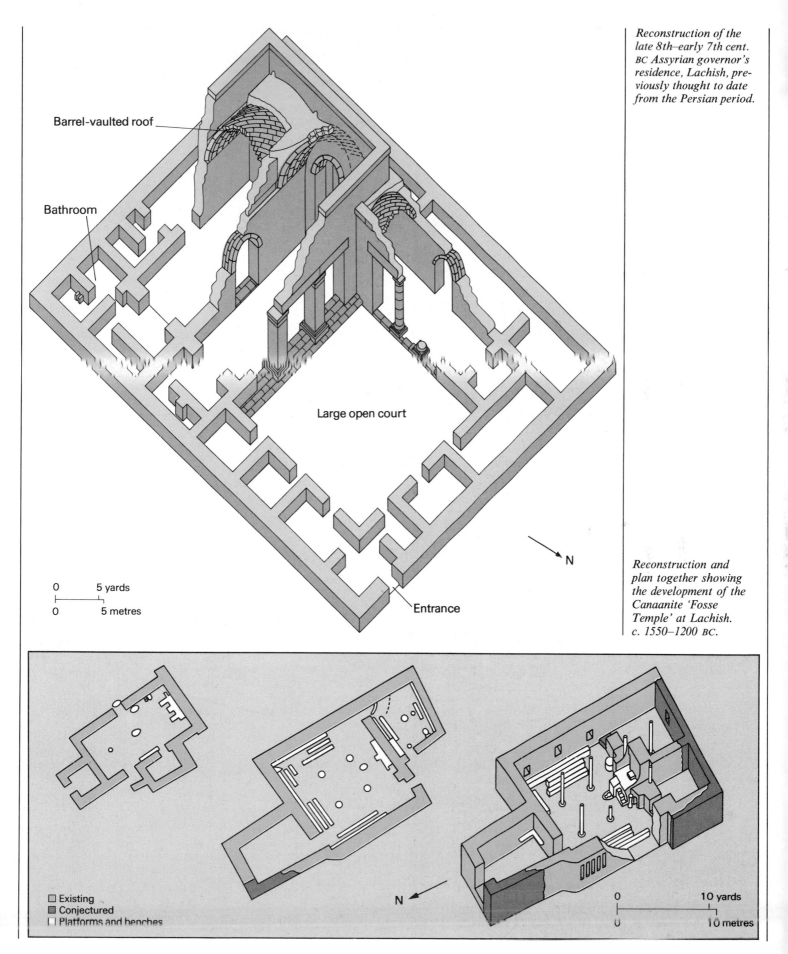

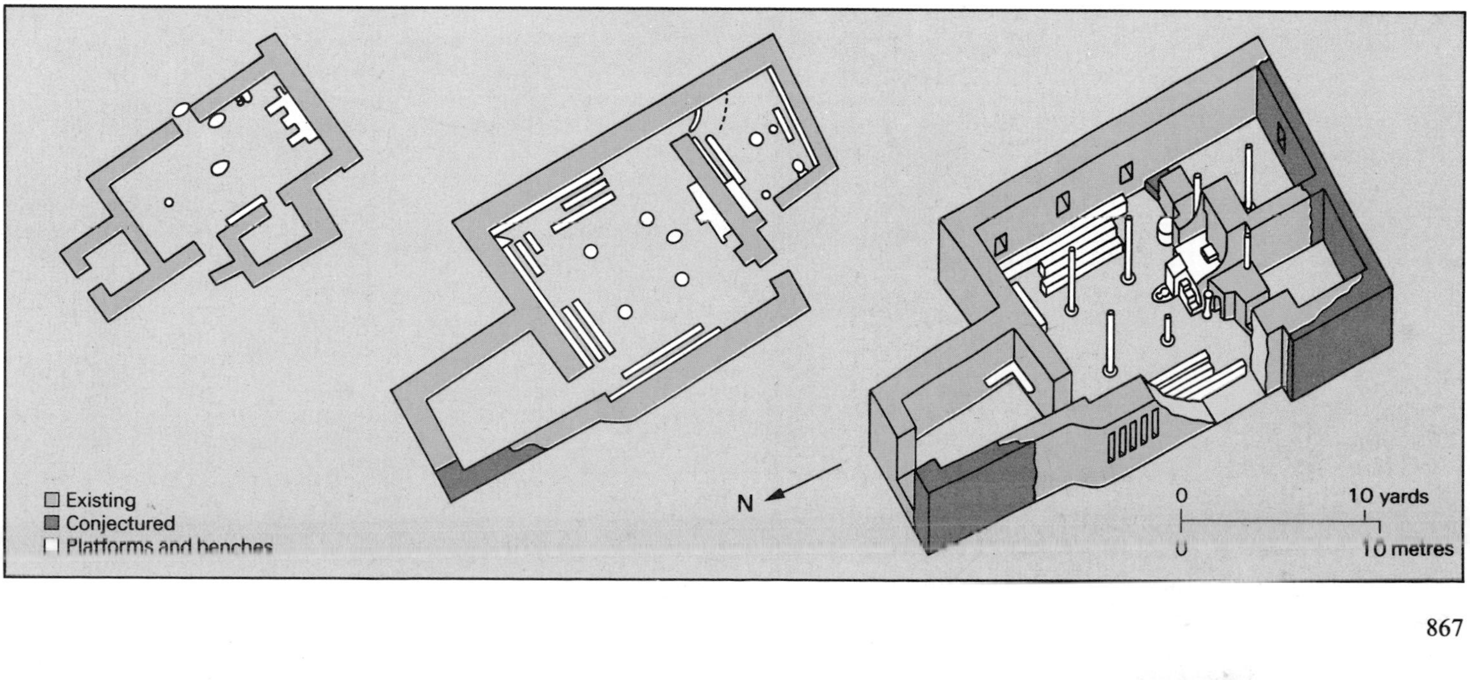

A reconstruction of the city of Lachish under siege by the army of Sennacherib, king of Assyria in 701 BC.

Hellenistic periods, after which the site was abandoned.

Inscriptions. A number of inscribed objects of the Bronze Age have been found at Lachish. Pictographic signs were incised on a dagger of *c.* 1700 BC and proto-Canaanite scripts appear on a sherd of *c.* 1600 BC, an ewer of *c.* 1250 BC and a bowl of the same date.

Inscriptions from the time of the Judaean monarchy are numerous and are most important for the history of Hebrew script. The first five letters of the Hebrew alphabet were found carved on one of the steps of a large building of *c.* 800 BC. A seal impression appears on a bulla from Lachish which had traces of papyrus fibres on the reverse, revealing that it had sealed a rolled papyrus document. The seal bore the name of * Gedaliah, the royal steward (Heb. 'who is over the house'), and may well be the person appointed governor over Judah by Nebuchadrezzar (2 Ki. 25:22; Je. 40:11–12). About seventeen other clay bullae and many jar handles bearing seal impressions with Hebrew names have also been found.

A total of twenty-one ostraca (inscribed potsherds) which were written during the last few weeks before Nebuchadrezzar's conquest in 588–587 BC were found in the gate house. Although the language is biblical Hebrew, the cursive script has been almost obliterated on many of the ostraca making reading impossible. The legible examples reveal that the collection is the correspondence of a subordinate, Hoshayahu, who is in charge of an outpost, to his superior, Yaush, who is the commanding officer of the garrison at Lachish. Hoshayahu commences the letters with the greeting 'May YHWH cause my lord to hear tidings of peace this day' before proceeding with the business which in most of the letters is answering the charge that he has read confidential letters from the king. In letter II, he replies in words reminiscent of those spoken by Mephibosheth to David (2 Sa. 9:8); 'Who is your servant (but) a dog . . . May YHWH afflict those who re[port] an (evil) rumour about which you are not informed.' It has been suggested that the ostraca were stored in the gate pending a trial, but it is more likely that the military command to which the letters were sent was situated in the gate building.

Letter IV concludes, 'we are watching for the signals of Lachish, according to all the indications which my lord has given, for we cannot see Azekah'. This recalls the situation mentioned by Jeremiah (34:7) when Azekah, Lachish and Jerusalem were the only fortified Judaean cities left. Azekah is 11 km NE of Lachish and the fact that Hoshayahu could not see its signals may indicate it had already fallen.

Letters III and XVI refer to 'the prophet'. His identity has been much debated. Jeremiah is one possibility. Uriah who fled to Egypt (Je. 26:20–22) during Jehoiakim's reign is another suggestion which requires the redating of the letters. Others believe him to be an unnamed prophet. Whatever the case the letter testifies to the recognition of prophets in ancient Israel and their participation in affairs of state. Letter III also mentions an expedition to Egypt by the commander of the army which may have been a last desperate attempt by Zedekiah to obtain Egyptian assistance to withstand the inevitable Babylonian attack. See also * WEIGHTS AND MEASURES, * WRITING.

BIBLIOGRAPHY. Excavation Reports: *Lachish I*, H. Torczyner, *The Lachish Letters*, 1935; *II*, O. Tufnell, *The Fosse Temple*, 1940; *III*, *The Iron Age*; *IV*, *The Bronze Age*. Also Y. Aharoni, *Lachish V*, 1975. C.J.D.

LADAN
See Libni, Part 2.

LADDER
See Fortification and siegecraft, Part 1.

LAHMI. A personal name found only in 1 Ch. 20:5 and applied to the brother of * Goliath the Gittite, who is there stated to have been slain by Elhanan. There is no valid reason why this should not be accepted, but it is possible that the reading may be a copyist's error for 'Bethlehemite' (*cf.* 2 Sa. 21:19), the last part of which is identical to 'Lahmi' in Hebrew. There is, however, no MS authority for this conjecture. G.W.G.

LAMB OF GOD. This expression occurs twice only in the NT (Jn. 1:29, 36). The word *amnos* is also found in Acts 8:32 and 1 Pet. 1:19, *arnos* occurs in Lk. 10:3, and *arnion* is found once in Jn. 21:15 and twenty-eight times in Revelation. The words 'Behold the Lamb of God, who takes away the sin of the world' (Jn. 1:29) are attributed to John the Baptist when acclaiming Jesus. Many possible interpretations of the word 'lamb' have been canvassed.

Some suggest that it refers to the lamb of the sin-offering, and the phrase 'who takes away the sin of the world' lends support to this. The fact that propitiatory ideas do not seem to be found elsewhere in the Fourth Gospel is not a sufficient reason for rejecting this.

Others believe there is a reference to the paschal lamb. The Jewish festivals have great significance in John, and Jn. 19:36 may well be alluding to the lamb of the Passover. But this would not explain the whole phrase, as the paschal lamb did not take away sins.

Some maintain that we have here a reference to the suffering servant of Is. 53. The word *amnos* occurs in the LXX of Is. 53:7. The Baptist quoted from Is. 40 the day before and he may have been meditating on those chapters. The sin-bearing function is clear in Is. 53. The suggestion that *amnos* is a mistranslation of the Aramaic *ṭalyā'* meaning 'servant' is ingenious, but it has not been proved.

Another possible reference is to the horned ram who led the flock. The 'lamb of God' would thus be the same as the 'king of Israel'. This view is acceptable only if it is claimed that *ho airōn tēn hamartian* has no propitiatory meaning.

It seems likely that, whatever the Baptist intended, the Evangelist intended his readers to think of the lamb offered in the Temple, the paschal lamb, and the suffering servant. The 'Lamb of God' also reminds us of God's provision of a lamb for Abraham (Gn. 22:8).

BIBLIOGRAPHY. Arndt; J. Jeremias, *TDNT* 1, pp. 338–340; R. Tuente, *NIDNTT* 2, pp. 410–414; standard commentaries on John's Gospel; C. H. Dodd, *The Interpretation of the Fourth Gospel*, 1953, pp. 230–238; L. Morris, *The Apostolic Preaching of the Cross*³, 1965, pp. 129ff. R.E.N.

LAMECH (Heb. *lemeḵ*, possibly from an Arabic word meaning 'a strong young man'; so Dillmann, Holzinger). **1.** A descendant of Cain (Gn. 4:18f.), who introduced polygamy. One of his sons was Tubal-cain, the first worker in metals, and Lamech's song in Gn. 4:23f. is sometimes thought to be a 'sword-lay' glorifying the weapons of war invented by his son. He boasts to his wives, Adah and Zillah, that he has killed men, and because of his superior strength due to his weapons, he has no need of God's protection like Cain. Jesus may be referring to this in Mt. 18:22, substituting forgiveness for revenge.

2. A descendant of Seth and father of Noah (Gn. 5:25–31; 1 Ch. 1:3; Lk. 3:36). From the fact that 'Lamech' and 'Enoch' occur in both Cainite (Kenite) and Sethite genealogies, and from other likenesses, it is held by many that they are variants of one original list according to J and P (*e.g.* G. von Rad, *Genesis*, 1961). But there are differences, notably in the character of this Lamech, who voiced the pious hope that Noah would reverse the curse of Adam (Gn. 5:29; *cf.* 3:17ff.). J.G.G.N.

LAMENTATIONS, BOOK OF. In the Heb. Bible Lamentations (called *'êḵâ*, the characteristic lament 'how!'; *cf.* 1:1; 2:1; 4:1) is included among the five scrolls, since it is read on the ninth of Ab, the day of mourning over the destruction of the Temple. The EVV follow the LXX (*thrēnoi*, 'wailings' or 'dirges') and the Vulg. (whose sub-title *Lamentationes* supplied the English name) in placing Lamentations after the book of Jeremiah.

I. Outline of contents and literary structure

The first four chapters are acrostic poems, each containing sixty-six lines, except ch. 4, which has forty-four. Ch. 3 is noteworthy because each of the twenty-two Heb. letters is used for three successive one-line verses. One purpose of an acrostic is to aid memorization. But in a collection of acrostics the alphabetic pattern would not help one remember which verse beginning with a given letter belongs in which chapter. This carefully wrought, highly artificial style seems to have a further purpose: 'to encourage completeness in the expression of grief, the confession of sin and the instilling of hope' (N. K. Gottwald, *Studies in the Book of Lamentations*, 1954, p. 28). The acrostic speaks to the eye, not the ear, and conveys an idea not merely a feeling. Gottwald stresses the cathartic role of the acrostic: 'to bring about a complete cleansing of the conscience through a total confession of sin' (*op. cit.*, p. 30). Though curbing spontaneity, the acrostic lends a restraint, a gentle dignity, to what could have become an unfettered display of grief.

The dirge-like rhythm of chs. 1–4 helps to convey the feeling of grief. Characteristic of Heb. elegies (*e.g.* 2 Sa. 1:19ff.; Am. 5:2), this *qînâ* rhythm drives home its message with short, sobbing lines. An important device in *qînâ* poetry is *dramatic contrast* in which the former state of the deceased or bereaved is described in glowing terms to sharpen the sense of tragedy (*e.g.* 1:1; 4:1–2; *cf.* 2 Sa. 1:19, 23).

Ch. 3, though written in *qînâ* rhythm, is an *individual lament* rather than a funeral dirge (*cf.* Pss. 7; 22; *etc.*), containing elements typical of this category: a figurative description of suffering (3:1–18) and an affirmation that God will answer the suppliant's plea (3:19–66), the climax of the book. Though the form is *individual* the intent is *national*; the author speaks for the nation. Ch. 5, neither acrostic nor *qînâ*, resembles closely in form the psalms of *communal lament* (*e.g.* Pss. 44; 80).

Fragment of Lamentations found in Qumran Cave IV. (4Q Lam.) A piece from the Dead Sea Scrolls. 1st cent. BC. (RM)

This lamp with its open bowl is unusual in having places for seven wicks (*as in Zc. 4:2*). *It shows a rare development from the earlier and common open-dish type. Length 26·7 cm. Palestine. 2nd cent. AD.* (BM)

II. Authorship and date

Though anonymous, Lamentations has been attributed to Jeremiah by the LXX, Vulg., and Jewish tradition (Targum at Je. 1:1; Talmud, *Baba Bathra* 15a), probably on the basis of 2 Ch. 35:25.

The evidences for and against a Jeremianic authorship approach a stalemate. S. R. Driver and E. J. Young cite similar lines of evidence and reach differing conclusions, Young voting *pro* and Driver *contra*. The chief arguments for the traditional view are the similarity in temperament between Lamentations and Jeremiah, their unanimity in attributing Jerusalem's destruction to God's judgment, and certain stylistic parallels. Against these one must consider the variation in alphabetic order of the acrostic poems (ch. 1, *s*, ‘, *p*; chs. 2–4, *s*, *p*, ‘), which may hint at multiple authorship, alleged conflicts in viewpoint, such as the author's apparent dependence on Egypt (*cf.* 4:17 with Je. 37:5–10) or his support of King Zedekiah (*cf.* 4:20 with Je. 24:8–10), and the contrast between Jeremiah's spontaneity and the stylized acrostics of Lamentations (see S. R. Driver, *LOT*, pp. 462–464, for details of the various arguments).

Attempts to attribute the first four poems to different times and authors have generally proved too subjective to gain wide acceptance. These chapters seem to be the work of an eye-witness of Jerusalem's calamity (*c.* 587 BC), who recorded his impressions while they were still fresh. Ch. 5 may date from a slightly later period when the intense anguish of the catastrophe had given way to the prolonged ache of captivity. No part of the book need be dated later than the return in 538 BC.

III. Message and significance

Lamentations is by no means barren theologically. Gottwald's analysis is convincing in its main thrusts if not in all details (*op. cit.*, pp. 47–110). Finding the central theme in the *tragic reversal*, the contrast between past glory and present degradation, he discusses the theology in terms of *doom* and *hope*.

The prophets had heralded Judah's doom, convinced that a righteous God would act in history to punish his people's sin. Lamentations continues this prophetic emphasis by seeing in the ashes of Jerusalem the vindication of God's righteousness (1:18). The city's destruction is no capricious coincidence; it is the logical and inevitable result of defying God's law. Even where God is chided (*e.g.* ch. 2) for his severity, the deep-seated sense of guilt which permeates the book is evident (2:14; *cf.* 1:5, 8–9, 18, 22; 3:40–42; 4:13, 22; 5:7). The sense of tragedy is heightened by the recognition that it was avoidable. The manifold picture of the wrath of God (*e.g.* 1:12ff.; 2:1–9, 20–22; 3:1–18; 4:6, 11) makes Lamentations a key source for any study of this aspect of God's nature.

Judah's plight is desperate but not hopeless. Though the aspects of her hope are not delineated, her reason for hope is cogently stated: the faithfulness of a covenant-keeping God (3:19–39). It was one thing for the prophets to forecast a better day before the disaster struck; it is another thing for our prophet to appropriate this hope in the midst of appalling circumstances. His recognition of the disciplinary role of suffering and its relationship to God's goodness (3:25–30) is cogent testimony to his prophetic insight.

Lamentations is a meeting-place of three great strands of Heb. thought: prophecy, ritual and wisdom. The priestly influence is evident in the liturgical forms of the poems. The wisdom emphasis is stressed in the willingness to contemplate the mysteries of God's ways with men, especially in regard to the timeless problem of suffering.

BIBLIOGRAPHY. I. Bettan, *The Five Scrolls*, 1950; H. L. Ellison, *Men Spake from God*², 1958, pp. 149–154; Max Haller, *Die fünf Megilloth*, J. C. B. Mohr, 1940; T. J. Meek, *Lamentations* in *IB*; T. H. Robinson, *The Poetry of the Old Testament*, 1947, pp. 205–216; N. K. Gottwald, *Studies in the Book of Lamentations*, 1954; B. Albrektson, *Studies in the Text and Theology of the Book of Lamentations*, 1963; R. Gordis, *The Song of Songs and Lamentations*, 1974; R. K. Harrison, *Jeremiah and Lamentations*, *TOTC*, 1973; D. R. Hillers, *Lamentations* in *AB*, 1972; W. Rudolph, in *KAT*, 1962.

D.A.H.

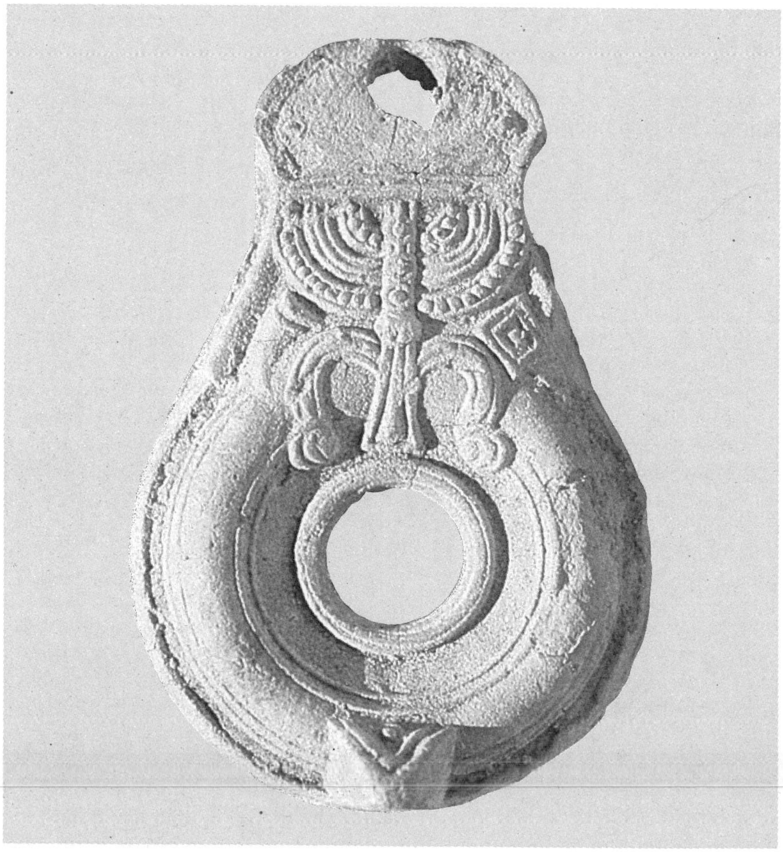

Pottery lamp decorated with the Jewish menorah *(branched candlestick). 2nd–3rd cent. AD.* (MEPhA)

LAMP, LAMPSTAND, LANTERN.

I. Design and development

Small open pottery bowls with one or more slight lips, which can be

Opposite page:
Top left:
Seven-spouted lamp from a tomb at Jericho. Maximum diameter 9·7 cm. Middle Bronze Age II. c. 1700 BC. (SAOS)

Top right:
Four-spouted lamp left alight in a tomb at Jericho. Maximum diameter 14.25 cm. Middle Bronze Age I. c. 1900 BC. (SAOS)

LAMMERGEIER

See Animals, Part 1.

Opposite page:
Bottom left:
Single-spouted lamp from Judah. Diameter 12·5 cm. Iron Age II. c. 700 BC. (ARM)

Bottom right:
Lamp from a Jericho tomb. Maximum diameter 11·85 cm. Middle Bronze Age IIB. c. 1650 BC. (SAOS)

Early Iron Age lamp from Gezer. c. 900 BC. (BM)

■ **LANCE**
See Armour, Part 1.

■ **LAND OF PROMISE**
See Promised land, Part 3.

identified as lamps (Heb. *nēr*, Gk. *lychnos*, *lampas*), first appear in the Middle Bronze Age. This simple form continued in use throughout the Iron Age, the lip becoming more pronounced. The final development took place in the Hellenistic period when the Greek style of lamp with inward curving rim became completely enclosed, a small central hole alone remaining for feeding the oil (*cf.* Mt. 25:4). These lamps were mass-produced from moulds, one making the base, the other the lid. A very long spout for the wick characterizes Hellenistic lamps; this was shortened in the Roman period. Small handles were sometimes added. The moulds for the lids were frequently impressed with floral and other patterns, and, in the Roman period when the lid became broad and concave, with pictures that appear in relief on the lamps. From the 3rd century AD Christian symbols (cross, fishes, alpha and omega) form decorative motifs, while the seven-branched candlestick (*menorah*) marks Jewish lamps. The standard Palestinian lamp of the Gospel period was plain, round, with a fairly wide flanged filling hole, and a flared nozzle for the wick, sloping downwards.

Lamps could be held in the hand, set on a shelf or placed on a stand (Heb. *mᵉnôrâ*, 2 Ki. 4:10; Aram. *neḇraštâ*, Dn. 5:5; Gk. *lychnia*, Mt. 5:15; *cf. ANEP*, no. 657, left edge). A simple wooden stand would serve most households, but some Iron Age lamps were provided with thick bases or separate hollow pedestals. Where brighter light was needed lamps with several spouts were employed, seven-spouted examples having been found in Palestine from this and earlier times, and many with provision for multiple wicks are known from the Roman era.

Pottery forms were copied in metal, although few examples survive from the OT period. In the tabernacle stood the elaborate golden lampstand (Ex. 25:31ff.). Three branches ending in flower-shaped lamp-holders protruded from either side of the main stem, which also supported a lamp-holder. Representations on certain Maccabean coins, a Herodian period drawing on stone found in Jerusalem and a relief on the arch of Titus supplement Hebrew descriptions, and it may be assumed the pattern given in Exodus was followed closely throughout. Ten similar lampstands were made for Solomon's Temple (1 Ki. 7:49).

The single lamps described burnt coarse olive oil or fat, and could stay alight for 2 to 4 hours, it seems, with an occasional trimming of the wick which was made of flax or other fibre (Heb. *pištâ*, Is. 42:3; 43:17). It might be allowed to die away at night, or be kept alight (1 Sa. 3:3; Pr. 31:18).

Out-of-doors lamps could be carried in pottery vessels, although no examples are known earlier than the Roman era. These were dome-shaped with a flat base, a handle at the top and an opening at one side for the light. Such may have been the 'lantern' of Jn. 18:3 (Gk. *phanos*), or it may have been a more elaborate metal form. Gk. *phanos* can also mean 'torch', and that could be the sense here. Gideon's men had torches at an earlier date (Heb. *lappîḏ*, Jdg. 7:16).

II. Symbolic uses

Lamps were placed in tombs from the first, partly, no doubt, to illuminate the chamber, at the same time very likely serving as a symbol of life. The expression 'his lamp' is so used metaphorically in the OT (Jb. 21:17; Pr. 20:20; 24:20; *cf.* 2 Sa. 21:17; 1 Ki. 11:36, *etc.*). From its purpose the lamp became a symbol of joy and prosperity, and of guidance: see Ps. 119:105; 2 Sa. 22:29; Pr. 6:20, 23, and personal names such as Neriyah, 'The Lord is my light'.

BIBLIOGRAPHY. D. M. Bailey, *Greek and Roman Pottery Lamps*, 1963; R. H. Smith, *BA* 27, 1964, pp. 1–31, 101–124; 29, 1966, pp. 2–27. A.R.M.

III. Symbolic and other uses in the New Testament

In the NT 'lamp' occurs 7 times in AV, on each occasion rendering *lampas*. RV renders *lampas* as 'torch' in Jn. 18:3 (following AV) and in Rev. 8:10, as 'light' in Acts 20:8 (following AV), and as 'lamp' in Mt. 25:1, 3–4, 7–8; Rev. 4:5 (following AV). RV renders *lychnos* (AV 'light' 6 times, 'candle' 8 times) as 'lamp' on every occasion.

The RV rendering must be accepted apart from the translating of *lampas* by 'lamp' in Mt. 25 and Rev. 4:5. In the latter RSV has 'torch'. In the parable of the virgins (Mt. 25:1–13) RVmg. should be followed, where 'torch' is read. The conventional lamp was for indoor use, and what was needed (and what is still sometimes used) at a wedding was a *torch. The rags which formed its wick needed to be soaked in oil. It seems that the foolish virgins had no oil at all (v. 3), and therefore when they lit their torches they went out instantly (v. 8). The wise had taken oil in separate containers ready for use at the appropriate moment. The difference between them seems to have been not in the quantity of oil that they possessed but in the fact of their possessing or not possessing any at all. The foolish could have gone and bought some had they acted in time.

lychnos is used frequently in a symbolic sense. It is the lamp which must be put on a stand to give light to all in the house (Mt. 5:15). John the Baptist was 'a burning and shining lamp' (Jn. 5:35), who came 'to bear witness to the light' (Jn. 1:7). It is Christ who is the light (*phōs*). In Mt. 6:22 the eye is called 'the lamp of the body' because it receives the light from outside.

lychnia is rendered 'candlestick' by AV *passim* and 'stand' by RV in the Gospels. RV translates this 'candlestick' in Heb. 9:2 and also 7 times in Rev., but gives 'lampstand' in mg. RSV has 'lampstand' throughout. The seven churches (Rev. 1:12–13, 20; 2:1, 5) and the two witnesses (Rev. 11:4) are symbolized by lampstands, similar to those used in the tabernacle (Heb. [illegible]

LANDMARK. Canaan was divided among the Israelite tribes, and to each family was given a plot of land to provide its livelihood. This was passed from father to son, or at least kept within the tribe (Nu. 27:1–11; 36), from which it was, theoretically, inalienable (see the story of Naboth, 1 Ki. 21). Inevitably many lost their land through debt, so that the situation in which every man owned his own plot was looked upon as an ideal (Zc. 3:10). The boundaries were defined by stone pillars or cairns. (In Babylonia inscribed stones recorded the size of important estates, Bab. *kudurru*, *ANEP*, nos. 519–522, contemporary with the Israelite settlement of Canaan.) To remove these was tantamount to removing a man's claim, and was a lawless act (Dt. 19:14; 27:17; Pr. 22:28; 23:10). (For an Egyp. parallel, *cf. ANET*, p. 422, ch. 6.) It was a sign of evil times when men dared to do so (Jb. 24:2; Ho. 5:10). A.R.M.

LANGUAGE OF THE APOCRYPHA. The so-called *'Apocrypha' comprise a heterogeneous group of books, so that to talk of its language is in fact to talk of the individual books and the problems of language which they pose. They have been preserved for us in MSS of the LXX and so lie before us like that translation in Greek. Their Greek varies widely: *e.g.* an evident 'translation Greek' in Tobit, Judith, Ben-Sira, 1 Maccabees; a relatively idiomatic Greek in 1 Esdras and Wisdom of Solomon 1–9, in which nonetheless may be perceived traces of its original; the rest of Wisdom and 2 Maccabees in a Greek uninfluenced by any other tongue, although these two works differ widely in their literary merit. In this Greek dress, then, the Apocrypha present instances of a variety of popular Greek works current among Jewish people in the three centuries immediately before Christ. The writings pose textual problems which fall within the general pattern of the textual criticism of the LXX.

It has often been assumed that Hebrew is the original tongue of those works in this group which are evidently based on a Semitic original. C. C. Torrey, however, in this as in the NT field, opened the pertinent question whether Aramaic is not the original language, at least in certain cases. His knowledge of Aramaic was vast and his contributions to biblical learning always challenging and stimulating, sometimes providing solutions to problems old and new, but not always convincing or even necessary (see the review by G. R. Driver of his posthumously published work on the Apocalypse: *JTS* n.s. 11, 1960, pp. 383–389). This must be borne in mind in evaluating his views on the language of the Apocrypha.

The Hebrew origin of a number of books is not controverted even by Torrey. 1 Maccabees has been translated from Hebrew by one better acquainted with Greek than Hebrew: signs of its origin are to be seen in, for instance, 1:28; 9:24; 14:28. Judith is plainly from Hebrew, as phrases such as *apo prosōpou, eis prosōpon*, and instrumentally used *en* show. The prologue to the Wisdom of Ben Sira,

Bottom left: The biblical 'landmark' could also refer to the title-deeds for the land. This 'boundary stone' (kudurru) *records the grant of the land by Nebuchadrezzar I of Babylon to Ritti-Marduk in return for military services. Height 0·65 m. c. 1110 BC.* (BM)

A 'landmark' or boundary-stone defining the extent of arable land, shown on an Egyptian painting in the tomb of Nebamun, Thebes, c. 1422–1411 BC. (BM)

or Ecclesiasticus, as it is often called, expressly states Hebrew to be the original, and a large part of this was discovered in the Cairo Geniza in 1896. The additions to Daniel are shown to be Hebrew in origin by passages such as the Prayer of Azariah 17 (3:40 in continuous Greek text) and Susanna 15. The Greek of the Prayer of Manasses is fluent, but the obscurities of vv. 4 and 7, for example, appear to derive from imperfectly expressed Hebrew locutions. Baruch displays in 4:5 evidence of a scribal error in the Hebrew (*zikrôn* read instead of *zikrû*) translated into Greek. 1 Esdras is a rendering of a known original, part Hebrew, part Aramaic: it is idiomatically rendered. Finally, within this group, the first nine chapters of the Wisdom of Solomon are now widely acknowledged to be based on a Hebrew original; they are translated by the author of the rest of the book, to whose original additions we should perhaps also attribute 6:22–8:1.

Tobit is generally conceded to be translated from some Semitic language. Pfeiffer admits that both Hebrew and Aramaic can be proposed but that the case for Aramaic is the stronger. Torrey proposed to find evidence for this latter hypothesis in the meaningless Manasses of 14:10 (MSS B and A), an original participle with objective suffix *m^enassēh*, 'the one who exalted him', 'his benefactor'. (Fragments of Tobit in both Hebrew and Aramaic have been identified among the Qumran texts.) The Epistle of Jeremy admits of debate: some still maintain a Greek original. A crucial point is 'the harlots on the roof' (v. 11). Torrey sees here evidence of a misrendering of *'al 'aḡrā*, 'for their hire', as *'al 'iggārā*. However, both readings in the Greek (*stegous/tegous*) may be understood as 'brothel', so that mistranslation seems to be an unnecessary hypothesis in this case. In the case of 2 Esdras (not extant in Greek) variant hypotheses have been advanced for both Hebrew and Aramaic originals. The question of the additions to Esther is larger than merely discussion of language: if the argument of Torrey that this represents the original form of the book be correct, then Aramaic may well have been its original. But this argument has not been accepted by most scholars.

Lastly, 2 Maccabees is a composition in Greek, a highly artificial attempt at the attainment of rhetorical heights. The letters which are found in chs. 1 and 2 may be original, and appear to be from a Semitic source, perhaps in Aramaic.

In these linguistic debates it may be well to bear in mind the remarks of G. R. Driver (*op. cit.*) to the effect that in the case of one author at least both Hebrew and Aramaic must be considered. As the one was spoken increasingly during the time of the composition of the Apocrypha and the other was still a literary medium and sometimes spoken, it may be that both have left their imprint upon the eventual Greek form of these books: and that this fact has led to the possibility of such different arguments upon a single matter.

BIBLIOGRAPHY. R. H. Charles, *The Apocrypha and Pseudepigrapha of the Old Testament*, 2 vols., 1913; C. C. Torrey, *The Apocryphal Literature*, 1945; R. H. Pfeiffer, *History of New Testament Times with an Introduction to the Apocrypha*, 1949; E. A. Speiser, 'The Hebrew Origin of the First Part of the Book of Wisdom', *JQR* n.s. 14, 1924, pp. 455–482; C. E. Purinton, 'Translation Greek in the Wisdom of Solomon', *JBL* 47, 1928, pp. 276–304; C. C. Torrey, 'The Older Book of Esther', *HTR* 37, 1944, pp. 1–40. J.N.B.

LANGUAGE OF THE OLD TESTAMENT.

I. Hebrew

Hebrew belongs to the W group of the Semitic languages (the word Semitic is formed from the name of Shem, Noah's eldest son). It is most closely related to the language of ancient Ugarit, and to Phoenician and Moabite. *Canaanite is known only from occasional words in the *Amarna Letters. Probably it was the parent of Hebrew. In the OT it is called the 'language (lit. "lip") of Canaan' (Is. 19:18), or Judaic (2 Ki. 18:26f.; *cf.* Is. 36:11ff. and Ne. 13:24). The designation 'Hebrew' first occurs in the Prologue to Ecclesiasticus (Ben Sira, *c.* 180 BC).

Characteristic of the Semitic languages is the triconsonantal root acting as a kind of frame for a series of vowel-patterns. The insertion of the vowel-pattern into the frame gives it its specific meaning. In *kōhēn*, for instance, *k-h-n* would be the consonantal frame and *o-e* would be the vowel-pattern. The force of the *o-e* is roughly equivalent to that of the present participle in English, thus *kōhēn*, 'ministering (one)'.

Hebrew script is a descendant of the N Semitic or Phoenician script (*WRITING). It consists of 22 consonants (later *š* and *ś* were distinguished, making 23). It is written from right to left. It contains various sounds not found in Indo-European languages; *e.g.* emphatic consonants (*ṭ*, *ḳ* [*q*], and *ṣ*) and the laryngal *'ayin* (ʿ). The latter was often transliterated into Greek by *gamma*, as for instance in 'Gomorrah'. When Hebrew was no longer widely current, systems of marks were inserted above, below and within the consonants to show the correct vowels (*TEXTS AND VERSIONS).

This vocalization represents an important synchronic stage in Hebrew, and it is the product of a highly enlightened and reliable tradition, as is shown, for instance, by the care with which it observes the distinction that originally obtained between certain vowels of 'substantival' and 'adjectival' verbs, where modifications of the consonantal frame reveal their primitive forms. There are also a number of extra-alphabetical and punctuation or intonation signs. For biblical Hebrew the pronunciation most commonly adopted is the Sephardic (Judaeo-Spanish).

The scribes scrupulously avoided making any change in the consonantal text. Where they presumed that there had been a transcriptional error, or where a word was no longer in polite use, they placed what they considered was the right or preferable word in the margin and the vowels of this word were added to the word in the text (over which a small circle was often placed). The consonants in the text are referred to as *K^etîḇ* ('the written'), those in the margin as the *Q^erē'* ('that which is to be read').

Hebrew possesses no indefinite article. The definite article (*ha-*) is prefixed to the noun. Its use differs in many details from that of the definite article in English. For example, demonstrative pronouns and adjectives take it when used attributively with a noun determinate in its reference (*e.g.* the book, the this; the man, the fat). It is also used with a member of a class or with something previously mentioned.

Nouns in Hebrew distinguish gender and number. Gender is

grammatical: inanimate as well as animate things are assigned gender. The feminine has usually a specific termination (-*â*). A number of feminine nouns, however, have no termination, but their gender is indicated by the agreement of adjectives and verbs. Hebrew also possesses a specific termination for the dual, largely confined to members of the body occurring in pairs; case-endings were discarded early, but a few traces remain.

There are two main classes of verbs: those with *substantival* cognates and those with *adjectival* cognates. Broadly speaking, the 'substantival' verb is dynamic, whereas the 'adjectival' (often called 'stative') is static. The verb primarily indicates the kind of the action, and distinguishes two main aspects: completed action (perfective) and incompleted (imperfective). For the perfective, the pronominal element is suffixed: for the imperfective it is prefixed. In the perfective, gender is distinguished in the 3rd person singular and in the 2nd person singular and plural, and in the imperfective also in the 3rd person plural. Hebrew has a number of verb-forms for particular categories of action, such as iterative, causative, tolerative, *etc.*

Nouns are formed in many ways: by a variety of vowel-patterns, and with or without the addition of certain consonants. When consonants are used they are usually prefixed, *m* and *t* being the most common. Wide use is made of the singular as a collective, with the result that the feminine termination is sometimes used as a kind of singulative ending, *e.g. śē'ār*, 'hair', *śa'*^{a}*râ* (fem.), 'single hair'. Zero forms, that is forms in which a morphological element common to a class is missing, are not uncommon; *ṣō'n* (fem.), 'flocks', *cf. ṣō'n 'ōḇ*^{e}*ḏôṯ*, 'lost sheep', where *ôṯ* indicates the element missing. The noun preceding a genitive has its vowels reduced to the minimum and omits the definite article. The group is treated virtually as an inseparable compound. Possessive pronouns appear as suffixes to the noun.

Adjectives may be used either predicatively, when they do not take the definite article and usually precede the noun, or attributively, when they follow the noun and take the definite article if the noun has it. The adjective may also take the definite article and be used independently, having the value of a substantive. Comparison is rendered by the use of the preposition *min*, 'from', equivalent to the English 'more . . . than'. The highest degree of a quantity is often left unexpressed, *e.g.* 'the good', namely 'the best', or the superlative is expressed by a phrase consisting of a singular form followed by a plural, *e.g.* 'song of the songs', *i.e.* the greatest or best song.

The use of the numerals shows several peculiarities. One and two agree in gender with their noun, but three to ten disagree. This may indicate a late introduction of grammatical gender.

The 'verbless' or nominal sentence in which the predicate consists of a noun, a pronoun, or adjective, is widely used. Usually we supply in translation some part of the verb 'to be', *e.g.* 'the servant of Abraham (am) I'. In sentences with a finite verb the word-order usually follows the pattern—verb, subject, object. Often with the accusative the particle *'eṯ* is used. If the object consists of a pronoun it can be appended to the accusative particle, or it can be added as an enclitic form to the verb. An indirect object consisting of a preposition and a pronominal suffix normally comes before the subject. If there is an adverbial extension it usually follows the object. Where English might use the impersonal 'one', *e.g.* in 'one says', Hebrew uses either the 2nd or 3rd singular masculine or the 3rd plural.

The most distinctive feature of Hebrew style is its syndetic or coordinative character, that is, the prevalence of the simple conjunction 'and', and the infrequent use of subordinating conjunctions. Compared with English, it might seem to be less abstract. Hebrew, for instance, makes extensive use of terms for physical attitudes to describe psychological states, or organs of the body are associated with mental attitudes. It is most difficult for anyone inured to Indo-European procedure to dissociate his mind from the original meanings; this is particularly so when a work is replete with them, as, for instance, in the Song of Songs.

The imagery of Hebrew is largely drawn from the things and activities of everyday life. It has, therefore, a universal quality and lends itself without difficulty to translation. Hebrew makes use of all the common figures of speech, parables (*e.g.* 2 Sa. 12), similes, metaphors, *e.g.* 'star' or 'lion' for hero, 'rock' for refuge, 'light' for life and for the divine revelation, 'darkness' for sorrow and ignorance.

Hebrew, in common with general linguistic usage, makes wide use of anthropomorphic expressions; that is, the transference or adaptation of terms for parts of the human body and for human activities to the inanimate world and other conditions to which they are not strictly attributable. These expressions have their origin in metaphor and come under the heading of 'extension of

Hebrew	Hebrew or Aramaic	Greek
1 Maccabees	Tobit	2 Maccabees
Judith	Epistle of Jeremy (or Greek?)	Wisdom of Solomon 9 to the end
Wisdom of Ben Sira (Ecclesiasticus)	(Part of) 1 Esdras	
Additions to Daniel; Susanna 15 Prayer of Azariah Prayer of Manasses	2 Esdras	
Baruch	Additions to Esther	
(Part of) 1 Esdras	2 Maccabees (the letters in chs. 1 and 2)	
Wisdom of Solomon 1-9		

Table of languages used for the original texts in the books of the Apocrypha.

meaning', a device essential apparently to mechanism of languages in general. They occur as frequently in other Semitic languages as in Hebrew. Akkadian, for instance, refers to the keel of a ship as the 'backbone', to which the 'ribs' are attached. Hebrew speaks about the 'head' of a mountain, the 'face' of the earth, the 'lip' (shore) of the sea, the 'mouth' of a cave, the 'going' of water (a verb often used elsewhere with the meaning of 'walking'). These and many other expressions had obviously become 'fossilized' metaphors. When such expressions are applied to the activities or attributes of God it would be indefensible on linguistic grounds to interpret them in a literal sense, or to base theories of beliefs on what are intrinsic modes of expression dictated by the very nature of linguistic communication.

Elliptical expressions, by which the semantic content of a full phrase is vested in a single member of the group, are not uncommon, *e.g.* the omission of 'voice' after 'to lift up' (Is. 42:2). Although one of the earliest references to semantic change occurs in the OT (1 Sa. 9:9), there is little evidence of change in Hebrew in the course of the centuries. It is likely, however, that many parts have been revised to a standard Hebrew, perhaps that of late pre-exilic Jerusalem. Traces of dialects may be found in some books, *e.g.* Ruth, parts of 2 Kings. Later forms of the language can be traced in Esther, Chronicles and other passages. In the nature of the case, it would not be easy to detect loan-words from cognate languages. Examples are *hêḵāl*, 'temple', from Akkad. *ekallu*, 'palace', which in turn was borrowed from Sumerian *e-gal*, 'great house'; *'argāmān*, 'purple', comes from Hittite.

Recovery of numerous ancient texts in cognate languages has brought a more precise understanding of some points. There is a danger that the excitement of new discoveries may give rise to ill-founded proposals that contravene in-built safeguards of the language which prevent ambiguity. Frequent appeal to Arabic in this way mars NEB (see J. Barr, *Comparative Philology and the Text of the Old Testament*, 1968). The great divergences between Hebrew and the other cognate languages, largely due to the action of semantic change, make it extremely hazardous to attempt on etymological grounds to assign meanings to Hebrew words of infrequent occurrence.

The high literary style of much of the OT would seem to indicate the early existence of literary models or of a 'grand style'. The ancient Near East offers examples of high styles continuing in use for many centuries. Much that has been written about divergences in Hebrew style is, in the absence of proper criteria, valueless.

While it is now clear that the influence of Hebrew on NT Greek is not as extensive as was formerly held by many scholars, nevertheless it has left its mark both on vocabulary and syntax. There are a number of loan-words and many loan-translations, *e.g. hilastērion* for the covering of the ark which, on the Day of Atonement, was sprinkled with blood, and an expression like 'Blessed art thou among (lit. "in") women', where the Greek follows the Hebrew use of the preposition.

The influence of Hebrew on European literature is incalculable, even though much of it may have come indirectly through the Vulgate. Among the many Hebrew loan-words in English are: sabbath, sack, Satan, shekel, jubilee, hallelujah, aloes (fragrant resin) and myrrh. The use of 'heart' as the seat of the emotions and will and of 'soul' for person are probably loan-translations.

BIBLIOGRAPHY. A. B. Davidson, *An Introductory Hebrew Grammar*[25], 1962; G. Beer and R. Meyer, *Hebräische Gram.*, 1, 1952; 2, 1955; 3–4, 1972; J. Weingreen, *Practical Grammar for Classical Hebrew*, 1959: T. O. Lambdin, *Introduction to Biblical Hebrew*, 1971; H. Bauer and P. Leander, *Historische Gram. der Hebräischen Sprache*, 1918–19; C. Bergsträsser, *Hebräische Grammatik*[29] (Gesenius-Kautzsch); W. Gesenius, *Hebrew Grammar* (tr. A. E. Cowley), 1910; F. Böttcher, *Lehrbuch der Hebräischen Sprache*, 1861; P. Joüon, *Grammaire de l'Hébreu Biblique*, 1923; E. König, *Lehrgebäude der Hebräischen Sprache*, 1881–1897; S. R. Driver, *Hebrew Tenses*, 1892; E. König, *Stilistik*, 1900; *idem*, *Rythmik*, 1914; C. Brockelmann, *Hebräische Syntax*, 1956; F. I. Andersen, *The Hebrew Verbless Clause in the Pentateuch*, 1970; *idem*, *The Sentence in Biblical Hebrew*, 1974; Gesenius–Buhl, *Handwörterbuch*, 1921; L. Koehler, W. Baumgartner, *Hebräisches und aramaisches Lexicon zum Alten Testament*, 1967ff.; *BDB*.

II. Aramaic

Aramaic, a close cognate, not a derivative, of Hebrew, is the language of Dn. 2:4–7:28; Ezr. 4:8–6:18; 7:12–26; Je. 10:11; two words in Gn. 31:47; and of the Targums (Aramaic translations of parts of the OT). In the 9th and following centuries BC, Aramaic and its script (taken from alphabetic Hebrew/Phoenician) rapidly became the international medium of commerce and diplomacy. Already in the 9th century BC, Israel and Damascus had merchants in each other's capitals (1 Ki. 20:34), and in 701 BC Hezekiah's officers sought to be addressed in Aramaic—understood by rulers or merchants, but not by (Hebrew) 'men in the street' (2 Ki. 18:26). In Assyria itself from *c.* 730 BC under Tiglath-pileser III, Aramaic steadily came into official use: Aramaic dockets on cuneiform tablets, Aramaic annotations by high Assyrian officials and Assyrian sculptures showing the recording of tribute by scribes who write (Aramaic) with pen on parchment as well as in cuneiform on clay tablets. (For full references, see R. A. Bowman, *JNES* 7, 1948, pp. 73–76, to which add the ostracon listing Hebrew exiles in Assyria found at Calah, J. B. Segal, *Iraq* 19, 1957, pp. 139–145, and Albright, *BASOR* 149, 1958, pp. 33–36.) Note here, too, the Aramaic letter of Adon of Ascalon to the pharaoh of Egypt in 604(?) BC (W. D. McHardy in *DOTT*, pp. 251–255 with bibliography). Unless it is a note to readers that Aramaic directly follows, the note in Dn. 2:4 'in Aramaic' when the Chaldeans address Nebuchadrezzar would fit in perfectly with Assyro-Babylonian court use of Aramaic. Besides examples above, Aramaic epigraphs occur on the very bricks used in constructing the great buildings of Nebuchadrezzar's Babylon and testify to the common use of that language there then (see R. Koldewey, *The Excavations at Babylon*, 1914, pp. 80–81, figs. 52–53).

Aramaic ('Reichsaramäisch') became the official medium of communication throughout the polyglot Persian empire—Ezra is the classic biblical example. This is vividly illustrated by Aramaic papyri from Egypt (5th century BC); for these see A. Cowley, *Aramaic Papyri of the Fifth Century BC*, 1923; H. L. Ginsberg in *ANET*, pp. 222–223, 427–430, 491–492; E. G.

Kraeling, *The Brooklyn Museum Aramaic Papyri*, 1953; G. R. Driver and others, *Aramaic Documents of the Fifth Century* BC, 1954 and abridged and revised, 1957.

The script is the same as Hebrew, and Aramaic has approximately the same phonological characteristics, including the position of the stress. The vowel-patterns are on the whole more attenuated and on occasions preserve more primitive forms. The consonantal shift between the two languages lacks the consistency of a law. Heb. *z* = Aram. *d* (*ḏ*), Heb. *š* = Aram. *t*, Heb. *ṣ* = Aram. *ṭ*, *etc.*, but the change of Heb. *ṣ* to Aram. *ʿ* and *q* is phonetically hard to explain.

The definite article is -*â* and is suffixed to its noun. The genitive relation can be expressed as in Hebrew, the noun preceding the genitive is shortened if possible and the group is treated as inseparable. The relationship is more often expressed by *dî*, originally a demon-

SEMITIC LANGUAGE FAMILY (all dates are approximate)

(N) – W SEMITIC		(N) – E SEMITIC		S SEMITIC	
'Eblaite' 2400 BC		Old Akkadian 2500 – 2000 BC			
Amorite 18th cent. BC		Old Assyrian = Akkadian = Old Babylonian 2000 – 1500 BC			
Ugaritic (Ras Shamra) 1450 – 1200 BC		Middle Assyrian 1500 – 1000 BC	Middle Babylonian		
Early Canaanite (Amarna Glosses) 14th cent. BC					
Canaanite	Aramaic				
Hebrew (Classical/Biblical) 1200 – 200 BC					
Phoenician/Punic 10th cent. BC – 2nd cent. AD	Old Aramaic dialects. 10th – 7th cent. BC	Neo-Assyrian 1000 – 600 BC	Neo-Babylonian 1000 BC		
Moabite 9th cent. BC					Ancient (Epigraphic) S. Arabic 8th cent. BC – 6th cent. AD Sabaean Hadramautic Minaean Qatabanian
	Classical/Imperial Aramaic. 7th – 3rd cent. BC. Includes Biblical Aramaic		Late Babylonian 625 BC – 1st cent. AD	N. Arabic 5th cent. BC – 4th cent. AD Dedanite Safaitic Lihyanic Thamudic	
	W. Aramaic	E. Aramaic			
	Jewish Palestinian Aramaic. 150 BC – 4th cent. AD	Hatrene 1st cent. BC – 3rd cent. AD			
	Nabataean 100 BC – AD 200				
	Palmyrene 100 BC – AD 200				
Hebrew, Mishnaic 1st – 4th cent. AD					Ancient Ethiopic (Ge'ez)
		Syriac 3rd – 13th cent. AD			
	Samaritan 4th cent. AD	Mandaean 3rd cent. AD onwards			
		Babylonian Aramaic 4th – 6th cent. AD		Classical Arabic 4th cent. AD	
	Christian Palestinian Aramaic 5th – 8th cent. AD	Neo-Syriac dialects			
					Harari Tigre Trigrina Amharic
Medieval Hebrew					
Modern Hebrew				Modern Arabic Dialects	Gurage

Chart showing the Semitic family of languages including biblical Hebrew and Aramaic.

strative pronoun, thus *ḥezwâ dî lēlyâ*, 'vision of the night'.

As in Hebrew, the noun has singular, dual and plural. There are two genders: masculine and feminine. The feminine termination is -*â*, but many feminine nouns are without any indication. Possessive pronouns are suffixed to the noun.

The verb possesses two tense-aspects: perfective (completed action) with pronominal elements suffixed, and imperfective (incompleted action) with the pronominal elements prefixed. The active participle is widely used to express present or future. There are some eight 'verb-forms' or conjugations: Primary Form, with modifications for active, passive and reflexive; Intensive; and the Causative, designated by either a prefixed *h*, *'* or *š*. The verb 'to be', *hᵃwâ*, comes to be used very much like an auxiliary verb.

The verbless sentence is common. In verbal sentences either the verb or the subject may come first, but the latter order seems more common. Word-order is less rigid than in Hebrew.

The Aramaic of the OT is a subject of dispute. S. R. Driver (*LOT*, pp. 502ff.) affirmed that the Aramaic of Daniel was a *Western* Aramaic dialect and hence late. When he wrote, the only material available was too late to be relevant. Subsequently R. D. Wilson, making use of earlier material that had come to light, was able to show that the distinction between E and W Aramaic did not exist in pre-Christian times. This was amply confirmed by H. H. Schaeder. Schaeder also drew attention to the fact that the static nature of 'Imperial Aramaic', as it has come to be called, precludes the possibility of dating documents in it, including Daniel and Ezra. He showed that the criteria adduced to assign to Daniel and Ezra a late date are merely the result of a process of orthographical modernization going on in the 5th century BC (see F. Rosenthal, *Aramaistische Forschung*, pp. 67ff.). From what we know from contemporary documents of the extent of trade and diplomatic contacts, we are not surprised to find loan-words in the most unexpected places.

Advancing knowledge based upon old and new discoveries shows arguments for dating the Aramaic of the OT after the Persian period are often groundless. Recent evidence on one matter must suffice here. In early Aramaic there was a sound *ḏ* (*dh*) which by Persian times had become identical with ordinary 'd' in pronunciation. In the W (Syria) this consonant was written as 'z' (even in a non-Aramaic name, as Miliz for Milid(h), 'Melitene' in Zakir's stele), and this persisted as a 'historical' spelling in the Aramaic papyri of the Persian empire. But in the E, 'dh' was already represented by the Assyrians as 'd' from the 9th century BC (Adad-idri for (H)adadezer). The real pronunciation 'd' in Persian times is betrayed by various hints: a remarkable Aramaic text in Egyptian demotic script, 5th century BC, writes 't'/'d' (J. A. Bowman *JNES* 3, 1944, pp. 224–225 and n. 17), while in some of the normal Aramaic papyri there are cases of false archaism in writing 'z' for original 'd' (not 'dh'), *cf.* E. Y. Kutscher, *JAOS* 74, 1954, p. 235 (*zyn wzbb*).

OT Aramaic writes a phonetically true 'd', not a W historic 'z'; this is no indicator of late date, but signifies one of two things. Either Daniel, Ezra, *etc.*, simply put Aramaic as spoken in 6th/5th-century Babylonia into a directly phonetic spelling, or else they used the historic spelling largely eliminated by a subsequent spelling-revision of rather later date.

BIBLIOGRAPHY. *Reallexikon der Assyriologie* (*s.v.* 'Aramu'); E. Y. Kutscher, in T. A. Seboek (ed.), *Current Trends in Linguistics* 6, 1970, pp. 347–412; R. D. Wilson, *Aramaic of Daniel*, 1912; *idem*, *Studies in the Book of Daniel*, 1917; H. H. Rowley, *The Aramaic of the Old Testament*, 1929; F. Rosenthal, *Aramaistische Forschung*, 1939; H. H. Schaeder, *Iranische Beiträge*, 1, 1930; K. A. Kitchen, in D. J. Wiseman (ed.), *Notes on Some Problems in the Book of Daniel*, 1965, pp. 31–79; *Grammars*—by H. Bauer and P. Leander, 1927; H. Strack, 1921; W. B. Stevenson, 1924; F. Rosenthal, 1961; *Lexicons*—those listed under *Hebrew* contain Aramaic supplements.

W.J.M.
K.A.K.

LANGUAGE OF THE NEW TESTAMENT.

I. General characteristics

a. The nature of 'common Greek'

The language in which the NT documents have been preserved is the 'common Greek' (*koinē*), which was the *lingua franca* of the Near Eastern and Mediterranean lands in Roman times. It had been established over this wide territory by the conquests and express cultural purpose of Alexander the Great, whose colonies provided *foci* for the continued use of the language. It exercised influence in vocabulary upon Coptic, Jewish Aramaic, rabbinical Hebrew and Syriac, and was spoken as far W as the Rhone valley, colonized from the province of Asia. It represents, as its morphology and accidence show, a mingling of the Attic, Ionic and W Greek dialects, which in the course of Greek political history before and after Alexander's conquests became fused together into a fully unified language with little trace of dialectal differentiation, so far as our records go. It is the direct ancestor of Byzantine and modern Greek which have recently been much utilized to cast light on its development and normative forms.

A number of the writers of the Roman period strove to attain the Attic ideal, and thus the living dialect is largely obscured in their works (Dionysius of Halicarnassus, Dio Chrysostom, Lucian); and even those who wrote in the *koinē* were inevitably influenced at times by their literary background (Polybius, Diodorus Siculus, Plutarch, Josephus).

The language of the NT, however, belongs to a style which is not moulded by formal literary education, but stands in a tradition of the presentation of technical materials and practical philosophy. The antecedents of this are in the scientific writings of Aristotle and Theophrastus, and in the medical writings of the Hippocratic school. Contemporary parallels to NT Greek are to be found in popular philosophical writings such as the discourses of Epictetus, in business and legal documents known to us from papyrus discoveries, and in various Hellenistic writers on medical and other technical matters. This style provided a convenient medium for the presentation of the matters of general interest which the early church desired to convey, in a language which was likely to be that which the non-Greek speaker learnt when he entered Graeco-Roman society. It had an intellectual tradition but was not the property of a sophisticated lettered class: it was not the colloquial daily speech but had links with that, as the cultivated literary language did not. The language of the NT, from the solecisms of the Apocalypse to the highly-wrought style of Luke or Hebrews, stands within this common tradition. It is not a separate dialect but draws its peculiarities from its subject-matter, from the background of the LXX and from the imprint of the mother tongue of most of its writers.

The *koinē* is characterized by the loss or attenuation of many subtleties of the classical period, and by a general weakening in force of particles, conjunctions and the *Aktionsart* of verbal conjugations. The extent and particular instances of this tendency to simplification naturally vary even within the NT, and much more within the whole range of the linguistic monuments of the dialect. The dual number has totally disappeared. The optative mood is little used and generally not strictly according to the canons of classical Attic. The distinction of perfect and aorist is sometimes not observed, a feature often reflected in variant readings. Certain particles, *e.g. te, hōs*, and even *ge*, are used as mere otiose supplements to others. Distinctions between different prepositions, *e.g. eis* and *en*, *hypo* and *apo*, are blurred; and similarly, the use of the same preposition (*e.g. epi*) with differing cases of the noun.

In vocabulary, compound verbs take the place of simple verbs, and thematic of non-thematic, while back-formations appear; in the noun there is a marked inclination to use diminutives without due implication of smallness. Similarly, the usage of such conjunctions as *hina* and *mē* has been greatly extended; and the pattern of conditional sentences (whether with *ei* or with a relative) has lost its clearly-defined nuances. This is not to imply that the language was in this form totally weakened and bereft of all its powers and subtleties—it remained a keen and precise instrument of expression—but without cognizance of the attenuating processes which were at work the expositor stands in danger of oversubtlety in exegesis.

During the period of our NT writings, under Roman domination, the *koinē* was exposed to the influence of Latin, and this has left its mark upon the language. However, this impression is mainly upon vocabulary and is to be seen in two forms, transliterated words (*e.g. kentyriōn*) and literally transposed phrases (*e.g. to hikanon poiein = satisfacere*). An attempt has been made to argue that the original tongue of Mark's Gospel was Latin, as some Syr. colophons say, and a plausible case erected; but the thesis has not met with acceptance, since much of its evidence may be paralleled either in the papyri or in modern Greek. It is in fact an unchallenged axiom of present-day scholarship in this field that that which is at home in modern Greek is the development of a natural Hellenistic locution, and in its appearance in the NT cannot be the result of a foreign influence upon NT Greek. As regards the language of Mark, it should also be noted that Latinisms of both kinds are to be found in Matthew and John and even in Luke, while the African Latin text, claimed as the original text, is in fact valuable for all four Gospels and not only for Mark.

b. Hebraisms in the New Testament

No local dialects are observable within the *koinē*, and in extant records there seems to be little local variation apart from pronunciation. A few 'Phrygianisms' and 'Egyptianisms' have been isolated. But in the NT writings we meet the particular problem of Semitisms, *i.e.* abnormal locutions which reveal an underlying or otherwise influencing Hebrew or Aramaic. We find that here we are dealing with an extremely subtle problem, in solving which a number of different types of influence and reflection may be discerned. Much that seemed curious to earlier scholars and was put down to Hebraism has, since the discoveries of the papyri, proved to be but the common Greek of the period. Yet certain features remain about which debate continues.

Hebraisms are mainly of Septuagintal origin. The Septuagint (LXX) was the Bible text chiefly known and used in the period of the formation of the NT. Its influence upon the NT writers varies. To trace this is again somewhat difficult, except in the case of explicit citation or phraseology, because of different strata in the LXX itself, some parts of which are written in idiomatic *koinē*, others in good literary *koinē*, while the Pentateuch and some other portions, largely for reverential reasons, closely adhere to the Heb. text, even when this entails a certain wrestling of the grammatical usage of Greek. Heb. phrases are rendered word for word into Greek, *e.g. pasa sarx*, 'all flesh'; *akrobystia*, 'uncircumcision', *enōpion tou kyriou*, 'before the Lord'; pronouns are much used, following Heb. usage; various verbal features of Hebrew, especially the infinitive absolute, are rendered as literally as possible into Greek, *e.g.* in this case by pleonastic participle or cognate noun in the dative case; various periphrastic prepositional forms are used in imitation of Hebrew, *e.g. en mesō, dia cheiros*. In some cases, for instance the last named, this represents simply an over-use of a development already observable in popular Greek of the period.

The Greek of the NT, however, is not translated from Hebrew; and where (citations, *etc.*, apart) Hebraism is observable, it is in works otherwise high in the scale of stylistic and literary elegance in the NT. These are Luke, whose Septuagintalism is probably the result of deliberate pastiche, and Hebrews, whose author is steeped in the LXX while himself being capable of a highly complex and subtle Greek style. In Revelation the author's Greek, basically *koinē*, has been moulded by his Semitic mother-tongue. For instance, the verbal pattern of Hebrew and Aramaic has been imposed thoroughly upon his usage of the Greek verb, and Hebrew influence may be seen in the numerals. The resultant style is thoroughly Semitized but distinct from Septuagintal styles.

c. The so-called 'Aramaic approach'

This approach is a method even more difficult to pursue than the tracing of Hebraism. This is due to many factors. First, there has been considerable debate over the appropriate dialect of the widespread Aramaic language, in which the sayings of Jesus may be presumed to have been uttered and preserved. In the upshot it would appear that the Palestinian Targum, the Aramaic portions of the Talmud Yerushalmi, and Samaritan Aramaic sources are probably the safest guide, with biblical Aramaic and Christian Palestinian Syriac as useful auxiliary aids. Secondly, whereas for Hebraisms we have a known translation from Hebrew to guide us, in the case of Aramaic there is no translated literature apart from the versions of biblical books known to have been translated from Aramaic, and various pseudepigrapha presumably translated; and only in the first of these cases have we the originals by which to control our understanding. Josephus' *Jewish War*, originally composed in Aramaic, has been skilfully rendered into Greek in a version which shows little or no trace of its original language. Thirdly, a number of alleged signs of Aramaic origin (*e.g.* asyndeton, parataxis, an extended use of *hina* said to be based on the Aramaic *d*[e]) are also to be found in the *koinē*, where simplicity of construction is often found and finer shades of meaning are sometimes lost.

In view of these difficulties, one needs to proceed with care. The more ambitious hypotheses which find all the Gospels and parts of Acts to be translations from Aramaic have failed to meet with general acceptance. More sober positions need to be taken up. We have to assess the probabilities largely by an 'un-Greek' preponderance of, or predilection for, certain locutions, or by means of patent ambiguities directly attributable to errors of translation. We find, then, that, broadly speaking, sayings and discourse material prove to be that which displays the most unambiguous signs of translation out of Aramaic: *viz.* sayings, complexes of sayings, parables, in the Synoptics; peculiarly Johannine discourse material; speeches in Acts. In these sections a number of ambiguities have been resolved by recourse to the syntax and style of Aramaic: this is the most securely established conclusion of this method. The majority of attempts to find flagrant mistranslations, however, in the *cruces interpretum* of the Greek, have not met with general agreement; each scholar tends to put forward his own suggestions, to the detriment of others and in criticism of theirs. In the case of John not all would be willing to find Aramaic sources even behind the discourses: rather, the work of a bilingual author has been postulated, in which the more natural Aramaic has left its indelible imprint on the more mannered Greek. This is certainly so in the case of Paul, whose rugged and vigorous *koinē* is marked throughout by his close acquaintance with the LXX and sometimes, perhaps, by his native Aramaic.

II. Individual stylistic features

Having thus summarized the general characteristics of NT Greek, we may give a brief characterization of each individual author. Mark is written in the Greek of the common man; our increased knowledge of the papyri has done much to illuminate his usage, though Aramaisms still remain, notably his impersonal use of the third person plural of the active verb to express a general action or thought. Matthew and Luke each utilize the Marcan text, but each corrects his solecisms, and prunes his style, in accordance with principles which we may find illustrated in their extreme form in Phrynichus. Matthew's own style is less distinguished than that of Luke—he writes a grammatical Greek, sober but cultivated, yet with some marked Septuagintalisms; Luke is capable of achieving momentarily great heights of style in the Attic tradition, but lacks the power to sustain these; he lapses at length back to the style of his sources or to a very humble *koinē*. In both Evangelists, of course, the Aramaic background of the material reveals itself again and again, especially in sayings. The first two chapters of Luke have led to some debate: it is common to describe them as a pastiche of the LXX, but it may be plausibly argued that they are translated directly from a Heb. source. John's Greek can be closely paralleled from Epictetus, but in the opinion of most scholars appears to be a *koinē* written by one whose native thought and speech were Aramaic; there may even be passages translated from that language. Certain qualities of his style, notably the 'I AM' type of theophanic declaration, are most closely to be paralleled from the Mandaean writings which have their roots in W Syria; this too underlines the description of the Gospel as markedly Semitic. Acts is clearly the work of Luke, whose style fluctuates here as in the Gospel, and in spite of his spasmodic achievements remains at the mercy of his sources.

Paul writes a forceful Greek, with noticeable developments in style between his earliest and his latest Epistles. The development in Ephesians and in the Pastorals is so striking as to have led to hypotheses of pseudonymous composition; it is naturally patient of other explanations in the view of conservative scholars (*PSEUDONYMITY). Hebrews is written in very polished Greek of one acquainted with the philosophers, and with the type of thought and exegesis exemplified in Philo, yet the LXX has affected the language and style as it has not in Philo's case. James and 1 Peter both show close acquaintance with classical style, although in the former some very 'Jewish' Greek may also be seen. The Johannine Epistles are closely similar to the Gospel in language, but are more uniform and, even, duller in style, though the wide differences of literary type and subject may well be the operative factor in this. Jude and 2 Peter both display a highly tortuous and involved Greek; the latter has in fact with some justification been accused of Atticizing, and has been described as the one NT writing which gains by translation. The Apocalypse, as we have indicated, is *sui generis* in language and style; its vigour, power and success, though a *tour de force*, cannot be denied.

III. Conclusion

So NT Greek, while showing a markedly Semitic cast in places, remains in grammar, syntax and even style essentially Greek. Semantically, however, it has come to be increasingly acknowledged that its terminology is as strongly moulded by the usage of the LXX as by its origins, etymology and usage in Greek. This realization has led to the *TDNT* founded by Kittel, and has made a major contribution towards the current investigations of biblical theology; readily accessible to the English reader, there is also the work of C. H. Dodd in this field, especially in *The Bible and the Greeks* and *The Interpretation of the Fourth Gospel*. Behind 'righteousness' and 'justification', behind 'faith' and 'to believe', behind 'knowledge' and 'grace', stand Heb. concepts which quite transform the Gk. significance and which must be comprehended if the gospel is not to be misunderstood. The lack of this knowledge affects even the best of patristic and mediaeval exegesis, and later theologians too have suffered from lack of it. The realization of it is one of our greatest gains from modern biblical research: but note the criticism of J. Barr.

In summary, we may state that the Greek of the NT is known to us today as a language 'understanded of the people', and that it was used with varying degrees of stylistic attainment, but with one impetus and vigour, to express in these documents a message which at any rate for its preachers was continuous with that of the OT scriptures—a message of a living God, concerned for man's right relation with himself, providing of himself the means of reconciliation. This gospel has moulded the language and its meaning so that even the linguistic disciplines of its analysis become ultimately parts of theology.

BIBLIOGRAPHY. R. W. Funk, *A Greek Grammar of the New Testament* (rev. of F. Blass and A. Debrunner, *Grammatik der neutestamentlichen Griechisch*), 1961; J. H. Moulton, *Grammar of New Testament Greek*, 1³, 1908; 2 (ed. W. F. Howard), 1929; 3, 1963; 4, 1976; F. M. Abel, *Grammaire du Grec Biblique*, 1927; M. Black, *An Aramaic Approach to the Four Gospels and Acts*², 1953; L. Rydbeck, *Fachprosa, vermeintliche Volkssprache u. Neues Testament*, 1967; G. Mussies, *The Morphology of Koine Greek*, 1971; C. F. D. Moule, *An Idiom Book of New Testament Greek*², 1959; *TDNT*; Walter Bauer, *Griechisch-Deutsches Wörterbuch zu den Schriften des Neuen Testament und der übrigen urchristlichen Literatur*⁵, 1957–8; W. F. Arndt and F. W. Gingrich, *A Greek–English Lexicon of the New Testament*, 1957 (translated and augmented from Bauer⁴); C. H. Dodd, *The Bible and the Greeks*, 1934, and *The Interpretation of the Fourth Gospel*, 1953; J. Barr, *The Semantics of Biblical Language*, 1961; *idem*, *Biblical Words for Time*, 1962.

J.N.B.

LAODICEA. A city of SW Phrygia, in the Roman province of Asia, in the W of what is now Asiatic Turkey. It was founded by the Seleucid Antiochus II in the 3rd century BC, and called after his wife Laodice. It lay in the fertile valley of the Lycus (a tributary of the Maeander), close to *Hierapolis and *Colossae, and was distinguished by the epithet 'on Lycus' from several other cities of the name. It was at a very important cross-road: the main road across Asia Minor ran W to the ports of *Miletus and *Ephesus about 160 km away and E by an easy incline on to the central plateau and thence towards Syria, and another road ran N to *Pergamum and S to the coast at *Attalia.

This strategic position made Laodicea an extremely prosperous commercial centre, especially under Roman rule. When destroyed by a disastrous earthquake in AD 60 (Tacitus, *Ann.* 14. 27) it could afford to dispense with aid from Nero. It was an important centre of banking and exchange (*cf.* Cicero, *ad Fam.* 3. 5. 4, *etc.*). Its distinctive products included garments of glossy black wool (Strabo, *Geog.* 12. 8. 16 [578]), and it was a medical centre noted for ophthalmology. The site had one disadvantage: being determined by the road-system, it lacked a sufficient and permanent supply of good water. Water was piped to the city from hot springs some distance S, and probably arrived lukewarm. The deposits still encrusting the remains testify to its warmth. The site of Laodicea was eventually abandoned, and the modern town (Denizli) grew up near the springs.

The gospel must have reached Laodicea at an early date, probably while Paul was living at Ephesus (Acts 19:10), and perhaps through Epaphras (Col. 4:12–13). Although Paul mentions the church there (Col. 2:1; 4:13–16), there is no record that he visited it. It is evident that the church maintained close connections with the Christians in Hierapolis and Colossae. The 'letter from Laodicea' (Col. 4:16) is often thought to have been a copy of our Ephesians which had been received in Laodicea.

The last of the Letters to 'the seven churches of Asia' (Rev. 3:14–22) was addressed to Laodicea. Its imagery owes relatively little to the OT, but contains pointed allusions to the character and circumstances of the city. For all its wealth, it could produce neither the healing

LANGUR
See Animals, Part 1.

LANTERN
See Lamp, Part 2.

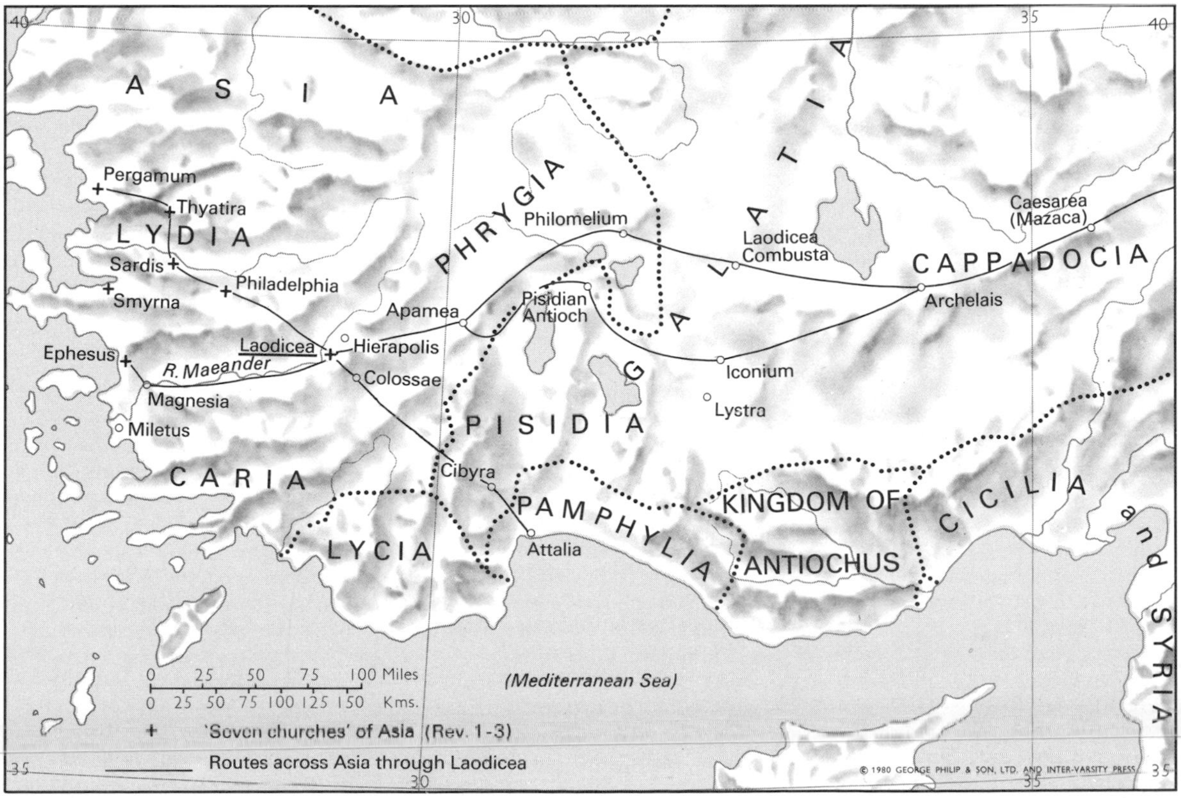

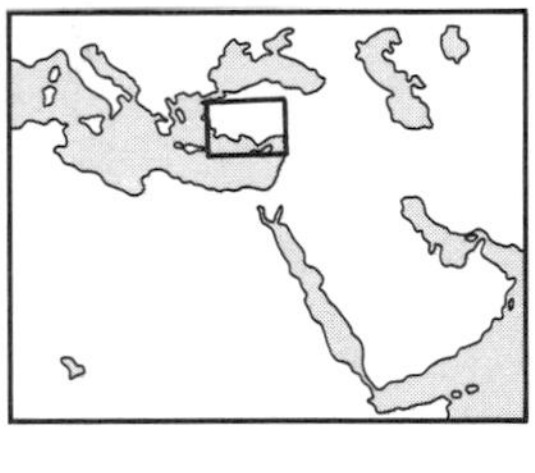

Map showing the strategic position of Laodicea in Asia Minor.

Ancient water-pipes at the site of Laodicea. They were constructed from blocks of stone, approximately 1 m across, and had become partially blocked by precipitated mineral matter. (CH)

LAPIS LAZULI
See Jewels, Part 2.

LAST SUPPER
See Lord's supper, Part 2.

LATCHET
See Dress, Part 1.

LATTER RAINS
See Rain, Part 3.

power of hot water, like its neighbour Hierapolis, nor the refreshing power of cold water to be found at Colossae, but merely lukewarm water, useful only as an emetic. The church was charged with a similar uselessness: it was self-sufficient, rather than half-hearted. Like the city, it thought it had 'need of nothing'. In fact it was spiritually poor, naked and blind, and needed 'gold', 'white garments' and 'eye-salve' more effective than its bankers, clothiers and doctors could supply. Like citizens inhospitable to a traveller who offers them priceless goods, the Laodiceans had closed their doors and left their real Provider outside. Christ turns in loving appeal to the individual (v. 20).

BIBLIOGRAPHY. W. M. Ramsay, *The Letters to the Seven Churches of Asia*, 1904; M. J. S. Rudwick and E. M. B. Green, *ExpT* 69, 1957–8, pp. 176–178; C. J. Hemer, *NIDNTT* 1, pp. 317–319; *idem*, *Buried History* 11, 1975, pp. 175–190.

M.J.S.R.
C.J.H.

LAPPIDOTH (Heb. *lappîdôṯ*, 'torches'). The husband of Deborah (Jdg. 4:4). Some Jewish commentators, taking it as a description of Deborah, would render the Hebrew as 'a woman of lightning flashes', but there is little evidence to support this view; other Jewish commentators (with equal lack of evidence) identified him with Barak (Jdg. 4:6), whose name means 'lightning'. J.D.D.

LASEA, presumably the same town as the Lasos mentioned by Pliny (*NH* 4. 59), has been identified with ruins some 8 km E of *Fair Havens. If this identification is correct, one of the disadvantages of Fair Havens as a winter harbour would be the distance of the town from it. K.L.McK.

LASHA. Probably *lešaʿ*, but written *lāšaʿ* in the interests of prosody in its sole occurrence, which is at the end of a verse (Gn. 10:19). It figures in the designation of the limits of the territory of Canaan in a context which suggests that one travelling from the Mediterranean coast would encounter it as the farthest inland of a group consisting of Sodom, Gomorrah, Admah and Zeboim. This points to a locality somewhere near the SE shore of the Dead Sea, but no site of this name is known there. Ancient tradition equated it with the hot springs of *Kallirrhoē*, modern Zarqa Maʿin SW of Madaba near the E coast of the Dead Sea, and some modern scholars prefer to identify it with *layiš* of *Dan, but neither of these can be substantiated. T.C.M.

LASHARON (RV 'Lassharon', AVmg. 'Sharon'). A Canaanite royal city mentioned with Aphek as taken by Joshua (12:18). LXX (B) reads 'the king of Aphek in Sharon'. However, Eusebius (*Onomasticon*, *s.v.* 'Saron') mentions a district called Sarona, between Mt Tabor and the Sea of Tiberias, and this ancient site, 10 km SW of Tiberias, may be the biblical Lasharon. J.D.D.

LATIN. The word is mentioned only twice in the NT (Lk. 23:38, RSVmg.; Jn. 19:20). An Indo-European language, it was spoken first in Rome and the contiguous Latian plain by racial elements which entered Italy, probably from the N, before 900 BC. Latin was confined to the Latian enclave by the alien Etruscan language to the N, and to the E and S by the allied languages, Oscan and Umbrian, which came with a later wave of immigrants, possibly across the Adriatic. Latin expanded with Rome, became the second speech of the W Mediterranean, fathered the Romance languages, and contributed major elements to the vocabularies of the Teutonic and Slavonic languages. Latin words appearing in the NT are: *as, charta, census, centurio, colonia, custodia, denarius, forum, flagellum, grabbatus, legio, lenteum, libertini, lolium, praetorium, quadrans, macellum, membrana, modius, raeda, semicinctium, sicarius, speculator, sudarium, taberna, titulus, zizanium.* E.M.B.

LAW.

I. In the Old Testament

a. Terminology

The term *tôrâ* is used in some instances in the OT for law in general. In the great majority of cases it is used for commandments in the vetitive ('you shall not do this'), imperative ('do this') and jussive ('you shall do this'). It is a commandment from a person of higher authority to a lower one. It could have originated in the family circle where it refers to the education given by a mother to her children. Closely related to *tôrâ* is *miṣwâ*. It is usually used as a direct command from a higher authority, *e.g.* the Lord, the king, the father, *etc.* These commandments are sometimes prohibitives and in other cases positively stated (German: *heischendes Präsens*). The term *ḥōq* or *ḥuqqâ* is used in a great variety of meanings. *ḥōq* is not something pronounced like *tôrâ* and *miṣwâ*, but established. It points occasionally to a newly-established stipulation. In the priestly sphere of meaning it means a cultic obligation, in the royal sphere of meaning a royal pronouncement. The term *d*^{e}*ḇārîm* is usually connected to the commandments of the Lord. Where law is sanctioned by the Lord, it becomes *d*^{e}*ḇārîm*. The term *mišpāṭ* has also a great variety of meanings, ranging from legal verdict to a fixed pattern of the legal community. From the meaning 'legal verdict of a judge' developed the meaning of a rule of law or customary law which becomes normative for future judges. In this sense it was used as a technical term for case or casuistic law. The term *'*^{e}*ḏûṯ* in the legal sphere means 'admonition' and *piqquḏîm* 'assignment'. In later Hebrew literature from the Persian period *dāṯ* is used to denote a royal decree or government law, but it is also used for the law of the Lord (cf., e.g., Ezr. 7.12, 14, 21). It is thus clear that the different terms originated as legal material from the pronouncement of a person in higher authority. In the religious sphere it is the Lord; in the legal sphere it might be the king, judge or elders (*z*^{e}*qēnîm*); in the family sphere it might be the father or mother.

b. Israelite law and the ancient Near East

Discoveries of ancient Near Eastern legal material make it clear that the legal tradition, as we also have it in the OT, started well back in the 3rd millennium BC. A fragmentary code of Ur-Nammu goes back to the 3rd dynasty of Ur, 2050 BC. It has a preamble like most of the other codes. The few readable stipulations are in the casuistic style. Another Sumerian code is that of Lipit-Ishtar of *c*. 1850 BC. It has a preamble and epilogue. The oldest code in Akkadian is the one of the city of Eshnunna probably from the time of Dadusha *c*. 1800 BC. It also has a preamble. A. Goetze, who has published the tablets, could in quite a few instances point to a remarkable similarity between these laws and certain laws of the Covenant code of the OT (Ex. 21–23). The first Near Eastern code to be discovered was that of Hammurapi, king of Babel. It originated in *c*. 1700 BC, if we follow the low chronology of Albright. It has a preamble and epilogue. Some of these laws have thrown fresh light on the legal material of the OT. This is by far the largest corpus of laws we have from the ancient Near East. The Middle Assyrian Laws come from the time of Tiglath-pileser I in *c*. 1100 BC. They also have a preamble and epilogue. The main characteristics are the Draconian approach and the detailed stipulations on marriage. Only one tablet has been found of the Neo-Babylonian Laws which originated from *c*. 600 BC. The Hittite Laws come from the time of Hattusilis III in *c*. 1280 BC. It is, however, clear that the code is much older than that. The main characteristic is that a difference is made between laws that are still in force and others that are antiquated. Along with these codes we have a wealth of legal material like contracts, court procedures, *etc*. In Egypt no corpus of laws has yet been discovered, but there we also have a large amount of legal material of which the marriage-contracts are the most significant.

The style generally used in the codes is casuistic and comparable to that of a large amount of legal material in the OT. The one exception is the Neo-Babylonian Laws where relative sentences are used and only in the subsections is the casuistic style applied. When we compare the OT casuistic laws with those of the ancient Near East, the similarity of subject-matter stands out clearly. At the same time there are certain differences in smaller detail. It is obvious that the Israelites have dealt in the same tradition as that of Mesopotamia. Legal traditions were conservatively handed over from one generation to another. Some of the Israelite casuistic material has its roots way back in Mesopotamia and points to a common heritage. This ties perfectly with the biblical record of Abraham's migration from Mesopotamia. Another similarity in form is the usage of the preamble and epilogue. In Mesopotamia the codes are accompanied by the preamble and epilogue to place the laws in a definite historical and religious framework. The name of the promulgator of the laws is mentioned as well as the gods to whom the laws are dedicated. The Covenant code has a similar framework where Moses is mentioned as the receiver of the laws and the Lord as the One who sanctioned them.

c. The style of Israelite law and its origins

A. Alt has made an important contribution to the understanding of Hebrew law with the distinction of certain formal types of law and their possible origin. He has distinguished three types of law: in the first place, apodictic law which consists of positive and negative commands ('you shall . . ., you shall not'). This type of law he has regarded as Yahwistic and of pure Israelite origin. In the second place, he has discovered a type of law consisting of participle clauses in which the command is given to kill the trangressor ('one doing such

An Old Latin (pre-Vulgate) translation of Gn. 5:4–6:2, written on vellum. Codex fragment, probably late 5th cent. AD. *Found at Oxyrhynchus, Egypt.* (BL)

A typical Hebrew scroll of the Law (Torah), the five books of Moses (Pentateuch). This example, with modern handles, was in use in a synagogue in Jerusalem for at least 200 years until withdrawn in 1924 owing to wear and the fading of the ink. (DJW)

and such shall be put to death'). He has regarded this kind of law as closely related to the apodictic form and thus also of Israelite origin. The third type is called casuistic ('if a man . . .'). The typical style is to start with *kî* or *'im* ('if') and to give the transgression in the protasis and the legal verdict in the apodosis. The major case is always introduced by *kî* and the subsections by *'im*. This is also the general style of the laws of the ancient Near East. Alt has held that the Israelites came into contact with these laws in Palestine and borrowed them from the Canaanites.

Meanwhile this view of Alt has been scrutinized from several angles. The so-called apodictic laws were studied by E. Gerstenberger on a much wider scale. Alt's research was more or less restricted to the Covenant code. Gerstenberger has widened his scope to include this genre of literature also in Wisdom Literature and elsewhere. He has proposed new nomenclature for these laws, *e.g.* vetitives and prohibitives ('you shall not'). Looking for the *Sitz im Leben* (life-setting) of these laws he is more inclined to regard it as an *Ethos* and more specifically as a *Sippenethos* (clan ethics). The *Sitz im Leben* of these laws is the family circle where the father gives certain commands according to the customs of the clan to which he belongs. The next step was taken by W. Richter who does not want to restrict the *Sitz im Leben* only to the clan, but to connect these types of law with the school situation. The attitude to widen the scope of the *Sitz im Leben* is to be welcomed. The situation as we have it in the OT shows that the vetitives and prohibitives can be given by a variety of persons in authoritative positions: the Lord (*cf.* Ex. 20), the king, the tribal leader, the teacher, the father, *etc.* An important question is whether we should regard the vetitives and prohibitions as law at all, or not. In the OT they are intermixed with other types of law. This could lead us to accept that they are indeed legal stipulations. But the laws are sometimes intermixed with kerygmatic material (*cf. e.g.* Ex. 22:27b, 26b in *MT*) which is of a religious nature and has nothing in common with legal material. We might, thus, regard the vetitives and prohibitives as policy. To regard the Decalogue as the Lord's policy and not as a cluster of laws is more satisfactory. It is observable that in the case of the vetitives and prohibitives no punishment is prescribed, as it is in the casuistic laws.

The latest studies have shown that the participial and relative clauses must be studied as a whole. H. Schulz has studied especially those with the death-penalty clause and has reached the conclusion that their *Sitz im Leben* is the tribal circle. In the tribal circle the tribal chief gave these kinds of death-penalty verdicts. The typification of these laws is still not settled. G. Liedke has recently suggested that these laws be called apodictic.

The casuistic material or case law is designated in the OT with *mišpāṭ* (*cf.* Ex. 21:1). These laws are verdicts of judges which became legal examples to be followed by later judges. And so it became customary law. The presence of the laws in legal codes does not mean that they have originated with the promulgation of the codes, but that they were regarded as typical legal examples to be followed. Recently Liedke has given careful attention to these laws. He has held that they are case law formed from customary law which were used as examples for the solution of civil cases.

d. The different Israelite codes

1. The Covenant code. This is by far the oldest code of Hebrew law; its core goes back to the time of Moses. It is even possible that some of the casuistic material might go back to the time of the patriarchs while they were in Mesopotamia. It is also true that later material was added and that existing material was altered in later times. It is to be expected that older legal material is continually adapted to new circumstances. In Exodus this code is placed in a definite historical framework, *viz.* the forming of the covenant at Sinai. These laws are, thus, intended as the stipulations of the covenant. The laws, however, do not cover all the possible judicial fields and show that they are merely a torso or an extract of laws. The most important characteristic of the Covenant code is that it is sanctioned by the Lord as his law for his people.

2. The Deuteronomic code. This is to be found in Dt. 12–25. Here we have the codification of old Hebrew laws in later times, possibly in the time of Josiah (*c.* 622 BC). It is wrong to assume that the promulgation of laws indicates the time of their origin, as we have seen. Many of the laws have an archaic character and some of them are similar to the laws in the Covenant code (*cf. e.g.* Ex. 23:15–16 and Dt. 22:23–29). It is thus quite probable that most of the stipulations of Deuteronomy may have an early date. As has been pointed out by various scholars, Deuteronomy has in some instances ancient material, but it is also probable that later material was added. This could have been the case in the time of Josiah. The old laws were then adapted to new circumstances and new laws added according to the need of later times.

3. The Holiness code. It is to be found in Lv. 17–26. This compilation of laws is called the Holiness code on account of the phrase 'for I the Lord, who sanctify you, am holy' (Lv. 21:8). The contents of this code mainly comprise stipulations in connection with the sanctuary, the priests and the covenant community. All the stipulations must be kept by the Israelites and regarded as holy and thus the property of the Lord. Although these laws could have been compiled in later times, the archaic character of some of them is obvious and they might go back to the time of the Exodus.

4. The final compilation of laws. Many of the legal compilations were not in the exact form as we have them in the Pentateuch. After the exile compilations were made, some laws were re-adjusted to new circumstances and other laws added. The different codes were then placed in the broad framework of the Pentateuch as we have it today. The final form of the Pentateuch was reached only in *c.* 450 BC, in the time of Ezra, when it was promulgated by being publicly read (*cf.* Ne. 8).

e. Types of Israelite laws

1. The lack of legal theory. One of the characteristics of Israelite law as well as the legal compilations of the ancient Near East is the lack of legal theory. It is *e.g.* difficult to find any rationale or any logical sequence in these laws. Sometimes we have a cluster of laws on a certain subject, *e.g.* the goring ox (Ex. 21:28–32, 35–36). In this case the goring ox is placed in the centre of the reasoning and not the kind of transgression. The subject-matter can suddenly change from the rape of a virgin (Ex. 22:16–17) to sorcery (Ex. 22:18), to bestiality (Ex. 22:19) and to idolatry (Ex. 22:20). There might have been a rationale behind this for the Semites, but to us it is totally lost.

2. Civil and criminal law. Another distinction which we make between civil and criminal law does not seem to have been made by the Semites. Recently A. Phillips has held that the so-called apodictic material is to be regarded as criminal law, but this cannot be upheld in the light of what we have said above. What we should regard as a criminal offence, *e.g.* theft, was regarded in Hebrew law as a civil case in which the transgressor must make amends for his deed by paying back the owner in kind. The whole rationale behind the stipulations is to redress the damage done to someone's property, *viz.* to restore the balance. Even in the case of the rape of a virgin the transgressor must pay her father the bride's price to redress his loss, because after her violation he could not ask the bride's price for his daughter.

(i) Murder and assault. It is noteworthy that in Hebrew law a difference is made between premeditated murder and unintentional manslaughter (Ex. 21:12–14). In the case of murder the penalty is death. In the case of unintentional manslaughter, which is described by the phrase 'God let him fall into his hand', or 'he met with an act of God', the person can flee to a place of asylum. Assault is also regarded as a grave offence. A distinction is made between assault on parents (Ex. 21:15), assault that leads to incapacitation (Ex. 21:18–19), assault on a pregnant woman (Ex. 21:22–25) and assault on slaves (Ex. 21:26–27). These cases are differently approached. As a result of the strong conviction of the value of family solidarity, the son who beats his parents is sentenced to death. The cases of incapacitation and of the pregnant woman are approached from the restitution angle. For the incapacitated man redress must be made for his medical expenses and for his loss of time; while in the case of the pregnant woman who has lost her foetus, a redress must be made to her husband for loss of his child, his property. Very interesting is the case of assault on one's own slaves. When a serious bodily injury is incurred, the slave receives manumission. This is a typical Hebrew law and not to be found in any legal compilation in the ancient Near East. This testifies to a unique humane approach to slaves.

(ii) Theft. This offence can broadly be viewed in three aspects: *viz.* kidnapping, theft of cattle and theft of movable property which is given in custody. Kidnapping is regarded with severity. Two proofs of guilt are mentioned, *viz.* when the thief sells the kidnapped person and when the kidnapped person is found in the possession of the thief. In this case the death penalty is prescribed (Ex. 21:16). In a nomadic and semi-nomadic society the possession of animals is regarded as very important. Theft of these animals is thus regarded as a grave offence. A good example occurs in Ex. 22:1–3. Restitution must be made by the payment of five cattle for one stolen and four sheep for one. In some cases the penalty is double payment in kind. The co-existence of these two kinds of penalty is an enigma. B. S. Jackson has held that the heavier penalty is the older one and that double restitution is a later reduction in penalty. This cannot be proved, however. Certain stipulations occur in which a depositor of movable property, like cattle, is protected against theft by the bailee. If such a theft can be proved, the bailee must pay double in kind (*cf.* Ex. 22:6–12).

(iii) Negligence and damage. Negligence is regarded all over the ancient Near East as a serious offence. In cuneiform law a technical term *egūm* occurs which is absent in Hebrew law, though negligence plays an important role in Hebrew jurisprudence. A good example is the goring ox. When the owner of the ox is aware of its habit to gore, or has been warned against it, and the ox kills a free man or woman, the owner and the ox are liable. Both must be killed (Ex. 21:29). Another case of negligence is where a well is dug and not properly covered. If an animal falls into the well, the owner of the well must compensate the owner of the animal with money.

(iv) Offences of a moral and religious nature. Under this subsection a great variety of offences can be classified. They range from cursing parents to the seduction of a virgin, combating sorcery, bestiality, idolatry, a variety of cultic prescriptions (especially in Lv.) and the ill-treatment of alien, widow and orphan. We want to single out the latter offence as example (Ex. 22:21–24). The principle of protecting a widow and orphan is a very old one. As early as the time of Urukagina (*c.* 2400 BC) this principle is propagated. Even in Egypt traces of this principle are present. In the case of the Hebrew commandment it is stated as the policy of the Lord for his people not to oppress widows and orphans.

(iv) Family law. In the OT world the family was regarded as very important. The father was the head of the family. In a certain sense his wife and children were his property. The most important laws on the family are those on marriage and on inheritance. In the first instance laws were made to forbid marriage in certain circumstances (*e.g.* Lv. 18), to prescribe the levirate marriage (*cf.* especially Dt. 25:5–10) and to prescribe divorce (*cf.* Dt. 24:1–4). The laws against beating and cursing parents point in the direction of family solidarity in which the authority of the father must be accepted without any question.

(vi) Slavery. As we have seen, a unique humane approach to slaves is visible in Hebrew law. A distinction must be made between Hebrew slaves and foreign slaves. It is not always clear to which form of slavery the laws refer. According to Ex. 21:2–6 a Hebrew slave who is taken into slavery by sale, possibly as a result of his debts, must be released at the end of 6 years of service. In Ex. 21:7–11 the case of the second woman is described which is regarded as a kind of slavery. Interesting in this case is that the rights of this woman are defended by law. It is thus clear, by and large, that the excesses of slavery are neatly combated in Hebrew law.

(vii) *Lex talionis.* In the Covenant code, the oldest Hebrew corpus of laws, the law of talion (retaliation) is awkwardly brought in. The previous law treats the case of assault on a pregnant woman. It is probable that the final editor of Exodus has reasoned that he must give in addition to this case of assault a general introduction to assault and single out those cases in which the *lex talionis* can be applied (Ex. 21:23–25). *Lex talionis* is there to restrict blood-revenge to certain prescribed cases, because of its danger to the prosperity of a society. It is not a primitive form of jurisprudence, but it is made to discourage homicide and wilful acts of assault.

3. International law. A long legal history of international law existed in the ancient Near East. Scores of tablets with treaties between various nations have been discovered. Two main types of contracts occur, *viz.* parity-treaty between equals and vassal-treaties. The Israelites were well aware of both for they formed a parity-treaty with the Phoenicians and a vassal-treaty with the Gibeonites. In the OT legal material the principles for forming a vassal-treaty are given in Dt. 20:10–14. The Israelites must offer the enemy peace (*šālôm*) which means a peaceful co-existence in which the enemy as minor partner must have certain obligations, *e.g.* to serve the major partner and to pay tax to him. We know from vassal-treaties that the major partner is also obliged to defend the minor partner when he is attacked by an enemy.

f. The religious nature of Israelite laws

It is clear from the OT laws, even from those with a purely secular character, that the Lord promulgated them in the interest of his people. In some instances the Lord is suddenly introduced in the third, second or first person to give force to the particular law (*e.g.* Ex. 21:13). Sometimes the kerygmatic element is clearly visible (*e.g.* Ex. 22:9). The laws are given to extol the mercy of the Lord. This characteristic in Hebrew law is unique in the legal tradition of the ancient Near East. It points to a direct involvement of the Lord in the laws of the covenant community. The binding of the laws to the covenant, and thus to the Major Partner of the covenant, ensures that the stipulations must be kept or else the covenant is broken and also the relationship with the Lord. The keeping of the laws is thus necessary to secure the blessing of the Lord. These laws have a twofold character: they are to promote love to the Lord and love to one's neighbour. The summary of the law given by Jesus (Mt. 22:35–40) is exactly in accordance with the twofold character as it is presented in the OT.

BIBLIOGRAPHY. A. Alt, 'The Origins of Israelite Law', in *Essays on Old Testament History and Religion*, 1968, pp. 101–171; W. Beyerlin, *Origins and History of the Oldest Sinaitic Traditions*, 1965; D. Daube, *Studies in Biblical Law*, 1947; Z. Falk, *Hebrew Law in Biblical Times*, 1964; F. C. Fensham, 'Widow, Orphan and the Poor in Ancient Near Eastern Legal and Wisdom Literature', *JNES* 21, 1962, pp. 129–139; *idem*, 'Aspects of Family Law in the Covenant Code', *Dine Israel* 1, 1969, pp. 5–19; E. Gerstenberger, *Wesen und Herkunft des 'apodiktischen Rechts'*, 1965; M. Greenberg, 'Some Postulates of Biblical Criminal Law', in *Y. Kaufman Jubilee Volume*, 1960; B. S. Jackson, *Theft in Early Jewish Law*, 1972; *idem*, *Essays in Jewish and Comparative Legal History*, 1975; L. Köhler, *Der hebräische Mensch*, 1953; G. Liedke, *Gestalt und Bezeichnung alttestamentliche Rechtssätze*, 1971; N. Lohfink, *Das Hauptgebot*, 1963; M. Noth, *The Laws in the Pentateuch and Other Studies*, 1966; G. Osborn, *Tora in the Old Testament*, 1945; S. M. Paul, *Studies in the Book of the Covenant*, 1970; A. Phillips, *Ancient Israel's Criminal Law*, 1970; G. J. Wenham, 'Grace and Law in the Old Testament', and 'Law and the Legal System in the Old Testament', in B. N. Kaye and G. J. Wenham (eds.), *Law, Morality and the Bible*, 1978; D. J. Wiseman, 'Law and Order in Old Testament Times', *Vox Evangelica* 8, 1973, pp. 5–21.

F.C.F.

II. In the New Testament

a. The meaning of the term

There is much flexibility in the use of the term 'law' (*nomos*) in the NT.

1. Frequently it is used in the canonical sense to denote the whole or part of the OT writings. In Rom. 3:19a it clearly refers to the OT in its entirety; Paul has quoted from various parts of the OT in the preceding context, and he must be understood as culling these quotations from what he calls 'the law'. But the flexibility of his use of the term is apparent. For, when he speaks of those 'under the law' in the next clause, 'law' in this instance has a different meaning. It is likely that this broader denotation comprising the OT as a whole is the sense in Rom. 2:17–27. It is likewise apparent in the usage of our Lord on several occasions (*cf.* Mt. 5:18; Lk. 16:17; Jn. 8:17; 10:34; 15:25).

But the term is also used in a more restricted canonical sense to designate a part of the OT. In the expression 'the law and the prophets' it will have to be understood as comprising the whole of the OT not included in 'the prophets' (*cf.* Mt. 5:17; 7:12; 11:13; 22:40; Lk. 16:16; Acts 13:15; Rom. 3:21b). In a still more restricted sense it is used to denote the Pentateuch as distinct from the other two main divisions of the OT (*cf.* Lk. 24:44). There are some instances in which it is uncertain whether 'the law of Moses' refers merely to the Pentateuch or is used in the more inclusive sense to denote the rest of the OT not included in 'the prophets' (*cf.* Jn. 1:45; Acts 28:23). It is possible that, since the simple term 'the law' can be used in a more inclusive sense, so 'the law of Moses' could even be understood as embracing more than was strictly Mosaic. This again is symptomatic of the flexibility of terms in the usage of the NT, arising, in this connection, from the fact that the expression 'the law and the prophets' is a convenient designation of the OT in its entirety.

2. There are instances in which the term designates the Mosaic administration dispensed at Sinai. This use is particularly apparent in Paul (*cf.* Rom. 5:13, 20; Gal. 3:17, 19, 21a). Closely related to this denotation is the use by Paul of the expression 'under the law' (1 Cor. 9:20; Gal. 3:23; 4:4–5, 21; *cf.* Eph. 2:15; 'of the law' in Rom. 4:16). This characterization, in these precise connections, means to be under the Mosaic economy or, in the case of 1 Cor. 9:20, to consider oneself as still bound by the Mosaic institutions. The Mosaic economy as an administration had divine sanction and authority during the period of its operation. This use of the term 'under law' must not be confused with another application of the same expression which will be dealt with later.

3. Frequently the term is used to designate the law of God as the expression of God's will. The instances are so numerous that only a fraction can be cited (Rom. 3:20; 4:15; 7:2, 5, 7, 8–9, 12, 16, 22; 8:3–4, 7; 13:8, 10; 1 Cor. 15:56; Gal. 3:13; 1 Tim. 1:8; Jas. 1:25; 4:11). The abiding obligation and sanctity of the law as the expression of God's character as holy, just and good lie on the face of such references. The obligation for men involved is expressed in terms of being 'under law' (1 Cor. 9:21, *ennomos*).

4. On occasion 'law' is used as the virtual synonym of law specially revealed in contrast with the work of the law natively inscribed on the heart of man (Rom. 2:12–14). It is to be understood that law in the other senses is law specially revealed. But in the instance cited attention is focused on this consideration because of the contrast respecting mode of revelation. There is no indication that a different law is in view. The emphasis falls upon the greater fullness and clearness of special revelation and the correlative increase of responsibility for the recipients.

5. In varying forms of expression 'law' is used in a depreciatory sense to denote the status of the person who looks to the law, and therefore to works of law, as the way of justification and acceptance with God. The formula 'under law' has this signification (Rom. 6:14–15, Gal. 5:18). As indicated above, this use of the formula is not to be confused with the same when applied to the Mosaic dispensation (*cf.* Gal. 3:23 and others cited). Interpretation of the NT, particularly of the Pauline Epistles, has been complicated by failure to recognize the distinction. The person who is 'under law' in the sense of Rom. 6:14 is in bondage to sin in its guilt, defilement and power. But this was not the consequence of being under the Mosaic economy during the period from Moses to Christ. Nor is 'under law', in this sense, to be confused with a similar term as it applies to a believer in Christ (1 Cor. 9:21). Of the same force as 'under law' in this depreciatory sense is the expression 'of the law' (Rom. 4:14; Gal. 3:18; Phil. 3:9); and the phrase 'by works of the law' (Rom. 3:20; Gal. 2:16; 3:2, 5, 10) refers to the same notion. 'Apart from works of law' (Rom. 3:28) expresses the opposite. Several expressions are to be interpreted in terms of this concept and of the status it denotes. When Paul says, 'the righteousness of God has been manifested apart from law' (Rom. 3:21), he means a righteousness apart from works of law, and therefore antithetical to a works-righteousness. When he says that we have been put to death to the law and discharged from the law (Rom. 7:4, 6), he refers to the breaking of that bond that binds us to the law as the way of acceptance with God (*cf.* also Gal. 2:19). Law as law, as commandment requiring obedience and pronouncing its curse upon all transgression, does not have any potency or provision for the justification of the ungodly. The contrast between law-righteousness, which is our own righteousness, and the righteousness of God provided in Christ is the contrast between human merit and the gospel of grace (*cf.* Rom. 10:3; Gal. 2:21; 5:4; Phil. 3:9). Paul's polemic in the Epistles to the Romans and Galatians is concerned with that antithesis.

6. Law is sometimes used in the sense of an operating and governing principle. In this sense Paul speaks of 'the law of faith' (Rom. 3:27, AV; RSV 'principle'), which is contrasted with the law of works. The contrast is that between the principle of faith and that of works. It is the same idea that offers the best interpretation of the word 'law' in Rom. 7:21, 23, 25b; 8:2.

There is thus great diversity in the denotation of the word 'law', and sometimes there is deep-seated difference in connotation. The result is that a meaning totally diverse from that intended by the NT speaker or writer would be imposed upon his words if we did not appreciate the differentiation which appears in the usage. There are instances, especially in Paul, where transition from one meaning to another appears in adjacent clauses. In Rom. 3:21, if we did not appreciate the two distinct senses of the word, there would be patent contradiction. In Rom. 4:14 the expression 'of the law' is exclusive of faith. However, in v. 16 'of the law' is not exclusive of faith, for those of the law are represented as having the promise made sure to them. Different senses are thus demanded. There are other classifications beyond those given above that other nuances of meaning and application would suggest. And on numerous occasions it is difficult to ascertain what the precise denotation is. In the main, however, when the distinctions given above are recognized, interpretation will be relieved of frequent distortions and needless difficulties will be resolved.

b. Law and gospel

The foregoing analysis makes it apparent how important is the question of the relation which a believer sustains to the law of God. To be 'under law' in one sense (Rom. 6:14) excludes a person from the enjoyment of the grace which the gospel imparts; to be 'under law' is the opposite of being 'under grace' and means that the person is the bondslave of the condemnation and power of sin. In this sense, therefore, it is by the gospel that we are discharged from the law (Rom. 7:6) and put to death to the law (Rom. 7:4)—'we are . . . dead to that which held us captive' (*cf.* Gal. 2:19). The gospel is annulled if the decisiveness of this discharge is not appreciated. In that event we have fallen away from grace and Christ becomes of no effect (*cf.* Gal. 5:4).

But this is not the whole account of the relation of law and gospel. Paul said also in the heart of his exposition and defence of the gospel of grace, 'Do we then overthrow the law by this faith? By no means! On the contrary, we uphold the law' (Rom. 3:31). As a believer he protests that he agrees that the law is good, that he delights in the law of God in his inmost self, that with the mind he serves the law of God (Rom. 7:16, 22, 25), and that the aim of Christ's accomplishment was that the righteousness of the law might be fulfilled in those who walk not according to the flesh but according to the Spirit (Rom. 8:4). An example of the law he had in mind is in Rom. 7:7. And no doubt can remain that in Rom. 13:9 he provides us with concrete examples of the law which love fulfils, showing thereby that there is no incompatibility between love as the controlling motive of the believer's life and conformity to the commandments which the law of God enunciates. The conclusion is inescapable that the precepts of the Decalogue have relevance to the believer as the criteria of that manner of life which love to God and to our neighbour dictates. The same apostle uses terms which are to the same effect as that of being 'under law' when he says, 'not being without law toward God, but under the law of Christ' (1 Cor. 9:21). In respect of obligation he is not divorced from the law of God, he is not lawless in reference to God. And this is validated and exemplified in his being bound to the law of Christ.

When Paul says that 'love is the fulfilling of the law' (Rom. 13:10) it is obvious that the commandments appealed to in the preceding verse are examples of the law in view. But by the words 'and any other commandment' he intimates that he has not enumerated all the commandments. The distinction is, therefore, that 'the law' is the generic term and the commandments are the specific expressions. Hence, although the apostle John does not speak in terms of fulfilling the law, the emphasis placed upon the necessity of keeping and doing the commandments (1 Jn. 2:3–4; 3:22, 24; 5:2–3) is to the same effect. And when he writes that 'whoever keeps his word, in him truly love for God is perfected' (1 Jn. 2:5), he is pointing to what he elsewhere defines as that of which the love of God consists, namely, that 'we keep his commandments' (1 Jn. 5:3). The sum is that the keeping of God's commandments is the practical expression of that love apart from which we know not God and our Christian profession is a lie (*cf.* 1 Jn. 2:4; 4:8). John's teaching is the reproduction of our Lord's, and it is John who records for us Jesus' corresponding injunctions (Jn. 14:15, 21; 15:10). It is also significant that our Lord himself should enforce the necessity of keeping commandments by appealing to his own example of keeping the Father's commandments and thus abiding in and constraining the Father's love (*cf.* Jn. 10:17–18; 15:10).

No NT writer is more jealous for the fruits that accompany and vindicate faith than James. The criterion by which these fruits are to be assessed is 'the perfect law of liberty' (Jas. 1:25). James, like other NT writers, is well aware that love is the motive power. The 'royal law' is 'You shall love your neighbour as yourself' (Jas. 2:8). But for James also neither love nor law is conceived of apart from the concrete examples of law and expressions of love in commandments, instances of which he provides (Jas. 2:11). It is by this law that we shall be judged (Jas. 2:12); it is in this law we are to continue (Jas. 1:25); it is this law we are to keep in each of its demands (Jas. 2:10); it is this law we are to perform (Jas. 4:11).

The reason for this sustained appeal to the law of God as the norm by which the conduct of the believer is to be judged and by which his life is to be governed resides in the relation of the law to the character of God. God is holy, just and good. Likewise 'the law is holy, and the commandment is holy and just and good' (Rom. 7:12). The law is, therefore, the reflection of God's own perfections. In a word, it is the transcript of God's holiness as the same comes to expression for the regulation of thought and behaviour consonant with his glory. We are to be holy in all manner of life because he who has called us is holy (1 Pet. 1:15–16). To be relieved of the demands which the law prescribes would contradict the relation to God which grace establishes. Salvation is salvation from sin, and 'sin is lawlessness' (1 Jn. 3:4). Salvation is, therefore, to be saved from breaking the law and thus saved to conformity unto it. Antinomian bias strikes at the nature of the gospel. It says, in effect, let us continue in sin.

A believer is re-created after the image of God. He therefore loves God and his brother also (1 Jn. 4:20–21). And because he loves God he loves what mirrors God's perfection. He delights in the law of God in his inmost self (Rom. 7:22). Obedience is his joy, disobedience the plague of his heart. The saint is destined for conformity to the image of God's Son (Rom. 8:29) and he is re-made after the pattern of him who had no sin and could say, 'thy law is within my heart' (Ps. 40:8).

BIBLIOGRAPHY. J. Durham, *The Law Unsealed*, 1802; S. H. Tyng, *Lectures on the Law and the Gospel*, 1849; W. S. Plumer, *The Law of God as Contained in the Ten Commandments*, 1864; P. H. Eldersveld, *Of Law and Love*, 1954; C. H. Dodd, 'Ennomos Christou' in *More New Testament Studies*, 1968, pp. 134–148; C. H. Dodd, *Gospel and Law*, 1953; E. F. Kevan, *The Evangelical Doctrine of Law*, 1955; H. N. Ridderbos, *When the Time Had Fully Come*, 1957; H.-H. Esser, *NIDNTT* 2, pp. 436–456; H. Preisker, *TDNT* 2, pp. 372f.; J. D. M. Derrett, *Law in the New Testament*, 1970. (* ETHICS, BIBLICAL). J.M.

LAWGIVER (Heb. *meḥōqēq*; Gk. *nomothetēs*). All six OT occurrences of the Heb. word are in poetry. In Gn. 49:10; Nu. 21:18; Ps. 60:7 (= Ps. 108:8) the rendering 'staff' or 'sceptre' makes better sense in context and with parallels. Dt. 33:21; Jdg. 5:14; Is. 33:22 ascribe judicial leadership to Gad, Manasseh and the Lord. James (4:12) rebukes censoriousness among his readers by reminding them that God alone is judge.

The idea of lawgiver in the NT, if not the word, is much more widespread. In particular, Christ is characterized as Lawgiver by his respect for the Mosaic Law (Mt. 5:17–18), and by comparison with Moses (Mt. 17:3; Jn. 1:17). The superiority of Christ is emphasized in his own pronouncements (Mt. 5:22ff.; 22:36–40) and elsewhere by stressing his status (Gal. 3:19; Heb. 7:11), the scope of his law (Rom. 10:4; 13:8ff.), and its spiritual nature (Rom. 7–8; Jas. 1:25, *etc*.). P.A.B.

The laws of Hammurapi, king of Babylon, c. 1792–1750 BC, inscribed on a diorite stele 2·25 m high. Above, the king receives the symbols of 'justice and truth' (law and order) from the god Marduk or the sun-god Shamash. (MC)

LAWYER. The NT title *nomikos* was used of the scribes synonymously with *grammateus* (scribe) and *nomodidaskalos* (teacher of the law). All scribes were originally students of Scripture, but by the 2nd century BC lay scribes had begun to expound the minutiae of the law without direct reference to Scripture. Lawyers had seats in the Sanhedrin (Mt. 16:21; Lk. 22:66; Acts 4:5). R.K.H.

LAYING ON OF HANDS. Actions with the * hands were an important part of ancient religious ritual, *e.g.* in prayer (1 Ki. 8:54; 1 Tim. 2:8) and invocation of divine blessing (Lv. 9:22; Ecclus. 50:20; Lk. 24:50). Jacob blessed the sons of Joseph by laying (*šîṯ*) his hands upon their heads (Gn. 48:8–20), and Jesus similarly blessed children brought to him (Mk. 10:16; Mt. 19:13–15; *cf. SB*, 1, pp. 807f.). Jesus also touched (*e.g.* Mk. 1:41; 7:33), or laid his hands on, the sick (Mk. 5:23; 6:5; 7:32; 8:23, 25; Mt. 9:18; Lk. 4:40; 5:13; 13:13), as did the apostles (Acts 9:12, 17; 28:8; Mk. 16:[18]; *cf.* 1 Qap Gen 20. 21, 28f. The action was symbolic of spiritual blessing flowing from one person to another (*cf.* Mk. 5:30).

I. In the Old Testament

On the Day of Atonement Aaron placed (*sāmaḵ*) his hands on the head of the goat which was to be sent into the wilderness and confessed the people's sins over it, thus putting them upon the goat (Lv. 16:21). A similar rite accompanied the burnt, peace, sin and ordination offerings (*e.g.* Lv. 1:4; 3:2; 4:4; Nu. 8:12), indicating the 'identification' of the people with their offering. (In Lv. 24:14 [*cf.* Susanna 34] the people who put their hands upon a blasphemer were probably 'thrusting' his guilt upon him.)

The Levites, who as priests represented the people before God, were ordained by the people placing their hands upon them (Nu. 8:10). Moses ordained his successor Joshua by placing his hands upon him and thus investing him with some of his authority (Nu. 27:18–23). This passage describes Joshua as 'a man in whom is the spirit' before his ordination, but Dt. 34:9 states that he was full of the spirit of wisdom because Moses had laid his hands upon him. The implication would appear to be that a worthy person, possessed of the divine Spirit, received additional spiritual gifts when commissioned for service by this rite. At the same time the rite indicated a transfer of authority.

II. In the New Testament

In the NT baptism and the reception of the Spirit were on occasion accompanied by the laying on of hands. In Acts 8:14–19 the gift of the Spirit was conferred only when baptism had been followed by apostolic laying on of hands. It is unlikely that the laying on of hands by Ananias in Acts 9:12, 17 (where it precedes baptism) is to be understood similarly. Acts 19:6 links laying on of hands with baptism and the gift of the Spirit expressed in tongues and prophecy, and Heb. 6:2 refers to teaching about baptisms and laying on of hands, probably as instruction given to new converts. Elsewhere, however, the gift of the Spirit was given without mention of laying on of hands, and once even before baptism (Acts 10:44–48), and it is unlikely that in the NT period baptism was always accompanied by laying on of hands.

Following the OT analogies and what may have been contemporary rabbinic practice, laying on of hands was also the rite of ordination for Christian service. After the congregation had chosen the seven helpers they (or possibly the apostles) prayed and laid hands on them (Acts 6:5f.; *cf. SB*, 2, pp. 647–661); similarly, the church at Antioch prayed and laid hands on Barnabas and Saul for mission work (Acts 13:3). In 1 Tim. 5:22 Timothy is urged not to be hasty in laying on of hands; this may refer to the ordination of elders or to the restora-

LAW OF CHRIST
See Liberty, Part 2.

LAW OF LOVE
See Liberty, Part 2.

LAWS OF HAMMURAPI
See Hammurapi, Part 2.

tion of backsliders to fellowship with an act of blessing. 2 Tim. 1:6 refers to Timothy's own reception of the gift of God for the work of the ministry by the laying on of Paul's hands. *Cf.* 1 Tim. 4:14, where, however, it is the 'presbytery' which laid hands on him. The simplest and best solution is that Paul and the local elders were associated in the act, but D. Daube thinks that the phrase in question means 'ordination to the rank of presbyter'. Such ordination, carried out under divine guidance (Acts 13:3; *cf.* 1 Tim. 1:18), was an outward sign that God gave to the person his gifts for some task of ministry, and by it the church acknowledged the divine commission and enabling and associated itself with the Spirit in commissioning and authorizing the minister for his task.

BIBLIOGRAPHY. G. W. H. Lampe, *The Seal of the Spirit*, 1951, ch. 5; E. Lohse, *Die Ordination im Spätjudentum und im Neuen Testament*, 1951; D. Daube, *The New Testament and Rabbinic Judaism*, 1956, pp. 224ff.; J. Newman, *Semikhah*, 1950; N. Adler, *Taufe und Handauflegung*, 1951; E. Ferguson, *HTR* 56, 1963, pp. 12–19; *JTS* n.s. 26, 1975, pp. 1–12; C. Maurer, *TDNT* 8, pp. 159–161; E. Lohse, *TDNT* 9, pp. 424–434; H.-G. Schütz, *NIDNTT* 2, pp. 148–153.

I.H.M.

LAZARUS AND DIVES. In the story, which occurs in Lk. 16:19–31, Dives (Lat. 'rich man') is nowhere named. He failed to take notice of the plight of Lazarus, the beggar at his gate. After death Lazarus went to *Abraham's bosom and Dives to Hades. It was impossible for any contact to be made between them. Nor was there any point in Abraham's sending Lazarus to the brothers of Dives, as they had sufficient in Moses and the prophets to bring them to repentance.

The story teaches the dangers of wealth in blinding men to the need of their fellows and the irrevocable decision of our eternal destiny in our life on earth. It does not suggest that poverty is a virtue and wealth a vice, for Abraham was a rich man. Dives failed to learn the unjust steward's lesson (Lk. 16:9). The reference to resurrection in 16:31 applies more naturally to that of Christ than to that of Lazarus of Bethany. (*GULF.)

BIBLIOGRAPHY. I. H. Marshall, *The Gospel of Luke*, 1978, pp. 632–639.

R.E.N.

LAZARUS OF BETHANY. Students of the NT know well the two sisters of the Bethany home, but they know nothing whatever about the character and the temperament of Lazarus. The theory that he may be identified with the rich young ruler is nothing more than a flight of fancy. (This theory first occurs in an apocryphal insertion between vv. 34 and 35 of Mk. 10, quoted in a letter ascribed to Clement of Alexandria; *cf.* M. Smith, *Clement of Alexandria and a Secret Gospel of Mark*, 1973.) He appears in the Gospel story, not because of any shining qualities in his personality nor because of any resounding achievement, but solely because of the amazing miracle that was wrought upon him. He was perhaps quite an undistinguished sort of man, 'scarcely heard of half a mile from home', and yet it was to him that the very wonderful thing happened.

The laborious attempts which have been made to explain, or to explain away, the miracle are condemned by their patent absurdity. To believe, as Renan did, that the disciples arranged with Lazarus to pretend to be dead in order that Jesus might gain renown by pretending to raise him from the dead, and that Jesus agreed to take part in such an imposture, is an astounding *tour de force* of ingenious scepticism. The story reads most naturally as a sober and convincing account of an actual happening.

The early part of John 11 reads like the writing of an eye-witness and ear-witness of what is recorded, one who was with Jesus on the E of Jordan and who wondered why he remained 2 days there after he had heard of the sickness of Lazarus (v. 6); one who can record striking sayings of Jesus, such as the one about the number of the hours (v. 9) or the tremendous claim reported in v. 25; one who knows the exact distance between Bethany and Jerusalem, no doubt because he had often walked that road (v. 18); one who can report words spoken by Thomas and the other disciples (vv. 8, 12–16). The facts mentioned form a small part of the many indications that the Fourth Gospel comes from one who saw the deeds of Jesus and heard his words, who was familiar with the thoughts, the fears and the difficulties of the disciples, because he was, almost certainly, one of them, who brings to us firsthand information.

If he narrates the events in the early part of the chapter faithfully and soberly, why should he be accused of romancing when he comes to the grave of Lazarus? The *Gospel of Peter*, in its fantastic account of the resurrection of Jesus, shows us what the inventive mind of man can accomplish when it attempts to describe an event which no human eye saw; on the other hand, the quiet sobriety of the story of what happened at the grave of Lazarus seems to prove that it comes from a man who is describing something that he saw, exactly as he saw it. The story is told, says A. T. Olmstead, 'with all the circumstantial detail of the convinced eyewitness. It is utterly alien in form to the literary miracle tale. As with so many accounts found in our best sources, the historian can only repeat it, without seeking for psychological or other explanations' (*Jesus in the Light of History*, 1942, p. 206).

Would a romancer who, according to sceptical theories, was intent on multiplying miraculous details, have been likely to represent Jesus as weeping, not long before he called Lazarus out of the grave? The mention of the tears of Jesus may be regarded as an indirect confirmation of the authenticity of the narrative, since 'a cold or stony-hearted raiser of the dead would belong to the region of fiction' (E. W. Hengstenberg).

It can fairly be said that the silence of the narrative is as impressive as its contents. Not a single word of Lazarus is recorded. Nothing is told us about his experiences during 'those four days', and no revelation is made concerning the conditions of life in the other world.

Unresolved questions have been raised about the relation of this Lazarus to the Lazarus of Lk. 16:19ff. who was *not* sent back from the dead; the statement in Jn. 12:10f. that the chief priests plotted Lazarus' death because so many believed in Jesus on his account might exemplify the pronouncement of Lk. 16:31: 'If they do not hear Moses and the prophets, neither will they be convinced if some one should rise from the dead.'

BIBLIOGRAPHY. J. N. Sanders,

'Those whom Jesus loved', *NTS* 1, 1954–5, pp. 29–41. A.R. F.F.B.

LEAH (Heb. *lē'â*, 'wild cow' ?). The elder daughter of the Aramaean, Laban. Through his deception she became the wife of Jacob, because of the local custom prohibiting the younger daughter from marrying before the elder (Gn. 29:21–30). She was, not unnaturally, jealous of her more attractive sister Rachel.

As the mother of Reuben, Simeon, Levi, Judah, Issachar, Zebulun and Dinah she was acclaimed with Rachel as one of the builders of the house of Israel (Ru. 4:11). Together they allied with Jacob against Laban, and when they went to meet Esau she was given a place in the middle of the procession.

Her burial took place at Machpelah, in Hebron, presumably before Jacob's descent to Egypt (Gn. 49:31). M.B.

LEAVEN (Heb. *ś^{e}'ōr*, 'leaven', 'leavened bread' in Dt. 16:4; *ḥāmēṣ*, 'anything leavened or fermented'; *cf. maṣṣâ*, 'without leaven', Lv. 10:12; Gk. *zymē*, 'leaven'; *cf.* Lat. *levare*, 'to raise').

In Heb. life leaven came to play an important part, not only in bread-making, but also in law, ritual and religious teaching. It was made originally from fine white bran kneaded with must; from the meal of certain plants such as fitch or vetch; or from barley mixed with water and then allowed to stand till it turned sour. As baking developed, leaven was produced from bread flour kneaded without salt and kept till it passed into a state of fermentation.

a. In bread-making

In bread-making the leaven was probably a piece of dough, retained from a former baking, which had fermented and turned acid. This was then either dissolved in water in the kneading-trough before the flour was added, or was 'hid' in the flour (Mt. 13:33) and kneaded along with it. The *bread thus made was known as 'leavened', as distinct from 'unleavened' bread (Ex. 12:15, *etc.*). There is no clear trace of the use of other sorts of leaven, although it has often been suggested that the Jews used also the lees of wine as yeast.

b. In law and ritual

The earliest Mosaic legislation (Ex. 23:18; 34:25) prohibited the use of leaven during the *Passover and the 'feast of unleavened bread' (Gk. *azymos*) (Ex. 23:15; Mt. 26:17, *etc.*). This was to remind the Israelites of their hurried departure from Egypt, when without waiting to bake leavened bread they carried dough and kneading-troughs with them, baking as they wandered (Ex. 12:34ff.; Dt. 16:3, *etc.*), much as the bedouin still do.

The prohibition on leaven, as that on honey (Lv. 2:11), was possibly made because fermentation implied disintegration and corruption, and to the Hebrew anything in a decayed state suggested uncleanness. Rabbinical writers often used leaven as a symbol of evil and of man's hereditary corruption (*cf.* also Ex. 12:8, 15–20). Plutarch echoes this ancient view when he describes leaven as 'itself the offspring of corruption, and corrupting the mass of dough with which it is mixed'. *fermentum* is used in Persius (*Sat.* 1. 24) for 'corruption'.

Doubtless for this reason it was excluded also from the offerings placed upon the altar of Yahweh, only cakes made from flour without leaven (*maṣṣôṯ*, Lv. 10:12) being allowed. (*SHOWBREAD.)

Two exceptions to this rule should, however, be noted (Lv. 7:13; *cf.* Am. 4:5). 'Leavened bread' was an accompaniment of the thank-offering, and leavened loaves were used also in the wave-offering —*i.e.* at the Feast of Pentecost.

c. In religious teaching

The figurative uses of leaven in the NT to a large extent reflect the former view of it as 'corrupt and corrupting'. Jesus utters warnings against the leaven of the Pharisees, Sadducees and Herodians (Mt. 16:6; Mk. 8:15): the Pharisees' hypocrisy and preoccupation with outward show (Mt. 23:14, 16; Lk. 12:1); the Sadducees' scepticism and culpable ignorance (Mt. 22:23, 29); the Herodians' malice and political guile (Mt. 22:16–21; Mk. 3:6).

The two Pauline passages in which the word occurs support this view (1 Cor. 5:6ff.; Gal. 5:9), with the former going on to contrast 'the leaven of malice and evil' with 'the unleavened bread of sincerity and truth', remembering the new significance of the old feast: that 'Christ, our paschal lamb, has been sacrificed'.

No such meaning attaches, however, to Jesus' brief but profoundly significant parable which (following that of the slow-growing mustard seed) compares the kingdom of God with 'leaven which a woman took and hid in three measures of flour, till it was all leavened' (Mt. 13:33; Lk. 13:21), clearly an allusion to 'the hidden, silent, mysterious, but all-pervading and transforming action of the leaven in the . . . flour' (*ISBE*, 3, p. 1862).

BIBLIOGRAPHY. *ISBE*; J. Lightfoot, *Horae Hebraicae*, 1659, 2, pp. 232–233; O. T. Allis, 'The Parable of the Leaven', *EQ* 19, 1947, pp. 254–273; R. S. Wallace, *Many Things in Parables*, 1955, pp. 22–25; H. Windisch, *TDNT* 2, pp. 902–906; G. T. D. Angel, *NIDNTT* 2, pp. 461–463. J.D.D.

LEBANON. A mountain range in Syria. The name is also more loosely applied to the adjoining regions (Jos. 13:5), and is also that of a modern republic.

I. Name

Heb. *l^{e}ḇānôn* is derived from the root *lbn*, 'white'. The range owes this name to two factors: the white limestone of the high ridge of Lebanon and especially the glittering snows that cap its peaks for 6 months of the year; *cf.* Je. 18:14. Lebanon is attested in ancient records from at least the 18th century BC onwards; see on history, below. The Assyrians called it *Lab'an*, then *Labnanu*; the Hittites, *Niblani*; the Egyptians, *rmnn* or *rbrn*; and the Canaanites themselves, *e.g.* at Ugarit, *Lbnn* just as in Hebrew.

II. Topography

The S end of the Lebanon range is a direct continuation of the hills of N Galilee, and is divided from them only by the deep E–W gorge of the lower reaches of the Litani river, which enters the sea a few km N of Tyre. The Lebanon range is a ridge almost 160 km long, following the SW to NE trend of the Phoenician coast from behind Sidon N to the E–W valley of the Nahr el-Kebir river (the river Eleutherus of antiquity), which divides Lebanon from the next N–S mountain range extending still farther N (Nuseiri or Ansariya Mts).

This ridge is marked by a series of peaks. From S to N, the principal ones are Gebel Rihan, Tomat

LEAD
See Mining, Part 2.

LEAGUE
See Weights and measures, Part 3.

LEAH TRIBES
See Tribes of Israel, Part 3.

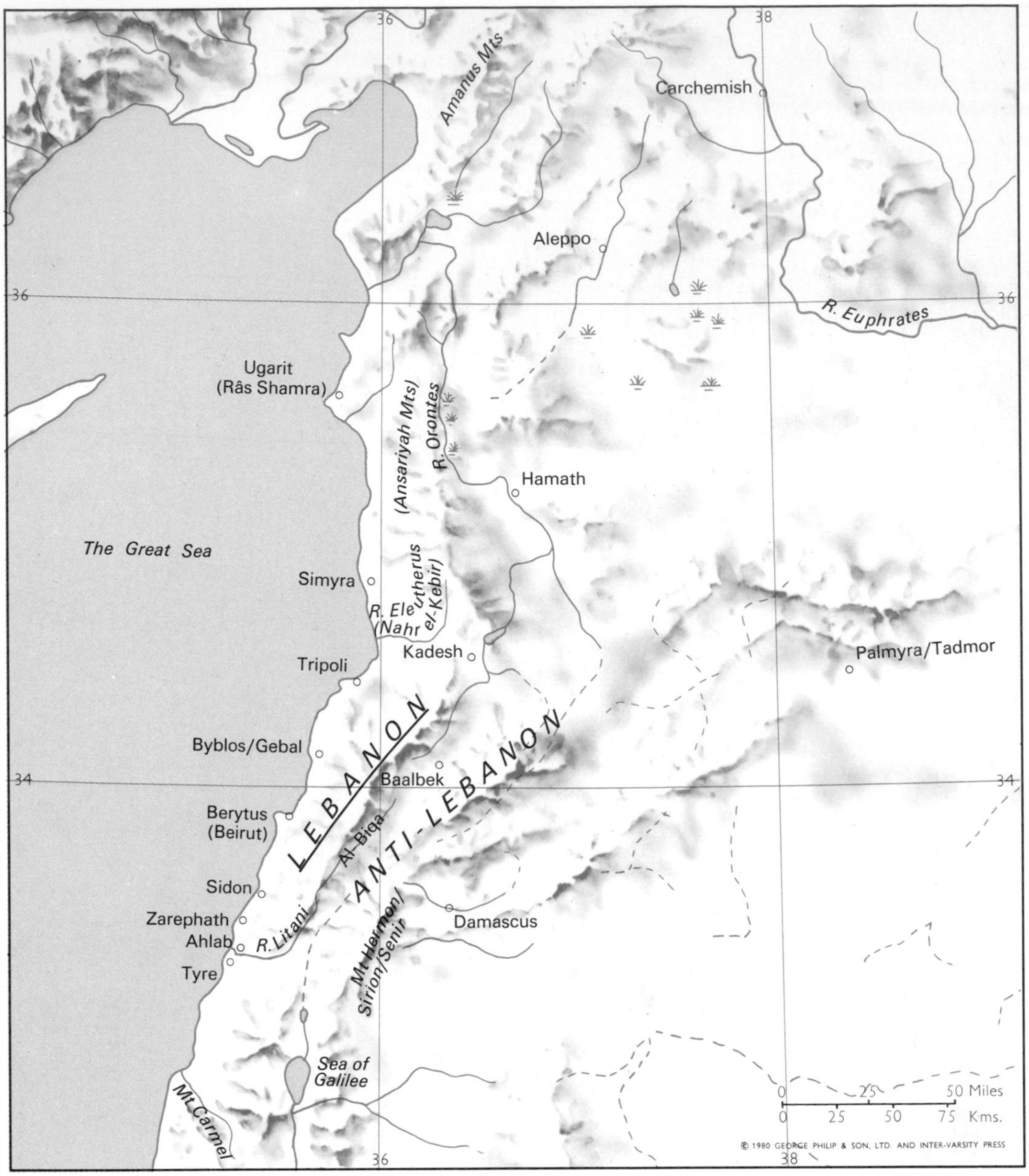

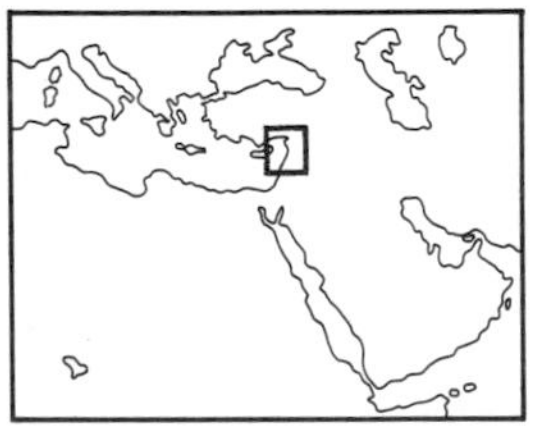

The Lebanon range of mountains.

and Gebel Niha (from over 1,630 m high to nearly 1,900 m) behind Sidon; Gebel Baruk, Gebel Kuneiyiseh and Gebel Sunnin (*c.* 2,200 m, 2,100 m and 2,600 m high respectively) behind Beirut; Qurnet es-Sauda, the highest at about 3,000 m, ESE of Tripoli; N is Qurnet Aruba, *c.* 2,230 m high. These high mountains and the coastal strip have a good rainfall, but in the 'rain-shadow' area Damascus and the N half of the Biqā' plain have less than 25 cm a year and must depend on stream water.

The W flanks of this range sweep right down to the Mediterranean, leaving only a narrow coastal plain for the Canaanite/Phoenician cities, and sometimes reach the sea, roads having had to be cut by man round such headlands. Typical of these is the headland of the Nahr el-Kelb just N of Beirut. The E flanks of Lebanon descend into the Biqā'. This plain, or broad vale, is highest in the vicinity of Baalbek, and it is the 'valley (*biq'aṯ*) of Lebanon' of Jos. 11:17. It descends N with the Orontes and S with the Litani and headwater streams of the Jordan. It is the classical *Coelesyria ('Hollow Syria') and is bounded along its E side by the corresponding mountain range of Anti-Lebanon. This latter range also runs from SW to NE and is broken in two by the plateau from which the Barada river descends E to water the incredibly rich oasis of Damascus. The highest peak is Mt Hermon (over 2,750 m) in the S half of the range. The structure of the whole region is clearly expressed in the diagram of D. Baly, *Geography of the Bible*, 1957, p. 11, fig. 3. For routes connecting the Biqā', Anti-Lebanon and Damascus, see *ibid.*, pp. 110–111.

Mt Hermon in Anti-Lebanon was called Sirion by the Sidonians (*i.e.* Phoenicians), and Senir by the Amorites (Dt. 3:9). Both names are independently attested in antiquity. Senir is mentioned as Saniru by Shalmaneser III of Assyria in 841 BC (*ANET*, p. 280b; *DOTT*, p. 48). Besides a Hittite mention of Sirion as Sariyana about 1320 BC (*ANET*, p. 205a), the use of the name Sirion for Hermon by the Canaanites/Phoenicians is confirmed by the Ugaritic texts of the 14th/13th centuries BC that picture Lebanon and Sirion as yielding timber for Baal's temple (*ANET*, p. 134a, § vi). Hermon is often thought to be the 'many-peaked mountain, mountain of Bashan' in Ps. 68:15; but Baly (*op. cit.*, pp. 194, 220, 222) suggests that it could equally well be the impressive peaks of the Gebel Druze. (*BASHAN, *HERMON, *SENIR, *SIRION.)

The biblical writers sometimes define the promised land in general terms as extending 'from the wilderness and Lebanon and from the River . . . Euphrates to the western sea' (Dt. 11:24; Jos. 1:4), *i.e.* within these S–N and E–W limits. For the Phoenician coastal cities, the Lebanon mountain ridge formed a natural barrier to invaders from inland. The Assyrian king Shamshi-Adad I reached Lab'an in the 18th century BC (*ANET*, p. 274b) and the Hittite emperor Suppiluliuma made it his SW boundary in the 14th century BC (Mt Niblani, *ANET*, p. 318b), without their disturbing the coastal cities to any extent.

III. Resources

Lebanon was above all famous for its former dense forest cover. The ample November and March rainfall and limestone ridges gave rise to many springs and streams flowing down to E and W (Ct. 4:15; Je. 18:14). The coastland, Biqā', and lower mountain-slopes support garden-cultivation, olive-groves, vineyards, fruit-orchards (mulberries, figs, apples, apricots, walnuts) and small cornfields (Rawlinson, *Phoenicia*, p. 17). Higher still rises the forest-cover of myrtles and conifers, culminating in the groves of mighty cedars, of which, alas, only one or two isolated groves survive (because of excessive deforestation), the main one being at Bsharreh SE of Tripoli (picture in L. H. Grollenberg, *Shorter Atlas of the Bible*, 1959, p. 13). The fertility and fruitfulness of the Lebanon region is reflected in scriptures such as Ps. 72:16; Ct. 4:11; Ho. 14:5–7, as well as in early inscriptions (Tuthmosis III, 5th and 7th campaigns, 15th century BC, *ANET*, p. 239a and b). Wild beasts also lurked there (*e.g.* 2 Ki. 14:9; Ct. 4:8).

The mighty cedars were apt symbols of majesty and strength in biblical imagery; *cf.* Jdg. 9:15; 1 Ki. 4:33; 2 Ki. 14:9 (= 2 Ch. 25:18); Pss. 92:12; 104:16; Ct. 5:15; Is. 35:2; 60:13. They were also symbols of earthly pride subject to divine wrath; *cf.* Ps. 29:5–6; Is. 2:13; 10:34; Je. 22:6; Ezk. 31:3–14; Zc. 11:1–2. These forests afforded a refuge (Je. 22:23). But above all, Lebanon's cedars and conifers (firs, cypresses, *etc.*) furnished the finest building timber in the ancient East, sought by the rulers of Egypt, Mesopotamia and Syria-Palestine alike. The most celebrated of such deliveries of timber were those sent to Solomon by Hiram I of Tyre for the Temple at Jerusalem (1 Ki. 5:6, 9, 14 (= 2 Ch. 2:8, 16); 7:2; 10:17, 21 (= 2 Ch. 9:20)). For the price in foodstuffs paid by Solomon for his timber, *etc.*, see *FOOD (Solomon's palace food-supplies). The firs of Lebanon and Anti-Lebanon (Sirion) provided ships for Tyre (Ezk. 27:5) and sacred barges for Egypt (*ANET*, pp. 25b, 27a; *c.* 1090 BC), as well as furniture (Ct. 3:9). Wood for the second Jerusalem Temple was also cut in Lebanon (Ezr. 3:7).

Snow-capped mountain ridges in the Lebanon with cedars at Kadesh. (MEPhA)

IV. History

The history of Lebanon is essentially that of the Phoenician cities on its littoral and the story of the exploitation of its splendid timber. From S to N, the Canaanite/Phoenician cities of Tyre, Ahlab, Zarephath, Sidon, Beirut, Byblos (Gebal, modern Jebail) and Simyra (N of Tripoli) all had the wealth of the Lebanon as their hinterland besides their maritime trade. For their detailed histories (except Beirut and Simyra), see separate articles; see also *CANAAN and *PHOENICIA.

The Lebanon timber-trade goes back to the earliest times. The 4th Dynasty pharaoh Snofru fetched forty shiploads of cedars as early as *c.* 2600 BC (*ANET*, p. 227a), and various of his successors followed suit in later centuries. Byblos in particular became virtually an Egyptian dependency and its princes thoroughly assimilated to Egyptian culture, even writing their Semitic names in hieroglyphs (*cf. ANET*, p. 229a). In exchange for timber, they received handsome gold jewellery from the 12th Dynasty pharaohs (*c.* 1900–1800 BC).

When the New Kingdom pharaohs conquered Syria they exacted a regular annual tribute of 'genuine cedar of Lebanon' (*ANET*, p. 240b: Tuthmosis III, *c.* 1460 BC), and a relief of Sethos I (*c.* 1300 BC) actually depicts the Syrian princes hewing down the timbers of Lebanon for the pharaoh (*ANEP*, p. 110, fig. 331, or Grollenberg, *Shorter Atlas of the Bible*, p. 14; *cf. ANET*, p. 254, § c, end). In later days (20th Dynasty) the pharaohs had to pay handsomely for such timber (*cf.*

Cedar trees in the Lebanon hills. (RS)

LEBBAEUS
See Thaddaeus, Part 3.

LECTURE HALL
See Tyrannus, Part 3.

LEECH
See Animals, Part 1.

LEEKS
See Vegetables, Part 3.

LEGATE
See Province, Part 3.

Cedars of Lebanon being felled by Syrian princes at the command of the Egyptian King Sethos I. Relief from N wall, Great Hall, Karnak, Egypt. c. 1300 BC. (BPK)

Solomon), as Wenamun, envoy of Rameses XI, found to his cost (*ANET*, p. 27a).

From Canaan itself in the 2nd millennium BC, the Ugaritic epics about Baal and Anath and Aqhat allude to 'Lebanon and its trees; Sirion, its choice cedars' providing timber for the house (*i.e.* temple) of Baal (*ANET*, p. 134a, § vi; C. H. Gordon, *Ugaritic Literature*, 1949, p. 34), and furnishing material for a bow (*ANET*, p. 151b, § vi; Gordon, *op. cit.*, p. 90).

The Assyrians, too, exacted a tribute of timber from Lebanon for temple-building—so Tiglath-pileser I, *c.* 1100 BC (*ANET*, p. 275a) and Esarhaddon about 675 BC (*ANET*, p. 291b)—but also often drew upon the Amanus forests farther N (*ANET*, pp. 276b, 278a); *cf.* here, 2 Ki. 19:23; Is. 37:24. Nebuchadrezzar followed their example (*ANET*, p. 307; *DOTT*, p. 87). Habakkuk (2:17) refers to Babylonian despoliation of Lebanon, which was also foreseen by Isaiah (14:8).

BIBLIOGRAPHY. In addition to works already cited above for particular points, see also P. K. Hitti, *Lebanon in History*, 1957, and his *History of Syria with Lebanon and Palestine*, 1951, and J. P. Brown, *The Lebanon and Phoenicia*, 1, 1969 (on ancient sources). K.A.K.
A.K.C.

LEB-KAMAI. An artificial word (Je. 51:1, RV), formed by the device known as Athbash (explained under * SHESHACH). The Heb. consonants *l-b-q-m-y* really represent *k-ś-d-y-m, i.e. kaśdîm*, 'Chaldeans'; *cf.* RSVmg. The vowels added by the Massoretes give the word a quasi-meaning, 'the heart of those that rise up against me' (*cf.* RVmg.). The verse mentions Babylon openly, so the device is here word-play rather than cipher. NEB with some scholars prefers to emend the text. D.F.P.

LEES (Heb. *š^{e}mārîm*, 'preserves', Is. 25:6; Je. 48:11; Zp. 1:12). The dregs at the bottom of wine-jars. See * WINE AND STRONG DRINK, and an excellent comprehensive article under 'Shemarim' in Kitto, *A Cyclopaedia of Biblical Literature*. The expression is used only figuratively in the OT. J.D.D.

LEG. 1. Heb. *k^{e}rā'ayim* occurs chiefly in ritual passages, *e.g.* Ex. 12:9; 29:17; Lv. 1:9, 13; 4:11, *etc.* In Lv. 11:21 it describes the bending hind-legs of locusts permitted for food, and provides an illustration of judgment in Am. 3:12.

2. *reḡel* normally means foot but is used of Goliath's legs in 1 Sa. 17:6.

3. *šôq* means the upper leg, and is synonymous with 'thigh'. It is used of men in Dt. 28:35; Ps. 147:10; Pr. 26:7; Ct. 5:15; Is. 47:2; Dn. 2:33. In Jdg. 15:8 it is translated 'hip'. It is also used with reference to animals. In several ritual passages, *e.g.* Ex. 29:22, 27; Lv. 7:32–34; 8:25–26; Nu. 6:20, *etc.*, it is translated 'thigh' in RSV, while in 1 Sa. 9:24 RSV translates as 'leg'. This was one of the choicest pieces of the animal, normally reserved for priests.

4. *šōḇel* is incorrectly translated 'leg' in AV of Is. 47:2 (RSV 'robe').

5. Gk. *skelos* occurs only in Jn. 19:31ff., when the legs of those crucified with Jesus were broken to hasten death. J.G.G.N.

LEGION. Gk. *legeōn* (from Lat. *legio*), used four times in the NT, was the main division of the Roman army and comprised between 4,000 and 6,000 men. It was divided into ten cohorts and these in turn into six centuries each. Sometimes a small cavalry division (*ala*) of about 120 was attached. In the 1st century AD three or four legions were normally on duty in Syria, but Palestine saw very few legionaries until the beginning of the first Jewish rebellion in AD 66; previously the policing had been done by auxiliary cohorts. The word is used in the NT to suggest a very great number, as in Mt. 26:53 (of angels) and in Mk. 5:9, 15; Lk. 8:30 (of the demons possessing the Gerasene demoniac). R.P.G.

LEHABIM. The third son of Mizraim (Gn. 10:13; 1 Ch. 1:11). The name (Heb. *l^{e}hāḇîm*) is unknown

Replica of a tile marked with the stamp of the Roman 10th Legion. Its task in Palestine, after the destruction of the Temple in AD 70, included preventing Jews from gaining access to the ruins. Original found in Jerusalem. (RP)

The 22nd Roman Legion was commanded by Caelius, depicted here on a grave stele. 1st cent. AD. (RS)

apart from these references, but many scholars would equate it with *lûḇîm* of 2 Ch. 12:3, *etc.* (* LUBIM), which is generally identified as referring to the Libyans. In support of this is the LXX reading *Labieim* and the fact that these people, who figure in the ancient Egyp. inscriptions as *rbw*, are not elsewhere mentioned in Gn. 10, unless *lûḏîm* (v. 13) is to be read for *lûḇîm*, as some scholars hold (* LUD, LUDIM). The matter therefore remains uncertain. T.C.M.

LEHI (Heb. *lᵉḥî*, *leḥî*, 'jawbone', Jdg. 15:9, 14, 19; 'Ramath-lehi' in Jdg. 15:17). The place in Judah where Samson slew 1,000 men with the jawbone of an ass. The site is unknown, but see F. F. Bruce, in *NBCR*, p. 271. J.D.D.

LEMUEL. King of * Massa, whose mother's instructions concerning good government and the dangers of sensuality and overindulgence in wine are recorded in Pr. 31:1–9. Modern scholars have not generally accepted the rabbinic tradition, which says that Lemuel and the names in Pr. 30:1 are attributes of Solomon, an attempt to credit Proverbs entirely to Solomon (*cf.* L. Ginzberg, *The Legends of the Jews*, 6, 1946, p. 277). See W. McKane, *Proverbs*, 1970, pp. 407–412. D.A.H.

LEVI. The third son of Jacob and Leah (Gn. 29:34). The name (Heb. *lēwî*) is here linked with the root *lāwâ* (to join), and a play upon this meaning is found in Nu. 18:2, 4.

The only detail of his life known to us, apart from those events common to all Jacob's sons, is his treacherous attack on Shechem in company with Simeon (Gn. 34:25–26). It should in fairness be noted that the natural meaning of Gn. 34:13, 27 is that the two brothers were acting with the connivance of all. The two were specially concerned because Dinah was their full sister. The two lads could carry out the massacre with the help of their father's slaves.

It has almost universally been taken for granted that Gn. 49:5–7 refers to this incident, but this is most doubtful. There is no validity in the versional variation in the last clause of v. 6 represented by AV, 'they digged down a wall'; the Heb. 'they houghed an ox' (RV) is seem-

LENDING
See Debt, Part 1.

LENTILS
See Vegetables (Leeks), Part 3.

LEONTOPOLIS
See Ptolemy, Part 3.

LEOPARD
See Animals, Part 1.

ingly contradicted by Gn. 34:28. It is better to take the tenses in v. 6 as 'perfects of experience' and render, 'For in their anger they slay men, and in their wantonness they hamstring oxen' (RSV). They are cursed for a life of violence and cruelty in which Shechem was merely an early and outstanding example. Later history was to show that the loyalty of Levi's descendants to Yahweh could turn the curse to a blessing, and their division and scattering in Israel was as his representatives. None the less, the curse seems to have hit Levi very heavily. The total census figure in Nu. 3:22, 28, 34 of males from a month upward is strikingly below all the tribal figures in Nu. 1 of males from 20 years upwards. No indication is given how this happened. Levi seems to have had only three sons, Gershon, Kohath and Merari, all born before he went down with Jacob to Egypt.

Modern critical scholarship has questioned the biblical account of the origin of the tribe of Levi in various ways, but most of them have by now fallen into disfavour. We need mention only the conjecture of Lagarde that the Levites were those Egyptians that 'joined themselves' to the Israelites at the Exodus, and that of Baudissin that they were those 'joined to', *i.e.* escorting, the ark—in other words priestly servants. Much more important is Hommel's linking of *lēwî* with *lawi'a*, meaning 'priest', in Minaean N Arabian inscriptions. The facts and a valuable discussion will be found in G. B. Gray, *Sacrifice in the Old Testament*, pp. 242–245. He points out that the Minaeans *might* have borrowed the term from Israel. In fact, an overwhelming majority of scholars agree that Gn. 49:5–7 is proof positive that Levi must have originated as a secular tribe. The mention of Aaron as 'the Levite' in Ex. 4:14 is difficult, perhaps best explained as a later scribal addition.

For Levi the son of Alphaeus, one of the Twelve (Mk. 2:13), see *MATTHEW. The name also occurs twice in the genealogy of our Lord (Lk. 3:24, 29). H.L.E.

LEVIATHAN is a transliteration of a Heb. word which occurs in only five passages in the OT. It is generally thought to be from a root *lāwâ*, *cf.* Arab. *lawā*, 'bend', 'twist'. Its literal meaning would then be 'wreathed', *i.e.* 'gathering itself in folds'. Some scholars have suggested that it may be a foreign loan-word, possibly of Bab. origin. The context of its use in the OT indicates some form of aquatic monster. In Ps. 104:26 it is clearly of the sea and is generally thought to be the whale, although the dolphin has been suggested. It is used twice symbolically in Is. 27:1, referring to the empires of Assyria (the 'fleeing' serpent is the swift-flowing Tigris) and Babylonia (the 'twisting' serpent is the Euphrates). In Ps. 74:14 it occurs in reference to Pharaoh and the Exodus in parallel with the Heb. *tannîn*, 'sea or river monster'. This word occurs again in Ezk. 29:3–5 symbolically of Pharaoh and the Egyptians, where the description of its scales and jaws makes it clear that the crocodile is intended.

Leviathan is referred to twice in Job. In 3:8 it is generally held to be the dragon which, according to popular ancient mythology, was supposed to cause eclipses by wrapping its coils around the sun. The longest description of Leviathan occupies Jb. 41:1–34, and most scholars agree that here the creature is the crocodile (*ANIMALS). Some have objected that the crocodile would not have been described as unapproachable and that there is no reference in the OT to crocodiles in Palestine. However, the author probably had in mind the crocodile of the Nile, and the description of the creature's invincibility is rhetorical. The only alternative interpretation of any significance regards Leviathan as a mythical monster, perhaps to be identified with the Bab. mother goddess Tiamat (father Apsu) who, in the Creation Epic, even in battle against Marduk 'recites charms and casts spells'. The word is cognate with Ugaritic *ltn*, the seven-headed monster whose description as 'the fleeing serpent, . . . the tortuous serpent' smitten by Baal is so reminiscent of the language of Is. 27:1.

BIBLIOGRAPHY. C. F. Pfeiffer, 'Lotan and Leviathan', *EQ* 32, 1960, pp. 208ff.; J. N. Oswalt, 'The Myth of the Dragon and OT Faith', *EQ* 49, 1977, pp. 163ff. D.G.S.

LEVITICUS, BOOK OF. The third book of the Pentateuch is referred to in Jewish usage as *wayyiqrā'* ('and he called'), this being the word with which it begins in Hebrew. In the Mishnah the book is variously named *tôra̱t kôhanîm*, 'priests' law', *sēp̄er kôhanîm*, 'priests' book', *tôra̱t haqqorbānîm*, 'law of the offerings'; these names refer to the contents of the book. In the LXX it is called *Leueitikon* or *Leuitikon* (*sc. biblion*), 'the Levitical (book)'. The Latin Vulg. entitles it *Leviticus* (*sc. liber*), which similarly means 'the Levitical (book)'; in some Latin MSS the name appears as *Leviticum*. The Peshitta calls it 'the book of the priests'.

It can be objected to the name Leviticus that the book has much less to do with Levites than with priests. But the priests in question are levitical priests (*cf.* Heb. 7:11, 'the Levitical priesthood'). The name Leviticus indicates clearly enough that the book has to do with the cult; this name may indeed have been chosen because 'Levitical' was understood in the sense of 'cultic' or 'ritual'.

I. Outline of contents

Leviticus consists mainly of laws. The historical framework in which these laws are set is Israel's residence at Sinai. The book may be divided as follows:

a. Laws concerning offerings (1:1–7:38).

b. The tabernacle service put into operation (8:1–10:20).

c. Laws concerning purity and impurity (11:1–15:33).

d. The great Day of Atonement (16:1–34).

e. Various laws (17:1–25:55).

f. Promises and warnings (26:1–46).

g. Appendix: valuation and redemption (27:1–34).

As may be seen from this outline, the contents consist largely of ritual law. At the same time it must be noted that the intention is to continue the narrative of Israel's experiences at Sinai. This is evident from the first words of the book, and from the repeated formula 'And the Lord said to Moses' (1:1; 4:1; 5:14, *et passim*), with which we should compare 'And the Lord spoke to Aaron' (10:8) and 'And the Lord said to Moses and Aaron' (11:1; *cf.* 13:1, *etc.*). The historical setting must not be forgotten. As part of the complete Pentateuch, the book occupies its own place in the Pentateuchal narrative.

At Mt Sinai the nation of Israel is equipped for its task, a task stated in the words 'And you shall be to me a kingdom of priests and a holy nation' (Ex. 19:6). Israel had already had committed to it the Decalogue, the Book of the Covenant and the regulations with regard to the tabernacle. This dwelling-place for the Lord had already been set up in the midst of the camp (Ex. 40). It is possible that the laws concerning the offerings (Lv. 1–7) once existed as a separate unit (*cf.* 7:35–38). But they fit very well into the Pentateuchal context in which they now appear. The history of sacrificial offerings, about which the book of Leviticus provides such important information, and in which Christians ought to take a special interest because we know how perfectly their inmost significance was fulfilled by the obedience of Jesus Christ, begins as early in the Pentateuch as Gn. 4:3–5. There are also other passages in the Pentateuch before the book of Leviticus in which sacrifices and offerings are mentioned. But in Leviticus the Lord regulates the whole sacrificial service and institutes a special form of it as a means of atonement for Israel. Lv. 17:11 states the reason for the ban upon eating blood ('the life of the flesh is in the blood'); the ban has already been imposed in 3:17 and 7:26f., but in neither of these places is the reason for it explicitly stated. It is in the light of 17:11 that the shedding of blood and sprinkling with blood prescribed in chs. 1–7 must be viewed. This is an indication of the unity of the book.

Another indication of its unity is the fact that 17:11 prepares us for the transition to the regulations regarding impurity, which come up for detailed treatment in chs. 11–15. Similarly, 10:10 looks forward to the transition to the detailed distinctions between clean and unclean which we have in ch. 11. Viewed in the light of the whole book of Leviticus, the laws concerning purity and impurity point to the necessity laid upon Israel to keep sin at a distance. It is sin which brings about separation between the Lord and his people, so that they have to approach him through the mediation of sacrifice (chs. 1–7) and priesthood (chs. 8–10). Lv. 16:1 follows close on 15:31 and refers back to 10:1f. In 20:25 we have a clear allusion to the law concerning clean and unclean animals in ch. 11; and this verse provides a closer link between the commandments of chs. 18–20 and those of chs. 11–15. This does not support the view of those who accept the existence at one time of a separate Holiness Code, preserved for us in chs. 17–26. In 21:1–22:16 expressions like those of 11:44f.; 19:2; 20:7 are repeated with reference to the priests (*e.g.* 21:8, 'I the Lord, who sanctify you, am holy'). Lv. 25:1 states that the words which follow were revealed to Moses on Mt Sinai, just as is stated of the laws summarized in 7:37f.

In the form in which we now possess Leviticus, it forms a well-knit and coherent whole. The historical portion is larger than one might think at first sight (*cf.* 10:1–7; 24:10–23; chs. 8–10 and the formula 'And the Lord said to Moses').

Attention is also paid to marriage and chastity, the sanctification of daily life, and Israel's attitude to the commandments of her God (*cf.* 18:3–5, 30; 19:1–3, 18, 37; 20:26; 22:31–33; 26 [illegible]).

In view of the character of its contents throughout, we can call Leviticus 'the book of the holiness of Yahweh', whose fundamental requirement is 'You shall be holy to me: for I the Lord am holy' (20:26).

II. Authorship and composition

The author of Leviticus is not named in the book. Yahweh does indeed speak repeatedly to Moses, to Moses and Aaron, or to Aaron; but no command is given to make a written record of what he says. We owe the contents of the book to divine revelation given at Sinai in the time of Moses (*cf.* 7:37f.; 26:46; 27:34); but that does not settle the question of the authorship of Leviticus. Moses is not named as the author of any single part of the book, as he is named with regard to certain sections of Exodus (*cf.* Ex. 17:14; 24:4; 34:27). It may be that a later writer set in order the Mosaic material of which Leviticus consists. It may equally well be that Moses himself set it in order in the form which has been handed down to us.

The question of authorship is bound up with the whole problem of the composition of the Pentateuch. Leviticus is commonly assigned to P (the Priestly Code). The objections to this documentary hypothesis in general are equally valid as regards their application to Leviticus. The name 'Holiness Code', given to Lv. 17–26, is due to August Klostermann, who in 1877 wrote for the *Zeitschrift für lutherische Theologie* an article entitled 'Ezechiel und das Heiligkeitsgesetz' ('Ezekiel and the Law of Holiness'), which was reprinted in his book *Der Pentateuch: Beiträge zu seinem Verständnis und seiner Entstehungsgeschichte* (*The Pentateuch: Contributions to its understanding and the history of its composition*), 1893, pp. 368–418. The name 'Holiness Code' came into wide vogue; many found it especially apt because of the explicit and repeated emphasis on holiness and sanctification in 19:2; 20:7–8, 26; 21:6–8, 15, 23; 22:9, 16, 32. It is not possible to debate the whole question here; reference should be made to the case for the separate existence of H, based upon distinctive features of style and language, as presented, *e.g.*, in S. R. Driver, *LOT*, pp. 47ff. A close relationship is pointed out between H and Ezekiel; indeed, some have seen in Ezekiel himself the author or redactor of H, while others hold the view that Ezekiel was acquainted with H. But the majority opinion is that H is earlier than Ezekiel.

None of the arguments for the view that Lv. 17–26 should be regarded as a separate law-code seems to be conclusive. We must not forget that here as elsewhere the investigator of the OT is greatly influenced by the attitude which he adopts to Holy Scripture as the Word of God. For example, the argument that Lv. 26 must be dated in the time of the Exile, because this exile is foretold in that chapter, is far from doing justice to divine revelation. The absence of a special superscription at the head of Lv. 17 is best explained by the view that here the book of Leviticus continues quite ordinarily.

III. Significance

Leviticus is a book of great significance from many points of view.

First of all, it provides us with a background to all the other books of the Bible. If we wish to understand references to sacrificial offerings and ceremonies of purification, or institutions such as the sabbatical year or the year of jubilee, it is this book that we must consult.

In the second place, it is of interest from a general religious viewpoint. Thanks especially to archaeological excavation, we can compare the institutions dealt with in Leviticus with those of other people, *e.g.* the Phoenicians, Canaanites, Egyptians, Assyrians, Babylonians and Hittites.

In the third place, orthodox Jews have to this day found their binding regulations—*e.g.* with regard to food—in this book. Hoffmann, a Jewish exegete of Leviticus, points out that other confessions which draw upon the OT chiefly select Genesis as the subject of their study, while Jews pay special attention to Leviticus.

Fourthly, Leviticus proclaims to us who are Christians the way in which the God of Israel combats sin in Israel. He combats it by means of his institutions of sacrifice and purification—social sin by means of the sabbatical year and year of jubilee, sexual sins by means of the laws of chastity—and also by means of his promises and warnings. And in this combating of sin the book of Leviticus presents to us Christ as the means of atonement, the means of purification, the great Priest, Prophet and Teacher, the King who rules us through his ordinances. That is the abiding significance of Leviticus. It is the book of sanctification, of the consecration of life (the burnt-offering stands in the forefront of the book), the book of the avoidance and atonement of sin, the combating and removal of sin among the people of the Lord. The Day of Atonement occupies a central place in it (Lv. 16); the ceremony of the two goats prescribed for that day reminds us that 'as far as the east is from the west, so far does he remove our transgressions from us' (Ps. 103:12). (*LAW.)

BIBLIOGRAPHY. A. A. Bonar, *Commentary on Leviticus*[4], 1861, reprinted 1959; S. H. Kellogg, *The Book of Leviticus*, *EB*, 1891; S. R. Driver and H. A. White, *The Book of Leviticus*, 1898; A. T. Chapman and A. W. Streane, *The Book of Leviticus*, *CBSC*, 1914; W. H. Gispen, *Het Boek Leviticus*, 1950; N. Micklem, *Leviticus*, *IB*, 2, 1955; H. Cazelles, *Le Lévitique, Bible de Jérusalem*, 2, 1958; L. G. Vink, *Léviticus*, 1962; J. L. Mays, *LBC*, 1963; K. Elliger, *HAT*, 1966; N. H. Snaith, *NCB*, 1967; M. Noth, *Leviticus*, E.T. 1968; W. Kornfeld, *Das Buch Leviticus*, 1972; B. Maarsingh, *Leviticus*, 1974; A. Ibáñez Arana, *El Levitico*, 1975; G. J. Wenham, *Leviticus*, 1978. W.H.G.

LIBERTINES. The Gk. of Acts 6:9 makes it difficult to determine whether the *Libertinoi*, the members of a Jewish synagogue at Jerusalem, worshipped by themselves or with the Cyrenians, the Alexandrians, the Cilicians and the Asiatics. The meaning of the name is equally uncertain, and this has given rise to a number of variants for this verse (notably the reading 'Libyans' for 'Libertines', which appears in the Armenian vss and the Syriac). Schürer suggests that the Libertines were Rom. freedmen (Lat. *libertini*, from which the Gk. word is borrowed) descended from Jews who had been prisoners of war under Pompey (63 BC) and subsequently released. Possibly only one synagogue is referred to here (then *kai Kyrēnaiōn . . . Asias* is epexegetic of *Libertinōn*), which was attended by Jewish freedmen or their descendants from the places mentioned (so F. F. Bruce, *The Acts of the Apostles*[2], 1952, p. 156). S.S.S.

LIBERTY. The biblical idea of liberty (freedom) has as its background the thought of imprisonment or slavery. Rulers would imprison those whom they regarded as wrongdoers (Gn. 39:20); a conquered nation might be enslaved by its conqueror, or a prisoner of war by his captor, or an individual might, like Joseph, be sold into slavery. When the Bible speaks of liberty, a prior bondage or incarceration is always implied. Liberty means the happy state of having been released from servitude for a life of enjoyment and satisfaction that was not possible before. The idea of liberty appears in Scripture in its ordinary secular application (*e.g.* Ps. 105:20; Acts 26:32); but it also receives a significant theological development. This sprang from Israel's realization that such freedom from subjugation by foreigners as she enjoyed was God's gift to her. In the NT liberty becomes an important theological concept for describing salvation.

I. Israel's liberty

At the Exodus God set Israel free from bondage in Egypt, in order that henceforth the nation might serve him as his covenant people (Ex. 19:3ff.; 20:1ff.; Lv. 25:55; *cf.* Is. 43:21). He brought them into the 'land flowing with milk and honey' (Ex. 3:8; *cf.* Nu. 14:7ff.; Dt. 8:7ff.), settled them there, and undertook to maintain them in political independence and economic prosperity as long as they eschewed idolatry and kept his laws (Dt. 28:1–14). This meant that Israel's freedom would not depend upon her own efforts in either the military or the political realm, but on the quality of her obedience to God. Her freedom was a supernatural blessing, Yahweh's gracious gift to his own covenant people; unmerited and, apart from him, unattainable in the first instance, and now maintained only through his continued favour. Disobedience, whether in the form of religious impiety or social injustice, would result in the loss of freedom. God would judge his people by national disaster and enslavement (Dt. 28:25, 47ff.; *cf.* Jdg. 2:14ff.; 3:7ff., 12ff.; 4:1ff.; 6:1ff.); he would raise up hostile powers against them, and would ultimately cause them to be deported into a land where no tokens of his favour could be expected (Dt. 28:64ff.; Am. 5; 2 Ki. 17:6–23; *cf.* Ps. 137:1–4).

The structure of the theological idea of liberty is here fully evident. Liberty, as the OT conceives it, means, on the one hand, deliverance from created forces that would keep men from serving and enjoying their Creator, and, on the other hand, the positive happiness of living in fellowship with God under his covenant in the place where he is pleased to manifest himself and to bless. Liberty is *from* slavery to powers that oppose God *for* the fulfilment of his claims upon one's life. Liberty is not man's own achievement, but a free gift of grace, something which apart from God's action man does not possess at all. In its continuance, liberty is a covenant blessing, something which God has promised to maintain as long as his people are faithful. Liberty does not mean independence of God; it is precisely in God's service that man finds his perfect freedom. Man can enjoy release from bondage to the created only through bondage to his Creator. Thus, the way that God sets men free from their captors and enemies is to make them his own slaves. He frees them by bringing them to himself (Ex. 19:4).

The Isaianic prophecies of the release from captivity and the restoration of Jerusalem gave added religious content to the idea of liberty by stressing that these events would herald a new and unprecedented experience of joyful and satisfying fellowship with Israel's gracious God (Is. 35:3–10; 43:14–44:5; 45:14–17; 49:8–50:3; 51:17–52:12; 54; 61:1ff., *etc.*; *cf.* Ezk. 36:16–36; 37:15–28).

Since all members of the liberated nation were, as such, God's servants (Lv. 25:42, 55), Israelites who through pressure of poverty sold themselves into household service were not to be treated like foreign slaves, as mere property, in their master's hereditary possession (Lv. 25:44ff.). Every 7th year they were to be released (unless they had voluntarily chosen to make their service permanent) in memory of God's release of Israel from Egyptian bondage (Dt. 15:12ff.). Every 50th year, in addition to a release of Israelite servants, alienated land was also to revert to its hereditary owner (Lv. 25:10). Jeremiah denounced the people because, having thus 'proclaimed liberty' for Hebrew servants, they went back on it (Je. 34:8–17).

II. The Christian's liberty

The full development of the idea of liberty appears in the Gospels and Pauline Epistles, where the enemies from whom God through Christ liberates his people are revealed to be sin, Satan, the law and death.

Christ's public ministry was one of liberation. He opened it by announcing himself as the fulfilment of Is. 61:1: '. . . he has anointed me . . . to proclaim release to the captives' (Lk. 4:16ff.). Ignoring Zealot hankerings after a national liberation from Rome, Christ declared that he had come to set Israelites free from the state of slavery to sin and Satan in which he found them (Jn. 8:34–36, 41–44). He had come, he said, to overthrow 'the prince of this world', the 'strong man', and to release his prisoners (Jn. 12:31f.; Mk. 3:27; Lk. 10:17f.). Exorcisms (Mk. 3:22ff.) and healings (Lk. 13:16) were part of this work of dispossession. Christ appealed to these (Lk. 11:20; *cf.* Mt. 12:28) as proof positive of the coming among men of the *kingdom of God (*i.e.* the promised eschatological state in which men effectively receive God's forgiveness and salvation and are effectively made subject to his will).

Paul makes much of the thought that Christ liberates believers, here and now, from destructive influences to which they were previously in bondage: from sin, the tyrannical overlord whose wages for services rendered is death (Rom. 6:18–23); from the law as a system of salvation, which stirred sin up and gave it its strength (Gal. 4:21ff.; 5:1; Rom. 6:14; 7:5–13; 8:2; 1 Cor. 15:56); from the demonic 'power of darkness' (Col. 1:13); from polytheistic superstition (1 Cor. 10:29; Gal. 4:8); and from the burden of Jewish ceremonialism (Gal. 2:4). To all this, Paul affirms, freedom from the remaining partial bondages to indwelling sin (Rom. 7:14, 23), and from physical corruption and death, will in due course be added (Rom. 8:18–21).

This freedom, in all its aspects, is the gift of Christ, who by death bought his people out of bondage (1 Cor. 6:20; 7:22f.). (There may be an allusion here to the legal fiction by which Greek deities 'bought' slaves for their manumission.) Present freedom from the law, sin and death is conveyed to believers by the Spirit, who unites them to Christ through faith (Rom. 8:2; 2 Cor. 3:17). Liberation brings with it adoption (Gal. 4:5); those set free from guilt become sons of God, and receive the Spirit of Christ as a Spirit of adoption, assuring them that they are in truth God's sons and heirs (Gal. 4:6f.; Rom. 8:15f.).

Man's response to the divine gift of liberty (*eleutheria*), and indeed the very means of his receiving it, is a free acceptance of bondservice (*douleia*) to God (Rom. 6:17–22), to Christ (1 Cor. 7:22), to righteousness (Rom. 6:18), and to all men for the sake of the gospel (1 Cor. 9:19–23) and of the saviour (2 Cor. 4:5). Christian liberty is neither an abolishing of responsibility nor a sanctioning of licence. The Christian is no longer 'under law' (Rom. 6:14) for salvation, but he is not therefore 'without law toward God' (1 Cor. 9:21). The divine law, as interpreted and exemplified by Christ himself, remains a standard expressing Christ's will for his own freed bondservants (1 Cor. 7:22). Christians are thus 'under the law of Christ' (1 Cor. 9:21). The 'law of Christ' (Gal. 6:2)—James' 'law of liberty' (Jas. 1:25; 2:12)—is the law of love (Gal. 5:13f.; *cf.* Mk. 12:28ff.; Jn. 13:34), the principle of voluntary and unstinting self-sacrifice for the good of men (1 Cor. 9:1–23; 10:23–33) and the glory of God (1 Cor. 10:31). This life of love is the response of gratitude which the liberating gospel both requires and evokes. Christian liberty is precisely freedom for love and service to God and men, and it is therefore abused when it is made an excuse for unloving licence (Gal. 5:13; *cf.* 1 Pet. 2:16; 2 Pet. 2:19), or irresponsible inconsiderateness (1 Cor. 8:9–12).

Paul wrote the Epistle to the *Galatians to counter the threat to Christian liberty which Judaizing theology presented. The basic issue, as he saw it, was the sufficiency of Christ for salvation apart from works of law. The Judaizers held that Gentiles who had put faith in Christ still needed circumcision for salvation. Paul argued that if this were so, then by parity of reasoning they would need to keep the whole Mosaic law for salvation; but this would be seeking justification by the law, and such a quest would mean a falling away from grace and from Christ (Gal. 5:2–4). The Christian, Jew or Gentile, Paul maintained, is free from all need to perform works of law for acceptance, for as a believer in Christ he is fully accepted already (Gal. 3:28f.), as the gift of the Spirit to him proves (Gal. 3:2f., 14; 4:6; 5:18). There is no reason why a Gentile convert should burden himself with Mosaic ceremonies (circumcision, the festal calendar [Gal. 4:10], *etc.*), which in any case belonged to the pre-Christian era. The redeeming work of Christ has freed him completely from the need to seek salvation through law (Gal. 3:13; 4:5; 5:1). His task now is, first, to guard his God-given liberty against any who would tell him that faith in Christ alone is not enough to save him (Gal. 5:1) and, second, to put his liberty to the best use by letting the Spirit lead him into responsible fulfilment of the law of love (Gal. 5:13ff.).

Paul makes a similar point elsewhere. The Christian is free from the need to work for his salvation, and he is bound neither by Jewish ceremonialism nor by pagan superstition and taboos. There is a large realm of things indifferent in which 'all things are lawful for me' (1 Cor. 6:12; 10:23). In this realm the Christian must use his liberty responsibly, with an eye to what is expedient and edifying and with a tender regard for the weaker brother's conscience (*cf.* 1 Cor. 8–10; Rom. 14:1–15:7).

III. 'Free will'

The historic debate as to whether fallen men have 'free will' has only an indirect connection with the biblical concept of freedom. Distinctions must be made to indicate the issues involved.

1. If the phrase 'free will' be taken morally and psychologically, as meaning the power of unconstrained, spontaneous, voluntary, and therefore responsible, choice, the Bible everywhere assumes that all men, as such, possess it, unregenerate and regenerate alike.

2. If the phrase be taken metaphysically, as implying that men's future actions are indeterminate and therefore in principle unpredictable, the Bible seems neither to assert nor to deny an indeterminacy of future action relative to the agent's own moral or physical constitution, but it does seem to imply that no future event is indeterminate relative to God, for he foreknows and in some sense foreordains all things. (*PROVIDENCE, *PREDESTINATION.)

3. If the phrase be taken theologically, as denoting a natural ability on the part of unregenerate man to perform acts that are good without qualification in God's sight, or to respond to the gospel invitation, such passages as Rom. 8:5–8; Eph. 2:1–10; Jn. 6:44 seem to indicate that no man is free for obedience and faith till he is freed from sin's dominion by prevenient grace. All his voluntary choices are in one way or another acts of serving *sin till grace breaks sin's power and moves him to obey the gospel. (*Cf.* Rom. 6:17–22; *REGENERATION.)

BIBLIOGRAPHY. Arndt; *MM*; H. Schlier, *TDNT* 2, pp. 487–502; J. Blunck, *NIDNTT* 1, pp. 715–720; *LAE*, pp. 326ff.; Calvin, *Institutio*, 3. 19. J.I.P.

LICTORS
See Police, Part 3.

LIBNAH (Heb. *liḇnâh*). **1.** An important town in the Shephelah, taken by Joshua and assigned to the priests (Jos. 10:29f.; 15:42; 21:13); revolted from Jehoram (2 Ki. 8:22); besieged by Sennacherib (2 Ki. 19:8, 35); the birthplace of Josiah's wife Hamutal. The identification by Bliss and Macalister with Tell es-Safi (the Crusader Blanchegarde), on a limestone outlier 7 km W of Azekah, is now widely contested; Sennacherib would hardly have passed it to attack Lachish first, and Jos. 15:42 suggests a site further SE. Alternatives are scarce. Tell Bornat (W. F. Albright, *BASOR* 15, p. 19) is too small; Tell Judeideh (Tel Goded), N of the Beit Guvrin basin, is attractive but unproved. See Kallai-Kleinmann, *VT* 8, 1958, p. 155; G. E. Wright, *BA* 34, 1971, pp. 81–85. **2.** An unidentified camping-place in the desert (Nu. 33:20; perhaps also Dt. 1:1). J.P.U.L.

LIBNI. A son of Gershon mentioned in Ex. 6:17; Nu. 3:18; 1 Ch. 6:17, 20. In 1 Ch. 6:29 Libni is listed as a son of Merari. The patronymic 'Libnites' is mentioned in Nu. 3:21; 26:58. Libni is 'Ladan' in 1 Ch. 23:7f.; 26:21. R.A.H.G.

LIBYA (LUBIM, AV). First occurs as *Rbw* (= Libu) in Egyp. texts of 13th–12th centuries BC, as a hostile Libyan tribe (Sir A. H. Gardiner, *Ancient Egyptian Onomastica*, 1, 1947, pp. 121*–122*). Libu as *lûḇîm* became a Heb. term for Libya, Libyans, and as *libys* became the general Gk. term 'Libyan' for the land and people W of Egypt. Thus the Heb. and Gk. terms cover other Libyans besides the tribe *Rbw*. During the 12th–8th centuries BC, Libyans entered Egypt as raiders, settlers or soldiers in Egypt's armies. Hence the prominence of Lubim in the forces of *Shishak (2 Ch. 12:3); of *Zerah (2 Ch. 14:9 with 16:8); and among the troops of the Ethiopian pharaohs that failed to protect No-Amon (Thebes) from Assyr. devastation (Na. 3:9). *Lubbîm*, Dn. 11:43, may be the same word. (*LEHABIM; *PUT.) K.A.K.

LIE, LYING (Heb. *šeqer*, 'falsehood', 'deception'; *kāzāḇ*, 'lie' or 'deceptive' thing'; Gk. *pseudos* and cognates). Essentially, a lie is a statement of what is known to be false with intent to deceive (Jdg. 16:10, 13). Biblical writers severely condemn aggravated forms of

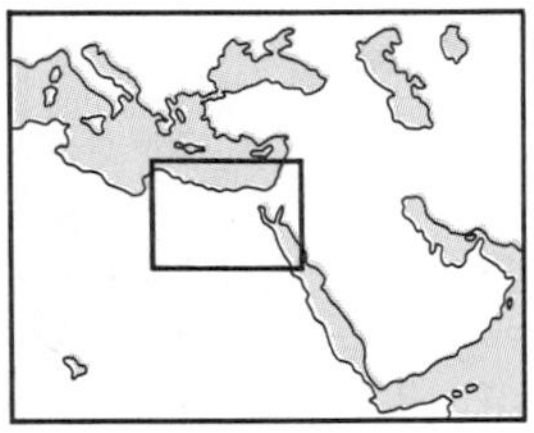

Ancient Libya and its neighbours.

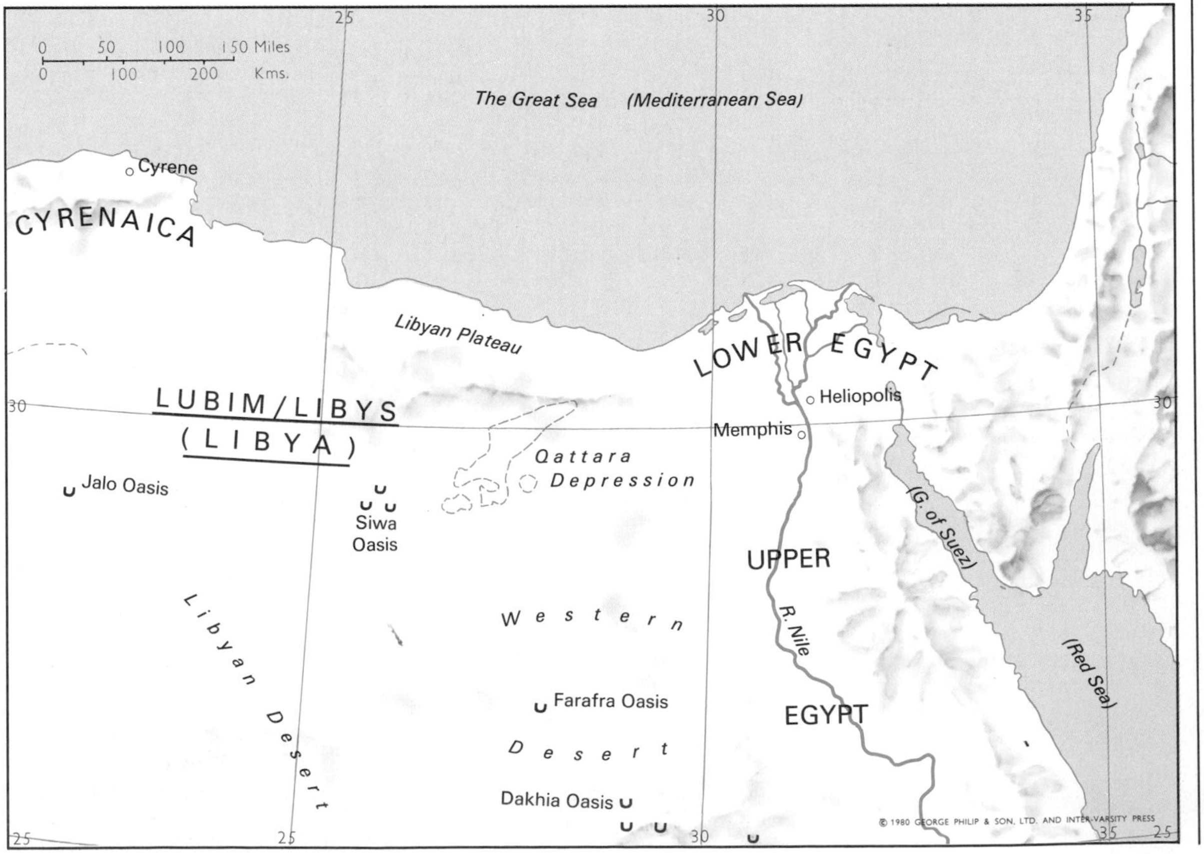

lying, *e.g.* those which perpetrate a fraud (Lv. 6:2–3) or secure wrongful condemnation (Dt. 19:15), and the testimony of false prophets (Je. 14:14). Lies may be expressed in words (Pr. 6:19), a way of life (Ps. 62:9), error (2 Thes. 2:11), or a false form of religion (Rom. 1:25). The prophets regarded lying as a specific expression of the principle of evil (Ho. 12:1). Lying is prohibited as repugnant to the moral conscience of Israel (Pr. 19:22), because of its anti-social effects (Pr. 26:28), and, above all, as incompatible with the divine nature (Nu. 23:19). Jesus declares that Satan is the father of lies (Jn. 8:44). All falsehood is forbidden in the Christian community (Col. 3:9).

Lying is characterized in various ways, *e.g.* Cain's evasive answer (Gn. 4:9), Jacob's deliberate falsehood (Gn. 27:19), Gehazi's misrepresentation of his master (2 Ki. 5:21–27), and the deception practised by Ananias and Sapphira (Acts 5:1–10). Lying is the sin of Antichrist (1 Jn. 2:22) and all habitual liars forfeit eternal salvation (Rev. 21:27).

1 Sa. 16:2 does not justify the expedient lie. God merely suggested an ostensible reason for Samuel's visit to Bethlehem, and the prophet was under no obligation to divulge his real purpose. Again, 1 Ki. 22:20–23 implies that God permitted a subterfuge that his righteous judgment should be enacted upon Ahab. In such passages as Gn. 12:10–20 it is clear that deception is not condoned nor recorded as an example to follow. (*TRUTH.)

BIBLIOGRAPHY. John Murray, *Principles of Conduct*, 1957, ch. 6; *HDB*, 3; H. Conzelmann, *TDNT* 9, pp. 594–603; U. Becker, H.-G. Link, *NIDNTT* 2, pp. 467–474.

A.F.

LIFE.

I. In the Old Testament

a. Terms and concepts

1. Inherent in 'life' (Heb. *ḥayyîm*) is the idea of activity. Life is 'that which moves' (Gn. 7:21f.; Ps. 69:34; *cf.* Acts 17:28) in contrast to the relaxed, dormant or inert state of non-life (*cf.* Rom. 7:8; Jas. 2:17, 20). Running water is 'living' (Gn. 26:19), and rapid labour in childbirth indicates the mother's 'aliveness' (Ex. 1:19). The word's frequently plural form emphasizes the intensity of the concept. Life is associated with light, gladness, fullness, order and active being (Ps. 27:1; Jb. 33:25ff.; Pr. 3:16; Gn. 1) and contrasted with the darkness, sorrow, emptiness, chaos and silence which are characteristic of death and inanimate being (Ec. 11:8; Ps. 115:17).

2. Soul (Heb. *nep̄eš*), as 'being' or 'self', is common to man and beast, living and dead (Lv. 21:11; Jb. 12:10; Rev. 8:9; 16:3). But its meaningful state is 'living soul' (*nep̄eš ḥayyâ*, Gn. 2:7) and, therefore, may simply mean 'life'. To die is to breathe out one's soul, and to revive is to have it return (Je. 15:9; 1 Ki. 17:21; *cf.* Acts 20:10); or, seated in the blood, it is 'poured out' at death (Lv. 17:11; La. 2:12; Is. 53:12). While the soul may continue in spilt blood (Rev. 6:9; Gn. 4:10) or, corporately, in one's name or descendants, 'life' and 'self' are so closely parallel that to lose one's life means virtually to lose one's self (Pedersen, pp. 151ff.; Jb. 2:4; Ezk. 18).

3. Similarly, spirit (Heb. *rûaḥ*) or breath (*n*ᵉ*šāmâ*), as the principle which distinguishes the living from the dead, often may be rendered life (1 Sa. 30:12; Jb. 27:3f.). To die is to lose one's breath or spirit (Jb. 27:3; Ps. 104:29f.; *cf.* Mt. 27:50); to revive is to 'have it come again' (*cf.* Lk. 8:55; Rev. 11:11; 13:15).

4. Life is given to man as a psychosomatic unity in which 'our own distinctions between physical, intellectual and spiritual life do not exist' (von Allmen, pp. 231f.); and the OT view of man may be described as 'animated body' (Robinson, p. 27). Thus soul may be paralleled with flesh (Ps. 63:1; *cf.* Mt. 6:25; Acts 2:31), life (Jb. 33:28) or spirit (Ps. 77:2f.; *cf.* Lk. 1:46f.), and all terms viewed as the self or 'I'. It is the 'I' which lives—and which dies (*cf.* Gn. 7:21; Ezk. 18:4).

b. Life unto death

1. What will man give for his life (Jb. 2:4; *cf.* Mk. 8:37)? Man is not only a unified being, he is a being threatened by death—mortal (Jb. 4:17), barred from the tree of life (Gn. 3:24), existing like cut grass or a morning's dew (Jb. 7:9; Pss. 39:4f.; 90:5f.; *cf.* 1 Pet. 1:24; Jas. 4:14). Death is at work in the midst of life, and life, therefore, is a battle against the dissolution of death, an ebb and flow, possessed in greater or less degree. The tired slave rests and is 'ensouled' (Ex. 23:12). Deliverance from sickness or an enemy or sorrow is deliverance from death, and to be sick or troubled is to be in Sheol (Nu. 21:8f.; Jos. 5:8; Ps. 30:2f.; *cf.* Pss. 71:20; 86:13). It is not that these are equated with death, but that anything threatening life is viewed as an invasion of death upon the soul. Thus, Adam and Eve 'died' when they disobeyed (Gn. 2:17); Abimelech, incurring God's displeasure, is a 'dead man' (Gn. 20:3); and Jonah (2:2) in the fish is in Sheol. Standing under threat of death, one may be viewed from that perspective (*cf.* Lk. 9:60).

2. Likewise long life as the gift of Wisdom or God (Pr. 3:16; Dt. 5:16) has implicit in it the idea of the good life. 'I have set before you . . . life and good, death and evil' (Dt. 30:15). 'Long live the king' (1 Sa. 10:24) does not mean merely length of life but a reign of peace, prosperity and well-being. The death of the righteous at an old *age and full of years is a blessing in that life has been lived to the full and a progeny blessed by God carries on the name (Gn. 25:8; Nu. 23:10).

3. Nevertheless, the present life is life unto death. 'What man can live and never see death? Who can deliver his soul from the power of Sheol?' (Ps. 89:48). Man is a thing moulded of clay; his breath goes back to God, man dies and returns to dust (Gn. 3:19; Jb. 10:9; Ps. 144:4; Ec. 12:7). One may continue to 'live' in his name or progeny (Ps. 72:17; Is. 66:22), and in a very real way these are viewed as a corporate extension of one's own soul (Pedersen, pp. 254ff.). But personal life ends and personal being belongs no more to the 'land of the living' (*cf.* Ps. 52:5; Je. 11:19). To live is to speak of *my* life; in death a man's plans perish and he returns to the common earth, gathered to and sleeping with the fathers (Gn. 25:8; 37:35; Dt. 31:16). Man's end is 'like water spilt on the ground, which cannot be gathered up again' (2 Sa. 14:14).

4. Death is not merely the momentary event of dying; it is the death state, *i.e.* Sheol. Sheol is 'in the dust' (Jb. 17:13ff.) and is probably best understood generically as 'the grave'. As a synonym for death it is the common goal and final leveller of all life: man and beast, righteous and wicked, wise and foolish (Jb. 3:13ff.; Ps. 49; Ec. 2:14; 3:19). It is a state of sleep, rest, darkness, silence, without thought or memory (Jb. 3:16f.; 17:13ff.; Ps. 6:5; Ec. 9:5, 10) in which one does not praise God and from which one does not return (2 Sa. 12:23; Jb. 7:9; Ps. 30:9; Is. 38:18). It is like an insatiable monster and its prospect, except in the most desperate straits, is one of foreboding (Hab. 2:5; *cf.* 2 Sa. 22:5f.).

A few times Sheol is pictured as a massive grave in which, amid the maggots, an enfeebled ghost-life continues (Ezk. 31–32; Is. 14:4ff.) and from which one's 'shade' may be called up (1 Sa. 28:8ff., AV). While the first two passages are obviously poetic symbolism, the medium of Endor séance reflects a common—though forbidden—practice. It is not representative of the general OT view, which sees life and death in utter opposition (*contra* Johnson, p. 89).

Although not strictly non-being, Sheol is the end of meaningful existence and is 'virtual annihilation' (Johnson, p. 93). 'The paths of glory lead but to the grave', and this conclusion to human life gives rise to the Preacher's refrain: 'Vanity of vanities, all is vanity' (Ec. 12:8; Ps. 89:47). To this victory of death the OT does offer a hopeful answer; it lies not in the nature of man but in the power of the living God.

c. The living God

1. The common formula for an oath, 'as the Lord lives' (*cf.* Nu. 14:21, 28; 1 Sa. 14:39), stresses that God is the God who speaks and acts because he is 'the living God'. This quality distinguishes Yahweh from all idols and attests not only his own vitality but his creative power and providential activity (Jos. 3:10; Je. 10:10; Is. 46:5ff.). He is the source and upholder of all life, the spring of living water (Je. 17:13; Ps. 36:9f.), who gives man breath and who, delivering from Sheol, leads one in the path of life (Gn. 2:7; Ps. 16:11; Pr. 5:6). God is the God who makes alive and who kills (Gn. 6:17; Dt. 32:39; Jdg. 13:3, 23; 1 Sa. 2:6; 2 Ki. 5:7).

2. Such is man's dependence upon God for life that man's breath or spirit may be called God's breath and God's spirit (Jb. 27:3f.; 33:4; Gn. 6:3; Is. 42:5). God gave manna in the wilderness that Israel might learn that even physical life is maintained by 'everything that proceeds out of the mouth of the Lord' (Dt. 8:3; *cf.* Mt. 4:4; Lk. 12:15, 20). God imparts breath and man lives (Gn. 2:7; *cf.* Rev. 11:11); if God 'should take back his spirit to himself, and gather to himself his breath, all flesh would perish together, and man would turn to dust' (Jb. 34:14f.; *cf.* Ec. 12:7; Pss. 90:3; 104:29f.). Man's life then is loaned to him at God's good pleasure, and true life consists not in the transient, even though prosperous, life of the wicked, but in having God as 'my portion for ever' (Ps. 73:17, 26). One's life is assured if he is 'bound in the bundle of the living in the care of the Lord' (1 Sa. 25:29).

3. Because life is 'life in relatedness to God', life and death are moral alternatives. The fate of the individual and nation, whether blessing and life or misfortune and death, hangs upon one's righteousness or sinfulness, obedience or disobedience to Yahweh (Dt. 30:15ff.; Jdg. 2:18ff.; Ezk. 18). Universal death is viewed (when viewed at all) as a judgment upon sin; because of disobedience man is barred from the 'tree of life' (Gn. 3:17ff.; *cf.* Jb. 14:1ff., 16f.; contrast Ps. 89:47). Although not always apparent, righteousness tends to life and evil to death (*cf.* Ps. 73:17; Pr. 11:19); righteousness is a 'way of life', and by it one is delivered from the threats of Sheol (Am. 5:4, 14; Pr. 6:23; Hab. 2:4).

4. God has no relationship to Sheol or to those in it. But this must not be confused with the mistaken notion that God has no power in Sheol. It is basic to the OT faith—as expressed in all strata of the literature—that Yahweh, the living God, reigns over death and/or Sheol. To heal (2 Ki. 5:7, 14), to raise the dead (1 Ki. 17:20ff.; 2 Ki. 4:16, 33ff.), to deliver Israel from national death (Jdg. 7:2ff.; Ho. 13:14; Ezk. 37), to cause life to bud in a barren woman (Gn. 17:15ff.; Jdg. 13:2f.; Sa. 1:19f.; 2:6)—all these reveal God's power over Sheol, for the maladies are themselves invasions of death into which God interjects resurrection power.

While God's power to deliver individuals from Sheol is implicit throughout the OT, his purpose to do so comes to explicit expression in comparatively few passages (*cf.* Is. 25:8; 26:19; Jb. 19:26; Pss. 16:8–11; 49:14f.; Dn. 12:2). When it does appear, however, the conviction is full-grown and seemingly is not an innovation (W. O. E. Oesterley, *The Jews and Judaism during the Greek Period*, 1941, p. 183). The concept is related to and perhaps an inference from: (i) God's expressed relationship to the righteous dead, and (ii) God's redemption of Israel understood within the framework of a 'corporate personality' in which the reality of the individual is preserved in the reality of the whole. In a later day Jesus Christ, as well as other rabbis, urged the former as a key to the proper understanding of the OT at this point (Mt. 22:31f.; Lk. 20:37f.; *cf. SB*, 1, pp. 893ff.): (i) God says to Moses, 'I am the God of Abraham.' (ii) Abraham is in Sheol. (iii) God is the God of the living and has no relationship with Sheol. (iv) Therefore, it is to be inferred that God will resurrect Abraham from Sheol.

5. Resurrection-life is pictured (as in intertestamental Judaism) in materialistic terms. It is restored life in which 'life', *i.e.* prosperity, peace and fullness, is multiplied and Sheol threats are removed (Is. 27; *cf.* Rev. 21–22). Its realization (in Is. 26:19; Dn. 12:2) belongs to the coming Messianic deliverance and, as creation life, it is solely the result of God's sovereign and gracious act. God, who by his creative word called man into being, again calls dust into life through resurrection.

II. In the New Testament

a. Terms and concepts

1. Life (Gk. *bios*), means 'course of life' or 'necessities of life maintenance' (Mk. 12:44; 1 Tim. 2:2; 1 Jn. 3:17). While *zōē* characteristically (and always in the Johannine literature) describes resurrection-life, it also denotes 'course of life' (Lk. 16:25; Phil. 1:20; *cf.* Lk. 15:13; Rom. 6:2), soul-life or natural vitality (Acts 8:33; 17:25; Phil. 1:20; 1 Tim. 4:8; *cf.* Jn. 4:50), and life duration (Jas. 4:14). Soul (*psychē*) and spirit (*pneuma*) continue their ambiguous role of 'self' and 'life'. As life, soul is simply 'being', 'natural-life' (Lk. 9:25; Mk. 8:36). It may be preserved to resurrection-life (Jn. 12:25), but at present it exists as natural vitality, lost at death (Mt. 2:20; Jn. 15:13; Acts 20:10; 1 Jn. 3:16) or, more importantly, as Adamic life, life of the old age, life under divine judgment (Lk. 12:20; *cf.* 1 Cor. 2:14; 15:44ff.; Jas. 3:15). While spirit can mean, as in ancient Israel, the vitalizing principle of Adamic life (Jn. 19:30; Acts 7:59), it tends to be associated with resurrection-life and, as such, to stand in contrast to soul-life, *i.e.* life under judgment (*cf.* Jude 19; Jn. 6:63; 1 Cor. 15:45).

2. As in the OT, man's life and being, although viewed from different aspects, is a psychosomatic unity (*cf.* Bultmann). The Gk. soul-body dualism is incidentally reflected in the parable of Lk. 16:19ff., but is not in accord with the general NT outlook or teaching.

b. Life under death

1. The OT view continues. (i) Life is borrowed, transitory, dependent upon and at the disposal of God (*cf.* Mt. 4:4). Man can neither prolong his soul-life nor destroy it (Mt. 6:25ff.; Lk. 12:25; Jas. 4:15); God can either forfeit it or redeem it to resurrection-life (Mt. 10:28; Lk. 12:20; 1 Cor. 15:44; 1 Jn. 5:16; *cf.* Jas. 5:20). (ii) Life is ebb and flow: to live is to live in health (Jn. 4:50).

2. In radical development of OT thought the moral quality of life as relationship to God comes into sharp focus. One related to God, although dead, may be viewed as 'living' (Lk. 20:38). On the other hand, soul-life alienated from the life of God (Eph. 4:18) is no life at all. Anyone in it—not only those under immediate threat of Sheol (Mk. 5:23; *cf.* Mt. 9:18)—may be regarded as 'dead' (Lk. 9:60; Rom. 8:10; 1 Jn. 3:14; Rev. 3:1; *cf.* Lk. 15:24). Even when called life, 'this life' is contrasted to real life (1 Cor. 15:19; 1 Tim. 6:19) and has meaning only in conjunction with the life of the coming age (Gal. 2:20; Phil. 1:22; 1 Tim. 4:8).

3. The cry of John the Baptist, 'Repent', sets the mood of the NT (Mt. 3:2; *cf.* Acts 11:18; 17:30f.). All life stands under imminent judgment, and decision is demanded of all who would share the life of the new age. Criminals suffering ignominious execution are not special sinners: 'unless you repent you will all likewise perish' (Lk. 13:3). Nor can prosperity be relied upon as a token of God's favour: in the midst of man's ease God speaks, 'Fool, this night your soul is required from you' (Lk. 12:20). While this (OT) view of the judgment of the soul-life by physical death is present, more often the *locus* of judgment shifts to the eschatological consummation—the parousia (Mt. 24:36ff.; 25:31ff.), the resurrection of judgment (Jn. 5:28f.), the second death (Rev. 21:8—in which God destroys 'soul and body' in hell (Mt. 10:28). Soul-life (*psychē*), in contrast to resurrection-life (*zōē*), is Adamic life, life under judgment, which without *zōē* must perish (Jn. 3:16). Indeed the 'soulish' man is one directing his life toward the perishing old age, the 'soulish' body one controlled by the Sheol-power dominating the old age (1 Cor. 2:14; 15:44; Jas. 3:15; Jude 19).

4. The judgment of death is executed corporately and representatively in Jesus Christ, the eschatological Adam (1 Cor. 15:45), who 'becomes sin' and voluntarily delivers his soul to Sheol as 'a ransom' (Mk. 10:45; Jn. 10:15; 2 Cor. 5:21; *cf.* Mk. 14:34; Is. 53:6, 10; Acts 8:32ff.; 1 Pet. 2:24) to give resurrection-life to the world (Jn. 6:51). However, Christ's soul is not left in Sheol; in resurrection victory he takes his soul again (Acts 2:31; Jn. 10:17). And by the power of an 'indestructible life' he becomes a 'life-giving spirit' who shares his victory and imparts resurrection-life to whom he will (Heb. 7:3; 1 Cor. 15:45; Eph. 4:8; Jn. 5:21; 17:2). Thereby, Christ removes for ever the Sheol threat to man's soul.

5. Man's soul life, then, need not be forfeited. If he loves it or seeks to preserve it, he will lose it, but if he loses it or gives it up for Christ, the gospel, or the brethren, it will be preserved, caught up in resurrection-life (Mk. 8:35f.; Jn. 12:25; 1 Jn. 3:16; 2 Cor. 12:15; Phil. 2:30; Rev. 12:11). To believe or to convert a sinner is to save a soul from death (Heb. 10:39; Jas. 1:21; 5:20; 1 Pet. 1:9). One who believes shall never taste real death (Jn. 8:51f.; 11:26; *cf.* Jn. 10:28; Mk. 9:1), for in Christ death is transformed into a temporary 'sleep in Jesus' (1 Thes. 4:14; *cf.* Mk. 5:39; Jn. 11:11). Both soul-life and resurrection-life are the life of the self, the whole man. The latter does not displace the former, but preserves it and transforms it.

c. Resurrection-life

1. The OT ideal of the good life has in the NT an eschatological fulfilment as resurrection-life (*zōē*). Since it is the only true life, it may be called simply 'life' (Acts 5:20; 11:18; Rom. 5:17; 2 Pet. 1:3; 1 Jn. 5:16). It is associated with light (Jn. 8:12), glory (1 Pet. 5:1, 4; *cf.* Jas. 1:12), honour (Rom. 2:7), abundance (Jn. 10:10), immortality (2 Tim. 1:10), resurrection (Jn. 6:40; 11:25), eternal life, the kingdom of God (Col. 1:13; Mt. 25), holiness (Rom. 6:22f.), joy (1 Thes. 2:19), spirit (Jn. 6:63; *cf.* 1 Cor. 15:45), the imperishable (Heb. 7:16; 1 Pet. 1:23); and is contrasted with darkness (Col. 1:13), dishonour (Rom. 2:7), death (1 Jn. 3:14), mortality (2 Cor. 5:4), destruction (Mt. 7:13f.), judgment (Jn. 5:28f.), corruption (Gal. 6:8), wrath (Rom. 2:7f.; Jn. 3:36), eternal punishment (Mt. 25:46). To have life is to 'abide' (Jn. 6:27). To lack it is to wither and be burnt as a severed branch (Mt. 7:13, 19; Lk. 3:9; *cf.* Jn. 15:6) and to be destroyed in hell (Mt. 10:28; Mk. 9:43ff.; Rev. 20:14f.).

2. As in the OT, life is properly the life of God, the Ever-Living One (Rom. 5:21; Rev. 4:9), who has life in himself and alone has immortality (Jn. 5:26; 1 Tim. 6:16). He can make alive and he can kill (Rom. 4:17; 2 Cor. 1:9; 1 Tim. 6:13; Mt. 10:28f.; Jas. 4:14f.; Lk. 12:20).

3. This life of God is manifest in Jesus Christ. In the Synoptic Gospels Jesus simply assures his followers of resurrection-life (Mk. 8:34ff.; 9:41ff.; 10:29f.; Mt. 25:46) and evidences his power to bestow it: to heal is to 'save souls' (Lk. 6:9) and death to 'life' (Mk. 5:41). Sheol itself is robbed by Christ's creative word (Mk. 5:39ff.; Lk. 7:14f.; *cf.* Jn. 11:43). The Fourth Gospel and the Epistles, written with Christ's resurrection in more deliberate perspective, are more explicit and elaborate: Christ is 'the true God, and eternal life' (1 Jn. 5:20; Jn. 1:4; 14:6), the 'Author of life' (Acts 3:15), to whom the Father has granted 'to have life in himself' (Jn. 5:26). He is 'the resurrection and the life' (Jn. 11:25), 'the bread of life' (Jn. 6:35), and his words are 'spirit and life' (Jn. 6:63). By his resurrection he manifests himself Lord and Judge over the living and the dead (Mt. 25:31ff.; Mk. 14:62; Jn. 5:27ff.; Acts 10:42; 17:31; Rom. 10:9f.; 14:9; 2 Tim. 4:1; *cf.* 1 Pet. 4:5; Rev. 11:18).

In Jesus Christ's resurrection immortal life has been actualized on the plane of history. His resurrection becomes the basis for all resurrection, and all resurrection is to be understood in terms of his (*cf.* 1 Cor. 15; Col. 3:4; 1 Jn. 3:2). No longer does the hope of resurrection rest, as in the OT, merely upon prophetic vision or upon inferences from God's covenant relationships. No longer is resurrection to be defined simply as renewed life out of Sheol. Resurrection-life now finds its meaning in the image of Jesus Christ (Rom. 8:29).

4. For man, then, true life is grounded in Jesus Christ who 'became a life-giving spirit' (1 Cor. 15:45; *cf.* Jn. 6:63; 2 Cor. 3:17). The core of the gospel proclamation is that he who was dead is 'alive for evermore' (Acts 2:31ff.; 1 Cor.

15:3ff.; Rev. 1:5, 18) and by the power of an indestructible life gives life to the world (Heb. 7:16; Jn. 6:33). If Christ has not been raised from death one must write over the Christian dead, *finis* (1 Cor. 15:18, 32). But Christ is risen and has the 'keys to Sheol'; because Sheol could not conquer him, neither can it prevail against his church (Mt. 16:18; Rev. 1:18). His Life is mediated to the believer through repentance, faith and baptism (Acts 11:18; Jn. 3:16; 11:25f.; Rom. 6:4); by it one is 'saved' (Rom. 5:10). In Christ's death and resurrection God pierces radically into the world of man to make him see the fatality of sin and the utter grace of the new life from God—an unfathomable, unexpected and freely-bestowed act of salvation.

5. Resurrection-life, like Adamic soul-life, is imparted and sustained by God's creative word. Man has no control over it. He may inherit, receive or enter it (Mk. 9:43ff.; 10:17, 30; Tit. 3:7; 1 Pet. 3:7). By evil deeds or rejection of the gospel he may judge himself unworthy of it (Acts 13:46; *cf.* Rom. 1:32) or, conversely, by the Spirit he may perform deeds yielding eternal life (Mk. 10:17ff.; Jn. 5:28f.; Rom. 2:7; 2 Cor. 5:10; Gal. 5:22; 6:8). Such deeds are possible only by a relationship to Christ through faith (Rom. 1:17; Jn. 20:31) which itself imparts life (Jn. 6:53f.; Rom. 6:23; Col. 3:3; 1 Jn. 3:14; 5:13). God gives life to those whom he wills (Jn. 1:13; 5:21), who are ordained for it, and who from the foundation of the world are written in the book of life (Acts 13:48; Rom. 9:11; Phil. 4:3; Rev. 17:8; 20:12ff.). The new life is a resurrection, a new birth, a sovereign and gracious act of the creator God (Jn. 5:24f.; Rom. 6:4; Col. 3:1ff.; Eph. 2:1ff.; Jn. 1:13).

6. In the Synoptic Gospels life is always viewed as future and associated with the coming kingdom of God (Mk. 10:17, 23; 9:43, 47; Mt. 25:46). The way to it is blocked by sin and found by few; yet to attain life is the highest possible goal and worthy of any sacrifice (Mk. 9:42ff.; Mt. 7:14; 13:44ff.), for only in this way can one's soul be preserved (Mk. 8:34ff.; *cf.* Jn. 12:25).

7. In the Johannine and Pauline literature this parousia perspective continues (Jn. 5:24, 28f.; 6:40; 11:24; 14:3, 6, 19; Rom. 5:10; 6:22; 2 Cor. 5:4; 13:4; Phil. 3:10f.; *cf.* 1 Cor. 15:52ff.), but resurrection-life is also viewed as a present possession of the believer. One passes 'from death to life' at conversion (1 Jn. 3:14; *cf.* Jn. 5:24; Eph. 2:1ff.), and one may even speak in the past tense of having been crucified, raised to life, brought into Christ's kingdom, glorified and made to sit in heaven (Gal. 2:20; Eph. 2:5f.; Col. 1:13; Rom. 8:30). However, in Paul (and probably in John) this is always viewed as a corporate participation in Christ's death and resurrection (Rom 6:4; 8:2; 2 Tim. 1:1; *cf.* Jn. 6:33, 51ff.) vouchsafed by the Spirit, the 'down-payment' of the new-age life (*cf.* 2 Cor. 4:12; 5:5). Our life is hid with Christ (Col. 3:3), and to have life means simply to have Christ (1 Jn. 5:11f.). Individually, resurrection-life is now being realized in ethical renewal and psychological transformation (Rom. 8:10; 12:1; Gal. 5:22f.; Col. 3:1ff., 9f.; Eph. 4:18ff.); but the self in its mortality remains under death. Only in the parousia is mortality 'swallowed by life' and Sheol's power vanquished (1 Cor. 15:26, 52ff.; 2 Cor. 5:4; *cf.* Rev. 20:13). At present the victory is actualized personally only in Jesus Christ, 'the first fruits of those who have fallen asleep', 'the first-born among many brethren' (1 Cor. 15:20; Rom. 8:29).

8. As in ancient Israel, the problem of death finds its answer neither in philosophical speculation about immortality nor in the sub-life of Sheol, but in deliverance from Sheol; to be a son of God is to be a son of the resurrection (Lk. 20:36). And it is the resurrected Son of God who imparts this victory to his church; in Adam all die, so in Christ all shall be made alive (1 Cor. 15:22). Not Bach's 'come, sweet death' but John's 'come, Lord Jesus' expresses the NT attitude towards death.

Resurrection-life is bodily life—the life of the whole man (Lk. 24:39ff.; Jn. 5:28f.; 1 Cor. 15; Phil. 3:21; Rev. 20:13). It is to be with Christ (Jn. 14:3; Col. 3:4; 1 Thes. 4:17), to have a full vision of God (1 Cor. 13:12; 2 Cor. 5:7; 1 Jn. 3:2; Rev. 22:4), to enter the kingdom (Mt. 25:34, 46), to enjoy the fulfilment of 'righteousness and peace and joy in the Holy Spirit' (Rom. 14:17; *cf.* Rev. 21–22) in which all Sheol-threats are removed.

Resurrection-life will be 'my life'. One's personal continuity does not rest, however, in the residual monad of Leibnitz nor in the escaping soul of Plato. It rests in God in whose mind 'all live' (Lk. 20:38) and 'who can bring the dead to life and can call to himself the things that do not exist as though they did' (Rom. 4:17, Williams).

BIBLIOGRAPHY. J.-J. von Allmen (ed.), *Vocabulary of the Bible*, 1958, pp. 231–237; R. Bultmann. *The Theology of the New Testament*, 1955, 1, pp. 191–227, 324–329; E. de W. Burton, *Spirit, Soul and Flesh*, 1918; H. C. C. Cavallin, *Life after Death . . . in 1 Cor. 15*, 1, 1974; 2, forthcoming; C. E. B. Cranfield, 'On Rom. viii. 19–21', in *Reconciliation and Hope*, ed. R. Banks, 1974, pp. 224–230; O. Cullmann, *Immortality of the Soul or Resurrection of the Dead?*, 1958; *idem*, *The Early Church*, 1956, pp. 165–173; C. H. Dodd, *The Interpretation of the Fourth Gospel*, 1954, pp. 144–150, 201ff.; E. E. Ellis, *Paul and his Recent Interpreters*, 1961, pp. 35–48; *idem*, *NTS* 10, 1963–64, pp. 274–279; *idem*, *Eschatology in Luke*, 1972; R. H. Gundry, *Sōma in Biblical Theology*, 1976; K. Hanhart, *The Intermediate State in the New Testament*, 1966; F. G. Lang, *2. Korintherbrief 5, 1–10 in der neueren Forschung*, 1973; H.-G. Link, *NIDNTT* 2, pp. 474–484; *TDNT* 2, pp. 832–872; 8, pp. 359–451; 9, pp. 617–656; A. R. Johnson, *The Vitality of the Individual in the Thought of Ancient Israel*, 1949; J. Pedersen, *Israel: Its Life and Culture*, 1, 1926, pp. 99–181, 453–496; H. W. Robinson, *Corporate Personality in Ancient Israel*, 1964.

E.E.E.

LIFE OF JESUS
See Jesus Christ, life of, Part 2.

LIGN ALOES
See Herbs, Part 2.

LIGURE
See Jewels, Part 2.

LILY
See Plants (Crocus, Lily), Part 3.

LILY-WORK
See Plants (Lily), Part 3.

LIGHT. The word is used in connection with joy, blessing and *life in contrast to sorrow, adversity and death (*cf.* Gn. 1:3f.; Jb. 10:22; 18:5f.). At an early time it came to signify God's presence and favour (*cf.* Ps. 27:1; Is. 9:2; 2 Cor. 4:6) in contrast to God's judgment (Am. 5:18). From this and other sources arises an ethical dualism between light and darkness, *i.e.* good and evil, which is quite marked in the NT (*cf.* Lk. 16:8; Jn. 3:19ff.; 12:36; 2 Cor. 6:14; Col. 1:12f.; 1 Thes. 5:5; 1 Pet. 2:9). Some, *e.g.* C. H. Dodd, have regarded Hellenistic parallels to be significant in this regard, but the presence of this usage in Judaism, *e.g. The War of the Sons of Light and the Sons of Darkness* in DSS, makes such an inference unnecessary and provides a more pertinent commentary on the NT concepts.

God's *holiness is expressed in terms of light, *e.g.* in 1 Tim. 6:16, where he is said to dwell 'in unapproachable light'; *cf.* 1 Jn. 1:5, where it is said that 'God is light', and other passages in that Epistle where the implications of this for the believer are worked out. The same thought is seen in the typically Heb. expression 'children of light' which is twice used by Paul (Eph. 5:8; *cf.* 1 Thes. 5:5; Jn. 12:36).

In John's Gospel the term light refers not so much to God's holiness as to the *revelation* of his love in Christ and the penetration of that love into lives darkened by sin. So Christ refers to himself as 'the light of the world' (Jn. 8:12; 9:5; *cf.* 12:46), and in the Sermon on the Mount applies this term to his disciples (Mt. 5:14–16). Similarly Paul can refer to 'the light of the gospel of the glory of Christ' and to God himself who 'has shone in our hearts' (2 Cor. 4:4, 6).

BIBLIOGRAPHY. Arndt; *ISBE*; C. H. Dodd, *The Interpretation of the Fourth Gospel*, 1954, pp. 201–212; D. Flusser, 'The Dead Sea Sect and Pre-Pauline Christianity', *Aspects of the Dead Sea Scrolls*, ed. C. Rabin and Y. Yadin, 1958, pp. 215–266; H. Conzelmann, *TDNT* 9, pp. 310–358; H.-C. Hahn *et al.*, *NIDNTT* 2, pp. 484–496. E.E.E.

LIGHTNING. 1. Lightning which accompanies *thunder is a well-known phenomenon in Palestine, especially in the cool season, with a maximum in November or December. The word is sometimes rendered 'glitter' or 'glittering' (Dt. 32:41; Jb. 20:25; Ezk. 21:15; Na. 3:3; Hab. 3:11). Lightning is a figure used for brightness of countenance (Dn. 10:6; Mt. 28:3) and of raiment (Lk. 24:4). In some passages the usage of 'fire' refers to lightning (*e.g.* Ex. 9:23; 1 Ki. 18:38; 2 Ki. 1:10, 12, 14; 1 Ch. 21:26; Jb. 1:16; Ps. 148:8). Lightning is poetically described with thunderstorms (2 Sa. 22:15; Pss. 18:14; 97:4; 135:7; Je. 10:13; 51:16).

2. Lightning is associated with theophanies as at Sinai (Ex. 19:16; 20:18), in Ezekiel's vision (Ezk. 1:13–14) and several times in the Apocalypse (Rev. 4:5; 8:5; 11:19; 16:18). It is regarded as an instrument of God's judgment (Ps. 144:6; Zc. 9:14; Lk. 10:18). J.M.H.

LILITH (Heb. *lîlîṯ*, Is. 34:14, RVmg., JB; LXX *onokentauros*; Symm., Vulg. *lamia* (Jerome, 'avenging fury'); AV 'screech owl'; AVmg., RV 'night-monster'; RSV 'night hag'; NIV 'night creatures').

This name appears in a description of the terrible desolation of Edom, and presents great difficulties of interpretation. At a time when Bab. and Persian influence was developing, Lilith appears evidently as a loan-word derived from the Assyr. female demon of the night, *Lilitu*.

It may, however, be misleading to regard the creature as necessarily associated with the night: the darkness which some demons were said to love was that caused by desert storms (*cf.* Sumerian *LIL.LÂ*, 'storm-wind'; and also a possible conclusion from Jerome's translation cited above). Some scholars regard it as the equivalent of the English vampire.

Later Jewish literature speaks variously of Lilith as the first wife of Adam, but she flew away and became a demon; as a fabulous monster which stole and destroyed newly-born infants; and as a demon against which charms were used to keep it from the haunts of men, lest it enter and bring disease.

There is, however, no real evidence for insisting on a mythological interpretation of the word, and it is perhaps significant that most of the other creatures listed in Is. 34 are real animals or birds. If the LXX rendering is understood as something akin to a tail-less monkey (*cf.* G. R. Driver, *loc. cit.*, p. 55), it seems an unlikely habitué of a desolate place. A similar objection applies also to both the tawny and the night owl, neither of which is a desert bird. Driver suggests a goat-sucker or nightjar (NEB), species of which are found in waste land.

BIBLIOGRAPHY. *JewE*; G. R. Driver, 'Lilith', *PEQ* 91, 1959, pp. 55–58. J.D.D.

LIME, LIMESTONE. Chemically, lime is calcium oxide, made by heating limestone in a kiln, of which there must have been many in ancient Palestine. The Heb. Bible uses three words, *śîḏ*, 'plaster', 'lime' or 'whitewash' (Dt. 27:2, 4; Is. 33:12; Am. 2:1), *gîr*, 'chalk' or 'lime' (Dn. 5:5) and *'aḇnê gîr*, 'stones of lime' (Is. 27:9, RSV 'chalkstones').

Limestone is abundant in Palestine. Geologically it was formed from the compacting together of shells, *etc.*, on the sea bed, which was then thrust up by earth movement. Palestine was under the sea more than once, at least in part. The bulk of the limestone visible today on both sides of the Jordan is from the Cretaceous period.

BIBLIOGRAPHY. D. Baly, *The Geography of Palestine*[2], 1974, pp. 17ff. J.A.T.

LINE. The commonest OT word is *qaw*, *qāw* or *qeweh*, denoting a measuring-line such as was used to measure the circumference of the

Simplified map showing areas of limestone in Palestine.

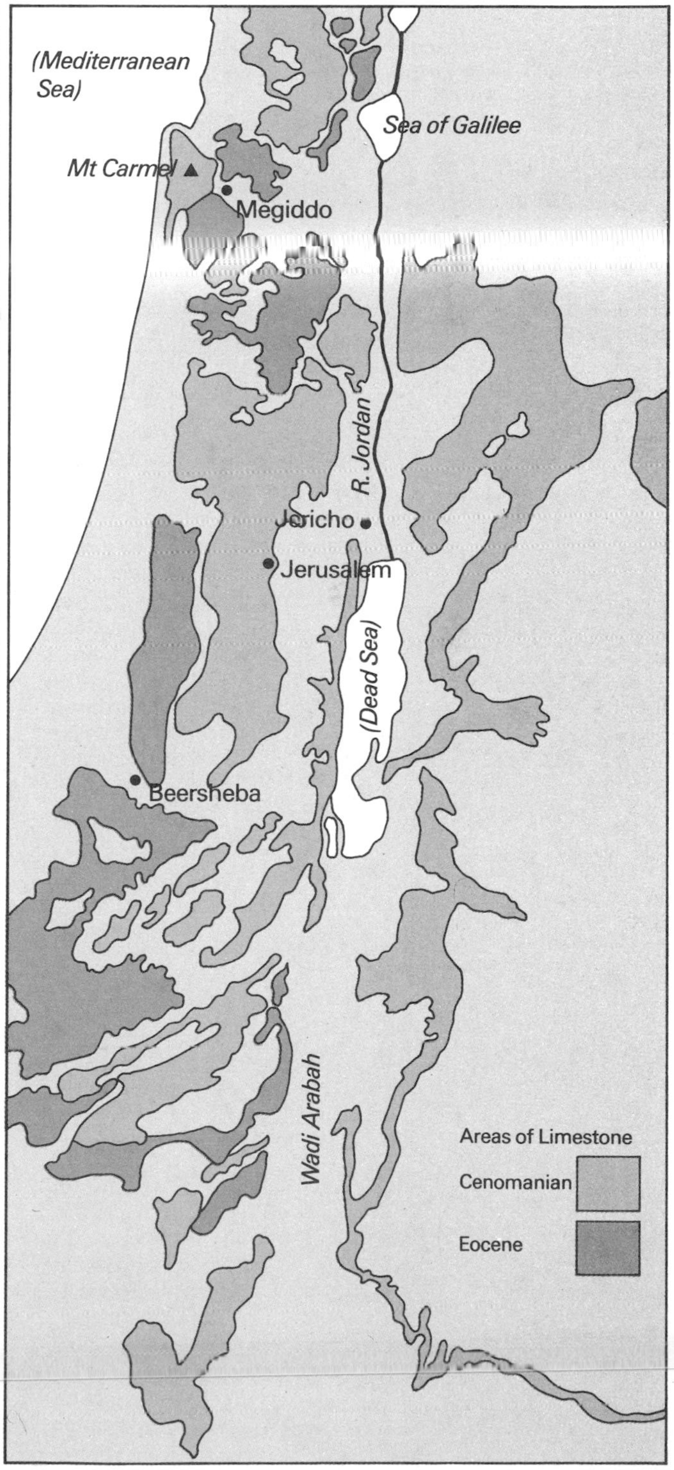

Temple laver (1 Ki. 7:23) or to mark out a city, or land for building (Is. 34:17; Je. 31:39; Zc. 1:16). It is used for measuring distances of 1,000 cubits from Ezekiel's Temple to test the water depth (Ezk. 47:3), and by an extension of meaning it is the plumbline used to check the integrity of a city or land (2 Ki. 21:13; Is. 28:17; 34:11; La. 2:8), or the lines of instruction of a teacher (Is. 28:10, 13, where the picture is one of children reciting the alphabet, *qāw* being an alternative way of naming the letter *qōp̄*).

The word *ḥeḇel*, 'cord' or 'rope', also refers to an instrument for dividing up land or an inheritance (Pss. 16:6, AV; 78:55, AV; Am. 7:17; Zc. 2:1). In 2 Sa. 8:2 it is used of the lines of Moabites drawn up by David, some destined for life and some for death.

The words *ḥûṭ* (1 Ki. 7:15), *pāṯîl* (Ezk. 40:3) and *śereḏ* (Is. 44:13) have special uses. Rahab's red cord is *tiqwâ* (Jos. 2:18, 21, AV). (*WEIGHTS AND MEASURES, *ARTS AND CRAFTS.) J.A.T.

LINEAR A AND B
See Crete, Part 1.

LINEN. The Heb. word *šēš* (Egyp. *sś*) is rendered 'fine linen'. The following Heb. words are rendered by 'linen': *baḏ*, *pištâ*, *bûṣ* and *'ēṭûn* (*cf.* Egyp. *'idmy*, 'yarn' in RV). The word *pištâ* means actually the flax of which linen was made. As early as the 14th century BC the word *pšt*, or plural *pštm*, was used in Ugarit for linen (*cf.* Virolleaud, *PRU*, Mission Ras Shamra 7, II). *bûṣ* is present only in later books (*cf.* Gk. *byssos*). RSV, AV translate the following Gk. words by linen: *sindōn*, *othonion* and *linon*.

Linen is made of flax (*Linum usitatissimum*). After treatment the thread of the rind gives linen and the seed linseed-oil. After the flax was treated it was spun by women and made into material (Pr. 31:13, 24). Flax was never extensively grown in Palestine in biblical times. According to Ex. 9:31; Ho. 2:5 and probably Jos. 2:6, it was, however, cultivated from early times. An extra-biblical witness is the Gezer calendar (*c.* 1000 BC), where we read in the fourth line: 'His month is hoeing up of flax' (Albright's translation in Pritchard, *ANET*^{2}). The great cultivator and exporter of flax was Egypt. In Pr. 7:16 we read of Egyptian linen (*cf.* Heb. *ḥ^{a}ṭuḇôṯ*, 'many coloured'). Red linen was especially precious in ancient Egypt and was called 'royal linen'. It is quite probable that linen (*cf.* Egyp. words *sś* and *'idmy* as possible loan-words in Hebrew and Canaanite) was imported from Egypt by the inhabitants of Palestine from the earliest times. We know from Egyp. documents that linen was exported from Egypt to Phoenicia (*cf.* also Ezk. 27:7) and especially Byblos through many centuries.

The use of linen in OT times was prescribed for priests (Ex. 28:39). The coat, turban and girdle must be of fine linen. This is, according to Ezk. 44:17, prescribed for the coolness of the material. The high priest used a woollen overcoat, but was draped in linen on the great Day of Atonement (Lv. 16:4, 23).

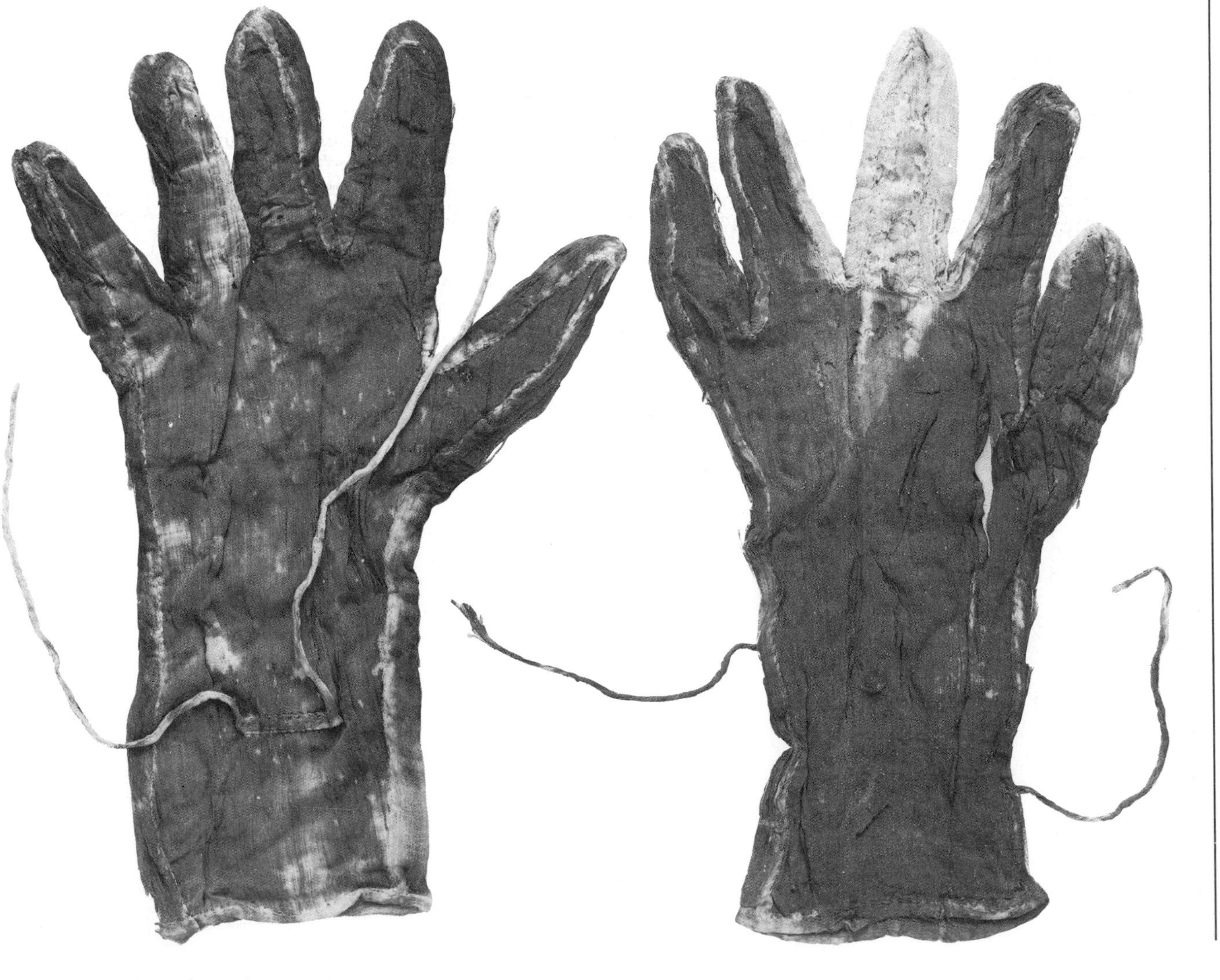

Linen tapestry-woven gloves belonging to King Tutankhamun. Valley of the Kings, Thebes. (Tomb of Tutankhamun.) c. 1340 BC. (GIO)

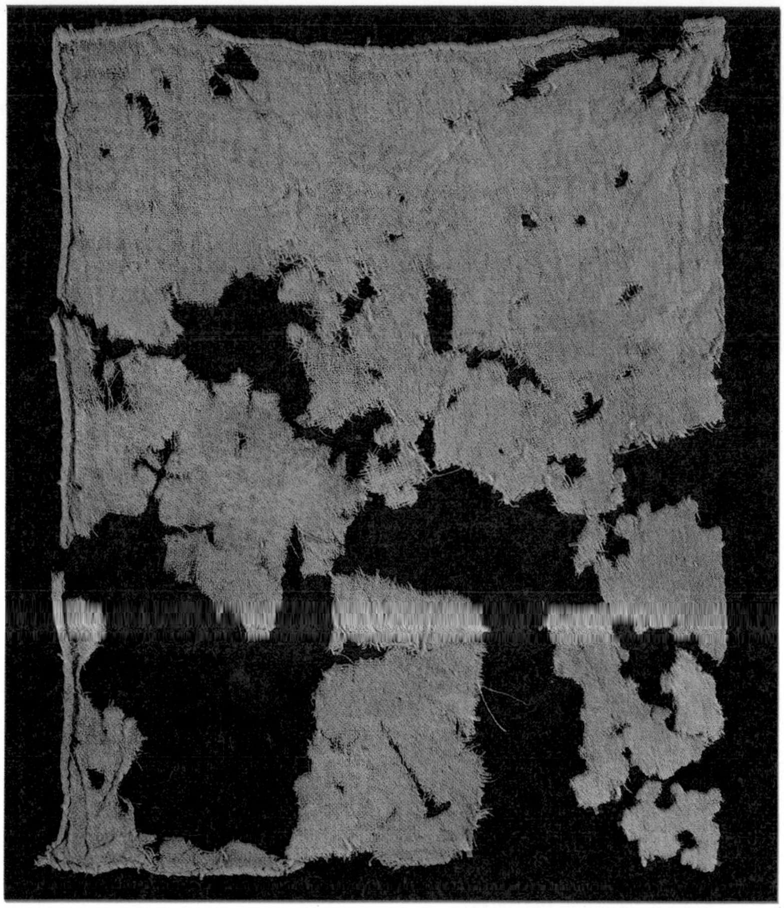

Linen cloth used as a cover or wrapper for one of the Dead Sea Scrolls. It was probably made locally on a vertical loom with warp weights. The cut edges were secured by rolling and whipping with thread. 33·6 cm × 26·7 cm. 1st cent. AD. (BM)

Linen the Israelites brought along from Egypt was used for the ten curtains of the tabernacle (Ex. 26:1), the veil (26:31) and the screen of the door of the tent (26:36). Samuel wore an ephod (*'ēp̄ôḏ*) of linen (1 Sa. 2:18); David danced in front of the ark draped in a linen ephod (2 Sa. 6:14). It seems as if the use of linen was associated with special, holy persons, *e.g.* the man with the writing-case in Ezk. 9:2 and the man Daniel saw in Dn. 10:5 and 12:6–7. Linen and fine linen were regarded as precious gifts to the woman a man loved. In Ezk. 16:10, 13 the Lord speaks to Jerusalem as a husband to his wife and reminds her how he has decked her with linen and fine linen. It is obvious from Pr. 31:22 that the use of linen by women was highly esteemed (as in *embroidery). It was a luxury (Is. 3:23). The word *bûṣ*, 'linen', is used in the later books as the material for the rich and important people, *e.g.* Mordecai went to the Persian king draped with a mantle of fine linen (Est. 8:15). Linen was commonly used for fine furnishings, sails and for protection of precious carpets.

The word linen is sparingly used in the NT. In the parable of the rich man and the beggar Lazarus the former is described as decked out in fine linen (Gk. *byssos*) and purple (Lk. 16:19). The young man who followed Jesus to Gethsemane lost his linen cloth (or sheet?) in his flight from the scene (Mk. 14:51). The body of Jesus was wrapped in linen according to Mt. 27:59 and parallel texts. According to Rev. 19:8, the Bride of the Lamb is clothed in fine linen, which is the righteous deeds of the saints. In Rev. 19:14 the eschatological armies are described as arrayed in fine white linen.

BIBLIOGRAPHY. L. M. Wilson, *Ancient Textiles from Egypt*, 1933; A. Bellinger, *BASOR* 118, 1950, pp. 9–11; G. M. Crowfoot, *PEQ* 83, 1951, pp. 5–31; *DEAD SEA SCROLLS. F.C.F.

LINUS. A Rom. Christian who greeted Timothy, 2 Tim. 4:21; for his relation to others *in loc.*, see *CLAUDIA. The name (a son of Apollo) is not common. Succession lists show a Linus, identified by Irenaeus (*Adv. Haer.* 3. 3. 2) and subsequent writers with Timothy's friend, as first bishop of Rome after the apostles. On the problems of such lists, *cf.* Lightfoot, *Clement I*, pp. 201–345; A. Ehrhardt, *The Apostolic Succession*, 1953. Writers dominated by later practice (*e.g.* Rufinus, Preface to *Clem. Recog.*) labour to reconcile the apostolic appointment of both Linus and *Clement. Linus made little further mark on tradition or legend. (*Cf. Liber Pontificalis*, ed. Duchesne, 1, pp. 53, 121, for meagre notices; Tischendorf, *Acta Apocrypha*, pp. xixf., for martyrdoms of Peter and Paul.) A.F.W.

LION OF JUDAH. An abbreviated form of one of Christ's Messianic titles found in Rev. 5:5, 'the Lion of the tribe of Judah'. An obvious allusion to Gn. 49:9, 'Judah is a lion's whelp', this title depicts Christ as the culmination of the courage, might and ferocity of the tribe of Judah. Like a lion Satan stalks the saints (1 Pet. 5:8), but Christ is the conquering lion, worthy to open the seven seals of judgment. The use of the term 'lion' (*ANIMALS) in connection with judgment may reflect passages like Is. 38:13; La. 3:10; Ho. 5:14; 13:8, where God's judgment is likened to a lion's attack. Emperors of Ethiopia, convinced that they stemmed from Judah as descendants of Solomon and the Queen of Sheba, proudly appropriated this title ('Conquering Lion of Judah') until the overthrow of Haile Selassie's regime in 1974. D.A.H.

LIP. Both the Heb. word *śāp̄â*, and (less frequently) the Gk. word *cheilos*, mean not only the human lip but also the brink or shore of the sea, or the bank of a river (Gn. 22:17; 41:3; Heb. 11:12) and, in the case of the Heb. word, edge of a

The lion was commonly used as a symbol of kingship in Judah and Assyria and occurs on seals of the royal administration. This imprint shows Ashurbanipal, king of Assyria, killing a lion as an expression of his supreme royal power. From Nineveh. Diameter of seal 1·75 cm. c. 650 BC. (BM)

LITTER
See Chariot, Part 1.

LIVING WATER
See Fountain, Part 1.

LIZARD
See Animals, Part 1.

LOAF
See Bread, Part 1.

LOAN
See Debt, Part 1.

LOCK
See Key, Part 2.

LOD
See Lydda, Part 2.

LODGE
See Vegetables (Cucumber), Part 3.

LOG
See Weights and measures, Part 3.

LOGIA
See Oracle, Part 2.

garment (Ex. 28:26), though the primary application is to lips. Another Heb. word *śāpām* refers to the upper lip or moustache, usually in respect of covering it, with the hand or garment, as a sign of grief or shame (Lv. 13:45). *Cf.* the reference to covering the face in 2 Sa. 19:4.

In the case of the lips we find clear examples of the Hebrew way of speaking whereby the organs seem to feel and act themselves, which is partly synecdoche, and partly due to the lack of physiological understanding of the nervous system (*BODY). However, the connection of the lips with the mind or heart is brought out in Pr. 16:23. For an explanation of this connotation, see *HEART.

The lips not only speak (Jb. 27:4) but shout for joy (Ps. 71:23), quiver (with fear) (Hab. 3:16), guard knowledge (Pr. 5:2), offer praise (Ps. 63:3), plead (Jb. 13:6) and possess ethical qualities of truthfulness or righteousness, or, conversely, sinning or speaking lies (Jb. 2:10; Pr. 12:19; 16:13). The parallelism with *tongue or *mouth is natural, and these are used in much the same senses (Pss. 34:13; 51:15). Just as with these words, lip can be extended to mean speech, words (Jb. 12:20) or language (Gn. 11:1; Is. 19:18). B.O.B.

LIVER. Only in the OT does this word occur. The Heb. *kāḇēḏ* is from a root meaning 'to be heavy', or by extension of meaning 'to be honoured'. So, it is the heavy organ. Of the 14 occurrences, 11 are in Ex. and Lv., referring to the liver of a sacrificial beast.

The 'appendage (AV 'caul') of the liver' (Ex. 29:13, *etc.*), always associated with the kidneys, was burnt on the altar. Josephus lists the parts burnt on the altar (*Ant.* 3. 228) 'the kidneys, the caul, all the fat along with the lobe of the liver'.

It is, however, unlikely that the 'caul', *yōṯereṯ*, refers to a lobe of the liver, but probably to fat upon it, or possibly the pancreas. The word literally means 'remainder' or 'appendage' (RSV), so it is not stated specifically that the liver itself was burnt on the altar, but the internal fat and the kidneys.

From Ezekiel (21:21) it appears that the liver was the material for a form of divination, based on the internal markings of the liver. Many artificial livers of clay have been unearthed in the Middle East, and were made for this purpose. A similar practice was known among the Etruscans, from whom it passed to the Romans (Lat. *haruspices* = 'liver diviners'). B.O.B.

LO-DEBAR. Where Mephibosheth lived before David recalled him (2 Sa. 9:4); E of the Jordan (*cf.* 2 Sa. 2:29; 17:27); possibly *DEBIR, 3. J.D.D.

LOGOS. A common Gk. word used in a quasi-technical sense as a title of Christ in the Johannine writings. It carries a large number of different meanings: its basic translation is 'word', *i.e.* meaningful utterance, whence develop its many senses 'statement, declaration, discourse, subject-matter, doctrine, affair' and, by another development, 'reason, cause, sake, respect'. As a grammatical term it means a finite sentence, in logic a factual statement, definition or judgment, in rhetoric a correctly constructed piece of oratory. As a term of psychology and metaphysics it was used by the Stoa, following Herakleitos, to signify the divine power of function by which the universe is given unity, coherence and meaning (*logos spermatikos*, 'seminal Word', which, like seed, gives form to unformed matter): man is made in accordance with the same principle, and is himself said to possess Logos, both inwardly (*logos endiathetos*, reason) and expressed in speech (*logos prophorikos*). The term is also used as the pattern or norm of man whereby he lives 'according to Nature'.

In the LXX Logos is used to translate Heb. *dāḇār*. The root of this signifies 'that which lies behind', and so when translated as 'word' it, too, means meaningful sound; it may also mean 'thing'. In accordance with a common feature of Heb. psychology a man's *dāḇār* is regarded as in some sense an extension of his personality and further as possessing a substantive existence of its own. The Word of God, then, is his self-revelation through Moses and the prophets; it may be used to designate *both* single visions and oracles *and* the whole content of the total revelation, and thus especially the Pentateuch. The Word possesses a like power to the God who speaks it (*cf.* Is. 55:11) and effects his will without hindrance. Hence the term may refer to the creative word of God. In the Wisdom literature the creative power of God is referred to as his wisdom, and in a number of passages is spoken of as an *hypostasis* distinct from him (see especially Pr. 8:22–30: Wisdom of Solomon 7:21ff.).

A clay model of a sheep's liver from Babylonia inscribed with omens for the use of diviners. 13·3 cm × 8·3 cm. 1830–1530 BC. (BM)

Influenced both by the OT and by Hellenic thought, Philo made frequent use of the term Logos, to which he gave a highly-developed significance and a central place to his theological scheme. He derived the term from Stoic sources and, in accordance with his discovery of Gk. thought in the Heb. Scriptures, made use of it on the basis of such passages as Ps. 33:6 to express the means whereby the transcendent God may be the Creator of the universe and the Revealer of himself to Moses and the Patriarchs. On the Gk. side he equates the Logos with the Platonic concept of the World of Ideas so that it becomes both God's plan and God's power of creation. On the side of biblical exegesis the Logos is identified with the Angel of the Lord and the Name of God, and is described by a variety of names as High Priest, Captain and Steersman, Advocate (Paraclete) and Son of God. It is termed a second God and, on the other hand, described as the Ideal Man, the Pattern of God's earthly creation of man. In spite of all this terminology of personification, however, the term remains—inevitably, in view of Philo's staunch Judaism (at least, in intention)—a philosophical and theological term and tool.

A further possible determining factor in the use of Logos in the passages which we need to review is the use of the term to signify the gospel message. The term is used absolutely (*e.g.* to preach the Word) and with a number of genitives (the Word of God, of Christ, of the cross, of reconciliation, of life, *etc.*). These show that the gospel story is seen in the NT as essentially a presentation of Jesus himself; he is the Word which is preached. But this is by no means always implicit in the phrase.

Three places are found at which the use of Logos in a technical sense has been concerned, *viz.* Jn. 1:1 and 14; 1 Jn. 1:1–3; Rev. 19:13.

Jn. 1:1 is the only unambiguous case. Here we have a highly metaphysical prologue to the Gospel in which the significance of the Christ is interpreted theologically. Divergence is found among scholars in the identification of the primary source of these verses and the chief meaning of Logos here. Attempts have been made to link the prologue primarily with the OT use of *dāḇār* alone, or with the rabbinical teaching concerning the Torah. These fail because these concepts are not sufficiently differentiated from the supreme Godhead to stand without alteration in v. 14. The figure of Wisdom provides more parallels but lacks identification in our sources with the Word: the teaching about the Primal or Heavenly Man which others have invoked is too conjectural to command much confidence. Only the Philonic Logos-teaching provides a clear theological scheme in which the Word possesses a like unity with God and a like distinction from him, and in which both creative and sustaining activity in the universe and revelatory activity towards man is ascribed to it. Further, the necessarily unique concept of incarnation is nevertheless a proper development of the identification of Philo's Logos with the Ideal Man. Either a direct use of a Philonic or a similar terminology in intellectual circles of Hellenistic Jewry may lie behind this.

In 1 Jn. 1:1 the phrase 'Word of life' is unlikely to bear the meaning of Logos in its technical theological sense; both context and construction are against this. Even if this be from the same pen as the Gospel (which some scholars regard as doubtful), the letter may date from a time prior to the adoption of a full-grown Logos-doctrine. The sense of 'Christian gospel' fits this context best.

In Rev. 19:13 the sense of 'gospel' may lie behind the ascription of the title Logos of God to the triumphant figure; compare 6:2, where in the view of some exegetes the mounted figure is the triumphant advancing gospel.

We may compare also the imagery of Wisdom of Solomon 18:15–16. But since in Revelation the figure is explicitly declared to be King of kings and Lord of lords, some more metaphysical meaning must be latent here. The literary genre of the book amply explains why this meaning is not developed here in the same fashion as in the Fourth Gospel.

All three places illustrate how the fullness of Christ consistently exhausts all preparatory imagery and thought; and how many places need an exegesis which draws on many sources for full exposition. Jesus gives fresh meaning to terminology which prior to him was expressive of lesser mysteries.

BIBLIOGRAPHY. Pauly-Wissowa, art. 'Logos'; C. H. Dodd, *The Interpretation of the Fourth Gospel*, 1954; A. Debrunner *et al.*, *TDNT* 4, pp. 69–143; H. Haarbeck *et al.*, *NIDNTT* 3, pp. 1078–1123.

J.N.B.

LOIS. Timothy's grandmother, presumably the mother of *Eunice (2 Tim. 1:5). Paul doubtless alludes to her Christian faith: had she been simply a godly Jewess, her devotion is less likely to have been known to him. The name is hard to parallel in the period.

A.F.W.

LORD'S DAY. The expression is found only once in Scripture. In Rev. 1:10 John discloses that the vision of the Apocalypse came to him while he was rapt 'in the Spirit on the Lord's day'. This is the first extant occurrence in Christian literature of *hē kyriakē hēmera*. The adjectival construction suggests that it was a formal designation of the church's worship day. As such it certainly appears early in the 2nd century (Ignatius, *Epistle to the Magnesians*, 1. 67).

Little support can be adduced for the theory that the term referred to Easter day, except, of course, in the sense that each Lord's day is a paschal recapitulation. But it must be noted that such reputable scholars as J. J. Wettstein, G. A. Deissmann and F. J. A. Hort, among others, prefer to interpret the verse as indicating that John was transported in his spiritual ecstasy to the great day of judgment itself (*cf.* Rev. 6:17; 16:14). J. B. Lightfoot believes that there are 'very good, if not conclusive reasons' for such a view (*The Apostolic Fathers*, 2, Section I, Part II, p. 129). The majority opinion, however, inclines to feel with H. B. Swete that such an interpretation is foreign to the immediate context and contrary to linguistic usage (LXX always has *hē hēmera tou kyriou* for the prophetic 'day of the Lord': *kyriakos* does not appear). It would seem reasonably safe, therefore, to conclude that as the actual location of John's vision is recorded in v. 9, so the actual occasion is recorded in v. 10.

Even if a late date for Revelation be accepted (*c.* AD 96), it is not necessary to assume with Harnack that *hē kyriakē hēmera* was not in use before the close of the 1st century. It may even have emerged as soon as AD 57 when Paul wrote 1 Corinthians. In 11:20 he speaks of *kyriakon deipnon* ('the Lord's supper'). It is interesting that Pesh. reads 'Lord's day' here. But it

LOINS
See Thigh, Part 3.

LONGSUFFERING
See Patience, Part 3.

LOOM
See Spinning, Part 3.

LOOPS
See Tabernacle, Part 3.

would hardly appear that the term was in current use, for later in the Epistle Paul has *kata mian sabbatou* (16:2).

Deissmann has thrown further light upon the title by showing that in Asia Minor and Egypt even before the Christian era the first day of each month was called Emperor's Day or *Sebastē*. This may eventually have been transferred to a day of the week, probably Thursday (*dies Iovis*). 'If these conclusions are valid,' comments R. H. Charles, 'we can understand how naturally the term "Lord's Day" arose; for just as the first day of each month, or a certain day of each week, was called "Emperor's Day", so it would be natural for Christians to name the *first day* of each week, associated as it was with the Lord's resurrection and the custom of Christians to meet together for worship, as "Lord's Day". It may have first arisen in apocalyptic circles when a hostile attitude to the Empire was adopted by Christianity' (R. H. Charles, *The Revelation of St. John*, 1, 1920, p. 23; *cf.* Deissmann, *Bible Studies*, pp. 218ff.).

'Lord' here clearly signifies Christ and not God the Father. It is Christ's own day. It belongs to him because of his resurrection, when he was 'designated Son of God in power' (Rom. 1:4). McArthur is surely right in claiming that the title ultimately derives from the Lordship of Jesus Christ which was made manifest in the resurrection on 'the first day of the week' (Mk. 16:2; see A. A. McArthur, *The Evolution of the Christian Year*, 1953, p. 21). Christian worship is essentially an *anamnēsis* (remembrance) of the Easter event which revealed the triumph of God's redemptive purpose. Hence the prevailing note of joy and praise. The first day was also appropriate, as it recalled the initial day of creation, when God made light, and the fact that the Christian Pentecost fell on Sunday. Furthermore, it may well have been the expectation of the primitive Christians that our Lord's return would take place on his own day.

The earliest piece of evidence relating to the Christian observance of the first day of the week lies in 1 Cor. 16:1–2, but there is no explicit reference to an actual assembly. Acts 20:7 is more specific and probably reflects the continued Christian use of the Jewish calendar under which the Lord's day would begin at sunset on Saturday. Alford sees in the readiness of Gentiles to accept this Jewish reckoning 'the greatest proof of all that this day was thus observed' (Henry Alford, *The New Testament for English Readers*[6], 1871, p. 788). On the other hand, there is no trace in the NT of any sabbatarian controversy. The Lord's day, while fulfilling all the beneficent purposes of God in the institution of the Sabbath for mankind, was kept 'not under the old written code but in the new life of the Spirit' (Rom. 7:6).

BIBLIOGRAPHY: H. P. Porter, *The Day of Light: the Biblical and Liturgical Meaning of Sunday*, 1960; W. Rordorf, *Sunday: the History of the Day of Rest and Worship in the Earliest Centuries of the Church*, E.T. 1968; R. T. Beckwith and W. Stott, *This is the Day*, 1978 (reply to Rordorf); S. Bacchiocchi, *From Sabbath to Sunday: A Historical Investigation of the Rise of Sunday Observance in Early Christianity*, 1977.

A.S.W.

LORD'S PRAYER, THE. The prayer which our Lord taught his disciples as the model prayer for their regular use. In Mt. 6:9–13 it is given as an integral part of the Sermon on the Mount. But in Lk. 11:2–4 it is given by our Lord in different circumstances. It is probable that since he meant this prayer to serve as a pattern for all his disciples at all times, he would have repeated it on different occasions.

In Mt. 6:9–13 he gives it as an example which complies with all the requisites which he himself had laid down as essential for true prayer: 'Pray then like this,' he said (v. 9). He was thus continuing to teach his disciples *how* to pray. After having warned them not to pray as hypocrites (v. 5) nor to 'heap up empty phrases' as the heathen do (v. 7), he taught them what sort of prayer is acceptable before God. But in Lk. 11:1–4, in response to the request of a disciple, he gives the prayer this time, not only as an example of a prayer which complies with his teaching, but as a definite prayer which must be prayed by his followers: 'When you pray, say . . .' (v. 2).

In Lk. 11:2–4 the prayer is given in a shorter form than in Mt. 6:9–13, as follows: 'Father, hallowed be thy name. Thy kingdom come. Give us each day our daily bread; and forgive us our sins, for we ourselves forgive every one who is indebted to us; and lead us not into temptation.'

The short form probably represents the compass of the prayer as Jesus originally phrased it: the simple address 'Father' corresponds to the form 'Abba' which he used himself (*cf.* Mk. 14:36) and which the early Christians followed his example in using (*cf.* Rom. 8:15; Gal. 4:6). The amplified Matthaean text has been adapted for Christian liturgical use, the address 'Our Father who art in heaven' being taken over from synagogue usage. Here we shall consider the full Matthaean text.

It is obvious that our Lord gave the prayer originally in Aramaic. By the time Matthew and Luke wrote their Gospels, however, the prayer would naturally have been used by Christians in Greek also. This probably explains why Mt. 6 and Lk. 11 have general agreement in language and both use the unique term *epiousios* (rendered 'daily') in the prayer.

By the opening words of the prayer—'Our Father who art in heaven'—we are taught the correct attitude and spirit in which we should pray to God. Addressing him as 'Our Father', we look up to him in love and faith, as to the One who is near us in perfect love and grace. By the words 'who art in heaven' we give expression to our holy reverence for him who is the Almighty Ruler over all. The introductory words of the prayer also remind us of the fact that all Christian believers are one in him, for we are to pray to him as '*Our* Father'.

The believer's heart being rightly attuned by the invocation, the first petitions are those concerning the glory and divine purpose of our heavenly Father. 'Hallowed be (*hagiasthētō*) thy name' is a prayer asking God to enable us and all men to recognize and honour him. His name, *i.e.* he himself in his self-revelation, is to be acknowledged as holy; and he is to receive all the honour and glory due to the One who perfectly loves us, our holy and omnipotent Creator. (*GOD, NAMES OF.) The petition 'Thy kingdom come' may, for general purposes, be used as a supplication that the divine dominion (*basileia*) of God will be extended 'here and now' (in this present age) in the heart of individuals as well as in the world as a whole. Primarily, however, this petition has an eschatological connotation; it is a supplication that the kingly rule of God may be established 'with power' (Mk. 9:1) at the glorious appearing of the Son of man. (*KINGDOM OF GOD.)

The third petition, 'Thy will be done on earth as it is in heaven', which is absent in the authentic text of Lk. 11:2, is practically an elaboration of the previous petition. In heaven, where the rule of God is gladly and unconditionally accepted by all, the will of God is continuously, spontaneously and joyfully obeyed by all. Believers should thus pray that God's will shall in the same way be obeyed by all on earth, and especially in their own lives. This petition has a partial reference to the present age, but it opens up vistas to the time when every knee shall bow before the King of kings and the powers of darkness will be finally destroyed. God will then be all in all and his will shall reign supreme (1 Cor. 15:25–28). The three imperatives *hagiasthētō* ('be hallowed'), *elthatō* ('come') and *genēthētō* ('be done') are all aorist and point to the final consummation.

The first three petitions having centred upon the glorification of God, the next three petitions are concerned with the physical and spiritual well-being of believers.

Believers should thus pray expressly for the aid and blessing of God regarding all aspects of life in this world. The petition 'Give us this day our daily bread' asks God as our heavenly Father to grant us the physical necessities of life. The word 'bread' here sums up all that we really need for our earthly existence. In view of the foregoing petitions, this is a supplication asking God continually to supply us with the material necessities of life so that we may most effectively sanctify his name, labour for the coming of his kingdom and do his will on earth. Our prayer for daily sustenance is thus not meant to be a selfish prayer, or a prayer for material luxury, but a prayer in which we confess our utter dependence on God and look to him in faith and love to supply us with all things which we really need to enable us to live according to his will.

The Gk. word *epiousios*, translated 'daily', occurs only in Mt. 6:11 and Lk. 11:3, and (reportedly) in one papyrus document (unfortunately no longer extant), where the neuter plural form *epiousia* appears to have meant 'daily rations'. Although finality has not yet been reached regarding its correct etymological derivation, and some prefer to translate it by 'for the coming day' or 'that is needful or sufficient', the translation 'daily' seems to be quite in order. The rendering 'supersubstantial bread' goes back to Jerome, as though the reference were to Jesus as the true bread of life. J. Jeremias relates this petition to the eschatological emphasis of its predecessors as though the reference were to 'eating bread in the kingdom of God' (*cf.* Lk. 14:15). But in the context, what is meant is the constant provision of what is really needed and adequate for us day by day in the realm of our physical, material existence.

The next petition, 'And forgive us our debts, as we also have forgiven our debtors', is both a prayer and a confession. For he who prays for forgiveness at the same time admits that he has sinned and is guilty. In Lk. 11:4 this petition reads: 'And forgive us our sins; for we ourselves forgive every one who is indebted to us.' The Gk. word *hamartias*, here rendered 'sins', has the primary meaning of 'missing the mark' and thus 'acting wrongly' and 'breaking the law of God'. In Mt. 6:12 *opheilēmata* ('debts') preserves the Aramaic idiom in which the word for 'debt' ($ḥ\hat{o}\underline{b}\hat{a}$) is also used in the sense of 'sin'. By sinning we have incurred a moral and spiritual debt to our Father and Creator, who has full authority over our lives. In this petition we therefore humbly ask him for a remission of our debts, seeing that we ourselves can never earn our forgiveness.

The words 'as we also [*hōs kai hēmeis*, 'in the same way also as we'] have forgiven [aorist] our debtors' (Mt. 6:12) and 'for we ourselves forgive [present indicative] every one who is indebted to us' (Lk. 11:4) do not mean that we are to ask forgiveness *on the ground* of our forgiving those who sin against us. We can receive forgiveness through grace alone. But in order to pray to God for forgiveness in sincerity and without hypocrisy, we must be free from all spirit of hatred and revenge. Only when God has given us the grace truly to forgive those who sin against us can we utter a true prayer for forgiveness. This was looked upon by our Lord as of such importance that he reiterated it in Mt. 6:14–15 (*cf.* Mt. 18:23–35; Mk. 11:25).

The final petition in Lk. 11:4 reads: 'And lead us not into temptation'. In Mt. 6:13, the words 'but deliver us from evil' (RSVmg. 'the evil one') follow. These additional words help to make the petition one of general application. Those who sincerely pray for forgiveness of sins long to be enabled not to sin again. Thus it is fitting that this petition follows the previous one. God never tempts anyone to do evil (Jas. 1:13), but he controls the circumstances of our lives. In this prayer we humbly confess that we are prone to sin and thus plead with him not to allow us to be brought into situations or conditions which involve grave temptation to sin. As a further elaboration of this there follows 'but deliver us from the evil one', *i.e.* shield, protect, guard (*rhyesthai*) us against the onslaughts of the devil (*tou ponērou*). This final petition, although applicable to every day in our lives, points very clearly to the consummation when our Lord will put an end to all that is evil, and establish his eternal kingdom of righteousness and holiness.

This brings us to the consideration that in the setting of Jesus' ministry this petition struck an eschatological note. The NEB rendering ('And do not bring us to the test') indicates this, albeit too cryptically. The test is that crucial test of the disciples' faith which, without divine strength, would prove too intense for them to resist. The form taken by that test was shown in the setting of Gethsemane (the final test also for Jesus himself). The exhortation to the disciples, 'Watch and pray that you may not enter into temptation' (Mk. 14:38) probably means 'Keep awake, and pray not to fail in the test'. This suggests that the petition in the Lord's Prayer means, 'Grant that we may not fail in the test' (*cf.* C. C. Torrey, *The Four Gospels*, 1933, p. 292). And today, over and above the general plea to be delivered from temptation, Christians may use the petition as a prayer for grace and power to keep them from failing when their faith is challenged by a supreme test.

In some ancient and many later MSS of Mt. 6:13 a doxology follows. In the AV it reads, 'For thine is the kingdom, and the power, and the glory, for ever. Amen.' Although the most authoritative MSS do not have the doxology, it has been used in the Christian church from the earliest times (*cf.* the *Didache* and the Western Text), and it is certainly a most suitable and worthy ending for the Lord's Prayer. That it does not, however, belong to the original text of Matthew is apparent from the fact that vv. 14 and 15 follow naturally after vv. 12 and 13a.

Someone has rightly said that the Lord's Prayer is Jesus' message of the kingdom of God summarized in prayer form. It is the prayer which all Christians should regularly offer to God in order to be enabled to live as his children ever more completely until the day when his sovereignty is perfectly established.

It should be noted that our Lord (when teaching his disciples this prayer) did not say, '*we* must pray' but '*you* pray'. The Lord's Prayer is the prayer which he taught, not one which he used. He does not appear ever to have used the expression 'Our Father' in such a way as to include his disciples with himself (*cf.* Jn. 20:17, 'my Father and your Father'), nor is there any hint that he ever felt the need to ask forgiveness for himself.

While the individual petitions in the Lord's Prayer are paralleled in various contexts in Jewish religious literature, nothing comparable to the prayer as a whole is found. The Lord's Prayer is unique, and unsurpassed even to this day—gathering in a few words all the essentials of true prayer.

BIBLIOGRAPHY. J. Jeremias, *The Lord's Prayer*, 1964 (reprinted in *The Prayers of Jesus*, 1967, pp. 82–107); E. Lohmeyer, *The Lord's Prayer*, 1965; T. W. Manson, 'The Lord's Prayer', *BJRL* 38, 1955–6, pp. 99–113, 436–448; B. M. Metzger, 'How Many Times does *epiousios* occur outside the Lord's Prayer?' in *Historical and Literary Studies*, 1968, pp. 64ff.; commentaries on Matthew and Luke.

J.N.G.
F.F.B.

LORD'S SUPPER, THE. It will be most convenient to set out the NT evidence for the Christian ordinance under the headings of 'The Last Supper'; 'The breaking of bread'; 'The Pauline Eucharist'; and 'Other NT material'.

I. The Last Supper

a. Was it the Passover?

The precise nature of the meal which the Lord shared with his disciples on the night in which he was betrayed is one of the most warmly debated topics of NT history and interpretation. Various suggestions have been made.

1. The traditional explanation is that the meal was the customary Passover feast, and this can claim the support of the Gospel records, both Synoptic (*e.g.* Mk. 14:1–2, 12–16) and Johannine (*e.g.* 13:21–30). There are features of the meal which students of Judaism (notably P. Billerbeck and G. H. Dalman) have noted as distinguishing features of the Paschal feast, *e.g.* reclining at the table (*ABRAHAM'S BOSOM), the distribution of alms (*cf.* Jn. 13:29), and the use of the 'sop' which is dipped in the special *ḥarōseṯ* sauce as a memorial of the bitterness of the Egyp. bondage. See the full details in G. H. Dalman, *Jesus–Jeshua*, E.T. 1929, pp. 106ff., and J. Jeremias, *The Eucharistic Words of Jesus*, E.T. ²1966, pp. 41ff. But the evidence is not so compelling as to exclude all other interpretations, although there is a tendency today, especially since the first publication of Jeremias' book in 1949, to give more respectful consideration to the Passover view than was formerly done. The earlier judgment was similar to that expressed by Hans Lietzmann, who dismissed the Paschal theory of the Supper as containing scarcely 'the least vestige of probability' (*Mass and Lord's Supper*, E.T. 1953, p. 173). There has been a reaction from this extreme negativism.

2. The data which caused some questioning of the traditional view are mainly derived from the Fourth Gospel, which apparently dates the events of the Supper evening and the passion a day earlier than the Synoptics. According to Jn. 13:1; 18:28; 19:14, 31, 42, the crucifixion happened a day before Nisan 15, which is the Synoptic reckoning, and the Last Supper was, of course, eaten on the evening before that. Thus it cannot have been the regular paschal meal, for the Lord died at the same time as the lambs for that meal were being immolated in the Temple ritual. Thus there is an apparent *impasse*, which is further complicated by the allegation that the Synoptic account is not consistent with itself; for instance, Lk. 22:15 may be read as an unfulfilled wish. For those scholars who prefer to support the Johannine dating (*e.g.* J. H. Bernard in the *ICC* on *John*) and believe that the last meal could therefore not have been the Passover, the question arises, what type of meal, then, was it? They answer this question by postulating a sabbath *Qiddūsh*, *i.e.*, according to this view, Jesus and his followers constituted a religious group which met on the eve of the sabbath and the Passover, and held a simple service in which a prayer of sanctification (*Qiddūsh*) over a cup of wine was said.

3. As a modification of this suggestion Hans Lietzmann put forward the idea that the meal was an ordinary one, and the Lord and his disciples, who shared it, formed a religious association called a *ḥaḇūrāh*, similar to the groups in which the Pharisees met. All these ideas have met with severe criticism, and there is apparent deadlock in the debate; though it is now being reopened through the investigation of the new evidence of the Qumran scrolls.

4. In the light of recent researches into the influence of separate calendars which were used for calculating feast-days, it is now possible to consider again the older submissions of P. Billerbeck and J. Pickl that the two strata of Gospel evidence may be harmonized on the assumption that both are understandable, with each reflecting a different tradition. Billerbeck and Pickl distinguished between the Pharisaic date of the Passover which Jesus used and the Sadducean dating a day earlier which lies behind the Fourth Gospel. This was dismissed by critics as lacking in supporting evidence, but the Dead Sea Scrolls show that there were divergent calendars in use in heterodox Jewry, and it is possible that separate traditions were, in fact, in vogue at the time of the passion. Mlle A. Jaubert has recently reconstructed the events on this basis so as to harmonize the data of the Gospels and early liturgical witnesses (in her book *The Date of the Last Supper*, E.T. 1965. See for an acceptance of her thesis, E. E. Ellis, *The Gospel of Luke*², *NCB*, 1974, pp. 249f. and Mlle Jaubert's later contribution in *NTS* 14, 1967–8, pp. 145–164.

Whether the date of the Supper will ever be conclusively determined is uncertain; but we may certainly believe that, whatever the exact nature of the meal, there were Passover ideas in the Lord's mind when he sat down with the disciples. The Jewish Passover, based on Ex. 12 and interpreted in the *Haggāḏāh* for Passover and the Mishnaic tractate *Pesaḥim*, provides the indispensable key to an understanding of the meal and also the meaning of the Lord's Supper in the early church. This conclusion is reinforced by recent studies in typology which have shown the importance of the OT events in their 'typological' significance for the NT writers; and no complex of saving events comes more decisively to the foreground in the thinking of early Christianity than the Exodus and redemption from Egypt (*cf.* H. Sahlin, 'The New Exodus of Salvation according to St Paul', in *The Root of the Vine*, ed. A. Fridrichsen, 1953, pp. 81–95; J. Daniélou, *Sacramentum Futuri*, 1950, Book IV, pp. 131ff.). Reference may also be made to the important contribution of T. Preiss, *Life in Christ*, E.T. 1954, p. 90, who shows the place of 'the totality of the events of the Exodus centring on the Passover' in both Jewish and Christian traditions).

b. The words of institution

We turn now to examine more closely the last meal in the upper room. Two questions immediately arise. What was the *form* of the words of institution, spoken over the bread and wine? And what was their *meaning*?

1. The original form of the words is not easily discoverable because there are several sets of variants, represented chiefly in the Marcan and the Pauline traditions respectively. Lk. 22:15–20 has peculiarities of its own, both textual and hermeneutical. There is a recent tendency to accept the longer recension of the Lucan text against the shorter readings of the Western MS D and certain Old Lat. and Syrian MSS which omit verses 19b and 20. The value of the Lucan *pericope* lies in its place as independent evidence of the same tradition as that used by Paul with the unusual order 'cup—bread' in Lk. 22:17–19 and 1 Cor. 10:16, 21 (*cf. Didache* 9); and the preservation in both accounts of the command to repeat the rite (Lk. 22:19b; 1 Cor. 11:25). The originality of the 'longer text' has been virtually established by H. Schürmann, *Bib* 32, 1951, pp. 364–392, 522–541. *Cf.* E. E. Ellis, *Luke*, pp. 254–256 (biblio.).

On the issue of Marcan versus Pauline form the arguments on both sides are inconclusive. Some scholars feel that Jesus could never have suggested that the disciples were to drink his blood, even symbolically, and the Pauline version, 'This cup is the new covenant in my blood' (1 Cor. 11:25), is more likely to be original, especially as the Marcan formula is liturgically symmetrical with that about the bread, and is aligned to Ex. 24:8 (LXX). Against this it has been contended by A. J. B. Higgins that the Marcan form is more primitive because of its harsh Semitisms in the Greek and the obvious dependence on the Servant passages in Isaiah, although Higgins would wish to excise some of the Marcan phrases. At all events, we may consider the following to be somewhere near the original: 'Jesus took a loaf, pronounced a blessing, broke it and said, This is my body. And he took a cup, blessed it and said, This cup is the new covenant in my blood (Paul), or, This is my blood of the covenant (Mark).' Then followed the eschatological pronouncement, [illegible] 'vow of abstinence', see J. Jeremias, *New Testament Theology*, 1, E.T. 1971, pp. 298f.

2. If we begin with the eschatological utterance this will be explained as the hope of the early believers, instructed by the Lord, that their fellowship with him will be fulfilled in the perfected kingdom of God; and this sets a *terminus ad quem* for the Pauline Eucharist, for when the Lord returns in glory to unite his people in fellowship the memorial table-fellowship will cease (*cf.* M. Dibelius, *From Tradition to Gospel*, E.T. 1934, p. 208).

The interpretative words over the elements have been variously estimated. There is no ground for a literal equivalence as in the doctrine of transubstantiation. The copula 'is' is the exegetical *significat* as in Gn. 41:26; Dn. 7:17; Lk. 8:11; Gal. 4:24; Rev. 1:20; and in the spoken Aramaic the copulative would be lacking, as in Gn. 40:12; Dn. 2:36; 4:22. The figurative, non-literal connotation 'ought never to have been disputed' (Lietzmann).

The words, 'body, blood', are sometimes taken in the sense that Jesus is referring to his impending death on the cross when his body was broken (but *cf.* Jn. 19:31–37) and his blood shed in violent death. The principal objection to this symbolic view is that the word over the bread was not spoken when it was broken but when it was distributed, and the wine had been poured out at an earlier part of the paschal meal. Also there is nothing unusual or unique in the fact that bread was broken. 'To break bread' was a common Jewish expression for the sharing of a meal.

Another view takes the Gk. term *sōma* (body) to denote the Aramaic *gûp̄*, which means not only 'body' but 'person', as though Jesus said, 'This is my person, my real self'; and points to his continuing fellowship as risen Lord with his people as they repeat the table-fellowship. Jeremias, however, has objected to this suggestion of Dalman (*op. cit.*, p. 143) by remarking that the true counterpart to 'blood' is not 'body', *sōma*, but 'flesh', *sarx*, for which the Aramaic is *bisrī*, 'my flesh'. But see E. Schweizer, *The Lord's Supper according to the New Testament*, E.T. 1967, pp. 14–17.

The most valuable clue to the meaning of the Lord's instituting words is to be found in the part which bread and wine play in the Passover ritual. Following Higgins' interpretation, we may take the words of the institution to be the Lord's own addition to the order of the paschal liturgy at two vital points, before and after the main meal. He tells his disciples, by his words and prophetic symbolism, that the original meaning of the paschal rite has now been transcended, inasmuch as he is the paschal Lamb fulfilling the OT prefigurement (1 Cor. 5:7). His words and action in taking the bread and the cup are parables which announce a new significance. The bread becomes under his sovereign word the parable of his body yielded up in the service of God's redeeming purpose (*cf.* Heb. 10:5–10); and his blood outpoured in death, recalling the sacrificial rites of the OT, is represented in the cup of blessing on the table. That cup is invested henceforward with a fresh significance as the memorial of the new Exodus, accomplished at Jerusalem (Lk. 9:31).

The function of the elements is parallel, then, to that of the Passover dishes. At the annual feast the Israelite is linked, in a realistic and dynamic way, with his forebears whom the Lord redeemed from Egypt. The bread on the table is to be regarded as though it were 'the bread of affliction' which the Jews of old ate (Dt. 16:3 as interpreted in the Passover *Haggāḏāh*); he is to account himself as though he personally was set free from Egyp. tyranny in that first generation of his nation long ago (Mishnah,

Pesaḥim 10. 5). At the Lord's Table which is genetically related to the upper room the church of the new Israel is gathered as the people of the new covenant (Je. 31:31ff.); is confronted afresh with the tokens of that once-offered sacrifice; and relives that experience by which it came out of the Egypt of sin and was ransomed to God by the precious death of God's paschal Victim. Further details of this 'dynamic' significance of the Lord's supper elements are given in R. P. Martin, *Worship in the Early Church*, 1974 ed., pp. 114ff.

II. The breaking of bread

In the early church of the Acts there are scattered references to table-fellowship, *e.g.* Acts 2:42, 46 where the phrase is 'breaking of bread'. In Acts 20:7 (but not 27:35, which describes an ordinary, non-cultic meal) there is a reference to a fellowship meal, using the identical phrase. The fact that no mention of the cup is ever made in Acts leads H. Lietzmann (see *ExpT* 65, 1953–54, pp. 333ff. for a clear, yet critical, statement of his theory) to the elaborate thesis that this Jerusalem communion in one kind is the earliest and most original form of the sacrament, though hardly deserving the name. It was, *ex hypothesi*, a fellowship meal beginning with the familiar Jewish custom of breaking of bread—a continuation, in fact, of the common meals of the Galilean ministry when the Lord fed the crowds and in which the Lord and his disciples formed a *ḥaḇūrāh*. The motif of the Jerusalem rite was not the death of Jesus, but the invisible presence of the exalted Lord in their midst. The Lord's Supper of 1 Cor. 11 with its emphasis on the atoning significance of the death of Christ was Paul's own new contribution, received by special revelation from the Lord in glory. So Lietzmann suggests.

But this elaboration is unnecessary. There is little suggestion that Paul was such an innovator. As A. M. Hunter remarks, 'It staggers belief that he could have successfully foisted his innovation . . . on the church at large' (*Paul and His Predecessors*², 1961, p. 75). The non-mention of the cup may not be significant; the name 'breaking of bread' may be a quasi-technical expression for the whole meal. What is significant about the early form of the Eucharist is the note of *joy* which stems directly, not so much from the Galilean meals as from the post-resurrection appearances, many of which are associated with a meal between the victorious Lord and his own (Lk. 24:30–35, 36–48; Jn. 21:9ff.; Acts 1:4 (RVmg.); 10:41; Rev. 3:20).

III. The Pauline Eucharist

The common meals of the Galilean ministry are more likely to find their fulfilment in the *agapē* or love feast of the Corinthian church (1 Cor. 11:20–34). At Corinth there were two parts of the cultic observance: a common meal, taken for the purpose of nourishment (*cf. Didache* 10. 1: 'after you are filled'), followed by a solemn rite of the Eucharist. (* LOVE FEAST.) There were serious excesses within the Corinthian assembly, such as greediness, selfishness, drunkenness and gluttony. Paul issued a grave warning, and the impression we gather is that it was his desire to have the two parts kept separate, as happened in the later church. Let the hungry eat at home, and come with reverence and self-examination to the Table, is his caution (11:22, 30–34).

Paul's distinctive eucharistic teaching serves to enhance the significance of the Supper by anchoring it firmly in God's redeeming purpose; so that it proclaims the Lord's death (1 Cor. 11:26) as the Passover ritual set forth (hence the title, *Haggāḏāh*, *i.e.* declaration, for which the Gk. equivalent would be the Pauline *katangellein* of 1 Cor. 11:26) the redeeming mercy of God under the old covenant. He also expounds the inner meaning of the Table as a communion (*koinōnia*) with the Lord in his death and risen life, signified in the bread and the wine (1 Cor. 10:16). Therein he discovers the unity of the church, for as the members share together the one loaf they sit down as the one body of Christ (*cf.* A. E. J. Rawlinson's essay in *Mysterium Christi*, ed. Bell and Deissmann, 1930, pp. 225ff.). There are eschatological overtones likewise, as in the evangelic tradition, with the forward look to the advent in glory. *Marānā-thā* in 1 Cor. 16:22 may very well be placed in a eucharistic setting so that the conclusion of the letter ends with the invocation 'Our Lord, come!' and prepares the scene for the celebration of the meal after the letter has been read to the congregation (*cf.* Lietzmann, *op. cit.*, p. 229; J. A. T. Robinson, 'The Earliest Christian Liturgical sequence?', *JTS* n.s. 4, 1953, pp. 38–41; but see C. F. D. Moule, *NTS* 6, 1959–60, pp. 307ff.). See, too, G. Wainwright, *Eucharist and Eschatology*, 1971. Further exposition of Paul's teaching on the Supper is offered in R. P. Martin, *op. cit.*, ch. 11.

IV. Other New Testament material

It is surely significant that there is little other *direct* NT witness to the sacrament apart from the references we have already given. This fact is especially important when it comes to an assessment of Paul's so-called 'sacramentalism'. The writer of 1 Cor. 1:16–17 could never have been one who regarded the sacraments as the last word about the Christian faith and practice; yet we must equally admit that, in C. T. Craig's words, 'Paul would not have understood an expression of Christian faith apart from a community in which the Lord's Supper was celebrated' (quoted by A. M. Hunter, *Interpreting Paul's Gospel*, 1954, p. 105). Adolf Schlatter, we believe, gives the truest estimate in his observation on the apostle's sacramental theology: Paul 'can express the word of Jesus, not in half measure but completely, without mentioning the sacraments at all. But if they come into view he connects with them the entire riches of the grace of Christ, because he sees in them the will of Jesus, not partially but fully expressed and effective' (*Die Briefe an die Thessalonicher, Philipper, Timotheus und Titus*, 1950, p. 262).

What is true of Paul is true of the other NT writers. There may be allusions to the Lord's Supper in such places as Heb. 6:4; 13:10; and John's Gospel contains the notable synagogue discourse which many scholars relate to the eucharistic tradition of the later church (Jn. 6:22–59); but we should not overpress these references, as O. Cullmann seems to have done in finding numerous subtle references to sacramental worship in the Fourth Gospel (see his *Early Christian Worship*, 1953, pp. 37ff., especially p. 106).

There is the witness of 2 Pet. 2:13 and Jude 12 to the *agapē* meal. Apart from these somewhat exiguous data and meagre details, the NT is silent about the ordering and observance of eucharistic worship in the primitive communities, mainly owing to the fact that what is generally received and practised is not usually the subject of ex-

LOSS
See Perdition, Part 3.

Opposite page. Top: Lot's family.

Opposite page: The journeyings of Lot, Abraham's nephew.

tended comment. For the development of the rite, and, it must be confessed, a fruitful source of heresy and confused doctrine, we must await the correspondence, epistles and liturgies of the 2nd and subsequent centuries, from *1 Clem.* 40. 2–4; Ignatius, *Smyrnaeans*. 8. 1; *Didache* 9–10, 14 onwards.

Bibliography. This article has mentioned some of the main works of importance. Of special value is A. J. B. Higgins, *The Lord's Supper in the New Testament*, 1952; and for the later development, J. H. Srawley, *The Early History of the Liturgy*, 1947. See also A. M. Stibbs, *Sacrifice, Sacrament and Eucharist*, 1961. Useful surveys of recent discussion of the NT evidence are books by E. Schweizer, *The Lord's Supper according to the New Testament*, E.T. 1967 (bibliography), and W. Marxsen, *The Lord's Supper as a Christological Problem*, E.T. 1970; see, for a more popular treatment, R. P. Martin, *Worship in the Early Church*, 1974. R.P.M.

LOT (Heb. *lôṭ*, 'covering' ?). The son of Haran, Abraham's youngest brother, and so Abraham's nephew. Apart from the account of his life in Genesis, his name is absent from the OT (except for references to his descendants in Dt. 2:9, 19; Ps.

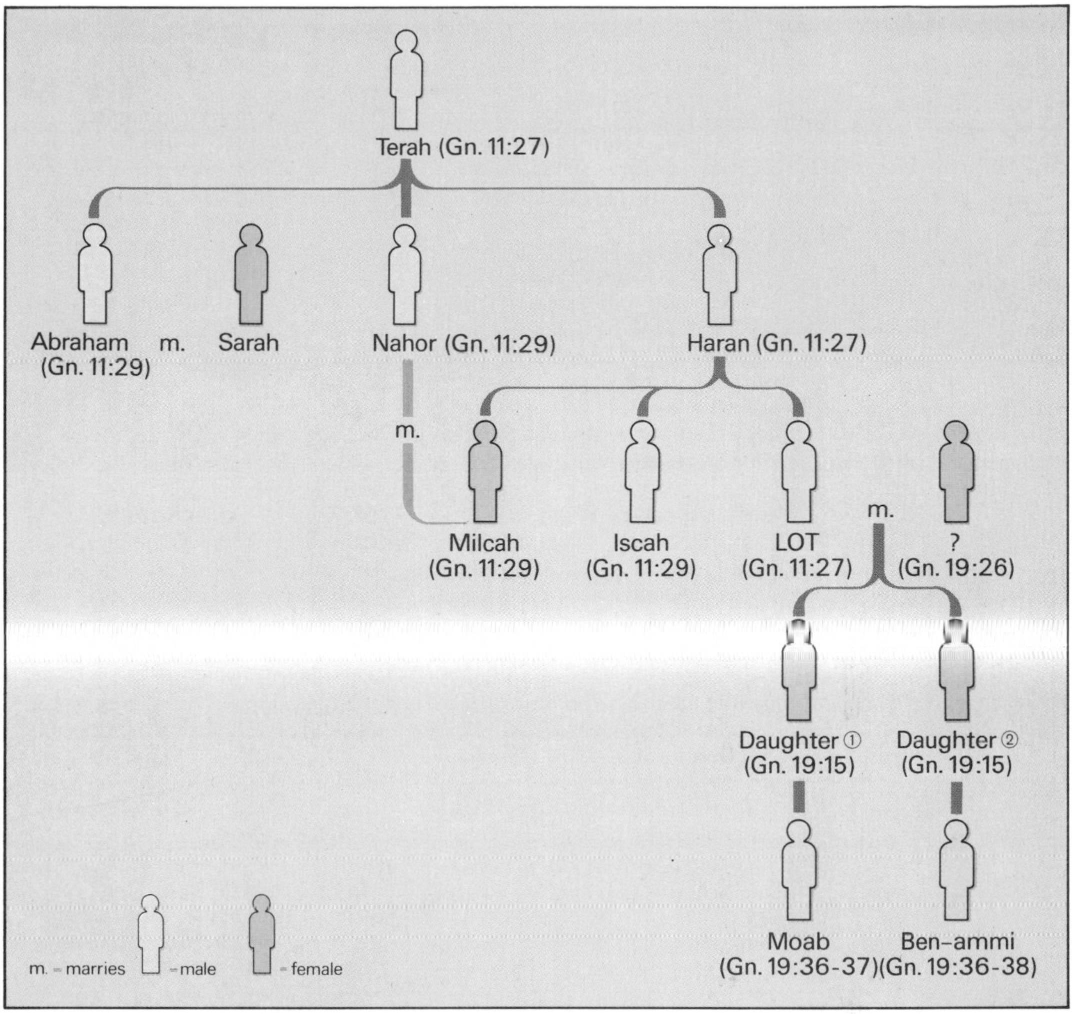

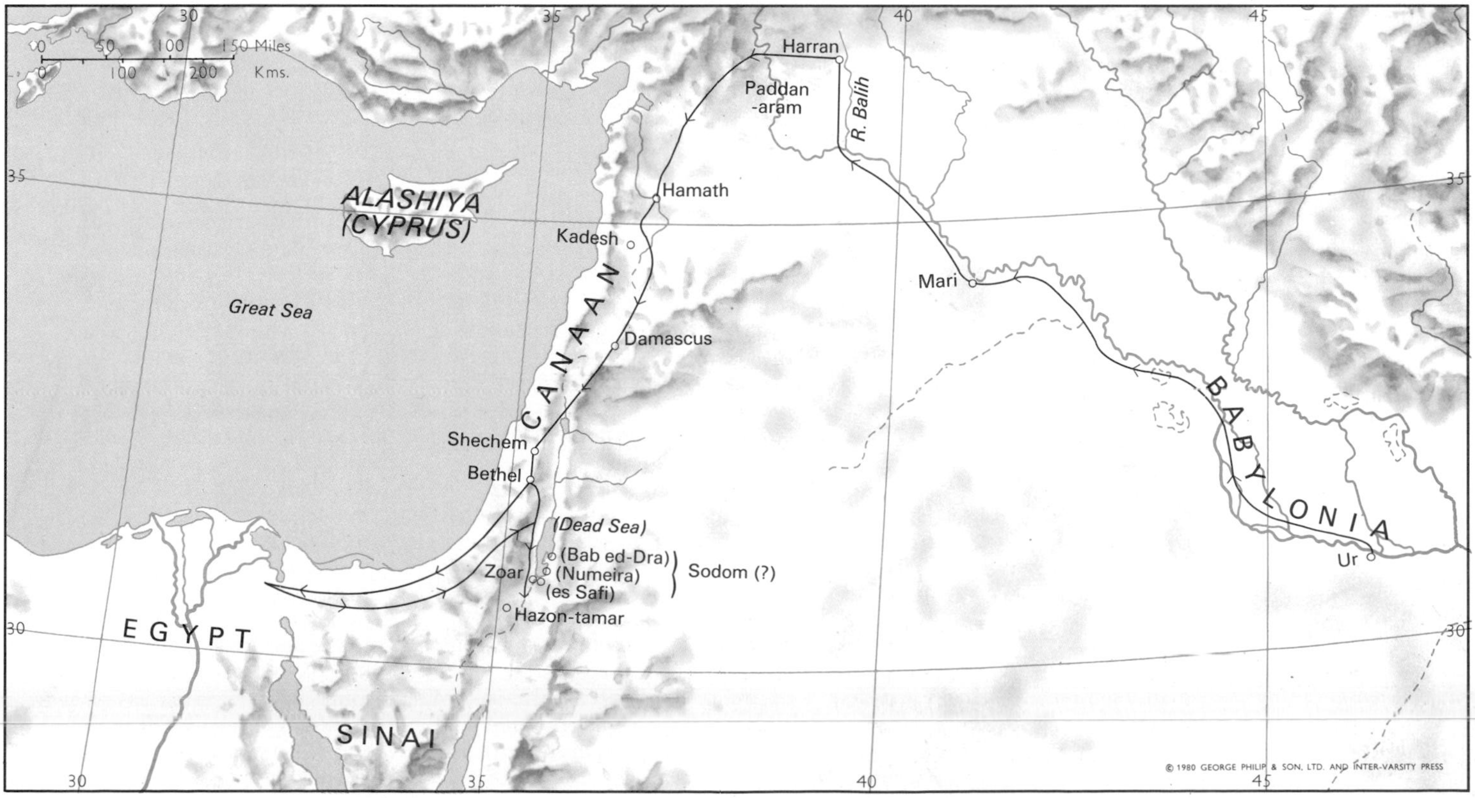

83:8), but he is mentioned by our Lord in Lk. 17:28–32 and also by Peter in 2 Pet. 2:7f.

He accompanied Terah, Abram and Sarai as they journeyed from Ur to Harran, and went on with Abram and Sarai into Canaan, down into Egypt and then out again into Canaan (Gn. 11:31; 12:4–5; 13:1). Flaws in his character first appear when he selfishly chose the well-watered Jordan valley (Gn. 13:8–13). This brought him into the midst of the wicked men of Sodom, and he had to be rescued from the results of his folly, first by Abraham (Gn. 14:11–16), and then by the two angels (Gn. 19). In the latter incident he revealed both his weakness and his inclination to compromise. His salvation from Sodom is expressly linked with God's remembrance of Abraham in Gn. 19:29.

Through his drunkenness his two daughters obtained children by him, and these became the ancestors of the Moabites and the Ammonites (Gn. 19:30–38; *cf.* Dt. 2:9, 19; Ps. 83:8).

Our Lord illustrated his teaching on the subject of his return from the story of Lot and his wife (Lk. 17:28–32), thus setting his seal upon its historicity, and 2 Pet. 2:7f. emphatically asserts his righteousness. It is probable that Peter is here deliberately alluding to Abraham's prayer for the 'righteous' in Sodom. G.W.G.

LOUSE
See Animals, Part 1.

LOVE, BELOVED.

I. In the Old Testament

a. Etymology

Love is the translation in the EVV primarily of the Heb. *'āhēḇ*, which is in every way as broad in its usage as the English word, and easily the most common word for every range of its meaning. Other Heb. words are *dôḏ* and *ra'yâ* (respectively of passionate love and its female object, especially in Ct.), *yāḏaḏ* (*e.g.* Ps. 127:2), *ḥāšaq* (*e.g.* Ps. 91:14), *ḥāḇaḇ* (only Dt. 33:3), *'āgaḇ* (*e.g.* Je. 4:30, of paramours) and *rāḥam* (Ps. 18:1).

In the OT love, whether human or divine, is the deepest possible expression of the personality and of the closeness of personal relations. In the non-religious sense *'āhēḇ* is most commonly employed of the mutual urge of the sexes, in which there is no restraint or sense of uncleanness (see Ct. for its most sublime expression). It is also used of a multitude of personal (Gn. 22:2; 37:3) and sub-personal (Pr. 18:21) relations which have no connection with the sexual impulse. Fundamentally it is an inner force (Dt. 6:5, 'might') which impels to performing the action which gives pleasure (Pr. 20:13), obtaining the object which awakens desire (Gn. 27:4), or in the case of persons to self-sacrifice for the good of the loved one (Lv. 19:18, 34), and unswerving loyalty (1 Sa. 20:17–42).

b. God's love for men

(i) *Its object.* This is primarily a collective group (Dt. 4:37, 'your fathers'; Pr. 8:17, 'those who love me'; Is. 43:4, 'Israel'), though the implication is clear that the individual shares in the divine regard for the group. Only in three places is God said in so many words to love an individual, and in each case it is a king (2 Sa. 12:24 and Ne. 13:26, Solomon; Is. 48:14, ?Cyrus). Here the special relationship may be because Israel's king is in some sense regarded as a son of God (*cf.* 2 Sa. 7:14; Pss. 2:7; 89:26f.), while Cyrus in the Isaianic passage may be a representative figure.

(ii) *Its personal nature.* Being rooted firmly in the personal character of God himself, it is deeper than that of a mother for her children (Is. 49:15; 66:13). This is most clear in Ho. 1–3, where (in whatever order the chapters are to be read) the relation between the prophet and his unfaithful wife Gomer is illustrative of the ultimate basis of the divine covenant in a deeper than legal relationship, in a love that is willing to suffer. God's love is part of his personality, and cannot be swayed by passion or diverted by disobedience (Ho. 11:1–4, 7–9; this passage is the nearest the OT approaches to a declaration that God is love). Israel's unfaithfulness can have no effect upon it, for 'I have loved you with an everlasting love' (Je. 31:3). The threat to 'love them no more' (Ho. 9:15) is best interpreted as one to be their God no more.

(iii) *Its selectiveness.* Dt. in particular bases the covenant relationship between Israel and God on God's prior love. Unlike the gods of other nations, who belong to them for natural and geographic reasons, Yahweh took the initiative and chose Israel because he loved her (Dt. 4:37; 7:6ff.; 10:15; Is. 43:4). This love is spontaneous, not evoked by any intrinsic worth in its object, but rather creating that worth (Dt. 7:7). The corollary is also true, that God hates those whom he does not love (Mal. 1:2f.). Although in various passages, notably Jon. and the Servant Songs of Is., a doctrine of universal love is foreshadowed, it nowhere finds concrete expression.

c. Love as a religious duty

(i) *Towards God.* Love for God with the whole personality (Dt. 6:5) is God's demand; though this is not to be understood as meaning merely a punctilious observance of an impersonal divine law but rather as summoning to a relationship of personal devotion created and sustained by the work of God in the human heart (Dt. 30:6).

It consists in the simple joyful experience of communion with God (Je. 2:2; Pss. 18:1; 116:1), worked out in daily obedience to his commandments (Dt. 10:12, 'to love him, to serve the Lord your God'; Jos. 22:5, 'to love the Lord your God and to walk in all his ways'). This obedience is more fundamental to the nature of love for God than any feeling. God alone will be the judge of its sincerity (Dt. 13:3).

(ii) *Towards fellow men.* Love is ordained by God to be the normal, ideal human relationship, and as such is given the sanction of the divine law (Lv. 19:18), though the parallel prohibition of hatred with its reference to the heart (Lv. 19:17) shows clearly that this too is deeper than a merely legal relationship. An enemy is never commanded to be loved, though he is to be helped (Ex. 23:4f.), even if for somewhat selfish motives (Pr. 25:21f.).

II. In the New Testament

a. Etymology

The commonest Gk. word in the NT for all forms of love is *agapē*, *agapaō*. This is one of the least frequent words in classical Greek, where it expresses, on the few occasions it occurs, that highest and noblest form of love which sees something infinitely precious in its object. Its use in the NT derives not directly from classical Greek so much as from the LXX, where it occurs in 95% of all cases where EVV translate the Hebrew by 'love', and in every case of love from God to man, man to God and man to his neighbour. The dignity which the word possesses in the NT has been contributed by its use as a vehicle of the OT revelation. It is pregnant with OT associations.

phileō is the alternative word to

agapaō. It is more naturally used of intimate affection (Jn. 11:3, 36; Rev. 3:19), and of liking to do things which are pleasant (Mt. 6:5). though there is considerable overlapping of usage between the two words. Much exegesis of Jn. 21:15–17 has turned on Peter's willingness to say *philō se* ('I am your friend', J. B. Phillips), and apparent reluctance to say *agapō se*. It is difficult to see why a writer of such simple Greek as John should have used the two words in this context unless he intended a distinction to be drawn between their meanings. The existence of any clear distinction, here or elsewhere, is, however, seriously disputed by scholars, and is not noticed by ancient commentators, except perhaps by Ambrose (*On Luke* 10. 176) and in the Vulg., which in this passage employs *diligo* and *amo* to translate *agapaō* and *phileō* respectively. (B. B. Warfield, 'The Terminology of Love in the New Testament', *PTR* 16, 1918; J. H. Bernard, *St John*, *ICC*, 2, 1928, pp. 701ff.)

b. God's love

(i) *For Christ.* The relationship between the Father and the Son is one of love (Jn. 3:35; 15:9; Col. 1:13). The word 'beloved' (*agapētos*), carrying with it a strong sense of 'only-beloved', is employed in the Synoptics only of the Christ, either directly (Mt. 17:5; Mk. 1:11) or by inference (Mt. 12:18; Mk. 12:6) (B. W. Bacon, 'Jesus' Voice from Heaven', *AJT* 9, 1905, pp. 451ff.). This love is returned and mutual (Jn. 14:31; *cf.* Mt. 11:27). Since this love is historically prior to creation (Jn. 17:24), it follows that, though known by men only as revealed in Jesus Christ and in redemption (Rom. 5:8), it is of the very nature of the Godhead (1 Jn. 4:8, 16), and that Jesus Christ, who is love incarnate and personified (1 Jn. 3:16), is God's self-revelation.

(ii) *For men.* Jesus is not recorded in the Synoptic Gospels as using *agapaō* or *phileō* to express God's love for men. Rather he revealed it by his countless acts of compassionate healing (Mk. 1:41; Lk. 7:13), his teaching about God's acceptance of the sinner (Lk. 15:11ff.; 18:10ff.), his grief-stricken attitude to human disobedience (Mt. 23:37; Lk. 19:41f.), and by being himself a friend (*philos*) of tax-collectors and outcasts (Lk. 7:34). This saving activity is declared in Jn. to be a demonstration of the love of God, imparting an eternal reality of life to men (Jn. 3:16; 1 Jn. 4:9f.). The whole drama of redemption, centring as it does on the death of Christ, is divine love in action (Gal. 2:20; Rom. 5:8; 2 Cor. 5:14).

As in the OT, God's love is selective. Its object is no longer the old Israel, but the new, the church (Gal. 6:16; Eph. 5:25). God's love and his choosing are closely connected, not only in Paul but clearly too by inference in certain sayings of Jesus himself (Mt. 10:5f.; 15:24). Those whom God's life-giving love does not reach are 'children of wrath' (Jn. 3:35f.; Eph. 2:3ff.) and of 'the devil' (Jn. 8:44). God's intention, however, is clearly the salvation of the whole world (Mt. 8:5; 28:19; Rom. 11:25f.), which is ultimately the object of his love (Jn. 3:16; 6:51), through the preaching of the gospel (Acts 1:8; 2 Cor. 5:19). Individuals are loved by God under the new covenant (Gal. 2:20), though response to his love involves fellowship in the people of God (1 Pet. 2:9f., a passage generally regarded as having a baptismal context).

c. Love as a religious duty

(i) *Towards God.* Man's natural state is to be God's enemy (Rom. 5:10; Col. 1:21), and to hate him (Lk. 19:14; Jn. 15:18ff.), this enmity being seen for what it is in the crucifixion. This attitude is transformed into one of love by the prior action of God in loving man (1 Jn. 4:11, 19). So closely related is God's love for man and man's for God that it is often difficult to decide whether the phrase 'the love of God' denotes a subjective or objective genitive (*e.g.* Jn. 5:42).

Jesus himself, though he accepted and underlined the Shema with his own authority (Mk. 12:28ff.), and expected men to love God and himself when there was ample opportunity for them not to (Mt. 6:24; 10:37f.; Lk. 11:42; Jn. 3:19), preferred to speak of the ideal man–God relationship as one of faith (Mt. 9:22; Mk. 4:40). The word love appears not to have sufficiently emphasized for him the humble trust which he regarded as vital in man's relationship to God. Accordingly, though love to God, worked out in service to one's fellows, is enjoined in the rest of the NT (1 Cor. 2:9; Eph. 6:24; 1 Jn. 4:20; 5:2f.), the writers more commonly follow Jesus' example and enjoin faith.

(ii) *Towards fellow men.* As in the OT, mutual love is to be the ideal human relationship. Jesus corrected contemporary Jewish thought in two directions. (*a*) He insisted that the commandment to love one's neighbour is not a limiting ordinance (Lk. 10:29), as in much rabbinic exegesis of Lv. 19:18, but rather means that the neighbour is to be the first object, because the nearest, of the love which is the characteristic of the Christian heart (Lk. 10:25–37). (*b*) He extended this demand for love to include enemies and persecutors (Mt. 5:44; Lk. 6:27), though none but the new people of God can be expected to have this attitude, for the demand belongs to a new time (Mt. 5:38f.), involves supernatural grace ('reward', Mt. 5:46; 'credit', Lk. 6:32ff.; 'more', Mt. 5:47), and is addressed to a group of 'hearers' (Lk. 6:27), who are sharply differentiated from sinners (Lk. 6:32ff.) and tax collectors (Mt. 5:46f.).

This new attitude is far from a sentimental utopianism, for it must issue in practical help to those who need it (Lk. 10:33ff.), nor is it a superficial virtue, for it involves a fundamental response of the heart (1 Cor. 13 *passim*) to the prior love of God (1 Jn. 4:19), and an acceptance of the Spirit's work in the depths of a man's being (Gal. 5:22).

The characteristic form of this love in the NT is love for the fellow Christian (Jn. 15:12, 17; Gal. 6:10; 1 Pet. 3:8; 4:8; 1 Jn. 2:10; 3:14), love for the outsider being expressed in the evangelistic outreach (Acts 1:8; 10:45; Rom. 1:15f.) and in the patient endurance of persecution (1 Pet. 2:20). The Christian loves his brother: (*a*) to imitate God's love (Mt. 5:43, 45; Eph. 5:2; 1 Jn. 4:11); (*b*) because he sees in him one for whom Christ died (Rom. 14:15; 1 Cor. 8:11); (*c*) because he sees in him Christ himself (Mt. 25:40). The very existence of this mutual love, issuing as it does in the unity of Christian people (Eph. 4:2f.; Phil. 2:1ff.), is the sign *par excellence* to the outside world of the reality of Christian discipleship (Jn. 13:35).

BIBLIOGRAPHY. J. Moffatt, *Love in the New Testament*, 1929; A. Nygren, *Agape and Eros*, Pt. 1, tr. P. S. Watson, 1953; W. Günther, C. Brown, *NIDNTT* 2, pp. 538–551; G. Quell, E. Stauffer, *TDNT* 1, pp. 21–55. F.H.P.

LOVE FEAST. The Christian duty to love one another has always been expressed in gatherings for fellowship. Such fellowship was realized from early times by participation in a common meal, and love feasts, *agapai*, are mentioned by Jude (v. 12; *cf.* 2 Pet. 2:13, RV). Among the Jews meals for fellowship and brotherhood were common, and similar convivial gatherings took place among the Gentiles. It was natural, therefore, that both Jewish and Gentile Christians should adopt such practices. The name *agapē* was later given to the fellowship meal. It is an anachronism, however, to apply it in its later sense to the conditions described in Acts and 1 Corinthians. 'The breaking of bread' referred to in Acts 2:42, 46 may describe a common meal which included both Agapē and Eucharist (see F. F. Bruce, *Acts of the Apostles*, 1951). St Paul's account (in 1 Cor. 11:17–34) of the administration of the Eucharist shows it set in the context of a fellowship supper. His farewell discourse at Troas which continued till midnight was delivered at a fellowship meal on the first day of the week which included the Eucharist (Acts 20:7ff.).

Although the common custom of fellowship meals among the Jews may have been sufficient ground for the primitive Agapē, some would trace the practice to the actual circumstances of the Last Supper. The sacrament was instituted at a Passover meal. Some scholars contend for another type of fellowship meal customary in the *qiddûsh* and *ḥaḇûrāh* gatherings. The early disciples probably reproduced the setting of the first Eucharist, preceding it with such a fellowship meal. The separation of the meal or Agapē from the Eucharist lies outside the times of the NT. The theory of Lietzmann that Eucharist and Agapē can be traced to two different types of sacramental observance in the NT is generally rejected (*LORD'S SUPPER).

For later development of Agapē and Eucharist, see Pliny's letter to Trajan, *Didache*, Justin Martyr, *Apol.* 1. 67, Tertullian, *de Corona* 3.

BIBLIOGRAPHY. J. H. Kelly, *Love Feasts: A History of the Christian Agape*, 1916; J. H. Srawley, *Early History of the Liturgy*, 1947; G. Dix, *Shape of the Liturgy*, 1944.

R.J.C.

LOVING-KINDNESS. One rendering of the Heb. word *ḥeseḏ* given prior to the 20th century in all EVV from the time of Coverdale. Most of its occurrences are in the Pss., but it comes seven times elsewhere in AV, which has ten other renderings, the most frequent being 'mercy', 'kindness' and 'goodness'. There have been many suggestions as to how it should best be translated, including 'leal-love' (G. Adam Smith), 'piety' (C. H. Dodd), 'solidarity' (*KB*) and 'covenant-love' (N. H. Snaith). RSV frequently, although not consistently, renders it 'steadfast love'. Its etymological origin is uncertain. An examination of the passages where it is found (*e.g.* Ps. 89, where it is rendered 'mercy' as well as 'loving kindness' in AV) reveals its close connection with the two ideas of covenant and faithfulness. Its meaning may be summed up as 'steadfast love on the basis of a covenant'. It is employed both of God's attitude towards his people and of theirs to him, the latter especially in Hosea.

BIBLIOGRAPHY. N. H. Snaith, *The Distinctive Ideas of the Old Testament*, 1944, pp. 94–130. G.W.G.

LOWEST ROOM
See Meals, Part 2.

LOWLAND
See Shephelah, Part 3.

LUCIFER (Lat. 'light-bearer'). This was the Lat. name for the planet Venus, the brightest object in the sky apart from the sun and moon, appearing sometimes as the evening, sometimes as the morning, star. In Is. 14:12 it is the translation of *hêlēl* ('shining one': LXX *heōsphoros*, 'light-bearer'; *cf.* the Arabic for Venus, *zuhratun*, 'the bright shining one'), and is applied tauntingly as a title for the king of Babylon, who in his glory and pomp had set himself among the gods. This name is appropriate, as the civilization of Babylon began in the grey dawn of history, and had strong astrological connections. Babylonians and Assyrians personified the morning star as Belit and Ištar. Some have considered that the phrase 'son of the morning' might refer to the crescent moon; *cf.* Gray in *ICC*, *ad loc.*; others (*e.g.* S. H. Langdon, *ExpT* 42, 1930–1, pp. 172ff.) argue for an identification with the planet Jupiter. The similarity of the description here with that of such passages as Lk. 10:18 and Rev. 9:1 (*cf.* 12:9) has led to the application of the title to Satan. The true claimant to this title is shown in Rev. 22:16 to be the Lord Jesus Christ in his ascended glory. D.H.W.

LUCIUS. Gk. *Loukios*, transcribing or imitating the Roman praenomen. *Loukas* (Luke) was a diminutive. (*Cf.* Ramsay, *BRD*, pp. 370–384, for inscriptions.)

1. A Cyrenian prophet and teacher of Antioch (Acts 13:1), probably one of its first missionaries (*cf.* Acts 11:19–21). A strange African quotation of Acts 13:1

Greek manuscript of Luke 9:45–10:1. Chester Beatty papyrus I. 3rd cent. AD. (CBL)

noted by Zahn (*cf. INT*, 3, pp. 28f.) adds 'who remains to this day'. Probably this writer, like Ephraem Syrus *in loc.*, identifies Lucius with the traditionally Antiochene Luke.

2. A companion of Paul in Corinth, sending greetings in Rom. 16:21. He is Paul's 'kinsman', *i.e.* a Jew (*cf.* Rom. 9:3). Origen *in loc.* mentions an identification with Luke.

That either is Luke is improbable. They were undoubtedly Jews; Luke was almost certainly a Gentile (see Col. 4:11, 14).

BIBLIOGRAPHY. H. J. Cadbury, *BC*, 1. 5, pp. 489–495. A.F.W.

LUD, LUDIM. In Gn. 10:22 and 1 Ch. 1:17 Lud is one of the descendants of Shem, and Josephus (*Ant.* 1. 144) refers to the Lydians (*LYDIA) as his descendants. Herodotus' account of the Lydians (50. 7) does not preclude a Semitic origin. In Is. 66:19 Lud is a Gentile nation characterized by the use of the bow (probably not true of Lydia); in Ezk. 27:10 and 30:5 they are allies of Tyre and of Egypt respectively, and as such Lydia (*Lūdu*) is mentioned in Neo-Babylonian annals.

Ludim appears in Gn. 10:13 and 1 Ch. 1:11 as a descendant of Ham, and in Je. 46:9 as a bow-bearing auxiliary of Egypt. This may be an unknown African nation, but some scholars emend to *Lubim* (Libya), and even the singular *Lud* to *Lub* in some passages. K.L.McK.

LUHITH, ASCENT OF. A place in Moab where the people fled from the Babylonians (Is. 15:5; Je. 48:5). Eusebius places it between Areopolis and Zoar, but it has not yet been certainly identified. J.D.D.

LUKE. Among the companions of Paul who send their greetings in his letter to Colossae there appears 'Luke (Gk. *Loukas*) the beloved physician' (Col. 4:14); the way in which he is described suggests that he had given medical care to Paul, no doubt during the latter's imprisonment. In Phm. 24, probably written at the same time, he is described as a fellow-worker of Paul, which suggests that his help in the work of the gospel was not confined to his medical skill. There is a third reference to him in what appears to have been one of Paul's last messages: 'Luke alone is with me' (2 Tim. 4:11), and this confirms the close link between the two men. He is generally thought to have been a Gentile, but E. E. Ellis (pp. 51–53) has argued that Col. 4:11 refers to a particular group within the wider circle of Jewish Christians, and that consequently Luke may have been a Jewish Christian of the Dispersion.

Irenaeus (*c.* AD 180) is the first person to refer clearly to Luke and to name him as the author of the third Gospel and Acts. The same tradition is found in the Muratorian Canon and the so-called anti-Marcionite Prologue to the Gospel of Luke. The last of these documents speaks of Luke as coming from Antioch in Syria, and as serving the Lord without the distractions of a wife or family until he died at the age of 84 in Boeotia, the earliness and reliability of this tradition are uncertain.

The tradition that Luke was the author of Lk. and Acts can probably be traced back to earlier in the 2nd century. The fact that Marcion, a fanatical follower of Paul's theology, chose Lk. as the one Gospel which he recognized, probably implies that he regarded it as the work of a companion of Paul. Acts contains a number of passages written in the 1st person plural which describe events from the point of view of a companion of Paul (Acts 16:10–17; 20:5–21:18; 27:1–28:16). The fact that the author of Acts made no attempt to rewrite these passages in the 3rd person is best explained by identifying him as their original author. Of the possible companions of Paul, known to us from his Epistles but not named in Acts, Luke stands out as the probable composer of Acts and hence of Lk. This identification is found in a variant reading of Acts 20:13 ('But I Luke, and those who were with me, went on board') which may go back to early in the 2nd century.

The argument from the internal evidence of Acts is strong. It is confirmed by the external evidence of 2nd-century tradition cited above, and especially by the fact that no other candidate for the authorship of Acts was ever suggested. The claim that the tradition rests on a deduction from the NT evidence and has no independent value is pure hypothesis. There is more force in the objection that the picture of the early church in Acts, and of Paul in particular, are not such as might be expected from a companion of Paul, but this objection can be answered (F. F. Bruce, *NBCR*, pp. 968–973).

The literary style of Lk. and Acts demonstrates that their author was a well-educated person with considerable gifts of expression. The traces of medical language and the interest in medical matters displayed in them are consistent with authorship by the 'beloved physician'. Luke's gifts as a historian have been recognized by many scholars who have viewed his work against its classical background and compared him favourably with the best of ancient historians.

Luke's admiration for Paul comes out clearly in the course of Acts. Through his close contact

The Greek text of Luke 16:16–21. Bodmer Papyrus codex. c. AD *180.* (FMB)

with him and with other Christian leaders, and as a consequence of his visits to Jerusalem and Caesarea (*cf.* Acts 21:17ff.), Luke had ample opportunities to gain first-hand knowledge about the life of Jesus and the history of the earliest Christian church. He could rightly claim in the prologue to his Gospel that he was well qualified for his task, having carefully and thoroughly investigated all the relevant facts, as they were handed down by responsible witnesses in the church (Lk. 1:1–4).

The picture which emerges is of a self-effacing man possessed of strong human sympathies who regarded himself as a servant of the Word. With his considerable literary, historical and theological gifts, he was well fitted to recount the story of the beginnings of Christianity in a new way, adapted to the needs of the second generation in the church.

BIBLIOGRAPHY. N. Geldenhuys, *Commentary on the Gospel of Luke*, 1950, pp. 15–50; F. F. Bruce, *The Acts of the Apostles*, 1951, pp. 1–40; C. K. Barrett, *Luke the Historian in Recent Study*, 1961; E. E. Ellis, *The Gospel of Luke*², 1974, pp. 2–62; E. Haenchen, *The Acts of the Apostles*, 1971. I.H.M.

LUKE, GOSPEL OF.

I. Outline of contents

a. Preface (1:1–4).

b. The birth and childhood of Jesus (1:5–2:52).

c. John the Baptist and Jesus (3:1–4:13).

d. The ministry in Galilee (4:14–9:50).

e. Progress towards Jerusalem (9:51–19:10).

f. The ministry in Jerusalem (19:11–21:38).

g. The passion and resurrection of Jesus (22:1–24:53).

II. The sources of the Gospel

In its general pattern Lk. is similar to the other two *Synoptic Gospels. It shares with Mt. an interest in the birth of Jesus, although the two Gospels tell this story from different angles. It follows the general outline of the ministry of Jesus found in Mk. (and also in Mt.), but has a considerably longer section on the progress of Jesus from Galilee to Jerusalem. Whether or not Mk. originally included some account of the resurrection appearances of Jesus, Lk. and Mt. each contain their own individual accounts of these appearances.

To a considerable extent the contents of Lk. are also shared with the other Gospels. It is generally agreed that one of Luke's major sources was Mk., and that like Matthew he drew the most part of his account of the ministry and deeds of Jesus from the earlier Gospel. Nearly all of Mk. has been incorporated in Lk., but it has been rewritten in Luke's more developed literary style. Luke also includes a good deal of the teaching of Jesus which is found in Mt. (but not in Mk.), and it is generally assumed that the two Gospels were dependent on some common source (or a collection of sources), written or oral. It is much less likely that one Gospel was dependent on the other for this material. Although the relation between the sources of Jn. and the other Gospels continues to be uncertain, it is clear that Lk. and Jn. reflect some use of common traditions, especially in the story of the passion and resurrection. In addition, there is a good deal of information about Jesus peculiar to Lk., much of it to be found in the account of Jesus' journey to Jerusalem. In some places where Luke is at first sight dependent on Mk., such as the account of the Last Supper, it is highly probable that he had access to other traditions also.

All this means that Luke was dependent upon a variety of sources of information for his Gospel and illustrates his own statement (Lk. 1:1–4) that many other persons had made earlier attempts to draw up accounts of what had happened. The same statement suggests that Luke was acquainted not only with written accounts of the ministry of Jesus but also with persons who had been eyewitnesses of it, and that he wrote his Gospel after careful research into his various sources of information.

III. Authorship, date and place of composition

The question of the authorship of Lk. is closely bound up with that of Acts. The two books are parts of one work, and attempts to deny their common authorship have not been successful. The traditional ascription of both books to *Luke still remains the most probable view. The evidence is basically derived from *Acts. So far as the Gospel is concerned, it contains little concrete evidence for or against the traditional ascription of authorship. The claim that it breathes the atmosphere of the subapostolic period (*i.e.* the time after Luke's death) is too subjective to carry any conviction.

What the modern discussion of authorship has brought out is that Luke was not a slavish imitator of Paul in his theological outlook. He had his own distinctive slant on the Christian faith. His Gospel, therefore, is in no way a Pauline reinterpretation of the story of Jesus, but represents his own, independent assessment of the significance of Jesus, based on traditions handed down from the early church. We do not know how Paul regarded the earthly life of Jesus, since he makes so little mention of him in his letters, and we have, therefore, no way of comparing his views with those of Luke. If we cannot ascertain the measure of their agreement, we are equally unable to posit any disagreement between them.

In one sense, identification of the author of the Gospel sheds little light on it, since we know scarcely anything about the author additional to what can be gleaned from Lk. and Acts. In another sense, however, the knowledge of the author's identity is valuable because it confirms that he was a person well qualified (in accordance with his own explicit claim) to learn the contents of the Gospel tradition and to reformulate them. The historical credentials of the Gospel are greater than if it was the work of some unknown figure from a later date.

We do not know when or where the Gospel was written. There are two serious possibilities regarding the date, either in the early 60s or in the later decades of the 1st century. A decision depends on the date to be assigned to Mk. and on whether Luke was writing after the fall of Jerusalem prophesied by Jesus. A date before AD 70 is certainly not to be ruled out for Mk. In the case of Lk. the comparatively frequent and more precise references to the fall of Jerusalem, while based on genuine prophecy by Jesus, may be thought to reflect interest in the fulfilment of the prophecy. On the other hand, the lack of interest in the fall of Jerusalem in Acts, and the way in which that book ends its story before the death of Paul, are strong indications of a date before AD 70. It is possible that the composition of the books was largely complete before that date, although the date of completion may have been later.

Although there is a tradition of uncertain date connecting the composition of the Gospel with Achaia, there is nothing in the writing itself to substantiate this view. It is more likely that we should connect the Gospel with Rome (where Mk. was available and where Luke was present with Paul) or with Antioch in Syria (with which Luke is also connected by what is probably a more reliable tradition, and where the 'Q' source which he shared with Matthew was probably compiled). Behind the Gospel, however, there ultimately lie traditions current in Palestine. Luke's connection with the early church in Palestine and Syria is ultimately of more significance than where he adventitiously happened to produce his Gospel.

IV. Purpose and character

We are singularly fortunate in that Luke has given us his own statement of intention at the beginning of the Gospel. At the same time we can draw certain conclusions from the character of the work itself. His concern was to present the story of Jesus in such a way as to bring out its significance and its reliability for those who believed in him; and he did this in the context of a two-part work which went on to tell the story of the early church so as to demonstrate how the message of the gospel spread, in accordance with prophecy and God's command, to the ends of the earth and brought salvation to those who responded to it. Luke was writing for people at some remove from the ministry of Jesus, both in geography and in time. He addresses himself to a certain *Theophilus, whose identity remains quite unknown, but clearly this is no more than a literary dedication to a friend of the author and the book was intended for a wider audience. The dedication suggests that it was meant for members of the church, and its contents reinforce this view, but at the same time it could be used both as a handbook and as a tool for evangelism; its outward form, conforming to that of historical and literary works of the time, strongly suggests that a wider audience was in view.

Luke wrote as a man of culture and education, and his work has much more of a claim to being a deliberate literary production than the other Gospels have. It is clear that the author was a man of letters, well acquainted with the OT in Gk. and also with the style of contemporary literature, who was able to produce a work that would commend the gospel by its literary quality. Even if E. Renan intended to damn rather than to praise when he described Lk. as 'the most beautiful book that was ever written', his comment is not without some truth. Here literary art is employed as a servant of the gospel.

At the same time, Luke writes specifically as a historian. The evidence for his historical interests and abilities is more obvious in Acts, but the Gospel too is meant as a historical work whose aim is to demonstrate the reliability of the traditions about Jesus. Where we can compare his story with its sources, Luke has faithfully reproduced them, although of course he does not follow them with slavish literalness.

Literary art and historical skill are, however, servants of a conscious evangelistic and theological purpose. Two important groups of words take us to the centre of Luke's interest. The first is the verb 'to preach the gospel' (*euangelizomai*), a word which characterizes the Christmas message (Lk. 1:19; 2:10), the preaching of John (Lk. 3:18), the ministry of Jesus (Lk. 4:18, 43; 7:22; *et al.*) and the activity of the early church (Acts 5:42; 8:4; *et al.*). The fact that the verb, found frequently in Paul, is virtually absent from the other Gospels (Mt. 11:5; the corresponding noun, however, is used more often) is an indication of its significance for Luke in describing the nature of the work of Jesus and the early church. The other keyword is 'salvation' (with its cognates). Particularly in the birth stories the thought of God bringing a Saviour, to his people is prominent (Lk. 1:47, 69, 71, 77; 2:11, 30); although the word-group is not so conspicuous elsewhere in Lk. and Acts, the opening emphasis on it gives the key to the nature of the gospel message, just as John's opening stress on the Word gives the key to his Gospel. By contrast with Mark, Luke brings out the nature of Jesus' message of the kingdom of God as salvation for the lost; and where Matthew tends to present Jesus as the Teacher of true righteousness, Luke lays more stress on his action as Saviour; these contrasts, however, can be misleading if taken too far.

Luke shows how the ministry of Jesus represents the fulfilment of OT prophecy (Lk. 4:18–21; 10:23f.; 24:26f., 44–47). The new era of salvation has dawned, characterized by the preaching of the good news of the kingdom (Lk. 16:16). Although the full realization of the reign of God belongs to the future (Lk. 19:11), nevertheless God has already begun to deliver men and women from the power of Satan and the demons (Lk. 11:20; 13:16), and sinners can enjoy forgiveness and fellowship with Jesus. In Jesus the saving power of God himself is manifested (Lk. 7:16; Acts 10:38).

The One through whom God acts in this way is clearly a prophet, anointed with the Spirit, but for Luke he is more than a prophet, more even than the unique prophet like Moses for whom the people were waiting (Lk. 24:19–21; Acts [illegible]). He is the anointed King who will reign in the future kingdom (Lk. 22:29f.; 23:42), and already he can be described as the 'Lord', the title which indicates the role of Jesus confirmed by his resurrection and exaltation (Acts 2:36). Behind these roles fulfilled by Jesus there lies his unique nature as the Son of God (Lk. 1:32).

In his presentation of the ministry of Jesus Luke draws particular attention to the concern of Jesus for outcasts; all the Gospels bear witness to this undoubted historical fact, but it is Luke who takes most delight in drawing attention to it (Lk. 14:15–24; 15; 19:1–10). He demonstrates how Jesus was concerned for women (Lk. 7:36–50; 8:1–3), for the Samaritans (Lk. 9:51–56; 10:30–37; 17:11–19) and for the Gentiles (Lk. 7:1–9); yet Luke respects the historical fact that Jesus' ministry was almost exclusively to the Jews by confining himself to hints of the wider spread of the gospel in Acts (Lk. 2:32; 13:28f.; 24:47). Another concern of Jesus to which Luke draws attention is his care for the poor and his warnings that the rich who have lived for themselves thereby shut themselves out of the kingdom of God. In the kingdom human values are subjected to a radical reappraisal. There is no room for the self-sufficient who think that worldly wealth will shield them from judgment (Lk. 6:20–26; 12:13–21; 16:19–31) or for the self-righteous who see no need for repentance (Lk. 18:9–14). On the contrary, entry to the kingdom is reserved for the poor, *i.e.*, those who know their poverty and therefore trust in God, and the repentant who recognize their sin and cast themselves upon the mercy of God. Such repentance means whole-hearted turning from sin and readiness to follow Jesus, whatever the cost (Lk. 9:23); and that cost may involve renunciation of one's possessions (Lk. 14:33; 19:8).

The picture of Jesus in Lk. is no doubt meant as an example and a pattern for his disciples. This can be seen from a comparison of the life of Jesus in the Gospel with Luke's description of the church and its members in Acts. Thus, just as the life of Jesus was governed by the plan of God, partly revealed in OT prophecy, so the life of the church is at every pointed guided and directed by God. As Jesus did his work in the power of the Spirit (Lk. 4:14, 18), so the early church was filled with the Spirit for its task of witness (Lk. 24:49). Similarly, just as Jesus was a man of prayer, drawing guidance and inspiration from his communion with God (Lk. 3:21; 6:12; 9:18, 28f.; 22:32), so the church is to be continuously in prayer to God (Acts 1:14).

Such—in broadest outline—is the characteristic Lucan picture of Jesus and his teaching. It has a number of significant features. First, it presents the story of Jesus in terms of fulfilment of prophecy. For Luke the category of promise and fulfilment is of great significance and it provides the structure of his historical thinking. Second, Luke strongly emphasizes the actual presence of salvation in the ministry of Jesus. The accent falls on what Jesus accomplished rather than on the future, although the future dimension is by no means lacking. Third, Luke links the ministry of Jesus to the rise of the early church and shows how the latter follows on from the former. He is aware that the beginning of Christianity included both of the areas covered in the Gospel and Acts.

The effect of these considerations is to show that for Luke the story of Jesus was a part of history. The most important modern discussion of Luke, that of H. Conzelmann, argues that Luke saw the ministry of Jesus as the mid-point of history (preceded by the history of Israel and followed by the period of the church). Conzelmann claims that this was a new understanding of Jesus and stood in contrast with earlier views. The earlier understanding of Jesus was as the proclaimer of the imminent kingdom of God. Luke wrote at a time when the church was beginning to enjoy a settled existence and the future consummation of the kingdom had proved to be a disappointing hope. In effect he remoulded Christian theology to fit it for the second and subsequent generations by virtually abandoning hope of the imminent end of the world and regarding the ministry of Jesus as the midpoint in the history of God's dealings with men rather than as the immediate prelude to the end. The Christian summons to repent before the imminent end was turned into a historical account of the coming of Jesus, and the period of the church, during which the Holy Spirit would lead its members in mission, replaced the hope of the future kingdom of God.

Like so many first statements of a case, Conzelmann's understanding of Luke is one-sided and exaggerated, but it has had the merit of demonstrating that Luke was a careful theologian and of encouraging other scholars to offer a more balanced understanding of his theology. The truth is rather that the message of Jesus and the early church was not as one-sidedly futurist as Conzelmann suggests, and that Luke is simply drawing attention to the present features in that message. 'Salvation history' was by no means an invention of Luke. At the same time, Luke by no means gives up the hope of the coming of the end, and his work retains that element of tension between present realization and future hope which is typical of early Christianity. The effect of his work, however, is to lead the church away from looking for apocalyptic signs of the coming of the end to a concentration on the task of spreading the gospel.

We have to draw a distinction between the factors which moulded Luke's work and the conscious purposes which governed his writing. Among the former we must number the need to re-present the story of Jesus in a way that brought it up-to-date for the church of his day. Among the latter the chief was the desire to present Jesus as the Saviour and to show how the Spirit of God had constituted the church as the witness to Jesus. In the combination of these factors and purposes we can find the key to the distinctive nature of this Gospel in which a historical record has become a means of equipping the church for evangelism.

BIBLIOGRAPHY. Commentaries on the English text: T. W. Manson, *The Sayings of Jesus*, 1949; J. N. Geldenhuys, *NIC/NLC*, 1950; A. R. Leaney, *BNTC*, 1958; F. W. Danker, *Jesus and the New Age*, 1972; E. E. Ellis, *NCB*², 1974; L. Morris, *TNTC*, 1974; on the Greek text: A. Plummer, *ICC*, ⁵1922; J. M. Creed (Macmillan), 1930; I. H. Marshall (Paternoster), 1978; in German: K. H. Rengstorf, *NTD*, 1937; W. Grundmann, *THNT*, ³1966; H. Schürmann, *HTKNT*, 1, 1969. J. Ernst, *Regensburger NT*, 1977; G. Schneider, *Ökumenischer Taschenbuchkommentar zum NT*, 1977.

N. B. Stonehouse, *The Witness of Luke to Christ*, 1951; H. Conzelmann, *The Theology of St Luke*, 1960; H. Flender, *St Luke: Theologian of Redemption History*, 1967; I. H. Marshall, *Luke: Historian and Theologian*, 1970; S. G. Wilson, *The Gentiles and the Gentile Mission in Luke–Acts*, 1973; C. H. Talbert, *Literary Patterns, Theological Themes and the Genre of Luke–Acts*, 1974; E. Franklin, *Christ the Lord*, 1975; J. Drury, *Tradition and Design in Luke's Gospel*, 1976. I.H.M.

LUST. The Eng. word was originally a neutral term describing any strong desire; hence its use in early translations of Gn. 3:16; Jn. 1:13; Nu. 14:8; Heb. 10:6. In its modern restricted sense of sexual passion it cannot adequately render many familiar contexts in AV.

The Heb. *nep̄eš* expresses craving or desire in Ex. 15:9 and Ps. 78:18, and carries the promise of satisfaction in Pr. 10:24. Gk. *epithymia* expresses any strong desire, the context or a qualifying adjective determining its nature, whether good or evil. Hence it is used of the intensely pure desire of Christ, Lk. 22:15, and of Paul's desire to be with Christ, Phil. 1:23, and of his longing to see his converts, 1 Thes. 2:17. Yet in 1 Pet. 4:3 it stands among a list of Gentile vices, and the adjectives 'worldly', 'evil', 'youthful' and 'deceitful' are attached to it in Tit. 2:12; Col. 3:5; 2 Tim. 2:22; and Eph. 4:22 respectively. The restricted reference to sexual passion is found in Eph. 2:3; 1 Jn. 2:16; 1 Pet. 2:11 (*cf.* LXX and Jos., *Ant.*). The strong desire of the Spirit is set over against that of the flesh in Gal. 5:17. Other cognate words are *pathos*, 'passion' (1 Thes. 4:5); *orexis*, 'strong desire' (Rom. 1:27), and *hēdonē*, 'pleasure' (Jas. 4:3). The word 'lusty' when used in Jdg. 3:29 (AV); Is. 59:10 (RV); Ps. 73:4 (Prayer Book) carries no derogatory tone, and simply means able-bodied or vigorous.

BIBLIOGRAPHY. Arndt; *HDB*; B. S. Easton, *Pastoral Epistles*, 1947, pp. 186ff.; *MM*; H. Schönweiss *et al.*, *NIDNTT* 1, pp. 456–461.

D.H.T.

LUZ. The ancient name of *Bethel, which was so named by Jacob after he had dreamed of the ladder from heaven to earth after spending the night near to the city (Gn. 28:19; 35:6; 48:3). It was the site of Jacob's sojourn near to the city, rather than the city itself, that received the name Bethel (Jos. 16:2), but this site later became so important that the name was applied to the city as well (Jos. 18:13; Jdg. 1:23). The city was, however, still known to the Canaanite inhabitants as Luz, because when the Israelites took the city at the time of the conquest a Canaanite whom they pressed to show them the entrance to it in return for his life escaped to the 'land of the Hittites' and founded another city of that name (Jdg. 1:24–26).

BIBLIOGRAPHY. F. M. Abel, *Géographie de la Palestine*, 2, 1938, p. 371.

T.C.M.

LYCAONIA, a territory in S-central Asia Minor, so called from the *Lykaones* who inhabited it, mentioned by ancient writers from Xenophon (early 4th century BC) onwards. In Pompey's settlement of W Asia Minor (64 BC) the W part of Lycaonia was added to Cilicia, the E part to Cappadocia, and the N part to *Galatia, which became a Roman province in 25 BC. E Lycaonia later became independent of Cappadocia and from AD 37 onwards formed part of the client kingdom of Antiochus, king of Commagene, and was known as Lycaonia Antiochiana. In the NT 'Lycaonia' denotes that part of the territory which constituted a region of the province of Galatia, Lycaonia Galatica. Lystra and Derbe are designated 'cities of Lycaonia' in Acts 14:6, in a context which implies that Iconium lay on the Phrygian side of the frontier separating Lycaonia Galatica from Phrygia Galatica. W. M. Ramsay has put it on record that it was this geographical note that led to his 'first change of judgment' with regard to the historical value of Acts. Paul and Barnabas on their first 'missionary journey' (AD 47–8) doubtless recognized that they had crossed a linguistic frontier between Iconium and Lystra, for in the latter place (near modern Hatunsaray) they heard the indigenous population speak 'in Lycaonian' (Acts 14:11, Gk. *lykaonisti*). Lycaonian personal names have been identified in inscriptions hereabout, *e.g.* in one at Sedasa which records the dedication to Zeus of a statue of Hermes (*cf.* Acts 14:12). When, after leaving Lystra, Paul and Barnabas came to Derbe (modern Kerti Hüyük) and planted a church there, they turned back; had they gone farther they would have crossed into the kingdom of Antiochus, but it was no part of their plan to evangelize non-Roman territory.

BIBLIOGRAPHY. W. M. Ramsay, *Historical Commentary on Galatians*, 1899, pp. 185f., 215ff.; M. H. Ballance, *AS* 7, 1957, pp. 147ff.; 14, 1964, pp. 139f.; B. Van Elderen, 'Some Archaeological Observations on Paul's First Missionary Journey', in *Apostolic History and the Gospel*, ed. W. W. Gasque and R. P. Martin, 1970, pp. 156–161.

F.F.B.

LYCIA. A small district on the S coast of Asia Minor containing the broad valley of the river Xanthus, mountains rising to over 3,000 m, and the seaports *Patara and *Myra (Acts 21:1; 27:5). Although

LUTE
See Music, Part 2.

LUXOR
See Thebes, Part 3.

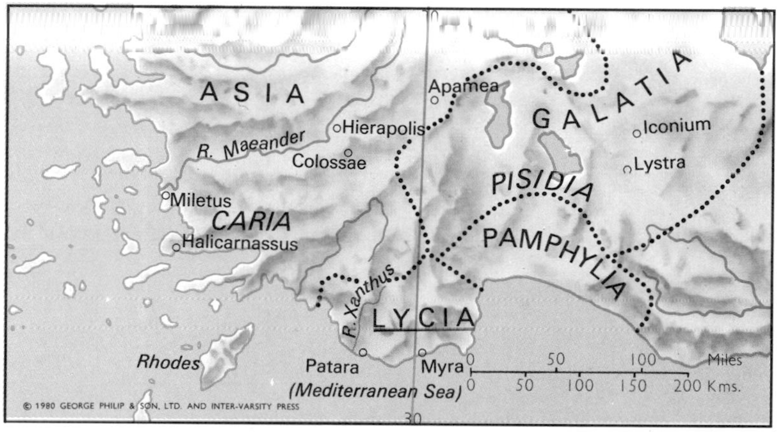

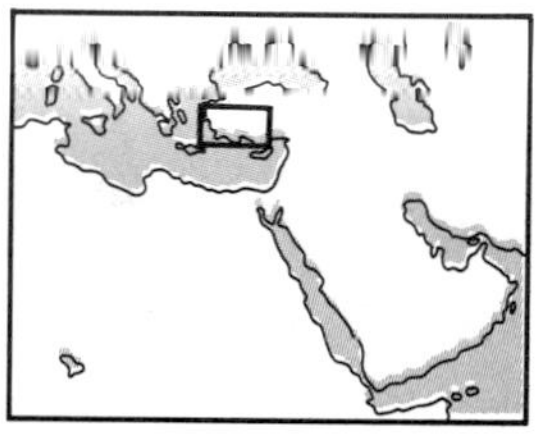

The Roman province of Lycia.

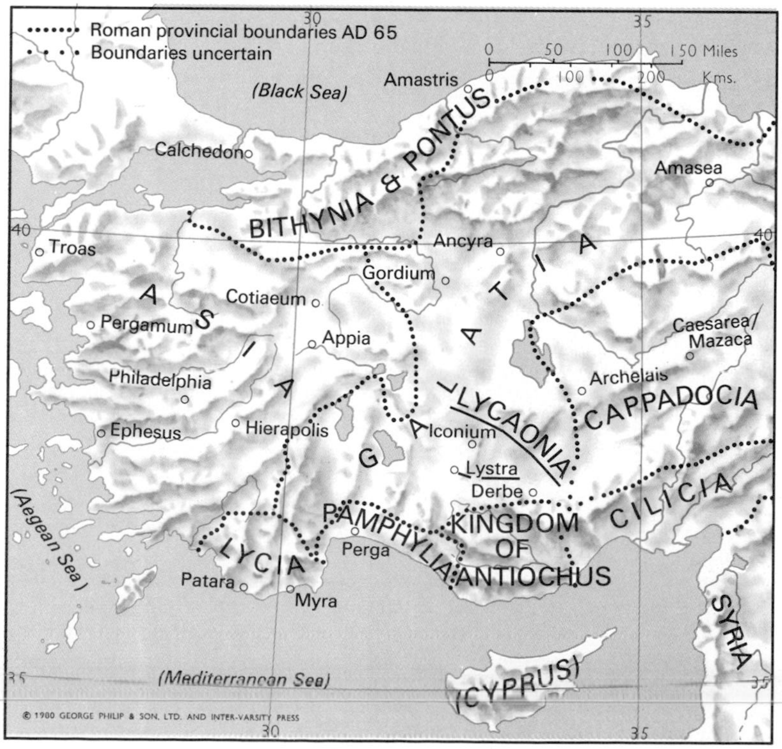

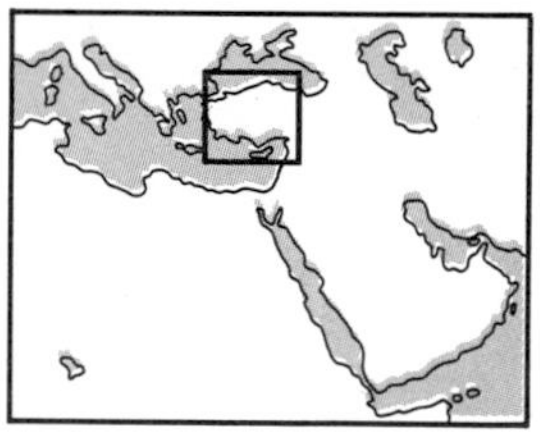

The location of Lystra and other places visited by Paul in Lycaonia.

A gold stater from Lydia, the first state to coin money. The lumps of metal of standard size were simply marked with punches. Diameter 15 mm. c. 600 BC. (RG)

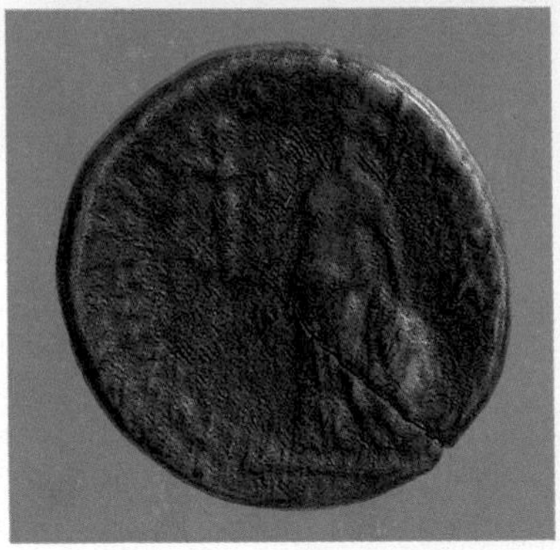

Coin, thought to be of Lysanias, king of the Ituraeans. Diameter 18 mm. 40–36 BC. (RG)

LYING
See Lie, Part 2.

LYRE
See Music, Part 2.

LYSIAS, CLAUDIUS
See Claudius Lysias, Part 1.

some sculptures and inscriptions have been preserved, the origin of the Lycian people is obscure. They alone of the peoples of W Asia Minor successfully resisted the Lydian kings, but they succumbed in 546 BC to the Persians.

Freed by Greeks in the following century, they were greatly influenced by Gk. civilization and eventually submitted voluntarily to Alexander. They adopted the Gk. language and script, and were thoroughly Hellenized by the time they came under Roman protection in the 2nd century BC. Claudius in AD 43 annexed Lycia to the province of Pamphylia, but apparently Nero restored their freedom, for Vespasian again reduced them to provincial status (Suetonius, *Vespasian* 8). Through these changes the federation of Lycian cities maintained its general political framework. K.L.McK.

LYDDA. A town some 18 km SE of the coast at Jaffa, in the Shephelah plain. It is almost certainly to be identified with the OT Lod, which is mentioned in the Karnak list of Thothmes III. In Israelite times it was a Benjaminite town; reoccupied after the Bab. Exile, it later fell to the authority of the governor of Samaria, and was not reclaimed by the Jews till 145 BC (1 Macc. 11:34). It was burnt down in Nero's reign. After the fall of Jerusalem (AD 70) it became a rabbinical centre for a period. It had a bishop in the early Christian centuries. Since then it has borne the names Diospolis, Ludd and Lod again (today). D.F.P.

LYDIA. A woman of Thyatira in Lydia, who at Philippi became Paul's first European convert and gave him hospitality, with Silas and Luke (Acts 16:14–15, 40). Lydia may be an adjectival form, 'the Lydian woman' (such ethnic names were common), but it was also a personal name (*e.g.* Horace, *Od.* 1. 8; 3. 9). Evidently a woman of rank (*cf.* Acts 17:4, 12), she was head of a household, and thus either widowed or unmarried. Lydian purple dye, in which she traded, was renowned (*cf.* Homer, *Il.* 4. 141). She was a Jewish proselyte, engaging in prayers and ablutions at the riverside on the sabbath; her connection with the Jewish faith probably went back to the colony in Thyatira. For the Christian church established there, *cf.* Rev. 1:11; 2:18–29. Lydia may be included in Paul's reference in Phil. 4:3, but since she is unmentioned by name she may have died or left the city. Her hospitality became traditional in the church there (*cf.* Phil. 1:5; 4:10). B.F.H.

LYDIA, a district in the centre of the W slope of Asia Minor, included the Caÿster and Hermus valleys, the most fertile and highly cultivated areas of the peninsula, and between them the mountains of Tmolus, rising to 2,000 m. Besides its natural wealth its position on the main routes from the coast to the interior of Asia Minor gave its cities (including *Sardis, *Thyatira and *Philadelphia) great commercial importance. Lydia was bordered by Mysia, Phrygia and Caria. Some of the coastal cities (including Smyrna and Ephesus) were sometimes reckoned as Lydian, sometimes as Gk.

The origins of the Lydian race are obscure, but there may have been Semitic elements (*LUD). Croesus, the last king of Lydia, dominated the whole of Asia Minor before he was conquered by Cyrus the Persian in 546 BC. The region was subsequently ruled by Alexander and his successors, and became part of the Attalid kingdom of Pergamum before becoming part of the Roman province of Asia in 133 BC. Some Lydian inscriptions of the 4th century BC have been discovered, but by the beginning of the Christian era Gk. had become the common language and, according to Strabo, Lydian was little used.

Lydia was the first state to use coined money and was the home of some innovations in music. K.L.McK.

LYSANIAS, listed in Lk. 3:1 as 'tetrarch of *Abilene', *c.* AD 27–8. So Josephus (*Ant.* 20. 138) speaks of 'Abila, which had been the tetrarchy of Lysanias'. His name appears on an inscription of Abila, dated between AD 14 and 29, recording a temple dedication by a freedman of 'Lysanias the tetrarch' (*CIG*, 4521). It is uncertain whether coins superscribed 'Lysanias tetrarch and high priest' refer to him or to an earlier Lysanias, 'king of the Ituraeans' (so Dio Cassius), executed by Antony *c.* 36 BC (Jos., *Ant.* 15. 92; *cf.* 14. 330). Two members of this family called Lysanias, of different generations, are named in *CIG*, 4523.

BIBLIOGRAPHY. F. F. Bruce, 'Lysanias of Abilene Inscriptions', in *Documents of NT Times*, ed. A. R. Millard (forthcoming). F.F.B.

LYSTRA. An obscure town on the high plains of Lycaonia (near modern Hatunsaray), singled out by Augustus as the site of one of a number of Roman colonies that were intended to consolidate the new province of Galatia. Its advantages are not known. Its remote position and proximity to the unsettled S mountains suggest defensive motives, as also does the considerable Latin-speaking settlement implied by surviving inscriptions. If it was the security of such a place that attracted Paul and Barnabas in their hasty retreat from Iconium (Acts 14:6) they were badly let down. Superstitious veneration, disabused by the apostles themselves, was converted by agitators into drastic hostility, which apparently secured official support for the stoning that was inflicted upon Paul (v. 19). There is no suggestion of Roman order or justice. Nor does the NT even disclose that it was a colony. There was plainly a substantial non-hellenic population (v. 11), as well as the usual Greeks and Jews (Acts 16:1). Nevertheless, a church was established (Acts 14:20–23) which provided in Timothy (unless, as is just possible, he came from the nearby Derbe, Acts 16:1–2) Paul's most devoted 'son'.

BIBLIOGRAPHY. B. Levick, *Roman Colonies in Southern Asia Minor*, 1967. E.A.J.

MAACAH, MAACHAH.
1. Maacah is used as a man's name for the following: the father of Shephatiah, one of David's henchmen (1 Ch. 27:16); the father of Hanun, one of David's warriors (1 Ch. 11:43); the father of Achish, king of Gath at the time of Solomon (1 Ki. 2:39).

2. It is also used as a woman's name for the following: the concubine of Caleb, mother of Sheber and Tirhanah (1 Ch. 2:48); the wife [illegible] 7:16); the wife of [illegible], or Jehiel, one of the ancestors of Saul (1 Ch. 8:29; 9:35); the daughter of Talmai, king of Geshur, who married David and was the mother of Absalom and Tamar (2 Sa. 3:3); the favourite wife of Rehoboam and the mother of Abijah and the daughter of Absalom (2 Ch. 11:20–22); the mother of Asa, the queen-mother of Judah until she was removed because of her idolatry (2 Ch. 15:16). (*QUEEN.)

3. The child of Nahor, the brother of Abraham, and his concubine Reumah, was called Maacah, but there is no indication as to sex (Gn. 22:24).

4. It is also the name for a small state to the SW of Mt Hermon, on the edge of the territory of the half-tribe of Manasseh (Dt. 3:14; Jos. 13:8–13) and possibly extending across the Jordan to Abel-beth-Maacah. At the time of David, its Aramaean king provided 1,000 soldiers for the Ammonite and Aramaean attempt to crush Israel. Following the defeat at Helam, Maacah probably became tributary to David (2 Sa. 10). Maacah was later absorbed into the kingdom of Damascus, which had been re-established during Solomon's reign (1 Ki. 11:23–25).

BIBLIOGRAPHY. B. Mazar, 'Geshur and Maacah', *JBL* 80, 1961, pp. 16ff. M.B.
A.R.M.

MAAREH-GEBA (Jdg. 20:33, RV; AV 'meadows of Gibeah'). Heb. [illegible] but LXX(A) *dysmōn* and Vulg. *occidentali urbis parte* suggest Heb. *ma'ᵃrāḇ*, 'west', which yields a better sense here. (*GEBA.) A.R.M.

MACCABEES. *Makkabaios* was the Gk. form of the surname of the Jewish hero Judas ben Mattathias (1 Macc. 2:4); its application has been extended to his family and his party. The derivation is quite obscure: 'the hammerer' or 'the eradicator' are perhaps the commonest modern interpretations. According to Josephus the family name seems to have been Ḥašmōn: hence the title 'Hasmonaeans' reflected in rabbinic literature.

I. The Maccabean revolt

Palestine was perennially a theatre for the power politics of the Seleucid and Ptolemaic heirs of Alexander the Great's empire. One result was the growth of a pro-Syrian and a pro-Egyptian party in Judaea, and tension between these groups was inextricably bound up with Jewish internal politics and family jealousies, and with a movement among 'liberal' Jews to adopt the customs and standards of the Gk. world. Resulting conflict brought about the decisive intervention of Syria. The Seleucid king, Antiochus IV (Epiphanes), who was mad, bad and dangerous, sold the high-priesthood to the highest bidder, one Menelaus, who was quite unentitled to it, and when, in 168 BC, his nominee was ejected, Antiochus sent his officer to sack [illegible]

Soon afterwards, Antiochus instituted a religious persecution of unprecedented bitterness. Sabbath-keeping and the practice of circumcision were forbidden under pain of death: pagan sacrifices and prostitution were established in the Temple; and law-loving Jews were subjected to every degradation and brutality (*cf.* Dn. 11:31–33). Doubtless many succumbed, but many endured heroic suffering (1 Macc. 1:60ff.; 2:29ff.; 2 Macc. 6:18ff.), and Antiochus could not have estimated the sober resilience of the Ḥasidim (or men of the covenant), who 'offered (themselves) willingly for the law' (1 Macc. 2:42). More drastic action began

MAALEH-ACRABBIM
See Akrabbim, Part 1.

MACAQUE
See Animals, Part 1.

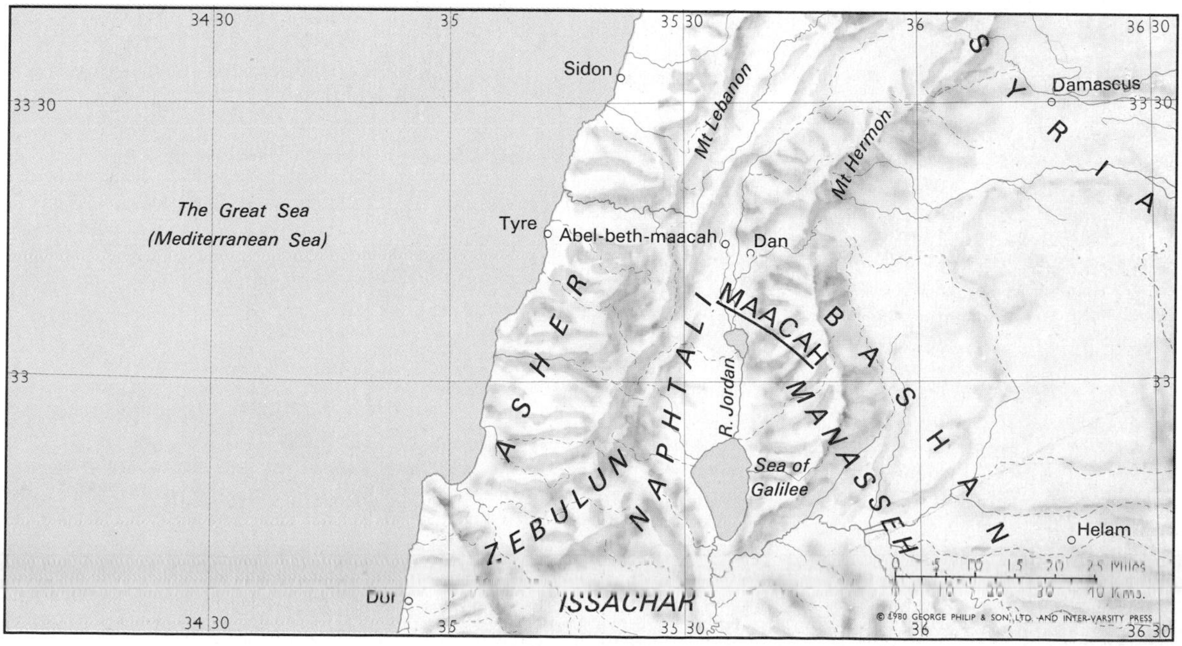

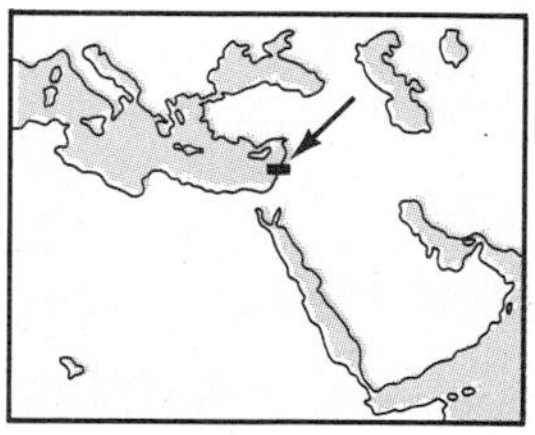

Maacah, a small state in David's time.

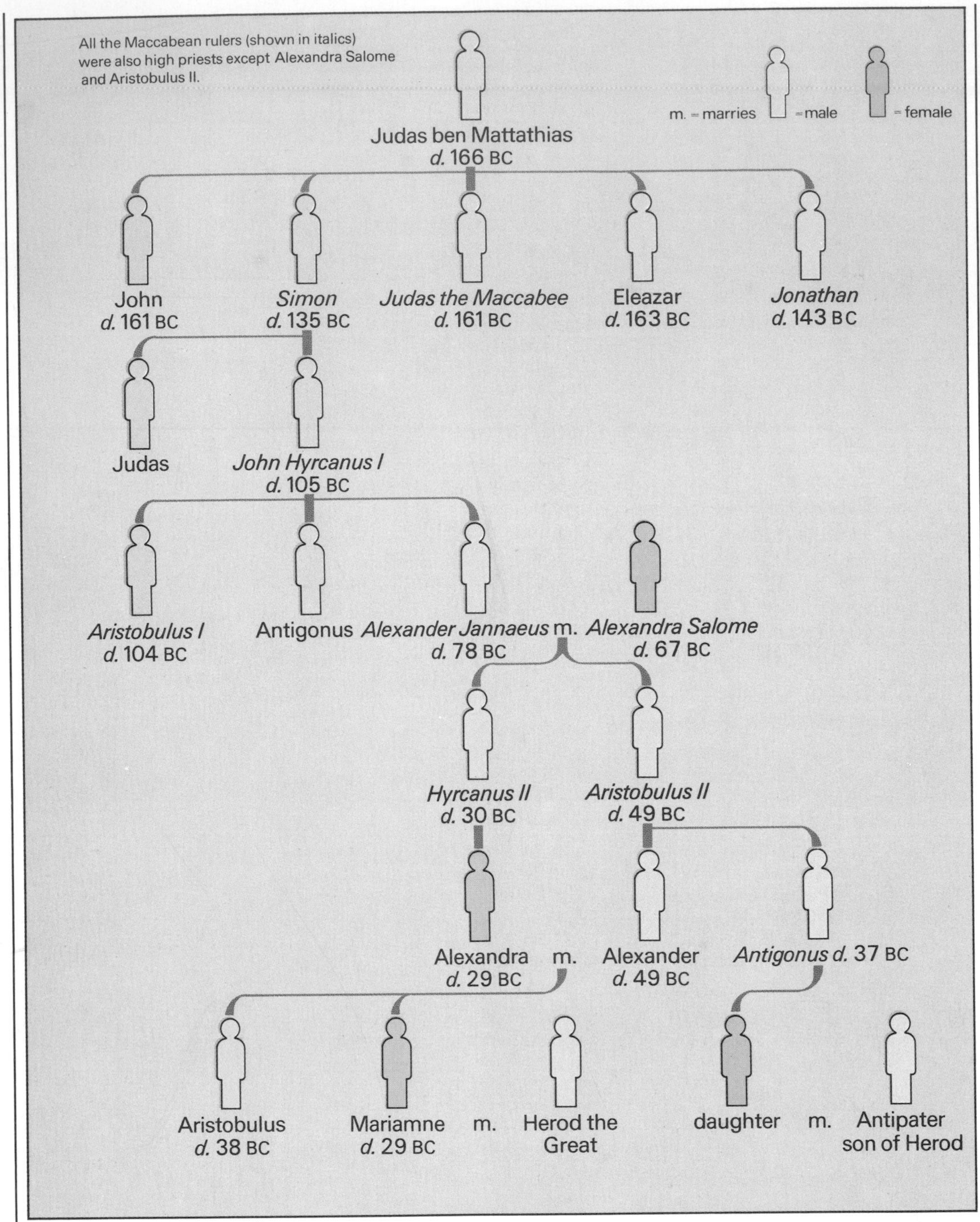

The family of the Maccabees.

in Modein, some 30 km from Jerusalem, where the aged Mattathias angrily killed a Jew who had come to sacrifice on the royal altar, and the Syrian officer who had come to supervise, and then called on everyone zealous for the Law to follow him and his five sons, John, Simon, Judas, Eleazar and Jonathan, to the mountains. The Maccabean revolt had begun.

II. Judas Maccabaeus

The Judaean hills were suited to guerrilla warfare. Mattathias and his sons were joined by many Ḥasidim, and at first were content with terrorizing apostates, destroying altars and enforcing the Law. Mattathias died, and his third son, Judas, proved a leader of Gideon's type and stature. Perhaps no army has ever had higher morale than the force with which he won his brilliant victories against numerically superior Syrian forces. Antiochus was occupied in larger wars with the Parthians, and his regent Lysias had no option but to conclude peace with Judas and withdraw the abominable decrees in 165 BC. Amid great rejoicing, Judas marched to Jerusalem, the Temple was solemnly cleansed, and the worship of God restored (1 Macc. 4)—an event commemorated by the Feast of Hanukkah, or the Dedication (Jn. 10:22).

Maccabean success had led to furious persecution of Jewish minorities in cities of mixed population. Judas raised the cry, 'Fight today for your brethren' (1 Macc. 5:32) and, with his brother Jonathan, carried out effective punitive expeditions in Transjordan, while Simon dealt similarly with Galilee. On the death of Antiochus Epiphanes in 164/3 BC Judas tried to seize the *Akra*, the Syrian fortress in Jerusalem, the symbol of Seleucid suzerainty: he was trapped, and was on the brink of disaster when political upheaval in Syria caused a diversion, and the Syrians had to be content with a treaty virtually securing the *status quo*.

Eventually Demetrius I (Soter) made good his claim to the throne, and he appointed a pro-Syrian high priest, Alcimus. Many Ḥasidim were prepared to support this man, since he was an Aaronite, but his outrageous actions played into Judas' hands. Judas took revenge on deserters, and a large Syrian force had to be called in. The Syrians were defeated at Adasa, but, after an interval, scattered the Jewish army at Elasa, where Judas was killed in battle in 161 BC.

III. Jonathan

Jonathan, youngest of the brothers, now headed the Maccabean party. For a long time he was reduced to guerrilla fighting in the hills, but internal faction had become endemic in the Seleucid empire, and he was more and more left to himself by the Syrians. In time he was the effective ruler of Judaea, and rival claimants to the Seleucid throne competed for his support. One such, Alexander Balas, appointed him high priest in 153 BC, and military and civil governor in 150. He continued to exploit Seleucid weakness until treacherously murdered by a pretended ally in 143 BC.

IV. Simon

Simon, the last survivor of the sons of Mattathias, showed a resolution not inferior to that of his brothers. He drove a hard bargain with Demetrius II whereby the latter virtually resigned the suzerainty of Judaea and 'the yoke of the Gentiles was removed from Israel' (1 Macc. 13:41). The Syrians were ejected from the *Akra*, Judaea was aggrandized at the expense of her neighbours at several points, and a period of relative peace and prosperity began, with Simon as high priest and unchallenged ruler.

V. The later Hasmonaeans

Simon died at the hand of his son-in-law in 135 BC. His son John Hyrcanus was forced into temporary submission to the disintegrating Seleucid empire, but at his death in 104 BC the Jewish realm was at its greatest extent since Solomon's time. His son Aristobulus (104–103 BC) formally claimed the title of king, and with him begins the sorry story of murder and intrigue and family jealousy which left the Jewish state a prey to the rising power of Rome. Antigonus, the last of the Hasmonaean high-priestly kings, was executed in 37 BC, and the pro-Roman *Herod the Great began a new era. Several later members of the house of Herod

Small bronze Maccabean coin, minted at the time of John Hyrcanus. Diameter 13 mm. 135–104 BC. (RG)

had Hasmonaean blood by the maternal side.

VI. The significance of the Maccabees

According to Dn. 11:34, the Maccabean revolt was to be only 'a little help' to God's people, for Daniel depicts events on the huge canvas of God's ultimate gracious purpose. Many Ḥasidim, looking for God to accomplish this, probably thought military action had gone far enough when the proscription of Judaism was abrogated and the Temple cleansed in 165 BC. At all events there are after that date increasing signs of Ḥasidim and Maccabees parting company. The assumption of the high-priesthood by Jonathan, and then Simon and his family, who were all of priestly but not Aaronic stock, must have been bitter to the Ḥasidim, and the latter's heirs, the Pharisees, were wholly alienated from the worldly and tyrannical Hasmonaean high-priest kings, who reached a grotesque climax in the drunken and unhinged Alexander Jannaeus (103–76 BC).

It would, nevertheless, be a mistake to divide Maccabean aims into the achievement first of religious liberty, and then of political liberty. Judas and his brethren were fighting for *Israel*, and desired, in the name of the God of Israel, to take away the 'yoke of the Gentiles'. The easy and natural process whereby the hereditary high-priesthood, which comprehended unquestioned civil leadership, assumed into itself the revived monarchy, is eloquent. John Hyrcanus and the Hasmonaean kings in their campaigns clearly have the ideal of the Davidic kingdom in mind, and there are records of some territories they conquered being forcibly Judaized.

In some respects, the Maccabees set the pattern of Jewish nationalism and Messianic thought for the NT period. Judas and his successors were invariably on good terms with the Romans, but in their day Rome was not yet ready to control Palestine. By NT times the Jews were firmly under 'the yoke of the Gentiles' once more, this time that of Rome. But the memory lingered of how Israel had once in the name of God defied another heathen empire, engaged her in single combat, and won; of how her borders had approached those of her Davidic glory. 'The ministry of Jesus falls . . . when the Jews of Palestine had still the memory of the Maccabean triumphs and no foreknowledge of the horrors of the siege under Titus' (T. W. Manson, *The Servant-Messiah*, 1953, p. 4).

W. R. Farmer has pointed to the preponderance of Maccabean names among anti-Roman agitators of NT times, and has associated the *Zealot party with Maccabean ideals, and the crowd's reaction to our Lord's triumphal entry with the deliberate recall of the triumphs of Judas and Simon.

The once fashionable habit of dating many Psalms in the Maccabean period has almost passed. For other literary questions, see *APOCRYPHA, *DANIEL, BOOK OF, *PSEUDEPIGRAPHA, *ZECHARIAH.

BIBLIOGRAPHY. 1 and 2 Maccabees (*APOCRYPHA); Josephus, *Ant.* 12–14; E. Schürer, *HJP*, 1, 1973, pp. 146–286; R. H. Pfeiffer, *History of New Testament Times*, 1949; E. Bickerman, *The Maccabees*, 1947; W. R. Farmer, *Maccabees, Zealots and Josephus*, 1956 (*cf. JTS* n.s. 3, 1952, pp. 62ff.). A.F.W.

Maccabean period architecture shown in the rock-cut 'Tomb of Zachariah' in the Kidron Valley, Jerusalem. 2nd–1st cent. BC. (RS)

MACEDONIA. A splendid tract of land, centred on the plains of the gulf of Thessalonica, and running up the great river valleys into the Balkan mountains. It was famous for timber and precious metal. Anciently ruled by cavalry barons under a hellenized royal house, its kings dominated Greek affairs

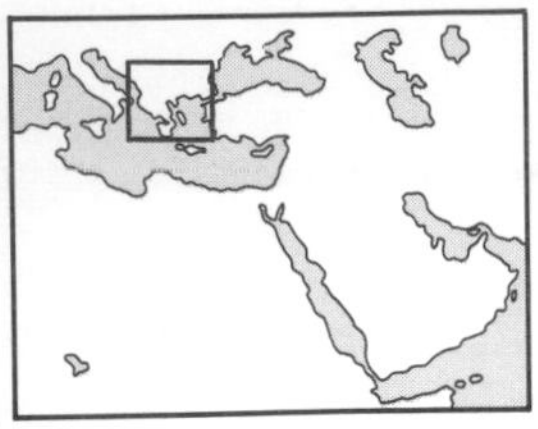

The location of Macedonia.

Macedonia, the Roman province, included 10 colonies, of which Philippi was one. Shown here are the ruins of the city visited by Paul (Acts 16:12). (PP)

from the 4th century BC, and after Alexander Macedonian dynasties ruled throughout the E Mediterranean until superseded by the Romans. The home monarchy was the first to go when in 167 BC Macedonia was constituted a series of four federations of republics (to which structure Acts 16:12 may refer), thus completing its hellenization. They were subsequently grouped under Roman provincial control, and, until the consolidation of Moesia and Thrace as provinces in NT times, were heavily garrisoned against the intractable N frontier. The province embraced the N part of modern Greece from the Adriatic to the Hebrus river, and was crossed by the Via Egnatia, the main land route from Italy to the E. After 44 BC the proconsul sat at Thessalonica, while the assembly of the Greek states met at Beroea, the seat of the imperial cult. The province included six Roman colonies, of which Philippi was one. There were also tribally organized communities. In spite of this diversity, the area is normally treated in the NT as a unit, following Roman usage.

Paul's vision of 'a man of Macedonia' (Acts 16:9) marks a distinct development in his methods of evangelism. At Philippi (Acts 16:37) for the first time he took advantage of his high civil station. He now enjoyed support in the cultivated circles to which he naturally belonged (Acts 16:15; 17:4, 12) in contrast to their hostility at earlier points on his route (Acts 13:50; 14:5). He looked back upon Macedonia with profound affection (1 Thes. 1:3; Phil. 4:1), and was always eager to return (Acts 20:1; 2 Cor. 1:16). The Macedonians were willing donors to his Jerusalem fund (2 Cor. 8:1–4), and several of their number were added to his regular retinue of assistants (Acts 19:29; 20:4). It was in Macedonia then, it seems, that Paul finally proved himself as an independent missionary leader.

BIBLIOGRAPHY. J. Keil, *CAH*, 9, pp. 566–570; J. A. O. Larsen, *Representative Government in Greek and Roman History*, 1955, pp. 103–104, 113–115; *idem* in T. Frank, *An Economic Survey of Ancient Rome*, 5, 1940, pp. 436–496. E.A.J.

MACHAERUS. A fortress E of the Dead Sea (modern el-Mekawar), near the S frontier of the region of

Macedonian coin from Philippi, struck in the time of Claudius I (AD *41–54*). (RG)

Peraea, built by Alexander Jannaeus (103–76 BC), destroyed by the Roman commander Gabinius (57 BC), rebuilt by Herod (37–4 BC), who appreciated the hot springs at Calirrhoe not far away (Wadi Zerka Ma'in). Here, according to Josephus (*Ant.* 18. 112, 119), Herod Antipas imprisoned John the Baptist and later had him put to death; here too Antipas' first wife, the daughter of the Nabataean king Aretas IV, broke her journey on her way home to her father's capital at Petra when Antipas divorced her for Herodias. When Peraea was added to the province of Judaea (AD 44), Machaerus was occupied by a Roman garrison, which evacuated the place on the outbreak of war in AD 66. It was then occupied by a force of Jewish insurgents, but surrendered to the governor Lucilius Bassus in AD 71.

BIBLIOGRAPHY. Josephus, *BJ* 7. 163–209. F.F.B.

MACHIR (Heb. *māḵîr*). **1.** A grandson of Joseph and son of Manasseh was named Machir (Gn. 50:23). We later learn that he was the father of Gilead, ancestor of the Gileadites (Nu. 26:29). His children later took Gilead, dispossessing the Amorites (Nu. 32:39–40). Gilead is later attributed to Machir (Jos. 17:1–3). For other references, *cf.* Dt. 3:15; Jos. 13:31; Jdg. 5:14; 1 Ch. 2:21–23; 7:14–17.

2. The son of Ammiel who protected Mephibosheth in Lo-debar (2 Sa. 9:4–5). Later Machir was one of those who brought provisions to David (2 Sa. 17:27–29). E.J.Y.

MACHPELAH. The name applied to the field, cave and surrounding land purchased by Abraham as a burial-place for his wife Sarah (Gn. 23). It was purchased from Ephron, a Hittite, for 400 shekels of silver (vv. 8–16). It lay E of Mamre (v. 17) in the district of Hebron. Here were later buried Abraham (Gn. 25:9), Isaac and Rebekah (Gn. 49:31) and Jacob (Gn. 50:13).

The Heb. (*hammaḵpēlâ*) implies that the name is in some way descriptive and the Gk. (*to diploun*, 'the double') is taken to describe the form of the cave in Gn. 23:17 (LXX). The reading of Shechem for Hebron in Acts 7:16 may be due to the summary nature of the record of this speech, which originally referred also to Joseph's burial at Shechem.

The modern site of the burial-cave (60 m by 34 m), now incorporated in the S end of the Ḥaram al-Ḥalîl at Hebron, is much venerated by Jews, Christians and Muslims. It is jealously guarded by massive stone walls, probably of Herodian work, though the antiquity of the cave itself and its furnishings has not been verified by archaeological research. The 'cenotaph of Sarah' is still to be seen among others in the mosque above the cave (see Vincent, Mackay and Abel, *Hébron, le Haram al Khalîl*, 1923).

The antiquity of the details of Abraham's purchase of Machpelah (Gn. 23) had been thought to find support in Middle Assyr. and Hittite laws prior to 1200 BC (*BASOR* 129, 1953, pp. 15–23), but this claim has now been questioned (*JBL* 85, 1966, pp. 77–84). D.J.W.

MADMANNAH (*maḏmannâh*). A town in SW Judah. At one time Calibbite (1 Ch. 2:49), it may have passed to Simeon and become known as Beth-marcaboth (*cf.* Jos. 15:31 with 19:5; Albright, *JPOS* 4, 1924, pp. 159f.). Khirbet umm Deimneh, 6 km SW of Dhahiriyah, and Kh. Tatrit, 2½ km further S, have been suggested as possible locations. J.P.U.L.

MADMEN. A town of Moab against which Jeremiah prophesied (48:2).

Since this place is otherwise unknown, it has been suggested, either that the Heb. text read *gm-dmm tdmm*, 'also thou (Moab) shalt be utterly silenced' (LXX, Syr., Vulg.), or that it stands for Dimon, a possible (but unlikely) rendering of the name of the capital *Dîbôn*. Modern Khirbet Dimneh may be the site. Madmen is unlikely to be the same as *Madmannah, which lay in the Negeb (Jos. 15:31; 1 Ch. 2:49), or *Madmenah, N of Jerusalem (Is. 10:31). D.J.W.

MADMENAH. A place mentioned only in Isaiah's description of the route whereby an invading army approached Jerusalem from the N (Is. 10:31). Shu'fat, 2 km N of Mt Scopus, is the supposed site. A.R.M.

MACHBENA
See Meconah, Part 2.

Machpelan, the traditional site of the patriarchal burial-caves, is now marked by a mosque containing shrines of the patriarchs, the Haram al-Halîl, at Hebron. (MEPhA)

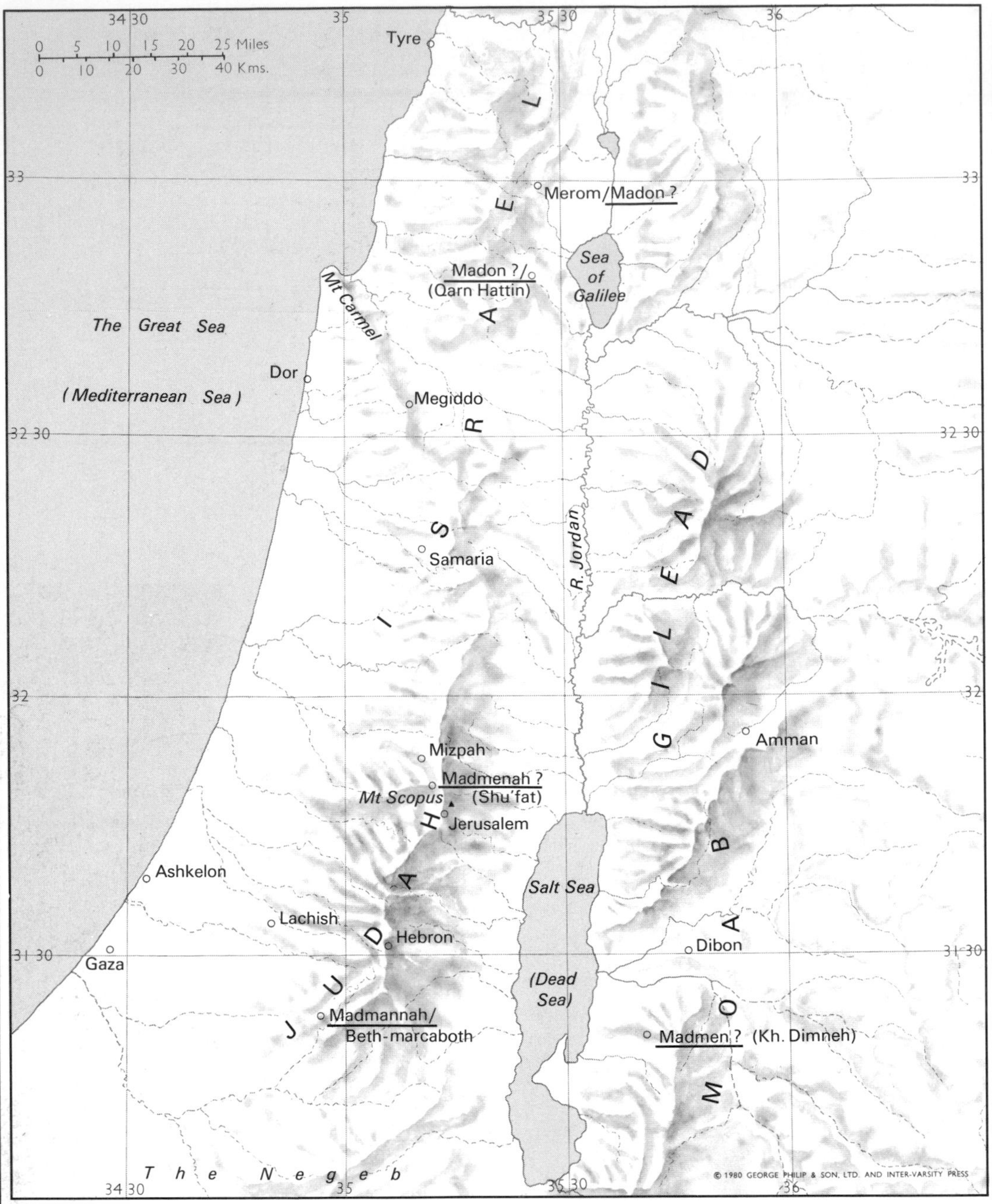

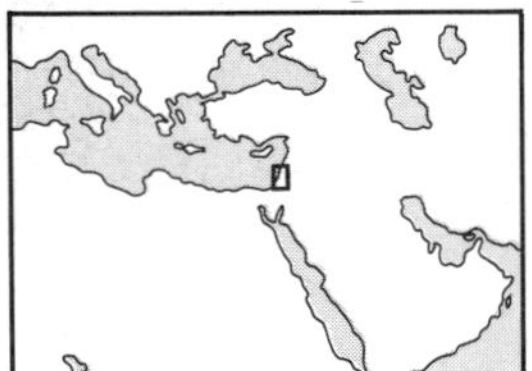

Proposed sites for Madmannah, Madmen, Madmenah and Madon.

MADON (Heb. *māḏôn*). A city of N Canaan (Jos. 11:1; 12:19; LXX *marrōn*, as in 11:7 for *Merom). If the names are identical (so *LOB*, pp. 106, 111, 206), *d* is a transcription error for *r*. *Mḏn* of Tuthmosis III list (no. 20) is not equivalent. For Kh. Madjan/Qarn Hattin see *Adamah. J.P.U.L.

MAGBISH. Either a town in Judah (*GTT*, p. 380) or the name of a clan. Ezr. 2:30 records that 156 of its 'sons' (or 'inhabitants') returned after the exile. It is inexplicably omitted from the parallel list in Ne. 7. D.J.A.C.

MAGDALA, MAGDALENE. The name 'Magdala' occurs only once in the NT (Mt. 15:39, AV), where the best MSS (followed by RSV, NEB) read 'Magadan'. Some MSS, however, also read 'Magdala' or 'Magadan' for *'Dalmanutha' (otherwise unknown) in Mk. 8:10. The town of Magdala (or Tarichaea) stood on the W shore of the Sea of Galilee, N of Tiberias and Hammath, and S of Capernaum. The name derives from the Heb. *miḡdāl*, 'tower'. It is probable that the modern Khirbet Mejdel stands on the site today. Magadan was the *locality* on the W shore of the lake to which Jesus crossed after feeding the crowds, and it probably included the town of Magdala. Evidently Mary called Magdalene came from this town or area. (For 'Mary Magdalene', see *MARY, **3**.) S.S.S.

MAGI. The term is used in Herodotus (1. 101, 132) of a tribe of the Medes who had a priestly function in the Persian empire; in other classical writers it is synonymous with priest. Complementing this, Daniel (1:20; 2:27; 5:15) applies the word to a class of 'wise men' or astrologers who interpret dreams and messages of the gods. In the NT the usage broadens to include all who practise magic arts (*cf.* Acts 8:9; 13:6, 8).

Both Daniel and Herodotus may contribute to the understanding of the Magi of Mt. 2:1–12. Apparently the Magi were non-Jewish religious astrologers who, from astronomical observations, inferred the birth of a great Jewish king. After inquiring of Jewish authorities, they came to Bethlehem to do homage. Whether 'the East' from which they came is Arabia, Babylon or elsewhere is uncertain.

The historicity of the visit of the Magi has been questioned on account of the silence of other sources concerning both the event and Herod's subsequent slaughter of the infants, and also because of what is regarded as the legendary character of parts of the narrative. While full weight must be given to the poetic descriptions in the story (*e.g.* the star standing over Bethlehem), descriptive symbolism neither affirms nor negates the historicity of the event involved. A literalist approach, either to dehistoricize the story or to exaggerate the miraculous, is out of keeping with the Evangelist's meaning. For Matthew the Magi's visit represents the Messiah's relationship to the Gentile world and is also a fitting introduction to other prophetically significant events of Christ's infancy. The story is in keeping with the 'royal' Messianic expectations of the Jews and with the character of Herod. Perhaps there is some astronomical confirmation of the *star in the conjunction of Jupiter and Saturn in 7 BC and in the report of a later (4 BC) evanescent star in Chinese records. But such parallels must be applied with caution.

Later Christian traditions regard the Magi as kings (because of Ps.

72:10; Is. 49:7; 60:3?) and number them at three (because of the gifts) or twelve. In the Christian calendar Epiphany, originally associated with Christ's baptism, reflects the importance of the Magi's visit for later Christendom. (*ANNUNCIATION; *MAGNIFICAT.) E.E.E.

MAGIC AND SORCERY.

1. The biblical view

Magic and sorcery attempt to influence people and events by supernatural or occult means. They may be associated with some form of *divination, though divination by itself is the attempt to use supernatural means to discover events without influencing them.

Magic is universal, and may be 'black' or 'white'. Black magic attempts to produce evil results through such methods as curses, spells, destruction of models of one's enemy and alliance with evil spirits. It often takes the form of witchcraft. White magic tries to undo curses and spells, and to use occult forces for the good of oneself and others. The magician tries to compel a god, demon or spirit to work for him; or he follows a pattern of occult practices to bend psychic forces to his will. There is no doubt that magic and sorcery are not always mere superstitions, but have a reality behind them. They must be resisted and overcome through the power of God in the name of Jesus Christ.

I. Biblical terms

The following root words are used in Scripture to denote magical practices and practitioners.

a. In the Old Testament

1. *kšp̄*. 'Sorcerer', 'sorcery', 'witch(craft)'. The root probably means 'to cut', and could refer to herbs cut for charms and spells (Ex. 22:18; Dt. 18:10; Is. 47:9, 12; Je. 27:9, *etc.*).

2. *ḥrṭm*. 'Magician'. This term derives from Egyp. *ḥry-tp*, 'chief (lector-priest)', the title borne by Egypt's most renowned magicians (Gn. 41:8; Ex. 7:11, *etc.*).

3. *ḥḇr*. 'Enchantment', 'charmer' (Dt. 18:11; Is. 47:9, 12, *etc.*). The root has the idea of binding, probably with amulets and charms.

4. *kaśdîm*. 'Chaldeans'. In Dn. the term is used racially (*e.g.* Dn. 5:30; 9:1) and of a special class linked with magicians (Dn. 2:2, 4, 10, *etc.*). The word is used in a similar sense by Herodotus (1. 181f.), and may have been current earlier with this special meaning. See A. R. Millard, *EQ* 49, 1977, pp. 69–71.

5. *qsm*. 'Divination', especially of future (Dt. 18:10; Ezk. 21:21). Of false prophets (Je. 14:14; Ezk. 13:6).

6. *lt*. 'Secret arts'. Pharaoh's magicians (Ex. 7:22).

7. *nḥš*. 'Enchantment' with spells (Nu. 23:23; 24:1).

8. *lḥš*. 'Expert in charms' (Is. 3:3). Snake charming (Ps. 58:5; Ec. 10:11; Je. 8:17).

b. In the New Testament

1. *magos* (and cognates). 'Magician', 'magic'; in Mt. 2, 'wise men'. Originally a Magian, a racial group in Media, it came, like 'Chaldean', to have a technical use (*e.g.* Acts 8:9, 11; 13:6, 8; found only in Mt. and Acts; *MAGI).

2. *pharmakos* (and cognates). 'Sorcerer', 'sorcery', 'witchcraft'. The root idea is that of drugs, potions (Rev. 9:21; 18:23; 21:8; 22:15; elsewhere only in Gal. 5:20).

Tomb model of implements for 'opening the mouth' in Egyptian mummification ceremonies. Probably New Kingdom. c. 1570–1085 BC. (BM)

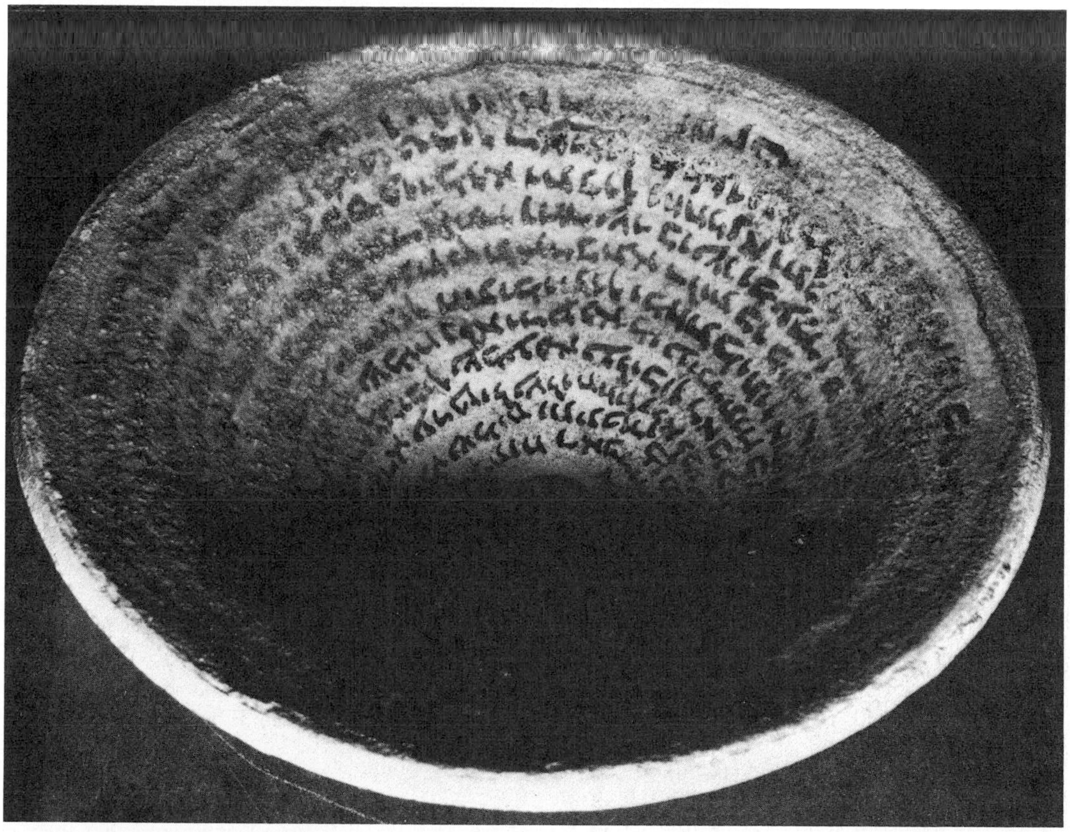

Magic formulae or spells were sometimes written on bowls to divert evil spirits from a corpse or house. This Aramaic inscription calls on Gabriel, Michael and other good spirits to protect the threshold and heal a client. Iraq. Pre-Islamic. (DJW)

3. *goēs*. 'Imposter' (AV 'seducer') (2 Tim. 3:13), it may also signify a spell-binding magician. It has the magical sense in classical and hellenistic Greek.

4. *perierga*. 'Magic arts', AV 'curious arts' (Acts 19:19). The adjective has the root idea of being exceedingly occupied, then of being occupied with other people's business, then of interfering with others by magical arts.

5. *baskainō*. In Gal. 3:1 metaphorically of Galatians bewitched into false beliefs.

II. The biblical judgment on magic

The references given in the first part of this article show that magic and sorcery are always condemned in Scripture. Magic is a rival to true religion, though it can be practised in conjunction with false religious ideas. True religion centres in the personal experience of the one God, with an attempt to live a life that is conformable to his will. The believer walks humbly with his God, prays to him, and is prepared to accept the circumstances of life as the sphere in which to glorify him. Magic, on the other hand, deals with lower supernatural beings, or attempts to force issues by using psychic forces, irrespective of whether the issues are for the glory of God. The following practices come under the specific condemnation of the Bible.

a. The wearing of charms

Among the list of women's ornaments in Is. 3:18–23 the word translated 'amulets' in v. 20 is the root *lḥš* (**I.** *a.* **8**, above); some consider that the word may originally have been *nḥš*, 'serpent', in which case the charm would have been a serpent figure. In this same passage there is a reference in v. 18 to 'crescents'. These are clearly moon-images, and the only other occurrence of the word (*śah*ᵃ*rōnîm*) is in Jdg. 8:21, 26, where they are worn both by camels and by the kings of Midian. The previous word in Is. 3:18 (*š*ᵉ*ḇîsîm*), translated 'headbands' (AV 'cauls') occurs only here in Scripture, but a similar word in the Ras Shamra tablets apparently denotes sun-pendants.

It is probable that there is a reference to charms in Gn. 35:2–4, where Jacob's household put away their 'foreign gods' and their 'ear-rings'. This is the normal word for ear-ring, but the association with idols here suggests that they were charms of some kind.

Bronze votive offering in the form of an aegis (breastplate) of the goddess Isis, patroness of Egyptian magic. 26th Dynasty. c. 664–525 BC. (BM)

b. Workers of magic; sorcerers; witches

Genesis and Exodus speak of the magicians of Egypt, and 2 Tim. 3:8 names two of them as Jannes and Jambres. The Exodus record says that the Egyp. magicians copied Moses in turning their rods into serpents (7:11), in turning water into blood (7:22), and in producing frogs (8:7), but failed to produce the lice (8:18–19), and were themselves incapacitated by the boils (9:11). The account leaves us free to decide whether they were clever conjurors or used occult methods.

There is little direct allusion to sorcerers and witches in Israel. It is incorrect to speak of the 'witch' of Endor (1 Sa. 28) since the Bible describes her as a medium, and not as a worker of magic. It is significant that Jezebel practised sorcery (2 Ki. 9:22), and Mi. 5:12 suggests that it was by no means rare in Israel. Manasseh personally encouraged it among other evils (2 Ki. 21:6).

There is an indication of magical practices in Is. 28:15, where people were initiated into some magical pact which they believed would give immunity from death.

The most striking reference to Heb. witchcraft is Ezk. 13:17–23. Here Heb. prophetesses were also practising magic arts for the preservation and destruction of individuals. In this they were going farther than the false prophets of Mi. 3:5, who gave messages of good or ill to individuals according to whether they were prepared to pay. The details of the magical practices here are not easy to follow. The armbands and veils are worn both by victims (18) and witches (20–21). Witchcraft practice suggests a psychic link between witch and client through interchange of material charged with good or evil spells. Alternatively, the veils are made to size (18), and maybe the witch made a veil of a size to represent one's enemy. The witch then wore it for a time and impregnated it with malevolent spells (*cf.* the use of doll figures). The wrist bands would bring luck to the wearers. J. G. Frazer, in his *Folk-Lore in the Old Testament*, suggests that the women professed to catch souls and bind them up in cloth bands. The imprisonment would cause the owner of the soul to waste away. The soul might be represented by some object from the victim, *e.g.* blood, hair or nails.

III. Does the Bible countenance magic?

We now deal with some of the passages where the Bible might seem to countenance magic and superstition.

a. The use of mandrakes

Down through the centuries E women have made use of mandrakes to ensure conception (*cf.* Gn. 30:14–18). Since modern investigations have shown that primitive medicines often contain some element that is really effective, it would be foolish to dismiss this example as magic.

b. Jacob and the peeled rods

In Gn. 30:37–41 Jacob was probably influenced by primitive ideas of the effect of seen objects upon the unborn young. But v. 40 indicates that the results really came about through selective breeding (see D. M. Blair, *A Doctor Looks at the Bible*, 1959).

c. Samuel and the water

This incident (1 Sa. 7:6) is often thought to denote sympathetic magic, the solemn pouring out of water to induce a storm. There is, however, not the slightest indication of this in the context. Water poured on the ground, according to 2 Sa. 14:14, is a symbol of human frailty and impermanence, and Samuel's action may best be interpreted as a sign of abasement and humiliation before God.

d. Samson's hair

Frazer and others have produced stories from all parts of the world in which the soul or the strength of someone resided in his hair, or even in some external object. The biblical story, however (Jdg. 16), shows that Samson's uncut hair denoted his faithfulness to the *Nazirite vow, and that the Spirit of God empowered him so long as he was faithful to this vow (*e.g.* Jdg. 13:25; 14:19). Those who wish to argue from a natural level may note that the loss of strength could be accounted for on psychological grounds when Samson realized his guilt. There are well-recognized cases of hysterical blindness, paralysis, *etc.*

e. Rousing up leviathan

Job asks that the day of his birth should be cursed by those who curse the day, who are ready to rouse up leviathan (Jb. 3:8). Some find here a reference to magicians who were thought to rouse up a dragon to swallow the sun at an eclipse. If this is correct, it is part of the extravagant language of Job, who calls upon everyone, bogus or true, who might claim to bring ill-luck on his birthday.

f. The power of blessing and cursing

The OT lays great stress on this. The Patriarchs bless their children, and Isaac cannot reverse what he has promised to Jacob (Gn. 27:33, 37). Balaam is called upon to curse Israel (Nu. 22f.). Throughout the rest of the OT there are other incidental references. It should be noted that the Bible does not visualize anyone's pronouncing an effective blessing or curse contrary to God's will. The Patriarchs believe that God is showing them the future of their descendants, and their blessing is declaratory of this. Balaam cannot effectively curse those whom God has blessed (Nu. 23:8, 20). The psalmist knows that God can turn the undeserved curse into a blessing (Ps. 109:28), while David's reluctance to interfere with Shimei is based on the fear that God may have inspired the curse for something that David had done (2 Sa. 16:10).

g. Miracles

The pagan world certainly regarded 'private' miracles as magic (Acts 8:9–11), but the Bible never treats divine miracles as superior magic, *i.e.* there is no use of incantations, invocation of spirits or spells. Moses did not silence Pharaoh's magicians by being a better magician, but acted solely as the agent of God, behaving when and how God instructed him. His rod was not a conjuror's magic wand, but the symbol of God's designation. It was 'the rod of God' (Ex. 4:20).

As regards exorcisms and healings, one need not be surprised to find linguistic resemblances between the Gospel records and pagan magic, since the vocabulary of demonology and illness is limited. But neither Christ nor the disciples are ever regarded as using the accompaniments of magical practice. For a full linguistic discussion see John M. Hull, *Hellenistic Magic and the Synoptic Tradition*, 1974. J.S.W.

2. Egyptian and Assyro-Babylonian

I. Ancient magic

Where the ordinary relationships and processes of life could readily be regulated through observation of obvious cause and effect, and by acting on an acquired modicum of knowledge and/or skill, this sufficed. But where mystery shrouded the causes of effects, and when ordinary means did not suffice to obtain desired results, then magic was appealed to. Magic was the exploitation of miraculous or occult powers by carefully specified methods to achieve ends otherwise unattainable.

Magic and religion were closely linked, in that whereas 'society' principally covers relationships between man and man, and 'religion' the relationship between deity and mankind, the powers of magic found application in both spheres. In general, *cf. Sources Orientales 7: Le monde du sorcier*, 1966.

II. Egyptian magic in the Bible

Learned in sacred writings, rituals and spells, trained in the 'House of Life' (temple 'schools' where this and other literature was composed, copied and taught), Egypt's greatest magicians were the chief lector-priests, in Egyp. *ḥry-ḥbt ḥry-tp*, later abbreviated by Moses' time (13th cent. BC) to *ḥry-tp*. This very title gave the Heb. *ḥarṭōm*, 'magician'. This essentially Egyp. term recurs in an Assyr. document (7th century BC), as *ḥar-ṭibi*, and as *ḥrtb* in 1st-century AD tales of magicians. (See A. H. Gardiner, *JEA* 24, 1938, pp. 164–165; and, more fully, J. Vergote, *Joseph en Égypte*, 1959, pp. 66–94, 206, with full references.) Thus the association of 'magicians' with 'wise men' generally in Gn. 41:8 and Ex. 7:11 reflects authentic Egyp. tradition; see paragraphs *a* and *c*, below.

BIBLIOGRAPHY. For a good formal analysis of Egyptian magic, see A. H. Gardiner in *ERE*, 8, pp. 262–269. Much material is collected (texts and pictures) in F. Lexa, *La Magie dans l'Égypte Antique*, 3 vols., 1925.

a. Magicians and dreams of Joseph's pharaoh

In Gn. 41:8, Joseph's pharaoh calls upon his magicians and wise men to interpret his dreams. This reflects the importance of dreams in ancient Egypt and the E; dreams and their interpretations were gathered into manuals, veritable handbooks of dream-interpretation. The original of one such MS, Papyrus Chester Beatty 3 (19th Dynasty, 13th century BC) may date back to the Middle Kingdom age, while the Papyri Carlsberg 13 and 14 of the 2nd century AD contain further collections from early sources. The common pattern is, that if a man sees himself in a dream doing or experiencing such-and-such, it is good or bad, and means that so-and-so will befall him. For this whole topic, see A. L. Oppenheim, *The Interpretation of Dreams in the Ancient Near East*, 1956; *Sources Orientales 2: Les Songes et leurs Interprétations*, 1959.

b. Joseph and divination

In Gn. 44:4–5, 15, Joseph play-acts the learned Egyptian, master of the divinatory art, before his brothers. Two interpretations of this incident are possible.

(i) Joseph had it said by his steward, according to the usual translations of v. 5, that he divined by means of his silver cup; this would imply knowledge of cup-divination (lecanomancy) in Hyksos-period Egypt, *c.* 1700 BC. By this technique, omens for interpretation were obtained by observing the movement or configuration of drops of oil upon water in a cup. This technique is of Mesopotamian origin, apparently already used by the Sumerians (*cf.* B. Meissner, *Babylonien und Assyrien,* 2, 1925, p. 284). A handbook to this technique is preserved on two cuneiform tablets dating from the 19th–17th centuries BC, *i.e.* within Joseph's general period.

In Egypt, however, cup-divination is attested only twice, once doubtfully. Two small statuettes of apparently Middle Kingdom date (*c.* 1900–1700 BC) each show a figure kneeling with chin on a cup held in the hands, and it is just possible that these depict cup-divination (J. Capart, *Chronique d'Égypte* 19, 1944, p. 263). Egypt offers no further example until the technique recurs in papyri of the 2nd century AD. But Bab. influence, including divination, was already felt in Palestine in the 2nd millennium BC. Bab. divinatory practice is attested at Hazor: in Temple II of the 15th century BC was found a clay model liver inscribed in cuneiform (see Y. Yadin, *BA* 22, 1959, p. 7 with fig. 5). Hence on this evidence there is no difficulty whatever in presupposing some knowledge of other forms of Mesopotamian divination such as lecanomancy in the Palestine of Joseph's day or in the immediately adjacent Egyp. E Delta, then under Hyksos (Semitic) control.

(ii) One may, on the other hand, render Joseph's steward's speech as 'Is it not from this cup that my lord drinks, and *concerning* which he will assuredly divine?', *i.e.* to unmask the theft. On this rendering Joseph's cup is solely a drinking-vessel, cup-divination would not be alluded to, and the form of his pretended divination remains wholly unspecified. This fits well with v. 15 when Joseph says to his brothers, 'Do you not know that such a man as I can indeed divine?', *i.e.* he pretends to have apprehended them in their theft by divination, to recover his cup. For this view, see J. Vergote, *Joseph en Égypte*, 1959, pp. 172–173.

c. Moses and the magicians

In Ex. 7:8–13, when Aaron at Moses' command casts down his rod as a serpent before Pharaoh, his magicians and sorcerers 'did in like manner with their enchantments' (v. 11). For this kind of conjuring, it would appear that the Egyp. cobra (Arab. *naja ḥaye*) can be rendered immobile (catalepsy) if pressure be applied to the muscles at the nape of the neck; *cf.* L. Keimer, *Histoires de Serpents dans l'Égypte ancienne et moderne* (*Mémoires, Institut d'Égypte*, 50), 1947, pp. 16–17. The serpent must first be charmed, then seized at the neck as shown on several ancient Egyptian scarab-amulets (Keimer, *op. cit.*, figs. 14–21) and thus be temporarily immobilized (*cf.* H. S. Noerdlinger, *Moses and Egypt*, 1956, p. 26; *EBr*[11], 6, p. 613). Aaron's serpent restored to a rod manifested the wholly-other omnipotence of God, however. On the plagues, see * Plagues of Egypt.

III. Assyro-Babylonian magic

a. Its role

Defensive and curative magic was mainly resorted to to obtain deliverance from affliction—illness, demon possession, *etc.*—which may originate with the sufferer. The exorcist might then often employ rites and spells from the 'handbook' *Šurpu*, 'Burning' (*i.e.* in purificatory rite), listing every conceivable fault the sufferer might have committed. Or affliction may have entered from without—some sorcerer's evil spell. To counter such, there was the companion 'handbook' of tablets, *Maqlu*, also 'Burning' (of wax or wooden effigies of sorcerers). 'As this image quivers, dissolves and melts away, even so may the sorcerer and sorceress quiver, dissolve and melt away!' (E. A. W. Budge, *British Museum: A Guide to the Babylonian and Assyrian Antiquities*, 1922, p. 201). Collections of prayers for release or absolution also exist. There is a full modern translation of *Šurpu* in E. Reiner, *Šurpu, A Collection of Sumerian and Akkadian Incantations*, 1958; of *Maqlu* in G. Meier, *Die Assyrische Beschwörungssammlung Maqlû*, 1937.

Prognostic magic, i.e. divination, was based on the conviction that any event, good or ill, may be announced or accompanied by some portent observable by men. Learned priests systematically compiled long series of omens with interpretations in veritable reference-manuals. Omens were either observed from signs in nature or sought by specific techniques.

[illegible] from the whole gamut of man's observation: haloes and eclipses of sun and moon, conjunctions of heavenly bodies, *etc.* (astrology); the flight of birds, actions and states of animals and insects; births of animals and humans, especially if abnormal—all in long series of omen-tablets. For a sick person, omens good or bad would determine their survival or decease (see R. Labat, *Traité Akkadien de Diagnostics et Prognostics Médicaux*, 2 vols., 1951). Is. 47:9–13 criticizes such proceedings.

2. Specific techniques of divination included observation of configurations of and on a sheep's liver (hepatoscopy, extispicy), and observation of patterns of oil on water (or vice versa) in a cup (lecanomancy). For translations of reports of the liver, see A. Goetze, *JCS* 11, 1957, pp. 89–105. This most famous form of Bab. divinatory magic penetrated among the Hittites of Asia Minor and the Canaanites in N Syria and Palestine alike (see Egyptian Magic, **II.***b*, above). *Cf.* also Ezk. 21:21–22. Dream-interpretation was as important as in Egypt. *Cf.* also *La divination en Mésopotamie ancienne* (*Rencontre, Strasbourg*), 1966; A. Caquot, M. Leibovici, *La divination*, 1–2, 1968.

c. Its practitioners

As in Egypt, magic was practised by priestly scholars attached to the temples. Exorcisms were performed by the *āšipu*-priest (*cf.* Heb. *'aššāpîm*, 'enchanters', Dn. 1:20) by virtue of the gods Ea and Marduk, the master-magicians. The elaborate apparatus of divination was the province of the *bārû*-priest; he had to be physically perfect, undertake long studies and be initiated. Those attached to the royal court were called upon at any time to interpret all manner of things. See G. Contenau, *Everyday Life in Babylon and Assyria*, 1954, pp. 281–283, 286–295.

BIBLIOGRAPHY. On Mesopotamian magic, see also briefly L. W. King, *ERE*, 4, 1911, pp. 783–786; 8, 1915, pp. 253–255. Useful notes can be found in É. Dhorme and R. Dussaud, *Les Religions de Babylonie et d'Assyrie . . . des Hittites, etc.*, 1949, pp. 258–298. Fully detailed surveys of magic and divination respectively, with copious translations from texts, can be found in M. Jastrow, *Die Religion Babyloniens und Assyriens*, 1–2, [illegible] G. Contenau, *La Magie chez les Assyriens et les Babyloniens*, 1940; B. Meissner, *Babylonien und Assyrien*, 2, 1925, pp. 198–282.

IV. Assyro-Babylonian magic in the Bible

a. Balaam

Balaam of Nu. 22–24 is apparently a diviner turned prophet under divine constraint. Thus Balak sent emissaries to hire Balaam 'with the fees for divination in their hand' (Nu. 22:7; *cf.* v. 18), and at first Balaam went 'to meet with omens', their nature unspecified (Nu. 24:1). Balak evidently required of Balaam evil omens wherewith to curse Israel. An astrological text was found at Qatna (*Revue d'Assyriologie* 44, 1950, pp. 105–112) and *bārû*-diviners in 18th- and 14th-century BC texts from Alalaḫ (D. J. Wiseman, *The Alalakh Tablets*, 1953, p. 158 *sub* '*bârû*'), both in N Syria. Further, an early 2nd millennium seal of one 'Manum the *bârû*(-diviner)' turned up at Beth-shan in Jezreel in levels of the 13th century BC, Balaam's own period, to which his oracles can be dated linguistically (W. F. Albright, *JBL* 63, 1944, pp. 207–233). It is therefore wholly in keeping with known facts that a Moabite ruler should hire a diviner from N Syria (Pethor by the River [Euphrates]), in the land of the sons of Amaw (Nu. 22:5; *cf.* Albright, *BASOR* 118, 1950, pp. 15–16, n. 13).

b. The law and magic in Canaan

The prohibitions in the Mosaic law against the magic and sorcery practised by other nations (*e.g.* Lv. 19:26; 20:27; Dt. 18:10–14) were very relevant to conditions in contemporary Canaan. For Bab. influence there, see above. The N Canaanite epics from * Ugarit/Ras Shamra (tablets of the 14th/13th century BC) show Danil kissing the growing plants and grain, invoking an oracular blessing upon Aqhat (*ANET*, p. 153: 60ff.); Puġat's activities are much less certainly connected with sorcery. That Ex. 22:18 expressly condemns sorceresses is also noteworthy.

*c. * Daniel*

In Dn. 1:4 the procedure for educating the well-favoured Heb. youths in Bab. learning as laid down by Nebuchadrezzar accurately reflects that which was usual for the *bārû* scholar-magicians.

To 'dissolve doubts' (Dn. 5:12, 16, 11), *i.e.* to dissipate anxiety caused by a (yet unexplained) dream or omen (*cf.* Dn. 4:5), was the purpose of interpreting or 'resolving' dreams. Then a good dream's benefits could be accepted and the threat from a bad one averted magically. On this, see A. L. Oppenheim, *The Interpretation of Dreams in the Ancient Near East*, pp. 218–220, 300–307. This emphasis on dreams is characteristic of the neo-Bab. kings, particularly Nabonidus, father of Belshazzar. For his dreams, see Oppenheim, *op. cit.*, pp. 202–206, 250, and, in part, T. Fish in *DOTT*, pp. 89f. New texts of, and new dreams by, Nabonidus and his venerable mother come from stelae of this king at Harran; see C. J. Gadd, *AS* 8, 1958, pp. 35–92 and pls. 1–16, especially pp. 49, 57, 63; *ANET*³, pp. 560–563. Closely parallel to Dn. 4 is the 'Prayer of Nabonidus' in the Dead Sea Scrolls in which an exiled Jewish sage (name not preserved) is granted to the king to explain the cause of the latter's affliction. E.T. in M. Burrows, *More Light on the Dead Sea Scrolls*, 1958, p. 400; text published by J.-T. Milik, *RB* 63, 1956, pp. 407–415; brief comments, D. N. Freedman, *BASOR* 145, 1957, pp. 31–32.

BIBLIOGRAPHY. 'Magic (Jewish)' in *ERE*; E. Langton, *Good and Evil Spirits*, 1942; *idem*, 'The Reality of Evil Powers Further Considered', *HJ* 132, July 1935, pp. 605–615; M. F. Unger, *Biblical Demonology*, 1952, pp. 107–164; A. D. Duncan, *The Christian, Psychotherapy and Magic*, 1969; D. Basham, *Deliver us from Evil*, 1972. K.A.K.

MAGI'S STAR
See Stars, Part 3.

MAGOG
See Gog and Magog, Part 1.

MAHALI
See Mahli, Part 2.

MAGISTRATE. In Ezr. 7:25 'magistrate' translates the Heb. *šôpēṭ*, 'judge'. In Jdg. 18:7, AV 'there was no magistrate in the land' is a paraphrase of the Heb, idiom *yāraš 'eṣer*, 'to possess restraint' (RSV 'lacking nothing'). Dn. 3:2–3 lists magistrates (Aram. *tip̄tāye'*, AV 'sheriffs') among officials summoned by Nebuchadrezzar.

In the NT Luke uses in his Gospel (12:11, 58) the words *archē* and *archōn* ('rule' and 'ruler') to refer to civil authorities in general. Paul was beaten, imprisoned and subsequently released by the magistrates at Philippi (Acts 16:20, 22, 35–36, 38). Here the Gk. word is *stratēgoi*, which literally means generals, or leaders of the host, but came to be used in a political context as an equivalent for Lat. *praetores*. This latter was the title found in some inscriptions as a popular designation for the leading men of the colony, though their correct title was *duoviri*. Evidence for the titles of the Philippian magistrates is to be found in *CIL*, 3. 633, 654, 7339, 14206^{15}. (*SANHEDRIN, *POLICE.) D.H.W.

MAGNIFICAT. Like other hymns in Lk. 1–2, the prophecy of Mary (Lk. 1:46–55) takes its name from the Lat. Vulg. Believing 'Mary' (Lk. 1:46) to be the secondary reading, some commentators accept the less well-attested reading 'Elizabeth' (*cf.* Creed). It may be that Luke originally wrote simply 'she said', and that both 'Mary' and 'Elizabeth' were attempts of copyists to assign the song to a particular person. The reading 'Mary' became universally accepted. Scholars are divided on the question of whether the contents of the hymn are more suitable to Mary or Elizabeth. The episode which forms the setting is, however, transitional from the annunciation to the birth stories; it stands in close conjunction with the former and continues its Messianic theme. Most probably, therefore, Luke viewed it as *Mary's* song regarding Christ.

This lyrical poem is modelled upon OT psalms and has also a special affinity to the Song of Hannah (1 Sa. 2:1–10). The sequence of the narrative is moulded by Luke's theme; and the hymn need not be regarded as Mary's spontaneous or exact reply. But neither should it be considered merely as an editorial reconstruction. Its significance for Luke lies in the fact that it is Mary's prophecy, *i.e.* that its contents sprang from her lips and express her mind and heart.

As this lyric forms a climax to the section, so also within the Magnificat itself the mood rises to a crescendo. It is divided into four strophes, describing (1) Mary's joyous exaltation, gratitude and praise for her personal blessing; (2) the character and gracious disposition of God to all who reverence him; (3) his sovereignty and his special love for the lowly in the world of men; and (4) his peculiar mercy to Israel. The cause of Mary's song is that God has deigned to choose her, a peasant maid of low estate, to fulfil the hope of every Jewish maiden. For it is probable that, in Judaism, that which gave deepest meaning and joy to motherhood was the possibility that this child might be the Deliverer.

The last part of the poem is a description of God's Messianic deliverance and is a virtual paraphrase of OT passages. This redemption is prophesied in terms of a national deliverance from human oppressors. This is a typical mode of expression of pre-Christian Messianism. The NT does not contradict it, but does transfer it to Messiah's parousia in the eschatological 'age to come' (*cf.* Acts 1:6ff.). As is often the case in OT oracles, these Messianic acts of God are viewed as though they were already accomplished: the promise of God has the efficacy of the act itself (*cf.* Gn. 1:3); his word is the word of power. The specific object of God's mercy is 'Israel his servant' (Lk. 1:54f.; *cf.* Acts 3:13, 26; 4:27, 30). Whether there is reflected here the OT distinction between the whole nation and the righteous remnant is uncertain; the concept is often left in an undifferentiated whole, and the contrast in vv. 51–53 may be only between the Jewish nation and the Gentile overlord. But in the mind of Luke—and in the mind of his first readers—certainly the distinctly Christian interpretation in such concepts as 'Israel' (*cf.* Lk. 24:21–26; Jn. 12:13; Acts 1:6; Rom. 9:6), 'servant', and 'the seed' (Jn. 8:39; Gal. 3:16, 29) is not absent, and it probably enters into his understanding and interpretation of Mary's prophecy. (*ANNUNCIATION; *BENEDICTUS.)

BIBLIOGRAPHY. J. M. Creed, *The Gospel according to St Luke*, 1942, pp. 21–24; R. Laurentin, 'Les Évangiles de l'enfance', *Lumière et Vie* 23, 1974, pp. 84–105. E.E.E.

MAGOR-MISSABIB (Heb. *māḡôr missāḇîḇ*, 'terror on every side'). A symbolic name that Jeremiah gave to Pashhur son of Immer (Je. 20:3, AV; see *PASHHUR, **1**). J.D.D.

MAHANAIM (Heb. *maḥᵃnayim*, 'two camps'). A place in Gilead where Jacob saw the angels of God before he reached Penuel and met Esau (Gn. 32:2). Appointed to be a levitical (Merarite) city from the territory of Gad (Jos. 21:38; 1 Ch. 6:80), Mahanaim was on the border of Gad with Gileadite Manasseh (Jos. 13:26, 30). It was briefly capital of Ishbosheth, Saul's son (2 Sa. 2:8, 12, 29), and later David's refuge from Absalom (2 Sa. 17:24, 27; 19:32; 1 Ki. 2:8), and then became the seat of a district-officer of Solomon's (1 Ki. 4:14). The location of Mahanaim is still uncertain; *cf.* J. R. Bartlett in *POTT*, p. 252, n. 47. It is usually placed in the middle of N Gilead at Khirbet Mahneh, 20 km N of the Jabbok river, but as the boundary of Gad is linked with the course of the Jabbok, Mahanaim is probably better located somewhere on (or overlooking) the N bank of the Jabbok. Mahanaim was at some distance from the Jordan, on the evidence of 2 Sa. 2:29, however 'Bithron' be interpreted. If (as is commonly taken) Bithron means 'cleft, ravine', Abner went from Jordan up the vale of the Jabbok E and through its narrow part before reaching Mahanaim. If the RSV reading be adopted, then 'the whole forenoon' was needed in any case for Abner's E flight. Hence perhaps Mahanaim was in the Jerash area, or up to 10–15 km SSW of Jerash, overlooking the N bank of the river Jabbok. See K.-D. Schunck, *ZDMG* 113, 1963, pp. 34–40. (*GAD, *GILEAD.) K.A.K.

MAHANEH-DAN (Heb. *maḥᵃnēh-ḏān*, 'camp of Dan'). Where Samson experienced the stirring of God's Spirit (Jdg. 13:25), and the first staging-post of the Danites in their quest for an inheritance (Jdg. 18:12). The geographical references given, 'between Zorah and Eshtaol' and 'W of Kiriath-jearim', cannot be reconciled, and the name itself suggests a temporary settlement.

As the Danites had no secure inheritance (Jdg. 18:1), probably due to Philistine pressure, there is no problem in two places bearing the same name. It is not surprising that no trace of such temporary encampments has survived. A.E.C.

MAHER-SHALAL-HASH-BAZ. A symbolical name ('speed the spoil, hasten the prey') given to one of the sons of *Isaiah to signify the speedy removal of Syria and Israel as enemies of Judah by the Assyrians. This removal was to take place before the child could lisp 'my father and my mother' (Is. 8:3–4). E.J.Y.

MAHLI (Heb. *maḥlî*, 'weak', 'sickly'). **1.** Eldest son of Merari and grandson of Levi (Ex. 6:19, AV 'Mahali'; Nu. 3:20; 1 Ch. 6:19, 29; [illegible] His descendants are mentioned in Nu. 3:33; 26:58. **2.** The son of Mushi, another son of Merari (1 Ch. 6:47; 23:23; 24:30); therefore nephew of **1,** above. J.D.D.

MAHOL (Heb. *māḥôl*, 'dance'). The father of certain sages whom Solomon excelled in wisdom (1 Ki. 4:31). But in 1 Ch. 2:6 they are said to be 'sons of Zerah'. 'Sons' may simply mean 'descendants' in either case. However, 'sons of Mahol' may be an appellative expression meaning 'sons of the dance' (*cf.* 'daughters of music' in Ec. 12:4). Such dancing would then be part of the ritual of worship, as in Pss. 149:3; 150:4 (*cf.* also the titles of Pss. 88–89). J.G.G.N.

MAKKEDAH (Heb. *maqqēḏâh*). A town in the Shephelah captured by Joshua (Jos. 10:28; 12:16); in the district of Lachish (15:41). Adonizedek and his allies hid in a cave nearby after their defeat (10:16ff.). Eusebius (*Onom.* p. 126) put Makkedah 8 Roman miles from Beit Guvrin; Khirbet el-Kheishum, NE of Azekah, seems to be too far, while Tell Bornat (Kallai-Kleinmann, *VT* 8, 1958, p. 155) is only 3 km from Beit Guvrin. El-Mughar, SE of Yibna, was once favoured but is unlikely.

BIBLIOGRAPHY. *GTT*, p. 273; F. M. Abel, *Géographie de la Palestine*, 2, 1937, p. 378; J. Garstang, *Joshua-Judges*, 1931, p. 181. J.P.U.L.

MAKTESH. A site in Jerusalem or near by (Zp. 1:11). The name means 'mortar' or 'trough'. The oldest suggestion is that it was the Kidron Valley; so says the Targum. But most scholars today believe it to have been some part of the Tyropoeon Valley, within the walls of the city, where foreign merchants gathered; *cf.* NEB 'Lower Town'. D.F.P.

MALACHI, BOOK OF.

I. Authorship, date and background

The LXX takes the word not as a proper name but as a common noun, and renders 'my messenger', which is the meaning of the Heb. word. Many scholars follow LXX, and believe that the name of the author is not given. But the analogy of the other prophetical books which give the author's name would support the view that the name is here intended to indicate the author. This is supported by the Targum, which adds the phrase 'whose name is called Ezra the scribe'.

From internal evidence the approximate date of the prophecy may be determined. Sacrifices were being offered in the Temple (1:7–10; 3:8). This implies that the Temple was standing; indeed, that it had been standing for some time, a fact which would point to the 5th century BC. This is substantiated by the reference in 1:8 to the *peḥâ* or Persian governor. Mixed marriages seem to have been practised (2:10–12). The phrase 'the daughter of a foreign god' means 'a woman of foreign religion'. Apparently this practice of marrying outside the covenant people was so widespread that the earlier prohibitions had long since been forgotten. Nor was great care exhibited in the offering of the sacrifices (1:7). The priests had despised the Lord in offering polluted bread. When blemished offerings are brought it is a sign of a lax attitude, and such an attitude would not well comport with the early zeal displayed by the returned exiles. This appears to have been accompanied by a neglect in paying the requisite tithes (3:8–10). The abuses which Malachi condemns are those which Nehemiah sought to correct.

It is impossible to date the book precisely, but it may be that it was composed during Nehemiah's visit to Susa. At least it would seem to come from approximately this time.

II. Outline of contents

The book falls into two main parts, and its purpose may best be ascertained through a study of its contents. The first part (chs. 1 and 2) deals with the sin of Israel, and the second part (chs. 3 and 4) with the judgment that will befall the guilty and the blessedness that will come upon those who repent.

We may analyse the book thus:

a. The superscription (1:1)

There is a connection between this heading and that found at the beginning of ch. 3. Whether or not Malachi is a proper name, it exemplifies the fact that he is a messenger of God.

b. The Lord's love for Israel (1:2–5)

God declares his love for the people in that he chose Jacob and rejected Esau. This fact is seen in that Edom is devastated and refugees from Edom will never be able to return and rebuild, whereas Israel is back in the promised land.

c. A delineation of Israel's sin (1:6–2:9)

In bold fashion the prophet now begins to delineate the chief and characteristic sins of the nation which were again bringing the wrath of God upon the nation's head. God is the Father of the people, for he has nourished and brought them up. A father deserves honour and love, but such have not been shown to God by Israel. This complaint is directed particularly to the priests who are the representatives of the people before God. These priests who should have set the example of godly fear in worship have, in fact, despised the name of the Lord. Unworthy worship had been characteristic of their predecessors in the 8th and 7th centuries until the Exile had been brought upon Judah. Now, however, the Exile is past, and its lessons have not yet been learnt. Restored to her land, able to worship in the Temple, Judah yet sins against the Lord in the same manner as before.

The accusation against Israel is carried on in the form of a dialogue. Against each charge of the Lord a question or challenge is raised. For example, God charges that the priests have offered polluted food. They reply, 'How have we polluted it? (1:7). It is thus

MAIL, COAT OF See Armour, Part 1.

brought out in clear-cut fashion that the priests have been bringing blemished sacrifices. This was in direct contravention of the law, which required that the offerings should be perfect. Instead, they had brought what was blind and lame, and in so doing had exhibited contempt for the Lord.

When such sacrifices come from their hands, how can they expect to be accepted as individuals and to find favour with him? (1:9). It would be better that the gates of the Temple were closed entirely than for such offerings to be brought (1:10). Both the offerer and his offering are unacceptable to the Lord, and the priests are despised by the people.

Such sacrifices are not desired by God, for even among the Gentiles his name will prove itself to be great so that pure sacrifices are offered to him (1:11). This does not refer to the offerings which the heathen nations bring to their gods, but to the time when the true gospel will be spread throughout the world and the true God worshipped by all peoples. Israel, however, had profaned the Lord's table, and found his service boring, resulting in a people who practised deception and were selfish.

If there is no repentance, then a curse will come upon the priests. In 2:5–7 the Lord makes clear the true duty of the priests, and thus there appears a great contrast between what the priest should be and what he actually was. Indeed, through his own poor example, he, instead of instructing others, has led them astray. He has been partial in instructing others (2:9b).

d. Condemnation of mixed marriages and divorce (2:10–17)

Israel had a common Father: God had created the nation. Therefore, it should have manifested unity. Instead of that, however, it had dealt treacherously. It had profaned the holiness of the Lord in the practice of mixed marriages. Those who had thus acted, however, were to be cut off. Divorce was also common, and the Lord hates divorce. These sins had been glossed over and rationalized. The Lord declares that the people have wearied him with their words. They have ignored him and acted as though he did not exist.

e. The coming Day of the Lord (3:1–6)

Malachi now breaks into the exalted language of prophecy in declaring that the messenger of the Lord will truly come and prepare the day for the Lord whom the people seek. He will appear as a refiner, to purify and purge the nation, and who can face the day of his coming? As a result of his work, the offering of Judah and Jerusalem will be pleasing to the Lord (3:4). Yet the coming will bring judgment, and this will fall upon those in the nation who are oppressing others. Nevertheless, Jacob will not be entirely wiped out, for the Lord does not change; he remains faithful to his promises (3:6).

f. Repentance and tithing (3:7–12)

The nation's apostasy is not new, but has continued from of old. For one thing, it has shown itself in withholding from God the tithes which had been commanded. This amounted to robbing God. If the nation would bring the tithes as it should, God would respond to its worship and pour upon it an overflowing blessing which would call forth comment from other nations.

g. A promise of deliverance for the godly (3:13–4:3)

The nation had been saying resentful things against God. It would seem that the people considered it did not pay them to serve God. But among them there were also those who 'feared the Lord', and they encouraged one another. These the Lord takes note of, and he will not only spare them but make them his own possession. The day of judgment will surely come, and it will consume the arrogant, but to those who fear the Lord's name righteousness will rise like a sun, and in its wings there will be healing, joy and victory.

h. Conclusion (4:4–6)

The prophecy closes with an exhortation to remember the law of Moses, and with the announcement that Elijah will come before there appears the great and terrible Day of the Lord.

BIBLIOGRAPHY. J. G. Baldwin, *Haggai, Zechariah, Malachi, TOTC*, 1972; D. R. Jones, *Haggai, Zechariah and Malachi, TBC*, 1962; J. M. P. Smith, in Mitchell, Smith and Bewer, *Haggai, Zechariah, Malachi and Jonah, ICC*, 1912.

E.J.Y.
J.G.B.

MALCAM. 1. A Benjaminite, son of Shaharaim by Hodesh (1 Ch. 8:9).

2. God of the Ammonites, possibly their chief deity (Am. 1:15, AV, RSV 'their king'), almost certainly to be identified with *Milcom (1 Ki. 11:5, 33; 2 Ki. 23:13), and *Molech or Moloch (Lv. 18:21; 1 Ki. 11:7; Je. 32:35, *etc.*). All these terms have the basic root *mlk* which conveys the idea of king, kingship. Both AV and RV translate *malkām* as 'their king' in Je. 49:1, 3 (RSV 'Milcom'). *Cf.* Zp. 1:5 (RSV 'Milcom').

J.A.T.

MALCHIAH
See Malchijah, Part 2.

MALCHIJAH ('Yah is King'). This is a common OT name, sometimes translated as Malchiah. It was the name of the following: **1.** A descendant of Gershom and ancestor of Asaph (1 Ch. 6:40); **2.** a priest, the father of Pashhur (1 Ch. 9:12; Je. 21:1); **3.** the head of a priestly course (1 Ch. 24:9), perhaps the same as **2**; **4**, **5**, **6**. three Israelites who had taken foreign wives in post-exilic times (Ezr. 10:25, 31). In 1 Esdras 9:26, 32 they are called Melchias, Asibias and Melchias respectively; **7.** 'the son of Rechab', who repaired the dung gate (Ne. 3:14); **8.** 'the goldsmith's son', possibly the same as **4**, **5**, **6** or **7**, who helped to repair the wall (Ne. 3:31).

9. One who stood beside Ezra at the reading of the Law (Ne. 8:4); **10.** one who sealed the covenant, perhaps the same as **9** (Ne. 10:3); **11.** a priest who took part in the purification of the wall (Ne. 12:42), perhaps the same as **9** and/or **10**.

12. The owner of the pit in which Jeremiah was imprisoned and probably a member of the royal family (Je. 38:6).

J.D.D.

MALCHUS (Gk. *Malchos* from Heb. *meleḵ*, 'king'). The high priest's servant whose ear Peter cut off when Jesus was arrested in the Garden of Gethsemane (Mt. 26:51; Mk. 14:47; Lk. 22:50; Jn. 18:10). Only John mentions the man's name, thus confirming his close acquaintance with the high priest Caiaphas and his household (*cf.* Jn. 18:15); and only Luke (22:51), with his interest in medical matters, mentions the healing of the ear. Malchus is a common Arab name in Nabatean and Palmyrene inscriptions.

J.D.D.

MALICE. In the NT this translates Gk. *kakia*, which has the following meanings: **1**. 'Wickedness', 'evil' (1 Cor. 14:20; Jas. 1:21; 1 Pet. 2:1, 16; and also in Acts 8:22, of an individual sinful act). 'Malice' in 17th-century (AV) English had primarily this meaning. **2**. 'Ill-will', 'spitefulness'; *i.e.* 'malice' in the modern sense of the word. **3**. 'Trouble', 'harm' (Mt. 6:34). In lists of sins (*e.g.* Rom. 1:29; Col. 3:8; Tit. 3:3), sense **2** is probably to be preferred, except, perhaps, in 1 Pet. 2:1 and Eph. 4:31, where 'all *kakia*' implies 'all kinds of wickedness'.

Malice characterizes the life of men under the wrath of God (Rom. 1:29). It is not only a moral deficiency but destroys fellowship (W. Grundmann, *TDNT* 3, pp. 482–484). For believers it belongs to the old life (Tit. 3:3); but there is still need for exhortation to 'clean it out' (1 Cor. 5:7f.) or 'strip it off' (Jas. 1:21, Col. 3:8). Christians are to be 'babes in evil' (1 Cor. 14:20), for Christian liberty is not lawlessness (1 Pet. 2:16). P.E.

MALTA (Gk. *Melitē*; Acts 28:1, AV 'Melita'). An island in the centre of the Mediterranean, 100 km S of Sicily and in area about 246 sq km (not to be confused with the island Mljet or Melitene off the Dalmatian coast; *cf.* O. F. A. Meinardus, 'St Paul Shipwrecked in Dalmatia', *BA* 39, 1976, pp. 145–147.) Here Paul's ship was driven from Crete by the ENE wind Euraquilo (27:14, RSV 'the northeaster'; * WIND). After being shipwrecked he spent 3 months on the island before continuing his journey to Rome *via* Syracuse, Rhegium and Puteoli (28:11–13). Paul performed acts of healing, and the party was treated with great respect.

Malta had been occupied from the 7th century BC by Phoenicians. The name itself means 'refuge' in that language (J. R. Harris, *ExpT* 21, 1909–10, p. 18). Later, Sicilian Greeks also came; there are bilingual inscriptions of the 1st century AD on the island. In 218 BC the island passed from Carthaginian to Roman control (Livy, 21. 51), later gaining the 'civitas'. Its inhabitants were *barbaroi* (28:2, 4) only in the sense of not speaking Greek. Luke may refer to one of their gods in v. 4 as *Dikē* (Justice). Publius, 'the chief man' (v. 7), probably served under the propraetor of Sicily. His title (Gk. *prōtos*) is attested by inscriptions (*CIG*, 14. 601; *CIL*, 10. 7495). The site of the shipwreck is thought to have been 'St Paul's Bay', 13 km NW of modern Valletta (*cf.* W. M. Ramsay, *SPT*, pp. 314ff.).

BIBLIOGRAPHY. J. Smith, *Voyage and Shipwreck of Paul*[4], 1880; W. Burridge, *Seeking the Site of St Paul's Shipwreck*, 1952; J. D. Evans, *Malta*, 1959; C. J. Hemer, 'Euraquilo and Melita', *JTS* n.s. 26, 1975, pp. 100–111. B.F.H.

MAMMON. This word occurs in the Bible only in Mt. 6:24 and Lk. 16:9, 11, 13, and is a transliteration of Aramaic *māmônâ*. It means simply wealth or profit, but Christ sees in it an egocentric covetousness which claims man's heart and thereby estranges him from God (Mt. 6:19ff.): when a man 'owns' anything, in reality it owns him. (*Cf.* the view that mammon derives from Bab. *mimma*, 'anything at all'.) 'Unrighteous mammon' (Lk. 16:9) is dishonest gain (F. Hauck, *TDNT* 4, pp. 388–390) or simply gain from self-centred motives (*cf.* Lk. 12:15ff.). The probable meaning is that such money, used for others, may be transformed thereby into true riches in the coming age (Lk. 16:12).

MALLOW
See Plants, Part 3.

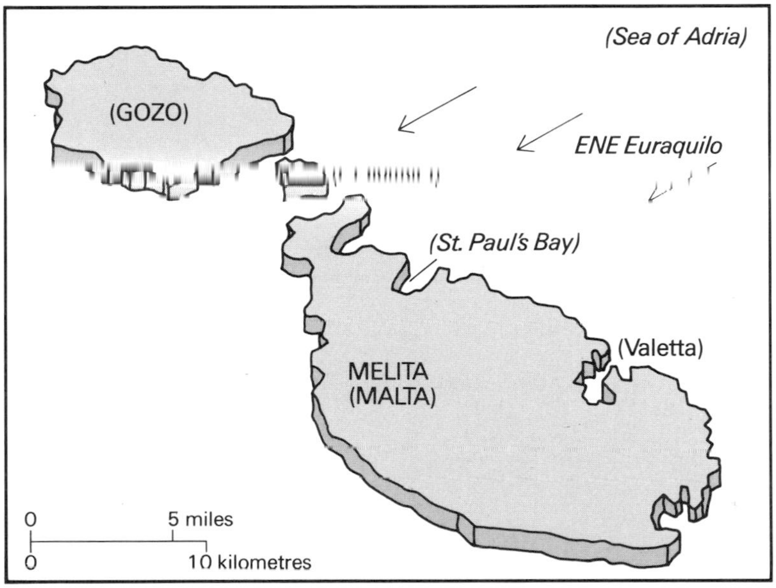

Malta, where Paul was shipwrecked (Acts 27:12ff.).

St Paul's Bay, Malta, the traditional site of the shipwreck in Acts 28:1. (FNH)

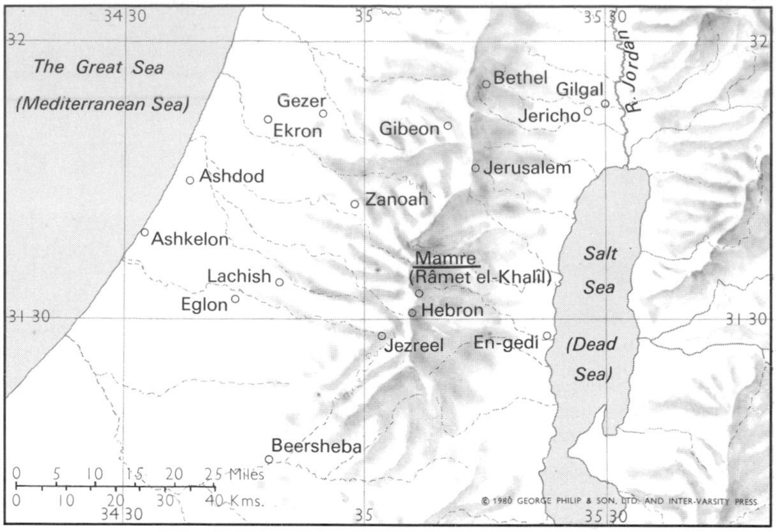

Mamre, identified with modern Râmet el-Khalîl.

Mamre, near Hebron. View of Herodian ruins. (MEPhA)

BIBLIOGRAPHY. C. Brown, *NIDNTT* 2, pp. 836–840; J. D. M. Derrett, *Law in the New Testament*, 1970. E.E.E.

MAMRE (Heb. *mamrē'*). **1.** A place in the Hebron district, W from Machpelah (Gn. 23:17, 19; 49:30; 50:13), associated with Abraham (Gn. 13:18; 14:13; 18:1) and Isaac (Gn. 35:27). Abraham resided for considerable periods under the terebinth of Mamre; there he built an altar, there he learnt of the capture of Lot, there he received Yahweh's promise of a son and pleaded for Sodom, and from there he saw the smoke of Sodom and its neighbour-cities ascend. The site has been identified at Râmet el-Khalîl, 4 km N of Hebron. Here Constantine built a basilica beside an ancient terebinth which was pointed out in his day (as by Josephus 250 years earlier) as the tree beneath which Abraham 'entertained angels unawares' (Gn. 18:4, 8). There was a shrine there under the Monarchy, but it was a sacred place before Abraham's time in the Early Bronze Age.

2. An Amorite chief at Mamre who with his brothers Eshcol and Aner joined Abraham's expedition against Chedorlaomer (Gn. 14:13, 24).

BIBLIOGRAPHY. E. Mader, *Mambre*, 2 vols., 1957. F.F.B.

MAN. The Genesis account of creation accords to man a supreme place in the cosmos. Not only is his creation the final work of God, but in it the work of the other 5 days finds its fulfilment and its meaning. Man is to possess the earth, make it serve him, and to rule the other creatures (Gn. 1:27–2:3). The same witness to man's dominion and centrality in creation is given elsewhere (Am. 4:13; Is. 42:5f.; Pss. 8:5f.; 104:14f.), and is supremely given in the incarnation (*cf.* Heb. 2).

a. Man in nature

It is emphasized throughout the Bible that man is part of nature. Being dust, and made from dust (Gn. 2:7), his biological and physical similarity to the animal creation is obvious in many aspects of his life (Gn. 18:27; Jb. 10:8–9; Ps. 103:14; Ec. 3:19–20; 12:5–7). Being 'flesh' he shares in the helpless dependence of the dumb creation on God's mercy (Is. 2:22; 40:6; Pss. 103:15; 104:27–30). Even in making nature serve him he has to serve nature, tend it, and bring it to fruition (Gn. 2:15). He is subject to the same laws as the natural world, and can find himself overwhelmed in the midst of the grandeur of the world in which he lives (Jb. 38–42).

Nature is not simply a neutral framework or background for man's life. Between nature and man there are deep and mysterious bonds. The natural world falls under the curse of corruption through the Fall of man (Gn. 3:17–18), and now suffers pain and death, waiting for the final redemption of mankind before it can expect its own (Rom. 8:19–23). Nature is regarded in the Bible as rejoicing in the events that lead to man's redemption (Ps. 96:10–13; Is. 35; 55:12–13) when it, too, shall enjoy deliverance (Is. 11:6–9; 65:25). Man, on his side, has an instinctive sympathy with nature (Gn. 2:19) and must respect its ordinances (Lv. 19:19; Dt. 22:9–10; Jb. 31:38–40), realize his dependence on it, and toil to gain from his natural environment sustenance for his life and enrichment for his culture (Gn. 3:17; 9:1–7).

b. Man's destiny

Yet man cannot find the true meaning of his life within this context. The animals can provide no 'helper fit for him' (Gn. 2:18). He has a history and a destiny to fulfil, unique among the rest of creation. He is made 'in the image of God' (Gn. 1:27). While some have suggested that this image is expressed in man's dominion over the earth, or in his power of reasoning, or even in his physical characteristics, it seems better to find it neither in man's relationship with the world nor in any static impress on man's being, but in his responsibility towards his Creator. In the Genesis account of creation God, when he creates man, is regarded as taking up an attitude of deeper personal concern for him (Gn. 1:26; *cf.* 1:3, 6, *etc.*), and an approach that involves himself in a closer relationship with man his creature (Gn. 2:7) than with the rest of creation. God approaches man and addresses him as a 'thou' (Gn. 3:9, AV), and man is made to respond to God's gracious word in personal love and trust. Only in this response can man be what he truly is. God's word by which he lives (*cf.* Mt. 4:4) offers him a relationship that lifts him above the rest of creation around him, and confers on him his dignity as a child of God, made in his image and reflecting his glory. This dignity, moreover, is not something he possesses as an isolated individual before God, but only as he also stands in responsible and loving relationship to his fellow-men. It is as man within his family and social relationships that he truly reflects the image of God (Gn. 1:27–28; 2:18).

c. Man's structure

Various words are used to describe man in his relationship to God and to his environment, and in the structure of his own being. These are: spirit (Heb. *rûaḥ*, Gk. *pneuma*), soul (Heb. *nep̄eš*, Gk. *psychē*), body (only in NT Gk., *sōma*), flesh (Heb. *bāśār*, Gk. *sarx*). These words are used according to the different aspects of man's activity or being which it is intended to emphasize, but they must not be regarded as describing separate or separable parts which go to make up what man is. The use of the word 'soul' may emphasize his individuality and vitality with emphasis on his inner life and feeling and personal consciousness. The use of the word 'body' may emphasize the historical and outward associations that affect his life. But the soul is, and must be, the soul of his body, and vice versa. Man is also in such a relation to the Spirit of God that he has spirit, and yet not in such a way that he can be described as spirit, or that spirit can be regarded as a third aspect of his identity. Man as 'flesh' is man in his connection with the realm of nature and with humanity as a whole, not only in its weakness but also in its sinfulness and opposition to God.

Other words are used to define the seat of certain particular aspects or functions of man. In the OT emotional impulses and feelings are attributed, really and metaphorically, to organs of the body such as the *heart (*lēḇ*), *liver (*kāḇēḏ*), *kidneys (*kᵉlāyôt*) and *bowels (*mē'îm*). The *blood is also regarded as being closely identified with the life or *nep̄eš*. It is especially the heart (*lēḇ*) that is the seat of a wide range of volitional and intellectual as well as emotional activities, and tends to denote the soul, or man viewed from his inward and hidden side. In the NT the same use is made of the Gk. word *kardia* (= *lēḇ*, heart). Two more words, *nous*, 'mind', and *syneidēsis*, 'conscience', are brought into use, and a clearer distinction is made between the 'inward' and 'outward' man, but these two aspects of the one man cannot be separated, and the future holds not the mere 'immortality of the soul' but the 'resurrection of the body', which means the salvation and renewal of the whole man in the fullness of his being.

d. Man's sin

The Fall of man (Gn. 3) involves his refusal to respond to God's word, and to enter the relationship in which he can fulfil the purpose for which he was created. Man seeks to find within himself the justification for his existence (Rom. 10:3). Instead of seeking to enter a true relationship with God and his fellow-men in which he can reflect God's image and glory, he seeks to find the meaning of his destiny merely in his relationship with the created world in the context of his immediate environment (Rom. 1:25). The result is that his life has become characterized by bondage (Heb. 2:14–15), conflict with evil powers (Eph. 6:12), frailty and frustration (Is. 40:6; Jb. 14:1), and he is so perverted and evil in his mind and heart (Gn. 8:21; Jb. 14:4; Ps. 51:5; Mt. 12:39; 15:19–20) that he turns the truth of God into a lie (Rom. 1:25).

e. Man in God's image

Yet in spite of the Fall, man under the promise of Christ must still be regarded as in the image of God (Gn. 5:1ff.; 9:1ff.; Ps. 8; 1 Cor. 11:7; Jas. 3:9), not because of what he is in himself, but because of what Christ is for him, and because of what he is in Christ. In Christ is now to be seen the true meaning of the covenant which God sought to make with man in the Word, and the destiny which man was made to fulfil (*cf.* Gn. 1:27–30; 9:8–17; Ps. 8; Eph. 1:22; Heb. 2:6ff.), for the unfaithfulness of man does not nullify the faithfulness of God (Rom. 3:3). Therefore in the sight of God, man, seen both in the individual (Mt. 18:12) and corporate (Mt. 9:36; 23:37) aspects of his life, is of more value than the whole realm of nature (Mt. 10:31; 12:12; Mk. 8:36–37), and the finding of the lost man is worth the most painful search and complete sacrifice on God's part (Lk. 15).

Jesus Christ is the true image of God (Col. 1:15; 2 Cor. 4:4) and thus the true man (Jn. 19:5). He is both the unique individual and the inclusive representative of the whole race, and his achievement and victory mean freedom and life for all mankind (Rom. 5:12–21). He fulfils the covenant in which God bestows on man his true destiny. In Christ, by faith, man finds himself being changed into the likeness of God (2 Cor. 3:18) and can hope confidently for full conformity to his image (Rom. 8:29) at the final manifestation of his glory (1 Jn. 3:2). In 'putting on' that image by faith he must now 'put off the old nature' (Eph. 4:24; Col. 3:10), which seems to imply a further renunciation of the idea that the image of God can be thought of as something inherent in the natural man, though even the natural man must be regarded as being created in the image of God (*cf.* 2 Cor. 5:16–17).

In the development of the doctrine of man, the church came under the influence of Gk. thought with its dualistic contrast between matter and spirit. Emphasis was placed on the soul with its 'divine spark', and there was a tendency to regard man as a self-contained individual entity whose true nature could be understood by the examination of the separate elements constituting his being. Emphasis was placed by some of the Fathers on the rationality, freedom and immortality of the soul as being the main element in man's likeness to God, though others found the image of God also in his physical being. Irenaeus regarded the image of God as a destiny which man was created to grow into. Augustine dwelt on the similarity between the Trinity and the threefold structure in man's memory, intellect and will.

An exaggerated distinction was also suggested between the meanings of the two words 'image' and 'likeness' (*ṣelem* and *dᵉmûṯ*) of God, in which man was said to be created (Gn. 1:26), and this gave rise to the scholastic doctrine that the 'likeness' (Lat. *similitudo*) of God was a supernatural gift given by God to man in his creation, *i.e.* an original righteousness (*justitia originalis*) and perfect self-determination before God, which could be, and indeed was, lost in the Fall. The 'image' (*imago*), on the other hand, consisted of what belonged to man by nature, *i.e.* his freewill, rational nature and dominion over the animal world, which could not be lost even in the Fall. This means that the Fall destroyed what was originally supernatural in man, but left his nature and the image of God in him wounded, and his will free.

At the Reformation Luther denied the distinction between *imago* and *similitudo*. The Fall radically affected the *imago*, destroyed man's freewill (in the sense of *arbitrium*, though not of *voluntas*), and corrupted man's being in its most important aspects, only a tiny relic of his original image and relationship to God being left. Calvin, however, also stressed the fact that the true meaning of man's creation is to be found in what is given to him in Christ, and that man comes to be in God's image as he reflects back to him his glory, in gratitude and faith.

In later Reformed dogmatics the concepts of *imago* and *similitudo* were again differentiated when theologians spoke of the essential image of God which could not be lost, and the accidental but natural endowments (including original righteousness) which might be lost without the loss of humanity itself. In more modern times Brunner has attempted to use the concept of the 'formal' *imago* consisting of the present structure of man's being, based on law. This has not been lost in the Fall, and is a point of contact for the gospel. It is one aspect of a unified theological nature of man which even in its perversion reveals traces of the image of God. 'Materially', however, for Brunner, the *imago* has been completely lost. R. Niebuhr has returned to the scholastic distinction between, on the one hand, the essential nature of man which cannot be destroyed, and, on the other hand, an original righteousness, the virtue and perfection of which would represent the normal expression of that nature.

Karl Barth, in formulating his doctrine of man, has chosen a path different from that followed by church tradition. We cannot know real man till we know him in and through Christ, therefore we must discover what man is only through what we find Jesus Christ to be in the gospel. We must not take sin more seriously than grace, therefore we must refuse to regard man as being no longer the one God made him. Sin creates the conditions under which God acts, but does not so change the structure of man's being that when we look at Jesus Christ in relation to men and mankind, we cannot see within human life analogical relationships which show a basic form of humanity corresponding to and similar to the divine determination of man. Though man is not by nature God's 'covenant-partner', nevertheless in the strength of the hope we have in Christ human existence is an existence which corresponds to God himself, and in this sense is in the image of God. Barth finds special significance in the fact that man and woman together are created in the image of God, and stresses the mutual communication and helpfulness of man to man as being of the essence of human nature. But only in the incarnate Son, Jesus Christ, and through his election in Christ, can man know God and be related to God in this divine image.

BIBLIOGRAPHY. H. Wheeler Robinson, *The Christian Doctrine of Man*, 1926; O. Weber, *Dogmatik*, 1, 1955, pp. 582–640; E. Brunner, *Man in Revolt*, E.T. 1939; K. Barth, *Church Dogmatics*, E.T. III/1, pp. 176–211, 235–249, and III/2, *Christ and Adam*, E.T. 1956; D. Cairns, *The Image of God in Man*, 1953; R. Niebuhr, *The Nature and Destiny of Man*, 1941; Gustaf Wingren, *Man and the Incarnation*, 1959; Günther Dehn, *Man and Revelation*, 1936, pp. 9–37; H. Heppe, *Reformed Dogmatics*, E.T. 1950, pp. 220–250; C. Hodge, *Systematic Theology*, 2, 1883, pp. 3–116; W. Eichrodt, *Man in the Old Testament*, E.T. 1951; C. H. Dodd, P. I. Bratsiotis, R. Bultmann and H. Clavier, *Man in God's Design*, 1952; R. P. Shedd, *Man in Community*, 1958; W. G. Kümmel, *Man in the New Testament*, 1963; K. Rahner, *Man in the Church* (= *Theological Investigations* 2), 1963; *idem*, *Theology, Anthropology, Christology* (= *Theological Investigations* 13), 1975; R. Scroggs, *The Last Adam: A Study in Pauline Anthropology*, 1966; W. Pannenberg, *What is Man?*, 1970; T. M. Kitwood, *What is Human?*, 1970; J. Moltmann, *Man*, 1971; R. Jewett, *Paul's Use of Anthropological Terms*, 1971; P. K. Jewett, *Man as Male and Female*, 1975; H. Vorländer, C.Brown, J. S. Wright in *NIDNTT* 2, pp. 562–572.

R.S.W.

MANAEN. The Gk. form of the Heb. name Menahem ('comforter'). Brought up with ('foster-brother of') Herod Antipas, Manaen's life took a very different turn from that of the tetrarch, and he is found as one of the Christian leaders at Antioch along with Paul and Barnabas (Acts 13:1). He may have been related to an earlier Manaen or Menahem, an Essene who, according to Josephus (*Ant.* 15. 373), was a friend of Herod the Great. J.D.D.

MANAHATH, MANAHATHITES. 1. Son of Shobal, son of Seir the Horite (Gn. 36:23; 1 Ch. 1:40), who was the eponymous ancestor of a clan of Mt Seir later absorbed by Edom.

2. The name of a city to which certain Benjaminites were carried captive (1 Ch. 8:6), and which seems to have been somewhere in the vicinity of Bethlehem (so *GTT*, p. 155). *ISBE* and Grollenberg suggest an identification with Manocho, a town in the hill-country of Judah listed in Jos. 15:59, LXX, and probably to be identified with the modern Malîha, SW of Jerusalem. Mahanath may also be the 'Nohah' of Jdg. 20:43, for both names mean 'resting-place'. Amarna Letter 292 (*ANET*, p. 489) mentions a Manhatu in the realm of Gezer which is probably the same place.

Manahathites, inhabitants of Manahath, are mentioned in 1 Ch. 2:52, 54. They were the descendants of Caleb. Half of them were the progeny of *Shobal, and the others of Salma (*SALMON). J.D.D.

MANASSEH ('making to forget'). **1.** Elder son of Joseph, born in Egypt of an Egyptian mother, *Asenath, daughter of *Potiphera, the priest of On (Gn. 41:51). Israel accepted Manasseh and Ephraim as co-equals with Reuben and Simeon, but Manasseh lost the right of *firstborn* ($b^e\underline{k}\hat{o}r$) in favour of his younger brother Ephraim (Gn. 48:5, 14). An interesting and early parallel is found in Ugaritic literature, *Keret Legend* (Tab. 128, 3. 15), 'The youngest of them I will make *firstborn* (*abrkn*).'

2. The tribe of Manasseh derived from seven families: one from Machir, and the remaining six from Gilead. They occupied land on both sides of Jordan; the E portion being granted by Moses, the W by Joshua (Jos. 22:7). After the crossing of Jordan and the settlement in the land, Joshua permitted the half-tribe of Manasseh, together with Reuben and Gad, to return to the conquered territory of Sihon, king of Heshbon, and Og, king of Bashan (Nu. 32:33). The E lot of the half-tribe of Manasseh covered part of Gilead and all of Bashan (Dt. 3:13). The W half of the tribe was granted good land N of Ephraim, and S of Zebulun and Issachar (Jos. 17:1–12). This W part was divided into ten portions: five to those families having male descendants, and five to Manasseh's sixth family, *i.e.* the posterity of Hepher, all females and daughters of Zelophehad (Jos. 17:3). W Manasseh included a chain of Canaanite fortresses and strong cities, among which were *Megiddo, *Taanach, *Ibleam and *Beth-shan.

These they failed to conquer but compelled their inhabitants eventually to pay tribute. Though the lot of Manasseh and Ephraim, the tribe of Joseph, was large, they lodged a complaint with Joshua for more land. In reply he advised them to show their worth by clearing the unclaimed forest areas (Jos. 17:14–18). Golan, a city of Bashan, in E Manasseh, was one of the six *'cities of refuge' (Jos. 20:8; 21:27; 1 Ch. 6:71).

The tribe was renowned for its valour; among its heroes was Gideon in the W (Jdg. 6:15), and Jephthah in the E (Jdg. 11:1). Some of the tribe of Manasseh deserted to David at Ziklag (1 Ch. 12:19–20), and also rallied to his support at Hebron (v. 31). Manassites were among those deported to Assyria by Tiglath-pileser (1 Ch. 5:18–26).

Difficulties have been found in the genealogies of the tribe of Manasseh, given in Nu. 26:28–34; Jos. 17:1–3; 1 Ch. 2:21–23; 7:14–19 (see *HDB* on 'Manasseh'). But if allowance is made for a corrupt text in 1 Ch. 7:14–15, then harmony can be restored. It is probable that the words 'Huppim and Shuppim' are glossed into v. 15 from v. 12, and possible that the word 'Asriel' is a dittograph.

A comparison of the Heb. text of these verses with LXX, Syr. Peshitta and Vulg. indicates that the original text may have had the following words: 'The son of Manasseh (Asriel) . . . whom his Syrian concubine . . . bore Machir the father of Gilead and Machir took a wife . . . and his sister's name Maacha and the name of the .. Zelophehad and Zelophehad had daughters . . .' Apart from these verses, the genealogies are consistent.

3. Son of Hezekiah and Hephzibah, he began his reign in Jerusalem at the age of 12 and reigned 55 years (2 Ki. 21:1; 2 Ch. 33:1); probably as co-regent with his father 696–686 BC, and as sole ruler 686–642 BC (E. R. Thiele, *The Mysterious Numbers of the Hebrew Kings*, 1951, pp. 154ff.). His reign was a time of religious retrogression, caused by terror of Assyria and a fascination for her cults. This resulted in a syncretism of Baalism, a cult of Astarte at the 'high places', astral worship, with spiritism and divination. His long reign was bloody and reactionary, and notorious for the introduction of illegal altars into the Temple courts, and 'the passing of his sons through the fire' in the valley of the son of Hinnom.

The name 'Manasseh, king of Judah' appears on the Prism of Esarhaddon (*Me-na-si-i šar Ia-ú-di*), and on the Prism of Ashurbanipal (*Mi-in-si-e šar Ia-ú-di*), among twenty-two tributaries of Assyria (*ANET*, pp. 291, 294). The Chronicler narrates Manasseh's deportation to Babylon, his repentance and release (2 Ch. 33:10–13). A parallel to this is the capture and the subsequent release of Neco I, king of Egypt, by Ashurbanipal (*Rassam Cylin-*

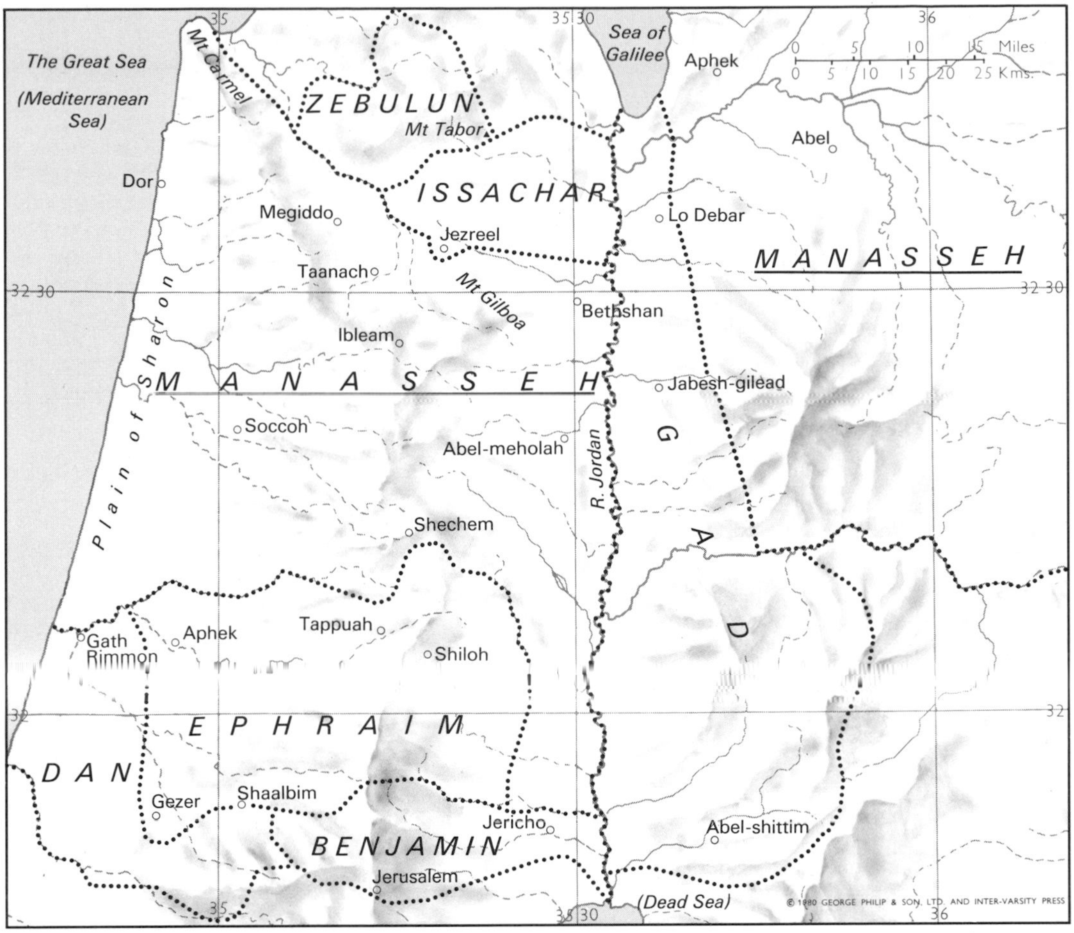

Top: Map showing the land allotted to the tribe of Manasseh.

Manasseh, king of Judah (Me-na-si-i šar Ia-ú-di), *is named on this clay prism among the rulers forced by Esarhaddon of Assyria to send materials for the building of his new palace at Nineveh. Nineveh. c. 673–672 BC.* (BM)

der, *ANET*, p. 295). Since a revolt against Assyria occurred in Manasseh's reign, in support of Shamash-shum-ukin, viceroy of Babylon, he may well have been involved in it (*ANET*, p. 298). His reformation appears to have been superficial and was swept away in the reign of his son. R.J.A.S.

MANGER. The feeding-trough for animals in a stall or stable, translated 'crib' in Jb. 39:9 (AV, RSV); Pr. 14:4 (AV); Is. 1:3 (AV, RSV). Gk. *phatnē* has an extended meaning of 'stall' (Lk. 13:15), and is used in LXX to translate various Heb. words, *'urwâ*, 'stall' (2 Ch. 32:28), *repet* (Hab. 3:17), *'ēbûs* (Jb. 39:9; Pr. 14:4; Is. 1:3). In the NT it occurs in Lk. 2:7, 12, 16; 13:15.

Mangers are known in other lands besides Palestine. In Palestine the stable or stall was attached to the owner's house and was furnished with a manger. The stables at *Megiddo, now dated to the Omrid dynasty, had hollowed-out limestone blocks for feed boxes. Christian tradition holds that Jesus was born in a cave in the neighbourhood of Bethlehem. In that case the manger may have been cut out of the rock walls. J.A.T.

MANDAEANS
See Nazarene, Part 2.

MANEH
See Weights and measures, Part 3.

Manger and hitching-post at Megiddo, dating from the time of Omri/Ahab. 9th cent. BC. (RS)

MANNA. A substance which was the Israelites' chief food during their 40 years' sojourn in the wilderness (Ex. 16:35). When Israel grumbled at the lack of food in the wilderness of Sin, God gave them 'bread from heaven' (Ex. 16:4; Ps. 78:23–24), and his provision did not cease until they crossed into Canaan and ate the food of that land (Jos. 5:12), despite their grumbling (Nu. 11:6; *cf.* Ne. 9:20). The Israelites were to collect an omer each for five days and double that amount on the sixth day to last them over the sabbath, as none would appear on that day. Usually it did not keep overnight but became maggoty and malodorous if left over, but the manna to be kept for sabbath use was preserved by being cooked or baked beforehand (Ex. 16:4–5, 16–30). Each morning after the dew had gone there was found on the ground a 'small, round thing' like hoar-frost, whitish, like coriander-seed and bdellium, with a honey taste; it could be ground and used in cooking and baking. The people said, 'What (Heb. *man*) is it?' and called it manna (*man*). Such are the data in Ex. 16:14–15, 31; Nu. 11:7–9. An omerful was preserved by Aaron at God's command as a witness for future generations (Ex. 16:33–34; Heb. 9:4).

Many have speculated on the precise nature of this manna, and several partial parallels are known. To the present time in Sinai, certain insects produce honeydew excretions on tamarisk-twigs seasonally every June for some weeks. At night these drops fall from the trees to the ground, where they remain until the heat of the sun brings forth the ants which remove them. These drops are small, sticky, light-coloured, and sugary-sweet, quite strikingly like the biblical descriptions in Ex. 16 and Nu. 11. Other honeydew-producing insects are known in Sinai and elsewhere, *e.g.* certain cicadas. However, these products do not fit the biblical description in all particulars. On them, see F. S. Bodenheimer, *BA* 10, 1947, pp. 1–6; for a photo of tamarisk-twigs with drops, see W. Keller, *The Bible as History*, 1956, plate between pp. 112–113. In S Algeria in 1932 and also about 70 years before, after unusual weather 'there were falls of a whitish, odourless, tasteless matter of a farinaceous kind which covered tents and vegetation each morning' (A. Rendle Short, *Modern Discovery and the Bible*[3], 1952, p. 152). Also in 1932, a white substance like manna one morning covered an area of ground 640 × 18 m on a farm in Natal and was eaten by the natives (H. S. Gehman in *WDB*, p. 375a). None of these phenomena satisfies the biblical data, and the provision of the manna remains ultimately in the realm of the miraculous, especially in its continuity, quantity and 6-day periodicity. The partial parallels cited above may indicate, however, the kind of physical bases used by God in this provision.

The manna was used by God to teach lessons for spiritual instruction as well as physical sustenance. Israel was told that with the failure of other food ('suffered thee to hunger'), his provision of manna was to 'make you know that man does not live by bread alone, but that man lives by everything that proceeds out of the mouth of the Lord' (Dt. 8:3, *cf.* v. 16). God used the provision of manna on 6 days and not the seventh to teach Israel obedience, and convicted them of disobedience (Ex. 16:19, *cf.* vv. 20, 25–30). Jesus Christ uses the manna, God-given 'bread from heaven', as a type of himself, the true bread of life, and contrasts the shadow with the substance: 'your fathers ate the manna in the wilderness, and they died' (Jn. 6:49), but he could say, 'I am the bread of life . . . which came down from heaven; if any one eats of this bread, he will live for ever' (Jn. 6:35, 51, and *cf.* vv. 26–59 *passim*). Eternal life was made available to man by the merits of Christ's death (v. 51). In Rev. 2:17 the 'hidden manna' represents spiritual sustenance imparted by the Spirit of Christ.

K.A.K.

MANOAH. Samson's father. The name is identical in form with a word meaning 'resting-place, state or condition of rest' from the root *nwḥ*, 'to rest' (*BDB*), and with the Wâdi el-Munâḥ, which runs into Wâdi Sarâr from Tibneh (= Timnah). Manoah was a Danite from Zorah (*ṣor'ā*) (Jdg. 13:2), and one name may be derived from the other. A connection with the Manahathites of 1 Ch. 2:54 is more dubious. These were a Calebite clan of Judah (1 Ch. 2:50ff.), and may have been among those Judahites who lived in Zorah in post-exilic times (Ne. 11:29). For a discussion of these coincidences, see C. F. Burney, *Book of Judges*, 1920, p. 341. Manoah is best known for the angelic annunciation of Samson's birth. He appears as a man of prayer and godly fear, and he tried to dissuade his son from marrying outside the covenant people (Jdg. 14:3). He predeceased his son (Jdg. 16:31).

A.G.

MANSIONS (AV) (Gk. *monai*, Vulg. *mansiones*, RVmg. 'abiding-places', RSV 'rooms'). Various speculations have been made about this figure of speech used by our Lord in Jn. 14:2 (*e.g.* B. F. Westcott, *The Gospel according to St John*, 2, 1908, p. 167). Most scholars agree that what is intended is that the Father will provide room and to spare in the eternal abode. The Gk. word elsewhere in NT occurs only in v. 23 of this chapter. See F. Hauck, *TDNT* 4, pp. 579–581.

J.D.D.

MAON, MAONITES. 1. Descendants of the Calebite branch of the tribe of Judah. Maon was the son of Shammai and the father of the inhabitants of Beth-zur (1 Ch. 2:45). The town Maon features in Judah in the list in Jos. 15:55. In this area David and his men sheltered from Saul (1 Sa. 23:24–25), and the churlish Nabal lived there (1 Sa. 25:2). The Maonites are mentioned in the official list of those who returned from Exile (Ezr. 2:50, AV 'Mehunim', RSV 'Meunim'; Ne. 7:52, 'Meunim'). Khirbet-el-Ma'în, 14 km S of Hebron and 20 km SW of Gaza, marks the ancient site. Traces of Early Iron Age I pottery and a remarkable late 4th–6th century AD synagogue with mosaics were found there. It is surrounded by pasture-lands, probably the 'wilderness of Maon' where David sought refuge from Saul (1 Sa. 23:24–25) and was saved by a Philistine raid (1 Sa. 23:27f.).

2. A hostile people in Transjordan, linked with Amalek and the Zidonians as oppressors of Israel (Jdg. 10:12); a pastoral people attacked by Hezekiah (RSV 'Meunim', 1 Ch. 4:41), and Uzziah (2 Ch. 26:7). Their association with Arabs and Ammonites (2 Ch. 20:1) suggests *Ma'ān*, SE of Petra, as their home.

J.A.T.

MARAH (Heb. *mārâ*, 'bitter'). This was the first named camp of the Israelites after the Red Sea crossing, called Marah because only bitter water was found there (Ex. 15:23; Nu. 33:8–9), and perhaps also by comparison with the sweet water of the Nile Valley to which they had been accustomed. On the likely assumption that the route from the crossing led to the mountains in the S of the Sinai peninsula, Marah is often identified with the modern Ain Hawarah, *c.* 75 km SSE of Suez. However, H. H. Rowley (*From Joseph to Joshua*, 1950, p. 104) and J. Gray (*VT* 4, 1954, pp. 149f.) identify Marah with *Kadesh, a view refuted by *GTT*, p. 252, n. 218; B. Rothenberg and Y. Aharoni, *God's Wilderness*, 1961, pp. 11, 93f., 142ff., present both views. (*WILDERNESS OF THE WANDERING.)

BIBLIOGRAPHY. B. S. Childs, *Exodus*, 1974, pp. 265–270.

J.D.D.
G.I.D.

MARANATHA. An Aramaic formula used in transliteration without explanation at 1 Cor. 16:22, AV. In the *Didache* (10. 6) it figures as part of the eucharistic liturgy. The phrase is probably to be resolved as *māranā tā*, 'our Lord, come!' (see G. H. Dalman, *Grammatik des jüdisch-palästinisch Aramäisch*, pp. 120, n. 2; 297, n. 2: also *Jesus–Jeshua*, 1929, p. 13, for the resolution *māran 'ᵉṯā* of identical meaning). The anticipation and longing expressed in this early Christian prayer may be seen reflected in 1 Cor. 11:26 (*cf.* the context in the *Didache*) and in Rev. 22:20. The occurrence of the phrase at 1 Cor. 16:22 derives from the idea of judgment implicit in v. 21, which is closely linked with the idea of the second coming (*cf.* the Old Latin MS g and the Ethiopic version, which render *maranatha* as 'at the coming of the Lord').

In Gk. MSS with accents and punctuation the phrase is often written as if it represented *māran 'ᵃṯâ*, 'our Lord has come'. This seems less likely in view of the ideas of the Eucharist and the judgment with which it is linked in the context, unless it be a reference to the Lord's manifestation of himself through the Eucharist.

BIBLIOGRAPHY. T. Zahn, *INT*, 1909, 1, pp. 303–305; K. G. Kuhn, *TDNT* 4, pp. 466–472; W. Mundle, C. Brown, *NIDNTT* 2, pp. 895–898; C. F. D. Moule, 'A Reconsideration of the Context of *Maranatha*', *NTS* 6, 1959–60, pp. 307ff.; Arndt, *s.v.*

J.N.B.

MARESHAH (Heb. *mārē'šâh*). A town in the Shephelah (Jos. 15:44), covering the road up the Wadi Zeita to Hebron; now Tell Sandahanna (Tel Maresha). The inhabitants claimed descent from Shelah (1 Ch. 4:21). Rehoboam fortified it, and in this area Zerah of Ethiopia was defeated by Asa; Eliezer the prophet was born here (2 Ch. 11:8; 14:9; 20:37). Later it was a Sidonian colony and an important stronghold of Idumaea (1 Macc. 5:66; 2 Macc. 12:35; Zeno, Cairo Museum pap. 59006; Josephus, *Ant.* 12. 353; 14. 75). The Parthians destroyed it in 40 BC (*Ant.* 14. 364); in its place rose Eleutheropolis, now Beit Guvrin or Jibrin, 1½ km to the N; a village to the W is now Khirbet Mar'ash. The name, probably derived from *rō'š* (head), was perhaps not unique (Rudolph on 1 Ch. 2:42).

J.P.U.L.

MARI. Excavations at Mari, mod. Tell Ḥarīri, in SE Syria, *c.* 12 km NNW of Abu Kemal by the Euphrates, were conducted in 1933–9 and 1951–64 by André

MAN OF LAWLESSNESS
See Antichrist, Part 1.

MANTLE
See Dress, Part 1.

MANURE
See Dung, Part 1.

MAPS
See Travel, Part 3.

MARA
See Naomi, Part 2.

MARCUS
See Mark (John), Part 2.

MARHESWAN
See Calendar, Part 1.

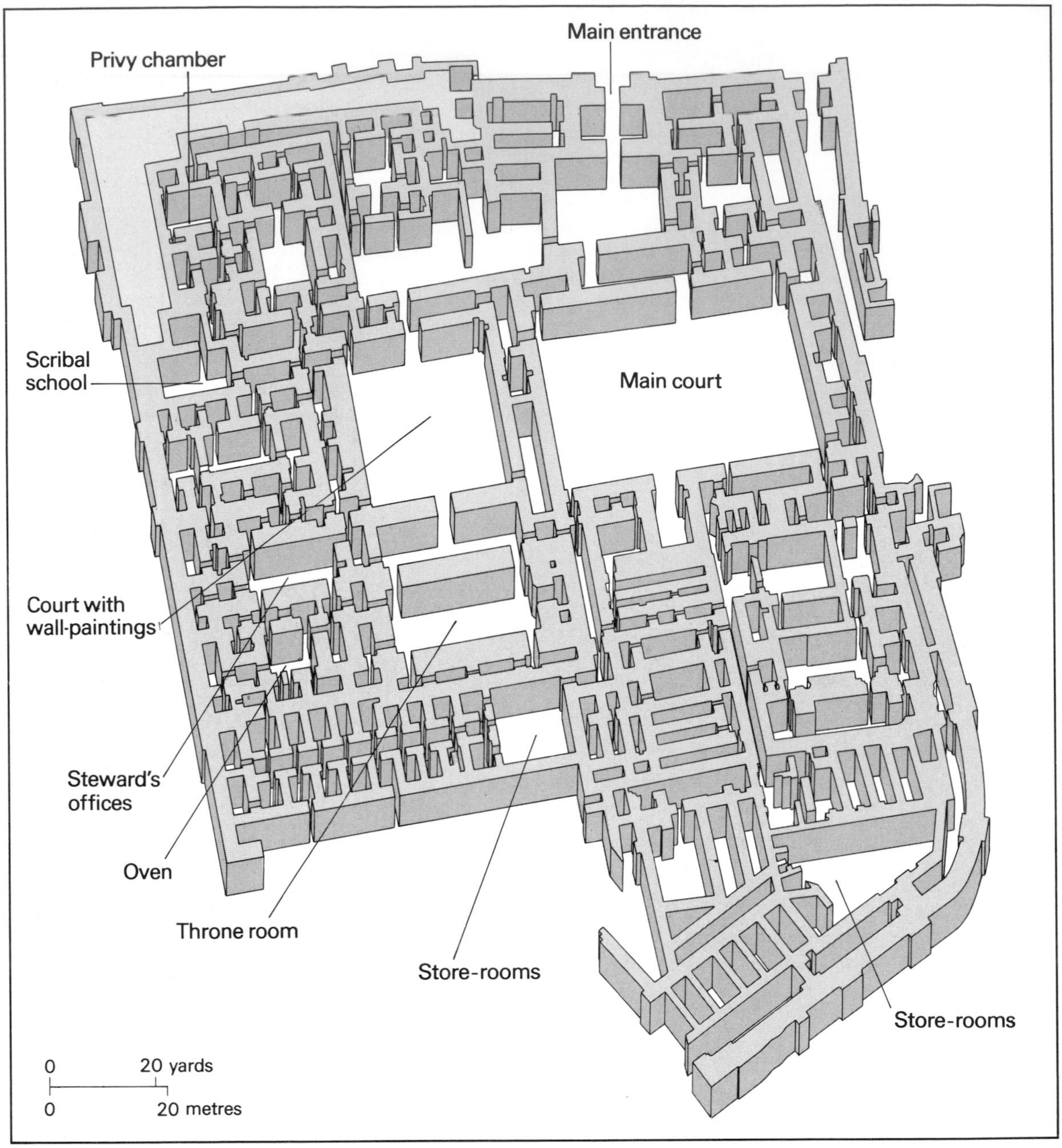

Axionometric projection of the palace of Zimri-Lim as excavated at Mari. c. 1775 BC.

Parrot for the Musée de Louvre. While not mentioned in OT, this strategic site proved to be the capital of a major *Amorite city-state in the 2nd millennium BC. More than 22,000 inscribed clay tablets, a quarter of them state letters, provide important information for the background of the *Patriarchal Age.

Founded in the 3rd millennium BC, Mari was already a powerful centre when it came for a while under the suzerainty of Ebrum of *Ebla and was later conquered by Sargon of Agade *c.* 2250 BC. Thereafter it was ruled by governors dependent on *Ur until freed by the Amorite Ishbi-Irra. About 1820 BC a strong ruling house under King Yahdun-Lim, son of Yaggid-Lim, controlled the region as far as the Mediterranean. He held the surrounding semi-nomad tribes in a firm but just hand, among them the Sutu, Amnanum, Ben-Yamini ('Benjaminites') and later Hapiru ('Hebrews'), not the same as their later biblical counterparts. His successors Yasmah-Adad and Zimri-Lim (*c.* 1775 BC), though powerful, found themselves hemmed in by the strong city-states of Aleppo (Yamhad), Assyria (Nineveh) and Babylon. The dynasty fell *c.* 1760 BC to *Hammurapi of Babylon, of whom one of Zimri-Lim's agents reported that 'there is no king really powerful in himself. Ten of fifteen kings go with Hammurapi of Babylon, the same number with Rim-Sin of Larsa, with Ibal-pī'el of Eshnunna and with Amut-pī'el of Watānum. Twenty go with Yarimlim of Yamhad.'

Diplomacy was a major subject of international correspondence and gifts between rulers (*Iraq* 18, 1958, pp. 68–110), equals addressed each other as 'brothers' and vassals referred to their overlords as 'father' or 'lord'. Tribal chiefs were designated 'fathers' and, as at Ebla, local administration was in the hands of sub-governors (*šāpiṭum*; *cf.* Heb. *šōp̄eṭ*, often mistranslated 'judge') responsible for law and order, collection of taxes, hospitality to passing dignitaries, *etc.*, much as the role adopted by Abra-

A votive statue of Ebih-il of Mari from the temple of Ishtar. He is clothed in a long fleece-like woollen skirt. Height 0·52 m. Mid-3rd millennium BC. (MC)

ham (*BS* 134, 1977, pp. 228–237). Relations with neighbours were regulated by written treaty or *covenant. These followed a pattern close to those in use in Syria, Mesopotamia and Palestine in the following centuries. At Mari some covenants were ratified in a ritual requiring the 'killing of an ass' (*hayaram qatālum*) which occurs also in Hebrew and seems to have been preserved by the Shechemite Bene Hamar ('sons of an ass', Jos. 24:13) who entered into covenant with Jacob (Gn. 33:14; 34:1–3). At Mari prophets, the *āpil(t)u*, 'male (or female) answerer', put questions to a deity, might function in a group, and received government maintenance. Others, *muhhû*, were low-ranking cult officials who were perhaps ecstatics and spoke for the god in the first person. Yet others were called 'speakers' (*qabbātum*) and were each attached to a god or temple. It was also known for lay persons to make divine pronouncements or report visions. In association with music some temple officials (*e.g. assinnu*) declared 'Thus says the god . . .'. One report from Itur-Asdu to King Zimri-Lim tells of a dream revelation in the temple of Dagan at Terqa. The message was not good, because the king had failed to report regularly to his god. 'If he had done so I would have delivered the sheiks of the Benjaminites into the hands of Zimri-Lim.' In this way too the king was told of the sacrifices required of him. Another prophet appears to have foretold the downfall of a city. This activity relied largely on divinatory and *magic techniques, dreams, the reading of the entrails of sacrificial animals and some astronomical observations. This is in marked contrast with the clarity, range, content and purpose of prophecies in Israel. At Mari, as in Israel, the census was of particular religious and ritual importance above any immediate political, military or economic significance (*cf.* 2 Sa. 24). While it involved political reform and questions of land tenure, it was thought to concern the purification of the people (Heb. *kōper*, Mari *tebibtum*), their enrolment (*pqd*, 'called to account'; *cf.* Ex. 30:13–14) and status. The many lists show personal names of a wide cosmopolitan range, some similar to, but not to be identified with, OT persons: Ariukku (*cf.* Arioch of Gn. 14:1), Abarama, Yaqub-'el, or the title *dawīdum*, 'chief' (*cf.* 'David'), now thought to be a word for 'defeat' (*JNES* 17, 1958, p. 130). Place-names mentioned in the texts include a number round Har(r)an, Nahur (Nahor), Til-Turahi (Terah) and Sarug (Serug; *cf.* Gn. 11:23–24). The only city of Palestine mentioned directly is *Hazor.

The texts provide a detailed insight into daily life, especially in the 300-room (15-acre) royal palace with its various archives recording not merely inter-state affairs but the detail of imports of wine, honey, oil, wool, ice and other commodities. Other notes detail the issues from the palace stores both for the royal hospitality and for the ritual feasts which were part of the worship of dead ancestors. The pantheon at Mari included the sun (Saps), moon (Sin, Yerah), the storm-god (Adad) as well as the goddess Ishtar, 'Attar, the god Dagan (*DAGON), Ba'al, 'El, Rasap (the underworld god) and many others (including Lim, 'the thousand gods'). All these could have been known to Terah (Jos. 24:2). Such an abundance of sources, including that for the position of women and the family, written in a Semitic dialect very similar to early books of the Pentateuch,

Wall-painting in the audience-chamber of the palace of Zimri-Lim at Mari, Syria, showing the goddess Ishtar receiving an offering. 18th cent. BC. (AP)

will yet throw much light on the practices of the patriarchal period.

BIBLIOGRAPHY. A. Parrot, *Mari, Capitale fabuleuse*, 1974; G. Dossin *et al.*, *Archives royales de Mari*, 1–15, 1941–78; J.-R. Kupper, *Les nomades en Mésopotamie au temps des rois de Mari*, 1957; B. F. Batto, *Studies in Women at Mari*, 1974. On the Mari prophecies, see *VT Supp*. 15, 1966, pp. 207–227; *VT Supp*. 17, 1969, pp. 112–138; *HTR* 63, 1970, pp. 1–28; *VT* 27, 1977, pp. 178–195; E. Noort, *Untersuchungen zum Gottesbescheid in Mari*, 1977. D.J.W.

MARIAM
See Mary, Part 2.

MARK, GOSPEL OF.

I. Outline of contents

a. Prologue (1:1–13)

The ministry of John (1:1–8); baptism and temptation of Jesus (1:9–13).

b. The earlier Galilean ministry (1:14–6:44)

The kingdom of God in Galilee (1:14–45); the beginning of conflict (2:1–3:6); conflict increases (3:7–35); division caused (parables of the Kingdom) (4:1–34); Jesus, bypassing the synagogue, communicates himself to Israel (4:35–6:44).

c. The later Galilean ministry (6:45–9:50)

Jesus, removing the barriers, communicates himself to Gentiles (6:45–8:10); the Pharisees are refused a sign and the disciples cannot see one when it is given (8:11–26); confession and transfiguration (8:27–9:10); the passion foretold (9:11–50).

d. The road to Jerusalem (10:1–52)

Debates in Peraea (10:1–34); the test of greatness (10:35–45); the healing of Bartimaeus (10:46–52).

e. The Jerusalem ministry (11:1–13:37)

Entry into Jerusalem (11:1–14); cleansing of the Temple (11:15–19); exhortation and debate (11:20–12:44); the *Olivet discourse (13:1–37).

f. Passion and resurrection (14:1–16:8)

The Last Supper (14:1–25); agony in Gethsemane (14:26–42); the arrest (14:43–52); Jesus before the Sanhedrin (14:53–72); Jesus before Pilate (15:1–15); the crucifixion (15:16–41); burial and resurrection (15:42–16:8).

(16:9–20 form a later addition to the Gospel.)

The scope of Mark's Gospel is thus identical with that of the primitive apostolic preaching, beginning with John the Baptist and ending with the resurrection (*cf.* Acts 10:36–43; 13:24–37). Those scholars who maintain that Mark originally ended at 13:37, at least in its 'first edition' (*e.g.* E. Trocmé), would say that verses like 9:9 assume the resurrection witness, so that the scope of the Gospel is still the same.

II. Authorship

This record of our Lord's ministry, the shortest and simplest of all the Gospels, was traditionally compiled by John Mark of Jerusalem, who at different times was a younger companion of Paul, Barnabas and Peter (*MARK (JOHN)). Other modern guesses have included Philip the evangelist.

a. Evidence of Papias

The earliest statement about the origin of this Gospel is that given by Papias (preserved in Eusebius, *EH* 3. 39): 'Mark, who was the interpreter of Peter, wrote down accurately all that he remembered, whether of sayings or doings of Christ, but not in order. For he was neither a hearer nor a companion of the Lord; but afterwards, as I have said, he accompanied Peter, who adapted his instruction as necessity required, not as though he were making a compilation of the Lord's oracles. So then Mark made no mistake when he wrote down thus some things as he remembered them; for he concentrated on this alone—not to omit anything that he had heard, nor to include any false statement among them.'

Papias' information (*c.* AD 140) is amplified a generation or so later in the anti-Marcionite prologue to Mark and in Irenaeus. The anti-Marcionite prologue, only part of which has survived, says that Mark 'was called "stumpy-fingered" (*kolobodaktylos*) because his fingers were short in relation to the rest of his body; he was Peter's interpreter, and after Peter's departure he committed his Gospel to writing in the parts of Italy'. Irenaeus (*Adv. Haer*. 3. 1. 1), after referring to Mark as having been written 'when Peter and Paul were preaching the gospel in Rome and founding the church there', adds that 'after their departure (*exodos*) Mark, Peter's disciple, has himself delivered to us in writing the substance of Peter's preaching'. Both of these authorities therefore suggest a date shortly after Peter's death, though later Fathers claim, perhaps tendentiously, that it was written in Peter's lifetime.

b. Influence of Peter

Mark's Gospel has sometimes been popularly called Peter's Gospel (to be distinguished from later heretical works with this or similar titles), not only because of the evidence of these 2nd-century writers but also since, even if the hand be Mark's, the voice is Peter's voice, to judge from the nature of the incidents, choice of matter, and manner of treatment. It is, however, only fair to say that alternative explanations can be found for all of these (see Nineham and Trocmé) taken individually: nevertheless, their cumulative evidence is strong. It may thus be no empty tradition that this is the written record of the preaching of Peter, originally delivered to Christian catechumens, whether at Rome, or in the Gk. East, and reduced to writing either on the death of its oral source or when the death became imminent. This would put the date of the Gospel somewhere in the second half of the 1st century, perhaps between the death of Peter in AD 65 and the fall of Jerusalem in AD 70, if ch. 13 was written before the fall, as seems most probable (unlike the parallel passages in Matthew and Luke). In any case, to allow use by Matthew and Luke, it could hardly be later than AD 75.

Others have chosen to describe it as the Gospel for the Romans (if it had the influence of the powerful Roman church behind it, then its rapid and apparently universal acceptance would be immediately explicable), or the Gospel for the Gentiles; but in the first of these identifications they may have been influenced more by the Lat. name borne by Mark, in addition to his Heb. name of John, and by the traditional place of origin of the Gospel, rather than by an examination of the contents of the book. Luke has more claim, in every way, to be regarded as the Gentile Gospel; and, while Peter was initially used by God for the conversion of the Gentile Cornelius (Acts 15:7), yet he was universally recognized in the early church as apostle to the circumcision (Gal. 2:8), not apostle to the Gentiles, as was Paul. Thus it is *a priori* unlikely that Peter's teaching forms would be initially aimed at, and adapted to, Gentile audiences. In any case, modern scholarship shows increasingly the thoroughly Jewish nature of *all* the Gospels, although it is true that Mark is at pains to explain Jewish words and customs, as though to a Hellenistic Gentile public.

III. Relationship to Matthew and Luke

For over a century, since Lachmann's day, the question of the literary relationship of Mark to the other Gospels has attracted the attention of W scholars. Apart from the Gospel of John, which in many ways stands by itself, it is obvious that some close link exists between the other three, usually called the Synoptic Gospels because, taken together, they present a very similar picture of the ministry and teaching of Christ. Source criticism is the scientific investigation of the assumed direct literary dependence of one Gospel upon another, or of both alike upon some third document, either present or hypothetical.

a. Primacy of Mark's Gospel

Most subsequent Protestant scholars have held firmly, with Lachmann, to the primacy of Mark, considering it to be the earliest of the three Synoptic Gospels, if not in its present form, at least in what might be called an early edition, possibly containing only chs. 1–13. Indeed, most modern scholars consider that Mark was the originator of the form of the *gospel*, a form which became very popular later (Lk. 1:1–3), by his combination of various unconnected sayings and miracles of Jesus, setting them in a framework of his own making. How far this framework is chronological, and how far it is theological, is disputed: and nowadays, some scholars hold that even this framework was traditional within the church. If this were true, Mark would underlie both Matthew and Luke as a principal source. A second presumed early written source was a mass of non-Marcan matter common to Matthew and Luke; this, when isolated, was denoted by the symbol 'Q', for German *Quelle*, 'source'. Mark and Q were thus two of the earliest strands in the Gospel tradition, although Matthew and Luke were acknowledged each to have their own peculiar material as well, for which suitable alphabetical symbols were adopted. Mark, under this system, was considered as a product of the years immediately preceding the fall of Jerusalem in AD 70, and the first Gospel to be written; some of its peculiarities were thus explained, as arising from its 'primitive' nature. The danger was that, if Matthew and Luke seemed to deviate from Mark, they would be considered as less reliable, as having controlled their source for some end of their own. But it is more and more apparent that even Mark selected his material from a vastly larger store (*cf.* Jn. 21:25) and arranged it with a theological purpose (even if it was that of the whole church) so that these strictures are unjustified. All the Evangelists stand or fall together, as far as the historicity of their material is concerned.

b. Primacy of Matthew's Gospel

Roman Catholic scholars for a long time would have none of this, although the situation is very different nowadays; for them it was an article of faith to believe in the primacy of Matthew, and they argued their case with great ingenuity, although without producing much conviction outside their own ranks. They could at least argue that the early church believed in the primacy of Matthew—else why put Mark as the second Gospel? But the principle of arrangement of books within the various sections of the NT is still too little understood to make such a psychological argument valid. Their view, if true, would make Mark only a secondary authority, and his words would tend to be treated as less weighty than those of Matthew. This is most unlikely: we can see reasons for Matthew's 'smoothing-out' or 'toning-down' of Mark, for instance, but no reasons at all for the reverse process taking place. The battle raged; mathematical symbols multiplied, and ultimately the multiplication of assumed literary sources led to fragmentation. Instead of Gospels, there were bundles of documents, and scholars were left in a morass of literary agnosticism. Was there a way out? As in contemporary OT scholarship, the literary hypothesis had broken down under its own weight.

c. Form criticism

Meanwhile, on the flank, a new force had arisen, which would in itself nullify and make meaningless the whole battle. This was form criticism, originated about 1920 by M. Dibelius, followed closely by R. Bultmann. This might be described as the abandonment of the study of the whole in favour of the study of the part, and, in origin, was purely a descriptive and classificatory science. The various incidents and sayings recorded in Mark (usually called 'pericopes', from the Gk. word for 'paragraph') were now examined, and classified by nature and content. So far, so good. This classification was made from a new angle, had the merit of freshness, and produced some positive and valuable results. But the next step was to examine the hypothetical circumstances and practical religious needs of the community that led to the preservation of each saying; and to make exegesis dependent upon hypothetical reconstruction is dangerous. In the case of extreme critics, this meant that the story was either created or moulded by the needs of the infant church; less extreme scholars would simply say that the story was selected and told with these needs in view. Thus, what had begun as a purely neutral movement ended by passing judgments on the historicity of the text of Scripture. In a sense, such a statement as the last phrase is meaningless to an adherent of this school, for documentary hypotheses have been abandoned in favour of oral tradition, exactly as in contemporary OT scholarship. It is doubtful, however, whether there is any ultimate difference between considering a particular mass of material as a written document or as a complex of oral tradition, especially in view of the fixity of oral tradition in the rabbinical world of the 1st century.

Nevertheless, this stress on form criticism and oral tradition has outdated rather than solved much of the old discussion. Further, it has made the question of the date of Mark's Gospel unanswerable, if not meaningless. The scholar may tentatively date the compilation of the tradition in its present literary form, but the origins of Mark lie much farther back, in the oral traditions of the generation of the crucifixion and resurrection. This, of course, has its good side, in that the reader is confronted directly with the recollections of those who had themselves been eyewitnesses of the events (Lk. 1:2). Much work along these lines has been constructive and cautious; and valuable results have emerged. In particular, it appears that many of the traditions used by Mark were 'church traditions' rather than 'individual traditions': the stories were already old when he used them, and represent the witness of a church (perhaps the Roman church?) to Christ.

d. History of tradition

A still more recent study is the attempt to discover by what means the oral tradition reached its present form, by delving further into the pre-literary history of the text. This, by its nature, is even more hypothetical. We can tell what a particular Marcan saying or incident became in Matthew or Luke, and we can suggest tentative reasons: but we have at present no way of getting behind the text of Mark except by guesswork. Ultimately, we must deal with the text that we have: the only Christ that we know is the Christ of the Gospels. To say that this is the Christ of faith is true: to deny that this is the Christ of history is unwarranted assumption.

e. Redaction criticism

Another recent movement concentrates on the contribution of the Evangelists themselves (redaction criticism). In the case of Mark's Gospel, this leads to an examination of Mark as a theologian. There is no doubt that the Evangelist has been selective in his use of material, but caution is needed to avoid the impression that he has imposed on it his own type of theology.

f. Liturgical approach

There has been an increasing tendency (probably representing the spirit of the times rather than any new discovery) to explain not only Matthew but also Mark as a 'church Gospel', and to see, for instance, his passion narrative as written around the 'holy week' observance of the primitive church. Sometimes this goes along with the belief that even the order of the Gospel may be linked with a primitive liturgic calendar. This, however, while not objectionable, seems too sophisticated for so early, especially outside Jerusalem: it sometimes goes along with the view that Mark was written by a 1st-century 'angry young man' to combat certain ecclesiological and un-missionary views in the early church. This again seems too modern a concept: young men did not act in that way in those days. In any case, Mark does not give the impression of being a brilliant individualist, but of a humdrum church member, faithfully reproducing the common tradition, whether in a liturgical context or not.

g. Recent discoveries

As against this swing towards oral tradition, a reaction in favour of early written documents as sources has been helped by the discovery in Egypt, during the last generation, of several early Gk. papyri containing portions of both canonical and uncanonical Gospels. By their early date, these have pushed back the emergence of written Gospels, in the modern sense of the word, to at least the end of the 1st Christian century. These finds, important as they are, have been overshadowed by the discovery in 1947 and the following years, in caves near Qumran, in the territory of Jordan, of caches of manuscripts in Heb., Aram. and Gk. These *Dead Sea Scrolls are largely of pre-Christian date, apparently the property of a semi-monastic community of Jewish sectaries. The very existence of these manuscripts proves that there is no *a priori* evidence against the existence of 1st-century Christian documents, Gk. or Aram., as sources of the Gospels, particularly collections of 'Messianic prophecies', or 'testimonies'.

h. Aramaic influences

Further, the discovery of such Sem. documents has raised again the issue, already live for half a century, as to whether Gk. or Aram. was the original language of the sources of the Gospels, and, in this instance, of Mark's Gospel. In the light of form criticism, this may well be a 'non-question': it all depends on what stage of the tradition we designate as 'sources' of the Gospel, since, the further back we go, the more likely they are to be in Aram., particularly in Galilee. This leads to the further question, as to how far the Gk. of Mark is not only *koinē* Gk., the *lingua franca* of the 1st-century Roman Mediterranean (*LANGUAGE OF THE NEW TESTAMENT), but actually 'translation Greek'. The many Semitisms in Mark would thus be due, not only to OT reminiscences, nor to influence by the 'translation Greek' of the Septuagint, the Gk. OT, nor even to Semitic speech-patterns persisting in the language of a Palestinian Jew (Mark's local knowledge can hardly be explained otherwise) even if he habitually spoke Gk. in later years at least, but directly to Aram. originals lying before the Evangelist. Indeed, to scholars pursuing this line, many difficult verses in Mark have appeared either as misunderstandings or mistranslations of a lost Aram. original, whether written or spoken. It appears certain that Aram. was the mother-tongue of the Lord and his apostles, to judge from the fossilized Aram. words and phrases that appear even in Gk. dress (*cf.* Mk. 5:41; 7:34; 15:34). While C. C. Torrey's theory of entirely translated Gospels has not generally commended itself to scholars, as being too extreme and involving too many forced arguments, yet few would deny the importance of the underlying Aram. substratum in every Gospel, and the value of considering Aram. vocabulary or idiom when the Gk. text presents difficulties. Recent and more cautious approaches in English have been made, especially by Matthew Black. There is traditional support for some such translation process in the evidence of Papias, preserved in Eusebius; but when he says that Mark was the 'interpreter' of Peter, he can hardly mean simply that Mark turned Peter's Aram. preaching into Gk. The Latinisms of Mark may support a Roman origin for the work: on the other hand, they may simply show the vulgar Gk. of the E part of the empire. In any case, they are not as significant as his Semitisms.

IV. Special characteristics

Basically, Mark is the most blunt and clipped of the Gospels; Matthew contains much of specifically Jewish interest nowhere to be found in Mark, and Luke has much of a 'medical' or of a 'human' interest not found in Mark, as for example the three famous parables of Luke 15. The abrupt ending of Mark is a problem in itself, although it is probably to be seen as a textual rather than a theological problem. The various alternatives put forward by the manuscripts suggest that the original ended abruptly at the same place, whether by accident or by design: this last is hard to believe. It will be objected that the above is a purely negative definition of Mark's nature and contents. Indeed, this was precisely why, in the heyday of source criticism, Mark was seen as the earliest and most primitive of the Gospels, and as a source for both the other Synoptists. But if all documentary sources alike disappear in a welter of oral tradition, what then? The basic observation as to the nature and style of Mark still holds good. Nor is this a purely subjective impression on the part of the 20th century; Papias of Hierapolis shows that the problem was felt equally keenly in the 2nd century. If Mark knew more facts about the Lord, why did he not recount them? Why does he omit so much that the other Evangelists record? Why, on the other hand, are his narratives commonly more detailed and more vivid than parallel accounts in the other Gospels? In addition, Mark appears on first sight to be constructed on a chronological framework of the Lord's life and thus to approach a 'biography' in the Hellenistic and modern sense of the word (although Mark himself warns us that it is a 'gospel', not a 'biography', Mk. 1:1). But is Mark so constructed? and, if not, is there any discernible principle of arrangement? In earlier days attempts were made to fit the other Gospels willy-nilly into Mark's assumed chronological framework. But this proved impossible, although Matthew and Luke do, broadly speaking, follow the same outline, and weave their own material into it—perhaps for the sake of convenience, or perhaps because the framework was already generally known and accepted.

Perhaps the answer is to be found in the cautious use of the new understanding of the nature and importance of oral tradition as underlying the present Gospel of Mark. For it is a plain fact that constant oral repetition leads not to diversity but to uniformity, especially when such repetition is by unimaginative and elderly teachers, whose aim is not to entertain but to instruct catechumens within the context of the church. Stories are not ramified but simplified, if told with a purely didactic end in view; events are boiled down to their bare bones. Variant stories do not grow from one original in such a tradition; if anything, the tendency is to assimilate original variants, all unconsciously. Scholars have not always recognized this, because they have too often considered the earliest custodians of Christian tradition in the light of professional story-tellers, Arabic, Celtic or Scandinavian, according to the culture-pattern the scholars already knew. The aged Sunday-school teacher in a country church might be a closer parallel, for with his continual practice of 'extempore prayer' he tends to become in such circumstances quasi-liturgical, and fixed in form. Seen in this light, Mark is not the most primitive and least developed of the Gospels. The second Gospel is not a bare recital of facts, to which other writers have added flowery details, as imagination prompted them. Rather, Mark is the most developed of the Gospels in the sense that it is threadbare with use, pared of all but significant fact, the record of teaching forms that have stood the test of time. After all, that is exactly what Papias said.

This does not say anything about the actual date of the writing of Mark in its present form; it is merely the empirical observation that it bears, more clearly than any other Gospel, the marks of being a virtual 1st-century Teachers' Handbook, a summary of facts, with all save what was deemed significant ruthlessly pruned. By contrast, Luke was specifically composed *de novo* as a written document, in the face of other existing written documents (Lk. 1:1–4), and in deliberate and pointed contrast to such disconnected instruction as Mark records. Luke, in fact, had claims to be regarded as a work of literature, as had Acts (Acts 1:1); Mark had none. He was not, in all probability, a well-educated man like Luke or Paul, and this may well account for some of the honest uncouthness of his Gospel. But his hearers were not well-educated men either, and his purpose was not to attain to literary excellence, but to communicate the truth. Even Matthew and John bear marks of careful arrangement, although on varying principles; but, for such matters as Mark contains, the principle of arrangement seems to be largely mnemonic. Stories and sayings are linked by keywords or similarity of subject rather than by strict chronological sequence. Where the order of incident varies, as against that given in Matthew and Luke, it is sometimes demonstrably because a different keyword or link is used.

All this would fit perfectly with the above sketch of the origin and nature of Mark, and when it is found to accord exactly with the earliest traditions about the Gospel the case becomes even stronger. For Papias, our oldest witness, in the extract quoted above, appears to be defending Mark against exactly the charges which a modern scholar might bring against him—omission of significant detail and lack of chronological arrangement. The defence is seen to lie in the very nature of the Gospel, which, says Papias, is but a permanent record of the teaching of Peter, thus preserved for posterity at a time when its primary source was passing away. Careful chronological order and full cataloguing of fact, says Papias, are not to be found in Peter because they were not his aim, which was purely practical and instructional; it is unfair to blame any man for failure to achieve something foreign to his purpose. If all this be so, Mark is absolved, along with Peter, and the reasons for many other aspects of his Gospel become apparent at once. (*GOSPELS.)

BIBLIOGRAPHY, Commentaries by A. Menzies, *The Earliest Gospel*, 1901; H. B. Swete, 1913; C. H. Turner, 1928; A. E. J. Rawlinson, 1936; V. Taylor, 1952; C. E. B. Cranfield, *CGT*, 1960; R. A. Cole, *TNTC*, 1961; D. E. Nineham, 1963; W. L. Lane, 1974; M. Black, *An Aramaic Approach to the Gospels and Acts*, 1946; G. R. Beasley-Murray, *A Commentary on Mark Thirteen*, 1957; N. B. Stonehouse, *The Witness of Matthew and Mark to Christ*, 1958; A. M. Farrer, *A Study in St. Mark*, 1951; É. Trocmé, *The Formation of the Gospel according to Mark*, E.T. 1975; R. P. Martin, *Mark—Evangelist and Theologian*, 1972.

A.C.

MARK (JOHN). Traditional author of the second Gospel, apparently a Jew and a native of Jerusalem. His Heb. name was the OT *yôḥānān*, 'Yahweh has shown grace' (*cf.* 2 Ki. 25:23, *etc.*), shortened in English to the familiar 'John'. The reason for his adopted Lat. name of 'Marcus' is uncertain; sometimes Jewish families that had been captured as slaves in war, and later freed, took, as 'freedmen', the name of the Roman family to which they had been enslaved; but this is unlikely in his case, the more so as Marcus is a praenomen, not a family name. It was not uncommon for 1st-century Jews to bear a Gk. or Rom. name in addition to their Heb. name, 'in religion'; see Acts 1:23 for another such 'surname', again Lat. and not Gk. in

Mark 8:10–26 on a fragmentary Greek papyrus of the 3rd cent. AD. *Chester Beatty papyrus I.* (CBL)

origin. The same phenomenon is common among Jews today. If his early nickname of *kolobodaktylos*, 'stumpy-fingered', is a genuine tradition (see the anti-Marcionite prologue to Mark, dating from the later 2nd century, which is the earliest evidence for it), then it may refer either to a physical peculiarity on the part of the author or to some strange stylistic features of the Gospel which have puzzled critics of all ages. It may, however, be only a late conjecture, due to the confusion of 'Marcus' with the Lat. adjective *mancus*, 'maimed'.

Scripture gives some very clear evidence about his family, and there are also several conjectures of varying degrees of probability. His mother, named Mary, was related to Barnabas (Col. 4:10), the wealthy Levite from Cyprus, who was a landowner (Acts 4:36) and, whatever his country of origin, was a resident of Jerusalem in the days of the opening chapters of Acts. Mary herself appears to have been a woman of wealth and position, as well as a Christian; certainly her house was large enough to house a number of people, boasted at least one maidservant and was used as a meeting-place by the apostolic church even in time of persecution (Acts 12:12). It is significant that Peter, released from prison, has no doubt as to where he will find the Christians gathered. John Mark's father is nowhere mentioned in Scripture, and, from the fact that the house of Acts 12:12 is called Mary's, it has been inferred, probably correctly, that he was dead by that date, and Mary a widow. To John Mark himself there is no certain early reference, although the young man of Mk. 14:51, who saved himself by ignominious flight, is usually taken to be Mark. (Was he sleeping in a hut on the family property, guarding the fruit?) It would be neither safe nor customary for an author to mention his own name in such circumstances (*cf.* Jn. 21:24 for similar deliberate anonymity). Less likely, as partly dependent on the above tentative identification, is the theory that the Last Supper of Mk. 14 actually took place in John Mark's house; the shadowy 'goodman of the house' of v. 14 would thus be John Mark's father, still alive then, although dead before the date of Acts 12:12.

John Mark apparently remained at home until brought to Antioch by Barnabas and Paul, who were returning from a relief mission to Jerusalem (Acts 12:25). When the two departed to Cyprus on the first missionary journey some time later he accompanied them, as travelling companion and attendant on the two older men (Acts 13:5). When, however, the party reached Perga, on the mainland of Asia Minor, John Mark left them, and returned to Jerusalem (Acts 13:13), while Barnabas and Paul continued alone. Paul apparently regarded this as desertion, and thus, when Barnabas suggested Mark as a travelling companion for the second journey, he refused point-blank (Acts 15:38). With both men, the attitude towards John Mark was no whim, but a point of principle (*cf.* Acts 9:27 and 11:25 for the character of Barnabas), so a separation was inevitable, Barnabas taking Mark back to Cyprus with him, and Paul taking Silas instead.

After that, Mark is lost to view in Acts, but appears spasmodically in the Epistles. By the date of Col. 4:10 he is in the company of Paul the prisoner, presumably at Rome; Paul is apparently intending to send him on a mission to Colossae, so that he must have forgiven and forgotten the past. Phm. 24 also mentions him among the same apostolic group, which includes Luke. By the time of writing 2 Tim. 4:11 Mark is now away with Timothy, but there has been no rift; presumably this means that Paul had sent Mark on the mission to Asia Minor envisaged above, if Timothy was indeed in Ephesus.

In the Petrine correspondence there is one significant mention, in 1 Pet. 5:13, where the wording shows the 'paternal' relationship existing between the older and younger disciples. If, as is probable, 'Babylon' in this verse stands for 'Rome', then the tradition of the Roman origins of Mark's Gospel may well be true. The tradition that Mark later founded the church of Alexandria (Eusebius, *EH* 2. 16) lacks support. As 'Mark' was the commonest of all Roman names, some have argued that the biblical references concern more than one person. But, in such cases, the Bible differentiates (*e.g.* Jn. 14:22), so we may reject the objection. For Bibliography, see *MARK, GOSPEL OF.

A.C.

Model of the market-place (agora) *at Athens in the 2nd cent.* AD. (ASCS)

The market-place (agora) at Athens below the temple of Hephaestos. 5th cent. BC *and later.* (SH)

MARKET, MARKET-PLACE. In the OT this translates Heb. *ma'ᵃrāḇ*, 'merchandise', in Ezk. 27:13, 17, 19, 25. In Is. 23:3 the word is *sāḥār*, 'emporium' (of Tyre). Both describe the trading centre of an E town.

In the NT the word used is *agora*, 'place of assembly', the chief place not only of trade but of public resort, often ornamented with statues and colonnades. Here the sick were brought (Mk. 6:56), children played games (Mt. 11:16; Lk. 7:32) and idlers waited to hire out their services (Mt. 20:3; *cf.* Acts 17:5, *agoraioi*, 'of the rabble'). In the market-places greetings were exchanged, according to social rank, and this the Pharisees particularly loved (Mt. 23:7; Mk. 12:38; Lk. 11:43; 20:46), but they were careful to remove any defilement (Mk. 7:4). Here also in Gentile towns preliminary trial hearings were held (Acts 16:19; *cf.* 19:38ff.) and philosophical or religious discussions took place, *e.g.* Paul in Athens (Acts 17:17–18). For an ancient description of this *agora*, *cf.* Pausanias 1. 2–17; for its modern excavation, Am. Sch. Class. Studs., *The Athenian Agora*, 1962. B.F.H.

MARKS. The variety of 'marks' mentioned in the Bible is reflected in the number of different Heb. and Gk. words which are used to describe them.

1. The various verbal forms which occur correspond to our Eng. verb 'to mark' in the sense of 'to consider' (Ps. 48:13), 'pay attention to' (Ps. 37:37), 'scrutinize with fixed gaze' (1 Sa. 1:12), 'observe closely' (Lk. 14:7), *etc.* With the meaning of 'to make a mark', Isaiah refers to the carpenter who draws a line with pencil and compasses (44:13), while Jeremiah speaks of Judah's sins being indelibly marked like a stain on cloth which neither lye nor soap can eradicate (2:22).

2. The first arresting use of 'mark' as a noun is found in Gn. 4:15. Here it is a translation of

MARK OF AUTHORITY See Seal, Part 3.

MARK OF CAIN See Marks, Part 2.

Heb. *'ôṯ*, which describes the mark on Cain's forehead. In the OT *'ôṯ* usually means 'sign', but it signifies also 'omens' (1 Sa. 10:7, 9), 'symbols' (Is. 8:18), 'miracles' (Ex. 7:3). However, underlying many of these different uses is the common idea of 'pledge', as, *e.g.*, of good (Ps. 86:17), of God's presence (Ex. 4:8f.), and of covenant (Gn. 9:12–13, 17). Hence *'ôṯ*, when used with reference to the mark on Cain's brow, should be understood in terms of a sign, a pledge or token, of the Lord's protection which would shield him from retribution. If this is correct, then *'ôṯ* might signify a token of some kind of covenant by which God promises to protect Cain (Gn. 4:15).

3. 'Mark' in the sense of 'target' is a rendering of the Heb. *maṭṭārā'* (1 Sa. 20:20). Job complains that God has made him a target at which he shoots his arrows (16:12; *cf.* La 3:12).

4. In Ezk. 9:4, 6, the Heb. word *tāw* is rendered 'mark' in the sense of 'sign'. This is the mark which is placed on the forehead of the righteous, and was an attestation that those who bore the sign were the Lord's people (*cf.* Jb. 31:35, RV, where *tāw* is rendered 'signature'), were distinguished from idolaters, and were therefore exempt from judgment because of the Lord's protection (*cf.* Ex. 12:22f.). Here 'mark' might have the meaning 'seal' (*cf.* Rev. 7:3; 14:1; 22:4).

5. Another word which is rendered 'mark' occurs only once in the Bible: *qa'ᵃqa'*. Its etymology is obscure, but in Lv. 19:28 it probably refers to tattoo marks which, along with 'cuttings in your flesh' (*i.e.* 'incisions' or 'lacerations'), the Israelites were forbidden to make. The prohibition probably points to their having pagan and magical associations.

6. In the well-known Pauline metaphor of 'pressing towards the mark' (*skopos*) in order to win the prize (Phil. 3:14, AV) 'mark' signifies the 'goal' (RSV). The apostle here uses the language of the chariot races to describe the intensity with which he concentrates on winning the crown—the honour of being called by God in Christ.

7. The next Gk. word rendered 'mark' is one that has entered the Eng. language without undergoing any alteration, *stigma*. Like *skopos*, it occurs only once (Gal. 6:17). The root means 'to prick', but probably Paul uses it in the sense of tattoo- or brand-marks with which slave-owners stamped their slaves for identification purposes. Paul was proud of being Christ's bondslave (*cf.* Rom. 1:1, RVmg.); for him no stigma attached to Christ's brand-marks with which he had been branded (Gal. 6:17) in the course of his Christian ministry (2 Cor. 11:23–27).

8. The last word, *charagma* (Rev. 13:16), is reminiscent of Heb. *tāw* in Ezk. 9:4, 6, but the circumstances are reversed. In Rev. 13:16 it is 'the mark of the beast', and is borne by the followers of Antichrist, who is the embodiment of apostasy. Whether a literal or a moral designation, this 'mark' may have stood for a travesty of God's 'seal' upon the Christians. J.G.S.S.T.

MARRIAGE. Marriage is the state in which men and women can live together in sexual relationship with the approval of their social group. Adultery and fornication are sexual relationships that society does not recognize as constituting marriage. This definition is necessary to show that in the OT polygamy is not sexually immoral, since it constitutes a recognized married state; though it is generally shown to be inexpedient.

I. The status of marriage

Marriage is regarded as normal, and there is no word for 'bachelor' in the OT. The record of the creation of Eve (Gn. 2:18–24) indicates the unique relationship of husband and wife, and serves as a picture of the relationship between God and his people (Je. 3; Ezk. 16; Ho. 1–3) and between Christ and his church (Eph. 5:22–33). Jeremiah's call to remain unmarried (Je. 16:2) is a unique prophetic sign, but in the NT it is recognized that for specific purposes celibacy can be God's call to Christians (Mt. 19:10–12; 1 Cor. 7:7–9), although marriage and family life are the normal calling (Jn. 2:1–11; Eph. 5:22–6:4; 1 Tim. 3:2; 4:3; 5:14).

Monogamy is implicit in the story of Adam and Eve, since God created only one wife for Adam. Yet polygamy is adopted from the time of Lamech (Gn. 4:19), and is not forbidden in Scripture. It would seem that God left it to man to discover by experience that his original institution of monogamy was the proper relationship. It

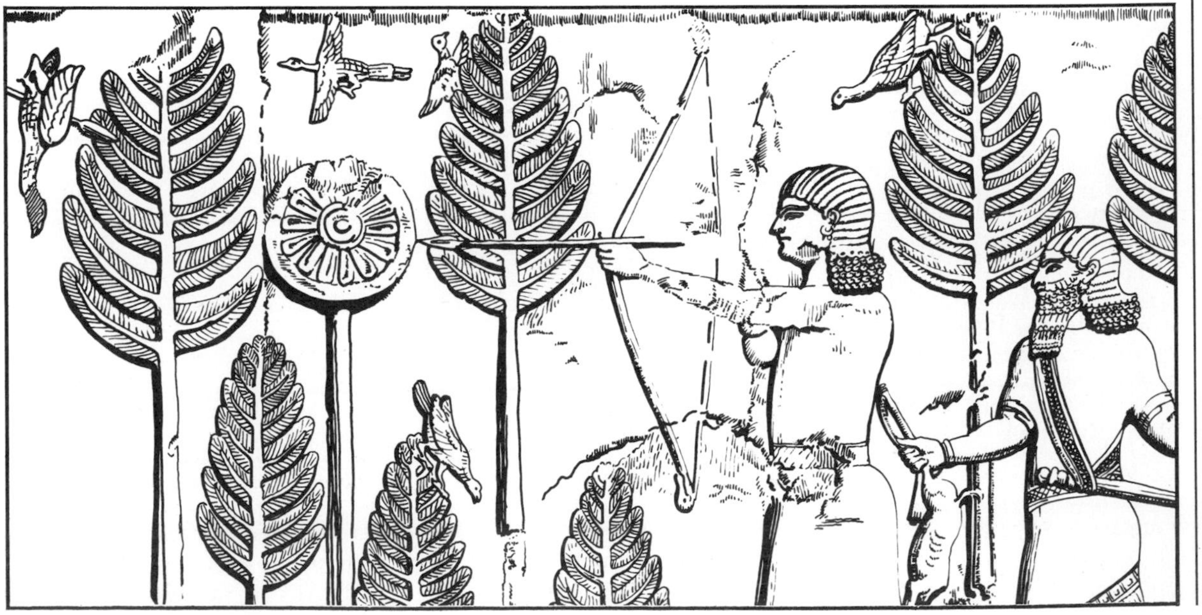

A mark or target (Heb. maṭṭārā'*) set up between trees by an Assyrian archer. Relief from the palace of Sargon II at Khorsabad (Dur-Sharrukin). 721–705 BC.*

is shown that polygamy brings trouble, and often results in sin, *e.g.* Abraham (Gn. 21); Gideon (Jdg. 8:29–9:57); David (2 Sa. 11; 13); Solomon (1 Ki. 11:1–8). In view of oriental customs Heb. kings are warned against it (Dt. 17:17). Family jealousies arise from it, as with Elkanah's two wives, one of whom is an adversary to the other (1 Sa. 1:6; *cf.* Lv. 18:18). It is difficult to know how far polygamy was practised, but on economic grounds it is probable that it was found more among the well-to-do than among the ordinary people. Herod the Great had nine wives at one time (Jos., *Ant.* 17. 19). Polygamy continues to the present day among Jews in Muslim countries.

When polygamy was practised the status and relationship of the wives can be gathered both from the narrative and the law. It was natural that the husband would be drawn to one rather than another. Thus Jacob, who was tricked into polygamy, loved Rachel more than Leah (Gn. 29). Elkanah preferred Hannah in spite of her childlessness (1 Sa. 1:1–8). In Dt. 21:15–17 it is admitted that the husband may love one wife and hate the other.

Since children were important to carry on the family name, a childless wife might allow her husband to have children by her slave. This was legal in civilized Mesopotamia (*e.g.* the Code of Hammurapi, §§ 144–147), and was practised by Sarah and Abraham (Gn. 16) and Rachel and Jacob (Gn. 30:1–8), though Jacob went farther and accepted Leah's maid also, even though Leah had already borne him children (Gn. 30:9). In these cases the rights of the wife are safeguarded; it is she who gives her maid to her husband for a specific occasion. It is difficult to give a name to the status of the maid in such a relationship; she is a secondary, rather than a second, wife, though, if the husband continued to have relations with her, she would have the position of concubine. This is perhaps why Bilhah is called Jacob's concubine in Gn. 35:22, while Hagar is not classed with Abraham's concubines in Gn. 25:6.

Wives would normally be chosen from among the Hebrews (*e.g.* Ne. 13:23–28). Betrothal and marriage would then follow a normal pattern (see below). Sometimes they were bought as Heb. slaves (Ex. 21:7–11; Ne. 5:5). It is commonly asserted that the master of a household had sexual rights over all his female slaves. No doubt there were flagrant examples of such promiscuity, but the Bible says nothing about them. It is noteworthy that Ex. 21:7–11 and Dt. 15:12 distinguish between an ordinary female slave, who is to be released after 7 years, and one who has been deliberately taken as a wife, or concubine, and who cannot claim her release automatically. Since her rights are here established by law, the head of the house or his son must have gone through some ceremony, however simple, of which the law can take cognizance. In speaking of her rights this passage does not make them depend upon her word against the word of the head of the house, nor even upon her having borne him or his son a child. It is difficult to say what her status was. No doubt it varied according to whether she was the first, second, or only 'wife' of the householder. Where she was given to the son of the house, she might well have full status as his wife. The fact is that this law, as the context shows, deals with her rights as a slave and not primarily as a wife.

Wives might also be taken from among captives after a war, provided that they were not Palestinians (Dt. 20:14–18). Some writers regard these captives as concubines, but the regulations of Dt. 21:10–14 regard them as normal wives.

There is no law dealing with concubines, and we do not know what rights they had. Obviously they had an inferior position to the wives, but their children could inherit at their father's discretion (Gn. 25:6). Judges records the rise to power of Abimelech, the son of Gideon's concubine (Jdg. 8:31–9:57), and also tells the tragic story of the Levite and his concubine (Jdg. 19). The impression given by 19:2–4 is that this concubine was free to leave her 'husband', and that the man relied on persuasion to bring her home. David and Solomon copied oriental monarchs in taking many wives and concubines (2 Sa. 5:13; 1 Ki. 11:3; Ct. 6:8–9). In the last two passages it seems that the concubines were drawn from a lower class of the population.

In normal marriages the wife came to the husband's home. There is, however, another form of marriage in Jdg. 14–15. This is practised among the Philistines, and there is no record of it among the Israelites. Here Samson's wife remains at her father's home, and Samson visits her. It might be argued that Samson had intended to take her home after the wedding, but went off alone in a rage after the trick that she had played on him. Yet she is still at her father's house in 15:1, even though in the meantime she has been married to a Philistine.

II. Marriage customs

The marriage customs of the Bible centre in the two events of betrothal and wedding.

a. Betrothal

In the Near East betrothal (Talmudic *'ērûsîn* and *qiddûšîn*) is almost as binding as marriage itself. In the Bible the betrothed woman was sometimes called 'wife' and was under the same obligation of faithfulness (Gn. 29:21; Dt 22:23–24; Mt. 1:18, 20), and the betrothed man was called 'husband' (Joel 1:8; Mt. 1:19). The Bible does not legislate for broken betrothals, but the Code of Hammurapi (§§ 159–160) stipulated that if the future husband broke the engagement the bride's father retained the bride-gift; while if the father changed his mind he repaid double the amount of the gift (see also the Law codes of Lipit-Ishtar, 29, and Eshnunna, 25). Presumably there was some formal declaration, but the amount of publicity would depend on the bridegroom. Thus Joseph wished to dissolve the betrothal to Mary as quietly as possible (Mt. 1:19).

God's love and faithfulness towards his people are pictured in terms of a betrothal in Ho. 2:19–20. The betrothal included the following steps:

(i) *Choice of a spouse.* Usually the parents of a young man chose his wife and arranged for the marriage, as Hagar did for Ishmael (Gn. 21:21) and Judah for Er (Gn. 38:6). Sometimes the young man did the choosing, and his parents the negotiating, as in the case of Shechem (Gn. 34:4, 8) and Samson (Jdg. 14:2). Rarely did a man marry against the wish of his parents, as did Esau (Gn. 26:34–35). The girl was sometimes asked whether she consented, as in the case of Rebekah (Gn. 24:58). Occasionally the girl's parents chose a likely man to be her husband, as did Naomi (Ru. 3:1–2) and Saul (1 Sa.18:21).

(ii) *Exchange of gifts.* Three types of gifts are associated with betrothal in the Bible: **1.** The *mōhar*, translated 'marriage present' in RSV and 'dowry' in AV (Gn. 34:12, for Dinah; Ex. 22:17, for a seduced maiden; 1 Sa. 18:25, for Michal). The *mōhar* is implied but not so named in such passages as Gn. 24:53, for Rebekah; 29:18, the 7 years' service performed by Jacob for Rachel. Moses' keeping of the sheep for his father-in-law may be interpreted in the same way (Ex. 3:1). This was a compensation gift from the bridegroom to the family of the bride, and it sealed the covenant and bound the two families together. Some scholars have considered the *mōhar* to be the price of the bride, but a wife was not bought like a slave. **2.** The dowry. This was a gift to the bride or the groom from her father, sometimes consisting of servants (Gn. 24:59, 61, to Rebekah; 29:24, to Leah) or land (Jdg. 1:15, to Achsah; 1 Ki. 9:16, to Pharaoh's daughter, the wife of Solomon), or other property (Tobit 8:21, to Tobias). **3.** The bridegroom's gift to the bride was sometimes jewellery and clothes, as those brought to Rebekah (Gn. 24:53). Biblical examples of oral contracts are Jacob's offer of 7 years' service to Laban (Gn. 29:18) and Shechem's promise of gifts to the family of Dinah (Gn. 34:12). In TB a contract of betrothal is called *šᵉṭar qiddûšîn* (*Moed Katan* 18b) or *šᵉṭar 'ērûsîn* (*Kiddushin* 9a). In the Near East today the contributions of each family are fixed in a written engagement contract.

b. Wedding ceremonies

An important feature of many of these ceremonies was the public acknowledgment of the marital relationship. It is to be understood that not all of the following steps were taken at all weddings.

(i) *Garments of bride and groom.* The bride sometimes wore embroidered garments (Ps. 45:13–14), jewels (Is. 61:10), a special girdle or 'attire' (Je. 2:32) and a veil (Gn. 24:65). Among the adornments of the groom might be a garland (Is. 61:10). Eph. 5:27; Rev. 19:8; 21:2 refer figuratively to the white garments of the church as the Bride of Christ.

(ii) *Bridesmaids and friends.* Ps. 45:14 speaks of bridesmaids for a royal bride, and we assume that lesser brides had their bridesmaids also. Certainly the bridegroom had his group of companions (Jdg. 14:11). One of these corresponded to the best man at our weddings, and is called 'companion' in Jdg. 14:20; 15:2, and 'the friend of the bridegroom' in Jn. 3:29. He may be the same as 'the steward (AV 'governor') of the feast' in Jn. 2:8–9.

(iii) *The procession.* In the evening of the day fixed for the marriage the bridegroom and his friends went in procession to the bride's house. The wedding supper could be held there: sometimes circumstances compelled this (Gn. 29:22; Jdg. 14), but it may have been fairly common, since the parable of the Ten Virgins in Mt. 25:1–13 is most easily interpreted of the bridegroom going to the bride's house for the supper. One would, however, expect that more usually the bridegroom escorted the bride back to his own or his parents' home for the supper, though the only references to this in Scripture are in Ps. 45:14f.; Mt. 22:1–14 (royal weddings), and probably in Jn. 2:9f.

The procession might be accompanied by singing, music and dancing (Je. 7:34; 1 Macc. 9:39), and by lamps if at night (Mt. 25:7).

(iv) *The marriage feast.* This was usually held at the house of the groom (Mt. 22:1–10; Jn. 2:9) and often at night (Mt. 22:13; 25:6). Many relatives and friends attended; so the wine might well run out (Jn. 2:3). A steward or friend supervised the feast (Jn. 2:9–10). To refuse an invitation to the wedding feast was an insult (Mt. 22:7). The guests were expected to wear festive clothes (Mt. 22:11–12). In special circumstances the feast could be held in the bride's home

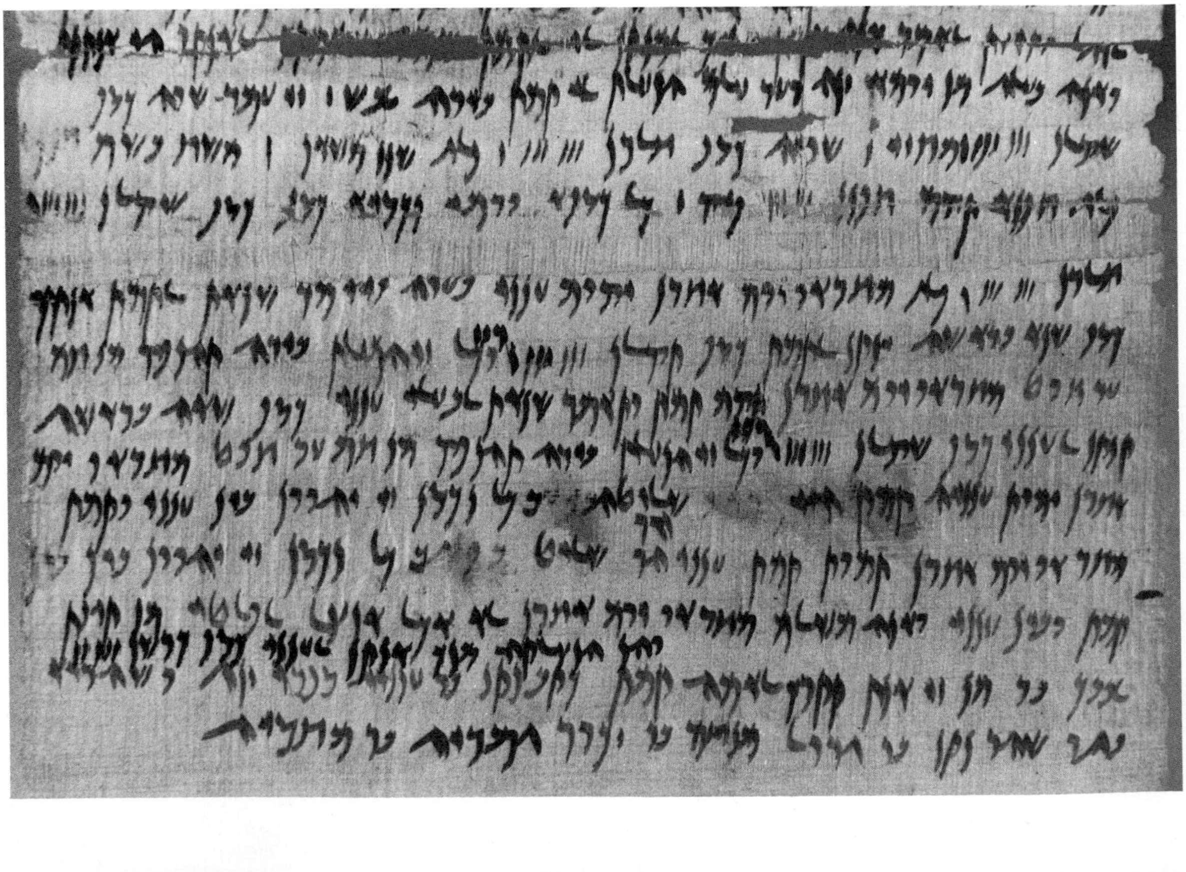

Part of an Aramaic marriage-contract on papyrus from Elephantine, Egypt. The terms include payment in the event of divorce and the disposition of property should either Ananiah or his wife Tamut die. 449 BC. (BrM)

(Gn. 29:22; Tobit 8:19) The glorious gathering of Christ and his saints in heaven is figuratively called 'the marriage supper of the Lamb' (Rev. 19:9).

(v) *Covering the bride*. In two cases in the OT (Ru. 3:9; Ezk. 16:8) the man covers the woman with his skirt, perhaps a sign that he takes her under his protection. D. R. Mace follows J. L. Burckhardt (*Notes on the Bedouin*, 1830, p. 264) in saying that in Arab weddings this is done by one of the bridegroom's relations. J. Eisler, in *Weltenmantel und Himmelszelt*, 1910, says that among the bedouin the bridegroom covers the bride with a special cloak, using the words, 'From now on, nobody but myself shall cover thee.' The Bible references suggest that the second custom was followed.

(vi) *Blessing*. Parents and friends blessed the couple and wished them well (Gn. 24:60; Ru. 4:11; Tobit 7:13).

(vii) *Covenant*. Another religious element was the covenant of faithfulness which is implied in Pr. 2:17; Ezk. 16:8; Mal. 2:14. According to Tobit 7:14, the father of the bride drew up a written marriage contract, which in the Mishnah is called *kᵉṯûḇâ*.

(viii) *Bridechamber*. A nuptial chamber was specially prepared (Tobit 7:16). The Heb. name for this room is *ḥuppâ* (Ps. 19:5; Joel 2:16), originally a canopy or tent, and the Gk. word is *nymphōn* (Mk. 2:19). The word *ḥuppâ* is still used among Jews today of the canopy under which the bride and bridegroom sit or stand during the wedding ceremony.

(ix) *Consummation*. The bride and groom were escorted to this room, often by the parents (Gn. 29:23; Tobit 7:16–17; 8:1). Before coming together, for which the Heb. uses the idiom 'to know', prayer was offered by husband and wife (Tobit 8:4).

(x) *Proof of virginity*. A bloodstained cloth or chemise was exhibited as a proof of the bride's virginity (Dt. 22:13–21). This custom continues in some places in the Near East.

(xi) *Festivities*. The wedding festivities continued for a week (Gn. 29:27, Jacob and Leah) or sometimes 2 weeks (Tobit 8:20, Tobias and Sarah). These celebrations were marked by music (Pss. 45; 78:63) and by joking like Samson's riddles (Jdg. 14:12–18). Some interpret Canticles in the light of a custom among Syrian peasants of calling the groom and bride 'king' and 'queen' during the festivities after the wedding and of praising them with songs.

III. Forbidden degrees of marriage

These are listed in Lv. 18 in detail, and less fully in Lv. 20:17–21; Dt. 27:20–23. They are analysed in detail by David Mace, *Hebrew Marriage*, pp. 152f. We presume that the ban held good both for a second wife during the first wife's lifetime and for any subsequent marriage after the wife's death, except for marriage with the wife's sister: for Lv. 18:18, in saying that the wife's sister may not be married during the wife's lifetime, implies that she may be married after the wife is dead.

Abraham (Gn. 20:12) and Jacob (Gn. 29:21–30) married within degrees of relationship that were later forbidden. The scandal in the church at Corinth (1 Cor. 5:1) may have been marriage of a stepmother after the father's death, but, since the woman is called 'his father's wife' (not *widow*), and the act is called *fornication*, it is more likely to be a case of immoral relationship with the man's young second wife.

IV. The levirate law

The name is derived from Lat. *levir*, meaning 'husband's brother'. When a married man died without a child his brother was expected to take his wife. Children of the marriage counted as children of the first husband. This custom is found among other peoples besides the Hebrews.

The custom is assumed in the story of Onan in Gn. 38:8–10. Onan took his brother's wife, but refused to have a child by her, because 'the seed should not be his' (v. 9), and his own children would not have the primary inheritance. This verse does not pass any judgment on birth control as such.

Dt. 25:5–10 states the law as applying to brethren who dwell together, but allows the brother the option of refusing.

The book of Ruth shows that the custom extended farther than the husband's brother. Here an unnamed kinsman has the primary duty, and only when he refuses does Boaz marry Ruth. A further extension of the custom here is that it is Ruth, and not Naomi, who marries Boaz, presumably because Naomi was too old to bear a child. The child is called 'a son to Naomi' (4:17).

The levirate law did not apply if daughters had been born, and regulations for the inheritance of daughters are given to the daughters of Zelophehad in Nu. 27:1–11. It might seem strange that vv. 9–11 seem to ignore, or even contradict, the levirate law. It could be argued that Dt. 25:5–10 had not yet been promulgated. On the other hand, when a law arises out of a specific occasion one must know the exact circumstances in order to judge what the law professes to cover. There would be no contradiction of the levirate law if Zelophehad's wife had died before he did, and the law here confines itself to similar cases. Nu. 27:8–11 would operate when there were daughters only, or when a childless wife had predeceased her husband, or when the late husband's brother refused to take the childless widow, or when the wife remained childless after the brother had married her.

In Lv. 18:16; 20:21 a man is forbidden to marry his brother's wife. In the light of the levirate law this clearly means that he may not take her as his own wife, whether she has been divorced during her husband's lifetime or has been left with or without children at her husband's death. John the Baptist rebuked Herod Antipas for marrying the wife of his brother Herod Philip (Mt. 14:3–4); Herod Philip was still alive.

In the NT the levirate law is used by the Sadducees to pose a problem about the resurrection (Mt. 22:23ff.).

V. Divorce

a. In the Old Testament

In Mt. 19:8 Jesus says that Moses 'allowed' divorce because of the hardness of the people's hearts. This means that Moses did not command divorce, but regulated an existing practice, and the form of the law in Dt. 24:1–4 is best understood in this sense. AV and RV imply a command in the second half of v. 1, but the RSV follows Keil, Delitzsch, S. R. Driver and LXX, in making the 'if' of the protasis extend to the end of v. 3, so that v. 4 contains the actual regulation. On any translation we gather from this section that divorce was practised, that a form of contract was given to the wife, and that she was then free to remarry.

The grounds of divorce here are referred to in such general terms that no precise interpretation can be given. The husband finds 'some uncleanness' in his wife. The Heb. words, *'erwaṯ dāḇār* (literally, 'nakedness of a thing'), occur elsewhere only as a phrase in Dt. 23:14. Shortly before the time of Christ the school of Shammai interpreted it of unfaithfulness only, while the school of Hillel extended it to anything unpleasing to the husband. We must remember that Moses is not here professing to state the grounds of divorce, but accepting it as an existing fact.

There are two situations in which divorce is forbidden: when a man has falsely accused his wife of pre-marital unfaithfulness (Dt. 22:13–19); and when a man has had relations with a girl, and her father has compelled him to marry her (Dt. 22:28–29; Ex. 22:16–17).

On two exceptional occasions divorce was insisted on. These were when the returned exiles had married pagan wives (Ezr. 9–10 and probably Ne. 13:23ff., although divorce is implied here, rather than stated). In Mal. 2:10–16 some had put away their Jewish wives so as to marry pagans.

b. In the New Testament

In comparing the words of Jesus in Mt. 5:32; 19:3–12; Mk. 10:2–12; Lk. 16:18, we find that he brands divorce and remarriage as adultery, but does not say that man *cannot* put asunder what God has joined together. In both passages in Matthew fornication (RSV 'unchastity') is given as the sole ground on which a man may put away his wife, whereas there is no such qualification in Mark and Luke. *Fornication* is commonly taken as here being equivalent to *adultery*; similarly, the conduct of the nation as Yahweh's wife is branded both as adultery (Je. 3:8; Ezk. 23:45) and as fornication (Je. 3:2–3; Ezk. 23:43); in Ecclus. 23:23 an unfaithful wife is said to have committed adultery in fornication (*cf.* also 1 Cor. 7:2 where 'immorality' is Gk. 'fornication').

The reason for the omission of the exceptive clause in Mark and Luke could be that no Jew, Roman or Greek ever doubted that adultery constituted grounds for divorce, and the Evangelists took it for granted. Similarly, Paul in Rom. 7:1–3, referring to Jewish and Rom. law, ignores the possibility of divorce for adultery which both these laws provided.

Other theories have been held about the meaning of Christ's words. Some refer *fornication* to pre-marital unfaithfulness, which the husband discovers after marriage. Others have suggested that the parties discover that they have married within the prohibited degrees of relationship, a thing which must have happened too rarely for it to be the subject of a special exception in Christ's words. Roman Catholics hold that the words sanction separation, but not remarriage. It is difficult to exclude permission to remarry from Mt. 19:9; and among the Jews there was no such custom as separation without permission to remarry.

Some have doubted the authenticity of Mk. 10:12, since a Jewish wife could not normally divorce her husband. But a wife could appeal to the court against her husband's treatment of her, and the court could compel the husband to divorce her. Moreover, Christ may have had Gk. and Rom. law in mind, and here the wife could divorce her husband, as Herodias had divorced her first husband.

There is a strong body of opinion both among Protestants and Roman Catholics that 1 Cor. 7:10–16 gives another ground for divorce. Here Paul repeats the teaching that the Lord had given when on earth, and then, under the guidance of the Spirit, gives teaching beyond what the Lord had given, since a new situation had arisen. When one party in a pagan marriage is converted to Christ he or she must not desert the other. But if the other insists on leaving the Christian 'a brother or sister is not under bondage in such cases'. This latter clause cannot simply mean that they are free to be deserted, but must mean that they are free to be remarried. This further ground, which on the face of it is of limited application, is known as the 'Pauline Privilege'.

In the present modern tangle of marriage, divorce and remarriage the Christian church, in dealing with converts and repentant members, is often compelled to accept the situation as it is. A convert who previously has been divorced, on sufficient or insufficient grounds, and who has remarried, cannot return to the original partner, and the present marriage cannot be branded as adulterous (1 Cor. 6:9, 11).

BIBLIOGRAPHY. W. R. Smith, *Kinship and Marriage in Early Arabia*, 1903; E. A. Westermarck, *The History of Human Marriage,* 3 vols., 1922; H. Granquist, *Marriage Conditions in a Palestinian Village*, 2 vols., 1931, 1935; M. Burrows, *The Basis of Israelite Marriage*, 1938; E. Neufeld, *Ancient Hebrew Marriage Laws*, 1944; D. R. Mace, *Hebrew Marriage*, 1953; J. Murray, *Divorce*, 1953; D. S. Bailey, *The Man–Woman Relation in Christian Thought*, 1959; R. de Vaux, *Ancient Israel*, 1961; E. Stauffer, *TDNT* 1, pp. 648–657; W. Günther *et al.*, *NIDNTT* 2, pp. 575–590; M. J. Harris, C. Brown, *NIDNTT* 3, pp. 534–543. J.S.W.
J.T.

MARS
See Nergal, Part 2.

MARSHAL. There are two Heb. words rendered 'marshal'. **1.** *sōp̄ēr* (Jdg. 5:14. 'they who wield the marshal's staff'). The word *sōp̄ēr* usually means 'writer' (so AV and Syr., Targ.; *cf.* LXX *grammateus*, 'scribe'). **2.** *ṭip̄sār* (Je. 51:27) or *ṭap̄sēr* (Na. 3:17). Probably from Akkad. *ṭupšarru*, 'tablet writer'; hence 'official', 'marshal'. For both these instances, *cf.* 1 Macc. 5:42, where Gk. *grammateus* means 'marshal'.

The seeming proper name * *Tartan* (Is. 20:1; 2 Ki. 18:17) is from the Akkad. *turtanu*, a title of high military rank which may be rendered 'marshal'. R.J.W.

MARTHA. The name derives from an Aram. form not found in Heb., meaning 'lady' or 'mistress'. It occurs only in the NT, and is used of only one person (Lk. 10:38–41; Jn. 11:1, 5, 19–39; 12:2). Martha was the sister of the Mary who anointed our Lord shortly before his death (Mt. 26:6ff., and parallels); and Lazarus, whom Jesus raised from the dead (Jn. 11), was their brother. According to Jn. 11:1 the family came from Bethany, a village probably about 4 km from Jerusalem on the road to Jericho. Luke seems to suggest by his placing of events that Martha's house was in Galilee (Lk. 10:38). This difficulty is removed, however, if we either allow the possibility that the Lucan incident is chronologically misplaced (so *HDB*, 3, p. 277) or, more reasonably, assume that this was one of the several journeys undertaken by Jesus to Jerusalem during the last 6 months of his earthly life (*cf.* Jn. 10:22).

Matthew, Mark and John all agree that our Lord was anointed in Bethany, and Matthew and Mark specify (presuming the same occasion is referred to) that it took place in the house of Simon the leper. Since Jesus was received into Martha's house in the Lucan record, and Martha served at the supper in Simon's house at Bethany during which Mary anointed our Lord, it has been supposed that Martha was the wife (or even the widow) of Simon. The lead she takes on both occasions suggests that she was the elder sister.

In Luke's narrative (10:38ff.) Martha is gently rebuked by Christ for her impatience with her sister, and her excessive concern for the practical details of the meal (v. 40). She was no less devoted to Jesus than Mary (*cf.* her faithful response to the Lord recorded at Jn. 11:27), but she failed to see the way of receiving him which would please him most—'one thing is needful'. Some of the oldest MSS read at this point, 'few things are needful, or only one' (so RSVmg.). 'Few' refers [illegible] 'one' to spiritual apprehension.

See J. N. Sanders, 'Those whom Jesus loved', *NTS* 1, 1954–5, pp. 29ff.; and the comment on Lk. 10:38–42 in E. E. Ellis, *The Gospel of Luke*², 1974, pp. 161f. (* MARY, 2.) S.S.S.

MARY. The name appears as *Maria* or *Mariam* in the NT. Both are Graecized forms of the Heb. name Miriam, which appears in LXX as Mariam (used of the sister of Moses), and may just possibly be derived from the Egyp. *Maryē*, 'beloved' (but see A. H. Gardiner, *JAOS* 56, 1936, pp. 194–197). In the NT the name is used to refer to the following:

1. Mary the mother of the Lord. Our information about the mother of Jesus is largely confined to the infancy narratives of Mt. and Lk. There we learn that when the angelic announcement of the birth of Jesus occurred, Mary was living at Nazareth, in Galilee, and was engaged to a carpenter named Joseph (Lk. 1:26f.). Luke tells us that Joseph was of Davidic descent (*ibid.*), and although no mention of Mary's lineage is made it is possible that she came from the same line, particularly if, as seems likely, the * genealogy of Christ in Lk. 3 is to be traced through his mother. The conception of Jesus is described as 'of the Holy Spirit' (Mt. 1:18; *cf.* Lk. 1:35), and his birth as taking place at Bethlehem towards the end of Herod the Great's reign (Mt. 2:1; Lk. 1:5; 2:4). (* VIRGIN BIRTH.)

It is recorded in both Mt. 2:23 and Lk. 2:39 that after the birth the holy family lived at Nazareth. Matthew alone mentions the flight into Egypt, where Joseph and Mary and the child Jesus took refuge from the jealous anger of Herod. Luke records Mary's visit to her cousin Elizabeth, who greeted her as 'the mother of my Lord' with the words 'Blessed are you among women' (1:42f.). Luke also has Mary's song of praise (1:46–55, where a few ancient witnesses read 'Elizabeth' for 'Mary' as the name of the speaker; * MAGNIFICAT). A single appealing glimpse of Christ's childhood is given to us by Luke (2:41–51), who records the typically anxious words of his mother at the discovery of the lost boy (v. 48), and the well-known reply, 'Did you not know that I must be in my Father's house?' (v. 49).

The remaining references to Mary in the Gospels are few and relatively uninformative. Apparently she did not accompany our Lord on his missionary journeys, although she was present with him at the marriage in Cana (Jn. 2:1ff.). The rebuke uttered by Jesus on this occasion, 'O woman, what have you to do with me?' (v. 4), reveals amazement rather than harshness (*cf.* Lk. 2:49, and the tender use of the same word *gynai*, 'woman', in Jn. 19:26; see also Mk. 3:31ff., where the Lord places spiritual fidelity above family relationship; with v. 35 *cf.* Lk. 11:27f.). Finally, we meet Mary at the foot of the cross (Jn. 19:25), when she and the beloved disciple are entrusted by him to each other's care (vv. 26–27). The only other explicit NT reference to Mary is in Acts 1:14, where she and the disciples are described as 'devoting themselves to prayer'.

The brief NT sketch of Mary and her relationship to our Lord leaves many gaps in the record which pious legend has not been slow to fill. But we are not able to press the Gospel records beyond their historical limit, and this means that we must be content at least to notice Mary's humility, obedience and obvious devotion to Jesus. And as she was the mother of the Son of God, we cannot say less about her than did her cousin Elizabeth, that she is 'blessed *among* women'.

BIBLIOGRAPHY. J. de Satgé, *Mary and the Christian Gospel*, 1976; R. E. Brown (ed.), *Mary*, 1977; J. McHugh, *The Mother of Jesus in the New Testament*, 1975.

2. Mary the sister of Martha. She appears by name only in Lk. and Jn. In Lk. 10:38–42 it is recorded that after the return of the Seventy Jesus came into 'a village' (identified subsequently in Jn. 11:1 as Bethany, about 2 km E of the summit of the Mount of Olives), where * Martha, who had a sister called Mary, received him into her house. In the account which follows Martha is rebuked by the Lord for complaining about her sister Mary, who listened to his 'word' rather than helping with the work.

Jn. 11 gives us the description of the meeting at Bethany between Jesus and the sisters Martha and Mary, on the occasion of the death of Lazarus their brother. Mary is now described (v. 2) as the one who 'anointed the Lord with ointment, and wiped his feet with her hair'; and after the raising of Lazarus by Jesus (11:43f.) we are told almost immediately of this anointing (12.1ff.).

All four Gospels contain an account of the anointing of Jesus by a woman (Mt. 26: 6–13; Mk. 14:3–9; Lk. 7:37–50; Jn. 12:1–8). The difficulty is to decide whether these four accounts report an identical occasion, and if not whether more than one woman is involved. Matthew and Mark more or less agree in their versions; the Lucan account differs widely (particularly in placing the event in Galilee while John the Baptist was in prison, rather than in Bethany shortly before the death of Christ); while the Johannine account is independent of all three. Only in John is the woman named, and there, as we have seen, she is clearly identified as Mary the sister of Martha. Luke alone adds that the woman was 'a sinner' (7:37); Matthew and Mark set the scene specifically 'in the house of Simon the leper'; and Matthew and Mark agree against Luke and John that it was the head and not the feet of Jesus that the woman anointed.

There have been various attempts to resolve these differences. One is to suggest that Luke describes a different occasion, but that it is the same woman who performs the anointing. The difficulty in this view (mostly held in the Latin church) is the earlier description 'sinner' for the saintly Mary of Bethany. It was this ascription indeed, together with the absence of further information, which led mediaeval scholars to identify the sinful woman of Luke's account

MARTIN
See Animals, Part 1.

with Mary Magdalene (for a discussion of which see below under 'Mary Magdalene'), and the Magdalene herself, by the further confusion just noted, with Mary of Bethany. Yet John could not have been unaware of the real identity of the two Marys, or been content to confuse his readers. There is really no justification for identifying Mary of Bethany with Mary Magdalene, and certainly none for associating either with the sinful woman of Lk. 7.

The second main view is that two anointings of our Lord occurred during his earthly ministry, one administered by a penitent sinner of Galilee, and the other by Mary of Bethany. In this case the description of Mary in Jn. 11:2, as the one who 'anointed the Lord', has a prospective reference. The only difficulty in this view is the repetition of what is evidently regarded by Jesus as an otherwise unique action, the singular character of which he clearly intends to underline by his commendation (Mt. 26:13; Mk. 14:9). This interpretation seems the most satisfactory one, however, and it solves more problems than it raises.Origen suggested that at least three anointings took place, involving either two or three different people.

The action of Mary is recognized as a spontaneous expression of devotion to Jesus, which in its character as well as its timing anticipates his death and is therefore associated with it.

3. Mary Magdalene. The name probably derives from the Galilean town of *Magdala. Her appearance prior to the passion narratives is confined to Lk. 8:2, where we read that among the women cured of possession by evil spirits who accompanied the Lord and his disciples during their evangelistic ministry was 'Mary called Magdalene, from whom seven demons had gone out' (*cf.* Mk. 16:9, in the longer ending).

It is not possible, at least from the biblical evidence, to limit the illness from which Mary was healed to one sphere alone, the physical, the mental or the moral. This is a further reason for resisting any identification between Mary Magdalene and the 'sinful woman' of Lk. 7 (see above, under **2**). If Luke had known that the Mary of ch. 8 was the same person as the sinner of ch. 7, would he not probably have made the connection explicit?

Mary reappears at the crucifixion, in company with the other women who had journeyed with our Lord from Galilee (see below, under **4**). In the Johannine account of the resurrection we have the description of the Lord's appearance to Mary alone. Mark's version, in the longer ending, is brief and not placed chronologically. Slight differences occur in the reports of the arrival of the women at the tomb. Mary sets out with the others (Mt. 8:1; Mk. 16:1), but apparently runs ahead of them and arrives first at the tomb (Jn. 20:1). She then tells Peter and the beloved disciple what has happened (Jn. 20:2), and is joined there by the other women (Lk. 24:10). She returns with Peter and the beloved disciple to the tomb, and lingers behind weeping after they have gone (Jn. 20:11). It is then that she sees two angels (v. 12), and finally the risen Christ himself (v. 14), who addresses to her the famous *noli tangere* injunction (v. 17). Clearly Mary's relationship to her Lord, following his resurrection, is to be of a different kind and to continue in another dimension.

4. Mary the mother of James; 'the other Mary'; Mary 'of *Clopas'. It is very probable that these three names all refer to the same person. Mary the mother of James and Joses is listed with Mary Magdalene among the women who accompanied our Lord to Jerusalem and were present at the crucifixion (Mt. 27:55f.). When Mary Magdalene and 'the other Mary' are described immediately afterwards (v. 61) as 'sitting opposite the sepulchre' after the burial it seems likely that the same Mary, the mother of James, is intended. 'The other Mary' again appears with Mary Magdalene on the resurrection morning (Mt. 28:1).

From the other Synoptists we learn further details. Mark refers to her (15:40) as 'Mary the mother of James the younger and of Joses', who was present at the crucifixion in the company of Mary Magdalene and Salome. In Mk. 15:47 she is called *Maria hē Iōsētos*, and in 16:1 she reappears (as 'Mary the mother of James') with Salome and Mary Magdalene as one who brought spices to the tomb on the morning of the resurrection to anoint the dead body of Jesus. Luke adds (24:10) that Joanna, as well as Mary Magdalene and Mary the mother of James, was among the women who had been onlookers at the passion of Christ, and who reported the events of the resurrection to the apostles.

John uses the descriptive term *Klōpa* ('of Clopas') for this Mary, when he records (19:25) that standing by the cross of Jesus were his mother and his mother's sister, Mary 'the wife of Clopas' and Mary Magdalene. It appears correct to translate the genitive *Klōpa* as '(wife) of Clopas', rather than as '(daughter) of Clopas'. Judging, then, by the list given in Mk. 15:40, and noted above, it seems fairly clear that Mary of Clopas (*pace* Jerome) is the same person as Mary of James. Hegesippus tells us (see Eus., *EH* 3. 11) that *Clopas (AV Cleophas) was the brother of Joseph, the husband of the Virgin Mary. (The 'Cleopas' of Lk. 24:18 is a different name.)

5. Mary the mother of Mark. The sole NT reference to this Mary occurs in Acts 12:12. After Peter's escape from prison (12:6ff.) it is to her house in Jerusalem, evidently a meeting-place for Christians, that he goes first. Since *Mark is described as the cousin of Barnabas (Col. 4:10), Barnabas was evidently Mary's nephew.

6. Mary greeted by St Paul. Her name appears among the 24 people listed in Rom. 16 to whom Paul sent greetings (v. 6). There she is described as one who 'worked hard' in (or for) the church. Otherwise nothing is known of her.

S.S.S.

MASH
See Meshech, Part 2.

MASON
See Arts and crafts, Part 1.

MASSA. The seventh of the twelve princes of Ishmael according to Gn. 25:14 and 1 Ch. 1:30, who apparently settled in N Arabia. Probably this tribe is to be identified with the Mas'a who paid tribute with Tema to Tiglath-pileser III (*ANET*, p. 283) and with the *Masanoi*, located by Ptolemy (5. 19, 2) NE of Duma. Perhaps Meshech in Ps. 120:5 should be emended to Massa, which more closely parallels Kedar. In Pr. 30:1 and 31:1 *hammaśśā'* ('the prophecy' in AV) should possibly be read as a proper name. If Agur and *Lemuel are Massaites, their collections of proverbs are examples of the international character of Heb. *wisdom literature, which on occasion was adopted and shaped by the Israelites to conform to their historic faith.

D.A.H.

MASSAH. According to Dt. 6:16 and 9:22, a place in the wilderness where Israel put God to the test: Massah (from *nissâ*, 'to test') means 'testing'. In Ex. 17:7 the name is coupled with Meribah (= 'quarrel, complaint', from *rîḇ* = 'strive, complain') in a story from the older Pentateuchal sources which shows the Israelites protesting because of lack of water at * Rephidim, close to Mt Horeb (v. 6). The two names again appear together in Ps. 95:8, a warning to later generations which could refer to this episode.

The name Meribah also occurs (without Massah) in conjunction with * Kadesh, both in a boundary-list (Ezk. 47:19) and as the location of a similar episode (mainly drawn from P), which results in both Moses and Aaron being denied the privilege of entering the promised land (Nu. 20:1–13 [*cf.* v. 24]; 27:14; Dt. 32:51; Ps. 106:32.

Both narratives are aetiological, *i.e.* imply that the names were given as a result of these events of the Mosaic period. But because of the legal connotations of the verb *rîḇ* it has often been suggested that Meribah was first of all a place where legal disputes were settled (*cf.* En-mishpat, 'well of judgment', another name for Kadesh [Gn. 14:7]). This can only be a hypothesis, but there are other reasons for wondering whether the straightforward explanation of the names is historically correct.

The attempt has frequently been made to separate out a Massah-story and a Meribah-story in Ex. 17:1–7, but, although there is a little unexpected repetition (vv. 2–3), it is not sufficient to justify analysis into two separate stories, deriving from different sources. The same must be said for Nu. 20:1–13. What is more likely is that, in both cases, there has been some amplification of the original account by a later author. In Ex. 17:1–7 this amplification may be responsible for the introduction of the allusion to Meribah (and perhaps Massah also) in vv. 2 and 7.

Dt. 33:8 and Ps. 81:7, where these names also occur, can scarcely refer to the same episodes, since here there is no hint of criticism and it is God, not the people of Israel, who is doing the 'testing'. The theme of God testing Israel is one that is encountered several times in Exodus (15:25; 16:4; 20:20). It seems likely that other events, perhaps mentioned elsewhere in the Bible (Ex. 32?), perhaps not, were at one time connected with these places. To date, no fully satisfactory correlation of the various passages has been made, and it may be that the literary and historical problems are insoluble. For some ingenious, if speculative, suggestions see H. Seebass, *Mose und Aaron*, 1962, pp. 61ff.

BIBLIOGRAPHY. B. S. Childs, *Exodus*, 1974, pp. 305–309.

G.I.D.

MASTER. The translation of five Heb. and seven Gk. words. In the OT the most common term is *'āḏôn*, 'lord', 'sir', found 96 times, particularly when the reference is to persons other than God—*e.g.* a master of servants (Gn. 24:14, *etc.*; *TDOT* 1, pp. 59–72). *ba'al*, 'owner', 'master', appears five times, generally denoting the master of a house (Jdg. 19:22; *cf.* Mt. 10:25, Gk. *oikodespotēs*; *TDNT* 2, p. 49; *TDOT* 2, pp. 181–200). (For the Phoenician god, see * BAAL.) *raḇ*, 'great', 'elder', occurs four times, notably in combination with another word—*e.g.* 'chief of the magicians' (Dn. 4:9; 5:11), 'chief eunuch' (Dn. 1:3). On two occasions the Heb. word is *śar*, 'prince', 'chief', 'commander' (Ex. 1:11; 1 Ch. 15:27), and once it is *'ēr*, 'to awake', 'to stir up' (Mal. 2:12), where RV and AVmg. render 'him that waketh' and RSV has 'any to witness' (reading *'ēḏ* for *'ēr*).

In the NT the most frequent term is *didaskalos* (*TDNT* 2, pp. 148–159), 'teacher', 'instructor', found 47 times, all in the Gospels except for Jas. 3:1. *despotēs* (*TDNT* 2, pp. 44–49) generally denotes a master over slaves, and is used five times (*e.g.* 1 Tim. 6:1–2). A word peculiar in this connection to Luke's Gospel and found there six times, always when the disciples are addressing Jesus, is *epistatēs* (*TDNT* 2, pp. 622–623), 'superintendent', 'overseer' (*e.g.* Lk. 5:5). *kyrios* (*TDNT* 3, pp. 1039–1095), 'lord', 'sir', is translated 'master' 14 times, often signifying God or Christ (*e.g.* Mk. 13:35; Eph. 6:9). Another word translated as master is *kathēgētēs*, 'a leader', 'a guide' (in the scholastic sense) (Mt. 23:8, 10). Gk. *rhabbi* (*TDNT* 6, pp. 961–965), * 'Rabbi', from Heb. *rabbî*, 'my master', is used of Jesus (*e.g.* Jn. 4:31) in 12 of its 15 NT occurrences. Finally, *kybernētēs* (*TDNT* 3, pp. 1035–1037), 'ship-master', 'pilot', is found twice (Acts 27:11; Rev. 18:17).

J.D.D.

MATTHEW. Matthew appears in all the lists of the twelve apostles (Mt. 10:3; Mk. 3:18; Lk. 6:15; Acts 1:13). In Mt. 10:3 he is further described as 'the tax-collector'. In Mt. 9:9 Jesus finds him 'sitting at the tax-office' and bids him follow him. In the parallel passages in Mark and Luke the tax-collector called from the tax-office is designated Levi, Mark adding that he was 'the son of Alphaeus'. The *Gospel of Peter* also speaks of Levi the son of Alphaeus as a disciple of Jesus. Subsequently, Jesus is a fellow-guest with many tax-collectors and sinners. Neither Mt. 9:10 nor Mk. 2:15 makes it clear at whose house the meal was held, but Lk. 5:29 states that 'Levi made him a great feast in his house'. From the evidence it is usually supposed that Matthew and Levi were the same person.

The statement of Papias that Matthew 'compiled the oracles' (*synegrapsato ta logia*) in Hebrew was taken by the early church as evidence that Matthew was the author of the Gospel which had been handed down as 'according to Matthew'. Most modern scholars believe that Papias was referring to a compilation by Matthew either of the sayings of Jesus or of Messianic proof-texts from the OT. It may be that the subsequent embodiment of some of these sayings or proof-texts in the Gospel was the reason why that document came to be styled 'according to Matthew' from the middle of the 2nd century. For Bibliography, * MATTHEW, GOSPEL OF.

R.V.G.T.

MATTHEW, GOSPEL OF.

I. Outline of contents

a. Events associated with the birth of Jesus the Messiah (1:1–2:23).

b. Jesus is baptized and tempted and begins his Galilean ministry (3:1–4:25).

c. The ethics of the kingdom of God are taught by Jesus by injunctions and illustrations (5:1–7:29).

d. Jesus demonstrates his power over disease, the devil and nature (8:1–9:34).

e. Jesus commissions the Twelve and sends them out as preachers (9:35–10:42).

f. Jesus commends John the Baptist, issues a gracious invitation to

MATERIALISM See Wealth, Part 3.

MATTANIAH See Zedekiah, Part 3.

the heavy laden, claims to be Lord of the sabbath day, argues that he cannot be Beelzebub and explains the qualifications for membership in his new family (11:1–12:50).

g. Jesus gives seven parables about the kingdom of heaven (13:1–52).

h. Jesus is rejected by his fellow-townsmen of Nazareth, and John the Baptist is martyred (13:53–14:12).

i. Further miracles are performed by Jesus, who is acknowledged to be the Christ by Peter. Later Jesus is transfigured before three disciples and predicts his coming death and resurrection (14:13–17:27).

j. Jesus teaches his disciples to be humble, careful in conduct, and very forgiving in practice (18:1–35).

k. Jesus travels to Jerusalem. On the way he gives teaching on divorce, the position of children, the snare of riches and the wickedness of God's people the Jews; he heals two blind men at Jericho (19:1–20:34).

l. After making a triumphal but humble entry into Jerusalem, Jesus shows his authority by cleansing the Temple, by cursing a fruitless fig-tree, and by attacking and counter-attacking the chief priests and Pharisees (21:1–23:35).

m. Jesus predicts the fall of Jerusalem and his own glorious second coming (24:1–51).

n. Jesus gives three parables on judgment (25:1–46).

o. Jesus is betrayed, tried, denied, mocked, crucified and buried (26:1–27:66).

p. Jesus is raised from the dead and is seen by his friends (28:1–10).

q. Jesus gives his final orders before returning to God in heaven (28:11–20).

II. Characteristics and authorship

In this Gospel the incidents in the life of Jesus which constituted 'the gospel' preached by the apostles are combined to a greater extent with the ethical teaching of Jesus than elsewhere in the NT; and it is this feature of the book, together with the orderly manner in which the material is presented, which made it from the earliest days the most widely read and in some respects the most influential of the four Gospels. Modern scholars hesitate to accept the tradition that its author was the apostle * Matthew, for he seems to have been dependent upon a document composed by a non-apostolic writer, the Gospel of Mark, to a degree improbable in an original apostle. For a full discussion of the question of authorship see the writer's Introduction to the *TNTC*.

III. The influence of Mark

It is clear that Matthew has included almost the whole of Mark, though he has greatly abbreviated the Marcan stories of the miracles to make space for the large amount of non-Marcan material he desires to insert (* GOSPELS; * MARK, GOSPEL OF). Along with the stories from Mark, the Evangelist inserts numerous sayings of Jesus, taken, it would seem, from a source common to himself and Luke; and he conflates these sayings with others found only in his Gospel, the resultant groupings constituting five blocks of teaching, chs. 5–7, 10, 13, 18 and 24–25, each block ending with the formula: 'When Jesus had finished these sayings.' The subject-matter of the Gospel is rendered complete by the addition of several narratives found nowhere else. These would appear for the most part to be elaborations of traditions used by Christians for apologetic purposes in defence against Jewish slanders. Evidence of style suggests that these particular narratives were first put in writing by the Evangelist himself (see G. D. Kilpatrick, *The Origins of the Gospel according to St. Matthew*, 1946).

IV. Differences from Mark's Gospel

The fact that this Gospel originated in a Gk.-speaking Jewish–Christian community accounts largely for the particular emphasis which it places upon the different elements that composed the primitive Christian preaching, and also for the manner in which the teaching of Jesus is presented. The note of *fulfilment* finds stronger emphasis here than in the Gospel of Mark. The author is most concerned to establish the truth that the earthly history of Jesus, in its origin and its purpose, and in the actual manner of its unfolding, was the activity of God himself, who was therein fulfilling his own words spoken by the prophets. No Gospel so closely links together OT and NT; and no document in the NT sets forth the person of Jesus, and his life and teaching, so clearly as the fulfilment of 'the law and the prophets'. Not only does the Evangelist add OT references to passages taken over from Mark, as, *e.g.*, at 27:34 and 43; but at various points in the narrative he introduces with the impressive formula 'this was to fulfil what was spoken by the prophet' some eleven special quotations from the OT, the cumulative effect of which is remarkable (see 1:23; 2:18; 2:23; 4:15f.; 8:17; 12:18ff.; 13:35; 21:5, and 27:9f.). Events are recorded as happening in the way they did because God had willed that it should be so. They were not freak events isolated and unexplained. They happened 'according to the scriptures', in which God's will had been expressed.

V. The story of Jesus

The record of the events in the life and death of Jesus which were of special importance and significance for the Christian gospel that we find presented in Matthew is for the most part Mark's story. Our Evangelist collects in chs. 8 and 9, in three groups of three, many of the Marcan narratives of the miracles; and in chs. 11 and 12 he combines from Mark and other sources stories about the relations of Jesus with prominent people of his day such as John the Baptist and the Pharisees. He makes no attempt to relate these incidents in chronological sequence. Such sequence is to be found only in the story of the passion, which, because it lay at the centre of the Christian gospel, was probably told in chronological form from very early days. Matthew, however, renders Mark's story of the life of Jesus more complete by prefacing it with a * genealogy and traditions about the infancy of Jesus and by following it with accounts of two of the appearances of the risen Jesus. The infancy narratives of Matthew do not contain an account of the birth of Jesus, which is mentioned only in passing in 2:1. The purpose of the Evangelist seems to be, by the genealogy, to show that Jesus, though born of a virgin-mother, was nevertheless legally of Abraham's seed and a son of the royal house of David; and, by the material contained in 1:18–25, to answer the calumny that Jesus was an illegitimate child of Mary, and to defend the action of Joseph. The subsequent story of the flight into Egypt is partly an answer to the Jewish cavil why, if Jesus, known as Jesus of Nazareth, was really born in Bethlehem, so much of his life was spent at Nazareth.

The two resurrection appearances peculiar to Matthew (28:9–10, 16–20) may be an attempt to round off the Marcan story. Certainly, the abruptness of Mark's ending is avoided by the statement that the women, instead of saying nothing to anybody of what they had heard and seen, at once obeyed the angel's command to report to the Lord's brethren that they were to go to Galilee where they would see him, and that, as the women were setting out on their errand, they met the risen Jesus. The momentous disclosure by the risen Jesus in Galilee that by his victory over death universal sovereignty had been given him, and his commission to the eleven disciples to embark upon a world-wide evangelistic mission with the assurance that he would be with them to the end of time, provide the climax of the Gospel of Matthew.

In these infancy and post-resurrection narratives Matthew is making definite additions to the story of Jesus as it had been set forth in Mark. Where he expands such Marcan stories as he embodies, it is usually by adding material which reflects interests that were of concern to the Christian church at the time he was writing. For example, the story of Peter walking over the waves to Jesus (14:28–31) and the famous Petrine passage in 16:18–19 were important at a time when that apostle was playing a leading part in the church; and the problem presented by taxation, especially after AD 70, when, on the destruction of the Temple, the tax for its upkeep was transferred to the temple of Jupiter Capitolinus, would receive some elucidation from the narrative recorded in 17:24–27. Moreover, as time went on, and biographical curiosity tended to increase, greater attention seems to have been paid to the secondary characters in the story of Jesus. Thus the Matthean account of the fate of Judas Iscariot (27:3–10) and the incident of Pilate's wife (27:19) would help to answer the puzzling questions, 'Why did Judas betray his Master?' and, 'Why did Pilate condemn Jesus?'

In his account of the crucifixion and resurrection Matthew makes four main additions to the Marcan narrative which at this point he is following closely. He relates that at the moment of Jesus' death an earthquake occurred accompanied by a resurrection of the saints, who had foretold the coming of the Messiah and who now rose to salute his death on Calvary (27:51–53). The three further additions of Matthew to Mark's resurrection narrative, *viz.* the special guarding and sealing of the tomb (27:62–66); the failure of these precautions due partly to the semi-mortification of the guards after another earthquake and partly to the presence of an angelic visitor who rolled the stone from the tomb (28:2–4); and the bribing of the guards to circulate the story, still current in the Evangelist's day, that the disciples of Jesus had come during the night and stolen the body (28:11–15)—are all of an apologetic nature. Their purpose is to dismiss the possibility that the body of Jesus could have been removed from the grave except in a supernatural manner. In many respects the Gospel of Matthew might be called an early Christian apology.

VI. The new Israel

The chief consequence of the life and death of Jesus emphasized in the Gospel of Matthew is the coming into being of the universal church of God, the new Israel, in which Gentiles as well as Jews find a place. The Gospel opens with the prophecy that Jesus is Emmanuel, God with us (1:23); and it closes with the promise that this same Jesus, now the risen Christ, will be with his disciples, drawn from all the nations, till the end of time. The note of universality, sounded at the beginning in the story of the manifestation of Jesus to the Magi, is re-echoed in the command with which the Gospel closes to go into all the world and make disciples of all nations. The Evangelist finds significance in the fact that the ministry of Jesus was exercised partly in 'Galilee of the Gentiles' (4:15); and describes him as God's servant who would 'proclaim justice to the Gentiles . . . and in his name will the Gentiles hope' (12:18, 21). The Christian church, universal in its membership, is, however, no new church. It is the old Israel transformed and widened because of Jesus' rejection by the majority of the Jews. It was to 'the lost sheep of the house of Israel' that Jesus confessed himself primarily to have been sent (15:24); and it was to the same lost sheep that he despatched his apostles to proclaim the arrival of the kingdom (10:6). But greater faith was found in a Roman centurion than in any in Israel (8:10); and in consequence the places at the Messianic banquet, unfilled by the Jew, would be thrown open to believers from E and W, while 'the sons of the kingdom' would remain outside (8:11–12). Because the Messiahship of Jesus had become to the Jews 'a stone of stumbling', the kingdom would be taken away from them and given to a nation 'producing the fruits of it' (21:42–43). The patriarchs of the new Israel, the apostles, would share in the Messiah's final victory, acting as his co-assessors in judgment, as Jesus makes clear in the words recorded by Matthew in 19:28, and as the Evangelist emphasizes by inserting the words 'with you' in the Marcan saying inserted at 26:29.

VII. Jesus as Judge

The fourth element in the primitive preaching was the call to repentance in view of the return of Jesus as Judge of living and dead. This call is sounded loudly in Matthew. John the Baptist in this Gospel calls Israel to repent in the same words as Jesus because they stand on the threshold of the Messiah's ministry (3:2); and at the close of the teaching of Jesus we read the parable of the great assize, found only in this

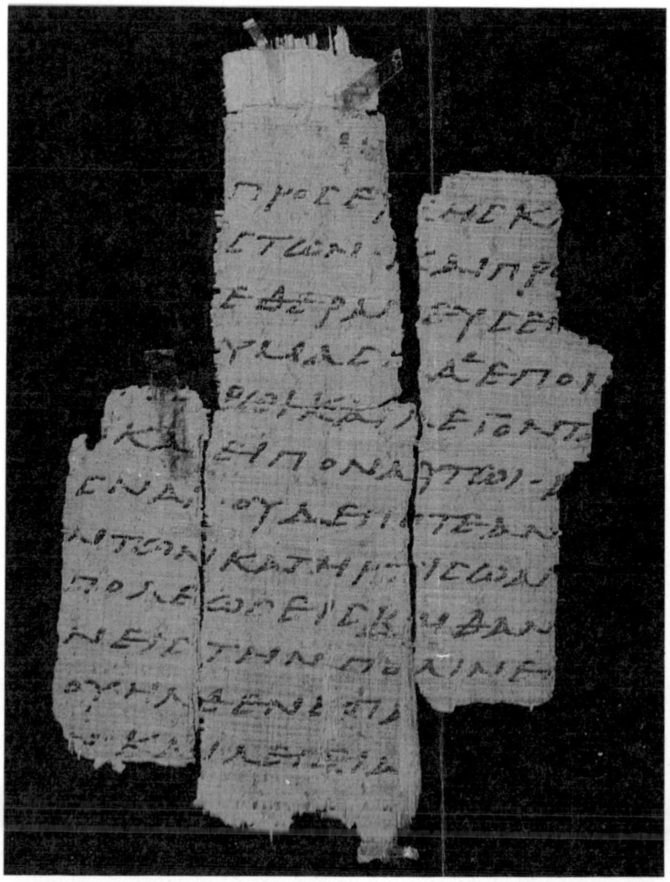

Fragment of Matthew's Gospel in Greek (Mt. 21:13–19). Part of a papyrus codex. 3rd cent. AD. Chester Beatty papyrus I. (CBL)

■ **MAZZAROTH**
See Stars, Part 3.

■ **MEAL**
See Bread, Part 1.

Gospel (25:31–46). This parable concludes a group of sayings and parables concerned exclusively with the coming of the Messiah in judgment. By the time the Gospel was written, perhaps in the early 80s of the 1st century, part of the divine judgment had already descended upon Israel in the fall of Jerusalem; and the words of 21:41 and 22:7 had indeed been fulfilled.

Many of the parables peculiar to Mt., such as the tares of the field, the unforgiving debtor, the guest without a wedding garment and the ten virgins, stress the inevitability and the serious nature of the divine judgment; and it is in them that we find constantly repeated the solemn phrases peculiar to this Gospel, 'the outer darkness', 'the close of the age' and 'the weeping and gnashing of teeth'. In the perspective of this Gospel this final coming of the Christ, though absolutely certain, is not pictured as immediate, because, as we have seen, the closing pronouncement of the risen Christ implies a period of indefinite duration, during which he is present and exercises his reign in his church, before his final appearance as Judge. It is probable, therefore, that in the light of the teaching of the Gospel as a whole we ought to interpret the two very difficult sayings in 10:23 and 16:28 as referring to the exaltation of Jesus to the right hand of God after the triumph of his resurrection, when he entered upon a more extended reign in the hearts of his followers. Otherwise we are forced to the unsatisfactory conclusion that either they remained unfulfilled, and were therefore false prophecies, or that they are not genuine sayings of Jesus.

VIII. Ethical teaching

The Gospel of Matthew is also remarkable for the extent to which and the manner in which the ethical teaching of Jesus is presented. To this Evangelist, as to Jewish Christians generally, and also to Paul (for the very phrase is his), there is such a thing as 'the law of Christ'. Some scholars have thought that the five groups of teaching in this Gospel were regarded by the author as comparable to the five books of the law. Be this as it may, it would seem clear that he presents Jesus as the great Teacher who proclaims a revised law for the new Israel from the mountain (5:1), even as Moses had spoken the divine law given to him on Mt Sinai. The Messiah calls Israel not only to repentance but to good works; and the desire to do them, and the willingness to suffer for doing them, render the doers blessed (5:6, 10). The righteousness of Christ's disciples must exceed that of the Pharisees (5:20). It is true that by their traditions, by their slavery to isolated texts and their failure to grasp the wider implications of the law, the Pharisees had rendered much of it void; but the law remained an integral part of divine revelation. It is this law which finds its fulfilment in Christ, who came not to destroy it but to supply what it lacked and to correct scribal misinterpretations of it (5:17). Accordingly, a large part of the Sermon on the Mount is taken up with an explanation of the Decalogue in which Jesus lays down the moral standards by which the conduct of his disciples is to be judged.

One of the major difficulties of this Gospel is that it presents Jesus as upholding the validity of the Mosaic law and also claiming authority so to 'fulfil' it that sometimes he has been thought to be contradicting it. That he regarded the OT as possessing permanent validity as the Word of God is explicit in the uncompromising saying of 5:17–19. At the same time, so strongly is the binding authority of Christ's own utterances stressed, that in certain instances the abiding nature of the old law *seems* to be denied. In view, however, of the categorical statement about the law's validity, the Evangelist cannot have meant his readers to infer that there was any real antithesis between the statements contained in it and Jesus' comments upon them. Six times in the Sermon on the Mount he appears to be setting his own pronouncements against what had been previously spoken, and in each instance what had been previously spoken consists of, or at least includes, a quotation from the Mosaic law.

It has, however, been well pointed out that the expressions in ch. 5, 'You have heard that it was said' or 'It was said', do not correspond exactly to 'It is written', which Jesus so often uses when he is appealing to the authority of Scripture. By them he is, in fact, drawing attention not only to what the law said but to what the people had been told by their teachers was its meaning. In Judaism the law occupied the supreme position. In Christianity that place is occupied by Christ himself. In the Jewish–Christian Gospel of Matthew Christ remains the dominant authority. It is significant that it is in this Gospel alone that we read his gracious but imperious invitation, 'Come to me, all who labour and are heavy laden, and I will give you rest. Take my yoke upon you, and learn from me; for I am gentle and lowly in heart, and you will find rest for your souls. For my yoke is easy, and my burden is light' (11:28–30).

BIBLIOGRAPHY. G. Bornkamm, G. Barth, H. J. Held, *Tradition and Interpretation in Matthew*, 1963; W. D. Davies, *The Setting of the Sermon on the Mount*, 1964; J. D. Kingsbury, *Matthew: Structure, Christology, Kingdom*, 1975. See also commentaries by W. F. Albright and C. S. Mann, 1971; F. V. Filson, 1960; H. B. Green, 1975; D. Hill, 1972; E. Schweizer, 1976; R. V. G. Tasker, *TNTC*, 1961. R.V.G.T.

MATTHIAS. The successor of Judas Iscariot, following the latter's defection from the Twelve (Acts 1:15–26). The fact and manner of his election have sometimes been called in question as hasty and unspiritual, and supervening on the place intended for Paul (*cf.*, *e.g.*, G. Campbell Morgan, *Acts*, 1924, *ad loc.*), but Luke gives no hint of such a view: the basis of the lot-casting, with its OT precedent (*cf.* 1 Sa. 14:41; *URIM AND THUMMIM), was that God had *already chosen* his apostle (v. 24), and it was fitting that the foundational apostolate should be complete at the outpouring of the Spirit on the church and its first preaching (*APOSTLE). That Matthias fulfilled the qualifications of vv. 21–22 makes the statement of Eusebius (*EH* 1. 12) that he was one of the Seventy not unlikely.

Of his later career nothing is known. His name was often confounded with that of Matthew, a process doubtless encouraged by the Gnostic groups who claimed secret traditions from him (Hippolytus, *Philos.* 7. 8). A book of so-called traditions was known to Clement of Alexandria (*Strom.* 2. 9; 3. 4; *cf.* 7. 17). Other apocryphal literature was fathered upon him.

The early identification of Matthias with Zacchaeus (Clement, *Strom.* 4. 6) may also arise from confusion with Matthew the tax-collector. The substitution of 'Tholomaeus' in the Old Syriac of Acts 1 is harder to understand.

The name is probably a contraction of Mattathias. A.F.W.

MATTOCK. Heb. *maḥ*^{a}*rēšā* in 1 Sa. 13:20 (end), 21, and the similar form *maḥ*^{a}*rešeṯ* (earlier in v. 20) represent cutting instruments (root *ḥrš*, 'to plough, engrave'), *i.e.* probably mattocks and hoes. Among other terms in these verses, the second one, Heb. *'ēṯ*, is a metal head: of an axe in 2 Ki. 6:5 and so perhaps of a ploughshare or more strictly a metal cap for a wooden plough (rather than AV's 'coulter'); *cf.* Is. 2:4 = Mi. 4:3; Joel 3:10, feasible adaptations as well as evocative. The third term in v. 20 (*qardōm*) is a pickaxe (AV 'axe').

In AV 'mattock' also translates Heb. *ma'dēr* in Is. 7:25, hoe, used in the vineyard terraces (*cf.* also Is. 5:6) and *b*^{e}*ḥarbōṯêhem* in 2 Ch. 34:6, which should probably be rendered 'in their ruins' with RV, RSV (from *ḥorbâ*).

For an iron mattock of about 10th century BC found at Tell Jemmeh in SW Palestine, see G. E. Wright, *Biblical Archaeology*, 1957, p. 92, fig. 57:3. (*ARTS AND CRAFTS.) K.A.K.

MEADOW. 1. Heb. *'āḥū*: AV 'meadow'; RV, RSV 'reed grass'. This Heb. word is a loan-word from Egyp. *'ḫ(y)* and, like it, means 'papyrus thicket(s)'. The picture of cattle pasturing in the papyrus thickets and marshes (Gn. 41:2, 18) is typically Egyptian: cattle are shown thus in tomb-scenes, while texts mention bringing 'best grass from the papyrus marshes' for livestock. In Jb. 8:11 *gōme'* and *'āḥū* are parallel: 'papyrus' or 'reeds' and 'papyrus thicket', which must have mud and water. In Ho. 13:15 it is possible to render *'aḥîm* as 'reed thickets' rather than 'brothers' (*cf.* RSV). See J. Vergote, *Joseph en Égypte*, 1959, pp. 59–66 (especially 62ff.) for full references; also *cf.* T. O. Lambdin, *JAOS* 73, 1953, p. 146, for other related Egyp. and Ugaritic terms.

2. In Jdg. 20:33 AV renders *ma'*^{a}*rēh-ḡeḇa'* as 'meadows of Geba'. This may be the 'bare place' by Geba, or perhaps a Maareh-geba close by, or even (with LXX) to be read as *ma'*^{a}*raḇ-geḇa'*, '(on) west of Geba' (RSV). K.A.K.

MEALS.

I. Non-biblical sources

What is probably the oldest banquet scene in the world has been preserved on a lapis-lazuli cylinder seal recovered from the mound at Ur in Mesopotamia. Now in the University of Philadelphia Museum, the artefact dates from the time of Queen Shub-ad (*c.* 2600 BC). It depicts a meal at which the royal guests are seated on low

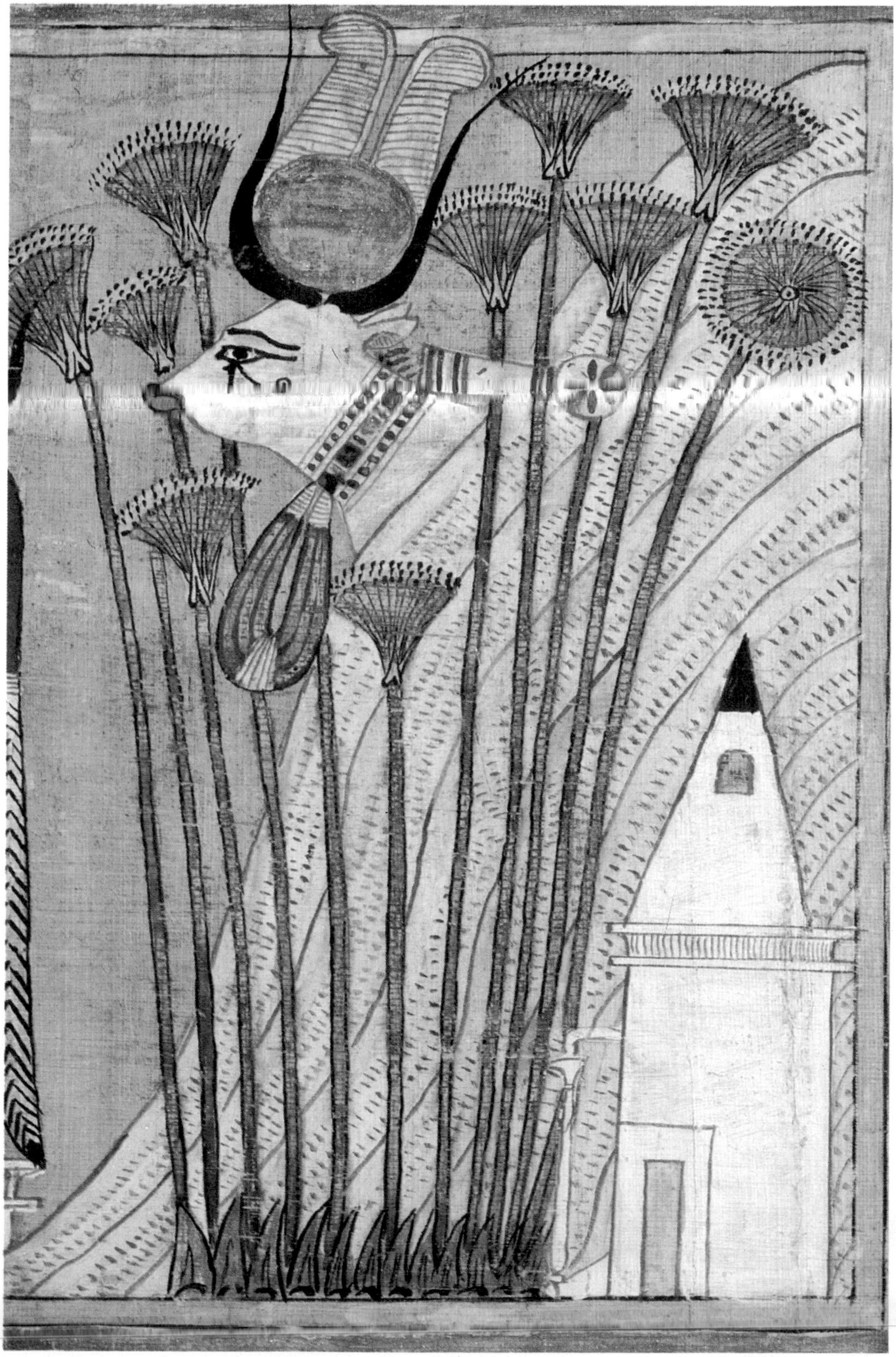

A meadow of papyrus as depicted on the Papyrus of Ani, Theban Book of the Dead. 19th Dynasty. c. 1250 BC. (BM)

stools and are being served with beakers of wine by attendants who wear skirts of fleece. Musical entertainment is provided by a harpist, while other servants employ fans in an attempt to cool the guests in the hot Mesopotamian air.

Similar scenes have been preserved by Bab. artists from subsequent periods, one of the more interesting of which is a large bas-relief from Assyria. King Ashurbanipal is seen eating with his wife in the garden of the royal palace at Nineveh. As the king reclines on a pillowed dining-couch he raises a bowl of wine to his lips. His wife is also shown drinking from an ele-

An Egyptian banquet. The guests, refreshed by ointment-cones on their heads, are entertained by a blind harpist. Painting in the tomb of the scribe Nakht at Thebes. 18th Dynasty. c. 1415 BC. (RS)

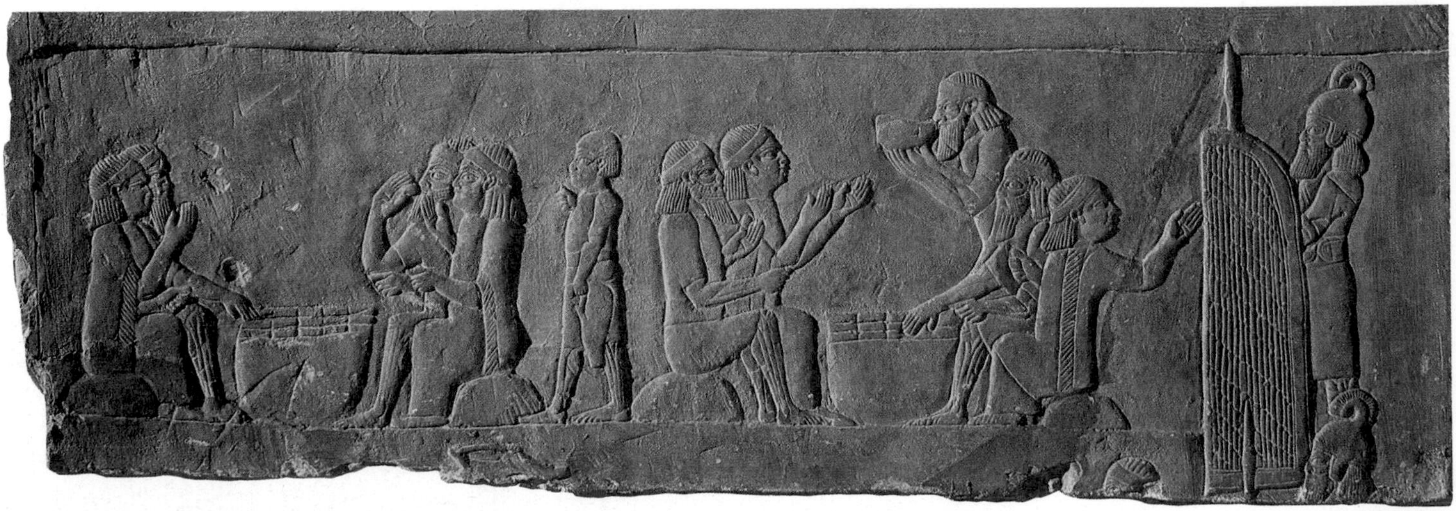

Elamite prisoners eating and drinking while guarded by an Assyrian soldier. Nineveh, palace of Ashurbanipal. c. 640 BC. (BM)

gant bowl, but she is seated upon a small chair which has a low shelf in the form of a foot-rest. As in the case of the Ur artefact, attendants stand ready with fans to cool the diners and dispel annoying insects. The relief shows a few musical instruments placed on the ground beside some vines and palm trees in readiness for the court musicians.

The earliest detailed menu of which we have any record relates to a feast given by Ashurnasirpal II at the dedication of his new palace at Nimrud. It was attended by 69,574 persons and lasted for 10 days. The details are given on a monument set up in 879 BC (see *IBA*, fig. 43).

II. Biblical references

a. Palace meals

The type of elegance mentioned above, which was characteristic of Mesopotamian antiquity, was far surpassed by the delicacy and expertise which surrounded the royal meals of ancient Egypt. Paintings on the walls of tombs and other buildings have furnished remarkable evidence of the splendour such a celebration as the palace birthday banquet of pharaoh in the time of Joseph (Gn. 40:20). On such occasions the guests, elegantly bewigged and perfumed, were seated on couches near to low tables. Their food would include a variety of roast fowl, vegetables, roast beef, a wide range of pastries and numerous sweetmeats. Popular beverages included beer brewed from barley, and wine. Representations on tomb walls show servants bringing in large containers of wine and handing the guests bent glass tubes which were then dipped into the jar. The guests drank until they were inebriated and fell to the floor near their dining-couches.

Banqueting customs in Persia in the 5th century BC have been preserved by the book of Esther, which describes no fewer than five such festive occasions at Susa. The first was a marathon feast lasting 180 days, given by the king in honour of the Persian and Median princes (Est. 1:3ff.). This was followed by a 7-day banquet in the royal gardens, to which all the palace staff were invited. The guests were shielded from the sunlight by awnings of blue, green and white, the royal Persian colours, while the dining-couches were inlaid with gold and silver. The other feasts mentioned included one for the palace women (Est. 1:9), the wedding feast of Queen Esther (2:16–18), the wine-banquet given to Ahasuerus and Haman (5:4; 7:1–8) and the festival period known as Purim (9:1–32).

By contrast the Heb. palace meals were austere until the days of Solomon. Guests and retainers were numerous even in the time of Saul, and the royal displeasure could be incurred by refusing an invitation to dine with the king (1 Sa. 20:6). The generosity of David was shown in the provision made at the royal board for Mephibosheth, the crippled son of Jonathan (2 Sa. 9:7). Solomon imitated the monarchs of surrounding nations in the elaborateness and splendour of his feasts. It has been suggested that Solomon would probably have his summer meals served in some such garden as that mentioned in Canticles. In the royal court at Samaria Queen Jezebel supported a retinue of 400 prophets of the Asherah and 450 Baal prophets (1 Ki. 18:19). The poverty of post-exilic Judaea contrasted sharply with the fare provided by Nehemiah the governor. He supported 150 Jews in addition to other guests, and the day's food included six sheep, an ox, numerous fowls, fruit and wine (Ne. 5:17–19).

b. Working-class meals

For the labouring classes in biblical times, however, the situation was very different. The day began early, and instead of eating a formal breakfast, the workers carried in their girdles or in other containers small loaves, goat's-milk cheese, figs, olives and the like, which they ate as they journeyed to work. The Egyptians apparently had their main meal of the day at noon (Gn. 43:16), but Heb. workers generally contented themselves with a light repast and a rest period (Ru. 2:14). Abstinence from this meal constituted fasting (Jdg. 20:26; 1 Sa. 14:24). Supper, the most important meal of the day, took place after the work had been done (Ru. 3:7). Once the food had been prepared,

An early banqueting-scene depicted on a cylinder-seal and its impression from Ur. The lower register includes a table laden with food and a musician to entertain the guests. c. 2600 BC. (UMUP)

the entire family dined together along with any guests who might be present. On festive occasions it was customary for entertainment to be provided, and this included riddles (Jdg. 14:12), music (Is. 5:12) and dancing (Mt. 14:6; Lk. 15:25). In the patriarchal period the diners sat in a group on the ground (Gn. 18:8; 37:25), but at a later time it became customary for them to sit at a table (1 Ki. 13:20; Ps. 23:5; Ezk. 23:41) after the Egyp. fashion, but perhaps in a semi-recumbent position (Est. 7:8).

c. Seating arrangements

In NT times meals were often eaten on a floor above that normally occupied by animals and domestic pets (*cf.* Mk. 7:28). Guests invariably reclined on couches, which were arranged on three sides of a square around a low table. Normally not more than three persons reclined on each couch, though occasionally this number was increased to four or five. Each couch was provided with cushions on which the left elbow rested and the right arm remained free, following the contemporary Graeco-Roman fashion. The guests so arranged themselves on the couches that each person could rest his head near the breast of the one who was reclining immediately behind him. He was thus reclining 'in the bosom' of his neighbour (Jn. 13:23; *cf.* Lk. 16:22), the close proximity of whom furnished adequate opportunity for an exchange of confidential communications. The place of greatest honour or 'highest couch' was the one immediately on the right of the servants as they entered the room to serve the meal. Conversely, the 'lowest room' was on the left of the servants, directly opposite to the 'highest couch'. The three guests on each couch were spoken of as highest, middle and lowest, a designation which was suggested by the fact that a guest who reclined on another's bosom always appeared to be below him. The most coveted seat (Mt. 23:6) was therefore the 'highest' place on the 'highest' couch. No questions of physical elevation were involved in such a usage of 'high' and 'low'.

d. The meal itself

The main meal of the day was generally a relaxed, happy occasion. Guests always washed their hands before partaking of food, since it was customary for all of them to eat from a communal dish. This was a large pottery container filled with meat and vegetables, and placed on a table in the centre of the couches. Only one instance is recorded in the OT of a blessing being pronounced before food was eaten (1 Sa. 9:13), but the NT mentions several occasions on which Christ pronounced grace before a meal commenced (Mt. 15:36; Lk. 9:16; Jn. 6:11).

While the general practice was for each guest to dip his hand into the common bowl (Mt. 26:23), there were occasions when separate portions were served to each guest (Gn. 43:34; Ru. 2:14; 1 Sa. 1:4–5). In the absence of knives and forks, small pieces of bread were held between the thumb and two fingers of the right hand to absorb the gravy from the dish (Jn. 13:26). They were also used after the fashion of spoons to scoop up a piece of meat, which was then conveyed to the mouth in the form of a sandwich. If a guest acquired a particularly delectable morsel by such means it was deemed an act of great politeness for him to hand it over to a companion (Jn. 13:26). When the meal was at an end it was customary for grace to be pronounced once again in compliance with the injunction of Dt. 8:10, after which the guests washed their hands a second time.

It would appear from instances such as those of Ruth among the reapers (Ru. 2:14), Elkanah and his two wives (1 Sa. 1:4–5), and the sons and daughters of Job (Jb. 1:4) that the womenfolk commonly partook of their meals in company with the men. But since it is probable that the task of preparing the food and waiting upon the guests normally devolved upon the women of the household (Lk. 10:40), they would doubtless be forced to take a somewhat more irregular and brief repast.

An ordinary family meal would not involve the preparation of more than one dish of food, so that when it had been served the member of the household who had cooked the meal would have no further work to do. This thought probably underlies the rebuke to *Martha (Lk. 10:42), when Christ suggested that only one dish was really necessary. In OT times, when the meal had been brought in by the person who had prepared it (1 Sa. 9:23), the head of the household allotted the various servings (1 Sa. 1:4), the size of which might well vary with the preference which he exercised towards individuals in the assembled group (Gn. 43:34; 1 Sa. 1:5).

e. Special meals

Special feasts celebrating birthdays, marriages or the presence of honoured guests were normally marked by an increased degree of ceremony. Visitors were received by the host with a kiss (Lk. 7:45) and provided with a refreshing footbath (Lk. 7:44). On certain occasions special clothing was furnished (Mt. 22:11) and the guests were decked out with floral wreaths (Is. 28:1). The head, beard, face and sometimes even the clothes were anointed with perfumes and ointments (Ps. 23:5; Am. 6:6; Lk. 7:38; Jn. 12:3) in celebration of an important festal occasion. The conduct of the banquet itself was under the direction of a special person known in NT times as the 'steward' of the feast (Jn. 2:8), to whom fell the task of sampling the various items of food and drink before they were placed on the table.

Guests were seated according to their respective rank (Gn. 43:33; 1 Sa. 9:22; Mk. 12:39; Lk. 14:8; Jn. 13:23), and were often served with individual portions of food (1 Sa. 1:4–5; 2 Sa. 6:19; 1 Ch. 16:3). Honoured guests were usually singled out by being offered either larger (Gn. 43:34) or more delectable (1 Sa. 9:24) portions than the others who were present at the banquet.

In the days of Paul the banquet was an elaborate meal which was generally followed by a symposium or intellectual discussion. On such occasions the discourse would often last far into the night, and would treat of such subjects as politics and philosophy.

f. Jesus' presence at meals

The NT records a number of occasions on which Jesus was a guest at an evening meal. The wedding feast at Cana (Jn. 2:1–11) was a festal occasion for which formal invitations had been issued, as was also the case in the parable of the king who gave a feast when his son was married (Mt. 22:2–14). The occasion on which Matthew was host at a banquet (Mt. 9:10) followed the more formal pattern of 1st-century AD Graeco-Roman meals. Jesus reclined at the table in company with his disciples, the tax-collectors and other invited guests. It is probable that the dining-room opened on to the street, with curtains placed near the entrance so that the guests would be shielded to some extent from the curious gaze of passers-by. The customs of the day, however, permitted people to look in through the curtains and gossip about those present at the feast. It was this practice which prompted the Pharisees to question the propriety of Christ's dining with publicans and sinners (Mt. 9:11).

On another occasion in a similar dining-room (Lk. 7:36–50) Jesus was noticed by a passing woman who returned with an alabaster cruse from which she poured ointment on the feet of Christ. Her action was interpreted as supplying the traditional unguent of hospitality which the host had neglected to furnish in honour of his guest. It would also appear that he had failed to provide a container of water in which the guest could wash his feet, an omission which constituted a grave breach of courtesy in those days. The meal served to Jesus in Jericho by Zacchaeus (Lk. 19:6) was probably of lavish proportions. More modest were the family gatherings in Bethany (Lk. 10:40; Jn. 12:2), and the interrupted meal at Emmaus (Lk. 24:30–33) on the first Easter day. Occasionally Christ omitted the traditional hand-washing as a preliminary to a meal in order to teach an important spiritual principle (Lk. 11:37–42).

g. Meals on journeys

Persons undertaking journeys to parts of the country where hospitality was uncertain usually carried an earthen bottle of water (Gn. 21:14) and items of food, such as cakes of figs or raisins, bread and parched corn. The plight of those who 'forgot to take bread' (Mk. 8:1–9, 14) could be very serious under certain circumstances.

III. Religious significance of meals

a. Among the Semites

The communal aspect of a meal was carried over into the religious sphere by all Semitic peoples. Archaeological discoveries at Ras Shamra (Ugarit) have shown the prevalence of such meals in Canaanite religious life. Baal temples were frequently dedicated amidst prolonged feasting and revelry. At Shechem the remains of a Hyksos temple indicated the presence of rooms for banquets consequent upon the performance of sacrificial rites. The Hebrews sought both divine fellowship and pardon by means of meals (*Passover, *Sacrifice, *Feasts) at which the blood and fat were the divine perquisite, while the priests and people received their appointed portions (Lv. 2:10; 7:6). Such sacrifices were common in the kingdom period (1 Sa. 9:11–14, 25; 1 Ch. 29:21–22; 2 Ch. 7:8–10), but were devoid of the licentiousness and debauchery which characterized Canaanite religious meals.

b. In Christianity

The principal sacred meal of Christianity was the *Lord's Supper, instituted by Christ just prior to his crucifixion (Mk. 14:22–25; Mt. 26:26–29; Lk. 22:14–20). In the early church the Agape, a communal meal denoting brotherly love among believers, frequently preceded celebrations of the Lord's Supper. (*Love Feast; *Food.)

Bibliography. EBi, 3, 2989–3002; E. W. Heaton, *Everyday Life in Old Testament Times*, 1956, pp. 81ff.; A. C. Bouquet, *Everyday Life in New Testament Times*, 1954, pp. 69ff. R.K.H.

MEAT MARKET (Gk. *makellon*; Lat. *macellum*). Jewish law forbade dealing in such pagan markets, which sold the flesh of ritually unclean animals. In 1 Cor. 10:25 Paul counsels his readers to avoid what in a later age was known as scrupulosity. On the meat market in Corinth see *JBL* 80, 1934, pp. 134–141. J.D.D.

MECONAH (AV, **MEKONAH**). A town near Ziklag occupied by the Jews under Nehemiah (Ne. 11:28). Simons (*GTT*, p. 155) equates it with Madmannah, but Grollenberg with Machbena, named separately from Madmannah as a Calebite settlement (1 Ch. 2:49). The site is unknown. J.P.U.L.

MEDAN. A son of Abraham by *Keturah (Gn. 25:2; 1 Ch. 1:32). The names of some of the other sons and descendants of Keturah, such as Midian and Dedan, were later known as those of N Arabian tribes (*Arabia), so it may be assumed that Medan likewise settled in this area, though the name is unknown outside the Bible. Medanites were associated with Midianites in the sale of Joseph, according to Gn. 37:36, *MT*. T.C.M.

MEDEBA (Heb. *mêḏᵉḇā'*, possibly 'water of quiet'). A plain and city of Reuben (Jos. 13:9, 16) N of the Arnon. An old Moabite town taken from Moab by Sihon (Nu. 21:21–30), it was used by the Syrian allies of Ammon as a camping-site after their defeat at the hand of Joab (1 Ch. 19:6–15). Thereafter it seems

MEASURES
See Weights and measures, Part 3.

MEATS OFFERED TO IDOLS
See Idols, meats offered to, Part 2.

MEDAD
See Eldad, Part 1.

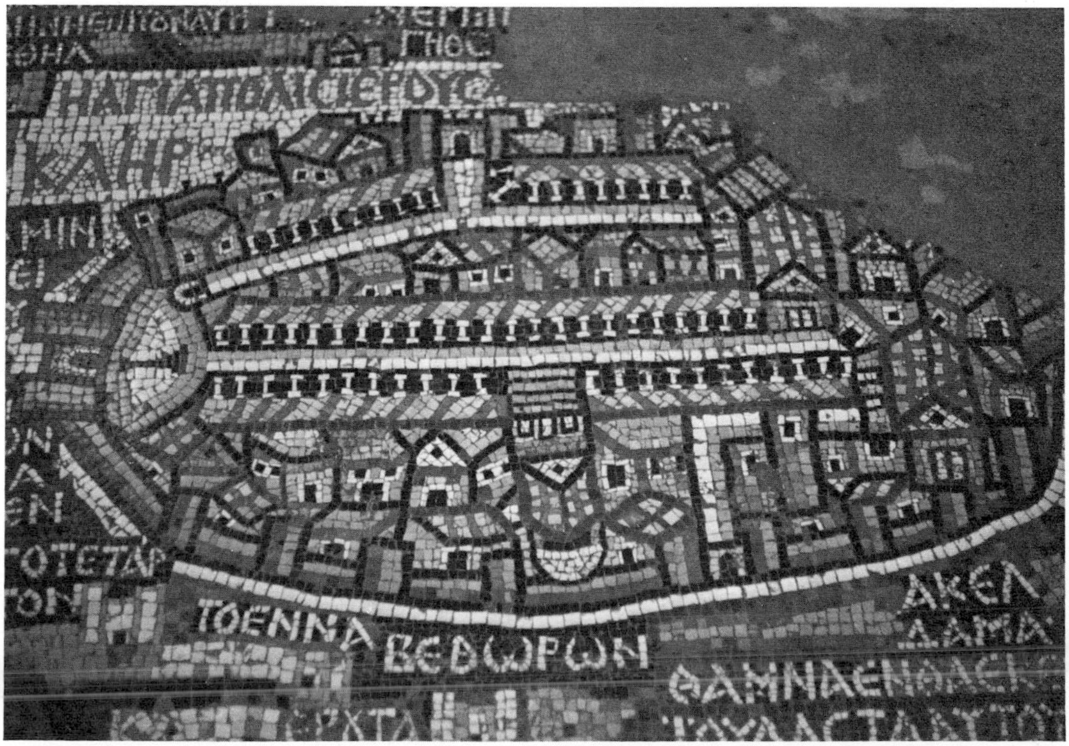

Part of a map made as a mosaic on the floor of St George's church at Medeba, Jordan. This section shows Jerusalem with its streets, gates and churches. 6th cent. AD. (SH)

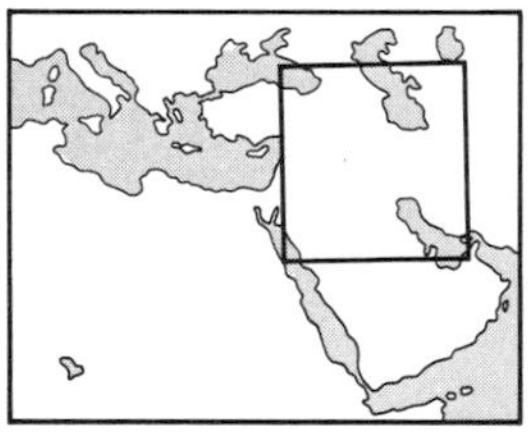

Media, later part of ancient Persia.

to have changed hands several times. It is mentioned in the *Moabite Stone as having been taken by Omri, perhaps from Moab, and as recovered by Mesha and fortified. Recaptured from Moab by Jeroboam II, it is again Moabite in Is. 15:2.

It figured also in the history of the intertestamental era (1 Macc. 9:36ff. as 'Medaba'; Jos., *BJ* 1. 63), before being captured by Hyrcanus after a long siege (Jos., *Ant.* 13. 11, 19).

The site, today called Mādabā, is 10 km S of Heshbon. There in 1896, during excavation of the site of a church, was discovered a 6th-century AD mosaic map showing part of Palestine from Beth-shan to the Nile. See M. Avi-Yonah, *The Madaba Mosaic Map*, 1954. In addition, there are considerable ruins, dating mainly from the Christian era, including a large temple and extensive cisterns. Tombs of Iron Age date have also been found. J.D.D.

MEDES, MEDIA (Heb. *madai*; Assyr. *(A)mada*; Old Pers. *Mada*; Gk. *Medai*).

Media was the name for NW Iran, SW of the Caspian Sea and N of the Zagros Mountains, covering the modern province of Azerbaijan and part of Persian Kurdistan. The inhabitants were called Medes or Medians and were Japhethites (Gn. 10:2), whose Aryan lineage is confirmed by Herodotus (7. 62), Strabo (15. 2. 8) and by the surviving traces of their language. The Medes were steppe-dwellers whose name is first mentioned by Shalmaneser III who raided their plains in 836 BC to obtain their famous, finely bred horses. Later Assyr. kings followed him and sought to keep the E passes open to the traders. Adad-nirari III (810–781 BC) claims to have conquered 'the land of the Medes and Parsua (Persia)', as did Tiglath-pileser III (743 BC) and Sargon II (716 BC). The latter transported Israelites to Media (2 Ki. 17:6; 18:11) after he had overrun the part of the land ruled by Dayaukku (Deioces), whom he exiled for a time to Hamath.

Esarhaddon bound his Median vassals by treaty (*Iraq* 20, 1958, pp. 1–91), but they soon rebelled and joined the Scythians (Ashguza) and Cimmerians against the declining power of Assyria after 631 BC. Under Phraortes there began the open attacks which culminated in the fall of Nineveh (612 BC) and Harran (610 BC) to Kyaxares of Media and his Bab. allies. The Medes controlled all lands to the N of Assyria and clashed with Lydia until peace was ratified in 585 BC.

In 550 BC *Cyrus of Anshan (*ELAM) defeated Astyages and brought Media under control, capturing the capital Ecbatana and adding 'King of the Medes' to his titles. Many Medes were given positions of responsibility and their customs and laws were combined with those of the Persians (Dn. 6:8, 15). Media was sometimes used to denote Persia but more usually combined with it as a major part of the new confederation (Dn. 8:20; Est. 1:19). The Medes, as seen by the prophets Isaiah (13:17) and Jeremiah (51:11, 28), took part in the capture of Babylon (Dn. 5:28). The new ruler of Babylon, *Darius, was called 'the Mede' (Dn. 11:1), being the son of Ahasuerus of Median origin (Dn. 9:1).

The Medes later rebelled under Darius I and II (409 BC). The history of the Jews in Media is recounted in Esther (1:3, 14, 18–19) and the Medians under Syrians (Seleucids) and Parthians are referred to in 1 Macc. 14:1–3; Josephus, *Ant.* 10. 232. Media was organized as the 11th and 18th Satrapies. The Medes are mentioned, with the Parthians and Elamites, in Acts 2:9. After the Sassanids Media was used only as a geographical term.

BIBLIOGRAPHY. G. Widengren, *POTT*, pp. 313ff. D.J.W.

MEDIATOR. The term occurs infrequently in the Scriptures (Gal. 3:19–20; 1 Tim. 2:5; Heb. 8:6; 9:15; 12:24; Jb. 9:33, LXX). But the idea of mediation and therefore of persons acting in the capacity of mediator permeates the Bible. The function of a mediator is to intervene between two parties in order to promote relations between them which the parties themselves are not able to effect. The situation requiring the offices of a mediator

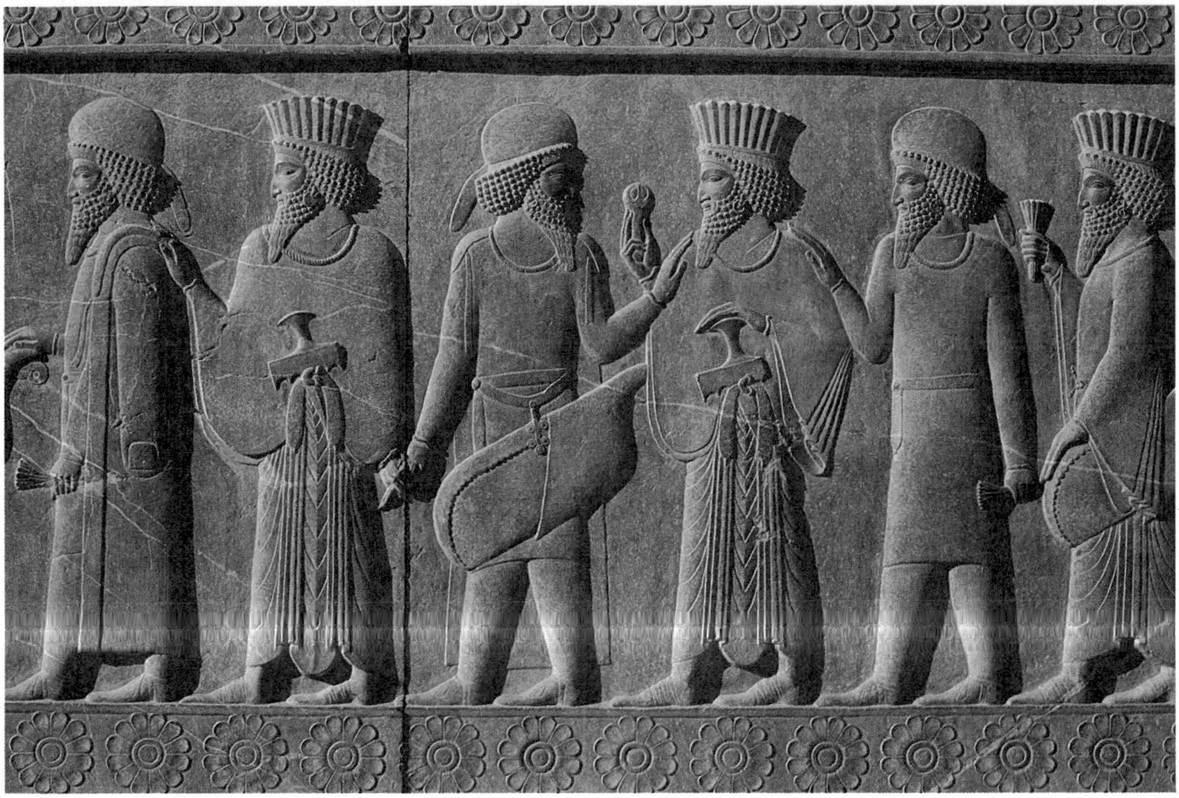

Medes wearing rounded hats and short tunics are distinguished from the Persians who wear high, fluted crowns and ankle-length robes on this relief from the Apandana, Persepolis, Iran. Height of figures c. 0·80 m. c. 485–465 BC. (BPL)

is often one of estrangement and alienation, and the mediator effects reconciliation. In the sphere of human relations Joab acted the part of mediator between David and Absalom (2 Sa. 14:1–23). Job expresses the need in regard to his relations to God when he said, 'There is no umpire (AV 'daysman') between us, who might lay his hand upon us both' (Jb. 9:33).

I. In the Old Testament

In the OT the prophet and the priest fulfilled, most characteristically, the office of mediator in the institution which God established in terms of covenant relations with his people. The prophet was God's spokesman; he acted for God in the presence of men (*cf.* Dt. 18:18–22). The priest acted on behalf of men in the presence of God (Ex. 28:1; Lv. 9:7; 16:6; Nu. 16:40; 2 Ch. 26:18; Heb. 5:1–4; *cf.* Jb. 42:8). In the OT, however, Moses, of all human instruments, was the mediator *par excellence* (*cf.* Ex. 32:30–32; Nu. 12:6–8; Gal. 3:19; Heb. 3:2–5). He was the mediator of the old covenant, because it was through his instrumentality that the covenant at Sinai was dispensed and ratified (*cf.* Ex. 19:3–8, 24:3–8; Acts 7:37–39). It is with Moses that Jesus as Mediator of the new covenant is compared and contrasted.

II. Christ as mediator

The designation 'Mediator' belongs pre-eminently to Christ, and even those men who executed mediatory offices in the OT institution were thus appointed only because the institution in which they performed these functions was the shadow of the archetypal realities fulfilled in Christ (*cf.* Jn. 1:17; Heb. 7:27–28; 9:23–24; 10:1). Jesus is the Mediator of the new covenant (Heb. 9:15; 12:24). And it is a better covenant (Heb. 8:6) because it brings to consummate fruition the grace which *covenant administration embodies. Christ is the 'one mediator between God and men' (1 Tim. 2:5). To invest any other with this prerogative is to assail the unique honour that belongs to him as well as to deny the express assertion of the text.

Though the title 'Mediator' is not often used, the Scripture abounds in references to the mediatory work of Christ.

a. Pre-incarnate mediation

As the eternal and pre-existent Son he was Mediator in the creation of the heavens and the earth (Jn. 1:3, 10; Col. 1:16; Heb. 1:2). This activity in the economy of creation is correlative with his mediatorship in the economy of redemption. The omnipotence evidenced in the former and the prerogatives that belong to him as Creator are indispensable to the execution of redemption. It is in redemption, however, that the extensiveness of his mediation appears. All along the line of the redemptive process from its inception to the consummation his mediacy enters.

Election as the ultimate fount of salvation did not take place apart from Christ. The elect were chosen in him before the foundation of the world (Eph. 1:4) and they were predestinated to be conformed to his image (Rom. 8:29).

b. Mediation in salvation and redemption

It is particularly in the once-for-all accomplishment of salvation and redemption that his mediatory action is patent (*cf.* Jn. 3:17; Acts 15:11; 20:28; Rom. 3:24–25; 5:10–11; 7:4; 2 Cor. 5:18; Eph. 1:7; Col. 1:20; 1 Jn. 4:9). The accent falls upon the death, blood and cross of Christ as the action through which redemption has been wrought. In the Scriptures the death of Christ is always conceived of as an event in which Jesus is intensely active in obedience to the Father's commandment and in fulfilment of his commission (*cf.* Jn. 10:17–18; Phil. 2:8). It is Jesus' activity as Mediator in the shedding of his blood that accords to his death its saving

MEDICINE See Health, Part 2.

efficacy. When salvation wrought is viewed as reconciliation and propitiation, it is here that the mediatory function is most clearly illustrated. Reconciliation presupposes alienation between God and men and consists in the removal of that alienation. The result is peace with God (*cf.* Rom. 5:1; Eph. 2:12–17). Propitiation is directed to the wrath of God and Jesus, as the propitiation, makes God propitious to us (*cf.* 1 Jn. 2:2).

c. Continued mediation

Christ's mediation is not confined to his finished work of redemption. His mediatory activity is never suspended. In our participation of the fruits of redemption we are dependent upon his continued intervention as Mediator. Our access to God and our introduction into the grace of God are through him; he conveys us into the Father's presence (Jn. 14:6; Rom. 5:2; Eph. 2:18). It is through him that grace reigns through righteousness to eternal life, and grace and peace are multiplied to the enjoyment of the fullness of Christ (*cf.* Rom. 1:5; 5:21; 2 Cor. 1:5; Phil. 1:11). The most characteristic exercises of devotion on the part of the believer are offered through Christ. Thanksgiving and prayer are not only exercised in the grace which Christ imparts but are also presented to God through Christ (*cf.* Jn. 14:14; Rom. 1:8; 7:25; Col. 3:17; Heb. 13:15). The acceptableness of the believer's worship and service springs from the virtue and efficacy of Christ's mediation, and nothing is a spiritual sacrifice except as rendered through him (1 Pet. 2:5). Even the pleas presented to others for the discharge of their obligations derive their most solemn sanction from the fact that they are urged through Christ and in his name (Rom. 15:30; 2 Cor. 10:1; *cf.* Rom. 12:1).

The continued mediation of Christ is specially exemplified in his heavenly ministry at the right hand of God. This ministry concerns particularly his priestly and kingly offices. He is a Priest for ever (Heb. 7:21, 24). An important aspect of this priestly ministry in the heavens is intercession directed to the Father and drawing within its scope every need of the people of God. Jesus is exalted in his human nature, and it is out of the reservoir of fellow feeling forged in the trials and temptations of his humiliation (Heb. 2:17–18; 4:15) that he meets every exigency of the believer's warfare. Every grace bestowed flows through the channel of Christ's intercession (Rom. 8:34; Heb. 7:25; *cf.* 1 Jn. 2:1) until the salvation which he has secured will reach its fruition in conformity to his image. The priestly ministry of Christ, however, must not be restricted to intercession. He is High Priest over the house of God (Heb. 3:1–6), and this administration involves many other functions. In his kingly office he is exalted above all principality and power (Eph. 1:20–23), and he will reign to the end of bringing all enemies into subjection (1 Cor. 15:25). This is Christ's mediatorial dominion, and it embraces all authority in heaven and in earth (Mt. 28:18; Jn. 3:35; 5:26–27; Acts 2:36; Phil. 2:9–11).

It is eschatology that will finally manifest and vindicate Christ's mediatorship; the resurrection and judgment will be wrought by him. All the dead, just and unjust, will be raised by his summons (Jn. 5:28–29). It is in him that the just will be raised to immortality and incorruption (1 Cor. 15:22, 52–54; 1 Thes. 4:16), and with him they will be glorified (Rom. 8:17; *cf.* Jn. 11:25; Rom. 14:9). The final judgment will be executed by him (Mt. 25:31–46; Jn. 5:27; Acts 17:31).

d. Conclusion

Christ's mediatorship is thus exercised in all the phases of redemption from election in God's eternal counsel to the consummation of salvation. He is Mediator in humiliation and exaltation. There is, therefore, multiformity attaching to his mediatorial activity, and it cannot be defined in terms of one idea or function. His mediatorship has as many facets as his person, office and work. And as there is diversity in the offices and tasks discharged and in the relations he sustains to men as Mediator, so there is also diversity in the relations he sustains to the Father and the Holy Spirit in the economy of redemption. The faith and worship of him require that we recognize this diversity. And the unique glory that is his as Mediator demands that we accord to no other even the semblance of that prerogative that belongs to him as the one Mediator between God and man.

BIBLIOGRAPHY. J. Calvin, *Institutes of the Christian Religion*, 2. 12; G. Stevenson, *Treatise on the Offices of Christ*, 1845; R. I. Wilberforce, *The Doctrine of the Incarnation of Our Lord Jesus Christ*, 1875, pp. 166–211; P. G. Medd, *The One Mediator*, 1884; W. Symington, *On the Atonement and Intercession of Christ*, Part 2, 1839; W. L. Alexander, *A System of Biblical Theology*, 1888, 1, p. 425, 2, p. 212; J. S. Candlish, *The Christian Salvation*, 1899, pp. 1–12; E. Brunner, *The Mediator*, 1934; H. B. Swete, *The Ascended Christ*, 1916, pp. 87–100; V. Taylor, *The Names of Jesus*, 1954, pp. 110–113; A. Oepke, *TDNT* 4, pp. 598–624; J. Guhrt, O. Becker, *NIDNTT* 1, pp. 365–376. J.M.

MEEKNESS. The high place accorded to meekness in the list of human virtues is due to the example and teaching of Jesus Christ. Pagan writers paid greater respect to the self-confident man. However, its roots lie in the OT. The adjective *'ānāw* is usually translated 'meek' in AV but by a variety of words in RSV related to its basic meaning, 'poor and afflicted', from which the spiritual quality of patient submission, humility, is derived, *e.g.* Pss. 22:26; 25:9; Is. 29:19. Meekness is a quality of the Messianic King (Zc. 9:9) and the theme of Ps. 37:11, 'the meek shall inherit the earth' (AV), is repeated by our Lord in the Beatitudes (Mt. 5:5). In meekness Moses, while maintaining strength of leadership, was ready to accept personal injury without resentment or recrimination (Nu. 12:1–3).

In the NT meekness (*prautēs* and adjective *praus*) refers to an inward attitude, whereas *gentleness is expressed rather in outward action. It is part of the fruit of Christlike character produced only by the Spirit (Gal. 5:23, AV). The meek do not resent adversity because they accept everything as being the effect of God's wise and loving purpose for them, so that they accept injuries from men also (as Moses above), knowing that these are permitted by God for their ultimate good (*cf.* 2 Sa. 16:11). The meekness and gentleness of Christ was the source of Paul's own plea to the disloyal Corinthians (2 Cor. 10:1). He enjoined meekness as the spirit in which to rebuke an erring brother (2 Tim. 2:25, AV), and when bearing with one another (Eph. 4:2). Similarly, Peter exhorted that the inquiring or arguing heathen should be answered in meekness (1 Pet. 3:15, AV). Supremely meekness is revealed in the character of Jesus (Mt. 11:29, AV; 21:5, AV), demonstrated in superlative degree when he stood before his unjust accusers without a word of retort or self-justification.

BIBLIOGRAPHY. F. Hauck, S. Schulz, *TDNT* 6, pp. 645–651.

J.C.C.

MEGIDDO. An important OT city which lay in the Carmel range some 30 km SSE of the modern port of Haifa.

I. Biblical evidence

The city of Megiddo (Heb. *m^e^giddô*) is first mentioned among the cities which Joshua captured during his conquest of Palestine (Jos. 12:21) and was subsequently allotted to Manasseh in the territory of Issachar (Jos. 17:11; 1 Ch. 7:29). Manasseh, however, did not destroy the Canaanites in the city but put them to menial labour (Jdg. 1:28). A curiously indirect reference is made to Megiddo in the Song of Deborah, where * Taanach is described as 'by the waters of Megid-

Model of the city of Megiddo in the 1st millennium BC*, showing storehouses, administrative buildings and gateway.* (NPAI)

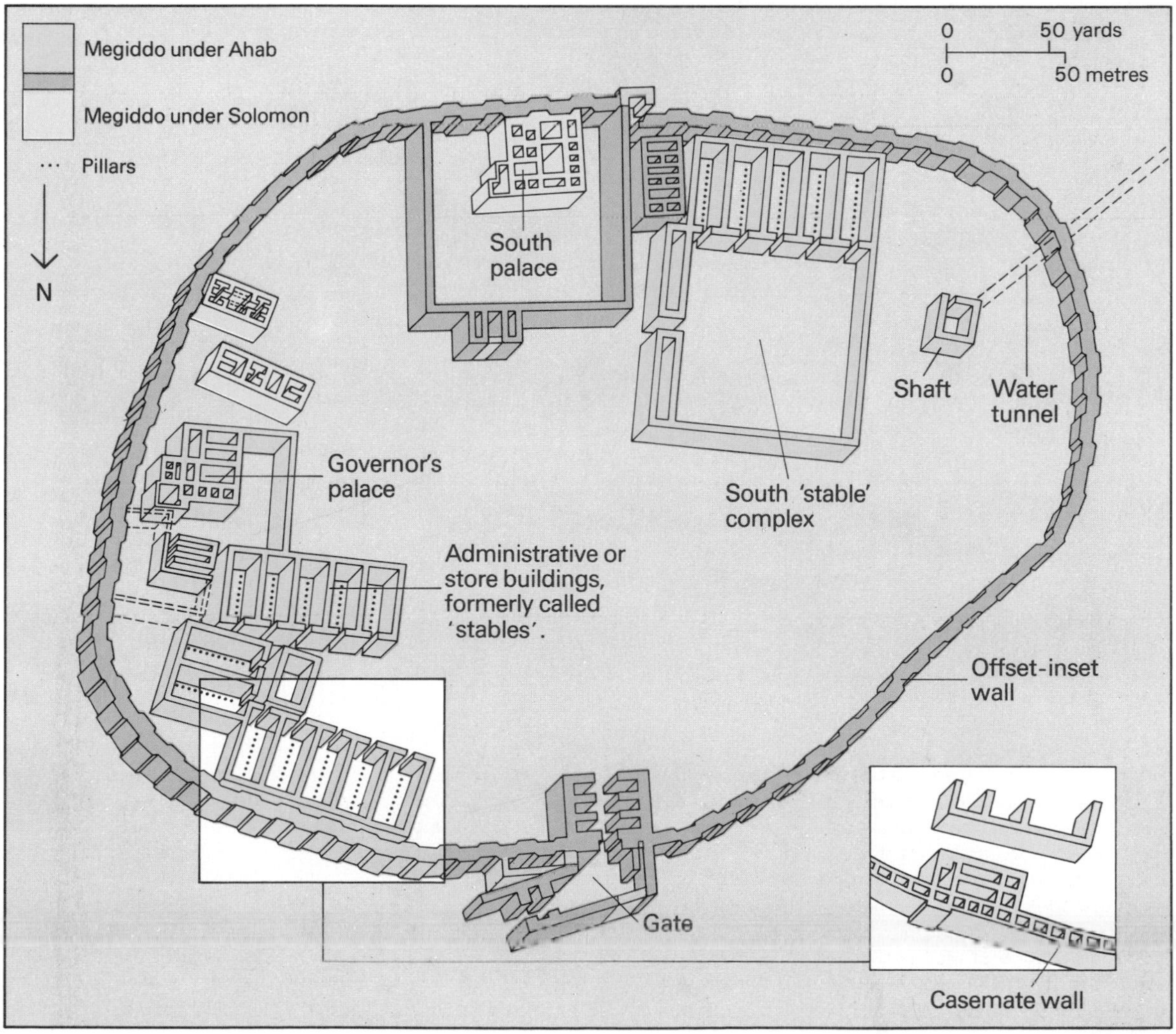

Megiddo, showing the excavated areas of the city in the times of Solomon and Ahab (Levels VA–IVB Solomon, IVA Ahab).

Megiddo. Ahab's 'stables', pillared buildings now considered to have been store-houses or barracks. Level IVA. 9th cent. BC. (SH)

Ivory box with lions and sphinx, Phoenician style. Part of the ivory hoard found at Megiddo. Height c. 6 cm. Mid-14th to 12th cent. BC. (IM)

do' (*'al-mê m^{e}ḡiddô*, Jdg. 5:19), but no mention of Megiddo as a city as opposed to the name of a water-course is made (*KISHON). The next reference to the city comes from the time of Solomon, when it was included in his fifth administrative district under Baana (the son of Ahilud) (1 Ki. 4:12) and was selected, with Hazor and Gezer, to be one of his main fortified cities outside Jerusalem, in which he had accommodation for chariots and horses (1 Ki. 9:15–19). Megiddo is briefly mentioned as the place where Ahaziah of Judah died after being wounded in his flight from Jehu (2 Ki. 9:27), and it was later the scene of the death of Josiah when he tried to prevent *Neco of Egypt from going to the aid of Assyria (2 Ki. 23:29–30; 2 Ch. 35:22, 24). The name occurs in the form *m^{e}ḡiddôn* in Zechariah (12:11), and it is this form which is used in the NT *Armageddon (Rev. 16:16), from *har-m^{e}ḡiddôn*, 'hill of Megiddo'.

This fragment of an Akkadian clay tablet, containing part of the Babylonian Epic of Gilgamesh, *was found near the gate at Megiddo. It illustrates early literary contacts between Palestine and Mesopotamia. 14th cent. BC.* (IM)

II. Extra-biblical sources

The site of ancient Megiddo has been identified with the modern deserted mound of Tell el-Mutesellim, which lies on the N side of the Carmel ridge and commands the most important pass from the coastal plain to the valley of Esdraelon. The tell stands nearly 21 m high, with an area on the summit of over 10 acres, and the earlier cities lower down in the mound were still larger than this. The first excavations were carried out by a German expedition under G. Schumacher from 1903 to 1905. A trench was cut across the top of the mound, and a number of buildings were found, but owing to the limited knowledge of pottery at the time little was learnt. The site was not excavated again until 1925, when the Oriental Institute of the University of Chicago under the direction of J. H. Breasted selected it as the first major project in an ambitious scheme of excavations all over the Near East. The work was directed successively by C. S. Fisher (1925–7), P. L. O. Guy (1927–35), and G. Loud (1935–9). The original intention was to clear the entire

Partial restoration of the 'stable' (or store-room) complex dating from the time of Ahab at Megiddo (Level IVA). Stones from the earlier and casemate wall were re-used by Ahab's builders. (OIUC)

mound, level by level, to the base, and to this end an area at the foot of the slope was excavated at an early stage to release it for the subsequent dumping of earth from the tell. War brought the work to an end, and though the lay-out of the entire city in Iron Age times had been revealed, the earlier levels were known only in a relatively small area. Further excavations were carried out in 1960, 1966–7 and 1971 by Y. Yadin to elucidate some problems outstanding from the previous campaigns.

Twenty main occupation levels were identified, dating back to Chalcolithic settlements in the early 4th millennium (levels XX, XIX). An interesting feature of level XIX is a small shrine with an altar in it. During the Early Bronze Age (3rd millennium) there was a considerable city at Megiddo (levels XVIII–XVI), one interesting feature of which was a circular platform of boulders approached by a flight of steps, which was covered with animal bones and broken pottery. It may be that this was a *bāmâ* or *'high place'. This platform continued in use in the Middle Bronze Age (levels XV–X; first half of the 2nd millennium), a period of Egyp. influence the start of which was marked by widespread rebuilding, in which the circular platform became the nucleus of three megaron-shaped temples with *altars. A fine triple-piered gateway, of a type which originated in Mesopotamia, was also found in these levels, and the necessity of such strong gates was shown by the evidence of a number of major destructions in the latter part of the period, culminating in a great devastation probably to be connected with the Egyp. reconquest of Palestine following the expulsion of the Hyksos from Egypt.

The evidences of periodical violence are less frequent in the Late Bronze Age (levels VIII, VII), and though this was a period of Egyp. domination the culture of Palestine reflected the Canaanite civilization of the N to a considerable extent. It was in this period that perhaps the most fully reported battle of antiquity was fought when Tuthmosis III routed an Asiatic coalition at Megiddo *c*. 1468 BC. Architectural remains of this period include a temple, a palace and a gate, and the N cultural influence is clearly seen in a great hoard of over 200 objects of carved ivory which was found in a subterranean treasury under the level VII palace. This is one of the earliest collections of a type of art which was well known in Iron Age times from *Samaria and from as far afield as Assyria, and though practically no examples have yet been discovered in Phoenicia it is probable that many of them were made either in Phoenician workshops or by expatriate Phoenician craftsmen. That there were contacts with Mesopotamia at this period is shown by the recent discovery on the edge of the mound of a fragment of the Bab. Epic of Gilgamesh which can be dated by its cuneiform script to the 14th century BC.

Another discovery, probably of this period, was the city water-supply systems. An unbuilt zone of the mound was excavated by a pit 37 m deep, the bottom section of which consisted of a shaft with a staircase round its side, cut into the rock at the base. From the foot of the shaft, the staircase entered a tunnel which, finally levelling off, led, some 50 m farther on, into a cave with a spring of water at the far end. It appeared that this spring had originally (VIA) given on to the slope outside the city, but at a later period the tunnel had been cut from inside the city and the cave was blocked and masked from the outside for strategic reasons.

Though there are signs of destruction towards the end of the 12th century, some time after the arrival of the Israelites, and evidence of a temporary abandonment following this destruction, the people responsible for resettling the mound (V) do not seem to have been Israelites. This would accord with the biblical statement that the inhabitants of Megiddo were not driven out at the time of the Conquest, and were later put to task work (Jdg. 1:27–28). A number of cult objects, limestone horned incense *altars, clay incense stands and braziers, from this and the following levels, are probably due to these Canaanites, who, contrary to God's command, were not destroyed. It is probably to the latter part of this and the beginning of the next level (VA–IVB) that a six-chambered city gate and associated casemate wall (*ARCHITECTURE) are to be assigned, as Y. Yadin has shown. These are almost identical in plan with examples found at Hazor and Gezer, and are probably with little doubt to be assigned to the time of Solomon, a fact which illuminates 1 Ki. 9:15–19.

The pre-war excavations uncovered an extensive series of stables, capable of accommodating up to 450 horses, and the excavators connected these with Solomon, who was known to have instituted a *chariot arm in his forces; but Yadin's investigations have shown that these stables date from the latter part of level IV (IVA), which was probably rebuilt after the destruction of the Solomonic city by the Pharaoh Sheshonq (*SHISHAK). The stables are therefore very probably the work of Ahab, who is known from the Annals of Shalmaneser to have had a chariot force of 2,000 vehicles. The final Israelite level (III) was probably destroyed in 733 BC by Tiglath-pileser III, when the city became the capital of an Assyr. province. With the decline in the fortunes of Assyria, this city (level II) came once more within the territory of Israel, and the defeat and death of Josiah there in 609 BC is probably marked by its destruction.

The excavations at Megiddo have shown what a formidable civilization the Israelites under Joshua had to encounter when they invaded the land.

BIBLIOGRAPHY. G. Schumacher and C. Steuernagel, *Tell el-Mutesellim*, 1, *Fundbericht*, 1908; C. Watzinger, 2, *Die Funde*, 1929; R. S. Lamon and G. S. Shipton, *Megiddo I: Seasons of 1925–34*, 1939; G. Loud, *Megiddo II: Seasons of 1935–1939*, 1948; H. G. May, *Material Remains of the Megiddo Cult*, 1935; P. L. O. Guy and R. M. Engberg, *Megiddo Tombs*, 1938; G. Loud, *The Megiddo Ivories*, 1939; W. F. Albright, *AJA* 53, 1949, pp. 213–215; G. E. Wright, *JAOS* 70, 1950, pp. 56–60; *idem*, *BA* 13, 1950, pp. 28–46; Y. Yadin, *BA* 33, 1970, pp. 66–96; *idem*, *Hazor* (Schweich Lectures, 1970), 1972, pp. 150–164; A. Goetze and S. Levy, 'Fragment of the Gilgamesh Epic from Megiddo', *'Atiqot*, 2, 1959, pp. 121–128; *IDBS*, 1976, pp. 583–585.

T.C.M.

MEKAL
See Nergal, Part 2.

MEKONA
See Mecona, Part 2.

MELCHIAS
See Malchijah, Part 2.

MELCHIZEDEK (Heb. *malkî-ṣeḏeq*, 'Ṣedeq is (my) king' or, as in Heb. 7:2, 'king of righteousness'). He was the king of Salem (probably Jerusalem) and priest of 'God Most High' (*'ēl 'elyôn*) who greeted Abram on his return from the rout of *Chedorlaomer and his allies, presented him with bread and wine, blessed him in the name of God Most High and received from him a tenth part of the booty which had been taken from the enemy (Gn. 14:18ff.). Abram thereupon declined the king of Sodom's offer to let him keep all the booty apart from the recovered prisoners, swearing by God Most High that he would allow no man to have the honour of making him rich (v. 22, where *MT*, but not Samaritan, LXX, or Pesh., adds *Yahweh* before *'ēl 'elyôn*, thus emphasizing that the two names denote one and the same God). The incident is probably to be dated in the Middle Bronze Age (*ABRAHAM). Melchizedek's name may be compared with that of a later king of Jerusalem, Adoni-zedek (Jos. 10:1ff.).

In Ps. 110:4 a Davidic king is acclaimed by divine oath as 'a priest for ever after the order of Melchizedek'. The background of this acclamation is provided by David's conquest of Jerusalem *c.* 1000 BC, by virtue of which David and his house became heirs to Melchizedek's dynasty of priest-kings. The king so acclaimed was identified by Jesus and his contemporaries as the Davidic Messiah (Mk. 12:35ff.). If Jesus is the Davidic Messiah, he must be the 'priest for ever after the order of Melchizedek'. This inevitable conclusion is drawn by the writer to the Hebrews, who develops his theme of our Lord's heavenly priesthood on the basis of Ps. 110:4, expounded in the light of Gn. 14:18ff., where Melchizedek appears and disappears suddenly, with nothing said about his birth or death, ancestry or descent, in a manner which declares his superiority to Abram and, by implication, to the Aaronic priesthood descended from Abram. The superiority of Christ and his new order to the levitical order of OT times is thus established (Heb. 5:6–11; 6:20–7:28).

A fragmentary text from Cave 11 at Qumran (11QMelch.) envisages Melchizedek as divinely appointed judge in the heavenly court, expounding Pss. 7:7ff.; 82:1ff. in this sense (*cf.* A. S. van der Woude, 'Melchisedech als himmlische Erlösergestalt', *OTS* 14, 1965, pp. 354ff.).

BIBLIOGRAPHY. Commentaries on Genesis, Psalms, Hebrews; F. F. Bruce, *The Epistle to the Hebrews*, *NIC*, 1964, pp. 94ff., 133ff.; H. H. Rowley, 'Melchizedek and Zadok', *Festschrift für A. Bertholet* (ed. W. Baumgartner *et al.*), 1950, pp. 461ff.; A. R. Johnson, *Sacral Kingship in Ancient Israel*, 1955; O. Cullmann, *The Christology of the New Testament*, 1959, pp. 83ff.; J. A. Fitzmyer, *Essays on the Semitic Background of the NT*, 1971, pp. 221–269; F. L. Horton, *The Melchizedek Tradition*, 1976; B. A. Demarest, *A History of Interpretation of Hebrews 7:1–10 from the Reformation to the Present*, 1976.

F.F.B.

MELZAR. The subordinate official in charge of Daniel and his companions, to whom Daniel appealed for a change of diet (Dn. 1:11–16). In AV it is translated as a proper name, as in Theodotion, Lucian, and in Syr., Vulg. and Arab. vss. LXX gives 'Abiesdri', and identifies him with the chief of the eunuchs in v. 3.

Most scholars now regard it as a title, probably a loan-word from the Assyr. *maṣṣāru*, 'guardian' (see *BDB*). Probably we should read 'steward' (RSV), 'overseer' (Nowack), or 'warden' (J. A. Montgomery, *Daniel*, *ICC*, 1926).

J.G.G.N.

MEMPHIS (Egyp. *Mn-nfr*; Heb. *Mōp̄* and *Nōp̄*). Situated on the Nile, at about 24 km from the apex of the Delta. It was a foundation of Menes (the White Walls), the pharaoh who united Upper and Lower Egypt. The name *Mn-nfr* is short for that of the temenos of the pyramid of Pepi (*c.* 2400 BC). It was the capital of Egypt during the Old Kingdom. It remained an important city up to the conquest by Alexander the Great (332 BC). Principal gods were Ptah, the demiurge, Sekhmet, Nefertem and Sokaris. The name *Hwt-k'-Ptḥ*, 'mansion of the Ka of Ptah', is the origin of the name Egypt. Very little remains of the city of the living (Mît-Rahîna); the necropolis

MELITA
See Malta, Part 2.

MELONS
See Vegetables, Part 3.

MEMPHIBAAL
See Mephibosheth, Part 2.

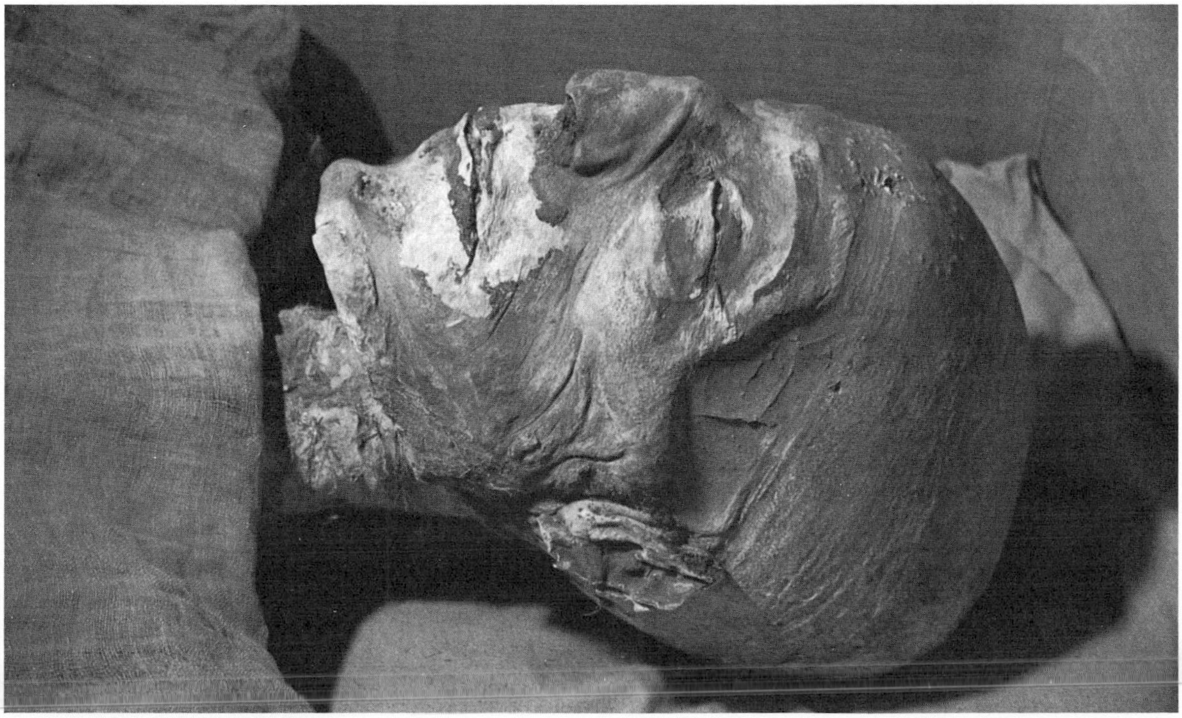

Mummy of Merenptah, a pharaoh (c. 1220 BC) who built extensively at Memphis. (PAC)

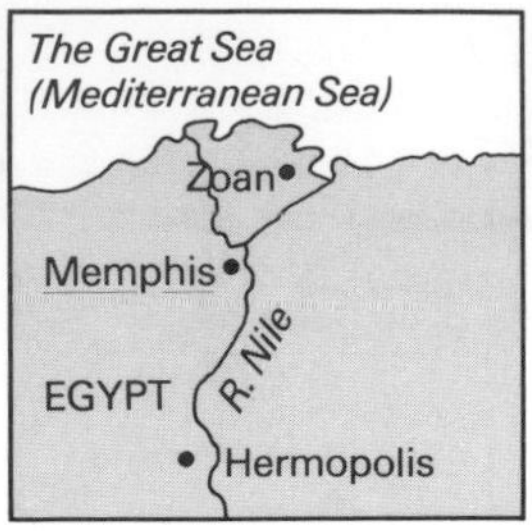

Plan of excavated temple areas at Memphis.

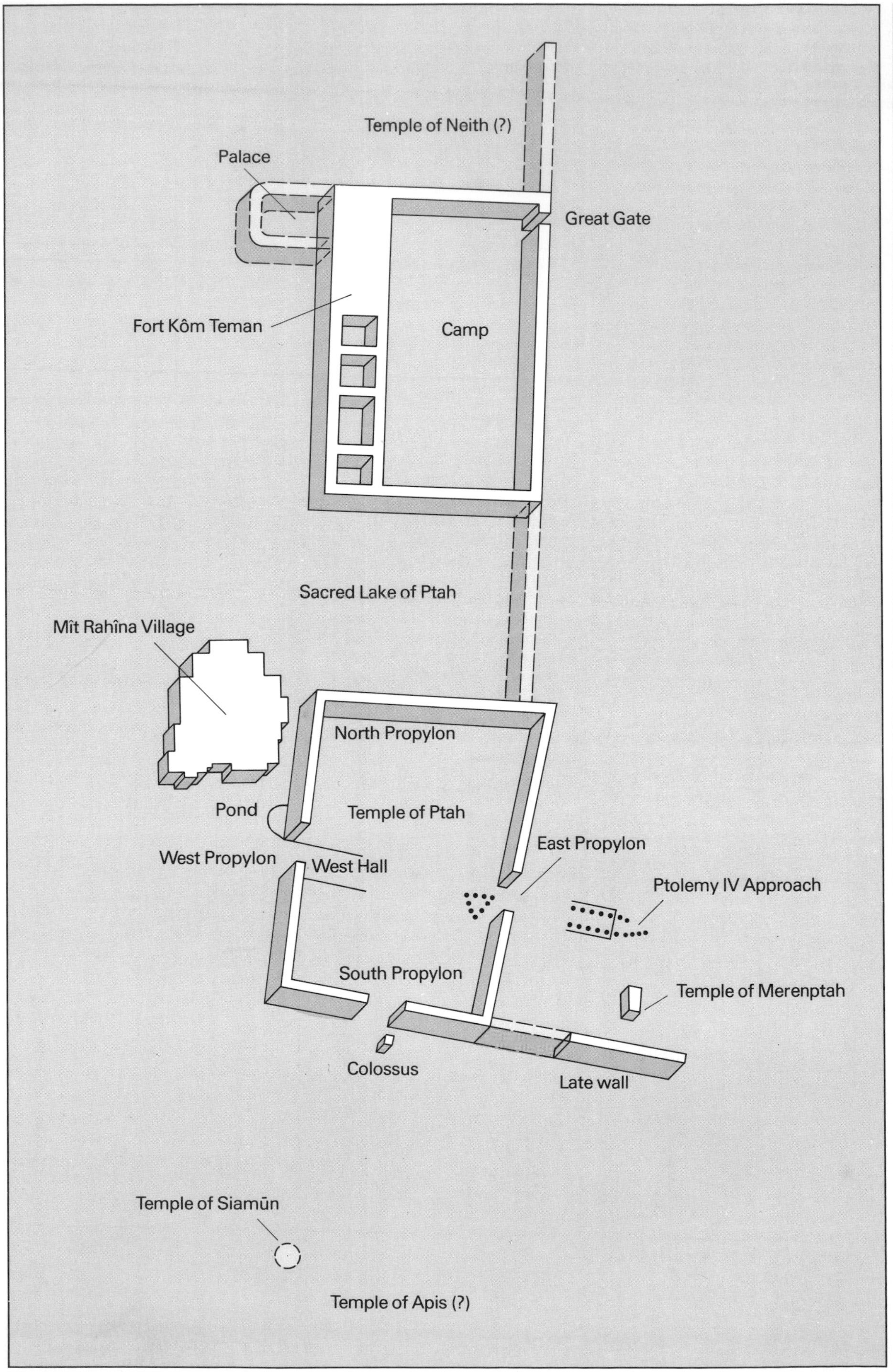

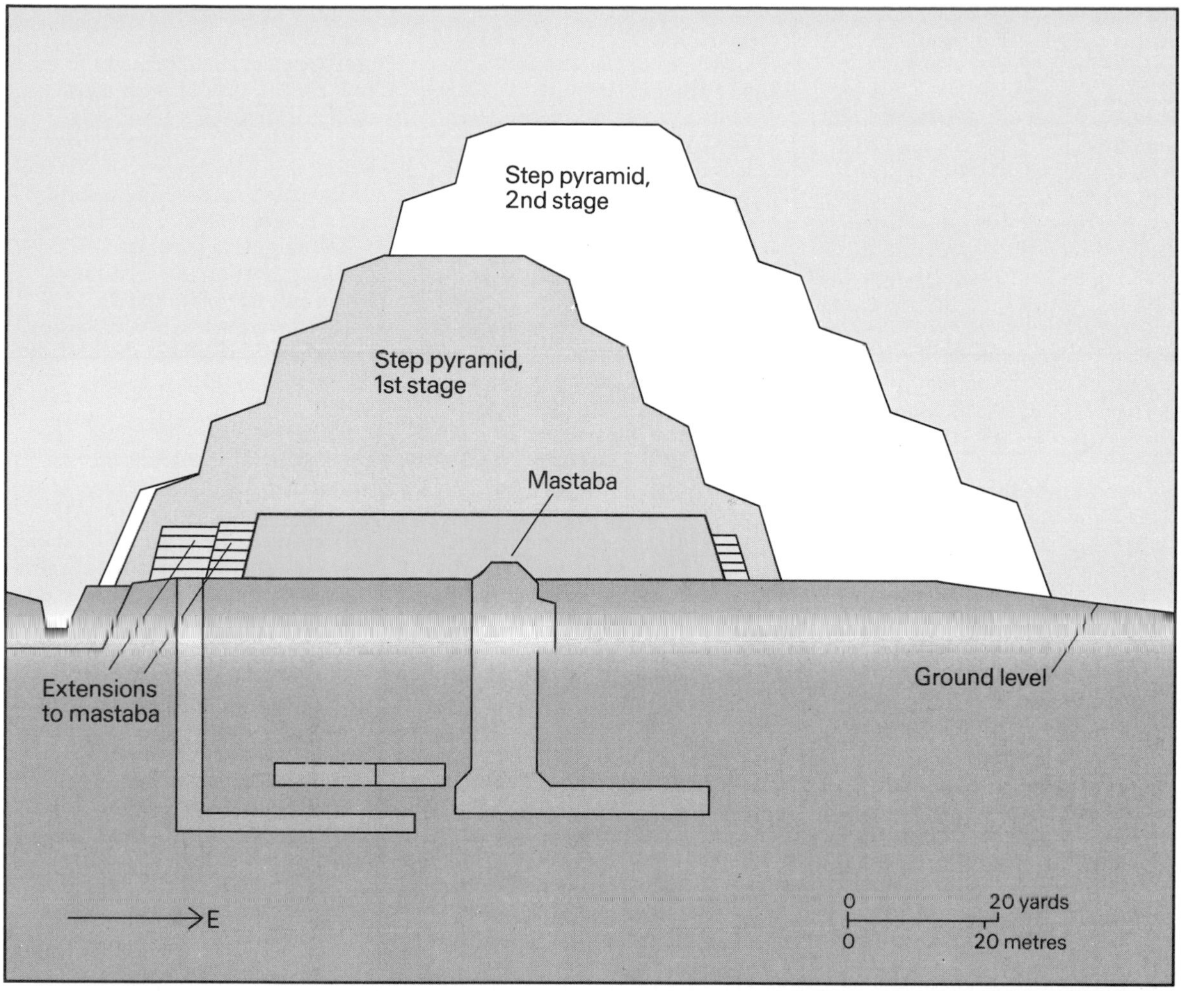

Section through the pyramid of Djeser at Memphis to show its development from a simple mastaba (bench tomb).

The pyramid of Djeser (Zoser), Memphis (Saqqara). Stages were added over the original mastaba (bench tomb) to form this first stepped pyramid. 3rd Dynasty (Old Kingdom). c. 2686–2613 BC. (PAC)

is better known with the important ruins of Djeser at Saqqara, the pyramid of Djedefrê at Abu Rawash, the pyramids of Kheops, Khephren and Mykerinos at Gîza, and those of the 5th Dynasty at Abusîr. Rameses II, Merenptah and Psammetichus pursued extensive building in the region. The temple is described by Herodotus (2. 153), and writers of old describe the place where the living Apis bull was kept. During the New Kingdom, as a consequence of Asiatic immigration, we find that foreign gods, such as Qadesh, Astarte and Baal, were worshipped at Memphis.

The city was taken by the Ethiopians (Piankhy 730 BC), the Assyrians (Esarhaddon 671, Ashurbanipal 666) and the Persians (Cambyses 525).

From the 7th century BC, colonies of foreigners established themselves in the place, and, after the destruction of Jerusalem, also Jews (Je. 44:1). The city is mentioned several times by the prophets (Ho. 9:6; Is. 19:13; Je. 2:16; 46:14, 19; Ezk. 30:13, 16).

BIBLIOGRAPHY. F. Petrie, *Memphis*, 1, 2, 3, 1909–10; Kees, in *RE, s.v.*; Porter and Moss, *Topographical Bibliography*, 3, 1931.

C.D.W.

MENAHEM (Heb. *m^{e}naḥēm*, 'comforter', 2 Ki. 15:14–22). The son of Gadi, and military governor of Tirzah, the older capital of Israel.

When *Shallum usurped the throne during a time of anarchy, Menahem resisted, attacked Shallum in Samaria, captured the city, put the usurper to death and was himself proclaimed king (*c.* 752 BC). Some opposition to him continued, and in the town of Tiphsah Menahem suppressed a serious rebellion, evidently with needless cruelty. To strengthen his position he became a vassal of Pul, king of Assyria (*TIGLATH-PILESER III; *DOTT*, pp. 53–58; *ANET*, p. 283). This privilege cost Menahem 1,000 talents, which he exacted from wealthy men in his realm. The alliance turned out to be a disastrous one for Israel, for it led eventually to an Assyrian annexation of the nation. Menahem's policy was resisted in Israel by an anti-Assyrian party, but he maintained his position till his death (*c.* 742/1) and was succeeded by his son Pekahiah. Menahem was the last king of Israel whose son followed him on the throne.

For the chronology of his reign, see H. Tadmor, *Scripta Hierosolymitana*, 8, 1961, pp. 248–266.

J.D.D.

Menahem is one of the names written in Aramaic on this ostracon, found at Calah (Nimrud), Iraq. The names are probably those of men taken there as exiles from Palestine or a neighbouring country. c. 700 BC. (BSAI)

MENE, MENE, TEKEL, UPHARSIN. The writing on the wall at Belshazzar's feast (Dn. 5:25, RSV 'MENE, MENE, TEKEL, and PARSIN', since the *u* of *u-pharsin* is the conjunction 'and', after which *p* becomes the spirant *ph* [*p̄*]). In Daniel's interpretation (vv. 26–28) *m^{e}nē'* is derived from Aram. *m^{e}nā'*, 'to number', indicating that the days of the Chaldean empire have been *numbered* and brought to an end; *t^{e}qēl* is derived from Aram. *t^{e}qal*, 'to weigh' (*cf.* Heb. *šāqal*, whence 'shekel'), indicating that Belshazzar has been *weighed* in the divine scales and found wanting; and the plural *parsîn* is replaced by the singular *p^{e}rēs*, which is derived from Aram. *p^{e}ras*, 'to divide', indicating that his empire is to be *divided* between the Medes and the Persians (*pārās*, with a further play on the root *prs*) (RSV, AV, NIV, 'PERES').

The mystery lay not in the decipherment of the Aram. words, but in their significance. On the surface they denoted a series of weights or monetary units, 'a mina, a mina, a shekel, and half-shekel' (Bab. *parisu*)—or, if the first word were regarded as imperative of the verb *m^{e}nā'*, 'number a mina, a shekel, and half-shekel'. But there was no context which could make these words seem relevant to the king or his wise men.

Various attempts have been made by several scholars to relate the specified units to successive rulers of Babylon, *e.g.* Nebuchadrezzar (a mina), Belshazzar (a shekel), Medes and Persians (divisions) (C. S. Clermont-Ganneau, A. H. Sayce); Evil-merodach and Neriglissar (two minas), Labashi-marduk (a shekel), Nabonidus and Belshazzar (two half-minas) (E. G. Kraeling); Nebuchadrezzar (a mina), Evil-merodach (a shekel), Belshazzar (one half-mina) (H. L. Ginsberg); Nebuchadrezzar (a mina), Nabonidus (a shekel), Belshazzar (one half-mina) (D. N. Freedman, who concludes from the Qumran *Prayer of Nabonidus* that the Daniel story originally knew these three Chaldean kings). These attempts are fascinating but inconclusive.

BIBLIOGRAPHY. Commentaries on Daniel by J. A. Montgomery, 1927, E. W. Heaton, 1956, A. Jeffery, *IB*, 6, 1956, and J. G. Baldwin, *TOTC*, 1978, *ad. loc.*; C. S. Clermont-Ganneau, *Journal Asiatique*, Series 8.1, 1886, pp. 36f.; A. H. Sayce, *The Higher Criticism and the Verdict of the Monuments*, 1895, pp. 530f.; E. G. Kraeling, *JBL* 63, 1944, pp. 11ff.; H. L. Ginsberg, *Studies in Daniel*, 1948, pp. 24ff.; O. Eissfeldt, 'Die Menetekel-Inschrift', *ZAW* 62, 1951, pp. 105ff.; D. N. Freedman, *BASOR* 145, February 1957, pp. 31f.

F.F.B.

MENICHAEANS
See Nazarene, Part 2.

MENORAH
See Lamp, Part 2.

Artist's reconstruction of the throne-room of the S citadel at Babylon, possibly that used by Belshazzar while regent for Nabonidus at the time of 'the writing on the wall'.

'MENE, MENE, TEKEL, and PARSIN' (mn' mn' tql prs), *written in the Aramaic script of the 6th–5th cent.* BC, *was interpreted by Daniel at Belshazzar's feast.*

MEONENIM, OAK OF. The RV rendering of the phrase *'ēlôn m^{e}'ôn^{e}nîm* in Jdg. 9:37, which is translated 'plain of Meonenim' in AV and 'Diviners' Oak' in RSV. The word *m^{e}'ôn^{e}nîm* is the intensive participle of the verb *'ānan*, 'to practise soothsaying', used, for instance, in 2 Ki. 21:6 = 2 Ch. 33:6 (RV 'observed times') and Lv. 19:26, where the practice is forbidden. The participial form, meaning 'soothsayer' or 'diviner' (*DIVINATION), occurs also in Dt. 18:10, 14 and in Mi. 5:12 (13, Heb.) but is treated only as a proper name by AV and RV in the passage in Judges. The reference is probably to a tree where Canaanite or apostate Israelite soothsayers carried out their business. The site is unknown.

T.C.M.

MEPHIBOSHETH. The original form of the name may have been Meribba'al, perhaps *'Baal is advocate' (1 Ch. 8:34; 9:40a), or Meriba'al, 'hero of Baal' (1 Ch. 9:40b). In the Lucianic recension of the LXX (except at 2 Sa. 21:8) the form is Memphibaal, perhaps 'one who cleaves Baal in pieces' (*cf.* Dt. 32:26). This transitional form was perhaps further modified by the replacement of *ba'al* with *bōše*ṯ, 'shame' (*cf.* Ishbosheth, Jerubbesheth in 2 Sa. 11:21, and the LXX 'prophets of shame' for 'prophets of Baal' in 1 Ki. 18:19, 25). See *BDB*; Smith, *ICC*, *Samuel*, 1899, pp. 284–285; S. R. Driver, *Notes on the Hebrew Text of the Books of Samuel*², 1913, pp. 253–255 with references. On the other hand, Mephibosheth and Meriba'al may have been alternative names (*ISHBOSHETH).

There were two men of this name. **1.** The son of Jonathan, Saul's son. When they were killed he was 5 years old and became lame owing to an injury sustained

MERCHANT SHIP
See Ships and boats, Part 3.

MEREMOTH
See Arad, Part 1.

MERI-BAAL
See Baal, Part 1.

MERIBA'AL
See Mephibosheth, Part 2.

in flight with his nurse (2 Sa. 4:4). David spared his life, gave him an honourable place at court for Jonathan's sake, and appointed Ziba, one of Saul's slaves, to serve him (2 Sa. 9; 21:7). Ziba's treachery and Mephibosheth's reconciliation with David at the time of Absalom's revolt are related in 2 Sa. 16:1–6; 19:24–30. **2.** Saul's son by his concubine Rizpah. He was among those executed by the Gibeonites to expiate Saul's massacre (2 Sa. 21:8). A.G.

MERAB. Saul's elder daughter (1 Sa. 14:49). She was promised to David but given instead to Adriel, the Meholathite (1 Sa. 18:17–20), an incident the LXX omits. Many scholars substitute Merab for Michal in 2 Sa. 21:8, regarding it as an ancient scribal error, saying that after her death her sons were hanged to atone for Saul's slaughter of the Gibeonites, a breaking of Israel's covenant (Jos. 9). M.B.

MERARI, MERARITES. Merari, third son of Levi, was founder of one of three great Levite families. His family was subdivided into the houses of Mahli and Mushi. In the wilderness the Merarites carried the tabernacle frames (boards), bars and sockets, and the court pillars, sockets, pins and cords. Four wagons and eight oxen were given them to help in the task. They encamped on the N side of the tabernacle. Their males over a month old numbered 6,200; those who actually served (age-group 30–50), 3,200 (Nu. 3:33–39; 4:42–45; 7:8). In the land they were assigned twelve cities (Jos. 21:7).

Under David's reorganization the Merarite family of Ethan (Jeduthun) shared in the Temple singing duties, while others were porters (1 Ch. 6:31–48; 25:3; 26:10–19). Merarites are mentioned as being present at the bringing up of the ark (1 Ch. 15:6), and again at the successive cleansings of the Temple under Hezekiah and Josiah (2 Ch. 29:12; 34:12). Some also are recorded as serving under Ezra (Ezr. 8:18–19) and Nehemiah (*cf.* Ne. 11:15 with 1 Ch. 9:14). D.W.G.

MERATHAIM (Heb. *m*ᵉ*rāṯayim*). A term found in Je. 50:21, having the dual meaning of 'double bitterness' or 'double rebellion'. Some hold that the dual expresses merely intensity of rebellion against the Lord (*cf.* v. 24); other scholars now suggest an identification of the word with Bab. *nār marrātu* (Persian Gulf) = S Babylonia (so *BDB*; *GTT*), but this is questionable. J.D.D.

MERCY, MERCIFUL. The tracing of the concept of mercy in the Eng. Bible is complicated by the fact that 'mercy', 'merciful' and 'have mercy upon' are translations of several different Heb. and Gk. roots, which are also variously rendered in other occurrences by other synonyms, such as 'kindness', 'grace', 'favour' (and cognate verbs). To picture this concept we would require a group of overlapping linguistic circles.

I. In the Old Testament

1. *ḥesed*: the etymological origin of this root is possibly 'keenness, eagerness' (Snaith). Its semantic core is best expressed by 'devotion'. Used nearly 250 times, it is translated in AV predominantly by 'mercy', but also by 'kindness', *'lovingkindness', 'goodness' (LXX, *eleos*; Luther, *Gnade*). Its range of meaning is: 'solidarity, kindness, grace' (G. Lisowsky, *Konkordanz*, 1958). It denotes devotion to a covenant, and so, of God, his covenant-love (Ps. 89:28). But God's faithfulness to a graciously established relationship with Israel or an individual, despite human unworthiness and defection, readily passes over into his mercy. 'This steady, persistent refusal of God to wash his hands of wayward Israel is the essential meaning of the Heb. word which is translated loving-kindness' (Snaith). RSV renders it often by 'loyalty', 'deal loyally', but chiefly by 'steadfast love'.

2. *ḥānan* is translated in AV chiefly as 'have mercy upon', be 'gracious', 'merciful'; and *ḥēn* by 'grace' and 'favour' (LXX mostly *charis*). 'It is the gracious favour of the superior to the inferior, all undeserved' (Snaith).

3. *rāḥam* may share common origin with *reḥem*, meaning 'womb', and hence denote 'brotherly' or 'motherly feeling' (*BDB*—*cf.* Is. 13:18; 49:15). AV 'have mercy' or 'compassion', and once (Ps. 18:1) 'love'. The plural *raḥ*ᵃ*mîm* is rendered 'tender mercies' (LXX *splanchna*, *oiktirmoi*, *eleos*). It expresses the affective aspect of love: its compassion and pity. 'The personal God has a heart' (Barth).

II. In the New Testament

In NT the meanings of *ḥesed* and *ḥēn* are largely combined in *charis*, *'grace'. The specific notion of mercy—compassion to one in need or helpless distress, or in debt and without claim to favourable treatment—is rendered by *eleos*, *oiktirmos* and *splanchnon* (and cognate verbs). Grace is concerned for man, as guilty; mercy, as he is miserable (R. C. Trench, *Synonyms of the New Testament*, pp. 166ff.).

God is 'the Father of mercies' (2 Cor. 1:3; Ex. 34:6; Ne. 9:17; Pss. 86:15; 103:8–14; Joel 2:13; Jon. 4:2). 'His compassion is over all that he has made' (Ps. 145:9), and it is because of his mercy that we are saved (Eph. 2:4; Tit. 3:5). Jesus was often 'moved with compassion' and he bids us to be 'merciful, as your Father also is merciful' (Lk. 6:36; Mt. 18:21ff.). Christians are to put on 'heartfelt compassion' (Col. 3:12). The merciful are blessed, and will receive mercy (Mt. 5:7; also Jas. 2:13, on which see R. V. G. Tasker, *TNTC*, *ad loc.*).

BIBLIOGRAPHY. N. H. Snaith, *The Distinctive Ideas of the Old Testament*, 1944; *TWBR*, ('Loving-kindness', 'Mercy'); Karl Barth, *Church Dogmatics*, 2, 1, 1957, section 30, pp. 368ff.; H.-H. Esser, *NIDNTT* 2, pp. 593–601. J.H.

MERODACH. The Heb. form of the Babylonian divine name Marduk. By the time of *Hammurapi (*c.* 1750 BC), on whose stela this god may be represented (*IBA*, fig. 24), the god Marduk (Sumerian *amar. utu*) had taken over many of the attributes of the god Enlil. Marduk was the primary deity of *Babylon and was later called by his epithet Bēl (Ba'al), so that his defeat was synonymous with that of his people (Je. 50:2) as was that of the earlier Canaanite *Ba'al'. The Babylonian epic of creation (*enuma eliš*) commemorates the god's victory over forces of evil and his honour as 'king of the gods'. Merodach occurs as the divine element in the Heb. rendering of Babylonian names, *Evil-merodach, *Merodach-baladan and *Mordecai. D.J.W.

MERODACH-BALADAN. Known from cuneiform texts as the name of Marduk-apla-iddina II, the king of Babylon who sent an embassy to

Hezekiah (Is. 39:1). The Heb. writing reflects the consonants of the name according to the methods of transcription used in the 8th and 7th centuries BC (*mrdkbldn*; 2 Ki. 20:12, Berodach-baladan, has a phonetic variant), the vowels being added by later tradition. His father, not named in cuneiform sources, could have been called Bēl-iddin, giving the same consonants as Baladan (*bldn*) when transcribed into Hebrew (Is. 39:1). See *TynB* 22, 1971, pp. 125–126.

He was a ruler of the Chaldean district of Bit-Yakin, N of the Persian Gulf, who claimed descent from Eriba-Marduk king of Babylon 782–762 BC. When Tiglath-pileser III entered Babylonia in 731 BC, Merodach-baladan brought presents to him at Sapia and supported the Assyrians against a rebellious sheikh Ukīn-zēr (*Iraq* 17, 1953, pp. 44–50). On the succession

Impression on a Neo-Babylonian seal showing a worshipper before the spade-symbol (marru) *of Marduk (Merodach) on the back of the god's dragon* (mušruššu). (BM)

Bottom left: A boundary-stone describing the property held by the official here shown receiving his land-charter from Marduk-apla-iddina II (Merodach-Baladan), king of Babylon (721–710, 705–703 BC). Above the two figures are emblems of four Babylonian deities on pedestals. Height 0·46 m. Black marble. (SMB)

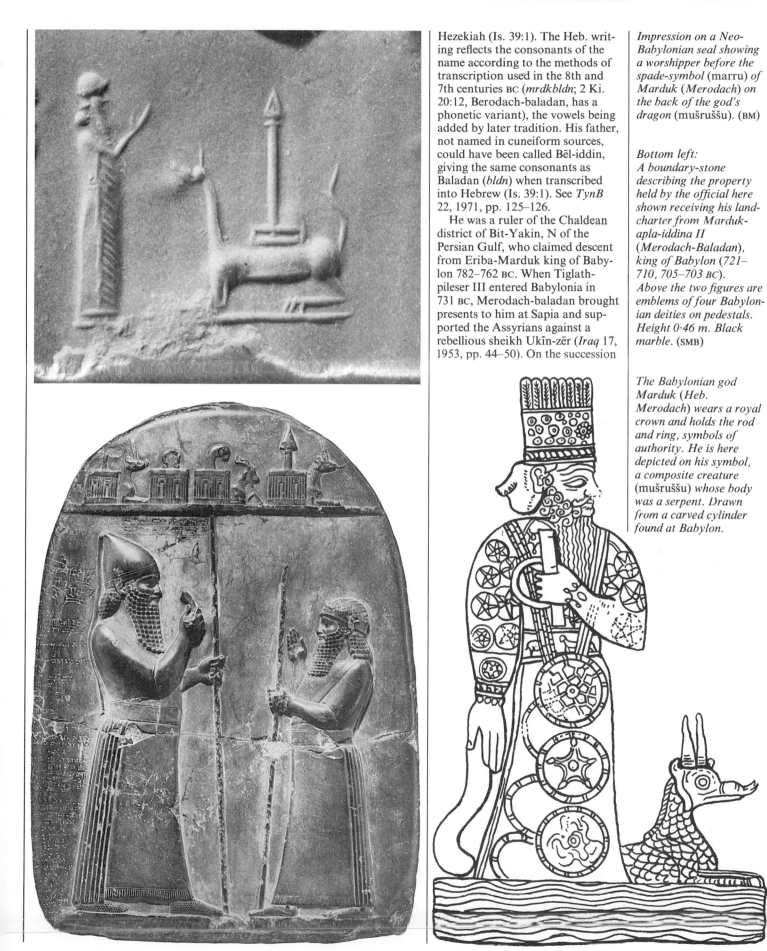

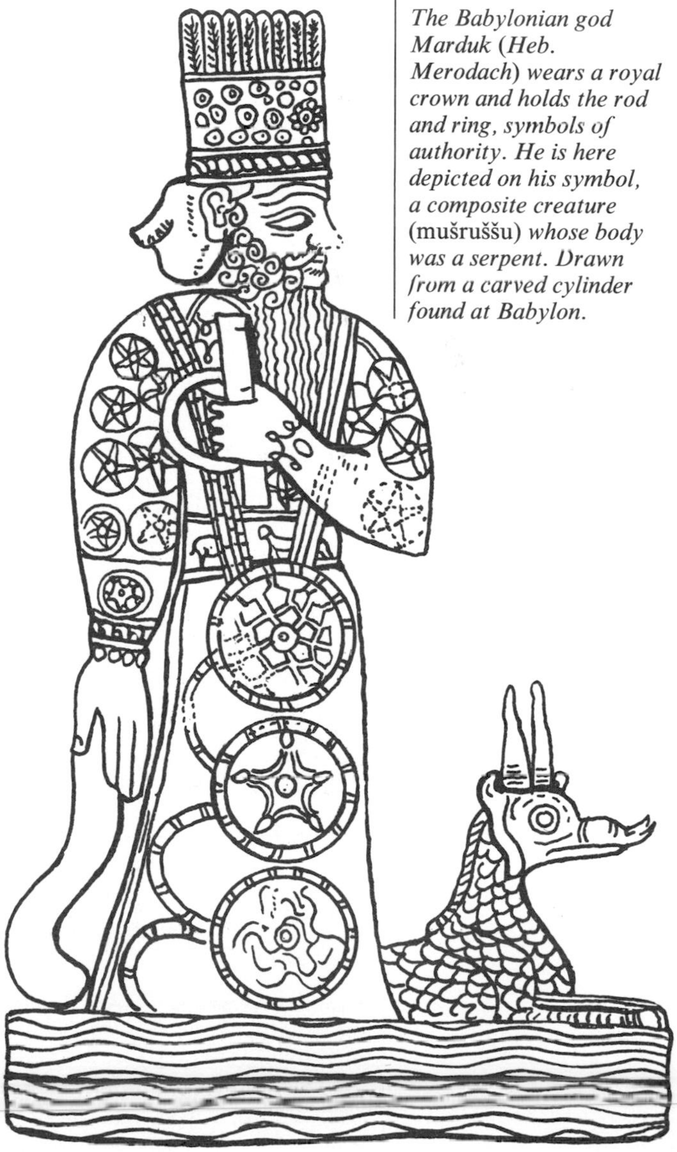

The Babylonian god Marduk (Heb. Merodach) wears a royal crown and holds the rod and ring, symbols of authority. He is here depicted on his symbol, a composite creature (mušruššu) *whose body was a serpent. Drawn from a carved cylinder found at Babylon.*

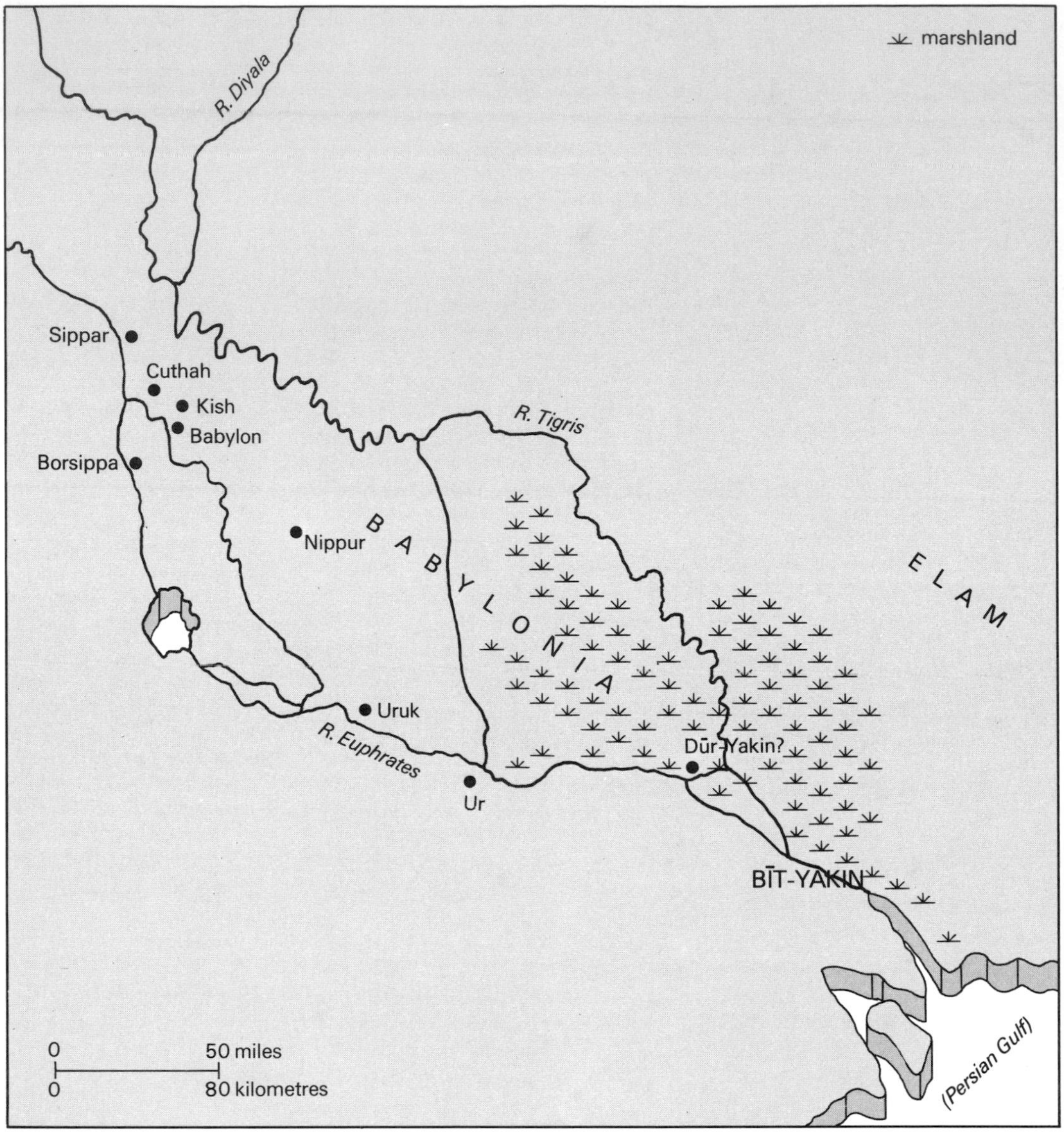

The region controlled by Merodach-Baladan (Marduk-aple-iddina II).

of Sargon in 721 BC Merodach-baladan entered Babylon and claimed the throne. The Assyrians reacted and attacked the Elamite allies of Babylon the following year. The outcome of the battle is obscure except in that Merodach-baladan remained on the throne until 710 BC, when Sargon, having previously neutralized the Elamites, entered Babylon unopposed. When the Assyrians moved S into Bit-Yakin, Merodach-baladan was retained as local ruler and did not openly oppose his overlord during the rest of his reign.

On Sargon's death in 705 BC, however, Merodach-baladan began to work for his independence from Assyria. It was probably at this time that he sent an embassy to Hezekiah, which was shown the resources of Judah (2 Ki. 20:12–19; Is. 39), with the aim of encouraging action against Assyria by the W. Not only did Isaiah's opposition to this scheme thwart Merodach-baladan's plan, but the Babylonians themselves forestalled him by setting up their own nominee, Marduk-zakir-šum, in 704 BC. He deposed the newly appointed king in Babylon and ruled from nearby friendly Borsippa. Despite the aid of Elamite troops under Imbappa sent by Šutur-Naḫundu, Sennacherib defeated the rebels in battles at Kutha and Kish and entered Babylon, where he set Bel-ibni on the throne. Bit-Yakin alone was despoiled, and Merodach-baladan fled to SW Elam, where he died.

BIBLIOGRAPHY. J. A. Brinkman, 'Merodach Baladān II', in *Studies presented to A. L. Oppenheim*, 1964, pp. 6–53. D.J.W.

MEROM, WATERS OF (Heb. *mērôm*). Rendezvous of the Hazor confederacy against Joshua, who surprised and routed them there (Jos. 11:5, 7). It is not clear whether Merom is (*a*) modern Meiron, a village 5 km WNW of Safed (Safat), near springs which feed the Wadi Leimun or W Meiron (M. Noth, *Josua*², p. 67); or (*b*) Maroun er-Ras, 15 km to the N, above a valley leading to the Huleh basin N of Hazor (*LOB*, pp. 205f.; J. Garstang, *Joshua–Judges*, 1931, pp. 191ff., 395). Whether or not it is the same as *Madon, Merom appears to have been an important site (Tuthmosis III list no. 85; *ANET*, p. 283); no such remains have been found at Meiron (E. Meyers, *BASOR* 214, 1974, pp. 2f.). J.P.U.L.

MERONOTHITE. Jehdeiah (1 Ch. 27:30) and Jadon (Ne. 3:7) were Meronothites. Ne. 3:7 seems to suggest that Meronoth was close to Gibeon and Mizpah, but Mizpah is a doubtful reading (*GTT*, p. 387). Grollenberg, *Atlas*, identifies it as Beitûniyeh, NW of Gibeon, following earlier studies. A.R.M.

MEROZ (Heb. *mērôz*), in Jdg. 5:23 a community (doubtfully identified with Khirbet Maruṣ, 12 km S of Barak's home at Kedesh-naphtali) on which Deborah pronounces a curse for its failure to take part in the campaign against Sisera. The bitterness of the curse suggests that Meroz was under a sacred obligation to obey Barak's summons. F.F.B.

MESHA. 1. King of Moab, succeeding his father who had reigned for 30 years and worshipped *Chemosh (Moabite Stone, 2–3). He rebelled after Ahab's death (2 Ki. 1:1; 3:5). Since an invasion of his territory by Judah, Israel and Edom failed, his breakaway may have occurred *c.* 853 BC while Ahab and Israel were engaging the Assyrians. The details of his reign on the *Moabite Stone record his building of towns and regulating the water-supply. His rebellion may have been an attempt to gain direct control of his considerable wool trade with Tyre (2 Ki. 3:4–5; *POTT*, pp. 235, 275).

2. Caleb's first-born son (1 Ch. 2:42, RSVmg.).

3. A Benjaminite born in Moab, son of Shaharaim by Hodesh (1 Ch. 8:9). D.J.W.

MESHA. A place mentioned as the limit of the territory of the descendants of Joktan (Gn. 10:30), the other limit being * Sephar. Some scholars would identify it with *maśśā'* in N Arabia (* MASSA), but the probable location of Sephar in S Arabia suggests a similar locality for Mesha, though no place of that name has been suggested in that region. T.C.M.

MESHACH (Heb. *mēšaḵ*). The name given to Mishael ('who is what God is'?), one of Daniel's companions in captivity at Babylon, by Nebuchadrezzar's chief eunuch (Dn. 1:7; 2:49, *etc.*). The most plausible meaning of the name suggested is the Bab. *mēšăku* ('I have become weak') perhaps given as similar to the Heb. name. D.J.W.

MESHECH (*MT mešeḵ*; LXX *Mosoch*). One of the sons of Japheth (Gn. 10:2 = 1 Ch. 1:5) here and elsewhere associated with Tubal. 1 Ch. 1:17 names him as a descendant of Shem by Aram, while the parallel passage (Gn. 10:23) gives the name as Mash. One of these is, presumably, an error, and LXX *Mosoch* in Gn. 10:23 suggests *k* has been lost there. The intermarriage implied by the presence of the same name among the children of Japheth and Shem, which such a view would involve, would not be impossible (* NATIONS, TABLE OF).

The descendants of Meshech are later mentioned as exporting slaves and copper (Ezk. 27:13), as a warlike people threatening from the N (Ezk. 32:26; 38:2–3; 39:1), and as typical of a barbarous society (Ps.

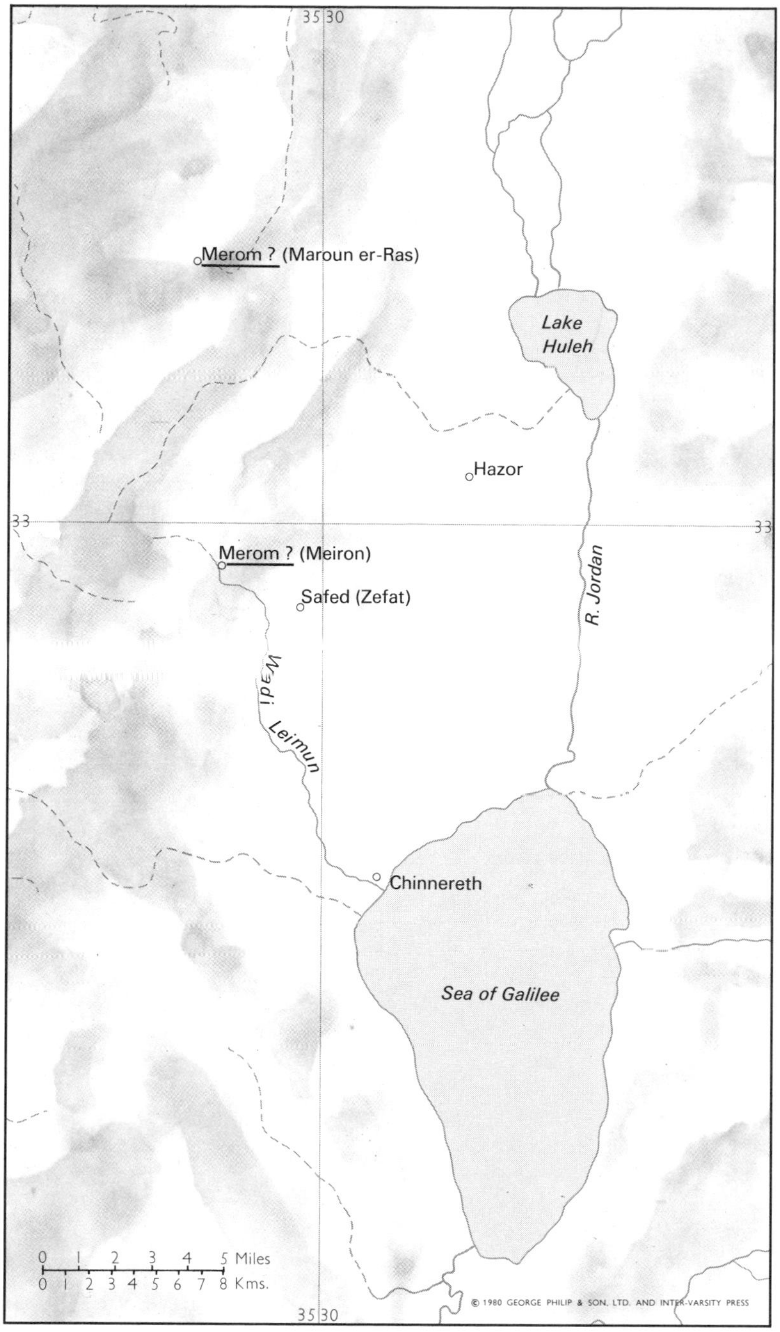

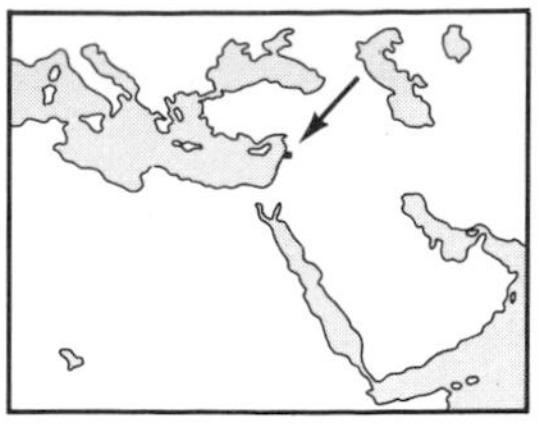

Possible sites of Merom.

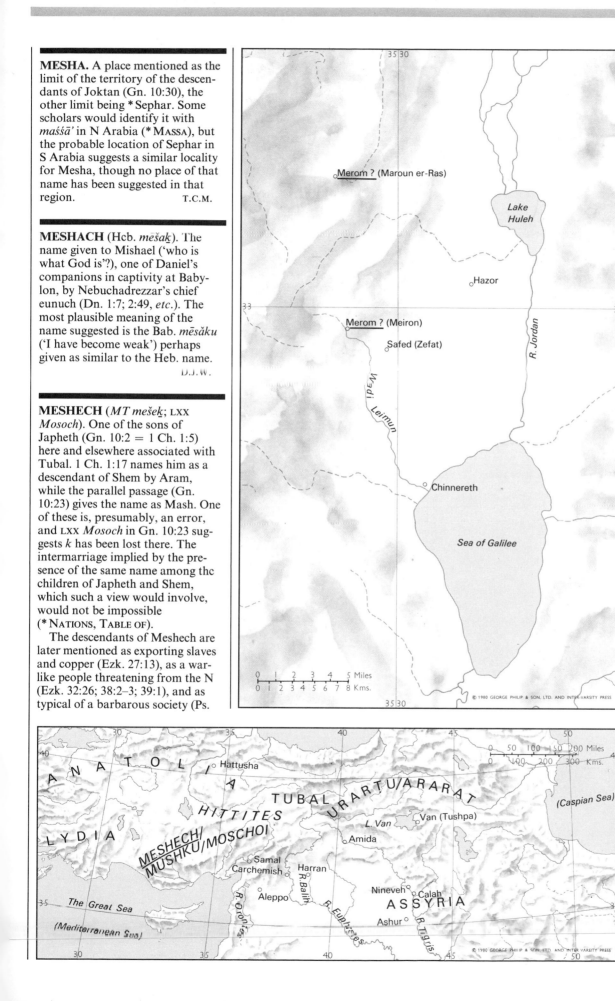

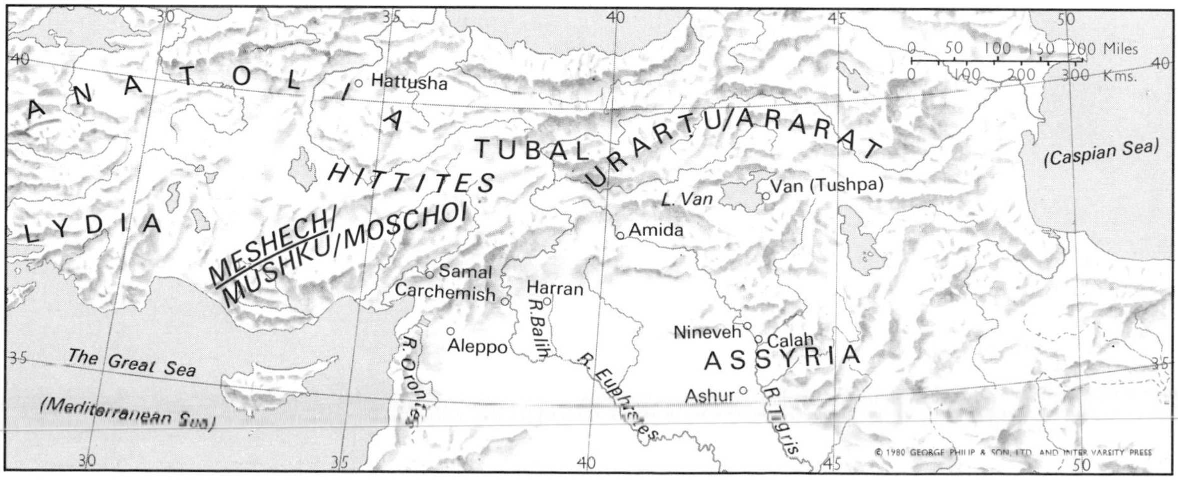

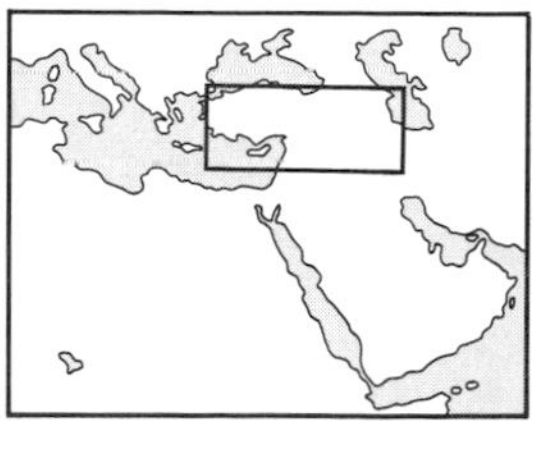

The location of Meshech.

MESHELEMIAH See Shallum, Part 3.

MESHULLAM See Shallum, Part 3.

Mesopotamia.

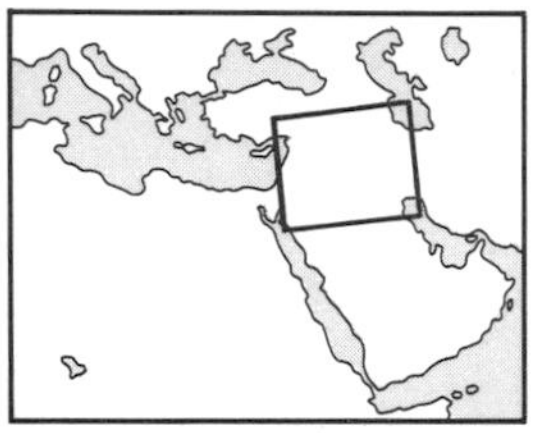

120:5). The close association of the name with Tubal renders likely their identification with the people often named together as *Tabâl* and *Musku* or *Mušku* in the Assyr. inscriptions and *Tibarēnoi* and *Moschoi* in Herodotus. The *muš-ka-a-ia* are first mentioned in the annals of Tiglath-pileser I (*c.* 1100 BC) as mounting an army of 20,000 men in the N, and it may be that they were already in the region SE of the Black Sea a century earlier when the Hittite texts mention one Mitas in that area, for this name is similar to that of the king of the Muški in the 8th century. They are mentioned in the annals of Tukulti-Ninurta II and Ashurnasirpal II in the 9th century and of Sargon in the 8th. This king gives their ruler's name as *mi-ta-a*, which some scholars suggest is to be equated with Midas of Phrygia, the kingdom which succeeded the Hittites in Asia Minor, and that the Muški are therefore to be equated with the Phrygians. The name Mušku is not mentioned in the Achaemenian inscriptions, but Herodotus names the Moschoi as falling within the 19th Satrapy of Darius (3. 94) and as forming a contingent in the army of Xerxes (7. 78). This information leads to the conclusion that Meshech refers to a people perhaps speaking an Indo-European language who entered the Near East from the N steppe, and imposed themselves as rulers upon the indigenous population of an area in E Anatolia.

BIBLIOGRAPHY. S. Parpola, *Neo-Assyrian Toponyms*, 1970, pp. 252–253; R. D. Barnett, *CAH*³, 1975, pp. 417–442; J. N. Postgate, *Iraq* 35, 1973, pp. 21–34. T.C.M.

MESOPOTAMIA. The Gk. *Mesopotamia*, 'between the two rivers', is AV borrowing from LXX to render the Heb. *'ᵃram nahᵃrayim* (except in the title of Ps. 60). This was the fertile land E of the river Orontes covering the upper and middle Euphrates and the lands watered by the rivers Habur and Tigris, *i.e.* modern E Syria–N Iraq. It includes Harran (to which Abraham moved after leaving Ur in Babylonia) and its surrounding townships, to which Eliezer was sent to find a wife for Isaac (Gn. 24:10). Mesopotamia was the original home of Balaam (Dt. 23:4;

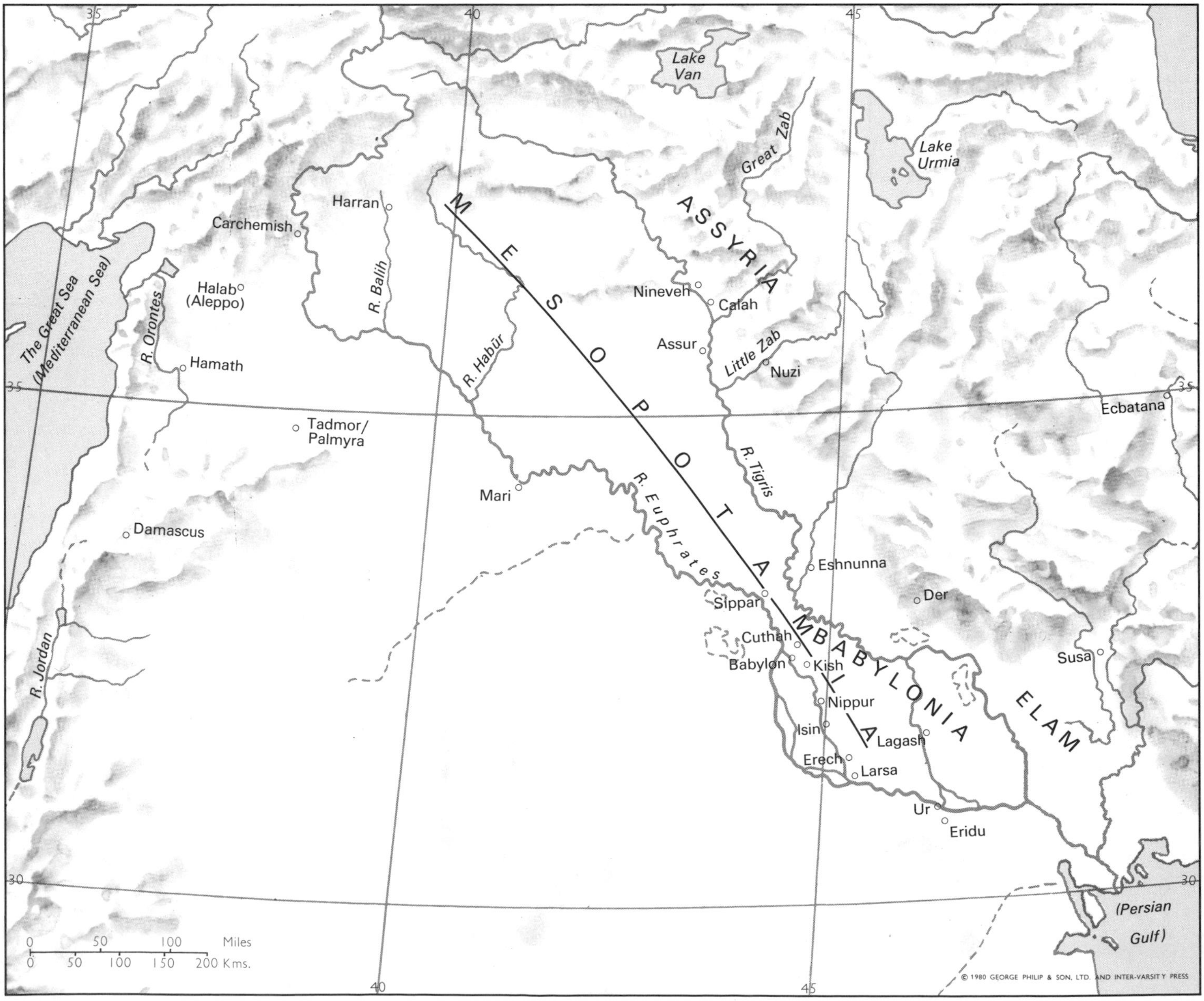

The river Euphrates flowing through E Syria, part of Mesopotamia. (MEPhA)

* PEOR) and was the country ruled by Cushan-rishathaim when he oppressed Israel (Jdg. 3:8–10). In David's time Mesopotamia provided charioteers and horsemen to support his Ammonite opponents (1 Ch. 19:6). This accords with the evidence for the occupation of this whole area by horse-rearing Indo-Aryan Mitanni and Hurrians (* HORITES) in the 2nd millennium.

Greek and Roman writers after the 4th century BC extended the use of 'Mesopotamia' to describe the whole Tigris–Euphrates valley, that is, the modern state of Iraq. Thus Stephen referred to Abraham's original home of Ur in Babylonia as in 'Mesopotamia, before he lived in Haran' (Acts 7:2). The inclusion of Mesopotamians with Parthians, Medes and Elamites may indicate that the Jews of the Diaspora in Babylonia were present in Jerusalem to hear Peter (Acts 2:9). Thus the NT follows the wider use of the geographical name which is still adopted by some modern scholars.

See also * ARAM, * SYRIA, and for the history of the region, * ASSYRIA and * BABYLONIA.

BIBLIOGRAPHY. J. J. Finkelstein, *JNES* 21, 1962, pp. 73–92.

D.J.W.

MESSIAH.

I. In the Old Testament

This word, used as the official title of the central figure of expectation, is in the main a product of later Judaism. Its use is, of course, validated by the NT, but the term is found only twice in the OT (Dn. 9:25–26).

The idea of * anointing and of the anointed person is a well-established OT usage. One particular example, which has sometimes caused difficulty to OT students, is in fact specially helpful in defining the term. In Is. 45:1 the Persian, Cyrus, is addressed as 'his (*i.e.* Yahweh's) anointed (*m^{e}šîḥô*)'. There are here five features which, in the light of the rest of Scripture, are clearly definitive of certain main lines of OT Messianism. Cyrus is a man of God's choice (Is. 41:25), appointed to accomplish a redemptive purpose towards God's people (45:11–13), and a judgment on his foes (47). He is given dominion over the nations (45:1–3); and in all his activities the real agent is Yahweh himself (45:1–7). The anointed status of Cyrus, as such, simply shows that there is a 'secular' (so to speak) usage of the terminology of Messiahship (*cf.* the 'anointing' of Hazael, 1 Ki. 19:15; and the description of Nebuchadrezzar as 'my servant', Is. 25:9). There could be no better summary of the OT view of the 'anointed' person; furthermore it is quite clear that these five points are pre-eminently true of the Lord Jesus Christ, who saw himself as the fulfilment of the OT Messianic expectations. In the light of this, the best and simplest plan for our study is to apply the word 'Messianic' to all those prophecies that place a person in the limelight as the figure of salvation (so Vriezen).

How old is the Messianic expectation? One major line of argument on this question (suggested by Mowinckel) is that the Messiah is an eschatological figure in the strict sense of the term: that is to say, not merely a figure of future hope, but emphatically belonging to the 'last days'. Consequently, since all properly defined eschatological passages look back upon the fall of the Davidic monarchy as a fact of past history, the Messiah must belong to post-exilic times, and is not found as a matter of prediction in pre-exilic documents. Seemingly Messianic passages belonging to monarchic times must be interpreted as simple addresses to the reigning king, and of no Messianic, that is, eschatological, significance. Later editing, it is urged, may have adapted them Messianically, and later Messianic writers may have drawn from them some of their imagery, but in themselves, and properly considered, they are not Messianic.

Against this it is urged (*e.g.* by Knight), with great weight, that it is hardly credible that the monarchs known to us in the books of Kings could have been seriously addressed or thought of in the terms used, for example, in the royal Psalms. We shall demonstrate this contention presently, and for the moment must be content to say that such passages point to a conception of Israelite kingship as such, and to an expectation resident in the kingly office itself. Even if Mowinckel has correctly insisted that Messiah must be an eschatological figure, by no means all OT specialists would agree that eschatology must be post-exilic (*cf.*, *e.g.*, Vriezen), but it may certainly be asked if he has not defined the concept of eschatology too rigidly. If, for example, he denies the description 'eschatological' to any passage which depicts the survival and life of a remnant after the divine intervention, the logical consequence of this is to deny that the Lord Jesus Christ is an eschatological figure, and thereby contradict the biblical view of the 'last days' (*e.g.* Heb. 1:2; 1 Jn. 2:18). It is much more satisfactory to define the Messiah as a 'teleological figure'. Unique in Israel was their apprehension of purpose in life. They possessed this awareness from the beginning (*cf.* Gn. 12:1–3), and this made them alone the true historians of the ancient world.

The specific attachment of this hope to a royal figure of the future is in no way dependent on the historical fall of the Monarchy, for the Davidic line was a failure from the start, and the expectation, even longing, for the royal Messiah need not be later than the time of Solomon. Our plan therefore will be to seek in the OT for a 'figure of salvation', and, by associating our search with Israelite teleology, rather than with a narrowly defined eschatology, we will find good reasons to hold that such a hope was early embraced by the chosen people, taking its rise from the famous 'protevangelium' of Gn. 3:15.

a. Messiah as the antitype of great historical figures

Israel's teleological view of life on earth, already mentioned, was rooted in the knowledge of the unique God who revealed himself to them. The faithfulness and self-consistency of their God provided them with a key to the future, in so far as it was necessary for faith to discern things to come. God had acted 'typically' and characteristically in certain great persons and events of the past, and, because God does not change, he will so act again. Three such persons of the past were specially woven into the Messianic pattern: Adam, Moses and David.

1. *The Messiah and Adam.* There are certain features of the Messianic future which are very clearly reminiscent of the Edenic state: for convenience we group them under the two headings of prosperity (Am. 9:13; Is. 4:2; 32:15, 20; 55:13; Ps. 72:16) and peace (the harmony of the world of living creatures: Is. 11:6–9; and of the world of human relations: Is. 32:1–8). Viewing the Fall in its effects purely upon this world, these were the things lost as God's curse took effect. When the curse is reversed and God's Man restores all things the Edenic scene reappears. This is not merely wishful thinking, but a logical and proper extension of the doctrine of creation by a holy God. All the passages cited above concern the Messianic King and the nature of his rule and kingdom. Here is the real recapitulation of the first man, who had 'dominion' over the rest of created things (Gn. 1:28; 2:19–20), but fell when he allowed his dominion to be usurped (*cf.* Gn. 3:13). Dominion will be restored in the Messiah. It may frankly be admitted that the notion of the Messiah as a new *Adam is neither lengthily nor specifically developed, 'but it is not unlikely that we have evidence that the royal ideology was sometimes influenced by the conception of the king of paradise' (Mowinckel). The NT doctrine of the 'Second Adam' has a clear OT root in the passages quoted.

2. *The Messiah and Moses.* It is not surprising that the Exodus and its leader should have so impressed the mind of Israel that the future was seen in this mould. As it was recorded and presented to succeeding generations of the nation, the pattern of the first Exodus constituted an eternal revelation of God (Ex. 3:15). The conception of the second Exodus is not always in a specifically Messianic setting. Sometimes the fact is stressed that God will do again what he did at the Exodus, only in a surpassing way, but without mentioning any man by whom God will so work as formerly he wrought by Moses (*e.g.* Ho. 2:14–23; Je. 31:31–34; Ezk. 20:33–44—note 'king' (RV, RSV) in v. 33: it may be that Moses is called 'king' in Dt. 33:5). Sometimes, however, the forecast of the second Exodus is Messianic, *e.g.* Is. 51:9–11; 52:12; Je. 23:5–8. Once again, it is only fair to notice that the matter is, at best, inferentially expressed. However, in the case of Moses we can take the study a stage farther, for we have his own prophecy recorded in Dt. 18:15–19 that the Lord will raise up a prophet 'like me'.

In general, the exegesis of this passage has tended to the exclusive advocacy of one or other point of view: either that the Messiah is here foretold or that the reference is simply to the providential provision of a continuing line of prophets. In recent work the latter has the support of the majority, although sometimes it has been allowed that the Messianic meaning may also, though secondarily, be admitted. However, the passage itself seems to require both interpretations, for some features in it can be satisfied only by the line of prophets, and others only by the Messiah.

Thus the context is very weighty for the former view. Moses insistently warning his hearers against Canaanite abomination stresses especially divinatory practices for ascertaining the future. The warning is buttressed by this prophecy of the Mosaic Prophet. Here, says Moses, is the Israelite alternative to divination; the living are not to consult the dead, for the God of Israel will speak to his people through a man raised up for that purpose. This seems to be a promise of continuous revelation; a prediction of a far-off Messiah would not meet the need for guidance of which Moses is speaking.

Again, vv. 21–22, supplying a test for prophets, may be seen as anticipating the situation which often arose in the days of the canonical prophets, and which caused such bitterness of soul to Jeremiah (23:9ff.). However, this consideration is not of equal weight with the foregoing, for it would not be at all improper that some test for the Messiah should be provided. A false Messiah is as likely as a false prophet and, indeed, to take the matter no farther, Jesus himself rested his claims on the coincidence of his words and works, and his Jewish opponents were continually pressing for an unequivocal Messianic sign.

If we take Moses' words as prophetic of a line of prophets, they were, of course, amply fulfilled. Every true prophet was 'like Moses', for he existed to teach Moses' doctrine. Both Jeremiah (23:9ff.) and Ezekiel (13:1–14:11) distinguish the true prophet from the false by the content of his message: the true prophet has a word to speak against sin, the false prophet has not. This is simply to say that the theology of true *prophecy derives from Sinai. This truth is taught also in Deuteronomy, for the question of false prophecy is raised in ch. 13, and it is precisely required that every prophet must be brought into comparison with the Exodus revelation (vv. 5, 10) and with the teaching of Moses (v. 18). Moses is the normative prophet; every true prophet, as such, is a prophet 'like Moses'.

But there is another side to the exegesis of this passage. According to Dt. 34:10, Moses is unique, and his like has not yet appeared. On any view of the date of Deuteronomy, this verse points to an understanding of Dt. 18:15ff. as Messianic: for if Deuteronomy is as late as some hold, or if 34:10 represents later editorial comment, then we are here being informed that no single prophet, nor yet the prophets collectively, fulfilled the prediction of 18:15ff.

Furthermore, when we come to the passage itself, special regard ought to be paid to the very precise terms of the comparison with Moses. The passage does not say, in a large and undefined way, that there will arise a prophet 'like Moses', but specifically a prophet who, in his person and work, may be compared with Moses at Horeb (v. 16). Now this comparison was not fulfilled by any of the OT prophets. Moses at Horeb was the mediator of the covenant; the prophets were preachers of the covenant and foretellers of its successor. Moses was an originator; the prophets were propagators. With Moses, Israel's religion entered a new phase; the prophets fought for the establishment and maintenance of that phase, and prepared the way for the next, to which they looked forward. The strict requirement of vv. 15–16, therefore, can be met only by Messiah.

How, then, are these two interpretations to be reconciled? We remarked above, relative to Israel's continuing need of the voice of God, that a far-off Messiah would not meet that need. In so saying, we spoke as if 20th-century information was at the disposal of the ancient Israelite. This passage certainly foretells the prophet-Messiah, but it says nothing about his being 'far off'. Only the actual passage of time could show that. Here, then, is the reconciliation: in respect of prophets, Israel was in exactly the same situation as in respect of kings (see further, below). The line of kings proceeded under the shadow of the promise of the coming great King, and each successive king was hailed in deliberately Messianic terms, both to remind him of his vocation to a certain type of kingship and to express the national longing that at last Messiah might have come. So too with the prophets. They likewise live under the shadow of the promise; they too have a pattern to fulfil. Each king must be, as best he can, like the king of the past (David) until the coming of the One who is able to reformulate the Davidic type and be the king of the future; so, too, each prophet must be, as best he can, like the prophet of the past (Moses) until the coming of the One who is able to reformulate the Mosaic type and be the prophet, lawgiver and mediator of the future, new covenant.

3. *The Messiah and David.* The dying Jacob is recorded (and there is no good reason for doubting the ascription) as prophesying about the future of his sons. The prophecy about Judah has deservedly attracted great attention (Gn. 49:9–10). Dispute has necessarily centred on the meaning of *'aḏ kî yāḇô' šîlôh*. Ezk. 21:27 seems to suggest the interpretation 'until he come, whose right it is', and this certainly is the most venerable approach to the problem. More recently the view has been taken that we have here an Akkadian loan-word meaning 'his (*i.e.* Judah's) ruler'. At all events, tribal rule is vested in Judah, and some pre-eminent Judahite ruler is foreseen as the consummation of the sovereignty. In an initial, and at the same time normative, sense, this came to pass in David of Judah, with whom all succeeding kings, for good or ill, were compared (*e.g.* 1 Ki. 11:4, 6; 14:8; 15:3, 11–14; 2 Ki. 18:3; 22:2). However, it is one thing to see that David, as a matter of fact, was the normative king; it is another matter altogether to say just why he should be the type of the king to come. The prophecy of Nathan (2 Sa. 7:12–16) does not precisely require a single king as its fulfilment, but rather predicts a stable house, kingdom and throne for David. We must presume that, as from Solomon's later years failure and declension set in, the days of David glowed brighter and brighter in Israel's memory, and hope crystallized into the 'David' of the future (*e.g.* Ezk. 34:23). This expectation is shown particularly by two groups of passages.

(i) The Psalms. There are certain psalms which centre on the king, and they depict a very precise character and career. Summarizing, this king meets world-opposition (2:1–3; 110:1), but, as a victor (45:3–5; 89:22–23), and by the activity of Yahweh (2:6, 8; 18:46–50; 21:1–13; 110:1–2), he establishes world-rule (2:8–12; 18:43–45; 45:17; 72:8–11; 89:25; 110:5–6), based on Zion (2:6) and marked by a primary concern for morality (45:4, 6–7; 72:2–3, 7; 101:1–8). His rule is everlasting (21:4; 45:6; 72:5); his kingdom is peaceful (72:7), prosperous (72:16) and undeviating in reverence for Yahweh (72:5). Pre-eminent among men (45:2, 7), he is the friend of the poor and the enemy of the oppressor (72:2–4, 12–14). Under him the righteous flourish (72:7). He is remembered for ever (45:17), possesses an everlasting name (72:17) and is the object of unending thanks (72:15). In relation to Yahweh, he is the recipient of his everlasting blessing (45:2). He is the heir of David's covenant (89:28–37; 132:11–12) and of Melchizedek's priesthood

(110:4). He belongs to Yahweh (89:18) and is devoted to him (21:1, 7; 63:1–8, 11). He is his son (2:7; 89:27), seated at his right hand (110:1), and is himself divine (45:6).

The Messianic pattern as deduced from Cyrus above is clearly here. It is inconceivable that such notions were entertained in any directly personal way concerning the line of monarchs who followed David in Judah. We have here, therefore, either the most blatant flattery the world has ever heard, or else the expression of a great ideal. Some comment is necessary on the ascription of divinity in Ps. 45:6. Unquestionably there are ways in which the address to the king as 'God' may legitimately be avoided (see Johnson), but such interpretations are not necessary in the light of the fact so clearly taught elsewhere in the OT that a divine Messiah was expected. It is no argument against this that v. 7 of the psalm, still addressing the king, speaks of 'God, your God'. Certainly we are intended to gather that there is some distinction between God and the king, even if the king can be spoken of as 'God', but this need occasion no surprise, because exactly the same thing occurs throughout Messianic expectation, as we shall see, and also in the case, for example, of the *Angel of the Lord, who is both himself divine and also distinct from God.

(ii) Isaiah 7–12, *etc.* The most sustained treatment of the Davidic–Messianic theme occurs in Isaiah 1–37 and in particular in the self-contained unit, chs. 7–12. From 745 BC onwards, pressure towards the W from the awakening imperialism of Assyria forced all the Palestinian states to look to their security. Aram and Israel (Ephraim) allied themselves for mutual defence and sought the additional strength of a united Palestinian front. When, as it seems, Judah stood aloof from this Syro-Ephraimite alliance, pressure was exerted to bring the S kingdom to a better mind. It is unnecessary to review the course of the events (*cf.* 2 Ki. 15:37–16:20; 2 Ch. 28); rather we must concentrate on sharing Isaiah's view of the matter. It is clear that he saw the threat as transitory (7:7, 16) but the moment as decisive for the future of the people of God. If in the face of this threat there should be a refusal to find security in Yahweh alone and a seeking of security in any sort of worldly pact, then in the prophet's view not just the current king (Ahaz) but the Davidic dynasty itself would be exposed as faithless; it would have rejected the promises and pleadings of its God in a decisive and final way and doom would follow. For this reason he identifies Ahaz with the dynasty (7:2, 13, 17), calls for a policy of total reliance on Yahweh (7:4, 'Take care that you do nothing'), warns that the issue of faith will settle the fortunes of the dynasty and nation (7:9), offers in Yahweh's name the provision of a sign of such magnitude as would virtually compel faith (7:10–11) and when this is rejected speaks of another sign, Immanuel, wherein the hope of the nation is seen as overwhelmed in the triumph of Assyria (7:14ff.).

There is a logic, therefore, about 7:1–25. There comes a moment when faith is decisively offered and beyond that offer lies only the doom which comes on unbelief. But for Isaiah this creates as many problems as it solves. It is one thing to say that the unbelieving Ahaz is doomed by his faithlessness, and dooms the dynasty and nation with him. But what of the promises themselves? Does God go back on his word? Does the promise of a Davidic king itself fail simply because Ahaz faithlessly refuses to enter into it? Is God's Messianic plan to that extent dependent on the choice of man? It is to this problem that Isaiah addresses himself in this section of his book and his treatment of it centres on the figure of Immanuel.

Immanuel must be approached first in relation to what is said of his birth: it is described as a 'sign' and as birth of an *'almâ*. On neither count is Isaiah's meaning uncontroverted. 'Sign' is used in the OT of a present persuader (as in 7:11; *cf.* Dt. 13:1) and of a future confirmation (*e.g.* Ex. 3:12). In which sense is Immanuel a 'sign'? Regarding Immanuel's mother, the majority opinion of specialists insists that the word *'almâ* means a young woman of marriageable age who, in this case, in the light of her pregnant state, must be assumed to be married and that if Isaiah had meant *virgo intacta* he must needs use another word, *bᵉtûlâ*. The issue, however, is not as settled as some commentators would suggest. 'From a survey of non-biblical evidence we may safely conclude that the word *'almâ*, in so far as may be ascertained, was never used of a married woman,' says E. J. Young (*Studies in Isaiah*, 1954, p.170); and of the eight other occasions on which the word is used in the Bible, there is no reason in any case to assume married state. The sequence of Gn. 24:14, 16, 43 is specially notable: Abraham's servant prays for a 'girl' (v. 14, *naᵃrâ*); when Rebekah comes he notes that she is marriageable but unmarried (v. 16, a *bᵉṯûlâ* whom man had not known); with this knowledge at his disposal he summarizes the whole story for Rebekah's family using *'almâ* (v. 43). In passing, it is important to ask why, if *bᵉṯûlâ* is virtually a technical term for 'virgin', it needs to be qualified on a number of significant occasions, as in Gn. 24:16 (*cf.* Lv. 21:3; Jdg. 11:39; 21:12). There is, in fact, strong ground for urging that Isaiah used *'almâ* because it is the nearest word in Hebrew which expresses *virgo intacta* and that Matthew practised no sleight of hand in accepting the rendering *parthenos* (1:23).

Secondly, Isaiah sets Immanuel in the context of the hope of Israel. Chs. 7–11 form an integrated unit of prophetic teaching in which 7:1–9:7 focuses on the S kingdom (Judah) and 9:8–11:16 on the N (Jacob, 9:8). Each section passes through the same four sub-sections: the moment of decision (7:1–17; 9:8–10:4), the judgment (7:18–8:8; 10:5–15), the remnant (8:9–22; 10:16–34) and the glorious hope (9:1–7; 11:1–16). As this sequence is followed through, the wonder-child, Immanuel (the possessor, 8:8, and security, 8:10, of his people) becomes, as the focus clarifies, the royal deliverer of 9:1–7 and the righteous king of 11:1–16. In each place he is a world-ruler (9:7; 11:10) and in each place the element of mystery regarding his person remains. In 9:6 he who sits on David's throne (v. 7) is also 'mighty God'—and in the light of the identical wording referring without equivocation to Yahweh in 10:21 it is exegetically unworthy to refuse either the translation or its clear implication here—and in 11:1, 10 he who springs out of the stock of Jesse is also the root of Jesse.

Thirdly, we must attempt to relate Immanuel and Maher-shalal-hash-baz (8:1–4). We noted above a problem whether, considered as a sign, Immanuel must be understood as a present persuader or a future confirmation. The implication of 7:15–17 that he would be born heir to the Assyrian devastations of Judah might appear to settle the point. Yet Isaiah seems, with a certain amount of emphasis and deliberation, to transfer the task of being an immediate sign to his own son (8:1–4) and in the rest of chs. 8–9 there is a plain contrast between this immediate child with a fourfold name of doom (8:1–4) and one whose birth comes 'in the latter time' (9:1) and who has a fourfold name of glory (9:6). Did Isaiah then change his mind about Immanuel and the date of his birth? Or how are we to understand this odd tension in the evidence? We come nearest to a solution if we assume that from the start Isaiah saw Immanuel's birth as a coming confirmation of the divine rejection of Ahaz and the Davidic dynasty as represented by him: the great, expected king would be born in the line of Ahaz to inherit an empty title, a meaningless crown, and a subjugated people. Were Immanuel to have been born there and then, that would have been the case; when, as we know, Immanuel was born, it was still the case. Isaiah gently eases the birth of Immanuel out of the present and into the undated future by the substitution of the birth of his own son and the open dating of 'the latter time' (9:1).

b. Other Messianic figures

1. *The Servant.* Isaiah 40–55 is dominated by the Messianic portrayal of the Servant (42:1–4; 49:1–6; 50:4–9; 52:13–53:12). The Servant is Yahweh's anointed (42:1), exercises the royal functions of 'judgment' (*mišpāṭ*, 42:1, 3–4) and dominion (53:12), displays prominently the marks of a prophet (49:1–2; 50:4), extends a ministry to Gentiles (42:1, 4; 49:6b) and to Israel (49:5–6a), is the agent in a world-wide revelation (42:1, 3–4) and salvation (49:6), and, not as priest but as victim, voluntarily submits to a death interpreted in the substitutionary terms of the levitical sacrifices (53:4–6, 8, 10–12).

The link between the first Servant Song and its context may be seen in the double 'behold' of 41:29; 42:1. The former verse is the climax of Isaiah's awareness of Gentile need; the latter is the introduction of one who will bring *mišpāṭ* to the Gentiles ('The religion of Jehovah regarded as a system of practical ordinances', Skinner, *Isaiah*, 1905, *ad loc.*). Both in relation to creation (40:12–31) and history (41:1–29) the God of Israel is the only God. This constitutes the ground for a word of comfort to Israel (40:1–11; 41:8–20) but it also exposes the plight of the larger part of the created and historical world (40:18–20, 25; 41:5–7, 21–24, 28–29). The Servant is divinely endowed (42:1) precisely to meet this need (42:1b, 3b–4).

Between the first and second Servant Songs a significant movement of thought develops. The first Song does not raise the question of the identity of the Servant but concentrates on his task. No sooner, however, has Yahweh confirmed this task as his will for his Servant (42:5–9) and committed himself to its accomplishment (42:10–17) than the prophet turns to an exposure of the plight of Israel (42:18–25). This significant passage must be deeply pondered by all who would understand this central section of the Isaianic literature: the nation of Israel is blind, deaf (vv. 18–19), enslaved (v. 22), under judgment for sin (vv. 23–25a) and spiritually unperceptive (v. 25b). In the sequence of the chapters, we have thus been informed that the Servant cannot be the nation. But Isaiah has not our preoccupation with the Servant's identity and proceeds (43:1–44:23) to indicate in promissory fashion that both the political (43:1–21) and spiritual (43:22–44:23) needs of Israel will be met by Yahweh. His provision in the former category is Cyrus (44:24–48:22), before whom Babylon falls (46:1–47:15) and by whom Israel leaves captivity (48:20–22).

A major preoccupation in Is. 48 is the sinfulness of Israel (vv. 1, 4–5, 7–8, 18, 22). Two things thus lie side by side: release from Babylon and continuance in sin. V. 22 is an apt climax and an equally apt introduction to the second Song. A change of address (from Babylon to home) is not a change of heart; the people may have come back to the land but they have yet to come back to Yahweh. That which has been promised of spiritual redemption (43:22–44:23) is to be fulfilled by the Servant who inherits the name they have forfeited (49:3; *cf.* 48:1) and, without loss of the task of bringing salvation to the Gentiles, adds the task of bringing Jacob to Yahweh (49:5–6).

The third Song in its content displays the Servant as the totally obedient one, suffering for obedience' sake, and in its context sets the Servant apart from even the faithful among the people of God. In contrast to Zion, despondent (49:14–26), and unresponsive (50:1–3), the Servant responds to Yahweh (50:4–5) with buoyant, optimistic faith (50:6–9) and becomes the Exemplar of all who would fear Yahweh (50:10): indeed, apart from the Servant, man is left to his own powers of self-illumination and under divine disapproval (50:11).

The command to watch ('Behold', 52:13) is in effect the climax of a number of addresses to the faithful (51:1, 4, 7) seen in their own persons or typified as Jerusalem/Zion (51:17; 52:1). Thus Isaiah continues to distinguish the Servant from the remnant until he stands out in terms 'unmistakably individual' (H. H. Rowley, *The Servant of the Lord*, 1965, p.52), internationally triumphant (52:13–15), rejected (53:1–3), sin-bearing (53:4–6), voluntarily the innocent sufferer of lawlessness, consigned to have 'his grave with wicked men, but with a rich man in his death' (53:7–9), yet living to dispense the fruits of his dying, the worthy recipient of the divine accolade, 'I will give him the many as his portion and he will take the strong as spoil' (53:10–12). And in all this, the universality of the Servant's redemptive work is not forgotten. The call goes first to the barren Zion (54:1–17) to enter peace (54:10) and to inherit righteousness (54:14, 17), and then to the whole world to enter a free salvation (55:1–2) and to enjoy the mercies promised to David (55:3).

The delineation of the Servant is thus straightforward and unified, but the person of the Servant retains its proper element of mystery: a man among men (53:2–3) who is also 'the arm of the Lord' (53:1). Aptly, Mowinckel brings out the proper emphasis: 'Who could have believed what we have heard? Who could have seen here the arm of Yahweh?' (53:1). For the 'arm of Yahweh' is none other than Yahweh himself (52:10) acting again as he acted at the Exodus and the Red Sea to redeem and ransom (51:9–11).

2. *The anointed Conqueror.* The third section of the Isaianic literature completes the Messianic forecast. Isaiah has shown in chs. 1–37 a world-wide king but yet without indicating how the Gentiles will be gathered in. In his delineation of the Servant he has foretold a world-wide salvation, bringing all

the redeemed under David's rule. Both these sections have included but without emphasis the exacting of vengeance on Yahweh's foes (*e.g.* 9:3–5; 42:13, 17; 45:16, 24; 49:24–26). This topic now predominates as one who, like the King (11:2, 4) and the Servant (42:1; 49:2), is anointed with the Spirit and the Word (59:21), steps on to the scene.

The vision of the world-wide house of prayer (56:1–8) is in danger of perishing under the weight of self-seeking princes (56:9ff.), religious corruption (57:3ff.), inability to rise to the heights of truly spiritual religion (58:1ff.) and to find the way of peace (59:1ff.). Under these circumstances, and in default of there being any other Saviour, Yahweh himself dons the garments of salvation (59:16–20) bringing a Redeemer to Zion. Mysteriously, however, the covenant which ensues is addressed to one endowed with Yahweh's Spirit and speaking Yahweh's words (59:21), but plainly this Zion-orientated work is world-wide for at once the universal call is issued (60:1ff.). In a manner reminiscent of the literary method of chs. 40–55, the affirmation that Yahweh will hasten the great vision to its fulfilment (60:22) merges into the testimony of one endowed with Yahweh's Spirit and Word to comfort (61:1–2a) and avenge (v. 2b). The work of comfort occupies the prophet until the end of ch. 62 and it is now the endowed One who dons the garments of Salvation (61:10–11) as formerly (59:16f.) did Yahweh himself. The mighty 63:1–6 relates the work of redemption to its counterpart in vengeance wherein one working alone (as Yahweh was alone, 59:16) treads the winepress and exacts a full penalty.

In his person, this Messianic Conqueror hardly differs from the king and the Servant. He has the same spiritual endowment; he is a man among men. But two other sidelights are given. First, he is described as the conqueror of Edom, a task accomplished by no other Israelite king but David (*cf.* Nu. 24:17–19). May we not see here the identity of the anointed Conqueror with the Davidic Messiah? Secondly, in the development of the theme it is he who at the last wears the garments of salvation and vengeance which Yahweh himself was seen to don (59:16ff.). Once more the prophet introduces the Messianic motif: the identity and the distinction of Yahweh and his Anointed.

3. *The Branch.* Under this Messianic label there is a beautifully unified series of predictions. Je. 23:5ff. and 33:14ff. are virtually identical. Yahweh will raise a Branch 'for David'. He is a king in whose days Israel will be saved. His rule is marked by judgment and righteousness. His name is 'Yahweh our Righteousness'.

The second of these passages associates the Branch prophecy with the assertion that the priests shall never want a man to offer sacrifice. This might seem somewhat extraneous were it not for the subsequent use made by Zechariah of the same Messianic figure. In Zc. 3:8 Joshua and his fellow-priests are declared to be a sign of Yahweh's purpose to bring forth 'my servant the Branch', who will accomplish the priestly work of removing the iniquity of the land in one day. Again, in 6:12ff., Zechariah returns to the Branch, who shall grow up in his place, build the Temple of Yahweh, be a priest upon his throne, and enjoy perfect, covenanted peace with Yahweh. The Branch is clearly, therefore, the Messiah in his kingly and priestly offices. He is the fulfilment of Ps. 110, with its designation of the king as an eternal Melchizedek-priest.

Having reached this point, it is now fair to refer to Is. 4:2–6. The Messianic reference of v. 2 is a matter of dispute, and is often denied, but, seeing that the following verses agree exactly with the use of the Branch in the passages already cited, the inference need not be resisted that the Messiah is found here too. He is the Branch of Yahweh, and he is associated with the priestly work of washing away the filth of the daughters of Zion (v. 4) and with the kingly reign of Yahweh in Jerusalem (vv. 5–6). The picture of the Branch summarizes in one figure what Isaiah elsewhere extended and analysed into the work of King, Servant and Conqueror. The Messianic motifs of humanity and divinity, and of identity and distinction in Deity, are present, for the Branch 'belongs to David' and yet is 'Yahweh's'—the very imagery speaking of origin and nature; he is 'my servant', and yet his name is 'Yahweh our righteousness'.

4. *The seed of the woman.* We have noticed throughout this study that the humanity of the Messiah is stressed. In particular, it is often through the mother that the human origin is described. It is easy to over-emphasize small details, but nevertheless it should be noted that both Immanuel (Is. 7:14) and the Servant (Is. 49:1) are cases in point. Likewise, Mi. 5:3 speaks of 'she who is in travail', and very likely the difficult Je. 31:22 refers to the conception and birth of a remarkable child. The most notable prophecy of the seed of the woman, and the one from which the whole notion may well have arisen, is given in Gn. 3:15. It has become almost an accepted thing to refuse any Messianic reference here, and to regard the verse as 'a quite general statement about mankind and serpents, and the struggle between them' (Mowinckel). But as a direct matter of the exegesis of these chs. in Genesis, it is unfair to isolate this verse from its context and to treat it aetiologically. In order to see the force of the promise made in 3:15, we must pay heed to the part played by the serpent in the tragedy of the Fall. Gn. 2:19 shows man's superiority over the animal creation. The Creator graciously instructs the man as to his difference from the mere animals: he can impose his order upon them, but among them is not found any 'help meet for him'. His like is not there.

But now, in Gn. 3, another phenomenon meets us: a talking animal, an animal which somehow has risen above its station, and presents itself as man's equal, able to engage him in intelligent conversation, and even as his superior, able to instruct him in matters wherein he was formerly misguided, to give him what purports to be a correct understanding of God's law and God's person. The serpent speaks as one well able to weigh God in the balances and find him wanting, to discern the inner thoughts of the Almighty and to expose his underhand motives! Even more, he displays open hostility to God; a hatred of God's character, a readiness to destroy his creation-plan, a sneering mockery of the Most High. It is simply not good enough to see in the serpent the spirit of man's irrepressible curiosity (Williams) or any such thing. The Bible knows only one who displays this ungodly arrogance, this hatred of God, and it is no wonder that the serpent in Eden becomes 'that ancient serpent, who is the Devil and Satan' (Rev. 20:2). But where sin abounds, grace superabounds, and so it is that at the very moment when Satan seems to have scored a signal triumph it is declared that the seed of the woman will crush and destroy Satan. He will be himself bruised in the process, but will be victorious. The seed of the woman will reverse the whole calamity of the Fall.

5. *The Son of man*. On Dn. 7, a passage which has aroused so much discussion and difference of opinion, it is only possible here, as throughout this article, to state one point of view. The essence of the vision is the judgment scene, wherein the Ancient of Days disposes of the worldly and hostile powers—we note in passing the reappearance of the kingly motif of Ps. 2—and there is brought to him 'with the clouds of heaven . . . one like a son of man' who receives a universal and everlasting dominion. It is clear that the general reference here must be associated in some way with the universal dominion already generally observed in the Messianic passages, but the question whether the 'one like a son of man' is the Messianic individual or is intended to be a personification of the people of God must not be thus summarily settled. It is urged that vv. 18 and 22 speak of judgment and the kingdom being given to the 'saints of the Most High', and that therefore reason demands that the same recipients must be intended by the single figure of vv. 13–14.

However, we may also notice that there is a double description of the beasts who are the enemies of the saints. V. 17 says 'these four great beasts . . . are four kings' and v. 23 says the fourth beast 'shall be a fourth kingdom'. The figures are both individual (kings) and corporate (kingdoms). We must adopt the same preliminary reference for the 'one like a son of man'. Next, we must view the king–kingdom relationship in its OT context. The king is prior, and the kingdom is derivative. It is not the kingdom which fashions the king, but the reverse. As for the beast-kings, they are the personal enemies of the kingdom of the saints, and they involve their kingdoms with them; equally the 'one like a son of man' receives universal dominion, and in this is implicated the dominion of his people (*cf*. the dominion of Israel in the dominion of the conqueror, Is. 60, *etc*.). On this ground it is urged that the 'one like a son of man' is the Messianic individual. As such, he fits into the general pattern found throughout the whole series of expectations: he is a king, opposed by the world, but achieving universal dominion by the zeal of the Lord, *i.e.* from the Ancient of Days, in Daniel's imagery; he is man, by the terms of his title, and yet he does not originate among men but comes 'with the clouds of heaven', a position characteristic of God (see, *e.g*., Ps. 104:3; Na. 1:3; Is. 19:1). Here is the same polarity of human and divine which is found almost without exception in OT Messianism, and which ought by now to occasion us no surprise.

6. *The anointed Prince*. It is something to say of any passage of the OT that it has attracted more interpretative enquiry and suggestion than any other, yet this is probably the case with Dn. 9:24–27. There is, however, a measure of appropriateness in attempting to urge one or two generalities in connection with it for, having begun our review with a secular 'anointed prince', Cyrus, it has at least the virtue of neatness to end it with the anointed Messiah himself.

The verses themselves fall into two unequal parts: clearly vv. 25–27 indicate a programme to be worked out in history. It starts with a command to rebuild Jerusalem (v. 25), from which a period of 62 weeks stretches until the coming of 'an anointed one, a prince'. V. 26 looks to what happens 'after the sixty-two weeks', and v. 27 brings matters to a 'decreed end'. V. 24, however, stands apart as offering a total statement of the purposes which are thus to be accomplished: three are negative, to finish transgression, put an end to sin and to atone for (*kipper*, to pay the atonement price) iniquity; three are positive, to introduce everlasting righteousness, to attest the veracity of vision and prophet and to anoint a most holy place (lit., a 'holiness of holinesses', elsewhere referring to the innermost shrine of the tabernacle, Ex. 26:33, the altar of burnt offering, Ex. 29:37, the tabernacle and all its furnishings, Ex. 30:29, the incense, Ex. 30:36, the priestly portions of the cereal-offerings, sin-offering, guilt-offering, Lv. 2:3, 10; 6:17, 25; 7:1, 6, the bread of the Presence, Lv. 24:9 (Nu. 4:7), and every 'devoted thing' including persons, Lv. 27:28). While there are in this statement of purpose a few difficulties with individual words and some unique expressions, the meaning of the whole cannot be in doubt: 'that the messianic age is to be marked by the abolition and forgiveness of sin, and by perpetual righteousness' (S. R. Driver, *Daniel*, 1900, p. 136).

It is very difficult to see how any such exalted purpose is explicable in terms of those interpretations which focus the prophecy on Antiochus Epiphanes: 7 'weeks' elapse between Jeremiah's prophecy (*cf*. Dn. 9:2) and the anointed prince, Cyrus; 62 weeks cover the history of Jerusalem to the high-priesthood of Onias III in 175 BC who was 'cut off', anointed one though he was, being assassinated and replaced by his brother. The 'prince' of v. 26 is Antiochus himself. But where, one might reasonably ask, is the finishing of transgression, the paying of the atoning price, the bringing in of everlasting righteousness?

To base the passage on the Lord Jesus Christ involves no greater [illegible] Antiochus-theory and, on the contrary, provides a more persuasive use of individual expressions and a complete satisfaction of the purposes stated in v. 24. The period between the decree and the anointed prince is in total 69 weeks (v. 25, lit. as NASB, 'From the issuing of a decree . . . [there will be] seven weeks and sixty-two weeks.') The division into two may well mark the period between Cyrus and Ezra–Nehemiah (a noteworthy point in the city's history) and between then and the coming of 'an anointed one, a prince'. During his 'week' the anointed one 'empowers a covenant with many' (v. 27) and causes sacrifice to cease—though, as we know, the meaningless, post-Calvary ritual slaughter of animals continued till the desolator brought the old Temple itself to an end.

It is one thing to wrest words into unnatural shapes to make them fit later knowledge. It is another altogether to refuse the aid of later light in trying to elucidate obscurities. That Daniel was instructed to expect one who would mean the end of sin's long reign, the eternal establishment of righteousness, and the inauguration of true religion, cannot be controverted, nor can it be controverted even remotely, that not until Jesus, nor with any necessity after him, has such been accomplished, nor in any other has the whole range of OT Messianism found its goal, the attestation of both vision and prophet.

BIBLIOGRAPHY. H. Ringgren, *The*

Messiah in the OT, 1956; A. Bentzen, *King and Messiah*, 1956; S. Mowinckel, *He that Cometh*, 1956; J. Klausner, *The Messianic Idea in Israel*, 1956; H. L. Ellison, *The Centrality of the Messianic Idea for the Old Testament*, 1953; B. B. Warfield, 'The Divine Messiah in the Old Testament', in *Biblical and Theological Studies*, 1952; H. H. Rowley, *The Servant of the Lord*, 1952; A. R. Johnson, *Sacral Kingship in Ancient Israel*, 1955; *IDB*, *s.v.* 'Messiah'; Y. Kaufmann, *The Religion of Israel*, 1961; G. A. F. Knight, *A Christian Theology of the Old Testament*, 1959; J. A. Motyer, 'Context and Content in the Interpretation of Is. 7:14', *TynB* 21, 1970; G. J. Wenham, '*B^{e}TULAH*, "A Girl of Marriageable Age"' *VT* 22, 1972, pp. 326–347; E. J. Young, *Daniel's Vision of the Son of Man*, 1958; P. and E. Achtemeier, *The Old Testament Roots of our Faith*, 1962. J.A.M.

II. In the New Testament

Christos, 'anointed', is the Gk. equivalent of Heb. *māšîaḥ*, Aram. *m^{e}šîḥā'* (transliterated as *messias* in Jn. 1:41; 4:25, in both cases glossed by *christos*). In the vast majority of NT uses, either alone or in the combination *Iēsous Christos*, it is apparently used as a name for Jesus without necessary reference to its original sense, as 'Christ' is in modern usage. Such uses (largely found in the NT letters, though some also in Acts and Rev., and a few in the Gospels) are not discussed in this article.

a. The Gospels

Particularly in the Gospel of John (1:20, 25, 41; 4:25, 29; 7:26f., 31, 41f.; 9:22; 10:24; 11:27) but also in the Synoptic Gospels (Mk. 8:29; 14:61; Lk. 2:11, 26; 3:15; 4:41) *christos* usually denotes the expected deliverer in a quite general sense. Such uses convey the impression of a widespread and eager expectation, without implying any specific figure or theme of OT hope. Sometimes, however, a nationalistic note is present when *christos* is used in connection with Jesus in the Gospels, particularly when it is linked with the title 'king of the Jews' (Mt. 2:4; 26:68; 27:17, 22; Mk. 12:35; 15:32; Lk. 23:2). While there were many strands to Messianic expectation in 1st-century Palestine, some of which find an echo in the NT (especially the prophet like Moses (above, **I.** *a.* 2) expected by Jews and Samaritans: see Jn. 6:14; *cf.* Mt. 21:11; Lk. 7:16; this expectation is the background also to Jn. 4:25), the dominant popular hope was of a king like David, with a role of political liberation and conquest, and it seems clear that this would be the popular understanding of *christos*.

It is against this background that we must understand Jesus' remarkable reluctance to apply the title *christos* to himself. The only time when he is recorded as doing so (apart from two passages where it seems to mean no more than 'I', and is probably an editorial addition, Mk. 9:41; Mt. 23:10) is with the Samaritan woman, to whom it would convey the idea of a prophet like Moses, not of a Jewish king (Jn. 4:25f.). His discussion of the status of the Messiah in Mark 12:35–37 does not explicitly claim the title for himself, and is aimed at dissociating it from the political connotations of 'son of David'.

Not that he denied that he was the Messiah. His constant stress on the fulfilment of OT hopes in his ministry (*JESUS CHRIST, **VII.** *b*, *c*) must carry this implication. John the Baptist, hearing of the works of the *christos*, asked if he was the 'coming one', and Jesus replied by pointing to his literal fulfilment of Isaiah 35:5f. and 61:1, the latter an unambiguously Messianic passage (Mt. 11:2–5). He declared at Nazareth that the same passage was fulfilled 'today' (Lk. 4:18ff.).

Yet when Peter acclaimed him as the *christos*, Jesus swore his disciples to secrecy, and went on to teach that his role was to suffer and be rejected, a role which Peter found quite incompatible with his idea of Messiahship; and the title he used to teach this was not *christos* but 'Son of man' (Mk. 8:29–33). When the high priest challenged Jesus to say whether he was the *christos*, he replied affirmatively (though the wording in Matthew and Luke suggests hesitation over the term used), but went on to speak of his role (as 'Son of man' not *christos*) as one of future vindication and authority, not present political power (Mk. 14:61f. and parallels).

All this indicates that Jesus' conception of his Messianic role was so much at variance with the popular connotations of *christos* that he preferred to avoid the title. His mission had been launched by God's declaration at his baptism (Mk. 1:11; *JESUS CHRIST, **IV.** *b*) whose words alluded to two key OT passages, the one (Ps. 2:7) marking out his role as Messianic king of the line of David, but the other (Is. 42:1) indicating that this role was to be accomplished through the obedience, suffering and death of the *Servant of the Lord. This declaration clearly moulded Jesus' understanding of his Messianic vocation, as may be seen from his careful selection of OT passages in explaining his mission, among which Is. 53, with its explicit portrayal of a Servant who would suffer and die to redeem his people, took pride of place (*JESUS CHRIST, **VII.** *g*). But he did not apply to himself the many predictions of a Davidic king (except by implication in Mk. 12:35–37, and there his intention was to play down this aspect of Messiahship), and avoided such titles as 'son of David' and 'king of Israel' which others used of him (*e.g.* Mk. 10:47f.; 15:2; Mt. 12:23; 21:9, 15; Jn. 12:13; 18:33ff.) as consistently as he did *christos*. The openly Messianic demonstration of the entry to Jerusalem (Mk. 11:1–10) was deliberately staged to call to mind Zechariah's prophecy of a humble king, bringer of peace not war (Zc. 9:9f.). But when the excited crowd wanted to make him a king of the more traditional nationalistic type he ran away (Jn. 6:15). It was only after his death and resurrection, when a misunderstanding of his mission as one of political liberation was no longer possible, that he referred to his mission of suffering explicitly as that of the *christos* (Lk. 24:26, 46).

On two significant occasions, as we have seen, while Jesus did not reject the suggestion that he was the *christos*, he quickly dropped the title in favour of 'Son of man'. That this was his chosen title for himself is indisputable in the light of its use in the NT (41 times, not counting parallels, in the Synoptic Gospels and 12 in John, *all* on the lips of Jesus; with no clear use as a title in the rest of the NT except in Acts 7:56), and is denied by radical scholarship only on the basis of large-scale excision of the relevant sayings as unauthentic. It is also clear that he applied this title to himself not only in his future glory (as its origin in Dn. 7:13f. would suggest), but in his earthly humiliation and particularly in his suffering and death. It was thus apparently his chosen term to convey the whole scope of his Messianic vocation as he conceived it, as distinct from the popular notion of the *christos*. This was because, apart from the special use of 'Son of man' in the *Similitudes of Enoch* (probably an isolated work, and possibly later than the time of Jesus; * PSEUDEPIGRAPHA, I), it was not in current use as a Messianic title. (For this point see R. T. France, *Jesus and the Old Testament*, 1971, pp. 187f.; Dn. 7:13f. was understood as a Messianic prophecy, but without turning the common Aram. phrase 'son of man' into a title.) Jesus could thus use it to carry his own unique conception of Messiahship without importing alien ideas already inherent in the title, as would have been the case with *christos* or 'son of David'. See further * JESUS CHRIST, TITLES OF.

b. Acts and Epistles

At the centre of the earliest Christian preaching as recorded in Acts is the declaration that Jesus, rejected and crucified by the Jewish leaders, is in fact the Messiah. This certainty is based on the resurrection, which has finally vindicated his claim: 'Let all the house of Israel therefore know assuredly that God has made him both Lord and Christ, this Jesus whom you crucified' (Acts 2:36).

This assertion was so improbable in the light of the popular conception of Messiahship that much attention was given to the scriptural ground for the rejection, death and resurrection of the Messiah (*e.g.* Acts 2:25–36; 3:20–26; 13:27–37; 18:28). In this apologetic and preaching activity among Jews the early Christians apparently had no inhibitions about using the actual term *christos*, and frequently in Acts it occurs in this context, not as a name of Jesus but as a title in its original sense of the expected deliverer (*e.g.* Acts 2:31, 36; 3:18, 20; 5:42; 9:22; 17:3; 18:5, 28). What had been during Jesus' ministry a misleading term was now, since his death and resurrection, no longer open to a political construction, and was taken up enthusiastically by his followers in presenting his claims to the Jews.

Their message was not only, or even mainly, that Jesus had been the Messiah while on earth, but that now, exalted to the right hand of God, he was enthroned as the Messianic King. Ps. 110:1, which Jesus had alluded to in this connection (Mk. 14:62), is taken up by Peter at Pentecost (Acts 2:34–36), and becomes perhaps the most quoted OT verse in the NT. Jesus is not a king on David's throne in Jerusalem, but, as David's lord, the ruler of an eternal and heavenly kingdom, waiting at God's right hand until all his enemies will be placed under his feet. The Messiah whose earthly humiliation was in such striking contrast with the political power of popular Messianic expectation now far transcends that popular hope of a merely national kingdom.

The triumphant proclamation of the first Christians that despite all appearances Jesus was indeed the *christos* seems quickly to have given way to such an unchallenged assumption of this truth within Christian circles that *Christos*, either alone or in combination with *Iēsous*, came to be used as a name of Jesus, and Jesus' followers could be known as *Christianoi* (Acts 11:26). Already by the time of the earliest letters of Paul *Christos* has ceased to be a technical term and has become a name. No doubt it was a name which continued to be full of deep meaning for a Jewish Christian, but it is remarkable that in the nearly 400 uses of *christos* in the letters of Paul (most of them written, of course, to predominantly Gentile churches) there is only one clear case of its use in its original technical sense (Rom. 9:5, significantly in a passage discussing the question of the Jews). The same is true, if less strikingly, of the other NT letters, though 1 Pet. 1:11 uses *christos* of the Messiah of OT prophecy, and 1 Jn. 2:22; 5:1 shows that the issue of whether Jesus was the *christos* was still a live one (though now in a different sense, probably, confronting Gnostic rather than Jewish opposition).

But if the technical sense of *christos* was quickly eclipsed by its use as a personal name, this does not mean that the church lost interest in the question of Jesus' fulfilment of OT hopes. Paul stressed that the basic elements of Jesus' work were 'according to the scriptures' (1 Cor. 15:3f.). This emphasis was not only necessary for effective preaching to Jews, but was clearly of absorbing interest to the Christians themselves; building on Jesus' expounding to them 'in all the scriptures the things concerning himself' (Lk. 24:27), they searched further in the OT for passages to throw light on his Messianic role. Beginning with the sermons in Acts 2, 7 and 13, they continued to draw together collections of relevant texts (*e.g.* Rom. 10:5–21; 15:9–12; Heb. 1:5–13; 2:6–13, *etc.*), and to explore OT themes which pointed forward to the ministry of Jesus (*e.g.* the recurring theme of the * 'stone', or the * Melchizedek priesthood of Ps. 110:4 which provides such rich material for the author of Hebrews, 5:5–10; 7:1–28). See further * QUOTATIONS.

Hebrews in particular, while it makes very sparing use of the title *christos*, consists largely of extended exposition of OT themes and their fulfilment in Jesus, who has come to bring in the new covenant and to provide the true reality of which the features of the OT dispensation were only shadows.

So if the term *christos* tended increasingly to be used simply as a name of Jesus, the fact that Jesus was the one through whom God was now working out his long-promised purpose of salvation remained of central importance in early Christian thought, as the NT writers went beyond the simple assertion of the fact of Jesus' Messiahship to explore more and more deeply the content and the meaning of that saving work.

BIBLIOGRAPHY. W. Manson, *Jesus the Messiah*, 1943; T. W. Manson, *The Servant-Messiah*, 1953; V. Taylor, *The Names of Jesus*, 1953; *idem*, *The Person of Christ in New Testament Teaching*, 1958; O. Cullmann, *The Christology of the New Testament*, 1959 (esp. ch. 5); R. H. Fuller, *The Foundations of New Testament Christology*, 1965; F. Hahn, *The Titles of Jesus in Christology*, 1969; F. F. Bruce, *This is That*, 1968; R. N. Longenecker, *The Christology of Early Jewish Christianity*, 1970; G. E. Ladd, *A Theology of the New Testament*, 1974, pp. 135ff., 328ff., 408ff. R.T.F.

METHEG-AMMAH. Apparent textual corruption in 2 Sa. 8:1 makes this name difficult to understand. No certainty seems possible, and at least three alternative interpretations present themselves.
1. That it is a place-name, evidently near Gath in the Philistine plain (*cf.* 'hill of Ammah', 2 Sa. 2:24).
2. That the RV translation, 'the bridle of the mother city', be preferred—*i.e.* regarding it as a figurative name for Gath, a chief city of the Philistines (*cf.* 1 Ch. 18:1).
3. That LXX be followed and the

METAL-WORK
See Art, Part 1.

METALWORKER
See Arts and crafts, Part 1.

METATRON
See Enoch, Part 1.

verse rendered as 'and David took the tribute out of the hand of the Philistines'. J.D.D.

METHUSELAH (Heb. *m*ᵉ*ṯûšᵉlaḥ*, meaning apparently 'man of [the deity] Lach'). The eighth Patriarch listed in the genealogy of Gn. 5. He was the son of Enoch and grandfather of Noah. He lived to the great age of 969 years according to the Heb. and the LXX (the Samaritan gives 720 years). Though they are both rendered in the LXX by *Mathousala*, there is no reason to assume that *m*ᵉ*ṯûšelaḥ* and *m*ᵉ*ṯûšā'ēl* (Methushael, Gn. 4:18) were the same person. T.C.M.

METHUSHAEL See Methuselah, Part 2.

MEZAHAB. The grandfather of Mehetabel who was the wife of Hadar, king of Edom (Gn. 36:39 = 1 Ch. 1:50). The form is that of a place- rather than personal-name (*mê zāhāḇ*, 'waters of gold'), but a man may sometimes be named after a place with which he is associated. T.C.M.

MICAH, MICAIAH ('who is like Yah?'). A common Hebrew name, variously spelt in both EVV and *MT*. Of the many men named with one of these forms, three are better known than the rest. **1.** Micah of Moresheth the prophet. (See next article.) **2.** Micah of Mt Ephraim, whose strange story is told in Jdg. 17–18, presumably to explain the origin of the sanctuary at Dan and incidentally relating the migration of the Danites to their new territory. **3.** Micaiah the son of Imlah, a prophet in Israel in the days of Ahab (1 Ki. 22:8–28; 2 Ch. 18:3–27). Nothing is known of him except for this single interview he had with Ahab, but we may infer that he had prophesied before and that Ahab was aware of his unfavourable messages. Probably he was brought out of prison to appear before Ahab, and there may be some truth in Josephus' tradition that he was the unknown prophet of 1 Ki. 20:35–43. J.B.Tr.

MICAH, BOOK OF (Heb. *mîḵâ*, abbreviated form of *mîḵāyᵉhû*, 'who is like Yahweh?').

I. Outline of contents

a. The coming judgment upon Israel (1:1–16).

b. Israel to be punished, then restored (2:1–13).

c. Condemnation of the princes and prophets (3:1–12).

d. The coming glory and peace of Jerusalem (4:1–13).

e. The suffering and restoration of Zion (5:1–15).

f. Prophetic and popular religion contrasted (6:1–16).

g. Corruption of society; concluding statement of trust in God (7:1–20).

II. Authorship and date

Authorship is usually attributed to Micah of Moresheth (1:1), whose home, identified with *Moresheth-gath in the Shephelah or lowlands of Judah, was the general locale of his prophetic activity (1:14). A younger contemporary of Isaiah, he uttered his sayings during the reigns of Jotham (*c.* 742–735 BC), Ahaz (*c.* 735–715 BC) and Hezekiah of Judah (*c.* 715–687 BC).

Some modern scholars have maintained that only Mi. 1:2–2:10 and parts of chs. 4 and 5 are the work of the prophet himself. While the last two chapters of the book have much in them that is akin to the work of Micah, critics have urged that the difference in background and style from earlier portions of the prophecy, and the comparatively subordinate position which they occupy in the book, require them to be assigned to a time later than the 8th century BC. In particular, 7:7–20 is held to be definitely post-exilic.

Other scholars have claimed that the forceful, descriptive style which is evident in each chapter of the prophecy, and the consistent revelation of divine judgment, compassion and hope, are powerful arguments for the unity of authorship of the prophecy. Arguments from style are never particularly strong at the best, since style can be altered so easily with a change of subject-matter. Furthermore, it is not easy to see why 7:7–20 should be assigned to a post-exilic period, since there is nothing in the content which is in the slightest degree at variance with the language or theology of the 8th-century BC prophets. The closing verses of the book are read each year by Jewish worshippers in the afternoon service on the Day of Atonement.

III. Background and message

Although he lived in rural surroundings, Micah was familiar with the corruptions of city life in Israel and Judah. His denunciations were directed particularly at Jerusalem (4:10), and like Amos and Isaiah he noted how the wealthy landowners took every advantage of the poor (2:1f.). He condemned the corruption rampant among the religious leaders of his day (2:11) and the gross miscarriages of justice perpetrated by those dedicated to the upholding of the law (3:10). The fact that all this was carried on in an atmosphere of false religiosity (3:11) proved for Micah to be the crowning insult.

Like his 8th-century BC contemporaries Amos, Hosea and Isaiah, Micah stressed the essential righteousness and morality of the divine nature. He was concerned also to point out that these qualities had pressing ethical implications for the life of the individual and the community alike. If the people of Israel and Judah were to take their covenant obligations at all seriously the justice which characterized the nature of God must be reflected in a similar state of affairs among the people of God.

Whereas Amos and Hosea had a good deal to say about the idolatry and immorality which were rampant in Israel and Judah as a result of the influence of pagan Canaanite religion, Micah confined his utterances to the problems arising from the social injustices perpetrated upon the small landowners, farmers and peasants. He warned those who wrongfully deprived others of their possessions that God was devising a drastic punishment for them. His denunciation of the rulers of Israel (3:1–4) and the false prophets (3:5–8) envisaged the ultimate destruction of Jerusalem because the corruption which they represented had permeated to the very core of national life.

Micah was in general accord with Amos, Hosea and Isaiah in his belief that God would use a pagan nation to punish his own guilty people. As a result he foretold the depredations of Shalmaneser V in the N kingdom, and the ultimate destruction of Samaria, capital of Israel (1:6–9). He did not view the collapse of the N kingdom in quite the same broad terms as did Isaiah, however. To Micah it brought the threat of invasion to the very doors of 'this family' (2:3), making the Assyr. invader Sennacherib the herald of a larger doom (5:5ff.).

There is a striking resemblance between the prophecies of devastation proclaimed for Samaria (1:6) and Jerusalem (3:12). A century after his death the words of Micah concerning the downfall of Zion were still remembered (Je. 26:18f.). On that occasion the prophet Jeremiah might well have been put to death for prophesying destruction for the Temple and the Holy City had not certain elders of the land recalled that Micah of Moresheth had said precisely the same thing a hundred years earlier. For Micah there could be no question as to the ultimate fate of the house of Judah. So pervasive and influential was the depraved religion of Canaan, and so widespread was the resultant corruption of society that nothing short of the exercise of divine judgment upon the S kingdom could avail for the ultimate salvation of the people of God. But before the remnant of Jacob could experience this saving grace it would be necessary for all idolatry and social corruption to be rooted out (5:10–15).

This experience would be one of tribulation and sorrow, during which the voice of prophecy would cease (3:6–7), and the sin of the nation would become evident (3:8). Consequent upon this would come the destruction of Jerusalem and the shame of captivity in the midst of other peoples (5:7–8). Restoration would be marked by a new universalistic religion in a restored Jerusalem. Under divine judgment swords would be beaten into ploughshares and spears into pruning-hooks (4:3), and the people of God would honour his name only (4:5). Prominent in the thought of Micah was the expectation of a Messiah to be born in Bethlehem (5:2). This personage would come forth from the common people, delivering them from oppression and injustice and restoring the remainder of the Israelite family to fellowship with the remnant in Zion.

Micah was at pains to point out that the saving grace of God could not be earned (6:6–8), either by pretentious sacrificial offerings or by indulgence in elaborate ritual forms of worship. Humility, mercy and justice must be an everyday experience in the life of the person who was to be well-pleasing to God.

BIBLIOGRAPHY. P. Haupt, *AJSL* 27, 1910, pp. 1–63; W. Nowack in *HDB*, 1900; J. M. P. Smith, *ICC*, 1911, pp. 5–156; G. A. Smith, *The Book of the Twelve Prophets*, 1, 1928, pp. 381ff.; S. Goldman in *Soncino Commentary*, 1948; R. K. Harrison, *IOT*, 1969, pp. 919–925; L. C. Allen, *The Books of Joel, Obadiah, Jonah and Micah*, *NIC*, 1976. R.K.H.

MICHAEL (Heb. *mîḵā'ēl*, 'who is like God?'—synonymous with Micaiah and Micah). The name of eleven biblical characters, only one of whom gets more than a passing reference. The exception is the *angel Michael, who in pseudepigraphic literature is regarded as the patron of, and intercessor for, Israel (*1 Enoch* 20:5; 89:76). In the book of Daniel he is more particularly the guardian of the Jews from the menace of the godless power of Greece and Persia (12:1), and is styled as 'one of the chief princes' and as 'your prince' (10:13, 21). In this capacity it is peculiarly fitting that he should be the archangel represented (Jude 9) as 'contending with the devil . . . about the body of Moses', that great leader of God's people to whom an angel (perhaps Michael) spoke in Mt Sinai (Acts 7:38). Michael further appears in Rev. 12:7 as waging war in heaven against the dragon. See R. H. Charles, *Studies in the Apocalypse*, 1913, pp. 158–161. J.D.D.

MICHAL (Heb. *mîḵal*) was Saul's younger daughter (1 Sa. 14:49). Instead of her sister *Merab she was married to David, for a dowry of a hundred Philistine foreskins (1 Sa. 18:20ff.). Her prompt action and resourcefulness saved him from Saul (1 Sa. 19:11–17). During his exile she was given in marriage to Palti(el), son of Laish, of Gallim (1 Sa. 25:44). After Saul's death, when Abner wanted to treat with him, David demanded her restitution—a political move to strengthen his claim to the throne (2 Sa. 3:14–16). Having brought the ark to Jerusalem, he danced before it with such abandon that Michal despised him (2 Sa. 6:12ff.). For this reason she remained childless for ever (2 Sa. 6:23). Five sons are mentioned (2 Sa. 21:8), but tradition holds that they were Merab's (so LXX and two Heb. MSS), and that Michal 'reared them'.

On one view David married Michal at Hebron 'to unite the tribes of Israel and the clans of Judah' (*EBi*); but the idea that she had one son, Ithream, her name being corrupted to Eglah (2 Sa.3:5), is without foundation. M.B.

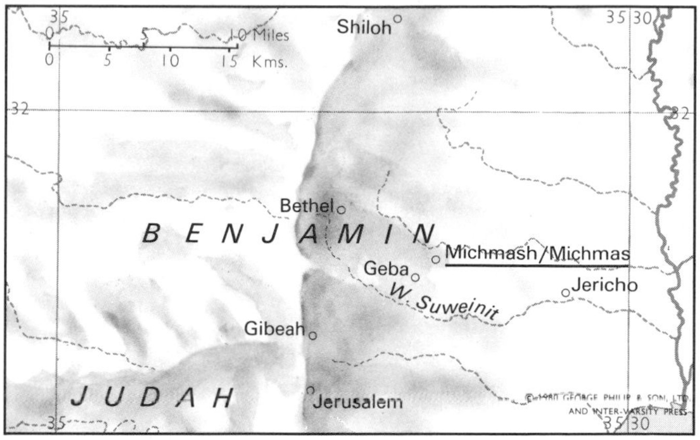

MICHMASH, MICHMAS. A city of Benjamin E of Bethel and 12 km N of Jerusalem, 600 m above sea-level, on the pass from Bethel to Jericho. In Geba, just S of this pass, Jonathan made a successful foray against the Philistine garrison (1 Sa. 13:3), whereupon the Philistines gathered a large well-equipped army and occupied Michmash, causing the scattered flight of the Hebrews (13:5ff.). Thereafter Saul's army camped at Geba (or Gibeah) with the Philistines on the other side of the pass (13:23).

Unknown to Saul, Jonathan and his armour-bearer descended from Geba and, ascending the S slope, surprised the Philistines and caused confusion in the enemy camp (for a description of this feat, see S. R. Driver, *Notes on the Hebrew Text of the Books of Samuel*², 1913, p. 106). Aided by Hebrew prisoners who had been in Philistine hands, by refugees from the previous defeat and by Saul's army, they put the Philistines to rout (1 Sa. 14:1ff.).

In his prophetic description of the coming attack on Jerusalem Isaiah (10:24, 28) represents the taking of Michmash by the Assyrians. After the Exile members of the Jewish community lived in Michmash (Ezr. 2:27; Ne. 7:31; 11:31), and it was later the residence of Jonathan Maccabeus (1 Macc. 9:73).

It is the present Mukhmâs, a ruined village on the N ridge of the Wadi Suweinit. J.D.D.

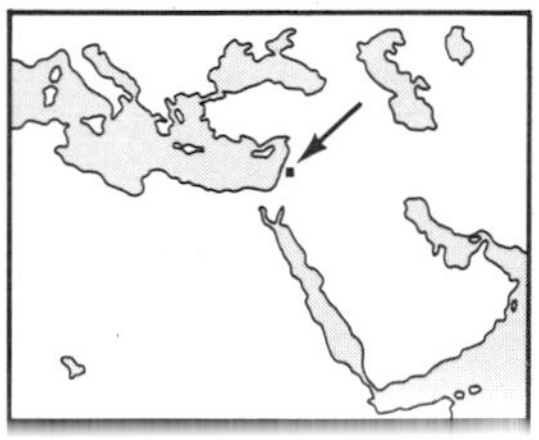

The location of Michmash.

MIDANITES. They consisted of five families, linked to Abraham through Midian, son of the concubine Keturah. Abraham sent them away, with all his other sons by concubines, into the E (Gn. 25:1–6). Thus the Midianites are

MIDAS
See Meshech, Part 2.

MIDGE
See Animals, Part 1.

MIDIAN, DAY OF
See Gideon, Part 1.

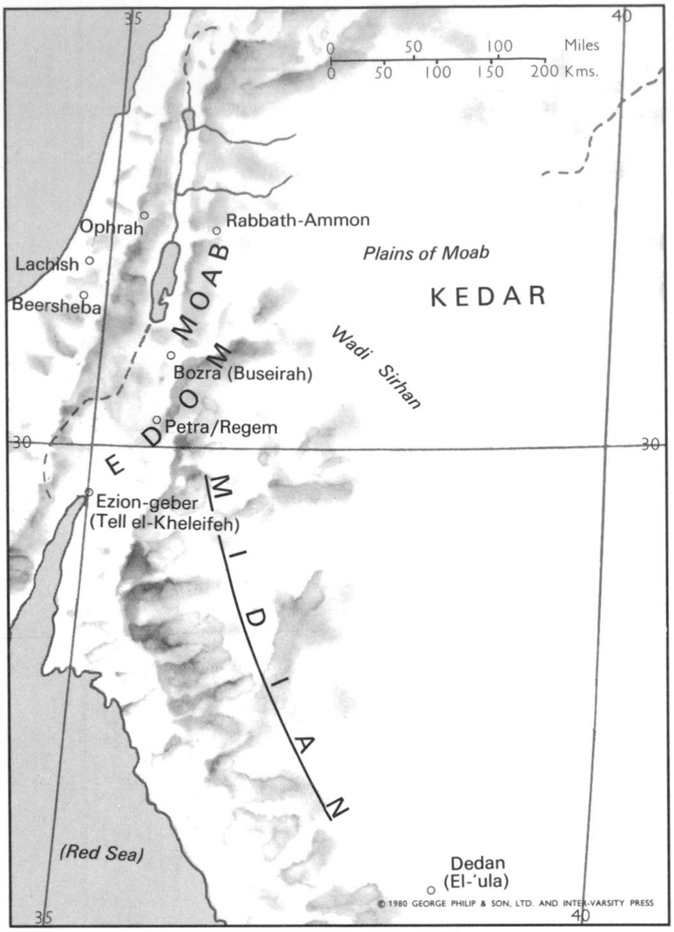

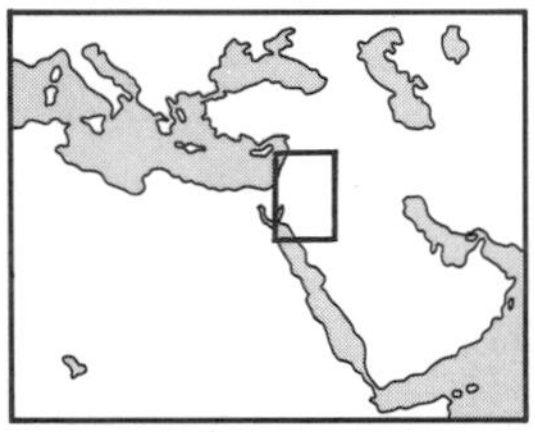

The territory of the Midianites.

found inhabiting desert borders in Transjordan from Moab down past Edom.

They were desert-dwellers associated with Ishmaelites and Medanites (Gn. 37:28, 36) when *Joseph was sold into Egypt; for the partial overlap of these three terms, *cf.* Jdg. 8:24, where the Midianites defeated by Gideon are said to have been Ishmaelites because of their use of gold ear- or nose-rings. Moses had a Midianite wife, Zipporah, father-in-law, Jethro/Reuel (Ex. 2:21; 3:1, *etc.*), and brother-in-law, Hobab (Nu. 10:29; Jdg. 4:11). As a man of the desert, Hobab was asked by Moses to guide Israel in travelling through the steppe (or 'wilderness') (Nu. 10:29–32).

Later, in the plains of Moab, the chiefs of Midian and Moab combined in hiring Balaam to curse Israel (Nu. 22ff.) and their people led Israel into idolatry and immorality (Nu. 25), and so had to be vanquished (Nu. 25:16–18; 31). The five princes of Midian were confederates of the Amorite king Sihon (Jos. 13:21). In the time of the judges, through Gideon and his puny band (Jdg. 6–8; 9:17), God delivered Israel from the scourge of camel-riding Midianites, Amalekites and other 'children of the east', an event remembered by psalmist and prophet (Ps. 83:9; Is. 9:4; 10:26). This at at present the earliest-known reference to full-scale use of camels in warfare (W. F. Albright, *Archaeology and the Religion of Israel*, 1953, pp. 132–133), but by no means the first occurrence of domesticated camels (*ANIMALS, Camel; and W. G. Lambert, *BASOR* 160, 1960, pp. 42–43, for indirect Old Babylonian evidence). The dromedaries of Midian recur in Is. 60:6. In Hab. 3:7 Midian is put in parallel with Cushan, an ancient term that probably goes back to *Kushu* mentioned in Egyp. texts of *c.* 1800 BC (see W. F. Albright, *BASOR* 83, 1941, p. 34, n. 8; *cf.* G. Posener, *Princes et Pays d'Asie et de Nubie*, 1940, p. 88, and B. Maisler, *Revue d'Histoire Juive en Égypte* 1, 1947, pp. 37–38; *ETHIOPIAN WOMAN.

K.A.K.

MIDWIFE (Heb. *m^{e}yalle${\underline{d}}$e${\underline{t}}$*, 'one who helps to bear'). The midwife helped at childbirth by taking the new-born child, cutting its umbilical cord, washing the babe with water, salting and wrapping it (Ezk. 16:4); news of the birth was

Fortress-tower (migdol) *forming a gateway to the temple of Rameses III (c. 1180 BC) at Medinet Habu, W Thebes, Egypt.* (KAK)

then brought to the father (Je. 20:15).

In Hebrew tradition, midwives are first mentioned in the time of Jacob, attending on Rachel (Gn. 35:17) and Tamar (Gn. 38:28); in the latter case the midwife tied a red thread to mark the first twin born, technically the eldest.

In Mesopotamia and Egypt and among the Hebrews women very often crouched in childbirth upon a pair of bricks or stones—the *'oḇnayim* of Ex. 1:16—or on a birthstool of similar pattern. All this can be well illustrated from ancient sources. The Egyptian Papyrus Westcar, written in the Hyksos period (*c.* 1700/1600 BC), records how three goddesses delivered a priest's wife of three sons: each took one child in her arms; they cut the umbilical cord, washed the children and put them on a cloth on a little brick bench, then went to announce the births to the waiting husband (M. Lichtheim, *Ancient Egyptian Literature*, 1, 1973, pp. 220–221). This text also illustrates the giving of punning names to children at birth as in Genesis and elsewhere. In Egyptian the two bricks or stones (and also birthstools) were called *ḏb't*, 'the brick(s)', or *msḫnt*, the latter word being followed in writing by the hieroglyph of a brick or of a pair of bricks, or of a birthstool (plan-view), *etc.* The Egyptian word *msi,* 'to give birth', was often followed by the hieroglyph of a crouching woman in the act of birth, and in one late text the figure is actually shown crouching on two bricks or stones. See W. Spiegelberg, *Aegyptologische Randglossen zum Alten Testament*, 1904, pp. 19–25; H. Rand, *IEJ* 20, 1970, pp. 209–212, pl. 47. K.A.K.

MIGDOL. The name is used of a Canaanite fort. Mentioned as a place-name in Ex. 14:2; Nu. 33:7; Je. 44:1; 46:14; Ezk. 29:10; 30:6. Several Migdols were built in the neighbourhood of the Egyptian border, but none of them can be accurately located. The Migdol of the Prophets, in the N of Egypt (possibly at Tell el-Her), is different from that in the S (P. Anastasi V), which is probably the Migdol of Succoth (Old Egyp. *ṯkw*). The Migdol in the N may be the Magdolum of *Itinerarium Antonini*, 12 Roman miles from Pelusium. (* ENCAMPMENT BY THE SEA.) C.D.W.

MIGRON. 1. A place mentioned in 1 Sa. 14:2 situated on the outskirts of Saul's home at Gibeah, where he remained during the first stage of the Philistine invasion after his election as king. It is possibly identical with **2**, a locality mentioned in the march of the Assyr. army in Is. 10:28, the modern Tell Miryam, N of Michmash. J.D.D.

MILCAH (Heb. *milkâ*, 'counsel'). **1.** The daughter of Haran (Abraham's brother) and wife of Nahor (Gn. 11:29). Her children are named in Gn. 22:20ff. Rebekah was her granddaughter (Gn. 24:15, 24, 47). **2.** One of the five daughters of * Zelophehad of the tribe of Manasseh. Because they had no brothers, they were given an inheritance when the land was divided (Nu. 26:33; 27:1; 36:11; Jos. 17:3). J.D.D.

MILCOM. In this form of spelling we have a distortion (or alternative form) of the name of the national deity of the * Ammonites. The basic root *mlk* enables an identification of the three biblical forms of the name (*milkōm, malkām, mōleḵ*). Solomon is described in 1 Ki. 11:5 as marrying an Ammonite princess and going 'after Milcom the abomination of the Ammonites'. Josiah broke down the high place which Solomon had erected for this god (2 Ki. 23:13).

In some passages in the OT, however, the term *mōleḵ* may refer to a sacrifice as in some Phoenician (Punic) inscriptions from N Africa. Certain OT passages may be read as saying that men caused children to go through fire for (or, as) a *mōleḵ* sacrifice. However in other passages the reference is to a deity. (* MALCAM, * MOLECH.)

BIBLIOGRAPHY. W. F. Albright, *Archaeology and the Religion of Israel*, 1953, pp. 162–164; D. R. Ap-Thomas in *POTT*, p. 271; R. de Vaux, *Studies in Old Testament Sacrifice*, 1964, pp. 52–90; A. R. W. Green, *The Role of Human Sacrifice in the Ancient Near East*, 1976. J.A.T.

MILETUS. The most S of the great Ionian (Gk.) cities on the W coast of Asia Minor. It flourished as a commercial centre, and in the 8th, 7th and 6th centuries BC established many colonies in the Black Sea area and also had contact with Egypt. Pharaoh Neco dedicated an offering in a Milesian temple after his victory at Megiddo in 608 BC (2 Ki. 23:29; 2 Ch. 35:20ff.). The Milesians resisted the expansion of Lydia, and in 499 BC initiated the Ionian revolt against Persia, but their city was destroyed in 494 BC. In its period of great prosperity Miletus was the home of the first

MIGHTY ACTS See Miracle, Part 2.

MIGHTY MAN See Giant, Part 1.

MILDEW See Plants, Part 3.

MILE See Weights and measures, Part 3.

MILESTONE See Travel, Part 3.

The theatre at Miletus, originally built in the 4th cent. BC and altered in Hellenistic and Roman times. (RVS)

Gk. philosophers Thales, Anaximander and Anaximenes, and of Hecataeus the chronicler. Its woollen goods were world famous.

After its Persian destruction the city had many vicissitudes, and when Paul called there (Acts 20:15; 2 Tim. 4:20) it was largely living on its past glories. At this time it was part of the Roman province of Asia, and due to the silting up of its harbour (nowadays an inland lake) by deposits from the river Maeander it was declining commercially. An inscription in the ruins shows the place reserved in the stone theatre for Jews and 'god-fearing' people. K.L.McK.

MILK (Heb. *ḥālāḇ*; Gk. *gala*). Milk was part of the staple diet of the Hebrews from patriarchal times, and where there was abundance of milk (Is. 7:22) it was possible to enjoy the added delicacy of cream or curdled milk (n*ḥem'â*, 'butter'). Hence the attraction of the land of Canaan as a land flowing with milk and honey (Ex. 3:8), for the rich supply of milk was an indication of the pasturage available. *ḥālāḇ* might be the milk of cows or sheep (Dt. 32:14; Is. 7:22), goats (Pr. 27:27), or possibly in patriarchal times of camels also (Gn. 32:15). It was contained in buckets, if RVmg. is the correct rendering of the *hapax legomenon* in Jb. 21:24, and in skin-bottles (Jdg. 4:19), from which it could conveniently be poured out for the refreshment of strangers (Gn. 18:8) or as a drink with meals (Ezk. 25:4). It is frequently coupled with honey, and with wine (Gn. 49:12; Is. 55:1; Joel 3:18), with which it may sometimes have been mingled as a rich delicacy (Ct. 5:1). The phrase 'honey and milk are under thy tongue' (Ct. 4:11) refers to the sweet conversation of the loved one.

Its metaphorical use to describe the land of Canaan has been men-

Plan of the site of ancient Miletus.

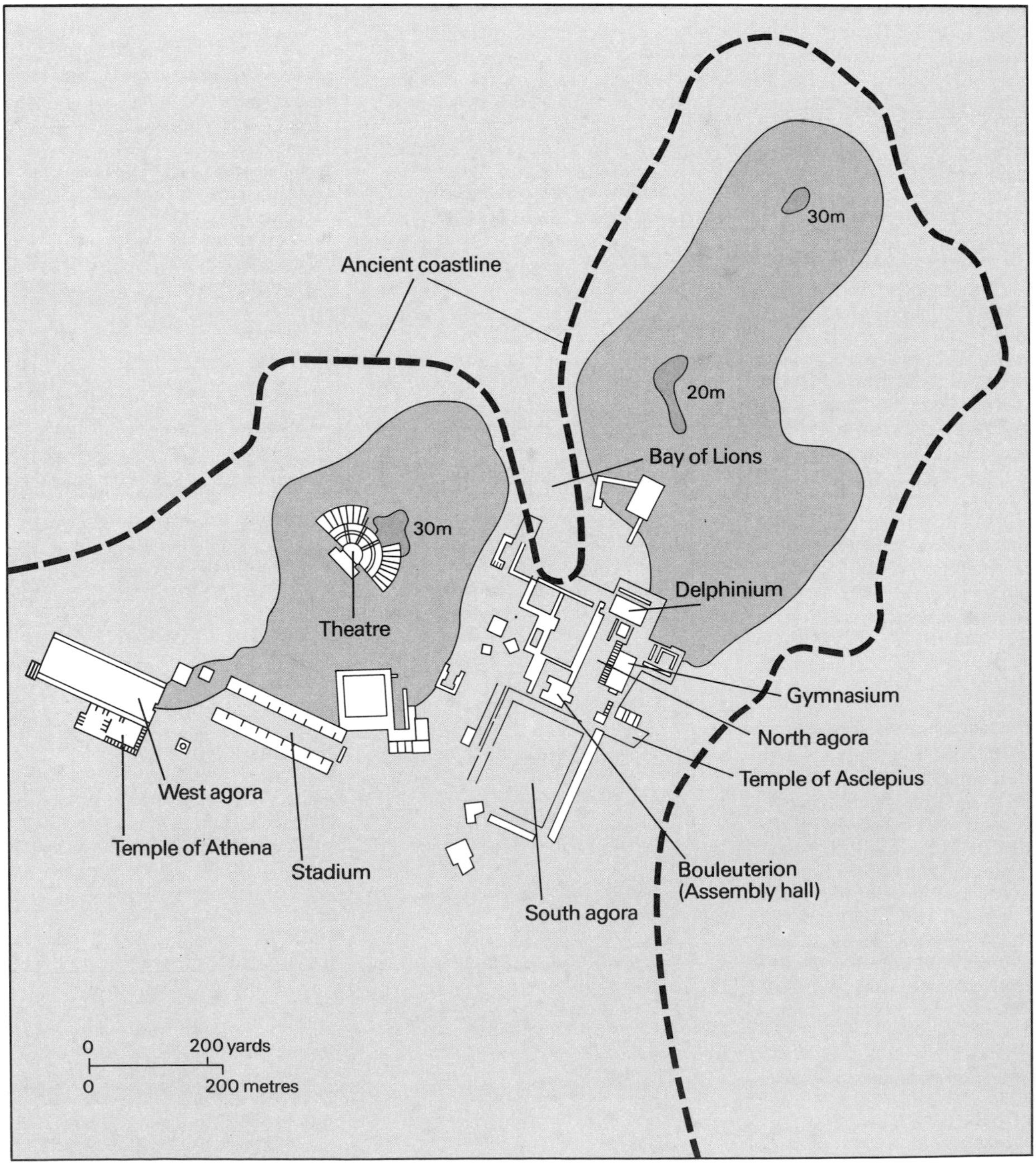

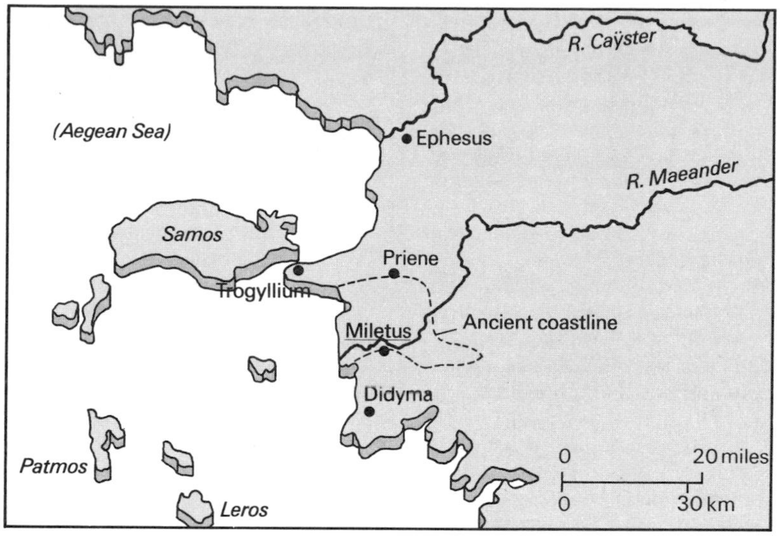

The location of the Greek city of Miletus.

tioned; Egypt was also so described by the embittered Israelites during the years of wandering (Nu. 16:13). Elsewhere it stands alone as a symbol of prosperity and abundance (Is. 60:16; Joel 3:18), and it is therefore not surprising that later Judaism compared it with the Torah. Kimchi says of Is. 55:1, 'As milk feeds and nourishes a child, so the law feeds and nourishes the soul.' This is a similar figure to that used in the NT of young converts imbibing the 'pure spiritual milk' (1 Pet. 2:2), though Paul carries the metaphor further and considers milk unworthy of mature disciples (1 Cor. 3:2; *cf.* Heb. 5:12f.).

The strange Mosaic prohibition of seething a kid in its mother's milk (Ex. 23:19; 34:26; Dt. 14:21) probably referred originally to a Canaanite ritual. On this verse, however, has been built the entire Jewish dietary law forbidding milk to be consumed at any meal at which meat is eaten, the cleavage between the two foods being so great that among orthodox Jews separate kitchen equipment has to be provided for the preparation and cooking of milk and meat dishes. J.B.Tr.

MILL, MILLSTONE. The oldest and most common method of grinding corn was to spread it on a flat stone slab and rub it with a round stone muller. Such stone querns have been found in the early Neolithic town at Jericho, together with stone *mortars (*PEQ* 85, 1953, pl. 38. 2; for an Egyptian model, see *ANEP*, no. 149). The rotary quern came into general use in the Iron Age. This consisted of two circular stone slabs, each about 50 cm across, the upper one (Heb. *reḵeḇ*, 'rider') pierced through to revolve on a pivot fixed to the lower (*cf.* the illustration of a potter's wheel). A wooden stick projecting from a hole near the outer edge of the upper stone was the handle. The grain was poured through the pivot-hole in the upper stone and crushed as this turned, so that the flour spilled from between the two stones (Heb. *rēḥayîm*) on to the ground. It was the woman's task to grind the corn (Ex. 11:5; Mt. 24:41), but it was also imposed upon prisoners as a menial service (Is. 47:2; La. 5:13). Larger types of rotary quern were turned by animals, or by prisoners (Samson, Jdg. 16:21) and were kept in a mill-house (Mt. 24:41, Gk. *mylōn*).

Since the Israelite depended on the hand-mill for his daily bread, he was forbidden to give it in pledge (Dt. 24:6). Cessation of the steady, constant sound of grinding was a sign of desolation and death (Je. 25:10; Rev. 18:22, a simile for the old man's teeth; Ec. 12:4). The upper stone was used on occasion as a missile in war (Jdg. 9:53; 2 Sa. 11:21) and as a weight (Mt. 18:6, Gk. *mylos onikos*, the largest sort of millstone, turned by an ass; Rev. 18:21). A.R.M.

MILLO. A place-name derived from the verb *mālē'*, 'to be full', 'to fill'. It is used in Jdg. 9:6, 20 of a place near Shechem, the 'house of Millo', perhaps a fortress; but its principal use is in connection with *Jerusalem, where it evidently formed part of the Jebusite city, for it was already in existence in the time of David (2 Sa. 5:9 = 1 Ch. 11:8). It was rebuilt by Solomon (1 Ki. 9:15, 24; 11:27; the 'breach' here referred to was probably a different thing) as part of his programme of strengthening the kingdom, and was again strengthened some 2½ centuries later when Hezekiah was preparing for the Assyrian invasion (2 Ch. 32:5). This verse is taken by some to indicate that Millo was another name for the whole city of David, but it can very plausibly be connected with a system of terraces, consisting of retaining walls with levelled filling, which have been discovered by Kathleen Kenyon on the E slope of Ophel Hill at Jerusalem. These terraces provided space for the construction of buildings on the slope.

Millo is otherwise mentioned as the place where Joash was murdered (2 Ki. 12:20). The LXX usually translates Millo by the name Akra, but this was a Maccabean structure. For a suggestion as to the type of construction indicated by the term *millô'*, see *ARCHITECTURE.

BIBLIOGRAPHY. J. Simons, *Jerusalem in the Old Testament*, 1952, pp. 131–144; K. M. Kenyon, *Digging up Jerusalem*, 1974, pp. 100–103. T.C.M.

MINAEANS. The people of the kingdom of Ma'īn which flourished in SW Arabia (in the N of modern Yemen) in the 1st millennium BC. The name is that of a tribe which became dominant in a state known from inscriptions to have been established with Qarnāwu as its capital by about 400 BC. It was active in establishing trade links with the N, having colonies along the Red Sea coastal route to Palestine, the best known being *Dedan. Late in the 1st century BC Ma'īn was absorbed by the expansion of its S neighbour Saba (*SHEBA, 7) and its N colonies lost their Minaean identity. The name does not occur with certainty anywhere in the Bible, though some scholars would see it in Jdg. 10:12 (Maonites); 1 Ch. 4:41 (AV 'habitation'); 2 Ch. 20:1 (altering Ammonites); 2 Ch. 26:7 (Mehunims); or Ezr. 2:50 = Ne. 7:52 (Mehunim). (*MAON; *ARABIA.)

BIBLIOGRAPHY. J. A. Montgomery, *Arabia and the Bible*, 1934, pp. 60–61, 133–138, 182–184; S. Moscati, *Ancient Semitic Civilizations*, 1957, pp. 184–194. T.C.M.

MINING AND METALS. The theatre of OT history is the so-called 'Fertile Crescent' (*i.e.* Mesopotamia, Syria, Palestine and the Nile Delta). The alluvial plains of the Tigris–Euphrates and Nile valleys provide but little stone. Much of Assyria's gypsum, indeed, comes from stone quarries near Mosul; and there is a worked vein of stone near Ur. But for the most part in those valleys clay bricks were used for building purposes in ancient times (Gn. 11:3; Ex. 1:11–14; 5:7–19).

The 'Crescent' is bounded on the N and E by high folded mountain chains consisting of rocks of many types and ages. The ranges are well mineralized and provide ores of gold, silver, copper, tin, lead and iron. On the S a complex of ancient rocks appears in which such types as granite, diorite and porphyry occur. This group extends along the E desert between the river Nile and the Red Sea, across the S half of the Sinai peninsula and E into the Arabian plateau. In some of these rocks occur gold, silver, iron, turquoise and other semi-precious stones, together with building stones of many kinds.

N of Sinai and the Arabian plateau lie the desert, Transjordan and Palestine. These are composed mainly of Cretaceous rocks (limestone, chalk and sandstone), but N and E of the upper Jordan are areas of newer volcanic basalts.

I. Non-metallic materials

a. Flint

Flint occurs abundantly in the chalk of the area and in gravels derived from the chalk. Flint is a close-grained hard rock which a steel blade will not scratch. It may be worked by percussion or pressure to produce a sharp cutting-edge. The earliest cutting tools available to man were made from flint. Stone-Age man made arrowheads, chisels, scrapers and knives of it, and it continued to be used well into the Bronze period. Zipporah, wife of Moses, circumcised her son with a flint knife (Ex. 4:25). Flint is referred to in Scripture to denote hardness, inflexibility, steadfastness (Dt. 8:15; Ps. 114:8; Is. 50:7; Ezk. 3:9).

b. Stone

Away from the alluvial plains of Mesopotamia and Lower Egypt supplies were plentiful. In Egypt limestone and sandstone were at hand in the river cliffs, and granite, diorite and other igneous rocks are found in outcrops. In Palestine limestone and sandstone occur throughout the hill country, and basalt is found E of the upper Jordan valley. The quarrying and erection of huge standing stones in Neolithic times gave experience for future quarrying and mining. Limestone is easily worked, being fairly soft, and was used for the excavation of cisterns and tombs, and the making of such things as water-pots (Je. 2:13; Mt. 27:60; Jn. 2:6). The term 'alabaster' as used in Mt. 26:7 properly refers to calcite (calcium carbonate), a much harder stone than English alabaster (calcium sulphate).

c. Marble

This is a close-grained crystalline limestone, usually white or cream in colour. It may be pink or veined in red or green. The best statuary marble in the Near East came from Paros (Minoa), but it also occurs on the W coast of the Gulf of Suez, in S Greece and in Assyria E of the river Tigris. 'Great quantities of marble' are mentioned in 1 Ch. 29:2, and may have been polished local limestone, but, considering that trade was vigorous and far-flung in David and Solomon's time, it may have been brought by sea or from the NE.

II. Metals and mining

The order in which the principal metals came into use was gold, copper (bronze) and iron. Gold is the first metal mentioned in Scripture (Gn. 2:11), and is thereafter closely associated with silver, the other *noble* metal of antiquity. All the above can occur in the native state, and as such they were first used. Silver is often found alloyed with gold. After the period when native metals were used, mainly for ornament (*Arts and Crafts), copper ores were won from outcrops at the surface, but mining began at a very early date and an advanced stage of the working of the metal (not mining) had been reached at Ur more than 1,000 years before Abraham's time. According to R. J. Forbes (*Metallurgy in Antiquity*, 1950, p. 297), 'it is certain that every form of mining from open-cut mining to the driving of galleries into the mountainside to follow up the copper-bearing strata was practised in Antiquity. But the details given on ancient mines are few.'

Mining for turquoise and for copper probably began in the time of the 1st Dynasty of Egypt *c.* 3000 BC at Magharah and Serabit el-Khadim in W Sinai, and evidence for large-scale copper working by Egyptians in the Ramesside period (13th century BC) has been found in the Arabah at Timna. Shafts more than 35 m in depth have been found in mines in Egypt. Tunnels, ventilated by shafts, were driven into hillsides, pillars being left in broad excavations to support the roof.

At first stone tools were used, but later bronze and stone continued to be used together. Wedges and fire were used to split the rock, and the ore was separated by crushing, washing and hand-picking. Smelting was usually done by feeding a charge of finely-ground copper ores and fluxes (iron oxides, limestone or sea shells) mixed with charcoal through the open top of the furnace on to the charcoal fire. As the ore was reduced the copper globules sank to the bowl-shaped bottom of the furnace. The slag which formed above the copper was drawn off into a slag-pit while still liquid and the copper ingot removed as soon as it had solidified. The ingot would need remelting in a crucible before it could be used for casting in a mould. Crucibles and slag-heaps are found at many old sites. Baskets were used for transporting the ore, and drainage tunnels constructed to get rid of surplus water. Moffatt's translation of Jb. 28:1–11 gives a vivid picture of mining in ancient times.

a. Gold

This occurs native, usually alloyed with silver in varying amounts. It is extremely malleable and ductile and does not tarnish. This property made it a very acceptable material for ornaments, such as beads and rings, even to Stone-Age man. Gold was prescribed for use in the most important furnishings in the Mosaic tabernacle (Ex. 25) and in Solomon's Temple (1 Ki. 6). The metal was especially abundant in the alluvium of the E desert of Egypt, and the Israelites must have removed large quantities of it at the Exodus. Other sources known to the ancient world were the W coast of Arabia, the mountains of Armenia and Persia, W Asia Minor, and the Aegean islands. Gold early became a valuable article of currency.

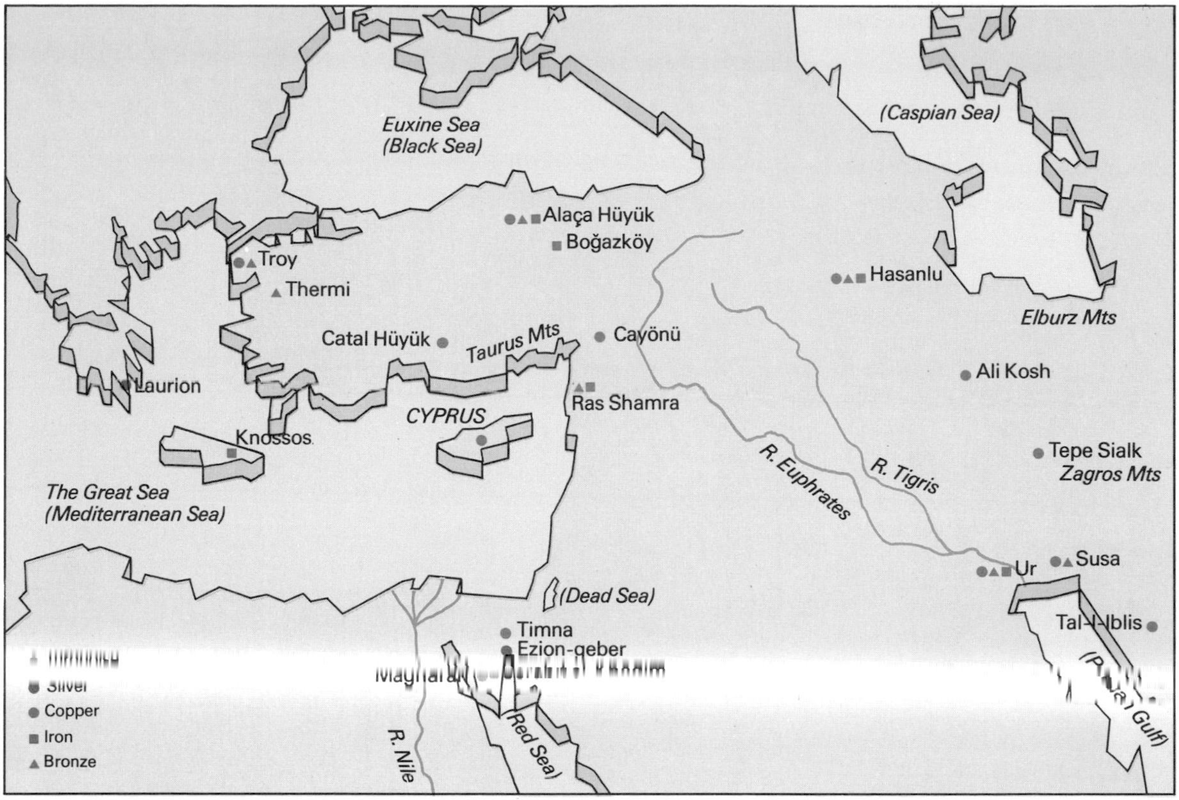

Some metal-working centres of the ancient Near East.

Egyptian metalsmiths refining copper prior to casting. Two men operate bellows with their feet to provide a forced draught to the furnace. From a wall painting in the tomb of Rekh-mi-rē', Thebes. c. 1470 BC. (SAOS)

Reconstruction of a copper-smelting furnace found at Timnah. Air is supplied by bellows; the removal of a plug allows the slag to run off, leaving the copper ore in the bottom of the furnace. This was retrieved by breaking open the furnace. Ramesside. c. 1250 BC.

A crucible found near the copper mines of Serabit el-Khadim, Sinai. It was used for melting and casting bronze. Diameter 19 cm, height 15 cm. c. 1500 BC. (UC)

b. Silver

This is ranked next to gold as a noble metal, with which it is often linked in Scripture. It does not tarnish in a pure atmosphere and will take a mirror-like polish. It is usually extracted from the sulphide ore of lead (galena), but may occur native. Silver was so plentiful in biblical times that the extraction and refining processes must have been known from an early date. Jeremiah (6:29–30) uses the failure of the refining process of lead and silver as an illustration of the refusal of the people to become obedient to God. Sources of the metal are the same as those for lead, namely, Asia Minor, the islands of the Aegean, Laurion in S Greece, Armenia and Persia, and 3 or 4 localities in the E desert of Egypt.

c. Lead

This occurs in Scripture in a few lists of metals. It was used occasionally as tablets for inscriptions (Jb. 19:24).

d. Copper (Bronze, Brass)

Heb. n^{e}*ḥōšeṯ* is translated 'copper' in Ezr. 8:27, AV, but elsewhere in AV is called 'brass'. Bronze is not mentioned in Scripture, but it was in common use from before patriarchal times (Abraham lived in the Middle Bronze Age). The 'brass' of Scripture may therefore be any of the three, except that true brass, an alloy of copper and zinc, came into use only at a late stage. Heb. *ḥašmal* in Ezk. 1:4 (AV, RV 'amber'; RSV 'gleaming bronze') may denote true brass. The first metal in general use was more or less pure copper, although the methods of production meant that some impurities were usually present, and eventually the alloy of copper and tin (bronze) was developed and produced deliberately. Some examples of brass (copper and zinc) are also known, but they were probably produced accidentally until the Romans began the production of brass for coinage and other uses about 20 BC. The ores of copper which appear at the surface are brightly coloured green and blue carbonates, and were used as eye paint or to produce a blue colour in glaze. Accidental heating of these ores could have led to the production of copper. There is no evidence in Egypt of the common use of native copper, although it was used at an early stage in the Palestinian copper industry. The ores were widespread around the 'Fertile Crescent' in Sinai, Midian, E Egypt, Armenia, Syria and Persia, and of course in Cyprus, which takes its name from the metal. The metal was used for a host of purposes. In addition to its use in the tabernacle and Temple, household articles, such as basins, ewers, idols, musical instruments, as well as armour, mirrors, *etc.*, were all made of it.

e. Tin

Tin is mentioned in Scripture only in lists of metals. It was often confused with lead in ancient times. A small percentage mixed with copper produces bronze. As tin often occurs in association with copper, the first bronze was probably made by accident. The dark heavy oxide ore, cassiterite, was taken mainly from stream-sands and was not mined, as were the other metals, until about Roman times.

Bellows (c. 1750 BC) excavated at Tell edh-Dhibai, Iraq. Diameter 44 cm, height 18 cm. A skin was fastened over the top of the bellows and was pumped up and down to force a draught out of the opening at the base into the furnace, as shown on this detail on an Egyptian wall-painting from the tomb of Rekh-mi-rē, Thebes. c. 1470 BC. (CD)

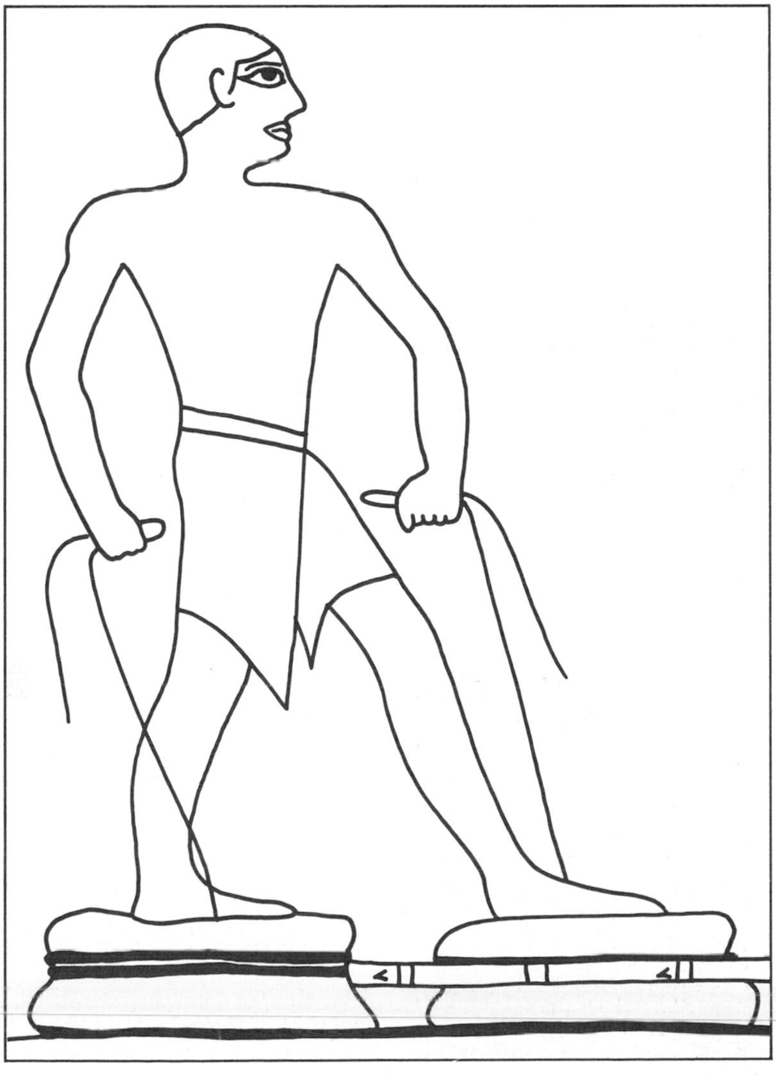

f. Iron

Rare and occasional uses of iron are known in very ancient times, but only in the native form, which has its origin in fragments of 'shooting stars' or meteors. This is probably the explanation of its early mention in Gn. 4:22, which belongs to a time long before the true Iron Age begins. Experiments with iron went on for a long time before tools could be made of it, since this depends for success on producing a metal with the properties of steel. The Hittites were the first people known to have used iron consistently, although on a limited scale, and when their kingdom came to an end the knowledge spread farther. The Philistines brought the art to Palestine, and the Israelites found themselves at a disadvantage in this respect (Jdg. 1:19; 1 Sa. 13:19–22). The balance was restored in the reigns of David and Solomon (1 Ch. 29:7). Iron was abundant along with copper in the Wadi Arabah between the Dead Sea and the Gulf of Aqabah. Iron ores were plentiful around Palestine and were to be found near Mt Carmel, Mt Hermon, SW Midian and the E Egyptian desert, in Syria, Cyprus, the Pontus coast of Asia Minor and in the Aegean Islands. The fact that both copper and iron could be mined within Solomon's realm near Ezion-geber was a literal fulfilment of Dt. 8:9.

Basalt mould for chisels and daggers from Brak, E Syria. 30 cm × 26·5 cm. 4 cm thick. c. 2300 BC. (BM)

Steel is mentioned in the AV of 2 Sa. 22:35 (= Ps. 18:34); Jb. 20:24; Je. 15:12, but the Heb. word is that for copper or bronze (*nᵉḥōšeṯ*); accordingly, RV renders 'brass' and RSV, more accurately, 'bronze'.

BIBLIOGRAPHY. R. J. Forbes, *Metallurgy in Antiquity*, 1950; L. Woolley, *Ur of the Chaldees*, 1938; W. A. Ruysch (ed.), *The Holy Land, Antiquity and Survival*, II, 2–3, 1957; T. Löw, *Die Mineralia der Juden*, 1935; A. Lucas (ed. J. R. Harris), *Ancient Egyptian Materials and Industries*, 4, 1962; A. Guillaume, 'Metallurgy in the Old Testament', *PEQ*, 1962, pp. 129–132; H. Hodges, *Technology in the Ancient World*, 1970; B. Rothenberg, *Timna*, 1972; R. F. Tylecote, *A History of Metallurgy*, 1976; Jane Waldbaum, *From Bronze to Iron*, 1978.

A.S.
J.Ru.

MINISTER. The Heb. term *mᵉšārēṯ* (LXX *leitourgos*) and its correlates normally refer to temple service, or else to the ministration of angels (Ps. 104:4); but in a more general sense Joshua is the *mᵉšārēṯ* or 'minister' of Moses (Ex. 24:13; Jos. 1:1), and Solomon's ministers (1 Ki. 10:5) are his domestic servants. In the NT the characteristic word is *diakonos*, at first in a non-technical sense, and then in Phil. 1:1 and in the Pastorals as the title of a subordinate church-officer. It refers to service in general, temporary or permanent, either by bond or free; but it has the special connotation of waiting at table (the corresponding verb is used in this sense, Lk. 12:37; 17:8, and Martha's trouble was excess of *diakonia*, Lk. 10:40). Christ appears among the disciples as *ho diakonōn*, 'one who serves' (Lk. 22:27), and he can be described as a *diakonos* of the circumcision (Rom. 15:8); following the example of this lowly service, the greatest of Christians should be a minister to the rest (Mt. 20:26; Mk. 10:43).

Thus we find the apostles and their helpers designated as ministers of God (2 Cor. 6:4; 1 Thes. 3:2), of Christ (2 Cor. 11:23; Col. 1:7; 1 Tim. 4:6), of the gospel (Eph. 3:7; Col. 1:23), of the new covenant (2 Cor. 3:6), of the church (Col. 1:25), or absolutely (1 Cor. 3:5; Eph. 6:21; Col. 4:7). But it is to be noted that Satan can also have his ministers (2 Cor. 11:15), and that there might be a minister of sin (Gal. 2:17); further, the secular power can be regarded as a minister of God (Rom. 13:4). The Seven were appointed to serve tables (*diakonein trapezais*, Acts 6:2); it is unlikely that the word is here used to denote a technical office, since it is immediately afterwards (v. 4) contrasted with the apostles' *diakonia* of the word, and in fact Stephen and Philip did the work of evangelists rather than of deacons; moreover, poor-relief at Jerusalem seems to have been managed by elders, not deacons (Acts 11:30). However, the Seven may in some sense have provided a prototype for the later assistants to the bishops, mentioned in Phil. 1:1, and characterized in 1 Tim. 3:8ff. as men of serious, honest, sober and faithful disposition. Their primary work seems to have been, not that of teaching, but visiting from house to house and relieving the poor and sick; deacons were thus the chief agents through which the church expressed its mutual fellowship of service. They seem also to have assisted at corporate worship.

It is uncertain whether 1 Tim. 3:11 refers to deacons' wives or to deaconesses; Phoebe is described (Rom. 16:1) as a *diakonos* (common gender) of the church at Cenchrea, but this perhaps means that she was a helper rather than that she held an official position; the two *ministrae* mentioned by Pliny in his letter to Trajan may have been deaconesses, but this office was not really developed until the 3rd century.

The lowliness of Christian service is emphasized even more strongly by the use of the word *doulos* or slave; it was the form of such a bond-servant that Christ assumed (Phil. 2:7), and, following his example, the apostles and their fellow-labourers are designated as the slaves of God or Christ (Rom. 1:1; Gal. 1:10; Col. 4:12; Tit. 1:1; Jas. 1:1; 2 Pet. 1:1).

Another term is *hypēretēs*, properly meaning an under-rower in a galley, and then anyone in a subordinate position. This word is used for the *ḥazzān*, a sort of verger in the Jewish synagogue, who had custody of the sacred books (Lk. 4:20); it also describes John Mark (Acts 13:5) when he acted in the capacity of batman to Paul and Barnabas. But Paul himself was proud to claim a similar position in relationship to Christ (Acts 26:16; 1 Cor. 4:1), and Luke (1:2) employs it as a generic term for the servants of the word.

Finally, the term *leitourgos* is taken over by the NT in a Christian sense. Originally it referred to public service, such as might be offered by wealthy citizens to the State; then it acquired a distinctively religious connotation, as in the LXX usage. Thus Christ appears as a *leitourgos* of the heavenly temple (Heb. 8:2), and the angels are 'liturgical', *i.e.* ministering spirits (Heb. 1:14). The corresponding verb is used when prophets and teachers minister to the Lord at Antioch (Acts 13:2); similarly, Paul describes himself as the *leitourgos* of Christ Jesus, ministering (*hierourgōn*) in the priestly service of the gospel of God (Rom. 15:16). But the NT terminology remains sufficiently fluid for the same word to be used of Epaphroditus as a minister to Paul's wants (Phil. 2:25), of Gentile assistance to Jews in material things (Rom. 15:27), and of the civil power as the servant of God (Rom. 13:6). In the Christian understanding of *ministry, whether official or otherwise, the minister renders a lowly but loving service to God or man.

BIBLIOGRAPHY. See under *MINISTRY. G.S.M.W.
R.T.B.

MINISTRY. To express the idea of professional or priestly ministration, the OT normally employs the verb *šāraṯ* and its correlates (LXX *leitourgein*), while *'āḇaḏ* (*latreuein*) refers rather to the religious service of the whole congregation or of an individual. In the NT the characteristic term is *diakonia*, which appears only in Esther among OT books, but is not there used of any priestly function; and the change in language implies a change also in doctrine, since ministry in the NT sense is not the exclusive privilege of a priestly caste. *leitourgia* is retained to describe the work of the Jewish priesthood (Lk. 1:23, RSV 'service'; Heb. 9:21, RSV 'used in worship'), and it is applied also to the more excellent ministry of Christ (Heb. 8:6); further, it can be applied, in a metaphorical sense, to the spiritual service rendered by prophets and preachers of the gospel (Acts 13:2; Rom. 15:16). But it remains true in general that the NT uses priestly language only in reference to the body of believers as a whole (Phil. 2:17; 1 Pet. 2:9).

I. Christ the pattern

The pattern of Christian ministry is provided by the life of Christ, who came not to receive service but to give it (Mt. 20:28; Mk. 10:45); the verb used in these texts is *diakonein*, which suggests something like waiting at table, and recalls the occasion when he washed the disciples' feet (Jn. 13:4ff.). It is significant that in the first recorded instance of ordination to the Christian ministry, the purpose of the office is stated to be that of 'serving tables' (Acts 6:2); and the same word is used in the same chapter (v. 4) to describe the service of the word exercised prior to this by the twelve apostles. The *minister of Christ, following the example of his Master, renders a humble but loving service to the needs of humanity at large, in the same spirit as that in which angels (Mt. 4:11; Mk. 1:13) and women (Mt. 27:55; Lk. 8:3) had ministered to the Lord on earth. Such service is reckoned as being done to Christ in the persons of the needy (Mt. 25:44); it is most frequently rendered to the saints (Rom. 15:25; 1 Cor. 16:15; 2 Cor. 8:4; 9:1; Heb. 6:10); but it is a mutual service within the fellowship of Christ's body (1 Pet. 4:10); and, as the ministry of the gospel (1 Pet. 1:12), it is in fact a ministry of reconciliation (2 Cor. 5:18) for the world.

The ability to perform such work is a gift of God (Acts 20:24; Col. [illegible] already in Rom. 12:7 it is being classified in a list of other spiritual gifts; and in 1 Tim. 3:8ff. the diaconate has become a recognized church office, probably open to women as well as men (*cf.* Rom. 16:1). But even so, the term is still being used in a wider sense; Timothy is to fulfil his ministry by doing the work of an evangelist (2 Tim. 4:5); and this work of service has as its great object the edification of the body of Christ (Eph. 4:12). In the words of Hort, Christ lifted 'every grade and pattern of service into a higher sphere . . . ministration thus became one of the primary aims of all Christian actions'; and the generic term is applied to all forms of ministry within the church.

II. Pastoral ministry

Christ is not only the pattern of the diaconate, but also, as the good Shepherd (Jn. 10:11), he is the great *Bishop of men's souls (1 Pet. 2:25, AV). In a sense, both of these offices originate from the example of Christ himself, while that of the *presbyter is a reflection of the ministry instituted by him in the apostolate (*cf.* 1 Pet. 5:1). But it would be wrong to stress these distinctions, since the terms bishop and presbyter are virtually synonymous, and the diaconate embraces many forms of assistant ministry. Pastoral care of the flock is an outstanding part of ministerial duty (Jn. 21:15–17; Acts 20:28; 1 Pet. 5:2), and is closely associated with the preaching of the word (1 Cor. 3:1–2) as the bread of life (Jn. 6:35), or pure nourishing milk (1 Pet. 2:2). The parable in Lk. 12:41–48 implies that some ministry of this character is to continue in the church until Christ's return.

III. Sacramental duties

The NT has comparatively little to say on the subject of sacramental duties; Paul regarded the administration of baptism as a subordinate activity, which he was accustomed to delegate to his assistants (1 Cor. 1:17; *cf.* Jn. 4:1f.; Acts 10:48); and although it is natural for an apostle, if present, to preside at the breaking of bread (Acts 20:7), the celebration of the Lord's Supper is nevertheless regarded as an activity of the entire congregation (1 Cor. 10:16f.; 11:25). However, a president must have been needed from the first; and in the absence of an apostle, prophet or evangelist, this duty would naturally fall to one of the local presbyters or bishops.

IV. Spiritual gifts

In its earliest form the Christian ministry is charismatic, *i.e.* it is a spiritual gift or supernatural endowment, whose exercise witnesses to the presence of the Holy Spirit in the church. Thus prophecy and glossolalia occur when Paul lays his hands on some ordinary believers after baptism (Acts 19:6); and the words there used imply that the occurrence was to some extent a repetition of the Pentecostal experience (Acts 2).

Three lists are provided in the Pauline Epistles of the various forms which such ministry may take, and it is notable that in each list administrative functions are included along with others more obviously spiritual (*Church Government). In Rom. 12:6–8 we have prophecy, *service (*diakonia*), teaching, exhortation, contributing (almsgiving), aiding and doing acts of mercy (?visitation of the sick and poor). 1 Cor. 12:28 lists apostles, prophets, teachers, together with those endowed with power to work miracles, heal the sick, help, administer, or speak with tongues. The more official catalogue in Eph. 4:11 mentions apostles, prophets, evangelists, pastors-cum-teachers, who all labour to perfect the saints in their Christian service, so that the whole church grows up in organic connection with her divine Head. Here, emphasis is laid on the ministration of the word, but the fruit of such ministry is mutual service in love. The various gifts listed in these passages are functions or ways of serving, rather than regular and stereotyped offices; one man might act in several capacities, but his ability to fulfil any depended on the prompting of the Spirit. All Christians are in fact called to minister, in their various capacities (Rom. 15:27; Phil. 2:17; Phm. 13; 1 Pet. 2:16), and it is for this ministry that the ministers of the word equip them (Eph. 4:11f.).

Not only the Twelve were included in the apostolate, but also Paul, James the Lord's brother (Gal. 1:19), who had also seen the risen Lord, Barnabas (Acts 14:14; 1 Cor. 9:5f.), who was Paul's fellow-evangelist, and Andronicus and Junias (Rom. 16:7). The primary qualification of an *'apostle' was that he had been an eye-witness of Christ's earthly ministry, particularly of the resurrection (Acts 1:21–22), and his authority depended on the fact that he had been in some way commissioned by Christ either in the days of his flesh (Mt. 10:5; 28:19) or after he was risen from the dead (Acts 1:24; 9:15). Apostles and elders might meet in council to decide a common policy for the church (Acts 15:6ff.), and apostles could be sent as delegates from the original congregation to superintend some new development in another locality (Acts 8:14ff.). But the picture of an apostolic college in permanent session at Jerusalem is quite unhistorical, and the great work of an apostle was to act as a missionary for the propagation of the gospel, in which capacity his labours should be confirmed by signs of divine approval (2 Cor. 12:12). Thus the apostolic ministry was not confined by local ties, though a division of labour might be made, as for example between Peter and Paul (Gal. 2:7–8).

The 'evangelist' exercised a similar ministry of unrestricted mission, and his work seems to have been identical with that of the apostle, except in so far as he lacked the special qualifications for the higher function; Philip, one of the original Seven, became an evangelist (Acts 21:8), and Timothy is called by the same title (2 Tim. 4:5), though he is by implication excluded (2 Cor. 1:1) from the rank of apostle.

Prophecy was by its very nature a gift of intermittent occurrence, but some individuals were so regularly endowed with it that they formed a special class of 'prophets'. Such men were found at Jerusalem (Acts 11:27), Antioch (Acts 13:1), and Corinth (1 Cor. 14:29); those mentioned by name include Judas and Silas (Acts 15:32), and Agabus (Acts 21:10), together with Anna (Lk. 2:36) and the pretended prophetess Jezebel (Rev. 2:20). Prophecy provided edification, exhortation and comfort (1 Cor. 14:3; *cf.* Acts 15:32), and might therefore be described as inspired preaching. The prophet could issue a specific direction (Acts 13:1–2) or on occasion foretell the future (Acts 11:28). Being delivered in a known tongue, his messages were more profitable than mere glossolalia (1 Cor. 14:23–25). But the gift was particularly liable to the danger of imposture, and although it should be controlled only by those possessing it (1 Cor. 14:32; 1 Thes. 5:19f.), its content must agree with the fundamental teaching of the gospel (1 Cor. 12:1–3; 1 Thes. 5:20; 1 Jn. 4:1–3), or else the prophet must be dismissed as one of the false pretenders whose coming had been foretold by Christ (Mt. 7:15).

'Pastors and teachers' (Eph. 4:11) are presumably to be identified with the local ministers instituted by the apostles (Acts 14:23) or their assistants (Tit. 1:5) to serve the needs of a particular congregation, and described indifferently as presbyters or bishops. 'Administrators' (AV 'governors') seems to be a generic name for those who administered the affairs of local congregations, while 'helpers' were engaged in works of charity, especially in attending to the sick and poor. Miraculous powers of healing and speaking with tongues were a marked feature of the apostolic age, and their renewal has been claimed at various periods from the Montanist revival onwards.

V. The origin of the ministry

There has been much debate over the precise relationship between the original and unrestricted mission of apostles and evangelists, on the one hand, and the permanent and local ministry of pastors, teachers, administrators and helpers, on the other. The latter class appears usually to have been appointed by the former; but if Acts 6 may be taken as describing a typical ordination, popular election played a part in the choice of candidates. Rom. 12 and 1 Cor. 12 might seem to imply that the church, as the Spirit-filled community, produces its own organs of ministration; on the other hand, Eph. 4:11 asserts that the ministry is given to the church by Christ. It may be suggested that, while Christ is the source of all authority and the pattern of every type of service, the church as a whole is the recipient of his divine commission. At all events, the NT is not concerned to indicate possible channels of transmission; its main preoccupation in this regard is to provide a doctrinal test for the orthodoxy of ministerial teaching.

BIBLIOGRAPHY. J. B. Lightfoot, 'Dissertation on the Christian Ministry', in *Philippians*, 1868, pp. 181–269; A. von Harnack, *The Constitution and Law of the Church in the First Two Centuries*, E.T. 1910; H. B. Swete, *Early History of the Church and Ministry*, 1918; B. H. Streeter, *The Primitive Church*, 1929; K. E. Kirk (ed.), *The Apostolic Ministry*, 1946; D. T. Jenkins, *The Gift of Ministry*, 1947; T. W. Manson, *The Church's Ministry*, 1948; J. K. S. Reid, *The Biblical Doctrine of the Ministry*, 1955; E. Schweizer, *Church Order in the NT*, E.T., 1961; L. Morris, *Ministers of God*, 1964; M. Green, *Called to Serve*, 1964; J. R. W. Stott, *One People*, 1969. G.S.M.W.
R.T.B.

MINNI. A people summoned by Jeremiah, with Ararat (Armenia) and Ashkenaz, to make war on Babylonia (Je. 51:27). The Mannai, whose territory lay SE of Lake Urmia, are frequently named in texts of the 9th–7th centuries BC. The Assyrians dominated them until 673 BC, when they were controlled by the Medes (v. 28). In the light of Jeremiah, it is interesting to note that the Mannai were allied with the Assyrians, their former enemies, against the Babylonians in 616 BC (Bab. Chronicle). They were probably present with the Guti and other hill-folk at the capture of Babylon in 539 BC. D.J.W.

MINNITH (Heb. *minnîṯ*). Mentioned in Jdg. 11:33 as the limit of Jephthah's invasion of Ammon. Eusebius (*Onom.* p. 132) indicates that it lay at the head of a natural route from the Jordan to the uplands between Rabbath-Ammon (Amman) and Heshbon. The exact site is unknown.

Ezk. 27:17 may refer to the same; but Cornill and others emend to 'spices' (*ICC*, *ad loc.*). J.P.U.L.

MIRACLES. A number of Heb., Aram. and Gk. words are used in the Bible to refer to the activity in nature and history of the living God. They are variously translated in the EVV by 'miracles', 'wonders', 'signs', 'mighty acts', 'powers'. Thus, for example, the Heb. word *môp̄ēṯ*, which is of uncertain etymology, is translated in RSV by 'miracle' (Ex. 7:9; Ps. 78:43), 'wonder' (*e.g.* Ex. 7:3; Dt. 4:34) and 'sign' (*e.g.* 1 Ki. 13:3, 5).

The words used by the English translators preserve in general, though not always in particular instances, the three distinctive emphases of the originals. These characterize God's activity as being:

1. Distinctive, wonderful; expressed by Heb. derivatives of the root *pl'*, 'be different', particularly the participle *nip̄lā'ôṯ* (*e.g.* Ex. 15:11; Jos. 3:5), by Aramaic *temah* (Dn. 4:2–3; 6:27), and by Gk. *teras* (*e.g.* Acts 4:30; Rom. 15:19).

2. Mighty, powerful; expressed by Heb. *g^{e}ḇûrâ* (Pss. 106:2; 145:4) and Gk. *dynamis* (*e.g.* Mt. 11:20; 1 Cor. 12:10; Gal. 3:5).

3. Meaningful, significant; expressed by Heb. *'ôṯ* (*e.g.* Nu. 14:11; Ne. 9:10), by Aramaic *'āṯ* (Dn. 4:2–3; 6:27), and by Gk. *sēmeion* (*e.g.* Jn. 2:11; 3:2; Acts 8:6).

I. Miracles and the natural order

A great deal of confusion on the subject of miracles has been caused by a failure to observe that Scripture does not sharply distinguish between God's constant sovereign providence and his particular acts. Belief in miracles is set in the context of a world-view which regards the whole of creation as continually dependent upon the sustaining activity of God and subject to his sovereign will (*cf.* Col. 1:16–17). All three aspects of divine activity—wonder, power, significance—are present not only in special acts but also in the whole created order (Rom. 1:20). When the psalmist celebrates the mighty acts of God he moves readily from the creation to the deliverance from Egypt (Ps. 135:6–12). In Jb. 5:9–10; 9:9–10 the word *nip̄lā'ôṯ* refers to what we would call 'natural events' (*cf.* Is. 8:18; Ezk. 12:6).

Thus when the biblical writers refer to the mighty acts of God they cannot be supposed to distinguish them from 'the course of nature' by their peculiar causation, since they think of all events as caused by God's sovereign power. The particular acts of God highlight the distinctive character of God's activity, different from and superior to that of men and more particularly that of false gods, almighty in power, revealing him in nature and history.

The discovery of, say, causal connections between the different plagues of Egypt, a repetition of the blocking of the Jordan, or increased knowledge of psychosomatic medicine could not of themselves contradict the biblical assertion that the deliverance from Egypt, the entry to Canaan and the healing works of Christ were mighty acts of God. 'Natural laws' are descriptions of that universe in which God is ever at work. It is only by an unwarranted philosophical twist that they are construed as the self-sustaining working of a closed system or the rigid decrees of a God who set the universe to work like some piece of machinery.

It has been argued by some philosophers and theologians that the working of miracles is inconsistent with God's nature and purpose. He is the Alpha and Omega, he knows the end from the beginning; he is the Creator who fashioned all things unhampered by any limitation imposed by pre-existent matter; he is the unchanging One. Why, then, should he need to 'interfere' with the working of the natural order?

This objection based on the character of God arises from a failure to grasp the biblical understanding of God as living and personal. His changelessness is not that of an impersonal force but the faithfulness of a person: his creative act brought into being responsible creatures with whom he deals, not as puppets but as other persons over against himself. Miracles are events which dramatically reveal this living, personal nature of God, active in history not as mere Destiny but as a Redeemer who saves and guides his people.

A fuller knowledge of the ways of God's working may show that some supposedly unique events were part of a regular pattern. It can, however, never logically exclude the exceptional and extraordinary. While there is no such radical discontinuity between miracles and the 'natural order' as has been assumed by those who have most keenly felt the modern doubts on the subject, it is clear

MINISTRY OF JESUS
See Jesus Christ, life of, Part 2.

MINT
See Herbs, Part 2.

[illegible]
See Money, Part 2.

that Scripture speaks of many events which are extraordinary or even unique so far as our general experience of nature goes.

II. Miracles and revelation

If it be granted that *a priori* objections to miracle stories are invalid, it still remains to ask what precise function these extraordinary events perform in the total self-revelation of God in history. Orthodox theologians have been accustomed to regard them primarily as the authenticating marks of God's prophets and apostles and supremely of his Son. More recently it has been argued by liberal critics that the miracle stories of OT and NT are of the same character as the wonder-stories told of pagan deities and their prophets. Both these views fail to do justice to the integral relationship between the miracle stories and the whole self-revelation of God. Miracles are not simply an external authentication of the revelation but an essential part of it, of which the true purpose was and is to nourish faith in the saving intervention of God towards those who believe.

a. False miracles

Jesus consistently refused to give a *sign from heaven, to work useless and spectacular wonders, simply to guarantee his teaching. In any case the simple ability to work miracles would have been no such guarantee. There is frequent reference both in Scripture and elsewhere to wonder-working by those who were opposed to the purposes of God (*cf.* Dt. 13:2–3; Mt. 7:22; 24:24; 2 Thes. 2:9; Rev. 13:13ff.; 16:14; 19:20). The refusal to do wonders for their own sake sharply marks off the biblical miracle stories from the general run of *Wundergeschichten.*

It is noteworthy that the word *teras*, which of all the biblical terms has most nearly the overtones of the English 'portent', is always used in the NT in conjunction with *sēmeion* to stress that only significant portents are meant. The only exception is the OT quotation in Acts 2:19 (but *cf.* Acts 2:22).

The mere portent or the false miracle is distinguished from the true by the fact that the true miracle is congruous with the rest of the revelation. It harmonizes with the knowledge which believers already possess concerning God, even where it also carries that knowledge farther and deeper. Thus Israel is to reject any miracle-worker who denies the Lord (Dt. 13:2–3) and thus also we may rightly discern between the miracle stories of the canonical Gospels and the romantic tales or ludicrous stupidities of the apocryphal writings and mediaeval hagiography.

b. Miracles and faith

The working of miracles is directed to a deepening of men's understanding of God. It is God's way of speaking dramatically to those who have ears to hear. The miracle stories are intimately concerned with the faith of observers or participants (*cf.* Ex. 14:31; 1 Ki. 18:39) and with the faith of those who will hear or read them later (Jn. 20:30–31). Jesus looked for faith as the right response to his saving presence and deeds; it was faith which 'made whole', which made the difference between the mere creation of an impression and a saving communication of his revelation of God.

It is important to observe that faith on the part of human participants is not a necessary condition of a miracle in the sense that God is of himself unable to act without human faith. Mk. 6:5 is often quoted to support such a view, but Jesus could do no mighty work in Nazareth, not because the people's unbelief limited his power—Mark tells us that he healed a few sick people there—but rather because he could not proceed with his preaching or with the deeds which proclaimed his gospel in action where men were unready to accept his good news and his own person. Wonder-working for the crowds or the sceptics was inconsistent with his mission: it is in this sense that he could not do it in Nazareth.

c. Miracles and the Word

It is a notable feature—in some cases the chief feature—of miracles that even where the matter of the event is such that it can be assimilated to the ordinary pattern of natural events (*e.g.* some of the plagues of Egypt), its occurrence is predicted by God to or through his agent (*cf.* Jos. 3:7–13; 1 Ki. 13:1–5) or takes place at an agent's command or prayer (*cf.* Ex. 4:17; Nu. 20:8; 1 Ki. 18:37–38); sometimes both prediction and command are recorded (*cf.* Ex. 14). This feature emphasizes yet again the connection between miracles and revelation, and between miracles and the divine creative Word.

d. The crises of the sacred history

Another connection between miracles and revelation is that they cluster about the crises of sacred history. The pre-eminently mighty acts of God are the deliverance at the Red Sea and the resurrection of Christ, the first the climax of the conflict with Pharaoh and the gods of Egypt (Ex. 12:12; Nu. 33:4), the second the climax of God's redeeming work in Christ and the conflict with all the power of evil. Miracles are also frequently noted in the time of Elijah and Elisha, when Israel seemed most likely to sink into complete apostasy (*cf.* 1 Ki. 19:14); in the time of the siege of Jerusalem under Hezekiah (2 Ki. 20:11); during the Exile (Dn. *passim*); and in the early days of the Christian mission.

III. Miracles in the New Testament

Some liberal treatments of the question of miracles draw a marked distinction between the miracles of the NT, particularly those of our Lord himself, and those of the OT. Both more radical and more conservative critics have pointed out that in principle the narratives stand or fall together.

The contention that the NT miracles are more credible in the light of modern psychology or psychosomatic medicine leaves out of account the nature miracles, such as that at the wedding-feast in Cana and the calming of the storm, the instantaneous cures of organic disease and malformation, and the raising of the dead. There is no *a priori* reason to suppose that Jesus did not make use of those resources of the human mind and spirit which today are employed by the psychotherapist; but other narratives take us into realms where psychotherapy makes no assertions and where the claims of spiritual healers find least support from qualified medical observers.

There is, however, evidence for regarding the miracles of Christ and those done in his name as different from those of the OT. Where before God had done mighty works in his transcendent power and revealed them to his servants or used his servants as the occasional agents of such deeds, in Jesus there confronts us God himself incarnate, freely active in sovereign authority in that world which is 'his own'. When the apostles did similar works in his name they acted in the power of the risen Lord with whom they were in intimate contact, so that Acts continues the story of the same things which Jesus began to do and teach in his earthly ministry (*cf.* Acts 1:1).

In stressing the direct presence and action of God in Christ we do not deny the continuity of his work with the previous course of God's dealing with the world. Of the list of works given by our Lord in answering the Baptist's inquiry (Mt. 11:5) it is the most wonderful, the healing of lepers and the raising of the dead, which have OT parallels, notably in the ministry of Elisha. What is remarkable is the integral relationship between the works and words of Jesus. The blind receive their sight, the lame walk, the deaf hear, and at the same time that gospel is preached to the poor by which spiritual sight and hearing and a power to walk in God's way are given to the spiritually needy.

Again, the frequency of healing miracles is far greater in the time of the NT than at any period of the OT. The OT records its miracles one by one and gives no indication that there were others unrecorded. The Gospels and the NT in general repeatedly claim that the miracles described in detail were but a fraction of those wrought.

Jesus' works are clearly marked off from others by their manner or mode. There is in Jesus' dealing with the sick and demon-possessed a note of inherent authority. Where prophets did their works in the name of God or after prayer to God, Jesus casts out demons and heals with that same air of rightful power as informs his pronouncement of forgiveness to the sinner; indeed, he deliberately linked the two authorities (Mk. 2:9–11). At the same time Jesus stressed that his works were done in constant dependence on the Father (*e.g.* Jn. 5:19). The balance between inherent authority and humble dependence is the very mark of the perfect unity of deity and humanity.

In general, it may be said of Jesus' works that in their integral relation to his mission, their frequency and their authoritative manner they are distinctively Messianic.

NT teaching on the virgin birth, the resurrection and the ascension emphasizes the newness of what God did in Christ. He is born of a woman in the genealogy of Abraham and David, but of a virgin; others had been raised from death, only to die again; he 'always lives' and has ascended to the right hand of power. It is, moreover, true of the resurrection as of no other individual miracle that on it the NT rests the whole structure of faith (*cf.* 1 Cor. 15:17). This event was unique as the decisive triumph over sin and death.

The miracles of the apostles and other leaders of the NT church spring from the solidarity of Christ with his people. They are works done in his name, in continuation of all that Jesus began to do and teach, in the power of the Spirit he sent from the Father. There is a close link between these miracles and the work of the apostles in testifying to the person and work of their Lord; they are part of the proclamation of the kingdom of God, not an end in themselves.

The debate continues over the contention that this function of miracle was of necessity confined to the apostolic age. But we may at least say that the NT miracles were distinct from any subsequent ones by virtue of their immediate connection with the full manifestation of the incarnate Son of God, with a revelation then given in its fullness. They do not, therefore, afford grounds in themselves for expecting miracles to accompany the subsequent dissemination of the revelation of which they formed an integral part.

BIBLIOGRAPHY. It is impossible to list here even a representative selection of the very extensive literature on the many aspects of the question of miracles. The following works represent points of view discussed above and will also provide references for further study: D. S. Cairns, *The Faith that Rebels*, 1927; A. Richardson, *The Miracle Stories of the Gospels*, 1941; C. S. Lewis, *Miracles, A Preliminary Study*, 1947; E. and M.-L. Keller, *Miracles in Dispute*, 1969; C. F. D. Moule (ed.), *Miracles: Cambridge Studies in their Philosophy and History*, 1965. M.H.C.

MIRIAM. (For derivation, see *MARY.) **1.** The daughter of Amram and Jochebed, and the sister of Aaron and Moses (Nu. 26:59). It is generally agreed that it was she who watched the baby Moses in the bulrushes and suggested her mother as his nurse. The term 'the prophetess' was used to describe her as she led the women in music, dancing and singing a paean of praise to celebrate the crossing of the Red Sea (Ex. 15:20f.).

Miriam and Aaron rebelled against Moses, supposedly because of his marriage to the Cushite woman, but in reality because they were jealous of his position. Divine judgment descended upon Miriam and she became leprous, whereupon Moses interceded for her and she was cleansed, but she was excluded from the camp for 7 days (Nu. 12).

She died at Kadesh and was buried there (Nu. 20:1). There is no record of her marriage in the Bible, but rabbinical tradition makes her the wife of Caleb and mother of Hur.

2. In his genealogy the Chronicler lists a Miriam as one of the children of Ezrah, of the tribe of Judah (1 Ch. 4:17). M.B.

MIRROR. During the OT period mirrors were made of metal, cast

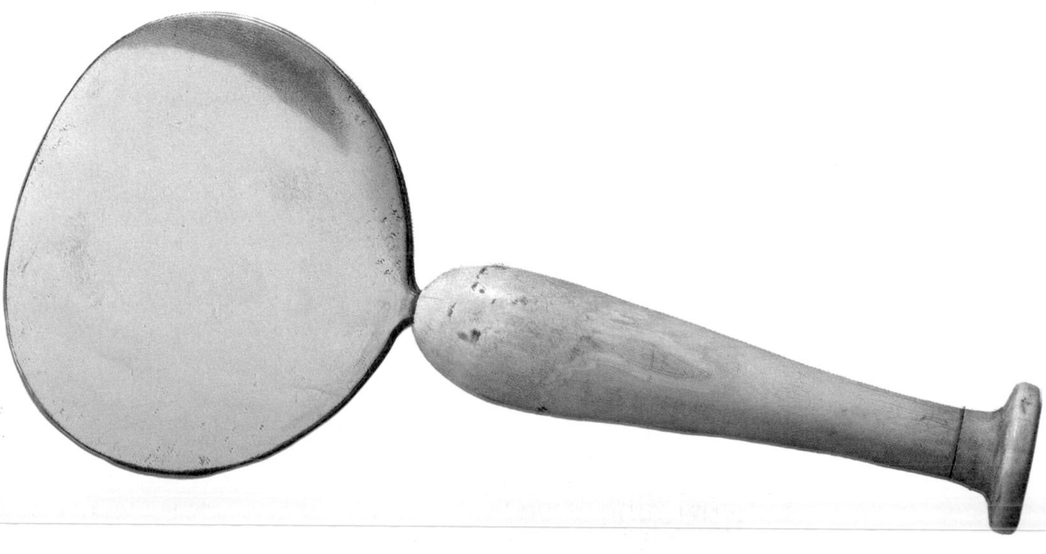

Polished bronze mirror with an ivory handle from the tomb of the scribe Ani at Thebes. New Kingdom. c. 1300 BC. (BM)

and highly polished (Jb. 37:18). Several bronze examples dating from the Middle Bronze Age onwards have been found in Palestine. These are of a form common throughout the Near East; *cf.* those used by the Israelite women in Ex. 38:8 (see *ANEP*, No. 71). The meaning of Heb. *gillāyôn* in Isaiah's list of finery (3:23, rendered 'tablet' in Is. 8:1) is uncertain; it may mean mirrors (Targ., AV, RV); others suggest garments of gauze (LXX, RSV). Glass mirrors were probably introduced in the 1st century AD. Whether of metal or glass, these mirrors never gave a perfect reflection (1 Cor. 13:12). It is probable that in 2 Cor. 3:18 (Gk. *hēmeis . . . katoptrizomenoi*) Paul's idea is that we see merely a reflection (AV); but it may be that we reflect (RV; see Arndt, pp. 425–426; R. V. G. Tasker, *2 Corinthians*, *TNTC*, 1958, pp. 67–68). James gives a simple illustration from the use of a mirror (1:23). A.R.M.

MISHAEL (Heb. *mîšā'ēl*, 'who is what God is'?). **1.** A son of *Uzziel, a Levite (Ex. 6:22) who, with his brother *Elzaphan, carried the bodies of Nadab and Abihu outside the camp after they had been killed for desecrating the altar (Lv. 10:1–5). **2.** A colleague of Daniel (Dn. 1:6, 11, *etc.*; 1 Macc. 2:59) whose name was changed to Meshach by the Babylonians (Dn. 1:7). D.W.B.

MISREPHOTH-MAIM (Heb. *miśrᵉpôṯ-mayim*). A limit of pursuit from *Merom (Jos. 11:8); the S border of Sidon (Jos. 13:6). If it was the rocky headland of Rosh Haniqra, Khirbet el-Mushreifeh (at the N end of the Acre plain) preserved the name; the gap in Late Bronze and Early Iron occupation would not be relevant. However, there were Israelite settlements to the N, and the river Litani is a possible identification (*LOB*, p. 216). J.P.U.L.

MISSION OF JESUS
See Jesus Christ, life of, Part 2.

MITE
See Money, Part 2.

MITHREDATH ('given by Mithra', the Persian god of light. *Cf.* Gk.–Lat. 'Mithridates'). **1.** The treasurer of Cyrus king of Persia, who in 536 BC restored to Sheshbazzar the sacred vessels confiscated by Nebuchadrezzar from Jerusalem (Ezr. 1:8). **2.** A Persian officer in Samaria, one of those who wrote in Aram. to Artaxerxes ('Longimanus') protesting against the rebuilding of the walls of Jerusalem (Ezr. 4:7). B.F.H.

MITRE (AV; Heb. *miṣnepeṯ*). One of the high priest's holy garments. From the use of the Heb. verb in Is. 22:18 it is thought to have been a kind of turban (RSV) wound round the head. It is described in Ex. 28:4, 36–39. On it was worn 'the plate of the holy crown' engraved 'Holy to

Aerial view of the harbour and town of Mitylene. (RVS)

the Lord' (Ex. 39:28, 30f.). Aaron wore it for his anointing (Lv. 8:9) and on the Day of Atonement (Lv. 16:4). To be uncovered was a sign of mourning (Ezk. 24:17) and uncleanness (Lv. 13:45; *cf.* 10:6) and was specifically forbidden to the high priest (Lv. 21:10–12)—*cf.* the 'bonnets' (AV) or 'caps' (Ex. 28:40; 29:9) (*miḡbā'ôṯ*) of inferior priests—so that Ezekiel (21:26) prophesies of the removal of the mitre because of the profanity of Israel, and Zechariah (3:5) sees Joshua invested with it (*ṣānîp̄*) as a sign of his cleansing and acceptance by God. Israel's ultimate renewal is symbolized by calling her a royal mitre (diadem) in the hand of God (Is. 62:3). P.A.B.

MITYLENE. An ancient republic of the Aeolian Greeks and the principal state of the island of Lesbos. Its situation on the trade routes of Europe and Asia frequently placed its political fortunes in jeopardy, until under the pax Romana it settled down as an honoured subordinate, highly favoured by the Romans as a holiday resort. A capacious harbour facing the mainland of Asia Minor across the straits made it a natural overnight stop for Paul's vessel on the S run to Palestine (Acts 20:14).

BIBLIOGRAPHY. R. Herbst, *RE,* 16. 2. 1411. E.A.J.

MIZAR. A hill mentioned in Ps. 42:6, in connection with Mt Hermon. It may be presumed that Hermon was visible from it; in which case it would have been in the Galilee region—note the reference to the Jordan. The word in Heb. (*miṣ'ār*) means 'smallness'. Some scholars emend the text of Ps. 42:6 slightly, making *miṣ'ār* an adjective, 'small', referring to Mt Zion. In this case the psalmist would be stating his preference for Zion rather than Hermon's great bulk. D.F.P.

MIZPAH, MIZPEH. The basic meaning of the word is 'watchtower', 'place for watching'. It is vocalized as *miṣpâ* and *miṣpeh*, and is found usually with the article. It is natural to look for places so named on high vantage-points. The following may be distinguished:

1. The place where *Jacob and Laban made a covenant and set up a cairn of stones as a witness (Galeed, *gal'ēḏ* in Hebrew, or *y^eḡar śāh^aḏûṯā'* in Aramaic). God was the watcher between them (Gn. 31:44–49).

2. Either the same place as **1** or a town in Gilead, E of the Jordan. The article is used both in Gn. 31:49 (*hammiṣpâ*), and in Jdg. 10:17; 11:11, 34. The place features in the story of Jephthah. When Ammon encroached on Gilead the Israelites assembled at Mizpah (Jdg. 10:17), the home of Jephthah, from which he commenced his attack and to which he returned to carry out his rash vow (Jdg. 11:11, 29, 34). Its identification with Ramoth-gilead is urged by some writers (J. D. Davis, *WDB*, p. 401), but is rejected by F. M. Abel and du Buit, who identify it with Jal'ûd. It is possibly the same as Ramath-mizpeh or height of Mizpeh (Jos. 13:26).

3. A place in Moab to which David took his parents for safety (1 Sa. 22:3), possibly the modern Rujm el-Meshrefeh, WSW of Madaba. **4.** A place at the foot of Mt Hermon (Jos. 11:3), referred to as 'the land of Mizpeh' or 'the valley of Mizpeh' (v. 8), the home of the Hivites. Opinions differ as to its identification, but Qal'at eṣ-Ṣubeibeh on a hill 3 km NE of Banias has much support. **5.** A town in the Shephelah (lowlands) of Judah named along with Joktheel, Lachish and Eglon (Jos. 15:38–39). The sites of Khirbet Ṣāfiyeh, 4 km NE of Beit Jibrin, and Ṣufiyeh, 10 km N, are possible choices for this Mizpeh.

6. A town of Benjamin (Jos. 18:26), in the neighbourhood of Gibeon and Ramah (1 Ki. 15:22). In the days of the Judges, when the Benjaminites of Gibeah outraged the Levite's concubine, the men of Israel assembled here (Jdg. 20:1, 3; 21:1, 5, 8). Here Samuel assembled Israel for prayer after the ark had been restored to Kiriath-jearim (1 Sa. 7:5–6). The Philistines attacked them, but were driven back (vv. 7, 11), and Samuel erected a stone of remembrance near by at Ebenezer (v. 12). Here also Saul was presented to the people as their king (1 Sa. 10:17). Mizpeh was one of the places visited by Samuel annually to judge Israel (1 Sa. 7:16).

King Asa fortified Mizpeh against Baasha of Israel, using materials his men took from Baasha's fort at Ramah, after Asa had asked the Syrian Ben-hadad to attack Israel (1 Ki. 15:22; 2 Ch. 16:6). After the destruction of Jerusalem by Nebuchadrezzar in 587 BC, Gedaliah was appointed governor of the remainder of the people, the governor's residence being fixed at Mizpeh (2 Ki. 25:23, 25). The prophet Jeremiah, released by Nebuzaradan, the captain of the guard, joined Gedaliah at Mizpeh (Je. 40:6), and refugee Jews soon returned (Je. 40:8, 10, 12–13, 15), Soon after, Ishmael of the royal seed slew Gedaliah and the garrison at the instigation of Baalis, king of Ammon. Two days later he murdered a company of pilgrims and threw their bodies into the great cistern Asa had built. He imprisoned others and sought to carry them to Ammon, but was frustrated by Johanan (Je. 41:1, 3, 6, 10, 14, 16).

Two references to a Mizpah in post-exilic times occur in Ne. 3:15, 19. It is possible that one or both of these refer to Mizpah in Benjamin though they may represent different places.

Mizpah was the scene of an important assembly in the days when Judas Maccabaeus called the men of Judah together for counsel and prayer (1 Macc. 3:46), 'because Israel formerly had a place of prayer in Mizpah'.

Two identifications are offered today—Nebi Samwil 7 km NW of Jerusalem, 895 m above sea-level and 150 m above the surrounding country, and Tell en-Nasbeh on the top of an isolated hill about 13 km N of Jerusalem. The evidence in favour of Tell en-Nasbeh is stronger than for Nebi Samwil, because it can be seen how the consonants *mzph* could become *nzbh* phonetically and the archaeological evidence supports the identification.

The site itself is ancient and was occupied in the Early Bronze Age, to judge from tombs in the area. It seems to have been deserted in the Middle and Late Bronze periods but was re-occupied in the Iron I period and continued during the years *c.* 1100–400 BC, so that it belongs to the period of Israelite settlement. In the days of the kings and during the Persian period the town was prosperous, as the relatively rich tombs suggest. Prosperity is also suggested by architectural remains, the massive gate, a large number of cisterns and silos, some dye-plants, numerous spinning-whorls, loom-weights, wine and oil presses, pottery, beads of semi-precious stones, pins, bangles and metal jewellery. The city ex-

MIXED MARRIAGES
See Foreigner, Part 1.

MIXED WOOL AND LINEN
See Wool, Part 3.

panded beyond its walls during the Iron II period, but began to decline in the 5th century BC. Fragments of Gk. pottery in the later city suggest trade with the Aegean areas. Numerous epigraphic discoveries, scarabs, stamped jar handles bearing the letters *MṢH* and *MṢP* (*i.e.* Miṣpah), a cuneiform inscription bearing the words *šar kiššati*, 'king of the universe', dating to the period *c.* 800–650 BC, and a beautiful seal bearing the inscription *ly'znyhw 'bd hmlk*, 'belonging to Jaazaniah, slave of the king', all attest the importance of the town.

BIBLIOGRAPHY. F. M. Abel, *Géographie de la Palestine*, 2, 1933, pp. 388–390; *LOB*, *passim*; D. Diringer, 'Mizpah', in *AOTS*, pp. 329–342; C. C. McCowan, *Excavations at Tell En-Nasbeh*, 2 vols., 1947.

J.A.T.

Moab and possible sites of the 'city of Moab'.

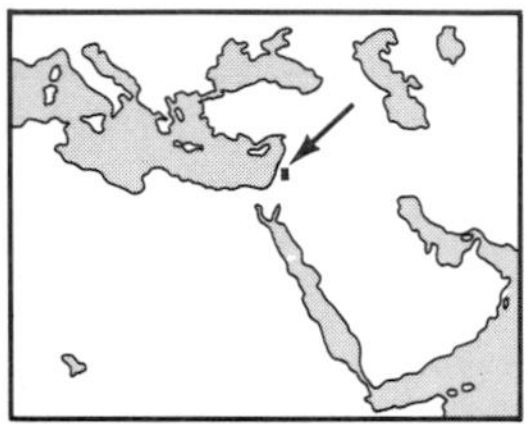

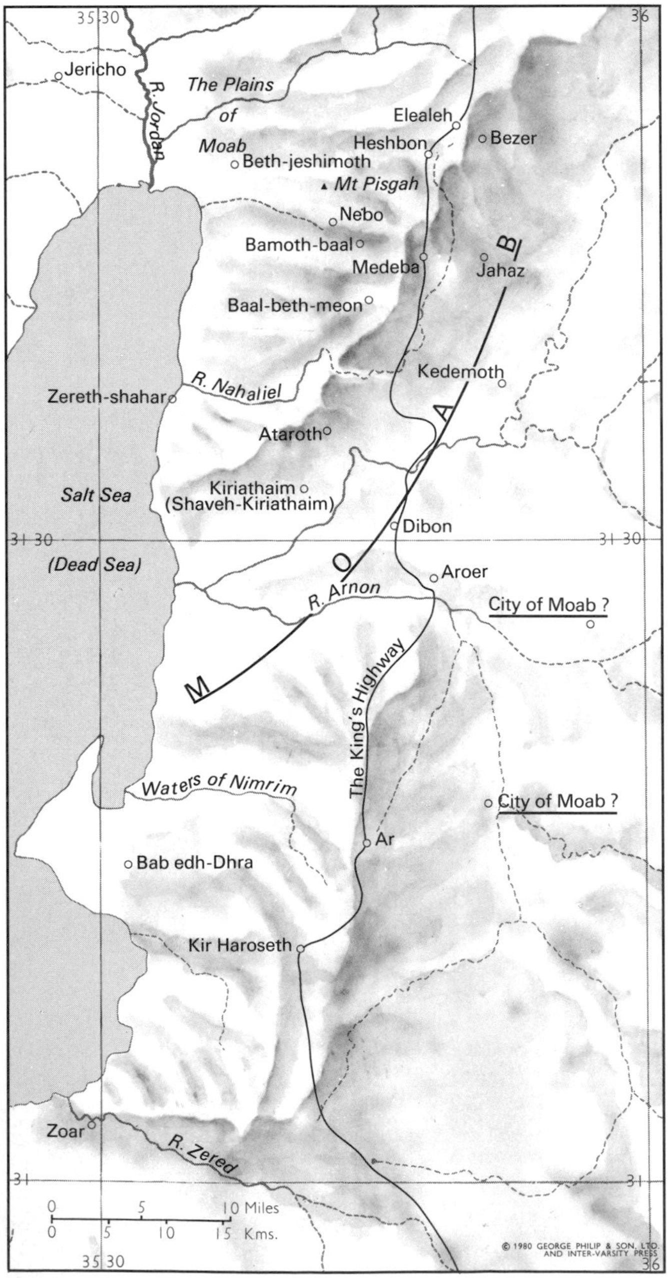

MIZRAIM. 1. Second son of Ham and progenitor of Ludim, Anamim, Lehabim, Naphtuhim, Casluhim and Caphtorim (Gn. 10:6, 13; 1 Ch. 1:8, 11). See *NATIONS, TABLE OF, and individual articles.

2. *miṣrayim* is also the regular Heb. (and common Semitic) term for Egypt. For details on this name, see *EGYPT (Name).

3. In 1 Ki. 10:28–29, it is possible to argue that the first *miṣrayim* is not Egypt but a land Muṣur in SE Asia Minor, and to render (modifying RSV) 'Solomon's import of horses was from Muṣur and from Que' (Cilicia), but this would require the *miṣrayim* of 2 Ch. 9:28 to be taken also as Muṣur and not Egypt. It is perhaps better to render *miṣrayim* as Egypt in these two passages as in all other OT references. See also P. Garelli, *Muṣur*, in *DBS*, 5, fasc. 29, 1957, cols. 1468–1474; H. Tadmor, 'Que and Muṣri', *IEJ* 11, 1961, pp. 143–150. K.A.K.

MNASON. 'An early (original) disciple'—*i.e.* at least from Pentecost—and Paul's host (Acts 21:16). Like Barnabas, he was a Jewish Cypriot. The name is Greek, and common.

Vulg., AV, RV, NEB understand the passage 'Caesarean disciples brought Mnason' (but why should they bring the prospective host?); RSV, TEV translate 'bringing *us* to the house of Mnason'. Neither is easy; probably *Mnasōni* has been attracted into the case of its relative (*cf.* A. T. Robertson, *Gram.*, p. 719). One would infer Mnason's residence in Jerusalem: a Hellenist host might not embarrass Paul's Gentile friends. The Western reading, valueless in itself, has 'reaching a village, we were with Mnason': perhaps a guess—the journey would require a night-stop—but perhaps correctly interpreting Luke. Mnason's house would then lie between Caesarea and Jerusalem: hence the escort, and the reference to Jerusalem in v. 17.

Luke's allusion may indicate Mnason provided source-material (*cf.* Ramsay, *BRD*, p. 309n.).

BIBLIOGRAPHY. H. J. Cadbury in *Amicitiae Corolla*, 1933, pp. 51ff.; F. F. Bruce, *The Acts of the Apostles*, 1951, *ad loc.* A.F.W.

MOAB, MOABITES. Moab (Heb. *mô'āḇ*) was the son of Lot by incestuous union with his eldest daughter (Gn. 19:37). Both the descendants and the land were known as Moab, and the people also as Moabites (*mô'āḇî*). The core of Moab was the plateau E of the Dead Sea between the wadis Arnon and Zered, though for considerable periods Moab extended well to the N of the Arnon. The average height of the plateau is 100 m, but it is cut by deep gorges. The Arnon itself divides about 21 km from the Dead Sea and several times more farther E into valleys of diminishing depth, the 'valleys of the Arnon' (Nu. 21:14). The Bible has preserved the names of many Moabite towns (Nu. 21:15, 20; 32:3; Jos. 13:17–20; Is. 15–16; Je. 48:20ff.).

In pre-Exodus times Moab was occupied and had settled villages until about 1850 BC. Lot's descendants found a population already there, and must have intermarried with them to emerge at length as the dominant group who gave their name to the whole population. The four kings from the E invaded Moab and overthrew the people of Shaveh-kiriathaim (Gn. 14:5). Either as a result of this campaign, or due to some cause unknown, Transjordan entered on a period of non-sedentary occupation till just before 1300 BC, when several of the Iron Age kingdoms appeared simultaneously. Moab, like the others, was a highly organized kingdom with good agricultural and pastoral pursuits, splendid buildings, distinctive pottery, and strong fortifications in the shape of small fortresses strategically placed around her boundaries. The Moabites overflowed their main plateau and occupied areas N of the Arnon, destroying the former inhabitants (Dt. 2:10–11, 19–21; *cf.* Gn. 14:5). These lands were shared with the closely related Ammonites.

Just prior to the Exodus, these lands N of the Arnon were wrested from Moab by Sihon, king of the Amorites. When Israel sought permission to travel along 'the King's Highway' which crossed the plateau, Moab refused (Jdg. 11:17). They may have had commercial contact (Dt. 2:28–29). Moses was forbidden to attack Moab despite their unfriendliness (Dt. 2:9), although Moabites were henceforth to be excluded from Israel (Dt. 23:3–6; Ne. 13:1).

Balak, king of Moab, distressed

by the Israelite successes, called for the prophet Balaam to curse Israel now settled across the Arnon (Nu. 22–24; Jos. 24:9).

As Israel prepared to cross the Jordan, they camped in the 'plains of Moab' (Nu. 22:1; Jos. 3:1) and were seduced by Moabite and Midianite women to participate in idolatrous practices (Nu. 25; Ho. 9:10).

In the days of the Judges, Eglon, king of Moab, invaded Israelite lands as far as Jericho and oppressed Israel for 18 years. Ehud the Benjaminite assassinated him (Jdg. 3:12–30). Elimelech of Bethlehem migrated to Moab and his sons married Moabite women, Orpah and Ruth. Ruth later married Boaz and became the ancestress of David (Ru. 4:18–22; Mt. 1:5–16). Saul warred with the Moabites (1 Sa. 14:47) and David lodged his parents there while he was a fugitive (1 Sa. 22:3–4). Later David subdued Moab and set apart many Moabites for death (2 Sa. 8:2, 12; 1 Ch. 18:2, 11). After Solomon's death, Moab broke free, but was subdued by Omri of Israel. (* Mesha, * Moabite Stone.) Towards the close of Ahab's life Moab began to break free again. Jehoram of Israel sought the help of Jehoshaphat, king of Judah, and the king of Edom to regain Moab, but the campaign was abortive (2 Ki. 1:1; 3:4–27). Later, Jehoshaphat's own land was invaded by a confederacy of Moabites, Ammon-

Rameses II receives two of his sons, bringing Moabite chiefs captive at the fortified town of Batora (shown above them). Luxor temple, Egypt. 13th cent. BC. (KAK)

Two captive Moabite chiefs from Batora shown between the two sons of Rameses II. Relief from Luxor temple. 13th cent. BC. (KAK)

ites and Edomites, but confusion broke out and the allies attacked one another so that Judah was delivered (2 Ch. 20:1–30).

In the year of Elisha's death, bands of Moabites raided Israel (2 Ki. 13:20). During the latter part of the 8th century BC Moab was subdued by Assyria and compelled to pay tribute (Is. 15–16), but after Assyria fell Moab was free again. Moabites entered Judah in the days of Jehoiakim (2 Ki. 24:2). At the fall of Jerusalem in 587 BC some Jews found refuge in Moab, but returned when Gedaliah became governor (Je. 40:11ff.). Moab was finally subdued by Nebuchadrezzar (Jos., *Ant.* 10. 181) and fell successively under the control of the Persians and various Arab groups. The Moabites ceased to have independent existence as a nation, though in post-exilic times they were known as a race (Ezr. 9:1; Ne. 13:1, 23). Alexander Jannaeus subdued them in the 2nd century BC (Jos., *Ant.* 13. 374).

In the prophets they are often mentioned and divine judgment pronounced on them (see Is. 15–16; 25:10; Je. 9:26; 25:21; 27:3; Ezk. 25:8–11; Am. 2:1–3; Zp. 2:8–11).

Places in Moab named in the Moabite Stone (Mesha inscription).

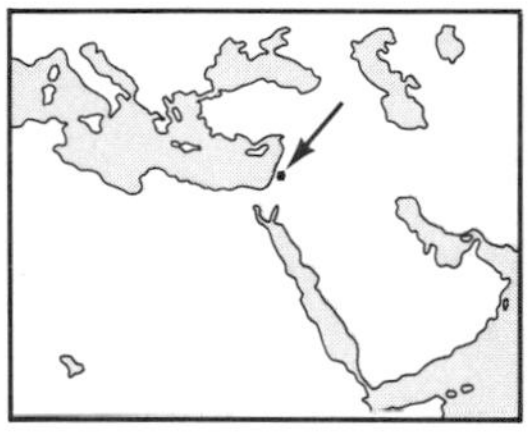

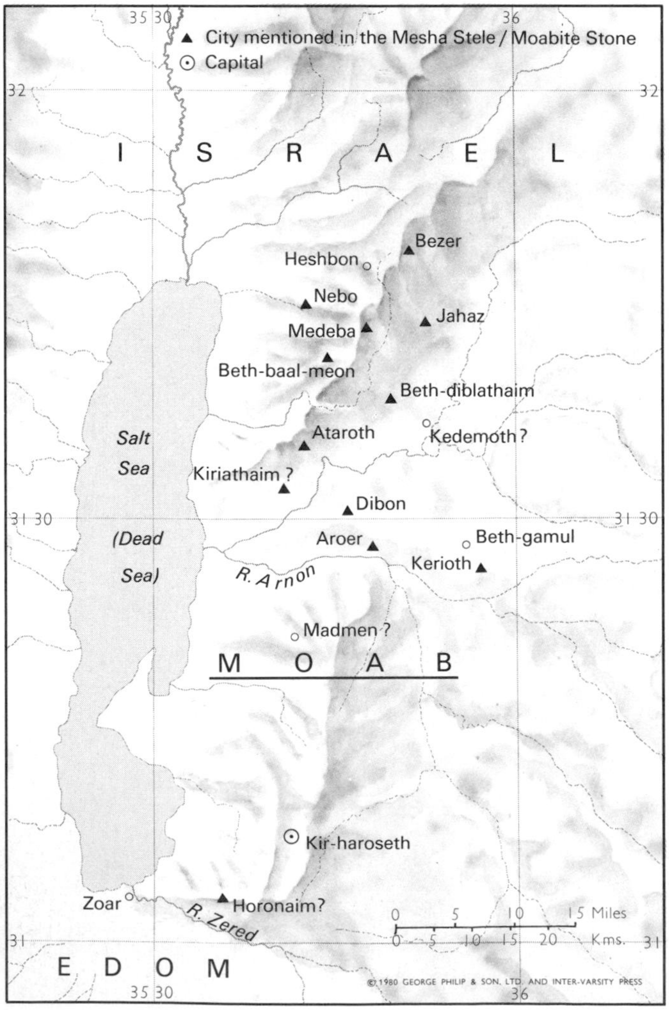

The archaeological story of Moab is slowly being unravelled. Excavation in Jordan has not proceeded as rapidly as it has in areas to the W of the Jordan, although in recent decades the programme has been increased. Important sites which have yielded significant results are Dibon, Aroer, Bab edh-Dhra and several sites in the area of the Lisan.

Our knowledge of Moab in early archaeological periods has been greatly expanded with new information about the transition between the Chalcolitic and the Early Bronze Age and the later transition between the Early and Middle Bronze Ages. At Bab edh-Dhra a vast cemetery of the Early Bronze Age has provided material from EB I to EB IV. The excavations at Aroer have given support to the theory that much of Moab was unoccupied during the greater part of the 2nd millennium. This site and the site of Dibon were typical of important Iron Age walled settlements contemporary with the period of the kings of Israel. At Dibon the important *Moabite (or Mesha) Stone was discovered. Sedentary life in these sites declined from the end of the 6th century BC down to the end of the 4th century.

BIBLIOGRAPHY. F. M. Abel, *Géographie de la Palestine*, 1, 1933, pp. 278–281; M. du Buit, *Géographie de la Terre Sainte*, 1958, pp. 142–143; Nelson Glueck, *The Other Side of Jordan*, 1940, pp. 150ff.; *idem*, *AASOR* 14–15, 18–19; G. L. Harding, *The Antiquities of Jordan*, 1967; A. D. Tushingham, *The Excavations at Dibon (Dhiban) in Moab*, *AASOR* 40, 1972; A. H. van Zyl, *The Moabites*, 1960; J. R. Bartlett, 'The Moabites and Edomites', in *POTT*, pp. 229–258; N. Avigad, 'Ammonite and Moabite Seals', in J. A. Sanders (ed.), *Near Eastern Archaeology in the Twentieth Century*, 1970, pp. 284–295

J.A.T.

MOABITE STONE. A black basalt inscription left by *Mesha, king of *Moab, at Dhiban (biblical *Dibon) to commemorate his revolt against Israel and his subsequent rebuilding of many important towns (2 Ki. 3:4–5).

The stone was found on 19 August 1868, by the Rev. F. Klein, a German missionary working with the Church Missionary Society. An Arab sheikh named Zattam showed him an inscribed slab some 120 cm high, 60 cm broad and 6 cm thick, rounded at the top and containing thirty-four lines of writing. Klein copied a few words and reported his find to Dr Petermann the German consul, who began negotiations to obtain the inscription for the Berlin Museum. Unfortunately, C. S. Clermont-Ganneau of the French Consulate sought to obtain it for the Paris Museum. He sent independent messengers to obtain a squeeze of the inscription, but a dispute arose and the messengers fled with the squeeze in several pieces. The Arabs, sensing the value of the stone, had forced the price up. When Turkish officials interfered the local Arabs kindled a fire under the stone and poured water over it to break it into fragments, which were carried away as charms to bless their grain. Clermont-Ganneau subsequently recovered several fragments, made fresh squeezes, and finally reconstructed the stone in the Louvre in Paris (see *IBA*, p. 54). Out of an estimated 1,100 letters, 669 were recovered, rather less than two-thirds, but the original squeeze, though somewhat marred, preserved the greater part of the story.

The inscription refers to the triumph of 'Mesha, ben *Chemosh, king of Moab', whose father reigned over Moab 30 years. He tells how he threw off the yoke of Israel and honoured his god Chemosh by building a high place at Qarḥoh (QRḤH) in gratitude. The account continues as follows—'As for Omri king of Israel, he humbled Moab many years [lit. days] for Chemosh was angry at his land. And his son followed him and he also said "I will humble Moab". In my time he spoke (thus) but I have triumphed over him and over his house, while Israel hath perished for ever! (Now) Omri had occupied the land of Medeba and (Israel) had dwelt there in his time and half the time of his son (Ahab), forty years; but Chemosh dwelt there in my time.'

This account seems to imply that Mesha broke free from Israel before Ahab's death and thus appears to clash with 2 Ki. 1:1. There need not be any contradiction, however, for during the last years of Ahab's life he was sore pressed by the Syrian wars and probably lost his control over Moab. From Mesha's angle, his freedom dated from then, but from Israel's viewpoint Moab could not be regarded as free till after the abortive campaign conducted by Ahab's son Joram (2 Ki. 3).

The stone continues with an account of the building of Baal-meon, Qaryaten, Qarḥoh, Aroer, Beth-bamoth, Bezer, Medeba, Beth-diblathen, Beth-baal-meon. Ataroth, built by the king of Israel for the men of Gad, was captured, its people slain and its chieftain Arel (or Oriel) dragged before Chemosh in Kerioth. Nebo was taken and 7,000 devoted to Ashtar-Chemosh. Yahaz, built by the king of Israel, and his centre during the fighting, was taken and attached to Dibon.

Mesha referred to the reservoirs and cisterns, the walls, gates, towers and the king's palace he constructed in Qarḥoh with Israelite slave labour. He also made a highway in the Arnon valley.

The great importance of this inscription linguistically, religiously and historically lies in its close relation to the OT. The language is closely akin to Hebrew. Both Chemosh the god of Moab and Yahweh the God of Israel are mentioned, and we have an interesting insight into Moabite beliefs, akin in some ways to those of Israel. Chemosh may be angry with his people, forsake them, deliver them to their enemies and finally save them. He might command Mesha in words like those that Yahweh used for his servants. The rite of *ḥērem* and the existence of sanctuaries in high places occur here as well as in the OT. Although the authenticity of the stone has been disputed, there are no adequate grounds for this. It must be dated towards the end of Mesha's reign, *c.* 830 BC.

For reproductions of the Stone see *IBA*, p. 54; *DOTT*, facing p. 198; *ANEP*, No. 274 (and alphabetic table in No. 286).

BIBLIOGRAPHY. W. F. Albright, *ANET*, pp. 320f.; *BASOR* 89, 1943, p. 16; F. I. Andersen, 'Moabite Syntax', *Orientalia* 35, 1966, pp. 81–120; G. A. Cooke, *A Text-Book of North-Semitic Inscriptions*, 1903, pp. 1–14; H. Donner and W. Röllig, *Kanaanäische and aramäische Inschriften*, I, 1962; S. R. Driver, *Notes on the Hebrew Text of the Books of Samuel*², 1913, pp. lxxxiv ff.; R. Dussaud, *Les monu-*

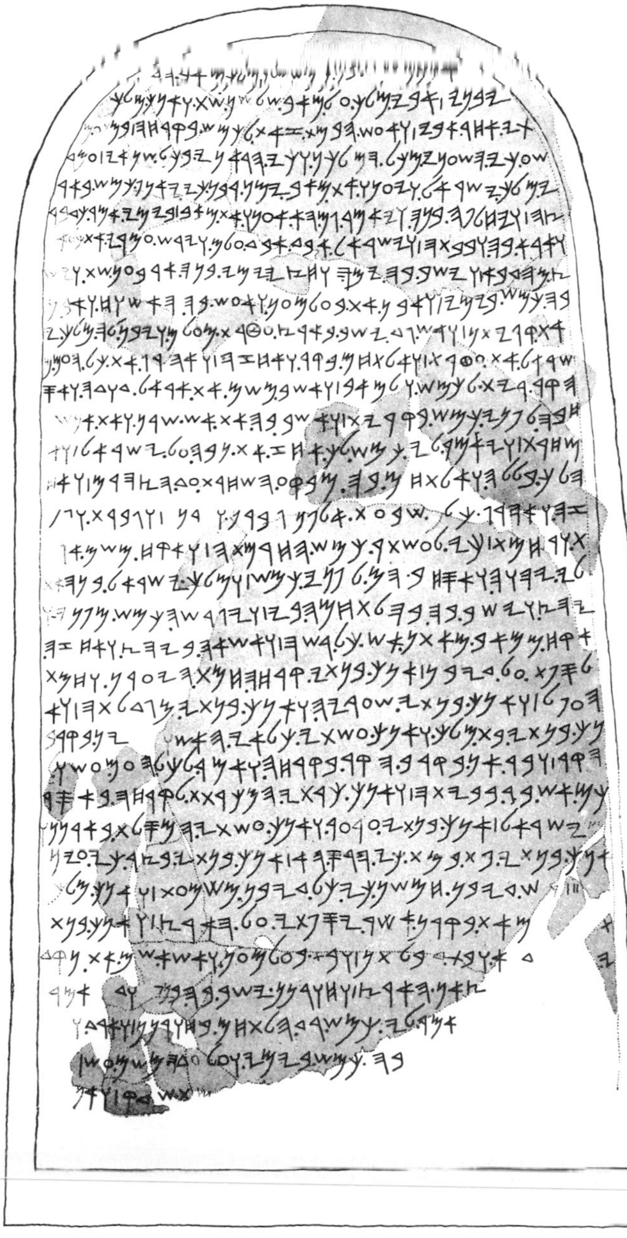

The Moabite Stone commemorates the revolt of Mesha, king of Moab, against Israel (see 2 Ki. 3:5ff.) and his rebuilding of several towns, e.g. Aroer, Medeba, Qarhoh, using Israelite slave labour. Black basalt. Height 1·0 m, breadth 0·60 m. c. 830 BC. (MC)

ments palestiniens et judaïque, 1912, pp. 4–22; E. Ullendorff in *DOTT*; A. H. van Zyl, *The Moabites*, 1960; J. R. Bartlett in *POTT*, pp. 229–258. J.A.T.

MOLADAH. A town of Simeon in the Negeb near Beersheba (Jos. 15:26; 19:2; 1 Ch. 4:28). Occupied by returning Judahite exiles (Ne. 11:26), it was later turned into an Idumean fortress. The site is not clearly identified. Tell el-Milḥ, SE of Beersheba, has regularly been identified with Moladah, but this mound is now thought to be Canaanite Arad. The more likely location is Khereibet el-Waṭen, E of Beersheba, which is possibly the Arabic equivalent of the Hebrew name.

BIBLIOGRAPHY. *LOB*, pp. 110, 298; *GTT*, p. 144. W.O.

MOLE
See Animals, Part 1.

MOLECH, MOLOCH. The OT often speaks of the fact that Israelites at times of apostasy made their children 'go through the fire to Molech' (2 Ki. 23:10; *cf.* Je. 7:31; 19:5). In some passages the reference is clearly to a deity to whom human sacrifice was made, particularly in the Valley of Hinnom on the SW of the Jerusalem hill (2 Ki. 23:10; Je. 32:35) at a site known as Topheth ('fire pit' in Syriac). The deity is associated with Ammon in 1 Ki. 11:7, where reference is made to 'the abomination of the Ammonites'. The worship of Molech seems to have been associated with the sacrifice of children in the fire (Lv. 18:21; 20:2–5; 2 Ki. 23:10; Je. 32:35; *cf.* 2 Ki. 17:31).

When we look more closely at the etymology of the word, some interesting facts emerge. Some commentators consider that the Heb. consonants of *meleḵ*, 'king', and the vowels of *bōšeṯ*, 'shame', were combined to form Heb. *môleḵ*, which expressed contempt for the heathen god. But there is another possibility which suggests that in some passages the term Moloch may not refer to a deity. Some Carthaginian–Phoenician (Punic) inscriptions from the period 400–150 BC imply that the word *mlk* (pronounced *molk* in Lat. inscriptions from Carthage about AD 200) is a general term for 'sacrifice' or 'offering', and a number of OT passages may be interpreted as saying that men caused children to go through the fire 'for a *môleḵ* sacrifice or votive offering'. In such passages as Lv. 18:21; 20:3–5; 2 Ki. 23:10; Je. 32:35 the translation must remain an open question.

These observations do not deny that a deity Molech is referred to in the Bible. (He is referred to in the AV twice as Moloch: Am. 5:26; Acts 7:43.) He is known as the national god of Ammon in 1 Ki. 11:7. He may be identified with the deity *muluk* worshipped at Mari about 1800 BC, and *malik*, known from Akkadian texts, and appearing in the compound forms Adrammelech and Anammelech in 2 Ki. 17:31. In some OT passages the word Molech carries the article suggesting that the word may have been an appellative for 'the one who rules' (Lv. 18:21; 20:2–5; 2 Ki. 23:10; Je. 32:35). In Je. 32:35 there seems to be a connection with Baal, whose name is also an appellative, and to whom, as Baal-melqart, human sacrifices were offered at Tyre.

The practice of offering children as human sacrifices was condemned in ancient Israel. Apart from general references to Molech in Je. 49:1, 3 and perhaps Am. 1:5, or to the cult of Molech in 1 Ki. 11:7, 33; Zp. 1:5 and some special passages noted above, the inference is clear in the OT that child-sacrifice was practised by some in Israel. The law of Moses demanded the death of anyone who offered his child to Molech or as a sacrifice (Lv. 18:21; 20:2–5). Solomon, however, built a high place for this god in 'the hill that is before (E of) Jerusalem', *i.e.* the Mount of Olives (1 Ki. 11:7). Several references in the OT to child-sacrifice, while not referred specifically to Molech, may be included here (Ps. 106:38; Je. 7:31; 19:4–5; Ezk. 16:21; 23:37, 39). King Ahaz, *c.* 730 BC, burnt his children in the fire (2 Ch. 28:3), and Manasseh did the same (2 Ki. 21:6). Samaria was judged for this sin (2 Ki. 17:17). Josiah, in Judah, destroyed the high places of Molech (2 Ki. 23:10, 13). Ezekiel was still condemning the practice early in the 6th century BC (Ezk. 16:20ff.; 20:26, 31; 23:37). The Exile seems to have put an end to this worship in Israel, but it lingered on in N Africa among the Carthaginian Phoenicians into the Christian era.

BIBLIOGRAPHY. W. F. Albright, *Archaeology and the Religion of Israel*, 1953, pp. 162ff.; H. Ringgren, *Religions of the Ancient Near East*, 1973, pp. 161f.; M. Weinfeld, 'The Worship of Molech and the Queen of Heaven', *UF* 4, 1972, pp. 133–154; A. R. W. Green, *The Role of Human Sacrifice in the Ancient Near East*, 1976, pp. 176ff. J.A.T.

MOLID. A name found in the genealogy of Jerahmeel (1 Ch. 2:29). Moladah may be connected, but evidence is lacking (*GTT*, pp. 48, 144). J.D.D.

MONEY.

I. In the Old Testament

Before the introduction of coinage in the late 8th century BC (see *c*, below) the medium of exchange in commercial transactions was a modified form of barter. Throughout the ancient Near East staple commodities, both those which

Electrum nugget, possibly used as unit of exchange in a pre-coinage era. Enkomi, Cyprus. Diameter 11 mm. c. 1100 BC. (BM)

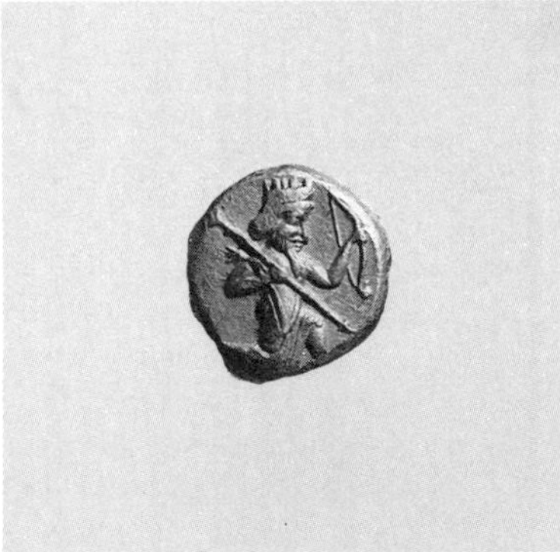

Gold daric. *Darius II, king of Persia, holding a sceptre and bow. Diameter 15 mm. Late 5th cent. BC.* (RG)

A silver quarter shekel, *struck by Jewish authorities of the Persian empire in Judaea. The Aramaic inscription reads* yhd (*Yehud or Judah*) *and the design shows a god seated on a winged wheel and holding a hawk. Diameter 16 mm. c. 350–332 BC.* (RG)

'Money' used by the Israelites may have been similar to the gold ring-shaped objects depicted in this Egyptian wall-painting from the tomb of Nebamun and Ipuky, Thebes. c. 1350–1300 BC. (BM)

Top left:
Tetradrachm *of Antiochus VI of Syria.* Obverse: *portrait of the king (145–144* BC*).* Reverse: *Castor and Pollux. Such Syrian coins circulated in Palestine. Diameter 32 mm.* (RG)

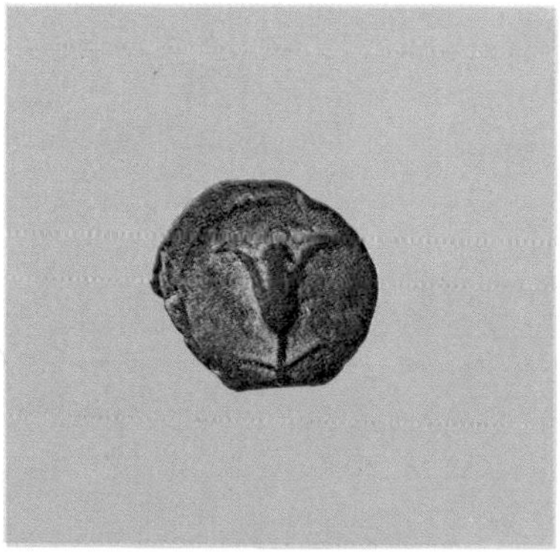

Left:
Coin, showing the lily, symbol of Judaea. This was struck on the authority of Antiochus III, 138–129 BC*. Diameter 14 mm.* (BM)

Right:
A bronze coin of Alexander Jannaeus shows an anchor with Greek inscription 'of King Alexander'. Diameter 15 mm. 103–76 BC. (RG)

A bronze coin of Matthias Antigonus, showing a seven-branched candlestick (menorah). *Diameter 17 mm. 40–37* BC. (RG)

A bronze coin of Herod I with a herald's wand (caduceus) *between a double cornucopia. Diameter 15 mm. 40–4* BC. (RG)

were perishable, such as wool, barley, wheat and dates, and those which were non-perishable, including metals, timber, wine, honey and livestock, served as 'exchangeable goods'. The texts show that from the earliest times periodic attempts were made to stabilize the values of these commodities with respect to each other. Thus wealth was measured by possession of cattle (Jb. 1:3) and precious metals. Abraham was 'very rich in cattle, in silver, and in gold' (Gn. 13:2).

a. Metal as an exchange commodity

Since silver (Heb. *kesep̄*) was the commonest precious metal available in Palestine (as in Assyria and Babylonia), it appears as the most frequently used (AV, RSV often translate *kesep̄* as 'money', *e.g.* Gn. 17:13). Thus in ordinary transactions the term silver is often omitted, as understood; Solomon purchased chariots at 600 (shekels weight of silver) and horses at 150 (1 Ki. 10:29; *cf.* Lv. 5:15). His revenue was reckoned in silver by talents (1 Ki. 10:14; *WEIGHTS AND MEASURES), for silver was as common in Jerusalem as stones (1 Ki. 10:27). Until post-exilic times the 'shekel' bears its literal meaning of a certain *weight rather than denoting a coin.

Silver was used for the purchase of real estate, such as the field purchased by Jeremiah at Anathoth for 17 shekels of silver (Je. 32:9), the cave at Machpelah bought by Abraham for 400 shekels of silver (Gn. 23:15–16), the village and hill of Samaria by Omri for 2 talents of silver (1 Ki. 16:24), or the threshing-floor of Araunah by David for 50 shekels (2 Sa. 24:24). Silver was also the basis of a dowry (Ex. 22:17) or a bride purchase-price (Ho. 3:2).

Gold, being more rarely obtained, often figures after silver in the payment of tribute. Thus Hezekiah paid Sennacherib in 701 BC 300 talents of silver and 30 talents of gold (2 Ki. 18:14), while Menahem had bought off the Assyrians for 1,000 talents of silver (2 Ki. 15:19). Gold played a prominent part in inter-state border transactions, and Hiram paid 120 talents of gold to Solomon for the villages ceded to him (1 Ki. 9:10–14).

In many transactions payment in goods might be agreed as a supplement or substitute for precious metal. Mesha of Moab offered

Bronze coin of Pontius Pilate, procurator of Judaea at the time of the crucifixion. Obverse: *a wreath, encircling the date 'Year 17'.* Reverse: *Lituus and a Greek inscription 'Tiberius Caesar'. Diameter 15 mm. AD 30.* (RG)

Silver tetradrachm *of Tyre, showing the head of Melqart, in use in Palestine from 125 BC to 70 AD . Since it was current at the time of the crucifixion a coin like this may have been a 'piece of silver' used to bribe Judas. The reverse shows an eagle. Diameter 23 mm. AD 37.* (RG)

Table relating three different systems of coinage used in biblical times to each other. An approximate value can be gauged from the fact that the drachmē/denarius *represented a labouring man's daily wage.*

△ Bronze/Copper coin
○ Silver coin
□ Gold coin

Scale	Jewish	Greek	Roman
1	1 lepton △		½ quadrans
2			1 quadrans △
8			1 as △
128		1 drachmē ○	1 denarius ○
512		1 statēr ○	4 denarii
3,200		25 drachmai	1 aureus □
12,800		1 mna ○	100 denarii
768,000		1 talent ○	240 aurei

sheep and wool (2 Ki. 3:4); Sennacherib was given precious stones, in addition to gold and silver, by Hezekiah according to the Assyr. annals, and the tribute of *Jehu to Shalmaneser III included blocks of antimony, lead, golden vessels and rare fruits. Barley (Ho. 3:2), spices (2 Ki. 20:13) or clothing might be part of the agreed price or gift (2 Ki. 5:23). Copper (AV 'brass') was another metal in use as currency (Ex. 35:5; 2 Sa. 21:16) of less value than gold (Is. 60:17).

To control the use of metals as currency they had to be weighed out (Heb. *šql*, hence 'shekel') by the purchaser and checked by the vendor in the presence of witnesses (Gn. 23:16; Je. 32:9–10). The standard of weight agreed was that in force by local standards called the 'silver of city X' or 'the silver (current with) the merchant' (Gn. 23:16; Bab. *kaspum ša tamqarim*). This agreed standard is also implied by payment 'in full weight' (Gn. 43:21). Thus merchants were 'weighers of silver'. Another check was made on the quality of the metal by marking it with its place of origin. Gold of Ophir (1 Ki. 10:11) or Parvaim (2 Ch. 3:6) was highly prized, while gold and silver were sometimes classified as 'refined' (AV 'pure, purified').

b. Forms of currency

To enable metal used as currency to be transportable it was kept either in the form of jewellery (often as arm-rings), of objects in daily use or in characteristic shapes. Thus Abraham gave Rebekah a gold ring (weighing) half a shekel and bracelets of 10 shekels (Gn. 24:22). Gold was often carried as thin bars or wedges (Heb. 'tongue'), like that weighing 50 shekels found by Achan at Jericho (Jos. 7:21) or the 'golden wedge of Ophir' (Is. 13:12). Gold and silver were also held as ingots, vessels, dust (Jb. 28:6) or small fragments, and could be melted and used immediately for many purposes. In these forms Joseph increased the revenue of Egypt (Gn. 47:14).

On a journey the small pieces of metal were carried in a pouch or bag of leather or cloth ('bundles of money', Gn. 42:35; Pr. 7:20) which, if holed, would easily lead to loss (Hg. 1:6). A talent of silver seemed to require two bags (2 Ki. 5:23). To guard against loss the money bags were often placed inside other sacks or receptacles (Gn. 42:35). Silver was also moulded into small drops or beads (1 Sa. 2:36, *ʾᵃgōrâ*) or lumps. It is probable that the half-shekel used for payment into the sanctuary was an unminted lump of silver (Ex. 30:13; 2 Ki. 12:9–16), though normally such temple dues as taxes could be paid either in silver or in kind (Dt. 26; Ne. 5:10).

Copper, being of less value than gold and silver, was transported as flat circular discs, hence the term *kikkār* ('a round', 'flat round of bread', Assyr. *kakkāru*) was used for the 'talent', the heaviest weight.

c. The introduction of coinage

Coinage, a piece of metal struck with a seal authenticating its title and weight so that it would be accepted on sight, first appears in Asia Minor in the mid-7th century BC. Though Sennacherib (*c.* 701 BC) refers to the 'minting of half-shekel pieces', there is no evidence that this refers to anything more than a bronze-casting technique, for no coins of this early period have been found as yet in Assyria, Syria or Palestine. The first known coins were struck in electrum (a natural alloy of gold and silver) in Lydia. Herodotus (1. 94) attributes the introduction of coinage to Croesus of Lydia (561–546 BC), his gold coins being called 'Croesides'. It would seem that coinage was introduced into Persia by Darius I (521–486 BC), whose name was used to denote the thick gold coin, or *daric*, which portrays the king, half-length or kneeling, with bow and arrow; with the die-punch mark in reverse (see Herodotus 4. 166). This daric weighed 130 gr., the silver *siglos* or shekel 86½ gr. It has been suggested (*PEQ* 87, 1955, p. 141) that Hg. 1:6 (520 BC) is the earliest biblical allusion to coined money.

The daric (AV 'dram') was known to the Jews in exile (Ezr. 2:69; 8:27; Ne. 7:70–71) and the reference to a daric in the time of David (1 Ch. 29:7) shows that the text at this point was giving the equivalent term at the time of compilation of this history. The change to payment of workmen in coin instead of in kind is attested by the Persepolis Treasury texts (*c.* 450 BC), confirming a ratio of 13:1 gold to silver. The spread of coinage to Judah seems to have been slow, perhaps because of the images they bore. It is therefore uncertain whether the silver shekels of Ne. 5:15; 10:32 were weights, as in the earlier period, or money in coin.

Phoenician traders quickly took up the use of coins, and mints were active by the 5th–4th centuries BC at Aradus, Byblos, Tyre and Sidon. The coinage of cities in Asia Minor and Greece, and of the kings of Ptolemaic Egypt and Seleucid Syria entered Judah and circulated there alongside coins of Persian kings. The Persian-approved Jewish governors were evidently allowed to issue small silver coins from about 400 BC. The designs of the half-dozen or so found follow Athenian patterns, but include the word *yhd*, 'Judah'. One also bears the name Hezekiah, perhaps the High Priest at the time of Alexander the Great.

After the independent Jewish state was established, Simon Maccabaeus was given the right to strike coins (1 Macc. 15:6), but does not seem to have used it (coins once attributed to him have been shown to belong to the First and Second Revolts, AD 67–70, 132–5). Alexander Jannaeus (103–76 BC) was probably the first Jewish ruler to strike coins. They are small bronze pieces bearing various designs, his name in Greek and Hebrew, and sometimes the words 'Yehonathan the high priest and the community of the Jews'. Following kings continued to strike small bronze coins, the Roman overlords retaining the prerogative to strike silver ones. Only in the Jewish Revolts were local silver coins issued.

BIBLIOGRAPHY. R. de Vaux, *Ancient Israel*, 1961, pp. 206–209; E. S. G. Robinson, 'The Beginnings of Achaemenid Coinage' in *Numismatic Chronicle* (6th Series) 18, 1958, pp. 187–193; Y. Meshorer, *Jewish Coins of the Second Temple Period*, 1967. D.J.W.

II. In the New Testament

During NT times money from three different sources was in circulation in Palestine. There was the official imperial money coined on the Roman standard; provincial coins minted at Antioch and Tyre, which held mainly to the old Gk. standard, and circulated chiefly among the inhabitants of Asia Minor; and the local Jewish money, coined perhaps at Caesarea. Certain cities and client-kings were also granted the right to strike their own bronze coins. With coins of so many different scales in circulation it is obvious that there was need of money-changers at Jerusalem, especially at feasts when Jews came from all parts to pay their poll-tax to the Temple treasury. On these occasions the money-changers moved their stalls into the Court of the Gentiles, whence Jesus expelled them (Jn. 2:15; Mt. 21:12; Mk. 11:15; Lk. 19:45f.) because of their avaricious practices.

Mt. 10:9 serves as a useful reminder that in those days, as now, money was coined in three principal metals, gold, silver and copper, bronze or brass. Bronze (Gk. *chalkos*) is used as a general word for money in Mk. 6:8 and 12:41, but as only the coins of smaller value, the Roman *as* (Gk. *assarion*) and

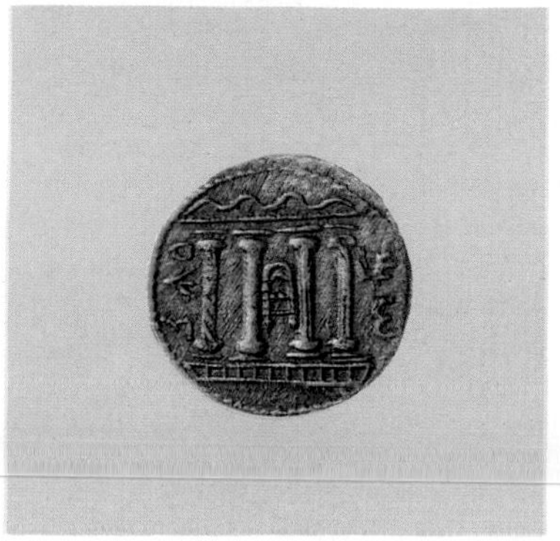

Top left:
A quadrans, *a small Roman coin (Mt. 5:26). Diameter 18 mm. This example (5 BC) dates from the reign of Augustus.* (RG)

Top right:
Silver denarius of the Roman Emperor Tiberius. This type of coin, common throughout the Empire, was the 'penny' brought to Christ (Lk. 20:24) and was equivalent to the daily wage of a labourer (Mt. 20:1–16). Diameter 16 mm. AD 14–37. (RG)

Centre left:
Bronze as *of Rome with a portrait of Tiberius. Diameter 30 mm. AD 22–23.* (RG)

Centre right:
Bronze sestertius *issued by Vespasian of Rome inscribed 'Judaea Capta', commemorating the capture of Jerusalem and Judaea (AD 67–70). The palm tree is a symbol of Judaea. Diameter 31 mm.* (RG)

Bottom left:
Silver 'shekel *of Israel', minted at the beginning of the first Jewish revolt. Diameter 17 mm. AD 66–70.* (BM)

Bottom right:
Silver tetradrachm (*the equivalent of a* shekel) *showing the Jerusalem Temple with, inside, a shrine containing a scroll of the law. Diameter 18 mm. AD 132–135.* (BM)

Jewish *lepton* were minted in bronze, the more common general term for money in the NT is silver (Gk. *argyrion*; see Lk. 9:3; Acts 8:20; *etc.*). The most common silver coins mentioned in the NT are the Attic tetradrachm and the Roman *denarius*. Gk. *chrysos*, gold, is most frequently used to refer to the metal itself, except in Mt. 10:9; Acts 3:6, possibly also Acts 20:33; 1 Pet. 1:18; Jas. 5:3; Mt. 23:16f., though these instances might equally well refer to gold vessels and ornaments.

Other general terms used for money in the NT are the common Gk. word *chrēma*, meaning property or wealth, as well as money (Acts 4:37; 8:18, 20; 24:26); *kerma*, or small change (from Gk. *keirō*, 'I cut up'), used in Jn. 2:15, and nearly always denoting copper coins; and *nomisma*, or money introduced into common use by law (*nomos*). This last is found only in Mt. 22:19, where the phrase *nomisma tou kēnsou* means the legal coin for paying the tax.

a. Jewish coins

In 141–140 BC Antiochus VII granted permission to Simon Maccabaeus 'priest and ethnarch of the Jews . . . to mint your own coinage as money for your country' (1 Macc. 15:6), and from that time Jewish coins were minted, mainly in bronze, as neighbouring cities produced an abundance of silver coins. Early Jewish coins heeded the second commandment, and so their devices adhered strictly to horticultural designs and inanimate objects. Coins minted under the Herods show one or two breaches of this rule, as they displayed sometimes the reigning emperor's head, sometimes their own, on the obverse (see Wiseman, *IBA*, p. 86). During the time of the First Revolt (AD 66–70) the Jews proudly coined their own silver for the first time, issuing silver shekels and quarter- and half-shekel pieces as well as their own bronzes. Following this revolt, the Temple treasures were seized, and so the Jews had no further supplies of metal to coin their own silver during the Second Revolt (AD 132–135). They therefore celebrated their independence by overstriking old foreign coins with Jewish dies containing the inscription 'deliverance of Jerusalem'.

The only Jewish coin mentioned in the NT is the bronze *lepton* (from Gk. *leptos*—'small, fine'). This is the widow's 'mite' (AV) of Mk. 12:42; Lk. 21:2, also called a 'farthing' in Lk. 12:59 (AV), where it stands for the smallest coin imaginable. It was equivalent to half the Roman *quadrans*, and so one-eighth of the *assarion* (see below). Such coins were minted locally by the procurator or tetrarch, and *Pilate appears to have introduced designs on his coins calculated to affront the Jews.

b. Greek coins

The basic Greek coin was the silver *drachmē*, of which there were 100 to the *mna*, or mina, and 6,000 to the talent. About 300 BC the drachm was the price of a sheep: an ox cost 5 *drachmai* (Demetrius Phalereus).

The *drachmē* is mentioned only in Lk. 15:8f., RSV 'silver coins', AV 'pieces of silver', which the woman in the parable may have worn as an ornament. It was regarded as approximately equivalent to the Roman *denarius* (see below).

The *didrachmon* or 2-drachm piece was used among the Jews for the half-shekel required for the annual Temple tax (Mt. 17:24). This regulation derived from the atonement-money prescribed in Ex. 30:11–16, which, according to Maimonides, later developed into a regular annual poll-tax (see Jos., *Ant.* 16. 160). After the fall of Jerusalem and the destruction of the Temple this tax had to be paid into the Roman treasury (Jos., *BJ* 7. 217). It seems most likely that the coins used for this tax would be those of Tyre, for the Talmudic law forbade the use of Antiochene money for the Temple treasury, not for any religious reasons, but because it did not contain enough silver.

The *statēr*, *tetradrachmon*, or 4-drachm piece, is found only in Mt. 17:27, where it is the coin which would pay the Temple tax for Jesus and Peter. As it was a more common coin than the didrachm, it would appear that Jews frequently united to pay the Temple tax in pairs by means of the tetradrachm. It was minted at Antioch, Caesarea in Cappadocia and in Tyre. Pompey fixed the rate of exchange of tetradrachms from Antioch and Tyre at 4 *denarii* (*c.* 65 BC), and Josephus refers to the same rate for the Tyrian tetradrachm in his day (*BJ* 2. 592). Antiochene tetradrachms were, however, tariffed by the imperial government at 3 *denarii* only. Most numismatists agree that this was the coin in which Judas received his thirty pieces of silver (Mt. 26:15). The use of the term *argyria hikana*, 'large silver-money', in Mt. 28:12–13 has been thought by some to suggest that the coins with which the Sanhedrin bribed the guards of the tomb were the large silver staters and not the smaller *drachmai* or *denarii*, though it is possible that the adjective here refers to quantity rather than size.

The *mna*, translated 'pound', occurs in the parable of Lk. 19:11–27.

The 'talent' was not a coin, but a unit of monetary reckoning. Its value was always high, though it varied with the different metals involved and the different monetary standards. The Roman–Attic was equivalent to 240 *aurei* (see below). It was mentioned by Jesus in two parables: in Mt. 18:24 'ten thousand talents' is figurative for a very large sum of money, and in the parable of the talents in Mt. 25:15–28 it is referred to in v. 18 as *argyrion*, which may suggest that our Lord had the silver talent in mind.

c. Roman coins

The basic Roman coin, mentioned above, was the silver *denarius*. There were 25 *denarii* to the golden *aureus*, the weight of which was fixed by Julius Caesar in 49 BC at 126·3 grs., though subsequent debasing of the coinage under Augustus and his successors brought the weight down to 115 grs. by Nero's time.

The *quadrans* (Gk. *kodrantēs*) was one-quarter of the copper *as* (see below). It is referred to by both Horace (*Satires* 2. 3. 93) and Juvenal (7. 8) as the smallest Roman coin: Mk. 12:42 states that the widow's 2 *lepta* (see *a*, above) were equivalent to a *quadrans*. Mt. 5:26 uses *quadrans* for the smallest coin, which must be paid to clear a debt in full, while the Lucan parallel (12:59) has *lepton*, except in the Western Text, which agrees with Matthew.

The copper *as* (Gk. *assarion*) was a quarter of the bronze *sestertius* and one-sixteenth of the silver *denarius*. It occurs in Mt. 10:29 and Lk. 12:6, where it is translated by the AV as 'farthing' and RV, RSV as 'penny', the price at which two sparrows are sold (Lk. has five sparrows for 2 farthings).

The *denarius* (Gk. *dēnarion*) gained its name (*deni* = ten at a time) from the fact that at first it was the equivalent in silver of 10 copper *asses*. From 217 BC it was worth 16 *asses*, when the weight of the latter coin was fixed at 28 gr. It was rendered consistently as 'penny' by the translators of the AV and RV (but see the note on Mt. 18:28 in the RVmg.), owing to the fact that British currency, modelled on that of Rome, used *d.* for *denarius* as the abbreviation for penny.

It would appear from the parable of Mt. 20:1–16 to have been the daily wage of a labourer, and 2 *denarii* was the sum paid by the good Samaritan to the innkeeper (Lk. 10:35): that should give some idea of its purchasing power. In Rev. 6:6 'a quart of wheat for a *denarius*, and three quarts of barley for a *denarius*' is an indication of famine prices (* WEIGHTS AND MEASURES).

From Mt. 22:19; Mk. 12:15; Lk. 20:24 we learn that it was the coin used to trick Jesus in the question concerning the payment of tribute-money. Silver *denarii* of the time have been discovered which carry the laureate head of the emperor Tiberius on the obverse, with his mother, Livia, in the role of Pax, holding a branch and sceptre, on the reverse (see *IBA*, p. 87, fig. 90).

The *aureus*, or *denarius aureus* (golden denarius), was a gold coin introduced by Julius Caesar in his financial reforms of 49 BC. It finds no mention in the Bible, but is referred to in Jos., *Ant.* 14. 147: it may be the 'gold' of Mt. 10:9.

d. Evaluation of money

The table on p. 1020 relates the three different systems of coinage to each other.

BIBLIOGRAPHY. K. A. Jacob, *Coins and Christianity*, 1959; R. G. Bratcher, 'Weights, Money, Measures and Time', *The Bible Translator* 10, No. 4, Oct. 1959, pp. 165ff.; Garnet R. Halliday, *Money Talks about the Bible*, 1948; G. F. Hill, *Catalogue of Greek Coins in the British Museum*, vol. on Palestine, 1914; E. Rodgers, *A Handy Guide to Jewish Coins*, 1914; Paul Romanoff, *Jewish Symbols on Ancient Jewish Coins*, 1944; F. A. Banks, *Coins of Bible Days*, 1955; A. Reifenberg, *Israel's History in Coins from the Maccabees to the Roman Conquest*, 1953; D. Kanael, *BA* 26, 1965, pp. 38–62; E. W. Klenowsky, *On Ancient Palestinian and Other Coins*, 1974; Y. Meshorer, *Jewish Coins of the Second Temple Period*, 1967.

D.H.W.

MONEY-CHANGERS. The 'exchangers' of Mt. 25:27 (AV) were regular bankers (*trapezitai*); *cf.* the saying commonly ascribed to our Lord, 'Be expert bankers'—*i.e.* trustworthy and skilled in detecting counterfeits. A specialized class of money-changers officiated in the Temple precincts, probably in the Court of the Gentiles—*kollybistai* (Mt. 21:12; Mk. 11:15; Jn. 2:15) or *kermatistai* (Jn. 2:14). The former title derived from a word of Semitic origin denoting exchange-rate or commission; the latter would, strictly speaking, relate to a dealer in small change. The trade arose from the fact that money for the Temple, including the obligatory half-shekel (Ex. 30:13; *cf.* Mt. 17:24, and see E. Schürer, *HJP*, 2, 1978) had to be in Tyrian standard coin, with its high level of silver purity, and not in the current Roman standard. A surcharge was made (Mishnah tractate *Sheqalim*, *passim*) and the way opened for various malpractices (add passages in *HHT* on Mt. 21:12 to those in *SB*). The Lord's cleansing of the Temple included the overthrow of the counters of these dealers at the (doubtless highly lucrative) Passover season.

A.F.W.

MOON. The creation of the moon is recorded in Gn. 1:16, where it is referred to as 'the lesser light' in contrast to the sun. It was placed in the heavens to rule the night, and with the other luminaries to be 'for signs and for seasons and for days and years' (1:14). Its appearance in regular phases in the night sky afforded a basis for early * calendars, and the word most commonly used for it (*yārēaḥ*) is closely related to *yeraḥ*, 'month'. The same word occurs in Akkad. ([*w*]*arḫu*), Ugaritic (*yrḫ*), Phoen. (*yrḥ*) and other Semitic languages. Another word, used less often for it, is *l*^e^*bānâ*, 'white one' (Ct. 6:10; Is. 24:23; 30:26).

The first day of each new month was considered holy. Hence the association in the OT of the monthly 'new moon' with the weekly sabbath (*e.g.* Is. 1:13). This fresh beginning was marked by special sacrifices (Nu. 28:11–15) over which the trumpets were blown (Nu. 10:10; Ps. 81:3). Amos depicts the merchants of his day anxiously awaiting the end of the new moon and of the sabbath so that they could resume their fraudulent trading. It seems therefore to have been regarded, like the sabbath, as a day on which normal work was not done. The reference may be, however, to the new moon of the 7th month, regarding which the law stated specifically that no servile work was to be done on it (Lv. 23:24–25; Nu. 29:1–6). 2 Ki. 4:23 suggests that both new moon and sabbath were regarded as providing opportunity for consulting the prophets, and Ezekiel marks out the new moon as a special day for worship (Ezk. 46:1, 3).

The moon is mentioned with the sun as a symbol of permanence (Ps. 72:5). It is quoted as a wonder of creation (Ps. 8:3), and as marking by its behaviour the coming of the Messiah (Mk. 13:24; Lk. 21:25). Ps. 121:6 suggests that it was recognized as capable of affecting the mind, and in the NT Gk. words meaning literally 'moon-struck' are used in Mt. 4:24 and 17:15.

The moon is named as an object of idolatrous worship in Jb. 31:26, and archaeology has shown that it was deified in ancient W Asia from early Sumerian to Islamic times. In Mesopotamia the Sumerian god Nanna, named * Sin by the Akkadians, was worshipped in particular at Ur, where he was the chief god of the city, and also in the city of

The Babylonian moon-god Sīn (Su'e) stands in a crescent-moon, his symbol. Agate Neo-Babylonian seal. c. 7th–6th cent. BC. (BM)

MONGOOSE
See Animals, Part 1.

MONKEY
See Animals, Part 1.

MONTH
See Calendar, Part 1.

A crescent was the symbol of the moon-god Sīn, as shown here on a stele of King Nabonidus of Babylon. He rebuilt the moon temple at Harran, one centre of the moon cult. 555–539 BC. (BM)

MOONSTONE
See Jewels, Part 2.

MORAL PURITY
See Clean, Part 1.

MORALS
See Ethics, biblical, Part 1.

Harran in Syria, which had close religious links with Ur. The Ugaritic texts have shown that there a moon deity was worshipped under the name *yrḫ*. On the monuments the god is represented by the symbol of a crescent moon (*AMULETS). At Hazor in Palestine a small Canaanite shrine of the late Bronze Age was discovered which contained a basalt stela depicting two hands lifted as if in prayer to a crescent moon, perhaps indicating that the shrine was dedicated to the moon god (see *IBA*, fig. 112).

T.C.M.

MORDECAI (Heb. *mordᵉḵay*; *mordᵒḵay*; Ezr. 2:2).

1. A leader of the exiles who returned with Zerubbabel (Ezr. 2:2; Ne. 7:7; 1 Esdras 5:8).

2. A Jewish exile who had moved to the Persian capital *Susa, where he was employed in the palace. He was a Benjaminite son of Jair and descendant of Kish, taken prisoner to Babylon by Nebuchadrezzar (Est. 2:5–6). He brought up his orphaned cousin Hadassah (*ESTHER) and was rewarded, by being mentioned in the royal chronicles, for revealing a plot against King Xerxes (Est. 2:7, 21–23). (Mordecai has been identified by some with a finance officer at Susa under Xerxes.)

He opposed the vizier Haman who plotted to kill all Jews (Est. 3). When this evil deed was turned against Haman, Mordecai succeeded him in office, being then next in rank to the king (chs. 5–6; 10). He used this position to encourage the Jews to defend themselves against the massacre inspired by Haman. In respect for Mordecai the Persian provincial officials to whom he wrote assisted in protecting the Jews. The celebration of this event by the annual feast of *Purim was later connected with the 'day of Mordecai' (2 Macc. 15:36).

Mordecai is probably the Heb. rendering of a common Bab. personal name Mardukaya. This is found in texts, including one *c.* 485 BC (*AfO* 19, 1959–60, pp. 79–81) and another concerning an official of Ushtannu, satrap of Babylon (*ZAW* 58, 1940–41, pp. 243ff.; *cf.* S. H. Horn, *BibRes* 9, 1964, pp. 14–25). D.J.W.

MOREH (Heb. *mōreh*, 'teacher', 'diviner'). **1.** The name of a place near Shechem mentioned in Gn. 12:6, where *'ēlôn mōreh* may be translated 'the teacher's oak' (or 'terebinth'). Dt. 11:30 makes reference to the 'oak of Moreh' in the district of Gilgal (*i.e.* the Shechemite Gilgal). It is recorded that Abraham pitched his camp there on arriving in Canaan from Harran, and it was there that God revealed himself to Abraham, promising to give the land of Canaan to his descendants (* MAMRE). This tree may also be the one mentioned in Gn. 35:4 where Jacob hid foreign gods, and a reference to the place also occurs in the story of Abimelech (Jdg. 9:37).

2. The hill of Moreh at the head of the N side of the valley of Jezreel, S of Mt Tabor, 2 km S of Nain, and *c.* 13 km NW of Mt Gilboa, is the modern Jebel Dahi; it features in Jdg. 7:1, where, in the encounter between Gideon and the Midianites, the Midianites encamped in the valley, by the hill of Moreh, to the N of Gideon's camp by the spring of Harod.

3. Moreh has a quasi-technical sense in the Qumran phrase *mōrēh ṣeḏeq*, commonly translated 'teacher of righteousness' and used as a designation of the first organizer of the Qumran community and possibly of each succeeding leader. There may be an allusion to Joel 2:23, where *mōreh liṣᵉḏāqāh* is rendered '(he hath given you) a teacher of righteousness' in AVmg., or to Ho. 10:12, where *yōreh ṣeḏeq* is rendered '(he will) teach (you) righteousness' in RVmg., as though the coming of the Qumran teacher were greeted as a fulfilment of these promises. *Cf.* F. F. Bruce, *The Teacher of Righteousness in the Qumran Texts*, 1957; J. Weingreen, *From Bible to Mishna*, 1976, pp. 100ff. R.A.H.G.
F.F.B.

MORESHETH-GATH. Hometown of the prophet Micah (Mi. 1:1; Je. 26:18) near the Philistine territory of Gath (Mi. 1:14); probably the modern Tell ej-Judeieh, 32 km SW of Jerusalem and 10 km NE of Lachish. Moresheth-gath (Mi. 1:14) is one of twelve cities listed by the prophet Micah, whose names are by word-play associated with the form of their imminent judgment through invasion. Lachish, so to speak, will have to give a parting bridal-gift or dowry (*cf.* 1 Ki. 9:16) to Moresheth (*môrešeṯ*, which sounds like *mᵉ'ôreśeṯ*, betrothed), as that city is lost to the enemy. N.H.

MORIAH. In Gn. 22:2 God commanded Abraham to take Isaac to 'the land of Moriah' (*'ereṣ hammōriyyâ*) and there to offer him as a burnt offering upon one of the mountains (*har*). The mountain chosen was 3 days' journey (22:4) from the land of the Philistines (21:34; the region of * Gerar), and was visible from a distance (22:4).

The only other mention of the name occurs in 2 Ch. 3:1, where the site of Solomon's Temple is said to be 'on mount Moriah (*bᵉhar hammôriyyâ*), on the threshing-floor of Ornan the Jebusite where God appeared to David (3:2). It should be noted that no reference is made here to Abraham in connection with this site. It has been objected that Jerusalem is not sufficiently distant from S Philistia to have required a 3 days' journey to get there, and that one of the characteristics of Jerusalem is that the Temple hill is not visible until the traveller is quite close, so that the correctness of the biblical identification is called in question. The Samaritan tradition identifies the site with Mt Gerizim (as though Moriah = Moreh; *cf.* Gn. 12:6), and this is claimed to fulfil the conditions of Gn. 22:4 adequately. However, the distance from S Philistia to Jerusalem is *c.* 80 km, which might well have required 3 days to traverse, and in Genesis the place in question is not a 'mount Moriah' but one of several mountains in a land of that name, and the hills on which Jerusalem stands are visible at a distance. There is no need to doubt therefore that Abraham's sacrifice took place on the site of later Jerusalem, if not on the Temple hill.

BIBLIOGRAPHY. F. M. Abel, *Géographie de la Palestine*, 1, 1933, pp. 374–375. T.C.M.

MORTAR AND PESTLE. This formed an alternative to the stone * mill. While in the wilderness the Israelites ground the * manna either in mills or in a mortar (Nu. 11:8; Heb. *mᵉḏōḵâ*), and olive oil was produced in the same way ('beaten

Stone mortars excavated at Capernaum. Basalt. 1st cent. BC *–7th cent.* AD (SH)

oil', Ex. 27:20). Pr. 27:22 shows that evil cannot be removed from a wicked man even if he were to be crushed small (Heb. *maktēš*, 'mortar'; *'ᵉlî*, 'pestle'). For Egyptians using mortar and pestle, see *ANEP*, no. 153, upper right, and 154, lower part. The mortar was either a hollowed stone or a deep wooden bowl, the pestle a stout wooden pole. A small hollow in the land could also be called 'mortar' from its form, so Jdg. 15:19; Zp. 1:11. (* MAKTESH.) A.R.M.

MOSERAH, MOSEROTH. A camp-site of the Israelites in the wilderness (Nu. 33:30f.), where Aaron died (Dt. 10:6). The name could mean 'chastisement(s)', with reference to the trespass at Meribah (*cf.* Nu. 20:24; Dt. 32:51). The site is unidentified, but may have been close to Mt * Hor, which also figures as the place of Aaron's death and burial. See J. A. Thompson, *Deuteronomy*, *TOTC*, 1974, p. 145. D.F.P.

MOSES. The great leader and lawgiver through whom God brought the Hebrews out of Egypt, constituted them a nation for his service, and brought them within reach of the land promised to their forefathers.

I. Name

In Ex. 2:10 it is said that 'she called his name *Mōšeh*: and she said, Because I drew him (*mᵉšîṯī-hû*) out of the water'. Most interpreters identify the 'she' as Pharaoh's daughter, and this has led many to assume an Egyp. origin for the name *Mōšeh*, Egyp. *ms*, 'child' or '(one) born' being the best possibility. However, the antecedent of 'she' could as easily be 'the woman', *i.e.* Moses' own mother and nurse, who '*had* called his name . . .' (so W. J. Martin). Ex. 2:10 clearly links the name of *Mōšeh* with his being taken from the waterside (*māšâ*, 'to draw forth'). This pun would come naturally to a Hebrew speaker but not to an Egyptian: which fact would favour the view just mentioned that it was Moses' own mother who first named him, rather than Pharaoh's daughter.

Mōšeh as it stands is an active participle meaning 'one who draws forth', and may be an ellipsis for some longer phrase. In the 14th/13th centuries BC Egyp. *ms*, 'child' (and the related grammatical form in such names as Ramose, 'Rē, is born') was pronounced approximately *măsĕ*, and there is no philological or other reason why Moses' Egyp. adoptive mother should not have assimilated a Semitic *māši* or *Mōšeh* to the common name-word *Măsĕ*, *Mōšeh* in her own tongue. Compare assimilations such as German Löwe to English Lowe in our own day. Hence Moses' name may simply be Semitic assimilated to Egyp. while in Egypt. The majority view, however, is that the daughter of Pharaoh called him *Mōse*, 'child' (or—less suitably—a theophoric name in *-mose*), which passed into Heb. speech as *Mōšeh*. This view, however, fails to account adequately for the Semitic pun, which there is no objective reason to reject as unhistorical, as it is a common practice in Egypt and elsewhere (including the OT) long before Moses; such a view, moreover, runs into real phonetic difficulties over Egyp. *s* appearing as *š* in *Mōšeh* but as *s* in Ra'amses and Phinehas in Hebrew, as was pointed out long ago by A. H. Gardiner, *JAOS* 56, 1936, pp. 192–194—a problem in no way solved by J. G. Griffiths, *JNES* 12, 1953, pp. 225–231, the best statement of this view.

II. Life and background

a. Ancestry

Moses belonged to the tribe of Levi, to the clan of Kohath, and to the house or family of Amram (Ex. 6:16ff.). That he was the distant descendant, not the son, of Amram by Jochebed is hinted at inasmuch as his parents are not named in the detailed account of his infancy (Ex. 2), and is made almost certain by the fact that Amram and his three brothers had numerous descendants within a year of the Exodus (Nu. 3:27f.). (* CHRONOLOGY OF THE OT, **III.** *b.*)

b. Egyptian upbringing

To save her baby son from the pharaonic edict ordering the destruction of Hebrew male infants, Moses' mother put him into a little basket of pitch-caulked reeds or papyrus among the rushes by the stream bank and bade his sister Miriam keep watch. Soon a daughter of Pharaoh came with her maidservants to bathe in the river, found the child, and took pity on him. Miriam discreetly offered to find a nurse for the child (in fact, his mother), and so Moses' life was saved. When weaned, he was handed over to his adoptive 'mother', the Egyptian princess (Ex. 2:1–10). Of Moses' growth to adult maturity in Egyptian court society no detail is given, but a boy in his position in New Kingdom period court circles could not avoid undergoing a substantial basic training in that 'wisdom of the Egyptians' with which Stephen credits him (Acts 7:22).

Modern knowledge of ancient Egypt yields a rich background for the early life of Moses in Egypt. The pharaohs of the New Kingdom period (*c.* 1550–1070 BC) maintained residences and *harîms* not only in the great capitals of Thebes, Memphis and Pi-Ramessē (Ra'amses) but also in other parts of Egypt. Typical is the long-established *harîm* in the Fayum, where the royal ladies supervised a hive of domestic industry (A. H. Gardiner, *JNES* 12, 1953, pp. 145–149, especially p. 149). One such *harîm* must have been Moses' first Egyptian home.

Anciently, children of *harîm*-women could be educated by the Overseer of the *harîm* ('a teacher of the children of the king', F. Ll. Griffith and P. E. Newberry, *El Bersheh*, 2, 1894, p. 40). In due course princes were given a tutor, usually a high official at court or a retired military officer close to the king (H. Brunner, *Altägyptische Erziehung*, 1957, pp. 32–33); Moses doubtless fared similarly.

Moreover, as a Semite in Egypt, Moses would have had no difficulty whatever in learning and using the twenty or so letters of the proto-Canaanite linear alphabet, especially if he had been submitted to the much more exacting discipline of a training in the scores of characters and sign-groups of the Egyptian scripts (though even these require only application, not genius, to learn them). The fact that Egypt, not Palestine, was his home would be no barrier to familiarity with this simple linear script. The 'proto-Sinaitic' inscriptions of the early 15th century BC are certainly just informal dedications, work-notes and brief epitaphs (for offerings) by Semitic captives from the Egyp. E Delta (or Memphis settlements) employed in the turquoise-mines (*cf.* W. F. Albright, *BASOR* 110, 1948, pp. 12–13, 22), and illustrate free use of that script by Semites under Egyptian rule nearly two centuries before Moses. Still more eloquent of the ready use of the linear script by Semites in Egypt is an ostracon from the Valley of the Queens at Thebes, some 560 km S of Palestine, Sinai, or the Delta (J. Leibovitch, *Annales du Service des Antiquités de l'Égypte* 40, 1940, p. 119, fig. 26, and pl. 16, 19:50); the one word fully preserved can be reasonably read *'mht*, 'maid-servants' (Albright, *op. cit.*, p. 12).

c. Foreigners at the Egyptian court

Semites and other Asiatics could be found at every level of Egyptian society in the New Kingdom. Besides thousands of prisoners brought from Canaan to be slaves (*cf. ANET*, pp. 246b, 247b), foreign artisans, Syrian warriors in Egyptian service (*e.g. ANEP*, fig. 157), Asian youths as attendants, fan-bearers, *etc.*, at court (R. A. Caminos, *Late-Egyptian Miscellanies*, 1954, pp. 117, 200–201), Semites in Egypt could rise to the highest levels of the social pyramid. They were couriers between Egypt and Syria (*ANET*, p. 258b), charioteers who themselves owned servants (J. Černý, *JEA* 23, 1937, p. 186), and merchants (Caminos, *op. cit.*, p. 26: 'Aper-Ba'al); the daughter of a Syrian sea-captain Ben-'Anath could marry a royal prince (W. Spiegelberg, *Recueil de Travaux*, 16, 1894, p. 64).

Under the Ramesside kings Asiatics were still more prominent. Thus, one of King Merenptah's trusted cupbearers was the Syrian Ben-'Ozen of Ṣûr-Bashan ('Rock-of-Bashan'), who accompanied the vizier in overseeing work on that pharaoh's tomb in the Valley of the Kings (*JEA* 34, 1948, p. 74). Further, at the very end of the 19th Dynasty, a Syrian very briefly took over control of Egypt itself: he was very possibly the immensely powerful Chancellor Bay (Černý in Gardiner, *JEA* 44, 1958, pp. 21–22).

In New Kingdom Egypt, Canaanite and other Asiatic deities were accepted (Baal, Resheph, 'Ashtaroth, 'Anath, *etc.*; *cf. ANET*, pp. 249–250); and as well as innumerable loan-words, Canaanite literary themes were current, either borrowed or assimilated to Egyp. ones (W. F. Albright, *Archaeology and the Religion of Israel*, 1953, pp. 197–198 (rape of 'Anath); T. H. Gaster, *BO* 9, 1952, pp. 82–85, 232; and G. Posener, *Mélanges Isidore Lévy*, 1955, pp. 461–478 (the greed of the Sea); and reference to a story of Qazardi, *ANET*, p. 477b). Some Egyp. officials prided themselves on being able to speak the lip of

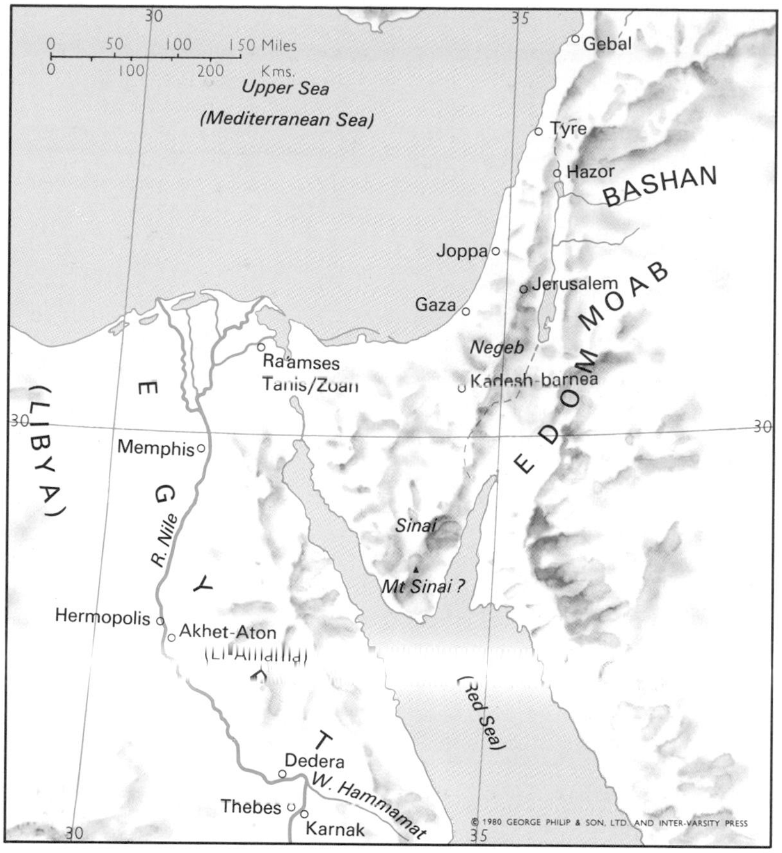

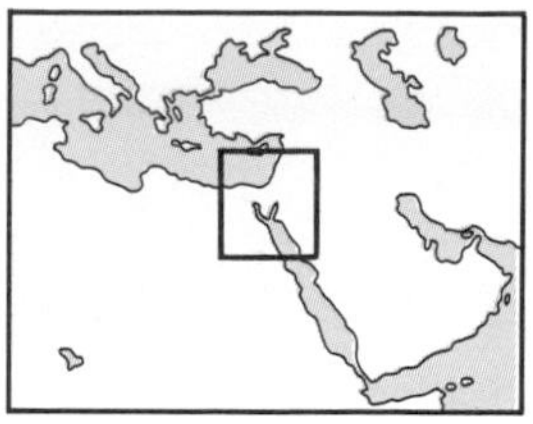

Map to illustrate the life of Moses.

Canaan as well as know its geography (*ANET*, p. 477b), not to mention those who had to learn Babylonian cuneiform for diplomatic purposes (*cf.* Albright, *Vocalization of the Egyptian Syllabic Orthography*, 1934, p. 13, n. 50, and *JEA* 23, 1937, pp. 191, 196–202).

d. In Midian and Sinai

Moses felt for his labouring brethren (*cf.* Acts 7:24) and slew an Egyp. overseer whom he found beating a Hebrew (Ex. 2:11f.); but the deed reached Pharaoh's ears, so Moses fled E over the border to Midian for safety (Ex. 2:15ff.). Flight over the E border was the escape chosen also by Sinuhe 600 years earlier (*ANET*, p. 19) and by runaway slaves later in the 13th century BC (*ANET*, p. 259b). Moses helped the daughters of a Midianite shepherd-priest Reuel/Jethro to water their flocks, and married one of them, Zipporah, who bore him a son, Gershom (Ex. 2:16–22).

Through the wonder of the burning bush that was not consumed came Moses' call from God, the God of ancestral Abraham, Isaac and Jacob (Ex. 3:6) and not just of his Midianite/Kenite in-laws, except in so far as they too were descendants of Abraham (*cf.* Gn. 25:1–6) and may have retained the worship of Abraham's God. After some procrastination, Moses obeyed the call (Ex. 3–4). Apparently Moses had omitted to circumcise one of his sons, perhaps under Zipporah's influence. At any rate, under threat of Moses' death by God's agency, she circumcised the boy, calling her husband 'a bridegroom of blood' (Ex. 4:24–26) because circumcision was binding on him and his people (but perhaps not on her people?). Moses may have gone on alone from this point, as later on Zipporah returns to Moses from Jethro's care (Ex. 18:1–6).

e. On the eve of the Exodus

After meeting his brother and the elders of Israel (Ex. 4:27–31), Moses with Aaron went before the pharaoh to request that he release the people to hold a feast to the Lord in the wilderness. But Pharaoh contemptuously dismissed them—there were already enough religious holidays and festivals on which no work was done, and this was just an excuse to be idle (Ex. 5:8, 17).

That Moses should be able to gain ready access to the pharaoh is not very surprising, especially if the pharaoh of the Exodus was Rameses II. P. Montet (*L'Égypte et la Bible*, 1959, p. 71) appositely

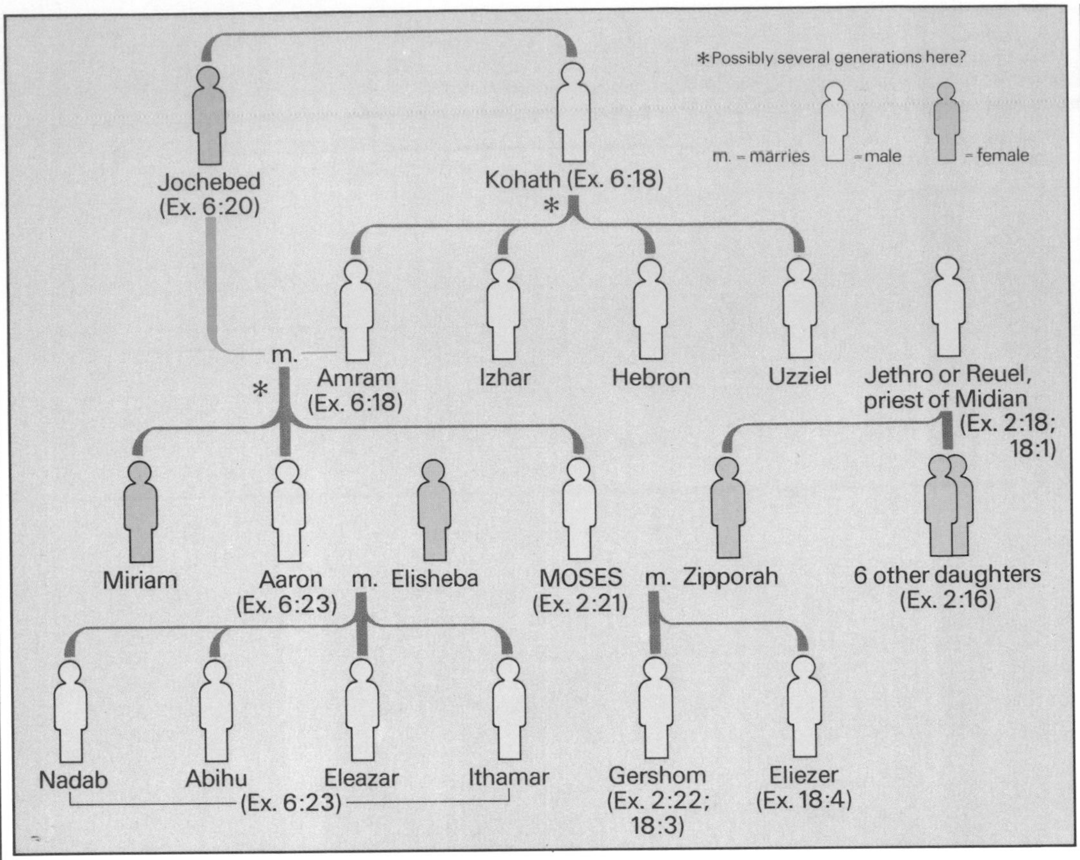

The family of Moses.

refers to Papyrus Anastasi III, which describes how the 'young people of (Pi-Ramessē) Great of Victories . . . stand by their doors . . . on the day of the entry of Wosermaetrē'-Setepenrē' (*i.e.* Rameses II) . . ., every man being like his fellow in voicing his petitions' (*i.e.* to the king), *cf. ANET*, p. 471b. For the brickmaking of the Israelites and use of straw, see * Brick. The organization of labour into gangs of workmen under foremen responsible to taskmasters is at once authentic and natural.

As for absence from work, Egyp. ostraca (* PAPYRI) include journals of work that give a day-to-day record of absenteeism, names of absentees and reasons. One ostracon shows that the workmen of the royal tomb were idle at one period for 30 days out of 48. One journal of absences takes note of several workmen, 'offering to his god' (A. Erman, *Life in Ancient Egypt*, 1894, pp. 124–125), and the laconic entry *wsf*, 'idle', is not infrequent in such journals. That the Hebrews should go 3 days' journey into the wilderness to celebrate their feast and not arouse Egyp. religious antagonism (Ex. 8:26f.; 10:9, 25f.) is, again, thoroughly realistic, as is pointed out by Montet (*op. cit.*, pp. 99–101 with references), in connection with sacred animals, especially the bull-cults in the Egyp. Delta provinces (* CALF, GOLDEN).

After the rebuff from Pharaoh, Moses was reassured by God that he would fulfil his covenant to their descendants, bringing them from Egypt to Palestine (Ex. 6:2–9). It should be noted that Ex. 6:3 does *not* deny knowledge of the name of YHWH to the Patriarchs, though it may possibly deny real knowledge of the significance of the name: see on this, W. J. Martin, *Stylistic Criteria and the Analysis of the Pentateuch*, 1955, pp. 16–19, and J. A. Motyer, *The Revelation of the Divine Name*, 1959, pp. 11–17. Successive * plagues demonstrated the God of Israel's power to Pharaoh in judgment (Ex. 7:14–12:36). On the eve of the last plague, the smiting of the first-born, the families of Israel had to kill a spotless lamb and mark the jambs and lintels of their house-doors with the blood, so that God should not destroy their first-born: 'the sacrifice of the Lord's passover' (Ex. 12:27). It has been suggested by B. Couroyer (*RB* 62, 1955, pp. 481–496) that the Hebrew *psḥ* is derived from the Egyptian *p(')-sḥ*, 'the stroke, blow' (*i.e.* of God), but this meaning does not fit all the Hebrew evidence, and so remains doubtful.

f. From Succoth to Sinai

On the date of the Exodus, see * Chronology of the OT; also J. J. Bimson, *Redating the Exodus and Conquest*, 1978; for its route from Ra'amses and Succoth out of Egypt, see * Encampment by the Sea, * Pithom; for travels in Sinai, see * Wilderness of Wandering. When Israel encamped by the *yam sûp̄*, 'sea of reeds', the pharaoh and his people imagined that the Hebrews were trapped (Ex. 14:1–9). For the figure of over 600 chariots (Ex. 14:7), compare the figures of 730 and 1,092 (*i.e.* 60 + 1032) Syr. chariots captured in Canaan on two campaigns by Amenophis II (*ANET*, pp. 246–247); on the role of chariots in the Egyptian army, *cf.* R. O. Faulkner, *JEA* 39, 1953, p. 43. But God divided the waters, led his people to safety and turned the waters upon the Egyp. forces. Then Moses and the Hebrews raised their song of God's triumph (Ex. 15).

Israel encamped at the foot of Mt Sinai and Moses went up to commune with God and receive the terms of the covenant (the 'ten commandments' of Ex. 20), which were the foundation of Israel's subsequent role as the people of God (he being their great King), and also the series of statutes carrying the commandments into effect (Ex. 21–23).

After the idolatrous lapse over the golden * calf and the restoration of the covenant so quickly violated (Ex. 32:1–35:3), the tabernacle, ark and furnishings were duly made and inaugurated for the worship of God (Ex. 35:4–40:33). The techniques used for the portable tabernacle reflect Moses' Egyp. training in so far as such techniques had been used in Egypt for portable structures (religious and otherwise) for over 1,000 years before his time (*cf.* K. A. Kitchen, *THB* 5/6, 1960, pp. 7–13). However, the representational and didactic nature of the tabernacle sacrifices stands out in marked contrast to Egyp. ritual. The Heb. sacrifices speak in picture-language of the offensiveness of sin in God's sight, and of the need of atonement for its cancellation, and were not merely a magically efficacious re-enactment of daily life needed to keep the god fed and flourishing as in Egyp. ritual.

At Sinai a census was taken, the manner of Israel's camp and marching order laid down. Levitical care for the tabernacle and its contents was arranged (Nu. 1–4) among other things on the eve of leaving Sinai (Nu. 5:1–10:10). The arrangement of the tribes by their standards in a 'hollow rectangle' round the tabernacle is also probably a mark of God's use of Moses' Egyp. training (*cf.* Kitchen, *op. cit.*, p. 11). The long, silver trumpets and their use for civil assembly and military and religious purposes (Nu. 10:1–10) is illustrated by contemporary Egyp. use of such trumpets (*cf.* H. Hickmann, *La Trompette dans l'Égypte Ancienne*, 1946, especially pp. 46–50). Ox-wagons were regularly used on campaigns in Syria by the pharaohs from Tuthmosis III (*c.* 1470 BC) onwards (*ANET*, p. 204a, 'chariot'), *e.g.* by Rameses II, *c.* 1270 BC, at Qadesh (C. Kuentz, *La Bataille de Qadech*, 1928/34, pl. 39, left centre). With Moses' wagons each drawn by a span of (two) oxen in Sinai, compare the ten wagons (Egyp. *'grt* from Heb. *'glt*, same word, in Nu. 7:3, 6–7) each drawn by six spans of oxen that carried supplies for 8,000 quarrymen of Rameses IV (*c.* 1160 BC) from the Nile valley into the deserts of Wadi Hammamat between the Nile and the Red Sea, in very similar conditions to Sinai (*ARE*, 4, § 467).

g. From Sinai to Jordan

In their 2nd year out from Egypt (Nu. 10:11), Israel left Sinai and reached Kadesh-barnea. Moses thence sent spies into Canaan. The land was a goodly one, but its inhabitants were powerful (Nu. 13:17–33). At this report, faithless Israel rebelled, but Moses pleaded with God to spare Israel (Nu. 14:5–19). Therefore the Lord decreed instead that Israel's travels in the wilderness should last 40 years until the rebellious generation had died and given place to a new one (Nu. 14:20–35).

It is very easy to forget that, prior to this tragic episode, Israel was intended to have crossed from Egypt—*via* Sinai—directly to the Promised Land within a few years; the 40 years in the wilderness was purely a commuted sentence (Nu. 14:12, 20–30, 33) and *not* part of God's 'first and best' plan for Israel. This should be remembered when reading the laws in Ex. 22–23, relating to agriculture, vineyards, *etc.*; Israel at Sinai had had 4 centuries living in Egypt amid a pastoral and agricultural environment (*cf.* Dt. 11:10), neither they nor their patriarchal forefathers were ever true desert nomads (*cf.* Gn. 26:12 and 37:6–8), and at Sinai they might well count themselves within striking distance of the land where these laws would find a speedy application. Israel had no need to settle in Canaan before such laws could be given, as is so often asserted (*cf.* Kitchen, *op. cit.*, pp. 13–14).

On the twin rebellion of Korah against the ecclesiastical role (Nu. 16:3), and Dathan and Abiram against the civil authority (Nu. 16:13), of Moses and Aaron, see *Wilderness of Wandering. This double revolt was followed by the threat of general revolt (Nu. 16:41–50). Back at Kadesh-barnea, where Miriam died, Moses himself and Aaron sinned blasphemously casting themselves in God's role: 'Hear now, you rebels; shall *we* [not God] bring forth water for you out of this rock?' (Nu. 20:10); their punishment was that neither should enter the Promised Land, and was one which Moses later felt very keenly (Dt. 3:24–27). The Edomites (Nu. 20:14–21; also Moab, *cf.* Jdg. 11:17) refused Israel passage through their territories so that Israel must go round their borders. At this time Aaron died and was buried in Mt Hor (Nu. 20:22–29). Yet again Israel rebelled. God punished them by sending serpents among them, and again Moses interceded for them. God commanded him to set up a bronze *serpent on a pole (Nu. 21:4–9), to which those bitten might look and live, through faith in the Healer. Thereafter Israel reached the Amorite kingdom of Sihon. Sihon marched—unprovoked—to attack Israel, into whose hand God then delivered him and his land; Og of Bashan, likewise hostile, met a similar fate (Nu. 21:21–35).

At last, Israel encamped in the plains of Moab (Nu. 22:1; 25:1). A second census was carried out, and preparations for apportioning the Promised Land were begun. A punitive war was conducted against Midian, and the tribes of Reuben, Gad and half-Manasseh were allowed to take Transjordan as their portion on condition that they would help their brethren beyond Jordan after Moses' death.

*Deuteronomy gives Moses' farewell addresses to his people; the covenant between God and Israel was renewed and placed under sanctions of blessing and cursing in a manner calculated to be widely understood in the 14th/13th centuries BC (as shown by *covenants or treaties from the contemporary Hittite state archives, *cf.* G. E. Mendenhall, *BA* 17, 1954, pp. 53–60 and *passim*). Finally, Moses saw to it that Israel had her covenant-law in written form, appropriately placed alongside the ark of the covenant (Dt. 31:24), left them a song to enjoin on them obedience to that law (Dt. 32, especially vv. 44–47), and laid upon them his dying blessing (Dt. 33) before ascending Mt Nebo to view the land he was not destined to enter, and being laid to rest in the land of Moab (Dt. 32:48–42; 34:1–8).

III. The work of Moses

a. Leader

As a leader of his people, Moses was not only equipped technically through his Egyp. upbringing and training (Acts 7:22), but was also, on a much more fundamental level, a supreme leader by being a close follower of his God by faith (Heb. 11:23–29; *cf.* Acts 7:23–37). Israel repeatedly failed to have faith in their God in all circumstances, broke the commandments, and rejected God's leadership in rebelling against Moses (sometimes Moses and Aaron) through whom that leadership was manifested (*e.g.* Nu. 14:4, 10; 16:41f.). Moses' own family let him down (Ex. 32:1ff., 21; Nu. 12:1f.). Great indeed was Moses' forbearance (Nu. 12:3); he was constantly interceding with God for sinning Israel (*e.g.* Nu. 14:13ff.; 16:46, *etc.*) and pleading with Israel to be faithful to their delivering God (*e.g.* Nu. 14:5–9). That he was a man of enduring faith in the invisible God (Heb. 11:27b) and so jealous for God's name (*cf.* Nu. 14:13ff.) can alone explain his achievement (*cf.* Phil. 4:13).

b. Prophet and lawgiver

As one especially prominent in declaring and teaching the will, commandments and nature of God, Moses was characteristically the model of all later true prophets until the coming of that One of whom he was forerunner (Dt. 18:18; Acts 3:22f.), to whom all the prophets bear witness (Acts 10:43). He was called by God (Ex. 3:1–4:17) not only to lead the people out of bondage but to make known God's will. Typical is Ex. 19:3, 7: God speaks to Moses, and he to the people.

MOSQUITO
See Animals, Part 1.

MOST HIGH
See God, names of, Part 1.

MOTE
See Speck, Part 3.

MOTH
See Animals, Part 1.

MOTHER-OF-PEARL
See Jewels, Part 2.

MOUFLON
See Animals, Part 1.

Moses communed with God long (Ex. 24:18) and often (*e.g.* Ex. 33:7–11), as did later prophets (*cf.* Samuel's life of prayer, 1 Sa. 7:5; 8:6; 12:23; 15:11). Just as the covenant was declared and renewed (Dt. 29:1) through Moses, so the later prophets in turn repeatedly reproved Israel for breaking the covenant and its conditions (*e.g.* 1 Ki. 18:18; 2 Ki. 17:15, 35–40; 2 Ch. 15:1f., 12; Je. 6:16, 19; 8:7f., 11:1–5, 6–10; Ho. 6:7; Am. 2:4; Hg. 2:5; Mal. 2:4ff.), though Jeremiah (31:31–34) could also look forward to a new covenant.

The term 'code' often given to various parts of the Pentateuch is misleading: Moses was not simply the promulgator of some kind of ideal, civil '*code Napoléon*' for Israel. Contemporary Near Eastern treaty-documents of the 13th century BC show that Moses was moved by God to express Israel's relationship to God in the form of a 'suzerainty' treaty or *covenant, by which a great king (in this case, God, the King of kings) bound to himself a vassal-people (here, Israel), the form in question being uniquely transmuted to the religious and spiritual plane. This was a kind of formulation that would be universally understood at the time. For Israel, the basic stipulations of their covenant were the Ten Commandments, in effect moral law as the expression of God's will; and the detailed covenant-obligations took the form of 'civil' statute rooted in the moral law of the Ten Commandments (*e.g.* Ex. 21–23; Dt. 12–26, *etc.*), and even of prescriptions governing the forms of permissible and authorized religious practice (*e.g.* Ex. 25:1ff.; 35:10ff.; Lv.); Israel's life in every way was to be marked by righteousness and holiness as issuing from obedience to the covenant, or, in other words, fulfilling the law. Attainment, however, waited upon further divine provision; *cf.* Gal. 3:23ff. (also 15–22, especially 21f.).

Because Israel's covenant was not merely a treaty of political obligations but regulated their daily life before God, its ordinances served also as a minimum basis of 'civil' law for the people. The existence of long series of laws promoted by individual heads of state from the end of the 3rd millennium BC onwards makes it superfluous to date the giving of the pentateuchal laws any later than Moses (13th century BC).

The number or quantity of 'civil' laws in the Pentateuch is in no way excessive or exceptional when compared with other collections. In Ex. 21–23 may be discerned about 40 'paragraphs', in Lv. 18–20 more than 20 'paragraphs', and in Dt. 12–26 nearly 90 'paragraphs', of very variable length from a chapter or half-chapter of the present-day text-divisions down to one short sentence; say, about 150 'paragraphs' in these sections altogether, leaving aside the more obviously religious prescriptions. This figure compares very reasonably with the 282 paragraphs of Hammurapi's laws, the 115 surviving paragraphs of the Middle Assyrian laws (many more being lost) or the 200 paragraphs of the Hittite laws.

c. Author

In modern times estimates of Moses' role as an author have varied over the whole range of conceivable opinion between the two extremes of either attributing to him every syllable of the present Pentateuch, or denying his very existence.

That Moses' name was attached to parts of the Pentateuch right from the start is clearly shown by the biblical text itself. Thus, at an utter minimum, Moses as a writer is undeniably credited with the following: a brief document on God's judgment against Amalek (Ex. 17:14); the 'book of the covenant' (Ex. 24:4–8; on the external parallels, this must include Ex. 20 and 21–23, the commandments and attendant laws); the restoration of the covenant (Ex. 34:27, referring to 34:10–26); an itinerary (Nu. 33:1f., referring to the document that furnished 33:3–40); the major part of Dt. to 31 (Dt. 31:9–13, 24ff., referring to renewal of the covenant and re-enforcement of its laws that precede ch. 31); and two poems (Dt. 32; *cf.* 31:22; and Ps. 90 by title, which there is no objective evidence to doubt). Later OT and NT references to Moses in this connection are collected by various scholars, *e.g.* by E. J. Young, *IOT*, 1949, pp. 50f.

The ability to write historical narrative, record laws and compose poetry in one man is not unique. An Egyp. example of this kind of ability 7 centuries before Moses is probably furnished by Khety (or Akhtoy), son of Duauf, a writer under the pharaoh Amenemhat I (*c.* 1991–1962 BC), who was apparently educator, political propagandist and poet. He wrote the *Satire of the Trades* for use in scribal schools, was probably commissioned to give literary form to the 'Teaching of Amenemhat I', a political pamphlet, and may have been author of a well-known Hymn to the Nile often copied out by scribes along with the other two works (*cf.* Gardiner, *Hieratic Papyri in the British Museum, Third Series*, 1935, 1, pp. 40, 43–44, and Posener, *Littérature et Politique dans l'Égypte de la XIIe Dynastie*, 1956, pp. 4–7, 19, n. 7, 72–73). However, beyond the 'utter minimum' already mentioned above, there is no objective reason why Moses should not have written, or have caused to be written (at dictation—hence third person pronouns), considerably more of the contents of the present Pentateuch, though just how much more must remain a matter of opinion.

d. Later fame

From Joshua (8:31; *cf.* 1 Ki. 2:3; 2 Ki. 14:6; Ezr. 6:18, *etc.*) to NT times (Mk. 12:26; Lk. 2:22; Jn. 7:23), the name of Moses was associated with the OT, especially the Pentateuch; note 2 Cor. 3:15, where 'Moses' stands *pars pro toto* for the OT. And it was Moses and Elijah, the representatives of OT law and prophecy, who stood with Christ on the Mount of Transfiguration (Mt. 17:3f.).

BIBLIOGRAPHY. O. T. Allis, *God Spake by Moses*, 1951; G. von Rad, *Moses*, 1960; H. H. Rowley, *Men of God*, 1963, pp. 1–36; *idem*, *From Moses to Qumran*, 1963, pp. 35–63; R. Smend, *Das Mosebild von Heinrich Ewald bis Martin Noth*, 1959; H. Schmid, *Mose, Überlieferung und Geschichte*, 1968. K.A.K.

MOUNT, MOUNTAIN. The topographical terms *giḇ'â* and *hār* in Heb., and *bounos* and *oros* in Gk., are best translated by the Eng. 'hill' and 'mountain' respectively. The term *giḇ'â*, 'hill', is specific, referring to an elevated site, slope or ascent. Its root meaning, 'bowl' or 'hump-backed', refers accurately to the rounded hills which form the backbone of central Palestine, carved out of the hard and folded arches of Cenomanian limestone. Their eroded form is distinct from the deep dissection of the soft Senonian limestones which flank the Judaean highlands, which are graphically described in AV as 'slippery places' (Dt. 32:35; Pr. 3:23; Je. 23:12; 31:9). Specific sites of the hills and mountains are personified in Scripture with descriptive titles. Such are: head (Gn. 8:5; Ex. 19:20; Dt. 34:1; 1 Ki. 18:42), ears (Jos. 19:34), shoulder (Jos. 15:8; 18:16), side (1 Sa. 23: 26; 2 Sa. 13:34), loins (Jos. 19:12), rib (2 Sa. 16:13), back—possible derivation of Shechem, backed by Mt Gerizim—and thigh (Jdg. 19:1, 18; 2 Ki. 19:23; Is. 37:24).

The term *hār*, generally translated 'mountain' in modern vss, is more general, used indiscriminately of a single mount, a mountain range, or a tract of mountainous terrain. In Eng. mountain and hill are relative terms associated with altitudinal differences, but AV regards the Heb. OT terms *giḇ'â* and *hār* as almost interchangeable. Similarly, in NT, Jesus, *e.g.*, is described as coming down the 'hill' (Lk. 9:37) which he ascended the previous day as the 'Mount' of Transfiguration. In the following passages AV would be better rendered 'mountain', as RSV: Gn. 7:19; Ex. 24:4; Nu. 14:44–45; Dt. 1:41, 43; 8:7; 11:11; Jos. 15:9; 18:13–14; Jdg. 2:9; 16:3; 1 Sa. 25:20; 26:13; 2 Sa. 13:34; 16:13; 21:9; 1 Ki. 11:7; 16:24; 20:23; 22:17; 2 Ki. 1:9; 4:27; Pss. 18:7; 68:15–16; 80:10; 95:4; 97:5; 98:8; 104:10, 13, 18, 32; 121:1; Lk. 9:37. On the other hand, Heb. *hār* is correctly termed 'hill country' (Jos. 13:6; 21:11; *cf.* Gk. *oreinē*, Lk. 1:39, 65, when applied to a regional tract of land such as Ephraim and Judah. It is also used of the land of the Amorites (Dt. 1:7, 19–20), of Naphtali (Jos. 20:7), of the Ammonites (Dt. 2:37) and Gilead (Dt. 3:12).

The identification of specific sites is therefore not always possible, as in the cases of the high mountain of temptation (Lk. 4:5), the mount of the Beatitudes (Mt. 5:1), and the Mount of Transfiguration (Mt. 17:1; Mk. 9:2; Lk. 9:28). Mt *Sinai cannot be identified if, as some have suggested, it was a previously active volcano (Ex. 19:16; Pss. 104:32; 144:5). The traditional location in the Sinai Peninsula (Jebel Mūsa) would in that case be impossible geologically, as the ancient rocks of the district show no evidence of recent volcanicity. Two pleistocene volcanic cones, perhaps active in historic times, occur on the E side of the Gulf of Aqabah, but some authorities cannot see how this fits with the route of the *Exodus described.

The mount of assembly mentioned in Is. 14:13 occurs in the boast of the king of Babylon, and may be an allusion to a probable Bab. legend relating to the dwelling of the gods (*cf.* Jb. 37:22; Ezk. 28:13f.).

Armageddon, Hebraicized Harmagedon in AV (Rev. 16:16), may refer to the mountain district of *Megiddo, *i.e.* Mt Gerizim, which overlooks the plain of Megiddo, the location of other apocalyptic scenes (*cf.* Zc. 12:11).

Mountains have great significance in the geography and history of *Palestine. Consequently they are frequently referred to in the Scriptures. They provide vistas—'go up to the top of Pisgah and lift up your eyes' (Dt. 3:27; *cf.* Lk. 4:5). Their influence on higher rainfall makes them a symbol of fertility (Dt. 33:15; Je. 50:19; Mi. 7:14), grazing-places (Ps. 50:10) and hunting-grounds (1 Sa. 26:20). They are associated with pagan sanctuaries (1 Ki. 18:17–46; Is. 14:13; 65:7; Ezk. 6:13). Their inaccessibility makes them places of refuge (Jdg. 6:2; 1 Sa. 14:21–22; Ps. 68:15, 22; Mt. 24:16).

Mountains are a symbol of eternal continuance (Dt. 33:15; Hab. 3:6) and stability (Is. 54:10). They are considered as the earliest created things (Jb. 15:7; Pr. 8:25), of ancient origin (Ps. 90:2) and objects of the Creator's might (Ps. 65:6) and majesty (Ps. 68:16). They are the scenes of theophanies, melting at Yahweh's presence (Jdg. 5:5; Ps. 97:5; Is. 64:1; Mi. 1:4) and shuddering at his judgments (Ps. 18:7; Mi. 6:1f.). They are called to cover the guilty from his face (Ho. 10:8; Lk. 23:30). When God touches them they bring forth smoke (Pss. 104:32; 144:5). They also rejoice at the advent of Israel's redemption (Ps. 98:8; Is. 44:23; 49:13; 55:12), leap at the praise of the Lord (Ps. 114:4, 6) and are called to witness his dealings with his people (Mi. 6:2).

Mountains are also symbols of difficult paths in life (Je. 13:16), obstacles (Mt. 21:21), and other difficulties (Zc. 4:7), the removal of which is possible to those of strong faith (Mt. 17:20). J.M.H.

MOUTH. Heb. *peh* with several other words occasionally translated mouth, and Gk. *stoma*. Both are used not only of the mouth of man or beast, or anthropomorphically of God, but are often translated 'edge', in the phrase 'edge of the sword'. *peh* is used also of the mouth of a well (Gn. 29:2), a sack (Gn. 42:27), or a cave (Jos. 10:22).

The general usage is very close to and almost interchangeable with *lip or *tongue. The hand laid upon the mouth, like the lip, was a sign of shame (Mi. 7:16). The mouth can sin (Ps. 59:12) or utter good. The tendency to speak of the mouth as acting independently, by synecdoche or ignorance of physiology, is not as marked as in the case of lip. This may be because the Heb. did not distinguish clearly between the supposed functions of the internal organs, and the mouth, being partly internal, was obviously connected with them (see *HEART and *cf.* Pr. 16:23 where *peh* is translated in RSV as 'speech').

Frequently the mouth is said to be filled with words of one kind or another, or a spirit which causes certain words to be spoken (1 Ki. 22:22; Ps. 40:3). By extension the word *peh* came to mean words or commandments (Ex. 17:1). B.O.B.

MUSIC AND MUSICAL INSTRUMENTS.

I. Music

It is evident from the frequent references in the OT that music played an important part in Heb. culture. According to tradition Jubal, the son of Lamech, who 'was the father of all those who play the lyre and pipe' (Gn. 4:21), was the inventor of music. The close relation between the pastoral and the musical arts is shown in that Jubal had an elder brother Jabal who was 'father of those who dwell in tents, and have cattle' (Gn. 4:20).

At a later stage music was consecrated to the service of the Temple worship, but found secular use also, from early times. Thus Laban reproached Jacob for stealing away without allowing him to cheer his departure 'with mirth and songs, with tambourine (AV tabret) and lyre' (Gn. 31:27). It was frequently used on occasions of rejoicing, when it was regularly linked with the *dance. There were songs of triumph after victory in battle (Ex. 15:1ff.; Jdg. 5:1ff.). Miriam and the women celebrated the downfall of Pharaoh and his horsemen 'with timbrels and dancing' (Ex. 15:20ff.), and Jehoshaphat returned victorious to Jerusalem 'with harps (AV psalteries) and lyres and trumpets' (2 Ch. 20:28). Music, singing and dancing were common at feasts (Is. 5:12; Am. 6:5). In particular, they

MOUNTAIN OF THREE LIGHTS
See Olives, Mount of, Part 2.

MOUNTAIN SHEEP
See Animals, Part 1.

MOUNT OF OFFENCE
See Olives, Mount of, Part 2.

MOVING CREATURE
See Animals, Part 1.

MULE
See Animals, Part 1.

MUMMIFICATION
See Burial and mourning, Part 1.

MUSHI
See Merari, Part 2.

ISRAELITE					
	Selected Bible references	Hebrew	AV	RSV	NIV
Stringed instruments					
Harp	1 Sa. 10:5	*nēḇel*	psaltery	harp	lyres
	Is: 5:12		viol	harp	lyres
	Is. 14:11; Am. 5:23; 6:5		viol(s)	harp(s)	harp(s)
(Zither?)	Pss. 33:2; 144:9	*nebel ʿāśôr*	psaltery and an instrument of ten strings	harp of ten strings; ten-stringed harp	ten-stringed lyre
Lyre	Gn. 4:21	*kinnôr*	harp	lyre	harp
Wind instruments					
Horn	Jos. 6:4	*qeren hayyôḇēl*	trumpets of rams' horns	trumpets of rams' horns	trumpets of rams' horns
	1 Ch. 15:28; 2 Ch. 15:14; Ps. 98:6	*šôp̄ār*	cornet, trumpet	the horn, trumpets	rams' horns, trumpets
	Ex. 19:13	*yôḇēl*	trumpet	trumpet	ram's horn
Trumpet	Nu. 10:2	*ḥ^{a}ṣōṣ^{e}râ*	trumpet	trumpet	trumpet
	Ezk. 7:14	*ʔtāqôaʿ*	trumpet	trumpet	trumpet
Vertical flute?	Gn. 4:21; Jb. 21:12; 30:31; Ps. 150:4	*ʿûgaḇ*	organ	pipe	flute
Double pipe (?)	1 Sa. 10:5; Is. 5:12; 1 Cor. 14:7	*ḥālîl*	pipe	flute	flutes
	1 Ki. 1:40		pipe	pipe	flutes
Percussion instruments					
Tambour or hand drum	Ex. 15:20; Ps. 81:2	*tōp̄*	timbrel	timbrel	tambourine
	Jb. 21:12		timbrel	tambourine	tambourine
	Gn. 31:27; 1 Sa. 10:5		tabret	tambourine	tambourine
	Is. 5:12		tabret	timbrel	tambourine
Cymbals	1 Ch. 15:19	*ṣelṣ^{e}lîm*	cymbals of brass	bronze cymbals	bronze cymbals
	2 Sa. 6:5; 2 Ch. 5:13; Ezr. 3:10; Ps. 150:5	*m^{e}ṣiltayim*	cymbals	cymbals	cymbals
Sistrum (?)	2 Sa. 6:5	*m^{e}naʿanʿîm*	cornets	castanets	sistrums
Bells	Ex. 28:33–34; 39:25–26	*pa^{ʿa}môn*	bells	bells	bells
	Zc. 14:20	*m^{e}ṣillâ*	bells of horses	bells of horses	bells of horses

BABYLONIAN					
	Selected Bible references	Aramaic	AV	RSV	NIV
Stringed instruments					
Horizontal harp?	Dn. 3:5, 7, etc.	*sabb^{e}ḵâ*	sackbut	trigon	lyre
Vertical harp?	Dn. 3:5, 7, etc.	*p^{e}sanṭērîn*	psaltery	harp	harp
Lyre	Dn. 3:5, 7, etc.	*qîṯrôs/qaṯrōs*	harp	lyre	zither
Wind instruments					
Horn	Dn. 3:5, 7, etc.	*qeren*	cornet	horn	horn
Double pipe	Dn. 3:5, 7, etc.	*maš̄rôqîṯâ*	flute	pipe	flute
Percussion?					
Drum?	Dn. 3:5, 7, etc.	*sûmpônyâ*	dulcimer	bagpipe	pipes

A Sumerian musician plays an 11-stringed lyre at a royal banquet. Part of the inlay on the 'Ur Standard'. The remains of similar bull-headed lyres were found in contemporary royal tombs at Ur. c. 2500 BC. (BM)

Opposite page: Table showing musical instruments mentioned in the Bible, with names used in three current translations.

Bronze cymbals from Luristan (Iran). 9th–7th cent. BC. (BM)

Reconstruction of a lyre found in the Royal Cemetery at Ur. The strings were attached to the cross-bar and fixed over a bridge on the wooden sound-box. The mosaic decoration is of lapis lazuli, shell and red limestone. Height 1·20 m. c. 2500 BC. (SI)

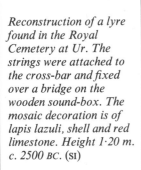

were features of the vintage festivals (Is. 16:10) and of marriage celebrations (1 Macc. 9:37, 39). Kings had their singers and instrumentalists (2 Sa. 19:35; Ec. 2:8). The shepherd boy also had his lyre (1 Sa. 16:18). The young men at the gates enjoyed their music (La. 5:14). Even the harlot increased her seductive powers with song (Is. 23:16).

Music was used at times of mourning as well as at times of gladness. The dirge (*qînâ*) which constitutes the book of Lamentations and David's lament over Saul and Jonathan (2 Sa. 1:18–27) are notable examples. It became the custom to hire professional mourners to assist at funerals. These regularly included flautists (Mt. 9:23). According to Maimonides, the poorest husband was expected to provide at least two flautists and one mourning woman for the funeral of his wife (*Mišnāyôṯ* 4).

As music formed an integral part of Heb. social life, so it had its place in their religious life. 1 Ch. 15:16–24 contains a detailed account of the organization by David of the levitical choir and orchestra. Apart from this passage there are only scattered and indirect references to the use of music in religious worship, and there is little evidence on which to form any clear impression of the character of the musical service of the Temple.

Of the nature of the music performed by the Heb. musicians we have no knowledge whatever. It is uncertain whether they had any system of notation. No identifiable system has survived. Attempts have been made to interpret the accents of the Heb. text as a form of notation, but without success. These accents were a guide to recitation rather than music and were, in any case, of late origin. Although we have no evidence regarding the instrumental music of the Temple, we can discover from the form of the psalms that they were intended to be sung antiphonally either by two choirs (Pss. 13; 20; 38), or by a choir and the congregation (Pss. 136; 118:1–4). It appears that after the captivity the choirs were formed of an equal number of male and female voices (Ezr. 2:65). But it is not clear whether each choir was of mixed voices or whether one was of male and the other of female voices. They probably chanted rather than sang, although the manner of their chanting is obscure and was certainly very different from modern ecclesiastical chanting.

From Mesopotamia comes written evidence (early 2nd millennium BC) on the stringing and tuning of harps, and musical instruments with a litany (6th century BC); *cf.* D. Wulstan, O. R. Gurney, *Iraq* 30, 1968, pp. 215–233; W. G. Lambert, in H. Goedicke (ed.), *Near Eastern Studies . . . W. F. Albright*, 1971, pp. 335–353. At Ugarit (from *c.* 1400 BC) was found a group of cuneiform tablets bearing hymns in the Hurrian language, accompanied by a form of musical notation; *cf.* A. D. Kilmer, *RA* 68, 1974, pp. 69–82; *ibid.* (with D. Wulstan), pp. 125–128) with earlier references. An attempt has been made to reproduce the harp-tuning and hymnology in musical form on a gramophone record; *cf.* A. D. Kilmer, R. L. Crocker, R. R. Brown, *Sounds from Silence*, 1977.

II. Musical instruments

We have a little more knowledge of the musical instruments of the Bible, although there is no definite information regarding their form or construction. Instruments have, however, been found belonging to other ancient nations of the Middle East, notably the Egyptians. The etymology of the Heb. words helps a little, and also the ancient vss, but still our knowledge is very slight. The instruments mentioned in the Bible can be divided into the three main groups: strings, wind and percussion.

a. Strings

(i) *Lyre*. The *kinnôr*, which is regularly rendered 'harp' by AV, is the first musical instrument mentioned in the Bible (Gn. 4:21) and is the only stringed instrument referred to in the Pentateuch. It is one of the instruments with which Laban the Syrian would have wished to send Jacob on his way, had he not departed so suddenly (Gn. 31:27). This allusion suggests that the instrument may have been of Syrian origin. There has been difference of opinion whether it was truly a harp or a lyre. The balance of opinion is in favour of the lyre, which word is used in RSV. That it was portable and therefore small is evidenced by the fact that it was one of the four musical instruments borne before the young prophets (1 Sa. 10:5). Ancient Egyp. tomb-paintings represent foreign-

Elamite musicians, playing a double pipe and vertical and horizontal harps, celebrate the accession to the throne of the refugee Elamite prince Ummanigash. SW palace, Nineveh. Ashurbanipal. c. 640 BC. (BM)

ers, Semites from Shutu (Transjordan), bearing lyres played with a plectrum in their hands. Nor is it clear whether the *kinnôr* was played with a plectrum or by hand. In 1 Sa. 16:23 'David took the lyre and played it with his hand'; but the absence of mention of a plectrum is no proof that the strings were plucked by the fingers alone. There is no certainty about the number of strings on the *kinnôr*. Josephus thought it had ten. Another suggestion, based on the association of the instrument with Heb. *šᵉmînîṯ* ('eighth', LXX *hyper tēs ogdoēs*) in 1 Ch. 15:21, is that it had eight strings; but the allusion in the passage is far from certain.

The *kinnôr* was a wooden instrument, David's being made probably of cypress (2 Sa. 6:5). Those which Solomon had made for the Temple were constructed of almug (1 Ki. 10:12), and were evidently very valuable. Josephus (*Ant*. 8. 94) records that their framework was fitted with electrum, *i.e.* either a mixed metal or amber.

The word 'harp' is used also by AV in translating Aram. *qîṯrôs* (RSV 'lyre'), which occurs only among the instruments of Nebuchadrezzar's orchestra in Dn. 3. It is the same root from which the European word 'guitar' has sprung.

A blind harpist on a relief from the tomb of Paatenemheb near Saqqara. c. 1350 BC. (RVO)

(ii) *Psaltery*. This word is derived from Gk. *psaltērion*, which denotes an instrument plucked with the fingers instead of with a plectrum. The Gk. verb *psallō* means to touch sharply or pluck. It is the word most often used to translate Heb. *nēḇel*, although occasionally the rendering 'viol' is found, and in the Prayer Book version of the Psalms the word 'lute' is used. In LXX *nēḇel* is variously rendered (*psaltērion*, *psalmos*, *kithara*, *nablion*, *nabla*, *nablē*, *naula* and *nablas*). It is generally accepted that it was a kind of harp, as it is rendered in RSV, although its exact description is uncertain. It is first mentioned in 1 Sa. 10:5, and this seems to confirm the opinion that it was of Phoenician origin, since there was little close contact between Israel and Phoenicia before this date. Attempts have been made to reconstruct the shape of the *nēḇel* by identifying it with a root meaning a skin-bottle, jar or pitcher. It has been suggested that it had a bulging resonant body at its lower end. This identification of the root has even led to the supposition that the instrument was a form of bagpipe. But these suggestions are mere conjecture.

Like the *kinnôr*, the *nēḇel* was made of cypress wood, and later of almug. It is clear that David was able to play the *nēḇel* as well as the *kinnôr*. As it is commonly linked in the Bible with other musical instruments, it is generally thought to have supplied the bass.

Heb. *'āśôr* is frequently linked with *nēḇel*. This word is from the root meaning 'ten', and is generally thought to indicate that the instrument had ten strings. This interpretation is found also in LXX and Vulg. (*psaltērion decachordon* and *psalterium decem chordarum*). In all probability the *nēḇel 'āśôr* was simply a variety of *nēḇel*.

The word 'psaltery' appears also in AV as a translation of Aram. *psantērîn* (Dn. 3:5ff.), another of the instruments in Nebuchadrezzar's orchestra. The Aram. word appears to be a rendering of Gk. *psaltērion*, and is translated in RSV 'harp'. J. Stainer (*The Music of the Bible*, pp. 40–55) argues at some length that the instrument referred to is in fact the dulcimer. It is, however, impossible to say more with confidence than that it was a stringed instrument.

(iii) *Sackbut*. This word occurs in AV only in Dn. 3 as a translation of Aram. *sabbᵉḵâ*. It was one of the instruments of Nebuchadrezzar's orchestra, and was therefore not a Heb. instrument. The AV translation is clearly wrong, as the sackbut was a wind instrument, being in fact a kind of bass trumpet with a slide rather like a modern trombone. The *sabb^{e}ḵâ* is usually identified with Gk. *sambykē*, by which it is translated in Dn. 3, LXX. This has been described as either a small triangular harp of four or more strings and high pitch, or a large, many-stringed harp. Whichever description is correct, it was a stringed and not a wind instrument. According to Strabo (10. 471) it was of barbaric origin. RSV more correctly renders 'trigon'.

(iv) *Dulcimer*. This is the AV translation of Aram. *sûmpônyâ*, which is generally regarded as a Gk. loan-word. It occurs in the Bible only in the orchestra of Dn. 3. The AV rendering is incorrect, as it is not a stringed instrument. It is now generally supposed to have been a form of bagpipe (as rendered in RV, RSV). The modern Italian rendering of the word is *sampogna*, a kind of bagpipe in current use in that country. Alternatively, it may derive from Gk. *ty(m)panon*, a kind of drum.

b. Wind instruments

(i) *Pipe*. This is Heb. *ḥālîl*, rendered 'pipe' in AV, 'flute' in RSV. The word occurs only six times in the OT. In the NT the pipe is Gk. *aulos*, used in LXX for the *ḥālîl*. Vulg. uses *tibia*. Both *aulos* and *tibia* are general terms covering both reed instruments, such as the oboe and the clarinet, and instruments played by blowing across or through a hole, such as with the flute.

The word *ḥālîl* derives from a root meaning to bore or pierce. The word *aulos* is from a root meaning to blow. But neither the derivation of *ḥālîl*, nor its rendering in LXX, gives any indication of the nature of the instrument. The balance of opinion seems to be in favour of the oboe rather than the flute, but there is no certainty on the matter. Just as today, it was apparently customary in ancient times for the player of a reed instrument to carry with him a supply of reeds in a box (Gk. *glōssokomon*). It was in fact a reed-box and not a 'bag', as AV renders it, which Judas used as a money-box (Jn. 12:6; 13:29).

The pipe was used in festival processions (Is. 30:29), at times of national rejoicing (1 Ki. 1:40), and also in mourning at funerals (Mt. 9:23). That it could produce a plaintive note is evidenced by the

Musicians playing the double reed-pipe, the long-necked lute (pandore) and the harp at an Egyptian banquet. The centre figure is dancing as she plays. Painting in the tomb of Nakht at Thebes. c. 1415 BC. (MEPhA)

Bronze figure of a trumpet player. From Caria (SW Turkey). Height 6 cm. c. 800 BC. (BM)

A lyre played with a plectrum by a Semite. Part of a procession of Asiatics painted on the wall of the tomb of Khnum-hotep, Beni-Hasan, Egypt. c. 1900 BC. (PAC)

allusion to it in Je. 48:36.

(ii) *Flute*. This is the AV translation of Aram. *mašrôqîṯâ*. It occurs only in Dn. 3, and is derived from the root *šāraq*, an onomatopoeic word meaning 'to whistle' or 'hiss'. The playing of most types of pipe or flute is usually accompanied by a hissing sound. It is therefore a reasonable supposition that the instrument referred to is of that class.

(iii) *Organ*. This word (Heb. *'ûḡāḇ*) occurs only four times in the OT. In Gn. 4:21 it is evidently a generic term covering all wind instruments, just as the parallel word in the verse, *kinnôr*, is the general term for all stringed instruments. In Jb. 30:31 it again occurs in association with the *kinnôr*, and in Jb. 21:12 it represents the wind section in parallel with members of the stringed and percussion families. We find it again in Ps. 150:4 among numerous other instruments. LXX gives no guide as to the nature of the instrument, for it uses three different words. (In Gn. 4:21 *kithara*, 'guitar'; in the two passages in Job *psalmos*, 'psaltery'; and in Ps. 150:4 *organon*, 'organ'.) The derivation of the Heb. word is uncertain. Some have linked it with a root meaning 'to lust', 'have inordinate affection', thus alluding to its sensuous or appealing tones; but this is no more than conjecture. The instrument must be some form of pipe or possibly a group of pipes.

(iv) *Horn*. This word (Heb. *qeren*) occurs frequently in the OT. Cognate with it are Gk. *keras* and Lat. *cornu*. It appears to have been used in biblical times for two purposes: as a flask for carrying oil and as a kind of trumpet. In this latter sense it occurs in only three passages. In Jos. 6 it is used synonymously with *šôp̄ār* ('trumpet', see (v) below) in the account of the capture of Jericho. In 1 Ch. 25:5 are listed those who were appointed by David to play it, and in Dn. 3 it is one of the instruments of Nebuchadrezzar's orchestra. The earliest trumpets were evidently made out of the horns of animals. These were later imitated in metal.

(v) *Trumpet*. There is frequent

A hand-drum, a rectangular lyre of five strings, cymbals and an eight-stringed lyre played by musicians in a military band. Height 0·37 m. Relief from Nineveh. c. 640 BC. (PP)

mention of the trumpet in the Bible. In AV it is used chiefly as a translation of two different Heb. words, *šôp̄ār* and *ḥᵃṣōṣᵉrâ*. It is used once also for Heb. *yôḇēl*, which means literally a ram's horn. LXX renders uniformly *salpinx*, which is used also in the NT.

The *šôp̄ār*, a long horn with a turned-up end, was the national trumpet of the Israelites. It was used on military and religious occasions to summon the people. The *šôp̄ār* is still used in Jewish synagogues today.

The *ḥᵃṣōṣᵉrâ* was a trumpet made of beaten silver. Moses was commanded by God to make two of them for summoning the congregation and for breaking camp. Nu. 10:1–10 contains God's instructions to Moses regarding the occasions for the blowing of the trumpet. It was principally a sacred and not a martial instrument.

(vi) *Cornet*. The word appears in AV as the translation of three different words. In Dn. 3 it is used for *qeren*, elsewhere translated 'horn' (see (iv) above). In four passages the Heb. word is *šôp̄ār*, which occurs frequently in the OT and is in all other instances translated 'trumpet' (see (v) above).

In 2 Sa. 6:5 the Heb. word is *mᵉna'an'îm*, which occurs only in this passage. It is used in conjunction with the cymbals (see *c* (ii) below) among other instruments on which David and the children of Israel played before the Lord. The root from which it is derived means 'to quiver', 'vibrate', and it is probable that the instrument was a kind of rattle. LXX renders *kymbala*, 'cymbals', and is therefore less accurate than Vulg. *sistra*, 'rattles' (Gk. *seistron* from *seiō*, 'shake', 'move to and fro'). RSV renders 'castanets'. Illustrations have been preserved of ancient Egyp. rattles consisting of an oval hoop on a handle, to which were affixed rods carrying loose rings which jangled together when the instrument was shaken.

c. Percussion

(i) *Bells*. Two Heb. words are rendered 'bells' in AV: *pa'ᵃmôn*, from a root meaning 'strike', occurs four times in Exodus, referring to the bells of gold on Aaron's high-priestly robes; the other word, *mᵉṣillâ*, is found only in Zc. 14:20. AVmg. follows LXX (*chalinoi*), reading 'bridles'. The Heb. word is from the same root as that rendered 'cymbals' in AV, and probably refers to the metal discs or cups fixed to the bridles of horses either as an ornament or in order to produce a jingling sound.

(ii) *Cymbals*. This word comes from Gk. *kymbalon*, which occurs once in the NT (1 Cor. 13:1) and also in LXX as a translation of Heb. *mᵉṣiltayim* and *ṣelṣᵉlîm*. *kymbalon* is derived from *kymbē*, which means a bowl or hollowed plate. The two Heb. words are derived from the same root, an onomatopoeic word meaning to whirr or quiver. *mᵉṣiltayim* seems to be a

Musicians playing a drum. Decoration on a Sumerian vase from Telloh (ancient Girsu). Height 12 cm. 22nd cent. BC. (MC)

later form of the word occurring about twelve times in the books of Chronicles and once each in Ezra and Nehemiah. The earlier form *ṣelṣ^{e}lîm* is found in the Psalms and once in 2 Samuel. In Ps. 150 the word is used twice in one verse with different adjectives. Two kinds of cymbals are known to have existed in ancient times. One kind consisted of two shallow metal plates held one in each hand and struck together. The others were cup-like in shape, one being held stationary while the other was brought down sharply against it. It has been suggested that in Ps. 150 these two kinds of cymbals are alluded to, but this is conjecture.

In all the passages where cymbals are mentioned they are used in religious ceremonies. Gk. *kymbalon* is used in 1 Sa. 18:6 LXX to translate Heb. *šālîš*, which is from the root meaning 'three'. The Vulg. renders *sistrum*, 'rattle'. Suggestions have been made that it was a triangle or a three-stringed instrument, but there is no certainty as to what is denoted.

(iii) *Timbrel* and *tabret*. These are each used eight times in AV, translating Heb. *tōp̄* (LXX *tympanon*). The instrument was a kind of tambourine held and struck with the hand. It was used as an accompaniment to singing and dancing (Ex. 15:20). It is always associated in the OT with joy and gladness, and is found accompanying the merriment of feasts (Is. 5:12) and the rejoicing of triumphal processions (1 Sa. 18:6).

BIBLIOGRAPHY. J. Stainer, *The Music of the Bible*, 1914; C. H. Cornill, *Music in the Old Testament*, 1909; *ISBE*; S. B. Finesinger, 'Musical Instruments in the Old Testament' in *HUCA* 3, 1926, pp. 21–75; K. Sachs, *A History of Musical Instruments*, 1940; H. Hartmann, *Die Musik der sumerischen Kultur*, 1960; T. C. Mitchell and R. Joyce in D. J. Wiseman (ed.), *Notes on some Problems in the Book of Daniel*, 1965, pp. 19–27; J. Rimmer, *Ancient Musical Instruments of Western Asia* (*British Museum*), 1969.

D.G.S.
K.A.K.

MYRA. With its port, about 4 km away, Myra was one of the chief cities of Lycia, a province on the SW tip of Asia Minor. There Paul and his centurion escort boarded an Alexandrian corn ship bound for Italy (Acts 27:5–6). Called

Dembre by the Turks, Myra displays some impressive ruins, including a well-preserved theatre.

J.D.D.

MYSIA. The homeland of one of the pre-hellenic peoples of Asia Minor, never a political unit in classical times, and therefore never precisely defined. It centred on the heavily forested hill country on either side of the main N road from Pergamum to Cyzicus on the Sea of Marmora, a tract which stretched from the border of Phrygia W to the promontory of the Troad. Troas itself, together with Assos and a number of other Gk. coastal states, and even Pergamum may be regarded as part of Mysia. It was the N portion of the Rom. province of Asia. Paul had reached its E limits on his way through Phrygia in Bithynia (Acts 16:7) when he was diverted through Mysia (v. 8) to Troas, probably following a route through the S of the region.

E.A.J.

MYSTERY.

I. In the Old Testament

The only OT appearance of the word is in the Aram. section of Dn. (2:18–19, 27–30, 47; 4:9), where LXX renders Aram. *rāz* by *mystērion* (AV, NEB 'secret'; RSV 'mystery'). In this context the word carries a specialized reference, and, as in the phrase 'there is a God in heaven who reveals mysteries' (2:28), it means primarily that which is hidden and still needs to be made known. Yet even here the meaning of the term is not unrelated to its NT use and significance, since the mysteries of which Daniel speaks in this chapter are contained within the eternal plan of God, and also made known by him in advance to his servants ('thoughts of what would be hereafter', 2:29).

Daniel's use of *rāz*, 'mystery', with the correlative *p^ešar*, 'solution', 'interpretation', was taken over by the Qumran sect, whose use of this terminology has provided an illuminating background for understanding the NT occurrences of the term *mystērion*.

II. In the New Testament

a. Meaning

The meaning of the term *mystērion* in classical Gk. is 'anything hidden or secret' (*HDB*, 3, p. 465), and it was used in the plural particularly (*ta mystēria*) to refer to the sacred rites of the Gk. mystery religions in which only the initiated shared. The root verb is *myō*, which means primarily 'to close the lips (or eyes)' (Lat. *mutus*). But whereas 'mystery' may mean, and in contemporary usage often does mean, a secret for which no answer can be found, this is not the connotation of the term *mystērion* in classical and biblical Gk. In the NT *mystērion* signifies a secret which is being, or even has been, revealed, which is also divine in scope, and needs to be made known by God to men through his Spirit. In this way the term comes very close to the NT word *apokalypsis*, 'revelation'. *mystērion* is a temporary secret, which once revealed is known and understood—a secret

The rock-tombs at Myra (modern Dembre) in Lycia, S Turkey. c. 4th cent. BC. (MEPhA)

no longer; *apokalypsis* is a temporarily hidden eventuality, which simply awaits its revelation to make it actual and apprehended (*cf.* 1 Cor. 1:7, for example, where *apokalypsis* is used, as so often, in reference to Christ himself; and Rom. 8:19, where Paul describes the creation as waiting with eager longing for its *apokatastasis* in the coming age of glory, which is to be revealed (*apokalyphthēnai*) at the *apokalypsis* of the sons of God themselves).

b. Usage

(i) *In the Gospels.* The single occurrence of the word *mystērion* in the Gospels is in Mk. 4:11 = Mt. 13:11 (plural) = Lk. 8:10 (AV 'mystery', RSV, NEB 'secret'). Here the term is used to refer to the kingdom of God, the knowledge of which, just because it is *God's* kingdom, is reserved for those to whom it is 'given'. As a result the unrevealed mystery is, for those 'outside' (*exō*), hidden in *'parables'.

(ii) *In the Pauline Letters.* Paul uses the word frequently, and indeed, apart from four occurrences of the word in Rev. and the three just noted in the Synoptic Gospels, the appearance of *mystērion* in the NT is confined to the Pauline Letters (21 times). The character of *to mystērion* in Paul's theology is fourfold.

1. It is eternal in its scope, in so far as it relates to the divine plan of salvation, the *Heilsgeschichte* itself. The 'mystery' is the good news which forms the content of God's revelation (*cf.* Eph. 6:19); it is the mystery of God himself, the focus of which is in Christ (Col. 2:2, reading *tou mystēriou tou theou, Christou*, with P⁴⁶, B, *et al.*; *cf.* 1 Cor. 2:1, where B, D, and other MSS read *martyrion* for *mystērion*). As such it is contained within God's everlasting counsels and hidden in him (Eph. 3:9), decreed 'before the ages' (1 Cor. 2:7) and declared as God's *sophia*, and veiled to human understanding, but awaiting its disclosure, throughout the ages (1 Cor. 2:8; Rom. 16:25, where the adjectival participle is *sesigēmenon*).

2. It is historical in its announcement. This mystery is also the 'mystery of Christ', announced historically and definitively by God in Christ himself (Eph. 1:9; 3:3f., where the *mystērion* is described as revealed to Paul *kata apokalypsin*; *cf.* Col. 4:3) when 'the time had fully come' (Gal. 4:4). It is precisely this mystery, centred and declared in the person of the Lord Jesus Christ, through whose death God reconciles us to himself (2 Cor. 5:18f.; *cf.* 1 Cor. 2:2), that Paul was commissioned to proclaim (Eph. 3:8f.; *cf.* 1 Cor. 4:1). In his letter to the Ephesians Paul considers particularly, against the background of a general and gradual movement towards a Christ-centred inclusiveness (see J. A. Robinson, *Ephesians*, 1903, pp. 238f.), the dominant and related notions of 'hope' and 'mystery'. Christ is the hope of men (1:12) and of the universe (1:10), and we possess as a result a hope which is both glorious (1:18) and real; already the Christian is saved, and raised with him (2:4–6, where the verbs are in the aorist). Not only so, but also—and this is the particular character of the *mystērion* which Paul has been sent to preach, and which in Eph. he is chiefly concerned to outline—the new hope, and thus also the new *life* in Christ, are available for Jew and Gentile alike (3:8; *cf.* Col. 1:27, where the content of the mystery is qualified as 'Christ in you, the hope of glory').

3. It is spiritual in its perception. We have seen already from the Synoptic Gospels that the mystery of the kingdom is spiritually perceived. Paul retains this idea when he regards the mystery of Christ (the focus of which is particularly 'the Gentiles as fellow-heirs') as revealed to apostles and prophets by the Spirit (*en pneumati*, Eph. 3:5; *cf.* also 1 Cor. 13:2; 14:2). In line with this must be understood the term as it is used derivatively by Paul in connection with Christian marriage (Eph. 5:32), and the 'man of lawlessness (or sin)' (2 Thes. 2:7). The divine significance of these 'mysteries' is apprehended by a conjunction of revelation and spiritual understanding (*cf.* also Rev. 17:3–7).

4. It is eschatological in its outcome. The mystery which has been revealed in time still awaits its divine consummation and fulfilment in eternity. This is the sense in which the term must be understood in Rev. 10:7: the 'mystery of God' already announced will be corporately fulfilled without delay, 'in the days of the trumpet call to be sounded by the seventh angel'. And this is equally true in terms of personal salvation—the 'mystery' of 'being changed' when the trumpet sounds, of mortality's being finally replaced by immortality (1 Cor. 15:51ff.). Such a mystery, even when it is made known, overwhelms us still with the depth of nothing less than the wisdom and the knowledge of God himself (Col. 2:2).

The use of the word 'mystery' with reference to the sacraments (Vulg. translates *mystērion* as *sacramentum*) is entirely post-biblical.

BIBLIOGRAPHY. E. Hatch, *Essays in Biblical Greek*, 1889, pp. 57–62; C. L. Mitton, *The Epistle to the Ephesians*, 1951, pp. 86–90; G. Bornkamm, *TDNT* 4, pp. 802–828.

S.S.S.

MYTH, MYTHOLOGY. Gk. *mythos*, 'story'; *mythologia*, 'story-telling'. In LXX the word-group appears rarely, and never in books translated from the Hebrew Bible. In Ecclus. 20:19 an ungracious man is compared to 'a story told at the wrong time (*mythos akairos*)'; in Baruch 3:23 the 'story-tellers (*mythologoi*) . . . have not learned the way to wisdom'. In NT *mythos* occurs only in the Pastoral Epistles and 2 Peter, and always in a disparaging sense. Timothy is told to discourage interest in 'myths and endless genealogies which promote speculations' (1 Tim. 1:4). There are similar references to 'godless and silly myths' (1 Tim. 4:7), 'myths' into which false teachers beguile hearers who have 'itching ears' (2 Tim. 4:4), and 'Jewish myths' to which Christians must lend no credence (Tit. 1:14). A mixture of judaizing and gnosticizing speculation is perhaps implied. Such 'myths' are set in contrast to gospel truth: 'we did not follow cleverly devised myths when we made known to you the power and coming of our Lord Jesus Christ, but we were eyewitnesses' (2 Pet. 1:16).

In modern usage the word-group has a wide variety of meaning.

1. *The 'myth and ritual' school.* The 'myth' is the story of which the ritual is the dramatic enactment. T. H. Gaster (*Thespis*, 1950) interprets the Ugaritic religious texts as 'myths' of seasonal rites of emptying and filling which he tries to reconstruct. The *Akitu* or New Year festival of Babylon has been thought to be an instance of a Near Eastern ritual pattern in which the king played the part of the dying and rising god, being regarded as his embodiment or as his mediatorial representative with the people.

In this sense a historical event, or series of historical events, could serve as the 'myth', as when the narrative of Ex. 1–15 is regarded as the *mythos* of the annually re-enacted Passover meal, or the passion narrative as the *mythos* of the even more frequently repeated Lord's Supper (*cf.* 1 Cor. 11:26).

2. *The 'demythologizing' programme*. This programme was launched in an essay by R. Bultmann (*New Testament and Mythology*, 1941) which maintained that, if the genuine 'offence' of the cross is to be presented effectively today, the gospel must be relieved ('demythologized') of features belonging to the world-view of those to whom it was first preached—not only the 'three-decker' universe but the concept of this world as being open to invasion by transcendent powers. Part of this mythological apparatus detected in the NT has been thought (on inadequate grounds) to belong to a redeemer myth of Iranian origin developed in various gnostic schools, especially in Mandaism.

3. *'Myth' in Theology*. This is the title of an essay by M. F. Wiles (*BJRL* 59, 1976–7, pp. 226ff.) which refers to another modern usage—that implied, *e.g.*, in the title of the symposium *The Myth of God Incarnate*, 1977 (to which Wiles is a contributor), in which a myth seems to be the pictorial and imaginative presentation of an ontological reality (such as the union of the divine and human at the heart of the human personality). The theological use of the word-group goes back to D. F. Strauss (*Life of Jesus*, 1835) but in wider parlance remains unacceptable because the dominant popular understanding of myth is something that is not simply factually untrue but positively misleading, like a mirage.

Quite different and much more adequate is the approach of C. S. Lewis and others, according to whom 'Myth became Fact' when God became man, so that the aspirations and insights of the human soul which formerly found mythological expression have been given a satisfying response in the historical events of the gospel, not least in the incarnation and redemption which it announces.

BIBLIOGRAPHY. H. W. Bartsch (ed.), *Kerygma and Myth*, 1, 1953; 2, 1962; F. F. Bruce, 'Myth and History' in C. Brown (ed.), *History, Criticism and Faith*, 1976, pp. 79ff.; *idem*, 'Myth', *NIDNTT* 2, pp. 643–647, with bibliography; D. Cairns, *A Gospel without Myth*, 1960; S. H. Hooke (ed.), *Myth, Ritual and Kingship*, 1958; G. V. Jones, *Christology and Myth in the New Testament*, 1956; C. S. Lewis, *Till we have Faces*, 1956; W. Pannenberg, 'The Later Dimensions of Myth in Biblical and Christian Tradition', *Basic Questions in Theology*, 3, 1972, pp. 1ff.; J. W. Rogerson, *Myth in Old Testament Interpretation*, 1974. F.F.B.

NAAMAH ('pleasant'). **1.** A daughter of Zillah and sister of Tubal-cain (Gn. 4:22). **2.** 'The Ammonitess', the mother of Rehoboam (1 Ki. 14:21). **3.** A city in lowland Judah (Jos. 15:41), probably identical to modern Nā'neh, 10 km S of Lydda. Zophar, one of Job's 'comforters', was a Naamathite, but it is unlikely that he originated from the same Naamah. G.W.G.

NAAMAN (Heb. *na'ᵃmān*, 'pleasant'). A common N Syrian name during the mid-2nd millennium as shown by texts from *Ugarit.

1. A dependant of Benjamin; forefather of the Naamite clan (Gn. 46:21; Nu. 26:40; 1 Ch. 8:4, 7).

2. A military commander of the Syrian army during the reign of *Ben-hadad I (2 Ki. 5). Although afflicted with leprosy, he still held his high position (v. 1). At the suggestion of an Israelite prisoner of war, he took a letter from his king, along with gifts, to the king of Israel, probably *Jehoram. He was referred to *Elisha who offered him a cure by bathing in the River Jordan, which Naaman indignantly refused until prevailed upon by his servants (vv. 8–14). Upon being cleansed, he took two mule-loads of earth, which he saw as a necessity for worshipping Yahweh, the one true god (vv. 15–17). Although a Yahwist, Naaman still needed to worship at the temple of *Rimmon, probably because of social obligation.

Jewish legend, recorded in Josephus (*Ant.* 8. 414) but unsubstantiated, identifies Naaman as the one who killed *Ahab by drawing 'his bow at a venture' (1 Ki. 22:34). He is also briefly mentioned in Lk. 4:27. D.W.B.

NABAL ('fool'). A wealthy inhabitant of Maon, SE of Hebron, of the tribe of Caleb, who pastured sheep and goats on adjacent *Carmel (**2**). During his exile in the reign of Saul, David heard that Nabal was shearing his sheep, a traditional time of hospitality, and sent ten of his men with the request that Nabal should provide David's force with hospitality on a feast-day in return for the protection from brigands David had given his flocks.

Nabal, whose aggressive *folly matched his name (1 Sa. 25:25), replied with insults, whereupon David with 400 men marched up. When Abigail, the beautiful and intelligent wife of Nabal, heard of the messengers' visit she arranged for food and wine to be sent on ahead and went to meet David. This prevented David from committing the crime of blood guilt upon Nabal.

On her return Abigail found her husband drunk. The following day Nabal suffered a paralytic stroke on hearing of his wife's action, and he died about 10 days later (1 Sa. 25). R.A.H.G.

NABATAEANS. Nebaioth, son of Ishmael and brother-in-law of Edom (Gn. 25:13; 28:9), is possibly to be considered the ancestor of the Nabataeans, who may also be the Nabaiate of inscriptions of Ashurbanipal of Assyria (*c.* 650 BC,

MYTH AND RITUAL SCHOOL
See Myth, Part 2.

NAAMITE
See Naaman, Part 2.

NAASHON
See Nahshon, Part 2.

View of the Khazneh from the Siq gorge leading into Petra, the Nabataean capital. (SH)

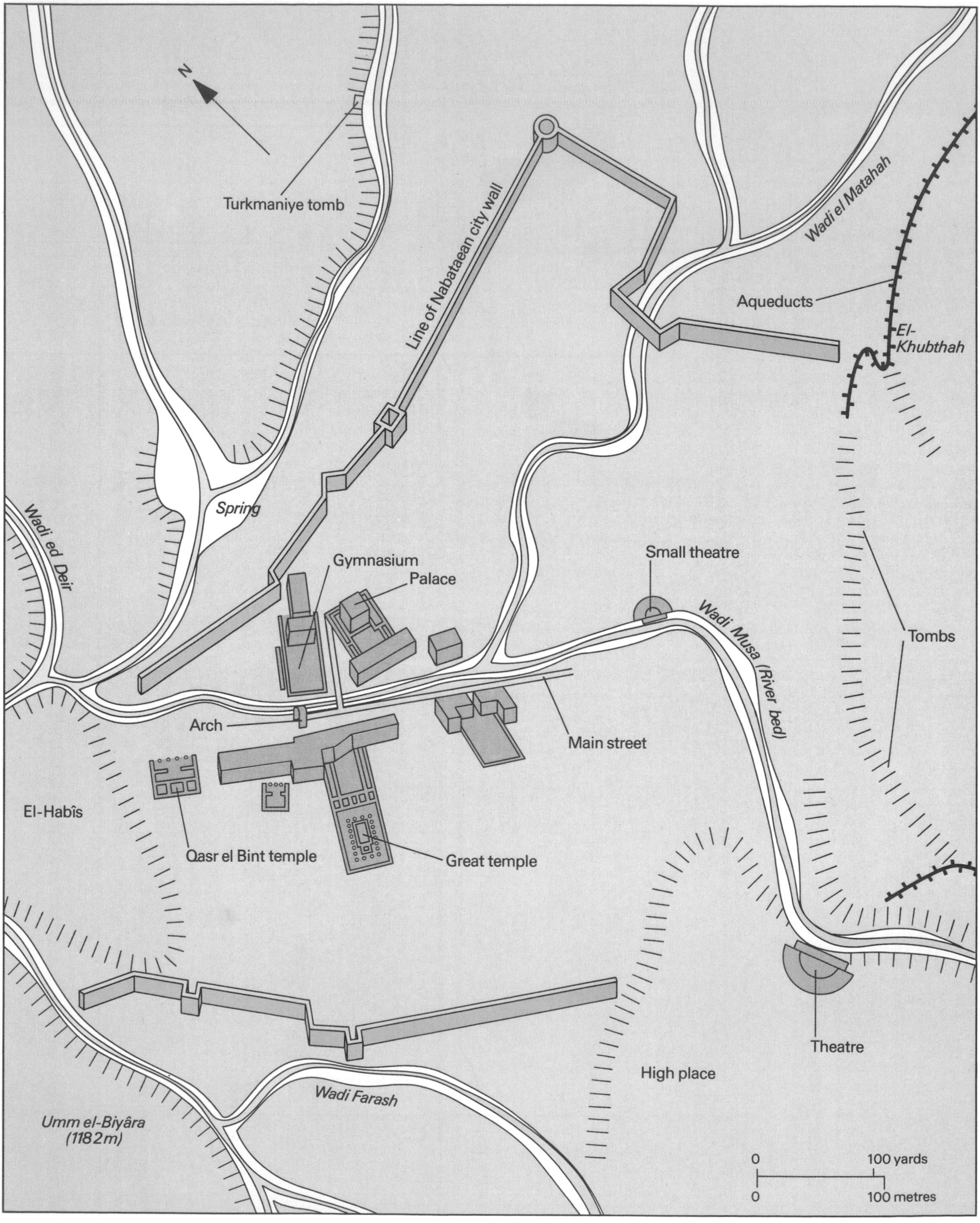
N
Turkmaniye tomb
Line of Nabataean city wall
Wadi el Matahah
Aqueducts
El-Khubthah
Spring
Wadi ed Deir
Gymnasium
Palace
Small theatre
Wadi Musa (River bed)
Tombs
Arch
Main street
El-Habîs
Qasr el Bint temple
Great temple
Theatre
High place
Wadi Farash
Umm el-Biyâra
(1182m)
0
100 yards
0
100 metres

Nabataean pottery fragments from Petra. The fine, thin fabric is painted with floral decoration of a high quality. 1st cent. BC – 1st cent. AD. (BM)

Street of façades in the Outer Siq, Petra. Early Nabataean tombs were topped with 'Assyrian-style' decoration. 1st cent. BC –1st cent. AD. (SH)

Opposite page: Plan of the Nabataean capital Petra, showing the layout of the city between hills.

ANET, pp. 298–299). A difference in spelling between these two names (with *tāw*) and the native *nbṭw* (with *ṭēth*) precludes certain identification. Diodorus Siculus (*c.* 50 BC) brings the Nabataeans into recorded history in his account of the end of the Persian empire and the career of Alexander. Quoting from an earlier source, he describes them as a nomadic Arab tribe who neither built houses nor tilled the soil. Their territory, the area S and E of the river Jordan, straddled the trade routes from the Orient to the Mediterranean, and their capital, Petra, 80 km S of the Dead Sea, formed a base from which caravans could be attacked. Antigonus, who gained power in Syria after Alexander's death, sent two expeditions to

The Deir, an elaborate tomb carved in the mountainside, is the largest surviving monument of Nabataean Petra. Façade, height 40·23 m, width 46·94 m. (RH)

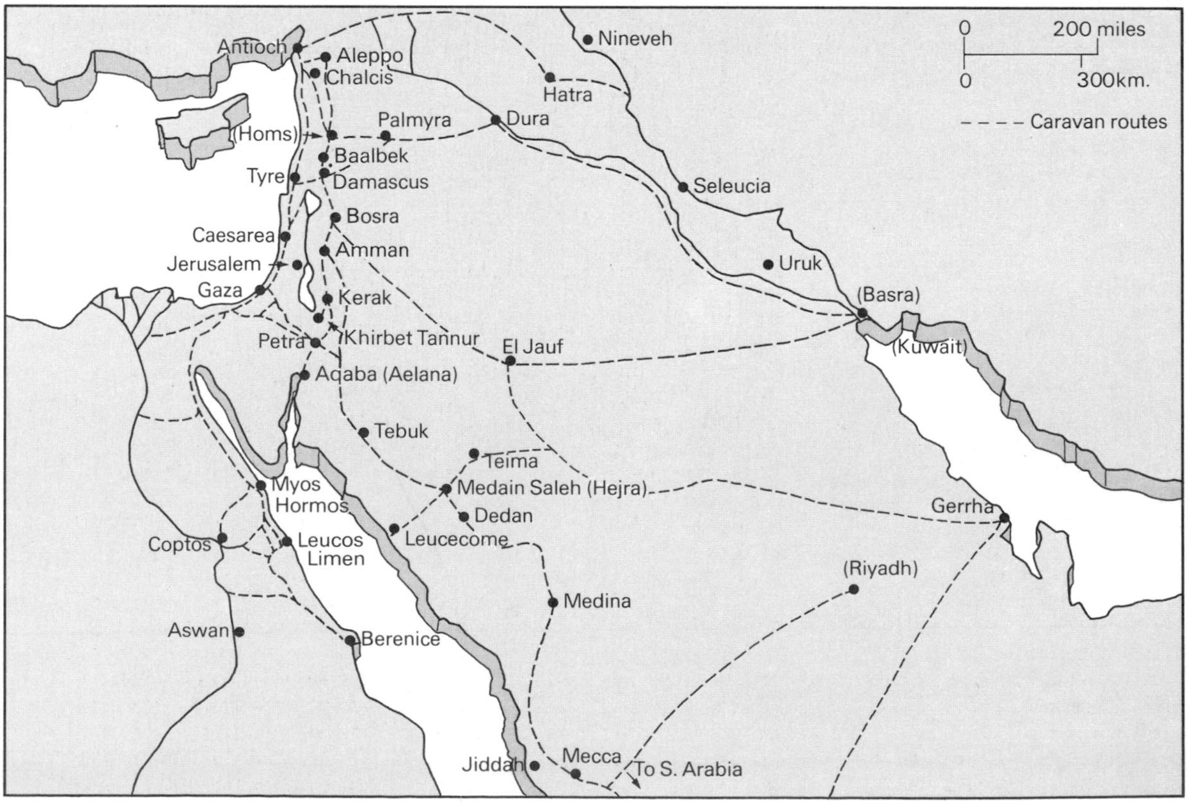

Caravan routes of Nabataean times.

Petra to subdue the Nabataeans and gain control of the trade (312 BC). Both were unsuccessful. It is clear that at this time Petra was at least a stronghold, and Gk. potsherds of *c*. 300 BC found there suggest a permanent settlement.

Contact with the settled communities of Palestine during the 2nd and 3rd centuries BC resulted in the development of Nabataean villages and towns and in intensive cultivation of formerly barren desert areas. This was aided by well-organized lines of frontier posts to guard against Arab marauders and by the skill of Nabataean engineers in constructing irrigation systems to conserve the scanty rainfall. Many of their dams and reservoirs are still usable. Petra is surrounded by high cliffs, pierced by narrow ravines, which form an almost impregnable defence.

When a Nabataean ruler arose (the earliest known king is Aretas I, *c*. 170 BC, 2 Macc. 5:8) who was able to safeguard the caravans, Nabataean merchants led trade from S Arabia and from the Persian Gulf to Petra, whence it was forwarded to the coast, particularly Gaza. Increased demands by the Rom. world for spices, silks and other luxuries from India and China swelled enormously the revenues of a power which could levy tolls on all goods passing through its territory. The redirection of the trade routes across the Red Sea to Egypt after Augustus' failure to conquer Arabia (25 BC) was an important factor in the decline of Nabataean prosperity.

Native records (coins and dedicatory inscriptions) are written in Aram. in a curiously heightened form of the 'square' script (*WRITING). Papyri from the Judaean desert and ostraca from Petra exhibit a cursive form of this writing from which the Arab. scripts are derived. Use of Aram. indicates a wide assimilation to the culture of neighbouring settled peoples. This is evidenced by Nabataean sculptures which contain features found in Syrian work and traceable in early Islamic ornamentation. It may be seen also in the acceptance of Syrian deities, Hadad and Atargatis (Astarte-Anat) into the Nabataean pantheon. These two may have been identified with Dushara and his consort Allat, the national deities. Many open-air shrines (*e.g.* the high place at Petra) and temples (*e.g.* Khirbet et-Tannur) have been discovered on isolated hill-tops. The gods worshipped were especially associated with weather and fertility. Nabataean *potters developed a distinctive ware of their own unsurpassed in Palestine.

Nabataean history, as reconstructed from incidental references by Jewish and Gk. authors, consists mainly of struggles to gain control of the Negeb in the S and of Damascus in the N. Aretas III (*c*. 70 BC) and Aretas IV (*c*. 9 BC–AD 40) succeeded in holding both these areas for a few years, so obtaining complete control of E–W trade. It was an officer (Gk. *ethnarchēs*) of Aretas IV who attempted to detain Paul in Damascus (2 Cor. 11:32). Malichus III and Rabbel II, the last Nabataean kings, moved the capital

The Khazneh (treasury) at Petra. Probably the work of Greek masons brought in by the Nabataeans in the 1st cent. AD. The name comes from a legend that the urn on top of the façade held a treasure. (RH)

Nabataean coin (tetradrachm) *bearing the head of Aretas IV* (*c.* 9 BC – AD 40). *Diameter 16 mm.* (RG)

NABONIDUS
See Belshazzar, Part 1.

NABU
See Nebuchadrezzar, Part 2.

NADDER
See Animals, Part 1.

from Petra to Bostra, 112 km E of Galilee. This became the capital of the Rom. province of Arabia following Trajan's conquests in AD 106. Petra enjoyed considerable prosperity during the 2nd century AD when many of the rock-cut façades were made. The rise of Palmyra diverted the trade which formerly went to Petra from the E, and that city gradually declined. The Nabataean people, subject to Arab raids, became absorbed in the surrounding population, although the script continued in use into the 4th century.

BIBLIOGRAPHY. J. Starcky, 'The Nabataeans: A Historical Sketch', *BA* 18, 1955, pp. 84–106; G. L. Harding, *The Antiquities of Jordan*, 1959; N. Glueck, *Deities and Dolphins*, 1966; Y. Meshorer, *Nabataean Coins*, 1975; S. Moscati, *The Semites in Ancient History*, 1959, pp. 117–119. A.R.M.

NABOTH. A Jezreelite who figures in a contrived legal process set in motion by Jezebel (1 Ki. 21). Naboth had refused to part with a vineyard to King Ahab, but following his judicial murder Ahab took possession of the vineyard. This implies, as 2 Ki. 9:26 suggests, that Naboth's heirs were executed with him. The crime of such magnitude is defined as: 'Naboth cursed God and the king' (1 Ki. 21:13). The legal process involved a selection procedure using * Urim and Thummim, at the end of which Naboth was left *b^{e}ro'š hā'ām*, 'at the head of the people' (RSV 'on high among the people' misses the point). What was regarded as divine disclosure of the criminal would normally call for confession (*cf.* Achan, Jos. 7:16ff., and Jonathan, 1 Sa. 14:40ff.), but in this contrived case Naboth will not confess, and witnesses are called to testify to an unspecified crime. His refusal, therefore, to accept the divine verdict is tantamount to 'making light of God and the king' and leads to his death (just as it did in Achan's case, and might have done for Jonathan).

The story forms part of the whole *Ahab-* Elijah complex with an ironic play on certain words. The sequel of the incident is the destruction of Jezebel and the entire house of Ahab (1 Ki. 22:34ff.; 2 Ki. 9:24, 33; 10:1–11). W.O.

NADAB (Heb. *nāḏāḇ*, 'generous', 'noble'). **1.** Aaron's eldest son (Nu. 3:2). Intimately present at Sinai (Ex. 24:1) and later a priest (Ex. 28:1), he transgressed the law (Ex. 30:9) with his brother Abihu in offering 'unholy fire' to God, for which they both died (Lv. 10:1–7; *cf.* Nu. 26:61). 'Unholy fire' may mean either fire or incense kindled elsewhere than at the altar (Lv. 16:12) or incense offered at the wrong time ('such as he had not commanded them'). Lv. 10:8–9 hints at the possibility that drunkenness was an element in the sin.

2. A son of Shammai, of the house of Jerahmeel, of the tribe of Judah (1 Ch. 2:28). **3.** A son of Gibeon, of the tribe of Benjamin (1 Ch. 8:30). **4.** A king of Israel, successor to his father, Jeroboam I. He reigned *c.* 915–914 BC, being assassinated and succeeded by Baasha while besieging Gibbethon (1 Ki. 14:20; 15:25–28). T.H.J.

NAHALAL, NAHALOL (Heb. *nah^{a}lol*). A town in Zebulun, but held by Canaanites (Jos. 19:15; 21:35; Jdg. 1:30). Probably not far from modern Nahalal, 9 km W of Nazareth. Simons (*GTT*, p. 182) favours Tell el-Beida to the S; Ma'lul to the NE ('Mahalul', Talmud *Megillah* 1. 1) is not old enough to be the actual site. Albright (*AASOR* 2–3, 1923, p. 26) suggested Tell en-Nahl near Haifa (*cf.* Gn. 49:13), but this is outside the tribal area. J.P.U.L.

NAHALIEL (Heb. *naḥ^{a}lî'ēl*, 'valley of God'). N of the Arnon (Nu. 21:19); now Wadi Zerka Ma'in; famous in Rom. times for its warm springs, which flow into the Dead Sea 16 km from the Jordan (Josephus, *BJ* 1. 657; 7. 185). J.P.U.L.

NAHASH (Heb. *nāḥāš*). **1.** An Ammonite king who attacked Jabesh-gilead in Saul's reign (1 Sa. 11–12). His relations with David were friendly (2 Sa. 10:2; 1 Ch. 19:1). **2.** Father of Abigail and Zeruiah, David's sisters (2 Sa. 17:25). LXX(B) and Origen support this reading against other Gk. MSS which give 'Jesse' (Driver, *Samuel*), perhaps assimilating to 1 Ch. 2:13–16. The Chronicler may mean that Abigail and Zeruiah were Jesse's step-daughters; their sons appear to have been of about David's age. J.P.U.L.

NAHOR. 1. Son of Serug, and grandfather of Abraham (Gn. 11:22–25; 1 Ch. 1:26).

2. Son of Terah, and brother of Abraham and Haran. He married his niece Milcah, Haran's daughter (Gn. 11:26–27, 29). Nahor probably journeyed to Harran with Terah, Abram and Lot despite the silence of Gn. 11:31 to this effect, for Harran became known as 'the city of Nahor' (Gn. 24:10; *cf.* 27:43). He was the progenitor of twelve Aramaean tribes which are listed in Gn. 22:20–24. This reflects the close relationship of the Hebrews and the Aramaeans. A place Nahur in the vicinity of Harran is named in the Mari tablets (18th century BC).

The two other passages where Nahor is mentioned need to be compared to reveal that Nahor was a devotee of the false god of his father Terah (Gn. 31:53; *cf.* Jos. 24:2). This implies that the consecration at Mizpah (Gn. 31:43ff.) took place in the presence of Yahweh and Terah's god.

See *BASOR* 67, 1937, p. 27. R.J.W.

NAHSHON (Heb. *naḥšôn*, possibly from *nāḥāš*, 'serpent'; Gk. *Naassōn*). Aaron's brother-in-law (Ex. 6:23; AV gives 'Naashon'), son of Amminadab and prince of Judah (Nu. 1:7; 2:3; 7:12, 17; 10:14; 1 Ch. 2:10). He is mentioned as an ancestor of David in Ru. 4:20, and of our Lord in Mt. 1:4 and Lk. 3:32. J.G.G.N.

NAHUM, BOOK OF.

I. Authorship and date

Nahum was a prophet from Elkosh, possibly in Judah. It is difficult to date his prophecy precisely, but we may note that the capture of Thebes (*i.e.* No-ammon) is regarded as already having taken place. This event occurred under Ashurbanipal in the years 664–663 BC. At the same time, Nineveh, the object of Nahum's preaching, is still standing. Nineveh fell in 612 BC, and so we may place the prophecy roughly between these two dates. More precise than this, however, it is impossible to be.

II. Summary of contents

Each of the three chapters is a unit in itself, and we may best understand the prophecy by considering these chapters one after another.

a. An acrostic poem and declaration of judgment, 1:1–15

Chapter 1 falls into three principal sections: the superscription (v. 1), the description of God's majesty (vv. 2–8), and the declaration of judgment to come (vv. 9–15). The superscription describes the message as a *maśśā'*, i.e. 'burden', a word which often denotes a message involving threatening. It also declares that the work is a 'book of the vision of Nahum', *i.e.* a book in which the vision received by Nahum is written down. The supernatural character of the message is thus early acknowledged.

The prophet immediately plunges into a statement of the jealousy of God. The zeal of the Lord is his determination to carry out his purposes both in the bringing in of his own kingdom and in the punishment of his adversaries. It is this latter aspect of God's jealousy which is here prominent. God is slow to anger, says the prophet (v. 3); nevertheless, he will take vengeance on his enemies. When these terms are applied to God we must understand that they are used anthropomorphically; they do not contain the sinister connotations that adhere to them when they are used of men. That God is able so to carry out his purposes is a matter that admits of no doubt. He can control the forces of nature, the storm, the rivers, the sea, Bashan, *etc.* For those who trust in him he is a stronghold, but for the wicked he is darkness.

The enemies of the Lord refuse to believe that he will smite them. Hence, God announces that in a time when they expect it not the enemy will be devoured as stubble that is wholly dry. Yet there is also to be an announcement of salvation, and Judah is commanded to keep her solemn feasts and to perform her vows.

b. The siege and sack of Nineveh, 2:1–13

In 2:1–6 Nahum describes the enemy who lay siege to Nineveh. These are the Medes who came from the plain of Persia and were turning their attention against the Assyrians of the Mesopotamian plain. They are described as those that dash in pieces (v. 1). In attacking the city they open the sluices so that the waters of the river may overflow and then they enter the city to destroy her palace.

Huzzab, a word which possibly designates the queen (*cf.* RSV 'its mistress'), is taken away into captivity, and her female attendants follow her. (NEB renders the word 'train of captives'; J. D. W. Watts suggests the pedestal of a temple image.) Nineveh, the object of attack, has become like a pool of water. Into her much trade has poured and many goods have been brought, so that she is now filled. Nevertheless, men will flee from

Quotations from Nahum 3:6–9 with commentary (4Q p.Nah, Col. III) referring to the 'Seeker-after-smooth-things'. Dead Sea Scroll from Qumran Cave 4. Late 1st cent. BC. (RM)

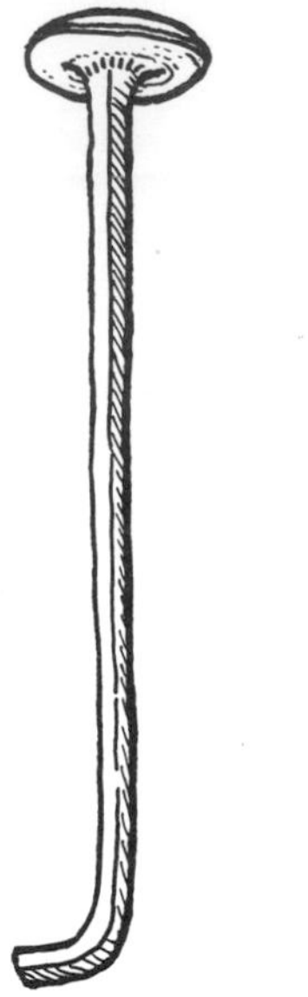

A bronze nail used for fixing the bronze reliefs depicting the campaigns of Shalmaneser III to the wooden frames of the gates of the temple of Imgur-Bel at Balawat, near Nineveh. c. 845 BC.

The location of Nain (Lk. 7:11).

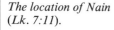

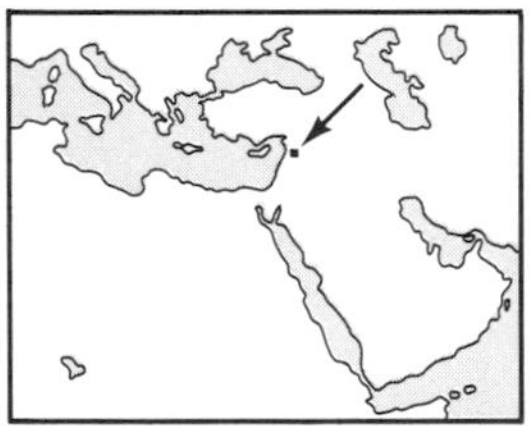

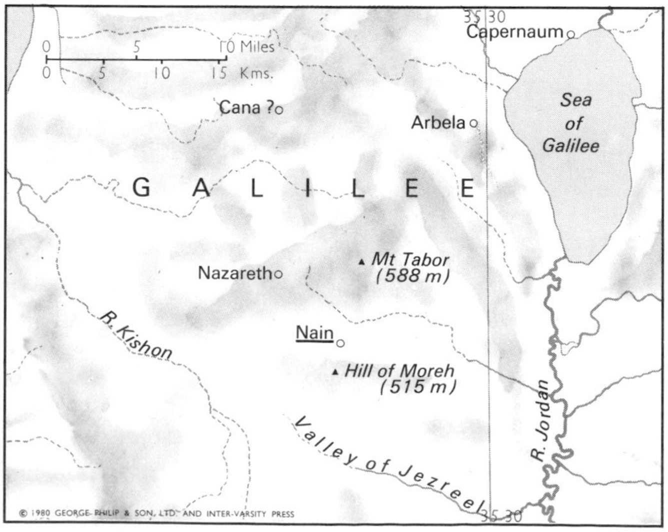

her, and those who cry 'Stand!' will not be able to stay those who would take refuge in flight. Plunder then begins in earnest, and the few survivors who remain behind look on in grief and terror as the city is despoiled.

Nineveh had once been a lion, a veritable den of lions. She had engaged in search for prey. Now, however, she is herself the object of such search and herself becomes a prey. What has become of Nineveh? The answer is that the Lord of hosts is against her, and he has determined to act in such a way as to remove her strength and power from her.

c. A description of the city and a comparison with Thebes, 3:1–19

Chapter 3 consists of a description of the wicked character of the city of Nineveh. She was a bloody city and full of cruelty. She was a warring city, and there were many that were slain. Through her whoredoms she sold nations and dealt in witchcrafts. Hence, the Lord had set himself against her and would expose her so that she would become a laughing-stock to all who looked upon her.

Nahum then makes a brief comparison with Thebes (3:8–15). Thebes, as the capital of Upper Egypt, had become strong, had revelled in her strength and acted as had Nineveh, yet her ruin had surely come. So also would it be with Nineveh. There could be no escape. Thus the prophet works up to a mighty climax, and announces that there is no healing for the bruise of Assyria, 'Your wound is grievous' (3:19a).

In this small prophecy of doom we learn that the God of Israel, the nation whom Assyria had despised, is truly the God who controls the destinies and the actions of all nations.

BIBLIOGRAPHY. A. Haldar, *Studies in the Book of Nahum,* 1947; Walter A. Maier, *Nahum,* 1959; J. H. Eaton, *Obadiah, Nahum, Habakkuk, Zephaniah, TBC,* 1961; J. D. W. Watts, *Joel, Obadiah, Jonah, Nahum, etc., CBC,* 1975.

E.J.Y.

NAIL. 1. Finger-nail (Heb. *ṣippōren*; Aram. *ṭᵉp̄ar*). Captive women were commanded to shave the head and pare the nails (Dt. 21:12). Nebuchadrezzar had 'nails like birds' claws' (Dn. 4:33; *cf.* 7:19).

2. A wooden tent peg (Jdg. 4:21, Heb. *yāṯēḏ*), used by Jael to slay Sisera. It was sometimes used for suspending objects as in Ezk. 15:3. Isaiah (22:25 AV; RSV 'peg') likened Eliakim to 'a nail in a sure place' on which the 'whole weight of his father's house' might hang. Such a nail was driven into a wall.

3. A metal nail or pin (*yāṯēḏ*) for driving into wood or other material to hold objects together, or left projecting to suspend objects. In the tabernacle the nails were of bronze (Ex. 27:19; 35:18; 38:20, 31; 39:40; Nu. 3:37; 4:32). Delilah used such a nail (pin) to bind Samson (Jdg. 16:14). The word *masmēr* refers to nails of iron (1 Ch. 22:3) or of gold (2 Ch. 3:9), driven into a wall (Ec. 12:11), or used to secure idols in their place (Is. 41:7; Je. 10:4). Nails have been found at many Palestinian sites including Tell Abu Hawam, an ancient harbour city near Mt Carmel.

4. In NT times victims were affixed to a *cross by nails driven through hands and feet (Gk. *hēlos,* Jn. 20:25).

J.A.T.

NAIN. Mentioned only in Lk. 7:11. There is a small village still bearing this name in the Plain of Jezreel, a few miles S of Nazareth, at the edge of Little Hermon, and it is generally accepted as the scene of the Gospel narrative. It is certainly to be distinguished from the Nain of Jos., *BJ* 4. 511, which was E of the Jordan. The name is perhaps a corruption of the Heb. word *nāʿîm,* 'pleasant', which adjective well describes the area and the views, if not the village itself. A problem is raised, however, by the reference to the city gate (Lk. 7:12); for the village today called Nain was never fortified, and so would never have had a gate in the proper sense of the word. But the word 'gate' may be used loosely, to indicate the place where the road entered between the houses of Nain. An ingenious suggestion solves the difficulty by proposing that the site was Shunem (as in the similar story of 2 Ki. 4), an original *synēm* becoming accidentally reduced to *nēm,* and then confused with Nain. Shunem, in any case, is in the same general area.

D.F.P.

NAIOTH. A place or quarter in Ramah where Samuel supervised a community of prophets and to which David fled from Saul (1 Sa. 19:18–19, 22–23). When Saul sent messengers there to seek David, each in turn 'prophesied'. Later, when Saul came in person he too 'prophesied' (v. 24), giving rise to a proverb: 'Is Saul also among the prophets?' The Heb. word *nāyôṯ* is related to *nāweh,* 'pasture ground' or 'abode', and is commonly translated 'habitation'.

J.A.T.

NAME. The Bible is no stranger to the custom, now virtually normative, of giving a name simply because it appeals to the parents. What else is likely to lie behind calling a little girl Deborah (meaning 'bee', Jdg. 4:4) or Esther (Heb. *hᵃḏassâ,* 'myrtle')? Even in cases where it offers some high-sounding, moralistic or religious sentiment, it would run beyond the evidence to assume without question that the name was conferred with that thought in mind rather than that the parents were indulging a preference for that rather than any other label. One can, for example, weave sad fancies round a name like Ahikam ('my brother has risen') as indicating a tragic earlier bereavement in the family which the subsequent birth of another son was seen to rectify, but Ahikam is a pleasant-sounding name and in default of evidence to the contrary may well have been chosen for no better reason.

Nevertheless, while we can be too high-minded in our approach to names and naming in the Bible, there is no question but that there is, throughout, a conceptual background which was very often given full play in the conferring of a name and which, even if it seemed to have no part (or none that we know) in the original naming yet in later life asserted its claim on the person concerned. Thus, for example, whereas Isaiah named his two sons with deliberation so that they would embody certain aspects of the word of God to his people (Is. 7:4; 8:1–4) his own name ('Yahweh saves'), as we should have to say, 'by coincidence', could not have been bettered as the name for this prophet above all. The Bible's view of names and naming would be offended by the idea of a mere coincidence or accident of parental choice: the link it sees between name and person is both too close and also too dynamic for that.

I. Significant naming

The general evidence dispersed throughout the Bible would insist that it is no coincidence that the great prophet of salvation is called by a theophoric name on the salvation theme. It would see the directive providence of God determining beforehand the whole course of the life; it would probably more typically see the name as embodying a word of God which would henceforth mould its recipient into the man whose life would express what the word declared. This, at any rate, is the dynamic view of names and naming which runs throughout Scripture and which differs so dramatically from our static view of a name as a differentiating label.

The following seven categories cover most of the dynamic name-giving situations:

a. The status-name. Of his new-found wife, the man said that she would be called 'Woman', thus according to her a co-equal (or, better, counterpart) status with her husband: he is *'îš*; she is *'iššâ*. In general in the Bible name-giving is an authority function: the imposition of the name 'Man' on the couple by their Creator (Gn. 5:2), the giving of animal names by the man, in his capacity as creation's lord (Gn. 2:19f.), the naming of children by parents (by the mother on 28 and by the father on 18 occasions), the naming of a conquered king (2 Ki. 23:34), *etc.* But in Gn. 2:23 the 'man' acknowledges his complementary equal, the one who, with him, shares the God-given dominion of the world (Gn. 1: 28ff.).

b. The occasion-name. The birth of her first-born is to Eve the significant moment of the fulfilling of the promise of a victorious seed; therefore 'along with Yahweh' as she said (Gn. 4:1)—he, fulfilling his promise, she bringing forth a child—she 'gained possession' (verb *qānâ*) of a child whom she therefore called 'Cain' (*qayin*).

c. The event-name. Sometimes names encapsulate a whole situation: *e.g.* Babel (Gn. 11:9) or Peleg (Gn. 10:25). Both these namings have the same quality, but we can see what was afoot more clearly in the fully-documented case of Babel: the name was in effect a word of God. Men had already discerned in themselves a tendency to separate or scatter (11:4) and they purposed by their technological advance (v. 3) to be their own saviours in this regard. The divine edict goes forth against man's confidence that his own cleverness can save him, and the word which imposes judicially on the human race the disability which it feared (v. 8) is succinctly built into the fabric of earthly things by the place-name 'Babel' ('confusion') which is to be henceforth the evil genius of the Bible story until the end (*cf.*, *e.g.*, Is. 13:1; 21:1–10; 24:10; Rev. 18:2; *etc.*; *BABYLON).

d. The circumstance-name. Isaac was named because of the attendant laughter of his parents (Gn. 17:17; 18:12; 21:3–7); Samuel, because of the prayer of his mother (1 Sa. 1:20); Moses, because his princess-mother drew him from the water (Ex. 2:10); Ichabod, because of the loss of the ark, seen as significant of the withdrawal of divine favour (1 Sa. 4:21); Jacob, because of the position of the twins at birth (Gn. 25:26). In many of such cases the Bible provides the evidence to show that such 'accidents' were truly symbolic: the victory at the Red Sea makes Moses pre-eminently the man who came up out of the water; the story of Samuel is precisely the story of the man who knew that prayer is answered, and so on. In other words, there is a continuing link between the idea of giving a name and the dynamism of the ever-potent word of God effecting that which it declares.

e. The transformation- or alteration-name. Names were bestowed in order to show that something new had entered the life of the person concerned, one chapter was complete and a new chapter was opening. Though this giving of a new name is usually hopeful and promissory, the category opens with the sad re-naming of *'iššâ* (Gn. 2:23) as Eve (Gn. 3:20), the name expressive of co-equality of status and complementariness of relationship becoming the name of function; the former name expressed what her husband saw in her (and was glad), the latter expressed what he would use her for, giving her domination in return for her longing (Gn. 3:16). But to the same category belongs the re-naming of Abram as Abraham, signifying the beginning of the new man with new powers: the childless Abram (whose name 'high father' was only a sour joke) becoming Abraham, which, though it does not grammatically mean 'father of many nations', has sufficient assonance with the words which would (at greater length) express that thought. Many significant names operate on just such a basis of assonance. Thus also on one and the same day Benoni became Benjamin (Gn. 35:18), the circumstance-name of pain and loss becoming the status-name of 'right-hand man'. The dominical bestowal of the name Peter (Jn. 1:42) has the same significance, *cf.* Mt. 16:18; as indeed does the (presumably) self-chosen change from Saul to Paul (Acts 13:9).

f. The predictive/admonitory-name. Isaiah's two sons are pre-eminent in this class. It is significant of the prophet's certainty of the word of God through him that he was willing to embody it in his sons who thus were, within their own time, 'the word become flesh', the greatest of the acted oracles (*PROPHECY) of the OT. *Cf.* Is. 7:3; 8:1–4, 18. See also 2 Ki. 24:17, where the name Zedekiah embodies the righteousness element (*ṣedeq*, 'righteousness') which Pharaoh thus warns the new king to practise. The Lord's naming of James and John as 'Boanerges' was equally a warning against the unacceptable element of fire in their zeal (Mk. 3:17; *cf.* Lk. 9:54) and once again the name proved itself to be an effective word of God.

g. Precative- and theophoric-names. A name like Nabal (*nāḇāl*, 'fool') (1 Sa. 25:25) can only have been given on the basis of a mother's prayer—'Let him not grow up to be a fool'—a prayer for which a cogent background could be provided without too much stretch of the imagination. It is likely that many theophoric names had this same element of prayer in them—or at the very least, most of those which are based on an imperfect tense of the verb: thus Ezekiel ('May God strengthen!'); Isaiah ('May Yah[weh] save!'). Even those which in direct translation make an affirmation (*e.g.* Jehoahaz, 'Yahweh has grasped') are most likely the product of pious parental aspirations—not always realized, as the sad case of Nabal (1 Sa. 25) may show, or the case of King Ahaz whose name is probably an abbreviation of 'Jehoahaz': it is fully in accord with the story of that politically astute, spiritually inept king to think that he deliberately dropped the theophoric element in his name.

The naming of the Lord Jesus Christ does not fit any single one of the foregoing categories. In its relation to OT prophecies (Mt. 1:23 with Is. 7:14; Lk. 1:31–33 with Is. 9:6f.) the name Jesus is a status-name, declaring the recipient to be God, born of a virgin and the promised king of David's line. It is a significant thing that the first person named in the NT receives (not a prediction-name but) a fulfilment-name: the purposes of God are being rounded out to completion. The name Jesus itself is a prediction-name looking forward to what he will himself do, and this is itself significant, for the prediction-names of the OT looked forward to what Yahweh would do and stood in relation to that act as external heralds or pointers. But Jesus is himself the fulfilment of what his name declares.

II. The name of God

Any and all evidence which helps to show that on the human level a name is a significant and indeed potent thing, not only labelling but moulding its recipient, finds its focus in the concept of the 'name of God' (*GOD, NAMES OF) which lies at the centre of the Bible. A 'divine name' is not, of course, a distinctively biblical notion. Amongst the ancient Greeks, for instance, Hesiod tried to enter more deeply into an understanding of the gods by a study of their names, an exercise which, *mutatis mutandis*, might well be seen as central to biblical theology.

There is a real sense in which the Bible is poised upon the revelation of the divine name. In the OT, the Patriarchs knew their God by titles (*e.g.* Gn. 14:22; 16:13; 17:1), among which was the so far unexplained 'Yahweh'. The significance of Moses and the Exodus is that at that point what had hitherto been no more than a label was revealed to be not a title, however exalted, but a personal name. The revelation enshrined in the name was opened up and confirmed in the Exodus events, the redemption of the people of God, the Passover and the Red Sea. In the NT the balancing event was the ministry and redemptive work of Jesus: the definitive 'name' of God as the Holy Trinity, Father, Son and Holy Spirit, coinciding with the public commencement of Jesus' ministry when at his baptism he began deliberately to be numbered with the transgressors (*cf.* Mk. 1:9–11). John sees the significance of this in his deliberate association of Jesus at his baptism with the Lamb of God (Jn. 1:29ff.). This comparison should warn against identifying the God of the OT ('Yahweh') with the NT revelation of God the Father. Yahweh is rather the Holy Trinity *incognito*.

In form the divine name *Yahweh* is either a simple indicative or a causative indicative of the verb 'to be', meaning 'he is (alive, present, active)' or 'he brings into being', and the formula in which the name is disclosed (Ex. 3:14, *I am who I am*) means either 'I reveal my active presence as and when I will' or 'I bring to pass what I choose to bring to pass'. In the setting of Ex. 3–20 this refers both to the events of the Exodus as those in which Yahweh is actively present (and which indeed he has deliberately brought to pass) and also to the preceding theological interpretation (Ex. 3:1–4:17; 5:22–6:8) of those events vouchsafed to Moses. Yahweh is thus the God of revelation and history and in particular reveals himself as the God who saves his people (according to covenant promise) and overthrows those who oppose his word.

Abundant though this revealed knowledge of God is, yet in the divine name there is a clear element of secrecy. The formula *I am who I am* in itself expresses no more than that God knows his own nature: it is a formula of the sovereignty of God in the revelation of himself. If anything is to be told, he must tell it; he will tell only what he pleases. *Cf.* Gn. 32:29; Jdg. 13:17. This is not in any way to be related to the concepts of magic. In the surrounding pagan world to know a god's name was supposed to confer some power over that god—a logical extension (as so much false religion is a logical embroidering upon a truth) of the idea that 'naming' is the act of a superior. Yahweh did not withhold any revelation of himself in fear lest man should gain power over him. Rather the revelation of himself belongs in a programme of privilege which he has designed for his people, whereby the somewhat 'external' relationship expressed in titles becomes the highly personal relationship to a God who has given his people the liberty to call him by name, and what is at that point held back is concealed only because the moment of supreme revelation is yet to come. Nevertheless what is already known is not a falsehood later to be set aside nor a partial truth (for *this is my name for ever*, Ex. 3:15) awaiting completion, but one way of expressing the whole truth which will yet achieve greater and fuller expression. The 'name' of God lies at the heart of progressive revelation.

But though the name does not confer 'power' in any magical sense (*cf.* Acts 19:13ff.), the knowledge of the name brings people into a wholly new relationship with God. They are his intimates, for this is the significance of 'knowing by name' (*cf.* Ex. 33:12, 18–19; Jn. 17:6). The initiation of the relationship thus described lies on the divine side: collectively and individually the people of God are 'called by his name' (*cf.* 2 Ch. 7:14; Is. 43:7; Je. 14:9; 15:16; Am. 9:12). Furthermore the motive which lies behind this divine outreach is often described as the Lord acting 'for the sake of his name' (*cf.* especially Ezk. 20:9, 14, 22, 44) by means of works through which he 'made for himself a name' (*e.g.* 2 Sa. 7:23; Ne. 9:10). The name is thus a summary way of stating what God is in himself (his name is all that is known to be true about him and his motives of action) and also what God is to others, allowing them to know his name (letting them into his truth) and sharing his name with them (letting them into his fellowship).

There are five aspects of this basic situation strongly enough attested in Scripture to warrant a brief statement of each, even though not all are evenly spread through the Bible.

a. It is a particularly Johannine emphasis to express the human side of the experience of God as 'believing in the name' (*e.g*. Jn. 3:18; 1 Jn. 3:23), *i.e*. personal commitment to the Lord Jesus as thus revealed in the essence of his Person and work.

b. Those who are of the people of God are 'kept' in his name (*e.g*. Jn. 17:11), taking up the distinctive OT picture of the name as a strong tower (*e.g*. Pr. 18:10) to which they may run for safety, and also the name given as a husband's name to a wife whereby provision and protection are guaranteed (*cf*. 'called by the name' above). When Christians are said to be 'justified in the name' (1 Cor. 6:11) the implication is the same: the name, as the unchangeable nature of Jesus and as the summary of all that he is and has done, is the ground of secure possession of all the implied blessings.

c. God's presence among his people is secured by 'making his name dwell' among them. *Cf*. Dt. 12:5, 11, 21; 14:23f.; 16:2, 6; 2 Sa. 7:13; *etc*. It has sometimes been foolishly pressed that there is a distinction if not a rift between a 'name-theology' and a 'glory-theology' in the OT, but these are two ways of expressing the same thing: *e.g*. when Moses sought to see Yahweh's glory, he found that the glory had to be verbalized by means of the name (Ex. 33:18–34:8). There is no sense in which the Deuteronomist is replacing a crude notion of indwelling glory by a refined notion of the indwelling name: it is rather that the 'glory' tends to express the 'sense' of God's real presence, including much that is rightly unapproachable and ineffable; 'name' explains why this is so, verbalizes the numinous, for nowhere does the God of the Bible deal in dumb sacraments but always with intelligible declarations.

d. The name of God is described as his 'holy name' more often than all other adjectival qualifications taken together. It was this sense of the sacredness of the name that finally led to the obtuse refusal to use 'Yahweh', leading as it has done to a deep loss of the sense of the divine name in EVV (with the notable exception of JB). The 'holiness' of the name, however, does not remove it from use but from abuse: this is the reason why the revelation of the divine name must never be confused with any thought of magical 'power with the divine'. Far from man being able to use the name to control God, it is the name which controls man, both in worship Godward (*e.g*. Lv. 18:21) and in service manward (*e.g*. Rom. 1:5). The 'name' is thus the motive of service; it is also the message (*e.g*. Acts 9:15) and the means of power (*e.g*. Acts 3:16; 4:12).

e. Throughout the Bible the name of God is the ground of prayer: *e.g*. Ps. 25:11; Jn. 16:23–24.

Distinctively the NT associates baptism with the name, either of the Holy Trinity (Mt. 28:19) or of the Lord Jesus (*e.g*. Acts 2:38): the distinction is that the former stresses the total reality of the divine nature and purpose and the totality of blessedness designed for the recipient, whereas the latter stresses the effective means of entry into these things through the sole mediation of Jesus.

BIBLIOGRAPHY. art. 'Name' in J.-J. von Allmen, *The Vocabulary of the Bible*, 1958; *IDB*, 1962, and Supp. Vol., 1976; *see also*, J. Pedersen, *Israel* 1 and 2, 1926, pp. 245–259; J. Barr, 'The Symbolism of Names in the OT', *BJRL* 52, 1969–70, pp. 11–29; L. Hartman, 'Into the Name of Jesus', *NTS* 20, 1973–4, pp. 432–440; J. A. Motyer, *The Revelation of the Divine Name*, 1959; R. de Vaux, 'The Revelation of the Divine Name YHWH', in J. I. Durham and J. R. Porter, *Proclamation and Presence*, 1970, pp. 44, 48–75; G. von Rad, *Studies in Deuteronomy*, 1953, pp. 37–44; G. T. Manley, *The Book of the Law*, 1957, pp. 33, 122ff.; H. Bietenhard, F. F. Bruce, *NIDNTT* 2, pp. 648–656.

J.A.M.

NAOMI (Heb. *no'ᵒmî*, 'my delight'). During the period of the Judges there was a famine in Bethlehem of Judah, which caused Elimelech, a citizen of that place, to take his wife Naomi, and their two sons, Mahlon and Chilion, to Moab. There she was widowed, and her sons married Moabite girls, Orpah and *Ruth, who were widowed in their turn.

Naomi decided to return to her own people alone, while her daughters-in-law remarried, but Ruth insisted on accompanying her. She told them that her name was now Mara (Heb. *mārā'*, 'bitter') (Ru. 1:20f.). At Bethlehem she planned a levirate marriage for Ruth with her near kinsman, Boaz. Their first child, Obed, was reckoned as hers, and he was the grandfather of David (Ru. 4:16f.).

M.B.

NAPHISH. The eleventh son of Ishmael (Gn. 25:15; 1 Ch. 1:31). His descendants have not been definitely identified, but may be the 'Naphish' of 1 Ch. 5:19; 'the sons of Nephisim' of Ezr. 2:50; and the 'Nephushesim' of Ne. 7:52.

J.D.D.

NAPHTALI (Heb. *nap̄tālî*, 'wrestler'). The sixth son of Jacob, and the second son of Bilhah, Rachel's maidservant; the younger brother of Dan, with whom he is usually associated (Gn. 30:5–8). In the Blessing of Jacob he is described as 'a hind let loose' which may allude to either his agility or his impetuosity.

In most of the administrative lists the tribe of Naphtali comes last (*e.g*. Nu. 1:15, 42f.; 2:29ff.; 7:78; 10:27). The Blessing of Moses commands Naphtali to 'possess the lake and the south' (Dt. 33:23) and following the settlement its tribal portion comprised a broad strip W of the Sea of Galilee and the upper Jordan, including the greater portion of E and central Galilee. This territory is roughly delineated in Jos. 19:32–39, including nineteen fortified cities. But the N boundary is undefined and since two of the cities mentioned, Beth-anath and Beth-shemesh, parts of a chain of Canaanite fortresses extending from the coast across upper Galilee, are noted in Jdg. 1:33 as not completely subjugated, it is probable that it varied considerably in the earlier period. Naphtali included also the largest Canaanite city, Hazor, covering about 80 hectares and dominating a vital trade route. Hazor, although destroyed by the Israelites under Joshua (Jos. 11:10f.), reasserted itself and, whilst never regaining its former prestige, it was not finally vanquished until well into the Judges' period (Jdg. 4:2, 23f.). Another important city was Kedesh, a levitical city and one of the cities of refuge (Jos. 20:7; 21:32).

The strong Canaanite element is reflected in Jdg. 1:33, 'Naphtali . . . dwelt among the Canaanites'. This would encourage syncretism and partly accounts for the relative insignificance, historically, of this tribe. But there were moments of glory. Barak, Deborah's partner in delivering Israel from Canaanite

NAMES OF GOD
See God, names of, Part 1.

domination, was a Naphtalite (Jdg. 4:6) and his tribe was conspicuous in the same campaign (Jdg. 5:18). A later generation served valiantly under Gideon (Jdg. 6:35; 7:23), and the Chronicler records their support for David (1 Ch. 12:34, 40). Thereafter, Naphtali, vulnerable because of its frontier situation, suffered from attacks from the N. During the reign of Baasha its territory was ravaged by Ben-hadad I of Syria (1 Ki. 15:20). Approximately 150 years later (734 BC) the tribe of Naphtali was the first W of the Jordan to be deported (2 Ki. 15:29). A probable reconstruction of Tiglath-pileser III's account of this campaign notes his annexation of the region, '. . . the wide land of Naphtali, in its entire extent, I united with Assyria'. Is. 9:1 alludes to the same event.

The territory of Naphtali included some of the most fertile areas of the entire land. During David's reign its 'chief officer' was Jeremoth (1 Ch. 27:19). It was one of the districts from which Solomon provisioned his court; at this time its governor was one of Solomon's sons-in-law, Ahimaaz (1 Ki. 4:15). Hiram, the principal architect of Solomon's Temple, was the son of 'a widow of the tribe of Naphtali' (1 Ki. 7:14). In Ezekiel's redistribution of the tribal allotments, Dan, Asher and Naphtali are assigned portions in the N, but the other N tribes, Issachar and Zebulun, are included further S (Ezk. 48:1–7, 23–29).

Jesus spent the greatest part of his public life in this area which, because of its chequered history of deportations and infusion of new settlers, was greatly despised by the Jews of Jerusalem, an attitude which partly explains why Galilee became the headquarters of the reactionary Zealots, bitterly opposed to Roman rule.

BIBLIOGRAPHY. Y. Aharoni, *The Settlement of the Israelite Tribes in Upper Galilee*, 1947; *idem*, *LOB*, pp. 201f., 238f. A.E.C.

NAPHTUHIM. Classed with Mizraim (Egypt), Gn. 10:13; 1 Ch. 1:11. Its identity is uncertain, but Lower Egypt, specifically the Nile Delta, would be appropriate alongside Pathrusim (*PATHROS) for Upper Egypt. Hence Brugsch and Erman emended the Heb. to fit Egyp. *p' t'-mḥw*, 'Lower Egypt'. Another Egyp. equivalent, without emendation, might be a *n'(-n-)/n'(yw-) p' idḥw*, 'they of the Delta (lit. marshland)', Lower Egypt(ians). Alternatively, *nap̱tuḥîm* may be an Egyp. *n'(-n-)/n'(yw-) p' t' wḥ'(t)*, 'they of the Oasis-land', *i.e.* the oases (and inhabitants) W of the Nile valley. K.A.K.

NARCISSUS. Paul salutes those 'who belong to the family of Narcissus' (Rom. 16:11). The phrase suggests the slaves of a prominent household. The rich freedman Narcissus, who brought about the fall of Messalina (Tacitus, *Annals* 11, *passim*), had committed suicide some little time before Rom. was written (*ibid.*, 13. 1); but his slaves ('Narcissiani' are mentioned in *CIL*, 3, 3973; 6, 15640) would pass to Nero and still be a recognizable entity. Though the name is also common outside Rome, it is tempting to see in Rom. 16:11 a Christian group within this body. A.F.W.

NATHAN (Heb. *nāṯān*, 'he [*i.e.* God] has given'). Of some eleven men of this name in the OT the following at least can be identified as separate individuals:

1. A prophet (Heb. *nāḇî'*) involved in the story of King David. He appears without introduction when David expresses his wish to build a temple (2 Sa. 7 = 1 Ch. 17). Nathan approves at first, but after speaking with God informs David that this task is for David's descendant, though David apparently arranges, at Nathan's instigation, the music for Temple worship (2 Ch. 29:25). When Adonijah plans to seize his father's throne,

The land occupied by the tribe of Naphtali.

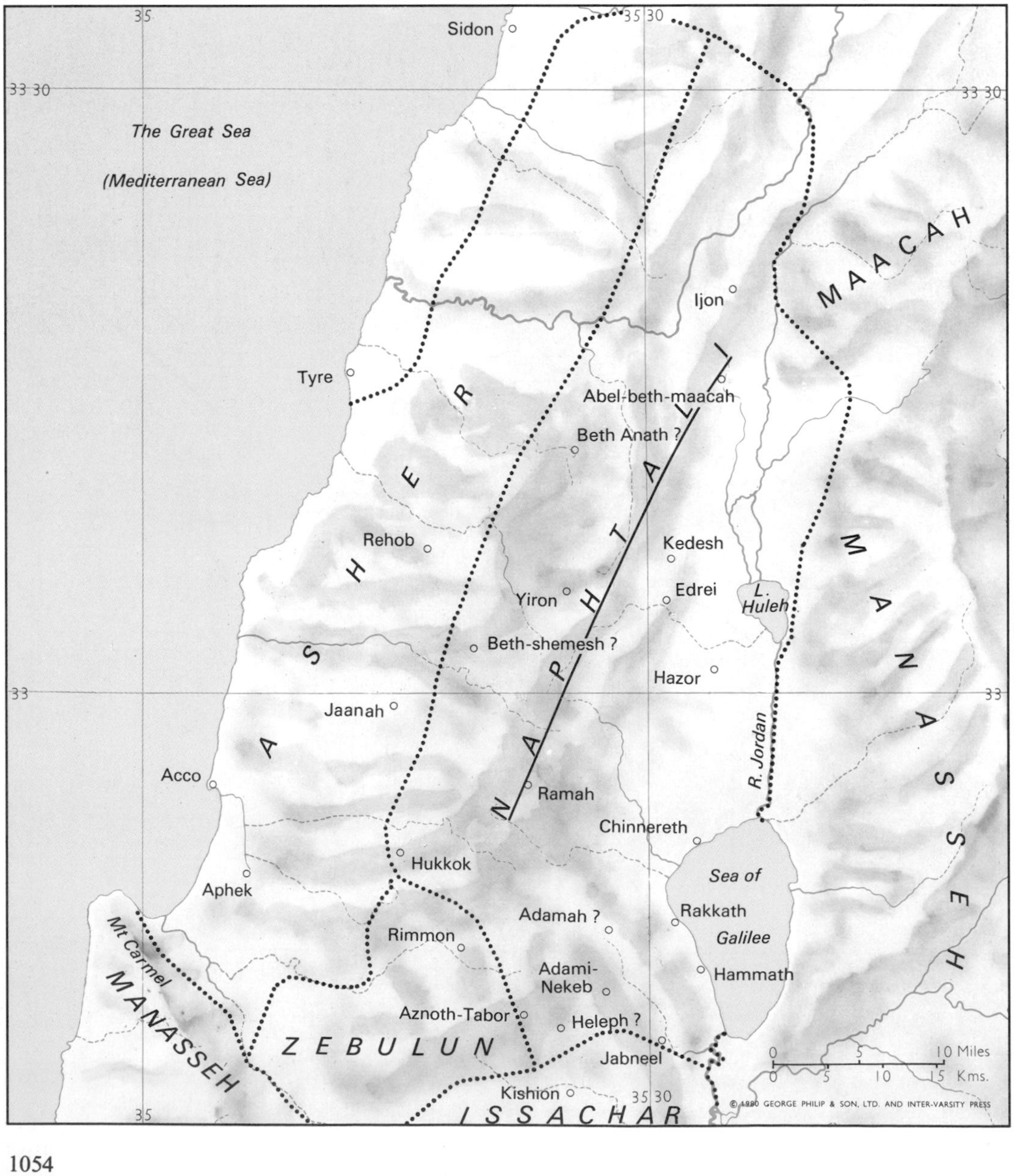

View of mountains near Safad in Naphtali, territory where Jesus taught. (FNH)

Nathan advises Bathsheba to remind David of his promise to name Solomon his successor. Supporting this reminder, Nathan is instructed to proclaim Solomon (1 Ki. 1:11–45). Nathan is best known for his fearless denunciation of David's double sin against Uriah the Hittite, and the parable in which it was couched (2 Sa. 12).

2. Relative of two of David's warriors (2 Sa. 23:36; 1 Ch. 11:38). **3.** Son of David, born in Jerusalem (2 Sa. 5:14). This line of descent is cited in Zc. 12:12 and in our Lord's genealogy in Lk. 3:31. Either this Nathan or the prophet is referred to in 1 Ki. 4:5. **4.** A man of Judah (1 Ch. 2:36). **5.** One of Ezra's companions to Jerusalem (Ezr. 8:16). **6.** Son of Bani, who put away his foreign wife at Ezra's instigation (Ezr. 10:39). T.H.J.

NATHANAEL. The name means 'gift of God', and it occurs only in Jn. 1:45–51; 21:2. He seems to be one of the Twelve and he has been variously identified, especially with Bartholomew. The name Bartholomew is a patronymic, and its bearer would have another name too. Bartholomew is next to Philip in the lists of the Twelve in the Synoptics (Mt. 10:3; Mk. 3:18; Lk. 6:14). Some, with but little justification, have identified Nathanael with Matthew, Matthias, John, Simon the Cananaean or Stephen. Others, with even less justification, have denied his real existence.

He was from Cana in Galilee and he was brought by Philip to Jesus, sceptical about the possibility of a Messiah from Nazareth. He was astonished that Jesus knew him already, having seen him under the fig tree. (This means a display of supernatural power, though the 'fig tree' may be symbolic of the study of the Law or of prosperity.) He confessed that Jesus was Son of God and King of Israel. This was the confession of an 'Israelite indeed, in whom is no guile', but it seems to limit the Messiahship to Israel. Christ promised him a greater vision, that of the Son of man as the link between heaven and all mankind (Jn. 1:45–51). He was one of those who saw Christ on his resurrection appearance by the Sea of Tiberias (Jn. 21:2).

BIBLIOGRAPHY. C. F. D. Moule, *JTS* N.S. 5, 1954, pp. 210f. R.E.N.

NATIONS, TABLE OF. An account, recorded in Gn. 10, and with a few minor variations in 1 Ch. 1:5–23, of the descendants of Noah by his three sons, *Shem, *Ham and *Japheth.

I. The Table

The table on p. 1057 represents the relationships by placing the names of the descendants of an individual below and to the right of the ancestor's name.

II. Position in Genesis

If Genesis is divided into sections by means of the recurring formula 'these are the *generations (Heb. *tôlᵉḏôṯ*) of . . .', the Table of Nations falls within the section Gn. 10:2–11:9, the formula occurring in Gn. 10:1 and 11:10. Different views are held as to whether these formulae constitute headings or colophons, but it does not affect the issue in the present case whether the Table of the Nations, together with the account of the tower of Babel, be regarded as part of the *tôl^eḏôṯ* of the sons of Noah (if 10:1 is the heading) or of Shem (if 11:10 is the colophon).

III. Arrangement

V. 32 summarizes the Table, stating that it gives the families (*mišpᵉḥôṯ*; * FAMILY, OT) of the sons or descendants (*bᵉnê*) of Noah, according to their genealogies (*lᵉṯôlᵉḏôt*; * GENERATION) in their nations (*bᵉḡôyīm*), and from these (*mē'ēlleh*, *i.e.* either the 'families' or the 'nations' making these up) the nations (*gôyim*) spread abroad on the earth (*'ereṣ*) after the Flood. While this verse forms a colophon to the Table as a whole, vv. 5, 20 and 31 form colophons to the subsections vv. 2–4, 6–19 and 21–30 which give the descendants of Japheth, Ham and Shem respectively. Their general tendency is the same as v. 32, but they further state that their lists give the names 'with reference to' their families (*mišpᵉḥôṯ*) and their languages (AV 'tongues', *lᵉšōnôṯ*; Japheth's colophon varies with 'each with his own language'), and in their lands and their nations (*gôyim*). In Japheth's colophon these are presented in a different order, and it is further stated that 'from these the coastland peoples spread'. Many commentators consider that this phrase applies to the descendants of Javan alone, since the designation 'coastland peoples' (AV 'isles') is not appropriate to the other members of the group. It is further suggested on the basis of the analogous statements in vv. 20 and 31 that the phrase 'these are the sons of Japheth' originally stood before 'in their lands . . .' in v. 5, and inadvertently dropped out in transmission. This view is adopted in the RSV and may be correct.

Within the three lineages the names are related to each other, either by the formula 'these are the sons of (*bᵉnê*) . . .' or '. . . became the father of (AV 'begat') (*yālaḏ*) . . .' (* GENEALOGY). The latter is not found in the list of Japheth's descendants, but under Ham is used of Nimrod, and the descendants of Mizraim and of Canaan, and under Shem is used of the section from Shelah to Jobab, that is, all the descendants of Arpachshad. One exception to these two formulae is found in the Philistines who 'came' or 'were begotten' (*yāṣā'*) from Casluhim (v. 14). The regular arrangement into three lists of names is modified by the insertion of other verses which give additional information, either in relating the names to each other, or in giving further information about individuals. The arrangement of the chapter may be summarized as follows:

- Heading (or colophon to previous section) (1)
  - Japheth's descendants (2–4)
    - Details concerning Javan (5a)
    - Colophon (5b)
  - Ham's descendants (6–7, 13–18a)
    - Details concerning Nimrod (8–12) and Canaan (18b–19)
    - Colophon (20)
  - Shem's descendants (22–29a)
    - Details concerning Shem (21), and Joktan (29b–30)
    - Colophon (31)
- Colophon to whole (32)

The order, in which Shem is given last, follows the usage of Genesis whereby the chosen line is treated after the collateral lines have been discussed. The genealogy in Gn. 11 carries on the line through Peleg to Abraham.

IV. Contents

Many of the names in the Table have been connected with names of peoples or regions known in the ancient inscriptions, and there is sufficient agreement on a number of these to make possible a general idea of the scope of the three lists.

a. Preliminary consideration

The names in the Table were probably the names of individuals, which came to be applied to the people descended from them, and in some cases to the territory inhabited by these people. It is important to note that such names could have different meanings at different points in history, so that the morphological identification of a name in Gn. 10 with one in the extra-biblical sources can be completely valid only if the two occurrences are exactly contemporary. The changes in significance of names of this kind are due largely to movements of peoples, in drift, infiltration, conquest or migration.

There are three principal characteristics of a people which are sufficiently distinctive to form some nuance of their name. These are race or physical type; language, which is one constituent of culture; and the geographical area in which they live or the political unit in which they are organized. Racial features cannot change, but they can become so mixed or dominated through intermarriage as to be indistinguishable. Language can change completely, that of a subordinate group being replaced by that of its rulers, in many cases permanently. Geographical habitat can be completely changed by migration. Since at times one, and at other times another, of these characteristics is uppermost in the significance of a name, lists in Gn. 10 are unlikely to have been drawn up on one system alone. Thus, for instance, the descendants of Shem cannot be expected all to have spoken one language, or even to have lived all in one area, or even to have belonged to one racial type, since intermarriage may have obscured this. That this could have taken place may be indicated by the presence of apparently duplicate names in more than one list, Asshur (* ASSYRIA), Sheba, Havilah and Lud(im) under both Shem and Ham, and probably Meshek (Mash in Shem's list; * MESHECH) under Shem and Japheth. Though these may indicate names that are entirely distinct, it is possible that they represent points where a strong people has absorbed a weaker.

It is necessary to observe that names have been adopted from this chapter for certain specific uses in modern times. Thus in language study the terms 'Semitic' and 'Hamitic' are applied, the former to the group of languages including Heb., Aram., Akkad., Arab., *etc.*, and the latter to the group of which (ancient) Egyp. is the chief. This is a usage of convenience, however, and does not mean that all the descendants of Shem spoke Semitic languages or all those of Ham Hamitic. Thus the entry of Elam under Shem, and Canaan under Ham, is not necessarily erroneous, even though Elamite was a non-Semitic and Canaanite was a Semitic tongue. In short, the names in Gn. 10 probably indicate now geographical, now linguistic, and now political entities, but not consistently any one alone.

b. Japheth

In this list the following identifica-

Japheth	Ham	Shem
Gomer	Cush	Elam
Ashkenaz	Seba	Asshur
Riphath	Havilah	Arpachshad
Togarmah	Sabtah	Shelah
Magog	Raamah	Eber
Madai	Sheba	Peleg
Javan	Dedan	Joktan
Elishah	Sabteca	Almodad
Tarshish	Nimrod	Sheleph
Kittim	Mizraim	Hazarmaveth
Dodanim	Ludim	Jerah
Tubal	Anamin	Hadoram
Meshech	Lehabim	Uzal
Tiras	Naphtuhim	Diklah
	Pathrusim	Obal
	Casluhim	Abimael
	Philistines	Sheba
	Caphtorim	Ophir
	Put (Phut)	Havilah
	Canaan	Jobab
	Zidon	Lud
	Heth	Aram
	Jebusite	Uz
	Amorite	Hul
	Girgashite	Gether
	Hivite	Mash
	Archite	
	Sinite	
	Arvadite	
	Zemorite	
	Hamathite	

Descendants of an individual are placed below and to the right of the ancestor's name

The Table of Nations, according to Gn. 10, showing the descendants of Noah's sons, Shem, Ham and Japheth.

tions receive general, though not universal, agreement: Gomer = Cimmerians; Ashkenaz = Scythians; Madai = Medes; Meshek = Muški, peoples who entered the ancient Near East from the N steppe. Javan = Ionians, and his descendants, including Elishah = Alašia (in Cyprus) and Dodanim [probably a corruption for Rodanim; *cf.* 1. Ch. 1:7, RSV] = Rhodes, were probably a W group of the N peoples who passed through Ionia to the islands and coastlands (*'iyyê*, v. 5) of the Aegean and Mediterranean. Thus it appears that the descendants of Japheth were people who in the 2nd millennium were found in the regions to the N and NW of the Near East.

c. Ham

Here the following identifications are accepted in general: Cush = Ethiopia; Sheba = Saba (in S Arabia); Dedan = Dedan (in N Arabia); Mizraim = Egypt; Ludim = Lydia (?); Philistines = Philistines; Caphtorim = Cretans; Put = Libya; Canaan = Canaan; Zidon = Sidon; Heth = Hittites; Amorite = Amorites; *Hivites = Hurrians; Hamathites = Hamathites.

Under *Nimrod an additional note is provided to the effect that the beginning of his kingdom was in *Shinar = Babylonia where he ruled in Babel = Babylon, Erech = Uruk, Accad = Agade, and *Calneh (possibly to be vocalized *kullānâ*, 'all of them'), the first three being important cities in S Mesopotamia, though the site of Agade is as yet unknown. From there he went to Asshur = Assyria (or 'Asshur went forth'; *cf.* AV) and built Nineveh, Rehoboth-ir, Calah = Kalḫu, and Resen. Nineveh and Kalḫu were Assyrian royal cities, but the other two names are unknown.

According to the situation revealed in the extra-biblical inscriptions, the statements that the inhabitants of Mesopotamia (Nimrod) came from Ethiopia, and that the Philistines and Cretans came from Egypt might appear to be erroneous, but the nature and origins of all the elements in the early population of Mesopotamia are still obscure, and Egypt's early connections with Crete and the Aegean area show the possibility of earlier unrecorded contacts. In general, the peoples to the S of the Near East are indicated in this list.

d. Shem

In Shem's list a few identifications are generally accepted: Elam =

Elam (the SE part of the Mesopotamian plain); Asshur = Aššur (or Assyria); Hazarmaveth = Ḥaḍramaut (in S Arabia); Sheba = Saba; Lud = Lydia (?); Aram = Aramaeans. These names suggest that the general area settled by the group stretched from Syria in the N, through Mesopotamia to Arabia.

V. Sources

The study of the ancient Near East gives some idea of the horizons of geographical knowledge of the 2nd millennium BC and earlier.

a. Mesopotamia

In the 4th millennium BC the evidence of pre-historic archaeology shows that at times a common culture flourished over an area stretching from the Persian Gulf to the Mediterranean. By about 3000 BC contacts through trade are attested with the Arabian peninsula, Anatolia, Iran and India. The cuneiform records take up the tale in the late 3rd and the 2nd millennia. Early rulers had business relations and other contacts with Iran, the Lebanon ('Cedar Forest'), the Mediterranean ('Upper Sea'), the Taurus ('Silver Mountain') and Anatolia (Burušḫatum) in the N, and in the S with Bahrain (Dilmun), where excavations have revealed a centre trading with Arabia and India. In the 18th century BC a colony of Assyr. merchants maintained themselves in Cappadocia (Kültepe), and from about this period a merchant's itinerary from S Mesopotamia to this station is known (*JCS* 7, 1953, pp. 51–72).

Movements in the 3rd millennium on the N steppe resulted in the arrival in the Near East during the early 2nd millennium of such peoples as the Kassites and later the rulers of Mitanni, who probably brought with them a knowledge of the N lands.

b. Egypt

In pre-historic times the inhabitants of the lower Nile had trading contacts with the Red Sea, Nubia, Libya and perhaps other places in the Sahara, and during the early Dynasties in the 3rd millennium regular expeditions were made to Sinai, and to Byblos on the Syrian coast. In the early 2nd millennium trade contacts with Cyprus, Cilicia and particularly Crete are attested by finds of objects at both ends. The Egyptians were given to listing names, and the Execration Texts of the 18th century and the lists of 'subject' cities and peoples of the pharaohs of the 15th show a geographical knowledge of Palestine and Syria. In the 14th century the archive of cuneiform tablets found at el-Amarna shows that one language (Akkadian) was used for diplomacy over the whole Near East and that a good knowledge of other areas was possible.

c. Literary criticism

It is believed by many scholars that the distinction between the *bᵉnê* and *yālaḏ* formulae in the arrangement of the Table betrays composite authorship. According to this, the main framework, making use of the *bᵉnê* formula, is to be ascribed to the Priestly Code (P), and the parts introduced by *yālaḏ*, together with other matter which gives additional information on some names in the lists, is derived from the earlier less scientific Yahwistic document (J) which was woven into their framework by the more methodical Priestly writers. The resulting division is: P = 1a, 2–7, 20, 22–23, 31–32; J = 1b, 8–19, 21, 24–30. This variation can be just as well understood, however, as the licence of style, and in the light of the geographical knowledge of the 2nd millennium BC it is no longer necessary to assume a date of composition as late as the early monarchy (J) and the post-exilic period (P). Indeed, the absence of Persia from the list would be difficult to explain if the Table was largely compiled and put into its final form by priests who owed their very return from exile to the tolerant policy of the Persians.

VI. Scope

Apart from those theories which would set the Table down as late and unreliable, there are two main views as to its scope. Some maintain that this Table names the peoples of the whole world, others that it mentions only those peoples of the Near East with whom the Israelites were likely to come in contact. This depends largely upon the word *'ereṣ* in v. 32. This is taken in EVV in the sense of '*earth', but it is a term whose significance could vary from 'the whole earth' through 'the known world' to a limited 'country' according to the context. The general view which can be obtained from the commonly accepted identifications of names in the Table supports the opinion that *'ereṣ* here means 'the known world'; but the fact that many of the names in the Table are as yet unidentified shows that the other view cannot be completely ruled out. To accept the former view does not imply that others besides Noah survived the flood, for, while the implication of Gn. 9:19 is that the earth was peopled by the descendants of Noah's three sons (*NOAH, *d*), the Table does not claim to name all of them.

VII. Authorship and date

The facts mentioned above show that the contents of the Table would not necessarily have been beyond the knowledge of a person educated in the Egyp. schools of the 15th or 14th century. Those who argue for a post-Mosaic date do so largely on the basis of the fact that such peoples as the Cimmerians, Scythians, Medes and perhaps Muški do not appear in the written documents until the 1st millennium and on the basis of this a date in the early 1st millennium is postulated. These peoples must, however, have existed as tribes or larger groups before they are mentioned in the extant records, and it is possible that such earlier invaders as the Kassites and the rulers of Mitanni, who had had contacts with the more N tribes, might have preserved a knowledge of them. It is also commonly held that the *Philistines (v. 14) did not appear in the biblical world until the 12th century, but various considerations point to the possibility of earlier contacts with these people. Likewise the S Arabian peoples mentioned in the Table, who do not appear in the written records until the 1st millennium, must have existed as tribes before then.

In brief, therefore, though there are some difficulties in the view, it is not impossible that the Table of Nations could have been compiled in the 13th century BC, perhaps by Moses.

BIBLIOGRAPHY. W. F. Albright, *Recent Discoveries in Bible Lands*, 1955, pp. 70–72; W. Brandenstein, 'Bemerkungen zur Völkertafel der Genesis', *Festschrift . . . Debrunner*, 1954, pp. 57–83; G. Hölscher, *Drei Erdkarten . . . .*, 1949, ch. 5; J. Simons, 'The Table of Nations (Gen. 10): Its General Structure and Meaning', *OTS* 10, 1954, pp. 155–184; D. J. Wiseman, 'Genesis 10: Some Archaeological Considerations', *JTVI* 87, 1955, pp. 14–24, 113–118 and *POTT*, pp. xv–xxi; E. A. Speiser, *Genesis*, 1964, pp. 64–73; most of the earlier views

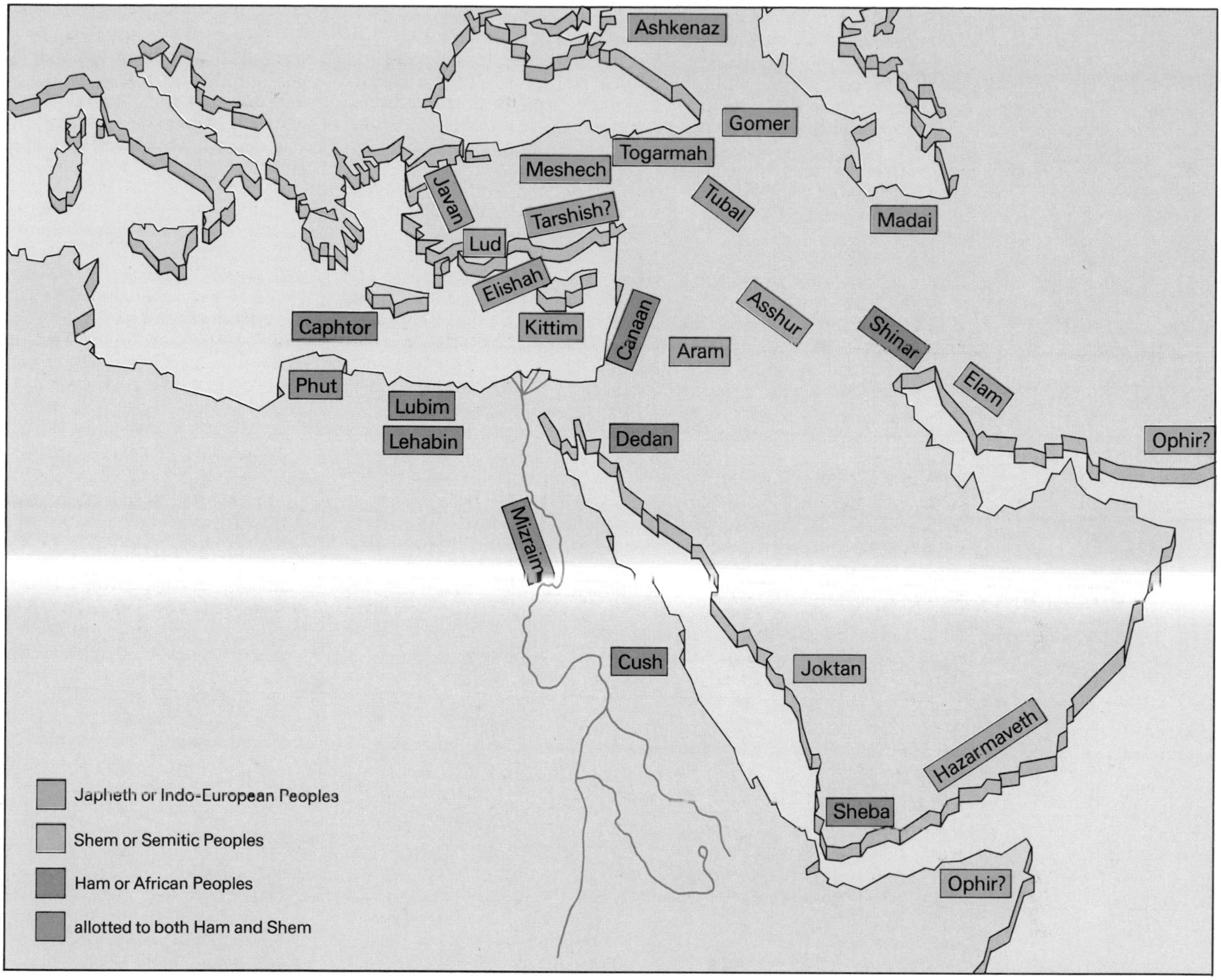

The location of the major groups in the Table of Nations.

are discussed in S. R. Driver, *The Book of Genesis*[12], 1926, pp. xxvi-xxvii, 112–132; G. R. Driver, *ibid.*, pp. 444–447; J. Skinner, *Genesis*[2], 1930, pp. 196–207. T.C.M.

NATURE. There are few words more dangerously ambiguous than 'nature'. It is impossible here to distinguish carefully all its various uses; the following analysis deals only with the words translated 'nature', 'natural', 'naturally' in AV and RSV. It is significant that even these spring from four distinct roots, one Heb. and three Gk.

1. The Heb. word *lēaḥ*, rendered 'natural force' at Dt. 34:7, has the root idea of 'freshness', 'moistness', and so of the vigour usually associated with the suppleness of youth.

2. The Gk. adverb *gnēsiōs* and the noun *genesis* stem from a root indicating 'birth', 'coming into being'. The former, although rendered 'naturally' in AV, Phil. 2:20, had lost its etymological sense in Hellenistic Greek and is better translated 'genuinely' (as RSV), 'sincerely' (*cf. MM s.v.* for the history of this change in meaning). The noun *genesis* occurs in the genitive case in Jas. 1:23; 3:6. In the first case RSV renders the genitive by 'natural', in the second 'of nature'. The idea is that of the successive birth, decay and new birth characteristic of the world around us. A man sees in a mirror the face which has come to be what it is through this process (1:23): 3:6 further brings out the sense of continuous process with the phrase 'the wheel' or 'course' of the changing world. There is abundant evidence in Philo for the contrast between *genesis*, the changing scene around us, and the eternity of God.

3. The word translated 'natural' in 1 Cor. 2:14; 15:44, 46 (AV) is the Greek *psychikos*. This adjective is used in the NT to refer to that which belongs to *psychē*, not in the most general sense of 'life', 'soul', but as it is distinguished from *pneuma*. *psychē* in this sense is the life of sensation, emotion, intellect apart from all conscious contact with God. The natural body of 1 Cor. 15 is a body which answers to the needs of this lower *psychē*; similarly, the spiritual body, otherwise undefined, will be a body not necessarily 'composed of spirit' but a fit 'vehicle', as it were, for the functioning of the spirit.

4. The words most frequently translated 'nature', 'natural', are *physis* and *physikos*. The basic meaning of *physis* is 'the process of growth' and hence that which

NATRON
See Nitre, Part 2.

Opposite page: A stone slab from Nazareth inscribed with a decree demanding the death penalty for anyone who broke the seals on a tomb and moved or stole a dead body. Some think this was set up in connection with charges against the disciples after the resurrection (Mt. 28:11–15). Height 0·61 m Nazareth. c. AD 50. (BN)

NATURE OF GOD
See God, Part 1.

NAZARAEANS
See Capernaum, Part 1.

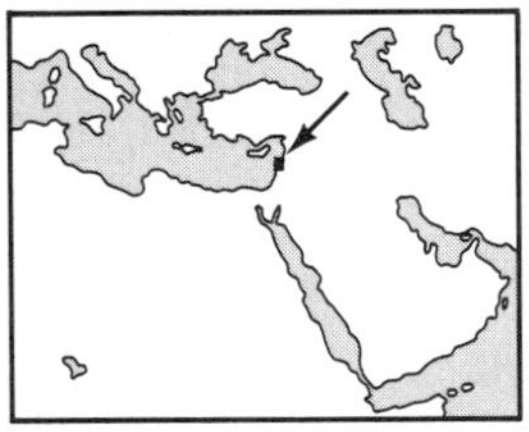

The location of Nazareth.

comes into being by such a process; *cf.* Rom. 11:21, 24 for the distinction between *physis*, the normal growth of a plant, and the results of grafting. Every order of beings has its own *physis*, Jas. 3:7 (*cf.* RV mg.); it is even possible to speak of the distinctive *physis* of God (2 Pet. 1:4), though no process of growth is conceivable within the divine Being itself.

The precise meaning of *physis, physikos*, is often determined by that with which *physis* is contrasted. Thus it may be regarded as characteristic of brute beasts as opposed to humanity (2 Pet. 2:12; Jude 10) or to be contrasted with that which is commonly but falsely believed (Gal. 4:8, Moffatt—'gods who are really', *physei*, 'no gods at all'; *cf.* 1 Cor. 8:5).

Of special importance are the Pauline uses of *physis* in contrast with (i) the perversions of Gentile society, (ii) the free grace of God in Christ and its consequences in man's life.

The former use is found in Rom. 1:26–27; sexual perversion is there viewed as a departure from the norm recognized by 'natural' man. The same idea is probably present in 1 Cor. 11:14, though here *physis* could have a reference to its primary sense 'the process of growth' and physiological facts about the length of uncut hair.

physis as distinguished from grace gives the Jew a place of comparative privilege (Gal. 2:15); it marks him off from the Gentile outside the covenant (Rom. 11:21, 24), though it does not of itself save. On the other hand, the Gentile, despite his not having the sign of the covenant and being, *ek physeōs*, uncircumcised, is sometimes able *physei* to do the works demanded by the law (Rom. 2:14, 27). Over against all privilege or good works, however, stands the fact that all men are *physei* children of wrath (Eph. 2:3). Thus *physis, physikos*, in these passages refer to all that belongs to the state of the world, Jewish and Gentile, apart from God's gracious act in Christ.

M.H.C.

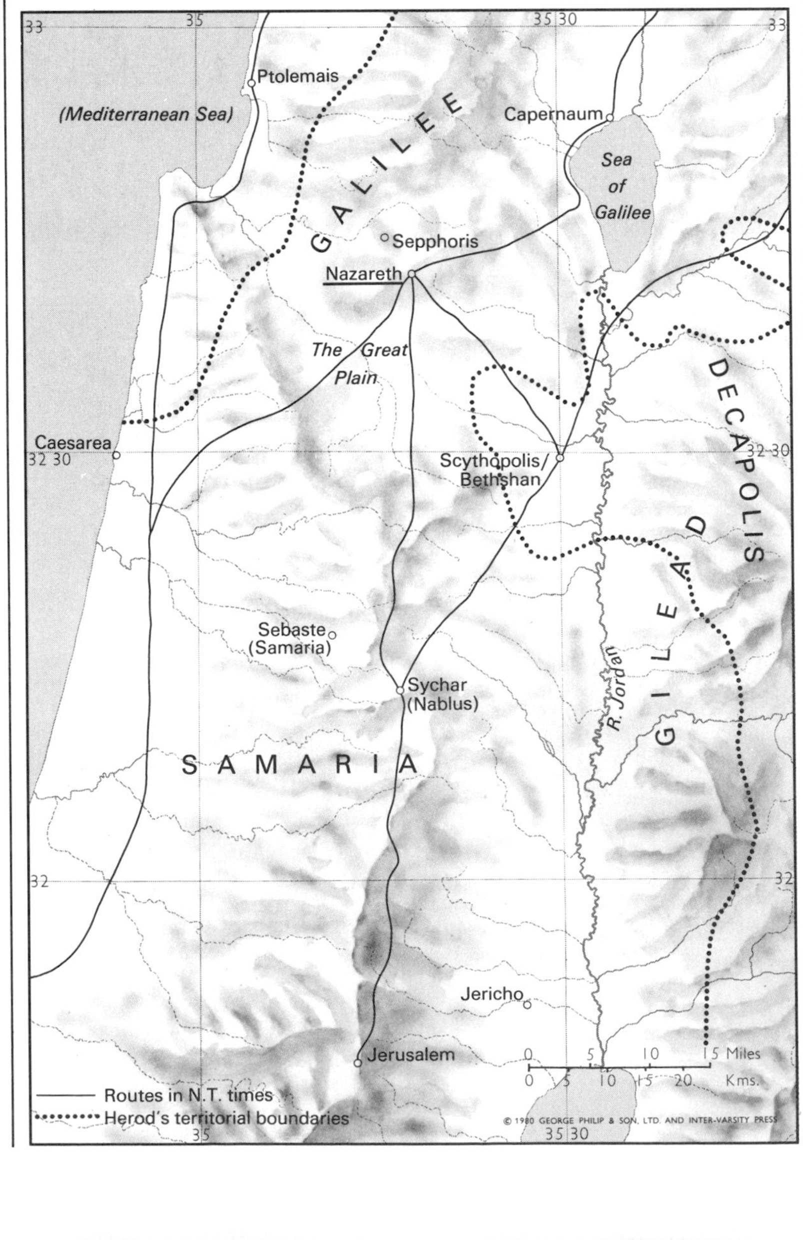

NAZARENE. According to Mk., the designation *Nazarēnos* was applied to our Lord by demons (1:24), the crowd (10:47), a domestic (14:67), and the messenger of the resurrection (16:6). It is used also in Lk. 4:34 (= Mk. 1:24) and Lk. 24:19 (the Emmaus disciples). But Mt., Lk. and Jn. normally employ *Nazōraios* (Mt. 26:71; Lk. 18:37; Jn. 18:5ff.; 19:19; Acts 2:22; 3:6; 4:10; 6:14; 22:8; 26:9). Both terms are translated in AV and RSV as 'of Nazareth'. *Nazōraios*, 'Nazarene', is applied also to Jesus in Mt. 2:23, and occurs as a popular designation of the Christian 'sect' in Acts 24:5. This is maintained in Jewish use (*cf.* the oldest Palestinian form of the *Shemoneh 'Esreh*, where at about AD 100 execration is pronounced on the *noṣrîm*) and in Arabic, apparently as a general designation for Christians (*cf.* R. Bell, *The Origin of Islam in its Christian Environment*, 1926, pp. 147ff.). The Christian Fathers knew of Jewish-Christian groups who called themselves 'Nazarenes' (Jerome, *De vir. ill.* 2–3, *Epist.* 20. 2) or 'Nazorenes' (Epiphanius, *Haer.* 29. 7, 9), and Epiphanius—never too reliable on such matters—mentions an aberrant Jewish sect, the Nasarenes (*Haer.* 1. 18).

In the NT the title is never applied to our Lord without the name 'Jesus', and to identify a man by his place of origin (*e.g.* John of Gischala) was a common Jewish practice. Linguistic objections have been raised, however, against deriving *Nazarēnos*, still more *Nazōraios*, from 'Nazareth', even issuing in a suggestion that Nazareth was created out of a misunderstanding of the title Nazorean (*cf.* E. Nestle, *ExpT* 19, 1907–8, pp. 523f.). These objections have been faithfully dealt with by G. F. Moore, but are still sometimes raised.

The allusion to *Nazōraios* as a title given to the Messiah in prophecy (Mt. 2:23) has been frequently taken as a reference to the 'Branch' (*nēṣer*) of Is. 11:1 and similar passages, or to the Nazirite (*nāzîr*, *cf.* Jdg. 13:7) in his character as God's holy one (*nāzîr* is used non-technically, and was perhaps interpreted Messianically, in Gn. 49:26; Dt. 33:16; see H. Smith, *JTS* 28, 1926, p. 60). Another ancient suggestion (Jerome, *in loc.*) is that Mt. alludes to the passages which speak of the Messiah as despised (*cf.* Jn. 1:46). At all events the different quotation formula in Mt. 2:23 from that in, *e.g.*, Mt. 1:22; 2:15, 17, suggests that a prophetic *theme*, not a specific prediction, is in mind.

The fact that the Mandaean Manichaean–Gnostic sect call themselves *Naṣorayya* has attracted attention. Moore has sufficiently disposed of the 'evidence' for a pre-Christian 'Nazarene' cult adapted to a Jewish *milieu*, but M. Black accepts Lidzbarski's derivation of *Naṣorayya* from *nāṣar*, 'to guard' (*sc.* the tradition), and points to the Mandaean claim to preserve the rites of John the Baptist. Rejecting on linguistic grounds any connection of *Nazōraios* with either *nēṣer* or *nāzîr*, he suggests the suitability of 'Nazarenes' as a title for the followers of John, that it is preserved by the Mandaeans and perhaps Epiphanius, and became applied to the 'Jesus-movement' which arose in the wake of John's. Ingenious as this is, it is perhaps over-subtle. It may be that word-play between *neṣer* or *nāzîr* or both and the name 'Nazareth' is all that is involved; and it is noteworthy that the Syriac versions, doubtless reflecting Aram. speech, spell Nazareth with *ṣ* not *z*. A different paronomasia is used in the Qur'an (*Sura* 3. 45; 11. 14), and yet another derivation has appeared in the Chenoboskion *Gospel of Philip*, Log. 47.

BIBLIOGRAPHY. G. F. Moore, *BC* 1, 1920, pp. 426ff.; W. O. E. Oesterley, *ExpT* 52, 1940–1, pp. 410ff.; W. F. Albright, 'The Names "Nazareth" and "Nazarene" ', *JBL* 65, 1946, pp. 397ff.; M. Black, *Aramaic Approach to the Gospels and Acts*[3], 1967, pp. 197ff. For the modern Mandaeans, see the works of Lady E. S. Drower, and especially *The Secret Adam*, 1960.

A.F.W.

NAZARETH. A town of Galilee where Joseph and Mary lived, and the home of Jesus for about 30 years until he was rejected (Lk. 2:39; 4:16, 28–31). He was therefore called Jesus of Nazareth. It is not mentioned in the OT, the Apocrypha, by Josephus, or in the Talmud. (The earliest Jewish reference to it is in a Hebrew inscription excavated at Caesarea in 1962, which mentions it as one of the places in Galilee to which members of the twenty-four priestly courses emigrated after the foundation of Aelia Capitolina in AD 135.) The

The valley between Nazareth and Cana. (SH)

Nazareth, situated among the southernmost hills of the Lebanon range. (RS)

reason for this was first geographical and later theological. Lower Galilee remained outside the main stream of Israelite life until NT times, when Rom. rule first brought security. Even then Sepphoris was the chief town of the area, a little to the N of Nazareth. But Nazareth lay close enough to several main trade-routes for easy contact with the outside world, while at the same time her position as a frontier-town on the S border of Zebulun overlooking the Esdraelon plain produced a certain aloofness. It was this independence of outlook in Lower Galilee which led to the scorn in which Nazareth was held by strict Jews (Jn. 1:46).

Nazareth is situated in a high valley among the most S limestone hills of the Lebanon range; it runs approximately from SSW to NNE. To the S there is a sharp drop down to the plain of Esdraelon. The base of the valley is 370 m above sea-level. Other hills rise on the N and E sides, while on the W side they reach up to 500 m and command an impressive view. Major roads from Jerusalem and Egypt debouched into the Esdraelon plain in the S; caravans from Gilead crossed the Jordan fords and passed below; the main road from Ptolemais to the Decapolis and the N, along which the Rom. legions travelled, passed a few kms above Nazareth. Such a location may have given rise to the name, which is possibly derived from the Aramaic *nāṣ^{e}raṯ*, 'watch-tower'. Another suggested derivation is from the Heb. *nēṣer*, 'shoot', advocated in Eusebius' *Onomasticon* and by Jerome (*Epist.* 46, *Ad Marcellam*). The mild climate in the valley causes wild flowers and fruit to flourish.

To judge by the rock-tombs, the early town was higher up the W hill than the present Nazareth. There are two possible water-supplies. The first, which is the larger, lies in the valley and has been called 'Mary's Well' since AD 1100, but there is no trace of early dwellings near by. The second is a very small fountain, called 'the New Well', in an angle formed by a projection of the W hill; the Byzantine church and town lay closer to this. The steep scarp of Jebel Qafsa, overlooking the plain, is traditionally but erroneously called 'the Mount of Precipitation', since this was not the hill 'on which their city was built' (Lk. 4:29).

BIBLIOGRAPHY. G. H. Dalman, *Sacred Sites and Ways*, 1935, pp. 57ff. J.W.C.

NAZIRITE (Heb. *nāzîr*, from *nāzar*, 'to separate, consecrate, abstain'; *cf. nēzer*, 'a diadem', the 'crown of God', sometimes identified with the Nazirite's uncut hair). In Israel the Nazirite was one who separated himself from others by consecration to Yahweh with a special vow.

The origin of the practice is pre-Mosaic and obscure. Semites and other primitive peoples often left the hair uncut during some undertaking calling for divine help, and thereafter consecrated the hair (*cf.* modern echoes of this among Arab tribes in A. Lods, *Israel*, 1932, p. 305; see also Jdg. 5:2).

I. Legislation in Numbers 6

Although chronologically not the first biblical reference to the subject, the rules for the Nazirite outlined in Nu. 6 provide the fullest and most convenient basis for discussion. The legislation has three sections.

a. Prohibitions

(i) The Nazirite had to abstain from wine and intoxicating drinks, vinegar and raisins. This may have been aimed at safeguarding the integrity and holiness of the Nazirite from possession by a spirit other than that of Yahweh (*cf.* Pr. 20:1). Like an officiating priest, the Nazirite renounced wine so as the more worthily to approach God. R. Kittel, however, sees in the abstention a protest against Canaanite culture, and a desire to return to nomadic customs (*Geschichte des Volkes Israel*[6], 2, 1925, p. 250).

(ii) He must not cut his hair during the time of consecration (*cf. nāzîr* = 'unpruned vine', Lv. 25:5, 11). The hair was regarded as the seat of life, 'the favourite abode of spirits and magical influences', to be kept in its natural state until its burning ensured its disappearance without fear of profanation.

(iii) He must not go near a dead body, even that of his nearest relation, a prohibition which applied also in the case of the high priest.

b. Violation

If the last-named rule were inadvertently broken, the Nazirite had to undergo closely-detailed purificatory rites, and to begin all over again. It is notable, however, that the terms of the Nazirite vow did not preclude the carrying out of other domestic and social duties.

c. Completion

At the end of his vow the Nazirite had to offer various prescribed sacrifices, and thereafter cut his hair and burn it on the altar. After certain ritual acts by the priest, the Nazirite was freed from his vow.

The distinctive features of the original Nazirate were a complete consecration to Yahweh, in which the body, not regarded merely as something to be restrained, was enlisted into holy service; an extension to the layman of a holiness usually associated only with the priest; and an individualistic character in contrast to groups such as * Rechabites.

II. Problems concerning the Nazirate

It is clear from the provisions in *c.* above that the Nazirate was for a fixed term only. But against that, and pre-dating the above legislation (for the dating of which, * NUMBERS, BOOK OF), there are instances during the pre-exilic era of parents dedicating children to be Nazirites all their lives. There is, for example, the consecration of Samuel (1 Sa. 1:11), who is not called a Nazirite in *MT* (but in a Qumran text, 4Q Sam^{a}, 1 Sa. 1:22 ends with the words, 'a Nazirite for ever all the days of his life'). There is also the express Nazirate of Samson (Jdg. 13), elements of whose story may date from the 10th century BC. That Samuel and Samson were Nazirites has been questioned (see G. B. Gray, *Numbers*, *ICC*, 1903, pp. 59–60). The Samson narrative conspicuously does not give the impression that he abstained from wine! It may be that the term 'Nazirite' was loosely applied to one devoted to Yahweh.

Absalom, moreover, has often been regarded as a type of perpetual Nazirite (for the cutting of the hair of such, see G. B. Gray, 'The Nazirite', *JTS* 1, 1900, p. 206). Amos, in whose day Nazirites appear to have been numerous, clearly speaks of Nazirites whom the people seek to deflect from their abstinence (2:11–12). During the whole pre-exilic period it is difficult to find direct evidence of temporary Nazirites.

III. Later developments

From the time of the Exile the Nazirate seems to have been for a fixed term only. Extraneous elements crept in, and no longer was the motive for taking the vow exclusively one of penitence and devotion. On occasion it was practised in order to gain certain favours from Yahweh (*cf.* Jos., *BJ* 2. 313, where Bernice undertakes a 30 days' vow), as a meritorious ritual activity, or even for a bet (Mishnah, *Nazir* 5. 5ff.). Wealthy Jews often financed the final sacrifice; Herod Agrippa I is said to have done so (Jos., *Ant.* 19. 293), and Paul was persuaded to perform this service for four members of the church of Jerusalem (Acts 21:23ff.; *cf.* 18:18 for Paul's personal undertaking of a Nazirite vow). Casuistry was inevitably introduced, and a special tractate of the Mishnah (*Nazir*) fixed the minimum duration of the Nazirate at 30 days.

From the references in Josephus it appears that Nazirites were a common feature of the contemporary scene. For the suggestion that John the Baptist and James the Lord's brother were Nazirites, and for the whole subject, see G. B. Gray, *JTS*, *art. cit.* J.D.D.

NEAPOLIS (the 'new city'). A town, mod. Kavalla, in Macedonia which served as the port of Philippi, 16 km inland. Originally thought to have been called Daton, it occupied a position on a neck of land between two bays, which gave it a useful harbour on both. Paul arrived here from Troas on his second missionary journey (Acts 16:11), after receiving his call to Macedonia. He may have visited it on his third journey also. J.H.P.

NEBAIOTH. The eldest son of Ishmael (Gn. 25:13; 28:9; 36:3; 1 Ch. 1:29). His descendants, an Arabian tribe mentioned in conjunction with Kedar in Is. 60:7 (the two are also named together in Assyr. records), are possibly to be identified with the later *Nabataeans (see *JSS* 18, 1973, pp. 1–16). J.D.D.

The symbol of the Babylonian god, Nabû (biblical Nebo). A wedge is here shown on a shrine base, as part of a boundary-stone of Nebuchadrezzar I. 12th cent. BC. (BM)

NEBAT. A name which occurs only in the phrase 'Jeroboam the son of Nebat' (1 Ki. 11:26, *etc.*), apparently to distinguish Jeroboam I from the later son of Joash. J.D.D.

NEBO (Heb. n^e*ḇô*). **1.** The Bab. deity Nabû, son of Bēl (Marduk), and thus descriptive of the power of Babylon itself (Is. 46:1). The name occurs as part of such appellatives as Nebuchadrezzar and perhaps *Abed-nego. Nabû was considered the god of learning and thus of writing, astronomy and all science. His symbol was a wedge upon a pole, signifying either the cuneiform script or a sighting instrument used in astronomy. He was the principal deity of Borsippa (12 km SSW of Babylon), but a temple Ezida ('the House of Knowledge') was dedicated to him in each of the larger cities of Babylonia and Assyria.

2. The (abbreviated?) name of the ancestor of Jews who married foreign women and thus incurred Ezra's displeasure (Ezr. 10:43). D.J.W.

NEBO. 1. Mt Nebo, from which Moses viewed the Promised Land, a prominent headland of the Transjordan plateau range, *Abarim, with which it is sometimes equated (Dt. 32:49; 34:1). Usually identified with Jebel en Neba, some 16 km E of the N end of the Dead Sea. It commands extensive views from Mt Hermon to the Dead Sea. Jebel Osha, about 45 km further N, is preferred by local Muslim tradition and some scholars (see G. T. Manley, *The Book of the Law*, 1957, pp. 163f.), but is outside the land of Moab. The original border was near Wadi Hesban (Nu. 21:26ff.; the *Moabite Stone also implies Jebel en Neba). (*Abarim, *Pisgah.)

2. A town in Moab (Nu. 32:3, 38; Is. 15:2), possibly Khirbet Ayn Musa or Khirbet el Mukkayet near Jebel en Musa. Taken by Mesha of Moab *c.* 830 BC.

3. A town in Judah (Ezr. 2:29; Ne. 7:33). G.G.G.

NEBUCHADREZZAR, NEBUCHADNEZZAR. The king of Babylon (605–562 BC) frequently named by the prophets Jeremiah, Ezekiel and Daniel, and in the his-

Mt Nebo (Jebel en Neba) in Jordan. (MEPhA)

tory of the last days of Judah. His name in Heb. (*n^{e}ḇūḵaḏre'ṣṣar*) transliterates the Bab. *Nabū-kudurri-uṣur*, meaning perhaps 'Nabû has protected the succession-rights'. The alternative Heb. rendering (*n^{e}būḵaḏne'ṣṣar*; *cf.* Gk. *Nabochodonosor*) is a not improper form of the name (*ZA* 65, 1975, pp. 227–230).

According to the Bab. Chronicle this son of the founder of the Chaldean dynasty, Nabopolassar, first commanded the Bab. army as 'crown-prince' in the fighting in N Assyria in 606 BC. In the following year he defeated Neco II and the Egyptians at Carchemish and Hamath (2 Ki. 23:29f.; 2 Ch. 35:20ff.; Je. 46:2). 'At this time he conquered the whole of Hatti' (*i.e.* Syria and Palestine, so Bab. Chronicle; 2 Ki. 24:7; Jos., *Ant.* 10. 86). Daniel was among hostages taken from Judah (Dn. 1:1), where Jehoiakim was in his 4th regnal year (Je. 36:1). While in the field Nebuchadrezzar heard of his father's death and rode across the desert to claim the Bab. throne, which he ascended on 6 September 605 BC.

In the following year, the first of his reign, Nebuchadrezzar received tribute in Syria from the kings of Damascus, Tyre and Sidon and others, including Jehoiakim, who was to remain his faithful vassal for

Kiln-fired brick, stamped with an inscription commemorating the rebuilding of the temples of Marduk (Esagila) and Nabū (Ezida) by Nebuchadrezzar II in Babylon (S Iraq). 602–562 BC. (BM)

only 3 years (2 Ki. 24:1; Je. 25:1). Ashkelon refused and was sacked. In the campaign of 601 BC the Babylonians were defeated by Egypt, whereupon Jehoiakim transferred his loyalty, despite the warnings of Jeremiah (27:9–11), to the victors. When his army had been re-equipped Nebuchadrezzar raided the Arab tribes of Qedar and E Jordan in 599/8 BC, as predicted by the same prophet (Je. 49:28–33), in preparation for subsequent reprisals on Jehoiakim and Judah (2 Ch. 36:6). Thus in his 7th year Nebuchadrezzar 'marched to Palestine and besieged the city of Judah which he captured on the second day of the month Adar' (= 16 March 597 BC). He then 'seized its king and appointed a king of his own choice, having received heavy tribute which he sent back to Babylon' (Bab. Chronicle B.M. 21946). This capture of Jerusalem and its king Jehoiachin (Jehoiakim's son and successor), the choice of Mattaniah-Zedekiah as his successor, and the taking of booty and prisoners, form the subject of the history recorded in 2 Ki. 24:10–17. Nebuchadrezzar removed the temple vessels to the temple of Bel-Marduk in Babylon (2 Ch. 36:7; 2 Ki. 24:13; Ezr. 6:5). The Judaean captives were marched off about April 597, 'in the spring of the year' (2 Ch. 36:10), which marked the beginning of his 8th regnal year (2 Ki. 24:12). Jehoiachin and other Jewish captives are named in inscriptions from Babylon dated in the years of this Bab. king (*ANET*, p. 308; *DOTT*, pp. 83–86).

In 596 BC Nebuchadrezzar fought with Elam (so also Je. 49:34), and in the next year mastered a rebellion in his own country. Thereafter Bab. historical texts are wanting, but in his 17th–19th years he campaigned again in the W. From his headquarters at Riblah he directed the operations which led to the sack of Jerusalem in 587 BC and the capture of the rebel Zedekiah (Je. 39:5–6; ch. 52). For a time the siege was raised when Apries, the successor of Neco II of Egypt, invaded Phoenicia and Gaza (Je. 47:1). In Nebuchadrezzar's 23rd year (582) a further deportation of Judaeans to Babylon was ordered (Je. 52:30). About this time also the 13-year siege of *Tyre was undertaken (Ezk. 26:7).

A fragmentary Bab. text tells of Nebuchadrezzar's invasion of Egypt in 568/7 BC (*cf*. Je. 43:8–13). Since little is yet known of the last 30 years of his reign, there is no corroboration of his madness which occurred for 7 months (or 'times') as recorded in Dn. 4:23–33. With the aid of his wife Amytis, he undertook the rebuilding and

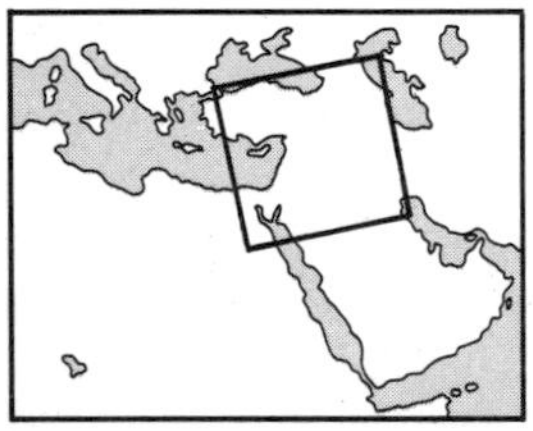

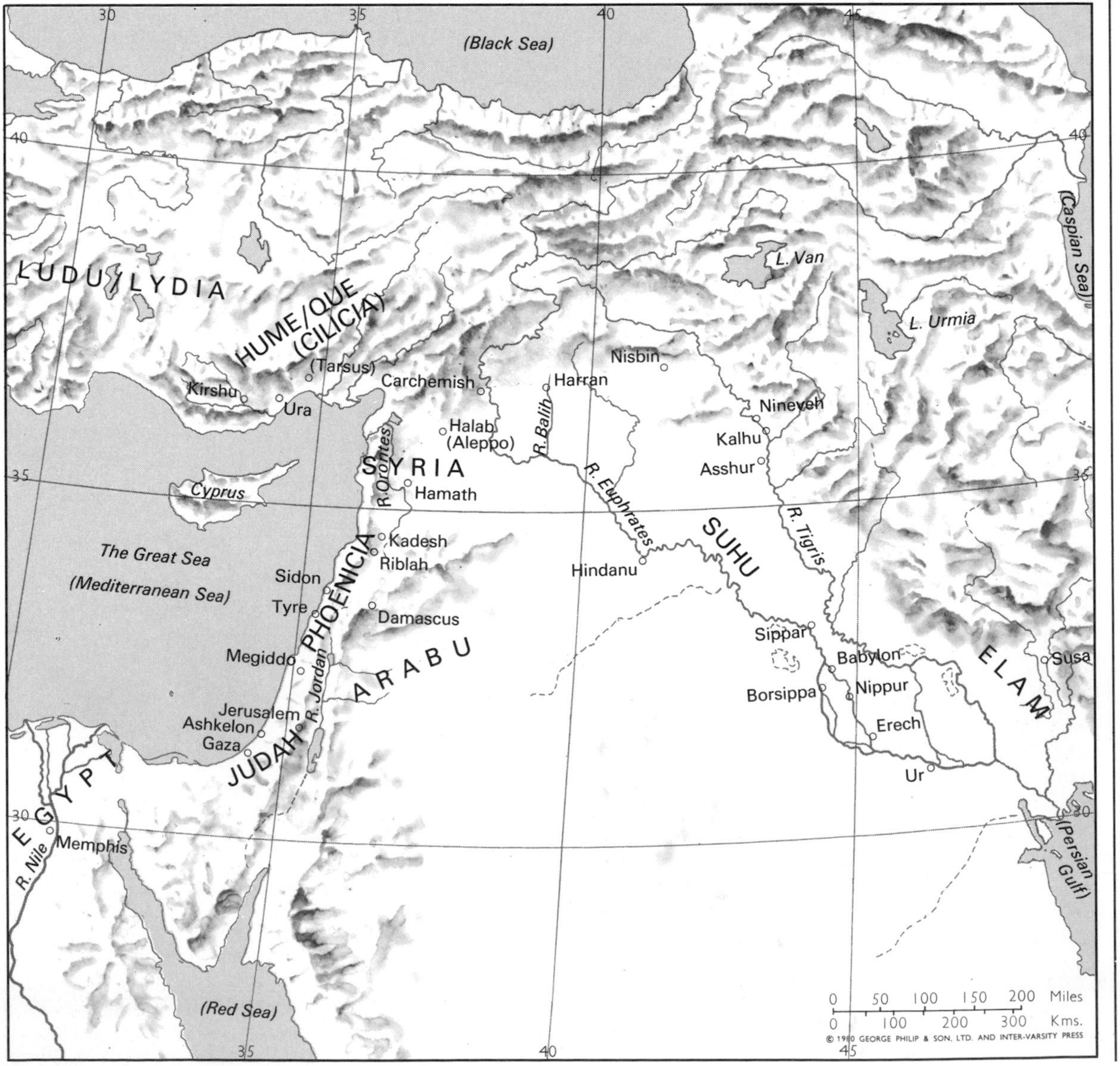

The area of Babylonian (Chaldean) influence in the time of Nebuchadrezzar II.

The Ishtar gate at Babylon of the time of Nebuchadrezzar II (605–562 BC*), reconstructed from the archaeological evidence.* (SAOB)

NEBUSHAZBAN See Sarsechim, Part 3.

embellishment of his capital Babylon. A religious man, he rebuilt the temples of Marduk and Nabû with many shrines in * Babylon and provided regular offerings and garments for the divine statues (*cf.* the golden image of Dn. 3:1). He also restored temples in Sippar, Marad and Borsippa and boasted of his achievements, especially in the two defence walls, the gateway of Ishtar, the ziggurat and the sacred processional way through his own city, which he provided with new canals (Dn. 4:30). Some of his architectural works were classed among the seven wonders of the world. Herodotus calls both Nebuchadrezzar and Nabonidus (556–539) by the name of Labynetus. Nebuchadrezzar died in August–September 562 BC and was succeeded by his son Amēl-Marduk (* EVIL-MERODACH).

BIBLIOGRAPHY. D. J. Wiseman, *Chronicles of Chaldaean Kings*, 1956; A. Malamat, 'A New Record of Nebuchadrezzar's Palestinian Campaigns', *IEJ* 6, 1956, pp. 246–256. D.J.W.

NECK. 1. Heb. *'ōrep̄* is used of the neck, or back of the neck; it is also translated 'back', when used of enemies turning their back in flight (*e.g.* Ex. 23:27). It is used of similar ideas in respect of conflict (Gn. 49:8; Jb. 16:12), and also in the descriptive metaphor of the hardened or stiffnecked, meaning obstinate or rebellious (Dt. 31:27; 2 Ki. 17:14; Is. 48:4).

2. Heb. *gārôn* is also used, meaning the front of the neck (Is. 3:16; Ezk. 16:11), or throat (Ps. 5:9; Je. 2:25), and so voice (Is. 58:1, 'cry aloud', lit. 'with your throat').

3. The commonest Heb. word is *ṣawwā'r*, used of the neck generally; bearing a yoke, symbolizing servitude (Gn. 27:40; Je. 30:8); wearing a necklace (Gn. 41:42); of falling on a person's neck in embrace (Gn. 33:4), or of the neck placed under the * foot of a conqueror (Jos. 10:24).

4. Gk. *trachēlos* is used of embrace (Lk. 15:20), of being under a yoke (Acts 15:10), or of wearing a millstone, a large flat stone with a hole in the centre, to weigh the body down (Mt. 18:6). Paul also speaks of risking the neck in respect of the custom of beheading (Rom. 16:4). From *trachēlos* comes the verb *trachēlizō*, 'to expose the neck or throat', used in the perfect participle passive in Heb. 4:13 in the sense of 'laid bare'. B.O.B.

NECO, NECHO. Egyp. *Nl-k'w*, Gk. *Nechao*. Pharaoh of Egypt *c.* 610–595 BC, and son and successor of Psammetichus I, the founder of the 26th Dynasty. In 609 BC, following his father's policy of maintaining a balance of power in W Asia (* EGYPT. History), Neco II marched into Syria to assist Aššur-uballiṭ II, last king of Assyria, against Babylon. But Josiah of Judah forced a battle with Neco at Megiddo; this delay of Egyp. help for the Assyrians sealed their fate at the cost of Josiah's own life (2 Ki. 23:29; 2 Ch. 35:20–24). On his return S, Neco deposed and deported Josiah's son Jehoahaz and appointed instead another son, Jehoiakim, as vassal-king in Jerusalem, which was obliged to pay tribute to Egypt (2 Ki. 23:31–35; 2 Ch. 36:1–4). Egypt claimed Palestine as her share of the former Assyr. empire, but in the battle of Carchemish, in May/June 605 BC, Nebuchadrezzar stormed that Egyp. outpost and pursued the remnants of the Egyp. forces through Syria as they scurried home to Egypt; Judah thus exchanged an Egyp. for a Bab. master (2 Ki. 24:1, 7).

Neco wisely desisted from any further Palestinian adventures. But the Bab. Chronicle shows that in 601 BC Nebuchadrezzar marched against Egypt; Neco met him in open battle, and both sides suffered heavy losses. Nebuchadrezzar therefore had to spend the next year at home in Babylon to refit his army. This Egyp. rebuff for the Babylonians perhaps tempted Jehoiakim to revolt against Baby-

lon as recorded in 2 Ki. 24:1, but no help came from neutral Egypt.

At home, Neco II followed his father's policy of fostering Egypt's internal unity and prosperity, granting trading-concessions to Gk. merchants to this end. He undertook the cutting of a canal from the Nile to the Red Sea, completed by Darius the Persian, and sent out a Phoenician fleet that circumnavigated Africa as recorded by Herodotus (4. 42), whose scepticism of this achievement is refuted by its cause, namely, that the voyagers reported that the sun eventually rose on their right hand.

Bibliography. For Neco, see Drioton and Vandier, *L'Égypte*, Coll. Clio, 1952; H. De Meulenaere, *Herodotos over de 26ste Dynastie*, 1951. For his conflicts with Babylon, see D. J. Wiseman, *Chronicles of Chaldaean Kings (626–556 BC)*, 1956. C.D.W.

NEGEB. Heb. *neḡeḇ*, 'the dry', refers to the S lands of Palestine. Misconceptions arise from its translation as 'the South' in both AV and RV, where some forty passages have described it inaccurately in this way. An indefinite region, it covers *c.* 1,200,000 hectares (4,520 sq. mls) or nearly half the area of modern Israel. The N boundary may be drawn conveniently S of the Gaza–Beersheba road, roughly the 20 cm-mean annual isohyet, then due E of Beersheba to the Dead Sea through Ras ez-Zuweira. The S boundary which merged traditionally into the highlands of the Sinai Peninsula is now drawn politically S of the Wadi el-Arish to the head of the Gulf of Aqabah at Eilat. The Wadi Arabah, now the political frontier with Jordan, is overlooked to the E by the Arabah escarpment, the traditional boundary. For the description of the geographical features to the Negeb, see *Palestine.

Mention of the Negeb is almost entirely confined to pre-exilic times, apart from allusions in Zc. 7:7 and Ob. 20. Five districts in the N Negeb are referred to: the Negeb of Judah, of the Jerahmeelites, of the Kenites (1 Sa. 27:10), of the Cherethites and of Caleb (1 Sa. 30:14). These occupied the grazing and agricultural lands between Beersheba and Bir Rikhmeh and the W slopes of the central highlands of Khurashe-Kurnub. This district was settled by the Amalekites (Nu. 13:29), the ruins of whose fortified

Pharaoh Neco II of Egypt is shown on a fragment of temple relief (lower right) *beneath the cartouche giving his name and titles. Limestone. Height of fragment 14·6 cm. Probably Lower Egypt. 26th Dynasty. 610–595 BC.* (WAG)

Opposite page:
Bronze beam-holder, inscribed in hieroglyphs with the name of Pharaoh Neco II of Egypt (610–595 BC). Height c. 20 cm. (BM)

NEEDLE'S EYE
See Eye of a needle, Part 1.

NEEDLEWORK
See Embroidery, Part 1.

Typical barren landscape of parts of the Negeb. (MEPhA)

Opposite page: Plan of Jerusalem under Nehemiah.

sites are still seen between Tell Arad (Nu. 21:1; 33:40), 32 km E of Beersheba and Tell Jemmeh or Gerar (Gn. 20:1; 26:1). At the Exodus the spies had been awed by their defences (Nu. 13:17–20, 27–29), which lasted until the early 6th century BC, when they were probably destroyed finally by the Babylonians (Je. 13:19; 33:13). The sites of the twenty-nine cities and their villages in the Negeb (Jos. 15:21–32) are unknown, only Beersheba ('well of seven', or 'well of oath', Gn. 21:30), Arad, Khirbet Ar'areh or Aroer (1 Sa. 30:28). Fein or Penon (Nu. 33:42), and Tell el-Kheleifeh or Ezion-geber, having been identified.

The strategic and economic importance of the Negeb has been significant. The 'Way of Shur' crossed it from central Sinai NE to Judaea (Gn. 16:7; 20:1; 25:18; Ex. 15:22; Nu. 33:8), a route followed by the Patriarchs (Gn. 24:62; 26:22), by Hadad the Edomite (1 Ki. 11:14, 17, 21–22), and probably the escape route used by Jeremiah (43:6–12) and later by Joseph and Mary (Mt. 2:13–15). The route was dictated by the zone of settled land where well-water is significant, hence the frequent references to its wells (*e.g.* Gn. 24:15–20; Jos. 15:18–19; Jdg. 1:14–15). Uzziah reinforced the defence of Jerusalem by establishing cultivation and defensive settlements in his exposed S flank of the N Negeb (2 Ch. 26:10). It seems clear from the history of the Near East that the Negeb was a convenient vacuum for resettlement whenever population pressure forced out migrants from the Fertile Crescent. Also significant was the location of copper ores in the E Negeb and its trade in the Arabah. Control of this industry explains the Amalekite and Edomite wars of Saul (1 Sa. 14:47f.) and the subsequent victories of David over the Edomites (1 Ki. 11:15f.). It also explains the creation by Solomon of the port of Ezion-geber, and, when it was silted up, the creation of a new port at Elath by Uzziah (1 Ki. 9:26; 22:48; 2 Ki. 14:22). The abiding hatred of the Edomites is explained by the struggles to control this trade (*cf.* Ezk. 25:12 and the book of Obadiah).

Between the 4th century BC and the beginning of the 2nd century AD, when the Nabataeans finally disappeared, these Semitic people of S Arabian origin created a brilliant civilization of small hydraulic works in the Negeb. Deployed across the strategic trade routes between Arabia and the Fertile Crescent, they waxed rich on the spice and incense trade of Arabia, and other exotic goods from Somaliland and India. Later, in the Christian era, the Negeb became a stronghold of Christianity. Glueck has identified some 300 early Christian Byzantine sites in the Negeb, dating from the 5th and 6th centuries AD.

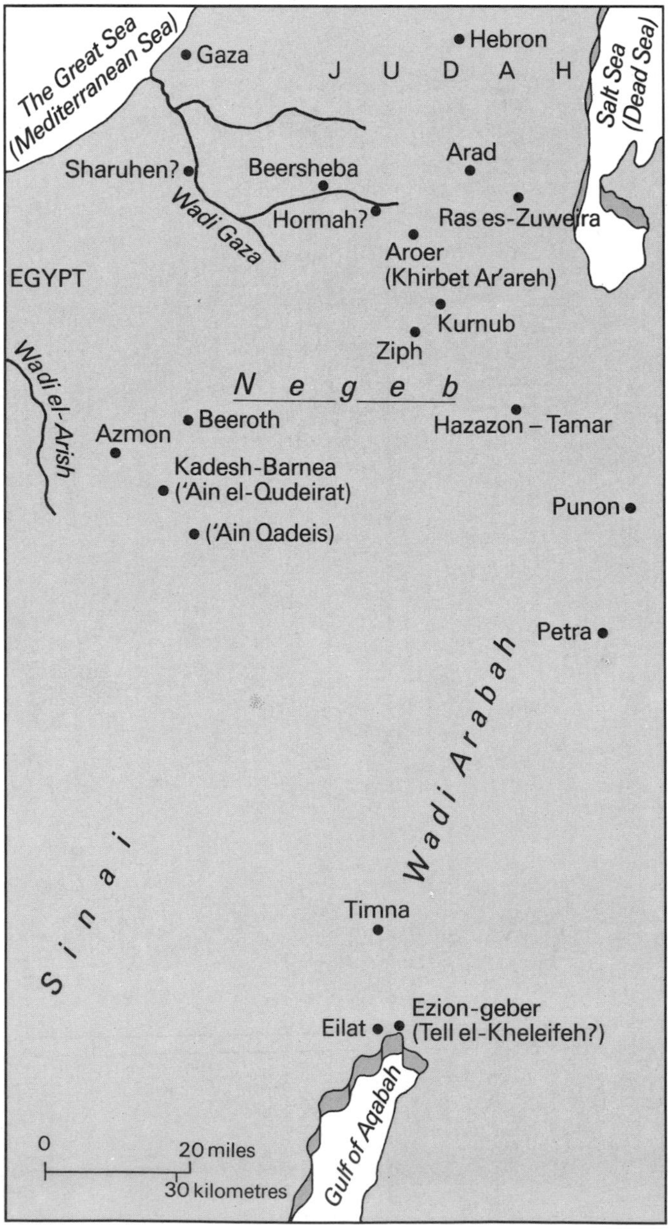

The Negeb.

BIBLIOGRAPHY, For the occupation of the Negeb at various archaeological periods, see *ARCHAEOLOGY; Y. Aharoni, *IEJ* 8, 1958, pp. 26ff.; 10, 1960, pp. 23ff., 97ff.; N. Glueck, *Rivers in the Desert*, 1959; *idem, Deities and Dolphins* (*The story of the Nabataeans*), 1966; C. L. Woolley and T. E. Lawrence, *The Wilderness of Zin*, 1936. J.M.H.

NEHELAM. Family name or place of origin of Shemaiah, a false prophet who withstood Jeremiah (Je. 29:24, 31f. The name is otherwise unknown. V. 24 AVmg. renders the word as 'dreamer', thus implying some connection with Heb. *ḥālam*, 'to dream'. M. F. Unger suggests a punning allusion to the dreams of the false prophets. J.D.D.

NEHEMIAH. Our only knowledge of Nehemiah comes from the book that bears his name. He was cupbearer to the Persian king, Artaxerxes I (465–424 BC). This was a privileged position. Since there is no mention of his wife, it is likely that he was a eunuch. On receiving news of the desolate state of Jerusalem (probably the result of the events of Ezr. 4:7–23), he obtained permission to go to his own country, and was appointed governor. In spite of intense opposition (*SANBALLAT, *TOBIAH), he and the Jews rebuilt the walls of Jerusalem in 52 days. He and the other Jews then called on Ezra to read the Law, and pledged themselves to observe its commands. During his absence in Persia, some of the abuses that he had put down reappeared, and on his return he had to carry out fresh reforms. His personal memoirs occupy a large part of the book of Nehemiah, and they reveal him as a man of prayer, action and devotion to duty.

For dating his movements we have the following references:

2:1. His appointment as governor in 445 BC.
5:14; 13:6. His return to Persia in 433 BC.
13:7. His return to Jerusalem 'after certain days' (AV).

The suggestion in 2:6 is that his first appointment was short, and he may have returned to Persia for a brief time between 445 and 433 BC. Since his absence from Jerusalem in 13:6 was long enough for considerable abuses to arise, and for the Levites to be driven out to work in the fields, we must conclude that the 'certain days' were at least 18 months, and possibly more. J.S.W.

NEHEMIAH, BOOK OF.

I. Outline of contents

a. Nehemiah's mission (1:1–7:73a)

i. Nehemiah hears news from Jerusalem (1:1–11).

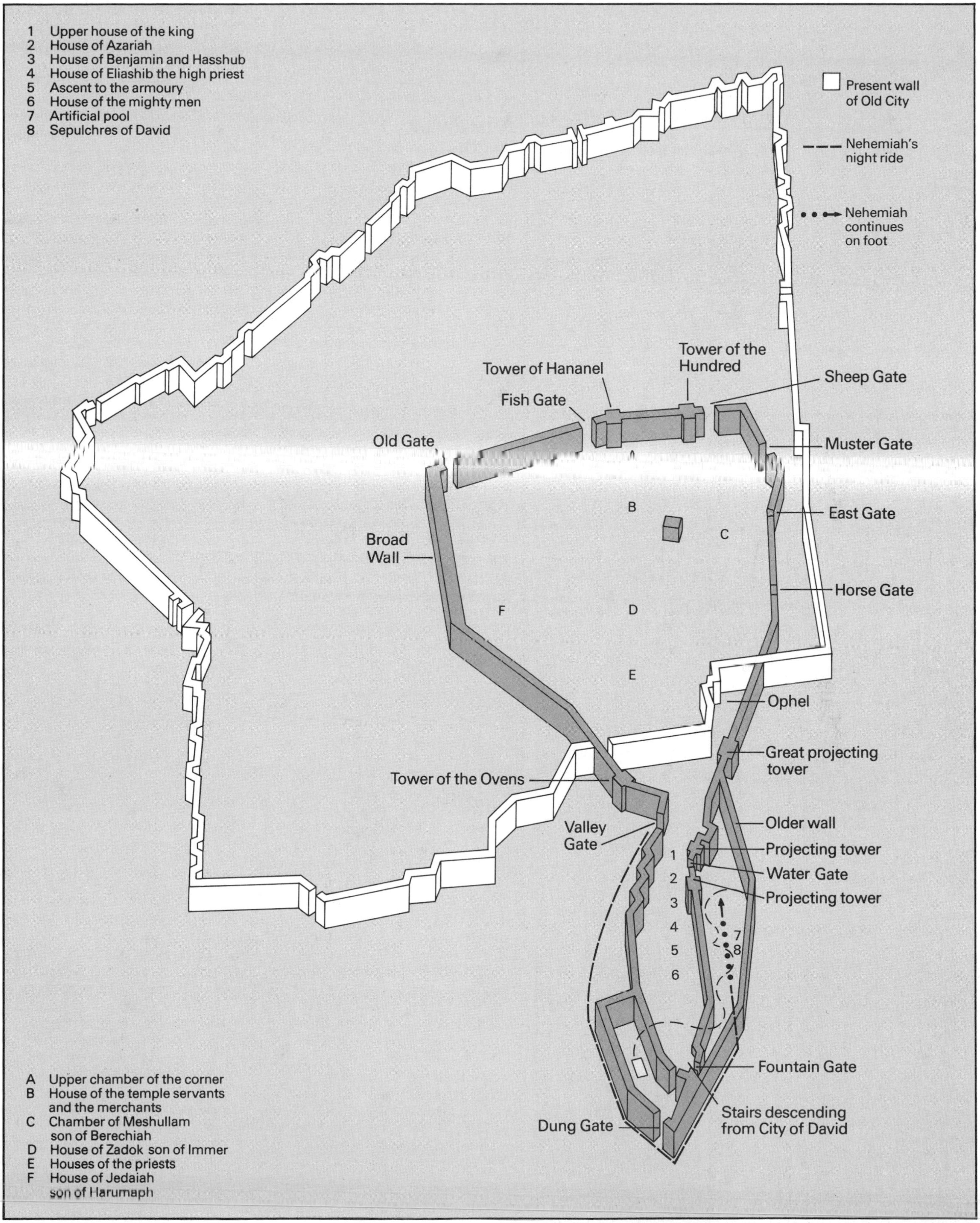
1 Upper house of the king
2 House of Azariah
3 House of Benjamin and Hasshub
4 House of Eliashib the high priest
5 Ascent to the armoury
6 House of the mighty men
7 Artificial pool
8 Sepulchres of David
Present wall of Old City
Nehemiah's night ride
Nehemiah continues on foot
Tower of Hananel
Tower of the Hundred
Sheep Gate
Fish Gate
Old Gate
Muster Gate
East Gate
Broad Wall
Horse Gate
Ophel
Great projecting tower
Tower of the Ovens
Valley Gate
Older wall
Projecting tower
Water Gate
Projecting tower
Fountain Gate
Stairs descending from City of David
Dung Gate
A Upper chamber of the corner
B House of the temple servants and the merchants
C Chamber of Meshullam son of Berechiah
D House of Zadok son of Immer
E Houses of the priests
F House of Jedaiah son of Harumaph

ii. He receives permission to visit Jerusalem (2:1–8).
iii. He arrives in Jerusalem, and makes plans to rebuild the walls (2:9–20).
iv. The list of wall-builders, with their allotted sections of wall (3:1–22).
v. Opposition from the Samaritans (4:1–23).
vi. Economic difficulties and Nehemiah's solution (5:1–13).
vii. Nehemiah's behaviour as governor (5:14–19).
viii. The wall is completed, in spite of plots against Nehemiah (6:1–19).
ix. Preparations for the re-peopling of Jerusalem (7:1–73a).

b. Ezra's work (continued from Ezr. 7–10) (7:73b–9:37)

i. Ezra's reading of the law (7:73b–8:12).
ii. Celebration of the festival of booths (8:13–18).
iii. A day of repentance and its penitential psalm (9:1–37).

c. Nehemiah's community (9:38–13:31)

i. The pledge of reform (9:38–10:39)
ii. The population of Jerusalem and Judaea (11:1–36).
iii. The clergy of the post-exilic community (12:1–26).
iv. The dedication of the wall (12:27–43).
v. An ideal community (12:44–13:3).
vi. Reforms during Nehemiah's second governorship (13:4–31).

II. Composition

It is commonly thought that the book of Nehemiah originally formed part of the Chronicler's work, which included also the books of 1 and 2 *Chronicles and *Ezra. Very little, however, of the book of Nehemiah was especially composed by the Chronicler (12:44–47 is probably one such passage), since he had ample source materials at his disposal.

Chief among these were the 'memoirs' of Nehemiah (Ne. 1:1–7:73a; 11:1–2; 12:31–43; 13:4–31), which may more properly be regarded as Nehemiah's formal record of his activities presented to God for his approval (note the places where Nehemiah appeals to God to 'remember' him: 5:19; 13:14, 22, 31). This first-person narrative is unique in the OT as a record made by a leading Jewish statesman about affairs he was personally involved in; though Nehemiah obviously looks at matters from his own point of view, there can be little serious doubt about the authenticity of this record. It has been subject to practically no editorial revision, and its simple and direct style marks it off quite clearly from the work of the Chronicler.

The other main source of the book is a section of the Ezra narrative (Ne. 8–9) which is inserted within the story of Nehemiah either because the activity of Ezra and Nehemiah overlapped or because the Chronicler has arranged his material thematically. The first explanation, though the most natural, creates the difficulty that though Ezra had been sent by the Persian emperor in 458 BC to proclaim the Pentateuchal law to the Jews, it was not until Nehemiah's arrival in 444 BC that he read it publicly to the people. The second explanation would imply that the Chronicler regarded the work of Ezra and Nehemiah as an integral whole; he then showed in his account that the community that came to live within the walls of rebuilt Jerusalem (Ne. 11:1–2) was united in its allegiance to the law of Moses (Ne. 8), penitent for its disobedience to that law (Ne. 9), and resolved to maintain its fidelity to the smallest detail of the law (Ne. 10).

Other sources used by the compiler of the book were lists of various kinds:

a. Wall-builders (Ne. 3). This may have been included in Nehemiah's 'memoirs'.

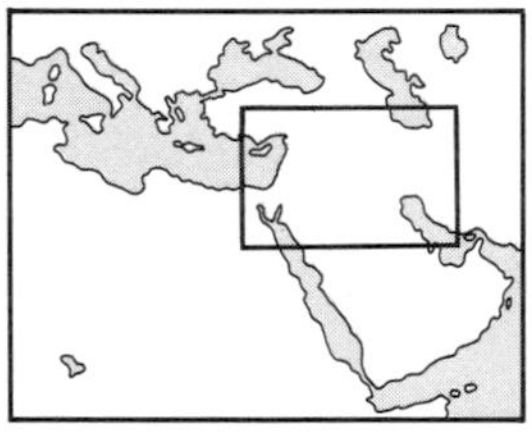

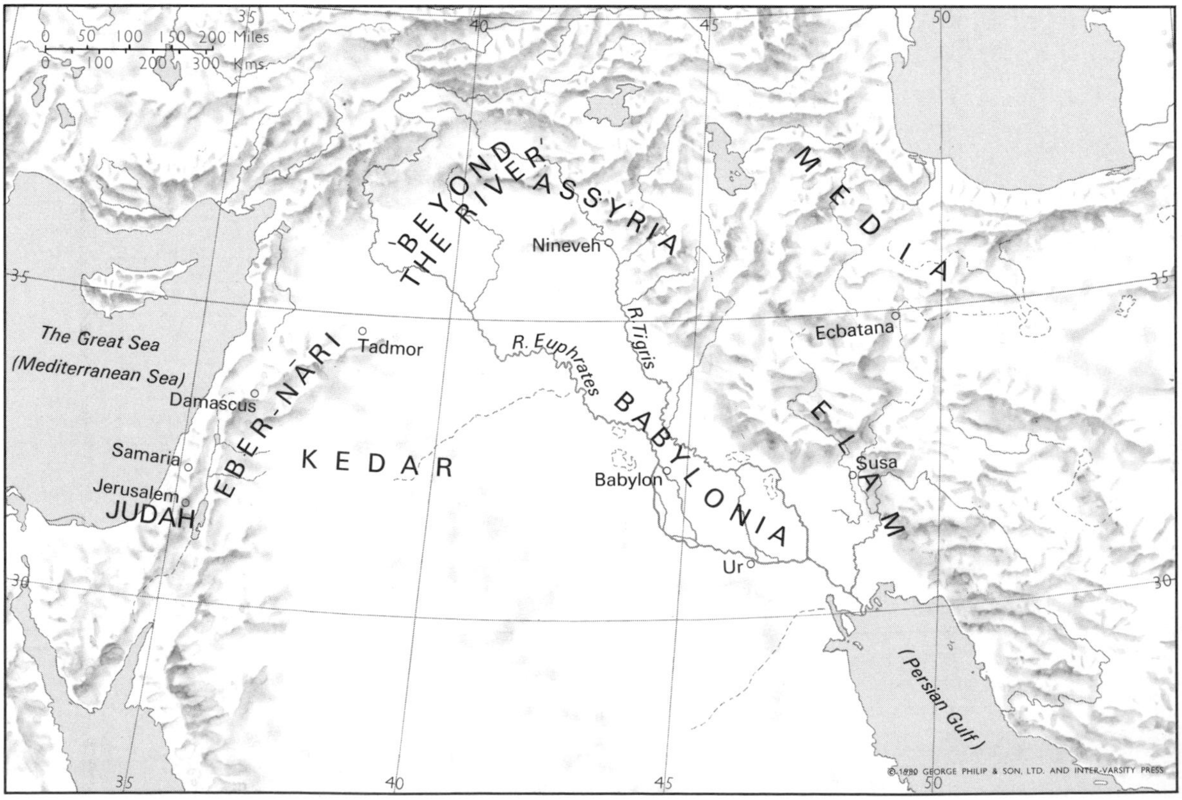

The Persian Empire at the time of Nehemiah.

Part of the wall of Jerusalem rebuilt by Nehemiah. (KK)

b. Returned exiles (7:6–73a). The same list, with minor variations, is found in Ezr. 2. It was apparently used by Nehemiah to prove the pure Jewish ancestry of the intended inhabitants of Jerusalem.

c. Signatories of the pledge to observe the Mosaic law (9:38–10:27), together with various particular interpretations of the law which the community bound itself to obey (10:28–39). This pledge seems to reflect reforms undertaken by Nehemiah during his second governorship (Ne. 13).

d. Family heads resident in Jerusalem (11:3–19).

e. Country towns with Jewish population (11:25–36).

f. Priests, Levites and high priests (12:1–26).

III. Message of the book

If, as most believe, Nehemiah formed part of the Chronicler's history (*CHRONICLES, BOOKS OF), its significance must be assessed within the context of the whole work. The Chronicler's purpose, broadly speaking, was to show that the Judaean community of his own time, probably the 4th century BC, was the legitimate heir of the promises made by God to Israel and to the Davidic dynasty. Although there was no longer a Davidic king, in the Chronicler's view the chief function of the Davidic kingship had been the establishment of the Temple and its worship; now that the Temple is restored, the worship of God can be carried on effectively by the community itself without the presence of a king. Characteristically, the Chronicler concludes his history proper with an almost idyllic picture of pure and joyful worship in the restored Temple, its clergy being willingly maintained by the tithes of the people (12:44–47). After his long story of Israel's disappointments, failures and grim periods of judgment, the finale to his history must have brought reassurance to his own community. Though they were only a tiny enclave in a vast Gentile empire, they could at least have the satisfaction of knowing that they were under the immediate leadership of men of God's choice and that they were fulfilling the purpose for which Israel had been created: the worship of God. Such a message can of course lead to self-congratulation and laxity. We have no way of knowing how the Chronicler's readers reacted to his encouragement, but it is worth while knowing that the people of God does not have to be always castigating itself, but is sometimes entitled to rejoice in what it has achieved.

As for the 'memoirs' of Nehemiah, which, apart from the lists, form the bulk of the book, their original purpose may well have been a kind of report such as a civil servant might make to his superior, in this case God. When Nehemiah's 'report' was read by others, they would have seen in it a revealing picture of a man of spirit, haughty and quick-tempered, and over-suspicious, no doubt, but passionately concerned for the well-being of his people (chs. 1–2), quick to respond to the appeals of brotherhood (ch. 5) and zealous for the purity of Jewish worship (13:4–9); above all, a leader who was the opposite of a self-made man, one who was always conscious of the 'good hand' and the 'fear' of his God upon him (2:8; 5:15; *cf.* 2:12, 18; 4:9, 14–15, 20; 6:9).

NEHUSHTAN
See Serpent, bronze, Part 3.

NEPHISIM
See Naphish, Part 2.

NEPHRITE
See Jewels, Part 2.

NEPHUSHESIM
See Naphish, Part 2.

NERIGLISSAR
See Nergal-sharezer, Part 2.

NERIYAH
See Lamp, Part 2.

BIBLIOGRAPHY. J. M. Myers, *Ezra, Nehemiah, AB*, 1965; U. Kellermann, *Nehemia. Quellen Überlieferung und Geschichte*, 1967; L. H. Brockington, *Ezra, Nehemiah and Esther, NCB*, 1969; P. R. Ackroyd, *I and II Chronicles, Ezra, Nehemiah, TBC*, 1973; D. Kidner, *Ezra and Nehemiah, TOTC*, 1979.
D.J.A.C.

NEHUSHTA (Heb. *neḥuštā'*). The wife of Jehoiakim and mother of Jehoiachin, a native of Jerusalem (2 Ki. 24:8) who was taken prisoner with her son when the Babylonians captured the city in 597 BC (v. 12; also Jos., *Ant.* 10. 84ff.). Her name may allude to her complexion (*cf.* Jb. 6:12) or to bronze (Heb. *neḥūšâ*) or even to the *serpent. Heb. personal names relating to colours, metals (*BARZILLAI) or to animals are typical of this period. D.J.W.

NEIGHBOUR. In the OT 'neighbour' translates the Heb. *šāḵēn*, *'āmîṯ*, *qārôḇ* and *rēa'*. In Lv. 19:18 LXX has *ho plēsion*. In the NT (in which this commandment is quoted eight times) Luke and John alone use the words *geitōn* and *perioikos*; elsewhere (and also Lk. 10:27–36; Acts 7:27) the LXX expression appears.

The Heb. *rēa'* is of more general application than English 'neighbour'. It is used, even of inanimate objects (Gn. 15:10), in the expression 'one *another*'; but it is also used in the sense of 'bosom friend' (Pr. 27:10), 'lover' (Ct. 5:16), even 'husband' (Je. 3:20). Like *'āmîṯ*, *rēa'* is almost exclusively used in contexts where moral principles are in question (*qārôḇ* and *šāḵēn* expressing mere geographical or physical proximity). Of passages where *rēa'* is defined in the context (*i.e.* refers to particular people) there are only three (1 Sa. 15:28; 28:17; 2 Sa. 12:11) which do not admit the translation 'friend', and these are all susceptible of ironical interpretation. Thus it is either used definitely, in which case it means one who has acted—or *surprisingly* has not acted (Ps. 38:11)—in the appropriate manner, hence a 'friend'; or indefinitely of those towards whom appropriate behaviour is due. *rēa'* is often found in parallel with *'āḥ*, 'brother', and the Bible uses this dichotomy of other people in a developing series of senses. Thus a relative is contrasted with another within the clan, a fellow Hebrew with a Gentile, and finally a fellow Christian with an unbeliever.

It is important to love those to whom one has a natural or covenanted obligation, but it is as important to love those with whom one's only contact is through circumstances: the distinct ideas *ḥeseḏ* and *'ahᵃḇâ* ('covenant' and 'elective' love—*cf.* N. H. Snaith, *Distinctive Ideas of the Old Testament*, 1944, pp. 94–95) merge in the NT into the one *agapē* required of a Christian both to those within and without the church. The Bible teaches this in the following ways:

1. It praises those who were exemplary neighbours to those whom they might have been expected to hate: particularly *cf.* Rahab's treatment of the spies (Jos. 2:1); Ruth's refusal to desert her mother-in-law, though in a sense free from obligation after the death of her husband (the whole story is most instructive in this connection, and it is perhaps no accident that 'Ruth' is the abstract noun from the same root as *rēa'*); the widow's entertainment of Elijah (implicity compared with the unclean birds [1 Ki. 17:6] who fed him: Zarephath was in the territory of Sidon from which Jezebel came).

2. It rebukes the proud independence of the Jew (*cf.* Am. 2:6ff.; Is. 1:17; Jonah *passim*; Jb. 12:2).

3. In the parable of the Good Samaritan an explicit epitome of biblical teaching is given which combines **1** and **2**. To the question, 'Who is my neighbour?' Jesus replies, 'Who proved neighbour to the man who fell among the robbers?' (Lk. 10:36).

BIBLIOGRAPHY. U. Falkenroth, *NIDNTT* 1, pp. 258f. J.B.J.

NEPHTOAH. Mentioned only in the expression 'the spring of the Waters of Nephtoah' (Jos. 15:9; 18:15). The context shows that it was on the borders of Judah and Benjamin. It is usually identified with Lifta, a village 4 km NW of Jerusalem. The linguistic equation Nephtoah = Lifta is very doubtful, but no other site seems to have strong claims. L.M.

NEREUS. A Christian greeted with his sister (not named, but conceivably Nereis) in Rom. 16:15. He is grouped with three others and 'the saints which are with them', perhaps because they belonged to the same house-church. The name (a Greek sea-god) is found in many areas, usually of freedmen and the lower orders (including slaves of 'Caesar's household'). Strangely, Paul's friend seems not to have been assimilated to the early Roman martyr commemorated in the Acts of SS. Nereus and Achilleus (*Acta Sanctorum*, 3, Maii, pp. 4f.; *cf.* Lightfoot, *Clement*, 1, pp. 42ff., especially p. 51n.). A.F.W.

NERGAL (Heb. *nērᵉḡal*; Sumerian U.GUR; Bab. *ner(i)gal*, 'Lord of the great city', *i.e.* the underworld). This Bab. deity had his cult-centre at Cuthah (modern Tell Ibrahim, NE of Babylon), where he was worshipped with his consort Ereshkigal, as lord of the underworld. Men from Cuthah continued to worship him as exiles in Samaria (2 Ki. 17:30), but, though he was the god of hunting, they feared the lion (his cult animal) sent by Yahweh (v. 26). Nergal was worshipped throughout Assyria and Babylonia as a deity having the sinister aspects of the sun, bringing plague, war, flood and havoc. He has been identified with Mekal, the god of *Bethshan and later with Mars. Temples at Larsa, Isin and Assur were dedicated to him. His name is commonly found as the divine element in personal names, as *Nergal-sharezer (Je. 39:3, 13).

BIBLIOGRAPHY. E. von Weiher, *Der babylonische Gott Nergal*, 1971. D.J.W.

NERGAL-SHAREZER. Heb. equivalent of Bab. *Nergal-šar-uṣur* (Gk. Neriglissar) meaning 'O Nergal, protect the king'. The name of a senior official with Nebuchadrezzar's army at Jerusalem in 587 BC (Je. 39:3, 13). It is possible that two persons of the same name are listed in v. 3; if so, the first may be the Neriglissar who was one of the Bab. army commanders, son of Bel-šum-iškun and married to Nebuchadrezzar's daughter. He succeeded to the throne at Babylon in 560 BC. The Nergal-sharezer qualified as *Rabmag seems to have held a position of lower rank. D.J.W.

NERO. Son of a distinguished family of the old Roman aristocracy, the Domitii, and on his mother's side the great-great-grandson of Augustus, he was adopted by Claudius as his heir and

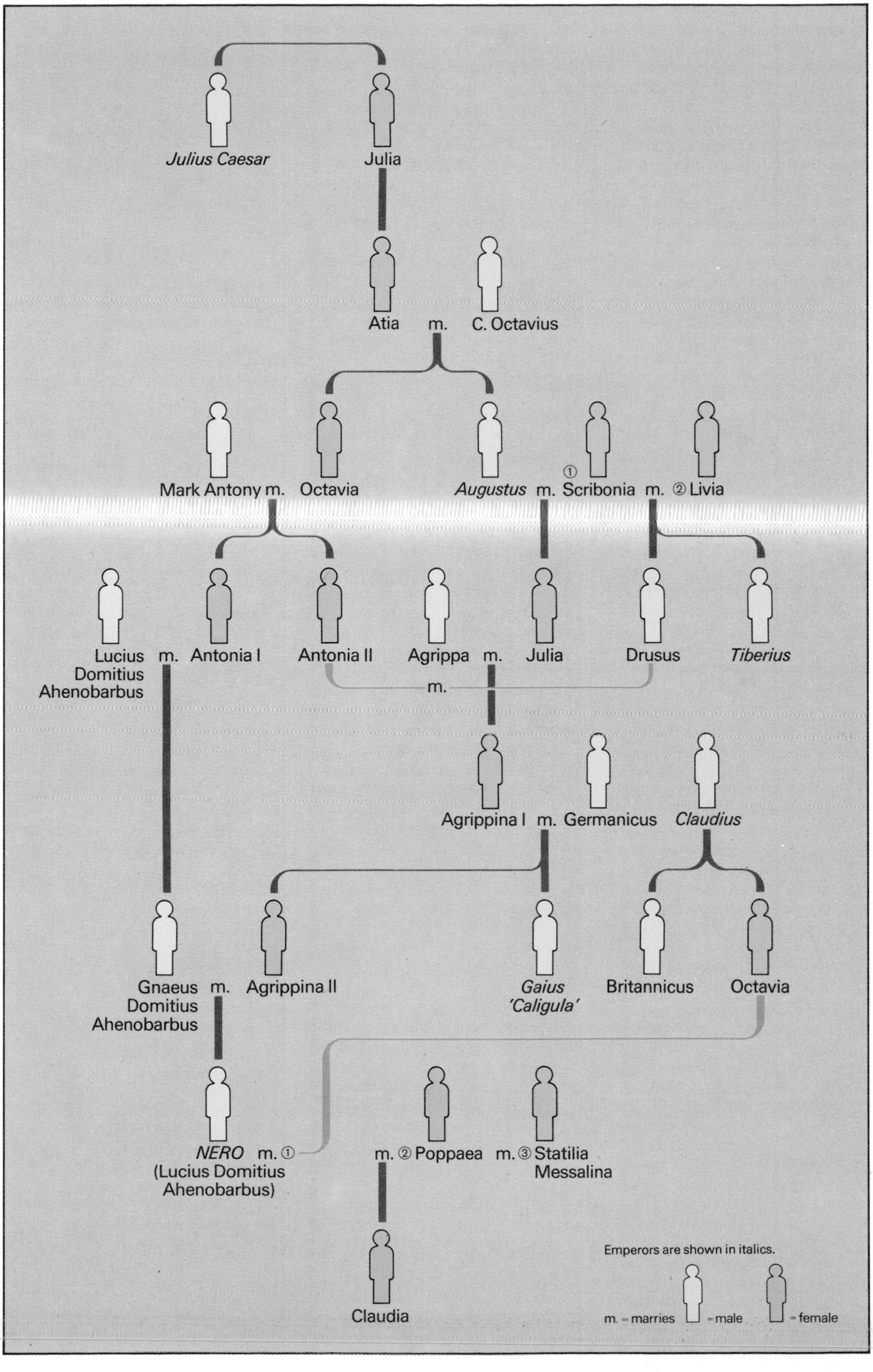

Simplified family tree of the Roman imperial house, showing the position of Nero in it.

duly took his place in the Caesarian succession in AD 54. His atrocities and feebleness finally destroyed the credit of his house, whose long ascendancy he finally brought to an end with his suicide in the face of the revolts of AD 68. A youth of exquisite taste, he fascinated and scandalized his contemporaries with his artistic pursuits. To the Greeks in particular he endeared himself; they never tired of flattering his longing for prizes in literary festivals; and he reciprocated this whimsy by abolishing Rom. control over the states of Achaia. After his premature death his legend flourished in the E, and his reincarnation was fervently expected, and even announced. On the other hand, within his domestic circle and among his aristocratic peers, his behaviour was monstrously sinister. The belief that his mother had murdered Claudius after marrying him to ensure her son's succession scarcely mitigated the horror when Nero himself had her done to death. Although there seems to have been a period of stable government while he remained under the influence of the senators Burrus and Seneca, he eventually freed himself from their restraints as well and was driven by his bloodthirsty suspicions to the inevitable end.

'Nero Caesar Augustus', inscribed on a gold aureus *of the emperor Nero to whom Paul appealed* (*Acts 25:11*). *Diameter 19 mm. AD 54–68.* (RG)

Nero, the Roman emperor, AD 54–68. (PP)

Nero is indirectly concerned with the NT at three points.

1. It was Nero to whose superior justice Paul appealed against the vacillations of his deputy, Festus (Acts 25:10–11), and Nero whose God-given authority he had studiously supported in writing to the Romans (Rom. 13:1–7). There is a horrible and tragic irony in this: 'he does not bear the sword in vain' (v. 4). We do not know the outcome of Paul's appeal, but the Christians of Rome were treated for their loyalty to one of the most barbaric pogroms in history.

2. In AD 64 much of the city of Rome was destroyed by fire. To divert the suspicion that he had started it for his own entertainment, Nero accused another party about whom the public were also prepared to believe the worst. Having forced a conviction for arson against certain Christians he conducted mass arrests, and among other tortures burnt his victims alive in public (Tacitus, *Ann.* 15. 44). The important things about this were that Christians were clearly distinguished from Jews (Nero's wife Poppaea was pro-Jewish), and that it was plausible to accuse them of such crimes. Although Tacitus makes it clear that the charges were a fabrication, and that they even attracted some sympathy to the Christians, he equally reveals that the public was profoundly suspicious of the morals of the Christians. Suetonius (*Nero* 16. 2), without mentioning the fire, lists the attack on the Christians with a number of other reforms that are put down to Nero's credit. What was disastrous for the Christians was that Nero's action had left a legal precedent for translating this popular odium into official action. The First Epistle of Peter reflects this kind of situation. Christians are in the agonizing position of being committed to honour the authorities, while knowing that any moral lapse may lead to legal proceedings against them, and that they may even be prosecuted on grounds of their membership in the Christian society alone.

3. In the closing years of Nero's régime his commanders in Palestine were drawn into the war that ended with the destruction of Jerusalem in AD 70, an event that finally set the Christian churches free from their Zionist orientation. Nero played no part in the campaigns, and was apparently oblivious of the issues involved: the critical year AD 67 found him engrossed in literary triumphs on the stages of Greece.

BIBLIOGRAPHY. J. H. Bishop, *Nero: the Man and the Legend*, 1964; B. H. Warmington, *Nero: Reality and Legend*, 1969; M. Grant, *Nero*, 1970. E.A.J.

[illegible] 'make a nest'; Gk. *kataskēnōsis*, 'place for roosting in'). The word is employed in its customary sense in Dt. 22:6; 32:11 (speaking of 'nestlings'); Jb. 39:27; Ps. 104:17; Pr. 27:8; Is. 16:2. It is found metaphorically (notably of a lofty fortress) in Nu. 24:21; Je. 49:16; Ob. 4; with reference to the secure home of Israel in Ps. 84:3–4; and of the Chaldeans' strong abode in Hab. 2:9. Job (29:18) speaks of his lost home as a 'nest'. In Gn. 6:14 'nests' (*qinnîm*, 'rooms') is used to describe the subdivisions within the ark. In Mt. 8:20; Lk. 9:58 Jesus contrasts his homeless situation with that of the * birds who have their nests (RVmg. 'lodging-places'). J.D.D.

NETHANIAH (Heb. *n*^{e}*ṯanyāhû*, 'Yahweh has given'; LXX *Nathanias*; *cf.* * NATHANAEL). **1.** The father of Ishmael, the murderer of Gedaliah (Je. 40:8, 14–15; 41:9). In 2 Ki. 25:23 the LXX reads *Maththanias*. **2.** An Asaphite, leader of the fifth group of the Temple choir (1 Ch. 25:2, 12). **3.** Father of Jehudi (Je. 36:14). **4.** A Levite accompanying the teaching mission sent by Jehoshaphat to Judah (2 Ch. 17:8). D.J.W.

NETHINIM (Heb. *n*^{e}*ṯînîm*, RSV 'temple servants'). Apart from 1 Ch. 9:2 (parallel to Ne. 11:3) these people are mentioned only in Ezra and Nehemiah (AV). They are listed among the returned exiles in Ezr. 2:43–58, where they are grouped with 'the sons of Solomon's servants'. When Ezra brings back a fresh party he sends to a place named Casiphia to obtain Levites and Nethinim (Ezr. 8:17, 20). In Jerusalem they had special quarters in the Ophel district near the Temple (Ne. 3:26, 31; 11:21). This may have been where they lived when they were on duty, since Ezr. 2:70; Ne. 7:73 refer to cities in which they lived; it is possible, however, that the reference here is to the period before the rebuilding of the Temple.

The name means 'those who are given', and Ezr. 8:20 says that David and the princes had given them for the service of the Levites. It has been held that they and the children of Solomon's servants were the descendants of Canaanite or foreign prisoners, like the Gibeonites of Jos. 9:27. The foreign [illegible] port this. In 1 Esdras 5:29 and Josephus (*Ant.* 11. 128) they are called 'temple slaves', *hierodouloi*. It has been supposed that Ezekiel protests against them in 44:6–8, but it is hardly likely that the Nethinim would have remained uncircumcised as Ezekiel here says, and their inclusion in the Ezra list, and the position given to them in Ezra-Nehemiah show that the rigoristic Chronicler had no objection to them. Similarly, the reference to the Canaanite in the house of the Lord in Zc. 14:21 is more likely to refer to Canaanite traders, as in Pr. 31:24.

BIBLIOGRAPHY. E. Schürer, *HJP*, 2, i. 273; L. W. Batten, *Ezra–Nehemiah*, *ICC*, 1913, p. 87; B. A. Levine, *JBL* 89, 1963, pp. 207–212. J.S.W.

NETOPHAH ('a dropping'). A city, or group of villages (1 Ch. 9:16; Ne. 12:28), near Bethlehem (Ne. 7:26). The inhabitants are called Netophathites in EVV. 'Netophathi' in Ne. 12:28, AV, should be 'the Netophathites' as RSV. It was the home of some of David's mighty men (2 Sa. 23:28–29). It is mentioned as a place to which returning exiles came (Ezr. 2:22). That it was near Bethlehem is clear, but it cannot be identified conclusively with any modern site. G.W.G.

NETS. Nets in the Bible are instruments of meshed strings for fishing or hunting, or reticulate designs or gratings.

a. Nets for fishing and hunting

Words from four Heb. roots are translated 'net' in the OT. **1.** From *yrš*, 'take', *rešeṯ* is a net to catch birds (Pr. 1:17) or water creatures (Ezk. 32:3), and is often used figuratively of the plots of evil men (*e.g.* Ps. 9:15, laid to catch the feet), or of God's judgments (*e.g.* Ezk. 12:13, cast over the prey). **2.** *ḥerem*, 'something perforated', is a large net which may be spread out on the shore to dry (Ezk. 26:5) and is used figuratively of an evil woman's heart (Ec. 7:26), of God's judgment of Pharaoh (Ezk. 32:3), of predatory individuals (Mi. 7:2), and of the Chaldeans' military power (Hab. 1:15). **3.** From the root *ṣûḏ*, 'hunt', *m*^{e}*ṣôḏâ* is a fish-net (Ec. 9:12), *māṣûḏ* and *m*^{e}*ṣûḏâ* are used of God's judgments (Jb. [illegible] 66:11), and *māṣôḏ* in Pr. 12:12 is perhaps a snare for evil men. **4.** From the root *kmr*, which in Arabic means 'overcome' or 'cover', Heb. *mikmōreṯ* is the net which Egyptian fishermen spread over the water (Is. 19:8), *mikmereṯ*, AV 'drag', RSV 'seine', is a symbol of the Chaldeans' army (Hab. 1:15), *mikmôr* is used to catch an antelope (Is. 51:20), and *mikmār* is figurative of the plots of the wicked (Ps. 141:10).

In the NT three Gk. words are translated 'net'. **5.** From *diktyō*, 'to net', *diktyon*, the most common and general word for net. This type of net was used by Jesus' disciples (Mt. 4:20–21); it was let down (Lk. 5:4) or cast (Jn. 21:6) in the water, and emptied into a boat (Lk. 5:7) or dragged to shore (Jn. 21:8). **6.** From *amphiballō*, 'cast around', *amphiblēstron*, 'a casting net', also used by the disciples of Jesus (Mt. 4:18). **7.** From *sassō*, 'fill', *sagēnē* (related to English 'seine'), a drag-net to which our Lord compared the kingdom of heaven (Mt. 13:47). It required several men to draw this large net to shore (Mt. 13:48).

The care of nets included washing (Lk. 5:2), drying (Ezk. 47:10) and mending (Mt. 4:21).

BIBLIOGRAPHY. G. Dalman, *Arbeit und Sitte*, 6, 1939, pp. 335–337, 343–363.

b. Nets as designs or gratings

Around the base of the brazen altar of burnt offering of the tabernacle was grating of net design (*rešeṯ*, Ex. 27:4–5) or net work (*ma'aśēh*

rešeṯ, Ex. 38:4). This grating may have had both artistic and practical purposes, since it would be lighter to carry than solid metal and allow draught for burning.

The capitals of the two pillars before Solomon's Temple were decorated with a net design (Heb. *śᵉḇāḵâ* from a root meaning 'interweave', 1 Ki. 7:17; Je. 52:22). Those who think these pillars were cressets point out that open net work would give air for burning inside the capital, but this feature is not mentioned in the Bible.

BIBLIOGRAPHY. H. G. May, *The Two Pillars before the Temple of Solomon, BASOR* 88, December 1942, pp. 19–27. J.T.

NEW TESTAMENT APOCRYPHA. The extent of the NT apocrypha is more difficult to determine than that of the OT. The term will here be confined to non-canonical works attributed to, or purporting to give extra-canonical information about, Christ or the apostles. Works written without such pretensions are thus excluded, even where they enjoyed quasi-canonical status in some churches for a time (*PATRISTIC LITERATURE); so are Christian attributions to (or Christianized versions of works attributed to) OT characters (*PSEUDEPIGRAPHA), and the interpolation or rehandling of NT texts with alien material (*TEXTS AND VERSIONS, NT section).

A huge literature remains, preserved partly in Gk. and Lat., but still more in Coptic, Ethiopic, Syriac, Arabic, Slavonic, and even in Anglo-Saxon and contemporary W European languages. Some works that we know to have been very influential have been almost lost, and many of the most important exist only in fragmentary state. New discoveries, however, often of much importance for early Christian history, are constantly being made. Complex literary problems are frequently met, for many of the apocryphal works lent themselves to re-telling, interpolation and plagiarization.

I. Forms

A large proportion of the apocryphal literature falls into one of the NT literary forms: Gospel, Acts, Epistle, Apocalypse. But this formal similarity is often accompanied by a huge difference in conception. This is particularly noticeable with the Gospels: we have Infancy Gospels, Passion Gospels, sayings documents and theological meditations; but (if we exclude the early fragmentary Gospels on which we are in any case ill-informed), it is hard to find works which, like the canonical Gospels, have any interest in the words and works of the incarnate Lord. Acts form a numerous and probably the most popular class, doubtless through the wide and non-sectarian appeal of many of the stories. Epistles are not common: despite the fact that nearly all the works in the NT sometimes said to be pseudepigraphic are Epistles. For apocalypses, there was Jewish precedent for attributing them to a celebrity of the past.

Another class of literature developed which took over some features of apocryphal literature: the Church Orders of Syria and Egypt. These collections of canons on church discipline and liturgy, of which the *Apostolic Constitutions* is the most popular, claiming to represent apostolic practice, came by convention to claim apostolic origin: and the most daring, the *Testament of our Lord*, purports to be a post-resurrection discourse of Christ. The custom was perhaps stimulated by its success in the 3rd-century *Didascalia*, and misunderstanding of the claim to apostolicity of the *Apostolic Tradition* of Hippolytus—two works which they plundered heavily—together with, in some cases, the popularity of the Clementine romance. (*Cf. Studia Patristica*, ed. K. Aland and F. L. Cross, 2, 1957, pp. 83ff.)

II. Motives

The creation of apocryphal literature had begun in apostolic times: Paul has apparently to authenticate his signature because of forgeries circulating (*cf.* 2 Thes. 3:17). In the 2nd century the literature comes into its own, and gathers momentum thenceforth, particularly in Egypt and Syria. It continues into the Middle Ages (where the older legends were still loved), and, occasionally, through sentiment, *parti pris* or sheer eccentricity, in our own day. The various motives behind it are thus related to the whole trend of Christian and sub-Christian history; but some of the motives operative at the beginning are particularly important.

a. Romance and the literary impulse

This shows itself in various forms. There is the desire to satisfy curiosity on matters of which the NT says nothing. A flood of worthless Infancy Gospels covers the silent years from Bethlehem to the baptism. As the Virgin Mary becomes more prominent in theology and devotion, pseudo-apostolic works describe her birth, life and, eventually, her assumption into heaven. A reader of Col. 4:16 felt it incumbent upon him to supply the apparently missing letter to the Laodiceans. It appears above all in the novelistic Acts and romances and some of the Gospels—bizarre, fetid, but packed with wonders and anecdotes, and many of them, with all their faults, having a certain animation. We best understand this movement as a branch of popular Christian literature, and, studied in this light, the earliest books reveal some of the issues which occupied congregations in the 2nd and 3rd centuries: relationships with the state, conformity with the Jews, debates on marriage and celibacy; and, by their belligerent insistence on miracles, reveal that the real age of miracles had passed. The productions are crude, even vulgar; but their authors knew their public. For many they must have replaced erotic pagan popular literature, and in many cases, with a real desire to edify. The authors would doubtless be hard put to it to differentiate their motives from those of the 20th-century author of *The Robe* or *The Big Fisherman*. There is no need to question the sincerity of the Asian presbyter who was unfrocked for publishing the *Acts of Paul* when he said that he did so 'for love of Paul', who had died 100 years before the presbyter wrote. This helps to explain how stories and whole books originating in heretical circles retained and increased their currency in orthodox quarters. It was heretical teachers who made the earliest effective use of this form of literature; and so successful was it that others transmitted, expurgated and imitated the forms designed as vehicles for their propaganda.

b. The inculcation of principles not, to the author's mind, sufficiently clearly enunciated in the New Testament books

Naturally, even in a work 'for love of Paul' any doctrinal disproportion or aberration of the author passed into his work; indeed part of his edificatory aim might well be to inculate the aberration: the Asian presbyter, for instance, had an

Opposite page: Nets and stakes carried by the servants of King Ashurbanipal during a hunt. Relief from Nineveh. c. 640 BC. (BM)

NEW BIRTH See Regeneration, Part 3.

NEW EXODUS See Typology, Part 3.

Opposite page: Stags and deer caught in nets. Relief from Nineveh. c. 650 BC. (BM)

obsession with virginity which makes his work, otherwise more or less orthodox, remote from evangelic spirit. But there are many works the aim of which is deliberately sectarian: to promulgate a body of doctrine to supplement or supersede that of the undisputed books. These were mainly the fruit of the two great reactionary movements of the 2nd century, *Gnosticism and Montanism. The Montanist 'Scriptures' arose almost by accident, and were not in our sense strictly apocryphal, for, though they claimed to preserve the living testimony of the Holy Spirit, they were not pseudonymous; they have virtually disappeared (but *cf.* those collected in R. M. Grant, *Second Century Christianity*, pp. 95ff.). Writings from the multiform expressions of Gnosticism, however, have survived in quantity. Such works as the *Gospel of Truth*, a meditation in Gnostic terms reflecting the language of the undisputed Scriptures, are less common than works which select, modify and interpret those Scriptures in a sectarian direction (*cf.* the Nag Hammadi *Gospel of Thomas*), those which blatantly profess to contain secret doctrine not available elsewhere (*cf.* the *Apocryphon of John*), and those which simply attribute to the Lord or the apostles the commonplaces of Gnostic teaching. And for all these purposes the apocryphal form became conventional.

The reason is not far to seek. In the sub-apostolic age and after, with the immense expansion of the church, the intensifying of the danger of persecution and the proliferation of false teaching, apostolicity became the norm of faith and practice: and, as the living memory of the apostles receded, apostolicity was increasingly centred in the Scriptures of our NT, over the majority of which there was unanimity in the church. If, therefore, a new form of teaching was to spread, it had to establish its apostolicity. This was commonly done by claiming a secret tradition from an apostle, or from the Lord through an apostle, either as a supplement to the open tradition of the Gospels or as a corrective. The favoured apostle varies: many sects had Judaic leanings, and James the Just and, curiously, Salome, are frequent sources of tradition; Thomas, Philip, Bartholomew and Matthias also appear constantly. In the *Gospel of Thomas*, for instance, it is Thomas who shows fullest understanding of the Lord's person (Matthew and Peter—perhaps as the apostles behind the church's first two Gospels—appear to their disadvantage). The still more weird *Pistis Sophia* envisages a sort of congress of the apostles and the women with the Lord, but indicates that Philip, Thomas and Matthias are to write the mysteries (*Pistis Sophia*, ch. 42, Schmidt). Local factors probably contribute something to the choice of apostle—all those named were associated with Syria and the East, some of the most fertile soil for literature of this type; and speculations about Thomas as the Lord's twin exercised an additional fascination. The process brought about a new emphasis on the post-resurrection period, in which discourses of the Lord were usually set; significantly, for little is said of this period in the undisputed Gospels, and it was a constant Gnostic feature to undervalue the humanity of the incarnate Lord. It is worth noticing that, while those syncretistic sects who adopted some Christian elements could get their revelations whence they would, Christian Gnosticism had to show that its knowledge was derived from an apostolic source.

c. The preservation of tradition

Inevitably in early days words of the Lord were handed down outside the canonical Gospels. Some were probably transformed out of recognition in the process, others tendentiously twisted. The celebrated preface of Papias (Eusebius, *EH* 3. 39), showing him collecting oracles of the Lord for his Expositions, reveals how conscious orthodox Christians in the early 2nd century were of this floating material and the problems of collecting it. Papias, whatever his shortcomings, was conscientious in scrutinizing his material: yet the results were not always happy, and perhaps not all his contemporaries had his compunction. Genuine material may thus sometimes have been preserved amid undisputed rubbish.

Similarly, memories of the lives and deaths of apostles would be likely to linger, and the apocryphal Acts, even when dubious theologically, may sometimes preserve genuine traditions, or reflect appropriate situations.

The desire to transmit such memories undoubtedly played its part in the production of the apocryphal literature; but it could not defeat the tendency to invent, elaborate, improve, or redirect. Any winnowing process is thus hazardous: and, as scholars like Origen knew, was already hazardous in patristic times. In consequence, the necessity of building squarely upon what was undisputed was universally recognized.

III. The apocryphal literature in the early church

The presence of such various writings under apostolic names when apostolicity was the norm made it urgent to be assured which the truly apostolic writings were, and the early Christian scholars were not deficient in insight and critical acumen (*CANON OF THE NEW TESTAMENT). But it is striking how little the generally received list of canonical books is affected by discussions over apocryphal literature. Some churches were slow in receiving books now regarded as canonical. Some gave high place to such works as *1 Clement* and the *Shepherd* of Hermas. But hardly any books in, say, M. R. James' *Apocryphal New Testament* were ever in any sense 'Excluded books of the NT'. They were beyond consideration. The Petrine literature caused more heart-searching than any other (*cf.* R. M. Grant and G. Quispel, *VC* 6, 1952, pp. 31ff.). By Eusebius' time the discussion, save on 2 Peter, is closed (*EH* 3. 3), but there is positive evidence that at least the *Apocalypse of Peter* was for a time employed in some areas (see below).

In this connection the letter of Serapion, bishop of Antioch, to the congregation at Rhossus about AD 190, is of interest (*cf.* Eusebius, *EH* 6. 12). The church had begun to use the *Gospel of Peter*. There had evidently been opposition to it, but Serapion, satisfied of the stability of the congregation, had, after a cursory glance, sanctioned its public reading. Trouble followed. Serapion read the Gospel more carefully and found not only that it was accepted by churches whose tendencies were suspect, but that it reflected at some points the Docetic heresy (denying the reality of Christ's manhood). He sums it up 'most is of the Saviour's true teaching', but some things (of which he appended a list) were added. He says, 'We accept Peter and the other apostles as Christ, but as men of experience we test writings falsely ascribed to them, knowing that such things were not handed down to us.'

In other words, the list of apostolic books was already traditional. Other books might be read, provided they were orthodox. The *Gospel of Peter* was *not* traditional: its use at Rhossus was the result of a specific request, and was not unopposed. At first Serapion had seen nothing to require prolonged controversy: if spurious, it was at least harmless. When closer examination revealed its tendencies its use in any form in church was forbidden.

The course of events seems best understood if, following the hint of Serapion's action, we recognize that the acknowledgment of a book as spurious did not necessarily involve complete refusal to allow its public reading, providing it had some devotional value and no heretical tendency: a sort of intermediate status analogous to that of the Apocrypha in the sixth Anglican Article. But even a heretical book, if it had other appeal, might still be read privately and laid under tribute. By these means the apocryphal literature came to have a lasting effect on mediaeval devotion and Christian art and story.

There is, however, nothing to suggest that it was an accepted part of catholic practice in the 1st or 2nd century to compile works in the name of an apostle, a process implied in some theories of the authorship of certain NT books (*cf.* D. Guthrie, *ExpT* 67, 1955–6, pp. 341f.), and the case of the author of the *Acts of Paul* is one example of drastic action against such publication.

Passing from any NT writings to the best NT apocrypha—the true creation of the early Christian community—one moves into a different world. If 2 Peter—to take the NT writing most commonly assigned to the 2nd century—be an apocryphon, it is unique among the apocrypha.

IV. Some representative works

A few representatives of different apocryphal forms may be given. They are, generally speaking, some of the more important older works. Few have a complete text: for some we are dependent on quotations from early writers.

a. Early apocryphal Gospels

A number of fragments from early Gospels are quoted by 3rd- and 4th-century writers. Debate continues on the nature and interrelationships of these Gospels. The *Gospel according to the Hebrews* was known to Clement of Alexandria, Origen, Hegesippus, Eusebius, and Jerome, who says (though he is not always believed) that he translated it into Gk. and Lat. (*De Viris Illustribus* 2) from Aramaic in Heb. characters, and that it was used by the Nazarenes, a Jewish–Christian group. Most people, he says, mistakenly thought it was the Heb. original of the Gospel of *Matthew mentioned by Papias, which recalls that Irenaeus knew of sects which used only Matthew (*Adv. Haer.* 1. 26. 2; 3. 11. 7). Some of the extracts we possess have certainly points of contact with Matthew; others reappear in other works, most recently the *Gospel of Thomas*. There is a strong Jewish–Christian tone, and a resurrection appearance to James the Just is recorded. Eusebius refers to a story, found both in Papias and in the *Gospel of the Hebrews*, of a woman accused before Jesus of many sins. This has been often identified with the story of the adulteress found in many MSS of Jn. 8.

The Gospel probably reflects the activity of Syrian Jewish Christians using Matthaean (the 'local' Gospel) and other local tradition, some of it doubtless valid. The Nazarenes called it 'The Gospel according to the Apostles' (Jerome, *Contra Pelag.* 3. 2)—a suspiciously belligerent title. (See V. Burch, *JTS* 21, 1920, pp. 310ff.; M. J. Lagrange, *RB* 31, 1922, pp. 161ff., 321ff.; and for its defence as a primary source, H. J. Schonfield, *According to the Hebrews*, 1937.)

Epiphanius, ever a confused writer, mentions a mutilated version of Matthew used by the Jewish–Christian sect he calls 'Ebionites'. This has been identified with the Hebrews Gospel, but the extracts given show a different view of the nativity and baptism, and the work is clearly sectarian and tendentious. It may be the same as the *Gospel of the Twelve Apostles* mentioned by Origen (*Lk. Hom.* 1; *cf.* J. R. Harris, *The Gospel of the Twelve Apostles*, 1900, pp. 11f.).

The *Gospel of the Egyptians* is known mainly through a series of quotations in the *Stromateis* of Clement of Alexandria. Some Gnostics used it (Hippolytus, *Philosophoumena* 5. 7), and it doubtless arose in an Egyptian sect. Extant portions relate to a dialogue of Christ and Salome on the repudiation of sexual relations. A document with the same title is included in the Nag Hammadi library, but is not related to the work known to Clement. It is an esoteric Gnostic tractate.

The papyri have yielded a number of fragments of uncanonical Gospels. The most celebrated, P. Oxy. 1. 654–655, will be considered later under the *Gospel of Thomas*. Next in interest comes the so-called *Unknown Gospel* (P. Egerton 2) published by H. I. Bell and T. C. Skeat in 1935, describing incidents after the Synoptic manner but with a Johannine dialogue and vocabulary. The MS, dated *c.* AD 100, is one of the oldest known Christian Gk. MSS. It has been held by some to draw on the Fourth Gospel and perhaps one of the Synoptics also, and by others to be an early example of Christian popular literature independent of these (*cf.* Lk. 1:1). (See H. I. Bell and T. C. Skeat, *The New Gospel Fragments*, 1935; C. H. Dodd, *BJRL* 20, 1936, pp. 56ff. = *New Testament Studies*, 1953, pp. 12ff.; G. Mayeda, *Das Leben-Jesu-Fragment Egerton 2*, 1946; H. I. Bell, *HTR* 42, 1949, pp. 53ff.)

b. Passion Gospels

The most important Gospel of which we have any substantial part is the (mid?) 2nd-century *Gospel of Peter*, of which a large Coptic fragment, covering from the judgment to the resurrection, exists (The Akhmim Fragment). It has been identified with the 'memoirs of Peter', perhaps mentioned by Justin (*Trypho* 106), but this is inappropriate. (*Cf.* V. H. Stanton, *JTS* 2, 1900, pp. 1ff.)

The miraculous element is heightened. The watch see three men come out from the tomb, two whose heads reach the sky and one who overpasses it. A cross follows them. A voice from heaven cries, 'Hast thou preached to them that sleep?' and a voice from the cross says, 'Yes' (*cf.* 1 Pet. 3:19). Pilate's share of blame is reduced, and that of Herod and the Jews emphasized: perhaps reflecting both an apologetic towards the state and controversy with the Jews.

Serapion's judgment (see above) did not err; most of it is lurid, but not dangerous. But there are telltale phrases: 'He kept silence as one feeling no pain', and the rendering of the cry of dereliction, 'My power, thou hast forsaken me', followed by the pregnant 'he was taken up', show that the author did not properly value the Lord's humanity. (See L. Vaganay,

L'Évangile de Pierre, 1930.)

The *Gospel of Nicodemus* is the name given to a composite work existing in various recensions in Gk., Lat. and Coptic, of which the principal elements are 'The Acts of Pilate', supposedly an official report of the trial, crucifixion and burial, an abstract of the subsequent debates and investigations of the Sanhedrin, and a highly-coloured account of the 'Descent into Hell'. There are various appendices in the different versions; one, a letter of Pilate to the emperor Claudius, may give the earliest example of 'Acts of Pilate'. Apologists like Justin (*Apol.* 35. 48) appeal confidently to the trial records, assuming they exist. Tertullian knew stories of Pilate's favourable reports to Tiberius about Jesus (*Apol.* 5. 21). Such 'records' would be constructed in time: especially when a persecuting government, *c.* AD 312, used forged and blasphemous reports of the trial for propaganda purposes (Eusebius, *EH* 9. 5). Our present 'Acts' may be a counter to these. The 'Descent into Hell' may be from rather later in the century, but both parts of the work probably draw on older material. The striking feature is the virtual vindication of Pilate, doubtless for reasons of policy. As the stories passed into Byzantine legend, Pilate became a saint, and his martyrdom is still celebrated in the Coptic Church.

There is no proper critical text. See J. Quasten, *Patrology*, 1, pp. 115ff. for versions.

c. Infancy Gospels

The *Protevangelium of James* had a huge popularity; many MSS exist in many languages (though none in Lat.), and it has deeply influenced much subsequent Mariology. It was known to Origen, so must be 2nd century. It gives the birth and presentation of Mary, her espousal to Joseph (an old man with children) and the Lord's miraculous birth (a midwife attesting the virginity *in partu*). It is clearly written in the interests of certain theories about the perpetual virginity. The supposed author is James the Just, though at one point Joseph becomes the narrator. (See M. Testuz, *Papyrus Bodmer 5*, 1958; E. de Strycker, *La forme plus ancienne du Protévangile de Jacques*, 1961.)

The other influential infancy Gospel of antiquity was the *Gospel of Thomas*, which tells some rather repulsive stories of the silent years. Our version seems to have been shorn of its Gnostic speeches. It is distinct from the Nag Hammadi work of the same name (see below); it is sometimes difficult to know to which work patristic writers refer.

d. The Nag Hammadi Gospels

In the Nag Hammadi library there are several Gospels in Coptic which were not previously known, besides new versions of others (*CHENOBOSKION).

One text opens 'The Gospel of Truth is a joy' (an *incipit*, not a title), and proceeds to a verbose and often obscure meditation on the scheme of redemption. Gnostic terminology of the type of the Valentinian school is evident, but not in the developed form we meet in Irenaeus. It alludes to most of the NT books in a way which suggests recognition of their authority. It has been commonly identified with the 'Gospel of Truth' ascribed to Valentinus by Irenaeus, though this has been denied (*cf.* H. M. Schenke, *ThL* 83, 1958, pp. 497ff.). Van Unnik has attractively proposed that it was written before Valentinus' break with the Roman church (where he was once a candidate for an episcopal chair), when he was seeking to establish his orthodoxy. It would thus be an important witness to the list of authoritative books (and substantially similar to our own) in Rome *c.* AD 140. (See G. Quispel and W. C. van Unnik in *The Jung Codex*, ed. by F. L. Cross, 1955; text by M. Malinine *et al.*, *Evangelium Veritatis*, 1956 and 1961; commentary by K. Grobel, *The Gospel of Truth*, 1960.) The most recent English translation is by G. W. MacRae in *The Nag Hammadi Library*, 1977.

The now famous *Gospel of Thomas* is a collection of sayings of Jesus, numbered at about 114, with little obvious arrangement. A high proportion resemble sayings in the Synoptic Gospels (with a bias towards Luke) but almost always with significant differences. These often take a Gnostic direction, and among other Gnostic themes the OT is minimized and the necessity for obliterating consciousness of sex is stressed. It has been identified with the Gospel used by the Naassene Gnostics (*cf.* R. M. Grant with D. N. Freedman, *The Secret Sayings of Jesus*, 1959; W. R. Schoedel, *VC* 14, 1960, pp. 225ff.), but its originally Gnostic character has been doubted (R. McL. Wilson, *Studies in the Gospel of Thomas*, 1961), and some are prepared to see independent traditions of some value in it. G. Quispel has found the variants similar in type to those in the Bezan ('Western') Text (*VC* 14, 1960, pp. 204ff.) as well as in Tatian's *Diatessaron* and the Pseudo-Clementines (see below). In a more recent article Quispel connects the *Gospel of Thomas* with the Encratites rather than the Gnostics (*VC* 28, 1974, pp. 29f.) The Oxyrhynchus Logia P. Oxy. 1. 654–655, including the celebrated 'Raise the stone and thou shalt find me', recur in a form which suggests that they were part of an earlier Gk. version of the book. Thomas (probably thought of as the twin of Jesus) plays the central role in the tradition (see above), but James the Just is said to become chief of the disciples—one of several indications that a Jewish–Christian source is under tribute.

Many problems beset this curious and inconsistent book, but so far it seems safe to place its origin in Syria (which may explain the Semitisms of the language), where there was always a freer attitude to the Gospel text and more contamination than elsewhere. (See text and translation by A. Guillaumont *et al.*, 1959; H. Koester and T. O. Lambdin in *The Nag Hammadi Library in English*, pp. 117–130; B. Gärtner, *The Theology of the Gospel of Thomas*, 1961; bibliography to 1960 in J. Leipoldt and H. M. Schenke, *Koptisch-Gnostische Schriften aus den Papyrus-Codices von Nag-Hamadi*, 1960, pp. 79f.)

The chief interest of the *Gospel of Philip* (Gnostic, though the sect is hard to identify) lies in its unusually developed sacramental doctrine, in which there are greater mysteries in chrism and the 'bridechamber' than in baptism (see E. Segelberg, *Numen* 7, 1960, pp. 189ff.; R. McL. Wilson, *The Gospel of Philip*, 1962, provides a translation and commentary. *Cf.* also *The Nag Hammadi Library in English*, pp. 131–151 [tr. by W. W. Isenberg]). The language is repulsive: interest in sexual repudiation amounts to an obsession.

e. The 'Leucian' Acts

The five major apocryphal Acts must serve as representatives of a large number. They were gathered into a corpus by Manicheans, who would inherit them from Gnostic sources. The 9th-century bibliophile Photius found the whole attributed to one 'Leucius Charinus' (*Bibliotheca*, 114), but it is probable that Leucius was simply the fictitious name of the author of the *Acts of John*, the earliest (and most unorthodox) of the corpus.

It belongs to about AD 150–160 and describes miracles and sermons (definitely Gnostic) by John in Asia Minor. It reflects ascetic ideals, but has some pleasant anecdotes amid more disreputable matter. It affects also to relate John's own accounts of some incidents with the Lord, and his farewell and death. Liturgically it is of some interest, and includes the first known eucharist for the dead.

The *Acts of Paul* is also early, for Tertullian knew people who justified female preaching and baptizing therefrom (*De Baptismos* 17). He says it was written ostensibly 'for love of Paul' by an Asian presbyter, who was deposed for the action. This must have happened before AD 190, probably before AD 160. The Acts reflect a time of persecution. There are three main sections:

(i) The Acts of Paul and Thecla, an Iconian girl who breaks off her engagement at Paul's preaching, is miraculously protected from martyrdom (winning the interest of 'Queen Tryphaena'—* TRYPHAENA AND TRYPHOSA), and assists Paul's missionary travels. There may have been some historical nucleus even if not a written Thecla source (so Ramsay, *CRE*, pp. 375ff.).

(ii) Further correspondence with the Corinthian church.

(iii) The martyrdom of Paul (legendary).

The tone is intensely ascetic (*cf.* Paul's Beatitudes for the celibate, ch. 5), but otherwise orthodox. There are many incomplete MSS, including a sizeable section of the original Gk. See L. Vouaux, *Les Actes de Paul*, 1913; E. Peterson, *VC* 3, 1949, pp. 142ff.

The *Acts of Peter* is somewhat later, but still well within the 2nd century. The main MS, in Latin (often called the Vercelli Acts), opens with Paul's farewell to the Roman Christians (perhaps from another source). Through the machinations of * Simon Magus the Roman church falls into heresy, but, in response to prayer, Peter arrives, and defeats Simon in a series of public encounters. There follows a plot against Peter initiated by pagans whose wives have left them as a result of his preaching, Peter's flight including the *Quo Vadis?* story, and his return to crucifixion, which was head downwards. A Coptic fragment and allusions to a lost portion suggest that other stories dealt with questions raised in the community about suffering and death. Like other Acts, it sees Peter's work and Paul's as supplementing each other: and the Roman church is a *Pauline* foundation. The ascetic tone is as intense as ever, but otherwise the Gnostic element is not often obtruded; we may, however, have expurgated editions. The place of origin is disputed, but it was almost certainly Eastern. See L. Vouaux, *Les Actes de Pierre*, 1922. It is worth noting that in the Nag Hammadi library the only two documents described as Acts are related to Peter. The Coptic *Acts of Peter* has some affinity with the Lat. *Acts of Peter*, but the latter is more extreme in its ascetic emphasis.

The Acts of (Judas) Thomas stand apart from the other Acts. They are a product of Syriac Christianity, and were almost certainly written in Syriac in Edessa in the early 3rd century. They describe how the apostles divided the world by lot, and Judas Thomas the Twin was appointed to India. He went as a slave, but became the means of the conversion of King 'Gundaphar' and many other notable Indians. Everywhere he preaches virginity and is frequently imprisoned in consequence of his success. Finally, he is martyred.

The Acts have certain Gnostic features: the famous 'Hymn of the Soul' which appears in them has the familiar Gnostic theme of the redemption of the soul from the corruption of matter—the king's son is sent to slay the dragon and bring back the pearl from the far country. There is clearly some relation, as yet unascertained, to the *Gospel of Thomas*: and the title of Thomas, 'Twin of the Messiah', is eloquent. The appeal for virginity is louder, shriller, than in any of the other Acts, but this was a characteristic of Syriac Christianity. Of Gnosticism in the sense of the possession of hidden mysteries there is little trace: the author is too much in earnest in preaching and recommending his Gospel.

There are complete versions in Syriac and Gk. The Acts seem to show some real knowledge of the history and topography of * India. (See A. A. Bevan, *The Hymn of the Soul*, 1897; F. C. Burkitt, *Early Christianity outside the Roman Empire*, 1899; A. F. J. Klijn, *VC* 14, 1960, pp. 154ff.; *idem, The Acts of Thomas*, 1962.)

The *Acts of Andrew* is the latest (*c.* AD 260?) and, in our MSS, the most fragmentary of the 'Leucian' Acts. It is closely related to the *Acts of John*, and its Gnostic character is mentioned by Eusebius (*EH* 3. 25). It describes preachings among the cannibals, miracles, exhortations to virginity, and, perhaps added from another source, martyrdom in Greece. An abstract is given by Gregory of Tours. (See P. M. Peterson, *Andrew, Brother of Simon Peter*, 1958; F. Dvornik, *The Idea of Apostolicity in Byzantium and the Legend of the Apostle Andrew*, 1958, pp. 181ff.; G. Quispel, *VC* 10, 1956, pp. 129ff.; *cf.* D. Guthrie, 'Acts and Epistles in Apocryphal Writings', in W. W. Gasque and R. P. Martin (eds.), *Apostolic History and the Gospel*, 1970.

f. Apocryphal epistles

The most important are the *Third Epistle to the Corinthians* (see *Acts of Paul*, above); the *Epistle of the Apostles*, really a series of early 2nd-century apocalyptic visions cast in the form of an address in the name of all the apostles, to convey post-resurrection teaching of Christ (important as one of the earliest examples of this form); the *Correspondence of Christ and Abgar*, in which the king of Edessa invites the Lord to his state, and of which Eusebius affords an early translation from the Syriac (*EH* 1. 13); the Latin *Correspondence of Paul and Seneca* (see Jerome, *De Viris Illustribus* 12), a 3rd-century apology for Paul's diction, evidently intended to gain a reading of the genuine Epistles in polite circles; and the *Epistle to the Laodiceans*, in Latin, a cento of Pauline language evoked by Col. 4:16. The Muratorian Fragment mentions Epistles to the Laodiceans, and to the Alexandrians, of Marcionite origin: of these there is no trace. The commonly quoted *Letter of Lentulus* describing Jesus and allegedly addressed to the Senate is mediaeval. (See H. Duensing, *Epistula Apostolorum*, 1925; J. de Zwaan in *Amicitiae Corolla* edited by H.G. Wood, 1933, pp. 344ff.; for all the pseudo-Pauline letters, L. Vouaux, *Les Actes de Paul*, 1913, pp. 315ff.)

g. Apocalypses

The *Apocalypse of Peter* is the

NEW WINE
See Wine, Part 3.

NICANOR'S DAY
See Purim, Part 3.

only strictly apocryphal work of which there is positive evidence that it held quasi-canonical status for any length of time. It occurs in the Muratorian Fragment, but with the accompanying note that some will not have it read in church. Clement of Alexandria seems to have commented on it as if it were canonical in a lost work (Eusebius, *EH* 6. 14), and in the 5th century it was read on Good Friday in some Palestinian churches (Sozomen, *Eccles. Hist.* 7. 19). But it was never universally accepted, and its canonicity was not a live issue in Eusebius' day (*EH* 3. 3). Its substantial orthodoxy seems certain. An old stichometry gives it 300 lines: about half of this appears in the main copy of the *Gospel of Peter* (see above). It contains visions of the transfigured Lord, and lurid accounts of the torments of the damned: with perhaps a confused reference to future probation. (See M. R. James, *JTS* 12, 1911, pp. 36ff., 362ff., 573ff.; 32, 1931, pp. 270ff.)

There were several Gnostic *Apocalypses of Paul*, one known to Origen, inspired by 2 Cor. 12:2ff. A version of one (which influenced Dante) has survived (see R. P. Casey, *JTS* 24, 1933, pp. 1ff.).

In the Nag Hammadi library Book V consists of four apocalypses, one of *Paul*, two of *James* and one of *Adam*. The *Apocalypse of Paul* in this collection is distinct from those previously known. All these works are Gnostic in their teaching. *Cf.* A. Böhlig and P. Labib, *Koptisch-gnostische Apocalypsen aus Codex V von Nag Hammadi*, 1963.

h. Other apocryphal works

The *Kerygmata Petrou*, or *Preachings of Peter*, is known to us only in fragments, mostly preserved by Clement of Alexandria. Origen had to deal with Gnostic scholars who employed it, and challenged them to prove its genuineness (in Jn. 13:17, *De Principiis* Pref. 8). It has been postulated as a source of the original Clementine romance (see below). The fragments we have claim to preserve words of the Lord and of Peter, and at least one accords with the *Gospel of the Hebrews*.

The *Clementine Homilies* and the *Clementine Recognitions* are the two chief forms of a romance in which Clement of Rome, seeking for ultimate truth, travels in the apostle Peter's footsteps and is eventually converted. It is probable that both derive from an immensely popular 2nd-century Christian novel, which may have used the *Preachings of Peter*. The literary and theological problems involved are very complex. The Homilies in particular command a Judaized sectarian form of Christianity. (See O. Cullmann, *Le Problème Littéraire et Historique du Roman Pseudo-Clémentin*, 1930; H. J. Schoeps, *Theologie und Geschichte des Judenchristentums*, 1949; E.T. of Homilies and Recognitions in Ante-Nicene Christian Library.)

The *Apocryphon of John* was popular in Gnostic circles, and has reappeared at Nag Hammadi. The Saviour appears to John on the Mount of Olives, bids him write secret doctrine, deposit it safely and impart it only to those whose spirit can understand it and whose way of life is worthy. There is a curse on anyone imparting the doctrine for reward to an unworthy person. It is to be dated before AD 180, probably in Egypt. (See W. C. Till, *Die Gnostischen Schriften des koptischen Papyrus Berol. 8502*, 1955; *cf. JEH* 3, 1952, pp. 14ff.) In the Nag Hammadi documents, an account is given of the creation, the Fall and the redemption of humanity.

The *Apocryphon of James* has also been discovered at Nag Hammadi. It is an exhortation to seek the kingdom, cast in the form of a post-resurrection discourse to Peter and James, who ascend with the Lord but are unable to penetrate the third heaven. Its interest lies in its early date (AD 125–150?), the prominence of James (the Just?), who sends the apostles to their work after the ascension, and, in van Unnik's opinion, its freedom from Gnostic influence. (See W. C. van Unnik, *VC* 10, 1956, pp. 149ff.) F. E. Williams in his introductory remarks to his translation of the Nag Hammadi text in *The Nag Hammadi Library in English*, p. 29, finds some evidence of Gnostic themes and suggests Christian Gnosticism as its source.

The *Pistis Sophia* and the *Books of Jeû* are obscure and bizarre Gnostic works of the 2nd or 3rd century. (See C. Schmidt, *Koptisch-gnostische Schriften*³, edited by W. Till, 1959; G. R. S. Mead, *Pistis Sophia*³, 1947, E.T.—*cf.* F. C. Burkitt, *JTS* 23, 1922, pp. 271ff.; C. A. Baynes, *A Coptic Gnostic Treatise*, 1933.)

General Bibliography. Critical editions of many of these works are still needed. Gk. and Lat. texts of the earlier Gospel discoveries are provided by C. Tischendorf, *Evangelia Apocrypha*, 1886, to be supplemented by A. de Santos, *Los Evangelios Apocrifos*, 1956 (with Spanish translations). The best collection of texts of the Acts is R. A. Lipsius and M. Bonnet, *Acta Apostolorum Apocrypha*, 1891–1903. Some newer texts and studies are provided in M. R. James, *Apocrypha Anecdota*, 1, 1893; 2, 1897. M. R. James, *ANT* (a splendid collection of English translations up to 1924); E. Hennecke–W. Schneemelcher (E.T. by R. M. Wilson), *New Testament Apocrypha*, 1, 1963; 2, 1965 (indispensable for serious study). Non-canonical sayings: A. Resch, *Agrapha*², 1906; B. Pick, *Paralipomena*, 1908; J. Jeremias, *Unknown Sayings of Jesus*, 1957; J. Finegan, *Hidden Records of the Life of Jesus*, 1969; F. F. Bruce, *Jesus and Christian Origins outside the New Testament*, 1974. Church orders: J. Cooper and A. J. Maclean, *The Testament of our Lord*, 1902; R. H. Connolly, *The So-Called Egyptian Church Order and its Derivatives*, 1917. A.F.W.

NICODEMUS. The name is Gk. and means 'conqueror of the people'. He is mentioned only in the Fourth Gospel, where he is described as a Pharisee and ruler of the Jews (*i.e.* a member of the Sanhedrin) who visited Jesus by night (Jn. 3:1–21). He seems to have been an earnest man attracted by the character and teaching of Jesus but afraid to allow this interest to be known by his fellow Pharisees. He could not understand the spiritual metaphors used by Christ. Nicodemus fades from the scene and we are left with Christ's word to a Judaism wrapped in darkness.

Nicodemus is mentioned again in Jn. 7:50–52, where he showed more courage in protesting against the condemnation of Christ without giving him a hearing. The final reference is in Jn. 19:40, where he is said to have brought a lavish gift of spices to anoint the body of Christ. Nothing more is known of him despite a large number of legends (*e.g.* in the apocryphal *Gospel of Nicodemus*). His identification with the wealthy and generous Naqdimon ben-Gorion of the Talmud is uncertain.

Bibliography. M. de Jonge,

'Nicodemus and Jesus', *BJRL* 53, 1970–71, pp. 337ff. R.E.N.

NICOLAUS, NICOLAITANS. Nicolaus of Antioch (Acts 6:5) is supposed to have given his name to a group in the early church who sought to work out a compromise with paganism, to enable Christians to take part without embarrassment in some of the social and religious activities of the close-knit society in which they found themselves. It is possible that the term Nicolaitan is a Graecized form of Heb. Balaam, and therefore allegorical, the policy of the sect being likened to that of the OT corrupter of Israel (Nu. 22). In that case the Nicolaitans are to be identified with groups attacked by Peter (2 Pet. 2:15), Jude (11) and John (Rev. 2:6, 15 and possibly 2:20–23), for their advocacy within the church of pagan sexual laxity. References in Irenaeus, Clement and Tertullian suggest that the group hardened into a Gnostic sect. E.M.B.

NICOPOLIS ('city of victory'). A town built as the capital of Epirus by Augustus on a peninsula of the Ambraciot Gulf, where he had camped before his victory at Actium in 31 BC. It was a Rom. colony, and derived some of its importance from the Actian games, also established by Augustus.

Although there were other towns named Nicopolis, this was the only one of sufficient standing to warrant Paul's spending a whole winter in it (Tit. 3:12), and its geographical position would suit its selection as a rendezvous with Titus. Paul may have planned to use it as a base for evangelizing Epirus. There is no ancient authority for the AV subscription to the Epistle to Titus. K.L.McK.

The ruins of the Odeon at the Roman colony of Nicopolis in Epirus, Greece, built by Augustus. (RH)

NILE.

I. Terminology

The origin of Gk. *Neilos* and Lat. *Nilus*, our 'Nile', is uncertain. In the OT, with a few rare exceptions, the word *yᵉʾôr*, 'river, stream, channel', is used whenever the Egyp. Nile is meant. This Heb. word is itself directly derived from Egyp. *itrw* in the form *i'r*(*w*) current from the 18th Dynasty onwards, meaning 'Nile-river, stream, canal', *i.e.* the Nile and its various subsidiary branches and channels. (A. Erman and H. Grapow, *Wörterbuch der Aegyptischen Sprache*, 1, 1926, p. 146; T. O. Lambdin, *JAOS* 73, 1953, p. 151). In AV the word *yᵉʾôr* is hidden under various common nouns, 'river, flood', *etc.* Just once the word *nāhār*, 'river', is used of the Nile as the river of Egypt in parallel with the Euphrates, the *nāhār*, 'river' *par excellence*, the promised land lying between these two broad limits (Gn. 15:18). *naḥal*, 'wadi', is apparently never used of the Nile, but of the Wadi el-'Arish or 'river of Egypt', while the Shihor is the seaward end of the E Delta branch of the Nile (*EGYPT, RIVER OF).

II. Course of the river

The ultimate origin of the Nile is the streams such as the Kagera that flow into Lake Victoria in Tanzania; from the latter, a river emerges N, *via* Lake Albert Nyanza and the vast Sudd swamps of the S Sudan, to become the White Nile. At Khartoum this is joined by the Blue Nile flowing down from Lake Tana in the Ethiopian (Abyssinian) highlands, and their united stream is the Nile proper. After being joined by the Atbara river some 320 km NE of Khartoum, the Nile flows for 2,700 km through the Sudan and Egypt N to the Mediter-

NIGER
See Simeon, Part 3.

NIGHT CREATURE
See Lilith, Part 2.

NIGHT HAWK
See Animals, Part 1.

NIGHTJAR
See Animals, Part 1.

ranean without receiving any other tributary; the total length of the river from Lake Victoria to the Mediterranean is roughly 5,600 km. Between Khartoum and Aswan, six 'sills' of hard granite rocks across the river's course give rise to the six cataracts that impede navigation on that part of its course.

Within Nubia and Upper Egypt, the Nile stream flows in a narrow valley which in Egypt is never much more than 20 km wide and often much less, bounded by hills or cliffs, beyond which stretch rocky deserts to E and W (*EGYPT, **II**). Some 20 km N of Cairo, the river divides into two main branches that reach the sea at Rosetta in the W and Damietta in the E respectively; between and beyond these two great channels extend the flat, swampy lands of the Egyptian Delta. In Pharaonic Egypt three main branches of the Delta Nile seem to have been recognized ('Western river', Canopic branch?; 'the Great river', very roughly the present Damietta branch; 'the Waters of Rē'', or Eastern, Pelusiac branch, Heb. Shihor), besides various smaller branches, streams and canals. Gk. travellers and geographers reckoned from five to seven branches and mouths of the Nile. See A. H. Gardiner, *Ancient Egyptian Onomastica*, 2, 1947, pp. 153*–170*, with map between pp. 131* and 134*, on this tricky question; also J. Ball, *Egypt in the Classical Geographers*, 1942; M. Bietak, *Tell El-Dab'a*, 2, 1975.

III. The inundation and agriculture

The most remarkable feature of the Nile is its annual rise and flooding over its banks, or inundation. In spring and early summer in Ethiopia and S Sudan the heavy rains and melting highland snows turn the Upper Nile—specifically the Blue Nile—into a vast torrent bringing down in its waters masses of fine, reddish earth in suspension which it used to deposit on the lands flooded on either side of its banks in Egypt and Nubia. Thus, until the perennial irrigation-system of dams at Aswan and elsewhere was instituted last century, those areas of the Egyptian valley and Delta within reach of the floods received every year a thin, new deposit of fresh, fertile mud. The muddy flood-waters used to be held within basins bounded by earthen banks, to be released when the level of the Nile waters sank again. In Egypt the Nile is lowest in May; its rise there begins in June, the main floodwaters reach Egypt in July/August, reach their peak there in

The Nile, showing the fertile land watered by it. (BPL)

September and slowly decline again thereafter. But for the Nile and its inundation, Egypt would be as desolate as the deserts on either hand; wherever the Nile waters reach, vegetation can grow, life can exist. So sharp is the change from watered land to desert that one can stand with a foot in each. Egypt's agriculture depended wholly on the inundation, whose level was checked off against river-level gauges or Nilometers. A high flood produced the splendid crops that made Egypt's agricultural wealth proverbial. A low Nile, like drought in other lands, spelt famine; too high a Nile that swept away irrigation-works and brought destruction in its wake was no better. The regular rhythm of Egypt's Nile was familiar to the Hebrews (*cf.* Is. 23:10; Am. 8:8; 9:5), and likewise the dependence of Egypt's cultivators, fisherfolk and marshes on those waters (Is. 19:5–8; 23:3). When then the prophet proclaimed judgment on Egypt in terms of drying up the Nile (Ezk. 30:12; *cf.* 29:10; Zc. 10:11), as other lands might be chastised by lack of rain (*cf.* *FAMINE). Jeremiah (46:7–9) compares the advance of Egypt's army with the surge of the rising Nile. On the inundation of the Nile, see G. Hort, *ZAW* 69, 1957, pp. 88–95; J. Ball, *Contributions to the Geography of Egypt*, 1939, *passim*; D. Bonneau, *La crue du Nil*, 1964.

IV. Other aspects

The Nile in dominating Egypt's agriculture also affected the form of her calendar, divided into three seasons (each of four 30-day months and excluding 5 additional days) called *'Akhet*, 'Inundation'; *Peret*, 'Coming Forth' (*i.e.* of the land from the receding waters); and *Shomu*, 'Dry(?)' or Summer season. The waters of the Nile not only supported crops but formed also the marshes for pasture (*cf.* Gn. 41:1–3, 17–18) and papyrus (*PAPYRI AND OSTRACA), and contained a wealth of fish caught by both line and net (Is. 19:8), *cf.* R. A. Caminos, *Late-Egyptian Miscellanies*, 1954, pp. 74, 200 (many sorts), and G. Posener *et al.*, *Dictionnaire de la Civilisation Égyptienne*, 1959, figures on pp. 214–215. On the plagues of a blood-red Nile, dead fish and frogs, *etc.*, *PLAGUES OF EGYPT. For Na. 3:8, *THEBES. The Assyrian's boast of drying up Egypt's streams (2 Ki. 19:24 = Is. 37:25) may refer to moats and similar river-defence

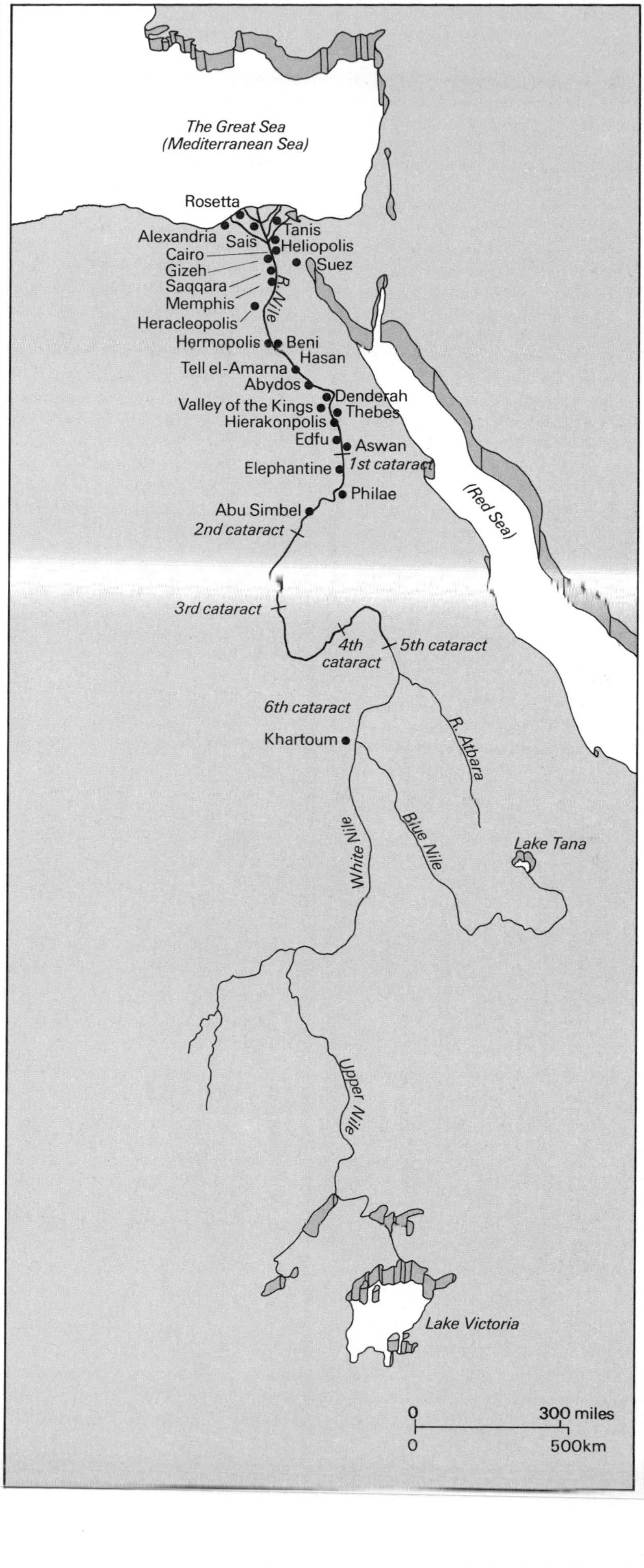

The course of the river Nile.

works. For Moses in the rushes by the Nile, * MOSES. The Nile was also Egypt's main arterial highway; boats could sail N by merely going with the stream, and could as readily sail S with the aid of the cool N wind from the Mediterranean. In the religious beliefs of the Egyptians the spirit of the Nile-flood was the god Ha'pi, bringer of fertility and abundance. K.A.K.

NIMRIM, WATERS OF. The waters of Nimrim are mentioned twice (Is. 15:6; Je. 48:34). In substantially identical terms the prophets tell of the overthrow of Moab; cries of anguish go up from the cities of Moab, and 'the waters of Nimrim are a desolation'. Both in Isaiah and (especially) in Jeremiah the sequence of place-names suggests a site in S Moab, the now-customary identification with Wadi en-Numeirah, 16 km S of the Dead Sea. This is to be distinguished from Nimrah (Nu. 32:3) or Beth-nimrah (Nu. 32:36) about 16 km N of the Dead Sea. J.A.M.

NIMROD. The name of the son of Cush, an early warrior, or hero (*gibbōr*), who lived in Babylonia, where his kingdom included Babylon, Erech and Akkad (Gn. 10:8–10; 1 Ch. 1:10). He was father or founder of Nineveh and Calah in Assyria (Gn. 10:11) and was famous as a hunter (v. 9). The land adjacent to Assyria was later referred to as the 'land of Nimrod' (Mi. 5:6).

His name is perpetuated in several place-names, including Birs Nimrud, SW of Babylon, and Nimrud in Assyria (* CALAH). This, with the legends concerning him preserved in Sumerian, Assyr. and later literature, implies a wider basis in the tradition than is provided in Genesis. Many scholars therefore compare him with Sargon of Agade, *c.* 2300 BC, who was a great warrior and huntsman and ruler of Assyria. He led expeditions to the Mediterranean coast and into S Anatolia and Persia, and the splendour of his age and achievements led to its being recalled as a 'golden age'. Since only the throne-name of Sargon is known, it is possible that he bore other names. Others see in Nimrod exploits attributed to such early rulers as Naram-Sin of Agade, Tukulti-Ninurta I of Assyria (*Eretz Israel* 5, 1958, pp. 32*–36*); or deities as Ninurta (Nimurda), the Bab. and Assyr. god of war, and the hunter, or Amar-utu, the Sumerian name of the god Marduk. No certain identification is yet possible.

D.J.W.

NINEVEH. A principal city, and last capital, of Assyria. The ruins are marked by the mounds called Kuyunjik and Nabi Yunus ('Prophet Jonah') on the river Tigris opposite Mosul, N Iraq.

I. Name

The Heb. *nînᵉwēh* (Gk. *Nineuē*; classical *Ninos*) represents the Assyr. *Ninuā* (Old Bab. *Ninuwa*), a rendering of the earlier Sumerian name *Nina*, a name of the goddess Ishtar written with a sign depicting a fish inside an enclosure. Despite the comparison with the history of Jonah, there is probably no connection with the Heb. *nûn*, 'fish'.

According to Gn. 10:11 Nineveh was one of the N cities founded by *Nimrod or Ashur after leaving Babylonia. Excavation 25 m down to virgin soil shows that the site was occupied from prehistoric times (*c.* 4500 BC). 'Ubaid (and Samarra) type pottery and pisée-buildings may indicate a S influence. Although first mentioned in the inscriptions of Gudea of Lagash who campaigned in the area *c.* 2200 BC, the texts of Tukulti-Ninurta I (*c.* 1230 BC) tell how he restored the temple of the goddess Ishtar of Nineveh founded by Manishtusu, son of Sargon, *c.* 2300 BC.

By the early 2nd millennium the city was in contact with the Assyr. colony of Kanish in Cappadocia, and when Assyria became independent under Shamshi-Adad I (*c.* 1800 BC) the same temple of Ishtar (called E-mash-mash) was again restored. Hammurapi of Babylon (*c.* 1750 BC) adorned the temple, but the expansion of the town followed the revival of Assyr. fortunes under Shalmaneser I (*c.* 1260 BC), and by the reign of Tiglath-pileser I (1114–1076 BC) it was established as an alternative royal residence to Assur and Calah. Both Ashurnasirpal II (883–859 BC) and Sargon II (722–705 BC) had palaces there. It was, therefore, likely that it was to Nineveh itself that the tribute of Menahem in 744 BC (2 Ki. 15:20) and of Samaria in 722 BC (Is. 8:4) was brought.

Sennacherib, with the aid of his W Semitic queen Naqi'a-Zakutu, extensively rebuilt the city, its defensive walls, gates and water-supply. He built a canal leading 48 km from a dam on the river Gomel to the N, and controlled the flow of the river Khasr, which flowed through the city, by the erection of another dam at Ajeila to the E. He also provided new administrative buildings and parks. The walls of his new palace were decorated with reliefs depicting his victories, including the successful

Opposite page: Bronze head of an Akkadian ruler, identified by some as Naram-Sin and by others as Sargon of Akkad. Both have been equated with the biblical Nimrod, but this must remain uncertain. Found at Nineveh. c. 2250 BC. (SI)

NIMRAH
See Beth-nimrah, Part 1.

Relief carving of a lion-hunt from the palace of Ashurbanipal (c. 640 BC). (BM)

siege of *Lachish. The tribute received from Hezekiah of Judah (2 Ki. 18:14) was sent to Nineveh, to which *Sennacherib himself had returned after the campaign (2 Ki. 19:36; Is. 37:37). It is possible that the temple of *Nisroch, where he was murdered, was in Nineveh. His account of his attack on Hezekiah in Jerusalem is recorded on clay prisms used as foundation inscriptions in Nineveh.

Ashurbanipal (669–*c.* 627 BC) again made Nineveh his main residence, having lived there as crown prince. The bas-reliefs depicting a lion hunt (British Museum), which were made for his palace, are the best examples of this form of Assyr. art. The fall of the great city of Nineveh, as predicted by the prophets Nahum and Zephaniah, occurred in August 612 BC. The Bab. Chronicle tells how a combined force of Medes, Babylonians and Scythians laid siege to the city, which fell as a result of the breaches made in the defences by the flooding rivers (Na. 2:6–8). The city was plundered by the Medes, and the king Sin-shar-ishkun perished in the flames, though his family escaped. The city was left to fall into the heap of desolate ruin which it is today (Na. 2:10; 3:7), a pasturing-place for the flocks (Zp. 2:13–15), which gives the citadel mound its modern name of Tell Kuyunjik ('mound of many sheep'). When Xenophon and the retreating Gk. army passed in 401 BC it was already an unrecognizable mass of debris.

At the height of its prosperity Nineveh was enclosed by an inner wall of *c.* 12 km circuit within which, according to Felix Jones' survey of 1834, more than 175,000 persons could have lived. The population of 'this great city' of Jonah's history (1:2; 3:2) is given as 120,000, who did not know right from wrong. This has been compared with the 69,574 persons in *Calah (Nimrud) in 865 BC, then a city of about half the size of Nineveh. The 'three days' journey' may not necessarily designate the size of Nineveh (Jon. 3:3) whether by its circumference or total administrative district. It could refer to a day's journey in from the suburbs (*cf.* 3:4), a day for business and then return. The Heb. translation by using *nînᵉwēh* in each case could not differentiate between the district (Assyr. *ninua[ki]*) and metropolis (*[al]ninuā*). There is no external evidence for the repentance of the people of Nineveh (Jon. 3:4–5), unless this is reflected in a text from Guzanu (*GOZAN) of the reign of Ashur-dān III when a total solar eclipse in 763 BC was followed by flooding and famine. Such signs would be interpreted by the Assyrians as affecting the king who would temporarily step down from the throne (Jon. 3:6). Such portents, including an earthquake about the time of Jonah ben Amittai (2 Ki. 14:25), could well have made the Ninevites take the step commended by Jesus (Lk. 11:30; Mt. 12:41).

III. Exploration

Following reports made by such early travellers as John Cartwright (17th century) and plans drawn by C. J. Rich in 1820, interest was reawakened in the discovery of the OT city. Excavation was at first undertaken by P. E. Botta (1842–

The fall of Nineveh in 612 BC to a combined force of Babylonians, Medes and Scythians (Ummanmanda) is recorded in this Babylonian Chronicle for 616–609 BC. (BM)

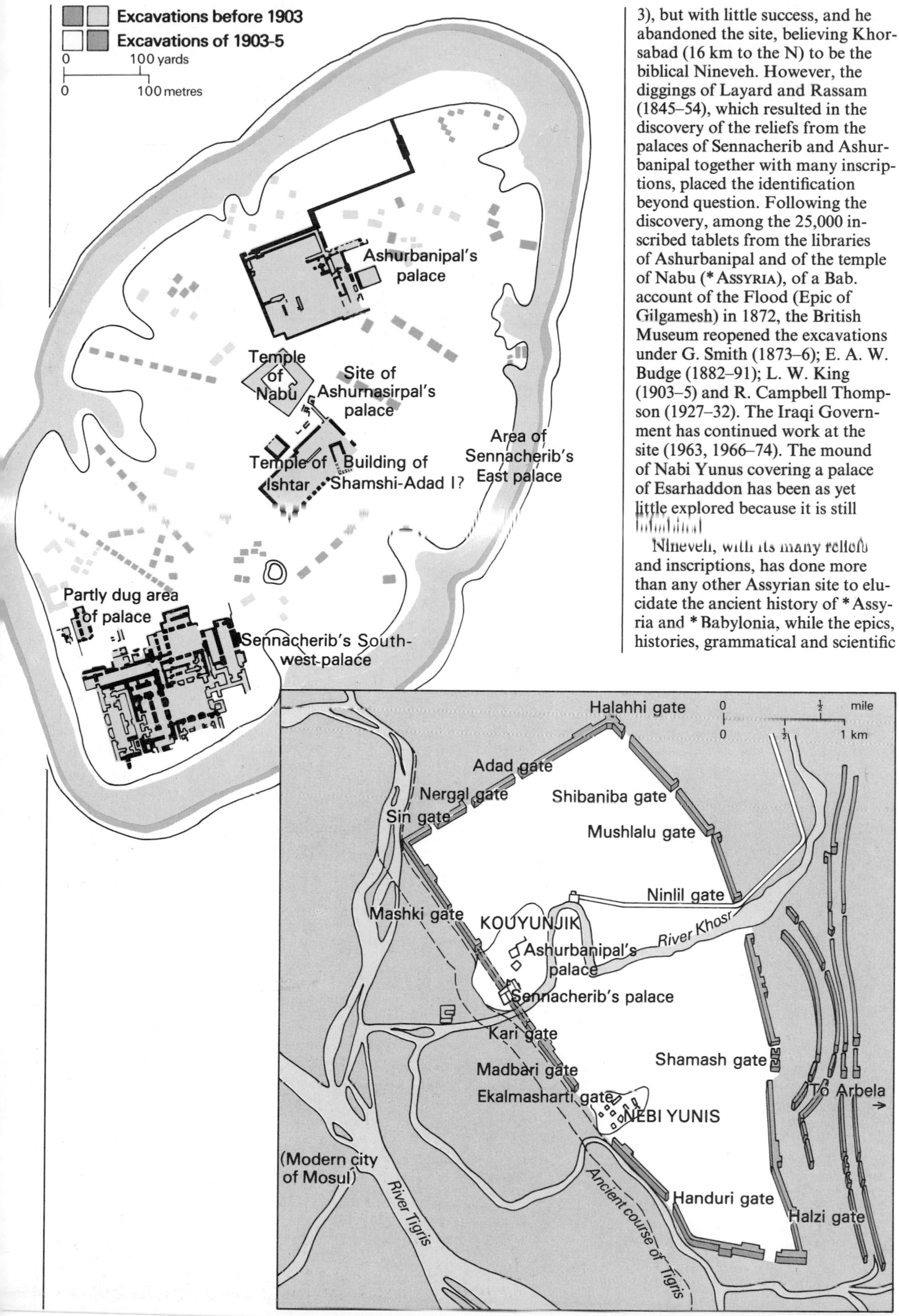

Plan of Nineveh.

3), but with little success, and he abandoned the site, believing Khorsabad (16 km to the N) to be the biblical Nineveh. However, the diggings of Layard and Rassam (1845–54), which resulted in the discovery of the reliefs from the palaces of Sennacherib and Ashurbanipal together with many inscriptions, placed the identification beyond question. Following the discovery, among the 25,000 inscribed tablets from the libraries of Ashurbanipal and of the temple of Nabu (* ASSYRIA), of a Bab. account of the Flood (Epic of Gilgamesh) in 1872, the British Museum reopened the excavations under G. Smith (1873–6); E. A. W. Budge (1882–91); L. W. King (1903–5) and R. Campbell Thompson (1927–32). The Iraqi Government has continued work at the site (1963, 1966–74). The mound of Nabi Yunus covering a palace of Esarhaddon has been as yet little explored because it is still inhabited.

Nineveh, with its many reliefs and inscriptions, has done more than any other Assyrian site to elucidate the ancient history of * Assyria and * Babylonia, while the epics, histories, grammatical and scientific

Part of the wall of Nineveh and the Shamash Gateway, rebuilt with some original stones. (DJW)

NIPPUR
See Calneh, Part 1.

NOADIAH
See Prophetess, Part 3.

texts and letters have made Assyr. literature better known than that of any ancient Semitic peoples except the Hebrews (*ARCHAEOLOGY, *WRITING).

BIBLIOGRAPHY. R. Campbell Thompson and R. W. Hutchinson, *A Century of Exploration at Nineveh*, 1929; A. Parrot, *Nineveh and the Old Testament*, 1955. The exploration of Nineveh is described in full by A. H. Layard, *Nineveh and its Remains*, 1849; G. Smith, *Assyrian Discoveries*, 1875; R. Campbell Thompson (and others), *Liverpool Annals of Archaeology and Anthropology* 18, 1931, pp. 55–116; 19, 1932, pp. 55–116; 20, 1933, pp. 71–186; *Archaeologia* 79, 1929; *Iraq* 1, 1934, pp. 95–105; *Sumer* 23, 1967, pp. 76–80. D.J.W.

NISROCH (Heb. *nisrōḵ*). The deity in whose temple Sennacherib was murdered by his sons as he worshipped (2 Ki. 19:37; Is. 37:38). The place of this assassination, which is mentioned also in Assyr. records (*DOTT*, pp. 70–73), is variously identified with one of the major cities, Nineveh, Assur or Calah. Nisroch may then be a rendering of the name of the Assyr. national god, Ashur (*cf.* LXX *Esdrach*, *Asorach*; *JRAS*, 1899, p. 459). A form of the god Nusku (assuming an original *nswk*) of Marduk, or a connection with the eagle-shaped army standards has also been suggested. D.J.W.

NITRE (Heb. *neṯer*). The modern name denotes saltpetre (sodium or potassium nitrate), but the biblical name refers to natron (carbonate of soda), which came chiefly from the 'soda lakes' of Lower Egypt. In Pr. 25:20 the effect of songs on a heavy heart is compared to the action of vinegar on nitre (RVmg. 'soda')—*i.e.* producing strong effervescence. RSV follows LXX: 'it is like pouring vinegar on a wound'. In Je. 2:22 nitre ('lye') is used in a purificatory sense: mixed with oil it formed a kind of *soap. (*ARTS AND CRAFTS, **III**. *h*.)

BIBLIOGRAPHY. R. J. Forbes, *Studies in Ancient Technology*, 3, 1955. J.D.D.

NOAH. The last of the ten antediluvian Patriarchs and hero of the *Flood. He was the son of Lamech, who was 182 (Samaritan Pentateuch, 53; LXX, 188) years old when Noah was born (Gn. 5:28–29; Lk. 3:36).

a. Name

The etymology of the name, *nōaḥ*, is uncertain, though many commentators connect it with the root *nwḥ*, 'to rest'. In Genesis (5:29) it is associated with the verb *nḥm* (translated 'comfort' in AV and RV; 'bring relief' in RSV), with which it is perhaps etymologically connected; though this is not necessarily required by the text. The element *nḥm* occurs in Amorite personal names and in the name Naḫmizuli which figures in a Hurrian fragment of the Gilgamesh epic found at Boğazköy, the Hittite capital in Asia Minor. The LXX gives the name as *Nōe*, in which form it appears in the NT (AV).

b. Life and character

Noah was a righteous man (Gn. 6:9, *ṣaddîq*), having the righteousness that comes of faith (Heb. 11:7, *hē kata pistin dikaiosynē*, lit. 'the according to faith righteousness'), and had close communion with God, as is indicated by the expression he 'walked with God' (Gn. 6:9). He is also described as without fault among his contemporaries (Gn. 6:9; AV 'perfect in his generations') who had all sunk to a very low moral level (Gn. 6:1–5, 11–13; Mt. 24:37–38; Lk. 17:26–27), and to them he preached righteousness (2 Pet. 2:5), though without success, as subsequent events showed. Like the other early Patriarchs, Noah was blessed with great length of years. He was 500 years old when his first son was born (Gn. 5:32), 600 when the *Flood came (Gn. 7:11) and died at the age of 950 (Gn. 9:28–29). According to the most likely interpretation of Gn. 6:3, together with 1 Pet. 3:20, when Noah was 480 years old God informed him that he was going to destroy man from the earth but would allow a period of grace for 120 years, during which time Noah was to build an * ark, in which he would save his immediate family and a representative selection of animals (Gn. 6:13–22). It was probably during this period that Noah preached, but there was no repentance, and the * Flood came and destroyed all but Noah, his three sons and their four wives (Gn. 7:7; 1 Pet. 3:20).

After the Flood Noah, who had probably been a farmer before it, planted a vineyard (Gn. 9:20; 'And Noah, the husbandman, began and planted a vineyard . . .', which is to be preferred to the EVV) and, becoming drunk, behaved in an unseemly way in his tent. * Ham, seeing his father naked, informed his two brothers, who covered him, but it is probable that Canaan, Ham's son, did something disrespectful to his grandfather, for Noah placed a curse on him when he awoke (Gn. 9:20–27).

c. God's covenant with Noah

The covenant implied in Gn. 6:18 might be interpreted as salvation for Noah conditional upon his building and entering the ark, which obligations he fulfilled (v. 22). On the other hand, it may be that this passage simply makes reference to the covenant which God made with Noah after the Flood, and which he sealed by conferring a new significance on the rainbow (Gn. 9:9–17; *cf.* Is. 54:9). The main features of this covenant were that it was entirely instituted by God, that it was universal in scope, applying not only to Noah and his seed after him but to every living creature, that it was unconditional, and that it was everlasting. In it God undertook from his own free lovingkindness never again to destroy all flesh with a flood.

d. Descendants

Noah had three sons, * Shem, * Ham and * Japheth (Gn. 5:32; 9:18–19; 10:1), who were born before the Flood, and accompanied him in the ark. We are told that after the Flood, from them 'was the whole earth (*'ereṣ*) overspread', or 'the whole (population of) the earth dispersed' (Gn. 9:19). Their descendants later spread out over a wide area, and an account is given of some of them in the Table of the * Nations in Gn. 10.

e. Cuneiform parallels

In the * flood accounts which have been preserved in Akkadian the name of the hero is Utanapishtim, which corresponds to the name Ziusuddu in a Sumerian account of the early 2nd millennium BC, which probably lies behind the Akkadian versions. Though in the principal version of the Sumerian king list only eight rulers are named before the Flood, of whom Ziusuddu is not one, other texts list ten rulers, the tenth being Ziusuddu, who is credited with a reign of 36,000 years. The same is found in a late account in Gk. by the Babylonian priest Berossos, whose flood hero Xisouthros is the tenth of his preflood rulers.

BIBLIOGRAPHY. J. Murray, *The Covenant of Grace*, 1954, pp. 12–16; E. A. Speiser, *Mesopotamian Origins*, 1930, pp. 160–161; H. B. Huffmon, *Amorite Personal Names in the Mari Texts*, 1965, pp. 237–239; E. Laroche, *Les noms des Hittites*, 1966, p. 125; T. Jacobsen, *The Sumerian King List*, 1939, pp. 76–77 and n. 34; F. F. Bruce, *NIDNTT* 1, pp. 601–603. T.C.M.

NOB. A locality mentioned in three passages of the OT, all of which may refer to the same place.

In 1 Sa. 22:19 it is referred to as a city of priests; presumably Yahweh's priests had fled there with the ephod after the capture of the ark and the destruction of Shiloh (1 Sa. 4:11). David visited Nob after he had escaped from Saul when Ahimelech was priest there and ate holy bread (1 Sa. 21:6). When Saul heard that the priest of Nob had assisted the fugitive David he raided the shrine and had Ahimelech, along with eighty-five other priests, put to death (1 Sa. 22:9, 11, 18–19).

Isaiah prophesied that the Assyrian invaders would reach Nob, between Anathoth, 4 km NE of Jerusalem, and the capital (Is. 10:32), and the city is also mentioned in Ne. 11:32 as a village which was reinhabited after the return from exile.

The latter two references indicate a locality near Jerusalem, probably the modern Râs Umm et-Tala on the E slopes of Mt Scopus, NE of Jerusalem (Grollenberg, *Atlas of the Bible*, 1956). S. R. Driver (*Notes on the Hebrew Text of the Books of Samuel*², 1913, p. 172) suggests perhaps a spot on the Rās el-Meshārif, under 2 km N of Jerusalem, a ridge from the brow of which (818 m) the pilgrim along the N road still catches his first view of the holy city (790 m). R.A.H.G.

NOBAH (Heb. *nōḇaḥ*). **1.** An Amorite locality settled and renamed by Nobah (see **2**) and his clan (Nu. 32:42). If the Amorite name Kenath indicates modern Kanawat (Eusebius' *Kanatha*), 96 km E of lake Tiberias, this can hardly be the Nobah of Jdg. 8:11, which must be in Mt Gilead.

2. A Manassite leader (Nu. 32:42). J.P.U.L.

NOD. A land E of, or in front of, Eden (*qiḏmaṯ-'ēḏen*, Gn. 4:16), to which Cain was banished by God after he had murdered Abel. The name (*nôḏ*) is the same in form as the infinitive of the verb *nûḏ* (*nwd*), 'to move to and fro, wander', the participle of which is used in Gn. 4:14 when Cain bemoans the fact that he will become a 'vagabond' (RSV 'wanderer'). The name is unknown outside the Bible, but its form and the context suggest that it was a region where a nomadic existence was necessary, such as is today found in several parts of the Middle East. T.C.M.

NODAB. A tribe which, among others, is mentioned in 1 Ch. 5:19 as having been conquered by Reuben, Gad and half-Manasseh, and about whom nothing more is definitely known. (* HAGARITES.) J.D.D.

NOMADS. A human group which changes its area of residence seasonally within a larger domain which is its home territory.

I. In the Bible

The word 'nomad' does not occur in EVV of the Bible, the nomadic groups being called by other names.

The first was * Cain, who was banished from his kindred to be a wanderer (Gn. 4). A number of nomadic groups are mentioned in the Table of the Nations in Gn. 10 (* NATIONS, TABLE OF). Among the descendants of * Japheth are * Gomer (Cimmerians), Madai (* MEDES), Meshek (perhaps Phrygians) and * Ashkenaz (Scythians), all peoples who probably came originally from the N steppe. Heth, among the children of Ham, may be the * Hittites of Asia Minor, though it is perhaps more probable that the reference is to the later Neo-Hittite states of N Syria. Among the descendants of Shem

NOAH'S ARK
See Ark, Part 1.

NOHAH
See Manahath, Part 2.

are listed *Aram (Aramaeans), and a number of Arabian tribes, some of them still nomadic in historical times, who stemmed from the Arabian peninsula.

The patriarchal period was largely a time of nomadism for God's chosen remnant. It is uncertain whether Abraham was actually living a sedentary life within the city of Ur when he was called by God. He is later called 'the Hebrew' (Gn. 14:13), and this may indicate that he was one of the Habiru (*HEBREWS) living outside the city in perhaps a client status. In such a situation he could still be a man of substance, as he undoubtedly was. How long he and his fathers had been at Ur is not stated, but when he left he began a nomadic life which was continued by Isaac and Jacob for two long generations, before the children of Israel settled to the sedentary life of Egypt (*cf.* Heb. 11:9). This was not the regular seasonal movement of nomads within a set territory, but a wandering from place to place; and, though Abraham had camels (*e.g.* Gn. 24; for the view of some scholars that patriarchal camels are anachronistic, see *CAMEL), his herds were largely of sheep and goats, and included asses (Gn. 22:3), so that some would class him as a semi-nomad or an 'ass-nomad'. Such a life would fit in well with the times as illuminated by the *Mari archives. Terah and his sons Nahor and Haran by remaining at Harran established affiliations with another nomadic group, the Aramaeans, as is shown by the reference to a 'wandering Aramaean' as the ancestor of the Israelites (Dt. 26:5).

After experiencing the luxuries of a sedentary life in Egypt, even though oppressed, the Israelites at the Exodus were reluctant to return to the rigours of wandering. The 40 years in the wilderness was a unique episode, for without the miraculous supply of food provided by God the numbers of the people would have been far too great to be supported by the natural resources of the area.

After the settlement in the Promised Land the true nomadic life ceased for the Israelites, but various reminiscences of it survive in the OT. For instance, in many cases a man's house is referred to as his 'tent' (*e.g.* Jdg. 20:8; 1 Sa. 13:2; 2 Sa. 20:1; 1 Ki. 12:16). To express the idea of rising early the verb *šāḵam* (in the Hiph'îl stem), which properly means 'to load the backs (of beasts)', is used (*e.g.* Jdg. 19:9; 1 Sa. 17:20). Certain metaphors used in poetry suggest a nomadic background: in Jb. 4:21 (RSV) the plucking up of a tent-cord signifies death; in Je. 10:20 the breaking of tent-cords indicates desolation, and conversely, a sound tent speaks of security (Is. 33:20); in Is. 54:2 a prosperous people is signified by an enlarged tent space.

The Israelites came in contact with various nomadic groups after they had settled in the land. The Aramaeans had by the 1st millennium largely settled in the city states of Syria, so that the nomadic threat came mostly from the E and S, where the *bᵉnê qeḏem*, 'the Children of the East' (*cf.* Ezk. 25:4) and such associated peoples as the *Midianites, *Amalekites, *Moabites, *Edomites, *Ammonites and *Kedarites would always take advantage of weakness in the settled territories. Solomon's commercial expansion in the 10th century brought contacts with *Arabia and the caravan traders of that area. In the 9th century Jehoshaphat was able to exact tribute from the Arabs (2 Ch. 17:11), but the family of Jehoram were carried off by this people in a raid (2 Ch. 21:16–17). Throughout the Monarchy, the Arabs are mentioned in various capacities (*e.g.* Is. 13:20; 21:13; Je. 3:2; 25:23–24; Ezk. 27:21).

After the return from the Exile the nomadic traders who were settling on the E fringes of Syria–Palestine are exemplified by *Geshem the Arab, who tried to hinder the rebuilding of Jerusalem (Ne. 2:19; 6:6). These people were followed in NT times by the *Nabataeans.

With the moral corruption which accompanied the settlement in the land, the prophets used the ideal of the nomadic life as a figure of spiritual health. They condemned the luxuries of city life (Am. 3:15; 6:8) and spoke of a return to the simplicity of the early days of Israel in the wilderness (Ho. 2:14–15; 12:9). It is probable that this call to the desert was put into practice from time to time, as is evidenced by the Qumran Community (*DEAD SEA SCROLLS) in the intertestamental period, and by John the Baptist, and Jesus Christ and his disciples in NT times. Though this was not nomadism in the strict sense, it was a manifestation of that value of nomadism which has always been held forth as an aim for God's people; to be pilgrims in this world, and to avoid the laying up of treasure upon earth. (*RECHABITES; *KENITES.)

II. Way of life

A nomadic group depends for its livelihood upon herds of animals such as the horse, camel, sheep, goat or ox, and the pasturing needs of the herds determine the movements of the community. This way of life is required by the terrain inhabited, which usually consists mainly of an area of steppe or plain which provides temporary pasture in the wet or cool season, and either oases or uplands to which a retreat is made in the dry season. Under normal conditions a nomadic tribe will have a recognized home territory, visiting different parts regularly in a seasonal cycle. Thus each tribe or, in more barren areas, smaller group visits annually its recognized tract of pasture, and returns annually to the same oasis or upland territory. Mobile dwellings are provided by tents of skins, felt or wool, and all equipment is strictly limited. There are variations from area to area. Some groups, mainly camel herders, abandon the plain for an oasis or upland only when compelled by drought; others, particularly shepherds, have semi-permanent dwellings at the oasis, even planting and raising crops, and go out on the plain only when the animals' needs for pasture compel it. Peoples of this latter type are sometimes called semi-nomads.

Such an economy is finely adjusted, and the natural increase of population disturbs the balance. In consequence, a growing group may encroach on a neighbour's traditional territory, and the weaker group be displaced, perhaps setting up a chain effect which may cause the fringe groups to look abroad. Sedentary farming communities fall an easy prey to the overspilling nomads who may set themselves as a military aristocracy over the less-vigorous population. A few generations, however, usually suffice for the interlopers to be absorbed by the dominant though less-aggressive culture of the settled peoples.

The most advantageous situation for a nomadic group is in a mixed country where city-states and their surrounding tilled territory are interspersed by less-intensively settled areas where the nomad can make his encampments and exploit the vulnerable settlements. This may be done either by mobile raids

Shosu *nomads, mentioned only in Egyptian sources at the time of the Exodus, here shown on relief at Memphis. Tomb of Horemheb. Saqqara, Memphis. c. 1330* BC. (RVO)

or by taking service either as mercenary troops or as labourers.

Certain values arise from the demands of the nomadic life. The mutual dependence of the members of a tribe, together with the consciousness of common descent, lead to great solidarity (*FAMILY) and to such concomitant practices as blood revenge (*AVENGER OF BLOOD) for murder or manslaughter. The need for mobility results in the reduction of property to that which is movable, wealth being accumulated in livestock. The rigours of life lead also to hospitality to the traveller and to chivalry, sometimes of a kind strange to the sedentary farmer.

III. The ancient Near East

There were two main areas supporting nomadic populations in ancient times, from which the more settled regions of the Near East suffered the influx of marauders. These were the peninsula of Arabia and the steppe of S Russia. Access from Arabia was easier than from the N, since the latter area lay across a mountain barrier, and for the nomads of N Arabia some of the oases visited seasonally lay on the very margins of the settled areas of Palestine and Syria.

a. The southern nomads

It is probable that Arabia was the immediate homeland of the Semites (Semitic speakers), and since from the earliest historical times in Mesopotamia the Semitic Akkadians formed part of the population, a continual influx of nomads from the Arabian peninsula may be inferred. Knowledge of the arrival of nomads from Arabia is very much conditioned by the surviving evidence. Written records are meagre from Palestine, intermittent from Syria, but more extensive from Mesopotamia. In Mesopotamia, however, the fullest records come from periods of political strength, when encroaching nomads could be most effectively resisted, and indeed, according to the records, the best-attested route of overt entry to Mesopotamia was from the N, though a peaceful infiltration into Babylonia from the W may be assumed. The early part of the 2nd millennium BC, following the fall of the 3rd Dynasty of Ur, was a period of weakness in Babylonia, and of consequent nomadic invasions from the N, the invaders, particularly the *'Amorites', finally establishing themselves as ruling dynasties in the cities of Babylonia. During the time of the greatest of these dynasties, the 1st of Babylon, the diplomatic archives discovered at the city of *Mari on the Middle Euphrates give a glimpse of the situation in N Mesopotamia–Syria, where the city-states were interspersed by territory occupied by nomadic groups. One group known as the Hanaeans (*Ḫanû*) provided the king of Mari with mercenary troops, and, though they lived in encampments, some of them were beginning to settle in permanent dwellings. A more troublesome group were the Yaminites (sometimes read Bini-Yamin; the writing is more likely to have been read *mārū yamīn*; *BENJAMIN, TUR [pl]-*ya-mi-in*), who spread through the steppe area between the Ḫabur river and the Euphrates and farther W, particularly in the vicinity of Harran, being frequently mentioned as raiding settlements and even attacking towns. The Sutaeans (*Sutû*) likewise raided farther S, particularly on the trade routes connecting the Euphrates with Syria. Another group of people, the Habiru (*HEBREWS), who are mentioned in the second half of the 2nd millennium in documents from Nuzi, Alalaḫ, Hattusas, Ugarit, El-Amarna and in native Egyp. documents, are already mentioned earlier (18th century BC) in the Mari letters and in documents of the same general period from Alalaḫ, Cappadocia and S Mesopotamia. These people seem to have been nomads or semi-nomads who are found now as raiders, now as settlers in the towns, serving sometimes as mercenary troops, and sometimes as labourers or even slaves.

These are the principal nomadic groups mentioned in the Mari archives from this period, but they were no doubt typical of peoples at other periods who menaced the isolated city-states, particularly of N Mesopotamia and Syria–Palestine. Some were probably more in the nature of travelling craftsmen than raiders, and such a group is depicted on a 19th-century BC wall

■ **NORTH-EASTER**
See Wind, Part 3.

■ **NOSE RING**
See Hook, Part 2.

■ **NUBIAN**
See Phineas, Part 3.

■ **NUBIAN IBEX**
See Animals, Part 1.

painting at Beni Hasan in Egypt (see *IBA*, fig. 25).

In the succeeding centuries another nomadic group which spread through Syria–Palestine and into *Egypt was the Hyksos, and again mainly during the 2nd millennium yet another body of nomads, the *Aramaeans, and a related group, the Aḫlamu, began to come into prominence. During the centuries around the turn of the 2nd to the 1st millennium, these people and their congeners flooded W Asia, putting a halt to the growing dominion of Assyria, and founding many city-states in the area of Syria and N Mesopotamia.

These groups of nomads are the principal ones known from the written documents, who probably came ultimately from the Arabian peninsula. More directly from the peninsula were groups of Arabs (*Arabia), who are mentioned in the Assyr. inscriptions and depicted in the bas-reliefs as riding camels and living in tents. Later in the 1st millennium such posts as Petra and Palmyra on the fringes of the sown were settled by Arab tribes who were able to profit from the caravan traffic.

b. The northern nomads

Access to the Near East was more difficult for the N nomads who inhabited the S Russian steppe; the principal route of entry was between the Caspian and the Black Seas and into Asia Minor and Iran. Signs of the influx of the N nomads are found already in the middle of the 3rd millennium at the 'Royal Tombs' of Alaca Hüyük in central Asia Minor, where a warrior aristocracy had imposed itself on the peasant population. These were predecessors of the Indo-European-speaking Hittites who established an empire in Asia Minor in the 2nd millennium. It is clear that, like the Hittites, many of the invaders from the N were Indo-European-speaking. In the 2nd millennium the Kassites in Babylonia and the rulers of Mitanni in N Mesopotamia betray, in their names and certain elements of vocabulary, their Indo-European origins. These people were among the first to introduce the *horse and *chariot to W Asia, and it is probable that this was a combination developed on the steppe. In the late 2nd millennium the Phrygians in Asia Minor repeated the pattern of a dominating warrior aristocracy, and later the Cimmerians are encountered as warlike raiders. In the 1st millennium the Medes and Persians came to prominence in Iran, the latter finally founding an empire which dominated the entire Near East. In the Assyr. inscriptions the earlier groups of the raiding warriors are known as Ummanmanda (*Assyria).

Bibliography. *General:* C. D. Forde, *Habitat, Economy and Society*[4], 1942, pp. 308–351. *Bible:* R. de Vaux, *Ancient Israel*, 1961, pp. 3–15, 519–520; D. J. Wiseman, *The Word of God for Abraham and Today*, 1959, pp. 10–12; *DBS* 6, coll. 541–550. *Ancient Near East:* F. Gabrieli (ed.), *L'Antica Società Beduina*, 1959; J. R. Kupper, *Les nomades en Mésopotamie au temps des rois de Mari*, 1957; S. Moscati, *The Semites in Ancient History*, 1959; T. T. Rice, *The Scythians*, 1958, esp. pp. 33–55; M. B. Rowton, 'Autonomy and Nomadism in Western Asia', *Or* 42, 1973, pp. 247–258; 'Dimorphic Structure and the Problem of the 'Apirû-'Ibrîm', *JNES* 35, 1976, pp. 13–20.

T.C.M.

NOSE, NOSTRILS (Heb. *'ap̄*, 'nose' or 'nostril'). The organ of breathing, used also of the face, perhaps by synecdoche, especially in the expression 'face to the ground' in worship or homage. The Hebrews apparently thought no further into the respiratory process, and no word for lung occurs in the Bible. The presence of breath in the nostrils was connected with *life (Gn. 2:7; Jb. 27:3), and the temporary nature thereof (Is. 2:22). The word also denotes the nose as the organ of smelling (Ps. 115:6; Am. 4:10). When breath was emitted visibly (called 'smoke', Ps. 18:8) it was connected with the expression of inner emotion, principally anger. By metonymy the word *'ap̄* often comes to mean 'anger' (Gn. 27:45; Jb. 4:9), and is used figuratively thus in the OT far more frequently than in the literal sense. It is apparent from cognate languages (*e.g.* Akkad. *appu*, 'face') that the physical designation is the original. The word is not found in the NT. B.O.B.

NUMBER.

I. General usage

Israel shared with most of her Mediterranean and Near Eastern neighbours, *e.g.* Assyria, Egypt, Greece, Rome and Phoenicia, the decimal system of counting. The numbers recorded in the Heb. text of the OT are written in words, as in the main are the figures in the Gk. text of the NT. Numbers are also written in word form on the Moabite Stone and the Siloam Inscription.

In Heb. the number one is an adjective. A series of nouns denote the numbers 2 to 10. Combinations of these numbers with 10 give 11 to 19. After 20 the tens are formed in a pattern similar to that used in Eng., *i.e.* 3, 30. A separate word denotes 100; 200 is the dual form of this, and from 300 to 900 there is again a pattern similar to that found in the Eng. numeral system. The highest number expressed by one word is 20,000, the dual form of 10,000.

Aram. papyri from Egypt from the 6th to the 4th centuries BC, Aramaic endorsements on cuneiform tablets from Mesopotamia and Heb. ostraca and weights provide evidence of an early system of numerical notation within the OT period. Vertical strokes were used for digits and horizontal strokes for tens, written one above the other for multiples of ten, often with a downward stroke on the right. A stylized *mem* represented 100 with vertical strokes for additional hundreds. An abbreviation of the word 'a thousand' was used to indicate this figure. It is considered that the Heb. material shows that a sign resembling a Gk. *lambda* represented 5 and a sign similar to an early *gimel* stood for 4. See Y. Yadin, *Scripta Hierosolymitana*, 8, 1961, pp. 9–25. (*Weights and Measures.)

H. L. Allrick (*BASOR* 136, 1954, pp. 21–27) proposes that originally the lists in Ne. 7 and Ezr. 2 were written in the early Heb.–Aram. numeral notation, and he suggests that an explanation of certain differences between the lists may be found in this fact. See A. R. Millard, *TynB* 11, 1962, pp. 6–7, for evidence of Heb. numerical signs.

The idea of using letters of the alphabet for numerals originated from Gk. influence or at least during the period of Gk. influence, and, as far as is known, first appeared on Maccabean coins. See however G. R. Driver, *Textus* 1, 1960, pp. 126f.; 4, 1964, p. 83, for indication of earlier origin. The first nine letters were used for the figures 1 to 9, the tens from 10 to 90 were represented by the next nine and the hundreds from 100 to 400 by the remaining four letters. The number 15, however, was denoted by a combination of *teth* (9) and *waw* (6), as the two letters *yod* (10) and *he* (5) were the consonants of Yah, a form of the sacred name Yahweh. Further numbers were denoted by a combination of letters. There are ordinal numbers in biblical Heb. from 1 to 10, after which the cardinal numbers are used. There are also words for fractions from a half to a fifth. Numbers in biblical Gk. follow the pattern used in Hellenistic Gk.

An indication of the mathematical concept of infinity may be found in the statement in Rev. 7:9 where the redeemed are 'a great multitude, which no man could number'. In a concrete image this concept is expressed in the OT as, *e.g.*, Gn. 13:16. *Cf.* also Gn. 15:5.

The elementary processes of arithmetic are recorded in the OT, *e.g.* addition, Nu. 1:17ff. and Nu. 1:45; subtraction, Lv. 27:18; multiplication, Lv. 25:8.

In certain passages it is evident that numbers are being used in an approximate sense. The numbers '2', '2 or 3', '3 or 4', '4 or 5' are sometimes used with the meaning of 'a few', *e.g.* 1 Ki. 17:12, where the widow of Zarephath says, 'I am gathering a couple of sticks', and also Lv. 26:8 'five of you shall chase a hundred'. Similar usages are found in 2 Ki. 6:10; Is. 17:6; for 'three or four', see Am. 1:3ff. and Pr. 30:15ff. From the NT we may quote the use of round numbers by Paul in 1 Cor. 14:19. 'Nevertheless in the church I would rather speak five words with my mind, in order to instruct others, than ten thousand words in a tongue.' *Cf.* also Mt. 18:22.

It would seem that '10' was used as the equivalent of 'quite a number of times', and we may instance Jacob's words in Gn. 31:7, where it is recorded that Laban changed his wages '10 times'; *cf.* also Nu. 14:22. That Saul, David and Solomon are recorded as having reigned for 40 years, and the recurring statement in the book of Judges that the land had rest 40 years (Jdg. 3:11; 5:31; 8:28) seem to indicate that 40 was used to stand for a generation, or quite a considerable number, or length of time. 100, *e.g.* Ec. 6:3, would equal a large number, and 1,000, 10,000 (Dt. 32:30; Lv. 26:8), and 40,000 (Jdg. 5:8) provide instances of round numbers which indicate an indefinitely large number. In the case of large numbers for the strength of armies, *e.g.* 2 Ch. 14:9, these are in all probability approximate estimates, as also seems to be the case with the number of David's census (2 Sa. 24:9; *cf.* 1 Ch. 21:5), and perhaps the 7,000 sheep sacrificed in Jerusalem (2 Ch. 15:11).

II. Large numbers in the Old Testament

The large numbers recorded in certain parts of the OT have occasioned considerable difficulties. These are concerned chiefly with the chronology of the early periods of OT history, where the problem is further complicated by the presence of differing figures in the various texts and versions, with the numbers of the Israelites at the time of the Exodus, and the numbers of warriors in various armies, and especially of the numbers of the [illegible] forces. With regard to the first problem one may instance that the Heb. text gives 1,656 years as the time between the creation and the Flood, the LXX 2,262 years and the Samaritan 1,307. Or for the age of Methuselah the Heb. text gives 969 years and the Samaritan 720. (*GENEALOGY; *CHRONOLOGY OF THE OLD TESTAMENT.) A similar problem exists in the NT regarding the number of persons on board the ship on which Paul travelled to Rome. Some MSS give 276 and others 76 (Acts 27:37). Again the number of the beast (Rev. 13:18) is given variously as 666 and 616.

An indication that numbers might suffer textual corruption in transmission is provided by differing numbers in parallel texts, *e.g.* the age of Jehoiachin at the beginning of his reign is given as 18 in 2 Ki. 24:8 and 8 in 2 Ch. 36:9.

Archaeological discoveries have contributed considerable background information to the age of the Exodus and the conquest of Palestine, and the contemporary population. Given that the Israelites were less in number than the Canaanites, as may be inferred from Ex. 23:29 and Dt. 7:7, 17, 22, the census numbers of Nu. 1 and 26 which imply a population of 2–3 million require investigation.

Divergent interpretations of the figures have been proposed, from acceptance at face value, *e.g. NBC*, 1953, p. 165, to J. Bright, *A History of Israel*², 1972, p. 130: 'these lists . . . represent a later period of Israel's history'. Attempts have been made to retranslate the figures and so reduce them. The Heb. word *'elep̄*, 'a thousand', can be translated 'family', 'tent group', or 'clan': *e.g.* Jdg. 6:15, 'my clan (*'alpî*) is the weakest in Manasseh'. The following may also be consulted: F. Petrie, *Egypt and Israel*, 1911, pp. 42ff.; G. E. Mendenhall, 'The Census Lists of Numbers 1 and 26', *JBL* 77, 1958, pp. 52ff.; C. S. Jarvis, *Yesterday and Today in Sinai*, 1936; R. E. D. Clark, 'The Large Numbers of the OT', *JTVI* 87, 1955, pp. 82ff.

J. W. Wenham (*TynB* 18, 1967, pp. 19–53), following R. E. D. Clark's repointing of *'elep̄* 'thousand' to *'allûp̄*, translated 'officer' or 'trained warrior', and interpreting *mē'ôṯ* 'hundreds' as 'contingents', suggests that the individual large numbers consist of a coalescence of these two terms in a specific ratio. The number of fighting men would then be reduced to 18,000 and, allowing for Levites and [illegible] old to fight, an estimated male population would total 36,000, consistent with the figure for first-born males (22,273) in Nu. 3:43. This figure, doubled to include women, gives a calculated Israelite population of 72,000.

Revocalization of *'elep̄* to *'allûp̄* 'officer', 'captain', provides a possible solution to the enormous numbers of fallen in battle, recorded in thousands, and is consistent with practice in ancient battles where mighty men did most of the fighting, *e.g.* David and Goliath.

III. Significant numbers

Numbers are also used with a symbolical or theological significance.

One is used to convey the concept of the unity and uniqueness of God, *e.g.* Dt. 6:4, 'The Lord our God is one Lord'. The human race stems from one (Acts 17:26). The entry of sin into the world is through one man (Rom. 5:12). The gift of grace is by one man, Jesus Christ (Rom. 5:15). His sacrifice in death is a once-for-all offering (Heb. 7:27), and he is the first-born from the dead (Col. 1:18), the first-fruits of the dead (1 Cor. 15:20). 'One' also expresses the unity between Christ and the Father (Jn. 10:30), the union between believers and the Godhead, and the unity which exists among Christians (Jn. 17:21; Gal. 3:28). 'One' further expresses singleness of purpose (Lk. 10:42). The concept of union is also found in the saying of Jesus concerning marriage, 'and the two

Opposite page: Table of numerals in use during the biblical period.

shall become one' (Mt. 19:6).

Two can be a figure both of unity and of division. Man and woman form the basic family unit (Gn. 1:27; 2:20, 24). Animals associate in pairs and enter the ark in twos (Gn. 7:9). Two people often work together in companionship, *e.g.* Joshua's spies (Jos. 2:1), and the Twelve and Seventy disciples were sent out in pairs (Mk. 6:7; Lk. 10:1). In addition, at Sinai there were two stone tablets, and animals were often offered for sacrifice in pairs. By contrast two is used with separating force in 1 Ki. 18:21, as it is also implied in the two 'ways' of Mt. 7:13–14.

Three. It is natural to associate the number 3 with the Trinity of Persons in the Godhead, and the following references among others may be instanced: Mt. 28:19; Jn. 14:26; 15:26; 2 Cor. 13:14; 1 Pet. 1:2, where this teaching is implied. The number 3 is also associated with certain of God's mighty acts. At Mt Sinai the Lord was to come down to give his Law on 'the third day' (Ex. 19:11). In Hosea's prophecy the Lord would raise up his people 'on the third day', probably meaning a short time (Ho. 6:2). There is a similar usage of 'three' in Lk. 13:32, where 'third day' is 'poetical for the moment when something is finished, completed, and perfected' (N. Geldenhuys, *Commentary on the Gospel of Luke*, 1950, p. 384, n. 4). Jonah was delivered (Jon. 1:17; Mt. 12:40), and God raised Christ from the dead, on the third day (1 Cor. 15:4). There were three disciples admitted to special terms of intimacy with Christ (Mk. 9:2; Mt. 26:37), and at Calvary there were three crosses. Paul emphasizes three Christian virtues (1 Cor. 13:13). A further instance of three being used in connection with periods of time is the choice offered to David of 3 days' pestilence, 3 months' defeat or 3 years' famine (1 Ch. 21;12). The deployment of Gideon's army furnishes an example of division into three (Jdg. 7:16), and the fraction, a third, is employed in Rev. 8:7–12.

Four, the number of the sides of a square, is one of symbols of completion in the Bible. The divine name Yahweh has 4 letters in Heb. (*YHWH*). There were 4 rivers flowing out of the garden of Eden (Gn. 2:10) and there are 4 corners of the earth (Rev. 7:1; 20:8), from whence blow the 4 winds (Je. 49:36; Ezk. 37:9; Dn. 7:2). In his vision of the glory of God, Ezekiel saw 4 living creatures (ch. 1), and with these we may compare the 4 living creatures of Rev. 4:6.

The history of the world from the time of the Babylonian empire is spanned by 4 kingdoms (Dn. 2; 7). Four is a prominent number in prophetic symbolism and apocalyptic literature, as the following additional references show: 4 smiths and 4 horns (Zc. 1:18–21), 4 chariots (Zc. 6:1–8), 4 horns of the altar (Rev. 9:13), 4 angels of destruction (Rev. 9:14). In addition, there are 4 Gospels, and at the time when the gospel was extended to the Gentiles Peter saw in a vision a sheet let down by its 4 corners.

Five and *ten*, and their multiples, occur frequently on account of the decimal system used in Palestine. In the OT 10 Patriarchs are mentioned before the Flood. The Egyptians were visited with 10 plagues and there were Ten Commandments. The fraction one-tenth formed the tithe (Gn. 14:20; 28:22; Lv. 27:30; 2 Ch. 31:5; Mal. 3:10). In the parable of Lk. 15:8 the woman possessed 10 coins, and in the parable of the pounds mention is made of 10 pounds, 10 servants and 10 cities (Lk. 19:11–27). Of the 10 virgins, 5 were wise and 5 foolish (Mt. 25:2). 5 sparrows were sold for 2 farthings (Lk. 12:6); Dives had 5 brothers (Lk. 16:28); the woman by the well had had 5 husbands (Jn. 4:18), and at the feeding of the 5,000 the lad had 5 loaves. There are 10 powers which cannot separate the believer from the love of God (Rom. 8:38f.) and 10 sins which exclude from the kingdom of God (1 Cor. 6:10). The number 10, therefore, also signifies completeness; 10 elders form a company (Ru. 4:2).

Six. In the creation narrative God created man and woman on the 6th day (Gn. 1:27). 6 days were allotted to man for labour (Ex. 20:9; 23:12; 31:15; *cf.* Lk. 13:14). A Heb. servant had to serve for 6 years before he was freed. The number 6 is therefore closely associated with man.

Seven has an eminent place among sacred numbers in the Scriptures, and is associated with completion, fulfilment and perfection. In the creation narrative God rested from his work on the 7th day, and sanctified it. This gave a pattern to the Jewish sabbath on which man was to refrain from work (Ex. 20:10), to the sabbatic year (Lv. 25:2–6), and also to the year of jubilee, which followed 7 times 7 years (Lv. 25:8). The Feast of Unleavened Bread and the Feast of Tabernacles lasted 7 days (Ex. 12:15, 19; Nu. 29:12). The Day of Atonement was in the 7th month (Lv. 16:29), and 7 occurs frequently in connection with OT ritual, *e.g.* the sprinkling of bullock's blood 7 times (Lv. 4:6) and the burnt-offering of 7 lambs (Nu. 28:11); the cleansed leper was sprinkled 7 times (Lv. 14:7), and Naaman had to dip 7 times in Jordan (2 Ki. 5:10). In the tabernacle the candlestick had 7 branches (Ex. 25:32).

Other references to be noted are: the mother of 7 sons (Je. 15:9; 2 Macc. 7:1ff.); 7 women for one man (Is. 4:1); a loving daughter-in-law preferable to 7 sons (Ru. 4:15). The Sadducees proposed a case of levirate marriage with 7 brothers (Mt. 22:25). The priests encompassed Jericho 7 times (Jos. 6:4). Elijah's servant looked for rain 7 times (1 Ki. 18:43). The psalmist praised God 7 times a day (Ps. 119:164), and Gn. 29:18; 41:29, 54 and Dn. 4:23 mention 7 years (times). The early church had 7 deacons (Acts 6:3) and John addresses 7 churches in the book of Revelation, where there is mention of 7 golden candlesticks (1:12) and 7 stars (1:16). At the miraculous feeding of 4,000 from 7 loaves and a few fishes (Mk. 8:1–9), the 7 basketsful collected afterwards may indicate that Jesus can satisfy completely. The complete possession of Mary Magdalene is effected by 7 demons (Lk. 8:2), while the dragon of Rev. 12:3 and the beast of Rev. 13:1; 17:7 have 7 heads.

Eight. 1 Pet. 3:20 records that 8 people were saved in the ark of Noah. Circumcision of a Jewish boy took place on the 8th day (Gn. 17:12; Phil. 3:5). In Ezekiel's vision of the new Temple the priests make their offering on the 8th day (43:27).

Ten. See *Five*.

Twelve. The Heb. year was divided into 12 months, the day into 12 hours (Jn. 11:9). Israel had 12 sons (Gn. 35:22–27; 42:13, 32) and there were 12 tribes of Israel, the people of God (Gn. 49:28). Christ chose 12 apostles (Mt. 10:1ff.). Twelve is therefore linked with the elective purposes of God.

Forty is associated with almost each new development in the history of God's mighty acts, especially of salvation, *e.g.* the Flood, redemption from Egypt, Elijah and the prophetic era, the advent of Christ and the birth of the church. The following periods of 40 days

	AKKADIAN	EGYPTIAN Hieroglyphic	EGYPTIAN Hieratic	EARLY HEBREW	PHOENICIAN	POST-EXILIC HEBREW	GREEK Before 200BC	GREEK After 200BC
1	𒁹	I	[illegible]	I	I	𐤀 א	I	A
2	𒈫	II	[illegible]	II	II	𐤁 ב	II	B
3	𒐈	III	[illegible]	III	III	𐤂 ג	III	Γ
4	𒐉	IIII	[illegible]	IIII	I III	𐤃 ד	IIII	Δ
5	𒐊	IIIII	[illegible]	˥	II III	𐤄 ה	Γ	E
6	𒐋	III III	[illegible]		III III	ו	ΓI	F
7	𒑂	IIII III	[illegible]		I III III	ז	ΓII	Z
8	𒑄	IIII IIII	[illegible]		II III III	ח	ΓIII	H
9	𒑆, 𒑆	III III III	[illegible]		III III III	ט	ΓIIII	Θ
10	𒌋	𓎆	[illegible]	Λ	¬	י	Δ	I
20	𒎙	𓎇	[illegible]	ᚷ	N, 3	כ	ΔΔ	K
30	𒌍			+	←N, −=	ל	ΔΔΔ	Λ
40	𒐏					מ	ΔΔΔΔ	M
50	𒐐			[illegible]		נ	𐅄	N
60	𒁹					ס	𐅄Δ	Ξ
70	𒁹𒌋					ע		O
80						פ		Π
90						צ		Ϙ
100	𒁹𒈨	𓍢	[illegible]		ש, א	ק	H	P
200			[illegible]			ר	HH	Σ
300						ש		T
400						ת		Υ
500						תק	𐅅	Φ
600	𒐙							X
700								Ψ
800								Ω
900								Ϡ
1,000	𒌋𒈨	𓆼	[illegible]		ר	תתר	X	/A
2,000			[illegible]					
3,600	𒊹							
10,000		𓂭	[illegible]				M	
20,000			[illegible]					
100,000		𓆐	[illegible]					
200,000			[illegible]					
1,000,000			[illegible]					
2,000,000			[illegible]					
5,000,000		𓁨						

NUMBERS AT EXODUS
See Wilderness of wandering, Part 3.

may be listed: the downpour of rain during the Flood (Gn. 7:17); the despatch of the raven (Gn. 8:6); Moses' fasts on the mount (Ex. 24:18; 34:28; Dt. 9:9); the spies' exploration of the land of Canaan (Nu. 13:25); Moses' prayer for Israel (Dt. 9:25); Goliath's defiance (1 Sa. 17:16); Elijah's journey to Horeb (1 Ki. 19:8); Ezekiel's lying on his right side (Ezk. 4:6); Jonah's warning to Nineveh (Jon. 3:4); Christ's stay in the wilderness prior to his temptation (Mt. 4:2), his appearances after his resurrection (Acts 1:3).

For 40 years, the general designation of a generation, the following may be quoted: the main divisions of Moses' life (Acts 7:23, 30, 36; Dt. 31:2); Israel's wandering in the wilderness (Ex. 16:35; Nu. 14:33; Jos. 5:6; Ps. 95:10); the recurring pattern of servitude and deliverance in the era of the judges (*e.g.* Jdg. 3:11; 13:1); the reigns of Saul, David and Solomon (Acts 13:21; 2 Sa. 5:4; 1 Ki. 11:42); the desolation of Egypt (Ezk. 29:11).

Seventy is often connected with God's administration of the world. After the Flood the world was repopulated through 70 descendants of Noah (Gn. 10); 70 persons went down to Egypt (Gn. 46:27); 70 elders were appointed to help Moses administer Israel in the wilderness (Nu. 11:16); the people of Judah spent 70 years of exile in Babylon (Je. 25:11; 29:10); 70 weeks, 'sevens', were decreed by God as the period in which Messianic redemption was to be accomplished (Dn. 9:24); Jesus sent forth the Seventy (Lk. 10:1); he enjoined forgiveness 'until seventy times seven' (Mt. 18:22).

666 (or *616*) is the number of the beast in Rev. 13:18. Many interpretations of this number have been proposed, and by *gematria*, in which figures are given the value of corresponding letters, the number 666 has been identified with the numerical values of the names of a variety of personalities from Caligula and Nero Caesar onwards, and with such concepts as the chaos monster.

For a full discussion, and of 'thousand', see commentaries on the book of Revelation, especially *NBCR*; H. B. Swete, *The Apocalypse of St. John*, 1906, pp. 175–176; J.-J von Allmen, art. 'Number' in *Vocabulary of the Bible*, 1958; D. R. Hillers, *BASOR* 170, 1963, p. 65.

Rev. 7:4; 14:1 records the number *144,000* 'which were sealed'. It is the number 12, the number of election, squared, and multiplied by 1,000, an indefinitely large number, and symbolizes the full number of saints of both covenants who are preserved by God.

Bibliography. E. D. Schmitz, C. J. Hemer, M. J. Harris and C. Brown, *NIDNTT* 2, pp. 683–704 (extensive bibliography).

R.A.H.G.

NUMBERS, BOOK OF. The synagogue named this book after its first word or after one of the first words (*way^e^ḏabbēr*, 'and he spoke'; or *b^e^miḏbar*, 'in the desert'). The Gk. translators called it *arithmoi*, 'numbers'. Where the four other parts of the Pentateuch are concerned, the Gk. names are commonly used; in this fifth part, in some countries the Gk. has been translated into the native language: 'Numbers', *etc.*; in other countries the Lat. translation of the Gk. name is used: *Numeri*. The title is given because the book's first few chapters (and ch. 26) contain many numbers, especially census-numbers.

I. Outline of contents

a. The numbering of the Israelites. The marshalling of the tribes (1:1–4:49).

b. The law regarding jealousy, legislation for the Nazirites and other laws (5:1–6:27).

c. The offerings for the consecration of the tabernacle (7:1–89).

d. The candlestick. The consecration of the Levites; their time of service (8:1–26).

e. The second Passover; the cloud; the two silver trumpets (9:1–10:10).

f. The departure from Sinai (10:11–36).

g. Taberah. The quails. The 70 elders (11:1–35).

h. Miriam and Aaron against Moses (12:1–16).

i. The twelve spies (13:1–14:45).

j. Miscellaneous commandments regarding, *inter alia*, meat and drink offerings, offerings where a person has sinned through ignorance, and commandments about sabbath-breaking (15:1–41).

k. Korah, Dathan and Abiram. The blossoming rod of Aaron (16:1–17:13).

l. The position of the priests and Levites (18:1–32).

m. The water of separation for purification of sins (19:1–22).

n. The death of Miriam. Meribah (20:1–13).

o. Edom refuses to give Israel passage. Death of Aaron (20:14–29).

p. The struggle at Hormah. The serpent of bronze. To the plains of Moab. The fight against Sihon and Og (21:1–35).

q. Balaam (22:1–24:25).

r. Baal-peor (25:1–18).

s. The second numbering of the Israelites (26:1–65).

t. The right of inheritance of daughters. The successor of Moses (27:1–23).

u. Commandments regarding offerings. Vows of the women (28:1–30:16).

v. Vengeance taken against the Midianites (31:1–54).

w. The allotment of the land on the E side of Jordan (32:1–42).

x. The places where Israel camped during their journeys through the desert (33:1–49).

y. Directions concerning the conquest of Canaan. The borders of Canaan. Regulations concerning the division of the land. The cities of the Levites. Cities of refuge (33:50–35:34).

z. The marriage of daughters having an inheritance (36:1–13).

II. Authorship and date

Many scholars today consider that the tradition according to which Moses is the author of the entire book must be seriously questioned. They draw attention to the following considerations. Only for ch. 33 is a literary activity of Moses mentioned (v. 2, *cf.* 5:23; 11:26); this is not mentioned for any other part of Nu.; for the contrary case, see *e.g.* Dt. 31:9. Various data point to a later time than that of Moses, or at least to another author than Moses; *cf.* 12:3; 15:22f. (Moses in the third person); 15:32; 21:14 (perhaps the 'book of the wars of the Lord' originates from the post-Mosaic time); 32:34ff. Nevertheless, the book repeatedly states that the regulations and the laws have been given through the agency of Moses (and Aaron), 1:1, *etc.*; it is also clear that the laws and regulations give the impression that they were enacted during the wanderings through the desert (5:17; 15:32ff., *etc.*). For that matter it is possible that the laws have gone through a process of growth: afterwards there may have been alterations made in them, *e.g.* for the purpose of adapting them to altered circumstances. Sometimes there are definite marks of these

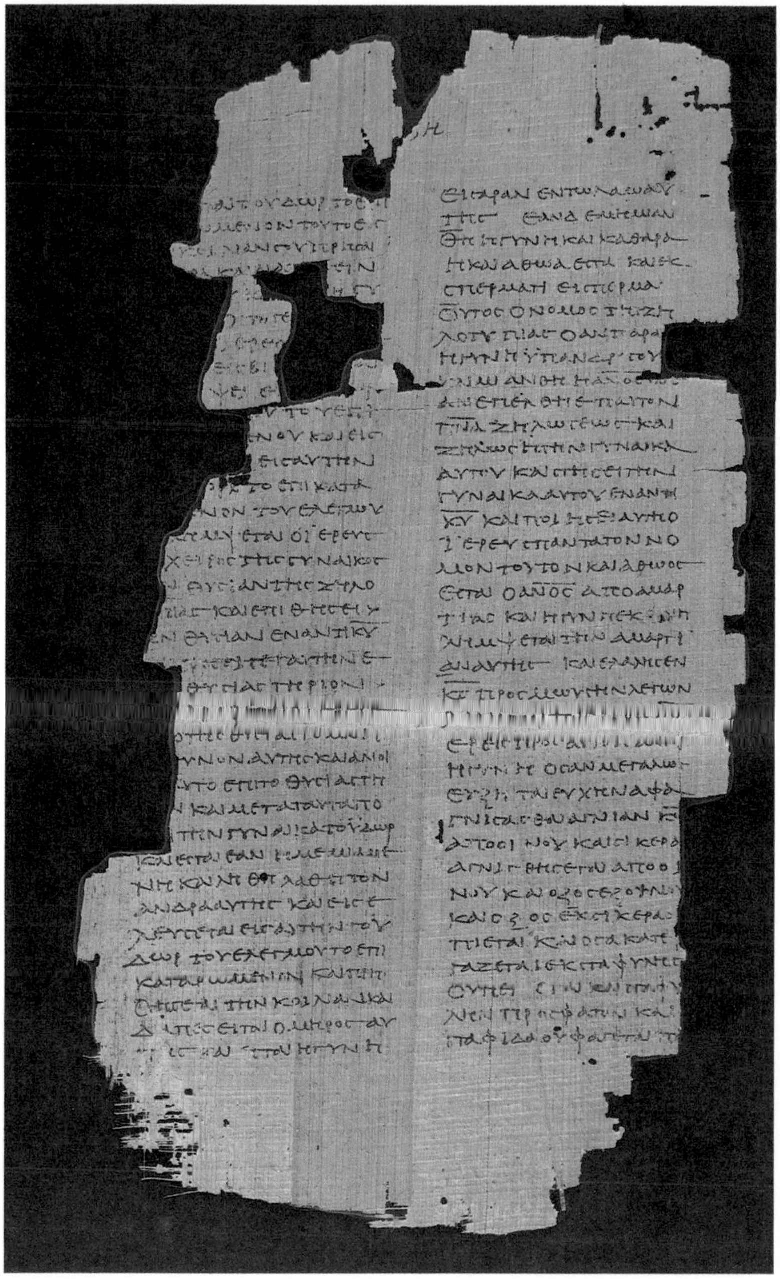

Greek papyrus of Numbers 5:22–6:4. 2nd–3rd cent. AD. *Chester Beatty papyrus VI.* (CBL)

processes; thus there are differences between Nu. 15:22–31 and Lv. 4:1f.; in addition, we note the fact that Nu. 15:22f. speaks about Moses in the third person, and it is not unlikely that Nu. 15:22–31 is a later version of Lv. 4.

We shall have to assume that the laws substantially originate from the Mosaic time. We can also assume that the noting down of both the laws and the stories was already begun during the Mosaic time. The time when the book received its final form is unknown to us. In the opinion of the present writer, it is a plausible view that the major points were already recorded in writing, *e.g.* in the early days of the Monarchy. It is significant that there are no *post-Mosaica* pointing unmistakably to a time much later than that of Moses.

Since the critical activity of Wellhausen and others, many scholars have adopted the view that Nu. belongs for the greater part to the so-called Priestly Code, which is said to have its origin in the post-exilic age. At present, however, scholars are inclined, more than Wellhausen was, to accept the view that Nu. contains material dating from old, even very remote, times, admitting that in Nu. 5:11ff. and ch. 19, ancient rites are described, and that other material points to a similar conclusion. Many scholars are willing to accept that the cult, as it is described in Nu., was in use, so far as concerns the main points, in pre-exilic Jerusalem. See also the articles on * PENTATEUCH, * MOSES, * WILDERNESS OF THE WANDERING, *etc.*, and articles under particular subjects such as * BALAAM, * CITIES OF REFUGE, *etc.*

III. Further summary of contents

1. The division of the Pentateuch into five books is not original. Thus, even though it is not without meaning that with Nu. 1:1 a new book begins (in which the first four chapters form the preparation for the departure from Sinai), this book nevertheless forms a unity with the preceding books. In the same way it may be said that Dt. is the continuation of Nu., but the separation between Nu. and Dt. is more fundamental than the separation of Lv. and Nu.

2. The history narrated in Nu. covers 38 years—the period between the 2nd year and the 40th year after the Exodus (see the definitions of the time in 1:1; 7:1; 9:1, 15; 10:11; 33:38; *cf.* Ex. 40:2; Dt. 1:3).

In the first part Israel is still staying near Mt Sinai (Ex. 19:1 tells of their arrival at Sinai). Nu. 10:11–12:16 deals with the departure from Sinai and the journey to Kadesh (*cf.* 13:26); in the 2nd year after the Exodus Israel had already arrived at Kadesh (*cf.* Dt. 2:14). Because Israel put faith in the defeatist words of the spies, there ensued a prolonged wandering in the desert (chs. 13–14). Little is known to us of the fortunes of Israel during the 38 years of their wanderings (15:1–20:13). We should reckon with the possibility that Kadesh was for a long time a sort of centre for Israel, while various groups of Israelites were wandering about the Sinai Peninsula. After these 38 years Israel leaves Kadesh for Canaan, marches round Edom, comes into the plains of Moab, and defeats Sihon and Og (20:14–21:35). The last part of the book describes the actions of Balaam, Israel's idol-worship of Baal-peor and the punishment of the Midianites.

3. Besides dealing with history, this book contains all kinds of regulations and laws. The relation between laws and history and between one law and another is often not very clear to us. Nevertheless, the author will, at least in many cases, have intended a connection. The simplest solution is to suppose that there is a chronological connection. Sometimes there is also a material connection; see, *e.g.*, how well 5:1–4 and ch. 18 correspond with what precedes, and 10:1–10 with what follows; after a survey of the journey through the desert has been given (33:1–49), the narrative continues (33:50–35:34) with regulations concerning the conquest of Canaan and laws for when they are dwelling in it. Finally, we should bear in mind that the construction of many OT books raises similar questions to those we have referred to here (*PSALMS, *PROVERBS, *ISAIAH, *etc.*).

Many laws (but not all of them) concern ritual matters. The Israelites did not distinguish between cultic, moral, juridical and social laws in the same way as we usually do. All the laws and regulations have as their object that Israel should be prepared to live in Canaan in the sight of the Lord, as an independent and well-conducted nation.

4. In Nu. Moses is again the dominant figure, depicted in all his greatness and weakness, and guiding the people in every respect. Through his mediation the Lord gives Israel a variety of laws and regulations, speaking to his servant 'mouth to mouth' (12:6–8). Over and over again Moses acts as intercessor for the people (11:2; 12:13; 14:13ff.; 16:22; 21:7). He was 'very meek, more than all men that were on the face of the earth' (12:3; *cf.* 14:5; 16:4ff.), yet he had his share of human failings. Contrary to the Lord's order he strikes the rock (20:10f.), and on occasion he makes temperamental complaints (11:10ff.; *cf.* 16:15). Next to Moses in prominence is Aaron (1:3, 17, 44; 2:1, *etc.*, especially chs. 12; 16–17).

IV. The message of the book

In Nu., as in the case of the whole Bible, the almighty and faithful God of the covenant reveals himself; it is this revelation that joins the different parts of Nu. into a unity. In the regulations and laws he imposes, God shows his care of his people. Israel frequently revolts against him. As a result the anger of the Lord is kindled: he does not allow the sin to go unpunished (11:1–3, 33f.; 12:10ff.; 14, *etc.*); Moses and Aaron are not allowed to enter Canaan (20:12f.). But the Lord does not repudiate his people; he remains faithful to his covenant. He guides Israel through the desert, so that the land promised to their fathers is reached. This is prevented neither by Israel's unfaithfulness nor by the power of the nations that turn against Israel.

Special attention should be paid to certain aspects of the revelation of God in Numbers.

1. The Lord is, indeed, unchangeable in his faithfulness (*cf.* 23:19), but this does not imply that he is an unmovable being (see especially the touching story in 14:11ff.). In this connection we should note the strong anthropomorphisms (see, *e.g.*, 10:35f.; 15:3, 'a pleasing odour to the Lord'; 28:2, 'my food', *etc.*); expressions which, while we must not take them in a strictly literal sense, show at the same time how deeply the Lord is involved in the doings of Israel.

2. God's holiness is specially emphasized. The stories do this (see, *e.g.*, 20:12f.), and so also, in a different way, do the laws and regulations: when a man approaches God he has to fulfil all kinds of prescribed rules, he has to be free from every uncleanness (*cf.* also 1:50ff., *etc.*).

3. Very detailed prescriptions are given in this book: God exercises his sovereign dominion over everything, even over the smallest details.

4. As soon as the children of Israel have arrived at the borders of the promised country they yield to the temptation to serve the gods of the new land. But the Lord is not only the Lord of the desert: he engages a heathen fortune-teller (22–24), and punishes Israel for their idol-worship (25), together with those who had seduced his people (31).

In what is said above, the Christological character of this book has already been mainly indicated. In Nu., as elsewhere, God reveals himself as the faithful God of the covenant. In other words, he reveals himself in the face of Christ. In addition, there is much in this book which has a typological meaning: in persons (especially Moses and Aaron), in occurrences, and in laws, the coming Christ casts his shadow before him (*cf.* Jn. 3:14; 1 Cor. 10:1ff.; Heb. 3:7ff.; 9:13; *etc.*).

BIBLIOGRAPHY. See various *IOT*s and the commentaries—*e.g.* G. B. Gray, *Numbers, ICC*, 1903 (1955); L. E. Binns, *The Book of Numbers, WC*, 1927; S. Fish, *The Book of Numbers*², 1950, in *The Soncino Books of the Bible*; J. Marsh, *Numbers, IB*, 2, 1953; W. H. Gispen, *Het boek Numeri*, 1, 1959; 2, 1964, in *Commentaar op het Oude Testament*; N. H. Snaith, *Leviticus and Numbers, NCB*, 1967; M. Noth, *Numbers, OTL*, 1968.

N.H.R.

NUNC DIMITTIS. The prophecies accompanying Christ's advent occur not (as with John the Baptist) at circumcision but at the rites of purification a month later. According to an ancient custom babies were brought to an old doctor or rabbi in the Temple for a blessing. Perhaps in this setting Simeon, taking the Lord Jesus, uttered his *nunc dimittis* (Lk. 2:29–35). Simeon is characterized as receiving a 'spirit which was holy', which in Jewish tradition is equated with the 'spirit of prophecy'. According to the rabbis the Spirit departed from Israel after the prophet Malachi, and his return was indicative of the Messianic age (*cf. SB, in loc.*). In the case of Simeon three specific 'acts of the Spirit' occur: (1) he receives by divine revelation assurance that he shall see the Lord's Messiah; (2) under the influence of the Spirit (*cf.* Rev. 1:10) he is led to encounter and recognize Jesus as Messiah (*cf.* 1 Sa. 16:6ff.); (3) he utters a prayer and prediction which, in Luke's context, is clearly to be regarded as prophetic.

Nunc Dimittis is divided into two parts, the first a prayer to God (liturgically, this alone came to be designated the 'Nunc Dimittis') and the second a prophecy spoken to Mary. Their mood and theme stand in stark contrast to each other. The prayer is joyful, expressing the Messianic hope of Judaism in its most exalted tone: in Messiah the Gentiles will receive the truth of God and thus, in him, Israel's glory as God's instrument of revelation and redemption will be fully manifest (*cf.* Is. 49:6; Acts 1:8; Rom. 15:8ff.). But, in the second section, as if to counterbalance the impression of the prayer, praise gives way to warning. The Messiah shall cause division and shall be rejected by many (*cf.* Rom. 9:33).

In Simeon's prophecy to Mary the concept of a suffering Messiah appears. Israel's destiny is glorious, but it is one of conflict. As a sign or pointer to the redemption of Israel Jesus shall be attacked and rejected (*cf.* Lk. 11:30), for the kind of redemption he represents will not be welcomed by all. Although this will bring anguish to Mary, through it men will be brought to decision and thus their real selves, their hidden selves, be uncovered. (* BENEDICTUS.)

E.E.E.

NURSE. 'Nurse' in the EVV may mean a wet-nurse, translating Heb. *mêneqeṯ*, used of Deborah (Gn. 24:59), of Moses' mother (Ex. 2:7), and of the nurse of the infant Joash (2 Ki. 11:2; 2 Ch. 22:11). Suckling is usually continued in the Near East for 2 years, and the nurse often remains with the family as a trusted servant, as in the case of Deborah (Gn. 35:8). The same word is used in a figurative sense of queens who will care for God's people in the glorious future (Is. 49:23). Paul compares his care for believers to that of a nurse (Gk. *trophos*) for her own children (1 Thes. 2:7).

In the more general sense of one who cares for children, 'nurse' translates Heb. *'ōmeneṯ*; for example, Naomi (Ru. 4:16) and the governess of 5-year-old Mephibosheth (2 Sa. 4:4) are so described. The masculine form of this Heb. word, *'ōmēn*, translated 'nursing father' AV, 'nurse' RSV, is used figuratively of Moses' care for the Israelites (Nu 11:12) and of kings who will serve the people of God (Is. 49:23). *Cf.* Acts 13:18, RVmg.

BIBLIOGRAPHY. H. Granquist, *Birth and Childhood among the Arabs*, 1947, pp. 107–117, 246–252; *RAC*, 1, pp. 383–385.

J.T.

NUZI. The excavations at Nuzi (Yorghan Tepe) and adjacent mounds near Kirkuk, Iraq, were carried out by E. Chiera and others between 1925 and 1931 through the co-operation of the American Schools of Oriental Research, the Iraq Museum and the Semitic Museum, Harvard. The earliest level of occupation was dated to the Ubaid period, while the latest traces came from Roman times. The two main periods of occupation were in the 3rd millennium BC when the site was known as Gasur, and in the 15th–14th centuries BC when the town was under Hurrian influence and known as Nuzi. In the palace and private homes more than 4,000 clay tablets were found, written in a local Hurrian dialect of Akkadian. These included several archives, among which those of Tehiptilla (*c.* 1,000 tablets), prince Shilwateshub and a successful business woman, Tulpunnaya, are the best known. The texts cover approximately five generations, thus providing a detailed picture of life in an ancient Mesopotamian community in a comparatively short period.

The tablets from Nuzi contain mainly private contracts and public records. Apart from lists of various kinds of goods and equipment, a wide range of topics is covered, including land, prices, family law, women, law and order, and slaves. Of particular importance are documents relating to various kinds of adoption, wills, marriage, lawsuits, antichretic security and exchange of persons, goods and land. Until comparatively recently several of the Nuzi text types were scarcely represented elsewhere, but excavation at Tell al-Fikhar (Kurruhanni), *c.* 30 km SW of Nuzi, has revealed similar material of comparable date, though it remains largely unpublished.

By contrast, the political history and religious life is poorly understood. Nuzi appears to have been situated within the Hurrian kingdom of Mitanni, though the extant texts make little reference to this or to the rising power of Assyria. Literature, including myths, epics, wisdom texts and scholarly documents, is also sparsely represented.

The Nuzi texts contain a significant number of points of contact with the OT, notably with the patriarchal narratives. These links between the customs and social conditions of the people of Nuzi and the biblical Patriarchs have led some scholars to argue for a similar 15th-century date for Abraham and his descendants, though there is evidence that many of these customs had already been observed for centuries. More recently attempts have been made to reduce considerably any connection between Nuzi and the Patriarchs (Thompson, van Seters). The examples listed below, however, indicate the existence of several significant parallels, and some of the customs concerned are also found elsewhere in Mesopotamia. Nuzi practice, in fact, followed mainly a Mesopotamian rather than a Hurrian pattern.

A large group of documents deals with *inheritance*. Throughout the ancient Near East an eldest son received a larger inheritance share than his brothers, though the exact proportion varied. The double share, which is most prominent at Nuzi and which also appears in other 2nd-millennium cuneiform texts, is closely paralleled in Dt. 21:17, though the Patriarchs seem to have followed a different practice (Gn. 25:5–6). The most frequent description of the eldest son at Nuzi (*rabû*, 'eldest'), also found at Ugarit, Alalaḫ and in Middle Assyrian texts, occurs in Hebrew (*raḇ*) in Gn. 25:23 instead of the usual *bᵉḵôr*.

It remains uncertain whether or not one's birthright could be exchanged at Nuzi, as in the case of Jacob and Esau (Gn. 25:29–34). Although several examples are known where at least part of an inheritance changed hands between brothers, in no instance can an eldest son be definitely identified in such transactions. In any case similar examples of the transfer of an inheritance occur in Assyria and Babylonia and are not confined to Nuzi.

However, any heir could be disinherited. Such drastic action was permitted only for offences against the family and the references to 'disrespect' and 'disobedience' towards parents provides a useful background to Reuben's demotion (Gn. 35:22; 49:3–4), though again similar examples can be found elsewhere.

The suggestion has been made that possession of the household gods in Nuzi formed an effective entitlement to an inheritance and that Rachel's theft of Laban's images, perhaps on Jacob's behalf, could be similarly explained (Gn. 31:19ff.). It is more probable, however, that the family deities could only be bequeathed by the father, normally to the first-born son, and that their theft did not improve an heir's claim.

Adoption also occupies an important place in the Nuzi texts. A man without an heir could adopt an outsider who would carry out certain responsibilities towards his adoptive parents, though of course similar customs are known from other Mesopotamian texts. The duties included the provision of food and clothing, particularly in old age, and ensuring proper burial and mourning rites, while in return the adoptee received an inheritance. It is quite possible that Abram adopted Eliezer in this manner prior to Isaac's birth (Gn. 15:2–4), especially since at Nuzi a son born subsequently usually gained a larger inheritance share than any adoptee and that the adoption of slaves is occasionally mentioned. The process of adoption at Nuzi

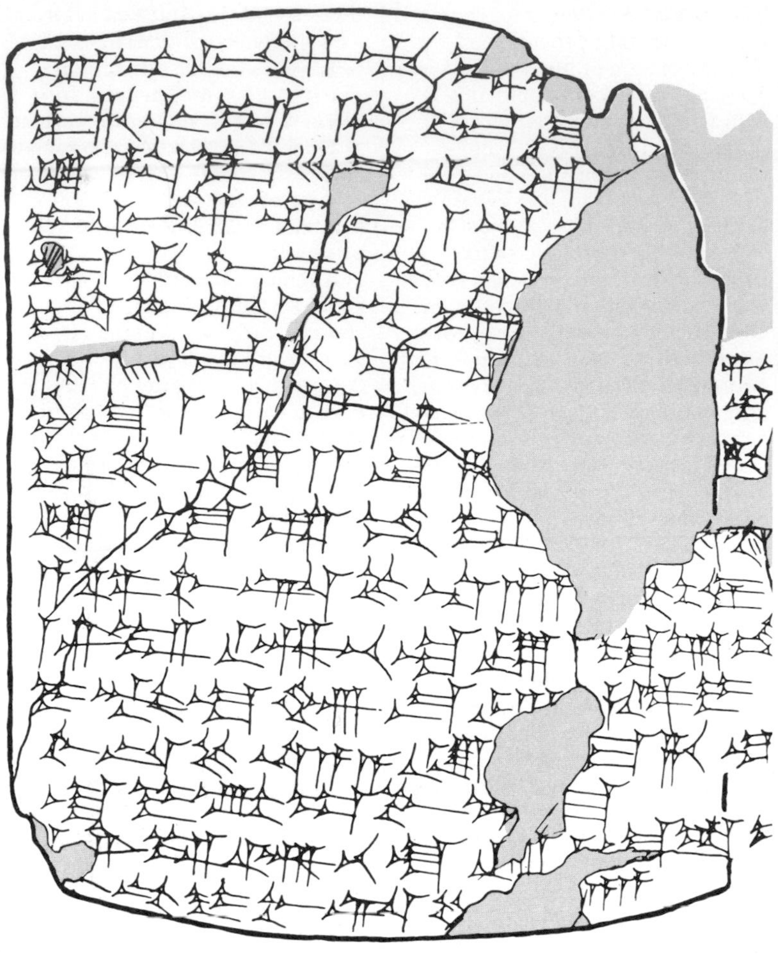

Transcription of the cuneiform text from Nuzi of a 'will' by which Hupitaya gives his wife full authority over her sons. The inheritance is divided so that the eldest son receives a double share (cf. Dt. 21:15–17). Near modern Kirkuk, Iraq. 15th–14th cent. BC. (HSM)

was also extended to become a fiction whereby property, apparently legally inalienable, could be sold. Tehiptilla, for example, was 'adopted' in this way some 150 times!

Apart from adoption, the Nuzi texts mention three further solutions for a childless marriage. The husband could remarry or take a concubine or the wife could present her own slave-girl to her husband. The latter custom, which afforded the barren wife some protection, parallels that of Sarah, Rachel and Leah (Gn. 16:1–4; 30:1–13), and though only one example occurs at Nuzi (*HSS* 5. 67), others are known from Babylonia and Assyria. A son born to a slave-girl in this way would normally have to be adopted or legitimated by the father according to Mesopotamian custom, though the Nuzi text is not specific on this point. *HSS* 5. 67 does indicate, however, that the wife maintained authority over her slave-girl's children and there are indications that Sarah, Rachel and Leah took responsibility for their slave-girls' offspring right from the naming of the children.

Although the Nuzi texts do not refer to a paternal blessing such as in Gn. 27:29, 33; 48:1ff., they do occasionally contain oral statements which were clearly regarded as having legal validity. One of these was made by a father to his son while the former lay ill in bed (*cf.* Isaac). In both Nuzi and Genesis such oral statements were supported by legal or customary safeguards, and symbolic actions involving the hands were frequently used.

Women are often mentioned in the Nuzi documents. The right of daughters to inherit property is attested, usually in the absence of sons, as in Babylonian contracts (*cf.* Nu. 27:8). Sometimes a marriage contract included a clause prohibiting the husband from marrying a second wife, a safeguard sought for Rachel by Laban (Gn. 31:50). Not every bride was so fortunate, however. A girl could be acquired by a man for optional marriage to himself or to his son (*cf.* Ex. 21:7–11), while the complaint of Laban's daughters that their father had held back their dowry (Gn. 31:15) is paralleled by an identical phrase (*kaspa akālu*) in five Nuzi texts.

Several Nuzi references to business transactions have some relevance to the OT. Land was sometimes apportioned by lot (Nu. 26:55f.; Jos. 18:2–10) and there was a periodic 'release' from debt (Dt. 15). Sale of land was sometimes confirmed by the seller lifting his foot and placing the buyer's on the soil, while shoes functioned as legal symbols in some transactions (*cf.* Ru. 4:7–8; 1 Sa. 12:3, LXX; Am. 2:6; 8:6). 1 Sa. 1:24 has been reinterpreted in the light of Nuzi evidence to read 'a bullock, three years old'.

Finally, the Nuzi references to *'apiru* (*habiru*), indicating various persons, many apparently foreigners who had accepted voluntary servitude, recalls the phrase 'Hebrew slave' and the derogatory use of 'Hebrews' by Egyptians and Philistines when referring to Israelites (Gn. 39:14; Ex. 1:15; 21:1–6; 1 Sa. 14:21).

BIBLIOGRAPHY. *Archaeology*: R. F. S. Starr, *Nuzi, Report on the Excavations at Yorghan Tepe*, 2 vols., 1939. *Texts:* E. Chiera *et al.*, *Joint Expedition at Nuzi*, 6 vols., 1927–39; E. R. Lacheman *et al.*, *Excavations at Nuzi*, 8 vols., 1929–62. *General:* C. H. Gordon, *BA* 3, 1940, pp. 1–12; H. H. Rowley, *The Servant of the Lord*², 1965, pp. 312–317; C. J. Mullo Weir, in *AOTS*, pp. 73–86; M. Dietrich *et al.*, *Nuzi-Bibliographie*, 1972; T. L. Thompson, *The Historicity of the Patriarchal Narratives*, 1974, pp. 196–297; J. van Seters, *Abraham in History and Tradition*, 1975, pp. 65–103; M. J. Selman, *TynB* 27, 1976, pp. 114–136.

M.J.S.

NYMPHA, NYMPHAS. Owner of a house in Laodicea (or possibly somewhere else near Colossae) in which a church met (Col. 4:15). Though many MSS read 'his house', as AV, most of the best read either 'her house' (*cf.* RSV, NEB) or 'their house' (*cf.* RV). The name is in the accusative and, unaccented, could represent a masculine Nymphas (pet-form for Nymphodōrus?) or a feminine Nympha (*cf.* J. H. Moulton, *Grammar*, 1, p. 48, for alleviation of the cause of Lightfoot's reserve). On either rendering the reading 'their house' is so hard to explain that it may well be correct. Perhaps it refers back to 'the brethren which are in Laodicea' (Lightfoot proposes a Colossian family there, or, alternatively, that *autōn* stands for 'Nymphas and his friends').

Nympha(s), like *Philemon and *Archippus, displays Paul's friendships (made in Ephesus?) in an area he had not visited (*cf.* Col. 2:1).

A.F.W.

OATHS. Heb. *šᵉḇû'â* and *'ālâ*; Gk. *horkos*. *'ālâ* is related to a verb whose basic meaning is 'to pronounce a contitional curse', or a *curse upon a person as yet unidentified (*TDOT* 1, pp. 261–266). A clear example occurs in 1 Sa. 14:24, where the wording of the oath is given: 'Cursed be the man who eats food until it is evening and I am avenged on my enemies.' In this case the oath served to reinforce a command (*cf.* Gn. 24:41). Similar oaths could be used in legal proceedings, where a dispute could not be resolved in the normal way (1 Ki. 8:31, 2 Ch. 6:22), and they also formed a regular part of treaties and covenants (Gn. 26:28; Ezk. 16:59; 17:13–19; Ho. 10:4), as is now well known also from contemporary ancient Near Eastern texts (*e.g.* *ANET*, pp. 201, 205, 538–541, 659–660; *cf.* D. R. Hillers, *Treaty-Curses and the OT Prophets*, 1964). Contrary to what is often asserted, such a curse was not irrevocable (*cf.* 1 Sa. 14:45; also Jdg. 17:1–2), and it owed its power not so much to any magical power believed to be inherent in the words uttered as to the sovereign response of God himself (1 Ki. 8:31f.; *cf.* A. C. Thiselton, *JTS* n.s. 25, 1974, pp. 283–299, esp. 295f.). In the other OT references to oaths, where the Heb. word is *šᵉḇû'â*, it is not at all certain that a curse of this kind was invariably involved, although it could be (Jdg. 21:18). In many cases 'solemn promise' would be a more adequate translation (*cf.* *THAT*, 2, pp. 858–859).

In taking oaths various means (Gn. 24:2; Dt. 32:40) and formulae (Gn. 31:50; Nu. 5:22; Jdg. 8:19; 2 Ki. 2:2; Je. 42:5; Mt. 5:34–36; 23:16) were adopted. Frequently the dire effects of non-fulfilment were not expressed (2 Sa. 3:9, but see Je. 29:22).

The seriousness of oaths is emphasized in the laws of Moses (Ex. 20:7; Lv. 19:12). Israelites were forbidden to swear their oaths by false gods (Je. 12:16; Am. 8:14). Ezekiel speaks as if perjury were punishable by death (17:16ff.), but in the law the false swearing by a witness, and the denial on oath regarding something found or received (Lv. 5:1–4; 6:1–3), could be atoned for by a sin-offering (Lv. 5:5ff.; 6:4ff.).

Christ taught that oaths were binding (Mt. 5:33). The Christian's daily conversation is to be as sacred as his oaths. He is not to have two standards of truth as certain Jews had when they introduced a sliding scale of values in regard to oaths. In the kingdom of God oaths will

OAR
See Ships and boats, Part 3.

Covenants, treaties and other documents were concluded with oaths or curses invoked by both parties to enforce the terms. In this vassal-treaty imposed by the Assyrian king, Esarhaddon, on his vassals, including Manasseh, at Calah, Nimrud in May 672 BC a series of over 60 oaths is listed. (SAOB)

finally become unnecessary (Mt. 5:34–37). Christ himself accepted the imprecatory oath (Mt. 26:63ff.), and Paul also swore by an oath (2 Cor. 1:23; Gal. 1:20).

Scripture also testifies that God bound himself by an oath (Heb. 6:13–18). What the Lord bound himself to perform was his promises to his covenant people: *e.g.* his promises to the Patriarchs (Gn. 50:24), to the Davidic dynasty (Ps. 89:19–37, 49), to the Messianic Priest-King (Ps. 110:1–4). The Guarantor of all these promises is Jesus Christ in whom they find the answering 'amen' (2 Cor. 1:19f.; *cf.* Is. 65:16, RVmg.). In his advent Jesus Christ fulfilled God's ancient oaths to Patriarchs (Lk. 1:68–73; 2:6–14), to David (Acts 2:30), and to the OT priest-king (Heb. 7:20f., 28).

BIBLIOGRAPHY. *TWBR*, pp. 159f.; M. R. Lehmann, *ZAW* 81, 1969, pp. 74–92; *THAT*, 2, pp. 855–863.

J.G.S.S.T.
G.I.D.

OBADIAH (*'ōḇaḏyāhû, 'ōḇaḏyâ*). A Heb. name meaning 'servant of Yahweh' or 'worshipper of Yahweh'. At least twelve men in the OT bear this name.

1. The steward, or major domo, in charge of the palace of King Ahab of Israel (1 Ki. 18:3–16). From his youth he was a devout worshipper of Yahweh. When Jezebel was persecuting the prophets of Yahweh, Obadiah hid 100 of them in two caves. During a drought while Obadiah was seeking grass for the royal horses and mules, Elijah met him and persuaded him to arrange a meeting with Ahab, which led to the contest between Elijah and the prophets of Baal. The TB (*Sanhedrin* 39b) mistakenly identifies him with the prophet Obadiah. An ancient Hebrew seal reading 'To Obadiah servant of the King' may have belonged to this man.

2. A descendant of David (1 Ch. 3:21). **3.** A chief of Issachar (1 Ch. 7:3). **4.** A descendant of Saul (1 Ch. 8:38; 9:44). **5.** A Levite (1 Ch. 9:16), identical with Abda (Ne. 11:17) and probably with Obadiah, a gatekeeper of the Temple (Ne. 12:25). **6.** A Gadite captain who joined David at Ziklag (1 Ch. 12:9).

7. A Zebulonite in the time of David (1 Ch. 27:19). **8.** One of the princes sent out by King Jehoshaphat to teach the law in the cities of Judah (2 Ch. 17:7). **9.** A Levite overseer of the repair of the Temple in the time of Josiah (2 Ch. 34:12). **10.** An Israelite leader who returned from Babylonia to Jerusalem with Ezra (Ezr. 8:9). **11.** A priest who sealed the covenant with Nehemiah (Ne. 10:5).

12. A prophet, presumably of Judah (Ob. 1). The Bible gives nothing directly about his life. Though some locate him before the Exile, it is more likely that he lived in the 5th century BC (see below, *OBADIAH, BOOK OF). If the latter view is correct it is chronologically impossible to identify him with Ahab's steward, as does the TB (*Sanhedrin* 39b), or with Ahaziah's captain (2 Ki. 1:13–15) as Pseudo-Epiphanius does in *The Lives of the Prophets*. The talmudic tradition that he was a proselyte of Edomite origin is improbable in view of his strong denunciation of Edom.

J.T.

OBADIAH, BOOK OF. The fourth of the Minor Prophets in the Heb. Bible and the fifth in the order of the LXX. For a note on the author, see the previous article (**12**).

I. Outline of contents

a. The judgment of Edom (vv. 1–14).

(i) Title (v. 1a).

(ii) Warning of Edom's doom (vv. 1b–4).

(iii) Completeness of Edom's destruction (vv. 5–9).

(iv) Reasons for Edom's judgment (vv. 10–14).

b. Universal judgment (vv. 15–16).

c. Restoration of Israel (vv. 17–21).

II. Historical background

a. Before the Exile

Jewish tradition in the Talmud (*Sanhedrin* 39b) placed Obadiah in the reign of Ahab in the 9th century BC, and the order of the Minor Prophets in the Heb. Bible includes Obadiah among the pre-exilic prophets. Some scholars have suggested that the background for the whole of Obadiah is the attack of the Arabians and Philistines on Judah in the reign of Jehoram mentioned in 2 Ch. 21:16–17 (so Keil), or the Edomite attack on Judah in the reign of Ahaz described in 2 Ch. 28:17 (so J. D. Davis). Many think that only the older oracle against Edom, which Obadiah embodies in vv. 1–6, 8–9, has a pre-exilic background. Arab raids on Palestine, and presumably on Edom, are recorded in the 9th century BC (2 Ch. 21:16–17) and in the 7th century BC (Assyr. Annals).

b. After 587 BC

Most scholars consider that the calamity to Jerusalem described in Ob. 11–14 is its capture by the Chaldeans in 587 BC. This is the only capture of Jerusalem in which it is recorded that Edomites participated (Ps. 137:7; 1 Esdras 4:45). The references to the sufferings caused by the fall of Jerusalem are so vivid that G. A. Smith would place Obadiah soon afterwards during the exilic period. Many, however, feel that the latter part of Obadiah reflects a post-exilic background. V. 7 states that the Edomites have been driven out of their old land (*cf.* Mal. 1:3–4). After the fall of Jerusalem Edomites under Arab pressure began moving into the Negeb (1 Esdras 4:50), which came to be called Idumaea, and by the late 6th century BC Arabs had largely pushed them out of the area of Petra, once the Edomite capital. Vv. 8–10 announce the future wiping out of the Edomites as a nation, and this prophecy must have been made before the fulfilment which took place in the Maccabean period (Jos., *Ant.* 13. 257). The territory occupied by the Jews according to vv. 19–20 is the area around Jerusalem, as in the days of Nehemiah (Ne. 11:25–36). Thus the latest clear indication of date in the prophecy is in the mid-5th century BC, about the time of Malachi.

III. Parallels in other prophecies

Other prophetic denunciations of Edom include: Is. 34:5–17; 63:1–6; Je. 49:7–22; La. 4:21–22; Ezk. 26:12–14; Joel 3:19; Am. 1:11–12.

The many identical phrases in Ob. 1–9 and Je. 49:7–22 suggest some literary relationship between the two passages. The different order of the phrases in the two prophecies makes it probable that they are both quoting some earlier divine oracle against Edom. Since some of the additional material in Jeremiah is characteristic of that prophet, and since the order is more natural in Obadiah, it is likely that the latter is closer in form to the original prophecy. Some scholars, however, hold that either Jeremiah (so Keil) or Obadiah (so Hitzig) made use of the other.

Several phrases are found in both Obadiah and Joel: Ob. 10 = Joel 3:19; Ob. 11 = Joel 3:3; Ob. 15 = Joel 1:15; 2:1; 3:4, 7, 14; Ob. 18 = Joel 3:8. In 2:32 Joel indicates by the words 'as the Lord has said' that he is quoting, probably from Ob. 17. Therefore Obadiah preceded Joel and doubtless influenced him in some of the other phrases common to the two prophets.

IV. Style

Obadiah, the shortest book of the OT, is marked by vigorous poetic language. The prevailing poetic metre is the pentameter (3 + 2), but other metres are used for variety (*e.g.* 3 + 3 and 3 + 3 + 3). Much of the prophecy consists of God's own words to personified Edom (vv. 2–15), and this feature gives a direct and personal quality to the book. Vividness is enhanced by the use of the prophetic perfect tense (v. 2) to describe a judgment yet to be fulfilled, and by the use of prohibitions (vv. 12–14) forbidding atrocities which had actually been perpetrated. Various striking comparisons and metaphors are used: the mountain fastness of Edom is like an eagle's eyrie (v. 4); the plunderers of Edom are compared to night thieves and gleaners of grapes (v. 5); the judgment of the nations is a bitter drink which they must swallow (v. 16); the avenging Israelites are called a fire, and the Edomites are called stubble (v. 18). Edom's crimes are listed in climactic order (vv. 10–14). The completeness of Israel's restoration is expressed by the specification of its expansion in the four cardinal directions (vv. 19–20). Sin and doom in vv. 1–16 are sharply contrasted with hope and victory in vv. 17–21. Obadiah proceeds from the particular to the general, from the judgment of Edom to the universal judgment, from the restoration of Israel to the establishment of the kingdom of God.

V. Literary analyses

Some hold that Obadiah was the original author of the whole prophecy (so Keil). Most scholars believe that he adapted an older oracle in vv. 1–6, 8–9. Some have found various other fragments, but the uniform historical background supports the literary unity of the remainder of the prophecy.

VI. Leading messages

1. *Divine inspiration.* Four times (vv. 1, 4, 8, 18) the prophet claims a divine origin for his words.

2. *Divine judgment.* The main message of this prophecy is God's moral judgment of nations. Edom is judged because of inhumanity to Israel, who also has been punished. Ultimately all nations will be judged in the Day of the Lord.

3. *The divine kingdom.* The final goal, according to Obadiah, is that 'the kingdom shall be the Lord's' (*cf.* Rev. 11:15). His hope for the restoration of his own people rises above mere nationalism, for in their victory he sees the establishment of the kingdom of God (v. 21). That kingdom will be characterized by 'deliverance' and 'holiness' (v. 17), ideas which are amplified in the NT.

Bibliography. *Commentaries* by E. B. Pusey, 1860; C. F. Keil in *Biblischer Commentar über das Alte Testament*, 1888; J. A. Bewer in *ICC*, 1911; H. C. O. Lanchester in *CBSC*, 1918; G. W. Wade in *WC*, 1925; G. A. Smith in *EB*, 1928; E. Sellin in *KAT*, 1929; T. H. Robinson in *HAT*, 1954; J. H. Eaton, *Obadiah, Nahum, Habakkuk, Zephaniah, TBC*, 1961; D. W. B. Robinson in *NBCR*, 1970; J. A. Thompson in *ID*, 1956; G. F. Wood in *The Jerome Biblical Commentary*, 1968; L. C. Allen, *The Books of Joel, Obadiah, Jonah and Micah, NIC*, 1976.

Special studies: G. L. Robinson, *The Sarcophagus of an Ancient Civilization*, 1930; W. Rudolph, 'Obadja', *ZAW* 8, 1931, pp. 222–231.

J.T.

OBED (Heb. *'ôḇēḏ*, 'servant'). **1.** The son of Ruth and Boaz (Ru. 4:17), and grandfather of David (Ru. 4:21f.; 1 Ch. 2:12; Mt. 1:5; Lk. 3:32). Obed's birth brought comfort to Naomi's old age. **2.** A Jerahmeelite (1 Ch. 2:37f.). **3.** One of David's mighty men (1 Ch. 11:47). **4.** A son of Shemaiah and grandson of Obed-edom, of the Korahite family (1 Ch. 26:7). **5.** The father of Azariah, a captain who served under Jehoiada (2 Ch. 23:1).

J.D.D.

OBED-EDOM (Heb. *'ōḇēḏ 'ᵉḏôm*, 'servant of [god?] Edom'). **1.** A Philistine of Gath living in the neighbourhood of Jerusalem. Before taking it to Jerusalem David left the ark in his house for 3 months after the death of Uzzah, during which time its presence brought blessing to the household (2 Sa. 6:10ff. = 1 Ch. 13:13f.; 15:25).

2. The ancestor of a family of doorkeepers (1 Ch. 15:18ff.; 16:38; 26:4ff.; 2 Ch. 25:24). **3.** A family of singers in pre-exilic times (1 Ch. 15:21; 16:5).

J.D.D.

OBEDIENCE. The Heb. verb translated 'obey' in EVV is *šāma' bᵉ*, lit. 'hearken to'. The verb used in LXX and the NT is *hypakouō* (noun, *hypakoē*; adjective, *hypēkoos*), a compound of *akouō*, which also means 'hear'. *hypakouō* means literally 'hear *under*'. The NT also uses *eisakouō* (1 Cor. 14:21), lit. 'hear *into*', *peithomai*, and *peitharcheō* (Tit. 3:1). The two latter words express respectively the ideas of yielding to persuasion and submitting to authority. The idea of obedience which this vocabulary suggests is of a hearing that takes place *under* the authority or influence of the speaker, and that leads *into* compliance with his requests.

For obedience to be due to a person, he must: (*a*) have a right to command, and (*b*) be able to make known his requirements. Man's duty to obey his Maker thus presupposes: (*a*) God's Lordship, and (*b*) his revelation. The OT habitually describes obedience to God as obeying (hearing) either his *voice* (accentuating (*b*)) or his *commandments* (assuming (*b*), and accentuating (*a*)). Disobedience it describes as not hearing God's voice when he speaks (Ps. 81:11; Je. 7:24–28).

According to Scripture, God demands that his revelation be taken as a rule for man's whole life. Thus obedience to God is a concept broad enough to include the whole of biblical religion and morality. The Bible is insistent that isolated external acts of homage to God cannot make up for a lack of consistent obedience in heart and conduct (1 Sa. 15:22; *cf.* Je. 7:22f.).

The disobedience of Adam, the first representative man, and the perfect obedience of the second, Jesus Christ, are decisive factors in the destiny of everyone. Adam's lapse from obedience plunged mankind into guilt, condemnation and death (Rom. 5:19; 1 Cor. 15:22). Christ's unfailing obedience 'unto death' (Phil. 2:8; *cf.* Heb. 5:8; 10:5–10) won righteousness (acceptance with God) and life (fellowship with God) for all who believe on him (Rom. 5:15–19).

In God's promulgation of the old covenant the emphasis was on obedience as his requirement if his people were to enjoy his favour (Ex. 19:5, *etc.*). In his promise of the new covenant, however, the emphasis was on obedience as his

OBAL
See Ebal, Part 1.

gift to them, in order that they might enjoy his favour (Je. 31:33; 32:40; *cf.* Ezk. 36:26f.; 37:23–26).

Faith in the gospel, and in Jesus Christ, is obedience (Acts 6:7; Rom. 6:17; Heb. 5:9; 1 Pet. 1:22), for God commands it (*cf.* Jn. 6:29; 1 Jn. 3:23). Unbelief is disobedience (Rom. 10:16; 2 Thes. 1:8; 1 Pet. 2:8; 3:1; 4:17). A life of obedience to God is the fruit of faith (*cf.* what is said of Abraham, Gn. 22:18; Heb. 11:8, 17ff.; Jas. 2:21ff.).

Christian obedience means imitating God in holiness (1 Pet. 1:15f.) and Christ in humility and love (Jn. 13:14f., 34f.; Phil. 2:5ff.; Eph. 4:32–5:2). It springs from gratitude for grace received (Rom. 12:1f.), not from the desire to gain merit and to justify oneself in God's sight. Indeed, law-keeping from the latter motive is not obedience to God, but its opposite (Rom. 9:31–10:3).

Obedience to divinely-established authority in the family (Eph. 5:22; 6:1ff.; *cf.* 2 Tim. 3:2), in the church (Phil. 2:12; Heb. 13:17), and in the state (Mt. 22:21; Rom. 13:1ff.; 1 Pet. 2:13ff.; Tit. 3:1), is part of the Christian's obedience to God. When claims clash, however, he must be ready to disobey men in order not to disobey God (*cf.* Acts 5:29).

BIBLIOGRAPHY. W. Mundle, *NIDNTT* 2, pp. 172–180. J.I.P.

ODED. 1. Father of Azariah the prophet (2 Ch. 15:1) in the reign of Asa. V. 8 has either included a marginal gloss or omitted 'Azariah the son of'. **2.** A prophet of Samaria (2 Ch. 28:9–15) who met the victorious army of the N kingdom

A high Assyrian officer stands before King Sargon II. Relief from the palace of Sargon II at Khorsabad. c. 710 BC. (BM)

OCCULT
See Magic, Part 2.

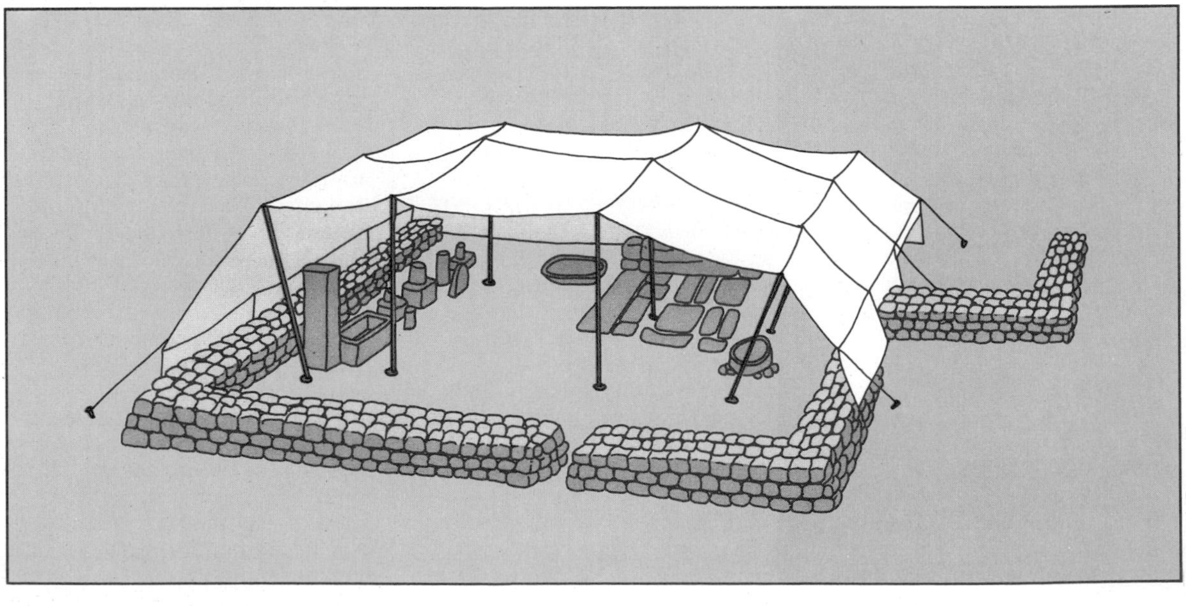

Reconstruction of the Midianite tent-shrine discovered at Timna. This was probably similar in concept to the Hebrew tabernacle and furnishes archaeological evidence for Oholibamah, 'tent of the high place'. Mid-12th cent. BC.

returning with a number of enslaved captives from Judah, and remonstrated with them to return the slaves. His pleadings, joined by those of some Samaritan leaders, were successful. M.A.M.

OFFICERS. A term used of various subordinate officials whether civil, judicial or military. The status of these officers as assisting and recording on behalf of their superiors originally may imply the ability to write (Heb. *šōṭēr*; *cf.* Akkad. *šaṭāru* 'to write'). The Egyptians used 'officers' to record the work of Hebrew slaves there (Ex. 5:6, 14), a practice attested in Egyp. records. Moses developed this in his employment of such officers as clerks to assist him and *judges by recording legal decisions (Nu. 11:16) and this became the later custom (Dt. 16:18; 1 Ch. 23:4; 2 Ch. 19:8; *cf.* Josephus, *Ant.* 4. [illegible]). These men had responsibilities also relating to call-up for war-service (Dt. 20:5; Jos. 1:10) and as military aides (Jos. 3:2). Their duties related them to the local governors and elders (Jos. 8:33; 23:2; 24:1). By the time of the Monarchy these were numerous (1,700) both in the Temple and civilian administration as well as in royal service (1 Ch. 26:29; 27:1) and as such were clearly distinguished in the time of Jehoshaphat (2 Ch. 19:11; 26:11; 34:13).

Officers were sometimes 'princes' (*sarîm*; Ezr. 7:28) with military duties (2 Ch. 32:3; Ne. 2:9) or were designated 'third man' or officer-in-charge of a *chariot crew (Ex. 14:7; 15:4, *šlš; cf.* Assyr. *šalšu*; J. V. Kinnier Wilson, *The Nimrud Wine Lists*, 1972). 'Officer' is also sometimes used to translate 'chief' (*rôš*, *râḇ*) as in Est. 1:8; Je. 41:1; Ezk. 23:15 or even 'eunuch' (*sarîs*; 2 Ki. 24:12).

An officer was an appointee (*pqd*) set to oversee all work on behalf of the king, whether in one region (Jdg. 9:28; Is. 60:17) or in a specific sphere (Ezk. 2:3). The term is also used of subordinates within the Temple organization (2 Ch. 21:11; Je. 20:1) including those on guard duties (2 Ki. 11:18). Sometimes the use of the Heb. term *nṣb* stresses that the official owed his appointment to the king (1 Ki. 4:5; 22:47; 2 Ch. 8:10).

In the NT an officer may denote the 'prison guard' (Lk. 12:58; *cf.* Mt. 5:25), the deputies (*hypēretēs*, lit. 'under oarsmen') who acted for the chief priests and Sanhedrin as bailiffs (Jn. 7:32, 45–46; *cf.* v. 36; *cf.* Acts 5:22, 26). Such officials served in Herod's court (Mk. 6:21) and Paul considered himself in similar relationship to God (1 Cor. 4:1). D.J.W.

OG (Heb. *'ôḡ*). An Amorite king of Bashan, of the giant race of Rephaim at the time of the Conquest of Palestine (Nu. 21:33; Jos. 13:12). His kingdom was a powerful one, having sixty cities 'fortified with high walls, gates and bars' (Dt. 3:4–5), extending from Mt Hermon to the Jabbok. These included two royal cities, Ashtaroth and Edrei, at the latter of which the Israelites defeated and slew him. His territory was given to the half tribe of Manasseh (Dt. 3:13), which remained E of the Jordan. His defeat was one of the signal victories of Israel (*cf.* Jos. 2:10; Ne. 9:22; Ps. 135:11; 136:20).

His bed (*'ereś*) was renowned as made of black basalt. Some have conjectured that it was in reality a sarcophagus, although the word nowhere else bears this meaning; but many such sarcophagi have been found in the region. It appears to have fallen into the hands of the Ammonites and was kept in Rabbah (Dt. 3:11). M.A.M.

OHOLIAB (AV **AHOLIAB**), a Danite, son of Ahisamach, specially gifted by God and appointed to assist *Bezalel in the design and construction of the tabernacle, its furniture and furnishings, and in teaching other craftsmen (Ex. 31:6; 35:34–35). D.W.G.

OHOLIBAMAH, OHOLAH, OHOLIBAH. Oholibamah was an Edomite name used for both men and women. It was the name of *Esau's second wife, a Canaanite woman, daughter of Anah and mother of Jeush, Jalam and Korah (Gn. 36:1–28). There was also an Edomite chief of this name (Gn. 36:41; 1 Ch. 1:52) which means 'tent of the high place'. In Gn. 36:34 and 1 Ch. 1:52 the name appears alongside Timna and it is interesting to note that a tent shrine has been discovered at Timna in the Negev, the region of ancient Edom. The shrine is dated to the Midianite period and is a parallel to the desert *tabernacle. The name suggests that some early *'high places' may have been tents (*cf.* Ezk. 16:16).

Oholah and Oholibah (AV Aholah and Aholibah) are allegorical names given to the N and S kingdoms in Ezk. 23. Both names mean 'tent worshipper' and were inspired by the term Oholibamah. They imply criticism of Israel's unfaithfulness to God. The two kingdoms are portrayed as sisters married to Yahweh but who have persisted in adultery by their entanglements with other nations. Oholibah is warned against following her sister's example and judgment is predicted. The sexuality of the imagery (*cf.* Ezk. 16; Ho. 1–3; Am. 5:1–2) is particularly appropriate as many of the neighbouring nations' religions involved fertility rites. J.T.W.

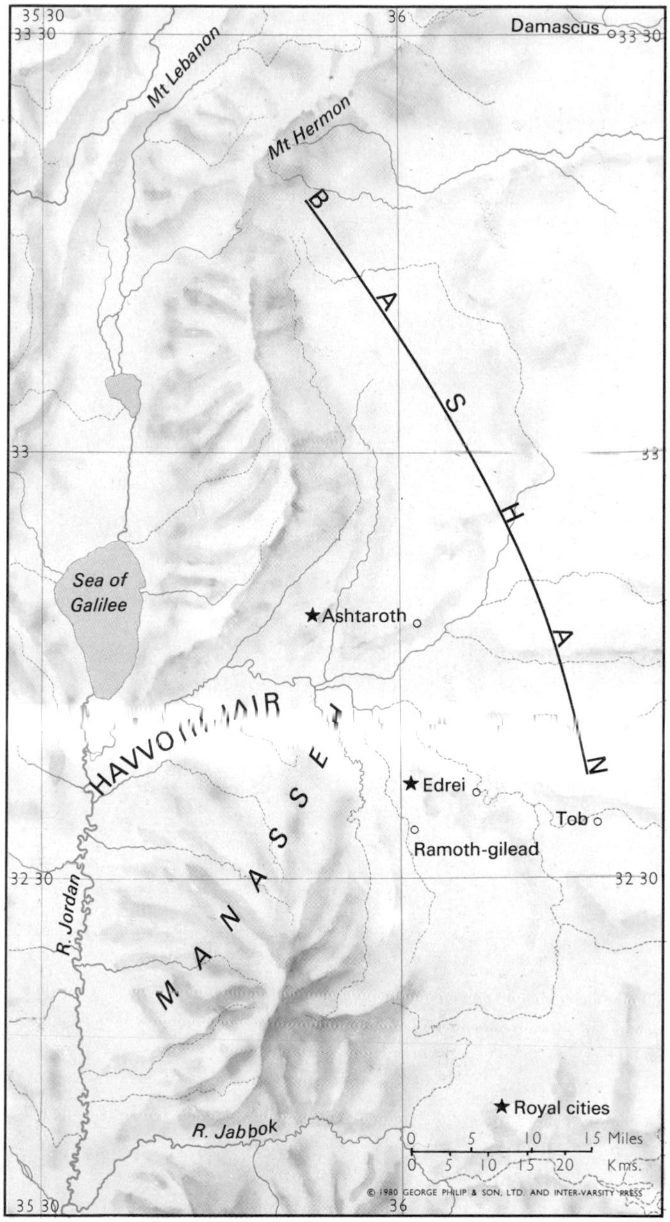

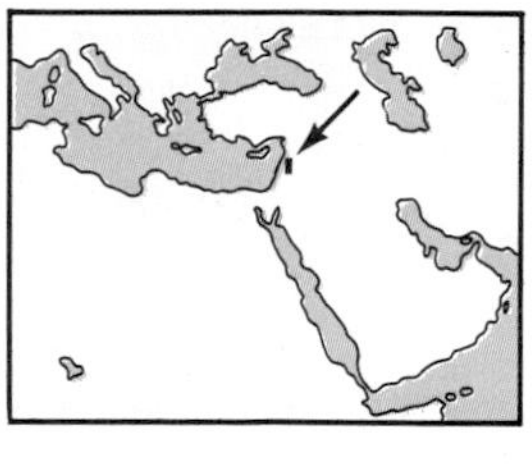

The region ruled by Og of Bashan.

OFFENCE
See Stumbling-block, Part 3.

Oil was extracted from the fruit of the olive tree (olea). (FNH)

OIL. Unless cosmetic ointments (Ru. 3:3; 2 Sa. 14:2; Ps. 104:15) or oil of myrrh (Est. 2:12) are indicated, all other biblical references to oil are to the expressed product of the *olive fruit. The abundance of olive-trees (*Olea europaea*) in ancient Palestine enabled a flourishing trade in oil to be carried on with Tyre and Egypt. Solomon supplied large quantities of oil to Hiram as part-payment for the construction of the Temple (1 Ki. 5:11; Ezk. 27:17), while Egypt imported substantial quantities of Palestinian oil (*cf.* Ho. 12:1), because the Egyp. climate is not conducive to successful cultivation.

As an important element of religious observances, oil was prominent among the firstfruit offerings (Ex. 22:29) and was also an object of tithing (Dt. 12:17). The meal-offerings were frequently mixed with oil (Lv. 8:26; Nu. 7:19), while the sanctuary lamp (Ex. 25:6) was replenished from a supply of freshly processed oil (Lv. 24:2). Oil was employed ceremonially at the consecration of priests (Ex. 29:2), at the purification of lepers (Lv. 14:10–18), during the daily sacrifice (Ex. 29:40), and at the completion

Cones of ointment were placed on the heads of guests at Egyptian banquets. The melting unguents provided a pleasant perfume. Tomb of Nebamun, Thebes. c. 1422–1411 BC. (BM)

of the Nazirite's vow (Nu. 6:15). But certain ceremonies were devoid of oil, such as the jealousy-offering (Nu. 5:15) and the sin-offering (Lv. 5:11).

Olive oil was widely employed in the preparation of food, replacing butter in cooking (1 Ki.17:12–16). An equally popular usage in the domestic sphere was that of a fuel for the small lamps found in abundance from an early period in Palestine. Both portable and other types of lamps generally had an indentation in the brim into which the wick of flax (Is. 42:3) or hemp was put. When the lamp was filled with olive oil the wick maintained a steady flame until the supply of fuel was depleted. When such lamps were being carried about it was customary in NT times for the bearer to attach a small container of olive oil to one finger by means of a string. Then if the lamp needed to be replenished at any time an adequate supply of oil was readily available (*cf.* Mt. 25:1–13).

Apart from the use of oil at the consecration of the priests (Ex. 29:2), it was an important ritual element in the ceremonial recognition of the kingly office (1 Sa. 10:1; 1 Ki. 1:39).

As a medicine olive oil was used both internally and externally. Its soothing protective qualities made it a valuable remedy for gastric disorders, while its properties as a mild laxative were also recognized in antiquity. Externally it formed a popular unguent application for bruises and wounds (Is. 1:6; Mk. 6:13; Lk. 10:34).

In OT times olive oil was produced either by means of a pestle and mortar (Ex. 27:20) or by grinding the olives in a stone press. Excavations at Taanach, Megiddo and Jerusalem have uncovered presses hewn out of the solid rock. A large stone roller manipulated by two people crushed the olives to a pulp, which was then either trodden out (Dt. 33:24) or subjected to further pressing. After impurities had been removed the oil was ready for use. The Garden of Gethsemane (*gaṯ-šemen*, 'oil press') received its name from the stone presses set up to extract oil from the berries gathered on the Mount of Olives.

Oil was commonly used for anointing the body after a bath (Ru. 3:3; 2 Sa. 12:20), or as part of some festive occasion (*cf.* Ps. 23:5). In ancient Egypt a servant generally anointed the head of each guest as he took his place at the feast. The anointing of the sick (Jas. 5:14) in NT times had become a quasi-sacramental rite. Josephus records as a peculiarity of the Essenes that they did not anoint themselves with oil, since they considered it 'defiling' (*BJ* 2. 123).

The presence of oil symbolized gladness (Is. 61:3) while its absence indicated sorrow or humiliation (Joel 1:10). Similarly oil was used as an image of comfort, spiritual nourishment, or prosperity (Dt. 33:24; Jb. 29:6; Ps. 45:7).

Bibliography. H. N. and A. L. Moldenke, *Plants of the Bible*, 1952, pp. 97f., 158ff.; A. Goor, 'The place of the olive in the Holy Land and its history through the ages', *Economic Botany* 20, 1966, pp. 223–243; A. Goor and M. Nurock, *The Fruits of the Holy Land*, 1968, pp. 89–120.

R.K.H.

OINTMENT (Heb. *mirqaḥaṯ*, *šemen*; Gk. *myron*). Unguent preparations of various kinds were widely used throughout the whole of the ancient Near East. Their primary use was cosmetic in nature, and they probably originated in Egypt. Toilet boxes, of which alabaster ointment containers formed a part, have been recovered in considerable numbers from Palestinian sites.

The Egyptians apparently found that the application of unguents was soothing and refreshing. It was their custom at feasts to place small cones of perfumed ointment upon the foreheads of guests. Bodily heat gradually melted the ointment, which trickled down the face on to the clothing, producing a pleasant perfume. This practice was adopted by the Semites (Ps. 133:2), and continued into NT times (Mt. 6:17; Lk. 7:46).

Other ancient peoples followed

Copy of a note scratched on a piece of broken pottery in ancient Hebrew 'for the king, 1000 [. . .] *of oil and 100* [. . . *from ? A*]*hiyahu'. Found at Tel Qasileh, near Tel Aviv. c. 700* BC.

Top left: Olive oil was used as a fuel for lamps. This one is from the Roman period. Jericho. 37–3 BC. (ZR) the Egyptians in using ointments to reduce chafing and irritation caused by the heat. In localities where water was frequently at a premium, aromatic unguents were employed to mask the odour of perspiration. At other times they were used along with cosmetics in personal toilet procedures. Ointments were compounded either by apothecaries (2 Ch. 16:14), perfumers (Ex. 30:35), priests or by private individuals, using a wide variety of aromatic substances.

The holy anointing oil (Ex. 30:23–25) prescribed for use in tabernacle rituals was required to be compounded according to the art of the perfumer. It consisted of olive oil, myrrh, cinnamon, calamus and cassia, the solid ingredients probably being pulverized and boiled in the olive oil (*cf.* Jb. 41:31). The manufacture of this preparation by unauthorized persons was strictly prohibited (Ex. 30:37–38).

According to Pliny, unguents were preserved most successfully in alabaster containers. Under such conditions they improved with age, and became very valuable after a number of years. Thus the alabaster box of ointment mentioned in the Gospels (Mt. 26:7; Mk. 14:3; Lk. 7:37) was a very costly one containing spikenard (*Nardostachys jatamansi*). This herb, related to valerian, was imported from N India and used widely by Hebrews and Romans alike in the anointing of the dead. The qualifying adjective *pistikē* in Mk. 14:3 and Jn. 12:3 may perhaps mean either 'liquid' or 'genuine'.

Ointments were employed in a quasi-sacramental sense when new kings were consecrated for their office. Thus Samuel anointed Saul (1 Sa. 10:1), Elijah anointed Jehu (2 Ki. 9:3), and Jehoiada anointed Joash (2 Ki. 11:12). Palestinian shepherds compounded an ointment of olive oil which they rubbed on to the bruised faces of sheep (*cf.* Ps. 23:5). In NT times the sick were often anointed during a religious rite (Jas. 5:14). Unguents perfumed with myrrh were used to anoint the dead (Lk. 23:56; Mk. 14:8).

BIBLIOGRAPHY. H. N. and A. L. Moldenke, *Plants of the Bible*, 1952, pp. 148f.; R. K. Harrison, *Healing Herbs of the Bible*, 1966, pp. 49–54. R.K.H.

OLD AGE
See Age, Part 1.

OLIVE (Heb. *zayiṯ*; Gk. *elaia*). One of the most valuable * trees of the ancient Hebrews, the olive is first mentioned in Gn. 8:11, when the dove returned to the ark with an olive branch. When the Israelites took possession of Canaan it was a conspicuous feature of the flora (*cf.* Dt. 6:11). At a later time the olive was esteemed with the vine as a profitable source of revenue (1 Sa. 8:14; 2 Ki. 5:26).

Although the botanical name of the olive is *Olea europaea*, the tree is thought to be a native of W Asia, being introduced subsequently into the Mediterranean region. Oriental peoples regarded the olive as a symbol of beauty, strength, divine blessing and prosperity. In harmony with the Noahic tradition, the olive and the dove have been venerated ever since as symbols of friendship and of peace (*cf.* Ps. 52:8).

In many parts of Palestine the olive, of which there are many varieties in the Near East, is still very often the only tree of any size in the immediate locality. The cultivated olive grows to about 6 m in height,

An olive grove in Greece. (BPL)

A characteristic olive tree (Olea). (FNH)

with a contorted trunk and numerous branches. The tree develops slowly, but often attains an age of several centuries if left undisturbed. If cut down, new shoots spring up from the root, so that as many as five new trunks could thus come into being. Moribund olives usually sprout in this manner also (*cf.* Ps. 128:3). Olive groves were chiefly valued for their potential * oil resources, although they were also highly esteemed as a shelter from the burning sun and as a place where one could meditate (Lk. 22:39).

In antiquity olive-trees were distributed profusely across Palestine. The groves on the edge of the Phoenician plain were particularly impressive, as were those in the plain of Esdraelon and the valley of Shechem. Bethlehem, Hebron, Gilead, Lachish and Bashan were all renowned in Bible times for their wealth of olive groves.

The berries borne by the olive ripened in the early autumn, and were harvested towards the end of November. The primitive and rather injurious method of gathering the olive berries described in Dt. 24:20, whereby the trees were either shaken or beaten with poles, is still widely employed. In antiquity a few berries were left on the tree or on the ground beneath it for the benefit of the poor. The olive harvest was normally transported to the presses in baskets on the backs of donkeys. The oil was usually extracted from the berries by placing them in a shallow rock cistern and crushing them with a large upright millstone. Occasionally the berries were pounded by the feet of the harvesters (Dt. 33:24; Mi. 6:15), but this was a rather inefficient procedure. After being allowed to stand for a time the oil separated itself from foreign matter, and was then stored in jars or rock cisterns.

The cherubim of the Solomonic Temple were fashioned from olive wood (1 Ki. 6:23), and since they were some 4·5 m high with the same wing-spread, it has been conjectured that they were composed of several pieces of wood joined together. While olive-wood is still used in Palestine for fine cabinet-work, the short gnarled trunks do

Round basin and press-stone (left) *used for crushing olives. En-Nashut, Golan Heights. c. 3rd cent. AD.* (JPK)

not provide very lengthy pieces of timber. After it has been seasoned for a number of years the rich amber-grained wood can be polished to a high gloss.

So prolific a tree as the olive was naturally turned to a wide variety of usages. It was deemed worthy of being called the king of the trees (Jdg. 9:8), and at coronations its oil was employed as an emblem of sovereignty. Olive boughs were used to construct booths during the Feast of Tabernacles (Ne. 8:15). Fresh or pickled olives eaten with bread formed an important part of ancient Palestinian diet. The oil constituted the base of many unguent preparations, and was also used as a dressing for the hair. In addition it did duty as a fuel (Mt. 25:3), a medicine (Lk. 10:34; Jas. 5:14) and a food (2 Ch. 2:10).

The olive-tree enjoyed wide symbolic usage among the Hebrews. The virility and fruitfulness of the tree suggested the ideal righteous man (Ps. 52:8; Ho. 14:6), whose offspring was described as 'olive branches' (Ps. 128:3). An allusion to the facility with which the olive sometimes sheds its blossoms is found in Jb. 15:33, where Eliphaz states that the wicked will 'cast off his blossom, like the olive-tree.' In Zc. 4:3 the two olive-trees were emblems of fruitfulness, indicating the abundance with which God had provided for human needs.

The olive mentioned in Is. 41:19 (Heb. *'ēṣ šāmen*; AV 'oil-tree') has been equated with the botanically unrelated *Elaeagnus angustifolia*, which yields an inferior oil; but the context favours the true olive.

The fruit of the olive in its wild state is small and worthless. To become prolific the olive must be grafted, a process by which good stock is made to grow upon the wild shrub. Paul uses this fact as a powerful allegory (Rom. 11:17) in showing how the Gentiles are under obligation to the true Israel, indicating that it is contrary to nature for the wild olive slip to be grafted on to good stock.

BIBLIOGRAPHY. W. M. Ramsay, *Pauline and Other Studies*, 1906, pp. 219ff.; H. N. and A. L. Moldenke, *Plants of the Bible*, 1952, pp. 157–160; A. Goor, 'The place of the olive in the Holy Land and its history through the ages', *Economic Botany* 20, 1966, pp. 223–243; A. Goor and M. Nurock, *The Fruits of the Holy Land*, 1968, pp. 89–120. R.K.H.
F.N.H.

OLIVES, MOUNT OF. Olivet, or the Mount of Olives, is a small range of four summits, the highest being 830 m, which overlooks Jerusalem and the Temple Mount from the E across the Kidron Valley and the Pool of Siloam. Thickly wooded in Jesus' day, rich in the olives which occasioned its name, the mount was denuded of trees in the time of Titus. All the ground is holy, for Christ unquestionably walked there, though particularized sites, with their commemorative churches, may be questioned. From the traditional place of Jesus' baptism, on Jordan's bank, far below sea level, Olivet's distant summit 1,200 m higher, a traditional site of the ascension, is clearly visible, for Palestine is a small land of long perspectives.

The OT references to Olivet at 2 Sa. 15:30; Ne. 8:15; Ezk. 11:23 are slight. 1 Ki. 11:7 and 2 Ki. 23:13 refer to Solomon's idolatry, the erection of high places to Chemosh and Molech, which probably caused one summit to be dubbed the Mount of Offence. In the eschatological future the Lord will part the Mount in two as he stands on it (Zc. 14:4).

Jews resident in Jerusalem used to announce the new moon to their compatriots in Babylonia by a chain of beacons starting on Olivet, each signalling the lighting of the next. But since Samaritans lit false flares, eventually human messengers had to replace the old beacons. G. H. Dalman considers the Mishnaic claim that this beacon service stretched as far afield as Mesopotamia perfectly feasible (*Sacred Sites and Ways*, 1935, p. 263, n. 7). The Mount has close connections with the red heifer (*CLEAN AND UNCLEAN) and its

The Mount of Olives seen from Jerusalem with ancient olive trees (foreground) and the Church of All Nations marking the area of Gethsemane. (MH)

ashes of purification (Nu. 19; *Parah* 3. 6–7, 11), as with other ceremonies of levitical Judaism. According to one legend, the dove sent forth from the ark by Noah plucked her leaf from Olivet (Gn. 8:11; Midrash *Genesis Rabba* 33. 6). Some believed that the faithful Jewish dead must be resurrected in Israel, that those who died abroad would eventually be rolled back through underground cavities (*Ketuboth* 111a), emerging at the sundered Mount of Olives (H. Loewe and C. G. Montefiore, *A Rabbinic Anthology*, 1938, pp. 660ff.). When the Shekinah, or radiance of God's presence, departed from the Temple through sin, it was said to linger for 3½ years on Olivet, vainly awaiting repentance (*Lamentations Rabba*, Proem 25; *cf.* Ezk. 10:18). The name 'Mountain of Three Lights' comes from the glow of the flaming Temple altar reflected on the hillside by night, the first beams of sunrise gilding the summit, and the oil from the olives which fed the Temple lamps.

Near the Church of All Nations, at the base of Olivet, are some venerable olive-trees, not demonstrably 2,000 years old. This is the area of Gethsemane, and the precise spot of the Agony, though undetermined, is close by. Half-way up the hill is the Church of Dominus Flevit. But why should our Lord weep there, half-way down? *HDB* cogently argues that he really approached Jerusalem by Bethany, round the S shoulder of Olivet, weeping when the city suddenly burst into view. A succession of churches of the ascension have long crowned the reputed summit of our Lord's assumption, and his supposed footprints are carefully preserved there as a tangible fulfilment of Zc. 14:4. Yet Luke's Gospel favours the Bethany area as the real scene of the Ascension. The visitor to Palestine learns the futility of pondering insolubles.

R.A.S.

OLIVET
See Olives, Mount of, Part 2.

OLIVET DISCOURSE. Sometimes known as the Synoptic Apocalypse, this is the last major discourse of Jesus recorded by Matthew, Mark and Luke (Mt. 24:3–25:46; Mk. 13:3–37; Lk. 21:5–36), and is the longest and most important section of teaching about the future in the Synoptics. The core is similar in each Gospel, but Matthew has the fullest form, adding at the end some parables and other teaching about the coming judgment. (References in this article will be to Mark's version, unless otherwise stated.)

I. Structure

The discourse is introduced by the disciples asking about (a) when Jesus' prediction of the destruction of the Temple will be fulfilled; (b) 'when these things are all to be accomplished' (v. 4). The wording in Matthew and the subsequent context in Mark suggest that 'all these things' include the end of the age and Jesus' second coming.

Jesus replies: **1.** Do not be misled by the appearance of false Christs, wars, earthquakes and famines: these are the beginning of sufferings, not an indication of the end (vv. 5–8). **2.** Be ready to endure bitter persecution as you witness to me (vv. 9–13). **3.** There will be a period of great distress when the 'desolating sacrilege' is set up (vv. 14–20). **4.** Do not be misled by the activities of false Christs (vv. 21–23). **5.** In those days after the distress the heavenly bodies will be shaken, and you will see the Son of man coming in power and gathering his elect (vv. 24–27). **6.** 'These things' are signs of the Lord's nearness and will happen in this generation (vv. 28–31). **7.** 'That day and hour' are unknown; so keep awake (vv. 32–37).

II. Problems of interpretation

The following are some of the most important points of interpretation on which there is dispute.

a. Particular exegetical problems

1. The phrase 'desolating sacrilege' (v. 14), one of the many OT allusions in the discourse, echoes Dn. 11:31; 12:11. In Daniel the primary reference is to the setting up of a pagan altar in the Jerusalem Temple in 168 BC by *Antiochus Epiphanes; but the intended meaning in the Synoptic Apocalypse is difficult to determine. The injunction 'let the reader understand' (probably to be taken as addressed to the reader of the Gospel, or possibly to the reader of Daniel) suggests that the phrase is deliberately cryptic. Some modern scholars associate it with the abortive attempt of the Roman emperor Gaius to have his statue set up in the Temple in AD 40. They argue that the prophecy derives from that time (so not from Jesus), and that it was unfulfilled. Others take the phrase to refer to the still future appearance of the *Antichrist in the last day, pointing to the similar description of the 'lawless one' in 2 Thes. 2. Others again see the fulfilment of the prophecy in the events leading up to the fall of Jerusalem in AD 70, a view apparently supported by Luke's slightly different version in 21:20. This last view seems the simplest, though it is possible to maintain that the prophecy has a double reference, both to the period of the Roman attack on Jerusalem in AD 66–70 and to the last days.

2. The reference in vv. 24–27 to the disturbances in the heavens and to the coming of the Son of man has been taken in at least two different ways. Some scholars argue that it is figurative language taken from the OT with a historical reference to the fall of Jerusalem: the coming of the Son of man is a coming in victory, not his return to earth, and the gathering of the elect by God's 'messengers' is the missionary outreach of the church. The more usual view is that the verses refer to the second coming, and this is supported by other similarly worded passages in the NT which undoubtedly refer to the parousia (*e.g.* Mt. 13:41ff.; 1 Thes. 4:14ff.).

3. The assertion 'this generation will not pass away before all these things take place' (v. 30) raises particularly difficult questions. Does it mean that the coming of the Son of man and everything else described in the discourse will take place within the lifetime of Jesus' contemporaries? If so—and if the coming referred to is the seond coming (see point **2** above)—then this is evidently a mistaken prediction. Some scholars accept it as such and maintain that the error was a reflection of Jesus' humanity. Many others have been unhappy about this view and have looked for alternative explanations. Some argue that the saying was not Jesus' at all but the teaching of the early church; this explanation probably creates as many difficulties as it solves. Others suggest that the word *genea* does not here mean 'generation' (so RSV and other versions) but 'race' or 'kind of people'. These proposed alternatives do not fit well into the context. A more satisfactory explanation based on the text is that 'these things' in v. 29 are the *signs* of the end, not the end itself; so 'all these things' in v. 30 may also be taken as a reference to the signs of the end. This view can claim support from v. 32; although this verse may simply be saying that Jesus is ignorant of the precise moment in 'this generation' when the Son of man will return, it may also be taken as a general disavowal of knowledge of the timing of 'that day' (= the last day in biblical terminology).Thus Jesus does know that the signs will take place within a generation, but he does not know when the end itself will come.

Even on this view the strong impression is still that the coming is near. Perhaps the best explanation of this strong sense of imminence, which pervades the whole NT, is to say that it is a theological awareness of the fact that, once Jesus has come, the parousia is near in God's plan, rather than a particular chronological conviction. The end began in Jesus, and ever afterwards we live in eager anticipation of the consummation.

b. More general questions

1. Many scholars have doubts about ascribing some or all of the discourse to Jesus. Many have felt, *e.g.*, that the apocalyptic teaching in the discourse is unlike Jesus' teaching elsewhere in the Gospels. T. Colani's famous *Little Apocalypse Theory*, propounded in 1864 and taken up with modification by many since, was that vv. 5–31 were a Jewish–Christian apocalyptic tract incorporated into the Gospel by the Evangelist. This theory was founded on a mistaken view of Jesus as one who taught eternal ethical truths and not an eschatological gospel. But although scholars today reject Colani's view of Jesus, some still argue that the teaching on signs contradicts Jesus' teaching elsewhere on the unexpectedness of the parousia (*e.g.* Lk. 17:20ff.). This view fails to take seriously the fact that in biblical apocalyptic teaching about suddenness and signs is regularly found together. Other objections to regarding the teaching as deriving from Jesus, *e.g.* that the OT quotations are based on the LXX and not on the Hebrew text, are equally indecisive.

2. There are important literary critical questions about the discourse. The differences between the Gospels force the critic to try to explain the relationship between the accounts; many scholars argue that two or more of the Evangelists had independent accounts of this discourse, and not simply that Matthew and Luke used Mark. Many also believe that one or more of the Evangelists has included in his version material that originally belonged in a different context; thus Matthew is thought to have imported 'Q' material into his account.

3. More important than the simply literary questions are questions about the theological teaching of the discourse in the three Gospels. One debated question is whether the prime intention is to give apocalyptic teaching about the signs of the end, or to exhort hearers and readers. The probability is that both purposes are present: Jesus taught his disciples that the rule (or * kingdom) of God had come with his ministry, but that it would be fully established in the future. Here he does give information about what will occur before the end, but his purpose is not so that anyone may draw up a timetable of future events but to prepare people practically for the future; thus the note of exhortation is very strong. Jesus' disciples are (a) not to get misled by false teachers and rumours before the end; (b) to endure hardship until the end; (c) to be awake for the return of Christ.

BIBLIOGRAPHY. G. R. Beasley-Murray, *Jesus and the Future*, 1954; W. Lane, *The Gospel according to St Mark*, 1974; C. E. B. Cranfield, *The Gospel according to St Mark*, 1959; D. Wenham, *TSFB* 71, 1975, pp. 6–15; 72, 1975, pp. 1–9; K. Grayston, 'The Study of Mark XIII', *BJRL* 56, 1973–4, pp. 371–387. D.W.

OLYMPAS. An otherwise unknown but influential Christian greeted by Paul in Rom. 16:15. As the name, probably an abbreviation of Olympiodorus, was common throughout the empire, its presence in this verse throws no light on the problem of the destination of Rom. 16. R.V.G.T.

OMRI (Heb. *'omri*). **1.** An officer from Issachar during David's reign (1 Ch. 27:18). **2.** Sixth king of the N kingdom of Israel and founder of a new dynasty after the death of *Elah. During the period of anarchy following the death of *Baashah, the army, besieging Gibbethon, proclaimed their leader Omri as king upon hearing of the [illegible] 16.15–17). He thereupon marched to the capital, *Tirzah, and besieged the town until Zimri committed suicide (v. 18). Tibni, another claimant to the throne, resisted Omri for 4 years but was finally defeated. Omri then reigned for 7 years, from the 31st to the 38th year of *Asa (vv. 23, 29), a total of 12 years (v. 23).

OMEGA
See Alpha, Part 1.

OMER
See Weights and measures, Part 3.

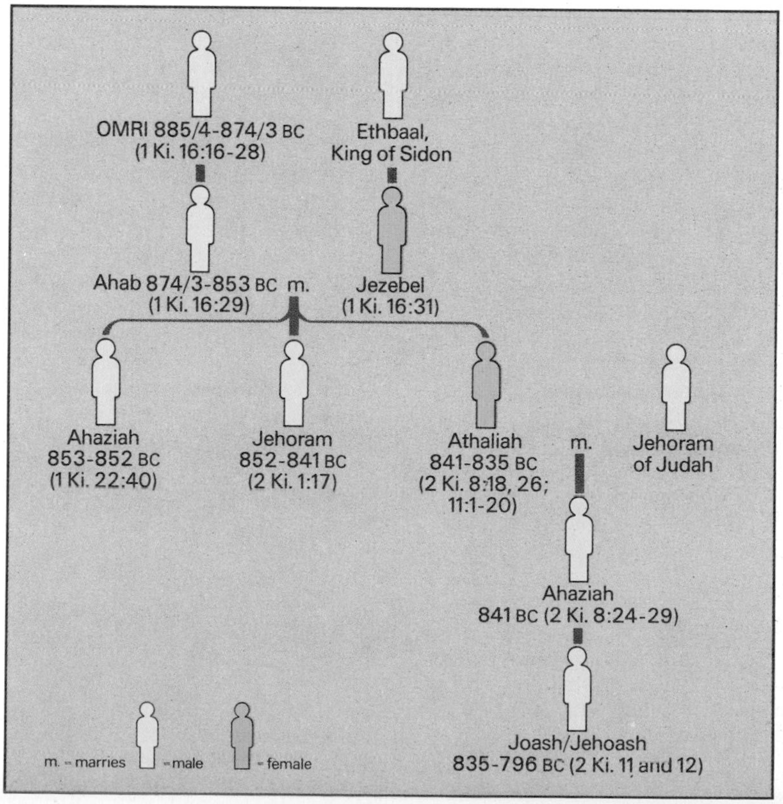

The dynasty of Omri, king of Israel (c. 885–874 BC).

Aram, which under *Ben-hadad I had been strong enough to annex part of Israel during Baasha's reign, still threatened Omri (*cf.* 1 Ki. 20:34). He allied himself with Ethbaal, king of Sidon, by taking his daughter *Jezebel for *Ahab, his son (16:31), thus averting some of the danger. He was strong enough to make Moab his vassal, as recorded by Mesha in the *Moabite stone (11:4–5) (*ANET*, p. 320; *DOTT*, p. 196; *cf.* 2 Ki. 3:4).

Omri is also remembered for his building activities. The most important of these was the new Israelite capital at *Samaria on a site purchased from Shemer, its previous owner (1 Ki. 16:24). The city had an excellent strategic position, and served as capital until the fall of Israel in 722 BC. Archaeological excavations at Megiddo and Hazor have also revealed buildings attributed to him.

Details of Omri's reign are sparse, but Assyrian sources show that until the reign of *Sargon II, Israel was also known as *māt/bīt Ḫumri*, 'the land/house of Omri' (*ANET*, pp. 281–285). Because he condoned pagan worship he was remembered as a bad king (1 Ki. 16:25–26). D.W.B.

ONAGER
See Animals, Part 1.

ONE
See Number, Part 2.

ON. 1. A venerable city, Egyp. *'Iwnw* ('city of the pillar'), Gk. Heliopolis, now represented by scattered or buried remains at Tell Ḥiṣn and Maṭariyeh, 16 km NE of Cairo. From antiquity it was the great centre of Egyp. sun-worship, where the solar deities Rēʿ and Atum were especially honoured, and the home of one of Egypt's several theological 'systems'. The pharaohs embellished the temple of Rēʿ with many obelisks—tall, tapering, monolithic shafts of square or rectangular section, each ending at the top in a pyramidally shaped point; such a 'pyramidion' represented the *benben* or sacred stone of Rēʿ, as first to catch the rays of the rising sun. Each pharaoh from the 5th Dynasty onward (25th century BC) was styled 'son of Rēʿ ', and the priestly corporations of On/Heliopolis were equalled in wealth only by that of the god Ptah of Memphis and exceeded only by that of the god Amūn of Thebes, during *c.* 1600–1100 BC.

The prominence of On is reflected in Gn. 41:45, 50; 46:20, where Joseph as Pharaoh's new chief minister is married to Asenath, daughter of *Potiphera, 'priest of On'. This title might mean that Potiphera was high priest there. His name, very fittingly, is compounded with that of the sun-god Rēʿ. *Cf.* A. Rowe, *PEQ* 94, 1962, pp. 133–142.

On next recurs in Heb. history under the appropriate pseudonym Beth-shemesh, 'House of the Sun', when Jeremiah (43:13) threatens that Nebuchadrezzar will smash 'the pillars of Beth-shemesh', *i.e.* the obelisks of On/Heliopolis. Whether Isaiah's 'city of the sun' (19:18) is On is less clear. Aven (Heb. *'awen*) of Ezk. 30:17 is a variant pointing of *'ôn*, 'On', perhaps as a pun on *'awen*, 'trouble, wickedness', in Ezekiel's judgment on Egypt's cities.

2. On, son of Peleth, a Reubenite chief, rebelled with Korah against Moses in the wilderness (Nu. 16:1). K.A.K.

ONAN (Heb. *'ōnān*, 'vigorous'). The second son of Judah (Gn. 38:4; 46:12; Nu. 26:19; 1 Ch. 2:3). On the death of his elder brother Er, Onan was commanded by Judah to contract a levirate marriage with Tamar, Er's widow. Onan, unwilling to follow this traditional practice, took steps to avoid a full consummation of the union, thus displeasing the Lord, who slew him (Gn. 38:8–10). Judah evidently attached some blame for his sons' deaths to Tamar herself (v. 11). For levirate marriage see *MARRIAGE, **IV**. J.D.D.

ONESIMUS. A runaway slave belonging to Philemon, an influential Christian at Colossae. He made the acquaintance of Paul, while the latter was a prisoner, either at Rome or Ephesus (according to the view which is taken of the provenance of Colossians). He was converted by the apostle (Phm. 10), and became a trustworthy and dear brother (Col. 4:9). His name, which means 'useful', was a common name for slaves, though not confined to them; and he lived up to it by making himself so helpful to Paul that the latter would have liked to have kept him to look after him as, Pauls feels, Philemon would have wished (Phm. 13). But the apostle felt constrained to do nothing without Philemon's willing consent; so he returned the slave to his former owner, with a covering note—the canonical *Philemon. In

Obelisk at the ancient site of On (Greek Heliopolis, Je. 43:13). Originally erected in the temple of the sun-god Rēʿ. (KAK)

this the apostle plays on the slave's name by describing him as 'once so little use to you, but now useful indeed, both to you and me'; and hints, tactfully but clearly, that he expects Philemon to take Onesimus 'back for good, no longer as a slave, but as more than a slave—as a dear brother, very dear indeed to me and how much dearer to you, both as man and as Christian' (Phm. 15–16, NEB). Nevertheless, Paul admits that sending him back is like being deprived of a part of himself (Phm. 12).

The mention of Onesimus is one of the links which bind together Colossians and Philemon, and shows that they were sent from the same place at the same time. Some scholars believe that the Onesimus known to Ignatius and described by him in his Epistle to the Ephesians as 'a man of inexpressible love and your bishop' was none other than the runaway slave. This hypothesis, though not impossible, would seem improbable on chronological considerations. It is urged in its support that it supplies a reason why Philemon was preserved as a canonical book. On the other hand, its close connection with Colossians, and its importance for the light it throws on the Christian treatment of slaves, would seem to provide adequate reasons for its canonicity.

BIBLIOGRAPHY. The role of Onesimus in Paul's letter is considered by P. N. Harrison, *ATR* 32, 1950, pp. 268–294. His later career has been made the subject of an elaborate theory by E. J. Goodspeed, *INT*, 1937, pp. 109–124, and J. Knox, *Philemon among the Letters of Paul*², 1959. For a criticism (with bibliography), see R. P. Martin, *Colossians and Philemon, NCB*, 1974, introduction. R.V.G.T.
R.P.M.

ONESIPHORUS. In the Second Epistle to Timothy, written by Paul to Timothy at Ephesus, the apostle sends greetings to the household of Onesiphorus (4:19), and prays that the Lord's mercy may rest upon it, and that Onesiphorus himself may find mercy from the Lord on the great day of judgment. This true Christian friend had often brought relief to the apostle in his troubles, and had taken pains to search out and find him in Rome, where Paul was now in prison. His conduct in this respect, Paul notices, stood out in marked contrast to other Asian Christians who had deserted Paul in his hour of need. Like Onesimus, Onesiphorus had lived up to his name, which means 'profit-bringer'. The apostle reminds Timothy that he knew better than Paul himself about the many services rendered by Onesiphorus to the Christians who lived at Ephesus (1:16–18).

BIBLIOGRAPHY. E. E. Ellis, *NTS* 17, 1970–71, pp. 437–452, 'Paul and his Co-Workers'; and for the view that Onesiphorus played a significant role regarding the collection in Galatia, and that the setting of 2 Tim. 1:16–18 is Pisidian Antioch, not Rome, see F. J. Badcock, *The Pauline Epistles*, 1937, especially pp. 150–158.

Problems to do with Paul's remembrance of Onesiphorus, who may or may not have been deceased when 2 Tim. 1:18 was written, are considered by D. Guthrie (*TNTC*, 1957) and J. N. D. Kelly (Harper-Black, 1963) *ad loc.* R.V.G.T.
R.P.M.

ONO. A town first mentioned in the lists of Thothmes III (1490–1436 BC). The Benjaminites rebuilt it after the conquest of Canaan (1 Ch. 8:12) and reoccupied it after the Exile (Ne. 11:31–35). Identified with Kafr 'Anâ, it lay near Lydda. The area was called the Plain of Ono (Ne. 6:2). D.F.P.

ONYCHA. Pungent component of holy incense made by Moses at God's command, by burning claw-shaped valves closing shell apertures of certain molluscs—Heb. *šᵉḥēleṯ*, Ex. 30:34 only. This is the Gk. accusative of *onyx*, meaning talon, claw, anything so shaped, the precious stone. The accusative form, misunderstood as nominative in Vulg., passed into EVV usage, thus conveniently distinguishing the specialized meaning in Ex. 30:34. R.A.S.

OPHIR (Heb. *'ôp̄ir*, Gn. 10:29; *'ôp̄îr*, 1 Ki. 10:11). **1.** The name of the son of Yoqtān in the genealogy of Shem (Gn. 10:29 = 1 Ch. 1:23). This tribe is known from pre-islamic inscriptions (G. Ryckmans, *Les noms propres sud-sémitiques*, 1934, pp. 298, 339f.). Their area lies between Saba in the Yemen and Ḥawilah (Ḥawlān) as described in Gn. 10:29. Islamic tradition equates Yoqtān with Qaḥtān, a son of Ishmael and 'father of all Arabs'.

2. The country from which fine gold was imported to Judah (2 Ch. 8:18; Jb. 22:24; 28:16; Ps. 45:9; Is. 13:12), sometimes in large quantities (1 Ch. 29:4), and with valuable almug(sandal?)-wood (1 Ki. 10:11), silver, ivories, apes and peacocks (1 Ki. 10:22), and precious stones (2 Ch. 9:10). It was reached by Solomon's fleet from Ezion-geber on the Gulf of Aqabah (1 Ki. 9:28) employing 'ships of Tarshish', which might be *ships normally used for carrying ore (1 Ki. 22:48). These voyages took 'three years', that is perhaps one entire year and parts of two others. The trade was sufficiently well known for Ophir to be synonymous with the fine gold which was its principal product (Jb. 22:24). In Is. 13:12 Ophir is paralleled with *'ôqir*, 'I will make precious' (*HUCA* 12–13, 1937–8, p. 61). A confirmation of this trade is found in an ostracon, found at Tell Qasileh NE of Tel Aviv in 1946, inscribed *zhb 'p̄r lbyt ḥrn* š =, 'gold from Ophir for Beth Horon 30 shekels' (*JNES* 10, 1951, pp. 265–267).

Various theories have been put forward for the site of Ophir.

a. S Arabia as in **1** above. R. North links (Š)ōpha(i)r(a) (= Ophir) with Parvaim (= Farwa) in Yemen as the source of Sheba gold (*cf.* Ps. 72:15; Is. 60:6).

b. SE Arabia: Oman. These are not far from Ezion-geber, and it is necessary to assume both that the 3-year voyage included laying up during the hot summer and that some commodities (*e.g.* apes) not commonly found in S Arabia were brought to Ophir as an entrepôt from more distant places.

c. E African coast: Somaliland, *i.e.* the Egyp. *Punt*, a source of the frankincense and myrrh and those items described as from Ophir (W. F. Albright, *Archaeology and the Religion of Israel*, 1953, pp. 133–135, 212; van Beek, *JAOS* 78, 1958, p. 146).

d. (S)upāra, 75 km N of Bombay, India. Josephus (*Ant.* 8. 164), LXX and Vulg. (Jb. 28:16) interpreted Ophir as India. In favour of this interpretation are the facts that all the commodities named are familiar in ancient India, and it is known that from the 2nd millennium BC there was a lively sea-trade between the Persian Gulf and India.

e. Other, more doubtful, suggestions include Apir, Baluchistan (possibly ancient Meluhha, *cf.*

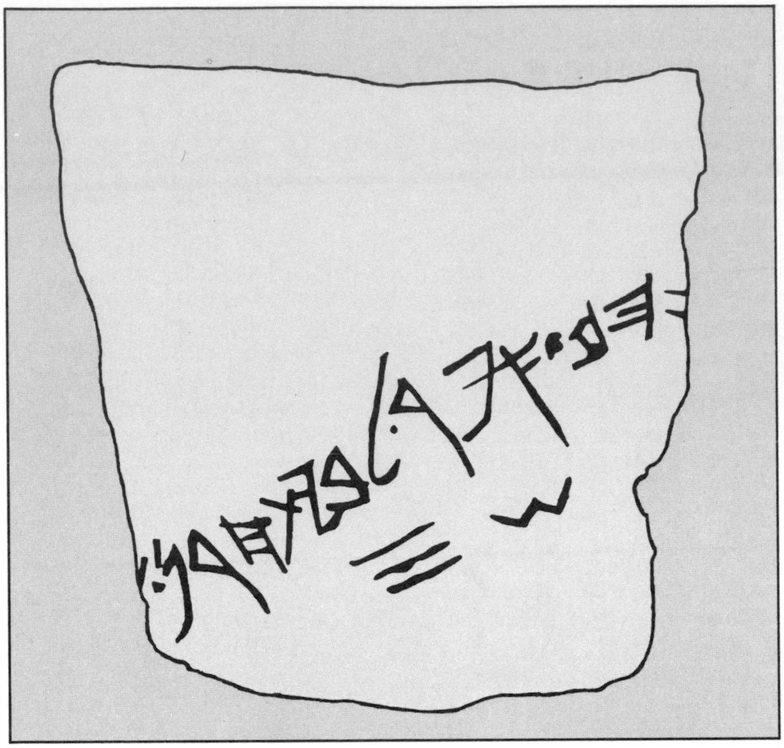

The inscription on this Hebrew ostracon found at Tell Qasileh, near Tel Aviv, reads zhb 'p̄r lbyt hrn š≡, *'gold of Ophir for Beth Horon, 30 shekels'. 8th cent.* BC.

BSOAS 36, 1973, pp. 554–587) and Zimbabwe, S Rhodesia.

BIBLIOGRAPHY. V. Christides, *RB* 77, 1970, pp. 240–247; R. North, *Fourth World Congress of Jewish Studies*, Papers, 1, 1967, pp. 197–202. D.J.W.

OPHRAH (Heb. *'op̄râh*). **1.** A town in Benjamin (Jos. 18:23; 1 Sa. 13:17, called Ephron (*Q^e^rē' 'ep̄raim*); 2 Ch. 13:19); modern et-Tayibeh, on a commanding height 9 km N of Michmash. Arabs often substituted *tayibeh* ('fortunate') where a place-name *'ofra* persisted in the Middle Ages, as it suggested black magic (Abel, *JPOS* 17, 1937, p. 38). It is doubtful whether *'op̄râh* developed into *Ephraim* (= Heb. *'ep̄raim*) of Jn. 11:54; see K.-D. Schunck, *VT* 11, 1961, pp. 188–200, and J. Heller, *VT* 12, 1962, pp. 339ff.

2. Ophrah of Abiezer in Manasseh, Gideon's home, where his altar of Jehovah-shalom (Jdg. 6:24, AV) was shown in later times. Possible sites are: (*a*) Fer'ata, W of Mt Gerizim (Conder), near Shechem but rather remote from the area of conflict, and probably *Pirathon of Jdg. 12:15; (*b*) et-Tayibeh, half-way between Beth-shan and Tabor (Abel), but well inside Issachar, and perhaps the Hapharaim of Jos. 19:19; (*c*) Afula, in the plain of Jezreel (Aharoni). Tell el-Far'a, 10 km NE of Shechem, was once considered, but is now known to be *Tirzah.

3. A town or family in Judah (1 Ch. 4:14). J.P.U.L.

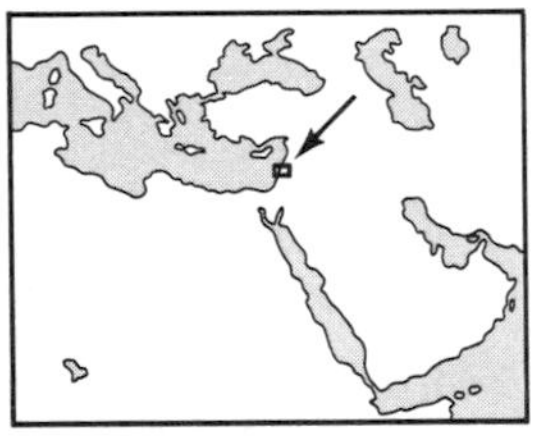

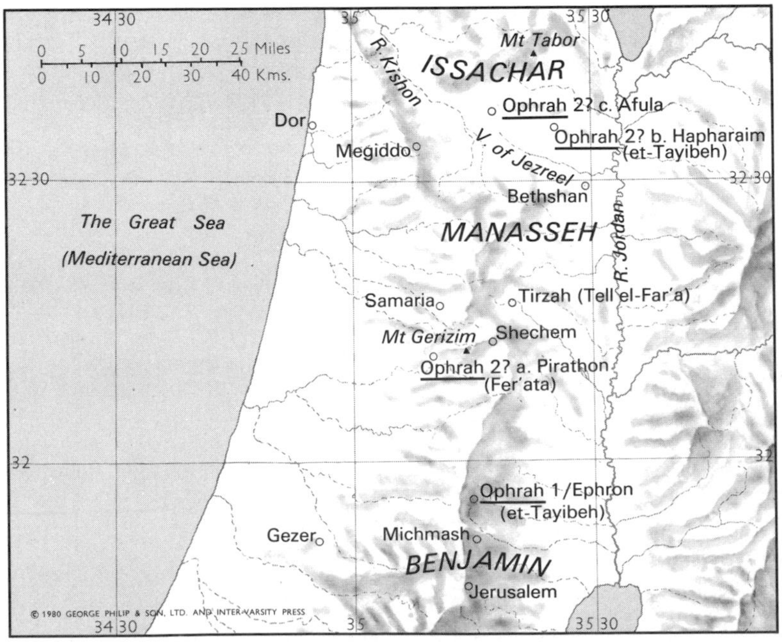

Possible locations for the site of Ophrah.

ORACLE. The translation 'oracle' occurs 17 times in the AV of the OT. Sixteen times it is the consistent mistranslation of the Heb. *d^e^ḇîr*, used exclusively of the inner shrine of Solomon's *Temple. The faulty derivation from *dibber*, 'speak', rather than from *dāḇar* in the sense of 'to be behind' stems from the translations of Aquila and Symmachus (who used *chrēmatistērion*, 'oracle') and the Vulgate (*oraculum*). That in heathen temples the chambers where the gods delivered their utterances (the oracular shrine of Apollo at Delphi was the most famous of these) were designated 'oracles' undoubtedly influenced the change as well.

In 2 Sa. 16:23 'oracle' translates the Heb. *dāḇār* and refers simply to the *word* or *utterance* of God without any specific indication of how this would be elicited; although some have here inferred a reference to the *Urim and Thummim (1 Sa. 28:6). In the RVmg. 'oracle' is sometimes used in place of 'burden' in the title of certain prophecies as a translation of the Heb. *maśśā'*.

In the NT 'oracles' translates the Gk. *logia*, meaning divine utterances and generally referring to the entire OT or some specific part of it. In Acts 7:38 the reference is either to the Decalogue or to the entire content of the Mosaic law. These oracles are said to be 'living', *zōnta*, that is, 'enduring' or 'abiding'. In Rom. 3:2 the reference is to all the written utterances of God through the OT writers, but with special regard to the divine promises made to Israel. The 'oracles of God' in Heb. 5:12, AV ('word', RSV) represent the body of Christian doctrine as it relates both to its OT foundation and to God's final utterance through his Son (Heb. 1:1). 1 Pet. 4:11 teaches that the NT preacher must speak as one who speaks the oracles of God, treating his words as carefully as if they were inspired Scripture.

The theological significance of the oracle is emphasized by B. B. Warfield who concludes that *ta logia*, as employed in the NT, are 'divinely authoritative communications before which men stand in awe and to which they bow in humility' (*The Inspiration and Authority of the Bible*, 1948, p. 403). R.H.M.

ORCHARD. Well known in various Bible lands throughout antiquity, these were plantations of fruit trees, specifically including pomegranates (Ec. 2:5, AV and Ct. 4:13 where 'orchard' renders Heb. *pardēs*). The *pardēs* of Ne. 2:8 furnished timber, and so is there rendered *'forest'. K.A.K.

ORDINATION. Considering the role played by the ministry throughout the history of the church, references to ordination are surprisingly few in the NT. Indeed, the word 'ordination' does not occur, and the verb 'to ordain' in the technical sense does not occur either. A number of verbs are translated 'ordain' in AV, but these all have meanings like 'appoint'. For example, *cheirotoneō* is used of the institution of elders in certain Galatian churches (Acts 14:23), but before we think of this as denoting 'ordination' in our sense of the term we must note its use in passages such as 2 Cor. 8:19, where it refers to the brother who was 'appointed by the churches to travel with us . . .'

The Twelve were chosen by Christ to be very near to himself and to be sent forth to minister (Mk. 3:14). But there is no word of any ceremony of ordination. Mark says that Jesus 'made (*poieō*)' twelve, and Luke that he 'chose (*eklegō*)' them (Mk. 3:14; Lk. 6:13). This was a very solemn occasion (Luke tells us that Jesus prayed all night before making his selection). But there is no 'ordination' mentioned. John speaks of the risen Lord as breathing on the ten, saying, 'Receive the Holy Spirit' (Jn. 20:22); but it is difficult to see an ordination in this. It is probably significant that when Matthias took the place of Judas there is again no mention of any ordination. Lots were cast, and when the choice of Matthias was known he was simply 'enrolled' or 'numbered' with the others (Acts 1:26). Similarly, prophets and others are called directly by God, though some at least are said to be 'for the work of ministry' (Eph. 4:12; the word 'ministry' here is, of course, used of service in a wide sense).

Luke tells us of the appointment of the Seven (Acts 6), and this is often understood as the institution of the diaconate. This may indeed be the case, but it is far from certain. Some think that the presbyterate is meant, and others deny that there is ordination to any ecclesiastical office. They think that Luke is describing nothing more than a temporary measure to meet a difficult situation. If the traditional view is accepted, then the essential thing about ordination is the laying on of hands with prayer. But in view of the uncertainties, and the wide use in antiquity of the laying on of hands, it is not possible to build much on this passage. Nor are we any better off when we read of elders as being appointed in the Galatian churches (Acts 14:23), for, while we may be tolerably sure that they were ordained in some way, nothing at all is told us of how this was done or what was expected of it.

Our most important information comes from the Pastoral Epistles. Paul counsels Timothy, 'Do not neglect the gift you have, which was given you by prophetic utterance when the council of elders laid their hands upon you' (1 Tim. 4:14). This passage yields us three items of information about Timothy's ordination. First, it meant the giving to him of a *charisma*, the spiritual *gift needed for the work of ministering. Secondly, this came to him 'by (*dia*) prophecy'. Thirdly, it came with (*meta*) the laying on of hands by the elders. The essential thing about ordination is the divine gift. Nothing can compensate for its lack. But there is also an outward act, the laying on of hands. It is possible that Paul refers to the same rite when he speaks of his own laying on of hands on Timothy (2 Tim. 1:6), though it should not be overlooked that some other rite may be in mind, perhaps something more akin to Anglican confirmation than to ordination. We might be able to make a better judgment if we knew when this took place, whether at the beginning of Paul's association with Timothy, or not long before the writing of the letter. If with most commentators we take this to refer to ordination, the meaning will be that Paul joined with the elders in the *laying on of hands, which in any case would be antecedently likely. It is probable that we have another reference to the same ordination in the words about 'the prophetic utterances which pointed to you' (1 Tim. 1:18).

Ordination is always a solemn affair, and it may be that the words 'Do not be hasty in the laying on of hands' (1 Tim. 5:22) emphasize this. But in view of the context it is perhaps more likely that they refer to the reception of penitents back into fellowship.

All this makes for a somewhat meagre harvest, which is all the more disappointing, since the Pastorals show us how important the *ministry was, especially the offices of presbyter and deacon. Titus, for example, is bidden 'appoint (*kathistēmi*) elders in every town' (Tit. 1:5), and much attention is paid to the qualifications for ministers. It is possible to suggest that the Christians took over the ordination of elders from the similar Jewish institution, but this does not get us far. All that we can say for certain is that the important thing for ministering is the divine gift, and that the essential rite in the earliest time appears to have been that of the laying on of hands with prayer. (*SPIRITUAL GIFTS.) L.M.

OREB (Heb. *'ōrēḇ*, 'raven'). **1.** A Midianite prince in the army routed by Gideon. **2.** The rock of Oreb, named after this prince, and remembered for the great defeat of Midian (Jdg. 7:25; Is. 10:26). The Ephraimites cut off the enemy's retreat at the Jordan fords, presumably opposite Jezreel; Bethbarah might be a ford (*'āḇar*, 'cross') some 20 km S of the Sea of Galilee. J.P.U.L.

ORNAMENTS. From Palaeolithic times ornament has been used by man to adorn the objects which surround him in his daily life. When the intention is right, the skill of the craftsman is a thing pleasing to God, and indeed for the building of the tabernacle Bezalel was filled with the spirit (*rûaḥ*) of God (Ex. 31:1–5), as were those who were to make the garments for the high priest (Ex. 28:3).

Archaeological discoveries have shown that in biblical times the carving of wood and ivory was done with great skill; weaving and embroidery reached a high stan-

ORCHESTRA
See Music, Part 2.

ORGAN
See Music, Part 2.

ORION
See Stars, Part 3.

dard; and the techniques involved in fine metalwork were well understood (*ARTS AND CRAFTS). Three main divisions of ornamented objects may be distinguished.

I. Personal

There is no evidence for the practice of ornamental tattooing in the ancient Near East, but clothing was often elaborately decorated, and jewellery was widely used. Though few examples of textiles have been recovered outside Egypt, the Assyrian and Persian sculptured reliefs and mural paintings at Mari on the Euphrates give, sometimes in great detail, representations of garments with fine embroidery. The Egyp. tomb-paintings likewise depict clothing in detail, and in one tomb at Beni-hasan a group of Asiatic nomads with brightly-coloured costumes (see *IBA*, fig. 25) gives an idea of the sort of ornamental clothing perhaps worn by the Patriarchs (*DRESS).

Many examples of jewellery (*JEWELS AND PRECIOUS STONES) have been found in excavations, perhaps the most outstanding being those from the 'Royal Tombs' at *Ur.

Various terms referring to objects of personal adornment are translated 'ornament', but their precise significance is in many cases uncertain. Among these are the following: **1.** *ḥ^{a}lî* (Pr. 25:12), perhaps from a Semitic root *ḥlh*, 'to adorn'; all EVV translate 'ornament'. The word also occurs in Ct. 7:1 where EVV translate it 'jewel'. **2.** *liwyâ* (Pr. 1:9; 4:9; lit. 'twisted thing'); RV renders 'chaplet' and RSV 'garland'. **3.** *'^{a}ḏî* (Ex. 33:4–6; 2 Sa. 1:24; Is. 49:18; Je. 2:32; 4:30; Ezk. 7:20; 16:7, 11; 23:40), derived from *'āḏâ*, 'to ornament', 'to deck oneself'; all EVV translate 'ornament'. **4.** *p^e'ēr* (Is. 61:10), from *pā'ar* in the Pi'el, meaning 'to beautify'; RV and RSV translate 'garland'. **5.** *ṣ^e'āḏâ* (Is. 3:20), of unknown etymology. It probably signifies an 'armlet' (so RSV); RV gives 'ankle chain'. **6.** *'eḵes* (Is. 3:18), perhaps connected with Arab. *'ikāsu*, 'to hobble (a camel)', from *'akasa*, 'to reverse, tie backwards', whence RV, RSV 'anklet'. The root occurs as a verb in Is. 3:16, where it is translated 'making a tinkling'.

Though on an occasion such as a wedding the putting on of ornaments and jewels by the participants is treated as right and proper (Is. 61:10), the immoderate use of personal ornament is roundly condemned (Is. 3:18–23; 1 Tim. 2:9). Is. 3 provides a catalogue of different kinds of ornaments which are translated variously in EVV. Some of these are *hapax legomena*, and little can be added to the RSV interpretation. The 'bracelet' (*šērâ*) of v. 19 is supported by the probable Akkad. cognate *šemēru* (*šewêru*) with this meaning. Likewise in v. 21, 'ring' (*ṭabba'aṯ*, RSV 'signet ring') is supported by Akkad. *ṭimbu'u*, *ṭimbûtu*, 'seal ring' (*SEAL). AV renderings which have been radically altered in the later versions are v. 20 'earring' (*laḥaš*; RV, RSV *'amulet'), v. 22 'wimple' (*miṭpaḥaṯ*; RV 'shawl', RSV 'cloak') and 'crisping pin' (*ḥārîṭ*; RV 'satchel', RSV 'handbag').

Among other articles of personal adornment were: **1.** *ḥāḥ*, usually a hook or ring for holding a man (2 Ki. 19:28) or animal (Ezk. 29:4) captive, but in Ex. 35:22 an ornament (AV 'bracelet', RV, RSV 'brooch'); **2.** *śah^{a}rôn*, probably a crescent-shaped object which was used on camels (Jdg. 8:21; AV 'ornament', RV 'crescent') and humans (Jdg. 8:26; Is. 3:18, AV 'round tire like the moon', RV 'crescent'); and many different kinds of chain ornaments, including **3.** *rāḇîḏ*, probably a twisted circlet for the neck (Gn. 41:42; Ezk. 16:11); **4.** *'^{a}nāq*, a more elaborate form made of plaited wire which might have pendants attached (Jdg. 8:26; Pr. 1:9; Ct. 4:9); **5.** *šarš^{e}râ*, probably a more flexible chain of the link type (Ex. 28:14, 22; 39:15; 1 Ki. 7:17; 2 Ch. 3:5, 16); **6.** *ḥārûz*, a necklace of beads strung on a thread (Ct. 1:10; RV 'string of jewels').

Another type of ornament, mentioned in 1 Macc. 10:89; 11:58; 14:44, is the 'buckle' (Gk. *porpē*, 'buckle pin', 'buckle brooch').

A special case of personal ornament is found in the garments of the high priest (*DRESS). The linen

A limestone slab from a threshold in Sennacherib's palace at Nineveh, c. 690 BC. The rooms were probably furnished with woven carpets, but as these would be damaged by the heavy wooden doors similar designs were carved in stone at the doorway. (BM)

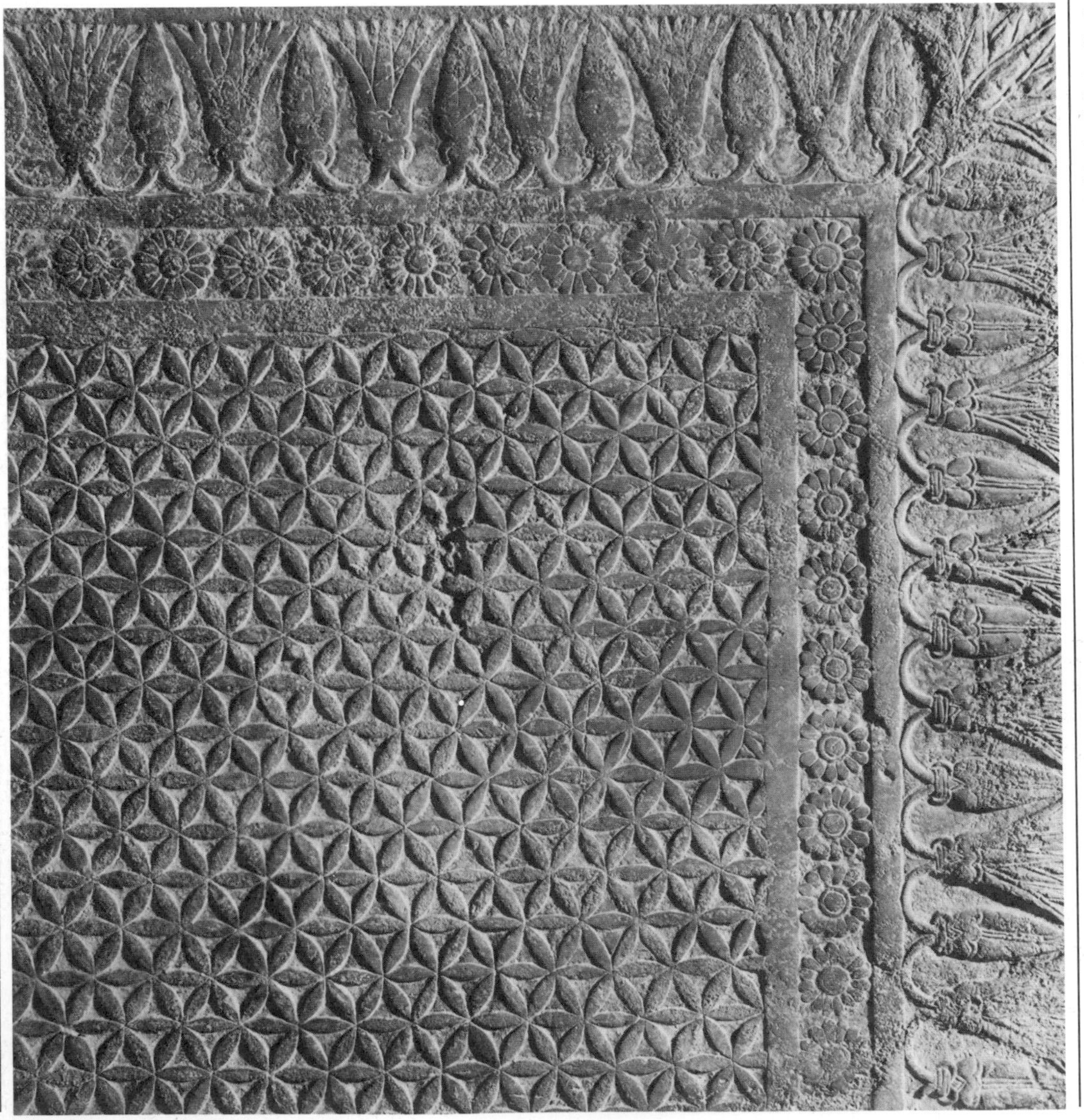

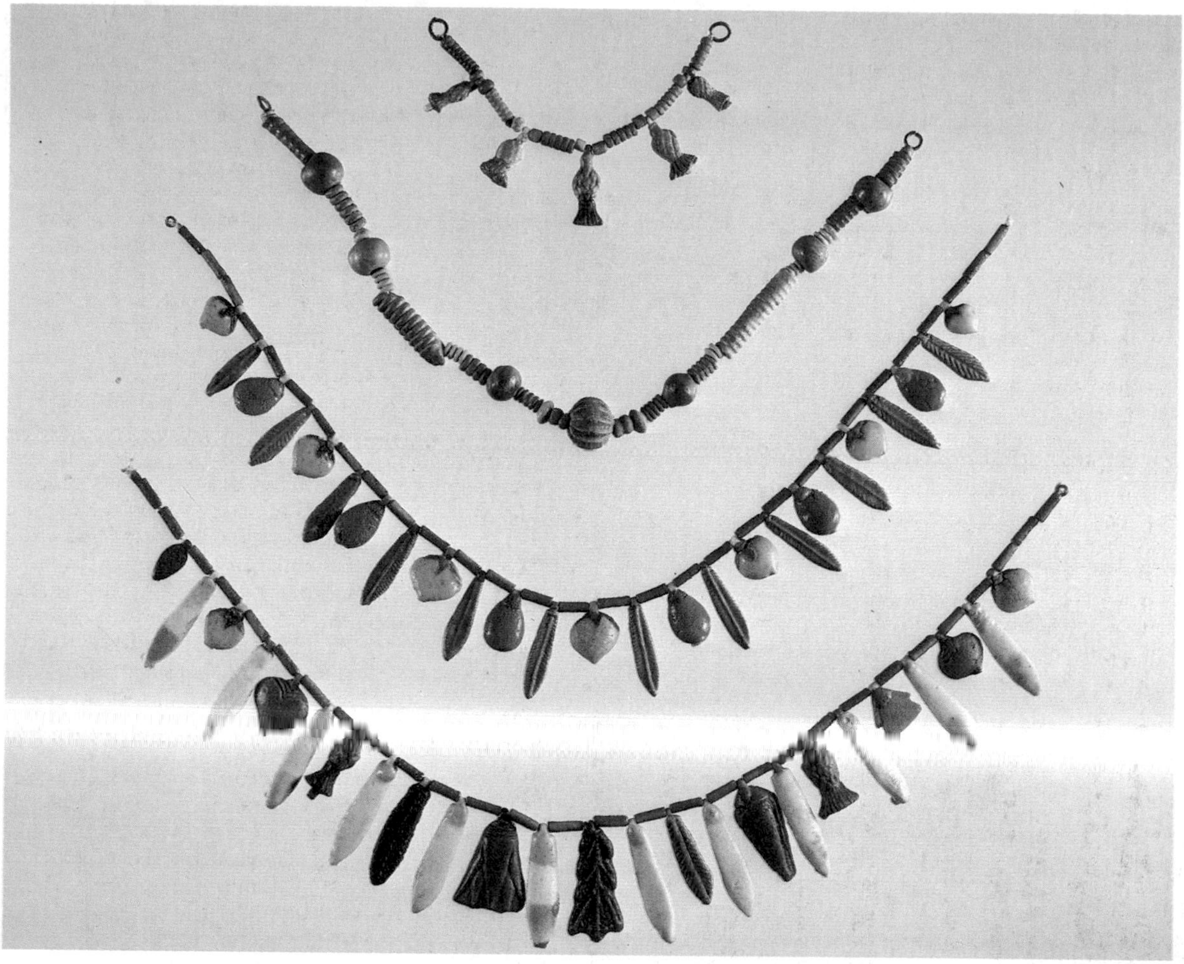

Egyptian jewellery from the New Kingdom period, found in houses at Tell el-Amarna. The glazed beads and pendants are modelled on flowers, leaves and fruit. c. 1350 BC. (BM)

Enamelled earthenware knobs from the Old Palace at Ashur, Iraq. Some of these ornaments may have been used for hanging trophies or other objects. Diameter 15·5 cm. Mid-9th cent. BC.

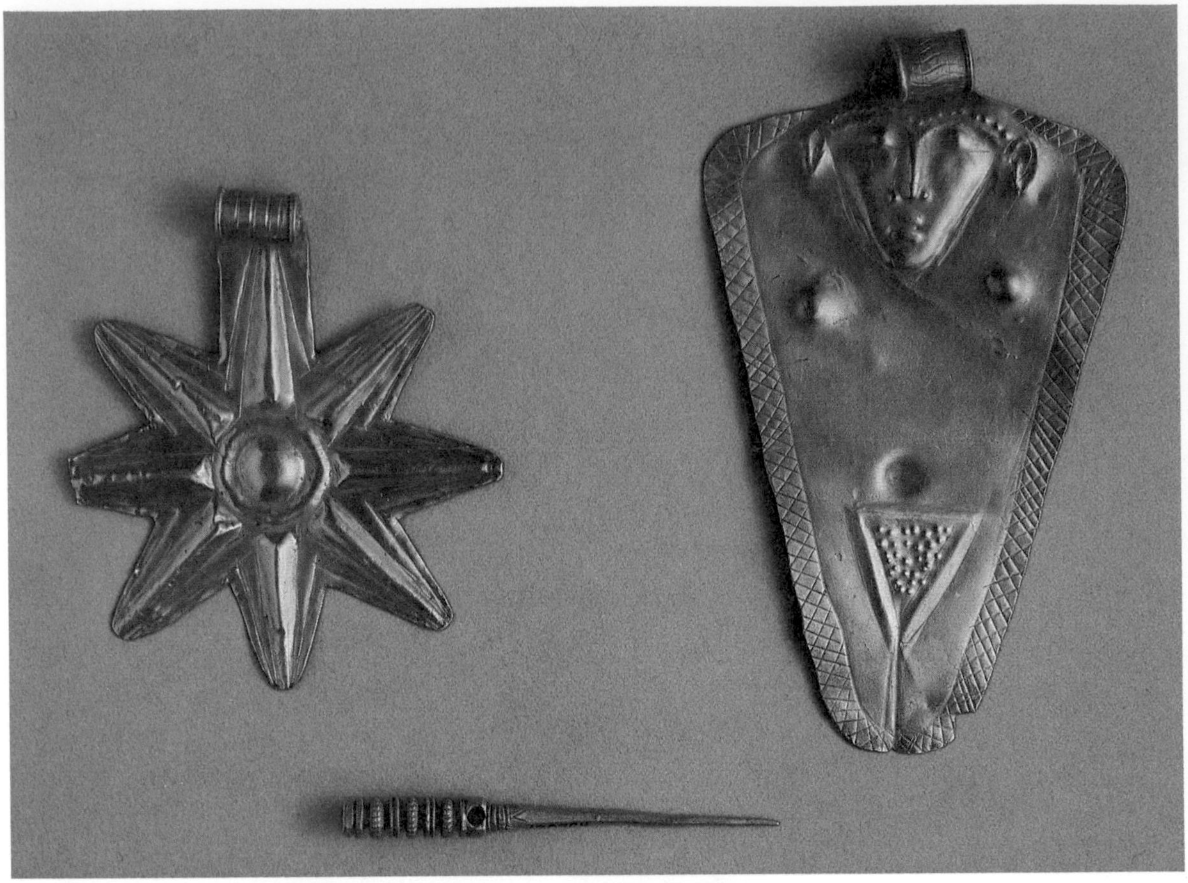

Gold jewellery—a toggle pin, an eight-pointed star amulet and a plaque representing the goddess Astarte—from Tell el-Ajjul, near Gaza. Middle Bronze Age. 16th cent. BC. (BM)

Gold ring, inlaid with lapis lazuli and cornelian. From Telloh, Babylonia. 2500–2370 BC. (MC)

coat was of an ornamental weave (Ex. 28:39, RV, RSV), the ephod and the girdle were decorative (Ex. 28:6, 8) and round the hem of the robe of the ephod were alternate bells and pomegranates (Ex. 28:31–35). In addition to these the breastplate (see *BREASTPIECE OF THE HIGH PRIEST) contained ornamental elements.

The ancient Hebrews, like their neighbours, probably wore *amulets and personal *seals for ornamentation.

In Ex. 13:16 and Dt. 6:8; 11:18 the word 'frontlets' (*ṭôṭāp̄ôṯ*) may refer to some ornament of the head. A connection with Akkad. *ṭaṭāpu*, 'to encircle', has been suggested, but this remains uncertain.

II. Movable objects

From very early times painted or incised decoration was used on *pottery, and though in historical times the abundance of other possessions resulted in absence of decoration, certain wares such as Mycenaean and that called 'Philistine' are easily distinguishable and provide useful criteria for dating to the archaeologist. *Archaeology has shown that tools and weapons had, on occasion, appropriate decorations, but the class of small object which often called forth the most elaborate and delicate ornamentation was that of cosmetic equipment. Boxes, jars for unguents, palettes for mixing pigments and mirror handles of elaborately carved bone and ivory have been excavated in Syria, Palestine, Mesopotamia and Egypt. Furniture, especially in royal palaces, was sometimes richly ornamented with carved ivory panels (*cf.* 1 Ki. 10:18; 2 Ch. 9:17; Am. 6:4 and * IVORY). That ornamental carpets were used is shown by stone paving slabs carved in replica of carpets from the Assyrian royal palaces. Elaborately ornamented horse harnesses are portrayed on the Assyrian palace reliefs and camel harness was also evidently decorated (Jdg. 8:21, 26).

The * tabernacle and its contents were ornamented, under the skill of * Bezalel, with cunning workmanship. This was also a common practice, as is shown by discoveries of temple furniture from Megiddo, Beth-shan and other sites, where incense and offering stands are decorated with birds, animals, serpents (symbol of fertility) and human figures. These were the common trappings of the pagan cults of the Israelites' neighbours, and often the most elaborate ornament was reserved for the casket of the deceased. Elaborately carved stone sarcophagi are known from Phoenicia and Egypt, and the discoveries in the 'Royal Tombs' at * Ur and in the tomb of Tutankhamūn show the wealth of ornamental riches that accompanied the dead to the grave.

III. Architectural

Buildings in antiquity, particularly palaces, were decorated both inside and out. The inside walls of important rooms in the palaces of the Assyrian kings at Nineveh and Khorsabad were adorned by carved bas-reliefs and the doorways guarded by great composite beasts (*IBA*, fig. 44). These reliefs were probably partially coloured in antiquity, being in fact glorified murals, examples of which from the Assyrian period were discovered at Til Barsip. In the early 2nd-millennium palace at Mari remains of several mural paintings were recovered suggesting that such decoration has not been discovered more often only on account of its perishable nature.

In Egypt, while the best-known mural paintings are found in rock-cut tombs, palaces with murals have been excavated at Malkata (Amenophis III) and el-Amarna (Amenophis IV). The great temples at Karnak and Luxor were decorated with carved and painted murals and hieroglyphic inscriptions, the hieroglyphs forming ornamental elements. * Ivory was probably used not only for the decoration of furniture but also for application to suitable parts of important rooms, as is suggested by caches of carved ivories found at Nimrud, Arslan Tash, Megiddo and Samaria (*cf.* 1 Ki. 22:39; Ps. 45:8; Am. 3:15).

Outside decoration, while in earlier periods it might consist of revetted walls, or in Assyria guardian beasts at gateways, reached a sumptuous level in Nebuchadrezzar's Babylon, where excavation has revealed great façades of coloured glazed bricks with animals and rosettes at intervals.

The Persians in the latter part of the 1st millennium BC recruited craftsmen from all over the Middle East to build and decorate the great ceremonial city of Persepolis, even employing men from as far afield as the Aegean. Aegean influences had already been felt in the 2nd millennium (Alalaḫ, Ugarit), and it is probable that the term *kap̄tôr* in Ex. 25:31–36; 37:17–22 (AV 'knop') and Am. 9:1; Zp. 2:14 (AV 'lintel') refers to some decorative architectural feature, perhaps a column capital, derived from Crete or the Aegean (* CAPHTOR).

The richly ornamented harness of King Ashurbanipal's horses. Relief from N palace, Nineveh. c. 640 BC. (BM)

ORYX
See Animals, Part 1.

OSHEA
See Joshua, Part 2.

OSNAPPAR
See Ashurbanipal, Part 1.

OSPREY
See Animals, Part 1.

OSSIFRAGE
See Animals, Part 1.

OSTRICH
See Animals, Part 1.

OVERSEER
See Governor, Part 2.

OWL
See Animals, Part 1.

There is reason to believe that under the Monarchy the kings and the wealthy would have followed the customs of the surrounding peoples, particularly the Phoenicians, in the decoration of their palaces and houses.

BIBLIOGRAPHY. No one work covers the whole subject. Relevant material is to be found incidentally in C. Singer, E. Holmyard and A. Hall, *A History of Technology*, 1, 1954, especially pp. 413–447, 623–703, and *passim* in H. Frankfort, *The Art and Architecture of the Ancient Orient*, 1954; W. S. Smith, *The Art and Architecture of Ancient Egypt*, 1958; and for Palestine, A. G. Barrois, *Manuel d'Archéologie Biblique*, 1–2, 1939–53; Y. Shiloh, *PEQ* 109, 1977, pp. 39–42 ('Proto-Aeolic' capital); K. R. Maxwell-Hyslop, *Western Asiatic Jewellery*, 1971. T.C.M.

ORPAH. A Moabitess, the daughter-in-law of Naomi, and Ruth's sister-in-law (Ru. 1:4). After their husbands died they came from Moab to Judah, but Orpah, following Naomi's advice, remained, to return to her former home and the worship of Chemosh (Ru. 1:15; 1 Ki. 11:33). Even so, Naomi commended her to Yahweh's protection. M.B.

ORPHAN, FATHERLESS (Heb. *yāṯôm*; Gk. *orphanos*). The care of the fatherless was from earliest times a concern of the Israelites, as of the surrounding nations. The Covenant Code (Ex. 22:22), and the Deuteronomic Code particularly, were most solicitous for the welfare of such (Dt. 16:11, 14; 24:17), protecting their rights of inheritance and enabling them to share in the great annual feasts and to have a portion of the tithe crops (Dt. 26:12). It is specifically stated, moreover, that God works on their behalf (Dt. 10:18), and that condemnation awaits those who oppress them (Dt. 27:19; *cf.* Mal.3:5).

Though many orphans would be aided by kindred and friends (Jb. 29:12; 31:17), there was a general failure to fulfil the provisions of the Codes, testified by the accusations and laments found in the prophets, in the Psalms, and in the book of Job. 'In you,' says Ezekiel (22:7), speaking of Jerusalem, 'the fatherless and the widow are wronged'. Justice, it is averred, is withheld from orphans; their plight is pitiable, for they are robbed and killed (Jb. 24:3, 9; Ps. 94:6; Is. 1:23; 10:2; Je. 5:28), making even more vivid the Psalmist's words against the wicked: 'May his children be fatherless . . . !' (109:9).

God, however, is specially concerned for the fatherless (Pss. 10:18; 68:5; 146:9; Ho. 14:3; *cf.* Jn. 14:18), especially when they look in vain to men for help (*cf.* Ps. 27:10).

The only NT occurrence of the word makes an integral part of true religion the visiting of 'orphans and widows in their affliction . . .' (Jas. 1:27).

BIBLIOGRAPHY. J. Pridmore, *NIDNTT* 2, pp. 737f.; H. Seesemann, *TDNT* 5, pp. 487f. J.D.D.

OTHNIEL (Heb. *'oṯnî'ēl*). **1.** A *Kenizzite, brother (or perhaps nephew) of Caleb ben Jephunneh (Jdg. 1:13; *cf.* Jos. 15:17); if 'son of Kenaz' is a patronymic, he and Caleb may have been brothers or half-brothers. Distinguishing himself in the sack of *Kiriath-sepher, he married Achsah, Caleb's daughter. Later he saw the beginnings of apostasy and the domination by *Cushan-rishathaim, against whom he led a successful revolt, becoming the first of the *judges. Jdg. 3:10 indicates that he was a charismatic leader, who restored order and authority ('judged' means this as well as deliverance; *cf.* 1 Sa. 7:15; 8:20).

2. A *Netophathite, whose descendant Heldai was one of David's officers (1 Ch. 27:15). J.P.U.L.

Reconstruction of Herod's palace at Jerusalem with the Antonia fortress on right 40–4 BC. (JPK) (HC)

PADDAN, PADDAN-ARAM. The 'field' or 'plain' of Aram (RSV *'Mesopotamia') is the name given in the area around Harran in Upper Mesopotamia, N of the junction of the rivers Ḫabur and Euphrates in Gn. 25:20; 28:2; 31:18, *etc.*, and is identical with Aram-naharaim, 'Aram of the rivers', of Gn. 24:10; Dt. 23:4; Jdg. 3:8. Abraham dwelt in this area before emigrating to Canaan. He sent his servant there to obtain a bride for Isaac, and thither Jacob fled from Esau. For a suggested identification of Paddan-aram, near Harran, see *AS* 2, 1952, p. 40; *POTT*, pp. 134f., 140. R.A.H.G.

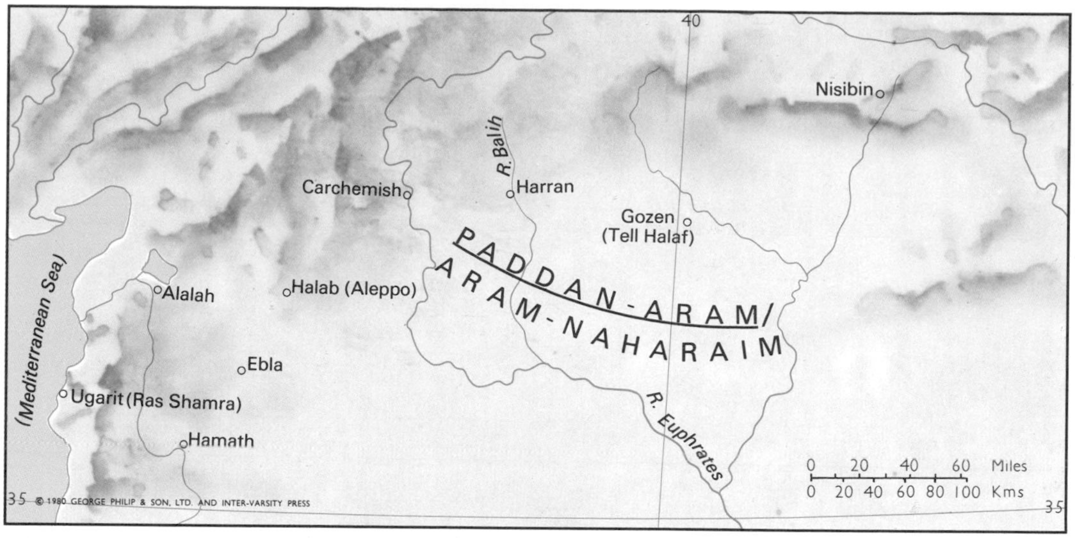

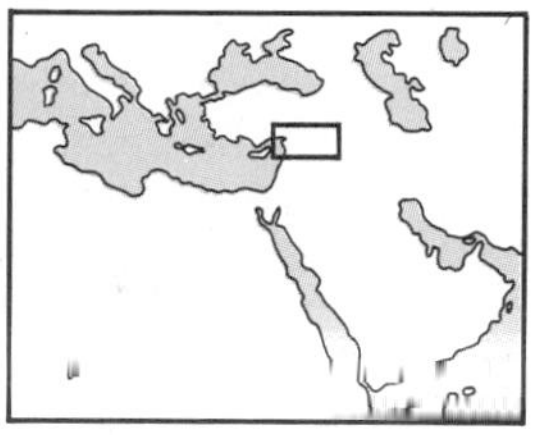

The location of Paddan-aram.

PAHATH-MOAB (lit. 'Governor of Moab'). Perhaps an ancestor had been a governor of Moab when Moab was subject to Israel. The name of a Jewish clan consisting of two families, Jeshua and Joab, 2,812 of whom returned to Judah with Zerubbabel (Ezr. 2:6. Ne. 7:11 gives the figure 2,818) and 201 with Ezra (Ezr. 8:4). Of this clan certain members are listed in Ezr. 10:30 as having married foreign women. Ne. 10:14 records that Pahath-moab among princes, priests and Levites set his seal to the covenant made on the return of the exiles to Jerusalem. R.A.H.G.

PALACE. The word designates a large residential building or group of buildings which accommodate a ruler and his administration. During the Israelite Monarchy, the administrative centre was called *'armôn*, AV 'palace', RSV 'citadel, palace, stronghold or castle'. A large portion of the nation's wealth was safeguarded in the citadel. Its capture was therefore the aim of a conquest and so substantial fortifications were constructed around the citadel so that the king and the loyal remnants of his army would be able to resist capture even when the remainder of the capital city

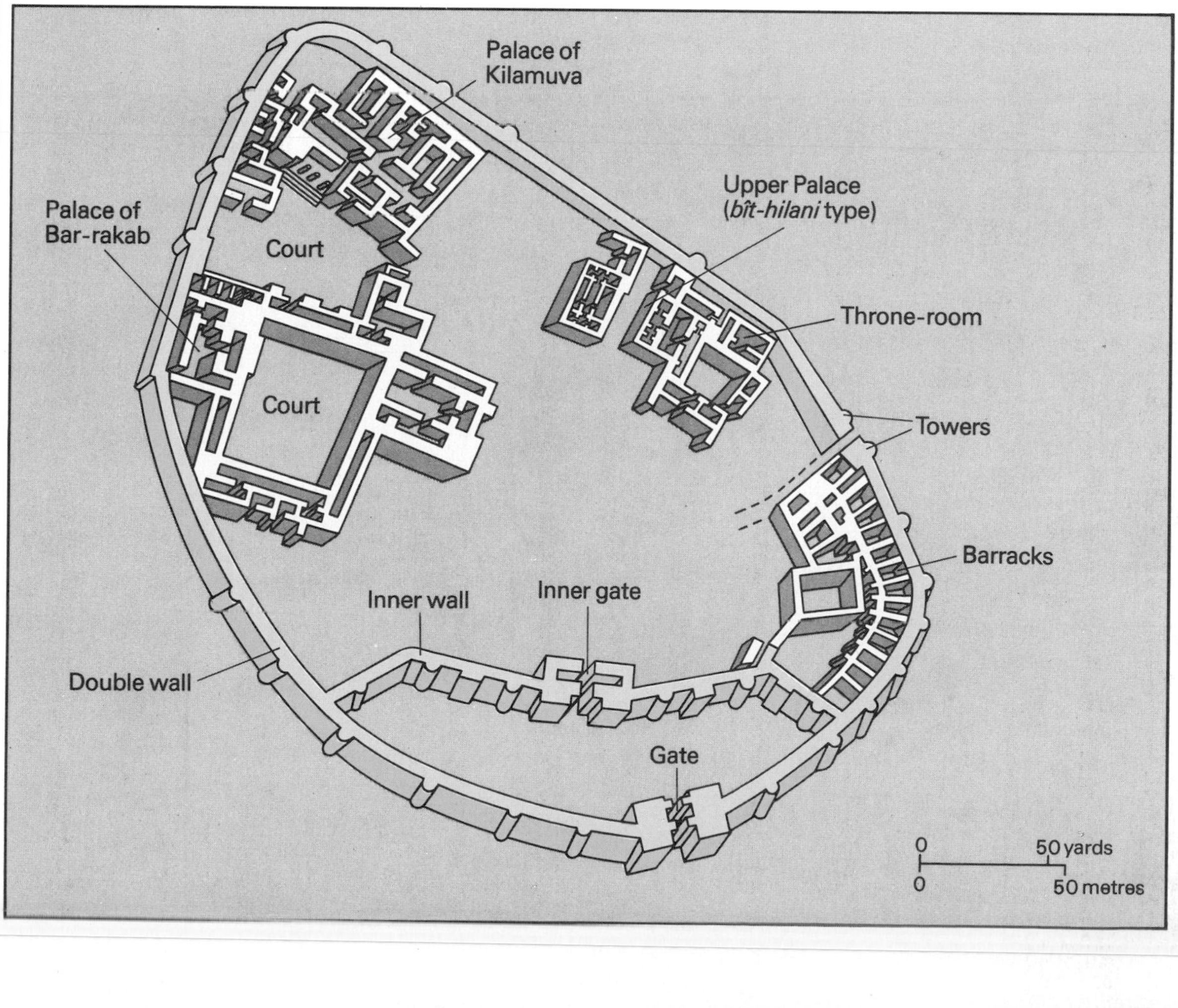

Plan showing the royal palaces on the citadel of Zinjirli (Sam'al) in Syria. c. 900–600 BC.

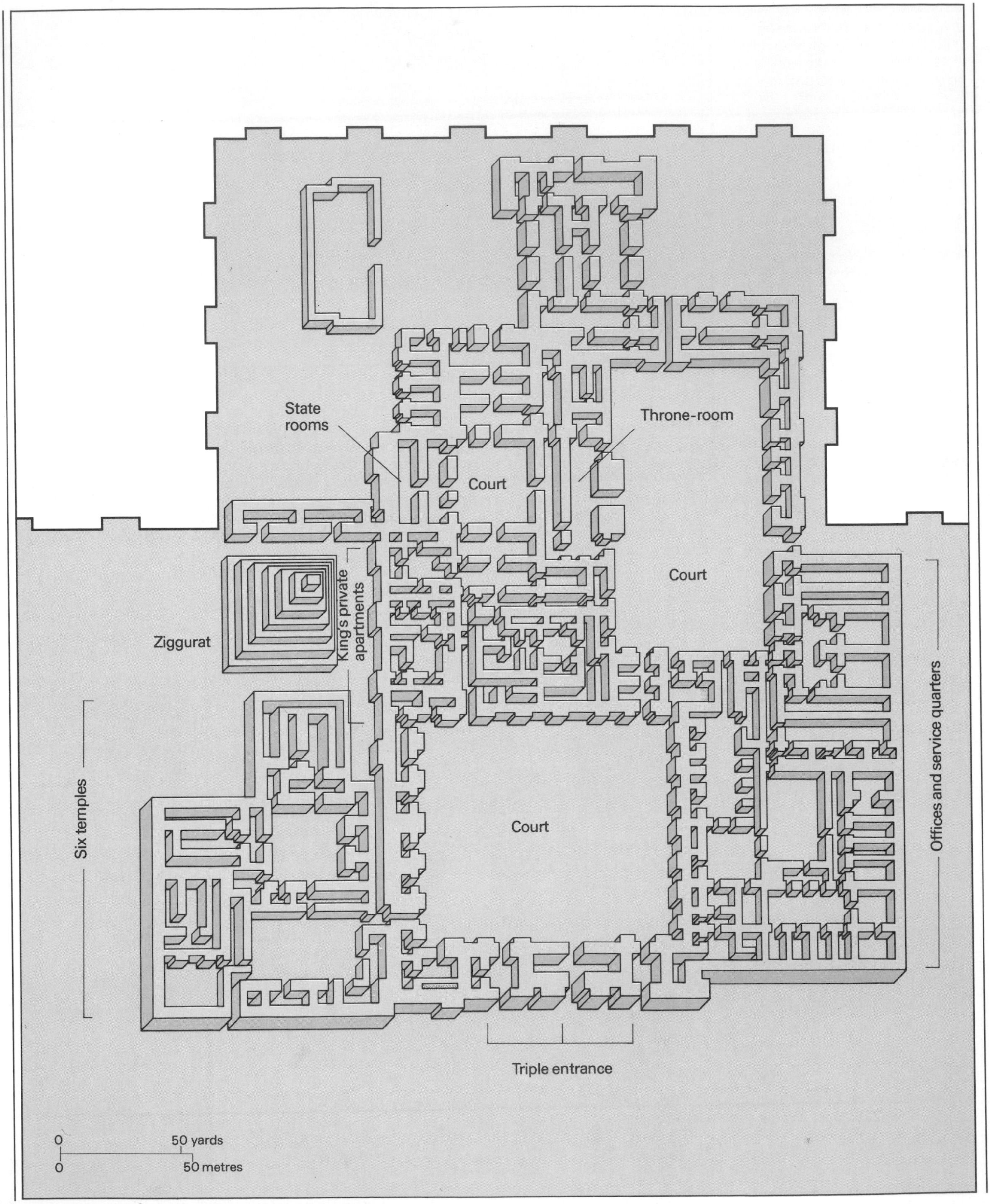
State rooms
Throne-room
Court
Court
King's private apartments
Ziggurat
Six temples
Court
Offices and service quarters
Triple entrance
0
50 yards
0
50 metres

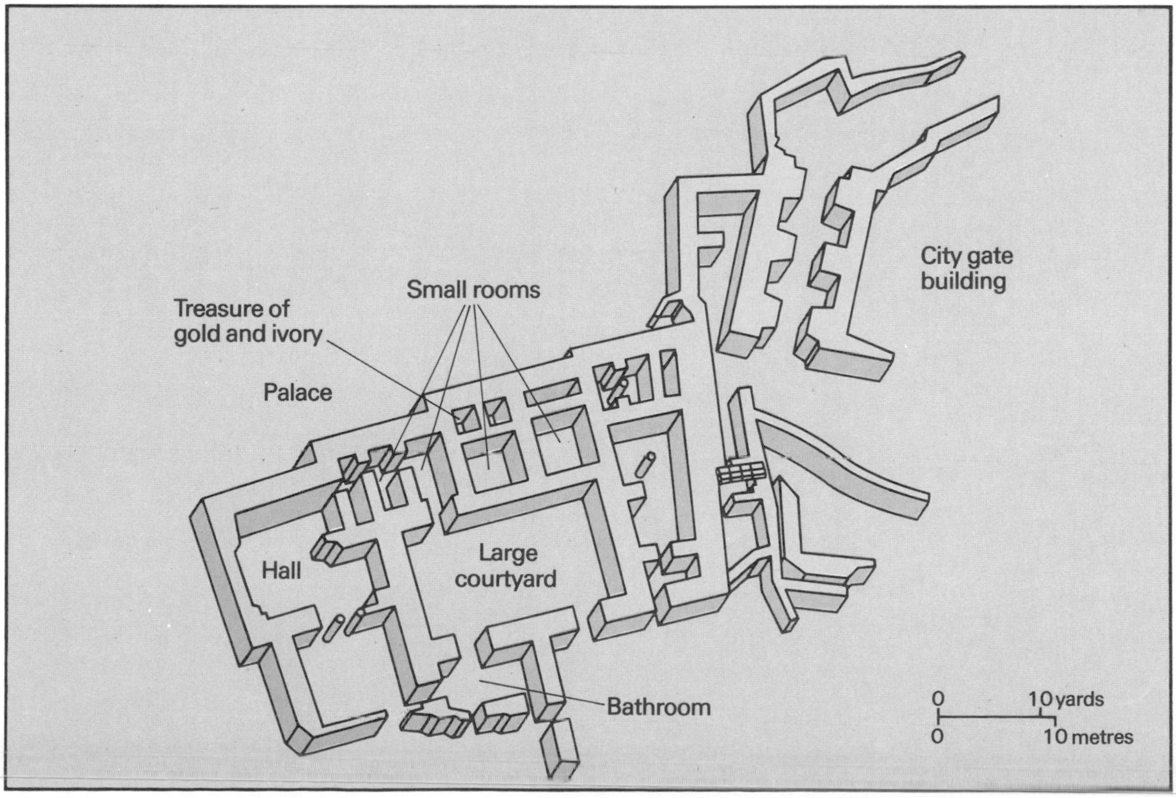

Remains of the columned throne-room (apadana) *of the palace of the Persian Kings Xerxes (c. 486–465* BC*) and Artaxerxes I (465–424* BC*) at Persepolis, Iran.* (BPL)

Opposite page: Plan of the palace of Sargon II built at Khorsabad (Dur-Sharrukin), Iraq. c. 710 BC.

Plan of the palace and the gate at Megiddo dating to the Late Bronze–Early Iron Age. The palace consists of a large courtyard, surrounded by small rooms, a hall and a bathroom. In one of the rooms a treasure of gold and ivory was found.

Reconstruction of the royal winter palace built by Herod the Great at Jericho.

had fallen. When predicting the overthrow of nations, the prophets specifically refer to the citadels of *Babylon (Is. 25:2), *Jerusalem (Is. 32:14; Je. 6:5; 9:21; 17:27; Am. 2:5), Damascus (Je. 49:27; Am. 1:4) and Edom (Is. 34:14; Am. 1:12). Amos also speaks about the destruction of the citadels of Gaza (1:7), Tyre (1:10), Rabbah (1:14), Moab (2:2) and *Samaria (3:11).

One of the most complete citadels in Syria/Palestine was excavated at Zinjirli (ancient Sam'al) used between *c.* 900 and 600 BC. Here three palaces and many storehouses were surrounded by walls and towers and the complex could be entered only after passing through two gates. In Palestine, only meagre remains of the citadel at *Samaria have been found. A similar but smaller citadel was built by King *Jehoiakim at Ramat Raḥel and is most probably referred to by Jeremiah (22:13–14). As at Samaria, the citadel was fortified with a casemate wall constructed with rectangular masonry and within the wall was a large courtyard, a storehouse and a palace.

Excavation has revealed that at the time of Solomon both *Hazor and *Megiddo had administrative buildings enclosed within citadel areas. Solomon chose a similar system at Jerusalem where the citadel embraced the *Temple, the king's palace (1 Ki. 3:1), the 'House of the Forest of Lebanon' (1 Ki. 7:2–5), halls and porches (7:6–7), a palace for Pharaoh's daughter (7:8; 9:24) and courts (7:12). One of the large buildings at Megiddo for which Solomon was probably responsible has been reconstructed as a *bīt-ḫilāni* (*PORCH), a style of palace which seems to have been adopted in the Hall of Pillars and the Hall of the Throne at Jerusalem (1 Ki. 7:6–7). The 'House of the Forest of Lebanon' was a hypostyle hall of 100 × 50 cubits. Its purpose was, at least in part, to display the kingdom's wealth (1 Ki. 10:17), but whether it was a banqueting-hall, as would be suggested by some of its contents (10:21), a magazine (Is. 22:8) or an entrance-hall is not clear. The royal residence (*bêṯ hammeleḵ*) would have been a number of storeys high, providing sufficient accommodation for the king, his wives and family and their advisers and servants.

Although the term 'great house' (Heb. *hêḵāl*) normally refers to a temple, it is also used of a palace (so Akkad. *ekallu*) when it is the principal building in a city. The palace of *Ahab at Jezreel (1 Ki. 21:1), the Assyrian king's palace at Nineveh (Na. 2:6) and the palaces at *Babylon (2 Ki. 20:18; Dn. 4:4, 29, *etc.*) and Susa (Ezr. 4:14) are described in this way. The palaces of Assyria, Babylon and Persia accommodated the administration for large empires and also considerable quantities of tribute. In addition to offices and magazines, temples were included in the palace

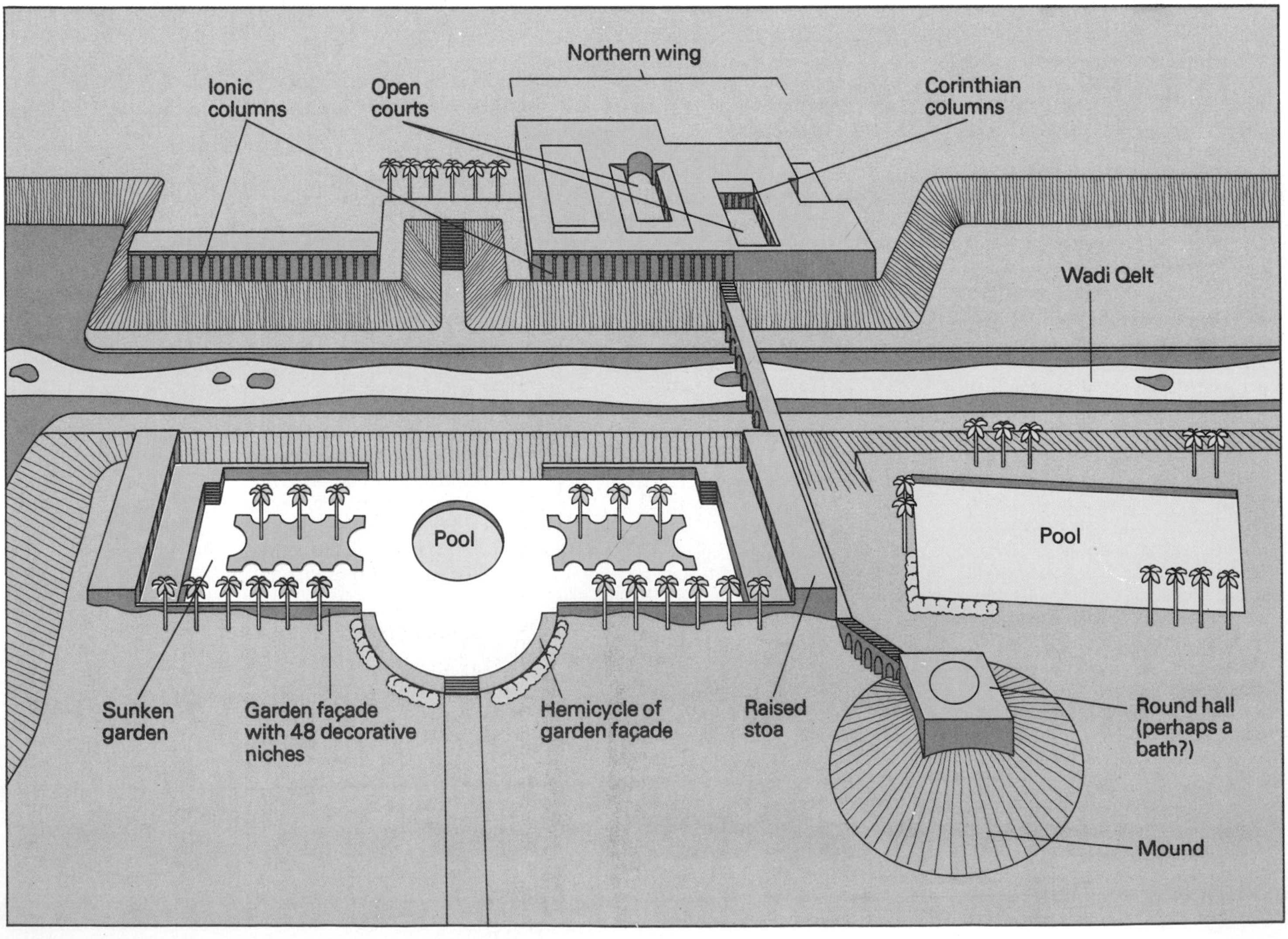

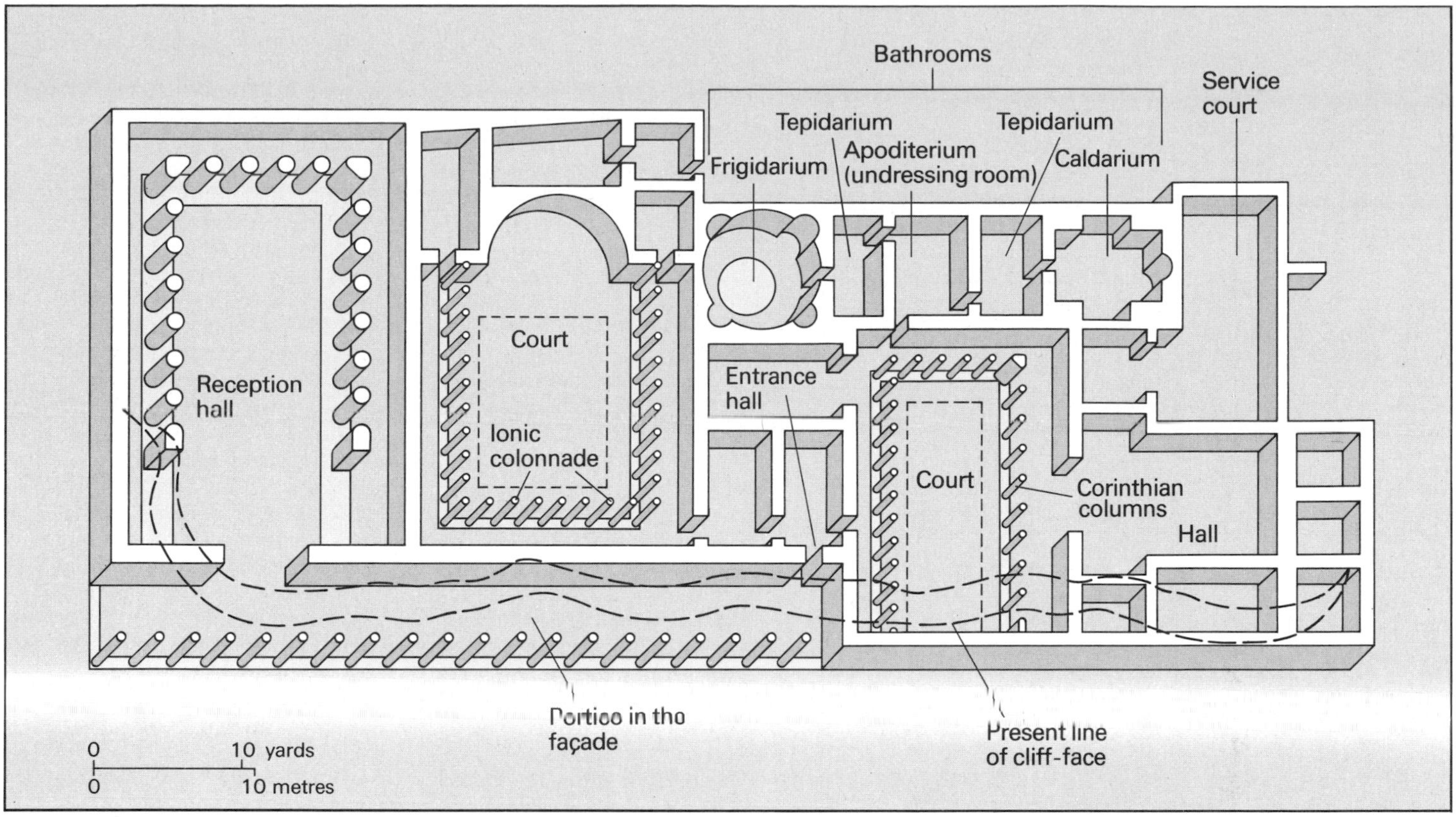

Plan of the N wing of Herod's winter palace, Jericho.

complex, thus enabling the king to fulfil his religious duties to ensure the favour of the gods. Senior officials each possessed their own residences and other parts of the palace housed schools (Dn. 1:4) for the princes, future civil servants and priests. The wealth of the king was suitably displayed to visitors and so public courtyards and the state rooms were richly decorated and lavishly furnished. Sometimes gardens of exotic plants were grown within the palace area (Est. 7:7–8).

After the Exile palaces are sometimes referred to as fortresses (Aram. *bîrâ*); palaces at Jerusalem (1 Ch. 29:1, 19; Ne. 2:8; 7:2), Susa (Dn. 8:2; Ne. 1:1, Est. 1:2, 5, *etc.*) and Ecbatana (Ezr. 6:2) are so described. Daniel (11:45) mentions the residence of the king of the N as *'appeḏen* (AV 'palace', RSV 'palatial tents') which is similar to the Old Persian word (*apadāna*) meaning columned hall and may in this case indicate large tents with many supports.

The palace (*aulē*) of the high priest (Mt. 26:3; Jn. 18:15) was probably a large hellenistic residence built around colonnaded courtyards. Jesus speaks about the need to guard such a palace which contains wealth (Lk. 11:21).

*Herod the Great built palaces at Jerusalem, *Machaerus, *Jericho, the Herodium near Bethlehem, and Masada. In Jerusalem he built a strongly fortified palace with three towers, named Hippicus, Phasael and Mariamne, by the corner gate. This building forms the foundations of the present-day Citadel. There were two palaces at Masada and both have been excavated and partially restored. The N palace is amazingly positioned on the cliff face of the flat-topped mountain which was fortified by Herod.

Palaces or citadels often represent the fortunes of a nation in the OT. The palace of the faithful nation possesses peace (Ps. 122:7), while that of a sinful nation is destroyed (Je. 17:27; Am. 2:5) and becomes deserted (Is. 34:13–14).

BIBLIOGRAPHY. D. Ussishkin, 'King Solomon's Palaces', *BA* 36, 1973, pp. 78–105; G. Turner, 'The State Apartments of the Late Assyrian Palaces', *Iraq* 32, 1970, pp. 177–213.

C.J.D.

PALESTINE. The term 'Palestine', originally applied to the territory of Israel's foes, the Philistines, was first used by Herodotus as a designation of S Syria. In the form of *Palaestina*, it was also used by the Romans. The older term 'Canaan' has a similar history. In the el *Amarna letters (14th century BC) Canaan was limited to the coastal plains, then with the Canaanite conquests of the interior it was applied to all the lands W of the Jordan valley. The terms 'land of Israel' (1 Sa. 13:19) and 'the land of promise' (Heb. 11:9) are associated with the Israelites in the same area, the latter usually connected with the area from Dan to Beersheba, N of the Negeb. The Israelite settlement of two-and-a-half tribes E of the Jordan seems to have resulted from unforeseen circumstances and the hold on that side of the valley appears to have been generally precarious. After the division of the kingdom, the name Israel was usually given to the N realm. In the Middle Ages, the term 'the Holy Land' was often adopted (*cf.* Zc. 2:12).

I. The position and highways of Palestine

The mediaeval perspective of Jerusalem as the centre of the earth is not so absurd as might be thought, for on the tiny Syrian corridor that unites the world island of Europe, Asia and Africa, the five seas of the Mediterranean, Black Sea, Caspian, Red Sea and the Persian Gulf narrow the greatest land mass of our planet into a single isthmus. All the important continental routes must go across this corridor, and the great sea-routes of antiquity between the Indies and the Mediterranean must in turn be linked by land communications across the Sinai Peninsula. The high mountain chains which run E from Asia Minor to Kurdistan and the deserts to the S and E further help to concentrate the routeways of 'the Fertile Crescent', which, sickle-shaped, runs from Palestine and S Syria to the alluvial valley basins of the Tigris and Euphrates. It is, of course, 'fertile' only in comparison with the surrounding desert and mountainous terrain, since most of it is either Mediterranean scrub or steppe. At either end of the Fertile Crescent a great locus of civilization developed in the lower basin of Mesopotamia and the lower Nile valley respectively, whose fortunes dominated the history of the Near East for almost two millennia.

Three great trade routes have always traversed Palestine. The great Trunk Road, perhaps described in Is. 9:1 as 'the way of the sea', runs along the low coast from Egypt to the Vale of Esdraelon. Then it is diverted inland by the Syrian mountains to skirt the W side of the Lake of Galilee, then through the Syrian Gate and central depression to Damascus, where it joins the desert caravan trails across to Mesopotamia. Two other routes are of great antiquity although of lesser importance. The *King's Highway follows the edge of the Transjordan plateau from the Gulf of Aqabah towards Damascus. It marks a zone of increased rainfall and was followed in part by the Israelites during the Exodus (Nu. 21–22), and all the towns enumerated in Nu. 21; 27–30 lie along it. The watershed of central Palestine is followed by another route, the shortest between Sinai and Canaan. In the N *Negeb it links an important series of wells, keeping W of the forbidding, barren depressions of the E Negeb that are still difficult to traverse. It links all the important historic centres from Kadesh-barnea and Beersheba to Hebron, Jerusalem, Shechem and Megiddo (see map). Heavily travelled from the Abramic (Middle Bronze I) period onwards, it was also made famous by the journey of Joshua and his fellow-spies. All these routes emphasized the N–S alignment of Palestine, which benefited from their fertilizing contacts of trade and culture. But Israel was rarely able to control these highways without upsetting the strategic interests of the great powers that dominated their terminals. Even in Solomon's day the coastal highway was too tightly controlled by the sea-powers to warrant interference there (1 Ki. 9:11; 10:22; Ezk. 27:17), while Edom was for long Israel's deadly enemy because it dominated the routes from the Gulf of Aqabah where Israel obtained its copper (Ob. 3).

A number of minor transverse routes have joined these parallel highways. Of these the most important have been: (1) Gaza–Beersheba–Petra; (2) Ashkelon–Gath–Helvan; (3) Joppa–Bethel–Jericho (*cf.* Jos. 10:6–14) and Joppa–Shechem–Adam–Gilead (Jos. 3:16); (4) Vale of Esdraelon–Megiddo–Gilead. Exposed to coastal sedimentation from the Nile, the coast of Palestine as far as Carmel has been unfavourable for port development, so the chief towns have been route centres at important road junctions, either in the strategic plain of Esdraelon or along the hilly dorsal of Judaea and Samaria. The sea was an unfamiliar medium of communication to the Hebrews (*cf.* Ps. 107), while the desert was also feared as 'a land of trouble and anguish' (Is. 30:6; *cf.* Dt. 8:15). Perched precariously between them, the Hebrew highlanders sought a protracted aloofness from both environments and their peoples. Thus autonomy of spirit became a major characteristic of the Israelites, despite their nodal position at the hub of the ancient world's trade routes.

II. The geological structure and relief

For some 675 km from the borders of Egypt to Asia Minor, the Levant consists of five major zones: (1) the littoral; (2) the W mountain chain (the Judaean–Galilean highlands, Lebanon and Ansariya mountains); (3) the rift valleys (Arabah, Jordan valley, Biqa' and Ghôr); (4) the E mountains (highlands of Transjordan, Hermon and Anti-lebanon); and (5) the deserts of Negeb, Arabia and Syria. But the contrasts between the N and S sections of these zones explain the individuality of Palestine. N of Acre, the mountains rise abruptly from the sea, limiting the narrow coastal plains to discontinuous stretches but providing the famous harbours of Sidon, Tyre, Beirut, Tripoli and Ras Shamra. The limited hinterlands of each unit have encouraged independent maritime city-states where 'the families of the Canaanites spread abroad' (Gn. 10:18). S of Mt Carmel, however, the coast opens into a broad continuous plain, harbourless except for artificial ports erected by the Philistines and later sea-peoples.

A second contrast is to be found in the Rift Valley sectors. In Syria the Biqa' depression is a broad, fertile plain between the lofty ranges of Lebanon and Anti-lebanon, with wide access to other rolling plains, and studded with historic centres such as Kadesh, Homs and Hamath. To the S, the depression blocked by recent basaltic lavas narrows into deep gorges before opening into the swamp of Lake Huleh, making N–S communication difficult. These features have tended to isolate Palestine from the N territory.

The rocks of Palestine are notably limestone, volcanics and recent deposits such as marls, gravels and sands. The Rift Valley represents an ancient planetary lineament that is traceable as far as the E African Lakes. Broadly speaking, it has operated like a hinge, so that the areas to the W of it have been mostly under the sea, whereas the Arabian block has been generally continental. Thus, W of the Rift the rocks are predominantly limestone laid down specially during the Cretaceous and Eocene eras. Some of these are hard and dolomitic (Cenomanian and Eocene), explaining the steep headland of Mt Carmel, the twin mountains of Ebal and Gerizim above Shechem, and generally all the rugged, higher relief of the Judaean–Galilean dorsal. But the Senonian is a soft chalk, easily eroded into gaps and valleys that breach the highlands, notably at Megiddo, the valley of Aijalon and the moat of Beth-shemesh which separates the Eocene foothills of the Shephelah from the Judaean plateau. These limestones have been upworked along the central dorsal and gently folded in a series of arches which become more complicated farther N in Samaria and Galilee. They occur, however, horizontal in Transjordan, resting upon the continental block beneath them. The ancient block is exposed in the SE in the high cliffs of the Wadi Arabah and in the Sinai Peninsula. Overlapping them are the so-called Nubian sandstones, whose desert

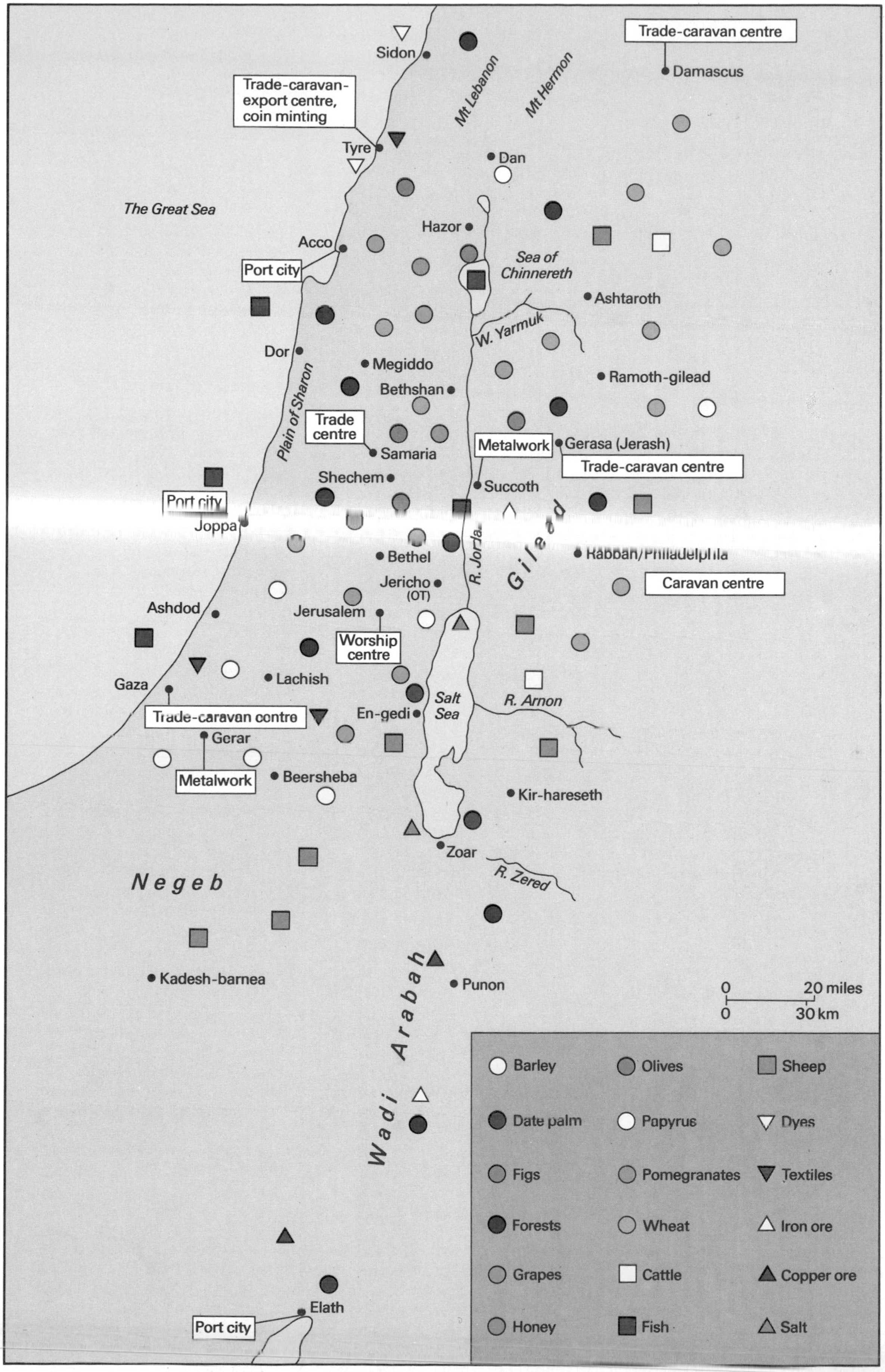
Trade-caravan centre
Damascus
Sidon
Trade-caravan-export centre, coin minting
Tyre
Mt Lebanon
Mt Hermon
Dan
The Great Sea
Hazor
Acco
Port city
Sea of Chinnereth
Ashtaroth
W. Yarmuk
Dor
Megiddo
Ramoth-gilead
Bethshan
Plain of Sharon
Trade centre
Samaria
Metalwork
Gerasa (Jerash)
Trade-caravan centre
Shechem
Succoth
Port city
Joppa
Gilead
R. Jordan
Bethel
Rabbah/Philadelphia
Jericho (OT)
Caravan centre
Ashdod
Jerusalem
Worship centre
Gaza
Lachish
Salt Sea
R. Arnon
Trade-caravan centre
En-gedi
Gerar
Metalwork
Beersheba
Kir-hareseth
Zoar
R. Zered
Negeb
Wadi Arabah
Punon
Kadesh-barnea
0 20 miles
0 30 km
Elath
Port city
Barley
Olives
Sheep
Date palm
Papyrus
Dyes
Figs
Pomegranates
Textiles
Forests
Wheat
Iron ore
Grapes
Cattle
Copper ore
Honey
Fish
Salt

Palestine: the economy.

- ☐ Alluvium
- ☐ Quaternary Red Sand
- ☐ Basalt
- ☐ Eocene Limestone
- ☐ Senonian Chert (Upper Cretaceous)
- ☐ Senonian Chalk (Middle Cretaceous)
- ☐ Cenomanian Limestone (Lower Cretaceous)
- ☐ Nubian Sandstone
- ☐ Granite
- ☐ Dune sand
- | Principal Faults

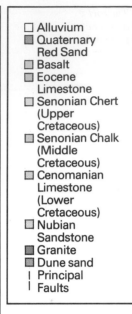

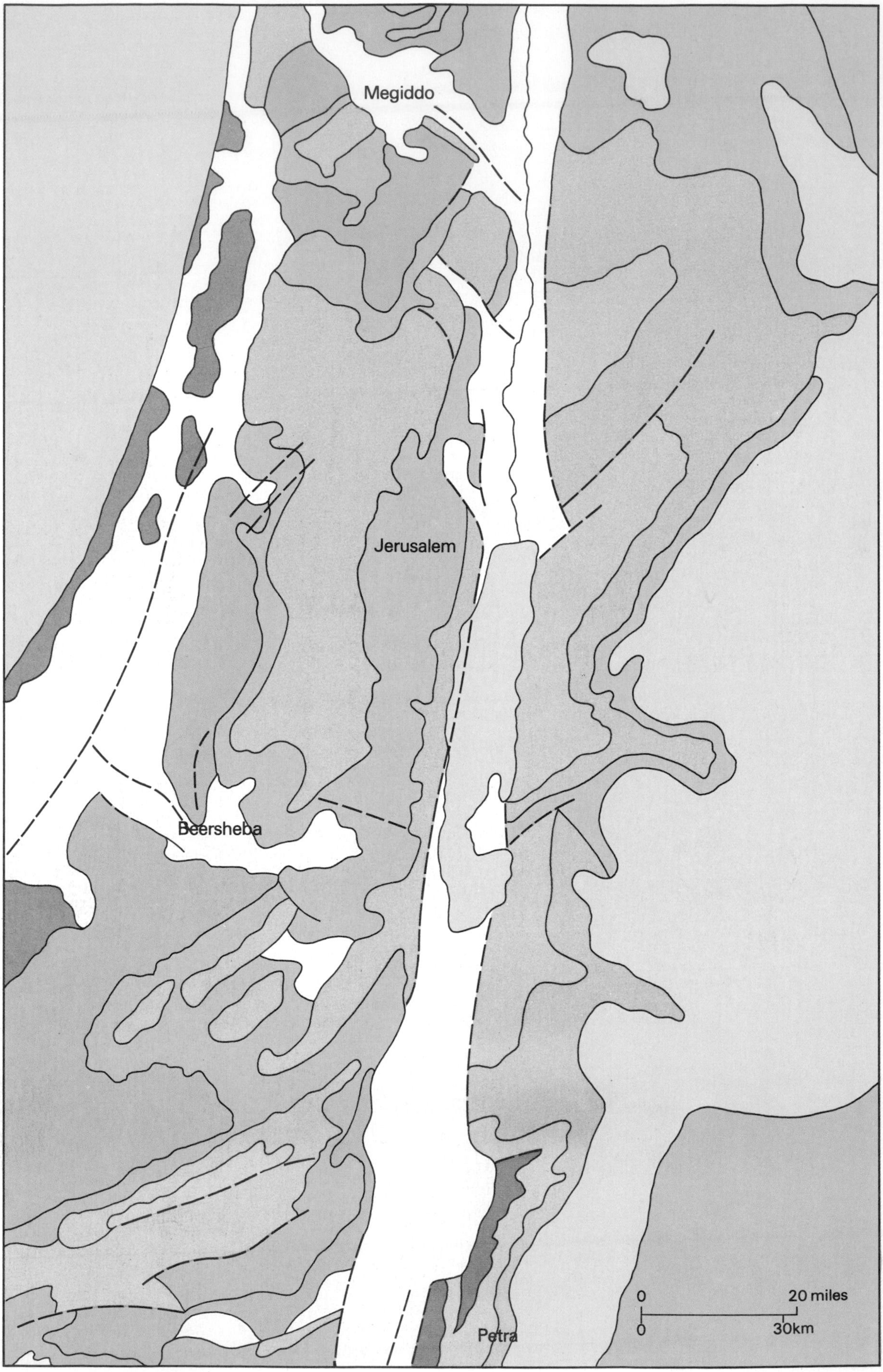

Palestine: geological structure.

The rocky Judaean desert beyond the fertile plain below Herodium, looking towards the Dead Sea. (SH)

Aerial view of the Wadi Makuk near Ai, surrounded by the Judaean hills ('badlands'). (SH)

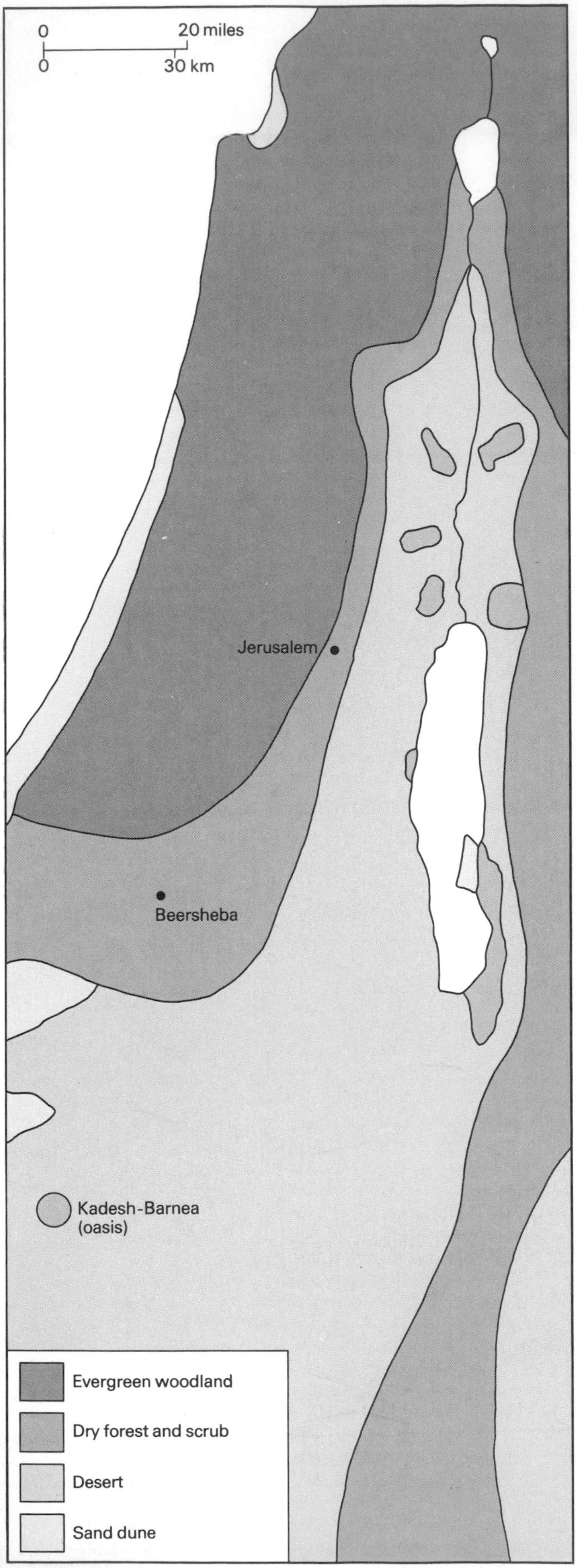

origin prolonged over vast geological periods explains the red colour from which Edom probably derives its name ('the red'). In the NE, recent basaltic lavas cap the limestones in the broad, undulating plateaux in the land of Bashan, and extending into the Jordan trough around the Lake of Galilee. These weather into the rich soils which attracted to the Galilean shores a high density of population from early times.

Palestine suffers from crustal instability. Volcanic eruptions have continued into historic times, notably in the cases of Harrat en-Nar, SE of the Gulf of Aqabah, which were active as late as the 8th and 13th centuries AD. It is tempting to equate the descriptions of Ex. 19:18 and Ps. 68:8 with volcanic manifestations, but the traditional site of Sinai is in an area of ancient, crystalline rocks where no recent volcanic action has occurred. The fate of Sodom and Gomorrah (Gn. 14:10; 19:23–28) is a memory of some kind of volcanic phenomena, associated probably with the intrusion of sulphurous gas and liquid asphalt. There are also the biblical records of earthquakes (Gn. 19:25; 1 Sa. 14:15; Am. 1:1) and geological faulting (Nu. 16:31–35). All these are associated with the Great Rift Valley of the Jordan and Dead Sea, or with the series of transverse faults that form the Vale of Esdraelon and divide Samaria and Galilee into a complicated series of highland blocks and depressions floored with sediments.

Under the semi-arid conditions, badland relief is typical, especially around the E and S rims of the Judaean highlands and the W edge of the Transjordan plateau. Within the deep Jordan valley, soft marls deposited by a lake more extensive than the present Dead Sea have been dissected to form the Ghôr in the middle of the trough, lying at more than 365 m below sea-level. The seasonal wadis that drain into the Arabah trough have also deeply dissected their slopes. Thus the AV references to the 'slippery places' are a characteristic feature of many parts of the Negeb and the Jordan (Dt. 32:35; Pr. 3:23; Je. 23:12; 31:9). Much of the Negeb is a rock waste of hammadas, and direct reference to the wind-borne loessial deposits is made (Ex. 10:20–23; Dt. 28:24; Na. 1:3).

III. The climate and vegetation

In the Levant three climatic zones may be distinguished: a Mediterranean, a steppe and a desert zone, each with its distinct type of vegetation. Along the coast as far S as Gaza, the Mediterranean zone has mild winters (53·6° F, 12° C, mean monthly average for January at Gaza) compared with the severer conditions of the interior hills (Jerusalem 44·6°F, 7°C, in January). But summers are everywhere hot (Gaza 78·8°F, 26°C, in July, Jerusalem 73·4°F, 23°C). The prolonged snow cover of the high Lebanon mountains (Je. 18:14) is exceptional, though snow is not infrequent in the Hauran. Elsewhere it is a rare phenomenon (2 Sa. 23:20). Less than one-fifteenth part of the annual rainfall occurs in the summer months from June to October; nearly all of it is concentrated in winter to reach a maximum in mid-winter. The total amount varies from about 35–40 cm on the coast to about 75 cm on Mt Carmel and the Judaean, Galilean and Transjordan mountains. In the Beersheba area to the S, and in parts of the Jordan valley and of the Transjordan plateau the climate is steppe, with only 20–30 cm of rain, though temperature conditions are comparable to those of the Judaean hills. The deep trough of the Jordan has sub-tropical conditions with stifling summer heat; at Jericho mean daily maxima remain above 100°F (38°C) from June to September, with frequent records of 110–120°F (43–49°C). The winter, however, has enjoyable conditions of 65–68°F (18–20°C) (January mean daily maximum). In the Negeb, the S part of the Jordan valley, and the country E and S of the Transjordan steppe the climate is desert, with less than 20 cm of rain a year.

There is no archaeological evidence that climate has changed since biblical times. Near the Gulf of Aqabah, a number of recently excavated Roman gutters still fit the springs for which they were constructed, and wherever the Byzantine wells of the Negeb have been kept clean and in constant use, the water still rises to the ancient levels. Thus the biblical narrative gives a convincing picture of the present climate. Distinction is made between the hot and cold seasons (Gn. 8:22; Am. 3:15), and the inception of the autumn rains is clearly described (Dt. 11:14; Ho. 6:3; Joel 2:23). Variability in the amount and distribution of rainfall is common (Am. 4:7), and the in-

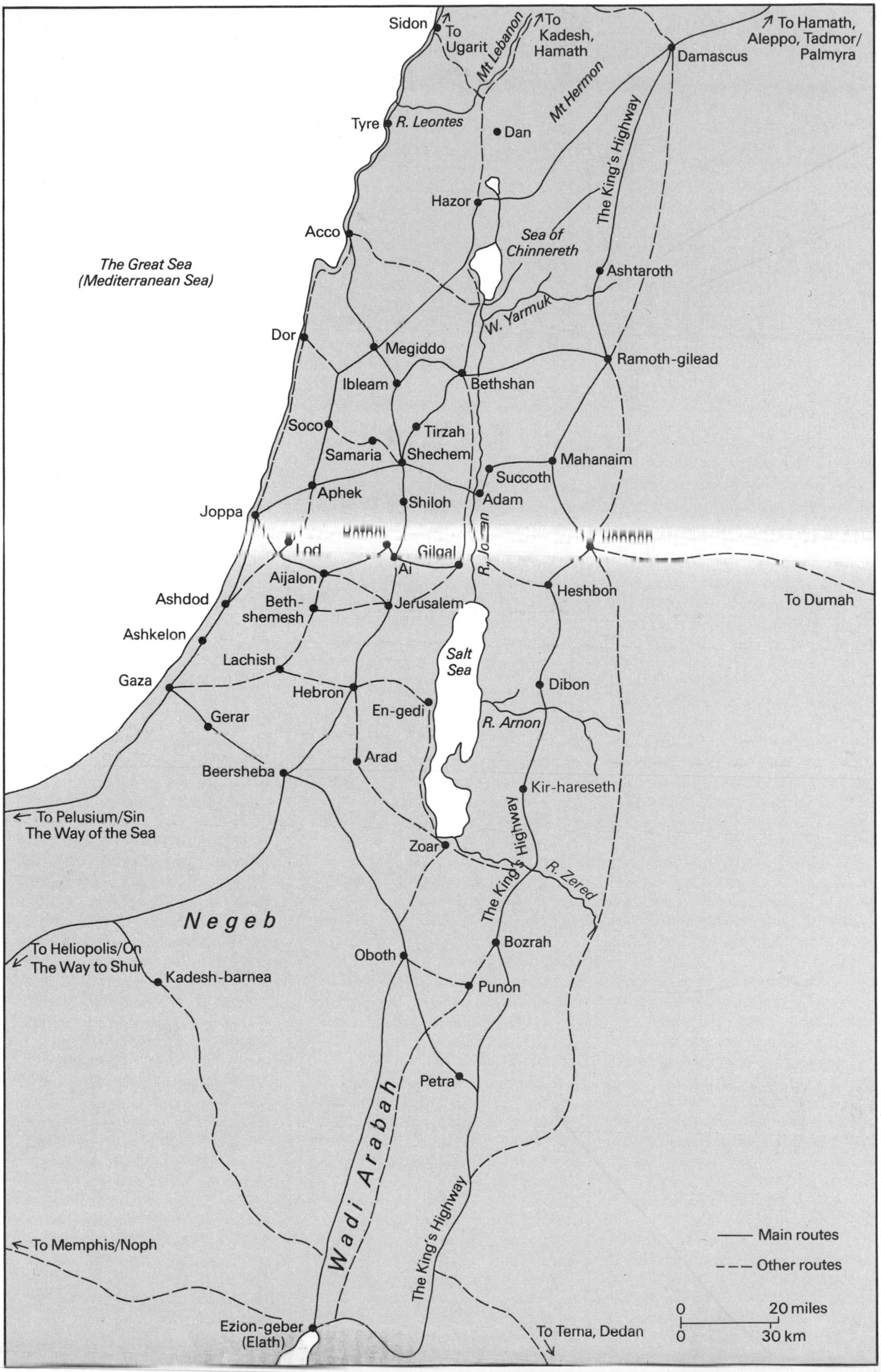
Sidon
To Ugarit
Mt Lebanon
To Kadesh, Hamath
To Hamath, Aleppo, Tadmor/ Palmyra
Damascus
Mt Hermon
Tyre
R. Leontes
Dan
The King's Highway
Hazor
Acco
Sea of Chinnereth
The Great Sea (Mediterranean Sea)
Ashtaroth
W. Yarmuk
Dor
Megiddo
Ramoth-gilead
Ibleam
Bethshan
Soco
Tirzah
Samaria
Shechem
Mahanaim
Succoth
Aphek
Adam
Shiloh
Joppa
Lod
Gilgal
R. Jordan
Ai
Aijalon
Heshbon
Ashdod
Beth-shemesh
Jerusalem
To Dumah
Ashkelon
Salt Sea
Lachish
Gaza
Hebron
Dibon
En-gedi
Gerar
R. Arnon
Arad
Beersheba
Kir-hareseth
To Pelusium/Sin The Way of the Sea
Zoar
The King's Highway
R. Zered
Negeb
Bozrah
To Heliopolis/On The Way to Shur
Oboth
Kadesh-barnea
Punon
Petra
Wadi Arabah
The King's Highway
Main routes
Other routes
To Memphis/Noph
0 20 miles
0 30 km
Ezion-geber (Elath)
To Tema, Dedan

Palestine: main routes.

Opposite page: Palestine: vegetation.

cidence of prolonged drought is recorded on a number of occasions (1 Ki. 17:7; Je. 17:8; Joel 1:10–12, 17–20).

Because of the contrasts of relief, from 1,020 m above sea-level near Hebron, to 390 m below sea-level at the Dead Sea, the flora of Palestine is very rich (about 3,000 vascular *plants) for such a small area. A large proportion of them are annuals. Few districts have ever had dense forests (*Trees), though remnants have been preserved in Mts *Hermon and *Lebanon with their cedars, firs, oaks and pines, and in the biblical Golan (Jaulan), where forests of pine and oak still exist. Lebanon has always been noted for its cedars. The Israelites had their share in deforestation of the Mediterranean woodland that once covered the central dorsal (Jos. 17:18), and today there are no traces of the woodlands that once existed at Bethel (2 Ki. 2:24), Ephraim (Jos. 17:15) and Gilead near the Jordan valley.

Oak forests long existed in Sharon, whose name means forest, but biblical prophecy states that three forested regions were to be turned into sheep pastures, the coastal Sharon, N Gilead and SE Galilee (see Is. 65:10). The development of pastoralism must be blamed for much of this forest clearance in Palestine (*cf.* 2 Ki. 3:4). But under Mediterranean conditions 'the pastures of the wilderness' are seasonally short-lived, so Rabbi Akiba (*c.* AD 100) observed shrewdly that 'those who rear small cattle and cut down good trees . . . will see no sign of blessing'. Deterioration of the woodland scrub had gone so far in Palestine before the establishment of the modern state of Israel in AD 1948 that most of the uncultivated land was a dreary expanse of *batha*, low scrub with open, rock outcrops. Towards the steppe and the desert, the colour of the landscape is governed more by the rocks than the plant cover, with only a few shrubby elements, such as wormwood, broom, saltwort and tufts of xerophytic grasses. Only along the banks of the Jordan is there a dense and wide gallery forest of various willows, poplar, tamarisk, oleander, *etc.*

But many of the Palestinian hill lands, eroded of their productive *terra vessa* soils, have been the graveyard of former civilizations, especially with the decay of terrace-cultivation. One estimate is that since Roman times 2,000–4,000 million cubic metres of soil have been worked off the E side of the Judaean hills, sufficient to make 4,000–8,000 sq. km of good farmland. This threat of soil erosion is possibly alluded to in Jb. 14:18–19, and the easy spread of fire during the summer drought is described (Ps. 83:13–14). These features of Mediterranean instability are recognized in the need for balance and restraint, in a land which lies so precariously between the desert and the sown (Ex. 23:29–30; Pr. 24:30–34). (*Dew, *Rain, *Wind.)

IV. Water-supply and agriculture

It is not by chance that the names of over seventy ancient sites in Palestine contain the word *'ain*, 'spring', and another sixty such sites the word *bîr*, 'well'. Apart from the Jordan, a few of its tributaries and four or five small coastal streams that are fed from springs, all the remaining rivers of Palestine are seasonal. Snow-fed streams account for their maximum volume in May–June (Jos. 3:15), but the majority dry up in the hot summer (1 Ki. 17:7; Jb. 24:19; Joel 1:20), notably in the Negeb (Ps. 126:4). With the autumn rains the sudden spate is graphically described (Jdg. 5:21; Mt. 7:27). Thus 'the fountain of living waters' was the ideal of the Israelite settler. The invention of a mortar which could be used in the construction of rain-collecting *cisterns (*c.* 1300 BC) may well have been a decisive factor in the rapid colonization of the highlands of Judaea by the Israelite settlers. *Wells dug for watering the stock are early alluded to (Gn. 26, *etc.*) and irrigation was well known (Gn. 13:10). Reservoirs too for the needs of the urban population are frequently mentioned (Ct. 7:4), some fed through imposing rock-cut tunnels (2 Ki. 20:20). The need for water often pointed a moral lesson to the Israelites (Dt. 8:7–10; 11:10–17; 1 Ki. 18; Je. 2:13; 14:22).

Before the rise of the Monarchy at least, the agricultural population of central Palestine consisted of small landowners, and the typical produce of the land is described in the presents given by Abigail to David (1 Sa. 25:18). The importance in Judaea of the barley crop rather than wheat because of its low rainfall, and the fame of Carmel for its vines and Ephraim and Galilee for olives, have been justified since biblical times. But droughts tend to introduce debt and servitude, so that despite the ideological democracy envisaged in the jubilee year (Lv. 25), crown-lands, large estates and forced labour already appear in the time of Saul (1 Sa. 8:16; 22:7; 25:2). In Transjordan and the Negeb it seems that the pastoral life has been traditionally supplemented by settled agricultural practices wherever wells and oases permitted. But the decline of agriculture has been constantly threatened by over-grazing by sheep and goats, apart from the more catastrophic incursions from the desert.

V. The settlements

A major problem in the historical geography of Palestine has been the identification of place-names. There are approximately 622 place-names W of Jordan recorded in the Bible. The lists of Tuthmosis III, Sethos I, Rameses II and *Shishak I at Karnak throw some light on Palestinian topography. The *Onomasticon* of Eusebius and Jerome is another valuable source. The work of R. Reland (1714) paved the way for the modern topographical work of Edward Robinson when he visited Palestine in 1838. He identified 177 place-names, few of which have been subsequently changed. In 1865 the Palestine Exploration Fund was established, and by 1927 about 434 place-names had been located; Conder in particular added 147 new names. A number of these are still disputed, and modern scholarship continues to debate a few of them.

The startling discoveries of Kathleen Kenyon at *Jericho show that there has been a semblance of urban life there since 6000–8000 BC with an 8-acre site occupied by some 3,000 inhabitants (*Archaeology). Indeed, the Jordan valley seems to have been from early times an area of dense settlement. N. Glueck notes some seventy sites there, many founded over 5,000 years ago, and over thirty-five of them still inhabited by Israelite times. It was only later that this valley which Lot found so attractive (Gn. 13:10) became more desolate, probably with the advent of malaria. It has been suggested that some of the Tells were artificial mounds built deliberately above the swampy ground, though added to by subsequent settlement. But everywhere water-supply has been the decisive factor of settlement. Fortified towns and castles were built at important perennial springs such as Jericho, Beth-shan and

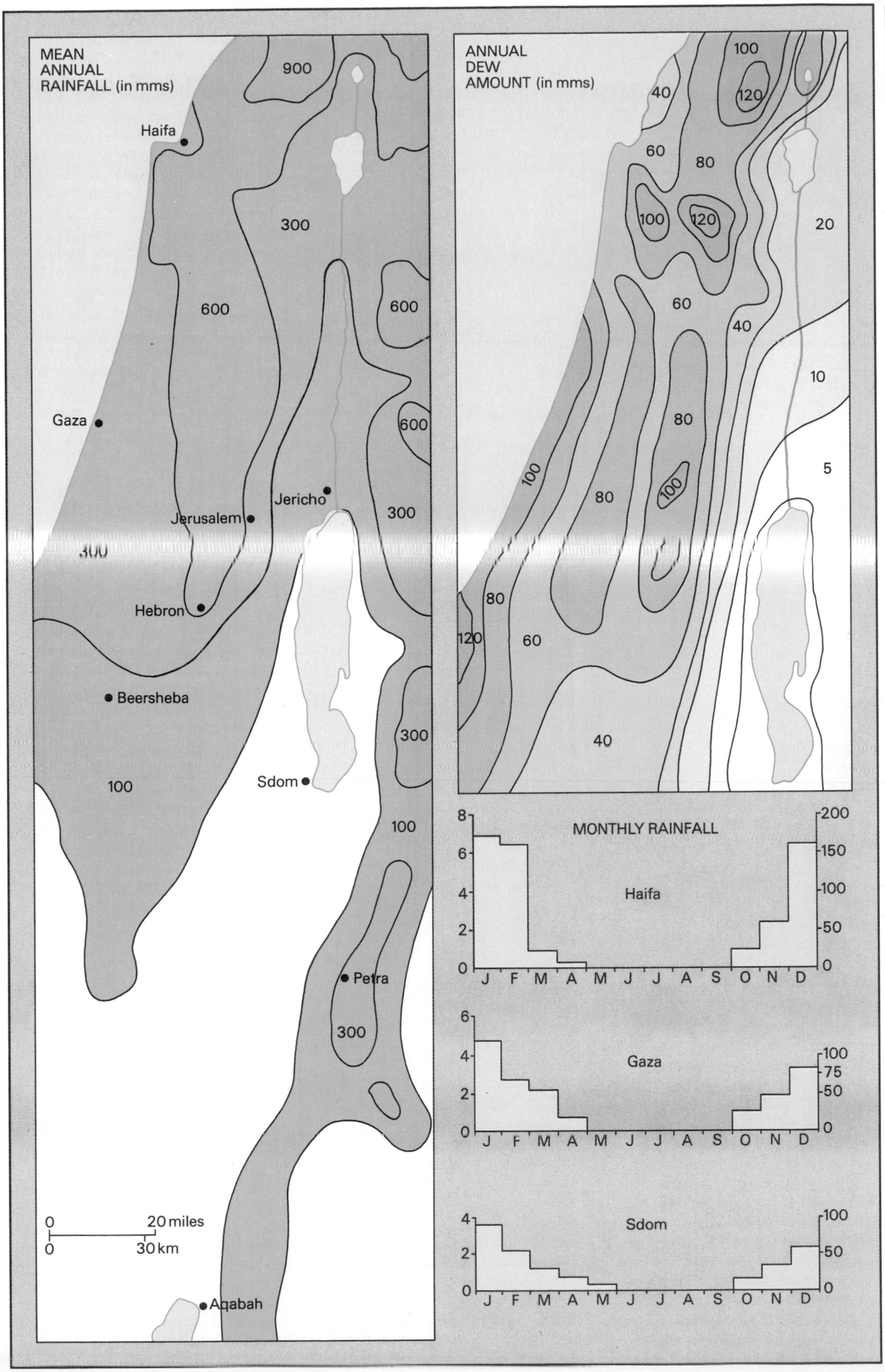

Left:
Palestine: rainfall.

Right:
Palestine: dewfall.

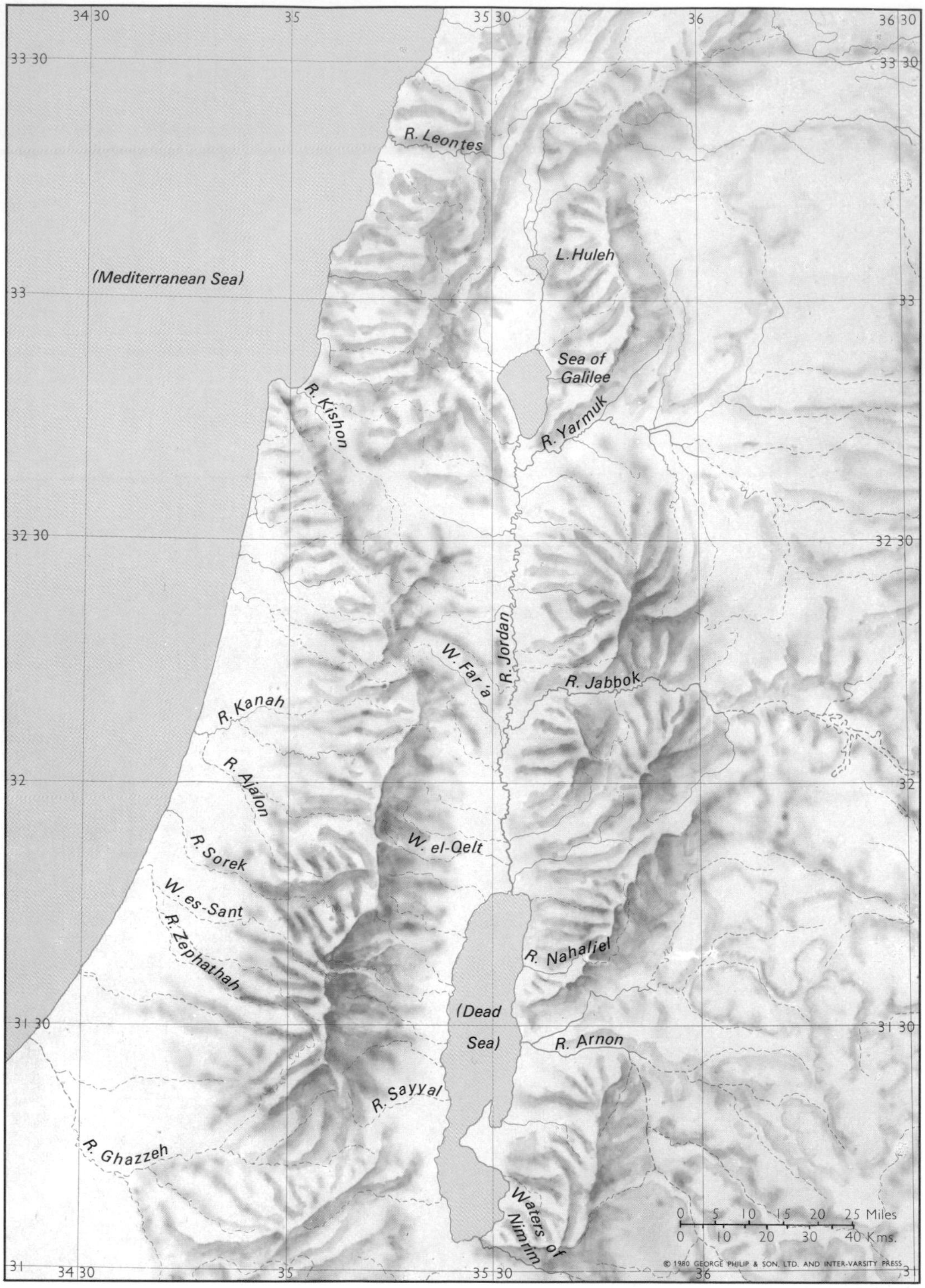

Palestine: principal water-courses.

PALM
See Weights and measures, Part 3.

PALMYRA
See Tadmor, Part 3.

Opposite page: Palestine: physical regions.

Aphek (famous from the wars of the Israelites with the Philistines). Indeed, it is a corollary that sites with abundant springs have usually had the most continuous settlement from remote times.

Along the coastal plain S of Carmel settlement has been relatively dense since antiquity, favoured by the ease with which wells could be dug through the sandy soils to the lenticular beds of clay that hold suspended water-tables. But farther N in the Vale of Sharon and Upper Galilee, where the water-supply is abundant, relatively dense woodland made human occupancy difficult until more recent centuries. In the basins of lower Galilee and Samaria population has for long been dense, scattered in numerous villages, but S of Jerusalem village sites become fewer and more nucleated, until around Beersheba settlement has been limited to strategic fortified well-sites. In Transjordan the edge of the plateau is marked by a number of fortresses such as Petra, Bozrah (Buseira) and Tophel (Tafileh). Beyond them to the E is the narrow stretch of agricultural land with its scattered villages along which ran the King's Highway. Within these patterns of settlement dictated largely by water conditions, the strategic and most important towns have grown up at cross-roads where the proximity of some defile enabled the transverse roads to link with the main N–S highways. Such were in biblical times Beersheba, Hebron, Jerusalem, Bethel, Shechem, Samaria, Megiddo, Beth-shan and Hazor. Hence the psalmist could exclaim: 'He led them by a straight way, till they reached a city to dwell in' (Ps. 107:7).

VI. The regions of Palestine

The geographer can create as many regions as there are problems worth studying, so it is absurd to suggest that the delimitation of areas within Palestine has a permanent validity. But certain regional units have appeared again and again in the history of Palestine, and should be recognized. The broad divisions already noted are distinct: the coastal plains, the central hill lands, the Rift Valley, the plateaux of Transjordan and the desert.

The coastal plains stretch for a distance of about 200 km from the borders of Lebanon to Gaza, interrupted by Mt Carmel in the N. To the N of it, the plain of Asher runs for 40 km to the ancient Ladder of Tyre, where the Galilean hills crowd close to the coast. It played no part in the life of Israel, but to the SE of it the valley of Jezreel and plain of Esdraelon have been of major significance. Stretching for 50 km into the interior and some 20 km at its widest, this formed the main road from Egypt to Damascus and the N. Along it were situated the strategic centres of Megiddo, Jezreel and Beth-shan, famous in many of Israel's wars (Jdg. 5; 7:1; 1 Sa. 29:1; 31:12) and the apocalyptic site of the future (Rev. 16:16). S of Carmel, which shelters the small plain of Dor, is the plain of Sharon with its five great Philistine strongholds of Ekron, Ashdod, Ashkelon, Gath and Gaza, merging E into the hill lands of the Shephelah, a buffer between Israel and Philistia. These hills were once heavily wooded with sycamores (1 Ki. 10:27; 2 Ch. 1:15; 9:27) and crossed transversely by narrow valleys which witnessed the early struggles of Israel from the times of the Judges to David, notably Aijalon (Jos. 10:10–15; 1 Sa. 14:31); Sorek (Jdg. 16), and Elah (1 Sa. 17:1–2).

The Central Hills run some 300 km from N Galilee to Sinai, made up of interlocking hills and plateaux. In the S, Judah has gently undulating folds except in the E, where the deeply dissected chalky relief of the Wilderness of Judah, or Jeshimon, descends steeply to the Rift Valley. This Judaean plateau runs N into the hill country of Ephraim with its easy transverse passages, but to the N the hills of Samaria decrease gently from the Judaean heights of over 1,000 m to an average of just over 300 m in the central basin, in which are situated the biblical sites of Gibeah, Shalem, Shechem and Sychar. Above it tower the heights of Ebal (945 m) and Gerizim (890 m). Together with other fertile basins, Samaria was exposed to outside influences, and its faith early corrupted. N of the plain of Esdraelon lies Galilee, divided into S or lower Galilee, which has a similar landscape to the lands of Samaria, and N or upper Galilee, where the mountains reach over 900 m. A number of basins, notably Nazareth, provide easy passage and rich cultivation between the coast and the Lake area, densely settled in our Lord's day.

Slicing across Palestine for over 100 km, the Jordan follows the great Rift Valley. Its N sector is occupied also by the lakes Huleh and Galilee, surrounded by high mountains, notably Hermon, the source of the Jordan (Dt. 3:9; 4:48). Below the basin of Huleh, the Jordan has cut through the basaltic dam that once blocked the depression in a gorge to enter the lake Tiberias or Sea of Galilee 200 m below sea-level. Beyond it the river Yarmuk adds its waters to the Jordan and the valley gradually widens S towards the Dead Sea trough. S of the cliffs of 'Ain Khaneizer commences the Arabah, stretching 160 km to the Gulf of Aqabah, a desert dominated by the great wall of the Transjordan tableland. W stretches the desolate hilly relief of the central Negeb and its steppe plains, towards Beersheba. E over the edge of the Transjordan plateaux extend a series of regions well known in Bible times: the tableland of Bashan dominated E by the great volcanic caves of Jebel Druze; Gilead situated in a huge oval dome 55 km by 40 km wide and famed for its forests (Je. 22:6; Zc. 10:10); the level steppes of Ammon and Moab; and S of the Zered valley (Dt. 2:13; Is. 15:7) the faulted and tilted block of Edom with its impregnable strongholds. Beyond to the E and the S are the deserts, tablelands of rock and sand, blasted by the hot winds. See also *Jordan, *Negeb, *Sharon, *Zin. For archaeology of Palestine, see *Archaeology and individual sites, for history, see *Canaan, *Israel, *Judah, *Philistines, *etc.*

Bibliography. F.-M. Abel, *Géographie de la Palestine*, 1937 (2 vols.); D. Baly, *The Geography of the Bible*[2], 1974; G. Dalman, *Sacred Sites and Ways*, 1935; M. du Buit, *Géographie de la Terre Sainte*, 1958; N. Glueck, *The River Jordan*, 1946; W. J. Phythian-Adams, 'The Land and the People' in *A Companion to the Bible* (ed. T. W. Manson), 1944, pp. 133–156; A. Reifenberg, *The Struggle between the Desert and the Sown in the Levant*, 1956; G. A. Smith, *The Historical Geography of the Holy Land*[25], 1931; *National Atlas of Israel* (in Hebrew), in course of publication since 1958.

J.M.H.

PALTITE, THE. The name given to the inhabitants of Beth-pelet, situated in the Judaean Negeb (Jos. 15:27; Ne. 11:26). Helez, one of David's 30 heroes, was a native of this town (2 Sa. 23:26). In 1 Ch. 11:27 and 27:10 he is called 'the *Pelonite'.

R.A.H.G.

PAMPHYLIA. A coastal region of S Asia Minor on the great bay of the Mare Lycium, lying between *Lycia and *Cilicia. It is mentioned in Acts 13:13; 14:24 and 15:38 in connection with Paul's first journey, a visit which Ramsay believed was cut short through illness and the enervating climate (*SPT*, pp. 89ff.). According to tradition, the area was colonized by Amphilochus and Calchas (or Mopsus, his rival and successor) after the Trojan War. Linguistic evidence confirms a mixed settlement. The chief towns were Attaleia, Paul's probable landing-place, founded by Attalus II of Pergamum after 189 BC with Athenian colonists; Aspendus, a Persian

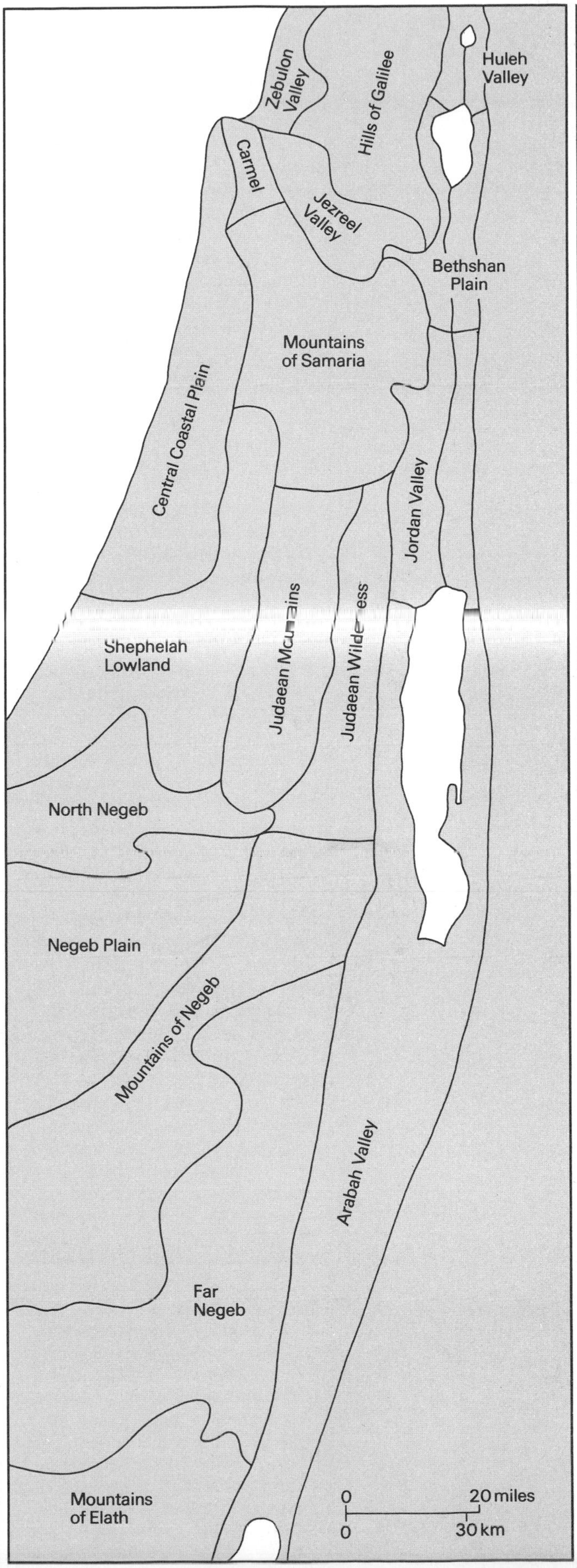

PANELLING See Art, Part 1.

naval base which claimed Argive foundation; Side, founded by Aeolian colonists; and *Perga. The region was under Persian rule until Alexander, after which, apart from brief occupations by Ptolemy I and Ptolemy III, it passed to the possession of the Seleucids of Syria. After the defeat of Antiochus III, C. Manlius took the region over for Rome and the main cities were associated in alliance. The Attalids at this time (189 BC) received the coastal strip, where they founded Attaleia. Many readjustments followed. From 102 BC Pamphylia was a part of the province of Cilicia, but about 44 BC was included in Asia. In 36 BC Antony made the territory over to his ally Amyntas, king of Galatia. Thanks to his timely desertion to Octavian before Actium, Amyntas retained possession until his death in battle against a highland tribe in 25 BC. From this date until AD 43 Pamphylia was part of the province of Galatia. In that year Claudius formed the province of Lycia-Pamphylia. There were later reorganizations under Galba and Vespasian. The church founded at Perga is the only one mentioned in the 1st century, but there were at least twelve foundations at the time of Diocletian's persecution in AD 304.

BIBLIOGRAPHY. A. H. M. Jones, *Cities of the Eastern Roman Provinces*², 1971, pp. 123ff. E.M.B.

PANNAG. A Heb. word, found only in Ezk. 27:17, denoting some type of merchandise, presumably edible. AV and RV transliterated, since the meaning was unknown. Scholars and EVV have often emended the Heb., either to *dônaḡ*, 'wax' (JB) or to *paggaḡ*, 'early figs' (RSV); but recent evidence from Hittite and Akkad. texts supports MT. 'Meal' (NEB), or some baked product, seems to be meant.

D.F.P.

PAPHOS. The name of two settlements in SW Cyprus in NT times, distinguished by scholars as Old and New Paphos. The former was a Phoenician foundation of great antiquity lying slightly inland from the coast. New Paphos grew up, after the Romans annexed the island in 58 BC, as the centre of Rom. rule, and it was here that Paul met the proconsul Sergius (Acts 13:6–7, 12) on his first missionary journey. Here, too, he had his encounter with Elymas the sorcerer (Acts 13:6–11). Old Paphos was the site of a famous shrine, probably of Phoenician or Syrian origin, but later devoted to the worship of Aphrodite. J.H.P.

PAPYRI AND OSTRACA.

I. Egyptian

a. Papyrus

(i) *Name.* The term papyrus applies to a large aquatic plant of the sedge family, to the writing material prepared from its pith, and to individual manuscripts made from this material. The origin of Gk. *papyros* (from which come 'papyrus', 'paper') is still uncertain. Some think that it derives from an assumed *papūro* in Coptic (last stage of the ancient Egyptian language), which would mean 'belonging to the king', reflecting the fact that production of papyrus was a royal monopoly in the Graeco-Roman epoch.

(ii) *The plant and its uses.* In antiquity, the *plant *Cyperus papyrus* L. grew throughout Egypt, especially in the Delta, in marshes and lakes; but the plant is not now found in the wild state N of the Sudan, although it still grows in the marshes of Lake Huleh in Palestine and is found in Sicily. From roots in the mud, the great stems, triangular in section, grew to heights of 3 to 6 m, ending in large, open, bell-shaped flowers. (See H. Frankfort, *Birth of Civilization in the Near East*, 1951, pl. 2, and for a representation in antiquity, W. Stevenson Smith, *Art and Architecture of Ancient Egypt*, 1958, plate 129A.) The graceful form of the papyrus was a favourite motif in Egyp. art and architecture. Heb. *gōme'* (AV 'bulrushes', 'rush', 'rushes') appears to signify the papyrus-plant. The biblical references to it tally well with the known nature and uses of papyrus. It indeed grew in the mire (Jb. 8:11) and fittingly symbolized luxuriant, swampy growth by contrast with the desert sands (Is. 35:7). The little basket or 'ark' in which the infant Moses was placed was of papyrus (Ex. 2:3); and in Egypt and Ethiopia papyrus vessels and skiffs were to be seen on the Nile and its marshes (Is. 18:2) as ancient pictures show (see, *e.g.* M. Murray, *The Splendour that was Egypt*, 1949, p. 83, pl. 19). Besides the manufacture of reed boats and baskets, papyrus was used for making ropes, sandals and some clothing, and its roots were even used as food for the poor.

(iii) *Papyrus 'paper'.* To make this, the plant-stems were stripped of their outer rinds, cut up into lengths of about 40–45 cm, and the fresh, pithy inner stem was cut into thin strips. These were laid out side by side, overlapping each other, on a hard wooden surface; more strips were similarly laid across these at right-angles; and the two layers were then welded into a whole simply by hard beating, *e.g.* with mallets. Trimmed and smoothed, the result was a sheet of whitish paper that was durable but yellowed with age. The side showing horizontal fibres was usually written on first (except for letters) and is called the recto; the 'back' with the vertical fibres is termed the verso. These sheets were pasted end to end, with slight overlaps, to form a papyrus roll. The standard length was twenty sheets, but this could be shortened by cutting or lengthened by pasting on more, as need arose. The longest known papyrus is the great *Papyrus Harris I*, *c.* 1160 BC, in the British Museum; it is some 40 m long. The height of a papyrus varied according to the use to which it was to be put: the larger sizes (maximum, 47 cm; usually 35·5 cm and 42 cm in Dynasties 18 and 19–20) for official and business papers and accounts (with long columns of figures); and the smaller ones (about 18 cm and 21 cm, but often less) for literary compositions.

(iv) *The use of papyrus.* This was governed by definite conventions. As Egyp. script usually runs from right to left, the scribes always began at the right-hand end of a papyrus and wrote to the left—at first in vertical lines (usual until *c.* 1800 BC), thereafter in horizontal lines of modest length, grouped in successive 'columns' or 'pages'. For scripts used, punctuation, writing equipment, manuscripts, *etc.*, see *WRITING; *TEXTS AND VERSIONS.

Papyrus was used from the beginning of Egyp. history (*c.* 3000 BC) down into the early Islamic period (7th century AD and later). The oldest (blank) rolls are of Dynasty 1, the first written ones are of Dynasty 5, *c.* 2500 BC. Large quantities were made and used in Egypt in the 2nd and 1st millennia BC for every kind of written record; but papyrus was not cheap, and the backs and blank spaces of old rolls were often used up, or an old text washed off to make room for a new one.

Before the end of the 2nd millennium BC, papyrus was being exported extensively to Syria–Palestine and doubtless beyond. About 1075 BC Zakarbaal, the prince of Phoen. Byblos, quoted timber-prices to the Egyp. envoy Wenamun from the rolls of accounts kept by his predecessors, and in Wenamun's part-payment for timber were included '500 (rolls of) finished papyrus' (*ANET*, pp. 27a, 28a). For the use of papyrus for Heb. and Aram., and in NT times, see separate sections below. On all aspects of papyrus as a writing-medium in Egypt, see J. Černý, *Paper and Books in Ancient Egypt*, 1952. For pictures of funerary and administrative papyri respectively, see *IBA*, pp. 36–37, figs. 30–31.

b. Ostraca

The plural of *ostrakon*, a Gk. word originally meaning 'oyster-shell', but applied by the Greeks to the potsherds on which they recorded their votes (hence English 'ostracize'). In Egypt this term is applied to slips of limestone or potsherds bearing ink-written inscriptions and drawings. Although such ostraca are known from most periods in Egyp. history and from various sites, the vast majority are of New Kingdom date (*c.* 1550–1070 BC) and come from Thebes in Upper Egypt, specifically from the Valleys of the Tombs of the Kings and the Queens and the village for the workers at these tombs (modern Deir el-Medineh). Most Egyp. ostraca are written in the cursive hieratic script; those in the more formal, pictorial hieroglyphic script are much rarer. The ostraca with drawings are often delightful, sketched by artists in their spare time. The inscribed ostraca fall into two classes: literary and non-literary. The former contain portions of Egyp. literary works (stories, poems, wisdom, hymns, *etc.*), written out as school exercises, test of memory, or for pleasure, these ostraca often preserve literary works (or parts of them) still unknown from any other source. Much more varied are the non-literary ostraca. These were the Egyptians' equivalent of memo-pads, jotters and scrap paper, and reflect every conceivable aspect of daily life: rosters of workmen with note of absentees, reports on work done (*cf.* Ex. 5:18–19), distribution of food-allowances and oil, innumerable accounts of bricks, straw, vegetables, vessels, *etc.*, lawsuits, marriage-contracts, bills of sale and demand-notes for debts, many letters and memoranda, and much else besides. The total of this material gives a vivid insight into Egyp. daily life during and after the time of Israel's sojourn and exodus and can provide useful background for the Exodus narratives. (*LACHISH, *SAMARIA.)

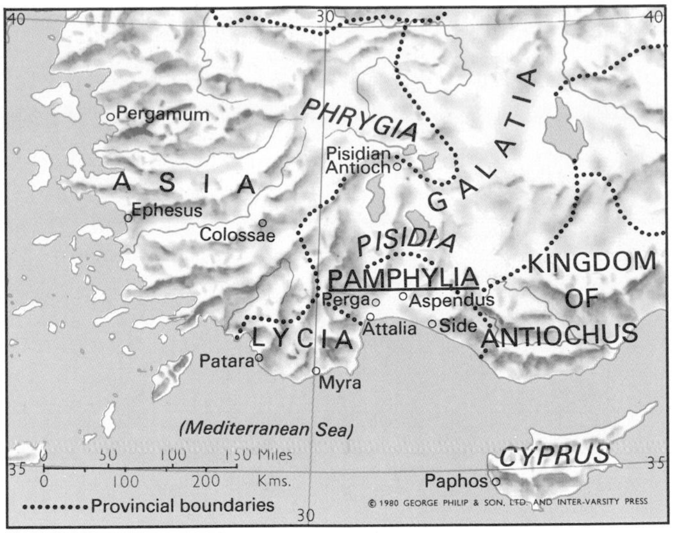

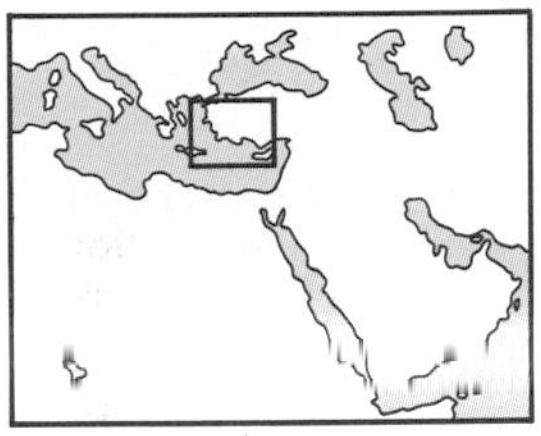

The location of Pamphylia in Asia Minor.

BIBLIOGRAPHY. On scope and importance of ostraca, see J. Černý, *Chronique d'Égypte*, 6/No. 12, 1931, pp. 212–224, and S. Sauneron, *Catalogue des Ostraca Hiératiques Non Littéraires de Deir el Medineh*, 1959, Introduction, pp. vi–xviii, who gives ample reference to other publications. In English, see W. C. Hayes, *The Scepter of Egypt*, 2, 1959, pp. 176–178, 390–394, 432. For pictures of typical ostraca, see Hayes, *op. cit.*, p. 177, fig. 98.

K.A.K.

II. Hebrew, Aramaic and Greek

a. Hebrew papyri

The oldest known Heb. papyrus (Mur 17) was discovered at Wadi Murabba'at by the Dead Sea in 1952. Mur 17 is a palimpsest written in palaeo-Hebrew script and dates from the late 8th or early 7th century BC. The original letter, of which a few words may still be read, was erased and a list of personal names superimposed. Most

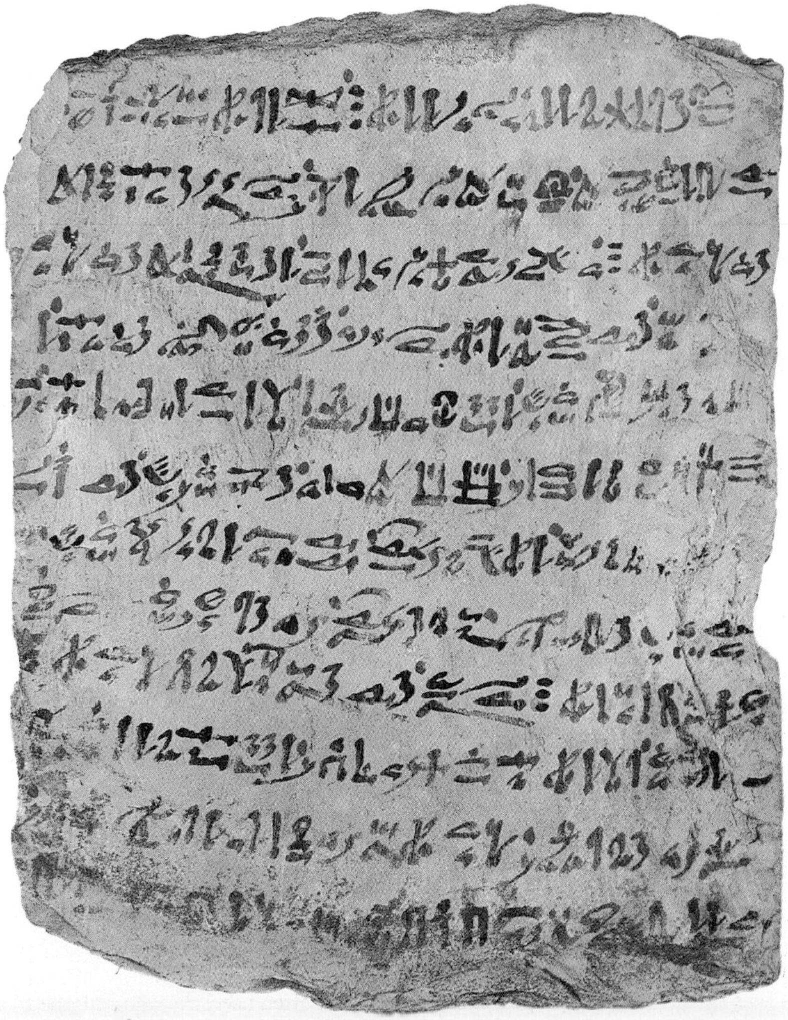

Limestone ostracon, inscribed in the Egyptian hieratic script with part of the 'Educational Instruction of the scribe Amennakhte to his apprentice, Hormin'. Red ink is used for the title and for points marking the beginning of phrases or verses. 19th Dynasty. (New Kingdom). c. 1250 BC. (BM)

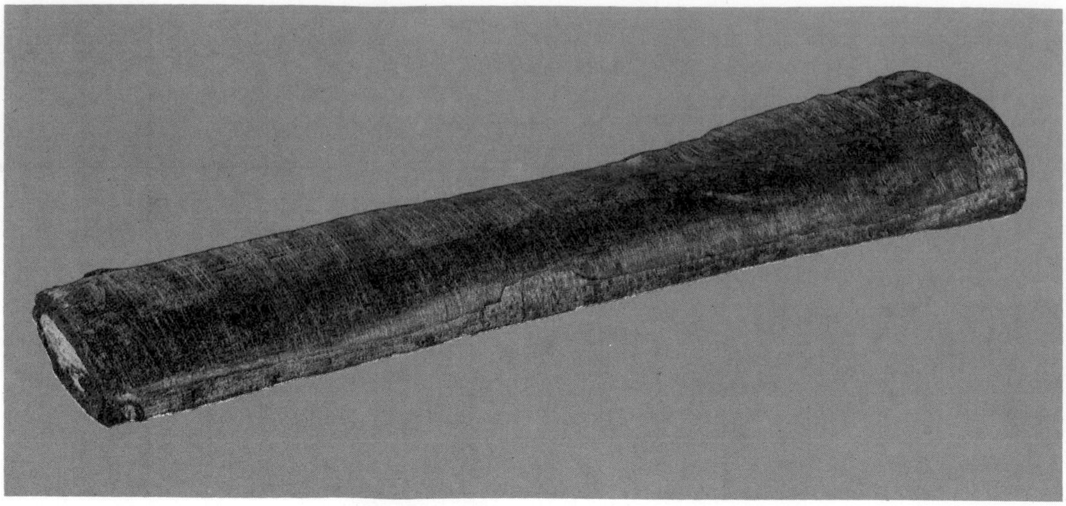

A rolled Egyptian papyrus, probably of Late Kingdom or Ptolemaic date (c. 1085–1080 BC). It is covered with pitch and has not been unrolled in modern times, so its contents remain unknown. (BM)

of the scrolls found at Qumran are of parchment but there are a few papyri worthy of mention. Cave 4 yielded papyrus fragments of *The Rule of the Community* and *The Thanksgiving Hymns*. Hundreds of papyrus pieces were found in Cave 6, among them fragments of the biblical books of Kings and Daniel written in a semi-cursive script. Before the Qumran discoveries the Nash Papyrus, containing parts of Dt. 5 and 6, had occupied a unique position as the oldest biblical Heb. MS extant; it is possibly to be dated as early as the 2nd century BC. Wadi Murabba'at has also produced assorted Heb. papyri from the time of the Bar Kokhba rebellion (AD 132–135). The most noteworthy finds were a couple of letters written by Bar Kokhba himself and containing his real name—Simeon Ben Kosebah.

b. Hebrew ostraca

Ostraca, being cheap and of limited use, tended to have only information of secondary importance inscribed on them. Nevertheless, ostraca bearing Heb. inscriptions have shed valuable light on the language and literature of the OT. The Samaria ostraca, discovered in the main during the Harvard excavations of 1908–10, are among the most important. They date from the time of the Jehu dynasty, possibly from the reign of Jehoahaz at the end of the 9th century. Discovered in a royal storehouse, they record information concerning the payment of oil and wine; it is possible that they refer to the produce from crown property in the vicinity of Samaria. In each case the regnal year is given and, though not uniformly, they contain many personal and place-names, the former including compounds of Yahweh, El and Baal. See *LOB*, pp. 315–327. Many ostraca inscribed in Aramaic, and some in Hebrew, have been discovered at Arad. The Hebrew-inscribed date from the late 7th century BC and concern supplies of wine, flour and bread which an official had to provide for travellers (troops?). Some smaller ostraca found in the temple ruins record names of priestly families, among them the Korahites (*bny qrḥ*). The Yavneh-Yam ostraca are dated to the same era. Special interest attaches to one of this collection which preserves an agricultural worker's plea for the return of his cloak which had been removed by an overseer who wrongly accused him of laziness (*cf.* Ex. 22:26–27). Of roughly similar date is the Ophel ostracon found in Jerusalem in the 1923–5 excavations. It contains a list of names and provenances in palaeo-Hebrew script. Probably best known of all are the Lachish ostraca, twenty-one of which were discovered on the site of the ancient city (mod. Tell ed-Duweir) in 1935 and 1938. These have a particular merit in that many of them can be dated with certainty to the year 587 BC. They are mostly letters and the name of Yaosh, military governor of Lachish, occurs as that of the addressee in some of them. The letters reflect the desperate situation in Judah as the Babylonians took city after city; there are some points of contact with the book of Jeremiah. Features of interest include the free use of the tetragrammaton and a reference to a prophet acting as postman. Some Heb.-inscribed sherds have also been discovered at Qumran, Wadi Murabba'at and Masada (where one with the name Ben Yair inscribed on it has aroused particular interest because of its probable connection with the Zealot leader Eleazar Ben Yair).

c. Aramaic papyri

Possibly the earliest extant papyrus written in Aramaic is that which was found in 1942 at Saqqarah in Egypt. It represents part of a letter from a king Adon to the pharaoh and would seem to have been written from somewhere on the Philistine or Phoenician coast. Thus the use of Aramaic in international diplomacy before the Persian era is illustrated, for the letter cannot have been written after the time of Nebuchadrezzar (d. 562 BC). But by far the most significant corpus of Aram. papyri is that which comes from the island of Elephantine in Egypt. Here and at Memphis and Hermopolis a large number of papyri written by Jews in the late 6th and 5th centuries BC have been

Papyrus growing in an Egyptian marsh. Painting from the tomb of Nebamun, Thebes. c. 1422–1411 BC. (BM)

Papyrus-gathering. Tomb of Ni-ankh-khum and Knum-hotep. Saqqara. c. 2400 BC. *Modern copy on papyrus.* (BM)

Head of the papyrus plant (Cyperus papyrus). (FNH)

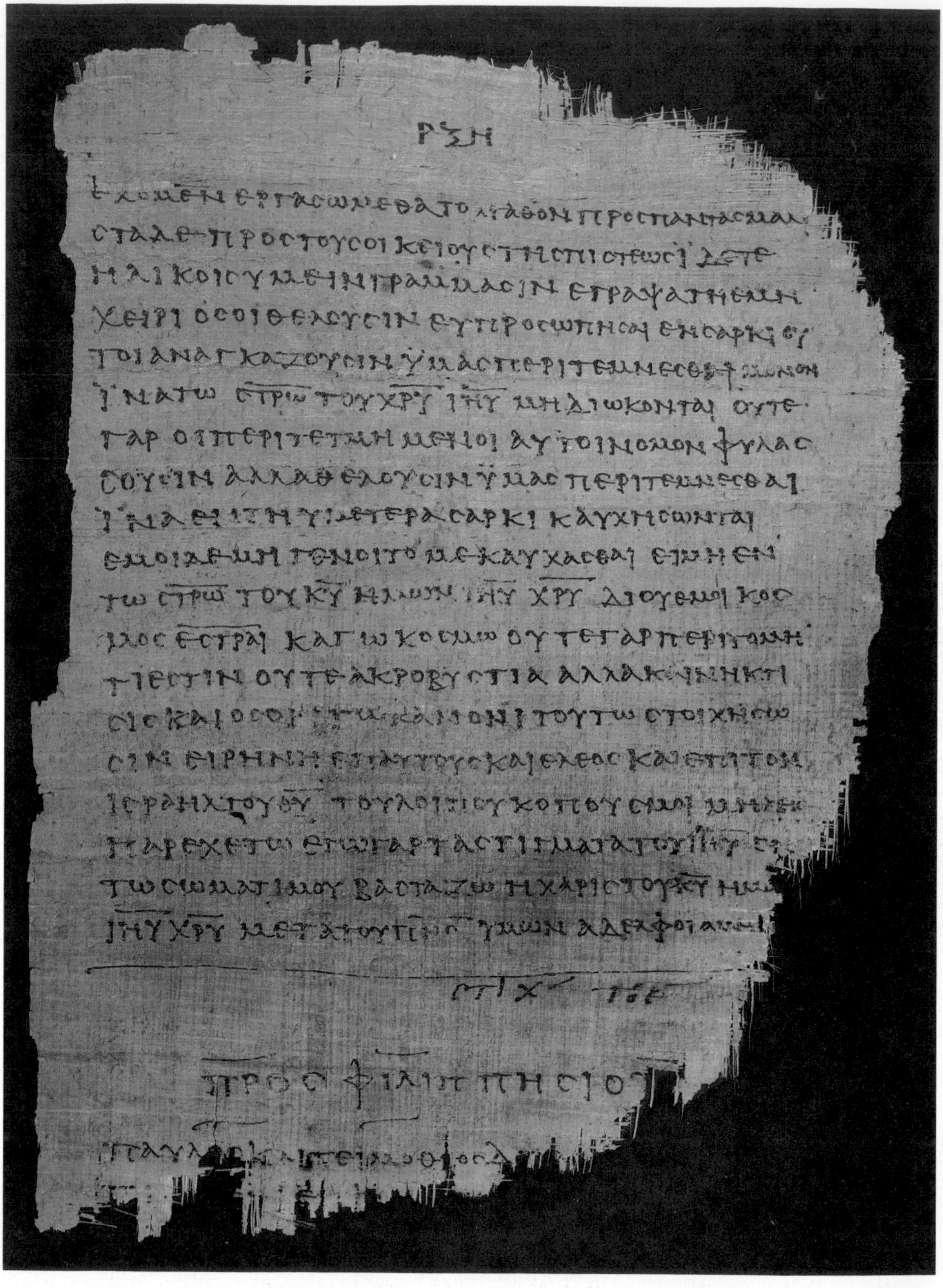

Greek papyrus of Gal. 6:10–18 and Phil. 1:1 from the Chester Beatty collection. 3rd cent. AD. (CBL)

preserved. Legal documents and private letters are well represented, and there is also a fragment of the oldest known version of the *Sayings of Ahikar*. The type of Aramaic is, as we should expect, rather like that in the biblical Ezra. These Jewish colonists had their own temple (despite Dt. 12:5–7) and went so far as to compound the name of the God of Israel with Canaanite divine names (*e.g.* Anath-Yahu, Anath-Bethel). Representing the 4th century are the papyri from Wadi Daliyeh, 19 km NW of Jericho. These were discovered in a cave and it is surmised that they were hidden there by refugees from Samaria where they were actually written. They are legal and administrative documents which were drawn up *c.* 375–365 BC; they may have been abandoned by people who had fled

Fragments of a papyrus scroll containing the oldest known copy of any book of the OT in Greek. Shown here are parts of Dt. 25:1–3; 26:17–19. Egypt. Mid-2nd cent. BC. (JR)

before Alexander the Great. Some Aram. papyri are included in the finds at Qumran (*e.g.* one containing OT genealogies, from Cave 4) and at Wadi Murabba'at (*e.g.* deeds of sale). Some Nabataean fragments have also been recovered in the vicinity of Wadi Murabba'at.

d. Aramaic ostraca

An early example is the letter on a potsherd found at Asshur and probably written in the 7th century BC. Aram. ostraca at Elephantine (*vid. sup.*) are mainly tax receipts. Fragments from the Persian period found at Tell al-Khalayfa evidently served as receipts for wine. Scores of Aram. sherds are among the finds at Arad. A few have turned up at Qumran and Wadi Murabba'at but they are of little significance. A fragment of a letter(?) at Wadi Murabba'at is dated to the early 1st century BC.

e. Greek Old Testament papyri

A considerable number are extant, though invariably they are in fragmentary condition. Perhaps the oldest is the John Rylands Pap. Gk. 458 containing parts of Dt. 23–28 and dating from the 2nd century BC. Pap. Fouad 266 is almost as old and preserves fragments of Gn. 7 and 38 and Dt. 17–33. The Chester Beatty Gk. OT papyri include parts of various OT books and range in date from the 2nd to the 4th centuries AD. From the 3rd century AD comes the Freer Gk. MS V, a papyrus codex of the Minor Prophets. Qumran Cave 4 has yielded fragments of Lv. 2–5, while in Cave 7 fragments containing Ex. 28:4–7 and the *Epistle of Jeremiah* 43–44 have been found. The Qumran finds may be given approx. dates in the 1st century BC.

BIBLIOGRAPHY (for Heb., Aram. and Gk. OT material): A. Cowley, *Aramaic Papyri of the Fifth Century BC*, 1923; E. G. Kraeling, *The Brooklyn Museum Aramaic Papyri*, 1953; *DOTT*, pp. 204–208, 212–217, 251–269; P. E. Kahle, *The Cairo Geniza*², 1959; P. Benoit *et al.*, *Discoveries in the Judaean Desert*, 2, 1961; F. F. Bruce, *The Books and the Parchments*³, 1963; S. Jellicoe, *The Septuagint and Modern Study*, 1968; B. Porten, *Archives from Elephantine*, 1968; K. Aland, *Repertorium der Griechischen Christlichen Papyri: I. Biblische Papyri*, 1976. R.P.G.

III. New Testament

a. Introduction

The discovery of the Gk. papyri in Egypt during the last century has had important results for NT studies. In the initial finds biblical papyri were rare, but with the commencement of systematic excavations by Grenfell and Hunt in 1896 large quantities of papyri came to light, including either portions of the NT books themselves or documents of the early centuries which helped our understanding of them. The most fruitful sites were in the Fayyûm and to the S, particularly at Oxyrhynchus, Hermopolis, Tebtynis, Aphroditopolis and Panopolis.

It had long been assumed by many scholars that NT Greek was *sui generis*, 'a language of the Holy Ghost', but there were some, such as Masson, Lightfoot and Farrar, who anticipated the fact soon to be proved, that the NT writers used the common tongue of the Gk. world in the 1st century AD, approximating more often to the spoken than to the literary form of *koinē* Greek. Thanks to the papyri, we now have illustrations of the contemporary 'secular' use of the vast majority of NT words. It is still true, in a restricted sense, that

This ostracon contains a message to Yaosh, the military governor of Lachish, written in 588 BC (?). It is an example of the use of the Early Hebrew script and language by Judaeans, also used in writing large parts of the OT. Lachish letter II. (BM)

the language is *sui generis*, because of the frequent substratum of Hebrew and Aramaic. 'The tension between the Jewish heritage and the Greek world vitally affects the language of the New Testament' (Hoskyns and Davey, *The Riddle of the New Testament*, 1931, p. 20). Another tendency corrected by the study of the papyri was the inclination of scholars to judge the NT by Attic standards of grammar and syntax, and also of literary taste. It was now made doubly clear that the *koinē* of the first Christian centuries was in a comparatively rapid state of evolution, which culminated in Byzantine and finally in modern Greek, and must therefore be evaluated in the light of this. It would be wrong to claim too much for these advances, but they have provided an indispensable aid to the study of the NT text, language and literature, and thus for its theological interpretation. In his Schweich Lecture of 1946 (published in 1953 as *The Text of the Epistles*) G. Zuntz makes a plea for the active conjunction of these two fields of study. 'The theologian who studies the New Testament must assume the quality also of the philologist' (p. 3). Perhaps the finest work exemplifying this is *TDNT*.

The original documents of the NT were all written on papyrus rolls (apart from one or two of the shortest Epistles, which may have been written on individual sheets of papyrus), and it may here be mentioned that the transmission of the text played an important part in the development of new techniques. In the rest of the Roman world papyrus codices did not begin to replace rolls until the 3rd century AD, but from Egypt we have evidence that the Christian communities developed the codex form considerably earlier. Ten Bible fragments have been found dated to the 2nd and early 3rd centuries, and of 111 fragments of the 3rd and 4th only twelve were in the form of papyrus rolls. The text of Romans would have required a roll of 4 m, Mark 6 m, Acts about 10 m (*cf.* 2 Tim. 4:13 referring to rolls and the parchment wrappings which protected them). But as the need arose for copies of the Gospels and Epistles in larger bulk, the use of codices naturally developed, *i.e.* leaves of papyrus folded and arranged in quires, much as in modern books. A single codex could now contain the four Gospels and Acts, or the whole of Paul's Epistles.

b. List of the most notable papyri

The latest tabulation, edited by K. Aland (1976), contains more than 241 entries, of which 68 are listed in the critical editions of the NT text. Many are comparatively small, but the importance of the more substantial texts is great.

P^1 (3rd or 4th cent.) contains Mt. 1:1–9, 12–20; P^4 (4th cent.) Lk. 1:74–80; 6:1–4; P^5 (3rd cent.) Jn. 1:23–31, 33–41 and 20:11–17, 19–25; it comprises the two leaves of a single quire, and illustrates the family from which the Codices Sinaiticus and Vaticanus later derived. P^8 (4th cent.) contains Acts 4:31–37; 5:2–9; 6:1–6, 8–15; P^{13} (3rd cent., written on the back of an Epitome of Livy) Heb. 2:14–5:5; 10:8–22; 10:29–11:13; 11:28–12:17; P^{20} (3rd cent.) Jas. 2:19–3:9; P^{22} (3rd cent.) Jn. 15:25–16:2, 21–32; P^{27} (3rd cent.) Rom. 8:12–22, 24–27, 33–9:3; 9:5–9; P^{37} (3rd cent.) contains Mt. 26:19–52; P^{38} (4th cent.) Acts 18:27–19:6; 19:12–16.

Of the Chester Beatty Papyri ($P^{45, 46, 47}$), Nos. 1 and 2 are of particular interest. P^{45} (early 3rd cent.) contains portions of 30 leaves out of a codex of 220 including the Gospels and Acts; it has parts of Matthew, Mark, Luke, John (17 leaves) and Acts (13 leaves). P^{46} (also early 3rd cent.) contains 86 leaves, found over a period in three groups, and has Romans, Hebrews, 1, 2 Corinthians, Galatians, Ephesians, Philippians, Colossians, 1, 2 Thessalonians, except for small gaps. It is notable that the concluding doxology of Romans here occurs at the end of ch. 15. P^{47} (3rd cent., 10 leaves) has Rev. 9:10–17:2; P^{48} (3rd cent., similar to P^{38}) has Acts 23:11–16, 24–29. P^{52} (the famous 'John Rylands' fragment, 9 cm by 6 cm) was identified by C. H. Roberts in 1935 as Jn. 18:31–33, 37–38 and belonging to the early 2nd cent. P^{64} (2nd cent.) contains portions of Mt. 26; P^{66} (*c.* AD 200), the 'Bodmer papyrus II', has 108 leaves in 5 quires, each 16 cm by 14 cm, and contains Jn. 1:1–14:26.

The textual relation of these and many lesser papyri to the most important vellum codices and early versions of the NT has been the subject of close study.

c. Effect on the textual study of the New Testament

To describe this, a brief sketch of the history of the Gk. text up to the papyrus discoveries is necessary. The AV of 1611 was based on the Gk. NT edition prepared by Stephanus (Robert Etienne) in 1550, the 'Textus Receptus', which itself drew largely on the edition of Erasmus published in 1516. Stephanus had made use of only fifteen MSS, all of them of late date, and representing the Byzantine or Eastern tradition of the text. The event which stimulated a serious search for all available MSS was the appearance in England in 1627 of the Codex Alexandrinus, a vellum codex of the 5th century AD. But it was not until the discovery of Codex Sinaiticus and the appearance of Tischendorf's edition of Vaticanus, in 1859 and 1867 respectively, that any great advance in textual study was possible. This came just as scholars began to realize the potential wealth of Egypt in papyri. Westcott and Hort published a revised Gk. text in 1881, which was used extensively in the Eng. RV of that year. These scholars postulated four main families of texts, Syrian, Neutral, Alexandrian and Western, and themselves gave most weight to the Neutral family, consisting of the Codices Vaticanus and Sinaiticus, the Coptic Versions and kindred MSS.

NT papyri have played a prominent part in the extension and modification of their results. Further study convinced scholars that Westcott and Hort's groups had been distinguished too sharply from each other; and B. H. Streeter, using the minuscule groups of MSS isolated by Ferrar and Abbott, and by K. Lake, together with the Koridethi MS (9th cent.) demonstrated the close relation these all bore to Origen's text of the NT, and postulated at any rate for the Gospel of Mark the 'Caesarean' family (Origen having spent his latter years at Caesarea). The text of the Gospels in the Freer MSS (the 'Washington Gospels') and the Chester Beatty papyri further showed that the 'Caesarean' family of texts probably originated in Egypt, and went from Alexandria to Caesarea with Origen. The Chester Beatty group, especially P^{46}, have been of immense value. They prove that the codex was early in use for collections of the Gospels and Pauline Epistles, the circulation of which greatly assisted towards the formation of the canon of the NT. Their firm dating to the 3rd century AD means that we now possess a line of textual evidence going beyond the great vellum codices of the 4th and 5th centuries, upon which scholars had depended so heavily, and earlier than the NT collections which Eusebius was ordered to produce for use in the churches, following the Edict of Milan in AD 313. Further valuable help has been provided by the Bodmer papyri, especially P⁶⁶, a late 2nd-century codex of John. Still earlier fragments, in particular the 'John Rylands' fragment of John's Gospel, take us into the first half of the 2nd century, *i.e.* to within a single generation of the last writings of the NT, the Johannine Corpus.

The general picture of the transmission of the text which emerges is that of many groups or families arising, as copies were made for public and private use, sometimes by trained scribes, but more often by untrained Christians. The need for a standard text had not yet arisen, and local attempts at the collation of different texts were never very widely used. We must also assume that in the persecutions, *e.g.* that of Decius in AD 250, many copies of the NT perished. The papyri have helped to reveal the complexity of this early stage of transmission; if we are still far from fulfilling Bentley's aim to make the text so undoubtedly true 'ut e manibus apostolorum vix purior et sincerior evaserit' ('that it could scarcely have come from the hands of the apostles themselves in a form purer or more free from corruption'), at least the story is one of continuous advance. (*Texts and Versions (NT).)

d. Effect on the study of New Testament language and literature

As noted above, the Gk. of the NT has affinities with both the literary and the non-literary forms of the *koinē*, principally the latter, which is now known so fully from papyrus documents of every type from Graeco-Roman Egypt—Imperial rescripts, judicial proceedings, tax and census papers, marriage contracts, birth, death and divorce notices, private letters, business accounts, and a host of others. There are without doubt many Semitisms in the NT, all the writers except one being Jewish, but their estimated number has been greatly reduced by the discovery of parallel expressions in the papyri. 'Even Mark's Semitisms are hardly ever barbarous Greek, though his extremely vernacular language makes us think so, until we read the less educated papyri' (Howard). An example is the expression *blepein apo* at Mk. 8:15. Many new word formations of NT Greek have been paralleled, *e.g.* substantives ending in *-mos*, *-ma*, *-sis*, *-ia*; adjectives ending in *-ios*, new compound adjectives and adverbs, new words with the privative *a-* prefix; foreign words, technical words used of the Roman army and administration. Problems of orthography have been settled, *e.g. genēma* (Mt. 26:29), *tameion* (Lk. 12:3), *sphyris* (Mt. 15:37); and of morphology, *e.g. gegonan* (Rom. 16:7), *elthatō* (Mt. 10:13), *ēlthan* (Mk. 3:8); and of syntax, *e.g.* the consecutive use of *hina* clauses (as in Jn. 17:3), the interchangeability of *eis* and *en* (as in Jn. 1:18; Mt. 18:19).

NT vocabulary was abundantly illustrated. Instead of the numerous *voces biblicae* of the older scholars, it became possible to show, as did Deissmann and Bauer, that only about 1 per cent of the vocabulary, about fifty words, was in fact peculiar to it. A better sense could be given to words like *hēlikia* (*e.g.* Lk. 2:52 = 'age'), *meris* (Acts 16:12 = 'district'), *anastatoō* (lit. 'drive out of hearth and home', used metaphorically in Acts 17:6 and Gal. 5:12), *hypostasis* (Heb. 11:1 = 'title-deeds', RSV 'assurance'), *parousia* (*passim*; = visit of royalty or other notable person), *arrhabōn* (*e.g.* Eph. 1:14 = 'deposit paid', RSV 'guarantee'), *leitourgia* (2 Cor. 9:12; of both private and public service). The common terms *adelphoi* and *presbyteroi* were

Chester Beatty papyrus fragment of John (10:31–11:10) in Greek. 3rd cent. AD. (CBL)

frequently illustrated, from social and religious fraternities and from village and temple officials.

At the time the NT was written a revised Atticism was popular, an essentially artificial movement which affected to recognize only 5th-century Attic Greek as the norm. But there were notable secular writers, such as Plutarch, Strabo, Diodorus Siculus and Epictetus, who shunned Atticism, and the NT itself represents a revolt against it by its use of the vernacular tongue. '*Koinē* is not, as it were, pure gold accidentally contaminated, but something more like a new and serviceable alloy' (Moule). The LXX had already set a precedent for such a use of popular Greek, and the writers, all of whom might have written in Aramaic, wrote in Greek from deliberate choice. The literary standard of their work of course varies enormously. 2 Peter most nearly approaches a fully literary level, and Luke and the author of Hebrews are also conscious stylists. But Luke and Paul, though obviously capable of speaking and writing Greek in its classical form (*cf.* the prefaces to Luke and Acts, and Acts 17:22ff.) did not hesitate to use highly colloquial forms. The extreme case is the Revelation, written in laboured and sometimes barbarous Greek, which clearly reflects the influence of Semitic terms and modes of thought. But it still remains true that 'the Greek in which the author expresses himself was more like the Greek of the Egyptian papyri' (A. Robinson). (*LANGUAGE OF THE NEW TESTAMENT.)

e. Ostraca

We have noted already that ostraca or 'potsherds' were used extensively in antiquity as the cheapest possible writing material. Their seeming insignificance (*cf.* Is. 45:9) caused them to be neglected as being of any value for the study of *koinē* Greek. As we might expect, among the large numbers found in Egypt, covering a period of nearly 1,000 years, the vast majority are documents, or fragments of them, belonging to the life of the lower classes. A few have been found bearing short literary texts, no doubt for use in schools, and we have ostraca with short passages of the NT inscribed on them (verses from Mk. 9 and Lk. 22) and one of the 6th century AD with a hymn to Mary influenced by Lk. 1. But more comprise brief letters, contracts, and, above all, tax receipts. Many languages are used, including Greek, Latin, Aramaic, Coptic and Old Egyptian.

Occasionally a NT expression is illuminated. Several ostraca give details of receipts dated to the day called *Sebastē*, meaning 'Emperor's Day', and perhaps parallel to the use by Christians of *kyriakē* as 'the *Lord's day'. The title *Kyrios*, 'Lord', appears on ostraca referring to the emperors Nero and Vespasian (*cf.* Jude 4). Receipts from Thebes dated to the 1st century have thrown light on the NT use of *logeia* (*e.g.* 1 Cor. 16:1–2 = 'collections') and also on the verb *apechō* signifying the receipt of a payment (*cf.* Mt. 6:2 = 'they have received their reward in full'). The common phrase *eis to onoma* ('in the name') is shown by ostraca to have been a regular legal formula, of the authority under which something is done. Ostraca thus supplement, on a comparatively minor scale, the evidence of the papyri as to NT language and idiom.

f. Apocryphal and non-canonical papyri

These deserve mention because of the assistance they have given to the understanding of the form and content of NT writings. Most notable are the *Logia* or Sayings of Jesus. The first of these (found at Oxyrhynchus in 1896 and 1897) was the leaf of a codex dated to the 3rd century, containing sayings some of which were familiar, others of a more mystical type; the second, of the late 2nd century, had the sayings written on the back of a roll about land surveys. A third contained fragments of a non-canonical Gospel, and another of this type was discovered in 1934; it comprises fragments of three leaves of a codex, assigned to *c.* AD 150, and narrates four incidents from Christ's life, similar to those in the Gospels. Then, among thirteen papyrus rolls found near Nag Hammadi in 1946 was the *Gospel of Thomas*, an important collection of Sayings in which Gnostic influence mingles with the Synoptic, Johannine and other traditions, evidently a Coptic version of the work of which the Oxyrhynchus Logia are fragments.

Several apocryphal works have been recovered in whole or in part. The Chester Beatty collection includes fourteen leaves of the *Book of Enoch*, from a 4th-century codex, and part of a homily by Melito of Sardis on the passion. One papyrus leaf of Gnostic origin has come to light (early 3rd century), out of the *Gospel of Mary*. At Akhmim fragments were found of the *Gospel* and *Apocalypse of Peter* (probably written in the 2nd century). The former has Docetic tendencies, and the latter is much inferior to the Revelation of John. In the Amherst collection is the major portion of the *Ascension of Isaiah*, and in the Hamburg State Library are eleven leaves of the *Acts of Paul*, a late 2nd-century 'religious romance'. Finally, the Oxyrhynchus papyri have provided some of the Gk. text of the well-known *Shepherd* of Hermas. This work later appears in full in the Codex Sinaiticus. (*CANON OF THE NEW TESTAMENT.)

BIBLIOGRAPHY (*listed according to above sections*).

a. F. G. Kenyon, *Our Bible and the Ancient Manuscripts*[5], 1958; E. G. Turner, *Greek Papyri*, 1968; C. H. Roberts, 'The Codex', *Proceedings of the British Academy* 40, 1954; A. Deissmann, *LAE*[4], 1929; F. F. Bruce, *The New Testament Documents: Are They Reliable?*[5], 1960.

b. K. Aland, *Kurzgefasste Liste der griechischen Handschriften des Neuen Testaments*, 1963, and subsequent additions; *idem*, *Repertorium der griechischen christlichen Papyri*, 1, 1976; J. van Haelst, *Catalogue des Papyrus Littéraires Juifs et Chrétiens*, 1976.

c. F. G. Kenyon, *The Text of the Greek Bible*[3], 1975; B. M. Metzger, *The Text of the New Testament*[2], 1968; *idem*, *A Textual Commentary on the Greek New Testament*, 1971.

d. A. Wikenhauser, *New Testament Introduction*[2], 1972, Part 2; Blass-Debrunner-Funk, *A Greek Grammar of the New Testament*[10], 1961; J. H. Moulton and G. Milligan, *Vocabulary of the Greek New Testament*, 1930; C. F. D. Moule, *An Idiom Book of New Testament Greek*[2], 1959.

e. Portions of NT found on *ostraca* are included in the papyri lists of *b.* above.

f. H. I. Bell and T. C. Skeat, *Fragments of an Unknown Gospel*, 1935; B. P. Grenfell, A. S. Hunt *et al.*, *The Oxyrhynchus Papyri* I–XLV, 1898–1977; R. M. Grant and D. N. Freedman, *The Secret Sayings of Jesus*, 1960; R. McL. Wilson, *Studies in the Gospel of Thomas*, 1960; J. Jeremias, *The Unknown Sayings of Jesus*, 1964.

B.F.H.

Acknowledgments

Acknowledgment of the sources of illustrations

The publishers have made every effort to trace the copyright holders of illustrations in this book. Should any have been inadvertently missed, copyright holders are asked to contact the publishers.

Diagrams, charts, line drawings and town plans

All diagrams, charts, line drawings and town plans in **The Illustrated Bible Dictionary** have been specially prepared for this work. The publishers are glad to acknowledge their indebtedness to a variety of sources as indicated below.
In acknowledging the source, 'After' indicates that the material remains essentially as it appears in the source acknowledged but has been redrawn. 'Based on' means that the substance of the source material has been retained but reinterpreted.
For abbreviations see pp.xii-xvi.

HAMATH, p.604
Based on E. Fugmann, *Hama, Fouilles et Recherches 1931-1938. II:I, L'architecture des périodes pré-Hellénistiques* (Foundation Carlsberg, Copenhagen, 1958), p.151, fig.185.

HAZOR, p.613
After *EAEHL*, vol.2, p.495.

HAZOR, p.614
Based on K. Crim (ed.), *IDB*, Supplementary volume (Abingdon Press, 1976), p.873.

HEROD, p.643
Based on S. Perowne, *The Later Herods* (Hodder and Stoughton, 1958), table I.

HIERAPOLIS, p.649
Based on E. Akurgal, *Ancient Civilizations and Ruins of Turkey* (Mobil Oil Türk A.Ş., Istanbul, 1970) pp.176f.

HITTITES, p.653
Based on *POTT*, p.203.

HOUSE (Ur), p.669
After material supplied by C. J. Davey.

HOUSE (villa), p.670
Based on W. F. Albright, *Archaeology of Palestine* (Penguin, 1947), fig.17.

HOUSE (Israelite), p.669
After material supplied by C. J. Davey.

HOUSE (T. beit Mirsim), p.670
Based on Y. Shiloh, *IEJ* 1970, p.187.

ISRAEL, p.708
Based on Y. Yadin, *The Excavation of Masada, 1963-4, Preliminary Report* (Israel Exploration Society, 1965).

JACHIN AND BOAZ, p.726
After *PEQ*, Jan.-June 1959, fig.9.

JERICHO, p.749
Based on P. R. S. Moorey, *Archaeology, Artefacts and the Bible* (Ashmolean Museum, Oxford, 1969), p.20.

JERUSALEM (David, Solomon and Herod), pp.754f.
Based on Walter de Gruyter (ed.), *Atlas of Jerusalem*, Maps 3:1, 3:2 and 3:6 (Jewish History Publications, 1973).

JERUSALEM (reconstruction) p.757
Based on Y. Yadin (ed.), *Jerusalem Revealed* (The Israel Exploration Society and Yale University Press, 1976), p.27.

JOT AND TITTLE, p.820
Supplied by A. R. Millard.

LACHISH, p.867
Based on *EAEHL*, vol.3, p.739.

LACHISH, p.867
Based on O. Tufnell, *Lachish III. The Iron Age* (Oxford University Press, 1953), pl.120.

MACCABEES, p.926
Based on S. Perowne, *The Life and Times of Herod the Great* (Hodder and Stoughton, 1956), p.6.

MARI, p.946
Based on A. Parrot, *Sumer* (Thames and Hudson, 1960), pp.257f.

MEGIDDO, p.973
Based on K. M. Kenyon, *The Bible and Recent Archaeology* (Colonnade Books), pp.63 and 71.

MEMPHIS, p.979
Based on L. V. Grinsell, *Barrow, Pyramid and Tomb* (Thames and Hudson, 1975), p.114.

MENE, p.981
Based on R. Koldewey, *Die Königsburgers von Babylon*, *WVDOG* 54 (Osnabrück, 1969), fig.4.

MENE, p.981
Supplied by A. R. Millard.

MILETUS, p.1000
Based on M. I. Finley, *ACA*, p.201.

MINING, p.1004
After material supplied by C. J. Davey.

MUSIC, p.1032
Based on J. Rimmer, *Ancient Musical Instruments of Western Asia* (British Museum, 1969), pp.50f.

NABATAEANS, p.1044
Based on *Supplément au Dictionnaire de la Bible*, vol.7 (Letouzey et Ané, Paris, 1966), cols.949f.

NERO, p.1075
After M. Grant, *Nero* (Weidenfeld and Nicolson, 1970), p.265.

NINEVEH, p.1091
After B. Mazar and M. Avi-Yonah *et al.* (eds.), *Views of the Biblical World* (International Publishing Co. Ltd, Jerusalem, 1960), vol.3, p.253 and R. Campbell Thompson, *Iraq I* (British School of Archaeology in Iraq, 1934), p.97, fig.1.

OHOLIBAMAH, p.1108
After B. Rothenberg, *Timna* (Thames and Hudson, 1972), p.152.

PALACE (Syrian), p.1127
Based on H. Frankfort, *The art and architecture of the Ancient Orient* (Penguin, 1954), p.170.

PALACE (Assyrian), p.1128
Based on *Ibid.*, pp.7f.

PALACE (Palestinian), p.1129
Based on W. G. Dever and S. M. Paul, *Biblical Archaeology* (Keter Publishing House, Jerusalem, 1973), p.44.

PALACE (Jericho), p.1131
Based on E. Netzer, *IEJ* 25, 1975, p.94.

PALACE (Jericho), p.1130
Based on *Ibid.*, p.98.

Photographs

The photographs in **The Illustrated Bible Dictionary** are reproduced by permission of the following persons or agencies. The initials provide a cross-reference from the captions. The numbers in the list are page references to the text.

AAI
Austrian Archaeological Institute/ M. Bietak, pp.579, 580.

ACL
A. C. L. Bruxelles, p.633.

AMO
Ashmolean Museum, Oxford, pp.861,862.

AP
A. Parrot, pp.603, 852, 947.

ARM
A. R. Millard, pp.649, 870.

ASCS
American School of Classical Studies at Athens, p.953.

AU
Andrews University, Michigan, pp.645, 646.

BL
Reproduced by permission of the British Library.
Hebrews Greek papyrus 1532, p.628.
Genesis papyrus 2052, p.883.

BM
Reproduced by Courtesy of the Trustees of the British Museum, pp.587, 588, 593, 598, 599, 602, 603, 605 (2), 607, 608, 621, 632, 642, 646, 647, 658, 659, 660, 661, 674 (2), 675 (2), 678 (3), 683, 684, 691, 723, 724, 737, 742, 749, 759 (2), 780, 781, 782, 784, 788, 846, 849, 866, 870, 872, 873 (2), 907 (2), 908, 931, 932, 943, 965, 966, 983, 1006, 1011, 1018, 1019 (2), 1021 (2), 1023, 1024, 1033 (2), 1035, 1038, 1045, 1064, 1065, 1068, 1078 (2), 1089, 1090, 1108, 1110, 1122, 1123, 1124, 1125, 1143, 1144 (2), 1145, 1147.

BN
Photograph Bibliothèque Nationale, Paris. B 11 591, p.1061.

BPK
Bildarchiv Preussischer Kulturbesitz. Ägyptisches Museum. Staatliche Museen Preussischer, Kulturbesitz, Berlin (West), p.894.

BPL
Barnaby's Picture Library, pp.594, 601, 971, 1086, 1112, 1129.

BrM
Courtesy of The Brooklyn Museum. Bequest of Miss Theodora Wilbour, p.956.

BSAI
British School of Archaeology in Iraq, pp.605, 724, 790 (2), 980.

CBL
Chester Beatty Library, pp.918, 952, 963, 1101, 1146, 1149.

CD
C. Davey, p.1005 (2).

CH
C. Hemer, p.882.

CP
Camera Press, pp.615, 660.

DJW
D. J. Wiseman, pp.758, 784, 884, 931, 1092.

DO
D. Oates, p.594.

FMB
Fondation Martin Bodmer, pp.583, 802, 919.

FNH
F. N. Hepper, pp. 579 (2), 590, 636 (2), 637 (3), 638 (3), 691 (2), 939, 1055, 1110, 1113, 1145.

GC
The Ny Carlsberg Glyptotek, Copenhagen, p.623.

GIO
Photograph, Griffith Institute, Ashmolean Museum, Oxford, p.906.

HC
The Holyland Corporation. Photos taken on the site of the reconstruction of Jerusalem at the time of the 2nd Temple (or Herod's time) in the grounds of the Holyland Hotel, Jerusalem, Israel, pp.673, 760, 1126.

HSM
Harvard Semitic Museum, p.1104.

IA
Institute of Archaeology. By permission of the Wellcome Trust, pp.743, 866.

IGS
Institute of Geological Sciences, pp.786 (2), 787 (4).

IM
Israel Museum, pp. 725, 739, 753, 783, 788, 849, 974, 975.

JCT
© John C. Trever, 1970, pp.596, 699.

JDH
J. D. Hawkins, pp.589, 596, 652 (3), 653.

JEF
Jericho Excavation Fund, pp. 671 (2), 748.

JLH
John L. Hillelson Photographic Agency Georg Gerster, p.647.

JPK
J. P. Kane, pp.607, 673, 750, 757, 760, 796, 830, 1114, 1126.

JR
John Rylands Library, pp.582, 1147.

KAK
K. A. Kitchen, pp.710, 998, 1015 (2), 1118.

KK
K. Kenyon, pp.736, 1073.

MC
Maurice Chuzeville/Louvre Museum, pp.595, 597, 602, 606, 612 (2), 619, 679, 727, 889, 947, 1017, 1040, 1124.

MEPhA
Middle East Photographic Archive, London, pp.614, 725, 871, 893, 929, 940, 987, 1037, 1041, 1065, 1069.

MH
M. Holford, pp.781, 1115.

MNAC
Museum of National Antiquities, Cairo, p.624.

NA
N. Avigad, p.743.

NMBL
National Museum of Beirut, Lebanon, p.615.

NPAI
National Parks Association, Israel, p.973.

OIUC
Oriental Institute, University of Chicago, pp.655, 722, 975.

P
Popperfoto Photographic Agency, p.810.

PAC
P. A. Clayton, pp.602, 724, 813, 977, 979, 1038.

PP
Picturepoint, London, pp.674, 721, 928, 1039, 1076.

PSR
Pacific School of Religion, p.725.

RC
Richard Cleave, Pictorial Archive, p.756.

RG
Ray Gardner, pp.676, 716 (3), 839, 924 (2), 927, 929, 1018 (2), 1019 (5), 1020 (4), 1021 (4), 1048, 1076.

RH
Robert Harding Picture Library, pp.1046, 1047, 1085.

RM
Rockefeller Museum, pp.664, 807, 869, 1049.

RP
R. Pitt, p.895.

RS
Ronald Sheridan's Photo-Library, pp.590, 593 (2), 614, 662, 723, 851, 893, 895, 927, 944, 966, 1062.

RVO
Courtesy of Rijksmuseum van Oudheden, Leiden, Netherlands, pp.617, 1036, 1095.

RVS
R. V. Schoder, pp.592, 999, 1012.

S
Shell U.K. Administrative Services, p.792.

SAOB
The State Antiquities Organisation, Baghdad, pp.1067, 1105.

SAOS
School of Archaeology and Oriental Studies, pp.870 (3), 1003.

SH
Sonia Halliday Photographs, pp.610, 641, 648, 650, 716, 789, 953, 969, 974, 1025, 1043, 1045, 1062, 1135 (2).

SI
Foto Scala Firenze, Italy, pp.595, 1034 (2), 1088.

SMB
Staatliche Museen zu Berlin/DDR Ägyptisches Museum, pp. 658, 738, 983.

SOAS
School of Oriental and African Studies. Photo D. S. Rice, p.609.

SZC
Sisters of Zion Convent, p.644.

TAU
Institute of Archaeology, Tel-Aviv University/Avraham Hay, p.690.

UC
Courtesy of the Petrie Museum, University College, London, UC 8901, p.1004.

UMUP
Reproduced by permission of the University Museum, University of Pennsylvania, p.967.

WAG
Walters Art Gallery, Baltimore, p.1069.

ZR
Zev Radovan, pp.821, 863, 1111.